The New York Times

SQUARE ONE
CROSSWORD DICTIONARY

Stanley Newman
and
Daniel Stark

TIMES

BOOKS

ISBN 0-8129-3043-6

Website address: www.puzzlesatrandom.com

Text design and typography by Daniel Stark
Manufactured in the United States of America

Introduction

A crossword dictionary has one purpose, and one purpose only: to be a comprehensive, authoritative source of answers to the crossword clues that you're looking for. Based on this bottom-line criterion, *The New York Times Square-One Crossword Dictionary* is <u>by far</u> the most useful crossword dictionary available anywhere. These introductory paragraphs should prove our case "beyond a reasonable doubt."

Over the past twenty years, American crosswords have undergone a tremendous change in content and style. Today's crosswords, as exemplified by *The New York Times*, are filled with the lively language of current events and popular culture, and are much less dependent on the "straight" dictionary definitions that used to predominate.

If you've used any other crossword dictionary recently, you know that, more times than not, the particular clue and answer you're looking for just isn't there. The reason: too many of the words in other crossword dictionaries seldom appear in today's crosswords, and they leave out too many of the clues and answers that do appear in today's crosswords all the time.

The result of five years of research and preparation, *The New York Times Square-One Crossword Dictionary* is the first crossword dictionary to fully reflect the clues and answers that appear most often in today's crossword puzzles. So you can see what we mean, let's describe the process by which this book came to be.

First, we examined many thousands of crosswords from a broad spectrum of contemporary sources, to determine puzzledom's "Hot List" – the words that appear most often, making up 50 percent of all crossword answers. Not surprisingly, the most popular crossword words are mostly three to six letters long and have mostly common letters – such as ALTER, COT, IRON, TAME, etc. In addition to everyday "dictionary" words, a host of abbreviations (like NOV and PTA), multiword phrases (like A BEE and IS TO), and proper names (like ELVIS and SHAW) made the list. What <u>did</u> surprise us about the list is the relative lack of "crosswordese," words that supposedly appear often in crosswords and seldom anywhere else. A few of these old standbys did poke up their heads, like ANOA and EDE, but today's crossword constructors and editors have largely succeeded in driving out obscurities.

Using the "Hot List," we then collected all the clues for these words from the thousands of puzzles we started with – which numbered <u>over 500,000 clues</u> in all. We examined each one of those clues, eliminating duplicates or near duplicates, as well as clues that we felt were too abstruse to merit inclusion. We also tightened up the wording of the clues that remained, and standardized the nomenclature for overall consistency.

Once we had finished deleting, we started adding. For example, we supplemented the listings for all "Hot List" words that were category names, such as birds, colors, moons, ores, and trees. So you'll find COLOR under "chartreuse" and "cerise," and TREE under "banyan" and "baobab," etc. We also added common synonyms of our words that somehow hadn't been used in the crosswords we examined. Clues from popular culture were added too, such as well-known celebrities from all fields, movie and song titles, and so forth.

When we were done, we had the approximately 150,000 entries that you'll find in this book, consisting of **the most important clues for the most popular crossword answers**. And, to be sure we had done our job right, we tested this book and the current leading crossword dictionaries against a recent group of America's most popular crosswords. The results? *The New York Times Square-One Crossword Dictionary* consistently had <u>more than twice as many</u> of the clues and answers than any other book.

While we're confident that these results are fully applicable to whatever your favorite crossword happens to be, it's important to keep in mind as you use this book that it is not, of course, an unabridged crossword dictionary. Our inclusion of the top 50 percent of crossword answers has led to some seemingly anomalous omissions. For example, under "coin toss call" you will find TAILS but not HEADS, because TAILS was on our "Hot List" and HEADS was not. This is nevertheless a useful bit of information for you as a puzzle solver, because you can conclude that TAILS is a more likely answer for "coin toss call" than HEADS.

For crossword fans seeking a more comprehensive book of puzzle answers, we can unabashedly recommend the recently updated edition of our previous book, *The New York Times Crossword Answer Book* (Times Books, $17.50 softcover, ISBN 0-8129-2972-1), an answers-only word finder with an unmatched <u>83 percent</u> of the answers in American crosswords.

For their help in the preparation of this book, we would like to thank Jon Delfin, Mark Frnka, Rebecca Kornbluh, Ellen Ripstein, Nancy Schuster and Tim Voss. Special thanks to Will Shortz, crossword editor of *The New York Times*, for his support and encouragement. At Times Books/Random House, thanks to Lisa Arrington, Mark Gottlieb, Eli Hausknecht, Nancy Inglis, Heidi North, Naomi Osnos, and Philip Turner. Finally, a "super kudos" to Roslyn Stark, for stepping in as deadlines approached and keeping us on schedule.

Your comments on any aspect of this book are most welcome, especially any clues you'd like us to include in future editions. Please keep in mind that the answers to your clues must be words already included herein. You may write to us at this address: Times Books Puzzles and Games, 201 East 50th Street, New York, NY 10022. E-mail: xwords@randomhouse.com. We will thank the first sender of any new clue we use in future editions by including his or her name in the introduction.

To use *The New York Times Square-One Crossword Dictionary* most effectively, we recommend you read the two-page "How to Use" section immediately following this introduction.

May all your crosswords be completely solved – with or without our help.

Stanley Newman

Daniel Stark

How to Use *The New York Times Square-One Crossword Dictionary*

Each standard clue has been indexed by its most important word, but many clues are listed multiple times under different keywords. So to use *The New York Times Square-One Crossword Dictionary* most effectively, look up the clue you're seeking under the word in that clue that seems the most important. If there seems to be more than one "important" word, chances are the clue is listed under each one. For example, the clue "false face" (for MASK) can be found both under "false" and "face." A tilde (~) is used in place of the headword in subsidiary listings under each headword.

HEADWORDS AND ALPHABETIZATION

A headword is a word, phrase, number, name, or title that is being used as an index. These are the words that are at the extreme left of each column. Headwords have been alphabetized on a letter-by-letter basis. Solid words precede hyphenated words or words with spaces, and lowercase letters precede capital letters. Headwords followed by a "fill in the blank" and headwords within quotation marks (such as titles, quotations and colloquial phrases) follow the same stand-alone headword.

Here's a sample headword sequence:

> flow
> flower
> flower __
> "Flower __"
> flowering
> "Flowering Peach, The"

ADDITIONAL ALPHABETIZATION RULES

Multiword personal names are generally listed "last-name first," such as "Foster, Jodie" and "Harris, Joel Chandler."

Headwords within quotation marks ignore initial articles, if any, as in "Forsyte Saga, The."

Fill-in-the-blank clues that start with the fill-in are alphabetized in their entirety, ignoring the fill-in, such as "__ the King's Men." The alphabetization for other fill-in-the-blank clues ends at the underscores showing the fill-in. So "Fort __, Calif." comes before "Fort Apache."

To make clues that start with numbers easy to find, they are sorted numerically at the beginning of the initial letter, considering how the number is spoken. So "500" is at the beginning of F, and "1998" is at the beginning of N. You will also find some clues under the spelled-out versions of smaller numbers, such as "five" and "nine." Years should be looked up under their full form (1936), not shortened form ('36).

Clues with "Ft.," "Mt." and "St." are spelled out – as "Fort" (listed under F), "Mount" (listed under M), and "Saint" (listed under S), respectively. Names of lakes that start with the word "Lake" are listed under L.

INFLECTED FORMS

To avoid needless repetition, most plural nouns have been "de-pluralized" for indexing. A clue containing "fathers" should therefore be looked up under "father." Similarly, most verbs are listed in infinitive form ("talk") rather than inflected form ("talks," "talked," or "talking"). Once you've found the answer you're looking for, it should be "re-inflected" accordingly.

FIRST OR LAST NAMES

Many crossword clues contain only first or last names, such as "actor Alda" (for ALAN), "Selleck and Seaver" (for TOMS), and "Bruce or Laura" (for DERN). Clues such as these will be found under each individual name, be it first or last, and not the occupation, if any.

FOREIGN WORDS

Clues for common foreign words are listed in two places – under the English meaning, and under the name of the foreign language. The clue "summer: Fr." can thus be found both under "summer" and "French." Because crosswords often use foreign places and names to clue foreign words (like "summer, to Yvette"), hundreds of such places and names are listed herein, and cross-referenced to the language. For example, you will find "see French" under "Marseille" and "Yvette."

CLUES BY EXAMPLE

Clues like "Man, for one" (for ISLE) and "linguine or rigatoni" (for PASTA) are crossword staples. Other signals such as "for example," "for instance," and "e.g." may also be used for this type of clue. These "clues by example" should be looked up individually. For example, PASTA will be found under both "linguine" and "rigatoni."

"STARTERS" AND "ENDERS"

Another type of crossword clue, such as "back starter" (for HORSE), "novel ender" (for ETTE) and "type of dance" (for BARN), gives a word to which another word (or prefix/suffix) must be added. When the answer forms a solid word with the clue, it is indexed with the indicator "starter" if added at the beginning, and "ender" if added at the end. When the answer is either hyphenated or has more than one word, it is indexed as a fill-in. So HORSE will be found under "back starter" and BARN will be found under "__ dance." Keep in mind that puzzle editors use many other keywords to indicate this type of clue, such as head, lead-in, opener, chaser, tail, add-on, etc.

Crossword answers are often word fragments (such as PRE, ENTO, and ISO), clued as "prefix," "suffix," or "combining form." We know that "prefix" and "combining form" are not synonymous, but for simplicity in lookup, all word-fragment answers that start words are herein called "prefixes" and all that end words are called "suffixes."

ABBREVIATIONS IN CLUES AND ANSWERS

Crossword clues whose answers are abbreviations are often, but not always, indicated by an abbreviation in the clue, or the word "abbr." When looking up abbreviations, be sure to check both the abbreviated word ("dr.") as well as its unabbreviated form ("doctor"), if needed.

POSSESSIVES IN CLUES

In order to keep related clues listed together, most clue possessives have been changed to the nonpossessive form. For example, "Frankenstein's assistant" is indexed under "Frankenstein." Possessives in titles and quotations have, of course, been retained.

"SEE ALSO"

To include as many different clues and answers as possible in this book, we have used cross-referencing to synonymous or nearly synonymous headwords. For example, you will find "see also canine" under "dog" and "see also Army, GI" under "military."

CLUE CAPITALIZATION

Crosswords generally capitalize the first letter of a clue, whether the word would be ordinarily capitalized or not. For clarity, we have separated headwords that are ordinarily capitalized from their noncapitalized counterparts. This should ease the confusion between clues like "Frost" (for POET) and "frost" (for RIME).

ANSWER WORDS

Answer words are given as they would normally be entered in crosswords – in capital letters, without any accent marks, punctuation, or spaces between words. Answer words are given alphabetically within a particular clue.

OTHER THINGS TO KEEP IN MIND

A word in parentheses at the end of a clue, such as "write (down)" (for JOT), is added to the answer word to give the indicated meaning – "jot down" means "write down."

The clue you're looking for will often be found at a related nearby entry, such as "topper" and "topping."

1

A

a ANY, PER
  ~ in code ABLE, ALFA
  ~ in French UNE
  ~ in German EIN, EINE
  ~ in Spanish UNA, UNO

a ___ (slightly) BIT

A TYPE
  ~ in communications ALFA
  ~ list ELITE
  ~ major KEY
  ~ minor KEY

A ___ "able" ASIN

A ___ "apple" ASIN

"A, ___ adorable..." YOURE

A-___ (elite) LIST

"A-___, The" TEAM

___ A (auto) MODEL

AA
  part of ~ ANON

A.A. ___ MILNE

A-1 TOPS

AAA
  ~ giveaway MAP
  ~ job TOW
  ~ opposite EEE
  ~ suggestion ROUTE, RTE

Aachen
  see German

aah
  ~ partner OOH

Aar
  city on the ~ BERN

aardvark ANIMAL
  ~ food ANT

Aaron BURR
  ~ brother MOSES
  ~ idol CALF
  ~ weapon BAT
  son of ~ ELI

AARP
  ~ members SRS
  part of ~ AMER, RET

AB TYPE

aba ROBE

ABA
  ~ member ATT, ATTY
  part of ~ AMER, ASSN, BAR

aback
  be taken ~ START
  take ~ ABASH, JAR

abacus
  ~ unit BEAD
  ~ user ADDER
  use an ~ ADD

Abadan
  ~ locale IRAN

"___ a Bad Mama Jama" SHES

abalone
  ~ eater OTTER

abandon ARDOR, CEDE, DASH, DESERT, DROP, ELAN, END, EXIT, LEAVE, SCRAP, STOP, YIELD

"Abandon ___!" SHIP

abandoned ALONE, BAD, LONE, LOOSE, LOST

"Abandon Ship"
  ~ director SALE

___ a barrel OVER

abase SHAME

abash AWE, SHAME, SNUB

abashed
  obviously ~ RED

abate CEASE, CUT, EASE, EBB, FLAG, REMIT, SINK, SLAKE, WANE

abatement WANE

Abaya LAKE

Abba EBAN
  ~ tune SOS

abbé TITLE

Abbe LANE

abbess NUN, RANK, TITLE

"Abbey ___" ROAD

Abbie
  ~ comic-strip partner SLATS

"Abbie an' ___" SLATS

abbot ABBE, DOM, RANK, TITLE

Abbott and Costello DUO, PAIR, TEAM

"Abbott and Costello ___ Frankenstein" MEET

abbreviate CUT, LOP, TRIM

abbreviated
  ~ version MINI

Abby
  ~ sister ANN
  ~ to Ann TWIN

"___ Abby" DEAR

ABC
  ~ rival CBS
  ~ sitcom ELLEN
  part of ~ AMER
  telephone's ~ TWO

"ABC's ___ World of Sports" WIDE

abdicate DESERT, LEAVE, YIELD

abdominous OBESE

Abdul PAULA

"Abdul Abulbul ___" AMIR

Abdul-Jabbar
  ~ alma mater UCLA

Abe
  ~ boy TAD
  like ~ HONEST

abecedarian BABE
  ~ phrase ASIN

abed
  ~ maybe ILL
  not ~ ASTIR

Abel ALAN, BOB, ELIE
  ~ brother CAIN, SETH
  ~ father ADAM
  ~ mother EVE
  ~ to Adam SON
  nephew of ~ ENOS

___ a bell RING

Abel, Rudolf SPY

Aberdeen CITY, PORT
  ~ boy LAD
  ~ miss LASS

~ native SCOT
~ river DEE
see also Scottish

aberrant ODD

aberration BLIP

abet AID, HELP

abettor
  actor's ~ AGENT

abeyance STOP
  be in ~ AWAIT, PEND
  hold in ~ DEFER

abhor HATE

abhorrent BAD, EVIL, VILE

Abib
  month before ~ ADAR

abide ALLOW, AWAIT, BEAR, LIE, LIVE, STAND, STAY, TAKE, WAIT
  ~ by ADHERE, KEEP, OBEY

abiding ETERNAL

___-abiding LAW

Abidjan CITY, PORT
  capital east of ~ ACCRA

Abie
  like ~'s Rose IRISH

"Abie's Irish ___" ROSE

"Abie's Irish Rose"
  ~ actress DRU

abigail GIRL, MAID

Abigail ADAMS
  ~ sib ANN

"___ a Big Boy Now" YOURE

___ a bill of goods SELL

abject BASE, LOW
  ~ fear PANIC

___ a blank DRAW

ablative CASE

ablaze
  set ~ LIT

able ADEPT, FIT
  isn't ~ to CANT
  is ~ to CAN

"Able ___ I..." WAS

able-bodied HALE

"Able to ___ tall buildings..." LEAP

"Able was I ___..." ERE, EREI

ablush RED

ablution BATH

ABM
 part of ~ ANTI

Abner LIL
 ~ creator CAPP

"___ Abner" LIL

abnormal ODD
 ~ (prefix) MAL, PARA

aboard
 ~ ship ASEA, ATSEA
 put ~ LADE

"___ aboard!" ALL

abode ESTATE, HOME, PAD, ROOF
 ~ in Spanish CASA
 Aleutian ~ IGLOO
 anchorite ~ CELL
 animal ~ DEN
 Arapaho ~ TEPEE
 canvas ~ TENT
 cozy ~ NEST
 craggy ~ AERIE
 dryad ~ TREE
 lofty ~ AERIE
 squirrel ~ TREE
 toad ~ POND

abolish ANNUL, END

A-bomb
 ~ scientist UREY

abominable BAD, EVIL, UGLY, VILE
 ~ snowman YETI

abominate ABHOR, HATE

abomination SIN

aboriginal EARLY, LOCAL, OLD

aborigine LOCAL
 ~ weapon SPEAR
 Japanese ~ AINU
 New Zealand ~ MAORI

"Abou ___ Adhem" BEN

"Abou Ben Adhem"
 ~ poet HUNT

abound TEEM

abounding AMPLE, RICH, RIFE
 ~ in (suffix) OSE

about AFTER, ASTIR, ASTO, INRE, NEAR, ORSO, SAY
 ~ (suffix) ISH
 ~ the same EVEN

about-___ FACE

___ about (approximately) ONOR

___ about (begin) SET

___ about (occur) COME

___ about (search) CAST

___ about (snoop) NOSE

___ about (worry) PUT

"About ___ Leslie" MRS

"About ___ Night..." LAST

"About a Quarter to ___" NINE

"___ About Eve" ALL

about-face TURN

"About Mrs. Leslie"
 ~ director MANN

"___ About Music" MAD

"___ about time!" ITS

___ about town MAN

"___ About You" MAD

above OVER
 ~ in German UBER
 ~ (prefix) EPI, SUR
 ~ to a poet OER

above ___ (primarily) ALL

above ___ (solvent) WATER

"Above ___ Beyond" AND

"___ Above All" THIS

aboveboard FAIR, HONEST, LEGAL, OPEN

aboveground
 ~ trains ELS

ab ovo NEW

"___ a Bowl of Tea" EAT

abrade ERODE, FILE, RASP, SAND, SKIN, WEAR

Abraham
 ~ grandson ESAU
 ~ nephew LOT
 ~ wife SARAH
 son of ~ ISAAC

abrasion SORE

abrasive EMERY, GRIT, RUDE, SAND

abreast EVEN

abri HAVEN

abridge CUT, ELIDE, EMEND, LOP, SLASH, TRIM
 ~ perhaps EDIT

abroad AFOOT, AWAY, OUT
 noise ~ POST, SAY

abrogate ANNUL

abrupt CRISP, RASH, RUDE, STEEP, TERSE
 ~ transition LEAP
 be ~ SNAP

abruptly BANG

"Absalom and Achitophel" POEM

"Absalom My ___" SON

abscind CUT, LOP

abscond ELOPE, FLEE, RUN

absence
 ~ of (prefix) DIS

absent AWAY, GONE, OUT
 ~ oneself LEAVE, MISS
 opposite of ~ HERE

absent-minded DAFT

"Absinthe Drinker"
 ~ artist MANET

absolute ENTIRE, ETERNAL, PURE, RANK, TOTAL, UTTER
 ~ ruler TSAR

absolute ___ ZERO

Absolute
 the ~ LORD

absolutely AMEN, CLEAN, SURE, YES

"Absolutely!"
 ~ in Spanish SISI

absolve CLEAR, REMIT

absorb AMUSE, ARREST, BLOT, GET, HOLD, LEARN, SOP
 ~ a book READ
 ~ as an expense EAT
 ~ as costs EAT

absorbed DEEP, RAPT
 ~ by INTO

___-absorbed SELF

absquatulate FLEE, HIE, RUN

abstain AVOID, DIET, FAST

abstemious SOBER

abstract CUT, IDEAL, LOP, PURE
 ~ painting OPART
 it may be ~ ART

abstract ___ ART

abstract art
 name in ~ KLEE

abstracted
 be ~ DREAM, MUSE

abstraction IDEA

abstractionist
 Swiss ~ KLEE

abstruse DEEP

absurd DAFT, INANE, MAD, RICH
 ~ art DADA

Abu Dhabi
 ~ denizen ARAB
 ~ leader AMIR, EMEER, EMIR

abundance EASE, MINE, OCEAN, PILE, SEA, STORE

abundant AMPLE, RICH
 ~ source MINE
 not ~ RARE

abuse HARM, MAUL

abutment PROP

abutting CLOSE, NEAR

abysmal DEEP, LOW, VILE

abyss DEEP, DROP, PIT, SPACE

abyssal DEEP

Abyssinian CAT
 word from an ~ MEOW, MEW

Ac ELEM
 89 for ~ ATNO

AC
 ~ supply ELEC
 part of ~ AIR, ALT

A/C
 ~ unit BTU
 peak ~ time AUG

acacia TREE

acad. INST

academic
 ~ climber IVY
 ~ specialty MAJOR
 Cambridge ~ DON

"___ Academic" ITS

academy
 ~ in French ECOLE
 ~ student CADET
 Annapolis ~ NAVAL

Academy
 ~ founder PLATO

Academy Award OSCAR

"___ a Camera" IAM

___ a candle to HOLD

Acapulco
 see Spanish

accede AGREE, DEFER, YIELD
 ~ to ADMIT, ALLOW

accelerate AID, REV, SPUR

accelerated FAST

acceleration
 unit of ~ GAL

accelerator GAS
 ~ item ATOM

accent PULSE, STRESS
 kind of ~ ACUTE
 Scottish ~ BURR

accept ABIDE, ADOPT, AGREE, BEAR, OBEY, OWN, TAKE
 ~ an applicant HIRE
 ~ an ovation BOW
 ~ as true ALLOW
 ~ without objection ABIDE
 vote to ~ ADOPT

acceptable GOOD, LEGAL, SOSO
 be ~ to SUIT
 is ~ GOES

accepts
 ~ an invitation GOES

access DOOR, ENTRY, GATE, LANE, ROAD
 authorize for ~ CLEAR
 collier's ~ ADIT
 floor ~ STAIR
 freeway ~ RAMP
 garden ~ GATE
 give ~ to ADMIT
 mailbox ~ DROP
 means of ~ ENTREE, RAMP
 subway ~ STILE

access ___ CODE

accessible NEAR, OPEN

accessories GEAR, RIG

accessory ALLY, EXTRA
  auto ~ ALARM

accident-___ PRONE

acclaim ECLAT, EXALT, HAIL, HONOR, LAUD

acclaimed NOTED

acclamation CRY, ECLAT

acclimate ADAPT, ENURE, INURE, ORIENT

acclivity RAMP, RISE, SLOPE, TILT

accolade HONOR, KISS

accommodate ADAPT, AID, FIT, HELP, HOLD, LEND, LOAN, SEAT, SERVE, SUIT

accommodating EASY, SWEET

accommodation BED
  arena ~ SEAT

accommodations ABODE, HOTEL, INN

accompaniment
  MS ~ SASE

accompany ATTEND, SEE, SHOW, USHER

accomplice AID, ALLY
  be an ~ ABET

accomplish WIN

accomplished ABLE, ADEPT, DONE, GOOD

accomplisher DOER

accomplishes DOES

accomplishment ACT, DEED, FEAT

accord AGREE, LOVE, PACT, PEACE, TUNE, UNION
  ~ with SUIT
  in ~ ASONE, ATONE, ONE
  reach ~ AGREE

accordance
  in ~ (with) ALONG

according
  ~ to ALA, PER

accordingly ERGO, THEN, THUS

accord signer
  ~ of 1978 SADAT

accost GREET, HAIL, MEET

account AUDIT, DEBT, LOG, NEWS, SAKE, TAB, TALE
  ~ abbr. BAL, INT
  ~ entry DEBIT, ITEM
  ~ exec REP
  ~ payable BILL
  ~ receivable IOU
  close an ~ CLEAR
  give an ~ RELATE
  keep an ~ LOG
  long ~ SAGA
  on no ~ NEVER
  take into ~ ALLOW, HEED, NOTE
  travel ~ LOG

turn to ~ AVAIL

accountant
  ~ activity AUDIT
  ~ at times ADDER
  ~ concern NET

accounting
  ~ entry DEBIT, ITEM
  ~ period YEAR

accounts
  check the ~ of AUDIT
  falsify ~ PAD
  settle ~ PAY

accouter ARM, ARRAY, ATTIRE, DRESS, FIT, GARB, RIG

accouterments DRESS, GEAR

Accra CITY, PORT

accredit CITE

accrete ADHERE, GROW

accroach TAKE

accrual
  IRA ~ INT

accrue ADD

acct. CPA
  long-term ~ IRA

accts.
  savings ~ CDS

accumulate AMASS, KEEP, PILE, SAVE

accumulation MASS, PILE, STORE, TOTAL
  rock ~ SCREE

accuracy CARE, RIGOR

accurate CLOSE, TRUE

accursed BAD, EVIL

accuse SUE
  ~ falsely LIBEL

accused
  ~ need BAIL

accustom ADAPT, ENURE, INURE, ORIENT, TRAIN

accustomed SET, USUAL
  get ~ ADAPT

ace ADEPT, CARD, PASS, PILOT, PRO, STAR
  ~ to Goren HONOR
  aria ~ DIVA
  within an ~ of CLOSE

ace in the ___ HOLE

acerbic ACID, ACRID, SOUR, TART, TESTY

acerbity TANG

"Aces High"
  ~ director GOLD

acetate ESTER, SALT

acetic ACID

acetous ACID, ACRID, SOUR, TART

acetylene GAS

acetylsalicylic ACID

___ a chance STAND

"___ a chance!" NOT

ache AIL, PAIN, YEARN
  ~ for MISS, PINE
  sharp ~ PANG

Achernar STAR

aches
  ~ and pains WOE

Acheson DEAN

achieve EARN, GAIN, GET, MAKE, TAKE, WIN
  ~ success ARRIVE

achieved DONE

achievement ACT, DEED, FEAT
  heroic ~ FEAT
  links ~ ACE
  pitcher's ~ SAVE
  symbol of ~ AWARD

achiever DOER

achieves DOES

Achilles HERO
  its hero is ~ ILIAD
  weak spot for ~ HEEL

aching SORE

"Achtung Baby"
  ~ producer ENO

achy SORE

aciculate ACUTE

acid ACRID, SOUR, TART
  ~ + alcohol product ESTER
  ~ neutralizer BASE
  ~ salt ESTER
  ~ solution BATH
  essential ~ AMINO
  protein ~ AMINO
  work with ~ ETCH

acid ___ RAIN, TEST

___ acid (organic compound) AMINO

acid-alcohol
  ~ compound ESTER

acidic SOUR, TART

acidity TANG

acid rain
  ~ watchdog org. EPA

acidulous SOUR, TART

acknowledge ADMIT, AVOW, NOD, OWN, REACT
  ~ a performance CLAP
  ~ applause BOW
  ~ a stimulus REACT
  ~ the band CLAP

acknowledgement NOD, NOTE

___ à clef ROMAN

ACLU
  part of ~ AMER, UNION

acme APEX, CAP, CREST, PEAK, TIP, TOP
  at the ~ of ATOP

"___ a cold..." FEED

acolyte
  ~ spot ALTAR

"___ a common proof..." TIS

Aconcagua
  ~ locale ANDES

"___ a consummation devoutly..." TIS

"___-A-Cop" RENT

acorn NUT, SEED
  ~ producer OAK

acoustic AURAL
  ~ organ EAR

acoustical
  ~ unit SABIN

acquaintance
  make ~ with MEET

"___ Acquaintance" OLD

acquainted
  become ~ with ADAPT
  be ~ with KNOW
  get ~ MEET

acquiesce AGREE, BEND, BOW, DEFER, NOD, THAW, YIELD
  ~ in ALLOW

acquiescent EASY, MEEK

acquire EARN, GAIN, GET, HAVE, TAKE, WIN
  ~ some color TAN

acquired
  ~ relative INLAW

acquisition TAKE

acquisitive AVID

acquisitiveness LUST

acquit ACT, CLEAR, FREE

acre
  anagram of ~ CARE, RACE
  one-quarter ~ ROOD

acre-___ (volume measure) FOOT

Acre CITY, PORT
  ~ locale ISRAEL

acreage AREA, LAND, SPACE

acres
  contiguous ~ TRACT
  plutocrat's ~ ESTATE

acrid ACID, SOUR

acrimonious ACID, RUDE

acrimony ANGER, EDGE, SPITE

acrobat
  ~ workplace RING

acrobatic
  ~ feat SPLIT

"___ a Crooked Shadow" CHASE

Acropolis
  ~ goddess ATHENA

___ a cropper COME

across
  come ~ MEET
  extend ~ SPAN
  get ~ TALK
  go ~ CUT
  put ~ SHOW
  reach ~ SPAN
  run ~ MEET
  sweep ~ COMB

___ across (accomplish) PUT

___ across (communicate) GET

___ across (find) COME

___ across (meet) RUN

"Across the ___ Missouri" WIDE

across-the-board TOTAL

acrylic PAINT

act DEED, EDICT, FAKE, FEAT, FIAT, LAW, POSE, SHAM, STIR
  ~ badly EMOTE
  ~ ender IVE
  ~ fresh SASS
  ~ funny AMUSE
  ~ grandmotherly DOTE
  ~ human ERR
  ~ hypocritical MASK
  ~ idly TOY
  ~ in concert UNITE
  ~ introducer EMCEE
  ~ like APE
  ~ like a baby BAWL
  ~ like a kid ROMP
  ~ of defiance DARE
  ~ of perdition RIOT
  ~ quickly LEAP
  ~ shocked START
  ~ snooty towards SNUB
  ~ starter INTER
  ~ (suffix) URE
  ~ surly SNARL
  ~ towards TREAT
  ~ uppity SNAP
  ~ worried PACE
  caught in the ~ SEEN
  deliberate ~ STEP
  disappearing ~ LAM
  do the disappearing
    ~ ELUDE, FLEE
  formal ~ RITE
  portion of an ~ SCENE
  prohibited ~ NONO
  put on an ~ FAKE
  read the riot ~ WARN
  rioter's ~ ARSON
  unlawful ~ TORT

act ___ hunch ONA

___ act CLASS

___-act (pretend) PLAY

acting
  ~ award OBIE, OSCAR, TONY
  ~ group CAST
  ~ job ROLE
  ~ up BAD

action ADO, DEED, PLAY, PLOT, STEP
  ~ starter INTER
  ~ (suffix) ENCE, ISM

___ action CLASS

___-action LIVE

actionable
  ~ wrong TORT

activate ENABLE, START
  ~ as a bomb ARM
  ~ as an alarm TRIP

active ABOUT, AGILE, ALIVE, LIVE
  ~ one DOER
  ~ starter OVER, RADIO, RETRO
  become ~ STIR
  not ~ IDLE, INERT
  very ~ AGILE

activist DOER
  ~ campus org. SDS
  ~ concern CAUSE

activity ADO, LABOR

"Act of the ___, The" HEART

actor DOER, LIAR, POSER
  ~ direction ENTER, EXIT
  ~ goal PART, ROLE
  ~ workplace SET, STAGE

actors CAST
  ~ org. SAG

acts DOES

"Acts of Faith"
  ~ author SEGAL

actual ALIVE, REAL, TRUE
  ~ performance DEED

actuality FACT

actuary
  ~ concern AGE, RATE

actuate AROUSE, IMPEL, MOVE

"Act your ___!" AGE

Acuff ROY

acumen SENSE, TACT, TASTE, WIT

acuminate EDGE, HONE

acupuncture
  life force, in ~ CHI

___ a customer ONETO

acute KEEN

acute ___ ANGLE

ad BILL
  ~ award CLIO
  ~ infinitum EVER
  ~ sign NEON
  ~ spiel HYPE
  ~ word FREE, NEW, SALE
  place the same ~ RERUN

ad ___ REM

___ ad WANT

A.D.
  ~ coiner BEDE
  part of ~ ANNO

"Ada"
  ~ director MANN

ADA
  ~ member DDS

adage GNOME, MORAL, MOT, SAW

adagio SLOW, TEMPO
  ~ cousin LENTO

Adah
  ~ husband ESAU

Adair RED

Adam ANT, BEDE
  ~ grandson ENOS
  ~ habitation EDEN
  ~ mate EVE
  ~ son ABEL, CAIN, SETH
  ~ to Ben SON
  bone taken from ~ RIB

Adam and Eve
  ~ locale EDEN

adamant STERN, STONE

adamantine STERN

"Adam Bede"
  ~ author ELIOT

"Adam had 'em"
  ~ author NASH

Adams DOC, DON, EDIE, SAM

Adam's
  ~ ale WATER

Adam's ___ APPLE

Adam's ___ (water) ALE

"Adam's ___" RIB

"___ Adams" ALICE

___ Adams ("Nearer, My God, to Thee" writer) SARAH

Adams, Ansel
  ~ tool CAMERA

Adams, Gerry
  ~ land EIRE
  ~ org. IRA

Adams, John
  ~ "excellent instrument" PEN

Adams, Nick
  ~ series, with "The" REBEL

Adamson
  ~ pet ELSA

Adams, Samuel BEER

"___ a Dancer" IAM

adapt EDIT, FIT, SUIT

adaptation
  mus. ~ ARR

"___ a Dark Shadow" CAST

"___ a day..., An" APPLE

ADC ASST
  part of ~ AIDE

add TOT
  ~ a fringe to EDGE
  ~ beauty to ADORN
  ~ bubbles to AERATE
  ~ embellishment ADORN
  ~ icing to TOP
  ~ liquor to LACE
  ~ more cells GROW
  ~ (on) TAG
  ~ oxygen to AERATE

~ some color TINT
  ~ to AMEND, PAD
  ~ to a database ENTER
  ~ to a scrapbook PASTE
  ~ to the payroll HIRE
  ~ to the pot ANTE
  ~ to, unnecessarily PAD
  ~ up SUM, TOTAL
  ~ water to THIN
  ~ years AGE

Addams JANE

Addams Family
  ~ cousin ITT

"Addams Family, The"
  ~ dance TANGO

added MORE, OTHER
  ~ cost EXTRA

addendum EXTRA, RIDER, TAG

adder ASP, SNAKE

Adderley
  ~ instrument ALTO, SAX

adder's-tongue FERN

Addis Ababa CITY
  ~ loc. ETH

Addison
  ~ partner STEELE

addition ELL, EXTRA, RIDER
  ~ column ONES, TENS
  ~ problem SUM
  architectural ~ ELL
  in ~ AGAIN, ALSO, AND, ELSE, MORE, OVER, PLUS, THEN, TOO, YET
  in ~ (prefix) SUR

additional ADDED, ELSE, EXTRA, MORE, NEW, OTHER
  ~ (prefix) SUR
  something ~ PLUS

additionally ALSO, AND, ELSE, YET

additive
  Chinese food ~ MSG

addle DAZE, SPOIL

addled ASEA, ATSEA

addlepated DAFT

add-on PLUS
  bill ~ RIDER
  diner's ~ TIP

address ABODE, HOME, MAIL, NAME, ORATE, TAG, TALK, WOO
  ~ abbr. AVE, HTS, RTE
  ~ abbrs. RDS, STS
  ~ for a knight SIR
  ~ for a lady MAAM
  ~ the villain BOO, HISS
  ~ to SEND
  Andover ~ SIR
  Army ~ SIR
  chairwoman's ~ MADAM
  change one's ~ MOVE
  courteous ~ MAAM
  formal ~ SIR
  Friend's ~ THEE
  general's ~ SIR
  how to ~ a lady MAAM

king's ~ SIRE
lady's ~ MADAM
majestic ~ SIRE
make an ~ ORATE
military ~ SIR
palindromic ~ MAAM
queen's ~ MAAM
respectful ~ MAAM, MADAM, SIR
Round Table ~ SIR
royal ~ SIRE
sahib's ~ SRI

adduce CITE

adduct DRAW

ade
~ starter LEMON, LIME, ORANGE

Adelaide CITY, PORT
see also Australian

Adele
~ to Fred SIS

Aden CITY, PORT

Adenauer
see German

adept ABLE, ACE, GOOD, NEAT

adeptness EASE

adequate ABLE, AMPLE, DUE, FAIR, OKAY, SOSO
be ~ SERVE
more than ~ AMPLE
not ~ SCANT

adhere BIND, GLUE, HOLD
~ to OBEY

adherent PASTE
~ (suffix) IST, ITE

adhesive GLUE, PASTE, SEAL

adhesive ___ TAPE

ad hoc
~ coalition BLOC

Adidas
~ rival NIKE

adieu
bid ~ LEAVE

"Adieu!"
~ in Hawaiian ALOHA
~ in Italian CIAO
~ in Latin AVE, VALE
~ in Spanish ADIOS

"Adios!"
~ in French ADIEU
~ in Hawaiian ALOHA
~ in Italian CIAO
~ in Latin AVE, VALE

adipose LARD, OILY
~ tissue FAT

Adirondacks RANGE

adit LANE

adjacent CLOSE, NEAR, NEXT
be ~ to ABUT

adjective
~ suffix ENT, EST, ILE, INE, ISH

adjoin ABUT, TAG

adjoining NEAR, NEXT

adjourn CLOSE, DEFER, STAY

adjt. ASST

adjudge AWARD, RATE

adjudicate HEAR, TRY

adjuration URGE

adjure ASK, BEG, BID, PLEAD, PRAY, SUE, URGE

adjust ADAPT, ALINE, ALTER, AMEND, FIT, RESET, SET, SUIT, TRUE, TUNE
~ the sails TRIM
~ the size ALTER

adjustable
~ loop NOOSE

adjusted
become ~ ADAPT

adjustments
make ~ ADAPT

adjutant AIDE
~ (abbr.) ASST

Adlai
~ opponent IKE
~ running mate ESTES

Adler LOU

Adler, Miss
~ (Sherlock's beloved) IRENE

ADM
~ branch USN

administer DEAL, USE
~ medicine to DOSE

administration REIGN, TERM
current ~ INS

administrator HEAD
~ briefly EXEC

admirable GOOD
~ act FEAT

admiral RANK
~ org. USN
WWI German ~ SPEE

___ admiral REAR

Admiralty ___ RANGE

admiration AWE
murmur of ~ OOH

admire ADORE, ESTEEM, HONOR, LIKE
~ maybe OGLE
~ oneself PREEN

admired
~ one HERO, IDOL

admirer BEAU, FAN

admissible LEGAL

admission ENTREE, ENTRY, SLIP
free ~ PASS
price of ~ FARE
select for ~ TAP

admission ___ FEE

admit ALLOW, AVOW, OWN
~ to LETON

admittance ENTREE, ENTRY

admitted
be ~ ENTER

admitting
~ customers OPEN
~ men and women COED

admonish RAP, URGE, WARN

admonisher
~ comment TSK

admonition
~ to Nanette NONO
parent's ~ DONT

ado FLAP, STIR

Ado ___ ("Oklahoma!" role) ANNIE

Ado Annie
what ~ "could" say YES

adobe CLAY
~ ingredient STRAW

"___: a Dog" LAD

adolescent KID, TEEN
~ affliction ACNE

Adolph OCHS

Adolphe SAX

"Adonais" POEM
last word of ~ ARE

Adonis
slayer of ~ BOAR

___-a-dope ROPE

adopt PASS, TAKE

adoption
~ org. SPCA

adorable CUTE

adoration AWE

adore EXALT, HONOR, LAUD, LIKE, LOVE

adored
~ one IDOL

Adorée RENEE

adorer
~ poem ODE

adorn ARRAY, ATTIRE, BEAD, DRAPE, DRESS, ROBE, TRIM
~ an i DOT

adornment LACE, PIN, TRIM
bit of ~ BEAD

___ a dozen, a DIME

Adrastea MOON

adrenaline
~ catalyst FEAR

Adrian POPE

Adriatic SEA
~ ctry. ALB
~ resort island LIDO

adrift LOST

adroit ABLE, CLEAN, DEFT, NEAT
~ starter MAL

adroitness ART, EASE, TACT

adscititious NEW

adulate ADORE

adulated
~ one IDOL

adulation LOVE

adult
~ male MAN

adulterate TAINT, THIN

adulterated CUT

adulteration TAINT

adult-to-be KID, TEEN

adumbrate BLUR

advance ASSERT, COME, GAIN, HELP, LEAD, LEND, LOAN, MOVE, NEAR, PASS, PAY, POSE, RISE, STEP
~ indication OMEN
~ info TIP
~ obliquely SIDLE
~ rudely ELBOW
cash ~ LOAN
go in ~ LEAD
in ~ AHEAD
in ~ (prefix) PRE

advanced
~ deg. MBA, PHD
more ~ in age ELDER

advantage ASSET, AVAIL, EDGE, ODDS, SAKE
put to ~ USE
set off to ~ ADORN
take ~ AVAIL
take ~ of ABUSE, USE
use to best ~ AVAIL

advantageous GOOD, UTILE
be ~ PAY

advantages INS

adventitious ALIEN, EXTRA

adventure CAPER, DARE, LARK, SAGA
~ story GEST, GESTE
grand-scale ~ SAGA
tale of ~ EPIC

"___ Adventure" ROME

"Adventures of ___ Juan" DON

"Adventures of ___ Munchausen, The" BARON

"Adventures of Huckleberry Finn"
~ director HUNT

"Adventures of Ichabod and Mr. ___, The" TOAD

"Adventures of Martin ___, The" EDEN

adventurous RASH
be ~ DARE
not ~ STAID

adverb
  ~ for a poet ANEAR, EEN, EER, ENOW, NEER, OER, OFT, YON
  archaic ~ ERST

adversary ENEMY, FOE

adverse AVERSE, BAD, ILL

adversity TRIAL, WOE
  overcome ~ WIN

advertence CARE

advertise BILL, BLARE, POST

advertisement SIGN

advertising
  ~ award CLIO
  ~ sign NEON
  ~ trademark LOGO
  extravagant ~ HYPE

advice TIP
  ~ columnist ANN
  ~ often DONT
  broker's ~ SELL
  piece of ~ STEER, TIP
  take ~ HEED

"Advice fo' Chillun"
  ~ cartoonist CAPP

Advil
  ~ target ACHE, PAIN

advisable WISE

advise ALERT, LEAD
  ~ against DETER

___-advised ILL

advisor AIDE, DEAN
  chief ~ ELDER
  fin. ~ CPA
  leg. ~ ATT, ATTY
  personal ~ GURU

advisory ALERT
  ~ group PANEL

advocate ASSERT, URGE
  ~ (suffix) IST, ITE
  author's ~ AGENT, REP
  auto-safety ~ NADER

advocates BAR
  ~ org. ABA

adytum ALTAR

adz AXE, HACK, TOOL

adzuki BEAN

A&E
  part of ~ ARTS

aedile ROMAN
  ~ garb TOGA

Aegean SEA
  ~ island COS, CRETE, KOS
  ancient ~ region IONIA

aegis ARMOR

Aeneas HERO
  ~ city ROME
  ~ home TROY
  lover of ~ DIDO

"Aeneid" EPIC, EPOS, POEM
  ~ locale TROY

aeonian ETERNAL

aerate AIR, FAN

aerator
  soil ~ ROOT

aerial
  ~ maneuver LOOP, SPIN
  ~ support MAST

aerialist
  ~ safeguard NET
  like an ~ AGILE

aerie LAIR, NEST

Aer Lingus
  ~ land EIRE, ERIN

aerobatic
  ~ maneuver LOOP

aerobic
  ~ measure PULSE

aerobics
  ~ center SPA
  ~ class aftereffect ACHE

aerodynamic SLEEK

aeronaut PILOT

Aerospatiale
  ~ product SST

AES
  ~ opponent DDE

Aesir
  ~ VIP ODIN
  like the ~ NORSE

Aesop
  ~ character ANT
  ~ lesson MORAL
  like ~'s grapes SOUR

aesthete
  ~ passion ARTS

aesthetic
  putting on ~ airs ARTY

afar APART
  not ~ ANEAR

___ a fashion (sort of) AFTER

AFC
  ~ division WEST

"___ a Few Dollars More" FOR

affability EASE

affable MILD, SUAVE

affair CASE, EVENT, LOVE
  ~ of honor DUEL
  evening ~ SOIREE
  fancy ~ FETE, GALA

"___ Affair" LOVE

affaire d'honneur DUEL

affaires d'___ ETAT

affairs
  state of ~ LIFE, PASS, SIZE

"Affair to Remember, An"
  ~ actress KERR

affect ADOPT, APE, FAKE, HIT, MOVE
  ~ emotionally GET

  ~ strongly STIR

affectation ACT, AIR, CAMP, POSE

affected ARTY, VAIN
  ~ manner AIRS

affectedness POSE

affection ESTEEM, LOVE
  evoke ~ ENDEAR
  lavish ~ DOTE
  show ~ KISS

affectionate
  ~ gesture KISS
  ~ sound COO
  ~ term DEAR

affiche BILL, SIGN

affidavit
  present an ~ ATTEST

affiliate ALLY, BAND, UNITE

affiliated AKIN

affiliation TIE
  pol. ~ DEM, IND, REP

affined KIN

affinity LOVE, TASTE
  have an ~ for LEAN

affirm ASSERT, ATTEST, AVER, AVOW, STATE

affirmation OATH
  terse ~ IDO

affirmative AYE, YEA, YES
  ~ gesture NOD
  astronaut's ~ AOK
  pilot's ~ ROGER
  sailor's ~ AYE
  slangy ~ SURE, YEAH, YEP

affix ADD, LASH, PASTE, PIN, TAG
  ~ a seal STAMP
  ~ one's name SIGN

afflict AIL, RACK, REND

afflicted AILED, ILL
  are ~ with HAVE

affliction BANE, CARE, EVIL, ILL, TRIAL, WOE

affluence EASE

affluent FAT, RICH

afford BEAR, SPARE
  ~ entrance to ADMIT

affray MELEE, RIOT

affright ALARM, COW, SCARE

affront ANGER, BARB, CUT, SLAP, SLUR, SNUB

affronted IRATE, SORE

afghan WRAP

Afghan
  ~ neighbor IRANI

Afghanistan
  ~ continent ASIA
  ~ neighbor IRAN

aficionado FAN, NUT

afire AVID, LIT

AFL
  part of ~ AMER, FED

afloat ASEA, ATSEA, AWASH
  stay ~ SWIM

aflutter
  all ~ AGOG

"___ a Fool" SHES

afoot
  it may be ~ GAME

afore ERE

aforementioned ABOVE, SAID, SAME

afoul
  run ~ of ANGER, IRK, PEEVE, RILE, UPSET

___ afoul of RUN

Afr.
  ~ nation ETH
  ~ neighbor EUR

A-frame
  ~ feature EAVE
  ~ site LOT

afreet DEMON

afresh ANEW, OVER

Africa
  ~ largest city CAIRO

"Africa"
  ~ band TOTO

African
  ~ antelope ELAND, GNU
  ~ beast HYENA, LION
  ~ capital ACCRA, CAIRO, DAKAR, RABAT
  ~ country MALI, TOGO
  ~ delta NILE
  ~ desert SAHARA
  ~ despot AMIN
  ~ fly TSETSE
  ~ gazelle ARIEL
  ~ lake CHAD
  ~ language BANTU, IBO
  ~ lily ALOE
  ~ linguistic group BANTU
  ~ menace CROC, TSETSE
  ~ native BANTU, IBO
  ~ river NIGER, NILE
  ~ ruminant OKAPI
  ~ snake ASP, COBRA
  ~ sorceress of fiction SHE
  ~ tribe BANTU
  ~ village STAD

"African Queen, The" BOAT
  ~ screenwriter AGEE

Afrikaner BOER

aft ASTERN, REAR
  farther ~ AFTER

AFT
  ~ rival NEA
  part of ~ AMER, FED

after LATER, PAST
  ~ a bit LATER
  ~ curfew LATE
  ~ in French APRES
  ~ (prefix) EPI

~ the style of ALA
~ the whistle LATE

__ after (resemble) TAKE

__ after (tend to) SEE

after a __ (haphazardly) SORT

after-bath
~ wear ROBE

"After Dark, My __" SWEET

"After Dark, My Sweet"
~ actress DERN

after-dinner
~ candy MINT
~ drink PORT

aftereffect SCAR, TRAIL

after-hours
~ joint BAR

aftermath EVENT, TRAIL, TRAIN

aftermost LAST

afternoon
~ gathering TEA
~ ritual NAP
early ~ ONE, TWO

afterpiece TAG

after-school
~ org. PTA
~ treat OREO

after-shave
~ powder TALC

aftershock TREMOR

after-shower
~ wear ROBE

aftertaste TANG

"After the __ Man" THIN

"After the Bath"
~ painter DEGAS

"After the Thin __" MAN

"...after they've __ Paree" SEEN

afterward LATER, NEXT, THEN

"Afton Water" POEM

AFTRA
~ cousin SAG

"__ a Fugitive From a Chain Gang" IAM

Ag ELEM
~ std. STER
47 for ~ ATNO

A.G.
part of ~ ATT, ATTY, GEN

aga RULER, TITLE

Aga __ KHAN

again ANEW, MORE, OVER
~ and again OFT, OFTEN
begin ~ RENEW

"__ Again (Naturally)" ALONE

against ANTI, AVERSE, CON
~ (prefix) ANTI

"...against __ of troubles" ASEA

"__ Against" (Dick Francis novel) ODDS

"Against All __" ODDS

"__ Against Harry, The" PLOT

"__ Against Thebes" SEVEN

"...__ against the dying of the light" RAGE

"__ Against Tomorrow" ODDS

Agamemnon
~ sister-in-law HELEN
~ to Atreus SON
Orestes, to ~ SON

agape LOVE, OPEN

Agassi ANDRE

Agassiz LAKE

agate TYPE
~ origin LAVA

Agatha
colleague of ~ ERLE

agave
~ fiber SISAL

agcy. ORG

age DATE, DAY, EPOCH, ESTATE, RIPEN
~ on the vine RIPEN
a coon's ~ YEARS
important ~ EPOCH, ERA
in this day and ~ NOW
more advanced in ~ ELDER
of ~ ADULT
of an ~ ERAL
proofs of ~ IDS
show one's ~ DATE

age-__ OLD

__ Age IRON, NEW, SPACE, STONE

aged OLD
~ person ELDER

ageless ETERNAL

agency ORGAN
~ worker TEMP

agenda BILL, LIST, PLAN
~ component ITEM
guide's ~ TOUR

agent CAUSE, FED, GMAN, REP, TMAN
~ cut TENTH
~ quest ROLE
anti-drug ~ NARC
bleaching ~ LEMON, OZONE
cleansing ~ SOAP
coloring ~ DYER, PAINT
DEA ~ NARC
double ~ MOLE, SPY
drain-unclogging ~ LYE
emulsifying ~ AGAR
federal ~ GMAN, NARC, TMAN
intelligence ~ SPY
IRS ~ TMAN
maturing ~ AGER
polishing ~ EMERY
ripening ~ AGER
secret ~ SPY
softening ~ ALOE

tanning ~ SUN
thickening ~ AGAR
Treasury ~ TMAN
U.N.C.L.E. ~ SOLO
undercover ~ MOLE, PLANT, SPY

__ agent FBI, FREE, IRS, PRESS

Agent
~ 86 SMART
~ 99's partner SMART

Agent __ ORANGE

agents
~ org. FBI
immunizing ~ SERA

"Age of Aquarius"
~ musical HAIR

ages EON
~ ago YORE
from ~ past OLD

"__ Ages" THREE

agglomerate AMASS, CLOT, WED

agglomeration MASS, PILE

agglutinate ADHERE, BIND

aggrandize EXALT, GROW, PAD

aggravate ANGER, FRET, IRK, PEEVE, RILE, TEASE, UPSET

aggravation BANE

aggregate ALL, AMASS, MASS, SUM, TOTAL
~ assets ESTATE

aggregation BAND, PILE

aggressive EAGER, GOGO, HARD
~ sort TIGER

aggressor ENEMY, FOE
Olympian ~ ARES

aggrieve CUT, PAIN

aggrieved SORE

aghast
stand ~ PALE

"__ a Gift" ITS

agile DEFT, FLEET, LITHE, SPRY

agin
~ cousin ANTI
not ~ FER

"__ a girl!" ITS

agitate ALARM, ANGER, AROUSE, BEAT, FAN, FRET, MOVE, RILE, ROIL, ROUSE, STIR, TOSS, UPSET

agitated IRATE, TENSE, UPSET
~ state SNIT
be ~ STEW

agitation ADO, FIT, YEAST

agitator REBEL

"Aglaura" POEM

agleam LIT

aglow LIT, LIVE, RED

agnate KIN

Agnes STE
see also French

__ Agnes' Eve SAINT

"Agnes of __" GOD

agnomen NAME

"Agnus __" DEI

"__ agnus Dei" ECCE

ago PAST
~ in German VON
~ in Scottish SYNE
long ~ EARLY, OLD, ONCE, PAST, YORE

__ ago LONG

agog AVID, EAGER, KEEN
all ~ KEEN

agonize FRET, STEW

agonizing HARD

agony PAIN, RACK

agora
~ wear TOGA
modern ~ MALL

Agra CITY
~ attire SARI

agraffe CLASP

"__ a grand old flag..." YOURE

agrarian RURAL

agree ADMIT, GIBE, NOD, SIT
~ on a contract SIGN
~ silently NOD
~ to ALLOW, LET
~ upon SETTLE
~ with SIDE, SUIT

agreeable EASY, NICE, SWEET

agreed
~ upon SET

"Agreed!" AMEN

agreeing ALIKE, ASONE, ATONE

agreement DEAL, PACT, SYNC, TUNE
~ component TERM
in ~ ASONE, ATONE, ONE, SOLID
in full ~ ATONE
nonverbal ~ NOD
rental ~ LEASE
security ~ LIEN
show ~ NOD
slangy ~ YEAH, YEP
word of ~ AMEN, AYE, YES

Agricola ROMAN

agricultural RURAL

agriculture
goddess of ~ CERES

Agri Dagi
~ to Turks ARARAT

Agrippa
see Latin

Agrippina ROMAN
Nero, to ~ SON

aground
  where ships run ~ REEF

agt.
  Secret Service ~ TMAN

ague
  ~ cousin FLU

"Aguirre: The Wrath of ___"
  GOD

Agulhas CAPE

"Ah ___" (Harte story) SIN

"Ah!" ISEE, OHO

"Ah! ___!" (Donnie Iris song)
  LEAH

"Aha!" ISEE

Ahab
  ~ god BAAL

"Ahab the ___" ARAB

___ a hand LEND

___ a handle on GET

ahead
  ~ of its time NEW
  ~ of schedule EARLY
  be ~ LEAD
  end up ~ WIN
  forge ~ LEAD, PRESS
  get ~ ARRIVE, RISE
  get ~ of LEAD, PASS
  go ~ MOVE, PASS
  go ~ with START
  look ~ PLAN
  move ~ slowly NOSE
  nudge ~ SPEED
  on ~ ALONG
  opposite of ~ ASTERN
  push ~ NOSE

___ ahead (succeed) GET

"___ a heart!" HAVE

"Ahem!" PSST, PST

Ahenobarbus CAESAR

"___ a hike!" TAKE

"Ah, me!" ALAS

Ahmed ALI

Ah Sin
  ~ creator HARTE

"Ah, Wilderness!"
  ~ character NAT

"Ah, Wilderness were Paradise ___!" ENOW

aid ABET, ASSET, EASE, ENABLE, HELP
  ~ in wrongdoing ABET
  ~ partner ABET

___ aid FIRST, LEGAL

___-Aid BAND

Aïda SLAVE

"Aïda" OPERA
  ~ opener ACTI
  ~ piece ARIA
  ~ stage set TOMB
  where ~ premiered CAIRO

aid and ___ ABET

aide
  ~ (abbr.) ASST
  Congressional ~ PAGE
  dictator's ~ STENO
  horror-film ~ IGOR
  pastry chef's ~ ICER
  Senate ~ PAGE

aide-de-___ CAMP

___ Aid Society LEGAL

aiguille CRAG

Aiken, Conrad POET
  see also poet

Aikman TROY
  ~ asset ARM

ail ACHE

aileron FLAP

ailing ILL, LOW
  ~ perhaps ABED

ailment FLU, ILL
  ~ ender ITIS
  eye ~ STY, STYE
  modern ~ STRESS
  winter ~ AGUE, FLU, STREP

aim CAUSE, END, ESSAY, EYE, GOAL, SAKE, TENOR, TRAIN, TRY, TURN
  ~ at SHOOT
  ~ (for) ANGLE
  ~ (to) MEAN

aimless IDLE

"Ain't ___ Sweet?" SHE

"Ain't No Way to ___ a Lady" TREAT

"Ain't She Sweet?"
  ~ composer AGER

"Ain't Too Proud to ___" BEG

Ainu ASIAN

air ARIA, AROMA, AURA, FEEL, GAS, LILT, MIEN, PSALM, RELATE, SONG, TUNE
  ~ anew RERUN
  ~ breather's organ LUNG
  ~ cooler FAN
  ~ freight MAIL
  ~ hero ACE
  ~ holder LUNG
  ~ hole NOSE
  ~ homophone ERE
  ~ in syndication RERUN
  ~ monitoring org. EPA
  ~ pollution SMOG
  ~ (prefix) AER, AERO, ATM
  ~ quality tester EPA
  ~ resistance DRAG
  ~ route LANE
  ~ strike RAID
  ~ to a poet ETHER
  ~ traveler's bane WAIT
  be up in the ~ PEND
  castle in the ~ DREAM
  earth's ~ env. ATM
  fight for ~ GASP
  fill the ~ RING
  fresh ~ OZONE

hot ~ GAS, TALK, TRASH
  in the ~ ABOUT, ALOFT
  lacking fresh ~ CLOSE
  live on ~ FAST
  mountain ~ YODEL
  navigate in ~ AVIATE
  put on the ~ RADIO
  something in the ~ ODOR
  stir the ~ FAN
  up in the ~ ABOVE, ALOFT, OPEN
  walking on ~ ELATED

air ___ BAG, BALL, BASE, HOLE, MAIL, MASS, RIFLE, TAXI

___ air HOT

___-air OPEN

air battle
  ~ star ACE

airborne
  ~ particulates ASH

Airbus PLANE

___ Air, Calif. BEL

air conditioned COOL

air conditioner
  ~ feature FAN

air conditioning
  ~ meas. BTU

aircraft PLANE
  ~ walkway AISLE

airfoil FIN

Air Force
  ~ missile THOR
  ~ org. SAC

"Air Force ___" ONE

Air Force One JET

Air France
  ~ destination ORLY
  ~ plane SST

air freshener
  ~ asset SCENT
  ~ brand GLADE
  ~ scent LILAC, PINE
  ~ target ODOR

air gun
  ~ ammo BBS

airhead DODO, DOLT

airline ANA, DELTA, ELAL, IBERIA, SAS, TWA
  ~ employee AGENT, PILOT
  ~ from Lod ELAL
  ~ to Jerusalem ELAL
  ~ to Stockholm SAS
  ~ to Tel Aviv ELAL
  ~ to Tokyo ANA
  European ~ IBERIA, SAS
  Israeli ~ ELAL
  St. Louis-based ~ TWA
  western ~ ALOHA

airliner JET, PLANE

airman RANK

airplane JET, LINER
  ~ access RAMP

~ maneuver LOOP
  ~ part FLAP, NOSE
  ~ tracker RADAR
  ~ walkway AISLE
  kind of ~ PROP
  model ~ TOY
  paper ~ part FLAP

airport
  ~ abbr. ARR, ETA
  ~ corridor RAMP
  ~ exit GATE
  ~ parking area APRON
  ~ queue CABS
  ~ shuttle BUS
  ~ transit CAB
  ~ vehicle LIMO
  Chicago ~ OHARE
  Paris ~ ORLY
  Windy City ~ OHARE

air pressure
  ~ meas. ATM, PSI

air pump
  ~ abbr. ATM, PSI

air raid
  ~ warning ALERT

airs
  one with ~ SNOB
  put on ~ POSE
  putting on aesthetic ~ ARTY

air show
  ~ maneuver LOOP

airtight
  it may be ~ ALIBI, CASE

air traffic
  ~ detector RADAR

airway LANE, ROUTE

airy OPEN, THIN

aisle ROW
  lead down the ~ USHER
  walk down the ~ MATE, WED

aisles
  they're between ~ SEATS
  walk the ~ USHER

Aisne
  ~ tributary AIRE

ait ISLE, ISLET
  ~ in French ILE

aitch
  ~ preceder GEE

Aix-en-Provence SPA

Aix-les-Bains SPA

ajar OPEN
  ~ to a poet OPE
  not ~ SHUT

Ajax HERO
  ~ foe DIRT

AK
  ~ once TER, TERR
  see also Alaska

AKA ALIAS

Akela
  ~ org. BSA

Akhmatova ANNA
"___ a Kick out of You" IGET
akimbo BENT
Akins, Claude
 ~ **TV role** LOBO
Akita CITY, DOG, PET, PORT
 ~ **comment** ARF
Akron
 ~ **locale** OHIO
 ~ **product** TIRE
Ak-Sar-Ben
 ~ **Coliseum site** OMAHA
Al CAPP, ELEM, GORE
 13 for ~ ATNO
 veep before ~ DAN
Al-___ ANON
AL
 ~ **stat** HRS, RBI
 see also Alabama
à la ___ CARTE
Ala.
 ~ **neighbor** FLA, MISS, TENN
 see also Alabama
Alabama BAND, STATE
 ~ **town** SELMA
alack
 ~ **partner** ALAS
alacrity FIRE, HASTE
Aladdin ARAB, HERO
"Aladdin"
 ~ **discovery** LAMP
 ~ **monkey** ABU
 ~ **parrot** IAGO
 ~ **prince** ALI
"___ a Lady" SHES
Alai RANGE
___ Alamitos, Calif. LOS
Alamo
 ~ **rival** AVIS
 ~ **st.** TEX
"Alamo, The" OATER
à la mode NEW
___ à la mode PIE
Alamogordo
 ~ **county** OTERO
 ~ **event** ATEST
___ Alamos, N. Mex. LOS
Alan ABEL, ALDA, LADD, PAGE, SUES
Alan Alexander ___ MILNE
alarm ALERT, FEAR, PANIC, SCARE, SIREN, UPSET
 ~ **button** RESET
 ~ **ender** IST
 cause for ~ ALERT
 cry of ~ EEK
 obey the ~ ARISE
 show ~ START
 sound the ~ AROUSE, WARN
 take ~ PALE, SHY

___ alarm FALSE, FIRE
alarm clock
 activate the ~ SET
alarmed
 be ~ **about** FEAR
alarming BAD, DIRE
alarms
 like some ~ FALSE
alarum ALERT
"Alas!" OHNO, WOE
"Alas! ___ Yorick..." POOR
Alas.
 see Alaska
Alaska STATE
 ~ **native** ALEUT
 ~ **vehicle** SLED
 first governor of ~ EGAN
 island off ~ ATTU
Alaskan ALEUT
 ~ **art form** TOTEM
 ~ **cape** NOME
 ~ **city** NOME
 ~ **glacier** MUIR
 ~ **language** ALEUT
 ~ **people** ALEUT
Alaskan king ___ CRAB
"___ a Latin From Manhattan" SHES
Alava CAPE
alb ROBE
Al B. ___ SURE
___ alba TERRA
Alba
 ~ **to Goya** MODEL
albacore TUNA
Alban BERG
___ Albán MONTE
Albania
 former president of ~ ALIA
Albanian-born
 ~ **nun** TERESA
Albany
 ~ **canal** ERIE
 ~ **father-in-law** LEAR
albatross BIRD, LOAD, ONUS
Albee
 "Tiny" ~ character ALICE
Albéniz ISAAC
 ~ **piano opus** IBERIA
albergo HOTEL
Albert BAND, BELLE, EDDIE, LAKE, SABIN
 green for ~ ACRES
___ Albert (Cosby character) FAT
Alberta
 ~ **hockey player** OILER
 ~ **native** CREE
Albert, Prince COAT

Albertville
 ~ **gear** SKI
 sight from ~ ALP
Albion
 ~ **neighbor** EIRE, ERIN
Ålborg CITY, PORT
Albright LOLA
album
 ~ **cover** LINER
albums
 old-fashioned ~ LPS
Albuquerque
 ~ **student** LOBO
Alcan Highway
 ~ **site** ALASKA
alchemist
 ~ **element** AIR, EARTH, FIRE, WATER
alchemy
 element, in ~ AIR
alcohol
 ~ **burner** ETNA
 acid + ~ product ESTER
 high in ~ HARD
alcoholic SOT
 ~ **beverage** ALE, BEER, LAGER, MEAD, PORT, RUM, RYE, SAKE, SAKI, WINE
Alcor STAR
Alcott AMY
 ~ **character** AMY, MEG
alcove ARBOR, BAY, NOOK
 harbor ~ INLET
 park ~ ARBOR
 vaulted ~ APSE
Alcyone STAR
Alda ALAN
 ~ **colleague** FARR
 ~ **series** MASH
Aldebaran STAR
___ al dente PASTA
alder TREE
 ~ **in Scottish** ARN
 scotch ~ ARN
Aldrich AMES
Aldridge IRA
Aldrin, Buzz
 ~ **alma mater** MIT
 ~ **craft** EAGLE
ale BEER, BREW
 ~ **carrier** TAP
 ~ **cousin** BEER, LAGER
 ~ **head** FOAM
 ~ **ingredient** MALT
 ~ **measure** PINT
 Adam's ~ WATER
 how ~ may be offered ONTAP
 Norfolk ~ NOG
 strong ~ NOG
___ ale ADAMS, PALE

___ aleck SMART
alehouse BAR, INN
 ~ **fixture** TAP
Alejandro REY
alembic POT
 ~ **locale** LAB
Alençon LACE
 ~ **department** ORNE
"...___ a lender be" NOR
Aleppo CITY
 ~ **ctry.** SYR
 ~ **land** SYRIA
alert ALARM, ALIVE, AROUSE, AWARE, WARN, WARY
 ~ **color** RED
 air-raid ~ SIREN
 golf ~ FORE
 highway ~ FLARE
 naval ~ SOS
 police radio ~ APB
 put on the ~ ALARM
 speaker's ~ AHEM
 theatrical ~ CALL
Alessandro
 see Italian
Aleta, Queen
 ~ **son** ARN
"___ a Letter, Darling" TAKE
Aleut
 ~ **carving** TOTEM
Aleutian
 ~ **abode** IGLOO
 ~ **island** ATTU
Aleutians RANGE
Alex SEGAL
Alexander HAIG, HALL, POPE, TSAR
 ~ **group** BAND
 ~ **stratagem** SIEGE
 adjective for ~ GREAT
"Alexander's Ragtime ___" BAND
"Alexander the ___" GREAT
Alexandre
 see French
Alexandria CITY, PORT
Alexei
 see Russian
Alexis KIM, TSAR
 see also Russian
ALF ALIEN
 ~ **and others** ETS
 ~ **covering** FUR
Alfa ___ ROMEO
alfalfa HAY
Alfalfa
 ~ **to Spanky** PAL
"Alfie"
 ~ **actor** CAINE
Alfonso REY
 ~ **mate** ENA

~ queen ENA
see also Italian

alforja BAG

Alfred ADLER

"Alfred"
~ composer ARNE

alfresco
place for ~ meals PATIO

alga PLANT

algebra MATH

Alger HISS

Algeria
~ neighbor MALI, NIGER

Algerian
~ governor DEY
~ port ORAN

Algiers CITY, PORT

Algol STAR

Algonquian CREE
~ language CREE

Algonquin
~ transport CANOE

Algonquin Round Table
~ member WIT

Ali
~ faith ISLAM
~ formerly CLAY
~ stat KOS
~ stung like one BEE
what ~ stung like ABEE

"Ali ___ and the Forty Thieves" BABA

___ alia INTER

alias AKA, NAME
~ for short NOM
~ in Spanish MOTE
Barge Canal's ~ ERIE
essayist's ~ ELIA
literary ~ SAKI

Ali Baba ARAB, HERO
~ command OPEN
locale for ~ CAVE

alibi OUT, TALE
~ guy IKE

Alibi ___ IKE

"___ Alibi" HER

Alicante
see Spanish

Alice
~ boss MEL
~ chronicler ARLO
~ restaurant MELS
like ~'s Hatter MAD

"Alice"
~ diner MELS
~ role FLO, VERA
~ spinoff FLO
diner owner on ~ MEL
she played Alice in ~ MIA

"Alice ___" ADAMS

"___ Alice" TINY

"Alice Doesn't ___ Here Anymore" LIVE

"Alice Doesn't Live ___ Anymore" HERE

"Alice in Wonderland"
~ cat DINAH

"Alice's Restaurant"
~ director PENN
~ name ARLO

___-Alicia ANA

alien EXILE, LONER
~ spacecraft UFO
Melmac ~ ALF
TV ~ ALF

"Alien"
~ director SCOTT

___ alienae RES

alienate REPEL

"Alienist, The"
~ author CARR

aliens ETS

"Aliens"
~ character NEWT

"___ a life!" GET

___ Alighieri DANTE

alight ARRIVE, LAND, LIT, SETTLE

align TRUE
~ the crosshairs AIM

aligned
~ with "in" AROW
properly ~ TRUE

alike BOTH, CLOSE, SAME
group that votes ~ BLOC
think ~ AGREE

aliment DIET, FARE, MEAL

alimentary ___ CANAL

alimony
~ recipients EXES

A-line
~ creator DIOR

___-a-ling DING

"___ a Little Prayer" ISAY

alive
~ and well SAFE
~ to AWARE
~ (with) RIFE

"___ alive!" ITS

"Alive"
~ author READ

"Alive!"
~ band KISS

"___ a Living" ITS

alkali LYE
~ opposite ACID

alkaline
~ derivative LYE

Alka-Seltzer
~ sound PLOP

alky SOT

all
~ in Spanish TODO
~ (prefix) OMNI
~ the time, to a poet EER
~ wound up TENSE
~ you own ESTATE
not at ~, to a poet NEER

all ___ (air-raid signal) CLEAR

all ___ (attentive) EARS

all ___ (completely wrong) WET

all ___ (done) OVER

all ___ (from the start) ALONG

all ___ (in sum) TOLD

all ___ (ready) SET

all ___ sudden OFA

all-___ (complete) OUT

all-___ (outstanding) STAR

___ all ABOVE, AFTER

___-all CURE, END

All
~ rival DASH, ERA, TIDE

"All ___" ATSEA

"All ___!" (court phrase) RISE

"All ___ and Heaven Too" THIS

"All ___ are off!" BETS

"All ___ day's work" INA

"All ___ Eve" ABOUT

"All ___ Heaven Allows" THAT

"All ___ Jazz" THAT

"All ___ that's going..." ASHORE

"All ___ the Watchtower" ALONG

All-___ BRAN

"All About ___" EVE, SOUL

"All About Eve"
Margo, in ~ BETTE

Allah LORD
worship of ~ ISLAM

"All Alone ___" AMI

"___ All Alone" WERE

all along the ___ LINE

Allan-a-___ DALE

___ Allan Poe EDGAR

"All at ___" SEA

allay ABATE, CALM, EASE, HELP
~ as thirst SLAKE

"All Creatures ___ and Small" GREAT

allege ASSERT, AVER, AVOW, CLAIM, SAY, STATE, URGE

Alleghenies RANGE

"Allegheny ___" MOON

allegiance
bear ~ ADHERE

allegiant TRUE

allegory TALE

"Allegory of Love, The"
~ author LEWIS

Allegret MARC

allegro RAPID, TEMPO

allele GENE

alleluia PSALM

allemande DANCE

all-embracing BIG, LARGE, TOTAL, VAST, WIDE

Allen ETHAN, FRED, LEWIS, MEL, STEVE, TATE, TIM
~ successor PAAR

___ Allen belt VAN

Allen, Ethan
~ brother IRA

Allen, Fred WIT
~ milieu RADIO

Allen, Gracie
~ heritage IRISH
~ milieu RADIO

Allen, Tim
~ movie character SANTA

Allentown
~ st. PENN

Allen, Woody
~ film ALICE

allergic
~ reaction ITCH, RASH

Allers ROGER

alleviate ABATE, ALLAY, EASE, HELP, SLAKE

alley LANE, PATH, ROAD
~ button RESET
~ challenge SPLIT
~ score SPARE
~ target PIN
bowling ~ LANE
see also bowling

alley ___ CAT

Alley, Kirstie
~ role HOWE

Alley Oop
~ kingdom MOO

"All Fall Down"
~ subject IRAN

All Fools' ___ DAY

all get ___ OUT

"all gone"
make ~ EAT

Allgood SARA

Allhallows ___ EVE

"All hope abandon, ye who ___ here!" ENTER

alliance AXIS, BAND, BLOC, PACT, TIE, UNION
former Mideast ~ UAR
former Pacific ~ SEATO
oil ~ OPEC
political ~ BLOC
post-WWII ~ NATO
W. Hemisphere ~ OAS
WWII ~ AXIS

Allie
~ TV friend KATE

"___ & Allie" KATE

allied
~ nations BLOC

Allies
~ opponent AXIS

alligator
~ on a shirt LOGO

alligator ___ PEAR

"All I Have to Do Is ___" DREAM

all-inclusive BIG, ENTIRE, LARGE, TOTAL
~ abbr. ETC

"All in the Family"
~ network CBS
~ producer LEAR

"___ all in this together!" WERE

Allison FRAN, ROE
~ on "Peyton Place" MIA

"All kidding ___..." ASIDE

all-knowing WISE

"___ All Mankind" FOR

"All My ___" SONS

"All My Children" SOAP
~ network ABC
~ role ERICA, OPAL
~ villainess KANE
Susan, on ~ ERICA

"All Night ___" LONG

all-nighter EVENT
pull an ~ CRAM

allocate ALLOT, DEAL, METE

allocation DOLE, SHARE

allocution TALK

allodium LAND

allonym ALIAS, NAME

all-or-___ NONE

allot DEAL, DOLE, METE

allotment DOLE, SHARE
~ adverb EACH
pill ~ DOSE

allotted
~ portion LOT, PART

all-out TOTAL, UTTER

"___ All Over" GLAD

allow AGREE, BEAR, LET, LOAN, OPINE
~ as a handicap SPOT
~ to enter ADMIT

~ to ride LETON
~ to use LEND

allowable LEGAL

allowance DOLE, LOT, REBATE, SHARE
scale ~ TARE, TRET

allowed
not ~ TABOO, TABU

allowing
~ a draft AJAR

alloy MELD, METAL
~ component METAL
copper-zinc ~ BRASS
iron ~ STEEL

"All praise to ___" ALLAH

all-purpose
~ abbr. ETC
~ truck UTE

all right OKAY

"All Right Now"
~ band FREE

All Saints' ___ DAY

"All Shook Up"
~ singer ELVIS

All Souls' ___ DAY

All-Star ___ GAME

Allstate
~ owner SEARS

"All systems go" AOK

all the ___ (nevertheless) SAME

all the ___ (popular) RAGE

"All the King's ___" MEN

"All the King's Men"
~ actress DRU

"All the news that's fit to print"
~ coiner OCHS

"All the President's ___" MEN

"All the Things You ___" ARE

"All the Way ___" HOME

"All the Way Home"
~ director SEGAL

"___ All the Way Home" IRAN

"All the world's a ___" STAGE

"All the Young ___" MEN

"All This ___ Heaven Too" AND

"All This and Heaven ___" TOO

"___ All True" ITS

allude HINT, REFER
~ to CITE

allurement BAIT

alluring SWEET
~ woman SIREN

allusion HINT

alluvial ___ FAN

alluvium OOZE, SILT

ally BAND
~ opposite ENEMY, FOE
~ (with) SIDE
Gulf War ~ SYRIA

"All your strength is in your ___" UNION

"All You Wanna Do Is ___" DANCE

Alma-___, Kazakhstan ATA

alma mater
~ visitor ALUM, GRAD

almanac
~ tidbit FACT

Almodóvar PEDRO

almond COLOR, NUT

almond ___ PASTE

Almond PAUL

almost CLOSE, NEAR
~ boil SCALD
~ (prefix) PARA
~ shut AJAR
~ to a poet ANEAR
~ up NEXT

alms DOLE
dispense ~ DOLE
seek ~ BEG

almsgiving AID, HELP

___ a load of GET

aloe PLANT

aloe ___ VERA

aloft ABOVE, AERIAL, OVER, RISEN
gone ~ ARISEN
hit ~ LOB

aloha
~ gift LEI

"Aloha!"
~ in French ADIEU
~ in Italian CIAO
~ in Latin AVE, VALE
~ in Spanish ADIOS

"Aloha Oe"
~ accompaniment UKE

Aloha State
~ city HILO
see also Hawaiian

alone APART, ONLY, SOLO, STAG
~ (prefix) MON

___ alone (don't bother) LEAVE, LET

___-alone STAND

"___ Alone" ALL, HOME, ONE

___ along (cooperate) PLAY

___ along (creep) INCH

___ along (fare) GET

___ along (follow) TAG

___ along (from the start) ALL

___ along (go) RUN

___ along (proceed) COME

___-along SING

"Along ___ a spider..." CAME

"Along ___ Jones" CAME

"Along Came Jones" OATER

along in ___ YEARS

"___ Along Little Dogie" GIT

alongside EVEN
~ (prefix) PARA

"Along the Navajo ___" TRAIL

"___ Along the Watchtower" ALL

"___ a Long Way to Tipperary" ITS

___ Alonzo Stagg AMOS

aloof APART, COOL, ICY
stand ~ SNUB

aloud
wonder ~ ASK

alp PEAK

Alp
~ ender INE

alpaca ANIMAL
~ cousin LLAMA
~ habitat ANDES, PERU

alpenstock CANE, ROD, STAVE

Alpert HERB
~ instrument HORN
~ instrumental RISE

alpha FIRST
~ and omega TOTAL
~ follower BETA
~ opposite OMEGA

alpha and ___ OMEGA

alphabet
~ ender ZEE
~ starters ABC
~ trio ABC, RST, STU

___ alphabet ROMAN

alphabetic
~ trio ABC, RST

alphabetize FILE, LIST, ORDER, SORT

alphabetizers
word ~ ignore THE

Alpha Centauri STAR

alpine TALL

Alpine
~ archer TELL
~ comeback ECHO
~ feature ARETE
~ gear SKI
~ music YODEL
~ river AAR, AARE, ISERE
~ surface SNOW

Alps MTS, RANGE

also AND, PLUS, THEN, TOO
~ known as ALIAS
~ not NOR

also-___ RAN

also-ran LAST, LOSER

"___ Also Rises, The" SUN

alt. ELEV

Alt CAROL, KEY
    emulate ~ MODEL, POSE

Altai RANGE

___-Altaic (language group) URAL

Altair STAR

Altamira CAVE

altar
    ~ activity RITE
    ~ constellation ARA
    ~ item ICON
    ~ neighbor APSE
    ~ robe ALB
    ~ utterance IDO
    path to the ~ AISLE

altar ___ RAIL

Altdorf
    ~ canton URI

"___ Alte" (Adenauer) DER

alter ADAPT, AMEND, EDIT, EMEND, SEW
    ~ by distortion COLOR
    ~ ego PAL
    ~ locks DYE

alter ___ EGO

altercation MELEE, ROW, SCRAP, SETTO, SPAT

alter ego
    fictional ~ HYDE

alternate OTHER

alternating current
    ~ pioneer TESLA

alternative
    ~ wd. SYN

alternatively ELSE

although YET

altiplano
    ~ beast LLAMA

altitudes HTS

Altman, Robert
    ~ film of 1970 MASH

alto RANGE

alto ___ SAX

altogether CLEAN
    in the ~ BARE, NUDE

___ Altos, Calif. LOS

altruistic GOOD

alts. HTS

alum GRAD

aluminum METAL
    ~ boat CANOE
    ~ foil alternative SARAN
    ~ source ORE

aluminum ___ PLANT

alumnus GRAD, MALE

alums
    next year's ~ SRS

Alvarado TRINI

Alvarez LUIS

Alvino REY

alway AYE, EER

always EVER
    ~ existing ETERNAL
    ~ to a poet EER

"___ Always a Woman" SHES

"___ Always Fair Weather" ITS

"___ always liked you best!" MOM

"___ Always Loved You" IVE

"___ always say..." ASI

Alworth LANCE

Aly
    ~ dad AGA

Aly ___ KHAN

Alysheba HORSE

___ alyssum SWEET

___-am PRO

Am ELEM
    95 for ~ ATNO

"Am ___ understand..." ITO

AM
    part of ~ ANTE
    when ~ meets PM NOON

AMA
    ~ member DOC
    ~ members DRS, MDS
    part of ~ AMER, ASSN, MED

"___ a Mad Mad Mad Mad World" ITS

"Amahl and the Night Visitors" OPERA

amain APACE

amalgamate BAND, GROW, MELD, UNITE, WED

Amalthea MOON

"...a man ___ mouse?" ORA

___ amandine SOLE

amanuensis PEN

"...___ a man with seven wives" IMET

amaranthine ETERNAL, RED

___ a march on STEAL

amaryllis AGAVE
    ~ family plant ALOE

___, amas, amat AMO

"___, amas, I love..." AMO

amass KEEP, LOG, PILE, SAVE, STORE

amateur LAY
    ~ opposite PRO

amateurish POOR

amateur radio
    ~ operator HAM

amatol
    ~ ingredient TNT

"___ Amatoria" ARS

amatory
    ~ writing ODE

amaze AWE, DAZE, STUN, WOW

amazed AGAPE, AGOG

amazement AWE
    show ~ GAPE
    word of ~ GEE

"Amazing Grace"
    ~ ending ISEE

Amazon
    ~ origin PERU
    arm of the ~ PARA
    how the ~ flows EAST

amazonite GEM

ambassador AGENT
    ~ asset TACT

amber COLOR, RESIN

"amber nectar" BEER

ambiance AIR, AURA, FEEL, MOOD, TONE

ambit LIMIT, PALE, ROUTE

ambition AIM, GOAL
    one without ~ IDLER

ambitious EAGER
    cry of the ~ MORE

amble PACE, ROVE, STEP

Ambler ERIC

amblygonite ORE

ambulance
    ~ crew mem. EMT
    ~ destinations ERS
    ~ letters EMS
    ~ sound SIREN

ambulate TREAD

ambush TRAP
    shoot from ~ SNIPE

amebas
    ~ have one CELL

Ameche ALAN, DON

Amedeo
    see Italian

ameliorate ALTER, AMEND, EASE, EMEND, HELP

amen
    ~ alternative YEA
    ~ corner PEW

amenable EASY, GAME, OPEN

amend ALTER, EDIT

amendment RIDER
    ~ letters ERA

___ Amendment (civil-rights safeguard) TENTH

amends
    make ~ ATONE, REMIT

Amenhotep IV
    ~ god ATEN, ATON

amenity
    motel ~ ICE, POOL, SAUNA

"___ Amen, Somebody" SAY

Amerada ___ HESS

amerce FINE

America
    England, to ~ ALLY

"America"
    ~ pronoun THEE
    third word of ~ TIS

___ America LATIN

"___ America" MISS

"___ America, The" OTHER

American
    ~ rival DELTA, TWA
    ~ seagoing letters USS

"American ___" HEART, PIE

"American ___ Wax" HOT

"___ American, The" UGLY

___-American AFRO, ALL

Americana
    ~ set ENC

"American Bandstand"
    ~ fan TEEN

American Beauty ROSE

American-born
    first ~ saint SETON

"___ American Cousin" OUR

"___ American Cowboy, The" GREAT

"American Gigolo"
    ~ actor GERE

"American Gladiators"
    ~ regular ICE

"American Graffiti"
    ~ drive-in MELS

"___ American Hero, The" LAST

___-American Highway PAN

"American in ___, An" PARIS

American League
    ~ division EAST, WEST

American Leaguer ANGEL, ORIOLE, TIGER, TWIN

American Legion
    ~ member VET

"American Madness"
    ~ director CAPRA

"American Psycho"
    ~ author ELLIS

American Revolution WAR

"American Tail, An"
  ~ **character** MOUSE

America's Cup AWARD
  ~ **craft** SLOOP

"America's Most Wanted"
  ~ **info** ALIAS

America's Uncle SAM

Ames
  ~ **and others** EDS
  ~ **state** IOWA

Ames, Aldrich
  ex-employer of ~ CIA

amethyst COLOR, GEM

ametrical
  ~ **bard** NASH

AMEX ASE
  ~ **overseer** SEC
  ~ **rival** NYSE
  ~ **unit** SHARE

ami MATE, PAL

___ ami MON

___ Ami BON

"Am I ___?" BLUE

amiable GOOD, MILD, NICE,
  SWEET, WARM
  ~ **look** GRIN, SMILE

amid AMONG

amidst AMONG

Amiens
  see French

amigo MATE, PAL

"___ Amigos" LOS

"___ am I in my speech..." RUDE

Amin EXILE, IDI

amino ___ ACID

amino acid
  ~ **suffix** INE

"___ a Miracle" ITS

Amish SECT

amiss AWRY, FALSE
  go ~ ERR

amity LOVE, PEACE

Amman CITY

ammo LEAD, SHOT
  air-gun ~ BBS
  blowgun ~ DART
  kiddie ~ PEA
  longbow ~ ARROW
  prankster's ~ EGG
  put ~ **in** LOAD
  shooter's ~ PEA
  toy gun ~ CAP

___ ammoniac SAL

ammunition BALL, LEAD, SHOT

Amneris
  ~ **slave** AIDA

Amnesty Intl.
  ~ **concern** MIA

amo, ___, amat AMAS

"Amo, ___, I love a lass" AMAS

amo, amas, ___ AMAT

amo, amas, amat LATIN

amoeba CELL

amok
  run ~ RIOT

Amonasro
  ~ **daughter** AIDA

among AMID
  ~ **in French** ENTRE
  ~ **in Spanish** ENTRE
  ~ **(prefix)** INTER

amongst AMID

"___ Among the Ruins" LOVE

Amor EROS, GOD, LOVE

___ amore CON

"Amores"
  ~ **poet** OVID

amorist BEAU

amorous
  ~ **gaze** LEER

Amos
  ~ **partner** ANDY

"Amos & Andrew"
  ~ **actor** CAGE

amount SIZE, SUM
  ~ **after expenses** NET
  ~ **borrowed** LOAN
  ~ **due** BILL, SCORE
  ~ **taken in** GATE
  ~ **to** COST, MAKE, RUN, TOTAL
  a fair ~ SOME
  bottom-line ~ NET
  break-even ~ COST
  determine the ~ **of** ASSESS
  drug ~ DOSE
  entire ~ SUM
  excessive ~ SPATE
  huge ~ LOTS, PILE, SLEW
  indefinite ~ ANY, SOME
  insignificant ~ CENT, MITE
  large ~ MINT, OCEAN, SCAD,
    SEA
  measured ~ DOSE
  minimal ~ HOOT, IOTA, TRACE
  outstanding ~ DEBT
  prescribed ~ DOSE
  red-ink ~ LOSS
  Rx ~ DOSE
  small ~ ATOM, BIT, DASH, DOT,
    DRAM, DROP, IOTA, MITE,
    SONG, TAD, TRACE
  smaller ~ LESS
  the whole ~ ALL
  tiny ~ BIT, JOT
  unspecified ~ ANY, SOME
  vague ~ SOME
  vitamin ~ DOSE
  wee ~ BIT

amour LOVE

amour-propre EGO

"___, a mouse!" EEK

___ a move on GET

AMPAS
  ~ **trophy** OSCAR

Ampère's ___ LAW

ampersand AND

amphibian EFT, NEWT, PLANE,
  TOAD

amphigoric DAFT, INANE

Amphion
  ~ **instrument** LYRE

amphitheater ARENA, HALL, OVAL
  ~ **section** TIER

amphora JAR, POT, URN, VASE

ample BIG, DUE, GOOD, LARGE,
  RICH

amplified
  ~ **beam** LASER

amplify ADD, GROW, RAISE

amplitude ROOM

AM-PM
  ~ **units** HRS

ampule VIAL

"Amscray!" SCAT, SCRAM, SHOO

Amsterdam CITY
  ~ **neighbor** EDE
  see also Dutch

amt.
  least ~ MIN
  recipe ~ TBS, TSP

Amtrak
  ~ **and others** RRS
  ~ **stop** STA
  ~ **track** RAIL
  see also railroad, train

amuck RABID

Amu Darya
  ~ **outlet** ARAL

Amundsen SEA
  ~ **quest** POLE
  like ~ NORSE

"___ a Murderer" ENTER

amuse PLEASE
  ~ **to the max** SLAY

amused
  ~ **reaction** HAHA
  look ~ GRIN

amusement BAG, GAME, PLAY
  ~ **center** ARCADE
  ~ **for short** REC
  playpen ~ TOY

amusement park
  ~ **feature** RIDE, SLIDE

amusing
  ~ **sort** WAG, WIT

Amy TAN

an ONE

Anabaptist
  ~ **sect** AMISH

___ Ana, Calif. SANTA

anaconda BOA, SNAKE

Anacreon POET
  ~ **subject** WINE
  see also poet

anacreontic POEM

anaglyph CAMEO

anagram
  ~ **for Emile** ELEMI

Anaheim Stadium
  ~ **player** ANGEL

Anaïs NIN
  see also French

analeptic TONIC

analgesic OPIATE
  ~ **target** PAIN
  need an ~ ACHE

analogist
  butterfly-bee ~ ALI

analogize RELATE

analogous AKIN, ALIKE, CLOSE,
  LIKE

analogy
  ~ **phrase** ISTO

analysis ASSAY, TEST

analyst
  ~ **concern** EGO, IDS

analyze ASSAY, SIFT, TEST
  ~ **grammatically** PARSE
  ~ **verse** SCAN

"___ a Name" IGOT

"___ an American Band" WERE

Ananias LIAR
  emulate ~ LIE

Ananke MOON

anapest FOOT
  ~ **kin** IAMB

anarchist REBEL

anarchistic LEFT

Anastasia
  ~ **father** TSAR
  see also Russian

anat. SCI

anathema BAN, BANE

anatomical
  ~ **hinge** KNEE
  ~ **passage** ITER
  ~ **pouch** SAC

anatomist
  early ~ GALEN

"Anatomy ___ Murder" OFA

ancestor ELDER, SIRE

ancestral
  ~ **home** ROOTS
  ~ **image** TOTEM

ancestry CASTE, CLAN, RACE,
  ROOTS

anchor ABIDE, LAND, MOOR, RIVET, SETTLE
~ domain NEWS
~ place DESK
~ race RELAY
botanical ~ ROOT
CNN ~ SHAW
drop ~ LAND
hoist ~ LEAVE
lay at ~ RIDE
lift ~ SAIL
ride at ~ REST
weigh ~ LEAVE

anchorage HAVEN, PORT

Anchorage
~ state ALASKA

anchoress LONER, NUN

anchorite LONER
~ abode CELL
like an ~ LONE

"Anchors Aweigh"
~ branch USN

anchovy
~ sauce ALEC

ancient AGED, EARLY, OLD, PASSE
~ Greek colony IONIA

ancilla MAID

ancillary EXTRA
~ (prefix) PARA

ancon ELBOW

Ancona CITY, PORT

and ALSO, PLUS

and ___ some THEN

"...and ___ grow on!" ONETO

"...and ___ the child" SPOIL

"...and ___ well!" ALLS

"And ___ for Something Completely Different" NOW

"And ___ Miguel" NOW

"And ___ the opposite shore will be" ION

"And ___ There Were None" THEN

___ and aah OOH

___ and abet AID

"...and a bottle of ___" RUM

___ and above OVER

"___ and Aeneas" DIDO

___ and aft FORE

___ and again NOW, TIME

___ and a half TIME

___ and a leg, an ARM

___ and all ONE

"And all ye ___ to know" NEED

Andalusia
see Spanish

___ and anon EVER

andante TEMPO
slower than ~ LENTO

"...and a partridge in a ___ tree" PEAR

"...and a time to ___" HEAL, LOSE, SEW

___ and away FAR

"___ and a Woman" AMAN

"___ and a Woman, A" MAN

___ and Bars STARS

"___ and Bear It" GRIN

"...and bells on her ___" TOES

"___ and Beyond" ABOVE

___ and board BED, ROOM

___ and bolts NUTS

___ and bothered HOT

___ and bounds LEAPS

___ and breakfast BED

___ and caboodle KIT

___ and carry CASH

"___ and Circumstance" POMP

___ and Clark LEWIS

"___ and Clark" LOIS

___ and clear LOUD

"___ and Cleopatra" CAESAR

___ and Coke RUM

___ and con PRO

"___ and Coo" BILL

___ and cranny NOOK

___ and cry HUE

___ and dance SONG

___ and dangerous ARMED

___-and-dart EGG

"___ and Death" LOVE

"___ and Death of Colonel Blimp" LIFE

"___ and Deliver" STAND

___ and desist CEASE

___ and die TOOL

___-and-dime FIVE

___ and dine WINE

"___ and Disorder" LAW

___ and don'ts DOS

___ and downs UPS

___-and-dried CUT

Andean
see Andes

___ and Eddie FLO

___ and effect CAUSE

___ and eggs HAM

___ and ends ODDS

___ and Entertainment Network ARTS

___ and error TRIAL

Andersen, Hans Christian DANE

Anderson IAN, LEROY, LONI

Anderson, Judith DAME

Anderson, Marian ALTO

Andersson ARNE

Andes RANGE
~ animal LLAMA
~ country PERU
~ shrub COCA
~ tuber OCA
former ~ denizen INCA

andesite LAVA

"___ and Essence" APE

___ and every EACH

"___ and Fall of Legs Diamond, The" RISE

"___ and Fall of the Third Reich, The" RISE

___ and far between FEW

"___ and farewell" HAIL

___ and fast HARD

___ and fauna FLORA

___ and feather TAR

___ and file RANK

___ and for all ONCE

___ and foremost FIRST

___ and found LOST

"___ and Future King, The" ONCE

"___ and Get It" COME

"___ and Get Me!" TRY

"___ and Glory" HOPE

___ and grill BAR

___ and groan MOAN

"___ and Harry McGraw, The" LAW

"And hast thou ___ the Jabberwock?" SLAIN

___ and haw HEM

___ and hearty HALE

___ and hiss BOO

___ and holler HOOT

___ and hounds HARE

"___ and I, The" EGG

"And I Love ___" HER

___ and improved NEW

"___ and Ivory" EBONY

"___ and Jake Wade, The" LAW

"___ and Janis" ARLO

___ and Jeremy CHAD

___ and jerk CLEAN

___ and Jerry TOM

"And Jill came tumbling ___" AFTER

___ and joy PRIDE

"___ and Juliet" ROMEO

___ and kicking ALIVE

___ and Leander HERO

___ and letters ARTS

"___ and Lovers" SONS

"___ and Mabel" CAIN

"___ and Me" ROGER

___ and mean LEAN

"___ and Meek" EEK

"___ and Mike" PAT

___ and mild MEEK

and more ETC

"___ and Mouse" CAT

"...and music in its ___" ROAR

___ and nail TOOTH

"___ and Nancy" SID

"...___ and not heard" SEEN

"And Now ___ Something Completely Different" FOR

___ and omega ALPHA

___ and on OFF

___ and only ONE

"___ and Order" LAW

and others ETAL

"___ and out" OVER

___ and outs INS

Andover
~ address SIR

"___ and Pain (and the Whole Damn Thing)" LOVE

___ and pains ACHES

___ and papa MAMA

___ and parcel PART

"___ and Peace" WAR

___-and-peck HUNT

___ and pepper SALT

___ and polish SPIT

___-and-pony show DOG

___ and pop MOM

___ and potatoes MEAT

"___ and Prejudice" PRIDE

"And pretty maids all in ___" AROW

___ and proper DUE, PRIM

___ and quiet PEACE

___ and rave RANT

André GIDE
~ ex MIA
see also French

"André"
~ star SEAL

André ___ GIDE

Andrea ___ Sarto DEL

"Andrea Doria" BOAT, LINER, SHIP

___ Andreas Fault SAN

___ and reel ROD

Andrei
see Russian

Andress, Ursula
~ film SHE
~ role SHE

Andre the ___ GIANT

Andretti MARIO, RACER
~ ex-duchess SARAH
~ sister ANNE

Andrew LANG, URE

Andrews DANA

Andrews, Julie
~ movie SOB, STAR

Andrews Sisters TRIO

"___ and Robbers" COPS

Androcles ROMAN, SLAVE
~ friend LION

"Androcles ___ the Lion" AND

"Androcles and the ___" LION

android
"Star Trek" ~ DATA

___ and run EAT, HIT

___ and running OFF

"___ and Satires" ODES

___ and sciences ARTS

___ and scrape BOW

___ and Sedition Acts ALIEN

___ and see WAIT

___-and-seek HIDE

"___ and Sensibility" SENSE

"___ and shine!" RISE

___ and shoulders above HEAD

___-and-shut case OPEN

"___ and Sixpence, The" MOON

___ and skittles BEER

"___ and Sober" CLEAN

___-and-socket joint BALL

and so forth ETC

"And so it ___" GOES

"And so to ___" BED

___ and soul HEART

"___ and Soul" HEART

___ and sound SAFE

___-and-sour SWEET

___ and square FAIR

"___ and Stacey" NED

___-and-stick PEEL

"And Still I ___" RISE

___ and Stripes STARS

___ and substance SUM

___ and switch BAIT

"___ and Sympathy" TEA

___ and tear WEAR

___ and tell KISS, SHOW

___-and-ten FIVE

___ and that THIS

"And that ___ hay!" AINT

"And that's the way ___" ITIS

"And the ___ Played On" BAND

"___ and the Art of Motorcycle Maintenance" ZEN

"___ and the Badman" ANGEL

"And the Band Played On"
~ actor GERE

"___ and the Beautiful, The" BAD

"___ and the Canary, The" CAT

"___ and the Crazy, The" COOL

"___ and the Cruisers" EDDIE

"___ and the Detectives" EMIL

"___ and the Dragon" BEL

"___ and the Fiddle, The" CAT

"___ and the Hawk, The" EAGLE

"___ and the King of Siam" ANNA

"And the Lord set a mark upon ___" CAIN

"___ and the Man" ARMS

"___ and the Marriage Broker, The" MODEL

"___ and the Minor, The" MAJOR

and then ___ SOME

___ and then NOW

"And Then ___ Were None" THERE

"And Then There ___ None" WERE

"And Then There Were ___" NONE

"___ and the Papas, The" MAMAS

"___ and the Pendulum, The" PIT

"___ and the Pussycat, The" OWL

___ and there HERE, THEN

"And thereby hangs a ___" TALE

"___ and the Swan" LEDA

"___ and the Tramp" LADY

"___ and the Wolf" PETER

___ and thread NEEDLE

___ and tittle JOT

"...and to ___ good night!" ALLA

___-and-toe HEEL

___ and tonic GIN

___ and trouble TOIL

___ and tuck NIP

___ and tucker BIB

___ and turn TOSS

___ and vigor VIM

___ and vinegar OIL

___ and void NULL

___-and-wear WASH

___ and weave BOB

___ and well ALIVE

___ and wide FAR

"___ and Winding Road, The" LONG

Andy BEAN, CAPP
~ aunt BEE
~ partner AMOS

Andy and Flo
~ mutual nickname PET

___ and yang YIN

"Andy Capp"
~ quaff ALE

"___, and ye shall receive..." ASK

"...and yet so ___" FAR

"Andy Griffith Show, The"
~ role BEE, CLARA, ELLIE, HELEN, OPIE, OTIS

ane
~ follower TWA

___ an ear LEND

anecdotal
~ collection ANA
~ knowledge LORE

anecdote TALE

___ Ane Langdon SUE

anemic PALE

___ anemone (woodland plant) RUE

anent ABOUT, ASTO, INRE

anesthetic ETHER, GAS

___ anesthetic LOCAL

anesthetized UNDER

anew AGAIN, OVER

Ang LEE

angel DONOR
~ accessory HALO
~ food CAKE

~ hair PASTA
~ instrument HARP

"Angel ___ the Badman" AND

"___ Angel" EARTH, TEEN

"___ Angel, The" BLUE

Angela
Broadway role for ~ MAME

"Angela's ___" ASHES

"Angel at My ___, An" TABLE

"___ Angelenos" LOS

___ Angeles LOS

angelfish PET

angel food CAKE

Angeli PIER

angelic GOOD, PURE
~ topper HALO

Angelico FRA

"Angel in the House, The" POEM

"Angelo, My ___" LOVE

"Angel on My Shoulder"
~ actor MUNI

___ Angelo, Tex. SAN

Angelou, Maya POET
see also poet

Angels TEAM, TEN

"Angels ___ Broadway" OVER

"___ Angels Have Wings" ONLY

"Angels in the Outfield"
~ director DEAR

angelus
pair on an ~ ALAE

anger BILE, ENRAGE, IRE, IRK, PEEVE, RAGE, RILE, SIN, UPSET
display of ~ SCENE
inclination to ~ BILE
internalize ~ STEW
unleash one's ~ ERUPT

angiosperm PLANT

angle BEND, BIAS, LEAN, PHASE, SKEW, SLANT, SLOPE, TILT
~ for SEEK
~ off BEND, SKEW, SLANT
~ starter PENT, TRI
at an ~ ATILT, AWRY
kind of ~ ACUTE
projecting ~ CANT
right ~ ELBOW, ELL
writer's ~ SLANT

angled BENT

___-angle lens WIDE

angler
~ action CAST
~ aid REEL
~ basket CREEL
~ buy BAIT, LURE
~ catch HAUL
~ device LURE
~ gear NET
~ hope BITE

angles

angles
~ **pole** ROD
see also fisherman

angles
at right ~ to the keel ABEAM

Anglo-Saxon
~ **bailiff** REEVE
~ **coin** ORA
~ **worker** ESNE

Angora CAT, GOAT

angry IRATE, MAD, SORE, UPSET, WARM
~ **look** GLARE
~ **mood** SNIT
~ **reaction** RISE
become ~ REACT
make ~ ENRAGE, IRE, PEEVE, RILE
short, ~ utterance SNAP

"___ Angry Man, The" LAST

"___ Angry Men" SEVEN

angry young ___ MAN

"Angry Young Men, The"
~ **author** AMIS

angst FEAR

Angström SWEDE

Anguilla rostrata EEL

anguilliform
~ **creature** EEL

anguish PAIN, RACK, STING, WOE
cry of ~ OHNO

angular
~ **letter** ELL

Angus STEER
~ **topper** TAM

anhydrous DRY

"___ a nice day!" HAVE

anigh
not ~ AFAR

anil DYE

anima LIFE, SOUL

animadvert CARP

animal BEAST
~ **category** BREED
~ **feed** BRAN
~ **pest** FLEA
~ **protection org.** SPCA
draft ~ MULE
see also beast

"___ Animal, The" MALE

animalcule AMEBA

"Animal House" FRAT
~ **brother** DDAY
~ **garb** TOGA

animalistic CRUEL

animal-rights
~ **org.** SPCA

animate ALIVE, FIRE, LIVE, ROUSE

animated ALIVE, GAY, LIVE, RACY, SPRY, WARM

animating
~ **principle** LIFE, SOUL

animation COLOR, LIFE, PEP, VIM

animosity ANGER, HATE, IRE, SPITE

animus HATE

anise HERB, SEED

Anita LOOS
see also Spanish

___ Anita SANTA

Anjou PEAR
~ **kin** BOSC

Anka PAUL
~ **tune** DIANA

Ankara CITY

ankh
~ **shape** TAU

ankle
~ **cover** SPAT

ankle-high LOW
~ **shoe** BAL

anklet
~ **feature** CLASP

anklets HOSE

ankylosaur
~ **feature** ARMOR

Ann CAPE
~ **to Abby** TWIN

Ann ___ ("That Girl" character) MARIE

Ann ___, Mich. ARBOR

___ Ann (Tomlin character) EDITH

Anna HELD, STEN
~ **kingdom** SIAM

Anna ___ Wong MAY

"Anna ___ the King of Siam" AND

___ Anna (Alamo victor) SANTA

"Anna and the King of ___" SIAM

"Annabel ___" LEE

"Annabel Lee" POEM
~ **poet** POE

Annakin KEN

Annapolis
~ **academy** NAVAL
~ **grad** ENS
~ **insignia** USN
~ **inst.** USNA

Anne MEARA, RICE
~ **to Margaret** NIECE

Anne de Beaupré STE

___-Anne-des-Plaines STE

"Anne of Green Gables"
~ **loc.** PEI

___-Anne of "Northern Exposure" RUTH

"Anne of the Thousand ___" DAYS

Annett PAUL

Annette OTOOLE

annex ADD, AMEND, ELL, TAG
build an ~ ADD

Annie
~ **to Warbucks** WARD
comment from ~'s dog ARF

"Annie ___" ALLEN, HALL

"Annie ___ Your Gun" GET

___ Annie ("Oklahoma!" role) ADO

"Annie Get Your ___" GUN

"Annie Hall"
~ **director** ALLEN

Annie Oakley PASS
like an ~ FREE

annihilate ANNUL, BLAST, SLAY, UNDO, WASTE

anniversary DATE, DAY, EVENT, GALA
~ **item** CAKE
1st ~ PAPER
4th ~ LINEN, SILK
6th ~ IRON
10th ~ TIN
11th ~ STEEL
12th ~ SILK
13th ~ LACE
14th ~ IVORY
30th ~ PEARL
35th ~ CORAL, JADE
50th ~ GOLD
tin ~ TENTH

Ann-Margret SWEDE

annotate EDIT

annotation NOTE

announce ASSERT, CALL, POST, RELATE, SAY, STATE, TELL, UTTER

announcement NEWS, SIGN

announcements
paid ~ ADS

annoy ANGER, EAT, FRET, GET, GRATE, IRE, IRK, NEEDLE, PEEVE, RAG, RILE, ROIL, TEASE, TRY, UPSET

annoyance TRIAL
be an ~ GRATE
exclamation of ~ RATS, TSK

annoyed IRATE, IRED, SORE, UPSET, WARM
~ **easily** TESTY
~ **state** SNIT

annoyer NAG

annoying BAD
~ **insect** GNAT
~ **one** PAIN, PEST

~ sensation ITCH

annual PLANT
~ **exhibition** FAIR
~ **visitor** SANTA

annuity
~ **alternative** IRA

annul ERASE, UNDO, VOID

annulus HALO

___ annum PER

anodize PLATE

anodyne BALM, OPIATE
~ **target** PAIN

anoint BLESS, OIL

anomalous ODD

anon LATER, NOW, SOON
~ **companion** EVER
ever and ~ OFT, OFTEN

anonym ALIAS, NAME

anonymous
~ **one** DOE, ROE

another NEW
~ **in Spanish** OTRA
~ **time** AGAIN, ANEW
at ~ time ANON, LATER
cover ~'s tracks ABET
in ~ direction AWAY
send to ~ PASS, REFER
to ~ place AWAY
with one ~ AMONG

"Another ___ Man" THIN

"Another ___ of the Forest" PART

"Another 48 ___" HRS

"Another Thin ___" MAN

"Another Woman"
~ **director** ALLEN

"Another World" SOAP

"Another year ___..." OLDER

Anouk AIMEE

Ansel ADAMS

anserine DAFT
~ **bird** GOOSE

Ansermet ERNEST

Anson CAP

answer NOTE, ORACLE, REACT, RSVP, SAY, SUM
~ **a charge** PLEAD
~ **back** SASS
~ **(for)** PAY
~ **to the Sphinx's riddle** MAN
~ **Trebek** ASK
affirmative ~ AYE, YEA, YES
defendant's ~ PLEA
get the same ~ AGREE
negative ~ NAY
quiz ~ FALSE, TRUE
sycophant's ~ YES

answering-machine
~ **option** ERASE
~ **sound** TONE

answers
    try to get ~ ASK

ant
    ~ at a picnic PEST

ant ___ BEAR, COW, LION

ant.
    ~ opposite SYN

___ ant ARMY, FIRE, SLAVE

Ant ADAM

Antaeus GIANT

antagonism SPITE

antagonist ENEMY, FOE
    ~ (prefix) ANTI

Antarctic OCEAN
    ~ sea ROSS
    of the ~ POLAR

Antarctica's ___ Ford Range
    EDSEL

Antares STAR

ante BET, BID, STAKE
    ~ amts. CTS
    ~ destination POT
    ~ follower DEAL
    ~ relative PRE
    ~ up PAY
    lowest ~ CENT
    penny ~ GAME
    up the ~ RAISE

ante- PRE

anteater ANIMAL

antecede LEAD

antecedents CAUSE

antediluvian EARLY, OLD

antelope ANIMAL, ELAND, GNU,
    GOA
    ~ playmate DEER
    female ~ DOE, EWE
    where the deer and the ~
        play RANGE
    young ~ KID

___ antelope GOAT

antenna AERIAL, ORGAN
    ~ cousin DISH
    ~ pole MAST
    TV ~ AERIAL

___ antenna DISH, UHF

anterior FORE, HEAD
    ~ limb ARM
    ~ (prefix) PRO

anteroom HALL

anthem SONG, TUNE
    ~ author KEY
    ~ preposition OER

anthill NEST

Anthony EARL, EDEN, MANN,
    PAGE

"Anthony Adverse"
    ~ author ALLEN
    ~ director LEROY

Anthony, Saint
    ~ cross TAU

Anthony, Susan B.
    ~ is on one COIN

anthracite COAL
    ~ deposit SEAM

anthropoid APE
    endangered ~ ORANG

anthropologist
    ~ in Samoa MEAD

anthropophagite OGRE

anti CON
    ~ opposite PRO
    ~ votes NOES, NOS

Antibes
    ~ neighbor NICE

antibiotic CURE
    ~ source MOLD

antibiotics
    candidate for ~ STREP

antic CAPER, DIDO, LARK

anticipate AWAIT, HOPE

anticipated DUE

anticipation HOPE
    in eager ~ AGOG

antidote CURE

anti-Dracula
    ~ device STAKE

antidrug
    ~ agent NARC
    ~ org. DEA

Antietam
    ~ general LEE

Antigone
    Creon, to ~ UNCLE

Antigua ISL

antiknock
    ~ number OCTANE

Antilles
    ~ island ARUBA

antimacassar SCARF

antimacassars
    make ~ TAT

antimony METAL

anti-mugger
    ~ weapon MACE

anti-narcotics
    ~ org. DEA

anti-nuke
    ~ org. SANE

Antioch
    ~ locale OHIO

antipasto
    ~ ingredient OLIVE

antipathetic AVERSE

antipathetical AVERSE

antipathy HATE, SPITE

antiphon PSALM

antipollution
    ~ org. EPA

anti-prohibitionist WET

___ Antiqua ARS

antiquate AGE

antiquated OLD, PASSE

antique EARLY, OLD, PASSE, RELIC
    ~ brooch CAMEO
    ~ car REO

antiquer
    ~ aid AGER

antiques
    work with ~ RESTORE

antique store
    ~ adjective OLDE

antiquing
    ~ medium AGER

antiquity ELD, PAST, YORE

anti-racketeering
    ~ org. FBI

antiseptic PURE, WASH

anti-slip
    ~ device CLEAT

antismoking
    ~ org. AMA

antisocial
    ~ type LONER

anti-sway ___ BAR

antithetical POLAR

antitoxin SERUM

antitoxins SERA

antivenins SERA

antler HORN
    ~ part TINE
    ~ wearer DEER, ELK, MOOSE,
        STAG
    budding ~ KNOB

antlered
    ~ animal DEER, ELK, MOOSE,
        STAG

Antofagasta CITY, PORT

Antoine
    see French

Antoinette MARIE
    see also French

Antonia BIRD

"Antonia & ___" JANE

Antonio
    ~ in "Evita" CHE
    see also Italian

___ Antonio Spurs SAN

___ Antonio, Texas SAN

Antony MARC, ROMAN
    ~ attendant EROS
    ~ paramour CLEO
    see also Latin

"Antony and Cleopatra"
    ~ character IRAS
    ~ servant EROS

Antony, Mark ROMAN

ant-sized TEENY

antsy TENSE

Antwerp CITY, PORT

Anubis
    ~ to Osiris SON

anvil BONE
    ~ site EAR

Anwar el-___ SADAT

anxiety CARE, FEAR, STRESS
    cause ~ to ALARM

anxious EAGER, TENSE

any EACH, SOME
    ~ day now ANON, SOON
    ~ miss HER, SHE
    ~ ship HER, SHE
    ~ thing NOUN
    at ~ time EVER
    hardly ~ FEW
    not ~ NARY, NONE, ZERO
    without ~ warning BANG

any ___ in a storm PORT

Anya SETON

anybody
    not ~ NOONE

"___ any drop to drink" NOR

"___ Any Girl" ASK

anyone
    not ~ NOONE
    not with ~ ALONE

**"Any Place I Hang My ___ Is
Home"** HAT

anything
    apart from ~ else PERSE
    before ~ else FIRST

"Anything ___" GOES

"___ Anything..." SAY

"Anything Goes"
    ~ name COLE, ETHEL, RENO

any way you ___ it SLICE

Aoede MUSE

Aoide MUSE

A-OK NEAT

AOL
    ~ customer USER
    ~ messages EMAIL

Aomori CITY, PORT

___ a one NARY

A-one ACE, BEST, TOP

aoudad ANIMAL

AP
    ~ erstwhile rival UPI

A&P
    part of ~ ATL, PAC

apace SOON

Apache TRIBE

"Aparajito"
~ **director** RAY

Aparicio LUIS

apart ALONE, ALOOF, LONE
~ **(from)** ASIDE
~ **from anything else** PERSE
~ **(prefix)** DIS
come ~ SPLIT, TEAR
fall ~ ROT
pull ~ REND, SPLIT, TEAR
set ~ ALLOT, ALLOW, ALONE,
SPACE
take ~ RAVEL, UNDO

___ **a part** ACT

apartment ABODE, FLAT, HOME,
PAD, UNIT
~ **heater** STEAM
~ **sign** TOLET
London ~ FLAT
take an ~ LET, RENT

"Apartment ___" ZERO

"Apartment ___ Peggy" FOR

apathetic DAMP

APB ALERT
~ **datum** AKA
part of ~ ALL

ape ANIMAL, ECHO
go ~ FLIP, RAGE
large ~ ORANG

ape-___ MAN

___ **ape** GREAT

"Ape and ___" ESSENCE

Apennines
~ **religious center** ASSISI

aperitif
~ **flavoring** ANISE
Honshu ~ SAKE, SAKI

aperture DOOR, EXIT, EYE, GAP,
HOLE, PEEP, SLOT
narrow ~ SLIT
tiny ~ PORE

apex ACME, CAP, CREST, NIB,
PEAK, SPIRE, TIP, TOP
at the ~ **of** ATOP

aphid PEST
~ **milker** ANT

aphonic MUTE

aphorism ADAGE, GNOME,
MORAL, MOT, SAW
mysterious ~ RUNE

aphrodisia EROS, LOVE, LUST

Aphrodite
~ **lover** ARES
~ **son** EROS
Eros, to ~ SON

Apia
~ **land** SAMOA

apian
~ **defense** STING

apiary HIVE
~ **resident** BEE

apical TOP

apiculture
~ **topic** BEE

apiece EACH, PER

A-plant
~ **cylinder** ROD

___ **a plea** COP

aplenty AMPLE, ENOW

aplomb POISE

APO
~ **addressees** GIS

apocalypse DOOM

"Apocalypse ___" NOW

"Apocalypse Now"
~ **actor** SHEEN

"Apocalypse Postponed"
~ **author** ECO

apod
~ **lack** FOOT

Apodes
~ **member** EEL

apogee ACME, APEX, CAP, CREST,
PEAK, TIP, TOP

Apollo GOD
~ **attendant** ERATO
~ **destination** MOON
~ **instrument** LYRE
~ **laurel, nowadays** MEDAL
~ **mother** LETO
~ **org.** NASA
~ **priestess** ORACLE
~ **shrine** ORACLE
~ **vehicle** LEM
Asclepius, to ~ SON
lover of ~ ARIA
son of ~ ION

Apollo ___ (Rocky's rival) CREED

Apollo 11
~ **module** EAGLE

Apollonian SERENE

Apollonius of Rhodes POET
see also poet

Apollyon SATAN

"Apologetic"
~ **Greek** PLATO

apologia PLEA

apologue TALE

apophysis NODE

apostate REBEL

apostatize DESERT

apostle PAUL, PETER

apostles
~ **had one** CREED

"Apostles, The"
~ **composer** ELGAR

apostrophe ASIDE

apostrophize ORATE

apothecary
~ **measure** DRAM

apothegm GNOME, MOT, SAW

apotheosis IDEAL

apotheosize ADORE, EXALT

___ **a powder** TAKE

Appalachian TRAIL

Appalachians RANGE

Appalachian Trail
~ **start** MAINE

appall REPEL, SCARE

appalling BAD, DIRE

appaloosa HORSE

apparatus GEAR, RIG, TOOL
breathing ~ LUNG
clothmaking ~ LOOM
playground ~ SLIDE

apparel ARRAY, ATTIRE, DRESS,
GARB, GEAR, SUIT, WEAR
put on ~ DRESS

apparent OVERT

___ **apparent** HEIR

apparition SHADE, SOUL

appeal ASK, CALL, CRY, PLEAD,
SUE, SUIT
~ **to** BEG, WOO
emotional ~ PLEA
lose ~ PALL
make an ~ ASK, PRAY
urgent ~ PLEA

___ **appeal** SEX, SNOB

"___ Appeal" MASS

appealing CUTE, NICE, SWEET

appear ACT, ARISE, COME,
EMERGE, LOOM, OCCUR, RISE,
SEEM, SHOW
~ **briefly** CAMEO
~ **imminent** LOOM
~ **indecisive** HAW, HEM
~ **stunned** GAPE
begin to ~ PEEP
charge to ~ CITE

appearance AIR, CAST, FACE,
IMAGE, MIEN, MODE, PHASE
brief ~ CAMEO
false ~ ACT, SHAM
general ~ AIR
make an ~ ARISE, ATTEND,
COME, ENTER
moon's ~ PHASE
outward ~ AIR
put in an ~ COME

appease ALLAY, ATONE, EASE,
SATE, SLAKE

appellation NAME, TAG, TITLE

appellative TAG

append ADD, AMEND, TAG

appendage ARM, PART, TAB, TAIL
animal ~ PAW

auto ~ AERIAL
caudal ~ TAIL
legislative ~ RIDER

appendix TAG

"___ appétit!" BON

appetite LUST, TASTE, WANT, YEN
~ **rouser** AROMA
whet the ~ LURE

appetizer PATE
~ **follower** ENTREE
wax-coated ~ EDAM

appetizing GOOD

___ **Appia (Roman road)** VIA

Appian Way
~ **terminus** ROME

applaud CLAP, EXALT, HAIL, REACT

applause NOISE
acknowledge ~ BOW
round of ~ HAND

apple PIE, TREE
~ **beverage** CIDER
~ **booster** EVE
~ **center** CORE
~ **drink** CIDER
~ **green** COLOR
~ **leftover** CORE
~ **of discord contender** HERA
~ **of one's eye** DEAR
~ **seed** PIP
~ **skin** PEEL
~ **spray** ALAR
~ **targeter** TELL
~ **tosser of myth** ERIS
~ **variety** MAC, ROME
early ~ **eater** ADAM

apple ___ PIE

___ **apple** ADAMS, CRAB, LOVE,
MAY

applecart
like the ~ UPSET

"Apple cider"
~ **girl** IDA

applejack
~ **ingredient** CIDER

apple of one's ___ EYE

apple pie
~ **maker** MOM
in ~ **order** NEAT, TRIM

apple pie à la ___ MODE

apple red ROSY

apples
like some crab ~ TART
search for ~ BOB

applesauce BLAH, PAP, POOH,
ROT, TRASH

appliance TOOL, UNIT
~ **button** RESET
~ **maker** AMANA
home ~ FAN, IRON
kitchen ~ OVEN, RANGE
living-room ~ **of old** RADIO
pizzeria ~ OVEN
self-cleaning ~ OVEN

appliances GEAR

applicability USE

applicable UTILE

applicant
  accept an ~ HIRE

application USAGE, USE
  ~ datum SEX
  job ~ entry NAME

applicator SWAB
  mascara ~ WAND

apply EXERT, USE
  ~ as plaster LAY
  ~ frosting ICE
  ~ gently DAB
  ~ lace TRIM
  ~ oneself LABOR
  ~ paint COAT, DAUB
  ~ pressure IMPEL, MAKE
  ~ to ASK
  ~ wax to SEAL

appoggiatura NOTE

appoint AWARD, ELECT, MAKE, NAME, POST, PUT

appointed
  ~ time DAY, HOUR
  before the ~ time EARLY
  finely ~ POSH

___-appointed SELF

appointment DATE, POST, TRYST
  make an ~ NAME
  make an ~ with DATE

appointment book
  ~ slot HOUR

appointments DECOR, GEAR

"Appointment With Danger"
  ~ director ALLEN

Appomattox
  ~ figure LEE
  ~ monogram REL
  part of an ~ signature ELEE

apportion ALLOT, DEAL, METE, SHARE

apportionment DOLE

appose ADD

apposite DUE, FIT, MEET

appraise ASSAY, ASSESS, EYE, RATE, TEST

appreciable ANY
  ~ effect DENT

appreciate DIG, ESTEEM, GET, HONOR, KNOW, LIKE, LOVE, NOTE, SAVOR, SENSE
  ~ jazz DIG

appreciation EYE
  murmurs of ~ AHS
  show ~ CLAP

appreciative
  ~ sound GEE, OOH, WOW

apprehend ARREST, GET, GRASP, KNOW, NAB, NAIL, SENSE, TAKE

apprehension ALARM, ARREST, FEAR, GRIP

apprehensive WARY

apprentice AIDE, HELP

apprise WARN

apprised AWARE
  ~ of INON

approach COME, DOOR, LINE, MODE, NEAR, PATH, PLAN, RAMP, ROAD, SLANT, STYLE
  ~ an end WANE
  ~ furtively SIDLE
  ~ the terminal TAXI
  hard ~ SELL
  reporter's ~ ANGLE, SLANT
  soft ~ SELL

appropriate ADOPT, ALLOT, APT, DUE, FIT, GRAB, MEET, NICE, ROB, STEAL, TAKE
  ~ period TIME

appropriation TAKE

approval
  flight ~ AOK
  gesture of ~ NOD
  implied, as ~ TACIT
  indicate ~ NOD
  mate's ~ AYE
  murmur of ~ AAH
  shout of ~ RAH
  show ~ CLAP
  sigh of ~ AAH
  silent ~ NOD
  slangy ~ AOK
  stamps of ~ OKS
  word of ~ AMEN, AYE, GOOD, YEA, YES

approvals OKS

approve ABET, AGREE, BLESS, CLEAR, ENACT, OKAY, PASS, SIGN, STAMP
  ~ enthusiastically LAUD
  ~ of ADMIT
  ~ wrongfully ABET
  refuse to ~ VETO

approved
  get ~ SELL

approves OKS

approx. EST

approximate CLOSE

approximately ABOUT, NEAR, ORSO, SAY
  ~ (suffix) ISH

approximating LIKE

appurtenance EXTRA

appurtenances GEAR

Apr.
  ~ payee IRS
  ~ predecessor MAR
  busy ~ worker CPA
  it starts in ~ DST

APR
  part of ~ RATE

après-ski
  ~ beverage COCOA

apricot COLOR, TREE

April
  ~ follower MAY
  ~ forecast RAIN

April 1
  ~ baby ARIES
  ~ trick RUSE

April 22
  ~ honoree EARTH

April Fools' ___ DAY

"April Love"
  ~ crooner BOONE

Apr.-Oct.
  ~ time DST

___ a profit TURN

apron
  ~ part BIB
  ~ strings TIES
  lady in an ~ MAID
  worker with an ~ CHEF

apropos APT
  ~ of ABOUT, ASTO, INRE

apse
  ~ table ALTAR
  path to an ~ AISLE

___ apso LHASA

apt ABLE, FIT, PRONE

apt.
  ~ dweller RES

apterous
  opposite of ~ ALAR

apteryx KIWI
  extinct ~ MOA

aptitude BENT

Apuleius ROMAN

Aqaba CITY, PORT

Aqua-___ LUNG

aqua fortis ACID

aquamarine BLUE, COLOR, GEM

aquarium TANK
  ~ fish EEL, SKATE, TETRA

Aquarius SIGN
  ~ tote EWER

aquatic
  ~ bird SWAN, TERN
  ~ mammal OTTER, SEAL
  ~ organism ALGA

"Aqua Velva ___" MAN

aqueduct CANAL, MAIN
  ~ contents AQUA

aqueous DAMP, WET

aquifer
  ~ feature PORE

Aquila
  constellation ~ EAGLE

ar
  ~ follower ESS

Ar ELEM
  18 for ~ ATNO

AR
  see Arkansas

Arab HORSE, STEED
  ~ boat DHOW
  ~ chieftain AMIR, EMEER, EMIR
  ~ combo from 1958-1961 UAR
  ~ garment ABA
  ~ grp. PLO
  ~ headband cord AGAL
  ~ name part IBN
  ~ noble AGA, AGHA
  ~ of song AHAB
  ~ prename ALI
  ~ robe ABA
  certain ~ OMANI

"Arabella" OPERA

arabesque ORNATE

Arabian DESERT, HORSE, SEA, STEED
  ~ appellation ALI
  ~ gazelle ARIEL
  ~ gulf ADEN
  ~ nation YEMEN
  ~ nobleman AMIR, EMEER, EMIR
  ~ peninsula ADEN
  ~ port ADEN
  ~ vessel DHOW
  bird of ~ myth ROC

"Arabian Nights"
  ~ bird ROC
  ~ character GENIE

Arabian Peninsula
  ~ port ADEN

Arabian Sea
  ~ gulf OMAN
  ~ territory GOA

Arabic
  father, in ~ ABU
  master, in ~ SAHIB

Arab League
  ~ headquarters CAIRO
  ~ member OMAN, YEMEN

arachnid MITE
  ~ flytrap WEB

"Arachnophobia"
  ~ actor SANDS

Arafat ARAB
  ~ birthplace CAIRO
  ~ grp. PLO

Arafura SEA

Aragón
  river through ~ EBRO
  see also Spanish

"___ a Rag Picker" HES

Aral SEA

Aramis
  ~ colleague ATHOS

Arapaho TRIBE
  ~ **abode** TEPEE
  ~ **enemy** UTE

arara MACAW

Ararat
  ~ **lander** ARK
  ~ **visitor** HAM, NOAH

arbalest BOW

arbiter
  sports ~ REF, UMP

arbitrate SETTLE

Arbor Day
  ~ **month** APRIL

arboreal
  ~ **Aussie** KOALA
  ~ **fluid** SAP
  ~ **home** NEST

arboretum
  ~ **specimen** TREE

___ Arbor, Mich. ANN

arborvitae TREE

Arbuckle, Jon
  ~ **dog** ODIE

Arbus DIANE

Arbuthnot SCOT

arc BOW

arc ___ LAMP, SINE

arcade MALL
  ~ **habitué** TEEN
  ~ **infraction** TILT
  video ~ **name** ATARI

Arcadian RURAL

Arcaro EDDIE
  ~ **prop** CROP

arch BEND, CAMP, ELFIN, LOOP, SLY
  ~ **over** SPAN
  ~ **site** FOOT
  ~ **support** PIER
  curved ~ OGEE

___ arch OGEE, ROMAN

archaeological
  ~ **datum** AGE
  ~ **site** DIG, RUIN

archaeologist
  ~ **find** BONE, IDOL, RELIC,
    RUIN, STELE

archaic EARLY, OLD, PASSE

archbishop RANK

archduchess LADY

archduke LORD, PEER

"Archduke ___" (Beethoven
  work) TRIO

arched
  ~ **recess** APSE

archer BOW
  ~ **need** ARROW
  ~ **skill** AIM
  ~ **weapon** ARROW, BOW
  Alpine ~ TELL

mythical ~ EROS

Archer ANNE, LEW
  the ~ SIGN

Archerd ARMY

Archer, Miles
  ~ **partner** SPADE

Arches National Park
  ~ **locale** UTAH

archetype IDEAL, MODEL

Archibald NATE

Archie MOORE, TEEN
  ~ **pal** MOOSE
  ~ **to Mike** INLAW

"Archie Bunker's Place"
  ~ **actress** MEARA

archimandrite ABBOT

Archimedes
  ~ **forte** MATH
  tool for ~ LEVER

archipelago
  ~ **component** ISLE
  ~ **sect.** ISL

architect
  glass pyramid ~ PEI
  John Hancock Building ~ PEI
  Mile High Center ~ PEI
  neoclassical ~ ADAM
  nineteenth-century British
    ~ NASH
  St. Paul's ~ WREN

architectural
  ~ **addition** ELL
  ~ **detail** DADO, OGEE
  ~ **drawing** PLAN
  ~ **order** IONIC
  ~ **pier** ANTA
  Greek ~ **style** IONIC

architecture
  first name in ~ EERO

Arco ARENA

arctic ___ TERN

Arctic OCEAN
  ~ **dwelling** IGLOO
  ~ **explorer** ROSS
  ~ **flier** TERN
  ~ **hazard** BERG, FLOE
  ~ **lights** AURORA
  ~ **native** LAPP
  ~ **surface** ICE
  ~ **trout** CHAR
  ~ **vehicle** SLED
  nineteenth-century ~
    explorer RAE
  of the ~ POLAR

Arcturus STAR

Arden EVE

___ Arden (Flash Gordon
  companion) DALE

Ardennes
  ~ **waterway** OISE

ardent AFIRE, AVID, EAGER, HOT,
  KEEN, WARM
  ~ **male** ROMEO

~ watcher FAN

Ardolino EMILE

ardor DASH, ELAN, FIRE, GLOW,
  HEAT, LOVE, ZEAL

arduous HARD, STEEP

are
  ~ **in French** ETES
  ~ **in Spanish** ESTA

"Are ___ Lonesome Tonight?"
  YOU

area BEAT, BELT, REALM, SITE, SIZE,
  SPACE, SPHERE, SPOT, TRACT,
  ZONE
  ~ **(abbr.)** REG
  ~ **behind a dam** LAKE
  ~ **in French** AIRE
  ~ **unit** ACRE
  in the ~**, to a poet** ANEAR
  poorly-drained ~ SINK

area ___ CODE, RUG

___ area REST

area code
  ~ **204** MAN
  ~ **205** ALA
  ~ **206** WASH
  ~ **207** MAINE
  ~ **208** IDA
  ~ **209** CAL
  ~ **210** TEX
  ~ **215** PENN
  ~ **216** OHIO
  ~ **217** ILL
  ~ **219** IND
  ~ **230** CAL
  ~ **254** TEX
  ~ **281** TEX
  ~ **302** DEL
  ~ **303** COL
  ~ **305** FLA
  ~ **308** NEB, NEBR
  ~ **309** ILL
  ~ **310** CAL
  ~ **312** ILL
  ~ **316** KAN
  ~ **317** IND
  ~ **319** IOWA
  ~ **323** CAL
  ~ **330** OHIO
  ~ **334** ALA
  ~ **352** FLA
  ~ **360** WASH
  ~ **402** NEB, NEBR
  ~ **403** ALB, ALTA
  ~ **407** FLA
  ~ **408** CAL
  ~ **409** TEX
  ~ **412** PENN
  ~ **413** MASS
  ~ **415** CAL
  ~ **419** OHIO
  ~ **423** TENN
  ~ **425** WASH
  ~ **435** UTAH
  ~ **440** OHIO
  ~ **501** ARK
  ~ **502** KEN
  ~ **503** ORE, OREGON
  ~ **508** MASS
  ~ **509** WASH

  ~ **510** CAL
  ~ **512** TEX
  ~ **513** OHIO
  ~ **515** IOWA
  ~ **530** CAL
  ~ **541** ORE, OREGON
  ~ **561** FLA
  ~ **562** CAL
  ~ **601** MISS
  ~ **605** SDAK
  ~ **606** KEN
  ~ **610** PENN
  ~ **614** OHIO
  ~ **617** MASS
  ~ **618** ILL
  ~ **619** CAL
  ~ **626** CAL
  ~ **630** ILL
  ~ **650** CAL
  ~ **701** NDAK
  ~ **702** NEV
  ~ **705** ONT
  ~ **707** CAL
  ~ **708** ILL
  ~ **712** IOWA
  ~ **713** TEX
  ~ **714** CAL
  ~ **717** PENN
  ~ **719** COL
  ~ **760** CAL
  ~ **765** IND
  ~ **785** KAN
  ~ **801** UTAH
  ~ **805** CAL
  ~ **806** TEX
  ~ **807** ONT
  ~ **812** IND
  ~ **813** FLA
  ~ **814** PENN
  ~ **815** ILL
  ~ **817** TEX
  ~ **818** CAL
  ~ **830** TEX
  ~ **831** CAL
  ~ **847** ILL
  ~ **850** FLA
  ~ **870** ARK
  ~ **901** TENN
  ~ **902** PEI
  ~ **903** TEX
  ~ **904** FLA
  ~ **907** ALAS, ALASKA
  ~ **909** CAL
  ~ **913** KAN
  ~ **915** TEX
  ~ **916** CAL
  ~ **925** CAL
  ~ **937** OHIO
  ~ **940** TEX
  ~ **941** FLA
  ~ **949** CAL
  ~ **954** FLA
  ~ **956** TEX
  ~ **970** COL
  ~ **972** TEX

"___ are a few of my favorite..."
  THESE

"___ a Real Nowhere Man" HES

"___ a Rebel" HES

areca PALM, TREE

"___ Are Gettin' Scarce" MEN

"___ Are My Lucky Star" YOU

"___ Are My Sunshine" YOU

arena REALM, RING, SPHERE, STAGE
~ accommodation SEAT
~ receipts GATE
circus ~ TENT
former Atlanta ~ OMNI
former Hawks ~ OMNI
hockey ~ RINK
jousting ~ LISTS
modern ~ DOME
naval ~ OCEAN, SEA

"___ Are Not Alone" YOU

aren't
~ out of HAVE

"___ are red..." ROSES

"___ Are Red, My Love" ROSES

Ares GOD
~ concern WAR
~ counterpart MARS
mother of ~ HERA
sister of ~ ERIS

arête CRAG, CREST

Aretha
~ music SOUL

"___ Are the Days" GONE

"___ are the jokes, folks" THESE

"___ Are There" YOU

"___ Are the Sunshine of My Life" YOU

"___ are the times..." THESE

___ a retreat BEAT

"Are we a ___?" PAIR

"Are we having fun ___?" YET

"Are we there ___?" YET

"Are you ___ or a mouse?" AMAN

"Are you a ___ a mouse?" MANOR

"Are you a man ___ mouse?" ORA

"Are you for ___?" REAL

argali ANIMAL

Argand
~ burner LAMP

argent METAL

Argentina
musical set in ~ EVITA
see also Spanish

Argentine
~ dance TANGO
~ dictator PERON
~ heroine EVITA

argentite ORE

argillite CLAY

"Argo" BOAT, SHIP

argon GAS
like ~ INERT

"Argonautica" EPIC
~ character MEDEA

Argonauts
~ patron HERA

argosy BOAT, FLEET, SHIP

argot CANT, IDIOM, SLANG

arguable OPEN

argue PLEAD, SCRAP, SPAR
~ for URGE

argument CASE, CON, ROW, SETTO, SPAT, TENOR
~ against CON
~ closer QED
~ for PRO
minor ~ SPAT

Argus DOG
one of ~ 100 EYE

Argus-eyed ALERT

argyles HOSE

aria AIR, SOLO, TUNE
~ ace DIVA

-arian
~ cousin IST, ITE, STER

Arias OSCAR

Arica CITY, PORT

arid DESERT, DRY, SERE

Ariel MOON

Aries AUTO, CAR, RAM, SIGN
~ mo. APR
~ month APRIL

arietta AIR, ARIA

ariette TUNE

Arikara REE, TRIBE

Arion HORSE
~ lifesaver LYRE

Ariosto
~ patron ESTE

arise EMERGE, ISSUE, OCCUR, STEM

"Arise, fair sun, and kill the envious moon"
~ speaker ROMEO

arisen
not ~ ABED

Aristide
~ realm HAITI
see also French

aristocracy CREAM, ELITE

aristocrat BARON, DAME, LORD, PEER

Aristotle
~ teacher PLATO
see also Greek

arithmetic
~ sign PLUS
~ sol. ANS
do ~ ADD, SUM

Ariz.
~ neighbor CAL, NEV, UTAH
~ once TER, TERR
see also Arizona

Arizona STATE
~ city MESA, TEMPE
~ elevation MESA
~ neighbor UTAH
~ river GILA, SALT
~ tribe HOPI

Arizona State
~ locale TEMPE

ark BOAT, SHIP
~ builder NOAH
~ landing site ARARAT
~ passenger HAM
scroll in an ~ TORAH

Ark
~ complement DUO, PAIR, TWO

Ark.
~ neighbor MISS, TENN, TEX
see also Arkansas

Arkansas STATE
city on the ~ TULSA

Arkhangelsk CITY, PORT
see also Russian

Arkin ADAM, ALAN

Arkin, Adam
~ dad ALAN

Arlene DAHL

Arles
see French

"Arli$$"
~ channel HBO

Arlington ___, Ill. HTS

Arlo
~ to Woody SON

arm BAY, NECK, PART
~ bone ULNA
~ bones RADII
~ in French BRAS
~ of the sea COVE, INLET
~ opposite LEG
~ starter FORE, TONE
at ~'s length ALOOF
bend of the ~ ELBOW
give one's right ~ PANT
one-armed bandit's ~ LEVER
starfish ~ RAY
take an ~ STEER
twist someone's ~ LEAD

___ arm (record-player part) TONE

armada FLEET
~ member BOAT, SHIP

armadas
of ~ NAVAL

armadillo ANIMAL
~ protection ARMOR

"Armageddon"
~ author URIS

Armand
see French

arm and a ___, an LEG

Armani
dressed by ~ CHIC

armed SET
~ swimmers OCTOPI

___-armed bandit ONE

Armendariz PEDRO

Armenia
~ once SSR
neighbor of ~ IRAN

armet ARMOR

armistice PEACE

Armistice ___ DAY

armless
~ garment VEST

armor MAIL, PLATE
equine ~ BARD

armor-breaking
~ weapon MACE

armored
~ car TANK
~ god ARES

"Armored ___ Robbery" CAR

armory
~ supply AMMO

arms CREST
~ of a sort RADII
~ of Morpheus SLEEP
~ recipient, maybe ALLY
call to ~ ALERT
clash of ~ WAR
comrade in ~ ALLY
rise up in ~ REBEL, RIOT
up in ~ IRATE, MAD

"Arms and the Man"
~ author SHAW

Armstrong BESS, NEIL, OTIS

Armstrong, Neil
~ program APOLLO
~ transport LEM

arm-twist MAKE

army ANT, HORDE, HOST, SEA
~ member ANT
coll. ~ program ROTC
join the ~ SERVE

army ___ ANT

army ___ (soldier's kid) BRAT

Army
~ address SIR
~ bed COT
~ command ATEASE
~ cops MPS
~ food MESS
~ leaders BRASS
~ mail addr. APO
~ need AMMO
~ off. COL, GEN, SGT
~ offender AWOL
~ officer MAJOR
~ outfit UNIT

Arn
- ~ outpost BASE, CAMP
- ~ status RANK
- ~ truant AWOL
- ~ vehicle TANK
- *see also* GI, military

Arn
- ~ domain, in "Prince Valiant" ORR

Arnaz DESI

Arndt, Felix
- ~ tune NOLA

Arnhem
- ~ neighbor EDE

"Arnie's ___" ARMY

Arno
- city on the ~ PISA

Arnold EDDY, TOM

Arnold, Matthew POET
- *see also* poet

"___ a Rock" IAM

aroma AURA, BALM, ESSENCE, NOSE, ODOR, SCENT

aromatic
- ~ compound ESTER
- ~ flavoring ANISE
- ~ fragrance BALM
- ~ herb MINT, SAGE
- ~ Himalayan plant NARD
- ~ lotion BALM
- ~ tree CEDAR, PINE
- burn ~ candles CENSE

___-a-Roni RICE

"___ a Rose" ONLY

around ABOUT, NEAR
- ~ (prefix) EPI
- ~ to a poet ANEAR

___ around COME, GET, HORSE, LOAF, SHOP, SIT

___ around (associate) PAL

___ around (discuss) TOSS

___ around (gridiron play) END

___ around (investigate) NOSE

___ around (linger) HANG

___-around ALL

"___ Around" IGET, SHOP

around the ___ BEND

"___ Around the Corner, The" SHOP

"Around the Fish"
- ~ painter KLEE

"Around the World in Eighty ___" DAYS

"___ Around Us, The" SEA

arouse ALARM, EVOKE, FIRE, MOVE, RAISE, STIR
- ~ wonder AWE

Arp
- ~ genre DADA

Arpád HERO

arpeggio RUN

arraign CITE, SUE

arraignment
- ~ offering BAIL, PLEA
- speak at ~ PLEAD

arrange CLASS, DRAPE, FILE, LAY, MAP, POSE, RANK, SORT, SPACE
- ~ alphabetically FILE
- ~ for an orchestra SCORE
- ~ gracefully DRAPE
- ~ the table SET

arranged SET

arrangement ARRAY, DEAL, ORDER, PLAN, SETUP
- ~ (abbr.) SYST
- business ~ DEAL

arranging
- flower ~ ART

arrant BALD

array ADORN, ATTIRE, DRAPE, DRESS, GARB, HOST, LINE, POMP, RANK, ROBE, SET, VEST
- cornfield ~ ROW

arrayed CLAD

arrears DEBT
- be in ~ OWE

arrest DETER, HALT, HOLD, NAB, NAIL, REIN, STAY, STEM, STOP
- place under ~ NAB

Arrested Development
- ~ offering RAP

Arrhenius SWEDE

Arrid
- ~ rival BAN

"___ 'Arris Goes to Paris" MRS

arrival
- Ararat ~ ARK

arrive COME, LAND
- ~ at EDUCE, MAKE
- ~ at a settlement AGREE

arrivederci ADIEU, ALOHA, TATA

"Arrivederci ___" ROMA

arriving DUE

arriviste YAHOO

arrogance PRIDE
- without ~ MEEK

arrogant VAIN

arrogate GRAB

arrow DART, SIGN
- ~ launcher BOW

arrowhead
- ~ part BARB

Arrowrock Dam
- ~ river BOISE

arrow-shooter
- mythological ~ EROS

"Arrowsmith"
- ~ author LEWIS

arrowy TRIM

arroyo GAP, WADI

"Ars Amatoria"
- ~ poet OVID

arsenal
- ~ stock AMMO, ARMS

arsenic METAL

"Arsenic ___ Old Lace" AND

"Arsenic and ___ Lace" OLD

"Arsenic and Old ___" LACE

"Arsenic and Old Lace"
- ~ director CAPRA

Arsenio HALL
- ~ buddy EDDIE

art
- ~ ender IST
- ~ figure NUDE
- ~ gallery SALON
- ~ in Italian ARTE
- ~ in Latin ARS
- ~ medium INK
- ~ nouveau STYLE
- ~ song LAY
- ~ stand EASEL
- ~ style DECO, GENRE
- ~ (suffix) SHIP
- ~ supporter EASEL
- absurd ~ DADA
- Alaskan ~ form TOTEM
- Altamira ~ site CAVE
- Byzantine ~ form ICON
- healer's ~ CURE
- iconoclastic ~ movement DADA
- pigment used in cave ~ OCHER, OCHRE
- put ~ on glass ETCH
- thespian ~ DRAMA
- transfer ~ DECAL
- work with ~ RESTORE

"art"
- modern ~ ARE
- Trump's ~ DEAL

art ___ SALON

art ___ (Erté's genre) DECO

___ art POP

Art SHELL

"Artaxerxes"
- ~ composer ARNE

art colony
- New Mexico ~ TAOS

Art Deco STYLE
- ~ artist ERTE

Artemis
- ~ equivalent DIANA
- ~ mother LETO
- ~ twin APOLLO
- ~ victim ORION
- companion of ~ AURA
- temple of ~ site IONIA

Artemus WARD

artery ROAD
- ~ clogger FAT
- large ~ AORTA
- Venetian ~ CANAL

art for art's ___ SAKE

artful ARCH, FALSE, SLY
- ~ dodge RUSE

Arthur ASHE, BEA, HERO, PENN

Arthurian
- ~ knight KAY
- ~ lady ELAINE, ENID
- ~ sword holder STONE

Arthur, King
- ~ foster brother KAY
- sister of ~ ANNE
- time of ~ YORE

artichoke
- ~ morsel HEART

article BIT, ESSAY, ITEM
- ~ of faith DOGMA, TENET
- loose ~ END
- news ~ ITEM
- useful ~ THE

articles
- cut out ~ CLIP
- stolen ~ LOOT, SWAG
- touch up ~ EDIT

articulate CLEAR, GLIB, RELATE, SAY, TALK, UTTER

articulated ORAL

articulation NODE

Artie SHAW
- ~ ex AVA, LANA

"Artie"
- ~ author ADE

artifact RELIC

artifice RUSE, WILE

artificial FAKE, FALSE, SHAM
- ~ fiber NYLON
- ~ fly LURE
- ~ gem PASTE
- ~ waterway CANAL
- outrageously ~ CAMP

artillery
- ~ need AMMO

artiodactyl DEER

artist
- ~ gum ERASER
- ~ headgear BERET
- ~ medium OIL
- ~ need EASEL
- ~ paste GESSO
- ~ rep AGENT
- ~ subj. ANAT
- abstract ~ ARP
- con ~ game SCAM

___ artist CON

artistic
- ~ category GENRE
- ~ expression STYLE
- ~ judgment TASTE
- ~ style IDIOM
- ~ work OPUS

"Artists ___ Models" AND

___ artium ARS

artless HONEST, NAIVE

"Art of Love, The"
~ **poet** OVID

"Art of the ___, The" DEAL

"Art of the Fugue"
~ **composer** BACH

arts
goddess of the ~ MUSE
one of the ~ DANCE, DRAMA

art school
~ **subj.** ANAT

art store
~ **buy** EASEL, PAINT

"Art thou a woman's ___..." SON

ARU
part of ~ AUDIO

Aruba
~ **(abbr.)** ISL

___-Aryan INDO

as LIKE
~ **previously** YET
~ **regards** INRE

as ___ (customarily) USUAL

as ___ (so far) YET

as ___ (united) ONE

as ___ (with regard to) FOR

as ___ to (biographer's credit)
TOLD

As ELEM
33 for ~ ATNO

"As ___ Goes By" TIME

"As ___ It" ISEE

"As ___ Like It" YOU

"As ___ on TV" SEEN

A's TEAM, TEN

as a ___ (usually) RULE

Asa GRAY

ASA
~ **cousin** ISO

___ as a button CUTE

___ as a fiddle FIT

___ as a goose LOOSE

___ as a hatter MAD

___ as a judge SOBER

___ as a March hare MAD

asana
~ **practicer** YOGI

ASAP APACE, SOON
~ **relative** STAT

___ as a rock HARD, SOLID

"___ as a Stranger" NOT

___ as a wet hen MAD

"...as a wild bull in ___" ANET

ascend ARISE, LOOM, RISE, SCALE, SLOPE, SOAR

ascendancy DAY, RULE, SWAY
have the ~ LEAD

ascent RAMP, RISE

ascertain LEARN, SEE, TRACE

ascetic STERN
ancient ~ ESSENE
Hindu ~ YOGI

Asclepius
~ **to Apollo** SON

ascorbic ACID

ascot SCARF, TIE

ascribe LAY

___ a secret INON

Asgard
~ **chief** ODIN
~ **resident** THOR

ash TREE
~ **holder** TRAY
glowing ~ EMBER

ashamed
be ~ of RUE
make ~ ABASH

Ashby ALAN, HAL

Ashcroft, Peggy DAME

ashen GRAY, GREY, PALE, WAN

___ a shine to TAKE

Ashley LAURA

ashore
go ~ LAND
not ~ ATSEA

___ a shot LIKE

ashram HAVEN

Ashtabula
~ **abuts it** ERIE
~ **state** OHIO

Ash Wednesday
~ **season** LENT

"Ash Wednesday" POEM
~ **monogram** TSE
~ **poet** ELIOT

ashy PALE, WAN

"As I ___ saying..." WAS

Asia
part of ~'s border URALS

Asia Minor
~ **region** IONIA

Asian
~ **antelope** GOA
~ **bean** SOY
~ **buffalo** ANOA
~ **capital** ADEN, HANOI
~ **cat** TIGER
~ **celebration** TET
~ **country** INDIA, IRAN, IRAQ, LAOS, NEPAL, TIBET
~ **country of old** SIAM
~ **cuisine** THAI

~ **desert** GOBI
~ **export** SILK
~ **garment** SARI
~ **holiday** TET
~ **honorific** KHAN, SRI
~ **island** JAVA
~ **land, slangily** NAM
~ **language** LAO, TAI, THAI
~ **monk** LAMA
~ **nanny** AMA, AMAH
~ **observance** TET
~ **ox** ANOA, YAK
~ **peninsula** ARABIA
~ **place-name suffix** STAN
~ **priest** LAMA
~ **princess** RANEE, RANI
~ **range** ALAI
~ **river** AMUR
~ **ruler** AMIR, EMEER, EMIR
~ **sea** ARAL
~ **seaport** HUE
~ **weight** TAEL
ancient ~ MEDE
divided ~ nation KOREA

Asian ___ FLU

aside APART, OFF
cast ~ SCRAP
lay ~ SAVE, TABLE
put ~ ALLOW, DEFER, ONICE, SAVE, STORE
set ~ ANNUL, SAVE
turn ~ AVERT, AVOID, VEER

___ aside LAY, SET

Asimov ISAAC

asinine DAFT, INANE

as it ___ WERE

"As I was going to St. ___..."
IVES

ask PLEAD
~ **a question** POSE
~ **desperately** BEG
~ **for** SEEK
~ **for an ID** CARD
~ **for help, in a way** PRAY
~ **on one's knees** PLEAD
~ **out** DATE

"Ask ___ Girl" ANY

"Ask ___ what your country..."
NOT

"Ask Any ___" GIRL

"Ask Dr. ___" RUTH

"___ Asked for It" YOU

"___ asked you?" WHO

___ a Sketch ETCH

askew ATILT, AWRY, BENT, OFF, WRY
~ **in Scottish** AGEE

asking
~ **price** COST

aslant
drive a nail ~ TOE

asleep
fall ~ NOD
still ~ ABED

___ as life BIG

"As Long ___ Needs Me" ASHE

"___ a Small World" ITS

"___ as Mistress, The" (Pergolesi work) MAID

Asner
~ **and others** EDS

"___ as 1, 2, 3" EASY

asocial
~ **one** LONER

Asoka
~ **continent** ASIA
~ **realm, today** INDIA

"___ a Song Go out of My Heart" ILET

___ a soul NARY

asp ADDER, SNAKE
~ **cousin** COBRA
~ **victim** CLEO

asparagus FERN
~ **shoot** SPEAR

"...a sparrow in the ___" EAVES

aspartic ACID

aspect AIR, ANGLE, FACE, MIEN, MODE, PHASE, SIDE

aspen TREE

Aspen
~ **asset** SNOW
~ **feature** SLOPE
~ **transport** TBAR
enjoy ~ SKI

asperity RIGOR

asperse TAINT

aspersion LIBEL, SLUR, SMEAR

aspersions
cast ~ SLUR

asphalt PAVE, TAR
~ **jungle** CITY
cover with ~ PAVE

aspic
~ **shaper** MOLD

aspidistra PLANT

___ as pie EASY

Aspin LES

aspiration DREAM, GOAL, HOPE

aspire AIM, HOPE, SOAR
~ **(to)** AIM, LONG

aspirin
~ **target** ACHE, PAIN
~ **unit** PILL

aspiring EAGER

as right as ___ RAIN

ass
emulate an ~ BRAY

Assad
~ **nation** SYRIA

assai PALM

assail BESET, HIT, LACE, PELT, RAID, SETON, SMITE
  ~ the ramparts STORM

assailant ENEMY, FOE

Assam
  ~ product TEA
  ~ silkworm ERI

assassinate SLAY

assault ONSET, RAID, STORM
  ~ the nostrils REEK
  blunt an ~ STEM

assault vehicle
  WWII ~ LST

assay RATE, TEST, TRY

assayer
  ~ concern ORE

assegai LANCE, PIKE, SPEAR

assemblage CREW, TOTAL, TROOP

assemble AMASS, CALL, ERECT, MAKE, MASS, MEET, SIT, UNITE
  ~ a film EDIT
  something to ~ KIT

assembly DIET, HOST, MASS, MEET, SALON, SYNOD
  ~ instruction STEP
  ecclesiastical ~ SYNOD
  requiring ~ APART

assembly ___ LINE

assent AGREE, NOD, YES
  ~ to ADMIT
  congregation's ~ AMEN
  informal ~ YEAH, YEP
  nautical ~ AYE
  refuse ~ DENY
  space-shuttle ~ AOK
  voiceless ~ NOD
  word of ~ AMEN, YEA

assert AVER, AVOW, CLAIM, SAY, STATE, URGE, UTTER

assertion CLAIM, SAYSO, STAND

assess ASSAY, RATE, TEST

assessment TOLL

asset PLUS
  ~ in Italian BENE

assets CDS, ESTATE
  aggregate ~ ESTATE

asseverate AVER, AVOW, CLAIM

assibilate LISP

assign ALLOT, AWARD, CAST, POST, PUT, SEND, SET
  ~ a "G" RATE
  ~ an "NC-17" RATE
  ~ an "R" RATE
  ~ an "X" RATE
  ~ a "PG-13" RATE
  ~ as blame LAY
  ~ roles CAST
  ~ to an errand SEND

assignation DATE, TRYST

assigned
  ~ function ROLE

assignment BEAT, POST, STINT, TASK
  conservatory ~ ETUDE
  English ~ ESSAY
  postman's ~ ROUTE
  teaching ~ CLASS

"Assignment to Kill"
  ~ actor ONEAL

assimilate ADAPT, GET, LEARN

as simple as ___ ABC

assist ABET, AID, ENABLE, HELP, SERVE, TIDE
  ~ in crime ABET

assistance AID, HAND, HELP
  ~ provider AIDE
  provide ~ AID
  without ~ ALONE, SOLO

assistant AIDE
  doctor's ~ NURSE
  lab ~ of film IGOR
  Senate ~ AIDE

assists STAT

assize EDICT

assn. ORG
  ~ to org. SYN

assoc. ORG
  lower than ~ ASST

associate ALLY, RELATE

associated
  one ~ with (suffix) EER

association BAND, RING
  Chinese ~ TONG

___ association FREE

assortment ARRAY, CROP

assuage ABATE, ALLAY, CALM, EASE, SLAKE

assume ADOPT, CLAIM, DON, FAKE, OPINE, POSE, TAKE

assumed SHAM
  ~ name ALIAS

assurance OATH, POISE, SEAL
  give ~ AGREE
  solemn ~ OATH
  state with ~ ATTEST, AVER, AVOW

assure
  ~ success ICE

___-assured SELF

assuredly AMEN

Assyrian
  ~ foe MEDE

Asta
  ~ mistress NORA

Astaire ADELE, FRED
  ~ hometown OMAHA
  ~ prop CANE

Astaire and Rogers DUO, PAIR, TEAM

Astaire, Fred
  ~ sister ADELE

like ~ SUAVE

asterisk STAR

astern AFT

asteroid CERES, EROS, IRENE
  ~ region BELT
  largest ~ CERES

as the ___ flies CROW

"As the World Turns" SOAP

as time ___ on WORE

"As Time Goes By"
  ~ requester ILSA
  ~ singer SAM

astir ABOUT, AFOOT

Astolat
  lily maid of ~ ELAINE

astonish AMAZE, AWE, DAZE, STUN

astonished AGOG
  ~ reaction WOW

astonishment AWE
  show ~ GAPE
  sound of ~ GASP

Astor
  ~ trade FUR
  part of ~'s inventory PELT

Astoria
  ~ locale ORE, OREGON

Astor, Nancy, ___ Langhorne NEE

astound AMAZE, DAZE, STUN, WOW

astounded AGAPE

astrakhan FUR

astral
  ~ influence FATE

astray LOST, WIDE
  go ~ ERR, SIN

astride ACROSS, ATOP

astringent ACID, ACRID, ALUM, SOUR, TART

Astrodome ARENA
  ~ home TEX

astrologer ORACLE, SEER

astrologers MAGI

astron. SCI

astronaut
  ~ affirmative AOK
  ~ Apollo BEAN, SCOTT
  ~ drink TANG
  ~ excursion EVA
  ~ milieu ETHER
  ~ vehicle LEM
  rotate, to an ~ YAW

astronauts
  ~ org. NASA
  number of Mercury ~ SEVEN

astronomer
  early ~ OMAR

astronomical
  ~ adjective LUNAR, SOLAR
  ~ unit YEAR

"Astrophel and Stella" POEM

Astros NINE, TEAM

Astroturf
  ~ component NYLON

astute ACUTE, CLEAR, KEEN, SMART

astuteness SENSE, WIT

Astyanax
  ~ to Hector SON

Asunción CITY, PORT
  see also Spanish

asunder APART
  ~ (prefix) DIS
  put ~ TEAR

Aswan DAM

Aswan Dam
  ~ site NILE

___ a swath CUT

"___ as we speak..." EVEN

asylum ARK, HAVEN
  ~ seeker ALIEN

"As you ___" WERE

"As You ___ It" LIKE

___ as you are COME

"As You Like It"
  ~ locale ARDEN
  ~ servant ADAM

at
  ~ liberty FREE
  ~ no cost FREE
  ~ no time, poetically NEER
  ~ some time EVER
  ~ that point THERE
  ~ this location HERE

at ___ (besides) THAT

at ___ (disagreeing) ODDS

at ___ (essentially) HEART

at ___ (finally) LAST

at ___ (free) LARGE

at ___ (hitting) BAT

at ___ (immediately) ONCE

at ___ (in jeopardy) STAKE

at ___ (in unison) ONE

at ___ (maximally) MOST

at ___ (minimally) LEAST

at ___ (nearby) HAND

at ___ (optimally) BEST

at ___ (perplexed) SEA

at ___ (relaxed) EASE, PEACE, REST

at ___ (wholesale) COST

at ___ end WITS

at ___ ends LOOSE

at ___ glance FIRST

at ___ length ARMS

at ___ rate ANY

___ at (attack) HAVE

___ at (bother) EAT, GNAW

___ at (censure) RAIL

___ at (charge) COME

___ at (criticize) SNIPE

___ at (dabble in) PLAY

___ at (draw a bead on) AIM

___ at (imply) HINT

___ at (malign) SNIPE

___ at (reach) GET

___ at (torment) GNAW

___ at (worry) EAT

At ELEM
   85 for ~ ATNO

"At ___ in the Fields of the Lord"
   PLAY

"At ___ Range" CLOSE

at a ___ for words LOSS

___-Ata ALMA

Atacama DESERT
   like the ~ ARID

Atahualpa INCA

Atalanta
   ~ fruit APPLE
   like ~ FLEET

"Atalanta in Calydon" POEM

at a later ___ DATE

"___ a tale told by an idiot" ITIS

at any ___ RATE

ataraxia PEACE

___-at-arms MAN

___-a-tat RAT

at-bat
   successful ~ HIT

at bats STAT

"At Close ___" RANGE

"___ at Diablo" DUEL

A-Team
   ~ member FACE, MRT

___ at ease ILL

atelier SHOP
   ~ item EASEL

"___ at End House" PERIL

___-à-terre PIED

at every ___ TURN

"___ at First Bite" LOVE

___ at first sight LOVE

at full ___ TILT

Athabaska LAKE

at hand
   not ~ AFAR

Athena
   ~ shield AEGIS, EGIS
   ~ symbol OWL

Athenian ATTIC

Athens CITY
   a, in ~ ALPHA
   see also Greek

"___ a Thief" ONCE

athirst EAGER

athlete's ___ FOOT

athletic AGILE, HALE, TRIM
   ~ event GAME, MEET
   ~ ring ARENA
   ~ trial HEAT
   gracefully ~ AGILE

Athletics TEAM, TEN

"___, a thousand times..." NONO

athwart ACROSS

"A-Tisket, A-Tasket"
   ~ name ELLA

Atitlán LAKE

Atkins CHET

Atkins, Dr.
   ~ plan DIET

Atl.
   ~ crosser SST
   ~ time zone EDT, EST

Atlanta
   ~ zone EDT, EST
   former ~ arena OMNI

Atlantic OCEAN
   ~ cape COD
   ~ fish COD
   ~ flier ERN, ERNE
   ~ st. DEL
   desert on the ~ SAHARA
   on the ~ ASEA, ATSEA

"Atlantic ___" CITY

Atlantic City
   ~ game FARO, KENO
   they're thrown in ~ DICE
   work in ~ DEAL

Atlantis
   ~ (abbr.) ISL
   ~ org. NASA

atlas POST
   ~ abbr. ATL, ISL, LAT, MTS, PAC,
      STR, TER, TERR
   ~ blowup INSET
   ~ datum AREA
   ~ dot ISLET
   ~ line ROAD, ROUTE
   ~ page MAP
   ~ section ASIA
   ~ unit MAP

Atlas GIANT, MOON, RANGE, TITAN

Atlas Mountains
   ~ desert SAHARA

"Atlas Shrugged"
   ~ author RAND

"___ at last!" ALONE

at long ___ LAST

at loose ___ ENDS

at low ___ EBB

ATM
   ~ code PIN
   ~ device CRT
   ~ key ENTER

atman SELF

atmo-
   ~ cousin AER, AERO

atmosphere AIR, AROMA, AURA,
   FEEL, MOOD, SKY, SPACE, TONE
   ~ (prefix) AER, AERO
   gloomy ~ PALL
   subtle ~ AURA
   unhealthy ~ SMOG
   upper ~ ETHER, SKY

atmospheric AERIAL, AIRY
   ~ layer OZONE
   ~ (prefix) AER, AERO

"___ at My Table, An" ANGEL

atoll REEF
   ~ material CORAL

atom BIT, IOTA, JOT, MITE, MOTE
   ~ ender ISM
   ~ ID ATNO
   charged ~ ION

"Atom ___" ANT

atomic SMALL, TINY, WEE
   ~ particle BETA

Atomic ___ AGE

"Atomic ___, The" CAFE

___ Atomic Dustbin NEDS

atomizer
   ~ output MIST

atomlike SMALL, TINY, WEE

atomy MOTE

___ at once ALL

at one's wits' ___ END

at one's wit's ___ END

___ at one's word TAKE

atop ABOVE, UPON
   ~ to a poet OER

"___ a Toy or a Treasure?" AMI

"At Play in the Fields of the ___"
   LORD

___ atque vale AVE

atrabilious SAD

Atreus
   Agamemnon, to ~ SON

atrocious BAD, EVIL, VILE

Atropos FATE

"___ at 6 A.M." ADAM

"___ at Sea" ALL, DAMES, SAPS

"At Seventeen"
   ~ singer IAN

AT&SF
   ~ and others RRS
   ~ stop STA

"___ at Sharkey's" STAG

AT&T
   part of ~ AMER, TEL, TELE

attach ADD, AMEND, BIND, LASH,
   NAIL, PASTE, PIN, RIVET, SEW,
   TAG, TIE
   ~ firmly GLUE

attaché AIDE
   ~ case BAG

attached
   be ~ ADHERE
   not ~ LOOSE

attachment LIEN

attack BESET, BOUT, HARM, HIT,
   ONSET, RAID, SETON, SIEGE,
   STAB, STORM
   ~ helicopter COBRA
   ~ in a way CLAW, STONE
   ~ viciously RIP
   ~ with snowballs PELT
   ~ word SIC
   olfactory ~ REEK
   sudden ~ RAID
   unlikely to ~ TAME
   verbal ~ SLAM

___ attack SNEAK

"___ Attack" DESERT

attacker ENEMY, FOE

"Attack of the 50 ___ Woman"
   FOOT

attacks
   where Shaq ~ NBA

attain GET, WIN
   ~ success ARRIVE

attainment ACT, DEED, FEAT

attar ESSENCE, SCENT

Attell ABE

attempt ASSAY, ESSAY, RISK,
   SHOT, TEST, TRIAL, TRY
   boldly ~ DARE
   brief ~ STAB
   failed ~ MISS

attempts
   like some ~ LAME

attend ENSUE, HEAR, SEE, SEETO,
   SERVE
   ~ a banquet EAT
   ~ a meeting SIT
   ~ carefully HEED
   ~ tables SERVE
   ~ to BEND, DEAL
   fail to ~ MISS

attendance GATE, ROLL

attendant MAN, PAGE
   bridegroom's ~ USHER
   flight ~ boss PILOT
   hospital ~ NURSE
   parking ~ VALET
   personal ~ VALET

attender
  reunion ~ ALUM, GRAD

attends GOES
  ~ **to** DOES

attention CARE, EAR, HEED
  at ~ ERECT
  bring to ~ SAY
  call ~ **to** NOTE, REFER, STRESS
  close ~, **for short** TLC
  hold, as ~ RIVET
  hold the ~ **of** ARREST
  let one's ~ **wander** MISS
  paying ~ ALERT
  pay no ~ **to** SLUR, SNUB
  pay ~ **to** ATTEND, HEAR, HEED, NOTE
  shower ~ DOTE
  undivided ~ EAR

attention ___ SPAN

___ **attention** PAY

"Attention!"
  opposite of ~ ATEASE

attention-getter AHEM, HEY, PSST, PST
  infant's ~ BAWL

attentions SUIT

attentive ALERT, WARY
  be ~ HEAR
  totally ~ RAPT

attenuate ABATE, THIN

attenuated THIN

attest AVER, STATE
  ~ **to** ASSERT

at the ___ **minute** LAST

at the ___ **of a hat** DROP

"At the ___**"** (1950s song) HOP

at the drop of a ___ HAT

___ **at the elbows** OUT

" ___ **at the Races, A"** DAY

"At the sound of the ___**..."** TONE

" ___ **at the Top"** ROOM

attic
  ~ **view** EAVE

Attic
  ~ **dialect** IONIC

Attica
  ~ **resident** CON

Atticism ADAGE

Attila
  ~ **follower** HUN

attire ARRAY, DON, DRESS, GARB, RIG, ROBE, SUIT, WEAR
  ~ **accessory** HAT
  business ~ SUIT, TIE
  don ~ DRESS
  formal ~ DRESS
  night ~ ROBE

attired CLAD

attitude AIR, MIEN, POSE, SET, TONE
  snobbish ~ AIRS
  strike an ~ POSE

attitudes
  group ~ ETHOS

attorney
  ~ **concern** LAW
  ~ **deg.** LLD
  ~ **income** FEE
  ~ **org.** ABA

attorney at ___ LAW

attorney general
  first female ~ RENO
  Reagan ~ MEESE

attorneys-at-law BAR

attract ARREST, BAIT, DRAW, ENDEAR, LURE, TAKE
  magnets ~ **it** IRON

attracted
  be ~ **to** WANT

attraction DRAW, LOVE, LURE
  center of ~ MECCA
  mutual ~ LOVE

attractions
  like some ~ ADDED

attractive CUTE, FAIR, NICE, SWEET
  find ~ LIKE

attribute OWE, TRAIT
  ~ **to** CITE

Attu
  ~ **(abbr.)** ISL
  ~ **resident** ALEUT

attuned
  perfectly ~ ATONE

atty.
  ~ **degree** LLD
  ~ **org.** ABA

Atty. ___ GEN

attys.
  some ~ DAS

ATV
  part of ~ ALL

" ___ **at will"** FIRE

___ **at windmills** TILT

atwitter AGOG

" ___ **at Work"** MEN

atypical ODD, RARE

au ___ PAIR

Au ELEM, GOLD
  79 for ~ ATNO

auberge INN

Auberjonois RENE

auburn BAY, COLOR, RED
  ~ **tint** HENNA

Auburn
  ~ **athlete** TIGER

A.U.C.
  part of ~ ANNO

Auckland CITY, PORT

au courant AWARE, HOT
  not ~ PASSE

auction SALE
  ~ **action** BID
  ~ **caveat** ASIS
  ~ **ender** EER, SOLD
  ~ **grouping** LOT
  ~ **off** SELL
  ~ **parcel** LOT
  ~ **shout** BID
  ~ **signal** NOD
  ~ **stipulation** ASIS
  ~ **unit** LOT
  ~ **word** GONE

auctioneer EMCEE
  ~ **cry** SOLD

audacious PERT
  be ~ DARE

audacity BRASS, FACE, NERVE, SASS

Auden, W.H. POET
  see also poet

audible ALOUD, CLEAR
  ~ **comeback** ECHO
  barely ~ SMALL

audibly ALOUD

audience EAR
  before an ~ LIVE
  break in the ~ AISLE
  give an ~ **to** HEAR

audio
  ~ **problem** ECHO
  ~ **receiver** EAR

audiophile
  ~ **equipment** STEREO

audit ___ TRAIL

auditing
  ~ **ace** CPA
  ~ **org.** IRS

audition READ, TEST, TRIAL
  ~ **attendee** ACTOR
  ~ **tape** DEMO

auditioner
  ~ **objective** PART, ROLE

auditioners
  successful ~ CAST

auditor
  ~ **letters** CPA

auditorium HALL
  ~ **sign** EXIT

auditory OTIC

Audrey
  ~ **to Jayne** SIS

Audubon
  of interest to ~ AVIAN

Auel
  ~ **subject** CLAN

Auerbach ARTIE, RED

au fait ABLE, ACE, ADEPT, SMART

___**-au-feu** POT

auf Wiedersehen ADIEU, ADIOS, BYE, CIAO, TATA

Aug.
  ~ **follower** SEPT
  ~ **hrs.** DST

Augean
  ~ **stables** MESS

auger BORE, TOOL

aught ANY, NIL, ZERO

augment ADD, EKE, GROW, PAD, RAISE

augmentation RISE

Augsburg
  see German

augur BODE, MEAN, ORACLE, SEER

augury OMEN, SIGN, TOKEN

august REGAL

August
  ~ **sign** LEO

Augusta
  ~ **state** MAINE

Auguste
  see French

Augustus CAESAR, ROMAN
  see also Latin

___ **au Haut** ISLE

auk BIRD

auks
  like ~ AVIAN

___ **au lait** CAFE

"Auld ___ **Syne"** LANG

"Auld Lang ___**"** SYNE

auld lang syne PAST, YORE

"Auld Lang Syne" POEM

auld sod
  the ~ ERIN

Auletta KEN

Aulis CITY, PORT

au naturel BARE, NUDE

aunt
  ~ **(abbr.)** REL
  ~ **in Spanish** TIA
  Mayberry ~ BEE

auntie
  fictional ~ MAME

"Auntie ___**"** MAME

Auntie Em
  ~ **st.** KAN

"Auntie Mame"
  ~ **character** AGNES

aunts KIN

au pair MAID

___ **au poivre** STEAK

___-au-Prince PORT

aura AIR, AROMA, HALO, MIEN, ODOR
  saint's ~ HALO

aural OTIC

Aurelian CAESAR, ROMAN

aureole HALO, RING

aureus COIN

au revoir ADIEU, ADIOS, ALOHA, BYE, CIAO, LATER, TATA

"Au revoir!" ADIEU, BYE, TATA
  ~ in Hawaiian ALOHA
  ~ in Italian CIAO
  ~ in Latin AVE, VALE
  ~ in Spanish ADIOS

"Au Revoir, ___ Enfants" LES

___ au rhum BABA

auricle EAR

auricular OTIC

auriculate EARED

aurochs ANIMAL

aurora
  ~ locale SKY

Aurora
  ~ counterpart EOS

aurum GOLD

auscultate HEAR

auslander ALIEN

auspice OMEN, SIGN

auspices AEGIS, EGIS, HELP

auspicious GOOD, RIPE

Aust.
  neighbor of ~ GER

Austen
  ~ novel EMMA

austere BARE, DOUR, SOBER, STERN

austerity RIGOR

Austin TERI
  ~ st. TEX

___ Austin, "The Six Million Dollar Man" STEVE

Austral.
  ~ island TAS

Australian
  ~ animal KOALA
  ~ bird EMU
  ~ island ADELE
  ~ jumper ROO
  ~ lake EYRE
  ~ mineral OPAL
  ~ native ABO
  ~ tree-dweller KOALA
  grounded ~ EMU

Australian English
  buddy, in ~ MATE

___ australis AURORA

Austria
  ~ largely ALPS
  ~ western boundary RHINE
  see also German

Austrian
  ~ composer BERG
  ~ mountains ALPS
  ~ peak ALP
  ~ psychologist ADLER
  see also German

Austronesian
  ~ language MAORI

authentic GOOD, REAL, SOLID, TRUE

authentication SEAL, TRIAL

author CAUSE, PEN, WRITE
  ~ concern PLOT
  ~ submissions MSS
  ~ unknown ANON

"author"
  prolific ~ ANON

authoritarian TSAR

authoritative SOLID
  ~ pronouncement FIAT
  ~ staff MACE
  ~ statement EDICT

authority ADEPT, ARM, SAYSO, SWAY
  challenge ~ REBEL
  diamond ~ UMP
  sports ~ REF
  staff of ~ MACE
  state with ~ ATTEST, AVER
  wield ~ RULE

authorization LEAVE, PAPER, PASS

authorize ALLOW, CLEAR, ENABLE, LET, OKAY

authorized LEGAL

authorizes OKS

auto CAR, MOTOR
  ~ accessory ALARM, BRA, PHONE, TIRE
  ~ appendage AERIAL
  ~ brand MAKE
  ~ classic REO
  ~ club letters AAA
  ~ document TITLE
  ~ financing letters APR
  ~ flop EDSEL
  ~ fuel GAS
  ~ gauge TACH
  ~ grille protector BRA
  ~ ID PLATE
  ~ inspection evidence DECAL
  ~ job LUBE
  ~ mishap mark DENT, DING
  ~ option AIR, LEASE
  ~ part AXLE, CAM, HORN
  ~ race INDY
  ~ race area PIT
  ~ safety advocate NADER
  ~ sound BEEP, TOOT
  ~ style SEDAN
  ~ testing org. EPA
  ~ tie-up JAM
  ~ track RUT

antique ~ AERO, CORD, NASH, REO
British ~ accessory TYRE
defective ~ LEMON
family ~ SEDAN
fast ~ GTO
imported ~ FIAT
onetime igloo-shaped
  ~ PACER
rickety ~ CRATE
ritzy ~ LIMO
skier's ~ adjunct RACK
souped-up ~ RACER
stretch ~ LIMO
  see also car

auto- SELF

autobahn PIKE, ROAD, ROUTE

autobiography LIFE

autochthonous EARLY, LOCAL, OLD

auto club
  ~ service TOW

autocrat TSAR

autograph SIGN
  ~ site CAST

automaker
  Italian ~ FIAT

automatic GUN

automatic ___ PILOT

automatic ___ processing DATA

automobile CAR, MOTOR
  ~ pioneer OLDS
  closed ~ SEDAN
  see also auto, car

autonomous FREE

___ Autonomous Republic of Russia TATAR

autostrada
  ~ place ITALY

Autry GENE
  ~ film OATER

autumn
  ~ beverage CIDER
  ~ bloom ASTER
  ~ fruit PEAR
  ~ mo. NOV, OCT, SEPT
  ~ tool RAKE
  like ~ leaves SERE
  like ~ weather CRISP

"___ Autumn" TIS

autunite ORE

auxiliary AID
  ~ verb ARE, BEEN

AV
  part of ~ AUDIO

Ava
  ~ ex ARTIE

avail AID, HELP, PAY, SERVE
  ~ oneself of TAKE, USE
  of some ~ UTILE

available FREE, ONTAP, OPEN
  no longer ~ TAKEN

not generally ~ RARE

availing UTILE

Avakian ARAM

Avalanche SIX, TEAM
  ~ milieu ICE, RINK
  ~ org. NHL

Avalon ISLE

avant-garde ARTY, NEW
  ~ artist ARP
  ~ prefix NEO

Avant Garde FONT

avarice LUST, SIN

avaricious AVID

avast STOP

ave. RTE

"Ave ___" MARIA

avec
  ~ in German MIT
  ~ opposite SANS

avenge GET

"Avengers, The"
  ~ name DIANA, UMA
  ~ role EMMA, PEEL, STEED
  Emma's successor on ~ TARA

avenue LANE, LINE, PATH, ROAD, ROUTE

aver ASSERT, AVOW, CLAIM, HOLD, SAY, STATE, URGE

average MEAN, NORM, PAR, SOSO
  ~ grade CEE
  ~ guy JOE
  below ~ POOR

___ average ONAN

Averno LAKE

averse
  ~ to mingling SHY

aversion HATE
  feel ~ toward ABHOR

avert AVOID, REPEL, TURN

Avery TEX
  ~ to Murphy SON

aves
  ~ have them ALAE

aves. RDS, STS

avg.
  ~ size MED

avian
  ~ domicile NEST

aviary CAGE

aviation
  ~ (prefix) AER, AERO
  ~ watchdog agcy. CAB

aviator PILOT

avid EAGER, HOT, KEEN, MAD
  ~ support ZEAL

Avignon
  see French

Avila
~ **saint** TERESA

___ **avion** PAR

avis
~ **pair** ALAE

___ **avis** RARA

Avis
~ **rival** ALAMO

___ **Aviv** TEL

avocado COLOR, TREE

avocation BAG

avocet BIRD

Avogadro's ___ LAW

avoid AVERT, BEG, ELUDE, EVADE, MISS, SHUN, SKIP, SNUB
~ **a big wedding** ELOPE
~ **a bogey** PAR
~ **an F** PASS
~ **cancellation** RENEW
~ **capture** ELUDE
~ **expiration** RENEW
~ **friction** OIL
~ **restaurants** EATIN
~ **summer school** PASS
in order to ~ LEST

avoiding
~ **others** SHY

avow ASSERT, AVER, STATE

avowal OATH

avril
~ **follower** MAI

A&W
~ **rival** DADS

await ABIDE, PEND

awaited DUE

awake ALERT, AWARE
stay ~ **nights** STEW

___**-awake** WIDE

"Awake and Sing!"
~ **playwright** ODETS

awaken ARISE, AROUSE, EVOKE, RAISE, RISE, ROUSE, STIR
~ **love** ENDEAR

___ **awakening** RUDE

award MEDAL
~ **an award** CITE
~ **for HBO** ACE
acting ~ OBIE, OSCAR, TONY
advertising ~ CLIO
Broadway ~ TONY
commercial ~ CLIO
director's ~ OBIE, OSCAR, TONY
film ~ OSCAR
French film ~ CESAR
mystery writers' ~ EDGAR
Olympian's ~ GOLD, MEDAL
playwright's ~ OBIE, TONY
rock-video ~ AVA
science-fiction ~ HUGO
service ~ TIP
theater ~ OBIE, TONY
"Village Voice" ~ OBIE
whodunit ~ EDGAR

awarded
be ~ LAND, WIN

aware ACUTE, ALERT, HEP, HIP, SMART
~ **of** INON, ONTO
become ~ ROUSE
become ~ **of** SENSE
be ~ **of** KNOW
make ~ **of** ALERT

awareness SENSE, TACT

away APART, ASIDE, FRO, OFF, OUT
~ **from (prefix)** APO
~ **in Italian** VIA

___ **away (cache)** HIDE, SALT

___ **away (escape)** GET, RUN

___ **away (reject)** TURN

___ **away (save)** LAY, PUT

___ **away (travel for free)** STOW

"___ Away" MOVE

awe
in ~ AGAPE, AGOG
inspire ~ AMAZE
regard with ~ GAPE
sound of ~ OOH
stand in ~ **of** FEAR

aweather
~ **opposite** ALEE

awed AGOG, RAPT

awesome RAD
~ **home** ESTATE

"Awesome!" WOW

awestruck AGAPE, AGOG, RAPT

awful BAD, DIRE
feel ~ AIL
feel ~ **about** RUE
find ~ HATE
something ~ LOSER

___ **a whack at** HAVE, TAKE

___ **a wide swath** CUT

awkward INEPT, MESSY

awl TOOL

awning ROOF, SHADE, TILT

AWOL
~ **pursuers** MPS
go ~ DESERT

"___ a Woman" IGOT, SHES

"___ a Wonderful Life" ITS

"___ a Wonderful World" ITS

awry AGEE, AMISS, OFF
go ~ ERR

"Aw, shucks!" PSHAW

axe CAN, HACK, HEW, SLASH, TOOL
~ **cousin** ADZE
~ **stroke** CHOP
prehistoric ~ **head** CELT
use an ~ HEW

axel LEAP
do an ~ SKATE
where to do an ~ ICE, RINK

axillary ALAR

axiom ADAGE, LAW, RULE, SAW, TENET

axis STEM
~ **extremity** POLE

axis ___ DEER

Axis
~ **once** ENEMY, FOE
~ **sub** UBOAT

Axl ROSE

axlike
~ **tool** ADZE

Ayatollah TITLE
~ **land** IRAN
~ **preceder** SHAH
~ **subject** IRANI
~ **title** IMAM

Ayckbourn ALAN

aye YEA, YES
~ **opposite** NAY
voting ~ FOR

"___ a yellow ribbon..." TIE

Ayesha
Haggard's ~ SHE

Aykroyd DAN

Ayn RAND

Ayres LEW

AZ
see Arizona

Azeem MOOR

Azerbaijan
~ **location** ASIA
~ **once** SSR

Azerbaijani
~ **neighbor** IRANI

azimuth ARC

Azinger
~ **org.** PGA

azo DYE

Azores
~ **essentially** LAVA
~ **loc.** ATL

Azrael ANGEL

azure BLUE, COLOR, SKY

azurite ORE

azygous ONE, SOLE

1

B ELEM, TYPE
   5 for ~ ATNO
   one of the musical ~'s BACH

B ___ "Baker" ASIN

B ___ "boy" ASIN

Ba ELEM
   56 for ~ ATNO

B.A.
   part of ~ ARTS

baa CRY, NOISE
   ~ relative MOO

"___ b-a-a-d boy!" IMA

baal IDOL

baba CAKE
   ~ ingredient RUM

Baba ALI

"___ Baba and the 40 Thieves"
   ALI

babassu PALM

"Babbitt"
   ~ author LEWIS

babble BLAB, GAB, NOISE, PRATE,
   RAVE, TALK, YAK, YAP

babe HON, TOT

Babe RUTH
   ~ word OINK
   home for ~ STY

"Babe"
   ~ band STYX

babe in the woods
   like a ~ NAIVE

babel DIN, NOISE

Babette
   see French

"Babette's Feast"
   ~ director AXEL

Babilonia TAI
   emulate ~ SKATE

babirusa HOG

"Babi Yar" POEM

baboon ANIMAL, APE

babushka SCARF

baby DOTE, KID, SPOIL, TINY, WEE
   ~ beaver KIT
   ~ bed CRIB
   ~ bird OWLET
   ~ blues EYES, ORBS
   ~ bouncer KNEE
   ~ carriage PRAM
   ~ cover BIB
   ~ cry MAMA
   ~ ender ISH, SIT
   ~ food PAP
   ~ fox KIT
   ~ goat KID
   ~ grand PIANO
   ~ kisser POL
   ~ place CRIB
   ~ seat LAP
   ~ soother TALC
   ~ sound COO
   ~ word DADA, GOO
   act like a ~ BAWL
   barn ~ CALF, OWLET
   barnyard ~ KID
   bush ~ ANIMAL
   ewe's ~ LAMB
   farm ~ CALF, FOAL, LAMB
   mind the ~ SIT
   seal ~ CALF
   stable ~ FOAL
   talk ~ talk LISP
   warning to ~ NONO

baby ___ BLUE

baby-___ SIT

___ baby TAR

Baby ___ (1930s film toddler)
   LEROY

Baby ___ (Milne character) ROO

"Baby ___" BOOM

"Baby ___ a Rich Man" YOURE

"Baby ___ Want You" IMA

"Baby ___ You" ITS

"___ Baby" ANGEL, TAR

"___ Baby" ("Hair" song) ABIE

"___ Baby" (Orbison tune)
   DREAM

"___-Baby" CRY

"___ Baby Baby" OOH

Baby Doc
   ~ country HAITI

baby-faced CUTE

baby grand PIANO

"Baby It's ___" YOU

Babylonia
   ~ neighbor ELAM
   ~ today IRAQ

baby powder
   ~ ingredient TALC

Baby Ruth BAR

"Baby's ___ Out" DAY

baby-sit TEND

baby sitter
   ~ bane BRAT

"Baby the ___ Must Fall" RAIN

Bacardi RUM

baccarat GAME
   ~ table item SHOE

bacchanal ORGY, REVEL

Bacchanalia ORGY, REVEL

Bacchus GOD
   ~ attendant SATYR
   bash for ~ REVEL

Bach
   ~ instrument ORGAN

bachelor MALE
   ~ home PAD
   ~ party STAG
   last words of a ~ IDO

bachelor-at-arms MAN

"Bachelor Party, The"
   ~ director MANN

Bach, J.S.
   ~ field MUS

bacillus GERM
   ~ shape ROD

back ABET, AFT, AGO, AID, FRO,
   HELP, STERN
   ~ biter FLEA
   ~ down REACT, YIELD
   ~ ender ACHE, BEAT, BITE,
     BONE, DATE, DROP, FIRE,
     HAND, HOE, LASH, LIST, LIT,

     LOG, PEDAL, SLAP, SLIDE,
     SPACE, SPIN, STAGE, STAIR,
     STOP, WARD, WASH, WATER
   ~ financially STAKE
   ~ from work HOME
   ~ in French DOS
   ~ in time AGO, ONCE, THEN
   ~ into a corner TREE
   ~ muscle, in the gym LAT
   ~ of the neck NAPE
   ~ out of DROP
   ~ part SMALL, STERN
   ~ starter CAMEL, FAST, FAT,
     FEED, HALF, HARD, HOG,
     HORSE, LAY, MOSS, OUT,
     PAPER, PAY, SHELL, TIE
   ~ street ALLEY
   ~ talk ECHO, LIP, SASS
   ~ then ONCE, PAST
   ~ there, on the ocean AFT
   ~ the wrong horse LOSE
   ~ tooth MOLAR
   ~ up CLOG, PRONE
   ~ way ALLEY
   answer ~ SASS
   at the ~ AFT
   a while ~ ONCE
   beat ~ REPEL, STEM
   be on a ~ burner PEND
   be on someone's ~ TEASE
   bounce ~ CAROM, ECHO
   break the ~ of TASK
   bring ~ RENEW, RESTORE
   bring ~ to snuff REHAB
   come ~ ARRIVE
   cut ~ ABATE, LOP, PARE, THIN
   draw ~ EBB, SHY, START
   drive ~ REPEL
   fall ~ EBB, LAPSE, REEL
   fight ~ REACT
   force ~ REPEL
   get one's ~ up IRE
   get someone's ~ up ANGER,
     IRK, PEEVE, RILE, UPSET
   give ~ ECHO, RESTORE
   go ~ and forth PLY
   go ~ on BELIE
   hang ~ LAG, TRAIL, WAIT
   hanging ~ SLOW
   hold ~ ARREST, DETER, HANG,
     LEASH, REIN, SAVE, SPARE,
     STAY, STEM
   in ~ of AFTER
   in the ~ REAR
   money ~ REBATE

move ~ and forth BOB, SWAY, WAG
neither front nor ~ SIDE
nurse ~ to health RESTORE
one of the ~ forty ACRE
pat oneself on the ~ BRAG, CROW, PREEN
pay ~ AVENGE, REBATE
pin one's ears ~ BEAT
push ~ REPEL
put ~ RESTORE
put on a ~ burner DEFER
put one ~ on one's feet CURE
put ~ on one's feet RESTORE
put ~ to zero RESET
send ~ to Congress VETO
set one ~ RUN
some time ~ AGO, ONCE
spring ~ REACT, SHY
take ~ DENY
take a ~ seat (to) DEFER
take the ~ roads MOTOR
talk ~ to SASS
thrust ~ REPEL
toward the ~ of the boat AFT, ASTERN
turn ~ REPEL
turned ~ on RELIT
turned the clock ~ RESET
turn one's ~ on CUT, DESERT
walk ~ and forth PACE
want ~ MISS
way ~ when ONCE, PAST, YORE

back ___ AWAY, OFF, OUT, ROOM, SEAT, TALK, YARD

back-___ driver SEAT

___ back (echo) PLAY

___ back (lag) HANG

___ back (reduce) CUT

___ back (regain) TAKE

___ back (reinvest) PLOW

___ back (restore) ROLL

___ back (restrain) HOLD

___ back (retreat) TURN

___ back (return) COME

___ back (return to normal) SNAP

___ back (sass) TALK

___-back (easygoing) LAID

"Back ___ to Heaven" DOOR

"___ Back, The" RIDE

backbiting LIBEL

backbone GRIT, METAL, NERVE, SAND
boat's ~ KEEL

backbreaker
camel's ~ STRAW

backcomb TEASE

"Backdraft"
~ crime ARSON
~ special effect FIRE

backdrop SCENE, SET
~ in westerns MESA

backer ANGEL, DONOR
~ favorite sign SRO
prefix for ~ LINE

backfire
~ sound BANG

backflow EDDY

backgammon
~ cube DIE
~ equipment DICE
~ impossibility TIE
~ piece STONE

background
~ noise DIN

backhoe SCOOP
use a ~ DIG

backing AID
picture ~ MAT
stamp ~ GLUE

"Back in the ___" USSR

"Back in the Saddle" OATER

backless
~ slipper MULE

"___ Back, Little Sheba" COME

backlog STORE
edit. ~ MSS

back-number DATED, OLD

backpack CAMP, HIKE
~ contents GEAR

backpacker
~ accessory TENT
~ stuff GEAR

back-pedal DENY, REACT

backroom
~ denizen POL

"___ Back Room, The" SMALL

backrub
need a ~ ACHE

back scratcher
~ target ITCH

backslide LAPSE, SLIP

backspace
~ perhaps ERASE

backspin
~ a tennis ball SLICE

"Backstage at the Kirov"
~ director HART

backstop CAGE

backstroke
do the ~ SWIM

backtalk ECHO, LIP, SASS

"___ Back the Clock" TURN

"___ Back the Dawn" HOLD

back-to-school
~ mo. SEPT

"Back to School"
~ name MELON

"Back to the Future III"
~ role CLARA

backup
make a ~ SAVE

backward ASTERN, FRO, SLOW
~ (prefix) RETRO
lean ~ ARCH
step ~ LOSS

backwards AFT, ASTERN

backwash LAP

backwater EDDY

backyard AREA
~ deck PATIO
~ structure SHED
~ swing part TIRE

Baclanova OLGA

bacon MEAT
~ unit STRIP
cook ~ FRY
cut of ~ SLAB

Bacon ROGER
~ product ESSAY

bacteria
~ for short STREP

bacteriologist
~ medium AGAR

bacterium GERM
~ type STREP

Bactria
~ today IRAN

Bactrian CAMEL

bad EVIL, MEAN, VILE
~ actor HAM, OGRE
~ blood ANGER
~ bottom line LOSS
~ deed SIN
~ egg CUR
~ end DOOM
~ feeling ANGER
~ guys THEM
~ humor ANGER
~ judgment ERROR
~ language OATH
~ mood PET
~ move ERROR
~ news OGRE
~ off POOR
~ (prefix) MAL, MIS
~ review PAN
~ sign OMEN
~ smell REEK
~ spell BOUT
~ temper ANGER, BILE, SNIT
~ thing BANE
~ treatment ABUSE
~ vibes OMEN
~ weather STORM
feel ~ ACHE, AIL
give a ~ name LIBEL
go ~ ROT, SOUR, SPOIL, TURN
not ~ FAIR, OKAY, SOSO
reaction to ~ news OHNO
throw good money after ~ WASTE
write ~ checks KITE

bad ___ HOP, NEWS

bad ___ day HAIR

___ bad (okay) NOT

"___ bad!" TOO

Bad ___, Germany EMS

Bad ___, Mich. AXE

"Bad ___" TASTE

"Bad ___, The" SEED

"Bad ___ at Black Rock" DAY

"Bad ___ Bears, The" NEWS

"Bad ___ of Missouri" MEN

"Bad ___ the Beautiful, The" AND

"B. A. D. ___" CATS

"___, bad, and dangerous to know" MAD

"Bad, Bad ___ Brown" LEROY

"Bad Behaviour"
~ actor REA

"___ bad boy!" IMA

"Bad Boys"
~ actor PENN

baddie
fairy-tale ~ GIANT, OGRE

Bad Ems SPA

Baden-Baden SPA

Badenov BORIS

___ Bader Ginsburg RUTH

___ bad example SETA

badge LABEL, SEAL, TOKEN
~ material TIN
~ of honor MEDAL
merit ~ org. BSA

___ badge MERIT

"___ Badge of Courage, The" RED

badger ANIMAL, BAIT, FRET, NAG, RAG, RIDE

___ Badger ("The Wind in the Willows" character) MAC

badges IDS

bad guys
~ nemesis POSSE

bad hair___ DAY

badinage TALK

Badlands
~ sight BISON

badly ILL
~ in French MAL
~ (prefix) MAL

"___ Bad Mama" BIG

bad-mannered RUDE

badminton GAME
~ call LET
~ need NET
~ stroke LOB

"Bad Moon Rising"
  ~ opening ISEE

badmouth ABUSE, DIS, LIBEL,
  OATH, RAP, SMEAR

badness EVIL, HARM, SIN

Bad News Bears
  the ~ TEAM

"Bad News Bears, The"
  ~ actress ONEAL

bad-tempered IRATE, MEAN,
  TESTY, UGLY

Baffin BAY

Baffin Bay
  ~ sight BERG

baffle ADDLE, DAZE, ELUDE, LOSE,
  POSE

baffled ASEA, ATSEA, LOST

baffling HARD
  ~ question POSER

bag EARN, GET, GRIP, LAND, NET,
  SACK, SCORE, SNARE
  ~ brand GLAD
  ~ ender PIPE
  ~ of bones NAG
  ~ starter BEAN, FEED, FLEA,
    GAS, HAND, MAIL, NOSE,
    SAND
  diamond ~ BASE
  ditty ~ KIT
  duffel ~ SACK
  grab ~ OLIO
  in the ~ ONICE, SAFE, SURE
  let the cat out of the ~ BLAB,
    LEAK, TELL
  medic's ~ KIT
  mixed ~ OLIO, STEW
  old-fashioned ~ GRIP
  school ~ KIT
  traveling ~ GRIP, KIT

___ bag AIR, GRAB, KIT, TEA, TOTE

"___ bagatelle!, A" MERE

"Bagdad ___" CAFE

Bagdasarian ROSS

bagel
  ~ feature HOLE
  ~ shop DELI

baggage GEAR, TRAPS
  ~ handler CART

___-bagger THREE, TWO

baggy LOOSE

Baghdad CITY
  ~ country IRAQ

Bagheera CAT

baglike
  ~ structure SAC

Bagnold ENID

bagpipe
  ~ player SCOT
  ~ sound DRONE

baguette GEM

"Bah!" FIE, POOH, PSHAW
  ~ in German ACH

___-Bah POOH

Baha'i
  ~ origin IRAN

Bahama
  ~ island CAT

Bahamas
  part of the ~ ISLE

Bahrain
  ~ native ARAB
  ~ ruler AMIR, EMEER, EMIR

baht COIN

Baikal LAKE

bail DIP, LADE, LADLE, SCOOP
  ~ out DESERT, EJECT, FLEE
  ~ out of DROP, LEAVE

bailer PAIL

Bailey FLEE, LEE, PEARL
  ~ bailiwick LAW

Bailey, Beetle
  ~ barracks-mate ZERO
  ~ superior SARGE

Bailey, F. Lee
  ~ occ. ATT, ATTY
  ~ org. ABA

Bailey, Pearl
  ~ middle name MAE

bailiff
  Anglo-Saxon ~ REEVE
  obey the ~ RISE

bailiwick AREA, REALM, SPHERE

bairn KID
  like a ~ WEE

bait ANGLE, LURE, RAG, RIDE,
  TRAP
  fish ~ LURE
  take the ~ BITE, REACT

Baiul, Oksana
  ~ jump AXEL
  ~ milieu ICE, RINK
  emulate ~ SKATE

Baja
  ~ neighbor USA
  see also Spanish

bake FIRE, HEAT, ROAST
  ~ ender WARE
  ~ pottery FIRE

bake-___ OFF

baked ARID, DRY, SERE
  ~ entrée HAM

baked ___ ALASKA

___-baked HALF

baker CHEF, OVEN
  ~ device OVEN
  ~ implement PEEL
  ~ ingredient EGG, YEAST

Baker ANITA, CHET, DIVA, WARD
  word before ~ ABLE

___, Baker, Charlie ABLE

Baker-Finch IAN

Baker, Janet DAME

Baker, Russell
  ~ specialty ESSAY

baker's ___ YEAST

Baker, Samuel White SIR

bakery
  ~ enticement AROMA, ODOR
  ~ fixture OVEN
  ~ item LOAF, PIE, ROLL, RYE,
    SCONE, TART
  ~ lure AROMA
  ~ worker ICER

bake sale
  ~ sponsor PTA

baking HOT
  ~ dish PAN
  ~ pan SHEET, TIN
  ~ potato IDAHO

baking ___ SODA

baking powder
  ~ ingredient ALUM

___-Bakr ABU

baksheesh ALMS, FEE, PAY, TIP

Bakst LEON

Balaam
  ~ beast ASS

Balaban BOB

balaclava CAP, HAT

"Balalaika"
  ~ actor EDDY

balance EVEN, PAR, POISE, REST,
  SCALE
  ~ beam EVENT
  ~ center EAR
  hang in the ~ PEND
  lose one's ~ SLIP
  off ~ AWRY
  throw off ~ UPSET

balance ___ BEAM, SHEET

Balance
  the ~ SIGN

balanced EVEN, SANE, SERENE,
  SOBER

balancer
  ball ~ SEAL
  fish ~ FIN

balance sheet
  ~ check AUDIT
  ~ guru CPA
  ~ item ASSET, DEBT
  ~ word LOSS

balas GEM

Balbinus
  see Latin

Balbo ITALO, PILOT

Balboa
  see Spanish

balcony
  ~ area LOGE

"Balcony, The"
  ~ painter MANET
  ~ playwright GENET

bald BARE, DRY
  ~ bird EAGLE
  ~ head DOME

bald ___ EAGLE

baldachin ROOF

bald eagle
  ~ look-alike ERN, ERNE

Balder
  brother of ~ THOR

balderdash POOH, ROT, TRASH

bald-faced
  ~ one LIAR

bald-faced ___ LIE

baldric BAND, BELT, STRAP

Baldwin ALEC, APPLE

bale BANE, ONUS
  ~ contents HAY

baleen BONE

baleful BAD, DIRE, EVIL, VILE

Bali ISLE

"Bali ___" HAI

Bali Ha'i ISLE

Balin INA

Balinese ASIAN, CAT

balk DETER, HALT
  ~ detector UMP

balk ___ LINE

Balkan SERB, SLAV

Balkans
  ~ map abbr. BOS

balky
  ~ beast ASS, BURRO, MULE

ball DANCE, GALA, ORB, SPHERE,
  TOY, WAD
  ~ attendee BELLE, DEB
  ~ balancer SEAL
  ~ caller UMP
  ~ club TEAM
  ~ ender ROOM
  ~ lightning GAS
  ~ of cotton WAD
  ~ of fire SUN
  ~ starter AIR, BASE, BEAN,
    CORN, CUE, EYE, FAST, FIRE,
    FOOT, HAIR, HAND, HARD,
    LOW, MEAT, MOTH, ODD, PIN,
    SNOW, SOUR, SPIT
  backspin a tennis ~ SLICE
  belle of the ~ DEB
  boot the ~ ERR
  conk with a ~ BEAN
  distance a golf ~ rolls RUN
  dropping the ~ ERROR
  drop the ~ ERR
  get the ~ rolling OPEN,
    START
  high ~ LOB
  inaugural ~ GALA
  miss at a ~ DEB

on the ~ ABLE, ACUTE, ADEPT, AGILE, ALERT, AWARE
rubber ~ TOY
the way the ~ bounces LOT
well-hit ~ LINER

ball __ GAME

ball-__ hammer PEEN

__ **ball** AIR, BEAN, CUE, FAIR, PLAY, TEA

__-ball LOW

ballad AIR, ARIA, LAY, POEM, SONG, TUNE
~ ender EER
~ subject LOVE

ballade LAY, POEM

balladmonger BARD, POET

"Ballad of __ Hogue, The" CABLE

"Ballad of East and West, The" POEM

Ballantine CARL, IAN
~ brew ALE, BEER

ballerina
~ asset TOE
~ costume TUTU
~ step PAS
prima ~ LEAD

ballerinas
painter of ~ DEGAS

ballet ART, DANCE
~ artist DEGAS
~ barre RAIL
~ bend PLIE
~ garb TUTU
~ lesson STEP
~ move LEAP, PAS
~ pivot TOE
Copland ~ RODEO

__ **ballet** WATER

"Ballet Class, The"
~ painter DEGAS

"__ Ball Express" RED

ballfield
~ bobble ERROR
~ protector TARP

__-ball foursome BEST

ballgame
~ arbiter UMP
~ stat ABS, ERA, HRS
~ stats BAS

ballgoer BELLE

Ball, Hugo
~ movement DADA

ballistic
~ missile THOR
go ~ RANT

Ball, Lucille
~ film MAME

"Ball of __" FIRE

balloon GROW, RISE, TOY
~ filler AIR, GAS

~ sound POP
go by ~ AVIATE
lead ~ DUD, LOSER
trial ~ TEST

__ **balloon** LEAD, TRIAL

"__ Balloon, The" RED

ballot
~ mo. NOV
cast one's ~ ELECT, POLL, VOTE
marks a ~ EXES

"__ Ballou" CAT

ballpark
~ entertainment ORGAN
~ figure EST, USHER
~ level TIER
~ official UMP
in the ~ CLOSE
New York ~ SHEA

ballpoint PEN
use a ~ WRITE

ballroom __ DANCE

"__ Balls of Fire" GREAT

Ball State U.
~ state IND

Ballston __, NY SPA

ballyhoo BLARE, DIN, HYPE, NOISE

balm OIL
~ of Gilead RESIN
natural ~ ALOE
reason for ~ ACHE

__ **balm** BEE, LEMON

balmoral CAP, HAT, SHOE, TAM

Balmoral Castle
~ river DEE

balmy DAFT, MAD, MILD, ODD

baloney LIE, POOH, ROT, TRASH

balsa TREE

balsam BALM, FIR, TREE

Balthazar
~ and others MAGI
like ~ WISE

Baltic SEA
~ capital RIGA
~ feeder ODER
~ island AERO
~ resident LETT
on the ~ ASEA, ATSEA

Baltimore CITY, PORT
~ ballplayer ORIOLE
~ paper SUN

Baluchistan DESERT

baluster POST

balusters RAIL

balustrade BAR

Bamako
~ country MALI

Bambi DEER
~ father STAG

~ mother DOE

"Bambi"
~ director HAND
~ doe ENA
aunt in ~ ENA

bambino KID

"Bambino, The" RUTH

bamboo CANE, REED
~ eater PANDA
~ stalk CANE
like ~ REEDY

bamboo __ SHOOT

bamboozle CON, DUPE, HAVE, SNOW

Bamm Bamm
~ to Barney SON

ban BAR, EDICT, ESTOP, EXILE, LAW, RULE, STOP, TABOO, TABU

Ban-__ LON

banal HACK, INANE, STALE, TRITE

banality TAG

banana TREE
~ bunch HAND
~ coat PEEL
~ oil ESTER

banana __ OIL, SEAT, SPLIT

__ **banana** TOP

"__ Banana" TOP

banana peel
~ mishap SLIP

bananas APE, LOCO, MAD
drive someone ~ IRK, PEEVE, RILE, UPSET

"Bananas"
~ director ALLEN

banana split
~ holder BOAT

Bancroft ANNE

band ARMY, BAR, BELT, CABAL, CLAN, CREW, GANG, HORDE, MOB, RING, STRIP, TAPE, TEAM, TIE, TROOP
~ booster AMP
~ ender STAND
~ engagement GIG
~ grouping SET
~ instrument BRASS, HORN, OBOE, SAX, TUBA
~ location SHELL
~ number TUNE
~ of a sort OCTET, TRIO
~ starter HAT, HEAD
~ together ALLY, TROOP, UNITE
acknowledge the ~ CLAP
coat-of-arms ~ ORLE
global ~ ZONE
heraldic ~ ORLE
leather ~ STRAP
one-man ~ SOLO
ornamental ~ SASH
palindromic ~ ABBA, AHA
sheriff's ~ POSSE

small ~ TRIO
spectrum ~ BLUE, ORANGE, RED
street ~ GANG
TV ~ UHF
waist ~ OBI, SASH
wedding ~ RING

band __ SAW, SHELL

__ **band** BIG, BRASS, STEEL

Band-__ AID

Banda SEA

bandage BIND, DRESS, TAPE
~ brand ACE
nature's ~ SCAB

bandana
~ cousin SCARF

bandeau BRA

banded
~ stone AGATE

__-banded armadillo NINE

Banderas, Antonio
~ role CHE

banderilla
~ item BARB

banderole FLAG

bandicoot ANIMAL
~ kin KOALA

"__ Bandido" AMOR

"bandit"
casino ~ feature ARM

"__ Bandits" TIME

Bando SAL

"Band on the __" RUN

bands
luminous ~ AURORA
radio ~ AMS

bandstand
~ equipment AMP

bandy TOSS, TRADE
~ words ARGUE, SPAR, TALK

Bandy MOE

bane
~ of pvts. SGT

baneful BAD, EVIL

Banff LAKE
~ burden SKI
~ prov. ALB, ALTA

bang CLAP, HIT, NOISE, POP, RAP, ROAR, SLAM
~ out TYPE
~ up DENT, MAR
get a ~ out of LIKE, LOVE

__-bang SLAM

"Bang a Gong (Get __)" ITON

Bangalore
see Indian

Bangkok CITY, PORT
~ cuisine THAI

~ native TAI, THAI
capital NE of ~ HANOI

Bangladesh
~ continent ASIA

Bangor
~ locale MAINE
~ neighbor ORONO

bangs HAIR

bangtail HORSE, NAG, RACER

___ bang theory BIG

bang-up AONE

Bani-Sadr IRANI
~ country IRAN

banish BAR, EJECT, EXILE, OUST

banister RAIL
~ post NEWEL
go down the ~ SLIDE

banjo
~ ancestor LUTE
~ cousin UKE
~ perch KNEE

"Banjo ___" (Eddie Cantor) EYES

"Banjo on My ___" KNEE

bank AMASS, CAROM, HEAP,
LEVEE, MASS, PILE, POOL, RISE,
SAFE, SAVE, SHORE, SLOPE
~ breaker RUN
~ claim LIEN
~ deal LOAN
~ dep. ACCT
~ draft NOTE
~ ender NOTE, ROLL
~ eponym CHASE
~ feature SAFE
~ holding LIEN
~ note CASH
~ offering IRA
~ offerings CDS
~ (on) RELY
~ pmt. INT
~ posting RATE
~ robber's nemesis ALARM,
CAMERA
~ service LOAN
~ stack ONES, TENS
~ starter DATA, SAND, SNOW
~ statement abbr. BAL
~ takeback REPO
~ worry RUN
gravel ~ BAR
modern place to ~ ATM
money in the ~ ASSET

___ bank DATA

"Bank ___" SHOT

___ Bank LEFT, WEST

banker
~ byword SAVE
ersatz ~ ATM

banking
~ convenience ATM

banknote PAPER

Bank One Ballpark ARENA

bankroll WAD

bankrupt NEEDY, POOR, RUIN,
SINK

banks
what ~ do LEND

Banks ERNIE

___ Banks, N.C. OUTER

bank statement
~ entry DEBIT

Banks, Tyra
emulate ~ MODEL, POSE

banned TABOO, TABU
~ act NONO
~ article of trade IVORY
~ fruit spray ALAR
~ pesticide DDT
something ~ TABOO, TABU

banner FLAG

Bannister MILER, ROGER
distance for ~ MILE
emulate ~ RACE, RUN

banquet DINE, EAT, FARE, FEED,
MEAL
~ course SALAD
~ official EMCEE
~ platform DAIS
attend a ~ EAT
do a ~ CATER
enjoy a ~ DINE
provide a ~ CATER

banshee DEMON

bantam ELFIN, SMALL, TINY

banter KID, PLAY, TALK

bantling BRAT

banyan TREE

banzai CRY

baobab TREE

baptism RITE

baptismal
~ area FONT

baptize NAME, TAG

bar BAN, BAND, CAKE, ESTOP,
EXILE, INGOT, LAND, LAW,
LEVER, REEF, ROD, SHUT, STOP,
TABOO, TABU
~ bill TAB
~ chaser SODA
~ ender HOP, KEEP, MAID,
WARE
~ food NUTS
~ legally ESTOP
~ mem. ATT, ATTY
~ mixer SODA, WATER
~ none ALL
~ of gold INGOT
~ order ALE, BEER, LAGER,
NEAT, RUM, RYE, SHOT,
SOUR
~ order, with "the" USUAL
~ pull TAP
~ rocks ICE
~ selection SALAD
~ shot SNORT
~ sign ONTAP
~ starter CROW, DRAW, SAND

car ~ AXLE
car with a ~ LIMO
handle the ~ TEND
horizontal ~ EVENT, RAIL
metal ~ INGOT
pry ~ LEVER
read ~ codes SCAN
sand ~ LAND, LEDGE, REEF,
SHOAL
soap ~ CAKE
wheel ~ AXLE

bar ___ CAR, CODE, NONE

___ bar CASH, PIANO, ROLL,
SALAD, SPACE, SWAY, WET

Bara SIREN, THEDA

Baracus, B.A.
~ group ATEAM

"Bar at the Folies-Bergère, A"
~ painter MANET

barb DART, GIBE

Barbados
~ export ALOE

Barbara ALLEN, EDEN, LUNA,
MAJOR, TRENT

Barbara ___ Geddes BEL

"___ Barbara" MAJOR

___ Barbara, Calif. SANTA

"Barbara Frietchie" POEM

barbarian ANIMAL, BEAST, BOOR,
HUN, YAHOO
behave like a ~ SACK

barbaric CRUEL

barbarous CRUEL, FERAL

Barbary
~ beast APE

barbecue HEAT, MEAL, ROAST
~ companion SLAW
~ favorite RIB
~ garb APRON
~ leftover ASH, EMBER
~ need COAL
~ offering STEAK
~ rocks LAVA
~ rod SPIT
~ spot PATIO

barbed ACUTE, TART

barbed ___ WIRE

barbell
~ material IRON
~ units LBS

barber
~ shout NEXT
~ sign POLE
~ stroke SNIP
~ sweepings HAIR

Barber RED

"Barber of Seville, The" OPERA

barbershop
~ call NEXT
~ quartet member TENOR
~ request TRIM
~ sound SNIP

~ symbol POLE

barbet BIRD

Barbie
~ boyfriend KEN

Barbra
~ "Funny Girl" costar OMAR

barcarole SONG

Barcelona CITY, PORT
~ bull TORO
see also Spanish

bard POET
~ work EPIC, POEM, TALE
see also poet

Bard
see Shakespeare

Bard of ___, The AVON

Bardot
see French

bare ARID, BALD, CLEAR, MERE,
NUDE, RAW, STRIP
~ one's teeth SNARL
~ peak TOR
~ rocky slope SCAR
lay ~ SHOW, SKIN
walk on ~ feet PAD

barefaced OPEN

barefoot
not ~ SHOD

"Barefoot Boy, The" POEM

"Barefoot Contessa, The"
~ actress AVA

Barents SEA

bare one's ___ TEETH

Baretta
~ bird FRED

barfly SOT

bargain DEAL, PACT, STEAL,
TRADE
~ maybe PLEA
in the ~ ALSO, EXTRA, TOO

___-bargain PLEA

bargain-hunt SHOP

bargain hunter
~ delight SALE

bargaining TRADE
~ group UNIT

bargaining ___ CHIP

barge BOAT, KEEL, SCOW
~ canal of song ERIE
~ into RAM
~ locale of old NILE
~ route CANAL

barge ___ (interrupt) INON

Barge Canal
~ alias ERIE

barghest DEMON

Baring EARL

barite ORE

baritone DEEP, MALE, RANGE
~ **fiddle** CELLO
~ **in "Marouf"** ALI
voice above ~ TENOR
voice under ~ BASS

barium METAL

bark BOAT, COAT, CRY, KEEL, NOISE, PEEL, RIND, SHIP, SKIN, SNARL, YAP, YELL, YELP
~ **boat** CANOE
~ **up the wrong tree** ERR
comic-strip ~ ARF
high-pitched ~ YAP, YELP

barkentine BOAT, SHIP

barker DOG
~ **of filmdom** ASTA, TOTO

Barker BOB
~ **and others** MAS

Barkin ELLEN

barking
~ **up the wrong tree** OFF

Barkley IRAN

barks
animal that ~ DOG, SEAL

bark up the wrong ___ TREE

Barlett DES

barley
~ **beard** AWN
~ **beverage** BEER
~ **bristle** AWN
~ **product** MALT

bar mitzvah RITE
~ **dance** HORA
~ **reading** TORAH

barn
~ **baby** CALF, OWLET
~ **bellow** MOO
~ **dance** REEL
~ **dweller** COW, EWE, GOAT, HORSE, OWL, RAM
~ **ender** YARD
~ **neighbor** SILO
~ **storage unit** BALE
~ **topper** VANE

barn ___ DANCE, OWL

"Barnaby Jones"
~ **actor** EBSEN

___ barnacle GOOSE

___ Barnacle (Mrs. James Joyce) NORA

barnburner EVENT

Barney LEM, REX
~ **buddy** FRED

"Barney Miller"
~ **actor** SOO

barnstorm TOUR

barnstorming
~ **feat** LOOP

barnyard
~ **animal** COW, EWE, HEN, HORSE, RAM, SOW
~ **baby** KID

~ **clucker** HEN
~ **cry** BRAY
~ **enclosure** PEN, STY
~ **female** COW, EWE, HEN, SOW
~ **fowl** GOOSE
~ **grub** FEED
~ **sound** BAA, MAA, MOO, OINK
~ **swinger** VANE

baron LORD, PEER, RANK, TITLE
~ **ender** ESS

Baron TITLE
~ **von Munchausen** LIAR

baroness DAME, LADY, TITLE

baronet PEER
~ **title** SIR
~ **wife** DAME, LADY

___ Baron, The RED

baroque ORNATE, STYLE
~ **composer** BACH
~ **instrument** LUTE, VIOL

Baroque ERA

"___ Barque" SOLAR

barracks BED, CAMP
~ **off.** SGT

barracuda
~ **habitat** OCEAN, SEA

barrage PELT, STREAM

barranca GAP

Barranquilla CITY, PORT

barre
ballet ~ RAIL
bend at the ~ PLIE

barred ___ OWL

barrel CASE, RACE, SPEED, VAT
~ **bottom contents** LEES
~ **component** STAVE
~ **diameter** BORE
~ **hoop wood** ELM
~ **into** RAM
~ **of laughs** RIOT
beer ~ KEG
open a ~ TAP

barrel ___ ORGAN, ROLL

barrelhouse BAR

"___ Barrel Polka" BEER

barrels ALOT

barren ARID, BARE, DESERT, DRY, POOR
~ **area** SAHARA

___ barrens PINE

Barrett RONA

barrette CLIP

barricade BAR, MOAT

barricades
mount the ~ REBEL

Barrie CHASE, MONA
~ **character** PAN, SMEE
~ **dog** NANA
J.M. ~ SIR

barrier BAR, GATE, GRATE, PALE
~ **island** CAY, KEY
farm ~ RAIL
flood ~ LEVEE
mosquito ~ NET
movable ~ GATE
race-winner's ~ TAPE
water ~ DAM
zoo ~ MOAT

___ Barrier Reef GREAT

barring SAVE

barrister
~ **occ.** ATT, ATTY
~ **org.** ABA

barristers BAR

Barron STEVE

"Barron's"
~ **subjs.** COS

barroom
~ **sign** ONTAP
~ **spigot** TAP

barrow CART, PILE

Barry DAVE, GENE, LEN

"Barry Lyndon"
~ **actor** ONEAL

Barrymore DREW, ETHEL

"___ Barry Turns 40" DAVE

bars
final ~ CODA

Bars
Stars and ~ FLAG

Bart STARR
~ **sister** LISA
~ **to Homer** SON
~ **to Lisa** BRO

Bartel PAUL

bartender
~ **need** ICE

bartenders
what ~ **check** IDS

barter DEAL, SWAP, TRADE

"Bartered Bride, The" OPERA

barterer
birthright ~ ESAU

Bartlett HALL, PEAR
~ **abbr.** ANON
~ **kin** BOSC

Bartok EVA

Bartók BELA

Bartoli
~ **performance** ARIA

Bartolomeo
see Italian

Barton CLARA, ENOS, NURSE

Barton, Clara NURSE

"Baruch: My ___ Story" OWN

baryon
~ **container** ATOM

Baryshnikov
~ **birthplace** RIGA

basalt LAVA

base BAD, BAG, BED, CAUSE, EVIL, FOOT, LEWD, LOW, MEAN, ROOT, SACK, SITE, VILE
~ **clearer** HOMER
~ **crew** CADRE
~ **ender** BALL, LESS, LINE
~ **food** MESS
~ **in baseball** BAG
~ **neutralizer** ACID
~ **starter** DATA
~ **VIPs** COS
baseball ~ HOME
be off ~ ERR
decimal ~ TEN
military ~ POST
off ~ AMISS, FALSE
off ~**, maybe** AWOL
reach ~ **headfirst** SLIDE

base ___ CAMP, HIT, PAY

___ base AIR, FIRST, HOME

baseball GAME, ORB, SPHERE
~ **base** HOME
~ **bat wood** ASH
~ **club** BAT
~ **coup** STEAL
~ **event** HIT, HOMER
~ **family name** ALOU
~ **feature** SEAM
~ **glove** MITT
~ **legend** RUTH
~ **maneuver** SLIDE
~ **record** STAT
~ **score** RUN
~ **shoe piece** CLEAT
~ **stat** ABS, ATBAT, ERA, HRS
~ **stats** BAS
~ **tag** OUT
~ **throw** PEG
~ **VIP** UMP
solid hit, in ~ LINER
up, in ~ ATBAT

baseballer
~ **wear** CAP
California ~ ANGEL
Cincinnati ~ RED
Detroit ~ TIGER
Minnesota ~ TWIN
NY ~ MET
San Diego ~ PADRE
San Francisco ~ GIANT
Santo Domingo-born ~ ALOU
Texas ~ ASTRO

___-base hit ONE, THREE, TWO

Basel
view from ~ RHINE

baseless IDLE, VAIN

baseline
~ **material** LIME

basement
~ **opposite** ATTIC
~ **reading** METER
in the ~ LAST

basements
like some ~ DAMP

basenji DOG

baserunner
~ **ploy** LEAD

bash BANG, BEAT, CHOP, GALA, HIT, LAM, SMITE
~ **Biblically** SMITE
big ~ FETE, GALA
celebrity ~ ROAST
throw a ~ HOST
Western ~ RODEO
see also party

bashes DOS

___ **Bashevis Singer** ISAAC

bashful SHY

Bashful
~ **colleague** DOC

Basho, Matsuo POET
see also poet

basic BARE, REAL
~ **(abbr.)** ELEM
~ **beliefs** ETHOS
~ **element** ROOT
~ **elements** ABCS
~ **nature** ESSENCE
~ **rule** LAW
~ **skills** ABCS
~ **unit** ATOM
bootlegger's ~ MASH

"Basic Instinct"
~ **actress** STONE

basics ABCS

Basie, Count
~ **instrument** PIANO

basil HERB

Basil TONI
~ **"Captain Blood" costar** ERROL
~ **successor** IVAN

basilica
~ **feature** APSE, NAVE, PEW
~ **treasure** ICON

basilisk OGRE

basin BATH, BAY, LAKE, SINK, TUB
~ **companion** EWER
cirque ~ TARN
holy-water ~ FONT

___ **basin** TIDAL

Basin
~ **and others** STS

___ **Basin (German region)** SAAR

___ **Basin (Western region)** GREAT

basinet ARMOR

Basinger KIM

basis CAUSE, PEG, ROOT

bask LOLL, SUN
~ **in** LIKE
~ **in the sun** TAN

basker
~ **acquisition** TAN

Baskerville FONT

basket
~ **filler** EGGS
fish ~ CREEL
make a ~ SINK
wicker ~ CREEL

basketball GAME, ORB, SPHERE
~ **coup** STEAL
~ **feed** PASS
~ **filler** AIR
~ **hoop** RIM
~ **path** ARC
~ **stratagem** PRESS
~ **target** NET
~ **team** FIVE
~ **throw** SHOT
~ **tourney** NIT
~ **venue** ARENA
defunct ~ **org.** ABA

basketballer
Boston ~ CELT
Indiana ~ PACER
Miami ~ HEAT
New Jersey ~ NET
Phoenix ~ SUN
San Antonio ~ SPUR
Seattle ~ SONIC

basketballers
like most ~ TALL

basket weaver
~ **material** OSIER

Baskin Robbins
~ **order** CONE

Basque
~ **bonnet** BERET

Basra CITY, PORT
~ **land** IRAQ

bass CLEF, DEEP, MALE, RANGE
~ **booster** AMP
~ **instrument** VIOL
higher than ~ TENOR

bass ___ VIOL

___ **bass** SEA

Bass
~ **(abbr.)** STR
~ **product** ALE

basset DOG
~ **features** EARS
comic-strip ~ FRED

" ___ **Basset"** FRED

bassinet BED, CRIB

basso DEEP

bassoon REED
~ **cousin** OBOE

baste BANG, BEAT, HIT, LAM, SEW

Bastille
~ **locale** PARIS

Bastille ___ DAY

___ **-basting** SELF

bastion AERIE, HAVEN

bat ANIMAL, CLAP, FLAP, HIT, REVEL
~ **feature** SONAR
~ **home** CAVE
~ **maker** LATHE

~ **navigational aid** ECHO
baseball ~ **wood** ASH
go to ~ **for** AID, HELP
move like a ~ FLIT
right off the ~ FIRST

"Bat, The" OPERA

batch CROP, HEAP, LOT, PILE, RAFT, RUN, SET

bated
with ~ **breath** AGOG

Bates ALAN

bath SPA
~ **aftermath** RING
~ **decor** TILE
~ **ender** MAT, ROBE, TUB
~ **powder** TALC
~ **starter** BIRD, SUN
Finnish ~ SAUNA
hot-air ~ SAUNA
kind of ~ DYE
long ~ SOAK
need a ~ REEK
steam ~ SAUNA
take a ~ WASH
take a sun ~ BASK
Turkish ~ SAUNA

bath ___ SALTS, WATER

___ **bath** EYE, STEAM

Bath SPA
~ **brew** TEA
~ **county** AVON
~ **state** MAINE
see also British, English

bathe CLEAN, DIP, LAVE, RINSE, WASH
~ **in color** DYE

bathhouse SAUNA

bathing
go ~ SWIM

bathing ___ CAP, SUIT

bathing suit
~ **top** BRA

bathmat RUG

bathroom
~ **device** SCALE
~ **feature** TILE
~ **fixture** TUB

Bathsheba
Solomon, to ~ SON

bathtub
~ **toy** BOAT

batik
~ **artisan** DYER
~ **need** DYE
make ~ DYE

Batman HERO
~ **creator** KANE
~ **portrayer** WEST
~ **wear** CAPE
headquarters for ~ CAVE

"Batman"
like TV's ~ CAMP

Batman and Robin DUO, PAIR

baton MACE, ROD
~ **passer's race** RELAY
magician's ~ WAND
wield a ~ LEAD

Baton ___, **La.** ROUGE

Baton Rouge
~ **sch.** LSU

___ **Bator** ULAN

bats LOCO, MAD

battalion ARMY

batten BAR, LATH, SLAT
~ **down** SEAL

battened
~ **down** FAST

batter ABUSE, BANG, BEAT, HARM, HIT, MAUL, RAM, SMASH
~ **down** RAZE
~ **goal** HIT
~ **ingredient** EGG, YEAST
~ **place** HOME, PLATE
~ **to the pitcher** FOE
face the first ~ START
hit the ~ BEAN
mix ~ BEAT, STIR

battering ___ RAM

battery ABUSE, STREAM
~ **chemical** ACID
~ **part** ANODE, CELL
~ **size** AAA
word on a ~ VOLT

___ **battery** SOLAR

batting
~ **order** CARD
~ **practice area** CAGE
~ **stat** RBI

batting champ
1954 ~ AVILA

battle SIEGE, WAR
~ **lineup** ARRAY
~ **of honor** DUEL
~ **site** ARENA
~ **the bulge** DIET
1813 ~ **site** ERIE
1836 ~ **site** ALAMO
1914 ~ **site** YSER
do ~ CLOSE
equip for ~ ARM
ready for ~ ARMED

"Battle ___**"** CRY

"Battle Cry"
~ **author** URIS

battlefield ARENA

battleground
~ **vehicle** TANK
1950s ~ KOREA
Santa Anna ~ ALAMO

"Battle Hymn of the Republic"
~ **author** HOWE

Battle, Kathleen DIVA
~ **offering** ARIA

battleship
~ **letters** USS
~ **of 1898** MAINE

battleship __
~ **to remember** MAINE

battleship __ GRAY

"Battleship Potemkin, The"
~ **locale** ODESSA

battle station
take a ~ MAN

batty DAFT, LOCO, MAD

bauble PIN, TOY

Baudelaire, Charles POET
see also poet

Bauhaus
~ **artist** KLEE

Baum
~ **beast** LION
~ **dog** TOTO

Baumé __ SCALE

bauxite ORE

Bavarian
~ **peak** ALP

bawdy LEWD, RACY

bawl CRY, HOOT, LOW, NOISE, SOB, WEEP
have a ~ WEEP

bawl __ (scold) OUT

Baxter ANNE, LES, TED
~ **role** EVE

bay COLOR, COVE, CRY, HAVEN, HORSE, INLET, NOISE, ROAN, TREE
~ **window** ORIEL
at ~ TREED
Florida ~ TAMPA
keep at ~ REPEL, STEM

bay __ LEAF, RUM

Bay
~ **St.** MASS

Bay __ Rollers CITY

"__ Bay" TIGER

__ Bay, Australia EMU

__ Bay Buccaneers TAMPA

Bayes NORA

Bayeux
~ **neighbor** STLO

Bayh EVAN

Bayley, Elizabeth SETON

Baylor University
~ **mascot** BEAR
~ **site** WACO

Bay of __ ACRE, URI

Bay of Biscay
~ **ocean** ATL

Bay of Fundy
~ **feature** TIDE

Bay of Pigs
~ **locale** CUBA

bayonet STAB

Bayonne CITY, PORT
see also French

__ Bay, Oregon COOS

bayou INLET, POOL

"__ Bayou" BLUE

Bayreuth
see German

Bay State
~ **cape** ANN

bay-windowed OBESE

bazaar FAIR
ancient ~ AGORA
indoor ~ MALL

bazooka
~ **target** TANK

BB
~ **propellant** AIR

BB __ GUN

B&B INN
part of ~ BED

BBC
~ **receiver** TELE

BBs AMMO

B.C.
~ **neighbor** ALB, ALTA, IDA

"B.C."
~ **cartoonist** HART
~ **character** THOR
~ **currency** CLAM

BCE
part of ~ ERA

__ B. Davis ANN

be LIVE
~ **a blowhard** BRAG
~ **a consumer** EAT
~ **a shrew** NAG
~ **a sport** TREAT
~ **at** ATTEND
~ **aware of** KNOW
~ **beholden to** OWE
~ **charitable** ENDOW
~ **close to** KNOW
~ **consistent** AGREE
~ **contrite** RUE
~ **deprived of** LOSE
~ **done with** END
~ **fearless** DARE
~ **frugal** EKE
~ **furious** BOIL, STEAM
~ **green around the gills** AIL
~ **gullible** BITE
~ **idle** LIE, REST, SIT, WAIT
~ **in accord** AGREE
~ **in a movie** ACT
~ **in a play** ACT
~ **indiscreet** BLAB
~ **in French** ETRE
~ **in harmony** AGREE
~ **in Italian** SER
~ **in knots** ACHE
~ **in Latin** ESSE
~ **in pain** ACHE
~ **in Spanish** SER
~ **in store** AWAIT
~ **mad about** ADORE, LOVE

~ **mistaken** ERR
~ **moribund** AIL
~ **of help** AVAIL
~ **on good terms with** KNOW
~ **philanthropic** AID
~ **solicitous** CARE
~ **sure of** KNOW
~ **the bellwether** LEAD
~ **too personal** PRY
~ **unoriginal** APE
~ **up** BAT
not ~ passive ACT

be-__ (hippie happenings) INS

Be ELEM
4 for ~ ATNO

"Be-__-A-Lula" BOP

beach LAND, SANDS, SHORE
~ **acquisition** TAN
~ **bird** ERN, ERNE
~ **ender** HEAD, WEAR
~ **find** SHELL
~ **near Cape Canaveral** COCOA
~ **near Venice** LIDO
~ **residue** GRIT
~ **surface** SAND
~ **toy** BALL, PAIL
cause of ~ erosion TIDE
D-Day ~ OMAHA, UTAH
enjoy the ~ BATHE
lie on the ~ BASK, SUN
on the ~ ASHORE
shade at the ~ TAN

beach __ BALL

"Beach __" RED

beach ball
~ **filler** AIR

Beach Boys
one of the ~ LOVE

__ Beach, Calif. LONG

beachcomber HOBO, NOMAD

beached ASHORE

__ Beach, Fla. COCOA, MIAMI, PALM

beachgoer
~ **goal** TAN
~ **item** RADIO

"__ Beach Story, The" PALM

beacon FLARE, LAMP
breakdown ~ FLARE

bead DROP, PEARL, TEAR
~ **material** CORAL, NACRE
draw a ~ AIM
get a ~ on TRAIN
rosary ~ AVE

beaded lizard
~ **cousin** GILA

__ beads LOVE

beagle
~ **feature** EAR

"Beagle" BOAT, SHIP

beak BILL, NEB, NIB, NOSE

beaker POT
~ **cousin** VIAL

be-all
~ **and end-all** SUM

beam GLOW, GRIN, LOG, PROP, RADIO, RAY, SHINE, SMILE
~ **ender** ISH
~ **fastener** RIVET
amplified ~ LASER
balance ~ EVENT
broad ~ GRIN
intense ~ LASER
make ~ ELATE
off the ~ BAD, FALSE, LOCO
penetrating ~ LASER, XRAY
railroad ~ TIE
ship ~ KEEL

__ beam LOW, TIE

Beame ABE

beamish ROSY

beamy LARGE

bean DOME, HEAD, NOB, NUT
~ **curd** TOFU
~ **ender** BAG, POLE
~ **hull** POD
~ **starter** SNAP
Asian ~ SOY
chili ~ PINTO
kind of ~ LIMA, PEA, PINTO
nutritious ~ SOY
soup ~ LIMA
tonka ~ TREE
tropical ~ COCOA

bean __ BALL

__ bean CHILI, COCOA, LIMA, PEA, PINTO, POLE, SHELL, SNAP

Bean ALAN, ANDY, ORSON, ROY

beanbag TOY

bean counter CPA

beanery
~ **fare** HASH
~ **list** MENU
~ **sign** EATS

beanfeast MEAL

beanie CAP, HAT

beans PIN
full of ~ FALSE
spill the ~ BLAB, LEAK, LETON, RAT, SING, TELL

beanstalk
~ **owner** GIANT

bear ABIDE, ANIMAL, CART, LUG, STAND, TAKE, YIELD
~ **advice** SELL
~ **allegiance** ADHERE
~ **constellation** URSA
~ **down** PRESS
~ **ender** ISH
~ **false witness** LIE
~ **foot** PAW
~ **(for)** HEAD
~ **fruit** GROW, RIPEN
~ **hair** FUR
~ **hard upon** COST
~ **home** DEN, LAIR

~ **in Latin** URSA
~ **in mind** HEED
~ **in Spanish** OSO
~ **off** SLANT
~ **of very little brain** POOH
~ **out** ATTEST, SHOW
~ **the expense** PAY, TREAT
~ **trap** SNARE
~ **upon** RELATE
~ **with patience** ABIDE
~ **witness** ATTEST, SAY
bring force to ~ IMPEL
bring to ~ EXERT, USE
cartoon ~ YOGI
CBer's ~ COP
cross to ~ ONUS
female ~ SOW
grin and ~ **it** BOW
heavenly ~ URSA
Jellystone Park ~ YOGI
polar ~ **country** ALASKA
teddy ~ TOY
what the traffic will ~ COST

bear ___ (confirm) OUT

___ bear ANT, POLAR

___ Bear BRER, PAPA, YOGI

___ Bear (George Halas) PAPA

beard DARE
~ **locale** CHIN
~ **of grain** AWN

bearded
~ **animal** GNU
~ **flower** IRIS
~ **one** GOAT, SANTA

Beard, James CHEF

bearer
coconut ~ PALM

___ Bearer (Aquarius) WATER

bearing AIR, CREST, GAIT, MIEN, POISE, SET, TENOR

___ bearing BALL

"Bearing gifts we traverse ___" AFAR

bearings
get one's ~ ORIENT

bearish EDGY, TESTY

bearlike
~ **mammal** PANDA
~ **marsupial** KOALA

bears
one that ~ **(suffix)** FER

Bears ELEVEN, TEAM
~ **org.** NFL

bearskin RUG

beast ANIMAL, OGRE
~ **of burden** ASS, BURRO, MULE, YAK
African ~ HYENA, LION
Andean ~ LLAMA
balky ~ ASS
Biblical ~ ASS
Bolivian ~ LLAMA
Borneo ~ ORANG
corrida ~ TORO

humped ~ BISON, CAMEL
man and bird and ~ LIFE
Middle Earth ~ ORC
Peruvian ~ LLAMA
Rue Morgue ~ APE
snouted ~ TAPIR
spiral-horned ~ ELAND
veldt ~ ELAND
Western ~ BISON
zodiac ~ LION, RAM
zoo ~ ELAND, GNU

beast ___ (type of long verse) EPIC

"Beast, The"
~ **love** BELLE

beastly ANIMAL, BAD, CRUEL, FERAL

"Beast of the ___, The" CITY

beasts
~ **of burden** OXEN
king of ~ LION
slow-moving ~ OXEN
the ~ **of the field** LIFE

beat ALLIN, CANE, CAP, FLAP, HIT, LACE, LAM, LASH, LILT, PULSE, ROUTE, SMASH, SPENT, SPHERE, STIR, STRESS, TAN, TEMPO, TIRED, TOP, TRIM, UPSET
~ **a hasty retreat** FLEE, RUN
~ **a path** TREAD
~ **a retreat** RUN
~ **around the bush** AVOID, EVADE, STALL
~ **as wings** FLAP
~ **at bridge** SET
~ **back** REPEL, STEM
~ **badly** CREAM, ROUT
~ **decisively** ROUT
~ **for a poet** METER
~ **in a way** CANE
~ **it** FLEE, LAM, RUN, SCAT, SCRAM, SHOO
~ **one's brains out** LABOR
~ **one's gums** CHAT, YAP
~ **out** WIN
~ **severely** CANE, CREAM
~ **the drum** BLARE, BRAG, CROW
~ **the drums for** SELL
~ **the offense** REPEL
~ **up** ABUSE, HARM, MAUL
~ **walker** COP
barely ~ EDGE, NIP, NOSE
get ~ LOSE
Latin-American ~ SALSA
music ~ STRESS
poetic ~ METER
vigorous ~ SALSA

beat ___ (defeat) OUT

"Beat ___ Clock" THE

"Beat ___ On, The" GOES

"___ Beat" TEEN

beaten
~ **path** TRAIL
it may be ~ EGG, PATH, RAP, RUG

beater
birdie ~ EAGLE
deuce ~ TREY

beatify BLESS

"Beat it!" AWAY, SCAT, SCRAM, SHOO

beatitudes
~ **verb** ARE

Beatle
~ **ender** MANIA

Beatles
~ **drummer** STARR
~ **film** HELP
~ **girl** RITA
~ **record label** APPLE
~ **tune** HELP

beatnik
~ **exclamation** MAN
~ **home** PAD
~ **topper** BERET

Beatrice
~ **beau** DANTE
~ **mother** SARAH

Beatrice d'___ ESTE

Beatrix
see Dutch

beats
~ **it** GOES

beat the ___ RAP

Beattie ANN

Beatty NED
Oscar-winning film for ~ REDS

Beatty, Ned
~ **"Superman" role** OTIS

Beatty, Warren
~ **film of 1981** REDS

beau DATE, DUDE, LOVE, MAN
~ **idéal** MODEL

beau ___ (paragon) IDEAL

Beau
~ **to Jeff** BRO

"Beau ___" GESTE, PERE

beaucoup ALOT

Beaufort SEA

Beaufort scale
0 on the ~ CALM
10 on the ~ GALE

Beau Geste HERO

"Beau Geste"
~ **author** WREN

Beaujolais WINE
~ **color** RED

Beaumont
~ **(Hammett detective)** NED

Beauregard
~ **boss** LEE
~ **org.** CSA

beaut GEM, LULU

beauteous FAIR

beautician
~ **sometimes** DYER

"___ Beauties" SEVEN

beautiful FAIR
~ **people** CREAM, ELITE
make more ~ ADORN

"Beautiful ___ of Somewhere" ISLE

"___ beautiful pea-green boat" INA

beautify ADORN

beauty ASSET
~ **aid** ROUGE
~ **parlor** SALON
~ **preceder** AGE
add ~ **to** ADORN
realm of ~ ART

beauty ___ SALON, SLEEP

Beauty
~ **beloved** BEAST

"Beauty ___ Sale" FOR

"Beauty ___ the Beast" AND

"Beauty and ___ Beast" THE

"Beauty and the ___" BEAST

"Beauty and the Beast"
~ **actress** EGAN
~ **director** WISE
~ **heroine** BELLE
Vincent's home, in ~ SEWER

___ Beauty apple ROME

beauty cream
~ **additive** ALOE

"Beauty for ___" SALE

beauty pageant
~ **accessory** SASH
~ **award** TIARA
~ **title** MISS

beauty parlor SALON
~ **application** DYE, HENNA, TINT
~ **item** NET
~ **treatment** PERM

Beaux-___ ARTS

beaver ANIMAL, ARMOR, FUR, HAT
~ **material** FELT
~ **project** DAM
baby ~ KIT
eager ~ DEMON
emulate a ~ GNAW
like a ~ EAGER

___ beaver EAGER

Beaver
~ **dad** WARD
~ **St.** ORE

Beaver State ORE, OREGON

Beavis TEEN

be-bopper CAT

because FOR, SINCE
~ **of** AFTER

"Because ___ Mine" YOURE

___-bêche TETE

Bechke ELENA

beck and ___ CALL

Becker BORIS
~ **barrier** NET

"Becket"
~ **actor** OTOOLE

Beckett
~ **home** EIRE

beckon ASK, BID, NOD, SIGN

beckoned BADE

becloud BLUR

become FIT, GET, SUIT
~ **concave** SINK

becoming MEET

"___ Be Cool" LADY

"___ Be Cruel" DONT

bed COT, SACK
~ **board** SLAT
~ **down** STALL
~ **ender** SIDE, STEAD, TIME
~ **frame** STEAD
~ **in slang** HAY
~ **linen** SHEET
~ **material** BRASS
~ **occupant** SEED
~ **of roses** EASE
~ **sheets** LINEN
~ **size** TWIN
Army ~ COT
baby ~ CRIB
care for a ~ WEED
coal ~ SEAM
day ~ SOFA
flower ~ PLOT
foldaway ~ COT
get out of ~ ARISE, RISE, ROUSE
go to ~ REST, SLEEP
it can hide a ~ SOFA
Japanese ~ MAT
military ~ COT
ore ~ RUN
out of ~ AFOOT, ARISEN, ASTIR
portable ~ COT
stable ~ STRAW

"bed"
entrée ~ RICE

___ bed DAY, SOFA

bed-and-breakfast INN

"___ be darned!" ILL

bedaub ADORN

bedazzle STUN

bedclothes LINEN

bedcover SHEET

bedding LINEN, SHEET

Bede ADAM

bedeck ADORN, ARRAY, ATTIRE, BEAD, DRAPE, DRESS, TRIM

bedecked CLAD

Bedelia
~ **home, in folk song** ERIN

bedevil TEASE

bedew BATHE, WATER

bedfellow ALLY

Bedfordshire
~ **river** OUSE

bedizen ADORN, ATTIRE, DRESS, GARB, TRIM

"Bedknobs ___ Broomsticks" AND

bedlam NOISE

bed of ___ ROSES

"Bed of ___" ROSES

bedog TAIL

Bedouin ARAB, NOMAD, TRIBE
~ **mount** CAMEL
~ **robe** ABA

bedraggle SOIL

"Bed Riddance"
~ **author** NASH

bedrock
~ **deposit** ORE

Bedrock
~ **abode** CAVE
~ **name** FRED
~ **pet** DINO

bedroll
~ **alternative** COT

"Bedroom at ___" ARLES

Bedrosian STEVE

bedsheets LINEN

bedside
~ **companion** NURSE
~ **furnishing** LAMP, TABLE

bedstead
~ **part** SLAT
light ~ COT

bedtime
~ **beverage** COCOA
~ **sound** SNORE
~ **story** TALE

"Bedtime Story"
~ **director** HALL

bee
~ **defense** STING
~ **ender** HIVE, LINE
~ **follower** CEE
~ **home** HIVE
busy ~ DEMON
male ~ DRONE
stingless ~ DRONE

bee ___ BALM, TREE

___ bee MASON

Bee AUNT
~ **to Andy** AUNT
~ **to Opie** AUNT

Bee ___, The GEES

Bee, Aunt
~ **grandnephew** OPIE

beech FERN, TREE

beef CARP, MEAT
~ **cut** CHOP, EYE, LOIN, ROAST, TBONE
~ **dish** STEW
~ **rating org.** USDA
~ **up** RAISE
half a ~ SIDE
large joint of ~ BARON
like some ~ LEAN
young ~ VEAL

beef bourguignon
~ **ingredient** WINE

beefcake
~ **model** STUD

beefy BIG, LARGE

Bee Gees TRIO

beehive
~ **cousin** AFRO

Beehive State UTAH
~ **athlete** UTE

Beelzebub DEMON, SATAN
~ **forte** EVIL

been
had ~ WAS, WERE

___-been HAS

"___ been had!" IVE

"___ been robbed!" IVE

"___ been thinking..." IVE

"___ Been Working on the Railroad" IVE

beep BLAST, PAGE, TOOT

beeper ALARM, HORN

beer BREW, LAGER
~ **and skittles** PLAY
~ **barrel** KEG
~ **buy** CASE
~ **container** STEIN
~ **cousin** ALE
~ **foam** HEAD
~ **head** FOAM
~ **ingredient** MALT, YEAST
~ **keg adjunct** TAP
~ **label word** LITE
~ **quantity** KEG
like bock ~ AGED
like some ~ ONTAP
low-calorie ~ LITE
make ~ BREW

___ beer ICE, NEAR, ROOT

beer on ___ TAP

Beersheba
~ **locale** ISRAEL

Beery NOAH

bees
~ **do it** STING

bee's ___, the KNEES

beet ROOT

Beethoven DOG, PET
~ **beat** METER, TEMPO
~ **birthplace** BONN
~ **honoree** ELISE
~ **treat** BONE
~ **wrote one** OPERA
command to ~ SIT, STAY

beetle DOR, HANG
Japanese ~ PEST

___ beetle WATER

"Beetle Bailey"
~ **character** SARGE
~ **dog** OTTO
~ **intellectual** PLATO
~ **organization** ARMY
~ **soldier** ZERO

beetlehead DOLT

befall COME, OCCUR

befit SUIT

befog ADDLE, BLUR

before AHEAD, TILL, UNTIL
~ **in German** VON
~ **in olden days** ERST
~ **(prefix)** ANTE, FORE, PRE, PRO
~ **the present** AGO
~ **the rest** FIRST
~ **to a poet** ERE

"Before ___ After" AND

"Before and ___" AFTER

___ before beauty AGE

"___ Before Dark" HOME

"___ Before Dying, A" KISS

beforehand EARLY

"___ Before Time, The" LAND

befoul SOIL, TAINT

befriend AID, HELP

befuddle ADDLE, DAZE

befuddled ASEA, ATSEA

beg ASK, CRY, PLEAD, PRAY

beg ___ OFF

beget HAVE, SIRE

begetter
first ~ ADAM

beggar
~ **request** ALMS

"Beggar Maid, The" POEM

"Beggar's ___, The" OPERA

"Beggar's Opera, The"
~ **author** GAY

begin ARISE, ENTER, OPEN, START
~ **again** RENEW
~ **business** OPEN
~ **in earnest** SETTO
~ **to appear** PEEP
to ~ with FIRST

Begin
~ **peace partner** SADAT

beginning ASOF, GERM, INTRO, NEW, ONSET, ROOT, SEED, TOP

"Beginning of the ___, The" END

beginnings START

"___ Beginning to Look a Lot Like Christmas" ITS

"___ Begins" LIFE

"___ Begins at Eight-Thirty" LIFE

"___ Begins at Forty" LIFE

"___ Begins for Andy Hardy" LIFE

"Begin the Beguine"
 ~ name COLE
 ~ recorder SHAW

Begley
 ~ and others EDS

"Begone!" AWAY, SCAT, SCRAM, SHOO

"___ Be Good" LADY

"Beg pardon..." AHEM

begrime SOIL, TAINT

beguile AMUSE, BAIT, LURE, WILE

beguine DANCE

begum LADY
 ~ spouse AGA, AGHA

behalf SAKE
 on ~ of FOR

Behan IRISH
 ~ land EIRE, ERIN

behave ACT
 ~ fatuously DOTE
 ~ like a barbarian SACK
 ~ like a siren LURE
 ~ theatrically EMOTE
 ~ towards TREAT

"___ Behaving Badly" MEN

behavior MIEN
 ~ pattern HABIT

behemoth GIANT

behest ORDER

behind AFT, AFTER, ASTERN, LATE, REAR, SEAT
 ~ (prefix) RETRO

behind ___ lines ENEMY

behind-the-___ SCENES

___ behind the ears WET

behind the eight ___ BALL

"___ Behind the Mask, The" FACE

behold EYE, SEE
 ~ in Latin ECCE

"Behold I will build me ___..." ANEST

behoof AVAIL

"Bei ___ Bist Du Schön" MIR

beige COLOR, ECRU, TAN

Beijing CITY
 ~ name MAO

being ESSE, ESSENCE, LIFE, SELF
 ~ in Latin ESSE
 bring into ~ MAKE
 folklore ~ ELF
 for the time ~ NOW
 have ~ ARE, LIVE
 heavenly ~ ANGEL
 human ~ MAN, SELF, SOUL
 reason for ~ CAUSE
 that ~ the case ERGO, THEN
 time ~ NONCE

"Being ___" THERE

Beirut CITY, PORT

"Be it ___ so humble..." EVER

bejewel ADORN

"Bel-___" AMI

belabor STRESS
 ~ a point ARGUE

Belafonte SHARI

belay LASH

belch
 ~ forth EMIT, ERUPT

Belch, Sir Toby SOT

beldam HAG

beleaguerment SIEGE

Belém CITY, PORT
 ~ once PARA

Belfast
 ~ org. IRA

belfry SPIRE
 ~ dweller BAT
 ~ sound PEAL, RING

Belg.
 neighbor of ~ GER

Belgian HORSE
 ~ city LIEGE
 ~ resort SPA
 ~ river OISE, YSER

Belgrade CITY
 ~ coin PARA

Belgradian SLAV

Belial SATAN

belief CAUSE, IDEA, STAND, TENET
 ~ (prefix) IDEO
 ~ system ISM
 false ~ ERROR
 firm ~ DOGMA
 group ~ TENET
 Mideast ~ ISLAM
 religious ~ CREED
 Shiite ~ ISLAM
 statement of ~ CREDO
 theologian's ~ DOGMA

beliefs
 basic ~ ETHOS
 set of ~ CREDO, CREED

believable SANE

believe DEEM, HOLD, HOPE
 hard to ~ TALL

make ~ ACT

___ believe MAKE

"Believe ___ Not!" ITOR

"Believe It or ___!" NOT

believer
 ~ (suffix) IST, ITE

"___ Believer" IMA, TRUE

belittle CARP, DIS, RIP, SHAME

Belize CITY, PORT
 see also Spanish

bell BAY
 ~ ender BIRD, HOP
 ~ sound DING, PEAL, TOLL
 ~ starter BAR, BLUE, COW, DOOR
 ~ the cat BEARD, DARE
 hit the ~ RING
 literary ~ town ADANO
 ring a warning ~ ALARM, ALERT

bell ___ JAR, METAL

Bell ELLIS
 ~ and others MAS
 Watson to ~ ASST

Bell ___ LABS

"Bell ___ Adano, A" FOR

___ Bell TACO

___ Bell (Brontë pseudonym) ELLIS

bell-bottoms
 like ~ MOD

"Bellboy, The"
 ~ director LEWIS

belle
 ~ époque ERA
 ~ friend BEAU
 ~ of the ball DEB

Belle STARR

"Bellefleur"
 ~ author OATES

Bellerophon HERO

"Belles on ___ Toes" THEIR

"Belles on Their ___" TOES

"Bell for ___, A" ADANO

bellhop PAGE

belli
 casus ~ EVENT

bellicose IRATE, UPSET
 ~ god ARES, MARS

belligerent IRATE, UPSET
 ~ god ARES

Belli, Melvin
 ~ bailiwick BAR, LAW
 ~ occ. ATT, ATTY
 ~ org. ABA

Bellingshausen SEA

Bellini
 ~ opera NORMA

bellow BAWL, BAY, BLARE, BLAST, CALL, CRY, HOOT, NOISE, RAGE, RAMP, ROAR, STORM, YELL

Bellow SAUL

bells
 sound of ~ PEAL

"Bells, The" POEM
 ~ author POE

"Bells ___ Ringing" ARE

bell-shaped
 ~ flower TULIP

bell the ___ CAT

bellum
 ~ starter ANTE

bellwether
 ~ mate EWE

belly CRAW
 ~ laugh ROAR
 ~ muscles ABS
 ~ up to NEAR

bellyache CARP, CRAB, MOAN

bellyful GLUT

Belmont Stakes RACE

belongings ESTATE, GEAR, TRAPS

beloved ADORED, BEAU, DEAR, LIFE, PET, SWEET
 make ~ ENDEAR

"Beloved ___" ENEMY

below AFTER, NEATH, UNDER
 ~ in French ABAS
 ~ to a poet NEATH

"___ Below, The" ENEMY

belowdecks
 put ~ STOW

belowground
 ~ critter MOLE

"Below the ___" BELT

belt AREA, BAND, BANG, BEAT, HIT, JAB, LACE, OBI, PASTE, PELT, SASH, SLAP, SMITE, SNORT, STRAP, TAN, ZONE
 ~ a tune SING
 ~ ender LINE
 ~ holder LOOP
 ~ out SING, YELL
 black ~ ACE, RANK
 brown ~ RANK
 decorative ~ OBI, SASH
 makeshift ~ ROPE
 quick ~ SNORT
 seat ~ STRAP
 tighten one's ~ SAVE, STINT
 white ~ RANK

___ belt FAN, RUST, SEAT

___ Belt CORN, SNOW, SUN

belted
 ~ constellation ORION

beltless
 ~ dress TENT

beltmaker
 ~ tool AWL

beluga
~ product ROE

Belushi
~ "killer" character BEE

bema
~ neighbor APSE

bemoan RUE, WEEP

bemused ASEA, ATSEA, LOST

"Be my guest!" YES

Ben UNCLE
~ of the Ponderosa LORNE
~ to Hoss PAW
like ~ BIG

"Ben"
Ben in the film ~ RAT

"Ben-___" HUR

Benaderet BEA

Benatar PAT

Benazir
~ father ALI

___ Ben Canaan ARI

bench PEW, SEAT, SETTEE, TABLE
~ warmer SUB
~ wear ROBE
ride the ~ SIT

bench ___ PRESS

Benchley PETER, WIT
~ novel, with "The" DEEP

benchmark NORM
golfer's ~ PAR

bend ANGLE, ARC, ARCH, ELBOW,
LEAN, LOOP, NOD, SAG, SKEW,
SWAY, TURN
~ at the barre PLIE
~ down DIP, KNEEL
~ in the middle SAG
~ in the road TURN
~ in the wind SWAY
~ of the arm ELBOW
~ over backward ARCH
~ someone's ear BORE, TALK
~ the head NOD
~ the knee to OBEY
ballet ~ PLIE
carrick ~ KNOT
fisherman's ~ KNOT
hawser ~ KNOT
plumbing ~ ELL, ESS
river ~ ELBOW
sharp ~ ELBOW

bend ___ ANEAR

bend ___ backward OVER

___ bend KNEE

bendable LITHE

bended
go on ~ knee PLEAD

bended knee
~ remark PLEA

bender SPREE, TEAR, TOOT
~ of a sort KNEE
elbow ~ SOT
eyeball ~ OPART

fender ~ DENT

___-bender ELBOW

Bendix, William
~ film role RUTH
~ TV role RILEY

___ Bend National Park BIG

"Bend of the River"
~ director MANN

___ bene NOTA

beneath UNDER

"Beneath the 12-___ Reef" MILE

"Beneath the 12-Mile ___" REEF

Benedict POPE, SAINT

___ Benedict EGGS

Benedictine
~ title DOM

benediction
~ windup AMEN
give a ~ BLESS

benefaction AID, ALMS, GOOD

benefactor ANGEL, DONOR
PBS ~ NEA

benefice SEE

beneficence ALMS, LOVE

beneficent BIG
~ one DONOR

beneficial GOOD, UTILE

beneficiary HEIR

benefit AID, ASSET, AVAIL, EVENT,
GAIN, GALA, GET, GOOD, PAY,
PERK, SAKE, SERVE, USE
~ by USE
fringe ~ ICING, PERK, PLUS

benefits
incr. in ~ COLA

benefitting FOR

Benelux
~ loc. EUR

Benét, William Rose POET
see also poet

benevolence LOVE

benevolent BIG, GOOD, GREAT,
NICE
~ guy ELK
~ household spirit LAR
~ order ELKS

Bengal
~ country INDIA
~ ender ESE

Bengals ELEVEN, TEAM
~ org. NFL

Ben-Gurion
~ airport client ELAL
~ contemporary MEIR

Ben-Hur SLAVE

"Ben-Hur" EPIC
~ costume designer ERTE
~ garb TOGA

benign GOOD

Benin
~ neighbor NIGER, TOGO
see also French

Benjamin ORR, WEST

Benjamin Moore
~ layer COAT

Benji DOG, PET

"Benji"
~ director CAMP

Bennett TONY
co-panelist of ~ ARLENE

"Bennie and the Jets"
~ name ELTON

Benny
~ bandstand rival ARTIE

Benny, Jack
~ to Rochester BOSS
39 for ~ AGE

Benson EZRA

bent BIAS, CAST, HABIT, TENOR,
TRAIT, TURN
~ elbows locale BAR
~ out of shape IRATE, UPSET
be ~ upon WANT
easily ~ LITHE
it may be ~ EAR

Bentley
~ sleuth TRENT

Bentsen, Lloyd
~, once SEN

benumb DAZE, STUN

Benvenuti NINO

benzene
~ base TAR

benzoate SALT

benzocaine ESTER

benzoic ACID

benzoyl peroxide
~ target ACNE

"Be our guest!" COME

Beowulf HERO

"Beowulf" EPIC, SAGA
~ beverage MEAD

"Be Prepared"
~ org. BSA

bequeath CEDE, ENDOW, LEAVE

berate LASH, RAG, RAIL, SCORE,
TWIT

Berber MOOR

Berberian ARA

bereavement LOSS

bereft ALONE, LONE

Berenstain STAN

beret CAP, HAT, TAM
~ site TETE

berg
~ feature TIP
~ portion FLOE

Berg MOE

Berg, Alban
~ opera LULU
like ~'s music ATONAL

bergamot PEAR

Bergen EDGAR

Berger SENTA

Bergman
~ role MEIR

Bergman, Ingmar SWEDE
~ film of 1968 SHAME

Bergman, Ingrid SWEDE
~ role ILSA
last ~ role MEIR

Berg, Moe SPY

bergschrund HOLE

Bering SEA
~ (abbr.) STR

Bering Sea
~ isle ATTU
~ sighting FLOE
~ swimmer SEAL

Bering, Vitus DANE

Berkow IRA

Berkshire
~ school ETON
~ town ETON
~ village ASCOT

Berle
~ inventory GAGS

Berlin CITY
~ composition SONG, TUNE
~ loc. GER
~ river SPREE
see also German

Berliner EMILE

Berlinger JOE

Berlin, Irving
~ org. ASCAP

Berman LEN, TED

Bermuda ISLE
~ ocean ATL

Bermuda ___ ONION

Bern
~ river AAR

Bernadette STE
see also French

Bernard ROSE, SHAW

___ Bernard SAINT

___ Bernardino, Calif. SAN

Bernardo
see Spanish

Bernard, Saint
~ home ALPS

Berne ERIC
  ~ river AARE

Bernese Alps
  ~ river AAR, AARE

Bernhardt SARAH
  ~ birthplace PARIS

Bernoulli's ___ LAW

Bernsen, Corbin
  ~ role ARNIE

Bernstein CARL, ELMER
  ~ composition MASS

Berra YOGI
  gear for ~ MITT

berry
  ~ tree ELDER

Berry KEN

berserk AMOK, MAD, RABID
  go ~ RAGE, RAMP, SNAP

Bert LAHR
  ~ friend ERNIE
  ~ sister NAN

berth BED, COT, SLIP, SPACE
  ~ place PIER, PORT
  camp ~ COT
  give a wide ~ AVOID
  wide ~ PLAY

Bertolucci, Bernardo
  ~ film of 1979 LUNA

Bertrille
  Sally's ~ NUN

beryl GEM

beryllium METAL

beseech ASK, BEG, BID, CRY,
  PLEAD, PRAY, SUE, URGE

beseechment PLEA

"___ Be Seeing You" ILL

beside ALONG
  ~ (prefix) PARA

besides ALSO, AND, ELSE, MORE,
  PLUS, THEN, TOO, YET
  ~ (prefix) EPI

besmear TAINT

besmirch LIBEL, SHAME, SLUR,
  SOIL, TAINT

bespangle ADORN

besprinkle WATER

Bessell TED

Bessemer, Henry SIR
  ~ product STEEL

best AONE, CAP, CREAM, ELITE,
  FIRST, IDEAL, TOP, TOPS
  ~ barely EDGE
  ~ bib and tucker ATTIRE
  ~ girl LOVE
  ~ man PAL
  ~ part CREAM, LEAD
  come out second ~ LOSE
  do one's ~ ESSAY, TRY
  roster of the ~ ALIST
  Sunday ~ DRESS

the ~ and the
  brightest CREAM, ELITE
  use to ~ advantage AVAIL
  wish the ~ for BLESS

best-___ foursome BALL

best-___ scenario CASE

"best-___ plans..., The" LAID

Best EDNA, PETE

"Best ___, The" MAN

"Best ___ Forward" FOOT

"Best ___ of Our Lives, The"
  YEARS

___ best friend MANS

bestial BAD, FERAL

best-liked PET

best man
  ~ offering TOAST

bestow AWARD, ENDOW, HEAP

bestowal AWARD

bestride SPAN

bestseller HIT

"Best Years of ___ Lives, The"
  OUR

bet ANTE, LAY, PLAY, PUT, STAKE
  ~ first OPEN
  ~ on HOLD
  ~ one's bottom dollar RELY
  amount ~ STAKE
  call a ~ SEE
  collect a ~ WIN
  make a ~ GAME, PLAY
  meet a poker ~ SEE
  parlay a ~ RIDE
  roulette ~ EVEN, ODD, RED
  you ~ SURE, YEP, YES

"___ bet!" YOU

beta
  ~ preceder ALPHA

___ Beta Kappa PHI

"Betcha by Golly, ___" WOW

bête ___ NOIRE

betel NUT, PALM

Betelgeuse STAR
  ~ constellation ORION

bête noire BANE, FEAR

Beth
  ~ sister AMY, MEG

be that ___ may ASIT

"___ Be There" ILL

Bethlehem
  ~ trio MAGI

"Bethune"
  ~ director TILL

betide COME, OCCUR

betimes ANON, EARLY, SOON

betoken BODE, MEAN

betray DESERT, SELL
  ~ a confidence BLAB

betrothed BEAU, LOVE

Betsy ROSS

"___ Betsy From Pike" SWEET

"Betsy's Wedding"
  ~ actor ALDA
  ~ director ALDA

"Bette Davis ___" EYES

better AID, ALTER, AMEND, CAP,
  HELP, TOP
  ~ half BRIDE, LADY, LOVE,
    MATE
  ~ than ABOVE
  ~ than better BEST
  ~ than OK FINE
  get ~ GAIN, HEAL, MEND
  get ~ in the bottle AGE
  get into ~
    condition RESTORE
  get the ~ of BEAT, ROUT
  go one ~ LEAD, TOP
  grow ~ HEAL
  make ~ MEND
  none ~ BEST, TOPS
  old enough to know
    ~ ADULT
  think ~ of RUE

better ___ HALF

better ___ than never LATE

better ___ than sorry SAFE

better late ___ never THAN

"___ better to have loved..." TIS

"___ Better Watch Out" YOU

betting
  ~ game FARO
  ~ parameters ODDS
  ~ setting RENO

bettor
  ~ note IOU
  ~ starter ANTE

Betty
  ~ White House
    predecessor PAT
  costar of ~ BEA

"Betty ___" COED

Betty Ford Center
  ~ purpose REHAB

between AMID, AMONG
  ~ in French ENTRE
  ~ in Spanish ENTRE
  ~ (prefix) INTER

between-meal
  ~ food NOSH

"Between the Devil and the
  Deep Blue ___" SEA

___ between the lines READ

___ Between the States WAR

"___ Between Two Lovers" TORN

betwixt AMID, AMONG

Betz CARL

"Beulah, ___ me a grape" PEEL

"Beulah, peel ___ grape" MEA

Bevans CLEM

bevel SLANT

beverage ADE, ALE, BEER, CIDER,
  COCOA, COLA, JOE, LAGER,
  MEAD, NOG, POP, PORT, RUM,
  RYE, SAKE, SAKI, TEA, WINE
  ~ cart locale AISLE
  ~ flavor COLA
  ~ flavoring ANISE
  ~ in French THE
  ~ suffix ADE
  alcoholic ~ ALE, BEER, LAGER,
    MEAD, PORT, RUM, RYE,
    SAKE, SAKI, WINE
  après-ski ~ COCOA
  autumn ~ CIDER
  barley ~ BEER
  bedtime ~ COCOA
  "Beowulf" ~ MEAD
  black ~ TEA
  brewed ~ ALE, BEER, LAGER,
    TEA
  Brighton ~ ALE
  carbonated ~ COLA, POP,
    SODA
  diner ~ JOE
  dinner ~ WINE
  eggy ~ NOG
  fermented ~ ALE, BEER,
    LAGER
  fruit ~ ADE, CIDER
  green ~ TEA
  herbal ~ TEA
  hops ~ ALE
  hot ~ COCOA, TEA
  iced ~ TEA
  Japanese ~ SAKE, SAKI
  malt ~ ALE, BEER
  tavern ~ ALE
  Yuletide ~ NOG
  see also drink

"Beverly Hillbillies, The"
  ~ actor BAER, EBSEN
  ~ actress RYAN

Beverly Hills
  Drive in ~ RODEO

"Beverly Hills ___" COP

"Beverly Hills Cop"
  ~ role AXEL
  Bronson Pinchot in ~ SERGE

"Beverly Hills 90210"
  ~ actor TATA
  ~ actress ELISE

bevy HOST, MOB, TROOP
  sheik's ~ HAREM

bewail CRY, MOAN, RUE, SOB,
  WEEP

"Beware the ___ of March" IDES

bewhiskered
  ~ animal CAT, OTTER, SEAL

bewilder AMAZE, DAZE, GET, STUN

bewildered ASEA, ATSEA, LOST

bewitch LURE

bewitched RAPT

bey RULER, TITLE
~ **robe** ABA

beyond ABOVE, ACROSS, AFAR, EXTRA, OUT, OVER
~ **in German** UBER
~ **(prefix)** PARA, ULTRA
~ **risqué** LEWD
~ **the horizon** AFAR

beyond the ___ PALE

"Beyond the ___" SEA

"___ Be You" NEVER

bezel SLANT

bezique GAME

BFA
part of ~ ARTS, FINE

"Bhagavad Gita" POEM

Bhutan
~ **locale** ASIA
neighbor of ~ ASSAM

Bhutanese ASIAN

bi-
~ **predecessor** UNI
~ **successor** TRI

Bi ELEM
83 for ~ ATNO

bialy ROLL

bias ANGLE, SKEW, SLANT, SWAY, TENOR, TILT

bias-ply TIRE

biathlon EVENT
~ **equipment** RIFLE
take part in a ~ SKI

bib
~ **wearer** TOT
best ~ and tucker ATTIRE, BEST

bibber SOT

Bible
~ **book** ACTS, AMOS, ESTHER, EZRA, HOSEA
fourth word of the ~ GOD
last word of the ~ AMEN
second word of the ~ THE

"Bible, The"
~ **role** ABEL, CAIN
she played Sarah in ~ AVA

Biblical
~ **beast** ASS
~ **boat** ARK
~ **brother** AARON, ABEL, CAIN, ESAU, SETH
~ **country** SHEBA
~ **garden** EDEN
~ **hunter** ESAU
~ **idol** BAAL
~ **king** ASA, HEROD
~ **kingdom** ELAM
~ **matriarch** LEAH, SARAH
~ **mountain** SINAI
~ **patriarch** ENOS, ISAAC
~ **peak** ARARAT
~ **pilgrims** MAGI

~ **preposition** UNTO
~ **priest** ELI
~ **prison escapee** PETER
~ **pronoun** THEE, THOU
~ **prophet** AMOS, HOSEA, MOSES
~ **scribe** EZRA
~ **shepherd** ABEL
~ **stargazers** MAGI
~ **topic** SIN
~ **travelers** MAGI
~ **tribe** LEVI
~ **trio** MAGI
~ **twin** ESAU
~ **verb ender** EST, ETH
~ **weed** TARE

bibliographic
~ **suffix** ANA

bibliography LIST
~ **abbr.** ETAL, IBID

bibliophile
~ **purchase** TOME

bibulous
~ **one** SOT

Bic PEN
~ **filler** INK

bicarbonate SALT

bicarbonate of ___ SODA

bice COLOR

Bichette DANTE

bichon
~ **frisé** DOG

bicker ARGUE, NAG, ROW, SPAR

bickering SPAT

Bickle, Travis
~ **drove one** TAXI

bicorne HAT

bicuspid
~ **neighbor** MOLAR

bicycle
~ **part** PEDAL, SEAT, TIRE
~ **path** TRAIL

"___ Bicycle Built for Two" ONA

bicyclist RIDER

bid ASK
~ **farewell** LEAVE
~ **first** OPEN
silent ~ NOD

bid and ___ ASKED

biddable MEEK

bidding ORDER
do someone's ~ OBEY

biddy HEN

bide AWAIT, STAY
~ **one's time** AWAIT, WAIT

bide one's ___ TIME

bid one ___ (depart) ADIEU

Biel LAKE

bien-___ ETRE

"___ bien!" ESTA, TRES

biennial EVENT, PLANT

biff BANG, BEAT, HIT, JAB, PASTE, SLAP, SMITE

bifold DUAL

biform DUAL

bifurcate PART, SPLIT

big AMPLE, LARGE, OBESE, TALL
~ **bang cause** TNT
~ **bash** BLAST, EVENT, FETE, GALA
~ **bill** CNOTE
~ **bird** EMU, RHEA
~ **blow** GALE, STORM
~ **blowout** BASH, BLAST
~ **boy** MAN
~ **burger** MAC
~ **chance** RISK
~ **cheese** LION, NAME
~ **deal** ADO
~ **difference** GAP
~ **do** EVENT, FETE, GALA
~ **eater** HOG
~ **family** CLAN, TRIBE
~ **gulp** BELT
~ **guy** GIANT, TITAN
~ **head** EGO
~ **hit** SMASH
~ **leaguer's concern** STAT
~ **lummox** APE
~ **name** STAR
~ **ox** OAF
~ **pig** HOG
~ **rig** SEMI
~ **sandwich** HERO
~ **shot** LION, NABOB, NAME, NOB
~ **top** TENT
~ **truck** RIG
~ **wheel** HEAD, NAME, NOB
make it ~ ARRIVE
no ~ thing BLIP
open one's ~ mouth BLAB
talk ~ BRAG, CROW, ORATE

big ___ BAND, BEAT, DEAL, GAME, GUN, LIE, NAME, SHOT, TIME, TOE, TOP

big ___ house ASA

___ big (brag) TALK

Big ___ APPLE, MAC, SUR

Big ___ (burger choice) MAC

Big ___ (college-sports conference) EAST

Big ___ (Cornell) RED

Big ___, Calif. SUR

Big ___ Conference EAST, TEN

Big ___ Era BAND

Big ___ National Park BEND

Big ___ Theory BANG

"Big ___" RED, SHOT, STEAL

"Big ___" (Kerouac novel) SUR

"Big ___, The" EASY, HEAT, PARADE, SKY, SLEEP, TRAIL

"Big ___!" DEAL

"Big ___ for the Little Lady, A" HAND

"Big ___ Mama" BAD

"Big ___ One, The" RED

"Big ___ on Madonna Street" DEAL

Big Apple
~ **neighborhood** SOHO
~ **player** MET
~ **stadium** SHEA

big as ___ LIFE

"Big Bad ___" MAMA

"Big Bad John"
~ **actor** DEAN, ELAM

big band
~ **name** ARTIE

Big Band ___ ERA

Big Ben
~ **three** III

Big Bertha GUN
~ **birthplace** ESSEN

Big Bird
~ **street** SESAME

Big Board
letters on the ~ RCA

"Big Combo, The"
~ **director** LEWIS

"Big Country, The"
~ **actor** IVES

Big Dipper LADLE
part of the ~ STAR

big-eared
~ **animal** ASS, BURRO

Bigfoot
~ **cousin** YETI

bigger
~ **than life** EPIC
get ~ GROW

bigger ___ a breadbox THAN

"Bigger ___ Life" THAN

"___ bigger and better things!" ONTO

"Bigger Than ___" LIFE

"___ bigger than a breadbox?" ISIT

"Bigger Than Life"
~ **director** RAY

"Biggest Little City in the World, The" RENO

biggin CAP

Biggs, E. Power
~ **forte** ORGAN

"Big Hand ___ the Little Lady, A" FOR

"Big Hand for the Little ___, A" LADY

"Big Heat, The"
~ director LANG

bighorn ANIMAL

Bighorns MTS, RANGE

big house PEN, STIR
~ resident CON

bight BAY, COVE, HAVEN, INLET

big-league PRO

big leaguer PRO

Big, Mr. LION

big-name NOTED

bigoted SMALL

bigotry BIAS, HATE

"Big Red ___, The" ONE

bigshot
mgmt. ~ CEO

Big Sky
~ team IDAHO

Big 10's ___ State PENN

Big Ten
~ team ILL, IND, IOWA, OSU

"Big Three"
~ site of 1945 YALTA

big-time MAJOR
~ operator DOER

big-voiced LOUD

bigwig EXEC, HEAD, NABOB, NAME, NOB
British ~ NOB
co. ~ CEO, PRES
corporate ~ EXEC
Eastern ~ AMIR, EMEER, EMIR
feudal ~ BARON
newspaper ~ EDITOR

bigwigs ELITE
Pentagon ~ BRASS

"Big Yellow ___" TAXI

bijou GEM, PEARL, STONE

bike
~ lane PATH
~ part GEAR, PEDAL, SEAT
~ path LANE
~ starter MINI, MOTOR
ride a ~ PEDAL
road ~ MOTOR
ten-speed ~ RACER

___ bike DIRT, TRAIL

biker
~ aid CLIP
~ selection SPEED

bikeway LANE

biking
go ~ PEDAL

bikini
~ part BRA

Bikini ATOLL
~ event ATEST, TEST

Biko STEVE

Bilbao CITY, PORT
see also Spanish

bile ANGER, IRE, SPITE

Biletnikoff FRED

bilge TRASH

bilk CLIP, CON, ROB, ROOK

Bilko ERNIE, NCO, SGT
~ command ATEASE
~ nickname SARGE

"___ Bilko" SGT

bill ACT, CASH, DEBT, FEE, LAW, NIB, NOSE, PEAK, SCORE
~ abbr. AMT
~ add-on RIDER
~ and coo NECK, PET
~ attachment RIDER
~ of exchange NOTE
~ of fare CARD, CARTE, MEAL, MENU
~ of sale PAPER
~ partner COO
~ starter HAND
bar ~ TAB
big ~ CNOTE
bird's ~ NEB
dollar ~ ONE
fill the ~ CATER, SERVE
five-dollar ~ FIN
foot the ~ PAY, TREAT
Hamilton ~ TEN
hundred-dollar ~ CNOTE
kill a ~ VETO
Lincoln ~ FIVE
lowest ~ ONE
monthly ~ PHONE
one-dollar ~ ACE
pass a ~ ADOPT, ENACT
pay the ~ TREAT
restaurant ~ TAB
small ~ ONE
telephone ~ TOLL
three-dollar ~ FAKE
util. ~ ELEC, TEL
Washington's ~ ONE

Bill DAY, GATES, NYE, TONY
partner of ~ in an "excellent adventure" TED

"Bill & ___ Bogus Journey" TEDS

"Bill & ___ Excellent Adventure" TEDS

Bill ___ (Charles Henry Smith) ARP

"Bill ___ Coo" AND

"Bill ___, the Science Guy" NYE

___ Bill (legendary cowboy) PECOS

"Bill and ___" COO

billboard SIGN
~ displays ADS

"Billboard"
~ entry SONG
~ listing HIT

billboards ADS

billed DUE
~ item CAP

billet BED, COT, LIVE

billet-doux NOTE
word in a ~ CHER

billfish GAR

billfold
~ filler FIN, ONE, TEN

billiards GAME, POOL
~ prop RACK
~ shot CAROM
~ stick CUE
glancing contact in ~ KISS

Billie
~ hubby FLO

billing
get top ~ STAR

billingsgate ABUSE

billion
~ ender AIRE
one ~ years, in geology EON

billions MINT
home to ~ ASIA

"Billions and billions..."
~ scientist SAGAN

billionth
~ (prefix) NANO

Bill, Mr.
~ cry OHNO

bill of ___ ENTRY, FARE, SALE

Bill of Rights
1944 ~ subjects GIS

billow ROLL

billowing
~ garment CAPE

bills
fat roll of ~ WAD
have ~ OWE
like new ~ CRISP
some ~ MOOLA

Bills ELEVEN, TEAM
~ org. NFL

bill-signing
~ souvenir PEN

billy GOAT

Billy IDOL, OCEAN, ROSE

Billy ___ Williams DEE

"Billy ___" (Waterhouse novel) LIAR

"Billy ___ Jumbo" ROSES

"Billy Don't Be a ___" HERO

billy goat MALE
~ feature BEARD

Billy Joel
~ instrument PIANO

Billy the ___ KID

Biloxi
~ st. MISS

bi-monthly ORGAN

bin CASE, CHEST, CRIB
dyeing ~ VAT
storage ~ CRIB, SILO

binary DUAL, PAIR, TWIN
~ digit ONE

binary ___ STAR

binate DUAL

binaural STEREO

bind BALE, CORD, HOLE, LACE, LASH, PASTE, STRAP, TAPE, TIE
~ anew RETIE
~ oneself AGREE
~ together ROPE

binder PASTE
model ~ GLUE
package ~ CORD
satchel ~ STRAP

Binder STEVE

binding BAND, CLOSE, STRAP
make ~ SIGN
not ~ LOOSE, NULL, VOID

bindlestiff HOBO, NOMAD

bine STEM

"___ bin ein Berliner" ICH

Bing DAVE
~ buddy in films BOB

binge ORGY, SPREE, TEAR, TOOT

"___ Bingle" DER

bingo GAME
~ cousin KENO

"Bingo ___ Traveling All-Stars & Motor Kings, The" LONG

"Bingo ___ Yale" ELI

"Bingo!" AHA

"Bingo Long Traveling ___-Stars & Motor Kings, The" ALL

"Bingo Long Traveling All-Stars & ___ Kings, The" MOTOR

binocular
~ lens OPTIC

bio
~ info AGE
final ~ OBIT

biography GENRE, LIFE, PAST

biol. SCI
~ branch ANAT

biology
~ subj. ANAT

Biondi MATT

biosphere EARTH

biota
some ~ FLORA

birch ALDER, BEER, LACE, ROD, TREE

birchbark CANOE

"Birches" POEM

"Birch Interval"
  ~ director MANN

bird AUK, CHAT, COOT, CRANE, CROW, DODO, DOVE, EAGLE, EGRET, EMU, ERN, ERNE, GOOSE, HEN, HERON, IBIS, KITE, KIWI, LARK, LOON, MACAW, MEW, MOA, MYNA, NENE, ORIOLE, OWL, PIE, RAIL, RAVEN, RHEA, ROC, SNIPE, STILT, SWAN, TERN, WREN
  ~ beak NEB, NIB
  ~ call CAW
  ~ claw TALON
  ~ crop CRAW
  ~ cry CAW
  ~ food SEED, SUET
  ~ home NEST
  ~ in Latin AVIS
  ~ Maoris once hunted MOA
  ~ of Arabian myth ROC
  ~ of Mauritius, once DODO
  ~ of passage HOBO, NOMAD
  ~ of peace DOVE
  ~ of prey BIRD, EAGLE, KITE
  ~ on a coin EAGLE
  ~ shed COTE
  ~ shelter NEST
  ~ sound COO
  ~ starter SONG
  ~ stomach CRAW
  ~ that has red meat EMU
  ~ that lays green eggs EMU
  ~ whose male hatches the eggs KIWI
  ~ with useless wings EMU
anserine ~ GOOSE
aquatic ~ COOT, SWAN, TERN
"Arabian Nights" ~ ROC
Australian ~ EMU
baby ~ OWLET
bald ~ EAGLE
beach ~ ERN, ERNE
big ~ EMU, RHEA
black ~ CROW, RAVEN
black-and-orange ~ ORIOLE
blue ~ HERON
brilliantly colored ~ MACAW
cattle ~ EGRET
Chesapeake Bay ~ TERN
Christmas ~ GOOSE
coastal ~ ERN, ERNE
colonel's ~ EAGLE
diving ~ AUK, COOT, LOON
domestic ~ HEN
down-under ~ EMU
ducklike ~ COOT
Egyptian sacred ~ IBIS
Eurasian ~ TERN
extinct ~ DODO, MOA
fabled ~ ROC
fish-eating ~ ERN, ERNE
flightless ~ EMU, KIWI, RHEA
flightless ~ of yore DODO
fork-tailed ~ TERN
Great Seal ~ EAGLE
hangar ~ PLANE
harsh-voiced ~ MACAW
Hawaii state ~ NENE
hieroglyphics ~ IBIS
imitate a ~ SING
lake ~ LOON

legendary ~ ROC
leggy ~ EGRET
like a worm-catching ~ EARLY
long-billed ~ HERON, IBIS, SNIPE
long-legged ~ HERON
long-necked ~ SWAN
long-plumed ~ EGRET
man and ~ and beast LIFE
marine ~ ERN, ERNE
marsh ~ EGRET, RAIL, SNIPE
Maryland state ~ ORIOLE
meadow ~ LARK
migratory ~ GOOSE
move like a ~ FLIT
mythical ~ ROC
Nile's sacred ~ IBIS
noisy ~ MACAW, PIE
ocean-going ~ ERN, ERNE
ostrichlike ~ MOA
outback ~ EMU
pampas ~ RHEA
rare ~ ONER
ratite ~ EMU
razor-billed ~ AUK
sea ~ ERN, ERNE, MEW
second-largest ~ EMU
shore ~ ERN, ERNE, HERON
singing ~ LARK
small ~ WREN
snowy ~ EGRET, OWL
strigiform ~ OWL
talking ~ MYNA
tall ~ CRANE
tropical ~ MACAW, MYNA
wading ~ CRANE, EGRET, HERON, IBIS, RAIL, SNIPE, STILT
water ~ COOT
web-footed ~ AUK
white ~ SWAN
wise ~ OWL
Wonderland ~ DODO
yellow-breasted ~ CHAT

bird ___ DOG

___ bird DODO, EARLY, GAME, SHORE, WATER

"___ bird!..." ITSA

Bird LANCE
  ~ milieu NBA

"Bird"
  ~ played it ALTO, SAX

"Bird ___ Wire" ONA

birdbath POOL
  ~ organism ALGA
  ~ slime ALGAE

birdbrain OAF, TWIT

birdbrained DAFT, MAD, SLOW

"Birdcage, The"
  ~ actor LANE

birdcall SONG

bird feeder
  ~ staple SUET

birdie
  ~ beater EAGLE
  ~ plus one PAR

birdlike AVIAN

birdman PILOT

bird of ___ PREY

"___ Bird of Youth" SWEET

"Bird on a ___" WIRE

bird-related AVIAN

birds
  ~ and the bees SEX
  ~ collectively AVES
  ~ do it ROOST, SING, SOAR
  ~ in Latin AVES
  ~ partner BEES
  for the ~ INANE
  like ~ ALATE
  of ~ AVIAN
  the ~ of the air LIFE
  with the ~ EARLY

birds ___ feather OFA

bird's-___ view EYE

birds and ___ BEES

bird's-eye ___ MAPLE

bird's-nest FERN

Birdsong OTIS

birdy AVIAN

bireme
  ~ equipment OAR
  ~ projection RAM

biretta CAP, HAT

birler
  ~ need LOG

Birmingham
  ~ st. ALA
  see also British

Birnbach LISA

birth ONSET, RISE, START
  give ~ to BEAR, DROP, HAVE
  high ~ RANK
  of ~ NATAL

"Birth ___ Nation, The" OFA

birthday EVENT
  ~ count YEARS
  ~ figure AGE
  ~ mail CARD
  have a ~ AGE

birthday ___ CAKE

birthday party
  ~ necessity CAKE

birthday suit
  in one's ~ BARE, NUDE

birthmark MOLE

birth month
  ~ symbol GEM, STONE

"Birth of a Nation" EPIC

birthplace HOME

birthright DUE
  ~ barterer ESAU

birthstone GEM
  May ~ AGATE
  October ~ OPAL

bis AGAIN, ANEW

Biscay
  Bay of ~ feeder LOIRE

Biscayne BAY

Biscayne Bay
  ~ site MIAMI
  county on ~ DADE

Bischoff SAM

biscotto
  ~ flavoring ANISE

biscuit ROLL
  Londoner's ~ SCONE

___ biscuit DOG, SEA, TEA, WATER

"Biscuit ___, The" EATER

bisect CUT, SAW, SPLIT

bisected HALF

bisector
  nave ~ AISLE

bishop MAN, RANK
  ~ domain SEE
  ~ of Rome POPE
  ~ starter ARCH
  ~ title ABBA
  Eastern ~ ABBA
  onetime TV ~ SHEEN
  South African ~ TUTU

Bishop, Joey EMCEE, HOST

"Bishop Orders His Tomb, The" POEM

bishopric SEE

bishops
  ~ council SYNOD

Bismarck OTTO, SEA
  ~ st. NDAK
  see also German

"Bismarck" BOAT, SHIP

bismuth METAL

bison ANIMAL

bisque COLOR

bistro BAR, CAFE
  ~ delicacy PATE
  ~ list MENU
  ~ menu CARTE
  patronize a ~ EAT

bit ACT, CHIP, DASH, DROP, JOT, MITE, PART, SCRAP, SHRED, SNIP, TAD, TINGE, TOOL
  ~ attachment REIN
  ~ part CAMEO
  the least ~ IOTA

bit ___ PART

___-bit TWO

bit by bit
  get ~ AMASS

bite EAT, GNAW, MEAL, NIP, SALT, SNAP, STING, TANG, TASTE
  ~ persistently GNAW
  ~ the dust LOSE
  have a ~ EAT
  just a ~ TASTE

not apt to ~ TAME
quick ~ NOSH
with a ~ RACY

biter
dog ~ FLEA

"___ Bites" LOVE

bite the ___ DUST

biting ACID, ACRID, KEEN, RAW, SOUR, TART
~ pest GNAT

"bit of talcum / is always walcum, A"
~ author NASH

bit part
~ performer EXTRA

___ bits (25 cents) TWO

___-bitten FLEA, HARD

"___ Bitten" ONCE

"___ bitten, twice shy" ONCE

bitter ACID, ACRID, ALE, SAD, SORE, SOUR
~ end LAST
~ medicinal RUE
~ order ALE
~ vetch ERS
it may be ~ END

bitter ___ ALOES, END, ORANGE

"Bitter ___" SWEET

"Bitter ___ of General Yen, The" TEA

bittern BIRD
~ cousin HERON

bitterness ANGER, SPITE, STING

Bitterroot RANGE

"Bitter Tea of General ___, The" YEN

"Bitter Tea of General Yen, The"
~ director CAPRA

bitumen COAL, TAR

bituminous
~ deposit COAL, SEAM

bivalve
~ mollusk CLAM

bivouac BED, CAMP, REST
~ quarters TENT

Biwa LAKE

___ biz SHOW

bizarre EERIE, EERY, ODD, OUTRE

Bizet
~ José DON
site in a ~ suite ARLES

Bjorn BORG
~ rival ILIE

Bk ELEM
97 for ~ ATNO

bks.-to-be MSS

blab SING, TALK, TELL, YAK

black BEAR, EBON, EVIL, INKY, JET, ONYX, SABLE, TEA
~ as night SABLE
~ belt ACE, RANK, SASH
~ beverage TEA
~ bird CROW, RAVEN
~ cat OMEN
~ cloud PALL
~ ender BALL, BIRD, CAP, MAIL, OUT, STRAP, TOP
~ eye TAINT
~ fruit OLIVE
~ fuel COAL
~ gem OPAL
~ gold OIL
~ goo TAR
~ hole, once STAR
~ humor GENRE
~ in French NOIR, NOIRE
~ look GLARE
~ mark LIBEL, SMUT, TAINT
~ plus white GRAY, GREY
~ racer SNAKE
~ starter BOOT, LAMP
~ tie DRESS
~ to a poet EBON
~ wood EBONY
deep ~ EBON, INKY, JET
glossy ~ RAVEN
in the ~ SOLID
jet ~ EBONY, ONYX
lustrous ~ EBON, RAVEN
penny ~ STAMP
pitch ~ UNLIT
pure ~ ONYX

black ___ BEAR, BELT, EYE, HOLE, ICE, MARIA, OAK, OUT, TEA, TIE

black ___ (kind of holly) ALDER

black ___ (oil) GOLD

black-___ pea EYED

black-___ Susan EYED

Black HUGO, NOEL, SEA
on the ~ ASEA, ATSEA

Black ___ (Dick Turpin's horse) BESS

Black ___ (paddy wagon) MARIA

Black ___ of Calcutta HOLE

"Black ___" ANGEL, HAND

"Black ___, The" ARROW, CAT, ROOM, SWAN, TULIP

"Black ___ Me" LIKE

black-and-___ BLUE

Black and ___ TAN

"Black and ___ Fantasy" TAN

black-and-orange
~ bird ORIOLE

black-and-white
~ diver AUK
~ snack OREO

Black Angus COW

blackball BAR, OUST, TABOO, TABU, VETO

Black Bears
home of the ~ MAINE, ORONO

Black Beauty HORSE

black-belt
~ move CHOP

"Blackberry Winter"
~ author MEAD

Black Bess HORSE

blackbird ANI, MERLE, ROOK
~ comment CAW

blackbirds
like ~ AVIAN

blackboard SLATE
~ accessory ERASER

Black Condor HERO

blacked
~ out UNLIT

blacken BLOT, CHAR, LIBEL, SEAR, SHAME, SLUR, SMEAR, SOIL

black-eyed ___ PEA

Black Flag
~ rival RAID
~ target ANT

Blackfoot TRIBE

blackguard BEAST, CAD, CUR, OGRE

Black Hawk SAC, WAR

Blackhawks SIX, TEAM
~ milieu ICE, RINK
~ org. NHL

black-hearted BAD, BASE, EVIL, LOW, MEAN

Black Hills
~ st. SDAK

black hole ABYSS

"Black Horse Troop, The"
~ composer SOUSA

black-ink
~ item ASSET

blackish
~ fish SABLE

"Black Is the ___ of My True Love's Hair" COLOR

blackjack GAME
~ card ACE, TEN
~ dealer's device SHOE
~ option STAY

blackjack table
work at the ~ DEAL

blackmail BLEED

Blackman HONOR

"Black Narcissus"
~ actor SABU

blackness
exemplar of ~ COAL

blackout ALERT, SKIT

Black Pearl
soccer's ~ PELE

Black Sea
~ port ODESSA

~ resort YALTA

blacksmith
~ tool RASP

blacksnake LASH

"Black Stallion, The"
~ boy ALEC
~ star RENO

blackthorn SLOE

blacktop PAVE

"Black Velvet ___, The" BAND

Blackwood
~ four-pointer ACE

bladder SAC

blade BEAU, CAD, DUDE, LEAF, MAN, SABER, STEEL
~ of yore SNEE
copter ~ ROTOR
fencing ~ EPEE
gay ~ DUDE
harrow ~ DISC
hussar's ~ SABER
Malay ~ KRIS
medieval ~ SNEE
three-sided ~ EPEE
turbine ~ VANE
windmill ~ VANE

blah DRAB, SOSO, TAME
a bit ~ TAME
visually ~ DRAB

blahs
having the ~ SAD
the ~ ENNUI

blain BOIL, NODE, SORE

Blaine, Rick
~ love ILSA

___ Blair (George Orwell) ERIC

Blair, Bonnie
~ milieu ARENA, ICE, RINK

Blake AMANDA

Blake, Colonel
~ aide RADAR

Blake, William POET
see also poet

Blakey ART

blame CARP, ONUS, PUT, RAP
~ deflector ALIBI
~ taker GOAT

"Blame ___ Rio" ITON

"Blame ___ the Bossa Nova" ITON

blamed
~ one GOAT

"Blame It on ___" RIO

"Blame It on the Bossa ___" NOVA

blameless CLEAN

"___ Blame Me" DONT

blameworthy BASE, LOW

Blanc ALP, MEL

Blanca ___, Colo. PEAK

blanch PALE, REACT, STEAM

blanche
carte ~ RUN
give carte ~ LET

___ **blanche** CARTE

blanched ASHEN

___ **blanco** OSO

___ **Blanco, Colo.** RIO

bland ARID, DRY, FLAT, INANE, MILD, STALE
~ **fare** PAP

blandish LURE

blank BARE, CLEAN, GAP
~ **look** STARE
~ **out** ERASE

Blank ___ ("Max Headroom" character) REG

blanket DRAPE, ROBE, SHEET
Mexican ~ SERAPE
wet ~ BORE, DRAG, DRIP

___ **blanket** WET

blare BLAST, BOOM, DIN, NOISE, ROAR, YELL

blaring LOUD

Blarney ___ STONE

Blarney Stone
~ **site** EIRE, ERIN
like the ~ IRISH

"___ Blas" GIL

___ **Blas (Caribbean gulf)** SAN

blasé TIRED
become ~ JADE
hardly ~ AWED

blasphemy OATH

Blass BILL

blast BLARE, BOOM, GALE, NOISE, PEAL, ROAR
~ **from the past** OLDIE
~ **off** LEAVE
~ **starter** ECTO, ENDO, SAND
~ **through** OPEN
fission ~ ATEST
gun ~ BANG
have a ~ REVEL
Ruthian ~ HOMER

blast ___ OFF

blaster
~ **need** TNT

blastoff START
~ **org.** NASA

blat NOISE

blatant BALD, OPEN, OVERT, RANK

blather PRATE, TALK, YAK

blaze FIRE, FLARE, GLARE, GLOW
~ **a trail** LEAD
~ **up** FLARE

blaze a ___ TRAIL

blazer COAT

Blazers FIVE, TEAM
~ **org.** NBA

blazing AFIRE, HOT, LIVE

"Blazing Saddles"
~ **singer** LAINE

blazon ADORN, TRIM

bldg.
~ **unit** APT

bleach FADE

bleached PALE

bleacher SEAT
~ **bum** FAN
~ **feature** ROW, TIER
~ **yell** RAH

bleacher ___ SEAT

bleacherite FAN

bleaching
~ **agent** LEMON, OZONE

bleak BARE, RAW, SAD

"Bleak House"
~ **girl** ADA

blear BLUR, DIM, MIST

bleary DIM

bleary-___ EYED

bleat BAA, BLAB, CRY, MAA, NOISE

bleater EWE

"Blecch!" UGH

bleed OOZE, SEEP, TAP
~ **as a color** RUN
~ **for** FEEL

bleep EDIT
~ **out** ERASE

blemish BLOT, MAR, MOLE, PIT, SPOT, TAINT
fender ~ DING
honor student's ~ CEE, DEE

blench FEAR, START
~ **from** HATE

blend BEAT, FUSE, MASH, MELD, MELT, OLIO, STIR, UNITE, WED
~ **together** STIR

blended
~ **whiskey** RYE

blender
~ **setting** CHOP, PUREE, SPEED

bless EXALT, LAUD

blessed
it may be ~ EVENT
not a ~ thing NONE

blessed ___ EVENT

"Blessed Damozel, The" POEM

"Blessed Event"
~ **director** RUTH

blessing ASSET

"Bless the Beasts ___ Children" AND

blether ADO

___ **bleu** BAS

blight BLAST, DASH, MOLD, ROT, TAINT
urban ~ SMOG

blighted BAD
~ **tree** ELM

blighter CAD

Blimp
~ **title** COL

blind RUSE
~ **tiger** BAR
~ **unit** SLAT
it may be ~ DATE
Venetian ~ SHADE

blind ___ ALLEY, DATE, SIDE, SPOT

blind ___ bat ASA

___ **blind** ROB

___**-blind** COLOR

Blind ___ MELON

"Blind Ambition"
~ **author** DEAN

blind as a ___ BAT

blinding LOUD

"___ Blind Mice" THREE

blinds
~ **component** SLAT

blink BAT
~ **at** AVOID
on the ~ OUT

blip
~ **on a polygraph** LIE
radar ~ ECHO
sonar ~ ECHO

bliss
bring ~ to ELATE

bliss ___ (exult) OUT

blissful ELATED, RAPT
~ **place** EDEN

"Bliss of ___ Blossom, The" MRS

blister SAC, SORE

blistering HOT

blithe GAY
~ **romp** LARK

"Blithe Spirit"
~ **director** LEAN

___ **blitz** MEDIA

blizzard GALE, SNOW, STORM
~ **maker** SNOW

bloated BIG, LARGE

blob MASS

Blob
move like the ~ OOZE

bloc RING, SECT
political ~ LABOR

Bloch ERNEST

block ARREST, BAR, CLOG, DAM, DETER, ESTOP, GAG, JAM, MASS, SHUT, STOP, TOY
~ **a broadcast** JAM
~ **ender** ADE, HEAD
~ **house** IGLOO
~ **illegally** CLIP
~ **of ice** FLOE
~ **out** PLAN
~ **part** CHIP
~ **print** CUT
~ **starter** ROAD
~ **unit** CELL
builder's ~ LOT
building ~ ATOM, UNIT
chip off the old ~ SON
chipped off the same ~ AKIN
illegal ~ CLIP
knock someone's ~ off BEAT
marble ~ SLAB
stumbling ~ BAR, SNAG
sun ~ SHADE

___ **block** PLATE, SUN

blockade BAR, CLOSE, SIEGE

blockage CLOG

blocker
river ~ DAM
UV ~ OZONE
x-ray ~ LEAD

___ **blocker** BETA

Blocker DAN

blockhead ASS, CLOD, DOLT, DOPE, IDIOT, LUG, OAF

blockheaded DAFT

Block, H&R
~ **staffer** CPA

blockish DENSE

blocks TOY

bloke CHAP, GENT, MALE
that ~ HIM
that ~'s HIS

blonde FAIR
~ **shade** ASH
go ~ DYE

"Blonde ___ Blue" OVER

Blondie
work like ~ CATER

"Blondie" STRIP
~ **kid** ELMO
~ **nickname** DAG

blood DUDE, GORE
~ **carrier** AORTA
~ **component** SERUM
~ **fluids** SERA
~ **grouping** ABO
~ **obstruction** CLOT
~ **relatives** KIN
~ **vessel** AORTA
bad ~ ANGER
blue ~ PEER

flesh and ~ CLAY, KIN, LIFE
make one's ~ run
  cold SCARE
make someone's ~
  boil ANGER, IRK, PEEVE,
    RILE, UPSET
sweat ~ STEW

blood ___ SERUM

blood ___ (fertilizer) MEAL

___ blood BAD, BLUE, NEW

"Blood ___ Poet, The" OFA

"Blood ___ Sand" AND

"___ Blood" WISE

"Blood and ___" SAND

blood bank
  ~ depositor DONOR
  ~ quantity UNIT

___-blooded HOT, RED, WARM

"Blood From the Mummy's ___"
  TOMB

bloodhound
  ~ trail ODOR, SCENT

bloodless PALE

bloodline RACE, TRIBE

"Blood of a ___, The" POET

"Blood on Satan's ___, The"
  CLAW

"Blood on the ___" MOON, SUN

"Blood on the Moon"
  ~ director WISE

bloods
  blue ~ ELITE

bloodstone GEM

Blood, Sweat and ___ TEARS

bloodthirsty CRUEL

blood-typing
  ~ system ABO

bloody RARE, RAW

bloom COLOR, OPEN, PEAK, SHINE

"___ Bloom" DESERT

"Bloom County"
  ~ Bill CAT
  ~ penguin OPUS

blooming ROSY

Bloom, Molly
  ~ last word YES

blooper ERROR, SLIP

Blore ERIC

blossom BEAR, GROW, OPEN,
  PEAK
  ~ support STEM

"Blossoms in the ___" DUST

"Blossoms in the Dust"
  ~ director LEROY

"___ Blossom Special" ORANGE

blot DAB, SLUR, SMEAR, SPOT,
  TAINT
  ~ on the escutcheon TAINT
  ~ out ANNUL, BLUR, ERASE,
    OMIT, SHADE
  ~ starter INK

blotch BLOT, SPOT, TAINT

blotter
  ~ spot INK
  name on a police ~ DOE, ROE
  place for a ~ DESK
  police ~ entry AKA, ALIAS

blouse TOP
  ~ adornment CAMEO, PIN
  ~ fabric SILK
  ~ part NECK
  make a ~ SEW
  sleeveless ~ SHELL

blow BANG, BLAST, CHOP, ERUPT,
  FLEE, GALE, HIT, PANT, SLAP,
  SPEND, STORM, WASTE
  ~ a gasket RAGE, RAMP, RANT
  ~ away AWE, STUN
  ~ cash SPEND, WASTE
  ~ hard BRAG
  ~ hole NOSE
  ~ hot and cold HANG
  ~ in ARRIVE, COME
  ~ it ERR, LOSE
  ~ one's cool RAGE, RAMP
  ~ one's horn BLARE, TOOT
  ~ one's mind AWE, DAZE,
    STUN
  ~ one's stack RAGE, STORM
  ~ one's top BOIL, ERUPT,
    RAGE, RAMP
  ~ one's trumpet BRAG,
    CROW, TOOT
  ~ over PASS
  ~ sky high BLAST
  ~ the chance MISS
  ~ the lid off LEAK, TELL
  ~ the whistle BLAB, RAT, TELL
  ~ to pieces BLAST
  ~ up BANG, BLAST, ERUPT, LIE,
    RAGE, RAMP, RANT
  big ~ GALE, STORM
  dull ~ THUD
  karate ~ CHOP
  low ~ DIG
  open-handed ~ SLAP
  powerful ~ SWAT
  severe ~ GALE
  verbal ~ LASH

blow ___ (extinguish) OUT

blow ___ (overwhelm) AWAY

blow ___ (subside) OVER

blow ___ steam OFF

blow-___ DRY

___ blow (unfair attack) LOW

Blow JOE

"Blow ___" OUT

blow a ___ FUSE

blower FAN
  use the ~ DRY

___ blower SNOW

blowgun
  ~ ammo DART

blown
  ~ over PAST
  it may be ~ off STEAM

blow off ___ STEAM

blow one's ___ COOL, TOP

blow one's ___ horn OWN

blow one's own ___ HORN

blowout BASH, BLAST, FLAT, GALA,
  REVEL
  big ~ BASH

blows
  come to ~ SCRAP
  exchange of ~ BOUT

"___ Blows at Midnight, The"
  HORN

blow the ___ off LID

blowup ROW, SCRAP
  cause of a ~ TNT

blow up
  ~ a photo ENL

"___ Blow Your Horn" COME

blubber BAWL, CRY, FAT, LARD,
  SOB, WEEP

blubberhead DOLT

blucher SHOE

bludgeon BEAT, SMITE

blue AZURE, COLOR, LEWD, LOW,
  RACY, SAD
  ~ bird HERON
  ~ blood PEER
  ~ bloods ELITE
  ~ dye ANIL
  ~ in a way ADULT
  ~ peter FLAG
  ~ point CAT
  ~ ribbon AWARD, FIRST
  ~ shade ALICE, ANIL, AQUA,
    AZURE, SKY, TEAL
  ~ spot on a map LAKE
  deep ~ PERSE
  deep ~ sea OCEAN
  earn a ~ ribbon WIN
  greenish ~ AQUA, NILE
  hoist the ~ peter SAIL
  light ~ AZURE
  purplish ~ AZURE
  shade of ~ AQUA, STEEL
  slightly ~ RACY
  the ~ SKY
  wild ~ yonder ETHER, SKY,
    SPACE

blue ___ CHIP, CRAB, FLU, LAW,
  MOON, NOTE, PETER

blue-___ law SKY

blue-___ special PLATE

___ blue ICE, NILE, SKY, SLATE,
  STEEL, TRUE

Blue BEN, RANGE
  ~ river NILE

Blue ___ NILE

"Blue ___" MOON, SKY

"Blue ___, The" ANGEL, LAMP

"Blue ___ Shoes" SUEDE

___ Blue BIG, DEEP

"___ Blue?" AMI

Bluebeard OGRE

"___ blue-bell or streamer"
  NEATH

bluebird
  ~ residence NEST

blue blood BARON, DAME, ELITE,
  LORD
  ~ org. DAR

bluebonnet CAP, HAT

bluebook
  ~ occasion ESSAY, EXAM,
    TEST

Blue Carbuncle
  Sherlock's ~ GEM

"Blue Chips"
  ~ actor NOLTE

bluecoat COP

Blue Eagle
  ~ org. NRA

bluefin TUNA

"Blue Gardenia, The"
  ~ director LANG

"___ Blue Gown" ALICE

Bluegrass
  ~ St. KEN

blue-green AQUA
  ~ organism ALGA

Blue Grotto
  ~ locale CAPRI

Blue Hen
  ~ St. DEL

blue in the ___ FACE

bluejacket GOB, SALT, TAR

bluejackets CREW

blue jay
  ~ topper CREST

Blue Jay
  ~ prov. ONT

Blue Jays TEAM, TEN

"___ Blue Line, The" THIN

blue moon
  like a ~ RARE

"Blue Moon"
  ~ lyricist HART

bluenose PRIG

blue-pencil ALTER, EDIT, EMEND,
  ERASE, OMIT
  ~ notation STET
  ~ wielder EDITOR

blueprint MODEL, PLAN

bluer
  litmus ~ BASE

blue-ribbon awarder FAIR

Blue Ridge RANGE

"Blue River"
  ~ actress DEY

blues GENRE, SONG
  baby ~ EYES, ORBS
  have the ~ MOPE
  having the ~ SAD

Blues SIX, TEAM
  ~ milieu ICE, RINK
  ~ org. NHL

"___ Blues" MIAMI, PARIS

"Blues in the Night"
  ~ composer ARLEN
  second word of ~ MAMA

"Blue Sky"
  ~ Oscar-winner LANGE

"Blue Tail Fly"
  ~ singer IVES

Blue, The UNION

blue-to-white
  ~ sun ASTAR

"Blue Velvet"
  ~ actress DERN

bluff CRAG, HONEST

___ Bluff, Ark. PINE

bluish
  ~ gray MERLE, SLATE, STEEL
  ~ green AQUA, JADE, TEAL

"Blume in ___" LOVE

"Blume in Love"
  ~ actor SEGAL

blunder BONER, ERR, ERROR, LAPSE, SLIP, TRIP
  ~ upon HIT

blunderbore OGRE

blunderbuss BOOR, GUN, OAF

blunderer BOOR, OAF

blunt ABATE, ALLAY, HONEST, RUDE, SNUB, TERSE
  ~ an assault STEM
  ~ end STUB

blur MIST

blurbs ADS

blurry DIM
  become ~ FADE

blurt
  ~ out BLAB, LEAK, TELL

blush COLOR, GLOW, REACT, WINE
  it makes you ~ ROUGE
  make ~ ABASH

blusher ROUGE
  ~ emotion, perhaps SHAME

blushing RED, ROSY, SHY

bluster BRAG, CROW, GAS, NOISE, RAGE, RANT, RAVE, STORM

blustering LOUD

blustery RAW

Bluto GOB, SALT, TAR

blvd.
  ~ cousin AVE, RTE
  ~ cousins RDS, STS

Blynken
  ~ shipmate NOD

Blyth ANN

Blyton ENID

BMI
  ~ rival ASCAP

BMOC LION
  ~ house FRAT
  part of ~ MAN

bo NOMAD, TREE

B&O
  ~ and others RRS
  ~ stop STA
  part of ~ OHIO

B.O.
  ~ sign SRO

boa SCARF, SNAKE, STOLE
  ~ sometimes PET

boar ANIMAL, HOG, MALE
  ~ mate SOW

board BEAM, DIET, ENTER, FARE, FEED, KEEP, MEAL, PANEL, PROP, SLAB, SLAT
  ~ by board ALONG
  ~ covering EMERY
  ~ ender ROOM
  ~ game CHESS, KENO, RISK
  ~ imperfection KNOT
  ~ insert PEG
  ~ member EXEC
  ~ member, often CEO, PRES
  ~ membership SEAT
  ~ partner BED, ROOM
  ~ starter ABOVE, BASE, BILL, CARD, CLAP, CLIP, CUP, DART, DASH, FOOT, FREE, HARD, HEAD, KEY, LAP, MOLD, OUT, OVER, PAPER, PASTE, PEG, SCALE, SCORE, SEA, SHIP, SIDE, SIGN, SKATE, SNOW, STAR, WASH
  ~ up SEAL
  bed ~ SLAT
  bring on ~ HIRE
  by the ~ GONE, LOST
  emery ~ FILE
  narrow ~ LATH
  pay for room and ~ LET, RENT, TENANT
  poster ~ PAPER
  put on ~ LOAD
  review ~ PANEL
  room and ~ KEEP
  stow on ~ LADE
  went off the ~ DOVE

board ___ FOOT, GAME

___ board EMERY, TOTE

boarder TENANT

board game CHESS, KENO, RISK
  ~ pair DICE
  whodunit ~ CLUE

boarding
  ~ device RAMP
  ~ place STOP
  ~ school PREP

boardinghouse
  ~ rental ROOM

boards
  gone by the ~ DATED, PASSE
  hit the ~ TREAD
  tread the ~ ACT, PLAY

boardwalk
  ~ structure PIER

Boardwalk
  ~ buy HOTEL

boast BRAG, CROW

boastful BIG

boastfulness PRIDE

boat KEEL, LINER, SHIP
  ~ backbone KEEL
  ~ ender BILL, LOAD
  ~ propeller OAR
  ~ runway RAMP
  ~ starter CAT, FLAT, ICE, LIFE, LONG, MOTOR, ROW, SAIL, SHOW, SPEED, STEAM, TUG
  ~ trip SAIL
  ~ wake WASH
  aluminum ~ CANOE
  animal ~ ARK
  any ~ HER, SHE
  Arab ~ DHOW
  bark ~ CANOE
  Biblical ~ ARK
  big ~ LINER, SHIP
  clumsy ~ ARK, SCOW, TUB
  dip out a ~ BAIL
  end of a ~ STERN
  flat-bottomed ~ RAFT, SCOW
  harbor ~ TUG
  Indian ~ CANOE
  "Jaws" ~ ORCA
  lake ~ CANOE
  land in a ~ NET
  lateen-rigged ~ DHOW
  narrow ~ CANOE
  off the ~ ASHORE
  on a slow ~ to China ASEA, ATSEA
  pea-green ~ passenger OWL
  racing ~ SHELL
  secure a ~ MOOR
  single-masted ~ SLOOP
  square-ended ~ PRAM
  tapered ~ CANOE
  that ~ HER, SHE
  tippy ~ CANOE
  toward the back, on a ~ AFT, ASTERN
  underwater ~ SUB
  WWII ~ LST
  see also ship

"___ Boat" SHOW

"___ Boat, The" LOVE

boater HAT, LID

boathouse
  ~ gear OAR

boating
  ~ hazard SNAG

"Boating"
  ~ painter MANET

boats
  letters on some big ~ USS

boatswain
  ~ whistle PIPE

boatwright
  early ~ NOAH

Boaz
  ~ wife RUTH

bob ANGLE, BEND, CLIP, CUT, LOP, PEND
  ~ up and down DANCE
  no siree ~ NAY
  plumb ~ LEAD

Bob ABEL, ARUM, ESTES, HOPE, KANE

"Bob & ___ & Ted & Alice" CAROL

Bob and ___ RAY

bobbin REEL, ROLL

bobble ERR, ERROR

Bobbsey, Bert
  ~ twin NAN

bobby COP

bobby ___ PIN

Bobby ORR, VEE
  ~ wife ETHEL

bobbysoxer GIRL, MISS, TEEN
  ~ dance HOP

"Bob & Carol & ___ & Alice" TED

"Bob & Carol & Ted & ___" ALICE

"Bob & Carol & Ted & Alice"
  Alice in ~ DYAN

bobcat ANIMAL

"Bob Newhart Show, The"
  ~ trains ELS

bobolink BIRD
  ~ cousin ORIOLE

bobtail
  ragtag and ~ MOB, ROUT

bobwhite BIRD

Boca ___, Fla. RATON

bocce GAME

bock BEER
  ~ cousin LAGER

___-bodied seaman ABLE

bodily ANIMAL, REAL

bodkin NEEDLE

Bodoni FONT

body CREW, MASS, TORSO
  ~ fluid SERUM
  ~ fluids SERA

~ of knowledge LORE
~ of laws CODE
~ of principles ETHIC
~ of soldiers TROOP
~ of water LAKE, OCEAN, POND, POOL, SEA, TARN
~ part ARM, HEAD, ORGAN
~ partner SOUL
~ politic STATE
~ rhythm PULSE
~ starter ANTI
Capitol ~ SENATE
celestial ~ (prefix) ASTRO
collective ~ (suffix) SHIP
Congressional ~ SENATE
DC ~ SEN
heavenly ~ MOON, ORB, SPHERE, STAR, SUN
human ~ CLAY
legislative ~ SENATE
main ~ MASS, TEXT
of sound ~ ABLE
of the ~, for short ANAT
political ~ UNION
troop ~ UNIT

body ___ SHOP

"Body ___" HEAT

"Body ___ Soul" AND

"Body and ___" SOUL

bodybuilder
~ concern ABS, TONE
~ iteration REP
~ pride ABS

bodybuilders
what ~ pump IRON

"Body Heat"
William Hurt, in ~ NED

___-body plane WIDE

body-shop
~ concern DENT
~ job DENT

"Body Snatcher, The"
~ director WISE

"___ Body Too Many" ONE

Boeing
~ product JET, PLANE

"Boeing Boeing"
~ director RICH
~ star LEWIS

Boeotian DENSE

Boer ___ WAR

Boesky IVAN

Boethius ROMAN

boffo
~ review RAVE
~ show HIT

"Bofors ___, The" GUN

"Bofors Gun, The"
~ director GOLD

Bofors guns AAS

bog FEN, MIRE, MOOR, SINK, WASH
~ down MIRE, STALL

~ material PEAT
peat ~ MOOR

___ bog PEAT

Bogan, Louise POET
see also poet

Bogart PAUL
~ film of 1943 SAHARA
~ movie ship CAINE
~ role SPADE

Bogdanovich PETER
~ film of 1985 MASK

bogey
~ minus one PAR
avoid a ~ PAR

bogeyman DEMON, OGRE

boggle DAZE

Bogg, Phineas
~ time travel device in "Voyagers" OMNI

Boggs WADE

boggy DAMP
~ land FEN

Bogosian ERIC

Bogotá CITY
see also Spanish

bogus BAD, FAKE, FALSE, SHAM

bogy DEMON, FEAR

bohea TEA

bohemian ARTY

"Bohemian ___, The" GIRL

Bohemian Forest RANGE

"Bohemian Girl, The"
~ director HORNE

Bohr, Niels DANE
~ concern ATOM

Boiardo, Matteo POET
see also poet

boil HEAT, RAGE, SORE, STEW
~ in oil FRY
~ over FLARE, RAGE
almost ~ SCALD
make someone's blood ~ ANGER, IRK, PEEVE, RILE, UPSET

___-boiled HARD

boiler TANK

boiler ___ ROOM

boilermaker
~ component BEER

boiling HOT
~ over MAD
keep the pot ~ EARN

Boise
~ county ADA
~ locale IDAHO
~ st. IDA

boisterous LOUD
hardly ~ TAME

Boitano
~ jump AXEL
emulate ~ SKATE

Bol.
neighbor of ~ ARG

bola ROPE

bold FREE, GAME, LOUD, PERT
~ look LEER
be ~ DARE
hardly ~ SHY
present a ~ front DARE

Bold
~ rival ALL, DASH, ERA

"Bold ___ the Brave, The" AND

boldface TYPE

boldness DASH, FACE, NERVE

"___ Bolena" ANNA

bolero DANCE

"Bolero"
~ composer RAVEL
instrument featured in ~ OBOE

Boleyn ANNE

Bolger RAY
~ costar LAHR

Bolivia
~ neighbor PERU
see also Spanish

Bolivian
~ beast LLAMA
~ buck PESO
~ export TIN
~ range ANDES

boll
~ cleaner GIN

bollard POST

bollix
~ up ERR

bologna
~ bread RYE
~ unit SLICE

Bologna
~ site ITALY
see also Italian

Bolshevik RED
~ founder LENIN
~ victim TSAR

Bolshevist RED

bolster AID, FEED, HELP, PAD, PROP

bolt AVOID, CLOSE, DART, DASH, DESERT, EAT, FLEE, PEG, RACE, RUN, SHUT, SIFT, SPEED, TBAR
~ down EAT, RIVET
~ fastener NUT
~ together ELOPE
~ up RISE
crossbow ~ ARROW
part of a ~ YARD
wheel ~ holder LUG

bolt from the ___ BLUE

bolts
bucket of ~ AUTO, CAR, CRATE, HEAP, LEMON, MOTOR

bolus PILL

bomb DUD, LOSER, SHELL
~ blast, in headlines ATEST
~ in a comedy act DIE
~ tryout ATEST
defective ~ DUD

___ bomb ATOM, SMART

bombard PELT, PLY, SHELL, SHOOT, ZAP
~ ender IER

bombast GAS, RANT

bombastic BIG, EPIC, LOUD
be ~ RANT

Bombay CITY, PORT
~ country INDIA
~ neighbor GOA
~ nursemaid AMA, AMAH
~ wear SARI
district south of ~ GOA
see also Indian

Bombeck ERMA, WIT

bomber
~ name ENOLA
~ org. SAC

bombinate DRONE

bombproof SAFE

bombs AMMO

bombycid MOTH

"Bomp-a-bomp"
~ singer BASS

bon
~ mot PUN
~ ton TASTE
~ voyage ADIEU

bon ___ MOT, TON

Bon CAPE

Bon ___ AMI

bona fide HONEST, REAL, SAFE, SOLID, TRUE

bonanza LODE, MINE, ORE
buyer's ~ SALE

Bonanza
~ st. NEV

"Bonanza"
~ brother ADAM, JOE
~ prop RIATA
Ben on ~ LORNE

Bonaparte
~ fate EXILE
~ island ELBA

bonbon DROP, TREAT

bond ASSET, BAIL, GLUE, MATE, PAPER, PASTE, SEAL, TIE, UNITE
~ rating AAA, BAA
~ return YIELD
~ servant SLAVE
~ slave SERF

___ bond

~ **starter** EURO
certain ~ MUNI
emotional ~ CORD
kind of ~ EURO
short-term ~ DEB

___ bond PAIR

bonded ONE

___ bonding MALE, PAIR

Bond, James AGENT, HERO, SPY
~ **alma mater** ETON
~ **portrayer** MOORE

bondman LIEGE

Bonds, Barry
~ **club** BAT

bondsman BAIL, LIEGE
feudal ~ SERF
medieval ~ ESNE
work for a ~ BAIL

bone
~ **of contention** CAUSE, ISSUE
~ **(prefix)** OSTE, OSTEO
~ **up** CRAM
~ **up on** READ
arm ~ ULNA
funny ~ ELBOW
leg ~ SHIN, TIBIA
postaxial ~ ULNA

bone ___ ASH

bone ___ (fertilizer) MEAL

bone ___ (study) UPON

bone-dry ARID, SERE

bonehead ASS, DOLT, IDIOT, OAF

boneheaded DAFT

boner ERROR, SLIP, TRIP
make a ~ ERR

boners ERRATA

bones DICE
~ **in Latin** OSSA
arm ~ RADII
bag of ~ NAG
feel in one's ~ SENSE
forearm ~ RADII
make no ~ **about** ADMIT
pelvic ~ ILIA
skin and ~ POOR, SPARE

___ bones BARE

Bones, Brom
~ **prey** CRANE

Bonet LISA

bonfire
~ **residue** ASH
started a ~ LIT

bong PEAL

Bonheur ROSA

boniface HOST
~ **place** INN

Boniface POPE

"Bonjour Tristesse"
~ **author** SAGAN

bonkers BATS, DAFT, LOCO, MAD, NUTS
go ~ **over** RAVE

Bonn
~ **loc.** GER
~ **river** RHINE
city near ~ ESSEN
see also German

bonne GIRL, MAID

bonne ___ IDEE

Bonner ELENA

bonnet CAP, HAT, HOOD
~ **bug** BEE
Basque ~ BERET
Brit's ~ HOOD
Scottish ~ TAM
see also hat

___ bonnet EASTER, WAR

Bonneville DAM

Bonneville ___ Flats SALT

Bonneville Salt Flats
~ **site** UTAH

Bonnie RAITT

"Bonnie ___ Clyde" AND

"Bonnie ___ Thing, The" WEE

"Bonnie and Clyde"
~ **director** PENN

bonny FAIR
~ **girl** LASS

___ bono PRO

Bono, Chastity
~ **mom** CHER

Bono, Mrs.
~ **once** CHER

bonsai ART, PLANT, TREE

bonus EXTRA, ICING, PAY, PERK, PLUS, TIP
buyer's ~ REBATE

bon voyage
~ **site** PIER

bony LANK, LEAN, THIN

bonze LAMA

Bonzo APE

boo GIBE, HISS, HOOT
~ **partner** HISS

"Boo!"
shout ~ SCARE

boob ASS, DOLT, OAF
~ **tube** SET

boo-boo BONER, ERROR, LAPSE, SLIP
~ **memento** SCAB
make a ~ ERR
moving-day ~ CHIP

Boo-Boo BEAR
~ **buddy** YOGI

boo-boos ERRATA
make ~ ERR

boob tube
~ **for short** TELE

booby BIRD, DOLT, IDIOT
~ **trap** MINE, SNARE

booby ___ TRAP

boodle LOOT, SWAG

boogie DANCE

boohoo CRY, SOB

boojum TREE

book ENTER, OPUS, TOME
~ **after Chronicles** EZRA
~ **after Daniel** HOSEA
~ **after Joel** AMOS
~ **after John** ACTS
~ **after Judges** RUTH
~ **after Nehemiah** ESTHER
~ **before Job** ESTHER
~ **before Joel** HOSEA
~ **before Nehemiah** EZRA
~ **before Obadiah** AMOS
~ **before Romans** ACTS
~ **div.** CHAP
~ **dropping sound** THUD
~ **ender** CASE, END, LET, LORE, PLATE, RACK, SHOP, STALL, STAND, STORE
~ **holders** ENDS
~ **illustration** PLATE
~ **lined room** DEN
~ **name** TITLE
~ **starter** CASE, CHAP, DAY, HAND, LOG, NOTE, OVER, PASS, PLAY, SCRAP, STYLE, YEAR
absorb a ~ READ
Bible ~ ACTS, AMOS, ESTHER, EZRA, HOSEA, RUTH
by the ~ LEGAL
captain's ~ LOG
cartographer's ~ ATLAS
church ~ ORDO
college ~ TEXT
crack a ~ READ
heavy ~ TOME
informative ~ TEXT
map ~ ATLAS
New Testament ~ ACTS
N.T. ~ COL, GAL, MATT, REV, ROM
Old Testament ~ AMOS, ESTHER, EZRA, HOSEA
O.T. ~ BAR, GEN, ISA, LAM, MAC, NAH
part of a ~ LEAF, PAGE
reference ~ ATLAS
serious ~ TEXT
telephone ~ LIST
world ~ ATLAS

___ book AUDIO, BLUE, MAKE, PHONE, TRADE

bookbinder
~ **leather** ROAN
~ **need** GLUE

bookie
~ **concern** BET
~ **quote** ODDS

booking GIG

bookish
~ **type** NERD

book jacket
~ **detail** TITLE
~ **feature** BIO
~ **part** FLAP

bookkeeping
~ **term** ASSET, DEBIT
~ **word** NET

booklet TRACT

Bookman FONT

"Book of Mormon"
~ **book** ALMA

"Book of Ruth"
~ **character** NAOMI

books
~ **expert** CPA
check the ~ AUDIT
five ~ **of Moses** TORAH
hit the ~ READ
it's on the ~ LAW
wipe off the ~ ANNUL

bookstore
~ **category** DIET

bookworm NERD

bookworms
what ~ **do** READ

"boola"
~ **cousin** RAH

"Boola Boola"
~ **singer** ELI

boom BANG, BAR, BEAM, BLAST, CRANE, GROW, MAST, NOISE, PEAL, POP, RISE, ROAR, ROLL, SPAR
~ **box** STEREO
~ **support** MAST
~ **times** UPS

___ boom SONIC

"___ boom bah!" SIS

boombox STEREO
~ **component** RADIO
~ **sound** BLARE, NOISE
abbr. on a ~ REC

"___ Boomer" HERES

booming BIG, LOUD

boon AID, ASSET
~ **companion** PAL

Boone PAT

Boone, Daniel HERO
region explored by ~ TENN

boor APE, CAD, LOUT, OAF, SLOB, YAHOO

boorish CRASS, RUDE

boost AID, ASSET, BOOM, HELP, HIKE, RAISE, RISE, ROB, STEAL, TAKE, TONIC
~ **in price** HIKE
give a ~ **to** AID

booster FAN, SHOT
~ **amount** DOSE

pot ~ ANTE
sound ~ AMP

booster ___ SHOT

Booster Club
~ **member** ALUM, GRAD

boot PAC, SACK, SHOE
~ **attachment** SPUR
~ **bottom** SOLE
~ **ender** LACE, LEG, STRAP
~ **feature** LUG
~ **out** EJECT, OUST
~ **part** TOE
~ **starter** FREE
~ **the ball** ERR
and something to ~ PLUS
Europe's ~ ITALY
fix a ~ SOLE
give the ~ **to** AXE, CAN, FIRE
to ~ ALSO, EXTRA, OVER, TOO

boot ___ CAMP

___ boot HIP, SKI

"___ Boot" DAS

boot camp
~ **sentence ender** SIR

booted SHOD

bootee SHOE

booth STALL, STAND
~ **offering** INFO

___ booth PHONE

___ Boothe Luce CLARE

Booth, Shirley
lost dog in a ~ film SHEBA

booties
make ~ KNIT

bootleg RUN, STEAL

bootlegger
~ **basic** MASH
~ **nemesis** FED, NESS

"Bootnose" ABEL
~ **Abel** SID

boots
shake in one's ~ FEAR

**"___ Boots Are Made for
Walkin'"** THESE

boot-shaped
~ **country** ITALY

booty HAUL, LOOT, SWAG, TAKE
Knave of Hearts' ~ TART

boozehound SOT

bop BEAT, HIT, LAM, SMITE

"Bop ___ You Drop" TIL

"___ Bop" SHE

Bo-Peep
call to ~ BAA
like ~'s charges OVINE

___-Bopp comet HALE

___-bopper TEENY

borate SALT

borax ORE

Bordeaux CITY, PORT, WINE
see also French

Borden
~ **cow** ELMER, ELSIE
~ **product** GLUE
~ **weapon** AXE

border ABUT, EDGE, HEM, LIMIT,
LINE, LIP, RIM
~ **line** METE
~ **on** ABUT
escutcheon ~ ORLE
fabric ~ HEM
ornamental ~ DADO
picture ~ MAT
shield ~ ORLE

"Border Incident"
~ **director** MANN

bordering CLOSE, NEAR, NEXT
desert ~ on the Nile SAHARA

Bordoni IRENE

bore DRAG, DRIP, HOLE, PALL, TIRE
broaden a ~ REAM
crashing ~ PEST

___ bore TIDAL

___ borealis AURORA

Boreas GOD
~ **mother** EOS

borecole KALE

bored
~ **feeling** BLAH
get ~ TIRE

boredom ENNUI

___ borer CORN

Borg, Bjorn SWEDE

Borge, Victor DANE
~ **instrument** PIANO

Borgia
~ **in-law** ESTE
see also Italian

Borgnine ERNEST

boric ACID

boring ARID, BLAH, DRAB, DRY,
FLAT, HARD, LONG, SLOW,
SOBER, TAME
~ **experience** DRAG
~ **person** PILL
~ **tool** AWL, BIT

Boris TSAR

"Boris Godunov" OPERA
~ **singer** BASS, BASSO

born NEE
~ **first** ELDER, OLDER
~ **in French** NEE
~ **in the US** AMER
~ **yesterday** NAIVE, RAW
be ~ COME, RISE

___-born FIRST

"Born ___" FREE

"Born ___, The" LOSER

born and ___ BRED

Bornean ASIAN

Borneo
~ **beast** ORANG
island near ~ BALI, JAVA

"Born Free"
~ **lioness** ELSA

"Born in ___ L.A." EAST

"Born in the ___" USA

bornite ORE

"Born on the Fourth of July"
~ **director** STONE
~ **setting** NAM

"Born to ___" DANCE

"Born to Dance"
~ **director** RUTH

"Born to Kill"
~ **director** WISE

Borodin
~ **subject** IGOR

borough
NYC ~ MAN

borrow RENT, STEAL
~ **opposite** LEND

borrowed
amount ~ LOAN

borrowed ___ TIME

borrower
~ **fig.** APR
~ **funds** LOAN

borscht
~ **ingredient** BEET

Boru, Brian
~ **land** ERIN

borzoi DOG

BOS
~ **abbr.** ARR, ETA

Bosc PEAR

bosh POOH, ROT, TRASH

Bosnian SERB
~ **peacekeeping org.** NATO

bosom CHEST, CLOSE

Bosox TEAM, TEN

boss COOL, EXEC, HEAD, LORD,
NEAT, NODE, RULE, RULER,
STUD
~ **demand** ASAP
~ **in Spanish** AMO
be the ~ RULE
co. ~ CEO
flight attendant's ~ PILOT
journal ~ EDITOR
Mafia ~ DON
prior's ~ ABBOT
reporter's ~ EDITOR
steno's ~ EXEC
store ~ OWNER
tabloid ~ EDITOR

___ boss PIT, STRAW

bossa ___ NOVA

bossa nova DANCE
~ **cousin** SAMBA

"Boss's ___, The" SON

"Boss's Son, The"
~ **director** ROTH

Bossy COW
~ **offspring** CALF
~ **refuge** BARN
~ **sound** LOW, MOO

Bostic EARL

Boston CITY, FERN, PORT
~ **basketball player** CELT
~ **cream** PIE
~ **entrée** COD, SCROD
~ **st.** MASS
~ **suburb** LYNN
~ **zone** EDT, EST

Boston ___ FERN, IVY

Boston ___ Party TEA

"Boston Blackie ___ Hollywood"
GOES

"___ Boston Blackie" MEET

Boston cream ___ PIE

Boston Garden ARENA
~ **player** CELT

Boston Harbor
~ **jetsam** TEA

Boswell SCOT

bot. SCI

botanist
~ **concern** FLORA

Botany BAY

botch ERR, ERROR, HASH, MAR,
MESS, RUIN, SPOIL

"Botch-___" AME

botched
~ **effort** ERROR

both DUO, PAIR
burn the candle at ~
ends LABOR
for ~ sexes COED
on ~ feet ERECT

"Both ___" SIDES

"Both ___ of the Law" SIDES

bother ADO, AIL, CARE, FRET, IRK,
PAIN, PEEVE, PEST, RILE, TEASE,
TODO, UPSET
~ **persistently** NAG

botheration ADO, PEST

bothersome BAD
~ **one** TWIT

"Both Sides ___" NOW

"Both Sides of the ___" LAW

Bothwell SCOT

bothy COT, HOME

Botticelli
~ **Venus** NUDE

bottle JAR, TREE
  ~ **capacity** LITER, PINT
  ~ **dweller** GENIE
  ~ **edge** LIP
  ~ **top** CAP, NECK
  ~ **up** SIEGE
  champagne ~ SPLIT
  get better in the ~ AGE
  shoemaker's ~ DYE
  small ~ VIAL
  spin the ~ GAME

bottle-___ dolphin NOSED

bottlebrush TREE

bottled
  ~ **creature** GENIE

bottleneck JAM, SNAG

bottom BASE, BASIS, BED, END, FOOT, NADIR
  ~ **feeder** CARP
  ~ **line** COST, TAKE, TOTAL
  ~ **of a paw** PAD
  ~ **of some scales** ONE
  bad ~ **line** LOSS
  bet one's ~ **dollar** RELY
  dress ~ HEM
  food-chain ~ ALGA
  from top to ~ OVER
  get to the ~ **line** ADD
  head for the ~ SINK
  hill ~ FOOT
  hit ~ SINK
  on the ~ DEEP
  river ~ BED
  rock ~ NADIR
  sea ~ BED
  send to the ~ SINK
  ship's ~ **timber** KEEL
  shoe ~ SOLE
  with a flared ~ ALINE

bottom ___ LINE, OUT

bottomless DEEP, RICH
  ~ **depths** ABYSS
  ~ **pit** ABYSS

bottomless ___ PIT

bottom line NET
  ~ **amount** NET, SUM, TOTAL

bottom-of-letter
  ~ **abbr.** ENC

bottoms LAND
  ~ **up** TOAST
  like some ~ FALSE

boudoir ROOM

___ bouffe OPERA

bough SPRIG
  stunted ~ SPUR
  take a ~ LOP

boughpot VASE

bought
  just ~ NEW
  opposite of ~ SOLD

___-bought STORE

bouillabaisse STEW

boulder DAM, STONE
  ~ **breaker** TNT

Boulder Dam
  ~ **lake** MEAD

boulevard PATH, ROAD, ROUTE
  ~ **liner** TREE

boulevardier DUDE

Boulogne CITY, PORT
  see also French

bounce CAPER, DROP, ECHO, EJECT, FIRE, LEAP, OUST, SKIP, SNAP
  ~ **across water** SKIP
  ~ **back** CAROM, ECHO
  ~ **over** CLEAR
  infield ~ HOP

bouncer
  ~ **demand** OUT
  baby ~ KNEE

bounces
  the way the ball ~ LOT

bouncy PERT
  ~ **gait** SKIP
  ~ **melody** LILT

bound CAPER, DART, DASH, HOP, LEAP, LIMIT, LOPE, SKIP
  ~ **over** CLEAR
  ~ **to happen** SURE
  furthest ~ LIMIT

___-bound HONOR

"Bound ___ Glory" FOR

"___ Boundaries" LOST

boundary EDGE, END, LIMIT, LINE, METE, RIM
  ~ **marker** RAIL, STAKE
  racetrack ~ RAIL
  ring ~ ROPE

bounder CAD, ROUE, YAHOO

bounding ___ MAIN

bounding main OCEAN, SEA
  on the ~ ASEA, ATSEA
  ride the ~ SAIL

boundless BIG, ETERNAL, GREAT, LARGE, VAST, WIDE

bounds PALE, SPHERE

bountiful AMPLE, FREE, RICH
  ~ **hairdo** MANE

Bountiful
  where ~ **is** UTAH

___ Bountiful LADY

bounty ALMS, LOOT, STORE

"Bounty" BOAT, SHIP

bouquet AROMA, BALM, ESSENCE, NOSE, ODOR, SCENT
  ~ **favorite** ROSE
  ~ **holder** VASE
  ~ **makers** FLORA
  wine's ~ NOSE

Bourbon
  ~ **and others** STS
  ~ **ruler** ROI
  see also French

bourgeois YAHOO

bourrée DANCE

bout MELEE, SETTO
  ~ **ender** TKO
  ~ **locale** ARENA
  long ~ SIEGE

boutique MART, SALON, SHOP, STORE

boutonniere
  ~ **site** LAPEL

Bouvier
  ~ **des Flandres** DOG, PET

Bouvier ___ Flandres (dog breed) DES

Bouvier, Jacqueline
  ~ **in 1947** DEB

Bova BEN

bovarism EGO

Bovary EMMA
  ~ **title** MME

bovine COW, DENSE, SLOW, STEER
  ~ **animals** OXEN
  ~ **group** HERD
  ~ **of ads** ELSIE
  ~ **sound** MOO
  shaggy ~ BISON
  wild ~ BISON
  young ~ CALF

bow ARC, ARCH, BEND, KNOT, LOOP, NOD, NOSE
  ~ **and scrape** BEND, KNEEL
  ~ **component** LOOP
  ~ **down** KNEEL
  ~ **down before** ADORE
  ~ **ender** FIN, HEAD, KNOT, LEG
  ~ **missile** ARROW
  ~ **opposite** STERN
  ~ **out** LEAVE
  ~ **out of** DROP
  ~ **starter** LONG, RAIN
  ~ **to** OBEY
  ~ **(to)** DEFER
  god with a ~ EROS
  make a ~ TIE
  take a ~ **out** UNTIE
  toward the ~ FORE

bow ___ OUT, SAW, TIE

Bow CLARA

bowdlerize EDIT, LOP
  ~ **perhaps** EDIT

Bowdoin College
  ~ **locale** MAINE

Bowe
  ~ **blow** JAB
  ~ **stat** TKO
  see also boxer

bowed BENT

bowed-down SAD

bowels
  ~ **of the earth** ABYSS
  in the ~ **of the earth** DEEP

bower
  shady ~ ARBOR

Bowes, Major
  ~ **medium** RADIO

"___ Bowes' Original Amateur Hour" MAJOR

bowfin AMIA

Bowie, David
  producer for ~ ENO
  wife of ~ IMAN

Bowie, Jim
  ~ **last stand** ALAMO

bowknot
  ~ **feature** LOOP

bowl ARENA, DISH, PIT, TANK
  ~ **along** RACE, RUN
  ~ **game prelude** PARADE
  ~ **of cherries, maybe** LIFE
  ~ **over** AMAZE, AWE, DAZE, STUN, WOW
  dust ~ DESERT
  pipe ~**, maybe** COB

bowl ___ (overwhelm) OVER

___ bowl DUST

___ Bowl HULA, ORANGE, PRO, ROSE

bowler HAT

bowline KNOT, ROPE

bowling
  ~ **alley** LANE
  ~ **button** RESET
  ~ **challenge** SPLIT
  ~ **milieu** ALLEY
  ~ **pin** MAPLE
  ~ **score** SPARE
  ~ **surface** LAWN
  ~ **target** PIN
  lawn ~ GAME

bowling ___ ALLEY, BALL

___ bowling LAWN

bowpot VASE

bow-shaped ARCED

bowsprit SPAR

bowstring
  like a ~ TAUT
  pull a ~ DRAW

bowwow ARF, CRY, NOISE

box BANG, BIN, CASE, CHEST, HIT, JAB, MILL, SMITE, SPAR, STALL, TILL
  ~ **buyer** FAN
  ~ **end** FLAP
  ~ **in** SIEGE, TRAP
  ~ **on a string** KITE
  ~ **social** EVENT
  ~ **starter** BAND, FIRE, GEAR, HAT, ICE, MAIL, SALT, SAND, SHOE, SKY, SOAP, TOOL
  ~ **top** LID
  boom ~ STEREO
  cache ~ SAFE
  drop in a letter ~ MAIL
  front-page ~ EAR
  idiot ~ SET
  in a ~ CASED
  large ~ CRATE

opera ~ LOGE
put in a ~ CASE
slotted ~ CRATE
witness ~ STAND

box ___ CAMERA, COAT, ELDER, KITE, PLEAT, SCORE, SEAT, STALL, TOP

___ box BOOM, FUSE, IDIOT, POOR, PRESS

boxcar
~ rider HOBO

boxed
~ in PENT

box elder
~ genus ACER

boxer DOG, PET
~ garb ROBE
~ jab LEFT
~ move JAB
~ place ARENA
~ punch CHOP
~ quest TITLE
~ stat KOS, TKO

Boxer
~ org. SEN

boxing
~ legend ALI
~ match BOUT, MELEE
~ official REF
~ venue ARENA, RING
1930s ~ champ BAER

Boxing Day
~ mo. DEC

box office
~ abbr. SRO
~ figure TAKE
~ smash HIT

box score
~ column heading HRS
~ entry ATBAT, ERROR, HIT, RBI, RUN

box social
~ action BID

boxtop
~ piece TAB

boy LAD, MALE, SON, TAD, TOM
~ ender ISH
~ starter ATTA, TOM

boy ___ door, the NEXT

___ boy ALTAR, BALL, BAT, BEST, BUS, MAMAS, POOR

"___ boy!" ATTA, ITSA

Boy
~ creator EDGAR

"Boy ___ Charlie Brown, A" NAMED

"Boy ___ Could Fly, The" WHO

"Boy ___ Feet Tall, A" TEN

"Boy ___ Girl" MEETS

"Boy ___ Sue, A" NAMED

"___ Boy" BEST

"___ Boy, The" ERRAND, STONE

"___ Boy" ("Tommy" song) ITSA

boyar LORD, PEER
see also Russian

boycott BAR

boyfriend BEAU, DATE, LOVE, MALE
~ in French AMI

boy-king
Egyptian ~ TUT

Boyle
study of ~ GAS

Boyle's ___ LAW

"Boy Meets ___" GIRL

"Boy Named ___, A" SUE

"Boy Named Sue, A"
~ singer CASH

___-boy network OLD

"Boy Next ___, The" DOOR

boys HES

"___ Boys" BAD

___ Boys (Manny, Moe & Jack) PEP

Boy Scout
~ act DEED
~ rank EAGLE, LIFE, STAR
~ wear SASH

"___ Boy Scout, The" LAST

Boy Scouts of America
~ founder BEARD

"Boys for Pele"
~ singer AMOS

"Boys in the ___, The" BAND

"___ Boy's Life" THIS

"Boys' Night ___" OUT

___ Boys of "Peter Pan" LOST

"Boys of Summer, The"
~ name CARL, GIL, ROY
~ shortstop REESE

"Boys on the ___" SIDE

"Boys on the Side"
~ director ROSS

Boys Town
~ site OMAHA
~ st. NEB, NEBR

"Boy Ten ___ Fall, A" FEET

"Boy! What a ___" GIRL

"Boy With the Green ___, The" HAIR

Boyz II ___ MEN

"Boyz N the ___" HOOD

Boz
~ boy PIP, TIM

BP
~ takers RNS

BPOE
~ member ELK
part of ~ ORDER

Br ELEM
35 for ~ ATNO

brace BEAM, BEAR, DUO, HOLD, PAIR, POST, PROP, SHORE, STAKE, STAY, TWO
~ (oneself) STEEL

bracelet
~ site ANKLE, ARM

bracer TONIC

brachium ARM

bracing CRISP, TONIC

bracken FERN

Bracken EDDIE, PEG

brackets
word often seen in ~ SIC

bract
~ cousin LEAF

bracteole LEAF

brad NAIL

Bradbury RAY

Braddock
~ dethroned him BAER

Bradlee BEN, EDITOR

Bradley BILL, OMAR
~ and others EDS
~ org., once SEN
~ rank GEN

Bradley Center ARENA

Bradstreet ANNE

Bradstreet, Anne POET
see also poet

___ Brady (Carl Reiner TV role) ALAN

Brady Bill
~ opponent NRA

"Brady Bunch, The"
~ actor REED
~ dog TIGER
~ housekeeper ALICE
~ mother CAROL
~ son PETER

Brady, Mrs. James SARAH

brae SLOPE

Braeden ERIC

brag CROW
nothing to ~ about SOSO
ready to ~ VAIN

braggadocio GAS, PRIDE

Brahe, Tycho DANE

"Brahma" POEM

Brahman CASTE

Brahmin HINDU, SNOB

braid COIL, LACE, PLAT, TAIL, TRESS

braided
~ cord ROPE

Braille
~ mark DOT
use ~ READ

brain ORGAN
~ ender PAN, STORM, WASH
~ part LOBE
~ passage ITER
~ starter BIRD, FORE, LAME

"___ Brain, The" GREAT

Brainard
~ (the Absent-Minded Professor) NED

brainchild IDEA
grifter's ~ SCAM

brains ASSET, SENSE
beat one's ~ out LABOR

brainstorm IDEA, IDEATE
~ in French IDEE

brainteaser POSER

brain wave
~ chart EEG

brainwork
bit of ~ IDEA

brainy ACUTE, KEEN, SMART

braise FRY, HEAT, STEW

brake HALT, SLOW, STOP
~ device SHOE
~ neighbor GAS
~ starter CANE
jockey's ~ REIN

brake ___ PAD, SHOE

___ brake AIR, DISC, FOOT

brake problems
have ~ SKID

brakes
put on the ~ SLOW, STOP

bramble BRIAR, NEEDLE

bran
~ source CORN, OAT, RYE

branch ANGLE, ARM, CLASS, PART, RILL, ROOST, RUN, SPRIG, STREAM, WAND
antler ~ TINE
dove's ~ OLIVE
family ~ SEPT
railroad ~ SPUR
small ~ SHOOT
union ~ LOCAL

___ branch OLIVE

___ Branch, N.J. LONG

brand LABEL, LIBEL, LINE, MAKE, SEAR, SORT, STAMP, STYLE
~ name LABEL

brand ___ NAME

brand-___ NEW

___ brand NAME

"Brandenburg Concertos"
~ composer BACH

branding
    use a ~ iron SEAR

branding ___ IRON

brandish WIELD

brand-new HOT, MINT

Brando, Marlon
    ~ adopted home SAMOA
    ~ birthplace OMAHA
    1966 ~ movie, with
        "The" CHASE

brandy
    ~ measure DRAM
    bit of ~ TOT
    French ~ MARC
    ready to sell, as ~ AGED
    store ~ AGE

Branigan LAURA

brannigan MELEE

brant GOOSE

Bras d'Or LAKE

brash PERT, RASH, SASSY

brashness SASS

brass FACE, METAL, NERVE
    ~ component ZINC
    ~ instrument HORN, TUBA

brass ___ BAND, HAT, RING

___ brass TOP

brassardo ARMOR

brassy LOUD, PERT
    ~ sound BLARE

brat IMP, KID, LAD, SNIP
    be a ~ SASS
    Christmas present for a
        ~ COAL

___ brat ARMY

brattle NOISE

bratwurst MEAT

"Brava!"
    ~ recipient DIVA

bravado RANT

brave DARE, FACE, MEET
    ~ it out BEAR, LAST, STAY
    ~ one HERO
    home for a ~ TEPEE

Brave
    Hall-of-Famer ~ AARON

"Brave ___, The" ONE

"Brave ___ World" NEW

"Braveheart"
    ~ award OSCAR
    ~ name MEL

"Brave Little Toaster, The"
    ~ director REES

"Brave Men"
    ~ author PYLE

bravery HEART, NERVE

Braves NINE, TEAM
    ~ home ATLANTA

~ loc. ATL

"Bravo!" CRY
    ~ in Spanish OLE

"___ Bravo" RIO

bravura DASH

brawl MELEE, RIOT, ROW, SCRAP,
    SETTO

brawn SINEW

brawny BIG, HALE, LARGE

Braxton TONI

bray BAWL, CRY, NOISE
    half a ~ HAW, HEE

brayer ASS, BURRO

Braz.
    ~ neighbor ARG

braze FUSE

brazen DARE, PERT

brazenness SASS

brazier
    ~ bit EMBER

Brazil
    ~ neighbor PERU
    state in ~ PARA

Brazil ___ NUT

Brazilian LATIN
    ~ border river ACRE
    ~ dance SAMBA
    ~ emperor PEDRO
    ~ macaw ARA
    ~ port NATAL, RIO
    ~ soccer star PELE
    ~ state ACRE, PARA
    ~ title DOM

Brazos
    city on the ~ WACO

Brazzaville CITY, PORT

breach GAP, HOLE, LAPSE, RENT,
    SPLIT
    ~ of contract TORT
    ~ of judgment LAPSE
    ~ of secrecy LEAK

bread CASH, FARE, GELT, MINT,
    MOOLA, ROLL, RYE
    ~ chamber OVEN
    ~ emanation AROMA
    ~ end HEEL
    ~ hunk SLAB
    ~ in French PAIN
    ~ in Italian PANE
    ~ in Japanese PAN
    ~ in Spanish PAN
    ~ need YEAST
    ~ spread JAM, OLEO
    ~ unit LOAF, SLICE
    ~ with a pocket PITA
    ~ with seeds RYE
    break ~ DINE, EAT
    brown ~ TOAST
    falafel ~ PITA
    like old ~ STALE
    make ~ BAKE, EARN
    Middle Eastern ~ PITA
    Reuben ~ RYE

Southern ~ PONE
    sweet ~ CAKE

___ bread CORN, PITA, RYE

"Bread ___ Chocolate" AND

bread-and-butter
    ~ letter NOTE

"Bread and Circuses"
    ~ author AGAR

breadbasket
    ~ st. ILL, KAN, NDAK, NEB,
        NEBR, SDAK
    ~ state IOWA

Breadbasket
    ~ prov. ALT, ALTA, MAN

breadth SPAN
    win by a hair's ~ NOSE

breadwinner
    be the ~ EARN

break DASH, GAP, HOLE, RENT,
    RUIN, SMASH, SPACE, STOP,
    TAME, TEAR
    ~ a bronc TAME
    ~ abruptly SNAP
    ~ a Commandment SIN
    ~ a fast EAT
    ~ apart REND, SPLIT
    ~ away PART
    ~ bread DINE, EAT
    ~ camp LEAVE, MOVE
    ~ down DIE, ERODE, ROT
    ~ down and cry BAWL
    ~ forth ERUPT, SPEW
    ~ ground PLOW, START
    ~ in ENTER, ROB, TRAIN, USE
    ~ in the audience AISLE
    ~ into OPEN
    ~ off CEASE, CHIP, DEFER,
        END, HALT, SNAP, STOP
    ~ out ERUPT, FLARE
    ~ out in a cold sweat PANIC
    ~ the back of TASK
    ~ the ice OPEN, START
    ~ the news LEAK, TELL
    ~ through PEEP
    ~ up DIG, PART, SPLIT
    coffee ~ REST
    kindergarten ~ NAP
    midday ~ NAP
    price ~ DISC
    sentence ~ DASH
    soldier's ~ LEAVE
    take a ~ CEASE, DEFER, HALT,
        REST

break ___ CAMP, DANCE, EVEN,
    INTO, OFF, OUT, RANK

break ___ ground NEW

"Break ___!" ALEG

"___ Break" FAST

"Break a ___!" LEG

breakaway
    ~ group SECT

breakdown
    ~ beacon FLARE

breaker
    circuit ~ FUSE

ground ~ HOE, SPADE
sound-barrier ~ SST

break-even
    ~ amount COST

breakfast DINE, EAT, MEAL
    ~ drink COCOA
    ~ fare HASH, OMELET, TOAST
    ~ food BRAN
    ~ fruit MELON
    ~ grain OAT
    ~ item EGG, OMELET
    ~ items, in Latin OVA
    ~ roll BAGEL
    ~ spread JAM
    Brooklyn ~ BAGEL

"Breakfast at Tiffany's"
    ~ actress NEAL

breakfaster EATER

breakfast in bed
    ~ prop TRAY

"Breakheart ___" PASS

"Breaking ___" AWAY

"Breaking Away"
    ~ vehicle BIKE

breaking-out RASH

"Breaking the Sound Barrier"
    ~ director LEAN

breakneck RAPID, RASH

breaks
    TV ~ ADS

break the ___ ICE

breakthrough GAIN

breakwater LEVEE, MOLE, PIER

"___ Breaky Heart" ACHY

Bream SID

___-breasted grosbeak ROSE

breastplate ARMOR, MAIL

breath
    ~ freshener MINT
    ~ holder LUNG
    brief ~ GASP
    every ~ you take AIR
    short ~ GASP
    take one's ~ away AMAZE,
        AWE, STUN, WOW
    with bated ~ AGOG

___ breath INONE

breathe ARE, HINT, LIVE, SAY
    ~ a word TELL
    ~ hard GASP, PANT
    ~ in DRAW
    ~ life into FIRE
    ~ new life into RENEW
    live and ~ ARE

breathe ___ EASY

breather LUNG, NOSE, REST
    take a ~ CEASE, DEFER, HALT,
        REST, STOP

breathing ALIVE, LIVE
    ~ organ LUNG
    ~ sound RALE

~ space PORE
~ spell PEACE, REST

breathing ___ ROOM, SPACE

breathless AGOG

"Breathless"
  ~ actor GERE
  ~ actress LANGE

bred-in-the-___ BONE

___ breeches KNEE

breechloader GUN

breed BEAR, GROW, ILK, LOT, MATE, ORDER, RACE, RAISE, REAR, SORT, TYPE
  mixed ~ MULE

Breeder's Cup
  ~ event RACE

breeding
  ~ place NEST

breeze AIR, EASY, SNAP
  ~ along MOVE
  ~ through ACE
  hang in the ~ DRY
  make a ~ FAN
  shoot the ~ BLAB, CHAT, GAB, PRATE, RAP, TALK
  stir up a ~ FAN

___ breeze SEA

"Breeze ___, The" ANDI

breezes
  filled with ~ AIRY
  gentle, as ~ MILD

breezeway HALL

breezy AIRY, COOL, PERT

Bremen CITY, PORT

Bremerhaven CITY, PORT

Brenda LEE, STARR

Brenneman AMY

Brenner ___ PASS

Breslau
  ~ river ODER

Breslow LOU

Brest
  see French

Bret HARTE

brethren KIN

Breton CAPE, CELT, HAT

breve NOTE

___ breve ALLA

breviloquent TERSE

brew ALE, BEER, BOIL, HEAT, LAGER, PERK, PLOT, STEEP, TEA
  witches' ~ need NEWT

___ brew HOME

brewed
  ~ beverage ALE, BEER, LAGER, TEA

brewer URN
  ~ kiln OAST
  ~ need MALT, YEAST
  ~ vat TUN

Brewer TERESA

Brewers NINE, TEAM

brewery
  ~ fixture VAT
  ~ ingredient MALT
  ~ product ALE, BEER, LAGER

brewing
  leaf for ~ PEKOE, TEA

brewski BEER

Brezhnev
  ~ domain USSR

Brian ENO

Brian Boru
  ~ land EIRE

"Brian's Song"
  ~ actor CAAN

briar PIPE

briard DOG

bribe BAIT, OIL, SMEAR, SOP

brick ADOBE, CLAY, COLOR, PAVE
  ~ carrier HOD
  ~ ender BAT, YARD
  ~ ingredient LOAM
  ~ material CLAY
  ~ worker MASON
  Southwestern ~ ADOBE

brick ___ RED

brickbat GIBE, LIBEL, SLAM

brick-colored BAY

Brickell EDIE

bricklayer MASON
  ~ implement HOD

brickmaker
  ~ need KILN, OVEN

brickmaking
  ~ mixture LOAM

Brickman PAUL

bricks
  ~ unit TON
  hit like a ton of ~ DAZE, STUN

Brickyard
  ~ event RACE

bridal
  ~ blossoms ORANGE
  ~ gown feature TRAIN
  ~ notice word NEE
  ~ path AISLE
  ~ path destination ALTAR
  ~ wear SATIN

"Bridal ___, The" PATH

bride LOVE, MATE
  ~ acquisition INLAW
  ~ destination ALTAR
  ~ new title MRS
  ~ of Christ NUN

~ response IDO
~ ride LIMO
~ walkway AISLE

"Bride ___ Black, The" WORE

"Bride Came ___, The" COD

bridegroom LOVE, MATE
  ~ attendant USHER

bridge GAME, SPAN
  ~ builder's concern STRESS
  ~ coup SLAM
  ~ designer ENG
  ~ fare TOLL
  ~ holding HAND
  ~ honor ACE
  ~ move RAISE
  ~ opening BID
  ~ option PASS
  ~ position EAST, WEST
  ~ response PASS
  ~ site NOSE
  ~ support PIER
  ~ team DUO, PAIR
  ~ toll unit AXLE
  American ~ engineer EADS
  beat, at ~ SET
  declare, in ~ BID
  electric ~ ARC
  place for a ~ GAP
  Saint Louis ~ EADS

___ bridge LAND, TOLL

"Bridge, The"
  ~ poet CRANE

"Bridge ___ Far, A" TOO

"___ Bridge" MRS

___ Bridge (Saint Louis span) EADS

"Bridge at ___" ARLES

"Bridge of ___" ASSES

"Bridge of San ___ Rey, The" LUIS

"Bridge of San Luis ___, The" REY

"Bridge on the River Kwai, The"
  ~ director LEAN
  ~ setting SIAM

Bridges ALAN, BEAU

Bridges, Beau
  ~ to Lloyd SON

Bridges, Jeff
  ~ film TRON

"Bridges of Madison County, The"
  ~ setting IOWA

Bridget
  ~ to Jane NIECE

"Bridge Too ___, A" FAR

"Bridge Too Far, A"
  ~ actor CAINE
  ~ author RYAN

bridle LEASH, LIMIT, REIN, STOP
  ~ part BIT, REIN
  ~ path TRAIL

bridle ___ PATH

Brie
  ~ covering RIND

brief NOTE, TERSE
  ~ appearance CAMEO
  ~ attempt STAB
  ~ breath GASP
  ~ farewell BYE
  ~ fashion FAD
  ~ letter NOTE
  ~ sample DEMO
  ~ statement NOTE
  ~ summary RECAP
  ~ swim DIP
  ~ treatise TRACT
  ~ trip ERRAND

briefcase
  ~ closer HASP

"Brief Encounter"
  ~ director LEAN

"Brief History of ___, A" TIME

brier NEEDLE

brig BOAT, HOLE, SHIP

brig. ___ GEN

brigade ARMY

___ brigade FIRE

brigadier RANK

brigantine BOAT, SHIP

Brigati EDDIE

Briggs CLARE

bright ACUTE, APT, CLEAR, GAY, KEEN, ROSY, SMART
  ~ color RED
  ~ spot RAY
  look on the ~ side HOPE
  not ~ DRAB

bright and ___ EARLY

bright-colored
  ~ fish OPAH, TETRA

brighten ADORN, COLOR, GLOW
  ~ up PERK

brightened
  ~ up LIT

brightest
  constellation's ~ star ALPHA
  second ~ star BETA
  the best and the ~ CREAM, ELITE

bright-eyed and bushy-tailed ALERT, EAGER, PERT

brightness GLARE
  ~ unit NIT
  lose ~ FADE, PALE

Brighton
  ~ beverage ALE
  see also British, English

Brigitte
  see French

brilliance ECLAT, FIRE, GLARE, POMP, SHEEN

brilliant ABLE, ACUTE, CLEAR, GEM, RICH, SMART, STONE
~ **display** RIOT
~ **ender** INE
be ~ GLOW, SHINE, STAR
not exactly ~ DENSE

"__ brillig and the slithy toves..." TWAS

Brillo
~ **rival** SOS

brim BILL, EDGE, LIP, PEAK, RIM

__-brim SNAP

brimful AWASH, LADEN

brimming LADEN, RIFE

Brindisi CITY, PORT
see also Italian

brine CURE, SALT, STEEP

bring TAKE
~ **about** CAUSE
~ **along** TOTE
~ **around** RESTORE, SELL, SWAY
~ **a smile to** AMUSE
~ **back** RENEW, RESTORE
~ **back to snuff** REHAB
~ **bliss to** ELATE
~ **cheer to** AMUSE
~ **down** ABASE, HEW, RUIN
~ **down a dogie** ROPE
~ **down the curtain** END
~ **down the house** RAZE, WOW
~ **force to bear** IMPEL
~ **forth** BEAR, EDUCE, EVOKE, MAKE
~ **forward** CITE, LAY
~ **forward as proof** CITE
~ **home** EARN, NET
~ **in** CLEAR, EARN, LAND, NET
~ **in a fish** LAND
~ **in the crops** REAP
~ **into being** MAKE
~ **into play** EXERT, USE
~ **legal action** SUE
~ **on** CAUSE
~ **on board** HIRE
~ **out** DRAW, EDUCE, EVOKE, SAY, TELL
~ **the food** CATER, SERVE
~ **the plane in** LAND
~ **through** HELP
~ **to** ADD
~ **to a boil** ENRAGE, HEAT
~ **to a halt** CEASE, END, STEM, STOP
~ **to an end** ANNUL, CEASE, RUIN
~ **to a standstill** ARREST
~ **to attention** SAY
~ **to bear** EXERT, USE
~ **together** AMASS, UNITE, WED
~ **to justice** SUE, TRY
~ **to light** AIR, BARE, LEAK, SHOW, TELL
~ **to mind** EVOKE
~ **to naught** DASH, RUIN, UNDO
~ **to one's knees** BEND

~ **to pass** CAUSE
~ **to ruin** UNDO
~ **to the firm** HIRE
~ **to trial** SUE
~ **under control** TAME
~ **up** BREED, RAISE, REAR, REFER, SAY, TELL
~ **up the rear** LAG, TRAIL

bring __ (accomplish) OFF

bring __ (reveal) OUT

bring __ halt TOA

bring __ the bacon HOME

bringing
~ **up the rear** LAST

"Bringing Up Buddy"
~ **aunt** IRIS

bring to __ BEAR, LIFE

bring to one's __ KNEES

bring up the __ REAR

brink EDGE, EVE, LIMIT, LIP, RIM
be on the ~ TEETER
on the ~ of ABOUT, NEAR

Brinker HANS

Brinkley
~ **partner** CHET

Brinkley, Christie
emulate ~ MODEL, POSE

Brinks truck
~ **protection** ARMOR

briny MAIN, OCEAN, SEA
~ **drop** TEAR
~ **septet** SEAS
on the ~ ASEA, ATSEA

brio DASH, ELAN, LIFE, PEP

__ brio CON

briolette GEM

Brisbane CITY, PORT
see also Australian

brisk AGILE, CRISP, FAST, RAPID, RAW, SMART, SPRY, WARM

brisket MEAT

briskness NIP

bristle AWN, BARB, HAIR, NEEDLE, SETA, TEEM
grain ~ AWN

bristlecone PINE

bristles BEARD

bristling RIFE

Bristol CITY, PORT
city near ~ BATH
river at ~ AVON
see also British, English

Brit.
~ **commercial abbr.** LTD
~ **currency symbols** LSD
~ **fliers** RAF
~ **legislators** MPS
~ **lexicon** OED
~ **military branch** RAF
~ **money** LSD

~ **pilots** RAF
~ **pound** STER
~ **reference work** OED

Britain
~ **to US** ALLY
ancient inhabitant of ~ CELT
neighbor of ~ EIRE
see also British, English

__ Britain GREAT

"__, Britannia" RULE

Britannica
~ **set** ENC

British
~ **auto accessory** TYRE
~ **bigwig** NOB
~ **bonnet** HOOD
~ **brew** ALE
~ **carbine** STEN
~ **cathedral town** ELY
~ **composer** ARNE
~ **conservative** TORY
~ **county** SHIRE
~ **county festival** ALE
~ **digs** FLAT
~ **dramatist** SHAW
~ **drink** TEA
~ **exclamation** ISAY
~ **farewell** TATA
~ **FBI** CID
~ **inc.** LTD
~ **lavatory** LOO
~ **legal society** INN
~ **maid** CHAR
~ **nobleman** EARL, PEER
~ **noblewoman** DAME
~ **political party** LABOR
~ **potato chip** CRISP
~ **prep school** ETON
~ **racecourse** ASCOT, EPSOM
~ **radial** TYRE
~ **raincoat** MAC
~ **resort** BATH
~ **royal, informally** ANDY
~ **scarf** ASCOT
~ **spa** BATH
~ **street** MEWS
~ **title** DAME, LORD, SIR
~ **TV** TELE
~ **verb ender** ISE
1950s ~ prime minister EDEN
buddy ~ MATE

British __ ISLES

British Airways
~ **plane** SST

British Commonwealth
member of the ~ MALTA

British Isle MAN

British Isles
~ **republic** EIRE

British Parliament
first woman in ~ ASTOR

British Protectorate
former ~ ADEN

Briton
ancient ~ CELT

Britt MAY

Brittain VERA

Brittany
see French

brittle CRISP

bro REL
~ **sib** SIS

broach OPEN, RAISE, TAP

broached OPEN

broad AMPLE, BIG, FAT, LARGE, LOOSE, WIDE
~ **jump** LEAP
~ **st.** AVE
~ **tie** ASCOT
~ **valley** DALE

broadcast AIR, CRY, EMIT, LEAK, NEWS, RADIO, RELATE, SEED, SEND, SOW
~ **component** AUDIO
~ **medium** RADIO
~ **pioneer** RCA
block a ~ JAM

"Broadcast __" NEWS

"__ Broadcast, The" BIG

broadcasting ONAIR

broaden FLARE
~ **a bore** REAM

broad-minded OPEN

broad-scope
~ **tale** SAGA

broadside BILL, FIRE, RAM, SIGN

Broadway
~ **angel's delight** HIT, SRO
~ **award** TONY
~ **backer** ANGEL
~ **brightener** NEON
~ **figure** ACTOR
~ **groom of 1922** ABIE
~ **hit** CATS, SMASH
~ **musical** ANNIE, CATS
~ **musical set in Argentina** EVITA
~ **offering** DRAMA, SHOW
1985 ~ show ASIS
big name in ~ history FLO
see also theater

"Broadway __" BILL, JOE

__-Broadway OFF

"Broadway Bill"
~ **director** CAPRA

"Broadway Danny __" ROSE

"Broadway Danny Rose"
~ **director** ALLEN

Broadway Limited TRAIN

"Broadway Melody of 1936"
~ **director** RUTH

Brobdingnagian BIG, GIANT, LARGE, VAST

"Broca's Brain"
~ **author** SAGAN

broccoli
~ **bit** SPEAR

___ broche ALA

brochette SPIT

brochure TRACT

Brock LOU
~ theft BASE

Brodie STEVE

brogan SHOE
~ bottom SOLE

brogue SHOE

broil BAKE, HEAT, RIOT, ROAST, ROW, SCRAP, SEAR

___-broil PAN

broiler OVEN

Brokaw TOM
~ beat NEWS
~ follower LENO

broke NEEDY, POOR
flat ~ POOR
go for ~ DARE, RISK

___-broke STONE

broken TAME
~ up APART
it may be ~ at parties ICE
not ~ ENTIRE

"Broken ___" ARROW, LANCE

broken-down OLD, SEEDY

brokenhearted LOW, SAD

brokenheartedness PAIN

broken mirror
~ maybe OMEN

broker AGENT
stock ~ directive SELL

brokerage PAY, RATE
~ term BEAR, CALL, MUNI, PUT, SHARE

bromate SALT

bromic ACID

bromide ADAGE, SAW, TAG

bromidic BANAL, STALE, TIRED, TRITE

bromo
~ target GAS

bronc HORSE, STEED
break a ~ TAME

bronchiole
~ locale LUNG

bronco ANIMAL, HORSE, STEED
~ buster TAMER
~ catcher LASSO, NOOSE

Bronco AUTO, CAR

broncobusters
~ meet RODEO

Broncos ELEVEN, TEAM
~ org. NFL

broncs
what ~ do REAR

Bronstein ENA

Brontë ANNE
~ heroine EYRE

"Brontë"
~ director MANN

Bronx
~ cheer HISS, HOOT
~ ender ITE

"Bronx ___, A" TALE

"Bronx? No, thonx!, The"
~ author NASH

"Bronx Zoo, The"
~ actor ASNER

bronze COLOR, IMAGE, MEDAL, METAL, TAN
~ coin CENT
~ component TIN
Roman ~ AES

Bronze AGE

Bronze ___ AGE, STAR

bronzed TAN

brooch CLASP, PIN
antique ~ CAMEO

brood ISSUE, MOPE, MUSE, NEST, SET, SIT, STEW

brooder HEN

broodmare DAM

brook ABIDE, ALLOW, BEAR, LET, RILL, RUN, STREAM, TAKE
small ~ RILL

brook ___ TROUT

Brook PETER

Brooke
~ groom ANDRE

Brooke, Rupert POET
see also poet

Brooklyn
~ breakfast BAGEL
~ ender ESE, ITE

Brooklyn Dodger
~ great REESE

Brookner ANITA

Brooks MEL

Brooks ___ RANGE

Brooks, Garth
~ birthplace TULSA

Brooks, Mrs. Mel ANNE

broom
~ material STRAW

Broom Hilda HAG

Brosnan, Pierce
~ role STEELE

brother ABBOT, MALE
~ address FRA
Cain's ~ SETH
madre's ~ TIO
padre's ~ TIO

___ brother BIG, SOUL

"Brother ___" RAT

"___ Brother, The" KID

brotherhood CLAN, LOVE, ORDER, PEACE, RING
~ of sorts FRAT
campus ~ FRAT

brother-in-___ LAW

"Brotherly ___" LOVE

___ Brothers (1950s singing group) AMES

___ Brothers (soap maker) LEVER

brougham CAB, MOTOR

brought
~ to light OUT, TOLD

brouhaha ADO, FLAP, MELEE, ROW, SCRAP, SETTO, SPAT, STIR, TODO

brow EDGE, LIP, RIM
~ starter LOW
sweat of one's ~ LABOR

browbeat CARP, COW, TREAD

brown FRY, HEAT, SAUTE, SEAR, TAN, TOAST
~ belt RANK
~ bread TOAST
~ brew ALE
~ oneself BASK
~ study MUSE
dark ~ SEPIA
do it up ~ ACE
dull ~ DRAB
get ~ TAN
light ~ ECRU, TAN
reddish ~ HENNA
shade of ~ COCOA

brown ___ BAG, BEAR, RICE

Brown LES, RON, TINA, TOM
~ rival YALE

___ Brown (Croce song subject) LEROY

Brown Adam HORSE

brown-bag
~ contents APPLE, MEAL

Brown, Charlie
~ exclamation RATS
~ toy KITE

Brown, Clarence
~ film of 1932 EMMA

___ Browne belt SAM

Brown, Father
~ house MANSE

brownie ELF, GNOME

Brownie CAMERA

Browning, Elizabeth Barrett POET
see also poet

Browning, Robert POET
see also poet

brownish ECRU

brownish-gray TAUPE

Brown, James
~ music SOUL

___ browns HASH

"___ Brown's Schooldays" TOM

Brownsville CITY, PORT

brown-tail ___ MOTH

Brown, Tina EDITOR

brown-winged
~ butterfly SATYR

"___ Brown You've Got a Lovely Daughter" MRS

brows
~ do it KNIT

browse CROP, DIP, FEED, ROAM, SCAN

Broz, Josip SLAV, TITO

Brubeck DAVE

Bruce DERN, LEE
~ daughter LAURA
Robert the ~ SCOT

Bruckner ANTON

Bruins SIX, TEAM, UCLA
~ hockey great ORR
~ milieu ICE, RINK
~ org. NHL

bruise ABUSE, MASH
~ easer ICE

bruised ACHY, SORE
easily ~ item EGO

bruiser APE, GIANT

bruit BLAB, CRY, NOISE, TALK
~ around AIR

brume MIST, SMOG

"___ Brummel" BEAU

Brummell, Beau DUDE

brunch EAT, MEAL
~ choice CREPE, OMELET, SALAD
have ~ EAT

Brunei
~ coin SEN
~ locale ASIA

Brünnhilde
~ mother ERDA

___ Bruno, Calif. SAN

Brunswick ___ STEW

brush CARESS, KISS
~ carelessly DAUB
~ ender FIRE
~ off SNUB
~ starter AIR, HAIR, NAIL, SAGE, TOOTH, UNDER
wield a ~ PAINT

brushed
~ hide SUEDE

brushoff SNUB
slangy ~ POOH

brushstroke
sloppy ~ SMEAR

brusque RUDE, TERSE
be ~ SNAP

Brussels CITY

Brussels ___ LACE

Brussels-based
~ grp. NATO

brut
~ relative SEC

brutal ANIMAL, BAD, CRUEL, FERAL, MEAN

brute ANIMAL, APE, BEAST, BOOR, LUG, OGRE, YAHOO

"___ Brute!" ETTU

brutish ANIMAL, CRUEL
~ person YAHOO

Brutus CAESAR, ROMAN
question to ~ ETTU
see also Latin

Bryan
emulate ~ ORATE

Bryant ANITA, BEAR

___ Bryant Ford EDSEL

Bryant, Paul
~ nickname BEAR

Bryant, William Cullen POET
see also poet

Bryan, William Jennings ORATOR

Bryce Canyon
~ site UTAH

Brynhild
~ brother ATLI

Brynner YUL
~ kingdom SIAM

bryophyte MOSS

BSA ORG
part of ~ AMER

___ B. Toklas ALICE

BTU
~ relative CAL
part of ~ UNIT

bub MAC

bubble AERATE, BEAD, BOIL
~ maker PIPE

bubble ___ BATH

___ bubble SOAP

bubbles FOAM
fill with ~ AERATE
minus ~ FLAT

"Bubbles in the ___" WINE

bubble wrap
play with ~ POP

bubbling ALIVE, ELATED
~ over AVID, KEEN

bubbly PERT, SODA
make ~ AERATE

Bubka, Sergei
~ catapult POLE

buccal ORAL

Buccaneers ELEVEN, TEAM
~ home TAMPA
~ org. NFL

Bucephalus HORSE, STEED

Buchanan EDGAR, EDNA, PAT

"Buchanan ___ Alone" RIDES

"Buchanan Rides ___" ALONE

Bucharest CITY
~ dance HORA

Buchwald ART

buck ANIMAL, CAD, DEER, DUDE, GOAT, MALE, ONE, ROE, STAG
~ ender AROO, EROO, EYE, HORN, SAW, SHOT, SKIN
~ mate DOE
~ the system REBEL
~ up AID, HELP
make a ~ EARN
pass the ~ REFER
pts. of a ~ CTS

___ buck FAST

Buck PEARL
~ character OLAN
~ partner ROY

"Buck Benny ___ Again" RIDES

"Buck Benny Rides ___" AGAIN

bucket CAN, PAIL, SCOOP
~ defect HOLE
~ handle BAIL
~ of bolts AUTO, CAR, CRATE, HEAP, LEMON, MOTOR
~ wood OAK
champagne ~ ICER
like a certain ~ OAKEN
use a ~ BAIL

bucket ___ SEAT

___ bucket ICE

"bucket of ashes"
Sandburg's ~ PAST

buckets ALOT
come down in ~ RAIN, STORM

buckeye TREE

Buckeyes
~ sch. OSU

Buckeye State OHIO

buckjump HOP

buckle BIND, CLASP
~ down START
~ holder STRAP

buckler ARMOR

Buckner NOEL

bucko MALE

Buck, Pearl
~ book, with "The" EXILE
~ heroine OLAN
~ novel SONS

"Buck Privates ___ Home" COME

"Buck Privates Come ___" HOME

bucks CASH, GELT, HES, MINT, MOOLA
~ starter MEGA
big ~, for short MIL
lots of ~ WAD
thousand ~ GEE

Bucks FIVE, TEAM
~ org. NBA

buckskin HORSE

Bucky DENT

bucolic RURAL
~ plot ACRE

Bucs ELEVEN, TEAM
~ org. NFL

bud GERM, LEAF, NODE, SHOOT
~ eventually LEAF
~ holder STEM, VASE
nip in the ~ ARREST, STAY, STOP
pickled ~ CAPER
pickled flower ~ CAPER
spud ~ EYE

___ bud TASTE

Bud BEER
~ partner LOU

Budapest CITY

Budd, Billy GOB, TAR
~ assent AYE

"Buddenbrooks"
~ author MANN

Buddha
~ attribute CALM

Buddhism REL

Buddhist
~ monk LAMA
~ sacred city LHASA
~ sect ZEN
sacred ~ mountain OMEI

budding NEW

buddy BRO, DUDE, MAC, MATE, PAL
~ in Australian English MATE
~ in British English MATE
~ in French AMI, AMIE
~ in Spanish AMIGO
good ~ BRO
shipboard ~ MATE

Buddy BAER, EBSEN, RICH
~ to Bill DOG, PET

buddy-buddy CLOSE

"Buddy Holly Story, The"
~ director RASH

budge MOVE, STIR
not ~ STAY

Budge DON

budgerigar BIRD, PET

budget
~ item RENT
~ limit CAP
~ subj. ECON

Budget
~ rival ALAMO, AVIS

Budweiser BEER

___ Buenaventura SAN

Buenos ___ AIRES

Buenos Aires CITY, PORT
~ loc. ARG
see also Spanish

"Buenos Aires"
~ musical EVITA

buff COLOR, CREAM, FAN, NUT, SAND, SHINE, TAN
in the ~ BARE, NUDE

___ buffa OPERA

buffalo ANIMAL, COW
~ cousin BISON
~ group HERD
Asian ~ ANOA

buffalo ___ ROBE

___ buffalo CAPE, WATER

Buffalo CITY, PORT
~ footballer BILL
~ lake ERIE
canal to ~ ERIE

"Buffalo ___" GALS

buffaloes
water ~ OXEN

buffer ___ STATE, ZONE

buffet BANG, BEAT, CLAP, HIT, LASH, MEAL, RAM, SLAP, TABLE
~ choice SALAD
~ patron EATER
enjoy the ~ EAT

buffoon CLOD, OAF

buffoonery
bit of ~ ANTIC

bug ANGER, FAN, FLEA, FLU, GERM, GET, IRK, NAG, NEEDLE, PEEVE, RIDE, RILE, TAP, TEASE, UPSET
~ in one's ear HINT
~ killer DDT
~ out LEAVE, START
bonnet ~ BEE
busy ~ ANT
catch a ~ AIL
June ~ DOR
pesky ~ GNAT
phone ~ TAP
strong ~ ANT
tiny ~ MITE

bug ___ (leave quickly) OFF, OUT

bug-___ EYED

___ bug LOVE

"___ Bug, The" LOVE, SATAN

bugaboo BANE, FEAR
student's ~ EXAM, TEST

bugbear BANE, OGRE

bug-eyed AGOG
~ monsters ETS

buggy AUTO, CAR, DAFT, LOCO, PRAM
~ drivers AMISH

~ **venue** DUNE
dune ~ MOTOR

___ **buggy** DUNE

bugle HORN
~ **call** TAPS

bugles
animal that ~ ELK

bugs
one who ~ PEST

Bugs BAER

Bugs Bunny HARE
~ **foil** ELMER
~ **voice** MEL
like ~ EARED

"Bugsy"
~ **wife** ESTA

Buick AUTO, CAR
~ **model** REGAL
~ **rival** OLDS

build ERECT, MAKE, RAISE, REAR
~ **a fire under** AROUSE, ROUSE
~ **an annex** ADD
~ **anew** RESTORE
~ **a road** PAVE
~ **a wing** ADD
~ **new tissue** HEAL
~ **(on)** ADD
~ **up** AMASS
something to ~ **on** LOT

build ___ egg ANEST

build a fire ___ UNDER

builder
~ **choice** SITE
~ **land** LOT
cell ~ BEE
character ~ GENE
colony ~ ANT
wall ~ MASON

building
~ **add-on** ELL
~ **block** UNIT
~ **block of nature** ATOM
~ **material** STEEL
~ **overgrowth** IVY
~ **regulations** CODE
~ **site** LOT
~ **support** BEAM
~ **wing** ELL
college ~ DORM
crude ~ SHED
farm ~ BARN, SILO
Little Pigs ~ **material** STRAW
nature's ~ **block** ATOM
Southwestern ~
material ADOBE
streetcar ~ BARN
tool ~ SHED
tumbledown ~ RUIN
utility ~ SHED

building ___ CODE

building block
~ **letters** DNA
nature's ~ CELL

building-site
~ **sight** CRANE

built
~ **for speed** SLEEK
~ **like a rock** SOLID
not ~ **up** OPEN

built-up
~ **area** CITY

Bujold
~ **film of 1978** COMA

bulb SEED
edible ~ LEEK, ONION
electric ~ LAMP
garden ~ IRIS, TULIP
gas in a ~ NEON
light ~, **symbolically** IDEA
like a low-watt ~ DIM

___ **bulb** DIM

Bulgarian SLAV
former ~ **king** BORIS

bulge NODE, START
battle the ~ DIET

bulk MASS, SIZE
the ~ MOST

bulky BIG, LARGE

bull ANIMAL, CANT, EDICT, LAW, LIE, MALE, TORO
~ **beloved** COW
~ **ender** DOG, HEAD, HORN, ISH, PEN, RING
~ **in Spanish** TORO
~ **session** TALK
~ **session site** DORM
~ **sound** SNORT
~ **weapon** HORN
papal ~ EDICT
shoot the ~ BLAB, CHAT, RAP, TALK, YAK
take the ~ **by the**
horns BEARD, DARE
young ~ CALF

bull ___ SNAKE

___ **bull** PIT

Bull
the ~ SIGN

"Bull"
emulate De Niro's ~ RAGE

Bull ___ MOOSE, RUN

Bull ___ Party MOOSE

Bulldog ELI

Bulldogs
~ **school** YALE

bulldoze COW, RAZE

bullet ACE, SHELL
poker ~ ACE

bullet ___ TRAIN

bulletin BILL, NEWS, NOTE, PAPER
police ~ ALERT
trooper's ~ APB

"Bullet in the ___, A" HEAD

"Bullet in the Head, A"
~ **director** WOO

bulletproof SAFE

bullets AMMO
sweat ~ STEW

Bullets FIVE, TEAM
~ **org.** NBA

"Bullets ___ Broadway" OVER

"Bullets Over Broadway"
~ **director** ALLEN

bull fiddle
~ **relative** CELLO

bullfight
~ **site** ARENA

"Bullfighter ___ the Lady" AND

"Bullfighter and the ___" LADY

bullion GOLD, INGOT, METAL
~ **shape** BAR

bullish
~ **sound** SNORT

bull market
~ **result** RISE

Bullock, Sandra
~ **film** SPEED
~ **film, with "The"** NET

bullpen
~ **fixture** PHONE
~ **standout** ACE

bull riding
~ **event** RODEO

bullring ARENA
~ **figure** TORO

Bull Run STREAM
~ **soldier** REB
~ **victor** LEE

bulls HES

Bulls FIVE, TEAM
~ **org.** NBA

bull's-eye
~ **hitter** DART
eye the ~ AIM
make a ~ HIT

bullwhip LASH

Bullwinkle MOOSE
~ **relative** ELK
~ **to Rocky** PAL
enemy of ~ BORIS

bully COW, RAG, TREAD

bullyrag COW, TEASE

bulrush REED, SEDGE

Bulwer-Lytton EARL
~ **heroine** IONE

bum BEG, DRONE, HOBO, NOMAD, STEAL
~ **around** LOAF, ROVE
bleacher ~ FAN
give someone a ~ **steer** LIE
on the ~ OUT

bum ___ RAP, STEER

___ **bum** SKI

Bumble Bee TUNA

bumbler ASS, BOOR, CLOD, LOUT, OAF
~ **cry** OOPS

bumbling INEPT

bummed
~ **out** LOW, SAD

bummer DRAG, LOSER

"Bummer!" ALAS

bump BANG, DENT, ELBOW, HIT, JAR, NODE, OUST, RAISE, RAM
~ **into** MEET
~ **on a log** NODE
~ **on a tree** KNOT
~ **on the scale** BLIP
~ **sound** THUD
~ **up against** ABUT

___ **bump** SPEED

bumper RICH
~ **blemish** DING
~ **item** CROP
~ **mark** DENT

bumpkin BOOR, LOUT, OAF, RUBE, YAHOO

bump on a log
like a ~ INERT

Bumppo, Natty HERO
~ **quarry** DEER

___ **bumps** GOOSE

bum's
give the ~ **rush to** OUST
the ~ **rush** SACK

"___ Bums" (Ebbets Fielders) DEM

Bumstead
~ **neighbor** ELMO, HERB
~ **nickname** DAG

bun HAIR, ROLL
~ **locale** NAPE

bunch BAND, GANG, GOB, HEAP, HERD, KNOT, LOT, MOB, PILE, RAFT, SET, SLEW, TON
~ **of people** TROOP
~ **together** AMASS, MASS
a whole ~ LOTS, SCAD
banana ~ HAND
honey ~ BEES
wild ~ MOB

bunches ALOT

bunco CON, SCAM

bund BLOC

bundle BALE, BIND, LOT, MASS, PILE, POT, WRAP
~ **of cash** WAD
~ **off** SEND, SHIP
~ **up** WRAP
hay ~ BALE
like a ~ **of nerves** EDGY, TENSE
worth a ~ RICH

Bundt CAKE

Bundy PEG
  ~ and others ALS

Bundy, Al
  ~ wife PEG

bung PEG, SEAL, STOP

bungalow ABODE, COT, HOME

bungle ERR, ERROR, HASH, SPOIL

bungler BOOR, IDIOT

bungling INEPT

bunk BED, CANT, COT, ROOM, ROT,
  SACK, TRASH
  ~ down (with) BED

bunker CHEST, TRAP
  ~ filler SAND

Bunker, Archie
  ~ wife EDITH

bunkhouse
  ~ item COT

bunkum TRASH

bunny HARE, PET
  emulate a ~ HOP

___ bunny EASTER

"Bunny ___" OHARE

bunnylike EARED

Bunsen
  ~ burner LAMP

bunting BIRD, FLAG

___ bunting SNOW

Buntline NED

Buntline, Ned ALIAS

Buñuel LUIS

bunya-bunya TREE

Bunyan GIANT, HERO, PAUL
  ~ blue ox BABE
  ~ cook OLE
  ~ tool AXE

bunyip FAKE, SHAM

"Buona ___" SERA

"Buona ___, Mrs. Campbell"
  SERA

"Buona Sera, ___ Campbell"
  MRS

buoy
  ~ up ELATE, HELP, PROP
  unlit ~ NUN
  where ~ meets gull OCEAN,
  SEA

buoyancy ELAN, LIFE, PEP

buoyant AIRY, GAY, RACY

buoyed
  be ~ up SWIM

buoys
  where the ~ are OCEAN, SEA

burble BOIL

"Burbs, The"
  ~ actor DERN

burden CARE, LADE, LOAD, ONUS,
  TASK, TENOR
  Banff ~ SKI
  beast of ~ ASS, BURRO, MULE,
  YAK
  beasts of ~ OXEN
  borrower's ~ LIEN
  busboy's ~ TRAY
  caddie's ~ BAG
  heavy ~ LOAD
  malamute's ~ SLED
  oxen's ~ PLOW
  Samoyed's ~ SLED
  shopper's ~ BAG, TOTE
  student's ~ TEXT
  traveler's ~ BAG
  waiter's ~ TRAY

burdened LADEN
  ~ Titan ATLAS

Burdette LEW

burdock WEED

Burdon, Eric
  ~ in the 1960s ANIMAL

bureau CHEST
  ~ projection KNOB
  farming ~ USDA

bureaucrat AGENT
  ~ ender ESE

bureaucrats
  what ~ follow SOP

burg CITY

burgeon GROW

burger
  ~ mate COLA
  ~ topper ONION
  big ~ MAC

Burger, Hamilton
  ~ nemesis MASON

Burghoff
  ~ costar ALDA, FARR
  ~ role RADAR

burglar
  ~ deterrent ALARM, DOG
  ~ goal SAFE
  ~ take LOOT

___ burglar CAT

burglarize LOOT, RIFLE, ROB

burgle LOOT, ROB

burgoo STEW

burgundy COLOR

Burgundy WINE
  ~ kingdom ARLES
  see also French

burin TOOL

Burke DELTA

"Burke ___ Wills" AND

"Burke's Law"
  Gene's ~ character AMOS

Burkina Faso
  ~ neighbor MALI, NIGER,
  TOGO

burl NODE

Burl IVES

burlap
  ~ carrier SACK
  ~ material HEMP

burlesque APE, PLAY
  ~ bit ACT, SKIT

Burlington Zephyr TRAIN

burly BIG, LARGE

Burma
  ~ neighbor ASSAM, LAOS
  ~ neighbor, once SIAM
  old capital of ~ AVA

Burma ___ ROAD

Burmese ASIAN, CAT
  ~ export TEAK
  ~ utterance MEOW, MEW

burn GLOW, HEAT, LOVE, SMART,
  STING
  ~ a joss stick CENSE
  ~ aromatic candles CENSE
  ~ candles to ADORE
  ~ cause LYE
  ~ (for) LONG, PANT
  ~ out PETER, TIRE
  ~ partner SLASH
  ~ remedy ALOE
  ~ slightly CHAR
  ~ someone up ENRAGE
  ~ the midnight oil CRAM,
  LABOR, SLAVE, TOIL
  ~ the outside of SEAR
  ~ treatment BALM
  ~ unsteadily FLARE
  ~ up ANGER, IRE, WASTE
  ~ up the road RACE, SPEED,
  TEAR
  ~ with liquid SCALD
  do a slow ~ ANGER
  money to ~ PILE

burn ___ (exhaust) OUT

___ burn SLOW

burned
  ~ up IRATE, SORE, UPSET

burned ___ crisp TOA

burned-out SPENT

burner
  ~ starter AFTER
  alcohol ~ ETNA
  Argand ~ LAMP
  be on a back ~ PEND
  Bunsen ~ LAMP
  gas ~ LAMP
  lab ~ ETNA
  put on a back ~ DEFER

___ burner (horse opera) OAT

Burnett CAROL
  ~ alma mater UCLA

___ Burnie, Md. GLEN

burning ACRID, AFIRE, AVID, HOT,
  IRATE, LIT, LIVE, RED
  ~ desire ARDOR
  ~ particle EMBER
  malicious ~ ARSON

burnish SHEEN, SHINE

burnoose CAPE, WRAP
  ~ wearer ARAB

burnout
  cause of ~ STRESS

Burns KEN, POET, SCOT
  ~ partner ALLEN
  cap for ~ TAM
  see also Scottish

Burns and ___ ALLEN

Burns and Allen DUO, PAIR, TEAM

Burns, Frank MAJOR

Burns, George
  ~ cigar PROP
  ~ role GOD

burnsides BEARD

Burns, Robert POET, SCOT
  see also poet

burnt SERE

burn the candle at both ___
  ENDS

burn the midnight ___ OIL

"Burnt Norton"
  ~ poet ELIOT

burnt-offering
  ~ spot ALTAR

burp ___ GUN

Burpee
  ~ offering SEED

Burr AARON
  ~ role MASON
  ~ to Hamilton FOE

burrito
  ~ cousin TACO

burro ANIMAL, ASS, MULE
  ~ comment BRAY
  go by ~ RIDE

burro's tail PLANT

Burroughs BEAT, EDGAR

Burroughs, Edgar Rice
  ~ character APE

burrow BORE, DEN, DIG, HOLE,
  HOME, LAIR, MINE
  ~ kin DEN

burrower MOLE

Burrows ABE

bursa SAC

burst CLAP, ERUPT, GALE, POP, RIP,
  SPLIT
  ~ forth FLARE
  ~ into tears BAWL
  ~ of activity SPATE
  ~ of energy SPASM

~ of laughter GALE
~ of speed RUN
~ open ERUPT
ready to ~ MAD
speed ~ DASH

Burstyn ELLEN

Burt
~ ex LONI

Burton LANE, TIM

Burton, Richard SIR
~ birthplace WALES

Burundi
it begins in ~ NILE

bury HIDE

**"Bury My Heart at Wounded
___"** KNEE

**"Bury my heart at Wounded
Knee"**
~ originator BENET

bus
~ alternative AUTO, CAB, CAR
~ depot STA
~ garage BARN
~ route LINE
~ sign LOCAL
~ starter MINI, OMNI
~ station DEPOT
~ station abbr. ARR, ETA
~ ticket price FARE
~ unit SEAT
small ~ VAN
take the ~ RIDE

bus.
~ abbr. ASSN, INC, LTD
~ concerns COS
~ deg. MBA
~ directive ATT
~ grp. ORG
~ leader CEO, EXEC
~ letter abbr. ATTN
~ orgs. COS
~ subj. ECON
~ VIP CEO

"Bus ___" STOP

busboy
~ burden TRAY

busby HAT

Buscaglia LEO

Busch MAE

Busch Gardens
~ city TAMPA

bush PLANT, TIRE
~ baby ANIMAL
beat around the ~ AVOID,
EVADE, STALL

bush ___ PILOT

"Bush Christmas"
~ director SMART

bushed ALLIN, BEAT, SPENT, TIRED

"Bushel ___ Peck, A" ANDA

bushels SCADS

Bushes'
~ Millie DOG, PET

Bush, George ELI, PRES
~ alma mater YALE
~ former org. CIA
~ in the 1940s ELI
~ to Yale ALUM
word in a ~ quote LIPS, READ

bushido CODE

bushmaster SNAKE

Bushmiller ERNIE

bushwa ROT, TRASH

bushy-tailed
bright-eyed and ~ ALERT,
EAGER, PERT

business CASE, GAME, LIFE, LINE,
PLANT, SHOP, STORE, TRADE
~ abbr. ASSN, INC, LTD
~ arrangement DEAL
~ attire SUIT
~ concerns COS
~ consideration COST
~ deg. MBA
~ directive ATT
~ expansion BOOM
~ grp. ORG
~ leader CEO, EXEC
~ letter abbr. ATTN
~ loss BATH
~ magazine INC
~ mogul BARON, TITAN
~ orgs. COS
~ partner, often SON
~ program AGENDA
~ subj. ECON
~ VIP CEO
begin ~ OPEN
bit of ~ DEAL
check of ~ records AUDIT
do ~ DEAL, TRADE
doing ~ OPEN
funny ~ ANTIC, CAPER
get down to ~ START
give someone the ~ BEAT
hum of ~ PRESS
mind other people's ~ PRY
minor ~ part COG
monkey ~ LARK, PLAY
newspaper ~ PRESS
out of ~ SHUT
risky ~ DARE

___ business BIG, MEAN, SHOW

business as ___ USUAL

business card
~ symbol LOGO

business letter
~ abbr. ATT, ATTN, ENC
~ encl. SASE
~ word SIRS

businessman
~ offer CARD
big ~ BARON, TITAN

business page
~ abbr. NYSE

business sign
~ abbr. EST

buskin BOOT, SHOE

Buson POET
see also poet

buss KISS

"Bus Stop"
~ playwright INGE

bust ARREST, CHEST, IMAGE,
LOSER, NAB, RAID, TAME
~ opposite BOOM
~ participant NARC

bustard BIRD

busted NEEDY, TAME

buster MAC
clod ~ HOE

"___ Busters, The" DAM

"Bustin' ___" LOOSE

"Bustin' Loose"
~ director SCOTT

bustle ADO, HASTE, STIR, TODO

bustling ALIVE, ASTIR, LIVE
~ about ADO

busts ART

busy ASTIR, ATIT, LIVE, ORNATE
~ activity ADO
~ as a bee ASTIR
~ bee DEMON
~ insect ANT, BEE
~ oneself with PLY
~ person DOER
~ place HIVE
~ with ABOUT
be ~ ACT, LABOR
not ~ FREE, IDLE, SLOW
very ~ ATIT

busy as ___ ABEE

busy as a ___ BEE

busybody HEN, YENTA
be a ~ PRY
like a ~ NOSY

busyness ADO

"busy old fool"
Donne's ~ SUN

but ONLY, SAVE
~ in Spanish MAS

but ___ (still) YET

"...but ___ itself" FEAR

"But ___ for Me" NOT

butane GAS

**"Butch Cassidy ___ the
Sundance Kid"** AND

**"Butch Cassidy and the
Sundance ___"** KID

butcher HACK, OGRE
~ cut TBONE
~ offering CHOP, LAMB, MEAT,
STEAK, VEAL
~ wts. LBS

butcher shop
~ fixture SCALE

___ but goodie OLDIE

"...but is it ___?" ART

butler HELP, MALE, MAN
~ teammate MAID

Butler, Rhett
~ love OHARA

butlers HELP

Butler, Samuel POET
see also poet

"___, but no cigar!" CLOSE

___ but not heard SEEN

___ but not least LAST

butt END, GOAT, PROD, RAM, STUB
~ in PRY

butte
~ cousin MESA
form a ~ ERODE

butter FAT, RAM
~ container TUB
~ ender BALL, CUP, FAT, NUT
~ serving PAT
~ substitute OLEO

butter ___ BEAN, CLAM

___ butter COCOA

butter-and-___ man EGG

butterbean LIMA

"Butterfield 8"
~ author OHARA
~ director MANN

butterfingered INEPT

butterfingers BOOR, CLOD, OAF
~ cry OOPS

butterflies FEAR

"Butterflies ___ Free" ARE

"Butterflies Are ___" FREE

butterfly
~ catcher NET
~ cousin MOTH
brown-winged ~ SATYR
do the ~ SWIM
emulate a ~ FLIT

Butterfly
~ sash OBI

butterfly-bee
~ analogist ALI

buttermilk ___ SKY

Buttermilk HORSE
~ rider DALE, EVANS

"___ Buttermilk Sky" OLE

butternut TREE

Butterworth MRS

buttery OILY

"___ But the Brave" NONE

"___ But the Lonely Heart"
NONE

**"But thy ___ summer shall not
fade"** ETERNAL

buttinskis
~ do it PRY

buttinsky PEST

button FERN
~ alternative SNAP
~ down PEG
~ material NACRE
~ word PRESS
appliance ~ RESET
blender ~ CHOP, PUREE
bowler's ~ RESET
computer ~ RESET
Dictaphone ~ ERASE
fax ~ SEND
furnace ~ RESET
ornamental ~ STUD
panic ~ ALARM
remote-control ~ MUTE
replace a ~ SEW
right on the ~ BANG
tape-deck ~ EJECT
telephone ~ ABC, HOLD, STAR
transceiver ~ SEND
VCR ~ EJECT, REC, RESET, STOP

___ button PANIC

buttonhole BORE, EYE, SLIT

buttonholer PEST

buttons
common ~ ONS
elevator ~ UPS
lift ~ UPS

Buttons RED

buttress ARM, PIER, PROP, SHORE, STAY

butyraceous OILY

Bux, Kuda
~ "the man with the ___ eyes" XRAY

Buxley MISS

buy AGREE, DEAL, GET, OWN, SPEND
~ alternative LEASE
~ into a poker game ANTE
~ opposite SELL
~ time STALL

buy ___ (bribe) OFF

buy ___ (secure one's share of) OUT

buy ___ (stall) TIME

buy-and-sell
~ place MART

buy a pig ___ poke INA

buyer OWNER
~ bonanza SALE
~ bonus REBATE
~ caution ASIS
find a ~ SELL

"Buy low, sell high" ADAGE

"___ Buy Me Love" CANT

buyout DEAL

buzz BLAB, CALL, DIAL, DRONE, NEWS, NOISE, PHONE, RING, RUMOR, STIR
~ off LEAVE, SCAT, SCRAM

buzz ___ SAW

buzz ___ (go) OFF

Buzz
~ capsule-mate NEIL

buzzard BIRD

Buzzards BAY

buzz-cut
~ opposite AFRO

buzzer ALARM
flying ~ BEE

Buzzi RUTH

buzzing ASTIR, NOISE
~ about ADO, ASTIR

"Buzz off!" SCAT, SCRAM, SHOO

B-vitamin
~ source YEAST

bwana
~ in India SAHIB

B'way
see Broadway

by ASOF, PER, VIA
~ any chance EVER
~ itself LONE
~ (prefix) PARA

by ___ FAR, HAND

by ___ (from memory) HEART, ROTE

by ___ and bounds LEAPS

by-___ LINE, NAME

___ by (acquire) COME

___ by (comply with) ABIDE

___ by (manage somehow) GET

___ by (save) PUT, SET

___ by (support) STAND

___ by (visit) DROP

by a ___ shot LONG

by a long ___ SHOT

by and ___ LARGE

___ by a nose WIN

"___ by any other name..." AROSE

"___ by any other name..., A" ROSE

"Bye-bye!" ADIEU, ALOHA, LATER, TATA
~ in French ADIEU
~ in Hawaiian ALOHA
~ in Italian CIAO
~ in Latin AVE, VALE
~ in Spanish ADIOS

Byelorussia
~ once SSR

___ by fire TRIAL

___-by-four TWO

bygone AGO, ELDER, OLD
~ days PAST
~ era THEN, YORE

"___ bygones be bygones" LET

"By gosh!" EGAD

"By Jove!" EGAD

___ by jury TRIAL

bylaw RULE

"___ by Me" STAND

"___ by Myself" ALL

___ Byng Memorial Trophy LADY

BYOB
part of ~ BEER, OWN

bypass AVOID, EVADE, SKIP

by-path TRAIL

by-play ASIDE

Byrd, Admiral
~ book ALONE
~ fox terrier IGLOO

Byrnes EDD

by-road LANE

Byron POET
~ daughter ADA
~ poem LARA
~ work ODE
see also poet

___ by storm TAKE

by-street LANE

byte
~ part BIT
~ starter MEGA

by the ___ BYE

by the ___ token SAME

___ by the bell SAVED

by-the-book STERN

"By the Light of the Silvery ___" MOON

by the same ___ TOKEN

"By the way"
~ line ASIDE

byway ALLEY, LANE, PATH, ROAD, TRAIL

byways
~ (abbr.) STS

byword ADAGE, MOT, TAG

"___ by Your Man" STAND

Byzantine
~ art form ICON
~ empress IRENE

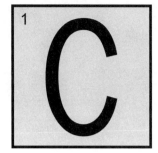

C CLEF, ELEM
~ **major** KEY
~ **minor** KEY
6 for ~ ATNO
high ~ NOTE
vitamin ~ ACID

C ___ **"cat"** ASIN

C ___ **"Charlie"** ASIN

"C' ___ **la vie!"** EST

C- ___ SPAN

Ca ELEM
20 for ~ ATNO

"Ça ___ **" (French revolutionary song)** IRA

CA
~ **clock setting** PDT, PST
~ **101** RTE
see also California

cab HACK, MOTOR, TAXI
~ **alternatives** ELS
~ **clock** METER
~ **cost** FARE
go by ~ RIDE
signal a ~ HAIL

cabal BAND, BLOC, CLAN, GANG, PLOT, RING

" ___ **Caballeros, The"** THREE

cabaret BAR
~ **number** SONG, TUNE

"Cabaret"
~ **actor** GREY
~ **lyricist** EBB
~ **role** EMCEE

cabbage CASH, GELT, MOOLA
~ **cousin** CRESS, KALE
~ **dish** SLAW
~ **in French** CHOU
~ **kin** KALE
~ **unit** HEAD

cabbagehead DOLT

cabbie HACK
~ **income** FARE, TIP

cabby HACK

Cabell ENOS

caber
~ **tosser** SCOT

cabernet WINE

cabin ABODE, CAMP, HOME
~ **material** LOG
~ **wood** PINE

cabin ___ CLASS

cabinet CASE, CHEST
~ **department** LABOR, STATE
~ **wood** ALDER

___ **cabinet** FILE

Cabinet
~ **dept.** INT
~ **post** LABOR
onetime ~ **dept.** HEW

Cabinet-level
~ **org.** USDA

cabinetmaker
~ **wood** EBONY

"Cabin in the ___ **"** SKY

cable CORD, LINE, ROPE, WIRE
~ **award** ACE
~ **car** TRAM
~ **ender** GRAM
~ **network** HBO, TBS, TNT, USA
~ **predecessor** AERIAL
install ~ LAY
power ~ LINE
premium ~ **channel** HBO

cable ___ CAR

cable stitch
make a ~ KNIT

cabochon GEM

caboodle
kit and ~ ALL, ENTIRE

caboose CAR, REAR
~ **position** REAR

Cabot
~ **(abbr.)** STR

Cabot ___ **("Murder, She Wrote" town)** COVE

Cabot Cove
~ **doc** SETH

Cabrini, Mother NUN

cabriolet AUTO, CAR, MOTOR

cacao TREE

___ **cacciatore** ALLA

cache HIDE, KEEP, STASH, STORE, STOW
~ **box** SAFE

cackle BLAB, CROW, CRY

cacoëthes MANIA

cacophony DIN, NOISE

cacti
suitable for ~ ARID, DRY

cactoid DESERT

cactus PLANT
~ **milieu** DESERT
kind of ~ AGAVE

cad HEEL, LOUSE, ROUE, YAHOO
~ **rebuke** SLAP

caddie
~ **bagful** IRONS
~ **burden** BAG
~ **offering** IRON, TEE

Caddoan Indian REE

caddy BIN, CASE, CHEST
~ **contents** TEA

___ **caddy** TEA

Caddy AUTO, CAR

cadence LILT, METER, PULSE, STRESS

cadet
~ **meal** MESS

cadge BEG

Cadillac AUTO, CAR

Cádiz CITY, PORT
where ~ **is** SPAIN
see also Spanish

cadmium METAL

caduceus ROD
org. with a ~ AMA

Caedmon POET
see also poet

Caen
~ **neighbor** STLO
~ **river** ORNE
see also French

caesar LORD, RULER, SALAD, TITLE

Caesar EDILE, ROMAN, SID
~ **city** ROME
~ **contemporary** BERLE
~ **lang.** LAT
~ **partner** COCA
~ **question** ETTU
~ **tongue** LATIN
duds for ~ TOGA
final day for ~ IDES
mo. named for a ~ AUG
opponent of ~ CATO
unlucky day for ~ IDES
see also Latin

Caesar ___ SALAD

" ___ **, Caesar!"** HAIL

Caesarea CITY, PORT

Caesar, Julius ROMAN
early post of ~ EDILE

" ___ **Caesar's ghost!"** GREAT

caesura GAP, LAPSE, REST

café
~ **alternative** THE
~ **attraction** AROMA
~ **customer** EATER
~ **handout** MENU

café ___ NOIR

café au ___ LAIT

cafeteria BAR
~ **item** TRAY
~ **patron** EATER

caffeine
~ **source** COLA

caftan ROBE, WRAP

cage PEN
elevator ~ CAR

___ **cage** RIB

cageling BIRD

cagers
~ **org.** NBA
defunct ~ **org.** ABA

cagey ARCH, SLY

Cagney COP
~ **imitator's word** RAT
~ **role** COHAN

"Cagney & Lacey"
   Mary Beth, on ~ TYNE

Cahuilla TRIBE

caiman
   ~ cousin CROC

Cain ELDEST
   ~ brother ABEL, SETH
   ~ dwelling place NOD
   ~ nephew ENOS
   ~ raiser ADAM, EVE
   ~ victim ABEL
   start of ~'s query AMI

___ Cain RAISE

caique BOAT, SHIP

cairn HEAP

Cairngorm RANGE

Cairo CITY
   ~ waterway NILE
   it ends at ~ OHIO
   opera that premiered in ~ AIDA

caisson
   ~ load AMMO

caitiff BASE, CAD, SNEAK

cajole LURE, URGE

Cajun
   ~ seasoning FILE

cake CLOT, MASS, SET, TREAT
   ~ cousin PIE, TART
   ~ decoration ICING
   ~ decorator ICER
   ~ ingredient YEAST
   ~ starter CUP, HOE, OAT, PAN, TEA
   Castile ~ SOAP
   decorate a ~ ICE
   first name in ~ SARA
   icing on the ~ PLUS
   make ~ BAKE
   nut ~ TORTE
   piece of ~ SLICE, SNAP
   rich ~ TORTE
   rum ~ BABA
   take the ~ WIN

___ cake HOT

___-Cake makeup PAN

cakes
   like many ~ ICED, RICH

"Cakes and ___" ALE

cakewalk DANCE, ROMP

cal.
   ~ notation APPT
   see also calendar

Cal ___ TECH

Cal.
   see California

Calabash MRS

calaboose STIR

Calais CITY, PORT
   see also French

calamine
   ~ ingredient ZINC
   ~ lotion BALM
   ~ target BITE, ITCH

calamitous BAD, DIRE

calamity BANE, EVENT, EVIL, ILL, RUIN, WOE
   financial ~ PANIC

"Calamity ___" JANE

calash HOOD

calaverite ORE

calcaneus HEEL

Calchas SEER

calcine BAKE

calcium METAL
   ~ oxide LIME

calculate ADD

calculated COOL

calculating ACUTE, KEEN

calculation AGE, AREA, RATIO, YIELD
   carbon-dater's ~ AGE
   carpet ~ AREA
   fertilizer-spreader's ~ AREA
   geometry ~ AREA
   interest ~ YIELD
   painter's ~ AREA
   price-earnings ~ RATIO
   seeder's ~ AREA

calculator
   ~ display LED
   ~ key COS, DOT, SIN, SINE, TAN
   ~ work MATH
   use a ~ ADD

___ calculator SOLAR

calculus MATH
   ~ pioneer EULER

Calcutta CITY, PORT
   ~ clothing SARI
   ~ locale INDIA
   Mother of ~ TERESA
   see also Indian

Caldwell, Erskine
   measure for ~ ACRE

calefaction HEAT

calendar AGENDA, BILL
   ~ abbr. APR, AUG, DEC, FRI, MAR, MON, NOV, OCT, SAT, SEPT, SUN, WED
   ~ division DATE, DAY, WEEK, YEAR
   ~ row WEEK
   ~ square DAY
   Chinese ~ animal DOG, GOAT, HARE, HORSE, RAT, SNAKE, TIGER
   Chinese ~ animals OXEN
   church ~ ORDO
   day of the Roman ~ IDES
   social ~ LIST

calendar ___ YEAR

calender PRESS

calends
   ~ follower IDES

calf ANIMAL
   ~ locale LEG
   ~ meat VEAL
   front of the ~ SHIN
   golden ~ IDOL
   look at with ~'s eyes OGLE

calf-length MIDI

calf-roping
   ~ event RODEO

Calgary
   ~ prov. ALB, ALTA

Calgary Stampede RODEO

Calhoun RORY

Caliban
   ~ tormentor ARIEL

calibrate
   ~ anew RESET

calico CAT

Calif.
   ~ neighbor NEV, ORE, OREGON
   ~ school UCLA
   ~ time PDT, PST
   see also California

California STATE
   ~ baseball player ANGEL, PADRE
   ~ city LODI
   ~ county LAKE, NAPA, ORANGE
   ~ fort ORD
   ~ peninsula BAJA
   ~ wine valley NAPA
   animal on ~ flag BEAR
   former ~ congressman BONO
   Northern ~ river EEL

___ California ALTA, BAJA

"___ California" HOTEL

California-Nevada
   ~ lake TAHOE

"California Suite"
   ~ actor ALDA
   ~ director ROSS

caliginous DIM

Caligula CAESAR, ROMAN
   ~ nephew NERO

caliph IMAM, MALE, RULER
   Shi'ite ~ ALI

Calixtus POPE

call DIAL, EVOKE, HAIL, LABEL, NAME, PHONE, ROUSE, STYLE, TAG
   ~ a bet SEE
   ~ a halt to END
   ~ attention to NOTE, REFER, STRESS
   ~ for NEED, PAGE, TAKE, WANT
   ~ (for) ASK
   ~ for takeout EATIN, ORDER
   ~ forth AROUSE, DRAW, EDUCE, EVOKE
   ~ in sick AIL, EVADE
   ~ it a day END, LEAVE, STOP
   ~ off, as a mission ABORT
   ~ on ASK
   ~ one's own ADOPT, HAVE
   ~ opposite PUT
   ~ out BAWL, CRY, YELL
   ~ the bookie BET
   ~ the shots BOSS, LEAD, RULE, RUN
   ~ the tune RULE
   ~ to arms ALERT
   ~ up EVOKE, RING
   ~ with chips SEE
   bird ~ CAW
   bugle ~ TAPS
   castaway's ~ SOS
   cat ~ MEOW, MEW
   cattle ~ MOO
   coin-toss ~ TAILS
   court ~ LET, OUT
   deli-counter ~ NEXT
   diamond ~ SAFE
   dogie ~ MAA
   drill sergeant's ~ HALT, HEP
   emergency ~ SOS
   farmer's wake-up ~ CROW
   grackle's ~ CAW
   hailing ~ AHOY
   intercom ~ PAGE
   naval ~ AVAST
   one way to ~ a waiter AHEM
   palms-down ~ SAFE
   put in a ~ DIAL, PHONE
   ref's ~ TKO
   roll ~ VOTE
   sailor's ~ AHOY
   sheepish ~ BAA
   tennis ~ LET, OUT
   umpire's ~ OUT, SAFE
   wake-up ~ ALARM

call ___ (cancel) OFF

call ___ (shout) OUT

call ___ (summon) FOR, UPON

call ___ day ITA

call ___ question INTO

___ call CLOSE, MAIL, ROLL, TOLL

"Call ___ cab!" MEA

calla ___ LILY

calla lily
   ~ family ARUM

callaloo
   ~ ingredient CRAB

Callao CITY, PORT
   ~ site PERU

Callas DIVA, MARIA
   song for ~ ARIA

called
   also ~ ALIAS
   formerly ~ NEE

"Called for his fiddlers ___" THREE

"___ Called Horse" AMAN

"___ Called Peter" AMAN

"___ Called Shenandoah" AMAN

caller
  identify a ~ TRACE
  sports ~ REF, UMP

"___ Call From a Stranger"
  PHONE

calligrapher
  ~ need INK, NIB, PEN

calligraphy
  ~ line SERIF

calling LINE, TRADE

calling ___ CARD

___-calling NAME

"___ Calling" PARIS

"Calling all cars..." APB

calliope
  ~ power STEAM
  ~ relative ORGAN, PIANO

Calliope MUSE
  ~ sister CLIO, ERATO

Callisto BEAR, MOON

"Call It ___" SLEEP

call it a ___ DAY

call it a day
  ~ on the set WRAP

"Call It Sleep"
  ~ author ROTH

"Call Me ___" ANNA, MADAM

"Call Me Madam"
  ~ director LANG
  inspiration for ~ MESTA

callous HARD

callow RAW

Calloway CAB

"___ Calloways" THOSE

call the ___ TUNE

"___ Call the Whole Thing Off"
  LETS

call-up
  ~ org. SSS
  ~ status ONEA

callus HORN

"___ call us..." DONT

calm ABATE, ALLAY, CLEAR, EASE,
  EVEN, HELP, MILD, ORDER,
  PEACE, SEDATE, SERENE,
  SETTLE, TAME
  ~ the fire DAMP

calmative OPIATE

"Calm down!" EASY

calmness REST

caloric
  less ~, in ads LITE

calorie
  ~ counters' retreat SPA
  ~ cousin BTU

calories
  ~ measure it HEAT

252 ~ BTU
count ~ DIET
loaded with ~ RICH

calotte CAP, HAT

calpac CAP, HAT

Calpurnia
  ~ husband CAESAR

Cal Tech
  ~ grad ENG
  ~ rival MIT

calumet PIPE

calumniate LIBEL, TAINT

calumny LIBEL, LIE, SLUR, SMEAR

Calvados
  capital of ~ CAEN

calve BEAR, DROP

Calvin
  ~ subj. REL

"Calvin and Hobbes"
  ~ bully MOE

Calvino ITALO

calvous BALD

Calypso MOON

calyx CASE, LEAF
  ~ leaf SEPAL

cam GEAR

Camacho AVILA

camarilla CABAL

Camay
  ~ rival DOVE

camber ARCH, BEND, BOW

Cambodia
  ~ continent ASIA
  ~ neighbor LAOS

Cambodian ASIAN
  ~ coin SEN
  ~ neighbor LAO, TAI, THAI

Cambrian ERA

Cambrian Mountains
  ~ site WALES

cambric LINEN, TEA

Cambridge
  ~ academic DON
  ~ grad ENG
  ~ quaff ALE
  ~ univ. MIT

camcorder
  ~ abbr. REC
  ~ format BETA
  use a ~ TAPE

Camden Yards ARENA
  ~ player ORIOLE
  ~ theft BASE
  see also baseball

came
  ~ to rest ALIT, LIT

"___ Came, The" RAINS

"___ came a spider..." ALONG

"___ Came Back" FIVE

"___ Came Bronson" THEN

"___ Came C.O.D., The" BRIDE

"___ Came Home" THREE

"___ Came Jones" ALONG

camel ANIMAL, TAN
  ~ backbreaker STRAW
  ~ country DESERT, SAHARA
  ~ cousin LLAMA
  ~ driver's command KNEEL
  ~ metaphorically SHIP
  ~ stop OASIS
  execute a ~ SKATE
  go by ~ RIDE

camelhair
  ~ fabric ABA

Camellia
  ~ St. ALA

Camelot
  ~ lady ENID

"Camelot"
  ~ (abbr.) MUS
  ~ actor NERO

camels
  where to watch ~ DESERT,
  ICE, RINK

camel's ___ coat HAIR

Camembert
  ~ cousin BRIE

cameo ROLE
  ~ role BIT
  ~ shape OVAL
  ~ stone ONYX

cameos
  do ~ ACT

camera
  ~ part IRIS, LENS
  ~ setting SPEED
  mug for the ~ POSE

Cameroon
  ~ neighbor CHAD

"___ Came Running" SOME

"___ Came You" THEN

Camiletti ROB

Camille
  see French

"Camino ___" REAL

camomile TEA

camouflage COLOR, HIDE

camp BASE, POST, REST
  ~ berth COT
  ~ bosses COS
  ~ craft CANOE
  ~ fixture TENT
  ~ meal MESS
  ~ out TENT
  break ~ LEAVE, MOVE
  opposite ~ ENEMY, FOE
  safari ~ BASE

___ camp BOOT, DAY

Camp JOE

Camp ___ Girl FIRE

___ Camp SPACE

campaign
  ~ donor PAC
  ~ for BOOM
  ~ issue ECON
  ~ pro POL
  ~ promise, often LIE
  ~ staffer AIDE
  ~ tactic SMEAR
  ~ topic ISSUE
  political ~ BID, RACE

campaign button
  ~ word ELECT, VOTE

campaigner
  corporate ~ ADMAN

campaign name
  ~ of 1936 ALF
  ~ of 1952 ADLAI, IKE
  ~ of 1956 ADLAI, IKE
  ~ of 1992 BILL, ROSS
  ~ of 1996 BILL, BOB, DOLE,
  ROSS

campaign poster
  ~ word ELECT, VOTE

Campanella JOE, ROY
  ~ teammate REESE

Campania
  ~ commune NOLA

Campbell EARL, GLEN, KIM, NAOMI
  ~ lid TAM

Camp David
  ~ conferee SADAT

camper ABODE, HOME, MOTOR
  ~ relative VAN

campfire
  ~ remains ASHES

Camp Fire ___ GIRL

camping
  ~ gear TENT

Campion JANE
  ~ film, with "The" PIANO

Campion, Thomas POET
  see also poet

"Camp Meeting, The"
  ~ composer IVES

campo LEA

camporee
  ~ unit TENT

"Camptown ___, De" RACES

campus
  ~ administrator DEAN
  ~ brotherhood FRAT
  ~ building DORM, HALL
  ~ cheer RAH
  ~ female COED
  ~ military org. ROTC
  ~ outcast NERD
  ~ sports org. NCAA
  big man on ~ LION
  militant 1960s ~ org. SDS
  see also college

campy BANAL
~ **perhaps** RETRO

can AXE, BIN, EJECT, FIRE, OUST, SACK, STOP, TIN
~ **covering** LABEL
~ **hold** TAKE
~ **of worms** MESS
~ **opener** TAB
~ **starter** ASH, OIL
do what one ~ TRY
like sardines in a ~ SOLID

___ **can** ASH, TIN

Can.
~ **neighbor** ALAS, AMER, USA
~ **police force** RCMP
~ **province** ALB, ALTA, MAN, ONT, PEI

Canaanite
~ **ancestor** HAM
~ **deity** BAAL

Canada
~ **baseballer** EXPO
~ **neighbor** ALAS, ALASKA, AMER
~ **prov.** ALB, ALTA, MAN, ONT, PEI
~ **river** OTTAWA
~ **tribe** CREE
capital of ~ OTTAWA

Canada ___ GOOSE

Canadian
~ **coin** CENT, DIME
~ **flag feature** LEAF
~ **flier** GOOSE, LOON
~ **Indian** CREE
~ **police force** RCMP
~ **prov.** ALB
~ **town-council official** REEVE
~ **tree** MAPLE

Canadian dollar
bird on a ~ LOON

Canadiens SIX, TEAM
~ **milieu** ICE, RINK
~ **org.** NHL

canaille MOB, ROUT

canal NECK
~ **locale** EAR
~ **site** ROOT
anatomical ~ ITER

___ **canal** EAR

___ **Canal** ERIE

canals
Great Lake ~ SOO

Canandaigua LAKE

canapé
~ **spread** PATE, ROE

canard LIE, RUMOR, TALE

canary BIRD, COLOR, DANCE, PET, WINE
~ **home** CAGE
imitate a ~ SING

Canary Islands
~ **owner** SPAIN

canasta GAME
~ **card** TREY
~ **cousin** GIN
~ **holding** MELD

Canaveral CAPE
~ **org.** NASA

Canberra
see Australian

can-can
~ **locale** PARIS

cancel ABORT, ANNUL, ERASE, REMIT, UNDO, VOID
~ **as a project** SCRAP
~ **debts** CLEAR
~ **suddenly** AXE
~ **the reservations** EATIN

canceled
~ **as a launch** NOGO

canceled check
~ **notation** PAID

cancellation
avoid ~ RENEW

Cancer
~ **symbol** CRAB
sign after ~ LEO

Cancún
~ **currency** PESO
see also Spanish

candelabra LAMP

Candice
~ **father** EDGAR

candid FREE, HONEST, NAIVE, OPEN

"Candid ___" CAMERA

"Candida"
~ **author** SHAW

candidate
~ **concern** ISSUE
~ **roster** SLATE
court-martial ~ AWOL
Dem. ~ **in 1928** AES
Dem. ~ **of the 1950s** AES
Emmy ~ ACTOR
five-time Presidential ~ DEBS
Oscar ~ ACTOR
shearing ~ EWE
Tony ~ ACTOR

candidates
successful ~ INS

"Candid Camera"
~ **request** SMILE

candied SWEET
~ **item** YAM

candle LAMP, TAPER
~ **circler** MOTH
~ **count** AGE
~ **holder** CAKE
burn the ~ **at both ends** LABOR
used a ~ LIT

___ **candle** ROMAN

___-**candle** FOOT

candleberry NUT

"Candle in the Wind"
~ **name** ELTON

candlelit DIM

candlemaker
~ **supply** SUET

candlenut TREE

Candler ASA

candles
burn aromatic ~ CENSE
burn ~ **to** ADORE
make ~ DIP

can-do ABLE

"___ Can Do" ALLI

candy SWEET, TREAT
~ **flavoring** ANISE
~ **maker** MARS, REESE
~ **shape** BAR, DROP
after-dinner ~ MINT
chocolate ~ BAR, KISS
foil-wrapped ~ BAR, KISS
half a ~ BON
hard ~ DROP
pillow ~ MINT

candy ___ CANE

___ **candy** EAR, HARD

___ **Candy (Wonder Woman's friend)** ETTA

"Candy is dandy"
~ **author** NASH

"Candyman"
~ **director** ROSE

"Candy-O"
~ **band** CARS

candy striper AIDE

cane BEAT, ROD, STAVE, STEM
~ **for Chaplin** PROP
~ **product** RUM

Canea
~ **locale** CRETE

___ **canem** CAVE

Canetti ELIAS

Canin ETHAN

canine DOG, TOOTH
~ **bane** FLEA
~ **category** TOY
~ **coat** FUR
~ **command** BEG, COME, HEEL, SIT, STAY
~ **comment** ARF
~ **cousin** MOLAR
~ **covering** CAP, ENAMEL
~ **in Oz** TOTO
~ **registry org.** AKC
~ **restraint** LEASH
~ **warning** SNARL
cinema ~ ASTA, TOTO
comics ~ OTTO
see also dog

Canio
~ **in "Pagliacci"** TENOR

Canis Major
~ **neighbor** ARGO

~ **owner** ORION

canister BIN, JAR

"___ Can I Turn To?" WHO

canned
~ **fish** TUNA

cannel COAL

cannelloni PASTA

"Cannery ___" ROW

"Cannery Row"
~ **actor** NOLTE
~ **character** DORA

Cannes
~ **cover** BERET
~ **thoroughfare** RUE
see also French

canning
~ **item** JAR

cannon GUN
~ **command** FIRE
~ **ender** ADE, EER
~ **roar** BOOM
march up to the ~**'s mouth** BEARD, DARE

___ **cannon** LOOSE, WATER

Cannon DYAN

cannonball TRAIN

"Cannonball Run"
~ **actor** ELAM

cannons
~ **(abbr.)** ARTY

"___ cannot wither her" AGE

canny ARCH, SLY

canoe BOAT
~ **anagram** OCEAN
~ **paddle** OAR

canola OIL

canon CODE, DOGMA, LAW, RULE, TENET
~ **composer** BACH

canon ___ LAW

cañon
~ **feature** TILDE

canonicals ROBE

canonize EXALT

canonized
~ **femme** STE
~ **ones** STS
~ **person** SAINT

canons CREED

canoodle CARESS, PET

can-opener
~ **target** LID

Canopus STAR

canopy ROOF, SHADE, TILT

"___ can say that again!" YOU

cant ARGOT, HEEL, IDIOM, LEAN, LIST, SLANG, SLOPE, TILT, TIP

Cantab
~ **rival** ELI

Cantabrian RANGE

Cantabrian Mountains
~ **location** IBERIA
~ **river** EBRO

Cantabrigian
~ **river** CAM

cantaloupe MELON

cantankerous MEAN, TESTY, UGLY
~ **one** CRAB

cantata SONG
~ **maestro** BACH
~ **tune** ARIA

"___ can't be!" THIS

"___ Can't Buy You Love" MAMA

"___ Can't Cheat an Honest Man" YOU

canted ATILT

canteen BAR
~ **initials** USO

canter GAIT, LOPE, PACE, POST, RUN, TROT

Canterbury
~ **locale** KENT

"Canterbury ___, A" TALE

"Canterbury Tales" POEM
~ **beverage** MEAD
~ **character** NUN, REEVE

"___ Can't Have Everything" YOU

"___ Can't Have You" IFI

canticle ODE, PAEAN, SONG

cantina
~ **snack** TACO

___ canto BEL

canton
Swiss ~ BERN, URI

Canton
~ **ender** ESE
~ **state** OHIO

cantonment CAMP

Cantor EDDIE
Mrs. ~ IDA

Cantrell LANA

"___ Can't Take It With You" YOU

Canucks SIX, TEAM
~ **milieu** ICE, RINK
~ **org.** NHL

Canute
~ **foe** OLAF, OLAV

canvas SAIL, SHEET
~ **abode** TENT
~ **cover** TARP
~ **holder** EASEL
~ **support** EASEL, MAST

___ canvas (in tents) UNDER

canvases ART

canvass POLL

canyon ABYSS, GAP
~ **edge** LIP, RIM
~ **phenomenon** ECHO
form a ~ ERODE

Canyon STEVE

canzone LAY, ODE, SONG

canzonet SONG

cap ACME, APEX, BERET, HAT, LID, LIMIT
~ **and gown** ROBE
~ **gun** TOY
~ **part** BILL
cloth ~ BERET
dunce ~ CONE
French ~ BERET
Groucho Marx ~ BERET
Guardian Angel ~ BERET
jaunty ~ BERET
kind of ~ KNEE
Picasso ~ BERET
polar ~ ICE
set one's ~ **for** WOO
Skye ~ TAM
soft ~ TAM
Special Forces ~ BERET
tasseled ~ TAM
tower ~ SPIRE
visorless ~ BERET

cap ___ GUN

___ cap ICE, INKY, POLAR

cap-a-___ PIE

Capablanca
~ **game** CHESS

capable ABLE, ADEPT, FIT, GOOD
~ **of** UPTO
~ **of (suffix)** ILE
isn't ~ **of** CANT
more ~ ABLER

capacious AMPLE, BIG, LARGE, WIDE

capacitate ENABLE

capacity LIMIT, ROLE, ROOM, SIZE, SPACE
have ~ **for** SIT
of large ~ AMPLE
unit of ~ LITER

___ Capades ICE

cap and gown
~ **wearer** GRAD

caparison ADORN, ARRAY, ATTIRE, FIT, GARB, TRAPS

cape LAND, NECK, NESS, SPIT, WRAP
Alaskan ~ NOME
Carolina ~ FEAR
Massachusetts ~ ANN, COD
New Jersey ~ MAY
Seward Peninsula ~ NOME
South American ~ HORN

Cape ___ HORN

Cape ___, Mass. ANN, COD

Cape ___, N.C. FEAR

Cape ___, N.J. MAY

"Cape ___" FEAR

Cape Canaveral
~ **org.** NASA
~ **st.** FLA
beach near ~ COCOA

Cape Cod
~ **sight** DUNE

"Cape Cod Lighter, The"
~ **author** OHARA

"Capeesh?" DIG

"Cape Fear"
~ **actor** NOLTE
~ **actress** LANGE

Capek
~ **drama** RUR

Capella STAR

Cape of ___ Hope GOOD

Cape of Good ___ HOPE

caper ANTIC, DANCE, DIDO, LARK, LEAP, PLANT, PLAY, ROMP, SKIP

Cape Roca
~ **region** IBERIA

Cape Town CITY
~ **mountain** TABLE

Cape Wrangell
~ **location** ATTU

___ capita PER

capital ACE, ASSET, FIRST, GOOD, GREAT, MAIN, MAJOR, NEAT, SEAT, TOPS
~ **ender** ISM
African ~ ACCRA, CAIRO, DAKAR, RABAT
ancient ~ **of Japan** EDO
Asian ~ HANOI
Calvados ~ CAEN
Canadian ~ OTTAWA
Canea is its ~ CRETE
cold-war ~ BONN
European ~ BERN, OSLO, PARIS, RIGA, ROME
former ~ **of Yemen** ADEN
France ~ PARIS
Gem State ~ BOISE
Ghana ~ ACCRA
Gold Coast ~ ACCRA
Idaho ~ BOISE
Italy ~ ROME
its ~ **is Lomé** TOGO
Latvia ~ RIGA
make ~ **out of** AVAIL, USE
Maldives ~ MALE
Manche ~ STLO
Mideast ~ SANA
Morocco ~ RABAT
Muscat is its ~ OMAN
Norway ~ OSLO
Oregon ~ SALEM
Peru ~ LIMA
Red River ~ HANOI
shogun ~ EDO
South American ~ LIMA
southwestern Asian ~ ADEN

Switzerland ~ BERN
Tibet ~ LHASA
Ukraine ~ KIEV
Vietnam ~ HANOI
Western Samoa ~ APIA
Yemen ~ SANA

capital ___ GAIN

Capitals SIX, TEAM
~ **milieu** ICE, RINK
~ **org.** NHL

capitation RATE

Capitol
~ **body** SENATE
~ **gofer** PAGE
~ **sight** MALL
~ **topper** DOME
~ **VIP** REP, SEN

Capitoline
~ **site** ROME

capitulate BEND, BOW, DEFER, YIELD

caplet PILL

"Cap'n ___" (Joseph Lincoln work) ERI

capo DON
da ~ AGAIN

capon BIRD, MALE, MEAT

Capone
~ **and others** ALS
~ **foe** NESS
~ **nemesis** IRS, NESS
where ~ **served time** ATLANTA

capote CAPE

Capp ANDY
~ **and others** ALS

Capp, Al
~ **adjective** LIL
~ **character** ABNER
~ **hyena** LENA

Capp, Andy
~ **wife** FLO

cappelletti PASTA

cappuccino
place for a ~ CAFE

Capri ISLE
~ **(abbr.)** ISL
island near ~ ELBA
see also Italian

Capriati
~ **foe** SELES

Capricorn GOAT, SIGN

"Capricorn ___" ONE

capriole LEAP

capri pants
~ **feature** SLIT

Caps SIX, TEAM
~ **milieu** ICE, RINK
~ **org.** NHL

Capshaw KATE

capsize KEEL, SINK, TIP, UPEND, UPSET

capstan CRANE

capstone ACME

capsule DOSE, PILL, SAC

___ capsule SPACE, TIME

capt.
~ **heading** ENE, ESE, NNE, NNW, SSE, SSW, WNW, WSW
~ **superior** COL

captain LEAD, RANK
~ **book** LOG
~ **command** AVAST
~ **destination** PORT
~ **heading** ALEE
~ **insignia** BAR
~ **milieu** MAIN, OCEAN, SEA
~ **of industry** BARON
~ **place** ASEA, ATSEA
~ **station** HELM
~ **superior** MAJOR
"20,000 Leagues" ~ NEMO
crazed ~ AHAB
fictional ~ NEMO
flight ~ PILOT
former Davis Cup ~ ASHE
obsessed ~ AHAB
"Show Boat" ~ ANDY

"Captain, The"
wife of ~ TONI

Captain ___ (Superman parody) NICE

Captain America HERO

Captain Blood HERO

"Captain Blood"
Basil's ~ **costar** ERROL

"Captain Carey, ___" USA

"Captain January"
Temple's ~ **dance partner** EBSEN

Captain Marvel HERO

Captain Midnight HERO

captain's ___ MAST

"Captains Courageous"
~ **character** TROOP

captious TESTY

captivate DRAW, ENDEAR, LURE, TAKE

captivated RAPT

captivating SWEET

captive
~ **worker** SLAVE
hold ~ TAKE

"Captive ___" HEART

capture ARREST, BAG, CAGE, GAIN, GET, GRAB, LAND, NAB, NAIL, NET, SNARE, TAKE, WIN
~ **in a way** ROPE
elude ~ HIDE

capuche HOOD

capuchin ANIMAL

Capulet
~ **to Montague** FOE

capybara ANIMAL

car AUTO, EDSEL, FIAT, GEO, LIMO, MOTOR, NASH, NEO, OLDS, REO, SEDAN
~ **ad abbr.** EPA
~ **bar** AXLE
~ **buyer need** LOAN
~ **coat** WRAP
~ **dealer sign** SOLD, USED
~ **dealer's offering** LEASE
~ **document** LEASE
~ **ender** HOP, LOAD, PORT
~ **engine part** HOSE
~ **fuel** GAS
~ **in a 1964 tune** GTO
~ **insurance case** DENT
~ **job** LUBE
~ **loan letters** APR
~ **metal** STEEL
~ **necessity** SPARE
~ **owner's dread** DENT
~ **parker** VALET
~ **part** AXLE, HOOD, MOTOR, TIRE
~ **path** ROAD
~ **scar** DENT
~ **security device** ALARM
~ **starter** FLAT, HAND, RACE, SIDE
~ **track** RUT
~ **trunk, in London** BOOT
~ **with a bar** LIMO
~ **with Teletouch transmission** EDSEL
armored ~ TANK
bar in a ~ AXLE
British ~ **part** TYRE
cable ~ TRAM
chauffeured ~ LIMO
classic ~ CORD, NASH, REO
closed ~ SEDAN
clunky ~ LEMON
coal ~ TRAM
defective ~ LEMON
drive the getaway ~ ABET
European ~ FIAT
exec's ~ LIMO
fast ~ RACER
Formula One ~ RACER
GM ~ GEO, OLDS
go by ~ MOTOR
hired ~ TAXI
Italian ~ FIAT
Italian sports ~, **informally** ALFA
luxury ~ LIMO
mine ~ TRAM
passenger ~ SEDAN
prowl ~ MOTOR
rundown ~ CRATE, HEAP
showroom ~ DEMO
sports ~ MOTOR
sports ~ **of old** GTO
star's ~ LIMO
stock ~ MOTOR, RACER
test ~ DEMO
touring ~ SEDAN
used ~ DEMO
VIP's ~ LIMO
see also auto

car ___ COAT, POOL, SEAT, WASH

___ car CABLE

Cara IRENE

"Cara ___" MIA

caracal CAT

Caracas CITY
see also Spanish

carafe
~ **kin** EWER

caramel
~ **custard** FLAN

carapace PLATE, SHELL

caravan PARADE
~ **animal** CAMEL
~ **halt** OASIS

caravansary HOTEL, INN
~ **site** OASIS

caravel BOAT, SHIP

caraway SEED
~ **holder** RYE

carbine GUN, RIFLE
British ~ STEN

carbo-___ LOAD

carbohydrate PASTA
~ **(suffix)** OSE

carbolic ACID

carbon
~ **compound** ENOL, ESTER
~ **deposit** SOOT
~ **dioxide** GAS
~ **monoxide** GAS
charge with ~ **dioxide** AERATE
form of ~ COAL

carbon ___ PAPER

carbon-___ DATE

carbonado MEAT

carbonate SALT

carbonated
~ **drink** COLA, POP

carbonated ___ WATER

carbonation GAS

carbon compound
~ **suffix** ENE

carbon dating
~ **calculation** AGE

carbon dioxide
add ~ AERATE

carbon-14
take a ~ **measurement** DATE

carbonic ACID

carbonize CHAR, HEAT

carbonized
~ **plants** PEAT

card COMB, NOTE, PANIC, RIOT, WAG, WIT
~ **catalog** LIST

car ___
~ **catalogue datum** TITLE
~ **collection** HAND
~ **combo** MELD, PAIR
~ **dealer's device** SHOE
~ **dealer's offering** CUT
~ **game** CANASTA, FARO, GIN, LOO, MONTE, PEDRO, SKAT, STUD, UNO, WAR
~ **game stake** ANTE
~ **player's yell** GIN
~ **spot** PIP
~ **up the sleeve** ACE
blackjack ~ ACE, TEN
canasta ~ TREY
clairvoyant's ~ TAROT
courtesy ~ PASS
drawing ~ LEAD, LURE, STAR
face ~ HONOR
high ~ ACE
honor ~ ACE, TEN
kids' ~ **game** WAR
low ~ TREY, TWO
lowest pinochle ~ NINE
low ~ **in skat** SEVEN
Monopoly ~ DEED
pinochle ~ TEN
playing ~ HEART, SPADE, TREY
poker ~ ACE, NINE, TREY
press ~ PASS
seer's ~ TAROT
select a ~ DRAW
top ~ ACE
winning ~, **in bridge** ENTRY

___ card CUE, FACE, HOLE, IDIOT, POST, SMART

cardboard PAPER
~ **cover** LINER
framer's ~ MAT

card-carrying HONEST

Cardiff CITY, PORT

cardigan
craft a ~ KNIT

cardinal BIRD, COLOR, FIRST, KEY, MAIN, MALE, POLAR, RANK, RED
~ **color** RED
~ **home** NEST
~ **point** EAST, WEST
~ **point suffix** ERN

cardinals
~ **(abbr.)** NOS

Cardinals ELEVEN, NINE, TEAM
~ **org.** NFL

cardiologist
~ **concern** AORTA, HEART

___-card monte THREE

cards
hand out ~ DEAL
in the ~ SURE
mystical ~ TAROT
three, in ~ TREY

Cards ELEVEN, NINE, TEAM
~ **org.** NFL

Carducci, Giosuè POET
see also poet

care HEED
~ **for** ATTEND, KEEP, LIKE,

LOVE, NURSE, SEETO, SERVE, SIT, TEND, TREAT
~ for a bed WEED
~ for animals WATER
~ for plants WATER
~ (to) LIKE
examine with ~ SIFT
freedom from ~ EASE
handle with ~ CARESS
personal ~ worker AIDE
take ~ of ATTEND, FEED, MEET, SEETO

___ care DAY, TAKE

CARE
~ package AID

___-care center DAY

careen HEEL, LEAN, LIST, TIP, VEER

careening ALIST

career LIFE, LINE, RACE, RUN, SPEED, TRADE
~ starter GRAD

carefree EASY
~ episode LARK

careful LEERY, WARY

"Careful, He Might ___ You" HEAR

"Careful, He Might Hear ___" YOU

___ care in the world NOTA

careless LOOSE, MESSY, RASH
become ~ NOD

"Careless Love"
~ author ADAMS

___ care of TAKE

caress FEEL, LOVE, NECK, PAT, PET

Carew ROD

Carew, Thomas POET
see also poet

Carey DIANE, DREW

Carey, Mariah
~ song HERO

"Car 54, Where ___ You?" ARE

cargo HAUL, LOAD
~ area HOLD
~ hauler VAN
~ ship OILER
~ unit TON
"Edmund Fitzgerald" ~ ORE
Great Lakes ~ ORE
load ~ STOW
take on ~ LADE
tanker ~ OIL
tram ~ ORE

Caribbean SEA
~ country CUBA, HAITI
~ liquor RUM
~ resort ARUBA
~ volcano PELEE

Cariboo RANGE

caribou ANIMAL, DEER
~ cousin DEER, ELK, MOOSE

caricature APE
~ feature NOSE

caring LOVE

carioca DANCE
~ relative SAMBA

Carioca
~ home RIO

Cariou LEN

caritas LOVE

Carl SAGAN
~ son ROB

Carla
~ in "Cheers" RHEA

___ Carlo MONTE

Carlos
see Spanish

Carlos Saavedra ___ LAMAS

Carlson ARNE

Carlton STEVE

car-maintenance
~ job LUBE

carmaker OLDS

Carman, Bliss POET
see also poet

Carme MOON

Carmelite NUN

Carmen ERIC
see also Spanish

"Carmen" OPERA
Don José, in ~ TENOR

"Carmen Sandiego"
~ feature MAP

Carmichael IAN

carmine COLOR, RED

Carnaby Street
~ locale SOHO

carnage GORE

carnallite ORE

carnation
~ spot LAPEL

carnauba PALM

Carnegie DALE

Carnegie ___ HALL, TECH

carnegiea
~ and others CACTI

carnelian GEM, SARD

Carnera
he KO'd ~ BAER

Carnes KIM

Carnesecca LOU

Carney ART

carnival FAIR
~ attraction RIDE
~ prop STILT

Carnival
~ locale RIO

"Carnival!"
~ character LILI

"___ Carnival, The" BIG

carnivore
~ quest MEAT
~ target PREY
large ~ LION, PUMA, TIGER
laughing ~ HYENA

carnotite ORE

carob TREE

carol NOEL, SING, SONG, TUNE
~ syllables FALA, LALA
~ word TIS

Carol ALT, KANE, REED

caroler ALTO, BASS, TENOR

Carolina
~ cape FEAR

Carolina ___ ASH, WREN

"Carolina ___" MOON

Caroline
aunt of ~ ETHEL, PAT

"Caroline in the City"
~ character DEL

Caroline Islands
one of the ~ YAP

caroling
go ~ SING

"___ & Carol & Ted & Alice" BOB

carom
light ~ KISS

Caron, Leslie
~ film LILI
see also French

"Caro nome" ARIA

___ carotene BETA

carousal SPREE, TEAR

carouse PLAY, REVEL

carousel RIDE

"___ Carousel" ONA

carp NAG, RAIL
~ starter ENDO

Carpathian
~ river ODER

Carpathians RANGE

"Carpe ___!" DIEM

carpenter ANT, BEE
~ garment APRON
~ groove DADO
~ in an 1859 novel BEDE
~ need NAIL
~ strip LATH
~ tool ADZE, PLANE, SAW
~ woe KNOT

Carpenter SCOTT

carpentry TRADE
~ machine LATHE

carpet PAPER, RUG
~ calculation AREA
~ feature NAP, PILE
kind of ~ SHAG
roll out the red ~ GREET

___ carpet RED

carpeting
install ~ LAY

carpet maker
~ need LOOM

carpus BONE
~ neighbor ULNA

carrack BOAT, SHIP

car radio
~ feature SCAN

car registration
~ datum COLOR

carrel DESK, STALL

car rental
~ name ALAMO, AVIS

Carreras TENOR

Carrere TIA

Carrey, Jim
~ in a 1997 movie LIAR

carriage AIR, GAIT, MIEN, POSE, SET
~ for two SHAY
~ horse HACK
~ part AXLE
baby ~ PRAM
Holmes ~ SHAY
horse and ~ RIG
horseless ~ AUTO, CAR
open ~ SHAY
two-wheeled ~ GIG

carriage ___ TRADE

carrick
~ bend KNOT

Carrie NYE

carried
~ away ELATED, LOST, RAPT

carrier
ale ~ TAP
brick ~ HOD
burlap ~ SACK
coal ~ CAR, SCOW
cold-weather ~ SLED
commuter ~ AUTO, BUS, CAR, TRAIN
fuel ~ OILER
letter ~ STAMP
letter ~'s beat ROUTE
Mideast ~ ELAL
ore ~ SCOW
purse ~ STRAP
sleeping-sickness ~ TSETSE
trait ~ GENE
water ~ HOSE, PAIL, PIPE

___ carrier BALL, MAIL

___-carrier SPEAR

carries
~ out DOES
one that ~ (suffix) FER

Carrillo LEO

Carroll LEO, LEWIS
~ **contemporary** LEAR
~ **heroine** ALICE

carrot ROOT
~ **family herb** ANISE
~ **on occasion** LURE

carroty RED

carry BEAR, CART, HAUL, KEEP, LUG, SELL, TAKE, TOTE
~ **away** CART
~ **off** STEAL, TAKE
~ **on** BEAR, EMOTE, RAGE, RAMP, RANT, RAVE, WAGE
~ **on a trade** PLY
~ **oneself** BEAR
~ **out** ACT, ENACT
~ **over** KEEP, SAVE
~ **the day** WIN
~ **the torch for** ADORE, PINE
~ **weight** RATE
runners ~ it SLED

carry __ (execute) OUT

carry __ (postpone) OVER

carry __ (transport) AWAY

carry __ (win) OFF

carryall TOTE

carrying
~ **a grudge** SORE
~ **a weapon** ARMED

__-carrying CARD

carry-on BAG

carryout MEAL

carry the __ BALL, DAY

cars
letters on some race ~ STP
line of ~ MAKE
railroad ~ TRAIN
street prohibiting ~ MALL

"Cars __ Ate Paris, The" THAT

"__ Cars" USED

Carson KIT
~ **predecessor** PAAR
~ **successor** LENO
composer of ~ theme ANKA

Carson City
~ **st.** NEV
lake near ~ TAHOE

Carson, Johnny EMCEE, HOST

Carson, Kit
~ **homesite** TAOS

"Cars That __ Paris, The" ATE

"Cars That Ate __, The" PARIS

"Cars That Ate Paris, The"
~ **director** WEIR

cart
~ **away** HAUL
~ **leader** HORSE
~ **part** AXLE
~ **pullers** OXEN

carte MENU
give ~ blanche LET

__ carte ALA

carte blanche RUN

carte du jour MENU

cartel BLOC, PACT, POOL, RING
oil ~ OPEC

Carter AMY, NELL

Carter, Benny
~ **sax** ALTO

Carter, Howard
~ **1922 discovery** TUT

Carter, Jimmy
~ **daughter** AMY
~ **middle name** EARL

Carter, Nick AGENT, SPY

Cartesian
~ **conclusion** IAM
~ **connection** ERGO
~ **line** AXIS

Carthage
ancient city near ~ UTICA
queen of ~ DIDO

cartogram MAP

cartographer
~ **abbr.** ALT, ATL, ISL, LAT, MTS, PAC, STR, TER, TERR
~ **product** ATLAS, MAP
~ **speck** CAY, ISLE, KEY

cartographic
~ **closeup** INSET

carton CASE

cartoonist
~ **need** ERASER, INK
nineteenth-century political ~ NAST

cartouche OVAL, SEAL, STAMP

cartridge SHELL

Cartwright ADAM, BEN, JOE

Cartwright, Ben
~ **eldest** ADAM
~ **portrayer** LORNE
~ **youngest** JOE

caruncle CREST, NODE

Caruso TENOR
solo for ~ ARIA

"__ Caruso, The" GREAT

carve ETCH, HEW, SCORE, SLICE
~ **up** ALLOT

"Carve __ Name With Pride" HER

carved
~ **gem** CAMEO
Crusoe ~ one CANOE

"Carve Her __ With Pride" NAME

"Carve Her Name With __" PRIDE

carver
~ **medium** JADE, SOAP

Carver STEVE

Carvey APER, DANA

carving
Aleut ~ TOTEM
Chinese ~ material JADE
genealogical ~ TOTEM
Hawaiian ~ material LAVA
Indian ~ TOTEM

car wash
~ **step** RINSE

Cary
~ **ex** DYAN

caryatid POST

casa
~ **material** ADOBE

casaba MELON

Casablanca CITY, PORT
port near ~ RABAT

"Casablanca"
~ **actor** LORRE, RAINS
~ **role** ILSA, SAM
~ **setting** CAFE

Casals PABLO
~ **instrument** CELLO

Casanova RAKE, ROMEO, ROUE, SATYR

"Casanova's __ Night" BIG

Casbah
~ **place** ORAN

cascade POUR, RUN, STREAM

Cascades RANGE
~ **peak** HOOD

Casco BAY

Casco Bay
~ **locale** MAINE

case BAG, CRATE, SUIT
~ **breaker** CLUE
~ **for a vet** LICE
~ **starter** SHOW, SLIP, STAIR, SUIT
attache ~ BAG
car insurance ~ DENT
conclude one's ~ REST
court ~ RES, TRIAL
decorative ~ ETUI
display ~ STAND
get on one's ~ NAG
gram. ~ NOM
hard-luck ~ LOSER
hear a ~ TRY
in ~ LEST
in that ~ THEN
jewelry ~ SAFE
needle ~ ETUI
notions ~ ETUI
nut ~ SHELL
personal-articles ~ ETUI
state one's ~ ARGUE, PLEAD
sundries ~ ETUI
that being the ~ ERGO, THEN
toiletries ~ ETUI
vanity ~ BAG

wind up a ~ SETTLE

__ case NUT, TEST

"Case of Samples, A"
~ **author** AMIS

cases
in many ~ OFT, OFTEN

__-case scenario BEST

Casey BEN
~ **club** BAT
~ **org.** CIA

"Casey at the __" BAT

cash ASSET, COIN, MOOLA
~ **advance** LOAN
~ **ender** IER
~ **machine** ATM
~ **on hand** ASSET
~ **register** TILL
~ **stash** IRA
~ **substitute** IOU
blow ~ SPEND
bundle of ~ WAD
Colombian ~ PESO
Cuban ~ PESO
Kyoto ~ YEN
petty ~ COIN
short of ~ NEEDY
Yiddish ~ GELT
see also coin, money

cash __ BAR, COW, CROP

Cash NORM, PAT

cash-back
~ **offer** REBATE

cashbox SAFE, TILL

cashew NUT, TREE

cashier EJECT, FIRE, OUST, SACK
24-hr. ~ ATM

cashless
~ **transaction** SWAP, TRADE

casing COAT, SKIN

casino
~ **action** BET
~ **city** RENO
~ **data** ODDS
~ **furnishing** TABLE
~ **game** FARO, KENO
~ **implement** RAKE
~ **maximum** LIMIT
~ **st.** NEV
Nevada ~ SAHARA, SANDS

"Casino Royale"
~ **heavy** LORRE

cask CASE, KEG, TUN, VAT
~ **part** STAVE

casmerodius albus EGRET

Caspar
~ **and others** MAGI
like ~ WISE

Caspian SEA
~ **neighbor** ARAL

Caspian Sea LAKE
~ **catch** CARP
~ **feeder** URAL
~ **land** IRAN

casque ARMOR

Cass MAMA

Cassandra SEER
   brother of ~ PARIS

Cassatt
   ~ contemporary DEGAS

casserole DISH, PAN
   ~ cover LID
   ~ ingredient TUNA
   cook a ~ BAKE

cassette TAPE
   ~ alternative DISC
   ~ starter AUDIO

cassette deck
   ~ button EJECT, REC, STOP

Cassidy TED

Cassidy, Hopalong HERO

Cassin RENE

Cassini OLEG
   ~ creation DRESS

Cassio
   ~ adversary IAGO

Cassiopeia
   ~ component STAR

cassiterite ORE

Cassius CLAY, ROMAN
   ~ and company CABAL

"___ Cassius Clay" AKA

cassock ROBE

cassowary
   ~ look-alike EMU

cast HUE, HURL, ILK, MIEN, MOLD,
   SORT, STAMP
   ~ around for HUNT, SEEK
   ~ aside SCRAP
   ~ down DASH
   ~ forth EMIT, SPEW
   ~ in the same mold as LIKE
   ~ member ACTOR
   ~ metal INGOT
   ~ off EGEST, PEEL, SAIL, SHED
   ~ one's ballot ELECT, POLL,
     VOTE
   ~ out EGEST, EJECT, EXILE
   ~ slot ROLE
   ~ starter FORE, MIS, OVER,
     TELE, TYPE
   be in a ~ ACT
   head the ~ STAR
   something to ~ LINE, ROLE,
     VOTE

cast ___ (discard) OFF

cast ___ (search) ABOUT

cast-___ stomach IRON

cast a ___ over PALL

"Casta Diva" ARIA

castaway
   ~ call SOS
   ~ home ISLE
   ~ transport RAFT

castaways
   where ~ are cast ASHORE

caste CLASS, ESTATE, ORDER
   ~ member HINDU

Castel Gandolfo
   ~ locale ITALY
   ~ resident POPE

Castellammare
   ~ di Stabia SPA

Castellammare di Stabia SPA

Castellaneta DAN

caster
   ~ need LINE, REEL, ROD

castigate LASH, RIP

Castile
   ~ cake SOAP
   city of old ~ AVILA
   see also Spanish

Castilla
   see Spanish

casting INGOT

casting out ___ NINES

castle ABODE, HOME, KEEP
   ~ defense MOAT
   ~ in chess ROOK
   ~ in Spain DREAM
   ~ in the air DREAM
   ~ section KEEP
   ~ worker SERF

___ castle SAND

Castle IRENE

"___ Castle" MANS

castle in ___ SPAIN

"Castle in the ___" DESERT

Castle, Nick
   ~ film of 1989 TAP

"Castle of Indolence, The" POEM

Castle of Saint ___ ELMO

castles
   where ~ move CHESS

"___ Castles" ICE

castoffs RAGS

"___ cast of thought" PALE

cast one's ___ with LOT

castor BEAN, HAT, OIL

Castor STAR
   ~ mother LEDA
   ~ slayer IDAS
   ~ to Leda SON
   ~ to Pollux TWIN

Castorini, Loretta
   ~ portrayer CHER

Castro
   ~ country CUBA
   see also Spanish

casual EASY, FREE, LOOSE, ODD
   ~ topper CAP
   ~ wear TEE

casually IDLY

casualness EASE

"Casualties of War"
   ~ locale NAM

casus belli EVENT

cat ANIMAL, GENET, LION, OCELOT,
   PET, PUMA, TIGER, TOM
   ~ call MEOW, MEW
   ~ coat FUR
   ~ doc VET
   ~ ender BIRD, BOAT, CALL, KIN,
     NAP, NIP, TAIL
   ~ fit SPASM
   ~ foot PAW
   ~ hangout ALLEY
   ~ in French CHAT
   ~ lives NINE
   ~ maneuver ARCH
   ~ murmur PURR
   ~ palm PAD
   ~ quarry MOUSE, RAT
   ~ starter BEAR, BOB, HEP,
     POLE, TOM
   ~ to a flea HOST
   ~ tormentor FLEA
   ~ toy YARN
   Asian ~ TIGER
   bell the ~ BEARD, DARE
   big ~ LION, OCELOT, PUMA,
     TIGER
   black ~ OMEN
   breed of ~ REX
   fat ~ NOB
   **let the ~ out of the
     bag** LEAK, TELL
   like an alley ~ FERAL
   male ~ TOM
   ring-tailed ~ GENET
   tawny ~ LION

___ cat ALLEY, FAT, HEP, TIGER

___-cat ONEA

"Cat ___ Hot Tin Roof" ONA

"Cat ___ Mouse" AND

"Cat ___ the Canary, The" AND

"Cat ___ the Fiddle, The" AND

"___ Cat" TOP

CAT ___ SCAN

Catalan
   **painter of ~
     landscapes** MIRO

Catalina
   ~ (abbr.) ISL

___ Catalina Island SANTA

catalog LIST, ROLL, SORT
   ~ items ADS
   ~ subject MODEL

___ catalog CARD

cataloguer
   early ~ SEARS

Catalonian
   ~ river EBRO

catalyst AGENT
   adrenaline ~ FEAR

catamaran RAFT

catamount ANIMAL, PUMA

cat and ___ MOUSE

Catania
   view from ~ ETNA

catapult HURL
   ~ missile STONE

cataract
   ~ site LENS

catastrophe EVIL, RUIN

catastrophic BAD

"Cat Ballou"
   **Stubby's singing partner in
     ~** NAT

catbird ___ SEAT

catcall GIBE, HISS, HOOT, NOISE

catch ARREST, BAG, CLASP, GAME,
   GET, GRAB, GRASP, HAUL, HEAR,
   LAND, NAB, NAIL, NET, SNAG,
   SNARE, TAKE, TRAP, TRIP
   ~ a bug AIL
   ~ as a criminal NAB
   ~ as a dogie LASSO
   ~ as game BAG
   ~ a wave RIDE
   ~ cattle ROPE
   ~ cold AIL
   ~ flies SHAG
   ~ forty winks NAP
   ~ holder CREEL
   ~ hold of GRAB
   ~ off guard AMAZE
   ~ on DIG, GRASP, SEE
   ~ on to GET, KNOW
   ~ phrase SAW
   ~ redhanded NAIL
   ~ sight of EYE, SEE, SPOT
   ~ someone's eye DRAW
   ~ some rays BASK, SUN, TAN
   ~ some z's NAP, REST, SLEEP
   ~ suddenly SPEAR
   ~ up GAIN
   angler's ~ HAUL
   dolphin-safe ~ TUNA
   fail to ~ MISS
   sniggler's ~ EEL

___ catch FAIR

"Catch a Falling ___" STAR

catchall
   ~ abbr. ETAL, ETC
   ~ category OTHER
   ~ term ETAL

catch-as-catch-can LOOSE

catcher
   ~ place RYE
   ~ protection PAD
   ~ spot HOME
   bronco ~ LASSO, NOOSE
   butterfly ~ NET
   cow ~ LASSO, RIATA
   fish ~ NET
   fly ~ WEB
   formula ~ BIB
   man behind the ~ UMP
   mouse ~ TRAP
   pass ~ END

"Catcher in the ___, The"
  quotable ~ YOGI
  tuna ~ NET
  wild-horse ~ LASSO, RIATA
  wind ~ SAIL

"Catcher in the ___, The" RYE

catching
  ~ some z's ABED
  start ~ up GAIN

___-catching EYE

catchpenny BASE, MEAN

catch some ___ RAYS

catch-22 BIND

"Catch-22"
  ~ character MAJOR, ORR

catchword MOT
  1960s ~ PEACE

catechism TEST

catechize ASK, TEST

categorical FLAT, UTTER

categorize FILE, LABEL, ORDER,
  PEG, RATE, SORT, TYPE

category CLASS, GENRE, ILK,
  RANK, SORT, TIER, TYPE
  ~ of artistic work GENRE
  catchall ~ OTHER

catena LINE

catenary ARCH, BOW

catenation LINE

cater FEED

caterpillar
  ~ construction TENT
  tent ~ PEST

___ caterpillar TENT

caterwaul BAWL, CRY, MEOW,
  MEW, NOISE

caterwauling DIN

catfight ROW, SETTO, SPAT

Catfish Row
  ~ resident BESS

Cathay
  ~ visitor POLO

cathedra SEAT

cathedral SEE
  ~ area APSE, NAVE
  ~ feature ARCH, ICON
  ~ head DEAN
  ~ seating PEW
  ~ topper SPIRE
  British ~ town ELY
  Spanish ~ town AVILA

Catherine PARR, STE

Catherine the Great
  ~ successor PAUL

cathode-___ tube RAY

Catholic
  ~ service MASS

"Cathy" STRIP

"Cat in the ___, The" HAT

"Cat in the Hat, The"
  ~ author SEUSS

catkins
  tree with ~ ALDER

catlike AGILE

catnap REST, SLEEP

catnip HERB

Cato ORATOR, ROMAN
  garment for ~ TOGA
  see also Latin

"Cat on a ___ Tin Roof" HOT

"Cat on a Hot ___ Roof" TIN

"Cat on a Hot Tin ___" ROOF

cat-o'-nine-tails LASH

cats
  like some ~ COOL, HEP
  mice, to ~ PREY
  rain ~ and dogs TEEM

cat's ___, the MEOW

cat's-___ PAW

cat's-___ marble EYE

"Cats"
  ~ inspiration ELIOT
  ~ monogram TSE

cat's-cradle GAME

cat's-eye GEM
  ~ alternative AGATE

Catskills RANGE

cat's-paw DUPE, KNOT, TOOL

catsup
  ~ sound PLOP

cattail REED

cattle HERD, STEER
  ~ bird EGRET
  ~ brand symbol BAR
  ~ call MOO
  ~ catcher LASSO, RIATA
  ~ country RANGE
  ~ enclosure PEN, YARD
  ~ genus BOS
  ~ group HERD
  ~ mover PROD
  ~ noise LOW
  ~ prod GOAD
  ~ stall CRIB
  catch ~ ROPE
  punch ~ HERD
  raise ~ RANCH
  some ~ OXEN
  wild ~ BISON

cattle ___ CALL, CAR, EGRET,
  PROD

"Cattle ___ and Little Britches"
  ANNIE

"Cattle Annie ___ Little Britches"
  AND

cattleman
  ~ spread RANCH

catty SNIDE
  ~ comment MEOW, MEW

Catullus, Gaius Valerius POET,
  ROMAN
  see also Latin, poet

Caucasian ARYAN

Caucasus RANGE

caucho ULE

caucus MEET
  ~ state IOWA
  Congressional ~ BLOC

cauda TAIL

caudal LAST
  ~ appendage TAIL

caudata
  ~ member NEWT

caudex STEM

caught
  ~ in the act SEEN
  be ~ off guard SLEEP

"Caught you!" AHA

cauldron POT, VAT
  ~ contents BREW

cause AGENT, BASIS, BREED,
  MAKE, ROOT, SAKE, SEED, YIELD
  ~ anxiety ALARM
  ~ confusion ADDLE
  ~ damage to MAIM
  ~ discomfort ACHE
  ~ for alarm ALERT
  ~ irritation GRATE
  final ~ END
  root ~ SEED

___ cause LOST

"Cause ___ Alarm" FOR

"Cause for ___" ALARM

causerie CHAT, TALK

causeuse SOFA

causeway ROAD, ROUTE

caustic ACID, ACRID, LYE, SNIDE,
  TART
  ~ remark NIP

cauterize CHAR, HEAT, SEAR

Cauthen STEVE

caution ALERT, CARE, HEED,
  WARN
  buyer's ~ ASIS
  color of ~ AMBER
  throw ~ to the winds DARE,
    RISK
  traffic ~ SLO

cautious ALERT, AWARE, LEERY,
  SLOW, WARY

cavalcade LINE, PARADE, TRAIN

cavalier BEAU

Cavaliers FIVE, TEAM
  ~ org. NBA

cavalry
  ~ weapon LANCE, SABER

cavalryman RIDER

cavatelli PASTA

cavatina AIR, ARIA

cave COVE, DEN, HAVEN, HOLE,
  LAIR
  ~ dweller BAT, LONER
  ~ in SAG, SINK, YIELD
  ~ sound ECHO
  pigment used in ~
    art OCHER, OCHRE

caveat EDICT
  buyer ~ ASIS
  issue a ~ WARN

cave-dwelling
  ~ fish EEL

caveman
  ~ discovery FIRE

Cavendish, Henry
  ~ birthplace NICE

cavern CAVE, COVE, LAIR
  ~ phenomenon ECHO

cavernous DEEP

Cavett, Dick
  ~ alma mater YALE
  ~ wife NYE

caviar EGGS, OVA, ROE
  ~ exporter IRAN
  ~ source SHAD

cavil ARGUE, CARP, NAG

cavity CAVE, DENT, HOLE, PIT,
  SPACE, VOID
  ~ detector XRAY
  ~ filler's deg. DDS
  bodily ~ SAC
  nasal ~ NOSE

cavort CAPER, LARK, LEAP, PLAY,
  ROMP, TRIP

Cavs FIVE, TEAM
  ~ org. NBA

cavy ANIMAL

caw CALL, CROW, CRY, NOISE

cay ISLE, ISLET, KEY

Cayce EDGAR

___ Cayes, Haiti LES

Cayuga LAKE, TRIBE

cayuse ANIMAL, HORSE

CB
  ~ word OVER
  emergency ~ channel NINE
  use the ~ RADIO

CBer
  ~ cousin HAM

CBS
  ~ eye LOGO
  ~ logo EYE
  part of ~ SYST

Cd ELEM
  48 for ~ ATNO

CD DISC
  ~ abbr. ASCAP
  ~ alternative TAPE
  ~ earnings INT
  ~ forerunners LPS

~ **maybe** IRA
~ **player maker** RCA
part of ~ DISC, ROM
put on ~ ENCODE

CD-___ ROM

CD player
~ **part** LASER

Ce ELEM
58 for ~ ATNO

C.E.
part of ~ ERA

cease END, HALT, REST, STOP
~ **starter** SUR
~ **to a sailor** AVAST

cease-fire PEACE

ceaseless ETERNAL

Cecil EARL

Cecilia STE

cedar TREE
~ **product** CONE

cedar ___ CHEST

Cedar Rapids
~ **college** COE
~ **state** IOWA
village near ~ AMANA

cede ALLOW, DEFER, YIELD
~ **starter** ANTE, INTER

Cedric ___ (Little Lord Fauntleroy) ERROL

cee
~ **as a grade** SOSO
~ **follower** DEE
~ **preceder** BEE

ceiling CAP, LID, LIMIT, ROOF
~ **device** FAN
hit the ~ ERUPT, RAGE, RANT, RAVE
price ~ CAP

"Ceiling ___" ZERO

celadon COLOR

celeb NAME, STAR
~ **vehicle** LIMO

Celebes SEA
~ **ox** ANOA

celebrant
homecoming ~ ALUM, GRAD

celebrate FETE, KEEP, LAUD
~ **boisterously** REVEL
~ **gustatorily** DINE

celebrated GREAT, NOTED, STAR

celebration FETE, GALA, LEVEE
~ **(suffix)** MAS
Asian ~ TET

celebratory GALA

___ célèbre CAUSE

celebrities
what some ~ like to be SEEN

celebrity LION, NAME, STAR
~ **bash** ROAST
~ **bit part** CAMEO

~ **dinner** ROAST
~ **perhaps** ICON

celeritous RAPID

celerity HASTE, PACE, SPEED

"Celeste Aïda" ARIA

celestial
~ **body** MOON, ORB
~ **hunter** ORION
~ **strings** HARP

celestial ___ POLE

celestite ORE

celibate ABBE

cell CADRE, CAGE
~ **builder** BEE
~ **component** GENE
~ **feature** BAR
~ **letters** RNA
~ **occupant** NUN
germ ~ SPORE
retina ~ CONE, ROD

cell ___ PHONE

___ cell DRY, NERVE, RED, WET

cellar CAVE
~ **contents** SALT, WINE
~ **selection** ROSE
in the ~ LAST

___ cellar ROOT, STORM, WINE

Cellini
~ **patron** ESTE

cellophane
~ **product** TAPE

cells
add more ~ GROW

cellular
~ **device** PHONE
~ **home** HIVE
~ **material** DNA, RNA

cellular ___ PHONE

Celsius SWEDE

celt AXE

Celt GAEL

Celtic
~ **great** BIRD
~ **group** CLAN
~ **instrument** HARP
~ **language** ERSE
~ **Neptune** LER
~ **poet** BARD
~ **sea god** LER
~ **tongue** GAEL
of ~ descent IRISH

Celtics FIVE, TEAM
~ **legend** BIRD
~ **org.** NBA

cement BIND, GLUE, PASTE
~ **section** SLAB
lay ~ POUR
packing ~ LUTE
spread ~ PAVE

cenobite ABBOT

cenotaph STONE

Cenozoic ERA

censor BAN, EDIT
Roman ~ CATO

censure BAN, CARP, SCORE, SLAM, TWIT

census POLL
~ **datum** AGE, SEX

cent COIN
mill, to a ~ TENTH

___ cent PER, RED

___ Centauri ALPHA

centenarian ELDER

centennial EVENT

Centennial
~ **St.** COL

center CORE, EYE, HEART, INNER, MIDST
~ **of operations** BASE
~ **of revolution** AXIS
~ **starter** EPI
in the ~ AMID, AMONG

___-centered SELF

centering
~ **point** NODE

centime COIN

centimeter-gram-second
~ **unit** ERG

centipede
~ **unit** LEG

central KEY, POLAR
~ **halls** ATRIA
~ **line** AXIS
~ **part** CADRE
~ **position** MIDST
~ **stage** ARENA

Central America
see Spanish

central processing ___ UNIT

cents
put one's two ~ in ADD, OPINE

"___ Cents a Dance" TEN

___-cent store TEN

centuries
untold ~ EON

centurion
see Latin

"___ Centurions, The" NEW

century
~ **plant** AGAVE, ALOE
~ **segment** YEAR

century ___ PLANT

Century Schoolbook FONT

Century 21
~ **rival** ERA

CEO EXEC
~ **calendar entry** APPT
~ **deg.** MBA
~ **often** PRES

part of ~ EXEC, OFF

"___-ce pas?" NEST

cephalopod
~ **defense** INK

ceramic
~ **square** TILE

ceramics CLAY, WARE

cerastes SNAKE

cerate BALM

Cerberus DOG

cereal PAP
~ **bristle** AWN
~ **fungus** ERGOT
~ **grain** CORN, OAT, RICE, RYE
~ **ingredient** BRAN
~ **sound** POP, SNAP
~ **spike** AWN, EAR
breakfast ~ BRAN
name in ~ POST

cereal box
~ **abbr.** LBS, RDA

cereal-eating
~ **tiger** TONY

cerebrate MUSE

ceremonial GALA, RITE, STATE
~ **club** MACE
~ **dinner** SEDER
~ **dress** ROBE
~ **practice** RITE

ceremonied
~ **drink** TEA

ceremony POMP
religious ~ MASS, RITE

___ ceremony TEA

Cerf, Bennett WIT
~ **specialty** PUN

cerise COLOR, RED

cerium METAL

Cermak ANTON

certain CLEAR, SURE

___ certain (surely) FOR

"Certainement!" OUI

"Certainly!" AYE, SURE, YES

certainty FACT, FATE
say with ~ AVER, AVOW

certificate NOTE, PAPER
owner's ~ DEED
silver ~ BILL

certified ___ MAIL

certifies OKS

certify ATTEST, AVER, AVOW, ENABLE, SEAL, STATE

certitude FACT

cerulean AZURE, COLOR, SKY

cerussite ORE

Cervantes
see Spanish

cervine
~ animal DEER

cesium METAL

cessation ARREST, END, HALT

Cessna
drive a ~ AVIATE

cesspool STY

"C'est ___" MOI

"C'est la ___!" VIE

cestus BAND, BELT

Cetera PETER

Cévennes RANGE

Cey RON

Cézanne
see French

Cf ELEM
98 for ~ ATNO

Chablis WINE
like ~ SEC

cha-cha DANCE

chaconne DANCE

Chad LAKE
~ neighbor NIGER

Chadwick SIR

chafe ABRADE, ANGER, BIND, ERODE, FRET, IRK, PEEVE, RILE, SMART, STEW, STING

chafed
~ place SORE

chaff GIBE, KID, STRAW, TRASH, WASTE
eliminate ~ SIFT

chaffer BLAB, DEAL

Chaffey DON

chaffinch BIRD, PET

chafing
~ dish PAN

Chagall MARC

chagrin ABASH, SHAME
feel ~ SMART

chain BIND, CABLE, LEASH, LINE, RANGE, ROW, RUN
~ mail ARMOR
~ unit STORE
clothing ~, with "The" GAP
dog's ~ LEASH
heavy ~ ROPE
mountain ~ RANGE

chain ___ GANG, MAIL, SAW

___ chain KEY

"___ Chain Don't Make No Prison" ONE

chains IRONS

chair LEAD, SEAT
~ mate TABLE
~ part ARM, LEG, SLAT
kind of ~ SEDAN
leave the ~ ARISE

offer a ~ to SEAT
take a ~ SIT
weave a ~ seat CANE

___ chair EASY

chairholders INS

chairman HEAD

Chairman ___ MAO

chairperson HEAD
~ concern AGENDA

chairs
musical ~ GAME
repair ~ CANE

chaise SHAY

Chaka KHAN

chalcedony AGATE, ONYX, SARD

chalcocite ORE

chalcopyrite ORE

Chaldean SEER

chalet
~ feature EAVE

Chaliapin BASSO

chalice AMA, CUP

chalk
~ target CUE

chalk ___ TALK

chalkboard
~ material SLATE

challenge DARE, FACE, TEST, TRY
~ authority REBEL
~ the polygraph LIE
bowling ~ SPLIT
climber's ~ ALP
Gordian ~ KNOT
gunslinger's ~ DRAW
lineman's ~ POLE
meet the ~ COPE
postman's ~ HAIL, ICE, RAIN, SLEET, SNOW
schoolyard ~ DARE
surfer's ~ CREST

challenger FOE
~ quest TITLE

challenging HARD

chamber CELL, ROOM
~ group OCTET
~ in Spanish SALA
~ starter ANTE
~ work OCTET
bread ~ OVEN
monastic ~ CELL
seraglio ~ ODA
underground ~ CAVE

___ chamber ECHO, STAR

"___ Chamber, The" STAR

Chamberlain SIR
~ foreign secretary EDEN
~ org. NBA

chamber-music
~ instrument CELLO

chambers ABODE, HOME
heart ~ ATRIA

chameleon
~ cousin IGUANA

chamfron ARMOR

chamois ANIMAL, COLOR

chamomile TEA

Chamonix
sight from ~ ALP

champ EAT, GNAW

champagne COLOR, WINE
~ bottle SPLIT
~ bucket ICER
~ descriptor SEC
~ ritual TOAST
~ title DOM
prepare ~ ICE

"Champagne ___ Caesar" FOR

"Champagne for ___" CAESAR

champ at the ___ BIT

champing
~ at the bit AVID, EAGER, KEEN

champion AID, HELP, HERO, RAVE
~ prize TITLE

Champion HORSE

championship AEGIS, EGIS, TITLE

Champlain LAKE

chance LOT, ODD, RISK, START, TIME, TURN
~ to play TURN
~ to speak SAY
~ upon HIT, LEARN, MEET
big ~ RISK
blow the ~ MISS
by any ~ EVER
contender's ~ SHOT
game of ~ KENO
hitter's ~ ATBAT
not a ~ NOPE
take a ~ BET, DARE, RISK

chance ___ (meet accidentally) UPON

___ chance MAIN

"___ chance!" FAT

Chance
~ teammate EVERS

"Chance ___ Lifetime" OFA

chancel
~ neighbor APSE, NAVE

chancellor RULER

___ Chancellor LORD

Chancellorsville
winner at ~ LEE

chances LOTS, ODDS
parimutuel ~ ODDS

"Chances ___" ARE

"___ Chances" SEVEN

chandelier LAMP

Chanel
~ product SCENT

Chaney LON

Chang
~ brother ENG
~ to Eng TWIN

change ADAPT, ALTER, AMEND, CASH, COIN
~ channels DIAL
~ color DYE
~ course CUT, TURN, VEER, YAW
~ for a C-note TENS
~ for a fifty TENS
~ for a fin ONES
~ for a fiver ONES
~ for a twenty TENS
~ maker EDITOR
~ one's address MOVE
~ one's ways MEND
~ positions RESET, STIR
~ purse BAG
~ shades DYE
~ starter INTER
~ text EDIT, EMEND
~ the clock RESET
~ the décor REDO
~ to suit ADAPT
~ with the times ADAPT
bit of ~ CENT
get used to ~ ADAPT
minimal ~ CENT
quick ~ LEAP
sm. ~ CTS
small ~ CENT, COIN, DIME
Tijuana ~ PESO

change ___ (alternate) OFF

___ change SEA, SMALL

"___ Change" SMALL

changeless ETERNAL, SAME

change of ___ HEART

"Change of ___" HABIT

change one's ___ TUNE

changer
hue ~ DYE

changes
make ~ to ADAPT, ALTER, AMEND, REDO

channel ARM, BED, CANAL, CUT, DIG, INLET, NECK, PASS, RACE, ROUTE, STREAM, STRIA
~ (abbr.) STR
~ control DIAL
~ designation UHF
~ surfers zap past them ADS
corporeal ~ AORTA
emergency CB ~ NINE
English ~ BBC

channel ___ BASS

channels
~ 14-83 UHF

channel-surf ZAP

Channing CAROL

chanson ARIA, SONG, TUNE

chanson de ___ GESTE

chant PSALM, SING, SONG

chantey AIR, SONG

chanticleer
  ~ summons CROW

"Chantilly ___" LACE

chaos MESS
  primal ~ ABYSS

Chaos
  goddess born of ~ GAEA

chaotic MESSY

chap DUDE, EGG, GENT, LAD,
  MALE, MAN
  ~ in Australian English MATE
  ~ in British English MATE
  well-bred ~ GENT
  young ~ LAD

Chapala LAKE

chaparral STAND

chapeau HAT
  slangy ~ LID

___ chapel LADY

___ Chapel (Padua site) ARENA

chaperone ATTEND

chaperoned
  ~ girl DEB

chapfallen LOW, SAD

Chapin, Harry
  ~ tune TAXI

chaplain PADRE

Chaplin OONA, SAUL
  ~ prop CANE

Chaplin, Charlie SIR
  ~ comedy, with "The" RINK

Chaplin, Geraldine
  ~ mother OONA

chapter PART
  ~ head DEAN
  ~ in a play ACT
  ~ of history ERA

Chapter 11
  ~ cause DEBT

"Chapter on Ears, A"
  ~ author ELIA, LAMB

"Chapter Two"
  ~ actor CAAN

Chapultepec
  see Spanish

char HEAT, SEAR

character AURA, BIRD, CARD,
  ETHOS, ILK, MAKE, ROLE, SIGN,
  TONE, TYPE
  ~ builder GENE

character ___ ACTOR

character-building
  ~ org. BSA

characteristic TRAIT
  ~ of LIKE

~ of (suffix) ILE, INE, ISH
  ~ quality SAVOR

characterize LABEL, STAMP

charade ACT, POSE

charades GAME

charbroil HEAT

charcoal COLOR, EBONY
  use ~ DRAW

chard BEET
  ~ kin KALE

chardonnay WINE

charge AERATE, ASSESS, BANG,
  CARE, COST, FARE, FEE, FINE,
  LOAD, ONUS, RATE, SPEED,
  STORM, TOLL, WARD, ZAP
  ~ alternative CASH
  ~ an obligation DEBIT
  ~ starter SUR
  ~ to appear CITE
  ~ with carbon
    dioxide AERATE
  answer a ~ PLEAD
  cabbie's ~ FARE
  criminal ~ RAP
  depth ~ MINE
  drover's ~ HERD
  false ~ SMEAR
  fish with a ~ EEL
  gardener's ~ PLANT
  get a ~ out of LIKE
  guardian's ~ WARD
  in ~ of OVER
  mudslinger's ~ LIAR
  mutual-fund ~ LOAD
  one in ~ HEAD
  road ~ TOLL
  service ~ FEE
  streetcar ~ FARE
  take ~ BOSS, LEAD, RULE,
    STEER
  take ~ of CARE
  teacher's ~ CLASS
  trucker's ~ SEMI
  Visa ~ DEBT
  without ~ FREE

charge ___ CARD

___ charge TAKE

charged HOT
  ~ atom ION
  ~ in a way LADEN
  ~ in physics IONIC
  ~ swimmer EEL
  electrically ~ LIVE

chargé d'affaires AGENT

"Charge of the Light Brigade,
  The" POEM

charger HORSE, PACER, STEED

Chargers ELEVEN, TEAM
  ~ org. NFL

charges BILL
  prefer ~ SUE

chariot
  ~ ender EER

"Chariots of ___" FIRE

charisma AURA

charitable
  ~ donation ALMS
  ~ one DONOR
  ~ org. CARE
  ~ undertaking CAUSE

charity AID, ALMS, DOLE, HELP,
  LOVE
  ~ sister HOPE

"___ Charity" SWEET

charlatan FAKE, LIAR

Charlemagne ROI
  Pope who crowned ~ LEO

Charles ATLAS, DANA, IVES, LAKE,
  LAMB, LANE, NORA, PEALE, RAY,
  READE
  ~ dog ASTA
  ~ princedom WALES
  ~ sib ANNE
  ~ sport POLO
  ~ to Elizabeth HEIR
  ~ to Philip SON
  alternative to ~ de
    Gaulle ORLY
  Mrs. Nick ~ NORA

___ Charles, La. LAKE

Charleston CITY, DANCE, IAN,
  PORT

Charles Wilson ___ PEALE

charley ___ HORSE

Charley PRIDE
  ~ Donna Lucia AUNT
  ~ had one AUNT

charley horse ACHE, SPASM

"Charley's ___" AUNT

Charlie PRIDE, ROSE, TUNA
  voice of ~ EDGAR

"Charlie and the Chocolate
  Factory"
  ~ author DAHL

"Charlie Brown"
  ~ opener FEE

"Charlie Chan at the ___" OPERA

"Charlie Hustle" ROSE

Charlie's Angels TRIO

"Charlie's Angels"
  ~ actress LADD
  ~ character KRIS

Charlotte RAE

charlotte russe CAKE

"Charlotte's ___" WEB

"Charlotte's Web"
  ~ character RAT

charm AMUSE, ASSET, ENDEAR,
  LURE, PLEASE

charmed RAPT

charmed ___ LIFE

charmer
  ~ partner COBRA
  ~ subject SNAKE

"___ Charmer, The" (Rousseau
  work) SNAKE

charming NICE, SWEET

Charon MOON
  ~ river STYX

charpoy COT

chart DRAW, LOG, MAP, PLAN, PLAT,
  PLOT, ROUTE, TABLE
  ~ indication TREND
  ~ shape PIE
  ~ topper HIT
  brain-wave ~ EEG
  genealogy ~ TREE
  Realtor's ~ PLAT
  town ~ PLAT

___ chart EYE, FLIP

___ chart (graph) BAR, PIE

___ chart (horoscope) NATAL

charter DEED, HIRE, LEASE, LET,
  RENT

Charteris
  ~ detective SAINT

chartreuse COLOR

chart-topper HIT

chartulary LIST

Chartwell
  ~ to Churchill ESTATE

chary ALERT, LEERY, SHY, WARY

Charybdis PERIL

chase ETCH, TAG, TRACE
  ~ away REPEL, SHOO
  ~ Bannister RACE, RUN
  ~ down HUNT
  ~ hounds RIDE
  anagram for ~ ACHES
  send on a wild-goose
    ~ STALL

Chase EDNA, HAL, ILKA

"___ Chase, The" PAPER

chase-away
  ~ word SCAT, SCRAM, SHOO

chaser
  ~ perhaps BEER
  bar ~ SODA
  convoy ~ UBOAT
  nymph ~ SATYR
  robber ~ COP
  without a ~ NEAT

chasing AFTER

chasm ABYSS, DROP, PIT, RENT,
  SPACE, SPLIT

chaste NICE, PURE

chastisement ROD

chasuble ROBE
  garment under a ~ ALB

chat BIRD, CHIN, GAB, RAP, TALK

château ABODE, HOME, KEEP
  ~ wall-hanging ARRAS

Chateaubriand STEAK
  ~ novel RENE

Château-Thierry
  see French

Chatham EARL

Chattanooga
  ~ st. TENN

"Chattanoogie ___ Shine Boy"
  SHOE

chattel SERF, SLAVE

chattels ESTATE, GEAR

chatter BLAB, CHAT, GAB, PRATE,
  TALK, YAK, YAP

___ chatter IDLE

chattering NOISE

Chaucer POET
  ~ pilgrim NUN, REEVE
  ~ Tabard INN
  ~ work TALE
  see also poet

chauffeured
  ~ car LIMO

Chavez CESAR

chaw WAD

cheap MEAN, POOR, SMALL
  ~ ender SKATE
  be ~ STINT

cheap ___ SHOT

___-cheap DIRT

"Cheap Detective, The"
  ~ actor CAESAR, LAMAS
  ~ director MOORE

"Cheaper by the Dozen"
  ~ director LANG

cheat CON, CRIB, DUPE, HAVE,
  LIAR, ROB, ROOK, STING
  ~ sheet CRIB, TROT

cheater CAD, LIAR
  ~ aid CRIB

"Cheaters, The"
  ~ director KANE

check ARREST, AUDIT, BILL, CEASE,
  DAMP, DETER, HALT, HOLD,
  LEASH, LIMIT, NIP, REIN, SCAN,
  SLOW, SNUB, STEM, STOP, TAB
  ~ in ARRIVE, COME
  ~ of business records AUDIT
  ~ out CASE, EYE, MOVE, OGLE,
    READ, TEST, VET
  ~ remainder STUB
  ~ someone out LEER
  ~ text EDIT
  item to ~ COAT, HAT
  monthly ~ RENT
  pick up the ~ PAY, TREAT
  put on one's ~ BILL
  rain ~ STUB
  redeem a ~ CASH
  send a ~ REMIT
  what bartenders ~ IDS
  word on a sample ~ VOID
  write a ~ DRAW
  write a bad ~ KITE

check ___ (examine) OUT, OVER

___ check BED, HAT, RAIN, SALES

___-check SPOT

check-cashing
  ~ needs IDS

checker MAN

Checker
  ~ maybe TAXI

checkers GAME
  ~ side RED
  Chinese ~ GAME

checkmate STOP

checkroom
  ~ item COAT, HAT

checkup EXAM, TEST
  ~ sounds AHS
  ~ word AAH

cheddar
  like good ~ AGED
  sharpen a ~ AGE

cheek FACE, LIP, NERVE, SASS
  ~ by jowl CLOSE, NEAR

cheeky PERT

cheep CRY, NOISE, PEEP, PIPE

cheer CRY, EASE, ELATE, HAIL, PEP,
  RAH, REACT, ROOT, YELL
  ~ for the bullfighter OLE
  ~ on URGE
  ~ opposite BOO
  ~ start SIS
  ~ up AMUSE, RAISE
  bring ~ to AMUSE
  Bronx ~ HISS, HOOT
  campus ~ RAH
  holiday ~ NOG
  rousing ~ YEA
  start of a ~ HIP

Cheer
  ~ rival ALL, ERA, TIDE

cheerful GAY, GLAD, RIANT, ROSY
  ~ song LILT
  not ~ BLUE, DOUR, LOW, SAD

cheerfulness GLEE

"___ Cheering" START

"Cheerio!" BYE, TATA, TOAST

cheerleader
  ~ feat SPLIT, YELL
  ~ quality PEP
  ~ shout RAH

cheerless DRAB, LOW, SAD

cheers TOAST

"___ cheers!" THREE

"Cheers"
  ~ actor REES
  ~ actress ALLEY, LONG
  ~ bartender SAM
  ~ character DIANE, ERNIE,
    HOWE, NORM, VERA
  ~ locale BAR
  ~ order ALE, BEER, BREW
  ~ prop STEIN
  Carla on ~ RHEA
  Norm's occupation on ~ CPA

Norm's wife on ~ VERA

"Cheers ___ Miss Bishop" FOR

"Cheers!" TOAST

"Cheers for ___ Bishop" MISS

cheery PERT
  ~ syllables ATTA

cheese BRIE, EDAM, FETA
  ~ coat RIND
  ~ in a mousetrap BAIT
  ~ it FLEE, RUN, SCRAM
  ~ lover MOUSE
  ~ unit SLAB, SLICE
  big ~ EXEC, LION, NABOB,
    NAME
  crumbly ~ FETA
  Dutch ~ EDAM
  French ~ BRIE
  goat's-milk ~ FETA
  improve ~ AGE
  like some ~ AGED, MILD
  mild ~ EDAM
  prepare ~ GRATE
  say ~ GRIN, POSE, SMILE
  soft ~ BRIE, FETA
  tray ~ EDAM
  white ~ FETA

___ cheese BIG, BLUE, CREAM,
  POT, RAT

Cheese ___ NIPS

cheesecloth NET

cheesy MEAN, POOR

cheetah ANIMAL, APE, CAT

Cheevy, Miniver
  like ~ LEAN

chef
  ~ accessory MITT
  ~ attraction AROMA
  ~ cry DONE
  ~ garment APRON
  ~ implement RICER
  ~ meas. TBS, TSP
  ~ need OVEN, PAN, POT
  ~ offerings MENU
  ~ phrase ALA
  ~ serving DISH
  ~ tool RICER
  ~ wear APRON
  pastry ~, at times ICER

Chef Boy-ar-___ DEE

chef's ___ SALAD

Chekhov ANTON

chela CLAW, ORGAN

Chelyuskin CAPE

chem
  ~ room LAB

chem. SCI

chemical
  ~ compound ENOL, ESTER
  ~ container VAT
  ~ prefix ISO
  ~ suffix ANE, ASE, ENE, INE,
    ITE, OSE
  agricultural ~ ALAR
  corrosive ~ ACID, LYE

lawn ~ LIME

chemical change
  undergo ~ REACT

chemin de ___ FER

chemise DRESS, SLIP

chemisette BIB

chemist
  ~ reagent ACID
  ~ vessel ETNA

chemistry
  ~ starter BIO

Chénier, André Marie de POET
  see also poet

Chenin Blanc WINE

Cher
  ~ ex BONO
  ~ film of 1985 MASK

Cherbourg CITY, PORT
  see also French

cherimoya TREE

cherish ADORE, CLASP, ESTEEM,
  LOVE

cherished DEAR, PET, SWEET
  ~ one PET
  make ~ ENDEAR

Chernobyl
  city near ~ KIEV

Cherokee TRIBE
  ~ kin ERIE

Cherokee ___ ROSE

cherries
  prepare ~ STEM

cherry COLOR, PIE, RED, SODA,
  TREE
  ~ leftover STEM
  ~ pit STONE
  ~ stone PIT

cherry ___ PIE

___ cherry SOUR

cherry picker
  ~ part BOOM

**"Cherry Pink and ___ Blossom
  White"** APPLE

cherrystone CLAM

chersonese CAPE

cherub ANGEL
  ~ with a bow AMOR
  mythical ~ EROS
  Valentine's Day ~ AMOR

chervil HERB

Cheryl LADD

Chesapeake BAY

Chesapeake and ___ OHIO

Chesapeake Bay
  ~ bird TERN

Cheshire ___ CAT

Cheshire Cat
  ~ expression GRIN

chess GAME
  ~ act MOVE
  ~ finale MATE
  ~ piece MAN, ROOK

chess ___ SET

Chessman
  ~ portrayer ALDA

chess piece MAN

chest CASE, SAFE
  ~ handle KNOB
  ~ material CEDAR
  ~ pounder APE
  ~ protector BIB, VEST
  ~ rattle RALE
  sacred ~ ARK

___ chest CEDAR, HOPE, WAR

Chester ___ Arthur ALAN

chesterfield COAT, SOFA

Chesterfield EARL, LORD

Chester White
  ~ home PEN, STY

chestnut BAY, COLOR, HORSE,
  NUT, RED, ROAN, TREE
  old ~ SAW

___ chestnut HORSE, WATER

"Chestnut ___ in Flower" TREES

chestnuts
  prepare ~ ROAST

**"Chestnuts roasting ___ open
  fire..."** ONAN

chest protector
  ~ wearer UMP

chevalier MALE, MAN

chevet APSE

Cheviot
  ~ cry BAA
  ~ home COTE, PEN
  ~ mama EWE
  ~ papa RAM

Chevrolet
  ~ division GEO

chevron
  ~ shape VEE

chevrotain DEER

Chevy AUTO, CAR, CHASE
  ~ rival OLDS

Chevy ___, Md. CHASE

chew BITE, EAT, GNAW
  ~ out RAG
  ~ the fat BLAB, CHAT, GAB,
    RAP, TALK, YAK
  ~ the scenery EMOTE

chew ___ (scold) OUT

___ chew DOG

Chewbacca ALIEN

chewer
  scenery ~ HAM

chew the ___ FAT, RAG

chewy HARD

Cheyenne TRIBE
  ~ home TEPEE
  ~ show RODEO

"Cheyenne" OATER

chez moi HOME

chi
  ~ follower PSI
  ~ preceder PHI

___ chi TAI

chia PLANT

Chiang
  ~ adversary MAO

Chianti WINE

chibouk PIPE

chic NEW, NOW, SMART, STYLE
  ~ shop SALON
  no longer ~ OUT, PASSE

Chicago BAND, CITY, PORT
  ~ airport OHARE
  ~ area LOOP
  ~ football player BEAR
  ~ hrs. CDT, CST
  ~ hub OHARE
  ~ lines ELS
  ~ planetarium ADLER
  ~ st. ILL
  ~ Union STA
  downtown ~ LOOP

"Chicago" POEM

Chicago Fire
  ~ starter COW

"Chicago Hope" DRAMA
  ~ actor BERG
  ~ extra EMT
  ~ extras RNS

"Chicago Sun Times"
  ~ critic EBERT

chicane RUSE

chicanery RUSE
  bit of ~ WILE

chichi ARTY, ORNATE

___ chi ch'uan TAI

chick BIRD
  ~ comment PEEP
  ~ ender PEA
  ~ home NEST
  ~ mother HEN
  ~ talk PEEP
  future ~ EGG

"Chickadee"
  W.C. Fields' ~ MAE

chickaree
  ~ morsel ACORN

Chickasaw TRIBE

chicken BIRD, MEAT
  ~ chow FEED
  ~ coop ROOST
  ~ feed COIN, MASH
  ~ of the sea TUNA
  ~ part LEG
  ~ seat ROOST
  ~ style KIEV

  ~ wire MESH
  clean a ~ DRESS

chicken ___ FEED, KIEV, OUT, WIRE

chicken ___ king ALA

chicken-hearted BASE

chicken pox
  ~ symptom ITCH

chickens
  ~ to chicken hawks PREY
  come home, as ~ ROOST

chickpea GRAM

chick-to-be EGG

Chico
  ~ brother HARPO

"Chico and the ___" MAN

chide RAG, RATE, TRIM

chief ARCH, BOSS, FIRST, HEAD,
  LEAD, MAIN, MAJOR, RULER,
  TOP
  ~ advisor ELDER
  ~ exec. PRES
  ~ group TRIBE
  ~ (prefix) ARCH
  ~ (suffix) ARCH

chiefdom LAND

chief of ___ STATE

chiefs
  magazine ~ EDS

Chiefs ELEVEN, TEAM
  ~ org. NFL

chieftain LORD
  ~ charge CLAN
  Middle East ~ AMIR, EMEER,
    EMIR

chien DOG

chiffon PIE

chiffonnier CHEST

chifforobe CHEST

chignon KNOT

Chihuahua
  ~ toon REN
  ~ wear SERAPE
  see also Spanish

Chihuahuas
  like ~ TINY

child BRAT, KID, MITE, SCION, TAD,
  TOT, TYKE
  ~ bed CRIB
  ~ cry MAMA
  ~ ender ISH, LIKE
  ~ getaway CAMP
  ~ in Spanish NINA, NINO
  ~ pleaser TOY
  ~ toy BALL, TOP
  annoying ~ BRAT
  brother's ~ NIECE
  female ~ LASS
  foster ~ WARD
  issei ~ NISEI
  like Monday's ~ FAIR
  misbehaving ~ BRAT

**naughty ~ Christmas
  gift** COAL
  sib's ~ NIECE
  talk like a ~ LISP

"Childe Harold's Pilgrimage"
  POEM

childhood
  be in one's second ~ DOTE

childish INANE

Child, Julia CHEF
  ~ instruction STIR
  ~ meas. TBS, TSP

childlike NAIVE

children ISSUE, SEED
  ~ game TAG
  Dr. for ~ SEUSS
  what ~ should be SEEN

"Children ___ Lesser God" OFA

"Children of a Lesser ___" GOD

"Children of Paradise"
  ~ director CARNE

"Children of the Albatross"
  ~ author NIN

children's book
  ~ pseudonym SEUSS

Childress, Alvin
  ~ role AMOS

child's
  ~ play EASY, SNAP
  play a ~ game HIDE

"Child's ___" PLAY

child support
  ~ recipients EXES

child welfare
  ~ org. PTA

chile
  ~ partner CARNE

Chile
  see Spanish

Chilean
  ~ island EASTER
  ~ money PESO
  ~ range ANDES

chili
  ~ bean PINTO
  ~ ingredient BEAN, CARNE
  ~ server LADLE

chiliad AGE

chili con ___ CARNE

chili pepper
  ~ dip SALSA

Chilkoot Pass
  ~ locale ALASKA

chill AGUE, COOL, ICE, NIP

"___ Chill, The" BIG

chilled ONICE

chilling EERIE, EERY, ICY

chills
  ~ and fever AGUE

chilly ALOOF, COOL, CRISP, ICY, RAW

chime PEAL, RING, TONE
~ **in** AGREE, TALK

chimera DREAM, OGRE

chimney PIPE
~ **coating** SOOT

chimp ANIMAL, APE
~ **cousin** ORANG
~ **expert Goodall** JANE
NASA ~ ENOS

chin CHAT, GAB, TALK
keep one's ~ **up** BEAR
take it on the ~ BEAR

chin-___ UPS

china CLAY, DISH
~ **buy** SET
~ **ender** WARE
~ **piece** CUP, DISH, PLATE
fine ~ BONE

___ china BONE

China
~ **locale** ASIA, ORIENT
~ **neighbor** LAOS, TIBET
~ **starter** INDO
desert in northern ~ GOBI
from ~ ASIAN
Great Wall of ~ **dynasty** CHIN
on a slow boat to ~ ASEA, ATSEA
tea in ~ CHA

China ___ ASTER, ROSE, SEA

"China ___" GATE, SEAS

"China Beach"
~ **extras** RNS

chinaberry TREE

China-Russia
~ **boundary** AMUR

chinchilla ANIMAL, FUR
~ **habitat** ANDES

Chinese ASIAN
~ **art material** JADE
~ **association** TONG
~ **checkers** GAME
~ **dynasty** CHI, CHIN, CHOU, HAN, TANG
~ **fabric** SILK
~ **gelatin** AGAR
~ **gooseberry** KIWI
~ **lantern** LAMP
~ **leader** MAO
~ **mammal** PANDA
~ **monetary unit** TAEL
~ **nanny** AMA, AMAH
~ **path** TAO
~ **pooch** PEKE
~ **premier** CHOU
~ **principle** YIN
~ **puzzle** POSER
~ **revolutionary** MAO
~ **river** HAN
~ **secret society** TONG
~ **tea** CHA
~ **zodiac animal** DOG, GOAT, HARE, HORSE, RAT, SNAKE, TIGER

~ **zodiac animals** OXEN
name in ~ **politics** ENLAI

Chinese food
~ **additive** MSG

Chinese-restaurant
~ **freebie** RICE, TEA

Chinese-restaurant syndrome
~ **cause** MSG

chink GAP, HOLE, RENT, SPLIT

Chinook TRIBE

chinquapin TREE

chintzy POOR

chip DENT, PEEP
~ **accompaniment** DIP
~ **away at** ERODE, PEG
~ **in** ADD, AID, ANTE, HELP, PAY
~ **in chips** BET
~ **ingredient** SALT
~ **off the old block** SON
~ **topping** DIP
Brit's potato ~ CRISP
hot ~ **dip** SALSA
starter ~ ANTE

chip ___ SHOT

chip ___ the old block OFF

___ chip BLUE, CORN

Chip
~ **partner** DALE

chipmunk ANIMAL
~ **snack** ACORN
cartoon ~ CHIP, DALE

chip off the ___ block OLD

chipped
~ **off the same block** AKIN

chipper PERT, SPRY

Chippewa TRIBE

chips
call with ~ SEE
chip in ~ BET
in the ~ RICH
make ~ FRY

"CHiPs"
Ponch, on ~ ERIK

Chips, Mr.
~ **portrayer** OTOOLE
what ~ **taught** LATIN

Chirac
see French

Chiricahua TRIBE

chiromancer SEER

chirp CALL, CRY, NOISE, PEEP, PIPE, SING

chirping SONG

chirrup PEEP

chisel CHIP, EDGER, HEW, ROB, ROOK, TOOL
~ **feature** EDGE
Neolithic ~ CELT

Chisholm TRAIL

Chisholm Trail
~ **town** ENID

Chisox TEAM, TEN

"Chisum" OATER

chit BRAT, IOU, NOTE, TAB

chitchat BLAB, PRATE, TALK

chiton ROBE

chits
have ~ **out** OWE

Chittagong CITY, PORT

"Chitty Chitty Bang Bang"
~ **screenwriter** DAHL

chivalrous
~ **deed** GEST, GESTE

Chivas ___ REGAL

chive HERB
~ **relative** LEEK

chivvy BAIT, CHASE, HUNT, NAG

chloride
sodium ~ SALT

chlorinate TREAT

chlorine GAS

chloroform
~ **cousin** ETHER

chlorophyll
~ **maker** PLANT
~ **respository** LEAF

chlorophyta
~ **bit** ALGA

chockablock SOLID

chockfull LADEN

chocolate COLOR, SWEET
~ **candy** BAR, KISS
~ **center** CREAM
hot ~ COCOA

"Chocolate ___, The" WAR

Choctaw TRIBE

choice ACE, BEST, ELECT, FINE, FIRST, GOOD, RARE, TOPS
~ **(abbr.)** SEL
~ **list** MENU

choices
list of ~ MENU
top ~ ALIST

choicest TOP
~ **part** CREAM

choir
~ **member** ALTO, BASS, BASSO, TENOR
~ **members** ALTI
~ **platform** RISER
area behind the ~ APSE
small ~ OCTET

choke CLOSE, DAMP, GAG, STALL
~ **up** CLOG, DAM

choke ___ (obstruct) OFF

choker
~ **fastener** CLASP

choler ANGER, BILE, IRE, RAGE

choleric BAD, IRATE, TESTY

___ cholesterol SERUM

chollas CACTI

chomp BITE, NIP
~ **on** EAT

choo-choo TRAIN

choose ADOPT, CAST, DRAW, ELECT, LIKE, OPT, PLEASE, SETTLE, TAKE
~ **(abbr.)** SEL
~ **actors** CAST
~ **a ticket** VOTE

chooser
~ **choice** EVENS, ODDS
~ **option** ELSE, THOSE

chop AXE, CUT, DICE, HACK, HASH, HEW, SLASH
~ **off** CHIP
kind of ~ LOIN, VEAL

chop-chop ASAP, STAT

chophouse
~ **order** RARE

Chopin
~ **by birth** POLE
~ **piece** ETUDE

chopine SHOE

chopped
~ **liver** PATE

chopper AXE
~ **topper** ROTOR
weed ~ HOE
wood ~ AXE

chopping
~ **tool** AXE

choppy
~ **sea** RACE

chops MEAT
mutton ~ BEARD
some ~ VEAL

choral
~ **ensemble** OCTET
~ **member** ALTO, BASS, BASSO, TENOR
~ **section** ALTI, ALTOS

chorale
~ **member** ALTO, BASS, BASSO, TENOR

chord
musical ~ TRIAD
touch a ~ MELT

chore ERRAND, LABOR, STINT, TASK
do a crime-scene ~ DUST
do a fall ~ RAKE
do a household ~ CLEAN, DUST, MEND, SEW, WASH
do a kitchen ~ MASH, PARE, PEEL
do a landscaping ~ MOW
do a laundry ~ IRON, SORT
do a postprandial ~ DRY
tug's ~ TOW

chorister ALTO, BASS, BASSO, TENOR

chortle SNORT

chorus SONG
~ **member** ALTO, BASS, BASSO, TENOR
~ **members** ALTI
~ **syllable** TRA
join the ~ SING
second ~ AGAIN

chorus ___ GIRL

"Chorus ___, A" LINE

"Chorus Line, A"
~ **song** ONE

chosen ELECT

chou
petit ~ LOVE

Chou ___ ENLAI

Chou En-___ LAI

chough CROW

chouse DUPE

chow EATS, MEAL
~ **down** EAT, FEED
Army ~ MESS
chicken ~ FEED
service ~ MESS
sow ~ SLOP

chow ___ LINE

chowder STEW
~ **ingredient** CLAM
~ **server** LADLE

chowderhead ASS, BOOR, CLOD, DODO, DOLT, OAF, SAP

chow mein
~ **additive** MSG

Chris EVERT

Chrissie EVERT

"Christabel" POEM

christen CALL, NAME, TAG

christening
~ **initials** USS

Christian DIOR, ERA, ROGER

___ Christian Andersen HANS

Christiania
~ **today** OSLO

Christianity REL

Christian Science
~ **founder** EDDY

Christie ANNA, LOU
~ **concoction** PLOT
~ **express** ORIENT
perform a ~ SKI

"___ Christie" ANNA

Christie, Agatha DAME
~ **locale** NILE

Christie, Julie
~ **role** LARA

Christie's
~ **action** BID
signal at ~ NOD

Christina
~ **father** ARI

Christine
~ **in film** CAR

Christmas NOEL, YULE
~ **bird** GOOSE
~ **ender** TIDE
~ **goodies** LOOT
~ **ornament** BALL
~ **pageant figures** MAGI
~ **pageant prop** HALO
~ **poem opener** TWAS
~ **predecessor** EVE
~ **quaff** NOG
~ **song** CAROL, NOEL
~ **travelers** MAGI
~ **tree** FIR, PINE
~ **trio** MAGI
naughty child's ~ **gift** COAL
white ~ **need** SNOW

Christmas ___ CARD, EVE, FERN, ROSE, SEAL, TREE

"Christmas ___, A" CAROL

Christmas card
~ **word** NOEL

"Christmas Carol, A"
~ **boy** TIM
~ **exclamation** BAH
last word of ~ ONE

"Christmas in ___" ASPEN

"Christmas Song, The"
~ **singer** COLE

Christmas tree
~ **base** STAND
~ **topper** ANGEL, STAR

Christ of the ___ ANDES

Christopher FRY, LEE, REEVE, WREN
~ **friend** POOH

"Christ Stopped at Eboli"
~ **novelist** LEVI

___ Christy Minstrels, The NEW

chroma TONE

chromium METAL

chromosome
~ **component** DNA, RNA
~ **factor** SEX
~ **part** GENE
having a Y ~ MALE
locate a gene on a ~ MAP

chronic
~ **malady (suffix)** ITIS
not ~ ACUTE

chronicle ENTER, LIST, SAGA
~ **entry** EVENT

"Chronicles of Clovis, The"
~ **author** SAKI

"Chronicles of Narnia, The"
~ **author** LEWIS

chronological
~ **division** ERA

chronology TIME
~ **element** EVENT

Chrysler AUTO, CAR

chrysoberyl GEM

chrysoprase GEM

chubby BIG, FAT, LARGE, OBESE

chuck BAIL, CAST, DROP, HURL, LOB, MEAL, STEAK, TOSS
~ **insert** BIT

chuck-a-luck GAME
~ **need** DICE

chuckhole PIT

chuckle HAHA, REACT

chucklehead DODO, DOLT, DOPE, OAF, SAP

chuckles
elicit ~ AMUSE

chuff BOOR

chug STEAM

chukka
~ **material** SUEDE

chukkers
game played in ~ POLO

Chulalongkorn
~ **locale** SIAM

chum BAIT, MATE, PAL
~ **in Australian English** MATE
~ **in British English** MATE
~ **in French** AMI, AMIE
~ **in Spanish** AMIGO

chummy CLOSE

chump DOLT, DOPE, LOUT, OAF

Chung
~ **network** CBS

chunk CHIP, CLOD, GOB, MASS, PART, SLAB, SLICE

chunk-light
~ **fish** TUNA

chunky BIG, LARGE

church
~ **area** ALTAR
~ **book** ORDO
~ **calendar** ORDO
~ **confab** SYNOD
~ **desk** AMBO
~ **feature** ORGAN, SPIRE
~ **figure** ICON
~ **honoree** SAINT
~ **officer** ELDER
~ **offshoot** SECT
~ **receptacle** FONT
~ **recess** APSE
~ **response** AMEN
~ **seat** PEW
~ **section** ALTAR, APSE, NAVE
~ **service** MASS
~ **song** PSALM
~ **teachings** DOGMA
~ **title** REV
~ **vestment** ALB

~ walkway AISLE
last word in ~ AMEN
not of the ~ LAIC

churchgoer LAIC

Churchill SARAH, SIR
~ **gesture** VEE
~ **prop** CANE
~ **successor** EDEN
"so few", to ~ RAF

Churchill Downs
~ **event** RACE

churchmouse
like a ~ POOR

churl BEAR, BOOR, CAD, LIEGE, LOUT, OAF, YAHOO

churlish BAD, MEAN, RUDE, SOUR, TART, TESTY, UGLY

churn BOIL, STIR
~ **up** ROIL

chute RACE, RUN, SLIDE
~ **material** SILK
~ **starter** PARA

chutzpah BRASS, NERVE

CIA
~ **forerunner** OSS
~ **operative** AGENT, AGT, SPY

"Ciao!" BYE, LATER, TATA
~ **in French** ADIEU
~ **in Hawaiian** ALOHA
~ **in Latin** AVE, VALE
~ **in Spanish** ADIOS

Ciardi, John POET
see also poet

cicatrix SCAR

Cicero ORATOR, ROMAN
emulate ~ ORATE
see also Latin

cicerone LEAD

cicisbeo BEAU

Cid
El ~ HERO

cider
~ **source** APPLE
~ **squeezer** BOOR
like some ~ HARD

cider-sweet
~ **girl** IDA

"Cielo e ___!" MAR

cigar
~ **end** STUB
~ **producer** CUBA
~ **residue** ASH
~ **slangily** ROPE
~ **tip** ASH

cigar box
~ **wood** CEDAR

cilantro HERB

Cilento DIANE

cilia HAIR

cilium LASH

cinch BELT, EASY, ICE, SEAL, SNAP
  a ~ EASY

Cincinnati HORSE
  ~ **baseballer** RED
  ~ **river** OHIO

Cincinnatus ROMAN

cinco
  ~ **- tres** DOS

cincture BAND, BELT

cinder ASH, EMBER, SLAG

Cinder
  ~ **ender** ELLA

Cinderella
  ~ **headpiece** TIARA
  like ~'s stepsisters UGLY

"Cinderella"
  ~ **setting** BALL

"Cinderella Liberty"
  ~ **actor** CAAN
  ~ **actress** MASON

cinders LAVA
  turn to ~ CHAR

"___ Cinders" (old comic) ELLA

cinema
  ~ **list** CAST
  ~ **sign** EXIT

cinematic
  ~ **technique** FADE, IRIS, PAN

cinematographer
  ~ **tool** CAM

Cinemax
  ~ **rival** HBO

cinereous ASHEN, GRAY, GREY

cinnabar ORE

cinnamon BEAR, FERN

cinque
  ~ **follower** SEI

cinquefoil
  ~ **feature** ARC

Cio-Cio-___ SAN

Cio-Cio-San
  ~ **to Yakusidé** NIECE
  accessory for ~ OBI

cipher ADD, CODE, NIL, SIGN, SUM,
  ZERO
  ~ **code** KEY
  put into ~ ENCODE

circa ABOUT, NEAR

Circe SIREN

circle BLOC, CLAN, GANG, HALO,
  LOOP, ORBIT, RING, SET
  ~ **dance** HORA
  ~ **measures** RADII
  ~ **of flowers** LEI
  ~ **overhead** HALO
  ~ **portion** ARC
  ~ **size** AREA
  ~ **to a poet** ORB
  flattened ~ OVAL
  full ~ LAP

inner ~ CADRE, ELITE
numbered ~ DIAL
tiny ~ DOT

___ circle DRESS, GREAT, INNER

circles
  going around in ~ LOST
  run ~ around BEAT, BEST,
  LEAD

circuit BEAT, LAP, LOOP, ORBIT,
  ROUTE, TOUR
  ~ **component** FUSE
  track ~ LAP

circuit ___ RIDER

circuit breaker FUSE
  attend to a ~ RESET

circular BILL, PAPER, SHEET
  ~ **current** EDDY
  ~ **word** SALE
  follow a ~ path ARC
  somewhat ~ OVAL

circular ___ FILE, SAW

circulars ADS

circulate ISSUE, NOISE, PASS,
  POST
  ~ **rumors** TALK

circulation AIR
  ~ **aid** FAN
  organ of ~ HEART

circulatory
  ~ **pump** HEART

circumambulate AVOID

circumference EDGE
  ~ **segment** ARC
  in ~ ABOUT

circumjacent ABOUT

circumscribe LIMIT, RING

circumscribed LOCAL

circumspect ALERT, LEERY, WARY

circumspection CARE

circumstance CASE, FACT
  ~ **partner** POMP

circumstances LOT
  in reduced ~ NEEDY
  under no ~ NEVER

circumvent AVERT, AVOID, ELUDE,
  EVADE

circumventor LIAR

circus ARENA
  ~ **animal** BEAR, DOG, FLEA,
  LION, SEAL, TIGER
  ~ **arena** TENT
  ~ **employee** TAMER
  ~ **feature** RING
  ~ **routine** ACT
  ~ **sound** ROAR
  ~ **walker** STILT

circus ___ ACT, TENT

___ circus FLEA

Circus Maximus ARENA
  ~ **official** EDILE

"Circus of Dr. ___, The" LAO

cirque
  ~ **basin** TARN

CIS
  ~ **predecessor** USSR

"Cisco ___" KID, PIKE

Cisco Kid
  ~ **movie** OATER

cistern TANK, VAT

citadel AERIE, HAVEN, KEEP

Citadel
  ~ **student** CADET

Citadel, The
  like ~, now COED

citation AWARD, MEDAL
  ~ **abbr.** ETAL
  give a ~ TAG
  invite a ~ SPEED

Citation HORSE

cite NAME, REFER, TAKE

cithara
  ~ **cousin** HARP

"Citizen ___" KANE

citizen of
  ~ **(suffix)** ITE

citizen's ___ ARREST

Citizens ___ radio BAND

"Citizen Tom Paine"
  ~ **author** FAST

"Citizen X"
  ~ **actor** REA

citrate ESTER, SALT

citric ACID

citron
  ~ **ender** ELLA

citrus LEMON, LIME, ORANGE, UGLI
  ~ **city** OCALA
  ~ **cover** RIND, SKIN
  ~ **drink** ADE
  Jamaican ~ UGLI

city
  like a ~'s population DENSE

city ___ DESK, EDITOR, HALL

city-___ STATE

___ city FAT, INNER

"City ___" GIRL, HALL

"City ___ Conquest" FOR

"City ___ Never Sleeps" THAT

"___ City" FAT, NEON, OPEN, SPIN

"___ City, The" (Rome) ETERNAL

___ City ("Another World"
  locale) BAY

___ City ("Bronk" setting)
  OCEAN

___ City, Ariz. SUN

___ City, Hawaii LANAI

City of ___ (New Haven, Conn.)
  ELMS

"City of ___" HOPE

"City of Hope"
  ~ **director** SALES

"City of Light, The" PARIS
  ~ **sight** SEINE
  ~ **slangily** PAREE

"City of New Orleans" TRAIN

"City of New Orleans, The"
  ~ **singer** ARLO

"City of the Kings" LIMA

"City of Trees, The" BOISE

___ City, Okla. DEL

___ City, Pa. OIL

___ City Rollers BAY

"City Slickers"
  ~ **actor** STERN

"City That ___ Sleeps" NEVER

"City That Never Sleeps"
  ~ **director** AUER

"___ City Woman" SWEET

civet ANIMAL, CAT

civic
  ~ **organization** ELKS

Civic AUTO, CAR

civic center ARENA

civil LAIC, MILD
  ~ **defense drill** ALERT
  ~ **disturbance** RIOT
  ~ **offense** TORT
  ~ **servant** AGENT

civil ___ LAW, WAR

"Civil Disobedience" ESSAY

"Civilization"
  ~ **director** WEST

___ Civilized Nations FIVE

civil rights
  ~ **org.** CORE

Civil War
  ~ **color** BLUE, GRAY
  ~ **general** LEE
  ~ **inits.** CSA
  ~ **monogram** REL
  ~ **nickname** ABE
  ~ **side** UNION
  ~ **soldier** REB
  ~ **veterans' org.** GAR
  ~ **weapon** SABER

Cl ELEM
  17 for ~ ATNO

clabber CLOT, SOUR

clabbered SOUR

clack CLAP, NOISE

claim ASSERT, AVER, DEBT, STAKE,
  STATE
  insurance ~ LOSS
  lawful ~ DUE

legal ~ LIEN
make a ~ ASSERT

___-claims court SMALL

___ claim to LAY

Clair RENE

Claire INA

"Claire's ___" KNEE

___ Claire, Wis. EAU

clairvoyance ESP, PSI

clairvoyant ORACLE, SEER
~ card TAROT
~ words ISEE

clam
~ ender BAKE

clambake MEAL

clamber RISE, SCALE

clammy DAMP, WET

clamor BAWL, BLARE, CRY, DIN,
NOISE, ROAR, ROW, TODO, YELL
~ (for) ASK

clamorous LOUD
~ multitude ROUT

clamp CLASP, CLIP

Clampett, Jed
~ portrayer EBSEN

clams
prepare ~ FRY, STEAM

clan KIN, TRIBE
~ division SEPT
~ emblem TOTEM
~ man SCOT

Clancy TOM
~ hero RYAN
~ subj. CIA

clandestine
~ org. CIA

clang BANG, BLARE, BLAST, BOOM,
DIN, NOISE, PEAL, RING

clanging LOUD

clangor BANG, BLARE, DIN, NOISE,
PEAL, ROW

clank NOISE

"Clan of the ___ Bear, The" CAVE

"Clan of the Cave ___, The"
BEAR

Clanton IKE
~ foe EARP

clap BANG, BOOM, PEAL
~ in cuffs ARREST
~ together HIT

clapperclaw ABUSE, LACE

clapping NOISE

Clapton ERIC
old ~ band CREAM

claptrap PRATE, ROT, TRASH

claqueur FAN

Clara BOW

___ Clara, Calif. SANTA

Clare, Angel
~ wife TESS

Clarence DAY, LION

"Clarence ___ Angel" AND

"Clarence and ___" ANGEL

"Clarence, the Cross-Eyed ___"
LION

Clare of ___ ASSISI

claret COLOR, RED, WINE

clarify CLEAR, RAVEL, SETTLE,
SORT

clarinet PIPE
~ cousin OBOE
~ part REED
~ sound TONE
kind of ~ ALTO
name in ~ players ARTIE

clarion CLEAR

"Clarissa Explains It All"
~ actress HART, HESS

Clark BOB, DANE, KENT, ROY
~ colleague LEWIS, LOIS
~ of Metropolis KENT

Clark, Dick EMCEE, HOST

Clarke ALAN, MAE

Clark, Kenneth SIR

clash BANG, JAR, ROW, SPAT
~ of arms WAR
doesn't ~ GOES

"Clash by Night"
~ director LANG

clashers
Hollywood ~ EGOS

clasp CARESS, GRAB, GRASP, GRIP,
HOLD, PRESS
~ starter HAND
metal ~ CLIP
place for a necklace ~ NAPE

___ clasp TIE

class CASTE, CHIC, CLAN, ESTATE,
GENRE, ILK, LOT, ORDER, RANK,
SORT, STYLE, TACT, TIER, TYPE
~ division ORDER
~ ender MATE
dominant ~ ELITE
head of the ~ BEST, FIRST,
TOPS
high-school ~ MATH, SHOP
Hindu ~ CASTE
in a ~ by itself RARE
in a ~ with LIKE
in the ~ of AMONG
lower ~ MOB
ruling ~ ELITE
working ~ LABOR

class ___ ACT

___ class FIRST

classic
~ starter NEO
popular ~ OLDIE

Classic
see Greek, Latin

classical ATTIC, STYLE
~ composer BACH
~ language LATIN
~ musical OPERA
~ starter NEO
~ theaters ODEA

classification ILK, TYPE
draft ~ ONEA
SSS ~ ONEA

classified ___ ADS

classified ad
~ abbr. APT, GAR

classify FILE, LABEL, LIST, ORDER,
PEG, RANGE, RATE, SORT, TYPE

classmate PEER

classroom
~ for Zeno STOA
~ furniture DESK
~ jotting NOTE
~ missile ERASER
~ sound PSST, PST
~ wall hanging MAP

classy CHIC, POSH, SMART

clatter CLAP, DIN, JAR, NOISE

Claude MONET, RAINS

Claude ___ (Jean Schopfer
pseudonym) ANET

Claudel, Paul POET
see also poet

Claudia
colleague of ~ ELLE

Claudia ___ Johnson ALTA

"Claudia ___ David" AND

"Claudia and David"
~ director LANG

claudication LIMP

Claudius CAESAR, ROMAN
~ home ROME
~ stepson NERO
~ successor NERO
year in ~ reign LII, LIV
see also Latin

Claus
~ employee ELF

___ Claus SANTA

clause
~ link NOR
escape ~ OUT
union-contract ~ COLA

"___ Clause, The" SANTA

clavicle BONE

clavier PIANO
composer for the ~ BACH

claw NAIL
bird's ~ TALON

claws
owl's ~ PLANT

clay DIRT, EARTH, SOIL
~ brick ADOBE
~ cooker KILN
~ pigeon BIRD
~ rock SHALE
~ square TILE
~ + straw + water ADOBE
~ target sport SKEET
work with ~ MODEL

___ clay FIRE

Clay
~ today ALI

claybank HORSE

Clayburgh, Jill
~ film LUNA

clay-colored BAY

clayey
~ deposit LOESS
~ soil LOAM

Clay, Henry ORATOR
emulate ~ ORATE

clay pigeon
~ launcher TRAP
~ shooting SKEET

Clayton MOORE

___ Clayton Powell ADAM

clean BATHE, DUST, ERASE, PURE,
RINSE, SWAB, WASH
~ a blackboard ERASE
~ a chicken DRESS
~ a fish SCALE
~ a pipe REAM
~ one's plate EAT
~ out STRIP
~ rugs BEAT
~ the deck SWAB
~ up BATHE, EDIT, EMEND,
LAVE
~ up copy EDIT
come ~ ADMIT, BARE
good ~ fun LARK
make a ~ slate ERASE
show a ~ pair of heels FLEE
wipe ~ CLEAR

clean ___ (exhaust) OUT

___ clean (confess) COME

___-clean DRY

"Clean ___ Sober" AND

clean air
~ org. EPA

"Clean and ___" SOBER

clean-cut NEAT, TRIM

cleaner
~ partner DYER
~ scent PINE
~ target SPOT
boll ~ GIN
ear ~ SWAB
house ~, in England CHAR
pipe ~ LYE, SNAKE
plate ~, often UMP
strong ~ LYE

___ cleaner PIPE

cleaning WASH
~ **cloth** RAG
~ **substance** LYE, SOAP
needing ~ MESSY

___-**cleaning oven** SELF

cleanse BATHE, CLEAR, LAVE, RINSE, SWAB

cleanser SOAP
heavy-duty ~ LYE

clean up one's ___ ACT

clean water
~ **org.** EPA

clear EARN, ERASE, FAIR, FINE, FREE, GAIN, NET, OPEN, PASS, PURE, RID, SERENE
~ **as profit** NET
~ **a tape** ERASE
~ **out** FLEE, RUN, SCAT, SCRAM, TEEM
~ **plastic** SARAN
~ **sailing** EASY
~ **sky** ETHER
~ **tables** BUS
~ **the way** AID, HELP
~ **up** CLEAR, RAVEL, SETTLE
become ~ GEL
get ~ **of** ELUDE, EVADE
in the ~ SAFE
it's not ~ BLUR
keep ~ **of** ELUDE, EVADE
make ~ OPEN, SHOW, STATE
not at all ~ DIM
steer ~ **of** AVOID, EVADE, SHUN

clear ___ **(leave)** OUT

clear ___ **bell** ASA

clear-___ CUT, EYED

___ **clear (air-raid signal)** ALL

clearance SALE
~ **phrase** ASIS

"Clear and Present Danger"
Ford role in ~ RYAN

Clearasil
~ **target** ACNE

"___ **Clear Day You Can See Forever"** ONA

cleared
~ **out** GONE

clearer
base ~ HOMER

clear-eyed SOBER

clearheaded ACUTE, SOBER

clearing GLADE

___ **clear of** STEER

clear the ___ AIR

Clearwater RANGE

cleave ADHERE, AXE, CHOP, CUT, GASH, LOP, PART, REND, RIP

cleaver AXE, HACK

Cleaver WARD

Cleaver, Beaver
word from ~ GEE

Cleaver, Wally
~ **buddy** EDDIE

clef BASS
~ **notation** REST
kind of ~ ALTO, BASS

cleft ABYSS, GAP, GASH, HOLE, PIT, RENT, SPLIT

Cleghorne ELLEN

clematis VINE

Clemens ROGER, SAM
~ **stat** ERA

clement MILD

Clement MOORE, POPE

___ **Clemente, Calif.** SAN

Clementi
~ **piece** ETUDE

Clementine
~ **shoe size** NINE
entrance for ~'s father ADIT

Clements RON

Clemson
~ **athlete** TIGER

clench CLOSE, GRASP, GRIP, GRIT

Cleo LAINE
~ **snake** ASP
~ **wooer** MARC

Cleopatra
~ **attendant** IRAS
~ **river** NILE
~ **serpent** ASP

"Cleopatra"
~ **setting** NILE

Cleopatra, Queen of the ___ NILE

Cleopatra's ___ NEEDLE

clepe CALL, NAME

clerestory ATTIC

clergy
~ **mem.** REV
not of the ~ LAIC, LAY

clergyman ABBE, DEAN, PADRE

cleric ABBOT, DEAN, PADRE
~ **home** MANSE
French ~ ABBE
Moslem ~ IMAM

clerical
~ **court** ROTA
~ **garment** ALB
~ **subj.** REL
~ **title** ABBE
not ~ LAIC

clerihew POEM

clerk PEN
~ **concern** FILE
~ **spot** DESK

Clermont
~ **(abbr.)** STR

"Clermont" BOAT, SHIP
~ **power source** STEAM

Cleveland ABBE
~ **lake** ERIE
~ **once** PRES
~ **state** OHIO
~ **time zone** EDT, EST
city near ~ AVON

clever ABLE, ACUTE, APT, CUTE, NEAT, SLY, SMART
~ **expression** PUN
~ **person** WIT
~ **trick** RUSE

cleverness ART, TACT

clew BALL, ROLL

Cliburn VAN

cliché SAW, TAG, TIRED

clichés
full of ~ STALE

click FIT, NOISE, SNAP

client USER
~ **mtg.** APPT

clientele TRADE

cliff CRAG
~ **debris** SCREE
~ **dweller** EAGLE, ERN, ERNE
~ **dwelling** AERIE
~ **edge** LIP
~ **feature** CRAG
precipitous ~ SCAR

Clifford ODETS

climate FEEL

"Climate ___ **Killing, A"** FOR

climatic
~ **uproar** STORM

climax ACME, APEX, CAP, CLOSE, CREST, HEAD, PEAK
~ **starter** ANTI

climb ARISE, RISE, SCALE, SHIN

climbed ROSE

climber PLANT
~ **challenge** ALP
~ **goal** ACME
~ **need** SPUR
~ **rest** LEDGE
academic ~ IVY
garden ~ IVY
social ~ SNOB
wall ~ VINE

climbing
~ **device** STAIR
~ **plant** IVY, LIANA, VINE

clinch CLASP, HOLD, ICE, RIVET, SEAL, TIE

cling ADHERE, HOLD

clinging
~ **vine** IVY

clinging ___ VINE

Clingmans Dome
~ **loc.** TENN

clingy
~ **clothing** KNIT

clinic
~ **worker** NURSE

clink NOISE, RING, SNAP, STIR
~ **glasses** TOAST
one in the ~ CON

clinker DUD, ERROR, LOSER

Clint
~ **"costar" Clyde** ORANG

Clinton BILL
~ **alma mater** YALE
~ **astrologically** LEO
~ **Cabinet member** ESPY, RENO
~ **hometown** HOPE
~ **idol** ELVIS
~ **instrument** SAX
~ **opponent of 1996** DOLE
~ **party** DEM
~ **st.** ARK
~ **veep** GORE

Clinton, Bill ELI

Clinton, Chelsea COED

Clinton, Hillary
~ **alma mater** YALE

Clinton, Hillary, ___ **Rodham** NEE

"Clinton's Big Ditch" ERIE

Clio AWARD, MUSE
~ **candidates** ADS
~ **sister** ERATO
~ **winner** ADMAN

clip BOB, CROP, CUT, JAB, LOP, NIP, PACE, PARE, PASTE, RATE, ROB, SLAP, SNIP, TEMPO, TRIM
~ **one's wings** LIMIT
at a good ~ APACE

___ **clip** ATA, GEM, NEWS, NOSE, PAPER

___ **clip (biker's gadget)** TOE

clipped TERSE

clipper BOAT, SHIP
on a ~ ASEA, ATSEA

clippers TOOL

Clippers FIVE, TEAM
~ **org.** NBA

clippety-clop STEP

clique BAND, BLOC, CABAL, CLAN, GANG, INNER, SET
power-seeking ~ CABAL

cloak BLUR, CAPE, DRAPE, MASK, ROBE, WRAP
sleeveless ~ ABA

"Cloak, The" OPERA

cloak-and-dagger
~ **org.** CIA

clobber BASH, BAT, BEAT, BELT, BOP, CREAM, LAM, PASTE, PELT, ROUT, SLAP
~ **a fly** SWAT
~ **old-style** SMITE

cloche HAT

clock TIME
~ **climber of rhyme** MOUSE
~ **component** GEAR
~ **face** DIAL
~ **in** COME
~ **nos.** HRS
~ **numeral** III, ONE
~ **part** FACE, HAND
~ **setting** CDT, CST, EDT, EST, MDT, MST, PDT, PST
~ **settings** AMS
cab ~ METER
change the ~ RESET
summer ~ **setting** DST
way to set a ~ AHEAD

___ **clock** ALARM, SHOT, TIME, WATER

"___ Clock, The" BIG

"Clockers"
~ **director** LEE

clock radio
~ **feature** ALARM

___ **clockwork** LIKE

"Clockwork ___, A" ORANGE

"Clockwork Orange, A"
~ **character** ALEX

clod ASS, BOOR, EARTH, LOUT, OAF
~ **buster** HOE

clodhopper BOOR, OAF

clog CLOSE, DANCE, GLUT, JAM, SHOE, STOP

cloisonné ENAMEL

cloister ARCADE, CELL, HAVEN, PATIO

"Cloister and the Hearth, The"
~ **author** READE

cloistered PENT
~ **vault** ARCH
~ **woman** NUN

clomp TREAD

clone DUPE, IMAGE, TWIN
~ **unit** CELL
Dolly the ~ EWE

clonk THUD

close ANEAR, DENSE, END, LIKE, NEAR, SAME, SHUT, STALE, STOP
~ **an account** CLEAR
~ **at hand** NEAR
~ **attention, for short** TLC
~ **by** ABOUT, LOCAL, NEAR
~ **by, to a poet** ANEAR
~ **call** SCARE
~ **down** END, HALT, SHUT
~ **forcefully** SLAM
~ **hermetically** SEAL
~ **in** COME
~ **in on** GAIN
~ **kin, for short** BRO, SIS
~ **one's eyes to** PASS
~ **starter** FORE
~ **the curtains** DRAW

~ **the defense** REST
~ **to** ABOUT
~ **to a solution** WARM
~ **to the ground** LOW
~ **up** SEAL, SHUT
at ~ **range** NEAR
be ~ **to** KNOW
come to a ~ STOP, WANE
cut too ~ SCALP
getting ~ WARM
hold ~ PRESS
make a ~ **study of** PORE
not ~ AFAR
tread ~ **upon** TAG
very ~ **relative** TWIN

close ___ CALL

close ___ (liquidate) OUT

close-___ KNIT, UPS

close call
~ **comment** PHEW

closed
~ **car** SEDAN
almost ~ AJAR
not ~ OPEN

closed-___ DOOR

"Closed" SIGN

"Close Encounters of the Third Kind"
~ **craft** UFO

closefisted NEAR, SMALL

___ **close for comfort** TOO

close-grained
~ **wood** MAPLE

close-minded SMALL

close-mindedness BIAS

close-mouthed MUTE, TACIT, TERSE
~ **one** CLAM

"Close My ___" EYES

closeness LOVE

closeout SALE

closer
~ **stat** ERA, SAVE
purse ~ SNAP
voting-booth ~ LEVER

close shave SCARE

closest NEXT

closet HIDE
~ **hanging** TIE
~ **items** ATTIRE, LINEN
~ **lining** CEDAR
~ **pest** MOTH
Fibber McGee's ~ MESS
put in the ~ HANG
water ~ BATH, LOO

close the ___ on DOOR

close to ___ HOME

"Close to My ___" HEART

"Close to the ___" EDGE

closeup
cartographic ~ INSET

closing END
~ **word** AMEN
letter ~ BEST

closing night
~ **partiers** CAST

closure END, LID
tight ~ SEAL

clot GORE, MASS, SET

cloth FELT, LINEN, NET, SATIN, SERGE
~ **border** HEM
~ **cap** BERET
~ **ender** IER
~ **fold** PLEAT
~ **measure** ELL
~ **worker** DYER
cleaning ~ RAG
cotton ~ LAWN
drop ~ SHEET
ground ~ SHEET
length of ~ YARD
make ~ SPIN
make out of whole ~ LIE
man of the ~ ABBE, PADRE
metallic ~ LAME
not of the ~ LAIC, LAY
old ~ **measure** ELL
scrap of ~ RAG
see also **fabric, material**

___ **cloth** DROP

clothe ARRAY, ATTIRE, DON, DRESS, GARB, RIG, ROBE, VEST

clothed CLAD

clothes ATTIRE, GARB, WEAR
~ **line** HEM, SEAM
~ **pole** TREE
~ **presser** IRON
~ **tree** RACK
dirty ~ WASH
evening ~ DRESS
iron ~ ARMOR, MAIL
nostalgic ~ **style** RETRO
old ~ RAGS
sister's ~ HABIT
wearing ~ CLAD

clothes ___ MOTH, RACK, TREE

clotheshorse MODEL

clothesline ROPE

clothespin PEG

clothing ARRAY, ATTIRE, DRESS, GARB, GEAR, WEAR
~ **problem** SNAG
~ **protector** APRON
~ **size** LARGE, SMALL
~ **specification** SIZE
~ **store** SHOP
clingy ~ KNIT
déjà-vu ~ **style** RETRO
iron ~ ARMOR, MAIL
make ~ SEW
wolf in sheep's ~ SHAM
work ~ APRON

clothmaking
~ **apparatus** LOOM

Clotho FATE

clotted SOLID

clotted ___ CREAM

cloud BLUR, DIM, MIST
~ **name starter** ALTO
~ **region** SKY
black ~ PALL
comet's gaseous ~ COMA
luminous ~ HALO
under a ~ LOW
white ~ PET

"Cloud, The" POEM

"Cloud ___" NINE

cloudburst RAIN, STORM

cloud chamber
~ **contents** GAS

clouded DIM

___ **cloud in the sky** NOTA

cloudless CLEAR, FAIR, SERENE

cloud nine
on ~ ELATED

clouds
move swiftly, as ~ SCUD
treat ~ SEED
up in the ~ ALOFT

cloudy DIM, GRAY, GREY
make ~ ROIL

clough DALE

Clouseau
~ **caper** CASE

clout BANG, BEAT, HIT, PELT, SLAP, SMITE
those with ~ INS

clove hitch KNOT

clover PLANT
in ~ RICH

___ **clover** SWEET

cloverleaf
part of a ~ EXIT, LOOP, RAMP

clown BOOR
~ **around** KID, PLAY
~ **prop** STILT
~ **white** PAINT
be a ~ AMUSE

"___ Clown" BEA

clowning
bit of ~ ANTIC

cloy GLUT, JADE, PALL, SATE

cloying SWEET
become ~ PALL

club ASSN, BANG, BEAT, HIT, MACE, ORDER, SMITE
~ **for short** ORG
~ **for vacationers** MED
~ **selection** IRON
~ **soda fillip** LIME
~ **together** BAND
ball ~ TEAM
baseball ~ BAT
ceremonial ~ MACE
college ~ FRAT

club ___
  fan ~ focus IDOL
  golf ~ IRON
  health ~ SPA
  men's ~ FRAT
  one ~, perhaps BID
  service ~ ELKS
  war ~ MACE

club ___ CAR, SODA, STEAK

___ club FAN, GLEE, KEY

Club ___ MED

clubs SUIT

cluck CRY
  disapproving ~ TUT

clucker HEN

clue HINT, KEY, LEAD, SIGN, TIP
  ~ in WARN
  bloodhound's ~ SCENT
  drop a ~ HINT
  eerie ~ OMEN
  Holmes ~ ASH
  "Name That Tune" ~ NOTE
  without a ~ ASEA, ATSEA

Clue GAME
  ~ room HALL
  ~ weapon ROPE

clueless ASEA, ATSEA, LOST

"Clueless"
  ~ character CHER

clump CLOD, CLOT, GOB, KNOT, MASS, SET, WAD
  ~ of turf SOD

clumsy INEPT, LAME, RUDE
  ~ boat SCOW, TUB
  ~ one APE, CLOD, OAF
  ~ one's comment OOPS
  ~ ship ARK

clunk NOISE, THUD

clunker AUTO, CAR, HEAP, LEMON, LOSER, MOTOR

Cluny LACE

cluster KNOT, SET

cluster ___ PINE

clutch CLASP, GRAB, GRASP, GRIP, HOLD, NAB, NEST

clutch ___ BAG

clutches GRASP, GRIP, SWAY

clutter MESS

cluttered MESSY

Clydesdale HORSE
  ~ feature MANE

Clytemnestra
  ~ mother LEDA
  ~ sister HELEN

Cm ELEM
  96 for ~ ATNO

CNN
  ~ anchorman SHAW
  ~ home ATLANTA
  ~ word LIVE
  part of ~ NEWS

C-note
  change for a ~ TENS

C-notes
  ten ~ GEE

co-___ (urban apartments) OPS

co. ORG
  ~ VIP CEO, PRES
  cousin of ~ LTD

Co ELEM
  27 for ~ ATNO

CO
  see Colorado

C&O
  ~ and others RRS

coach BUS, MOTOR, STAGE
  ~ and four RIG
  Little League ~, usually DAD

"Coach"
  ~ network ABC

coachman RIDER
  ~ strap REIN

coachwhip SNAKE

coact BAND

coagulate CAKE, CLOT, GEL, SET

coagulated SOLID

coagulum CLOT

coal EMBER, OIL
  ~ bed SEAM
  ~ car TRAM
  ~ carrier CAR, SCOW
  ~ deposit SEAM
  ~ hauler TRAM
  ~ holder HOD
  ~ measure TON
  ~ mine PIT
  ~ product OIL, TAR
  ~ repository BIN
  ~ scuttle HOD
  ~ size PEA
  European ~ region SAAR
  gem-grade ~ JET
  German ~ region SAAR
  hot ~ EMBER

___ coal HARD, PEA

coal-black EBON, EBONY, RAVEN, SABLE

coalesce FUSE, GEL, MELD, UNITE

coalition AXIS, BLOC, RING, UNION
  bygone ~ UAR

"Coal Miner's Daughter"
  ~ subject LYNN

coals
  haul over the ~ ROAST

coarse BLUE, CRASS, LEWD, RACY, RAW, RUDE
  ~ corundum EMERY
  ~ file RASP
  ~ person BOOR, OAF, YAHOO
  ~ tobacco SHAG
  ~ wool fabric ABA

coast IDLE, LAND, ROLL, SAIL, SHORE, SLIDE

Coast SOAP
  ~ rival DIAL

___ Coast GOLD, IVORY

coastal LOW
  ~ flyer ERN, ERNE
  ~ phenomenon TIDE
  ~ recess COVE

coaster BOAT, SHIP, SLED, TRAY

Coast Guard
  ~ alert SOS
  ~ off. CPO, ENS
  woman of the ~ SPAR

coastline SHORE

coat DAUB, HAIR, PAINT, PELT, PLATE, RIND, SHEET, SKIN, SMEAR, WRAP
  ~ fabric SERGE
  ~ fastener SNAP
  ~ fold LAPEL
  ~ for a house PAINT
  ~ part ARM
  ~ rack TREE
  ~ starter BLUE, GREAT, OVER, RAIN, RED, TOP, TURN, UNDER
  ~ style ALINE
  ~ with metal PLATE
  animal ~ FUR, PELT
  banana ~ PEEL
  Camelot ~ MAIL
  cheese ~ RIND
  expensive ~ SABLE
  lose one's ~ SHED
  outer ~ SKIN
  pedicurist's ~ ENAMEL
  remove the ~ PARE
  seed ~ ARIL
  shaggy ~ HAIR
  squash ~ RIND

___ coat CAR, FUR, PEA, SEED

coati ANIMAL

coating SCALE, SHEET
  chimney ~ SOOT
  cooking-utensil ~ ENAMEL
  cookware ~ LARD
  decorative ~ ENAMEL
  downy ~ NAP
  protective ~ ENAMEL
  rustproof ~ ZINC
  slippery ~ SLIME

coat of ___ ARMS, MAIL

coat of arms CREST
  ~ band ORLE
  ~ figure BEAST

coax EGG, NAG, URGE

coaxial ___ CABLE

cob ANIMAL, BIRD, HORSE, MALE, SWAN
  ~ mate PEN

cobalt BLUE, METAL

cobble HEEL, PAVE, RESTORE, SOLE

cobbler PIE
  ~ concern SOLE
  ~ form LAST

~ tool AWL

Cobb, Ty TIGER
  ~ surpasser ROSE

___ Cob, Conn. COS

cobra SNAKE
  ~ comment SSS
  ~ cousin ASP

cobweb NET
  ~ site ATTIC

cobwebby FINE, THIN

Coca
  ~ cohort CAESAR

"Coca-___ Kid, The" COLA

"Coca-Cola ___, The" KID

cochineal RED

cochlea
  ~ site EAR

Cochran, Johnnie
  ~ forte LAW
  ~ occ. ATT, ATTY
  ~ org. ABA

cock BIRD, MALE
  ~ crown COMB

cock-a-doodle-doo CRY, NOISE

cockamamie DAFT, INANE

cock-and-bull
  ~ story ALIBI, LIE, TALE

cockatiel BIRD

cockatoo BIRD
  ~ feature CREST
  ~ kin MACAW

cockatrice OGRE, SNAKE

cockcrow
  until ~ LATE

cocker DOG, PET

Cocker JOE

cockeyed AGEE, AMISS, ATILT, DAFT, INANE, LOCO

cockles of one's ___ HEART

cockloft ATTIC

cockpit
  ~ abbr. ALT
  ~ VIP PILOT

cockroach PEST

Cock Robin
  like ~ SLAIN

cockscomb CAP, CREST, HAT

cockscrow
  at ~ EARLY

cocksure SMUG

cocktail
  ~ counter BAR
  ~ garnish OLIVE
  ~ lounge BAR

"Cocktail"
  ~ locale BAR

cocktail-party
~ **concoction** DIP, SOUR

"Cocktail Party, The"
~ **author** ELIOT
~ **monogram** TSE

cocky
~ **racer** HARE

Coco
~ **competitor** ESTEE
~ **concern** STYLE

coco-de-mer PALM

coconut OIL, PALM
prepare ~ GRATE

"Cocoon"
~ **craft** UFO

cod
~ **alternative** SOLE
~ **cousin** HAKE

Cod CAPE

C.O.D.
part of ~ CASH

coda
~ **place in a score** END

___ **Cod cottage** CAPE

coddle DOTE, SPOIL

coddled
~ **item** EGG

code RULE
~ **breaker** KEY
~ **carrier** GENE
~ **inventor** MORSE
~ **of conduct** ETHIC
a, in ~ ABLE, ALFA
cipher ~ KEY
communications ~
word ALFA
"D" in ~ DELTA
first ~ **word** ABLE
legal ~ LAW
Morse ~ **word** DAH, DASH, DIT, DOT
part of a ~ LAW

code ___ NAME

___ **code** AREA, BAR, DRESS, MORSE

codeine OPIATE

"Code of Scotland ___, The" YARD

codes
read bar ~ SCAN

codfish SCROD

codger COOT

codicil RIDER, TAG

codling ___ MOTH

cod-liver OIL

codswallop ROT

Coe MILER

coed
~ **quarters** DORM

Coen ETHAN

coerce BEND, MAKE, PRESS

Coe, Sebastian MILER
emulate ~ RACE, RUN

Coeur d'___, Ida. ALENE

Coeur d'Alene
~ **st.** IDA
~ **state** IDAHO

coextensive EVEN

coffee BEAN, BREW, JAVA, JOE
~ **accompaniment** ROLL
~ **additive** CREAM
~ **alternative** TEA
~ **break** REST
~ **emanation** AROMA
~ **fruit** BEAN
~ **grind** DRIP
~ **grinder** MILL
~ **in French** CAFE
~ **lightener** CREAM
~ **maker** POT, URN
~ **serving** CUP
kind of ~ DRIP, ICED, IRISH
make ~ BREW, PERK
spill ~ **on, perhaps** SCALD

coffee ___ MILL, SHOP, TABLE

coffee-___ book TABLE

___ **coffee** DRIP, IRISH

coffee beans
prepare ~ ROAST

"Coffee Cantata"
~ **composer** BACH

coffeehouse CAFE

"Coffee or ___?" TEA

coffer BIN, CASE, CHEST, SAFE, TILL

cog CAM, TOOTH

cogent CLEAR, SANE, SOLID

Coghlan, Eamonn MILER

cogitate MUSE

"Cogito, ___ sum" ERGO

"Cogito, ergo sum"
"sum" in ~ IAM

cognate KIN

cognizant AWARE
~ **of** ONTO

cognize LEARN

cognomen NAME

cogwheel GEAR

Cohan
part of ~**'s signature** GEO

Cohan, George M.
~ **ancestors** IRISH

Cohen ROB

cohere BIND, UNITE

coherent CLEAR, SOBER

cohort ALLY, ARMY, PAL

cohune PALM

coif AFRO, HOOD, STYLE, UPDO
curly ~**, for short** FRO

coiffure
kind of ~ UPDO

coil BEND, LOOP, RING, ROLL

___ **coil** TESLA

coin CASH, MINT
~ **catalogue rating** FINE
~ **collector** SLOT
~ **cutter** DIE
~ **factory** MINT
~ **finish** MAT, MATTE
~ **in a fountain** CENT, LIRA
~ **producer** MINT
~ **stamp** DIE
~ **substitute** TOKEN
~ **toss call** TAILS
ancient Roman ~ AES
Anglo-Saxon ~ ORA
Asian ~ SEN
Belgrade ~ PARA
bird on a ~ EAGLE
bronze ~ CENT
Brunei ~ SEN
Cambodian ~ SEN
Canadian ~ CENT, DIME
Common Market ~ EURO
copper ~ CENT
Danish ~ ORE
five-franc ~ ECU
French ~ SOU
Ginza ~ YEN
Indian ~ ANNA
Indonesian ~ SEN
Irani ~ RIAL
Israeli ~ AGORA
Japanese ~ SEN
Java ~ SEN
Kennedy ~ HALF
Kyoto ~ SEN
Old French ~ ECU
Peruvian ~ SOL
poker ~ CHIP
Pretoria ~ RAND
small ~ CENT
smallest US ~ DIME
south-of-the-border ~ PESO
Spanish Main ~ REAL
$10 ~ EAGLE
Thailand ~ ATT
thin ~ DIME
toss a ~ FLIP
Trevi Fountain ~ LIRA
Uruguayan ~ PESO
worthless ~ SOU
Yugoslavian ~ PARA
see also money

coin-___ (vending machines) OPS

coincide AGREE, FIT

coincidental
almost too ~ EERIE, EERY

coin of the ___ REALM

coin-op
~ **feature** SLOT

coin-operated PAY

coins
make ~ MINT

sm. ~ CTS

"___ Coins in the Fountain" THREE

Coke COLA, POP, SODA

col PASS

col.
~ **subordinate** SGT
~ **superior** GEN

Col.
~ **neighbor** KAN, NEB, NEBR
see also Colorado

cola POP, SODA
~ **buy** CAN, LITER

"___-Cola Kid, The" COCA

Colchis
its destination was ~ ARGO

cold ALOOF, ARID, DRY, ICED, ICY, STERN
~ **cubes** ICE
~ **cut** HAM, MEAT, SALAMI
~ **dish** SALAD, SLAW
~ **drink** COLA, POP, SODA
~ **duck** WINE
~ **feet** FEAR
~ **kin** FLU
~ **one** BEER, BREW
~ **precipitation** SLEET
~ **shoulder** SNUB
~ **spell** AGUE, SNAP
bitterly ~ RAW
blow hot and ~ HANG
break out in a ~ **sweat** PANIC
catch ~ AIL
damp and ~ RAW
down ~ PAT
have a ~ AIL
have ~ **feet** FEAR
make one's blood run
~ SCARE
out in the ~ ALONE
protection from ~ WRAP
put in ~ **storage** DEFER
roughen from ~ CHAP
sharp ~ NIP

cold ___ CALL, CASH, CREAM, CUT, FEET, SNAP, WAR, WATER

___**-cold** ICE

Cold ___ WAR

"Cold ___ Tree" SASSY

cold-blooded CRUEL

cold cuts
~ **store** DELI

cold-shoulder CUT, SHUN, SNUB

"Cold Turkey"
~ **director** LEAR

Cold War
~ **capital** BONN
~ **initials** USSR
~ **news agcy.** TASS
~ **pres.** HST
~ **spin-off** NATO

cold water
~ **fish** SMELT

cold weather
  ~ **carrier** SLED
  ~ **drink** COCOA
  ~ **malady** FLU

cole ___ SLAW

Coleco
  ~ **rival** ATARI

Coleridge POET
  ~ **composition** POEM
  ~ **poem** LOVE
  ~ **work** ODE, RIME
  friend of ~ ELIA
  schoolmate of ~ LAMB
  see also poet

coleslaw SALAD, SIDE
  make ~ SHRED

Colette
  see French

colewort KALE

Colgate
  ~ **rival** AIM, CREST

coliseum ARENA

coll.
  ~ **course** STAT
  ~ **grad** ALUM
  see also college

collaborate BAND, HELP, POOL

collaborative
  ~ **group** TEAM

collaborator ALLY

collage OLIO
  ~ **need** GLUE

collapse DROP, RUIN, SAG, SINK
  ~ **slowly** SINK

collapsed FLAT

collar ARREST, BAND, ETON, GET,
  GRAB, LAND, NAB, NAIL
  ~ **extension** LAPEL
  ~ **fastener** STUD
  ~ **insert** STAY
  ~ **straightener** IRON
  ~ **style** ETON
  ~ **victim** FLEA
  hot under the ~ IRATE, IRED,
    SORE, UPSET
  put the ~ **on** ARREST
  what a ~ **covers** NAPE, NECK

___ **collar** DOG, ETON, FLEA,
  HORSE

___-**collar** BLUE

"___ **Collar**" BLUE

collate SORT

collateral
  ~ **maybe** LIEN

collation MEAL
  ~ **serving** TEA

colleague PEER

collect AMASS, GET, RAISE
  ~ **a bet** WIN
  ~ **as luggage** CLAIM
  ~ **ender** IVE
  ~ **leaves** RAKE

  ~ **sap** TAP
  ~ **wages** EARN

collected CALM, COOL, SEDATE,
  SERENE
  ~ **sayings** ANA

collectedness POISE

collectibles
  some ~ ART

collection ARRAY, SET
  ~ **of anecdotes** ANA
  designer's ~ LINE
  fed. ~ **org.** IRS

collective TOTAL

collective ___ NOUN

collectively ASONE

collector
  ~ **suffix** ANA
  ~ **word** RARE
  coin ~ SLOT
  dust ~ RAG
  lint ~ SERGE
  nectar ~ BEE, HIVE

colleen GIRL, LASS, MISS
  ~ **home** EIRE, ERIN

Colleen MOORE

college
  ~ **army prog.** ROTC
  ~ **book** TEXT
  ~ **building** DORM
  ~ **choice** MAJOR
  ~ **club** FRAT
  ~ **concentration** MAJOR
  ~ **Connecticut** YALE
  ~ **course** ART, DRAMA, MATH
  ~ **cred. units** HRS
  ~ **declaration** MAJOR
  ~ **degs.** ABS, BAS, MAS
  ~ **department** ART, DRAMA,
    MATH
  ~ **entrance exam** PSAT, SAT
  ~ **founded by a king** ETON
  ~ **freshman, usually** TEEN
  ~ **grad** ALUM
  ~ **maj.** BIO, ECO, ECON, ENG,
    GEO, MUS
  ~ **major** ART, DRAMA, MATH
  ~ **official** DEAN
  ~ **party site** FRAT
  ~ **party staple** KEG
  ~ **room** DORM
  ~ **sports event** NIT
  ~ **sports org.** NCAA
  ~ **woman** COED
  junior ~ **degs.** AAS
  rel. of ~ **boards** PSAT
  word in some ~
    nicknames TECH

college ___ TRY

___ **college** COW

"**College**"
  ~ **director** HORNE

colleges
  like most ~ COED

"**College Widow, The**"
  ~ **author** ADE

collegian
  certain ~ COED

collegiate
  ~ **starter** INTER

collide
  ~ **with** HIT, RAM

collie
  fictional ~ LAD

colliery MINE
  ~ **exit** ADIT

collies
  ~ **do it** HERD

collimation LINE

collins
  ~ **ingredient** LIME

Collins PHIL

___ **Collins** TOM

collision HIT, SMASH
  ~ **result** DENT

colloid GEL

collop CHIP, SLICE

colloquial
  ~ **phrase** IDIOM

colloquialism SLANG

collude
  ~ **in crime** ABET

Colo.
  ~ **neighbor** KAN, NEB, NEBR
  see also Colorado

cologne SCENT
  ~ **characteristic** ODOR
  ~ **container** VIAL

Cologne CITY
  ~ **loc.** GER
  ~ **river** RHINE
  city near ~ ESSEN
  eau de ~ SCENT
  see also German

Colombia
  ~ **neighbor** PERU
  see also Spanish

Colombian
  ~ **cash** PESO

colon
  ~ **in analogies** ISTO
  half a ~ DOT

Colón CITY, PORT

colonel RANK
  ~ **bird** EAGLE
  ~ **command** ATEASE

___ **colonel** BIRD

colonial ERA
  ~ **dance** REEL
  ~ **descendants' org.** DAR
  ~ **loyalist** TORY
  ~ **starter** NEO
  onetime ~ **power** SPAIN

colonies
  one of the 13 ~ DEL

colonize PLANT, SETTLE

colonizer
  small ~ ANT, BEE

colonnade ARCADE
  Greek ~ STOA

colonus SERF

colony
  ~ **member** ANT
  bee ~ HIVE
  wasp ~ NEST

color AQUA, BELIE, BLUE, BRAG,
  CORAL, CREAM, DYE, ECRU,
  HUE, IVORY, LIE, LIME, LOAD,
  ORANGE, PAINT, RED, SLANT,
  TAN, TINGE
  ~ **starter** TRI

"**color**"
  music whose name means
    ~ RAGA

color-___ CODE

___ **color** LOCAL

Colorado DESERT, STATE
  ~ **city** AURORA
  ~ **county** OTERO
  ~ **neighbor** UTAH
  ~ **peak** ESTES
  ~ **resort** ASPEN
  ~ **tribe** UTE
  ~ **tributary** GILA

Colorado Springs
  ~ **acad.** USAF
  ~ **student** CADET

colorant DYE, TINT

coloratura
  ~ **perhaps** DIVA
  ~ **piece** ARIA

___-**colored glasses** ROSE

"___ **Colored Sky**" ORANGE

colorfast
  wasn't ~ BLED, RAN

colorful LIVE
  ~ **expression** IDIOM, SLANG

coloring
  ~ **agent** DYER, PAINT
  hair ~ DYE
  slight ~ TINT

colorist DYER

colorless ASHEN, ASHY, DRAB,
  WAN

colors FLAG
  it ~ **the eye** IRIS
  profusion of ~ RIOT
  sail under false ~ FAKE, LIE,
    MASK
  troop the ~ PARADE

"___ **Colors**" TRUE

colossal BIG, EPIC, GIANT, LARGE,
  VAST

Colosseum ARENA
  ~ **denizen** LION
  ~ **honoree** CAESAR
  ~ **setting** ROME

colossus GIANT, TITAN

colt ANIMAL, FOAL, HORSE, MALE
~ **mother** DAM, MARE

Colt AUTO, CAR, GUN, SAM

Colt .45
onetime ~ ASTRO

Coltrane
~ **instrument** SAX

Coltrane, Roscoe
~ **deputy** ENOS

Colts ELEVEN, TEAM
~ **org.** NFL

coltsfoot PLANT

Columba, Saint
site of ~ **monastery** IONA

Columbia CAPE
~ **athlete** LION

Columbia River
~ **feeder** SNAKE

"Columbia, the ___ of the Ocean" GEM

columbite ORE

Columbo COP, TEC
~ **caper** CASE

"___ Columbo" MRS

Columbus
~ **home** GENOA
~ **locale** OHIO
~ **sch.** OSU
~ **ship** NINA
~ **sponsor** SPAIN

Columbus ___ DAY

Columbus Day
~ **event** SALE
~ **mo.** OCT

column ARMY, LINE, PARADE, PIER, POST, RANK, ROW, TRAIN
~ **ender** IST
~ **next to ones** TENS
~ **part** DADO
~ **style** IONIC
addition ~ ONES, TENS
box-score ~ RBI
cal. ~ FRI, MON, SAT, SUN, WED
kind of ~ IONIC
rightmost ~ ONES, UNITS
sched. ~ ARR
standings ~ LOSS
wall ~ ANTA

columnists PRESS

Colum, Padraic POET
~ **work** POEM
see also poet

coma SLEEP

Comanche TRIBE

"Comancheros, The" OATER

comb CREST, RAKE, RAVEL
~ **impediment** SNAG
~ **manufacturer** BEE, HIVE
~ **out** DRESS
~ **projection** TOOTH
go over with a fine-tooth ~ HUNT, SEEK

combat DUEL, WAR
~ **vehicle** TANK
~ **zone** ARENA
hand-to-hand ~ MELEE
join ~ CLOSE
place for knightly ~ LISTS

combatant FOE

combe DALE

combine ADD, BAND, FUSE, MELD, POOL, RING, UNITE, WED

combined TOTAL

combo BAND, DUO, OCTET
card ~ PAIR
musical ~ TRIO
pinochle ~ MELD

"___ Combo, The" BIG

combusted AFIRE

combustible
~ **substance** COAL, GAS, OIL

combustion FIRE
~ **residue** ASH
criminal ~ ARSON

come ARRIVE
~ **about** ARISE, OCCUR
~ **across** MEET
~ **across as** SEEM
~ **after** HUNT, TAIL
~ **and go** PASS
~ **apart** SPLIT, TEAR
~ **around** AGREE
~ **ashore** LAND
~ **back** ARRIVE
~ **before** LEAD
~ **by** GET
~ **by honestly** EARN
~ **clean** ADMIT, BARE
~ **close** NEAR
~ **down** LAND
~ **down hard** POUR, RAIN, STORM, TEEM
~ **down with** GET, HAVE
~ **down with the flu** AIL
~ **face to face with** MEET
~ **first** LEAD
~ **forth** EMERGE, ISSUE, RISE
~ **from** RISE, STEM
~ **from the shadows** EMERGE
~ **home** SCORE
~ **home, as chickens** ROOST
~ **in** ENTER
~ **in first** WIN
~ **in handy** HELP
~ **in horizontally** SLIDE
~ **in last** LOSE
~ **in second** LOSE
~ **into** ENTER
~ **into contact with** MEET
~ **into existence** ARISE, EMERGE, LIVE
~ **into port** LAND
~ **into view** EMERGE, LOOM, RISE, SHOW
~ **last** LAG
~ **near** DRAW
~ **next** ENSUE
~ **off** PEEL
~ **off second best** LOSE
~ **open** UNDO

~ **out of hiding** EMERGE
~ **out on top** ACE, WIN
~ **out second best** LOSE
~ **out the same** AGREE
~ **out with** SAY, UTTER
~ **to** ATTEND, COST, TOTAL
~ **to a close** CEASE, END, HALT, WANE
~ **to a point** TAPER
~ **to a standstill** CEASE, HALT, STALL, STOP
~ **to blows** SCRAP
~ **to fruition** RIPEN
~ **together** CLOSE, FIT, GEL, HERD, MASS, MEET, MESH, UNITE
~ **together sharply** CLAP
~ **to grief** LOSE
~ **to grips with** FACE, MEET
~ **to light** ARISE, EMERGE
~ **to mind** ARISE
~ **to pass** ARRIVE, ENSUE, OCCUR
~ **to terms** AGREE, CLOSE, DEAL, SETTLE
~ **to the fore** EMERGE
~ **to the plate** BAT, HIT
~ **to the rescue** AID, HELP, SAVE
~ **unglued** RAGE, RANT, RAVE, SNAP
~ **up** ARISE, EMERGE, OCCUR, RISE
~ **up against** ABUT
~ **up for air** EMERGE
~ **up in the world** RISE
~ **upon** MEET
~ **up short** LOSE, MISS, OWE
~ **up with a plan** IDEATE
hard to ~ by RARE, SPARSE
in days to ~ LATER
not ~ off LOSE
sign of things to ~ OMEN

come ___ (affect) OVER

come ___ (appear) OUT

come ___ (find) ACROSS, UPON

come ___ (get) INTO

come ___ (happen) ABOUT, TRUE

come ___ (own up) CLEAN

come ___ (proceed) ALONG

come ___ in the wash OUT

come ___ one's own INTO

come ___ to roost HOME

come-___ ONS

"Come ___ About Me" SEE

"Come ___ Get It" AND

"Come ___ Spring" NEXT

"Come ___ With Me" LIVE

"Come and ___ It" GET

comeback
audible ~ ECHO
comic ~ ADLIB

"Come Back, Little ___" SHEBA

"Come Back, Little Sheba"
~ **author** INGE
~ **director** MANN
~ **wife** LOLA

"Come Blow Your ___" HORN

"Come-come!" POOH

comedian CARD, WAG
~ **date** GIG
~ **familiarly** COS

come down the ___ PIKE

comedy GENRE, PLAY
~ **routine** SKIT
bit of ~ GAG
musical ~ GENRE

___ comedy (slapstick) LOW

come from ___ AFAR

come-hither
~ **look** PASS

come home to ___ ROOST

come in ___ (get) FOR

come into one's ___ OWN

"Come, let us ___ Him" ADORE

comely FAIR

"comely ___ man as busie as a bee, A" OLDE

come on ___ OVER

come-on BAIT, LINE, LURE
~ **artist** SIREN
advertising ~ FREE
angler's ~ BAIT, LURE
manufacturer's ~ REBATE

"Come on in!" ENTER

come-ons ADS

come out in the ___ WASH

"Come Rain or Come Shine"
~ **composer** ARLEN

comes
one who ~ out DEB

"Come See ___ Me" ABOUT

"___ Come She Will" APRIL

"___ Comes Mr. Jordan" HERE

"Come Softly ___" TOME

"___ Comes Santa Claus" HERE

"___ Comes the Groom" HERE

comestibles DIET, EATS, FARE, FEED, MEAL

comet
~ **head** COMA
~ **part** TAIL
~ **path** ARC

"___ Come the Waves" HERE

come to ___ LIFE, PASS, TERMS

come to a ___ HEAD

come up ___ ROSES

comeuppance DESERT, DUE
gain ~ AVENGE
masher's ~ SLAP

comfort AID, BALM, EASE, HELP
~ **companion** AID
expression of ~ AAH

"Comfort ___ Joy" AND

comfortable ATEASE, EASY

comforting
~ **word** THERE

comic WAG, WIT
~ **comeback** ADLIB
~ **exaggeration** CAMP
~ **offering** GAG
~ **reward** HAHA
~ **sketch** SKIT
it may be ~ OPERA

comic ___ OPERA, STRIP

comical RICH

comic book
~ **squeal** EEK

"Comic Book Confidential"
~ **director** MANN

Comice PEAR
~ **cousin** BOSC

comic-page
~ **item** STRIP

comic strip
~ **bark** ARF
~ **dog** ODIE, OTTO
~ **exclamation** EEK
~ **girl** ANNIE, ETTA, LULU
~ **possum** POGO
musical based on a ~ ANNIE

coming DUE
~ **next** AFTER
~ **starter** HOME
~ **up** NEXT
have ~ EARN
say you're ~ RSVP
what's ~ to one DESERT

"Coming ___" HOME

"___ Coming" (Three Dog Night song) ELIS

"Coming Home"
~ **actor** DERN
~ **subject** NAM

coming of age
~ **period** TEENS

"Coming of Age in ___" SAMOA

"Coming of Age in Samoa"
~ **author** MEAD

"Comin' Thro' the ___" RYE

"Comique"
~ **actor** TATI

Comiskey Park ARENA
~ **home** CHI

comity TACT

command ARM, ASK, BID, BOSS, FIAT, HEAD, LEAD, ORDER, RULE, SWAY, TELL
~ **ender** ANT, EER
~ **the troops** LEAD
~ **to a dog** BEG, COME, HEEL, SIC, SIT, STAY

~ **to a mule** GEE, HAW
~ **to kitty** SCAT, SHOO
cannon ~ FIRE
computer ~ EDIT, ENTER, ERASE, SAVE, SORT
dentist's ~ RINSE
E-mail ~ SEND
evangelist's ~ HEAL
general's ~ ARMY
gunslinger's ~ DRAW
high ~ BRASS
Kapitän's ~ UBOAT
MD's ~ STAT
military ~ ATEASE, FIRE
nautical ~ AVAST
parade ~ HALT
rider's ~ WHOA
sea captain's ~ AVAST
sentinel's ~ HALT
sergeant's ~ ATEASE
word-processing ~ CUT, PASTE, SAVE

"___ Command" LOST

"___ Command, The" LAST

commanded BADE

commandeer CLAIM, GRAB, ROB, STEAL, TAKE

commander RANK
former NATO ~ HAIG

commander-in-chief RULER

commanding GREAT

commandment FIAT, LAW
~ **number** TEN
~ **starter** THOU
break a ~ SIN
last ~ TENTH

"___ Commandments, The" TEN

commando
~ **action** RAID

comme ci, comme ça FAIR, SOSO

commedia dell' ___ ARTE

commemorate KEEP

commemoration EVENT

"Commemoration ___" ODE

commemorative STAMP
~ **feast** SEDER
~ **stone** STELE
~ **verse** ODE

commence ARISE, ENTER, OPEN, START

commencement ONSET, ROOT, START
~ **wear** CAP

commend CITE, LAUD

commendable GOOD

commensal CAT, DOG, PAL, PET

comment NOTE
biting ~ BARB
unprepared ~ ADLIB

commentary ESSAY, NOTE

commentator
sports ~'s patter COLOR

commerce TRADE

commercial
~ **award** CLIO
~ **coloring** DYE
~ **writer** ADMAN
TV ~ SPOT

commercial ___ CODE, PAPER, ZONE

commercialism TRADE

commercials ADS
skip past ~ ZAP

commingle UNITE, WED

comminute MILL

commiserate FEEL

commiseration BALM

commissary AGENT

commission ACT, DEED, ENABLE, FEE, LET, LOAD, RATE, SEND
out of ~ IDLE

commissioner
Forum ~ EDILE

commit TIE
~ **a faux pas** ERR
~ **matrimony** WED
~ **to memory** LEARN
refuse to ~ HEM

commitment TIE

committee PANEL
kind of ~ ADHOC

commix UNITE, WED

commodious AMPLE, BIG, LARGE

commodity WARE

commodity exchange
~ **area** PIT

commodore RANK

common BANAL, BASE, LOW, MERE, RIFE, STALE
~ **abbr.** ETAL, ETC

common ___ LAW, NOUN, ROOM, SENSE

Common ___ ERA

"Common ___" SENSE

common cause
~ **group** BLOC

Common Cause
~ **founder** NADER

___ common denominator LEAST

commoners MOB

commonly OFT, OFTEN

Common Market
~ **coin** EURO
~ **money** ECU, EURO
~ **prefix** EUR, EURO

Common Mkt.
~ **locale** EUR

commonplace BANAL, MERE, STALE, TAME, TIRED, TRITE, USUAL
~ **(abbr.)** ORD
be ~ REIGN

commons FARE, MEAL

commonwealth LAND, STATE

Commonwealth
sign of a ~ corp. LTD

commorancy ABODE

commotion ADO, DIN, DUST, FLAP, MELEE, NOISE, RIOT, ROW, SCENE, STIR, TODO, YEAST

communal
~ **word** OUR, OURS

communicate RAP, RELATE, SAY, TALK, TELL, WRITE
~ **silently** NOD, SIGN
~ **with a medium** RAP

communication MAIL
dolphin's ~ SONAR
office ~ MEMO
PC ~ EMAIL
silent ~ ESP, NOD
wordless ~ ESP

communications
~ **co.** ITT
~ **device** PHONE
~ **logo** RCA
~ **outlets** MEDIA
~ **starter** TELE

communion RITE
~ **table** ALTAR

communiqué NEWS, NOTE
interoffice ~ MEMO

Communist RED
~ **hero** LENIN
old ~ state SSR

communistic LEFT

community ___ CHEST

commute ALTER
~ **starter** TELE

commuter RIDER
~ **carrier** AUTO, BUS, CAR, TRAIN
~ **handhold** STRAP
~ **line** RAIL

Como LAKE
where ~ is ITALY

"¿Cómo ___ usted?" ESTA

Como, Perry
~ **label** RCA
~ **song** MORE

Comorin CAPE

compact AUTO, AXIS, CAR, DEAL, DENSE, SMALL, SOLID, TERSE, TRIM
~ **mass** WAD
~ **material** ROUGE

compact ___ CAR, DISC

compactor
~ **input** TRASH

compadre AMIGO

compañera
  ~ in French AMIE

compañero AMIGO
  ~ in French AMI

companion MATE, PAL
  bedside ~ NURSE

companionless ALONE, LONE, SOLO, STAG

companionway HALL

company ARMY, BAND, CAST, CLAN, CREW, GANG, HORDE, HOST, MASS, TEAM, TROOP
  ~ abbr. INC
  ~ honcho CEO

"___ company" TWOS

"Company, The" CIA

"___ Company" BAD

Compaq
  ~ rival APPLE, MAC

comparable AKIN, ALIKE, CLOSE, LIKE, SAME

comparative
  ~ size RATIO
  ~ words ASA

compare
  ~ notes CHAT, GAB, RAP, TALK
  beyond ~ SOLE

compare ___ NOTES

comparison
  ~ words ASA
  numeric ~ RATIO
  word of ~ BEST, LESS, THAN, WORSE

comparison-___ SHOP

compartment BAY, CELL, ROOM, STALL
  driver's ~ CAB
  elevator ~ CAB, CAGE, CAR
  small ~ STALL
  spacecraft ~ POD
  till ~ ONES, TENS
  warehouse ~ BIN

compás
  ~ point ESTE

compass AREA, EDGE, LIMIT, PALE, RANGE
  ~ direction EAST, WEST
  ~ drawing ARC
  ~ pointer NEEDLE
  ~ reading ENE, ESE, NNE, NNW, SSE, SSW, WNW, WSW
  use a ~ ORIENT

compassion HEART, RUTH
  feel ~ ACHE
  Tibetan embodiment of ~ TARA

compatible
  be ~ AGREE, SUIT

compatriot ALLY

compel BIND, MAKE, ORDER

compendium ANA, SUM, TOME

compensate ATONE, PAY

compensation FEE
  worker's ~ RAISE
  workmen's ~ DOLE

"___ Compères" LES

compete PLAY, RACE, RUN, START, VIE

competent ABLE, ADEPT, FIT, GOOD, SANE
  more ~ ABLER
  not ~ INEPT

competition EVENT, GAME, MEET, RACE
  ~ component LAP, LEG
  athletic ~ MEET
  cowboy ~ RODEO
  fencing ~ DUEL

competitor FOE
  ranked ~ SEED

compilation ANA

compile AMASS, LOG

complacency EASE, PRIDE

complacent SMUG

complain CARP, CRAB, FRET, HARP, MOAN, NAG
  ~ angrily RAGE, RANT, STORM, YELL
  ~ constantly CARP, HARP, NAG

complainer CRAB

complaint ACHE, MOAN, PEEVE

complaisance EASE

complaisant EASY, MEEK, SWEET

complement ADD, MATE
  Ark ~ DUO, TWO
  full ~ LOAD
  Muse ~ NINE
  Supreme Court ~ NINE

complete ALL, CAP, DONE, END, ENDED, ENTIRE, SOLID, TOTAL, UTTER
  ~ a "j" DOT
  ~ an "i" DOT
  ~ a salad DRESS
  ~ dispersal ROUT
  ~ easily ACE
  ~ (prefix) TEL

completed DONE, ENDED, OVER
  ~ to a poet OER

completely ALL, CLEAN, CLEAR, FLAT, OUT

completes DOES

completion END

complex DEEP, HARD
  edifice ~ MALL

complexion CAST, COLOR, MIEN, TONE
  ~ woe ACNE
  dark ~ OLIVE
  kind of ~ FAIR

compliance
  in ~ with ALONG

compliant MEEK

complicate SNARL

complicated DEEP, HARD, UGLY
  make ~ RAVEL

complication SNAG

compliment
  ~ extravagantly EXALT
  ~ in a way APE
  react to a ~ BEAM, SMILE
  return the ~ PAY

complimentary FREE
  ~ ticket PASS
  ~ word COOL, FINE, GOOD

compline HOUR

comply ADAPT, BEND, DEFER, OBEY
  ~ with ADHERE, AGREE, KEEP, MEET, OBEY

component COG, PART, UNIT

components
  addr. ~ STS

comport
  ~ oneself ACT, LIVE

comportment MIEN

compos
  ~ mentis FIT, SANE
  non ~ mentis DAFT, MAD

compose EDIT, MAKE, PEN, WRITE
  ~ for printing SET

composed CALM, CLEAR, COOL, EVEN, SEDATE, SERENE

composer
  ~ output OPUS

composers
  ~ org. ASCAP

composing ART

composite TOTAL
  flower of the ~ family ASTER

composition ESSAY
  ~ for eight OCTET
  metric ~ POEM
  musical ~ OCTET, OPUS, SONG
  numbered ~ OPUS
  short ~ ESSAY

___ compos mentis NON

compost ROT
  ~ item PEEL, RIND

composure CALM, POISE

compote
  ~ cousin JAM
  ~ ingredient PEAR

compound MELD, PALE

comprehend DIG, GET, GRASP, KNOW, LEARN, SEE

comprehensible CLEAR, EASY

comprehension GRASP, GRIP, KEN
  kind of ~ AURAL
  words of ~ ISEE, OHS

comprehensive BIG, LARGE, TOTAL, UTTER

"Comprende?" DIG, SEE

compress CRAM, WAD

compressed DENSE

compressed ___ AIR

comprise HAVE, TOTAL

compromise AGREE, BEND, SETTLE

Compton ANN

comptroller
  ~ task AUDIT

compulsion MANIA, URGE, YEN

compulsive
  ~ behavior HABIT

CompuServe
  ~ correspondence EMAIL
  ~ patron USER

compute ADD, TOTAL

computer
  ~ abbr. RAM, ROM
  ~ accessory MOUSE
  ~ acronym RAM, ROM
  ~ button RESET
  ~ capacity MEG
  ~ command EDIT, ENTER, ERASE, SAVE, SORT
  ~ company APPLE
  ~ component CHIP
  ~ correspondence EMAIL
  ~ czar GATES
  ~ data FILE
  ~ datum BIT
  ~ device MOUSE
  ~ ender ESE
  ~ fodder DATA
  ~ key ALT, ARROW, DEL, ENTER, HOME
  ~ knockoff CLONE
  ~ language ADA, BASIC
  ~ list MENU
  ~ memory CORE, RAM, ROM
  ~ message ERROR
  ~ messages EMAIL
  ~ owner USER
  ~ perch LAP
  ~ pictograph ICON
  ~ screen CRT
  ~ sound BEEP
  ~ storage device DISC
  ~ whiz, impolitely NERD
  Apple ~ MAC
  brand X ~ CLONE
  central ~ HOST
  early home ~ ATARI
  fictional ~ HAL
  kids' ~ language LOGO
  old ~ memory CORE
  Taiwanese ~ company ACER

___ computer HOME

computer printer
  ~ device LASER

computer screen
  ~ image ICON
  ~ listing MENU

comrade ALLY, MATE, PAL
  see also Russian

"___ Comrades" THREE

Comstock ADA, LODE
~ **deposit** LODE, ORE
~ **entrance** ADIT

Comstock Lode
~ **st.** NEV

Comte de la Fere ATHOS

"Comus"
~ **composer** ARNE

con ANTI, DUPE, HAVE, LEAD, LEARN, TAKE
~ **artist's game** SCAM
~ **country-style** AGIN
~ **cubicle** CELL
~ **job** SCAM, STING
~ **opposite** PRO
~ **votes** NAY, NOES, NOS

con ___ AMORE, GAME, MAN

___ con carne CHILI

concatenation LINE, TRAIN

concave LOW
become ~ SINK

concavity DENT, HOLE

conceal HIDE, MASK, PALM

concealed
~ **by, to a poet** NEATH

concede ADMIT, AGREE, ALLOW, OWN

conceit DREAM, EGO, IDEA, PRIDE

conceited SMUG, VAIN

conceive BEAR, DREAM
~ **of** IDEATE

___-conceived ILL

concentrate ESSENCE, MUSE

concentrated DENSE, TERSE
~ **beam** LASER

concentrating RAPT

concentration GAME, PILE

concept IDEA, IMAGE
~ **(prefix)** IDEO
form a ~ IDEATE

conception IDEA, PLAN

conceptualize IDEATE

concern ALARM, CARE, FEAR, LOVE
~ **for a poet** METER

concerned
~ **with** INTO
one ~ with (suffix) EER

concerning ABOUT, ASTO, INRE, OVER

concert
~ **hall equipment** AMP
~ **income** TAKE
~ **proceeds** GATE
act in ~ UNITE
in ~ ASONE, ATONE

concerted ASONE

concert halls ODEA

concerto
~ **conclusion** CODA
~ **instrument** HORN, PIANO

"Concerto for the Left Hand"
~ **composer** RAVEL

concession SOP
~ **ender** AIRE
small ~ BONE

conch HORN, SHELL
~ **liner** NACRE

concha APSE

"___ Conchos" RIO

concierge
~ **place** HOTEL

conciliate ATONE

conciliatory MILD

concise TERSE

conclude CAP, CEASE, DRAW, END, HALT, SETTLE, STOP
~ **negotiations** AGREE
~ **one's case** REST

concluded DONE, OVER
~ **to a poet** OER

concluding
~ **passage** CODA

conclusion CLOSE, END, TAG, TAIL
~ **preceder** ERGO
Cartesian ~ IAM
draw a ~ EDUCE
geometry-proof ~ QED
in ~ THUS
mass ~ AMEN
musical ~ CODA
prayer ~ AMEN
reach a quick ~ LEAP

conclusive CLEAR, LAST

concoct BREW, MAKE, PLAN, SPIN

concoction BREW, LIE, TALE
culinary ~ DISH
egg ~ NOG, OMELET
kelp ~ AGAR
meat-and-potatoes ~ HASH
prof's ~ EXAM, TEST

concord LOVE, PEACE, TUNE

concordat PACT

Concorde JET, PLANE, SST

"Concord Hymn" POEM

"Concord Sonata"
~ **composer** IVES

concours MEET

concourse ROAD, ROUTE

concrete SOLID
~ **foundation** SLAB
lay ~ PAVE

concupiscence LUST

concupiscent LEWD

concur AGREE, FIT, HEED, NOD
~ **with** ADMIT

concurrence
word of ~ AMEN, YEA

concurring ATONE

Condé NAST

condemn DOOM

condensation DEW, STEAM, WATER

condense CUT, RECAP

condensed SMALL

condescending
~ **type** SNOB

condign MEET

condiment CAPER, SALT
Mexican ~ SALSA

condition CASTE, ESTATE, STATE, TERM, TONE
~ **of life** ESTATE
~ **(suffix)** ENCE, ISM, NESS, SHIP, URE
get into better ~ RESTORE
in good ~ FIT, HALE, TRIM
in mint ~ NEW
perfect ~ MINT
sales ~ ASIS
the human ~ LIFE

conditional
~ **word** MAY

conditioner RINSE
~ **ingredient** ALOE
soil ~ LIME, PEAT

___ conditioner AIR

conditions IFS

condominium ABODE, HOME, UNIT

condor BIRD, COIN
~ **country** PERU
~ **nest** AERIE
emulate a ~ SOAR

conduct ACT, BEAR, HOLD, LEAD, MIEN, SHOW, STEER, TAKE, USHER, WAGE
~ **a meeting** HOLD
~ **oneself** LIVE
disorderly ~ RIOT
path of virtuous ~ TAO
rule of ~ LAW

conductor METAL
~ **concern** TEMPO
electrical ~ WIRE
good ~ METAL
heat ~ COIL

___-conduct pass SAFE

conduit CANAL, MAIN, PIPE
underground ~ SEWER
water ~ MAIN

cone
~ **partner** ROD
~ **producer** ALDER, CEDAR, FIR, PINE, TREE
~ **unit** SCOOP
snow ~ ICE

___ cone NOSE, PINE, SNOW

cone-bearing
~ **tree** ALDER, CEDAR, FIR, PINE

cone-shaped
~ **heater** ETNA

"Coney Island"
~ **director** LANG

confab CHAT, MEET, TALK
church ~ SYNOD

confabulate CHAT

confection DROP, JAM, KISS, SWEET, TORTE

confectionary SWEET

confectioner CHEF

confederacy RING

Confederacy
~ **opponent** UNION

confederate ALLY

Confederate
~ **general** LEE
~ **soldier** GRAY, REB

confederation AXIS, BAND, PACT

confer CAST, ENDOW, MEET, TALK
~ **ender** ENCE
~ **honors** AWARD

conference TALK
~ **questioners** MEDIA, PRESS
~ **site** HOTEL
WWII ~ site YALTA

conference ___ CALL, ROOM

___ conference NEWS, PRESS

confess ADMIT, AVOW, LETON, OWN, TELL
~ **all** BARE

confession
~ **starter** MEA

"Confession"
~ **director** MAY

confessional
~ **item** SIN

"Confessions of ___ Turner, The" NAT

"Confessions of Felix Krull"
~ **author** MANN

confetti
make ~ SHRED

confidence EASE, POISE
betray a ~ BLAB, TALK, TELL

confidence ___ GAME, MAN

confident CLEAR, SURE
feel ~ HOPE

___-confident SELF

"Confidential ___" AGENT

confiding NAIVE

configuration CUT, MODE

confine CAGE, HEM, LIMIT, PEN, SHUT, TIE

confined LOCAL, PENT

confinement
place of ~ CELL

confines LIMIT

confining CLOSE

confirm ATTEST, AVER, AVOW, STATE

confirmation RITE, SEAL

confiscate GRAB, TAKE

confiture JAM

conflagration FIRE

conflate MELD

conflict DUEL, JAR, ROW, WAR
  ~ site ARENA
  classic ~ DUEL

___ conflict ARMED

conform ADAPT, AGREE, FIT, SUIT, TUNE
  ~ with AGREE, MEET, OBEY

conformable MEEK

conformist
  ~ starter NON

confound ABASH, ADDLE, AMAZE, BLAST, DASH, DAZE, GET, LOSE

"Confound it!" DARN, DRAT

confrere PEER

confront BEARD, DARE, FACE, MEET, SEE

confronting ACROSS

Confucian
  ~ principle TAO

Confucius SAGE

confuse ADDLE, SNARL
  totally ~ LOSE

confused ASEA, ATSEA, LOST, MESSY
  ~ fight MELEE
  make ~ ADDLE

confusion ADO, DAZE, MELEE, STIR
  cause ~ ADDLE
  state of ~ MESS

confute DENY

conga DANCE
  **where the ~
  originated** CUBA

con game
  sidewalk ~ MONTE

congé LEAVE

congeal CAKE, CLOT, COOL, GEL, SET

congealed SOLID

congenial NICE, SWEET, WARM
  not ~ ALOOF, COOL, ICY

conger EEL

congeries MASS, PILE

congest CLOG

congestion SNARL

___ congestion NASAL

conglobation BALL

conglomerate UNITE
  ~ letters ITT

conglomeration MASS, MOB, OLIO, PILE

Congo
  ~ language BANTU, IBO

"Congo, The" POEM

congou TEA

congratulate
  ~ oneself BRAG, PREEN, PRIDE

congregate AMASS, HERD, MASS, MEET

congregating
  place for ~ NAVE

congregation
  ~ response AMEN

congress DIET

Congress
  ~ creation LAW
  ~ mem. REP, SEN
  first name in ~ NEWT
  law passed by ~ ACT
  send back to ~ VETO

Congressional
  ~ body SENATE
  ~ caucus BLOC
  ~ employee AIDE
  ~ mtg. SESS
  ~ output ACT, LAW

congressman
  former California ~ BONO

Congressman
  ~ (abbr.) REP

conical
  ~ dwelling TEPEE
  ~ kiln OAST

conifer CEDAR, FIR, PINE, TREE
  ~ part CONE, NEEDLE

conjecture IDEA, OPINE

conjoin ABUT, ALLY, MESH

conjointly ALSO, ASONE, TOO

conjunction AND, NOR
  in ~ with ALONG, PLUS
  uncommon ~ LEST

conjure EVOKE
  ~ up DREAM, EVOKE

conjurer SEER
  ~ prop WAND

conk BANG, BEAT, BOP, HIT, SMITE
  ~ off REST, SLEEP
  ~ out DIE, STALL
  ~ with a ball BEAN

con man
  ~ forte SCAM

Conn.
  ~ neighbor MASS
  ~ zone EDT, EST
  see also Connecticut

connect ABUT, ADD, RELATE, SPAN, TIE
  ~ points on a graph PLOT

connect ___ TIME

connected KIN, ONE
  not ~ APART

Connecticut STATE
  ~ campus YALE
  ~ collegian ELI

connection KIN, TIE

connections INS, KIN

connective AND, NOR

connector AND, NOR, TIE
  narrow ~ NECK
  wheel ~ AXLE

connectors ORS

connect-the-___ DOTS

Connelly MARC

Connery SCOT, SEAN

Conniff RAY

conniption FIT, SPASM
  have a ~ RAGE

connive
  ~ at ABET

conniver
  ~ quest ANGLE

conniving FALSE

Connors
  ~ colleague EVERT
  ~ rival ASHE

connotation SENSE, TENOR, USAGE

connote MEAN

Conoco
  ~ rival ESSO

conquer BEAT, BEST, TREAD, UNDO, WIN

conquering ___ HERO

"Conqueror Worm, The"
  ~ author POE

___ conquers all LOVE

conquistador
  ~ quest ORO

Conrad
  ~ setting SEA

Conried HANS

Conroy PAT

consanguineous AKIN, KIN

conscience
  without ~ AMORAL

conscious AWARE
  ~ of ONTO
  become ~ ROUSE

___-conscious SELF

consciousness SELF, SOUL
  ~ component EGO

conscript PRESS

conscription
  ~ agcy. SSS

consecrate BLESS

consensus PULSE

consent AGREE, NOD
  ~ to ABIDE, ALLOW, LET
  word of ~ AYE, YES

consenting
  ~ words IDO

consequence END, ISSUE, NOTE
  be a ~ of ATTEND

consequences
  like some ~ DIRE
  suffer ~ PAY

consequently ERGO, THEN, THUS

conservative SAFE, SLOW, STAID
  ~ starter NEO, ULTRA
  British ~ TORY

conserve KEEP, SAVE, SPARE, STINT, STORE

consider DEEM, ESTEEM, HEED, HOLD, MUSE, RATE, SEE, TRY

considerable AMPLE, BIG, LARGE, MAJOR, PILE

considerably ALOT

considerate MILD, NICE
  be ~ of SPARE

consideration CARE, PAY
  in ~ of FOR

___-considered ILL

consign LEAVE, SEND
  ~ to damnation DOOM

consist
  ~ ender ENT

consistent EVEN

consolation BALM

console EASE, HELP

consolidate CAKE, MELD, UNITE

consort MATE
  knight's ~ LADY
  mom's ~ POP

conspicuous LOUD, OVERT
  be ~ SHINE

conspirators CABAL, RING

conspire CABAL, PLOT

Constance LAKE

constant ETERNAL, EVEN, SAME, SOLID, TRUE
  be ~ ABIDE, ADHERE

"Constant Craving"
  ~ singer LANG

constantly EVER
  ~ to a poet EER

constellation
  ~ Aquila EAGLE
  ~ Grus CRANE
  ~ Lepus HARE

~ **near Hydra** LEO
~ **unit** STAR
altar ~ ARA
bear ~ URSA
belted ~ ORION
Betelgeuse ~ ORION
brightest star in a ~ ALPHA
Northern ~ SWAN
Regulus ~ LEO
Rigel ~ ORION
second brightest star in a
   ~ BETA
Southern ~ ALTAR, ARGO
zodiac ~ LEO

consternation ALARM, AWE, FEAR

constituent PART, UNIT

constitute ERECT

"Constitution" BOAT, SHIP
~ **commander Hull** ISAAC

constitutional LEGAL

Constitution Hall
org. at ~ DAR

constrain IMPEL, LEASH, LIMIT,
REIN, STOP, TIE, URGE

constraint ARREST

constrict BIND, TAPER

constricting CLOSE

constrictor BOA, NOOSE
boa ~ SNAKE

___ **constrictor** BOA

construct ERECT, MAKE, RAISE,
REAR

construction
~ **area** SITE
~ **machine** CRANE
~ **piece** TBAR
~ **site** LOT
~ **site tray** HOD
caterpillar ~ TENT

construction ___ PAPER, SITE

constructs
Freudian ~ IDS

construe READ

consul
Roman ~ CATO

consult REFER, SEE

consume BITE, EAT, ERODE,
SPEND, TAKE, USE
don't ~ FAST

consumed RAPT, SPENT
be ~ **with desire** LUST

consumer EATER, USER
~ **draw** SALE
~ **gds.** MDSE
~ **lures** ADS
~ **watchdog org.** FDA

___**-consuming** TIME

consummate ARCH, BEST, FIRST,
GREAT, IDEAL, PURE

consummation END, GOAL, PEAK

consumption USE

contact GET, LENS
~ **via pager** BEEP
come into ~ **with** MEET
make ~ **with** HIT

___ **contact** EYE

"Contact"
~ **author** SAGAN
~ **characters** ETS

contain HAVE, HOLD

___**-contained** SELF

container BAG, BIN, CAN, CASE,
CHEST, CRATE, DISH, EWER,
FLAT, JAR, KEG, KIT, MOLD, PAIL,
PAN, POD, POT, SAC, SACK,
SKIN, STEIN, TANK, TIN, TRAY,
TUB, TUN, URN, VASE, VAT, VIAL
baryon ~ ATOM
beer ~ KEG, STEIN
butter ~ TUB
chemical ~ VAT
flour ~ SACK
flower ~ URN, VASE
fluid ~ SAC
food ~ CAN, TIN
freight ~ CAR
fuel ~ TANK
garden ~ POD
gas ~ TANK
glass ~ JAR
gold ~ POT
grain ~ BIN
Jell-O ~ MOLD
jelly ~ JAR
lab ~ VIAL
large ~ VAT
nail ~ KEG
nursery ~ FLAT, POT, TRAY
packing ~ CRATE
paint ~ CAN
pea ~ POD
pharmacist's ~ VIAL
pop ~ CAN
preserves ~ JAR
quark ~ ATOM
seed ~ POD
seedling ~ FLAT, TRAY
soda ~ CAN
tiny ~ VIAL
tomato ~ CAN
water ~ EWER, PAN, POT
weight of a ~ TARE
wine ~ SKIN, TUN, VAT

contaminate SPOIL, TAINT

contaminated BAD

contamination BANE, TAINT

conte TALE

contemn ABHOR

contemplate FACE, MUSE, SEE

contemplative NUN

contemporary NEW, NOW, PEER

contempt
beneath ~ SAD
express ~ HISS, POOH, SNORT
expression of ~ BAH
treat with ~ DIS

vent ~ SNEER

contemptible BAD, BASE, EVIL,
LOW, MEAN, UGLY, VILE
~ **one** CAD, CUR, HEEL, TOAD

contemptuous RUDE
~ **look** SNEER
~ **remark** BAH, HAH, PAH,
PSHAW

contend ARGUE, COPE, PLAY, VIE

contender
~ **chance** SHOT
be a ~ START

content EASE
~ **starter** DIS, MAL
sigh of ~ AAH
substantial ~ MEAT

contented GLAD
~ **sound** AAH, PURR
~ **sounds** AHS

contention
bone of ~ CAUSE, ISSUE
item of ~ BONE
still in ~ ALIVE

contentious IRATE, TESTY
be ~ ARGUE

contentment EASE, PEACE
express ~ AAH, PURR
inner ~ PEACE

contents LOAD

contest BOUT, DUEL, EVENT,
GAME, MEET, RACE, TILT, VIE,
WAR
~ **of words** BEE
~ **submission** ENTRY
~ **venue** ARENA
faked ~ SETUP
"Ivanhoe" ~ TILT
judicial ~ SUIT
no ~**, maybe** PLEA
Olympic ~ EVENT
qualifying ~ HEAT
speed ~ RACE
spelling ~ BEE
track ~ MEET
try a ~ ENTER

contestant
become a ~ ENTER

contestants
rank ~ SEED

contested
sharply ~ CLOSE

contiguous CLOSE, NEAR, NEXT
~ **acres** TRACT

continent ASIA, LAND
~ **(abbr.).** EUR

Continent
~ **dividers** URALS

continental
~ **divider** OCEAN, SEA, URALS
~ **drifter** PLATE
~ **prefix** AFRO, EUR, EURO

Continental
~ **rival** DELTA
~ **to a Redcoat** ENEMY, FOE

Continental ___ **(Washington's**
men) ARMY

contingencies IFS

contingent
be ~ **upon** AWAIT, HANG

continual ETERNAL

continually EVER

continue ABIDE, GOON, KEEP,
LAST, STAY

continuity TRAIN

continuous ENTIRE, SOLID
~ **flow** STREAM

continuously EVER

continuum LINE

contorted WRY
~ **smile** SNEER

contortionist
like a ~ LITHE

contour LINE

contour ___ LINE, MAP

contour map
~ **line** ALT

contra ANTI

___**-contra affair** IRAN

contrabassoon
~ **cousin** OBOE

contract AGREE, DEAL, GET,
LEASE
~ **add-on** RIDER
~ **issue** RAISE
~ **negotiator** AGENT, REP
~ **proviso** TERM
~ **with** HIRE
diplomatic ~ PACT

contraction SPASM
~ **for a poet** EEN, EER, NEATH,
NEER, OER, TIS, TWAS
common ~ ARENT, CANT,
DONT, ILL, ISNT, ITS, IVE
nonstandard ~ AINT
"The Star-Spangled Banner"
   ~ OER

contractor
~ **estimate** BID

contradict BELIE, DENY

contradiction
in ~ AJAR

contralto
~ **colleague** BASS, BASSO,
TENOR

contrary ALIEN, OTHER, POLAR,
WRY
~ **one** ANTI
on the ~ AGAIN

contravene BELIE, DENY

contribute ADD, AID, HELP, LEND

contribution ALMS
pot ~ ANTE
small ~ MITE

contributor DONOR
  pol. ~ PAC

contrite
  feel ~ RUE

contrivance ART, RUSE, TOOL, WILE

contrive ANGLE, BREW, MAKE, PLAN, RIG

contrived FALSE, MADE, PAT

control BOSS, GRIP, OWN, RULE, RUN, SAY, STEER, SWAY, TAME, WIELD
  ~ a 747 AVIATE
  ~ a cutter STEER
  ~ device REIN
  firm ~ GRIP
  go out of ~ RAGE
  have ~ of RULE
  keep under ~ LEASH
  lose ~ PANIC, RAVE, SKID, SNAP
  out of ~ AMOK, MAD
  TV ~ DIAL, KNOB
  under ~ COOL

control ___ PANEL, ROOM

___ control GUN

___-control SELF

controller
  jockey's ~ REIN

controlling LEAD, OVER

controls
  like some ~ DUAL

control-tower
  ~ device RADAR
  ~ dot BLIP

controversy ROW, SPAT

controvert BELIE, DENY

contumely ABUSE

conundrum KNOT, POSER

convalesce HEAL, MEND

convalescence CURE

convene CALL, MEET, SIT

convenience
  banking ~ ATM

convenience ___ STORE

convenience store
  ~ item COLA, POP, SODA

convenient PAT
  ~ excuse ALIBI

convent
  ~ attire HABIT
  ~ dweller NUN
  ~ room CELL

convention HABIT, RULE, USAGE
  ~ site ARENA, HALL, HOTEL

conventional BANAL, STALE, USUAL
  ~ (abbr.) STD

conventionality TASTE

conventual ABBOT

converge
  ~ on MOB, NEAR

conversant AWARE
  ~ with UPON
  be ~ with KNOW

conversation TALK
  ~ filler ISEE
  ~ starter HELLO
  center of ~ TOPIC
  make idle ~ CHAT, CHIN, GAB, RAP, YAK

conversational ORAL
  ~ pauses ERS

converse CHAT, GAB, RAP, TALK, YAK

conversely AGAIN

conversion
  lane ~ SPARE

conversion ___ VAN

convert ADAPT, ALTER, TURN
  ~ to currency CASH
  ~ to leather TAN
  ~ to machine language ENCODE

converted ___ RICE

convertible AUTO, CAR, MOTOR
  ~ maybe SOFA

convexity BOW

convey CART, HAUL, LADLE, LUG, PASS, SEND, SHIP, TAKE, TOTE

conveyance
  city ~ CAB
  Huck Finn's ~ RAFT
  Iditarod ~ SLED
  instrument of ~ DEED
  musher's ~ SLED
  Old West ~ HORSE, STAGE
  see also vehicle

conveyor BELT, PIPE

conviction IDEA, RAP, TENET
  state with ~ AVER, AVOW
  voice a ~ ASSERT

convince LEAD, SELL, SWAY

convinced CLEAR, SURE

convincing
  be ~ SELL

convocation DIET

convoke CALL

convolution COIL, LOOP

convoy FLEET, TRAIN
  ~ chaser UBOAT
  ~ component SEMI

convulse RACK

Conway TIM

cony ANIMAL, HARE

coo CRY, NOISE
  bill and ~ NECK, PET

cooee CALL

"Coogan's Bluff" OATER

cook BAKE, BOIL, BREW, CHEF, FRY, HEAT, MAKE, ROAST, SAUTE, SCALD, STEAM, STEW, TOAST
  ~ accessory MITT
  ~ cookies BAKE
  ~ ender OUT, WARE
  ~ for a crowd CATER
  ~ garment APRON
  ~ in water BOIL
  ~ measure TBS, TSP
  ~ over water STEAM
  ~ quantity DASH
  ~ up BREW
  ~ up a cabal PLOT
  ~ vessel PAN
  ~ with steam SCALD
  gourmet ~ CHEF

cook-___ OFF

Cook
  ~ (abbr.) STR
  ~ and others MTS
  ~ book COMA
  ~ offering TOUR

cookbook
  ~ amt. TBS, TSP
  ~ direction ADD, BASTE, BEAT, BOIL, CHOP, DICE, FRY, HEAT, PUREE, ROAST, SAUTE, SCALD, STEAM, STEW, STIR, TOAST
  ~ phrase ALA

Cooke SAM

cooked DONE
  lightly ~ RARE
  not ~ RAW

cooker
  clay ~ KILN
  food ~ OVEN, PAN, POT

cookie
  ~ flavoring ANISE
  ~ holder JAR
  ~ ingredient NUT, OAT
  ~ name OREO
  ~ nugget CHIP
  ~ sheet TIN
  ~ topping ICING
  crisp ~ SNAP
  gingery ~ SNAP
  kind of ~ BAR
  the way the ~ crumbles FATE, LOT

cookie ___ JAR, SHEET

cookiemaker
  ~ need OVEN
  famous ~ AMOS

Cookie Monster
  ~ cohort ERNIE

cookies
  cook ~ BAKE

cooking
  ~ direction BAKE, BASTE, BEAT, BOIL, FRY, HEAT, ROAST, SAUTE, SCALD, STEAM, STEW, STIR
  ~ ingredient LARD
  ~ odor AROMA
  ~ pot OLLA

cooking oil
  ~ source CORN, OLIVE

cook one's ___ GOOSE

cookout FRY, MEAL
  ~ intruder ANT
  ~ requirement FIRE
  ~ residue ASH
  ~ site PATIO, YARD
  fish ~ FRY
  Hawaiian ~ LUAU

Cook, Robin
  ~ book COMA

cookware
  ~ coating LARD

cool ALOOF, CALM, CHIC, EVEN, FAN, FINE, HEP, HIP, NEAT, POISE, RAD, SEDATE, SERENE, STOIC
  ~ and refreshing ICY
  ~ down ICE
  ~ drink ADE, COLA, POP, SODA
  ~ dude CAT
  ~ flavor MINT
  ~ it CEASE, STOP
  ~ million PILE
  ~ off FAN
  ~ one's heels WAIT
  ~ one's heels, perhaps WADE
  ~ someone off CALM
  ~ spot SHADE
  blow one's ~ BOIL, RAGE, RAMP

"cool"
  jitterbug's ~ HEP

cool ___ cucumber ASA

___-cool AIR

Cool ___ Bell PAPA

"Cool ___ Luke" HAND

"Cool ___ the Crazy, The" AND

cooler ADE, FAN, ICE, PEN, STIR
  ~ contents COLA, SODA
  air ~ FAN
  drink ~ ICE
  in the ~ ONICE
  lemon ~ ADE
  lime ~ ADE
  one in the ~ CON
  room ~ FAN
  sommelier's ~ ICER
  summer ~ ADE, ICE, POP, SODA
  water ~ ICE
  wine ~ ICE

___ cooler WATER, WINE

cool-headed CALM, SANE, SOBER

Coolidge RITA
  ~ nickname CAL
  like ~ TERSE

cooling
  ~ capacity unit BTU

Coolio
  ~ music RAP

Cool, Mr.
  hardly ~ NERD

"Cool Tombs" POEM

coon cat
~ **origin** MAINE

coonskin CAP, HAT

coop CAGE, PEN, YARD
~ **dweller** HEN
~ **group** EGGS
~ **sound** COO, PEEP
chicken ~ ROOST
flown the ~ GONE
fly the ~ FLEE, RUN, SKIP
pigeon ~ COTE

co-op ABODE, HOME, STORE

cooped
~ **(up)** PENT

cooper
~ **tool** ADZE

Cooper ALICE, PAT
~ **deadline** NOON
~ **novel, with "The"** SPY
~ **role** DEEDS, GESTE
word in a ~ **title** LAST

cooperate AGREE, BAND, HELP
~ **with criminals** ABET

Cooper, J.F.
~ **novel, with "The"** SPY

Cooperstown
~ **name** AARON, BABE, OTT, RUTH, YOGI

co-opt ELECT

coordinate MESH

coordinated
~ **group** TEAM
~ **outfit** SET

Coors BEER

Coos BAY, TRIBE

coot BIRD

cooties LICE

cop ROB, STEAL, TAKE
~ **milieu** BEAT
~ **out** DESERT, EVADE
~ **route** BEAT
~ **show wailer** SIREN
drug ~ NARC
"French Connection"
~ NARC
recognize, as an undercover
~ MAKE
undercover ~ AGENT, NARC

cop ___ (renege) OUT

cop a ___ PLEA

Copacabana
~ **city** RIO

copacetic AOK, FINE

copal RESIN

"Cop and the ___, The" KID

cope
~ **with** FACE, MEET
~ **(with)** DEAL

"Cope Book"
~ **aunt** ERMA

Copenhagen CITY, HORSE
~ **native** DANE

copier APER
~ **additive** TONER
~ **button** RESET

coping ___ SAW

copious AMPLE, BIG, LARGE, RICH

Copland AARON
~ **ballet** RODEO

Copley TERI

copper COIN, COLOR, METAL, TAN
~ **coin** CENT
~ **source** ORE
~ **tone** RED

copper-colored BAY

Copperfield, David
~ **first wife** DORA
~ **mother** CLARA
prop for ~ WAND

copperhead SNAKE

Copper River
where the ~ **flows** ALASKA

copper-zinc
~ **alloy** BRASS

coppice STAND

cops LAW
Army ~ MPS

"Cops ___ Robbers" AND

copse STAND

copter
~ **blade** ROTOR

copula CORD

copy APE, CLONE, DUPE, ECHO, IMAGE, ISSUE, NEWS, REPRO, STEAL, TRACE
~ **a drawing** TRACE
~ **briefly** STAT
~ **editor's concern** STYLE
~ **once** DITTO
~ **runner** PAGE
clean up ~ EDIT
magazine ~ ISSUE

copy ___ DESK

___ copy HARD

copycat APE, APER

copy machine
~ **need** TONER

copyread EDIT

copyright
~ **letter** CEE

coquette TEASE
act the ~ OGLE, TEASE

coquina CLAM

coquito PALM

coral COLOR, GEM, RED, SEA
~ **formation** ATOLL, REEF
~ **island** CAY, KEY
~ **reef** CAY, KEY, LEDGE

coral ___ REEF, SNAKE

Coral CAPE, SEA

Corby ELLEN

cord BAND, CABLE, LINE, ROPE
~ **starter** RIP
braided ~ ROPE
extension ~ WIRE
fishing ~ LINE
kaffiyeh ~ AGAL
thick ~ ROPE

___ corda UNA

cordage CABLE, LINE, ROPE
~ **fiber** SISAL

Corday
~ **victim** MARAT
see also French

___ corde TRE

corded
~ **fabric** REP

Cordelia
~ **father** LEAR
~ **sister** REGAN

Cordero ANGEL

cordial NICE, SWEET, WARM
~ **flavoring** ANISE
not ~ ALOOF, ICY

cording LACE

cordite
co-inventor of ~ ABEL

Córdoba CITY
see also Spanish

cordon BAND, LACE

Cordon Bleu
~ **graduate** CHEF
~ **phrase** ALA

corduroy
~ **ridge** RIB, WALE

cordwood
~ **measure** STERE

core BASE, BASIS, ESSENCE, GIST, HEART, MIDST, TENOR
~ **group** CADRE
inner ~ SOUL
revolutionary ~ CADRE

___ core HARD

Corelli
~ **close** CODA

Coretta ___ King SCOTT

corgi DOG, PET

coriaceous HARD

coriander SEED

Corinth
see Greek

Corinthian ORDER
~ **alternative** IONIC

Coriolanus HERO, ROMAN

"Coriolanus"
~ **attire** TOGA

cork LID, SEAL, STOP, TREE
~ **sound** POP

pop the ~ OPEN

Cork
~ **loc.** IRE
~ **locale** EIRE, ERIN
from ~ IRISH

corker LULU, PIP

corkwood BALSA

Corleone, Sonny
~ **portrayer** CAAN

corm SEED

Corman ROGER

cormorant BIRD

corn CAMP, CURE, HORN, NODE, OIL, SALT
~ **bin** CRIB
~ **bread** PONE
~ **crib** BIN
~ **ender** FED, MEAL, ROW
~ **holder** CAN, COB, CRIB
~ **lover** CROW
~ **product** OIL, OLEO
~ **serving** EAR
~ **st.** KAN
~ **starter** TRI, UNI
~ **tassel** SILK
~ **waste** COB
bearing ~ EARED
ear of ~ COB

corn ___ CHIP, DOG, MEAL, OIL, PONE, SILK, SNAKE, SNOW

___ corn SWEET

Corn ___ BELT

Corn Belt
~ **state** ILL, IOWA, KAN, NEB, NEBR

corncob
~ **kin** BRIAR

corncob ___ PIPE

cornea
~ **cover** LID

corned beef
~ **dish** HASH

Cornelia ROMAN

Cornelia ___ Skinner OTIS

Cornell EZRA

corner ANGLE, HOG, HOLE, NOOK, TRAP, TREE
~ **in geometry** ANGLE
~ **shape** ANGLE
~ **sign** STOP
~ **starter** CATER
amen ~ PEW
around the ~ NEAR
back into a ~ TREE
infield ~ BASE
off in a ~ APART
tight ~ PASS

___ corner AMEN

"Corner ___, The" BAR

___ Corner POOH

___-cornered CATER

"___-Cornered Moon" THREE

corners
cut ~ STINT

___ corners CUT

"___ Corners" FIVE

cornerstone BASE, BASIS
~ abbr. EST
~ feature DATE
lay the ~ START

cornet HORN

cornfield
~ array ROW
~ cry CAW
~ preyer CROW
~ sight EAR

Cornhusker
~ St. NEB, NEBR

Cornhusker State
~ city OMAHA

corniness CAMP

Cornish GENE

Cornishman CELT

corn on the ___ COB

cornrows
~ alternative AFRO

cornstalks
like mature ~ EARED

cornstarch
~ name ARGO

cornu HORN

cornucopia HORN

Cornwallis
~ alma mater ETON

corny BANAL, TRITE

corolla
~ part PETAL

corona GAS, HALO, RING
~ part PETAL

Coronado
see Spanish

coronet TIARA

corporal RANK
~ punishment, with
"the" ROD

___ corporal LANCE

corporate
~ abbr. INC, LTD
~ bigwig EXEC
~ department LEGAL, SALES
~ icon LOGO
~ problem DEBT, IMAGE
~ VIP CEO, PRES

corporate jet
~ name LEAR

corporeal REAL
~ channel AORTA
~ joint KNEE

corps BAND, CREW, TEAM

corpulent BIG, LARGE, OBESE

corpus
~ juris CODE, LAW

corpuscle ATOM

corral PALE, PEN, YARD

correct ALTER, AMEND, CURE,
EDIT, MEND, NICE, TRUE
~ a correction STET
~ a manuscript EMEND
~ a mistake ERASE
~ proofs EDIT
~ the time RESET

corrections ERRATA
make ~ to AMEND, EMEND

correctness TASTE

Correggio
~ creations ART

correlative AND, NOR

correspond AGREE, WRITE
~ ender ENCE, ENT

correspondence MAIL, NOTE
computer ~ EMAIL
numerical ~ RATIO

correspondent
author's ~ EDITOR

___ correspondent WAR

correspondents PRESS

corresponding ALIKE, SAME
~ to LIKE

corrida
~ beast TORO
~ floor ARENA
~ shout OLE

corridor AISLE, HALL, PASS
airport ~ RAMP

corrigenda ERRATA

corrigendum ERROR

corroborate ATTEST

corroboration TRIAL

corroboree DANCE

corrode EAT, ERODE, ETCH, FRET,
WASTE, WEAR

corrosion WEAR

corrosive ACID

corrugate PLEAT

corrupt BAD, BASE, EVIL, LOW,
SOIL, TAINT, UGLY, VILE

corruption EVIL, TAINT

corsair BOAT, SHIP

corselet ARMOR
~ half BRA

corset
~ stiffener BONE, STAY

Corsica
~ (abbr.) ISL
~ neighbor ELBA, SARD
see also French

cortege LINE, PARADE, TRAIN

Cortés
see Spanish

cortex COAT, PEEL, RIND, SKIN

Cortez
see Spanish

Cortland APPLE

corundum EMERY

coruscate BEAM, FLARE

Corvair
~ critic NADER

Corvus CROW

Cos ___, Conn. COB

cosecant
~ reciprocal SINE

"Così ___ tutte" FAN

"Così fan tutte" OPERA

cosine RATIO

___ cosine ARC

cosmetic CREAM, LINER, ROUGE
~ ingredient ALOE
~ purchase DYE, LINER,
RINSE, SOAP, TALC, TINT,
TONER
~ safety org. FDA

cosmetics PAINT
~ applicator WAND
~ company AVON
~ name ARDEN, AVON, ESTEE
plant used in ~ ALOE

cosmic ___ DUST, NOISE, RAY

"Cosmic ___, The" EYE

"Cosmo" MAG

cosmonaut
~ home MIR

cosmopolitan CHIC
not ~ RURAL

"Cosmopolitan"
~ rival ELLE

cosmos ALL, SPACE

"Cosmos"
~ author SAGAN
~ host SAGAN

cossack RIDER

cosset PET

cost BILL, FARE, FEE, RATE, RUN,
TAB
~ in a way BITE
~ per unit RATE
added ~ EXTRA
long-distance ~ TOLL
old phone-call ~ DIME
set a ~ ASK

___ cost UNIT

___ cost (free) ATNO

costa RIB

Costa ___ RICA

Costa ___, Calif. MESA

Costa ___ Sol DEL

Costa del ___ SOL

Costa, Michael
~ oratorio ELI

cost an arm ___ leg ANDA

costard APPLE

Costa Rica
see Spanish

Costa Rican
~ leader ARIAS

Costello ELVIS, LOU

costly DEAR, RICH, STEEP

Costner, Kevin
~ role EARP, HOOD, NESS

costs
absorb, as ~ EAT
cut ~ SAVE

costume ATTIRE, DRESS, GARB,
RIG
~ jewelry PASTE
ballerina's ~ TUTU
ghost ~ SHEET

cot BED, SACK

cote HOME, SHED
~ dweller DOVE, EWE, LAMB,
RAM
~ sound BAA, COO, MAA

Côte d'Azur
~ resort NICE

coterie BAND, BLOC, CABAL, CLAN,
GANG, SET
criminal ~ MOB

cotillion DANCE, GALA
~ attendee DEB

Cotswold
~ cry BAA

___ cotta TERRA

cottage ABODE, COT, HOME

cotter KEY

cotton
~ fabric LAWN, TOILE
~ mesh LENO
~ processing machine GIN
~ thread LISLE
~ to AGREE, LIKE
~ unit BALE
ball of ~ WAD
like unginned ~ SEEDY

Cotton ___ BELT

cotton gin
~ name ELI

cottonmouth SNAKE

cottonseed OIL

cottontail ANIMAL, HARE

Cottontail PETER

cottonwood ALAMO, TREE
~ cousin ASPEN

Coty RENE

cotyledon LEAF

couch PUT, SEAT, SETTEE, SOFA
 left the ~ AROSE

couchant PRONE

couch potato IDLER
 ~ choice CABLE
 ~ device DISH
 ~ domain SOFA
 ~ spot DEN
 like a ~ INERT

cougar ANIMAL, CAT, PUMA
 ~ cousin LION, OCELOT

Cougar AUTO, CAR

cough HACK
 ~ up ANTE, PAY

cough drop
 ~ flavoring ANISE, LEMON, MINT

could
 ~ possibly MAY

"__ Could Get Killed" AMAN

"__ Couldn't Take It" SHE

coulee GAP

couloir GAP

coulomb
 ~ per second AMP

Coulomb's __ LAW

Coulter __ PINE

council DIET, PANEL
 bishops' ~ SYNOD
 post-Reformation ~ TRENT
 Roman ~ SENATE
 Wash. ~ SEN

__ council CITY

Council
 sixteenth-century ~
 city TRENT

Council Bluffs
 ~ neighbor OMAHA

Council of __ PISA

counsel LEAD, WARN
 ~ (abbr.) ATT, ATTY
 ~ perhaps WARN

counsellor-at-__ LAW

counselor DEAN
 ~ (abbr.) ATT, ATTY

counselors BAR

count ADD, CAST, LORD, POLL, RANK, RATE, TITLE
 ~ British equivalent EARL
 ~ ender ESS
 ~ in England EARL
 ~ noses POLL
 ~ tree rings DATE
 candle ~ AGE

Count TITLE

countdown
 ~ delay HOLD
 ~ end ZERO
 ~ number ONE
 ~ start TEN

discontinue the ~ ABORT

countenance ABET, BLESS, FACE, LET, MIEN, SMILE

counter TABLE
 ~ to ANTI
 calorie ~'s retreat SPA
 KO ~ REF
 lunch ~ BAR
 mah-jongg ~ TILE
 religious ~ BEAD
 words at the deli ~ TOGO

__ counter (accountant) BEAN

counteract UNDO

counteractive CURE

counterculturist REBEL

countercurrent EDDY

counterfeit ACT, APE, BAD, BASE, FAKE, FALSE, PASTE, SHAM, STEAL

counterfeiters
 ~ nemesis TMAN

"Counterfeiters, The"
 ~ author GIDE

counterflux EDDY

counterfoil STUB

countermand ANNUL, UNDO, VOID

counterpart MATE

counterpoint
 master of ~ BACH

countersink REAM

countertenor ALTO

countervail ATONE

countess LADY, RANK, TITLE
 ~ husband EARL

counting
 not ~ SAVE

countless GREAT

"Count of __ Cristo, The" MONTE

"Count of Monte Cristo, The"
 ~ director LEE

countrified RUDE, RURAL

country GENRE, LAND, STATE
 ~ addr. RFD, RTE
 ~ addrs. RRS
 ~ home ESTATE
 Eur. ~ ALB, DEN, ENG, GER, IRE, ITAL, NOR, ROM

country __ HAM, MILE

__ country OLD

"Country"
 ~ actress LANGE

"Country __" LIFE

"Country __, The" GIRL

"__ Country" AFAR

"__ Country, The" BIG, FAR

country club
 ~ cry FORE
 ~ instructor PRO

"Country Girl, The"
 ~ playwright ODETS

country music
 ~ superstar CASH, LYNN, REBA

countryside LAND
 of the ~ RURAL

county __ AGENT, FAIR, SEAT

County Cavan
 river through ~ ERNE

"County Chairman, The"
 ~ author ADE

County Donegal
 ~ islands ARAN

coup ACT, DEED, FEAT, MOVE

coup d'__ ETAT

coupe AUTO, CAR, MOTOR
 ~ cousin SEDAN

couple CLASP, CLIP, DUO, MATE, PAIR, TWO, UNITE
 new ~ ITEM
 one of a ballroom ~ LEAD

"__ Couple, The" ODD

coupled DUAL
 ~ with AND, PLUS

Couples FRED
 ~ org. PGA

couplet DUO, PAIR, TWO

coupon
 ~ sites ADS

coupons
 save, as ~ CLIP
 use ~ SAVE

courage GRIT, HEART, NERVE, SAND
 show ~ DARE

"Courage __ Fire" UNDER

courageous GAME

"Courage Under __" FIRE

courant
 au ~ AWARE

course BEAT, CHASE, CLASS, CUT, HUNT, ORBIT, PATH, PLATE, POUR, RACE, ROAD, ROUTE, STREAM, TENOR, TRAIL, TREND
 ~ deviation YAW
 ~ finale EXAM, TEST
 ~ for an MD-to-be ANAT
 ~ length TERM
 ~ listing MENU
 ~ of action LINE
 ~ of events TIDE
 ~ of thought TENOR
 ~ reading TEXT
 change ~ TURN, VEER, YAW
 coll. ~ BIO, ECO, ECON, ENG, GEO, MATH, MUS, SCI, STAT
 college ~ ART, DRAMA
 dinner ~ ENTREE, SALAD
 down a ~ EAT

Eng. ~ LIT
 go off ~ VEER
 half the golf ~ NINE
 H.S. ~ ALG, BIO, ECON, ENG, GEO, LIT, MATH, MUS
 in the ~ of ALONG, AMID, AMONG
 main ~ ENTREE, MEAT
 main ~ of study MAJOR
 map out a ~ PLOT
 math ~ ALG, TRIG
 matter of ~ HABIT
 of ~ FINE, OKAY, SURE, YES
 par for the ~ NORM
 pursue one's ~ WEND
 race ~ OVAL
 run its ~ END, PASS, STOP
 shape a ~ PLAN
 through the ~ of AMID

courser HORSE, MARE, PACER, STEED

court ABODE, CHASE, DATE, PATIO, SEE, WOO, YARD
 ~ action SUIT, TRIAL
 ~ break BYE
 ~ call ADIN, LET, OUT
 ~ case RES, TRIAL
 ~ concern CASE, LAW
 ~ decision AWARD, LET
 ~ declaration PLEA
 ~ defense ALIBI
 ~ divider NET
 ~ ender IER
 ~ evidence, sometimes DNA
 ~ fig. ATT, ATTY
 ~ great ASHE, BORG
 ~ grp. ABA
 ~ matter RES
 ~ official REF
 ~ offs. DAS
 ~ order LAW, WRIT
 ~ org. NBA
 ~ reporter STENO
 ~ session TRIAL
 ~ sight NET
 ~ winner ACE
 clerical ~ ROTA
 drag into ~ HAUL, SUE
 introduce in ~ ENTER
 kid at ~ PAGE
 motor ~ INN
 pay ~ to WOO
 take to ~ SUE
 see also tennis

court __ ORDER

courteous SUAVE
 not ~ RUDE

courtesy
 ~ env. SASE

"Courting at Burnt Ranch, The"
 ballet subtitled ~ RODEO

courtly REGAL

court-martial TRY

Courtney LOVE

court of __ LAW

courtroom
 ~ drama TRIAL
 ~ phrase IDO

~ **ritual** OATH

courts
central ~ ATRIA
system of ~ BAR

courtship SUIT

"Courtship of Miles Standish, The"
~ **character** ALDEN

courtyard
modern ~ PATIO

courtyards ATRIA

couscous PASTA

___ **cousin** FIRST

Cousteau
~ **bailiwick** MER, OCEAN, SEA

Cousy BOB, CELT

couter ARMOR

couturier
French ~ DIOR

cove ARM, BAY, HAVEN, INLET, NOOK

Coveleski STAN

covellite ORE

covenant PACT

"Covenant" BOAT, SHIP

Covent Garden
~ **offering** OPERA
~ **performer** DIVA
~ **song** ARIA

Coventry
send to ~ SHUN, TABOO, TABU

cover BATHE, COAT, DRAPE, LID, MASK, PAINT, SMEAR, SPAN, TOP, WRAP
~ **another's tracks** ABET
~ **center field, perhaps** ROVE
~ **ground** HIE, MOVE, RACE, RUN, SPEED, STEP, TROT
~ **inscription** TITLE
~ **story** ALIBI
~ **the inside of** LINE
~ **the walls** PAINT, PAPER
~ **thickly** SLAB
~ **up** HIDE
~ **with asphalt** PAVE
~ **with fabric** DRAPE
album ~ LINER
ankle ~ SPAT
baby ~ BIB
canine ~ CAP
Cannes ~ BERET
canvas ~ TARP
cardboard ~ LINER
car grille ~ BRA
casserole ~ LID
citrus ~ RIND, SKIN
cornea ~ LID
engine ~ HOOD
eye ~ LID
floor ~ RUG
from cover to ~ CLEAN, OVER
fruit ~ PEEL, RIND
furniture ~ TARP
ground ~ LAWN, PLANT, SOD

head ~ CAP, HAT
infield ~ TARP
kumquat ~ RIND
lamp ~ SHADE
mayonnaise ~ LID
nutmeg ~ ARIL
onion ~ SKIN
orange ~ PEEL, RIND
pillow ~ SHAM
pond ~ ALGAE
table ~ SCARF
wheel ~ MAG
words on the ~ TITLE
wound ~ SCAB

cover ___ CROP, SLIP

cover-___ UPS

___ **cover** AIR, DUST, TAKE, UNDER

"Cover ___" GIRL

coverage PRESS
rug ~ AREA

covered CLAD
~ **by, to a poet** NEATH
~ **passageway** ARCADE
~ **walkway** STOA
~ **with water** AWASH, WET
not ~ OPEN

covered wagon
~ **direction** WEST

coverer
pajama ~ ROBE

cover girl MODEL, POSER

covering CASE, COAT, HIDE, LID, OVER, RIND, SHEET, SKIN
~ **(prefix)** EPI
board ~ EMERY
cake ~ ICING
can ~ LABEL
canine ~ ENAMEL
dais ~ DRAPE
eye ~ LID
floor ~ MAT, RUG, TILE
foot ~ BOOT, HOSE, PAC, SHOE
frank ~ SKIN
hard outer ~ SHELL
head ~ BERET, CAP, HAIR, HAT, HOOD, SCARF, TAM
hot-dog ~ SKIN
house ~ PAINT
mattress ~ SHEET
outer ~ DRESS
peak ~ SNOW
Pompeii ~ ASH
pond ~ ALGAE
pool-table ~ FELT
protective ~ ARMOR, TARP
pupil's ~ UVEA
seed ~ ARIL
snake ~ SCALE
spud ~ SKIN
wall ~ PAINT
window ~ DRAPE, SHADE

coverless BALD, OPEN

covers
under the ~ ABED
what a collar ~ NAPE

covert DEN, HAVEN, LAIR, STAND
~ **org.** CIA

cover-up ALIBI
rain-delay ~ TARP
tot's ~ BIB

covet LONG, LUST, WANT

covetousness SIN

Covington WES
~ **st.** KEN

cow ANIMAL, AWE, SHE
~ **bellow** BAWL, LOW, MOO
~ **catcher** LASSO, RIATA
~ **ender** BIRD, GIRL, HAND, HIDE, PEA, SLIP
~ **genus** BOS
~ **home** BARN
~ **pony** NAG
sacred ~ IDOL
trademark ~ ELMER, ELSIE
young ~ CALF

___ **cow** ANT, CASH, SEA

Coward NOEL

cowardice FEAR

cowardly BASE

Cowardly Lion
~ **portrayer** LAHR

Coward, Noel SIR

cowboy RIDER
~ **charge** HERD
~ **companion** HORSE
~ **competition** RODEO
~ **flick** OATER
~ **gear** ROPE
~ **home** RANCH, RANGE
~ **nickname** TEX
~ **rope** LASSO, RIATA
~ **strap** REIN
~ **sweetie** GAL
~ **thumbs-up** YEP
~ **wear** BOOT, SPUR
film ~'s **nickname** HOOT

cowboy ___ BOOT, HAT

"Cowboy and the Señorita, The" OATER

Cowboys ELEVEN, TEAM
~ **org.** NFL

cower FEAR

"___ Cowgirls Get the Blues" EVEN

cow-headed
~ **goddess** ISIS

cowhide TAN
~ **puncher** AWL

cowl HOOD

cowlick HAIR

coworker MATE

Cow Palace ARENA

Cowper, William POET
see also poet

cowrie
~ **protector** SHELL

cows
bunch of ~ HERD

Cox ALEX

coxcomb BEAU, DUDE

coxswain PILOT
~ **charges** CREW
obey a ~ OAR

coy ARCH, SHY, SLY

coyote ANIMAL, DOG

Coyote
~ **St.** SDAK

Coyotes SIX, TEAM
~ **milieu** ICE, RINK
~ **org.** NHL

Coyote, Wile E.
~ **mail-order company** ACME

coypu ANIMAL

coze CHAT

cozen DUPE

Cozumel
see Spanish

cozy WARM
~ **dwelling** NEST
~ **place** DEN
~ **place to sit** LAP
~ **spot** NOOK

CPA ACCT
~ **concern** ACCT
~ **employer** IRS
~ **forte** NOS
do a ~ **job** AUDIT
part of ~ ACCT

cpl. NCO
~ **boss** SGT
like a ~ ENL

CPR
~ **expert** EMT

CPU
part of ~ UNIT

Cr ELEM
24 for ~ ATNO

crab BEAR, NAG
~ **dish** LEGS
~ **feature** CLAW
~ **grass** WEED
move like a ~ SIDLE

crab ___ APPLE

Crab
the ~ SIGN

crab apple TREE

crabbed ACID, BAD, EDGY, MEAN, UGLY

crabby SOUR, TESTY, UGLY

___-crab soup SHE

crack ABLE, ACE, ADEPT, BEST, CHAP, GAP, GASH, HOLE, LEAK, MAR, OPEN, RENT, SHOT, SLOT, SNAP, SPLIT, STAB, TOPS
~ **a book** READ
~ **and redden** CHAP
~ **down on** HALT, STOP

crackbrained
~ ender POT
~ off CHIP
~ the whip GAME, LEAD
~ up AMUSE
at the ~ of dawn EARLY
open a ~ AJAR
take a ~ at ESSAY, TRY
till the ~ of doom EVER
tough nut to ~ POSER

crackbrained DAFT

cracked
~ in a way AJAR
it may be ~ SAFE, SMILE
liquor over ~ ice MIST

cracker
~ box SAFE
~ shape ANIMAL
~ spread BRIE, PATE
~ starter NUT
~ topping DIP, PATE

___ **cracker** ANIMAL, SODA

crackerjack ABLE, ACE, ADEPT, AONE

crackers LOCO, MAD

"___ Crackers" ANIMAL

cracking
get ~ HIE, RUN, SPEED, START

crackle
~ partner POP, SNAP

___! crackle! pop! SNAP

crackpot LOON, MAD, NUT

cracks
creep through the ~ OOZE, SEEP

cradle BED, CRIB

"Cradle of Love"
~ singer IDOL

"Cradle of Texas Liberty, The" ALAMO

craft BOAT, CANOE, DHOW, LINER, MAKE, RAFT, SHIP, SLOOP
~ a cardigan KNIT
~ of myth ARGO
~ partner ART
~ (suffix) SHIP
~ to remember MAINE
Indian ~ CANOE
lateen-rigged ~ DHOW
Martian ~, maybe UFO
motorless ~ CANOE, RAFT, SLOOP
Prudhoe Bay ~ OILER
racing ~ SHELL
ungainly ~ TUB
water ~ BOAT, CANOE, DHOW, LINER, RAFT, SHIP, SLOOP
WWII ~ LST
see also boat, ship

crafts
wood used in ~ BALSA

crafty ACUTE, ARCH, SLY, SMART

crag PEAK, TOR

craggy
~ abode AERIE

crake BIRD

cram GLUT, JAM, LOAD, PRESS, RAM, STOW

cram-full LADEN, SATED

crammed DENSE

cramp SPASM
muscle ~ KNOT

cramp one's ___ STYLE

cranberries
like ~ TART

cranberry RED

crane BIRD
~ cousin EGRET, HERON, IBIS, RAIL
~ operator's perch CAB

Crane BOB, HART, LES

Crane, Hart POET
see also poet

Crane, Roy
~ Captain EASY

crank NUT, TURN
~ up REV, START

crank ___ (produce) OUT

crankcase
~ contents OIL

cranky BAD, IRATE, MEAN, ODD, TESTY

cranny GAP, HOLE, NOOK, SPLIT
~ partner NOOK

Cranston ALAN
~ once (abbr.) SEN

craps GAME
~ action BET
~ pair DICE
natural, in ~ SEVEN
shoot ~ PLAY

crash BANG, DIN, PEAL, RAM, REST, ROAR, SLAM, SLEEP, SMASH
~ diet FAST
~ into HIT, RAM
a place to ~ BED, PAD

crasher
tea-party ~ ALICE

crashing LOUD
~ bore PEST
~ one BORE

crass RAW
~ one BOOR, OAF

Crassus ROMAN

Cratchit TIM
like young ~ TINY

Cratchits'
~ dinner GOOSE

crate AUTO, BIN, CAR, CASE, MOTOR

crater HOLE, PIT
~ contents LAVA

Crater ___ LAKE

Crater Lake
~ setting OREGON
~ st. ORE

Craters of the ___ (national monument) MOON

cravat REP, SCARF, TIE
~ cousin ASCOT
fix a ~ RETIE

crave ACHE, ITCH, LONG, LUST, NEED, WANT, YEARN

craven BASE

Craven WES

craving EAGER, ITCH, LOVE, LUST, MANIA, TASTE, URGE, WANT, YEN

craw CROP
stick in one's ~ IRK, PEEVE, REPEL, RILE

Crawford, Cindy
~ ex GERE
emulate ~ MODEL, POSE

Crawford, Joan
~ film of 1932 RAIN

crawl DRAG, ITCH, SWIM
do the ~ SWIM
make one's flesh ~ ALARM, REPEL, SCARE

crawler TOT
black ~ ANT
desert ~ SNAKE
red-orange ~ EFT

Crawley, Rebecca, ___ Sharp NEE

Crayola
~ choice BLUE, COLOR, HUE, ORANGE, RED, SHADE

crayons
use ~ COLOR

craze FAD, MANIA, MODE, RAGE
1920s ~ YOYO

crazed AMOK, LOCO

craziness
epitome of ~ LOON

crazy DAFT, LOCO, MAD
~ about INTO
~ bone ELBOW
~ like a fox SLY
~ quilt OLIO
be ~ about ADORE, DOTE, LOVE
go ~ FLIP
like ~ ALOT
plumb ~ LOCO
wild and ~ guy YAHOO

crazy ___ BONE

crazy ___ loon ASA

___ crazy (a lot) LIKE

___-crazy STIR

Crazy ___ HORSE

"Crazy ___" MAMA, MOON

"Crazy ___" Hirsch LEGS

"___ Crazy" GET, GIRL, GUN, STIR

crazy as a ___ LOON

"___ Crazy Love" THIS

"___ Crazy Summer" ONE

creak NOISE

cream BALM, COLOR, FOAM, MASH, OIL, ROUT, SODA
~ of the crop AONE, BEST, ELECT, ELITE, TOPS
Boston ~ PIE
ice ~ TREAT
ice ~ treat CONE, MALT, SODA
like some ~ SOUR
shaving ~ FOAM
shaving ~ additive ALOE
skin ~ TONER
soothing ~ BALM
sour ~ DIP

cream ___ SODA

___ cream EGG, ICE, SOUR

cream cheese
~ partner BAGEL

creamer
~ relative EWER

cream puff
~ sometimes CAR

creamy RICH

creamy-white IVORY

crease LINE, PLEAT

create MAKE, START
~ a word COIN
~ mentally IDEATE

"Creation, The"
~ role ADAM, EVE

creative
~ drive EGO
~ input IDEA
~ skill ART

creature ANIMAL, BEAST

"___ Creature, The" SHE

"___ creature was stirring..." NOTA

crèche
~ trio MAGI

credibility ___ GAP

credible HONEST, SANE

credit LOAN, MERIT
~ letters IOU
~ opposite DEBIT
college ~ HOUR, UNIT
coll. ~ units HRS
extend ~ LEND, LOAN
get ~ OWE
give ~ for ALLOW
letter of ~ NOTE
use ~ OWE

credit ___ CARD, LINE, UNION

credit card
~ color GOLD

creditor
~ right LIEN

credo DOGMA, TENET

credulous NAIVE

Cree TRIBE

creed DOGMA, ISM, TENET
~ **ender** AMEN

___ **Creed ("Rocky" role)** APOLLO

creek INLET, RIA, RILL, RUN, STREAM
cross a ~ WADE

Creek TRIBE

creep CLOD, DRAG, EDGE, INCH, LOSER, SLIP, SNEAK, STEAL
~ **through the cracks** OOZE, SEEP

creeper IVY, PLANT, TOT, VINE

creeping SLOW

creeps
give one the ~ ALARM, REPEL, SCARE
the ~ FEAR

creepy EERIE, EERY

Creighton University
~ **site** OMAHA

crème ___ crème DELA

crème caramel FLAN

crème de la crème ELITE

Cremona
~ **violinmaker** AMATI

crenel SLIT

Crenshaw BEN, MELON
~ **org.** PGA

Creole
~ **vegetable** OKRA

Creon
~ **to Antigone** UNCLE

creosote
~ **source** TAR

crepe ___ PAPER

crepitate SNAP

crepuscular DIM

crescendo RISE

crescent ARC, BOW, MOON

crescent ___ MOON, ROLL

___ **Crescent** RED

crescent-moon
~ **end** HORN

crest ACME, APEX, CAP, COMB, PEAK, SEAL, TOP
mountain ~ ARETE
on the ~ ATOP

Crest
~ **rival** AIM

crestfallen BLUE, LOW, SAD

Crete
~ **peak** IDA

Creusa
son of ~ ION

crevasse ABYSS, HOLE, PIT, RENT, SPLIT

crevice ABYSS, GAP, HOLE, LEAK, RENT, SPACE, SPLIT

crew BAND, GANG, HELP, LOT, MOB, TEAM
~ **implement** OAR
~ **member** HAND
hire a ~ MAN
skeleton ~ CADRE

crew ___ NECK

crew cut
~ **opposite** AFRO
give a ~ CROP

crewel
~ **tool** NEEDLE

crewman GOB, SALT, TAR

crib BED, BIN, COT, PEN, RACK, ROB, STALL, STEAL, TAKE, TROT
~ **contents** CORN
~ **cry** MAMA
corn ~ BIN

crib ___ SHEET

cribbage GAME
~ **marker** PEG
jack, in ~ NOB

Crichton, Michael
~ **film of 1978** COMA

crick ACHE, PAIN, PANG

Crick
~ **concern** DNA

cricket GAME
~ **piece** BAT
~ **sides** ONS
~ **squad** ELEVEN
~ **term** BYE
~ **wicket** END

"___ Cried" SHE

cries OHS
~ **of delight** AHS

"Cries ___ Whispers" AND

crime EVIL, SIN
aid in ~ ABET
defamer's ~ LIBEL
firebug's ~ ARSON
organized ~ MOB
pyromaniac's ~ ARSON

"Crime ___ Punishment" AND

Crimea
see Russian

Crimean TATAR, WAR
~ **port** YALTA

"Crime and Punishment"
~ **actor** LORRE

crimebuster COP, GMAN, NARC, TMAN

"Crimes and Misdemeanors"
~ **actor** ALDA
~ **actress** AARON
~ **director** ALLEN

criminal BAD, EVIL
~ **charge** RAP

~ **combustion** ARSON
~ **group** MOB, RING
~ **slang** ARGOT

criminal ___ LAW

criminals
cooperate with ~ ABET

crimp PLEAT

crimson COLOR, RED

Crimson
~ **rivals** ELIS

Crimson ___ TIDE

Crimson Tide
~ **st.** ALA

"Crimson Tide"
~ **director** SCOTT

cringe SHY

crinkled
~ **fabric** CREPE

"___ Cripple Creek" UPON

crippled LAME

crisis HEAD, NEED
financial ~ PANIC

crisp HARD, TERSE
~ **cookie** SNAP
no longer ~ STALE

Crispin
~ **product** SHOE

Cristo
Sangre de ~ RANGE

___ **Cristo** MONTE

Cristobal CITY, PORT

___ **Cristóbal, Venezuela** SAN

criterion NORM, RULE, TEST
~ **(abbr.)** STD
financial-aid ~ NEED

critic
~ **unit** STAR
Corvair ~ NADER

critical ACUTE, DIRE, KEY
~ **reaction** RAVE
~ **remark** BARB

critical ___ MASS

criticism
constant ~ ABUSE
harsh ~ SLAM

criticize BASH, BLAST, CARP, LASH, NAG, PAN, RAIL, RAP, RIP, SCORE, SNIPE, TRASH

critique BARB

"Critique of Judgment"
~ **author** KANT

"Critique of Practical Reason"
~ **author** KANT

"Critique of Pure Reason"
~ **author** KANT

critter ANIMAL, BEAST

croak NOISE

Croat SLAV
~ **neighbor** SERB

crochet KNIT, LACE, NOTE

crock DISH, EWER, JAR, POT

Crockett
~ **beat** MIAMI

Crockett, Davy HERO
~ **last stand** ALAMO

crockpot
~ **recipe** STEW

crocodile
~ **tears** POSE
like ~ **tears** FAKE, FALSE

"Crocodile Rock"
~ **name** ELTON

crocodiles
home for some ~ NILE

crocus
~ **cousin** IRIS

Croesus
like ~ RICH

croft ABODE, HOME

Crofts
~ **partner** SEALS

Cro-Magnon
~ **home** CAVE

crone HAG
like a ~ ANILE

Cronkite
~ **network** CBS

Cronus TITAN
daughter of ~ HERA
mother of ~ GAEA
wife of ~ RHEA
Zeus, to ~ SON

crony ALLY, MATE, PAL

crook BEND, ROD
~ **one's finger** SIGN
~ **story** ALIBI
assist a ~ ABET

crooked AGEE, AWRY, BAD, BENT, WRY
~ **gate of nursery rhyme** STILE
~ **letter** ESS
~ **scheme** CON, SCAM

crookedly AWRY

"Crooklyn"
~ **director** LEE

croon SING

crooner
~ **of the 1950s** COMO

crop BOB, CLIP, CUT, FEED, LOP, NIP, PARE, SNIP
~ **unit** ROW
~ **up** ARISE, EMERGE, RISE
bird's ~ CRAW
cream of the ~ BEST, ELITE
insect ~ CRAW
Iowa ~ CORN
paddy ~ RICE
root ~ YAM

crop-___

crop-___ DUST, EARED

___ crop CASH, ROOT

cropland
~ **measure** ACRE

crops
bring in the ~ REAP
treat ~ DUST

croquet GAME
~ **site** LAWN, YARD

croquette MEAT

Crosby NORM

Crosby and Stills
partner of ~ NASH

Crosby, Bing
~ **costar** HOPE
~ **song** AMOR, DINAH

crosier ROD
~ **carrier** ABBOT

Crosland ALAN

cross BAD, IRATE, MEAN, ROOD, RUDE, SPAN, TESTY, UGLY, UPSET
~ **a creek** WADE
~ **ender** BAR, BEAM, BILL, BOW, BREED, CUT, FIRE, ROAD, TALK, TIE, WISE
~ **one's mind** OCCUR
~ **out** DELE, EMEND, ERASE, OMIT
~ **over** CUT, SPAN
~ **swords** ARGUE, CLOSE
~ **the plate** SCORE
~ **the threshold** ENTER
~ **to bear** ONUS
align the ~ hairs AIM
kind of ~ TAU

___ cross IONA

Cross AMANDA, BEN

___ Cross RED

crossbow
~ **bolt** ARROW
ready a ~ AIM

___ cross bun HOT

cross-check TEST

cross-country
~ **runner** RACER
go ~ HIKE

crosscurrent EDDY

crosscut ___ SAW

___-crossed STAR

___-crossed lovers STAR

crosser
Hollywood Boulevard ~ VINE
picket-line ~ SCAB
Rubicon ~ CAESAR

cross-examine ASK

crossing
~ **the ocean** ASEA, ATSEA
rural ~ STILE

"Crossing the Bar" POEM

cross-legged
~ **exercises** YOGA

"Cross my ___ with silver" PALM

"Cross of ___" GOLD, IRON

crosspiece BAR

cross-purposes ODDS

crosswalk LANE

crosswise AWRY
~ **at sea** ABEAM

crossword
~ **solver's need** ERASER

crotchety BAD, MEAN, TESTY
~ **one** COOT

croton PLANT

crouch BEND, DROP, SIT

crouching LOW

croup HIP, REAR

croupier
~ **tool** RAKE

crow BIRD, BRAG, CRY, LEVER, NOISE, ROOK
~ **ender** BAR
~ **foot** LINE
~ **sound** CAW
~ **starter** SCARE

___ crow EAT

Crow TRIBE
~ **home** TEPEE

crowbait HORSE, NAG

crowbar LEVER
use a ~ PRY

crowd ARMY, BAND, CLAN, CREW, GANG, HERD, HORDE, HOST, JAM, LOAD, LOT, MASS, MOB, PRESS, SET, TROOP
~ **around** MOB
~ **in** TROOP
~ **noise** RAH, ROAR
~ **pleaser** PARADE
~ **proverbially** THREE
cook for a ~ CATER
in a ~ AMID, AMONG
large ~ ARMY, MOB, SHOAL, TROOP
member of a ~ scene EXTRA

crowded CLOSE, DENSE

crowds
like some ~ UGLY

crowing ELATED, GLAD

crown ACME, APEX, BEAT, COIN, CREST, HIT, PATE, SMITE, TIARA, TOP
~ **topper** ENAMEL
at the ~ ATOP
cock's ~ COMB
earn the ~ WIN
rotunda's ~ DOME
wear the ~ REIGN, RULE

crown ___ ROAST

crowned
~ **head** LORD, RULER

get ~ REIGN, RULE

crowning TOP
~ **point** ACME, APEX, PEAK

crown-of-thorns PLANT

crow's-___ NEST

crow's-nest
~ **cry** AHOY, LAND
~ **site** MAST

___ Cruces, N. Mex. LAS

crucial ACUTE, DIRE, KEY, POLAR

crucible TRIAL

"Crucible, The"
~ **setting** SALEM

crucifix ROOD

"Crucifixion"
~ **artist** DALI

cruciverbalist
~ **direction** ACROSS

crud DIRT

crude BAD, CRASS, LEWD, OIL, RACY, RAW, RUDE
~ **building** SHED
~ **dude** BOOR
~ **metal** ORE

crude ___ OIL

crude oil
~ **component** ETHANE

crudités
~ **companion** DIP
like ~ RAW

cruel FERAL, HARD, MEAN, STERN
~ **one** BEAST, OGRE

"Cruel ___, The" SEA

"Cruel ___ Kind" TOBE

"cruellest month"
Eliot's ~ APR, APRIL

cruelty
exemplar of ~ SADE

cruet EWER
~ **contents** OIL

cruise BOAT, ROAM, ROVE, TRIP
~ **along** MOTOR
~ **destination** ALASKA, RIO
~ **ship** LINER
~ **stop** ISLE, PORT
go on a ~ SAIL
taking a ~ ASEA, ATSEA

Cruise TOM

"___ Cruise" SEA

cruiser
highway ~ SEMI

cruising ASEA, ATSEA

crumb BIT, CAD, IOTA, ORT, PART, SCRAP

crumble CHIP, ERODE, ROT, SMASH

crumbles
the way the cookie ~ FATE, LOT

crumbling OLD

crumbum LOUSE

crummy POOR, SEEDY

crumpet
~ **accompaniment** TEA

crumple WAD

crunch BITE, EAT, GNAW, MILL, SMASH
~ **benefactors** ABS
~ **into** HIT, RAM

cruncher
no. ~ ACCT, CPA

crunchy CRISP, HARD
~ **snack** CHIP

crusade WAR

"Crusade in Europe"
~ **author** IKE

crusader
~ **destination** EAST, SYRIA
consumers' ~ NADER

Crusader Rabbit
~ **partner** RAGS

cruse JAR, POT

crush BEAT, HOST, MASH, MILL, MOB, PRESS, ROUT, RUIN, STAMP, STAVE, TREAD
~ **grapes, old-style** TREAD
~ **of people** MOB
have a ~ on ADORE, LOVE

crushed BLUE, LOW, SAD

crushing BAD, SAD

Crusoe
~ **carved one** CANOE
like ~ before Friday ALONE

crust CAKE, HEEL, NERVE, RIND, SCALE, SKIN
pie ~ SHELL
section of earth's ~ PLATE
upper ~ CREAM, ELITE

crusty HARD, TESTY
~ **bread** RYE
~ **dessert** PIE, TART

crutch CANE, PROP

crux GIST, HEART, MEAT, SUM

"___ Cruz" VERA

cruzado COIN

___ Cruz, Calif. SANTA

cruzeiro COIN

cry BAY, MOAN, NOISE, REACT, SOB, WEEP, YELP
~ **for "poor Yorick"** ALAS
~ **of alarm** EEK
~ **of discovery** AHA
~ **of dismay** ALAS
~ **of surprise** EEK, LORD, OOH
barnyard ~ BAA, BRAY, CROW, MOO, OINK
bird's ~ CAW
country-club ~ FORE
derisive ~ BOO
discoverer's ~ OHO

exultant ~ AHA, HAH
gloater's ~ OHO
guard's ~ HALT
mouse-hater's ~ EEK
nautical ~ AHOY, AVAST
nursery ~ MAMA
pep-rally ~ RAH
Shakespearean ~ FIE
sorrowful ~ MOAN, SOB
triumphant ~ AHA, HAH
ump's ~ OUT, SAFE

cry ___ UNCLE

cry ___ (renege) OFF

cry ___ spilled milk OVER

___ cry AFAR, WAR

"Cry"
~ singer RAY

"Cry ___ River" MEA

"Crying ___, The" GAME

"Crying Game, The"
~ actor REA

"___ crying out loud!" FOR

"___ Cry, It's Only Thunder" DONT

cry one's ___ out EYES, HEART

cryptogram CODE
make a ~ ENCODE

cryptograph CODE

cryptographer
~ concern CODE

crystal
~ plane FACE
rock ~ GEM

crystal-___ CLEAR

crystal ball
~ gazer SEER
~ phrase ISEE

Crystal, Billy EMCEE, HOST
~ sitcom SOAP

crystal-filled
~ rock GEODE

crystalline CLEAR, SOLID
~ rock SPAR

crystallize GEL

crystals
natural ~ SNOW

"Cry Terror"
~ director STONE

"___ Cry Tomorrow" ILL

"___ Cry Wolf" NEVER

Cs ELEM
55 for ~ ATNO

CSA
~ fighter REB
~ monogram REL
end of a ~ signature ELEE
where the ~ was formed ALA

C-SPAN
part of ~ CABLE

CST
part of ~ STD

Ct.
~ neighbor MASS
see also Connecticut

C-to-C
~ sequence SCALE

CTRL
neighbor of ~ ALT

Cu ELEM
29 for ~ ATNO

___ Cuarto, Argentina RIO

cuatro
~ preceder TRES
twice ~ OCHO

cub BRAT, KID, TOT
~ home DEN, LAIR
~ parent BEAR, LION

Cuba
~ (abbr.) ISL
~ neighbor HAITI
see also Spanish

Cuban
~ cash PESO

Cuban ___ HEEL

Cubbins, Bartholomew
one of ~ 500 HAT

cubbyhole CELL, NOOK

cube CHOP, DICE, DIE

cube ___ ROOT, STEAK

cubes DICE
cold ~ ICE

cubic SOLID
~ meter STERE

cubicle CELL, ROOM, STALL

cubit
~ relative SPAN

Cubs NINE, TEAM
~ loc. CHI
~ org. BSA

Cub Scout
~ group DEN

cuckoo ANI, BATS, BIRD, DAFT, LOCO, MAD

cuckoopint ARUM, PLANT

___ cucumber SEA

cuddle CARESS, CLASP, HOLD, LOVE, PET

cudgel BANG, BAT, BEAT, ROD

cue CLUE, HINT, LEAD, NOD, SIGN
~ game POOL
answering-machine ~ BEEP
use a ~ CAROM

cue ___ BALL, CARD

Cuéllar, Pérez de
~ home PERU

cuff BANG, BAT, BEAT, HIT, PELT, SLAP, SMITE

cufflink STUD

cuffs
slap the ~ on ARREST

Cugat
~ ex ABBE, LANE

cuirass ARMOR, MAIL

cuisine
Asian ~ THAI
Greek ~ item FETA, OLIVE
mainstay of Greek ~ LAMB

cuisinier CHEF

cuisse ARMOR

Cujo
wound from ~ BITE

Culbertson ELY

cul-de-___ SAC

cul-de-sac ALLEY

culet ARMOR

culinary
~ by-product AROMA
~ concoction DISH
~ directive BASTE, BEAT, BOIL, CHOP, COOL, DICE, FRY, HEAT, ROAST, SAUTE, SCALD, STEAM, STEW, STIR, TOAST, WARM
~ lure AROMA

Culkin, Macaulay
like ~ in a 1990 film ALONE

cull SORT, TAKE

Cullen, Countee POET
see also poet

culm COAL, STEM

culminate CLOSE, CREST, PEAK

culmination ACME, APEX, CREST, END, TOP

___-culotte SANS

___ culpa MEA

cult SECT
~ follower ISM, IST, URE

cultivar PLANT

cultivate DIG, DRESS, GROW, HOE, PLANT, PLOW, RAISE, REAR, TEND, TILL
~ patience WAIT

cultivation BED

cultivator HOE

cultural
~ character ETHOS
~ precepts ETHIC
~ pursuit ARTS
~ theater OPERA

Cultural Revolution
~ leader MAO

culture
~ medium AGAR
~ starter AQUA
sign of ~ POISE, TASTE

cultured FINE, NICE
superficially ~ ARTY

culvert SEWER

Cumberland ___ GAP

Cumbrian RANGE

cumin HERB

cummerbund BAND, BELT, SASH

cummings POET

Cummings BOB

cummings, e.e. POET
~ construction POEM
~ play HIM
see also poet

cumulate AMASS

cumulus
~ starter ALTO

cunctatious LATE

cunctatory LATE

cunning ACUTE, ARCH, ART, FALSE, SLY, SMART
~ bit WILE

Cuomo MARIO

cup
~ edge LIP, RIM
~ handle EAR
~ to a caddy HOLE
~ up DIP
eighth of a ~ OUNCE
one's ~ of tea BAG
pass the ~ BEG
something 'twixt ~ and lip SLIP

"___ Cup" TIN

cupbearer PAGE

cupboard CHEST
~ item CAN, TIN
~ part DOOR, KNOB

cupel HEAT

Cupid AMOR, EROS
~ master SANTA
~ missile DART
~ target HEART
~ weapon ARROW, BOW

cupidinous AVID

cup of ___ TEA

cupola DOME
~ topper VANE

cuppa TEA

cuprite ORE

cups
two ~ PINT

cur DOG

curaçao
~ ingredient PEEL

Curaçao
~ neighbor ARUBA

curate ABBE, PADRE

curative TONIC

curb BIT, HALT, LEASH, LIMIT, REIN, RIM, STEM, STOP

curbside
  ~ cry TAXI

curd CLOT, PASTE
  bean ~ TOFU

___ curd BEAN

curdle CLOT, SOUR, TURN

curdled SOUR

cure DRY, HEAL, HELP, MEND, SALT
  ~ leather TAN
  ~ starter EPI
  something to ~ HAM

cured
  it may be ~ MEAT

curfew
  ~ maybe ELEVEN
  after ~ LATE

Curie EVE, MARIE, POLE
  ~ title MME
  see also French

Curie, Marie POLE
  ~ daughter IRENE

curio RELIC

curiosity
  ~ victim CAT
  indulge one's ~ ASK

"___ Curiosity Shop, The" OLD

curious NEW, NOSY, ODD
  be ~ ASK

"Curious George"
  ~ author REY

curium METAL

curl BEND, COIL, LOOP, ROLL, SET
  ~ a lip SNEER
  ~ one's hair AMAZE, SCARE
  long ~ TRESS

___ curl PIN, SPIT

curlew BIRD

curlicue COIL, ESS

curling GAME
  ~ period END
  ~ target TEE

curling ___ IRON

curls HAIR

curly
  ~ coiffure AFRO

Curly
  ~ colleague MOE

"Curly ___" SUE

curmudgeon BEAR
  ~ word BAH

curmudgeonly BAD, MEAN, SOUR

currency BILL, CASH, COIN, NOTE, PAPER
  convert to ~ CASH

current CHIC, EDDY, HEP, HIP, LIVE, NEW, NOW, STREAM, TENOR, TIDE
  ~ administration INS
  ~ amt. BAL

  ~ discharge ARC
  ~ events NEWS
  ~ medium CABLE, WIRE
  ~ rage FAD
  ~ terminal ANODE
  ~ unit AMP
  ~ with UPON
  circular ~ EDDY
  in ~ condition ASIS
  make ~ RENEW

currently NOW

curricle CART

curriculum CLASS
  ~ section UNIT

curried HOT

Currier NAT
  ~ partner IVES

curry BEAT, CANE, COMB
  ~ favor WOO
  loaded with ~ HOT

Curry TIM

currycomb
  ~ target MANE

curse ABUSE, BAN, BANE, BLAST, OATH, RACK
  ~ one's folly RUE

"Curse of the ___" DEMON

"Curse of the ___ People" CAT

"Curse of the Cat People"
  ~ director WISE

"Curses!" DRAT

cursor
  ~ mover MOUSE

cursory RAPID

curt RUDE, TERSE
  be ~ SNAP

curtail CLIP, CUT, ELIDE, LIMIT, LOP, PARE, SLASH, STEM, TIE, TRIM

curtain BLUR, DRAPE
  ~ fabric LACE
  ~ holder ROD
  ~ line TAG
  ~ material IRON
  ~ raiser ACT, EVENT, INTRO
  bring down the ~ END

curtain ___ CALL, ROD, TIME

___ curtain DROP, IRON

"___ Curtain" TORN

curtain raiser ACTI

curtains END
  close the ~ DRAW
  put up ~ HANG

Curtin JANE
  ~ role ALLIE

Curtis DAN, TONY

curtsey BOB, BOW, DIP

curvature ARC, ARCH, BOW

curve ARC, BEND, BOW, ESS, LOOP, SNAKE, TURN
  double ~ ESS, OGEE

  overhead ~ ARCH
  river ~ BEND
  señorita's ~ TILDE
  sigmoid ~ ESS
  slalom ~ ESS
  throw a ~ DUPE

curve ___ BALL

___ curve SINE

curved BENT
  ~ arch OGEE
  ~ entrance ARCH
  ~ letter ESS
  ~ line ARC
  ~ molding OGEE
  ~ nail CLAW
  ~ pipe TRAP
  ~ roof DOME
  ~ steel tool ADZE
  travel a ~ path ARC, ORBIT, RING

curvet LEAP

curvy ARCED

cushion MAT, PAD, SEAT
  ~ starter PIN

___ cushion AIR

cushy EASY

Cussler
  ~ bestseller SAHARA

cussword OATH

custard FLAN
  ~ base EGG

Custer
  ~ colleague RENO

Custer's Last ___ STAND

custody CARE
  one in ~ WARD
  release from ~ BAIL
  take into ~ ARREST, NAB, NAIL

custom HABIT, MODE, STYLE, USAGE, USE

custom-___ MADE

customary SET, USUAL
  ~ line of travel ROUTE
  ~ practice HABIT, RITE, RULE

customers
  admitting ~ OPEN
  like some ~ IRATE

customs ORDER

cut CHOP, CLIP, EDIT, EMEND, GAP, HACK, HEW, ILK, LANCE, LOT, MAIM, OMIT, PASS, SAW, SHARE, SKIP, SLICE, SNIP, STAB, TRIM
  ~ and paste EDIT
  ~ and run DESERT, FLEE
  ~ a rug DANCE
  ~ as a picture CROP
  ~ away CLEAR
  ~ back ABATE, LOP, THIN, TRIM
  ~ back on PARE, TRIM
  ~ closely CROP
  ~ corners STINT
  ~ costs SAVE
  ~ down ABASE, ABATE, HEW, LOG, PARE

  ~ down trees LOG
  ~ drastically SLASH
  ~ flower STEM
  ~ hay MOW
  ~ into ETCH, OPEN, SCORE
  ~ into metal ETCH
  ~ in two SPLIT
  ~ loose FREE, REVEL
  ~ of bacon SLAB
  ~ of beef LOIN, ROAST
  ~ off ALONE, APART, CLIP, CROP, END, LONE, LOP, NIP, TRIM
  ~ off from DENY
  ~ of lamb CHOP
  ~ of some jeans SLIM
  ~ old-style SNEE
  ~ open LANCE
  ~ out AVOID, BORE, CEASE, FLEE, LEAVE, OMIT, SPLIT, STOP
  ~ out articles CLIP
  ~ partner PASTE
  ~ prices TRIM
  ~ short ABORT, BOB, CLIP, CROP, END, LOP, NIP, STOP, TRIM
  ~ starter CREW
  ~ the grass MOW
  ~ through SLICE
  ~ through red tape AID, HELP
  ~ timber HEW, LOG, SAW
  ~ to fit ADAPT, TRIM
  ~ too close SCALP
  ~ to the quick STING
  ~ up CHOP, DICE, PLAY, SHRED
  ~ wood HEW, SAW
  agent's ~ TENTH
  beef ~ CHOP, LOIN, TBONE
  cold ~ HAM, MEAT, SALAMI
  cutlet ~ VEAL
  deep ~ GASH
  dressmaker's ~ BIAS
  garment ~ ALINE
  gemstone ~ PEAR
  loin ~ TBONE
  narrow ~ SLIT
  pants ~ SLIM
  pork ~ LOIN
  price ~ SLASH
  short ~ BOB, LANE, PATH
  slanting ~ BIAS
  steak ~ LOIN, TBONE
  stylish ~ ALINE
  veal ~ CHOP

cut ___ LOOSE, OFF, OUT

cut-___ RATE

___ cut CREW

___-cut CLEAN, CLEAR

cut a ___ RUG

cut a ___ swath WIDE

cut and ___ PASTE

cut and paste EDIT

cut-and-slash
  ~ sword SABER

cutaway TAILS

cutback DROP

cut down to ___ SIZE

cuticle SKIN

cutie ___ PIE

cutis SKIN

cutlass
~ **cousin** EPEE, SABER
~ **material** STEEL

cutlery
~ **metal** STEEL

cutlet CHOP, MEAT
~ **cut** VEAL

___ cutlet VEAL

cut no ___ ICE

cutoff
salary ~ CAP

cutoff ___ (fielder) MAN

cut one's ___ on TEETH

cutout
originator of ~ dresses ERTE

cuts
side that ~ EDGE

cutter AXE, BOAT, SHIP, SLED
~ **cousin** SLOOP
coin ~ DIE
control a ~ STEER
film ~ EDITOR
pipe ~ SAW
tree ~ AXE, SAW

___ cutter PAPER

cutthroat OGRE, TROUT

cutting ACID, ACUTE, KEEN,
PLANT, SCION, SHOOT, SLIP,
SPRIG, TART
~ **as a remark** SNIDE
~ **edge** LEAD

~ **remark** BARB, DIG
~ **tool** AXE, DIE, SAW
it may be ~ EDGE

cutting ___ EDGE, HORSE, ROOM

cutting room
~ **figure** EDITOR

"Cuttings" POEM

cuttlefish
~ **defense** INK
~ **pigment** SEPIA
like ~ secretion INKY

"Cutty Sark" BOAT, SHIP

cutup CARD, IMP, WAG

Cuxhaven
~ **river** ELBE

Cuzco
~ **inhabitant** INCA
~ **locale** PERU
see also Spanish

cyber
~ **tycoon** GATES

cyberspace
~ **conversation** CHAT
~ **frequenter** USER
~ **messages** EMAIL

"Cybill"
~ **character** IRA

Cyclades
~ **neighbor** CRETE

cyclamate SALT

cyclamen PLANT

cycle AGE, BIKE, EPOCH, ERA,
ORBIT, PEDAL, RING
~ **part** PHASE

~ **starter** EPI, MEGA, MOTOR,
TRI, UNI
dishwasher ~ RINSE
Gregorian ~ YEAR
laundry ~ RINSE, SOAK, SPIN,
WASH
sleep ~ REM
solar ~ YEAR
wash ~ RINSE, SOAK, SPIN

___ cycle LIFE

cyclic
~ **in a way** TIDAL

cycloid ARCH
~ **section** ARC

cyclone GALE, STORM
~ **center** EYE

Cyclones
~ **home** AMES, IOWA

cyclopean BIG, LARGE

Cyclops GIANT, OGRE
~ **had one** EYE

cyclotron
~ **target** ATOM

Cyd
~ **hubby** TONY

cygnet SWAN
~ **home** NEST

Cygnus SWAN
star in ~ DENEB

cylinder ROLL
A-plant ~ ROD

cylindrical
~ **instrument** OBOE
~ **structure** SILO

"Cymbeline"
~ **start** ACTI

Cynewulf POET
see also poet

cynical SOUR
~ **look** SNEER

cynosure IDOL

Cynthia MOON, SCOTT

"Cynthia" POEM

cypress TREE
~ **growth** KNEE

Cypress Gardens
~ **st.** FLA

Cyprus
~ **(abbr.)** ISL

Cyrano
~ **prominent feature** NOSE

cyst NODE, SAC

Cy Young AWARD

czar LORD, MALE, RULER
computer ~ GATES
industrial ~ BARON
Russian ~ IVAN
see also Russian

czardas DANCE

czarevna LADY

czarina LADY

Czech SLAV
~ **river** ELBE, ODER
play written in ~ RUR

Czerny CARL

Czinner PAUL

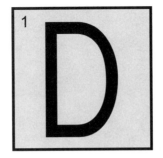

1 D

007 AGENT, SPY
~ **alma mater** ETON
~ **portrayer** MOORE

D CELL
~ **flat's neighbor** CEE
rating a ~ POOR

"D"
~ **in code** DELTA

D ___ "Delta" ASIN

D-___ DAY

"___ D" (Dallas) BIG

___-D THREE

da YES
~ **capo** AGAIN
~ **in French** OUI
~ **opposite** NYET

DA
~ **org.** ABA
~ **staffer** ASST
degree for a ~ LLD
part of ~ ATT, ATTY

Daalder RENEE

dab BIT, DROP, IOTA, JOT, MITE, PAT,
SPOT, TINGE
~ **hand** ACE, ADEPT
~ **on** PAT

"___ Daba Honeymoon, The"
ABA

dabble DIP

dabchick BIRD

daboia
~ **kin** ASP

d'Abruzzo, Alphonso
~ **stage name** ALDA

___ da capo ARIA

Dacca CITY

dacha ESTATE

dachshund DOG, PET

"___ Dachshund, The" UGLY

dachshundlike LOW

dactyl FOOT, TOE

dad MALE, PAPA, POP
~ **in French** PERE

"___ Dad" MAJOR

dada PAPA
~ **artist** ARP, ERNST
~ **ender** ISM

Dada
~ **co-founder** ARP
name in ~ ERTE

da-DAH IAMB

daddums PAPA

daddy PAPA

"Daddy ___ Legs" LONG

___ Daddy BIG

"Daddy Long ___" LEGS

"Daddy's ___ A-Hunting" GONE

"Daddy's Girls"
~ **actor** MOORE

Dade County
~ **city** MIAMI
~ **st.** FLA

dado DIE

dads PAS

Daedalus
Icarus, to ~ SON

___-da-fé AUTO

d'affaires
chargé ~ AGENT

daffodil COLOR

daffy BATS, LOCO

Daffy Duck
talk like ~ LISP

daft MAD

da Gama
stop for ~ INDIA

dagger SNEE, STEEL
~ **handle** HILT
~ **thrust** STAB
Malay ~ KRIS
wavy-bladed ~ KRIS

daggers
look ~ GLARE

"Dagnabbit!" DARN, DRAT

Dagwood
~ **frequent request** RAISE
~ **neighbor** ELMO, HERB
~ **sweetheart before
Blondie** IRMA

dah
~ **partner** DIT

Dahl ARLENE

"___ Dahlia, The" BLUE

Dahlin BOB

dahoon TREE

dahs
dits and ~ CODE

Dailey DAN

daily ORGAN, PAPER, SHEET
~ **delivery** MAIL, PAPER
~ **drama** SOAP
~ **grind** RUT
~ **report** NEWS
~ **routine** HABIT

daily double BET

Daily Planet
~ **reporter** KENT, LANE, LOIS,
OLSEN

daimyo LORD, PEER

dainty ELFIN, FINE, NICE

daiquiri
~ **ingredient** LIME, RUM

dairy
~ **animal** COW
~ **measure** PINT
~ **product** CREAM
~ **section, perhaps** AISLE
~ **sound** MOO
~ **starter** NON

dairy case
~ **buy** OLEO

Dairy Queen
~ **order** CONE

dais STAGE
~ **covering** DRAPE
~ **VIP** EMCEE, HOST
do ~ **duty** ORATE

daisy
~ **look-alike** ASTER

Daisy ___ MAE

Daisy Mae
~ **boyfriend** ABNER
~ **creator** CAPP
~ **mate** ABNER
~ **son** ABE

Dakota TRIBE
~ **dialect** TETON
~ **digs** TENT, TEPEE
~ **tribe** REE

Dalai ___ LAMA

Dalai Lama RANK
~ **city** LHASA
~ **country** TIBET

dale VALE

Dale EVANS
~ **hubby** ROY
~ **partner** CHIP

Daley
~ **city** CHI

Dalgliesh ADAM

Dali
~ **colleague** MIRO
like ~**'s watches** LIMP
see also Spanish

Dallas
~ **sch.** SMU

"Dallas" SOAP
~ **mom** ELLIE
~ **network** CBS
~ **role** PAM
~ **setting** RANCH

Dallas County
~ **city** SELMA

"___ Dalloway" (Woolf work)
MRS

dally DRAG, LAG, PLAY, TOY, WAIT

Dalmatian
~ **feature** SPOT

dalmatic ROBE

Dalrymple IAN, SCOT

Dalton
~ **gang victim** TRAIN

"Daltons, The" GANG

Daly TYNE

dam HORSE, MAMA, MARE, STOP, WEIR
~ **agcy.** TVA
~ **mate** SIRE
~ **opener** GATE
~ **up** CLOG, STEM
Egyptian ~ ASWAN

damage ABUSE, COST, HARM, MAR, SPOIL, TAINT
~ **a reputation** LIBEL
cause ~ **to** MAIM
irrevocable ~ RUIN
minor ~ DENT

damages FEE, RATE
~ **often** AWARD

damaging BAD, EVIL

___, Daman, and Diu GOA

Damascene ARAB

Damascus
~ **country** SYRIA
~ **loc.** SYR
big man in ~ ASSAD

Damascus ___ STEEL

damask LINEN, ROSE

damask rose
~ **product** ATTAR

d'Amato
~ **and others** ALS

dame GAL, LADY, TITLE
grande ~ LADY

Dame TITLE

"Dames ___" ATSEA

dame's rocket PLANT

daminozide ALAR

Damita LILI

___ Damme ("Timecop" star) VAN

damn OATH
give a ~ CARE

damnation
consign to ~ DOOM

"Damn Yankees"
~ **character** JOE, LOLA, SATAN
~ **composer** ADLER
~ **lyricist** ROSS
~ **siren** LOLA
~ **song** HEART

damoiselle GIRL, LASS

Damon
~ **to Pythias** PAL

"D'amor sull'ali rosee" ARIA

___ d'amour OBOE

damp RAINY, RAW, WET

dampen BATHE, DASH, MUTE, WET
~ **flax** RET

dampened WET

damper PALL
put a ~ **on** SLAKE

throw a ~ **on** DASH

damsel GIRL, LASS, MAID, MISS
~ **saver** HERO

dan ACE

Dan
fancy ~ DUDE

Danaë
Perseus, to ~ SON

Danakil DESERT

dance ART, BALL, CLOG, GALA, HOP, HORA, HULA, PROM, REEL, SALSA, SAMBA, SHAG, TANGO
~ **about** CAPER
~ **genre** TAP
~ **in French** BAL
~ **in wooden shoes** CLOG
~ **lesson** STEP
~ **maneuver** DIP
~ **partner** SONG
~ **site** BARN
~ **syllable** CHA
~ **to chants** HULA
Argentine ~ TANGO
bar-mitzvah ~ HORA
barn ~ REEL
bobbysoxer's ~ HOP
Brazilian ~ SAMBA
Bucharest ~ HORA
circle ~ HORA
colonial ~ REEL
fiery ~ TANGO
folk ~ REEL
formal ~ BALL, PROM
grass-skirt ~ HULA
gym ~ HOP
half a ~ CAN, CHA
Hawaiian ~ HULA
Highland ~ REEL
high-school ~ HOP, PROM
hippy ~ HULA
Israeli ~ HORA
June ~ PROM
Latin ~ SALSA, SAMBA, TANGO
1930s ~ SHAG
1950s ~ HOP
pantomime ~ HULA
Polynesian ~ HULA
pregraduation ~ PROM
Rio ~ SAMBA
Romanian ~ HORA
round ~ HORA
school ~ PROM
song and ~ TALE
storytelling ~ HULA

dance ___ HALL

___ dance BARN, SLAM, SNAKE, SUN, TAP, TEA, TOE, WAR

"___ Dance" LETS

"Dance of Life, The"
~ **author** ELLIS

"Dance on Little Girl"
~ **singer** ANKA

dancer
disco ~ GOGO
erstwhile sun ~ UTE
like a ballet ~ LITHE
rain ~ HOPI

___ dancer GOGO, TAP, TAXI

Dancer
~ **handler** SANTA

"Dancer at the Bar"
~ **painter** DEGAS

dancers
half the square ~ GALS
snake ~ HOPI

"Dances With Wolves"
~ **animal** BISON
~ **home** TEPEE

___ dancing ICE, SLAM

"___ Dancing" SLOW

"Dancing Class, The"
~ **painter** DEGAS

"___ Dancing Daughters" OUR

"Dancing Queen"
~ **band** ABBA

dandelion WEED, WINE

dander ANGER, IRE, IRISH, RAGE
get one's ~ **up** ANGER, PEEVE, RILE

dandiprat RUNT

dandruff SCALE

dandy AOK, BEAU, DUDE, PIP, PRIG
~ **accouterment** CANE
~ **partner** FINE

___ Dane GREAT

Daneyko KEN

"Dang!" DRAT, OATH

danger PERIL, RISK
~ **signal** ALARM, ALERT, RED
free from ~ SAFE
not in ~ **of** ABOVE
out of ~ SAFE
response to ~ FEAR

Danger CAVE

"___ Danger" CRY

Dangerfield
~ **persona** LOSER
~ **stock-in-trade** GAGS

dangerous ACUTE, BAD
~ **fly** TSETSE
~ **group** MOB
~ **partner** ARMED
~ **to drive on** ICY
~ **whale** ORCA
not ~ SAFE

"___ Dangerous Game, The" MOST

"Dangerous Liaisons"
~ **actress** CLOSE

"Dangerous When ___" WET

"Dangerous When Wet"
~ **actor** LAMAS
~ **name** ESTHER

dangle DRAPE, FLAP, HANG, LOLL, PEND, TRAIL

dangling LOOSE

___ dancer GOGO, TAP, TAXI

Daniel BOONE, MANN, STERN
~ **was put in one** DEN
book after ~ HOSEA

"Daniel"
~ **name** ELTON

Daniel ___-Lewis DAY

"Daniel Boone"
~ **actor** AMES
~ **poet** BENET

"Daniel Deronda"
~ **author** ELIOT

Danielle STEEL

Danish
~ **coin** ORE
name for ~ **kings** ERIC

dank DAMP, WET

"Danny Boy"
~ **setting** GLEN

Dan Patch
emulate ~ TROT

danseur MALE

Danson TED
~ **sitcom** INK

Dante JOE, POET
~ **land** ITALY
see also Italian, poet

Danube
~ **city** ULM
~ **feeder** INN

Danza TONY
~ **sitcom** TAXI

Daphne OREAD
lover of ~ APOLLO

Daphnis
god offended by ~ EROS

dapper AGILE, CHIC, NEAT, SMART, TRIM
~ **fellow** DAN

Dapper ___ DAN

dapple DOT, HORSE, SPOT

dapple-___ GRAY

dappled PIED
~ **feline** OCELOT

DAR
part of ~ AMER, REV

d'Arc, Jeanne ~ STE

dare FACE, RISK
~ **to** ASK
gunfighter's ~ DRAW

___ dare ONA

daredevil RASH
~ **need** NERVE

daresay HOLD

Dar es Salaam CITY, PORT

daring DASH, GAME, NERVE
~ **motorcyclist** EVEL

Darío, Rubén POET
see also poet

Darjeeling TEA

dark BAD, DEEP, DIRE, EBON, EBONY, EVIL, INKY, JET, SABLE, SAD, UNLIT
~ **and handsome companion** TALL
~ **bread** RYE
~ **brown** SEPIA
~ **complexion** OLIVE
~ **forces** EVIL
~ **grayish-green** FIR
~ **green** OLIVE
~ **lush fur** SABLE
~ **orange-yellow** AMBER
~ **purple fruit** SLOE
~ **shadow** PALL
~ **side of the Force** EVIL
~ **to a poet** EBON
~ **yellow** OCHER, OCHRE
in the ~ UNLIT
keep ~ HIDE
not in the ~ AWARE
piece of ~ **meat** LEG
shot in the ~ BET, STAB
the ~ **side** EVIL

dark ___ HORSE

Dark ___ AGE, AGES

"Dark ___" EYES

"Dark ___, The" ANGEL, PAST

"Dark ___ of the Street, The" END

"___ Dark" NEAR

___, dark, and handsome TALL

"Dark at the ___ of the Stairs, The" TOP

"Dark at the Top of the Stairs, The"
~ **author** INGE
~ **director** MANN

darken DIM, SHADE, TAN

"___ Dark House, The" OLD

"Dark Intruder"
~ **director** HART

"Dark Lady"
~ **singer** CHER

"___ Dark, My Sweet" AFTER

Darkness
Prince of ~ SATAN

"Dark of the ___" SUN

"Dark Past, The"
~ **director** MATE

darkroom
~ **abbr.** ENL
~ **solution** TONER

"Dark Shadows" SOAP

"___ Darlin'" LIL

darling DEAR, HON, LOVE, PET, SWEET

"Darling ___" LILI

Darlings'
~ **dog** NANA
~ **friend** PAN, PETER

darn MEND, RESTORE, SEW
~ **socks** MEND
give a ~ CARE

"Darn!" DRAT, NUTS, RATS
~ **in German** ACH

"___ Darn Cat!" THAT

darndest BEST

darner NEEDLE

"___ Darn Hot" TOO

darning ___ (dragonfly) NEEDLE

"Darn it!" SHOOT

Darnley LORD

Darnley, Lord SCOT

Darrow ANN

dart ARROW, DASH, FLIT, MOVE, PELT, PLEAT, RACE, RUN, SAIL, SHOOT, TEAR
~ **shooter** EROS

d'Artagnan
~ **friend** ATHOS
~ **prop** EPEE

dartboard
~ **wood** ELM

darts GAME

dart-thrower
~ **quaff** ALE

___ Darya SYR

Daryl HALL

"Das ___" BOOT

"Das Boot"
~ **craft** SUB, UBOAT

dash CHIC, DART, DROP, ELAN, FIRE, HIE, HINT, IOTA, LIFE, LINE, NERVE, PELT, PEP, RACE, RUN, SHADE, SHOOT, SIGN, SLAM, SLAP, SMASH, SPEED, STYLE, TEAR, VIM
~ **against** BEAT, RAM
~ **around** FLIT
~ **lengths** EMS, ENS
~ **off** HIE, RUN, WRITE
~ **partner** DOT
~ **sizes** ENS
~ **starter** SLAP
~ **to pieces** RUIN
Morse's ~ DAH

Dash
~ **rival** ALL, ERA, TIDE

dashboard
~ **abbr.** MPH
~ **device** DIAL
~ **dial** TACH
~ **feature** RADIO
~ **reading** MPH, RPM

Dashiell
~ **contemporary** ERLE
~ **dog** ASTA

dashing SMART

Dasht-e-Kavire DESERT

Dasht-e-Lut DESERT

"Das Lied ___ der Erde" VON

"Das Rheingold" OPERA
~ **goddess** ERDA

Dass RAM

dastard CAD, CUR, HEEL, SNEAK

dastardly BASE, VILE

data DOPE, FACT, INFO
~ **(abbr.)** NOS
~ **unit** BIT
input ~ ENTER
seek ~ ASK

database
~ **function** SORT

date AGE, BEAU, DAY, PALM, TIME, TRYST
~ **(abbr.)** APPT
~ **producer** YEMEN
~ **regularly** SEE
~ **starter** ANTE, PRE
~ **tree** PALM
at an early ~ ANON, SOON
comedian's ~ GIG
guy's ~ GAL
lad's ~ LASS
March ~ IDES
on a ~ OUT
on that ~ ASOF
to ~ YET
years to ~ AGE

date ___ LINE, PALM

___ date DUE, RAIN, SETA

"___ date!" ITSA

___-date UPTO

datebook
~ **duration** YEAR

dated OLD, PASSE, STALE

dateless ALONE, STAG

date-setting
~ **phrase** ASOF

"Dating Game, The"
~ **host** LANGE

dative CASE

datum FACT, STAT

daub SMEAR

daughter GIRL, KID, SHE

daughter-in-___ LAW

"Daughters of the ___" DUST

"Daughters of the Dust"
~ **director** DASH

daunt ALARM, AWE, COW, DETER, SCARE

dauntless GAME

dauntlessness HEART, NERVE

dauphin SON, TITLE

Davao CITY, PORT

Dave
~ **singing partner** SAM

davenport SOFA
~ **cousin** SETTEE

Davenport
~ **setting** IOWA

"Dave's World"
~ **network** CBS
~ **secretary** MIA

David CAMP, CONE, HAL, LEAN
~ **army commander** ABNER
~ **co-anchor** CHET
~ **great-grandmother** NAOMI
~ **instrument** HARP
king before ~ SAUL
song of ~ PSALM

David ___-Gurion BEN

David ___ Roth LEE

David ___ Stiers OGDEN

"David ___ Lisa" AND

___ David CAMP

"David and ___" LISA

"David Copperfield"
~ **character** DORA

David Lee ___ ROTH

Da Vinci Airport
~ **locale** ROME

Davis BETTE, ERIC, ERIN, MAC, OSSIE, PETER

Davis Cup
former ~ **captain** ASHE

"___ Davis Eyes" BETTE

Davis, Jefferson
~ **org.** CSA

Davis, Jim
~ **dog** ODIE

Davis, Judy
1994 ~ **film, with "The"** REF

Davis Love ___ III

Davis, Miles
~ **accessory** MUTE

davit CRANE

Davos
enjoy ~ SKI

Davy
~ **invention** LAMP

Davy Jones
~ **locker** OCEAN, SEA

daw CROW
~ **cousin** ANI

Dawber PAM

dawdle IDLE, LAG, STAY, WAIT

dawdling SLOW

dawn ARISE, AURORA, FIRST, ONSET, RISE, START
~ **goddess** AURORA, EOS
at the crack of ~ EARLY
met the ~ AROSE
until ~ LATE

"___ Dawn" DELTA

___ Dawn Chong RAE

"___ Dawn I Die" EACH

dawning ONSET

dawnward EAST

Dawson ANDRE, LEN

day DATE, ERA, TIME
~ **after day** OFT, OFTEN
~ **bed** SOFA
~ **before** EVE
~ **divs.** HRS
~ **in Latin** DIEM
~ **light** SUN
~ **of the Roman calendar** IDES
~ **of the wk.** FRI, MON, SAT, SUN, WED
~ **one** ONSET, START
~ **saver** HERO
any ~ now ANON, SOON
call it a ~ LEAVE, STOP
carry the ~ WIN
curse the ~ RUE
face the ~ RISE
field ~ SPREE
forever and a ~ EON
greet the ~ ARISE, RISE
in this ~ and age NOW
it's saved for a rainy ~ TARP
make one's ~ ELATE
midmonth ~ IDES
parade ~ EASTER
pass the time of ~ CHAT
plain as ~ OVERT
seize the ~ LIVE
start the ~ ARISE
time of ~ HOUR, NOON
work ~ and night LABOR

day ___ BED, CAMP, CARE, ONE, ROOM

day ___ day AFTER

___ day RAINY

___ day (2/29) LEAP

"Day ___ Night" FOR

___ Day ARBOR, EARTH, LABOR, MAY

"___ Day Afternoon" DOG

day and ___ AGE

"___ Day and Age" THIS

___ day at a time ONE

"___ Day at Black Rock" BAD

"Day at the ___, A" RACES

daybook LOG

daybreak
at ~ EARLY
until ~ LATE

day care
candidate for ~ TOT, TYKE

Day, Doris
1949 ~ tune AGAIN

daydream IDEATE, MOON, MUSE

"Daydreamer, The"
~ **director** BASS

daydreamers
limit, to ~ SKY

day-in-day-out OFT, OFTEN

"___ Day in Harlem, A" GREAT

day in June
like a ~ RARE

"Day in the ___, A" LIFE

Day Lewis, Cecil POET
see also poet

daylight SUN

daylight saving ___ TIME

___ day now ANY

day of ___ REST

days ERA
~ **of yore** ELD
bygone ~ PAST, YORE
in olden ~ AGO
in the old ~ ONCE
in ~ to come LATER
jolly ~ YULE
of former ~ AGO
one of these ~ ANON, SOON
seven ~ WEEK
the old ~ YORE

___ days DOG, SALAD

___ Days EMBER

"___ Days" RADIO

"___ Days in May" SEVEN

"___ Day's Journey Into Night" LONG

"___ Day's Night, A" HARD

days of ___ YORE

"Days of ___ and Roses" WINE

"Days of ___ Lives" OUR

"Days of Grace"
~ **author** ASHE

"Days of Heaven"
~ **actor** GERE

"Days of Our Lives" SOAP
~ **town** SALEM

"___ Days of Pompeii, The" LAST

"___ Days of the Condor" THREE

"Days of Wine ___ Roses" AND

"Days of Wine and ___" ROSES

"___ Days to Noon" SEVEN

___ days' wonder NINE

"Day the ___ Caught Fire, The" EARTH

"Day the ___ Stood Still, The" EARTH

"Day the Earth ___ Still, The" STOOD

"Day the Earth Caught ___, The" FIRE

"Day the Earth Stood Still, The"
~ **director** WISE

daytime
~ **TV fare** SOAP

Dayton
city north of ~ LIMA

Daytona RACE

___-day vitamins ONEA

"___ Day Will Come" OUR

daze JAR, STUN
in a ~ ASEA, ATSEA

"Dazed ___ Confused" AND

___ d'Azur COTE

dazzle AMAZE, AWE, DAZE, ECLAT, GLARE

dazzling
~ **light** GLARE
~ **success** ECLAT

DC
~ **agent** GMAN, TMAN
~ **body** SEN, USS
~ **clock setting** EDT, EST
~ **figure** PRES, REP, SEN
~ **gun lobby** NRA
~ **hostess** MESTA
~ **hundred** SENATE
~ **lobby** PAC
~ **party** DEM, REP
~ **record-keeping org.** GSA
~ **subway** METRO
~ **tax org.** IRS
~ **type** POL

"D.C. ___" CAB

"D.C. Cab"
~ **actor** MRT

DC Comics
~ **superhero, with "The"** ATOM

DC-10 PLANE
~ **device** RADAR

D-Day
~ **beach** OMAHA, UTAH
~ **city** CAEN
~ **cmdr.** DDE
~ **craft** LST
~ **figure** IKE
~ **site** CAEN
~ **town** STLO

DDE GEN, IKE, PRES
~ **milieu** ETO
~ **opponent** AES
~ **predecessor** HST

DDS
~ **org.** ADA

DDT-banning
~ **org.** EPA

de ___ ("Justine" novelist) SADE

"De ___ Poetica" ARTE

DE
see Delaware

DEA
~ **officer** NARC
~ **operative** FED

deacon RANK, TITLE
~ **scarf** STOLE

dead
~ **center** MIDST
~ **giveaway** SIGN
~ **heat** DRAW, TIE

dead ___ END, HEAT

dead ___ (broadcast interruption) AIR

Dead ___ SEA

"Dead ___" CALM, END

"Dead ___, The" POOL, ZONE

"Dead ___ Kids" END

"Dead ___ on a Merry-Go-Round" HEAT

"Dead ___ Society" POETS

"Dead ___ Walking" MAN

deadbeat DRONE

deaden BLUR, CALM, DAMP, MUTE

deadeye SHOT
~ **prowess** AIM

deadfall PIT, SNARE

deadhead CLOD, OAF

"Dead Heat ___ Merry-Go-Round" ONA

dead in the ___ WATER

"Deadlier Than the ___" MALE

deadline
before the ~ EARLY
past the ~ LATE

"Deadline ___" USA

deadlock HANG, TIE

deadlocked EVEN

deadly BAD, DIRE

"___ Deadly Sin, The" FIRST

"Dead Man's Hand"
~ **pair** ACES

"Dead Man Walking"
~ **role** NUN
Susan's ~ costar SEAN

"Dead Men Don't ___ Plaid" WEAR

"Dead of Winter"
~ **director** PENN

"Dead Poets Society"
~ **director** WEIR

dead ringer TWIN

"Dead Ringers"
~ **actor** IRONS

Dead Sea LAKE
~ **land** ISRAEL
~ **monastic** ESSENE

Dead Sea Scrolls
~ **writer** ESSENE

"Dead Toreador, The"
~ **painter** MANET

"Dead Zone, The"
~ **gift** ESP

deaf
   turn a ~ ear to DENY
___-deaf TONE
deafening LOUD
deafeningly ALOUD
deal PACT, TRADE
   ~ in SELL
   ~ maker AGENT, REP
   ~ out ISSUE, SHARE
   ~ (out) METE
   ~ preceder ANTE
   ~ with REACT, TREAT
   ~ (with) COPE
   ~ with knots UNTIE
   a great ~ LOTS
   bank ~ LOAN
   big ~ ADO
   cashless ~ SWAP, TRADE
   flea-market ~ RESALE
   great ~ ALOT, HEAP, MASS, PILE, STEAL
   one-for-one ~ SWAP, TRADE
   retail ~ SALE
   settle a ~ ICE
   sports ~ TRADE
   used-car ~ RESALE
___ deal RAW
"___ deal!" BIG, ITSA
___ Deal FAIR, NEW
"___ Deal" RAW
dealer
   ~ concern ANTE
   ~ offer REBATE
   ~ show FAIR
   ~ take-back REPO
   card ~ device SHOE
   card ~ offering CUT
   car ~ offering LEASE
dealing
   ~ with ABOUT
dealings
   have ~ with KNOW
"___ Deal on Madonna Street" BIG
dean ELDER
   ~ of St. Paul's INGE
Dean, James IDOL
   ~ film GIANT
   ~ persona REBEL
   ~ role CAL
dean's ___ LIST
dear CLOSE, RICH, STEEP, SWEET
   ~ in French CHER
   ~ in Italian CARA
   ~ one LOVE, PET
   hold ~ ADORE, DOTE, LIKE, LOVE
"Dear"
   ~ one SIR
"Dear ___" HEART
"Dear ___ or Madam..." SIR
dearest PET

"Dear Heart"
   ~ director MANN
dearie HON
___ dear life FOR
"Dear me!" ALAS
"Dear mother Ida, harken ___ die" EREI
"Dear old"
   ~ guy DAD
dearth NEED, WANT
"Death ___, The" KISS
"Death ___ a Holiday" TAKES
"Death ___ Salesman" OFA
"Death ___ the Maiden" AND
"___ Death" TILL
"Death Becomes ___" HER
"Death Be Not Proud"
   ~ poet DONNE
death-defying RASH
"Death in the Family, A"
   ~ author AGEE
"Death in Venice"
   ~ author MANN
"Death on the ___" NILE
"Deathtrap"
   ~ actor CAINE, REEVE
Death Valley DESERT
"Death Valley ___" DAYS
debacle EVIL, ROUT, RUIN
debar AVERT, BAN
debark ARRIVE, LAND
debase SHAME, TAINT
debased VILE
debasement TAINT
debatable OPEN
debate ARGUE
   ~ side ANTI, CON, FOR, PRO
   ~ squad TEAM
debauch ORGY
debauched LEWD
   ~ one ROUE
debauchee RAKE, SATYR
Debbie ALLEN
Debby BOONE
debenture IOU
debilitate SAP, TIRE
debit
   ~ ink RED
debonair GAY, SUAVE
De Bont, Jan
   ~ film of 1994 SPEED
Deborah KERR
   ~ dancing partner YUL

   ~ role in "The King and I" ANNA
debris TRASH
   cliff ~ SCREE
   incinerator ~ ASH
debt
   ~ letters IOU
   ~ security LIEN
   settle a ~ PAY
debtor
   ~ note IOU
debts
   cancel ~ CLEAR
   discharge, as ~ PAY
   have ~ OWE
debus ARRIVE
debussed ALIT
Debussy
   ~ piece ETUDE
   see also French
debut ARRIVE, BALL, INTRO, ONSET
debutante BELLE, LASS
dec-
   ~ halved PENT
Dec.
   ~ predecessor NOV
decade TEN
   ~ fraction YEAR
decadence ROT
decamp CUT, DESERT, EXIT, FLEE, MOVE, RUN
___-de-camp AIDE
"De Camptown ___" RACES
decant POUR
decanter EWER
decathlon
   ~ part EVENT
decay ROT, RUIN, SPOIL, WASTE
   cause to ~ ERODE
decayed BAD
deceit
   bit of ~ LIE, TALE
deceitful BAD, FALSE
deceive BELIE, CON, DUPE, HAVE, LIE, MASK, SNOW
   ~ by flattery SNOW
deceiver FAKE, LIAR
decelerate SLOW
   ~ on signs SLO
December
   ~ 24 EVE
   ~ 26th sign SALE
   ~ 31 EVE
   ~ song CAROL, NOEL
   ~ temp SANTA
   January to ~ YEAR
"December ___" BRIDE

decent CLAD, CLEAN, FAIR, HONEST, MORAL, NICE
deception ART, ERROR, LIE, RUSE, SCAM, SHAM, TALE, WILE
deceptive
   ~ one LIAR
   ~ scheme SETUP
___-de-chambre ROBE
___ de chat PAS
___ de cheval PAS
___ de chine CREPE
decide DEEM, ELECT, OPT, SETTLE, VOTE
   ~ in favor of AWARD
   ~ on OPT
   ~ to compete ENTER
   ~ upon ELECT, TAKE
   unable to ~ TORN
decided CLEAR, SET
   ~ on SET
   not ~ TIED
   yet to be ~ OPEN
deciding
   ~ factor KEY
decimal
   ~ base TEN
   ~ point DOT
decipher RAVEL, READ
decision EDICT
   court ~ AWARD
   formal ~ ACT
   hand down a ~ RULE
   make a ~ ACT, DEEM, RULE
   NASA ~ NOGO
   reach a ~ ACT
   render a ~ RULE
   ring ~ DRAW, TKO
   ump's ~ CALL, FAIR
decision-making
   ~ power SAYSO
decisive
   be ~ ACT, OPT
deck ADORN, GARB, RIG, TIER, TRIM
   ~ hands CREW
   ~ member TREY
   ~ out ADORN, ARRAY, ATTIRE, DRESS, ROBE
   ~ quartet ACES
   ~ worker HAND
   backyard ~ PATIO
   clean the ~ SWAB
   fortuneteller's ~ TAROT
   hit the ~ ARISE, RISE
   on ~ NEXT
   part of a ~ CARD
   shy of a full ~ LOCO
deck ___ HAND
___ deck SUN, TAPE
decked
   ~ out CLAD
deckhand GOB, MATE, SALT, TAR
   exp. ~ ABS

decks KOS

"Deck the Halls" CAROL, NOEL
   ~ contraction TIS
   ~ syllables FALA, LAS

declaim ORATE, RANT, TALK
   ~ (against) RAIL

declaimer ORATOR

declamation TALK

declaration EDICT, OATH
   college ~ MAJOR
   court ~ PLEA

declare ASSERT, ATTEST, AVER,
   AVOW, CLAIM, SAY, STATE, TELL,
   UTTER
   ~ false DENY
   ~ illegal BAN
   ~ in bridge BID
   ~ null and void ANNUL

"___ declare!" IDO

decline ABATE, DENY, DIE, DIP,
   DROP, EBB, FADE, FLAG, PINE,
   SAG, SINK, SLIDE, SLIP, SLOPE,
   WANE
   ~ as stock prices SAG
   period of ~ EBB
   Wall Street ~ DIP

declivitous STEEP

declivity DROP, RAMP, SLOPE, TILT

deco
   art ~ STYLE

___ deco ART

decoct BOIL

decode READ
   ~ grammatically PARSE

___ de coeur CRI

___ de Cologne EAU

decompose ROT, SPOIL

decomposed BAD

decontaminate CLEAN

decor MODE, STYLE
   bath ~ TILE
   stage ~ SET

décor
   change the ~ REDO

decorate ADORN, DRESS, TRIM
   ~ a cake ICE
   ~ again REDO
   ~ a gift WRAP
   ~ a room PAPER
   ~ as a cake ICE
   ~ as leather TOOL
   ~ nails PAINT
   ~ the tree TRIM

decorated ORNATE
   ~ metalware TOLE

decoration AWARD, LACE, MEDAL,
   TRIM
   cake ~ ICING
   furniture-leg ~ EAR
   Halloween ~ BAT
   military ~ MEDAL
   object of ~ FIR, HERO, TREE

onyx ~ CAMEO
rearview-mirror ~ DICE
wall ~ ARRAS, DADO

decorative
   ~ belt SASH
   ~ case ETUI
   ~ coating ENAMEL
   ~ fabric LACE
   ~ molding TRIM
   ~ paper CREPE
   ~ sticker SEAL
   ~ top EPI
   ~ vase URN
   overly ~ ORNATE

decorator
   ~ asset TASTE
   cake ~ ICER

decorous MEET, NICE, PURE,
   SEDATE, STAID

decorticate PARE

decoy LURE, RUSE, TRAP

decrease ABATE, EBB, FLAG,
   REMIT, SLAKE, SLIP, THIN, WANE
   ~ gradually TAPER, WANE
   ~ in importance PALE
   ~ pressure EASE
   ~ slightly DIP

de-crease IRON

decreasingly LESS

decree ACT, BID, EDICT, ENACT,
   FIAT, LAW, ORDER, STATE

decreed LEGAL

decrepit OLD, SEEDY

decretal EDICT

decry CARP

___ de dents MAL

___ de deux PAS

dedicate BLESS

dedicated AVID, TRUE
   ~ to FOR

dedicatory
   ~ work ODE

___ de Dios CASA

deduce DRAW

deduction REBATE
   ~ from revenue DEBIT
   weight ~ TARE

deductions
   after ~ NET

deed ACT, CLAIM, FACT, FEAT,
   PAPER, TITLE, TURN
   ~ holder OWNER
   bad ~ SIN
   chivalrous ~ GEST, GESTE
   do a good ~ HELP
   felon's ~ ARSON
   hold the ~ to OWN

"Deed ___" IDO

"Deed I Do"
   ~ singer HORNE

deeds ACTA

"deed without ___, A" ANAME

deejay
   ~ alternative BAND
   ~ disk DEMO
   ~ material CDS, LPS

deem ESTEEM, HOLD, OPINE,
   RATE, TAKE
   ~ likely HOPE

deep BASS, LOW, SEA
   ~ black EBON, INKY, JET
   ~ blue PERSE
   ~ blue sea OCEAN
   ~ cry ROAR
   ~ cut GASH
   ~ devotion ARDOR
   ~ freeze CUT
   ~ hole PIT
   ~ pink MELON, ROSE
   ~ respect AWE
   ~ sleep COMA
   ~ space ABYSS
   ~ voice BASS
   go ~ into PORE
   the ~ ABYSS, OCEAN, SEA
   the denizens of the ~ LIFE

deep ___ SPACE

deep-___ DISH, FRY, SEA, SET,
   WATER

deep-___ (toss overboard) SIX

___-deep KNEE, SKIN

"Deep, The"
   ~ actor NOLTE

deep-colored RICH

deep-dish PIE

deepen GROW

deeper
   pile it higher and ~ BRAG

deep-felt ACUTE

"Deep in the ___" HEART

deep knee ___ BEND

deep orange
   ~ quartz SARD

deep-seated SET

deep-six CAN, SCRAP

"Deep Space Nine"
   ~ station OPS

deep-toned BASS

deep-voiced
   ~ lady ALTO

deer ANIMAL, ROE
   big ~ ELK
   Disney ~ ENA
   female ~ DOE
   half the ~ STAGS
   large ~ ELK, MOOSE
   male ~ HART, STAG
   **where the ~ and the
      antelope play** RANGE

___ deer AXIS, MOUSE, MULE, ROE

Deere
   ~ rival TORO

deerstalker CAP, HAT

Dee, Ruby
   ~ husband OSSIE

deescalate SLOW

DEF
   telephone's ~ THREE

deface MAIM, MAR, RUIN, SCAR,
   SPOIL, TAINT

defacement TAINT

defamation LIBEL, LIE, SLUR

defame LIBEL, SHAME, SLUR,
   SMEAR, TAINT
   ~ in writing LIBEL

Defarge MME
   emulate ~ KNIT

default LOSE
   security against ~ LIEN

defeat BEAT, BEST, LOSS, MATE,
   STOP, TOP, TRIM, UNDO, UPEND,
   UPSET, ZAP
   ~ by a narrow margin NOSE
   ~ completely ACE
   ~ decisively CREAM
   ~ soundly ROUT, SKIN
   barely ~ EDGE, NIP
   disastrous ~ ROUT
   suffer ~ LOSE

defeated BEAT
   ~ one's cry UNCLE
   be ~ LOSE
   not yet ~ ALIVE

___-defeating SELF

defeatist
   ~ word CANT

defect BLOT, CHIP, DESERT, SCAR,
   SPOT

defective AMISS, BAD
   ~ bomb DUD
   ~ (prefix) PARA
   ~ purchase LEMON

defects
   ~ and all ASIS

"Defence of the ___" REALM

defend ASSERT

defendant
   ~ answer PLEA
   ~ excuse ALIBI

defended SAFE

defender
   ~ in bridge columns EAST

"Defending Your ___" LIFE

defense ALIBI, ARMOR, PLEA
   ~ acronym NATO
   ~ acronym of old SEATO
   ~ ploy ALIBI
   ~ system initials SAC
   1980s ~ strategy SDI
   apian ~ STING
   castle ~ MOAT
   civil ~ drill ALERT
   close the ~ REST
   court ~ ALIBI

fence ~ BARB
fortress ~ MOAT
legal ~ ALIBI
like an octopus's ~ INKY
nuclear ~ acronym SAC
octopus ~ INK
skunk's ~ ODOR
suspect's ~ ALIBI

___-defense SELF

Defense Dept.
~ org. USAF

defensive
~ effort STAND
~ spray MACE
~ tennis shot LOB

defer REMIT, TABLE
~ ender ENCE
~ to BOW, HONOR

deferments
having no ~ ONEA

defiance
act of ~ DARE

"Defiant" BOAT, SHIP

"Defiant ___, The" ONES

deficiency WANT

deficient BARE, LAME, SCANT, SHY, THIN

deficit DEBT, LOSS

___ deficit TRADE

defile COVE, DALE, GAP, PASS, SOIL, TAINT

defiled BAD

defilement TAINT

define LIMIT, SET

definite CLEAN, CLEAR, SURE

definitely
~ in Spanish SISI

"Definitely!" AYE, SURE, YES

definition
by ~ PERSE

definitive SURE

Def Jam
~ record RAP

deflate ABASE, SHAME

deflated FLAT

deflating
~ sound SSS

deflator
~ maybe PIN

deflect AVERT, BEND

deflection BEND

deflector
blame ~ ALIBI

___ de foie gras PATE

___ de force TOUR

De Forest LEE

deform MAR

___ de France ILE

defraud DUPE, REAM, ROB, ROOK, SCAM

defray PAY

defrost MELT, THAW

deft ABLE, ADEPT, AGILE, CLEAN, NEAT

deftness ASSET, EASE

defunct GONE, PAST

defuse CALM

defy BEARD, DARE, ELUDE, FACE, REBEL, RISE

Degas EDGAR
~ contemporary MANET

___ de gato UNA

de Gaulle
see French

de Gaulle, Charles
alternative to ~ ORLY

degauss
~ a tape ERASE

DeGeneres ELLEN

___ de Graaff generator VAN

degradable
~ starter BIO

degradation TAINT

degrade ABASE, TAINT

degree PEG, STEP, UNIT
~ holder ALUM, GRAD
~ (suffix) NESS
advanced ~ PHD
bus. ~ MBA
exec. ~ MBA
extreme ~ NTH
give the third ~ ASK
greatest ~ MOST
judo ~ DAN
med. ~ DDS
slight ~ SHADE, TINGE
to a smaller ~ LESS
to some ~ (prefix) DEMI
to the same ~ ALIKE

___ degree NTH, TOA

degrees
coll. ~ ABS, BAS, MAS
move by ~ INCH

"___ Degrees of Separation" SIX

___ de guerre NOM

degust TASTE

dehisce ERUPT, GAPE, OPEN, SPLIT

dehydrated ARID, DESERT, DRY, SERE

deice THAW
~ in a way SALT

deified
desire ~ EROS

deify EXALT

Deighton LEN
~ character SPY

Deimos MOON
~ orbits it MARS
father of ~ ARES

deity GOD

___ de Janeiro RIO

déjà-vu
~ clothing style RETRO

dejected BAD, LOW, SAD

déjeuner MEAL

"Déjeuner sur l'herbe"
~ painter MANET

"___ de Jour" BELLE

___ de Jouy TOILE

deke
~ in hockey FAKE

de Klerk BOER
~ title PRES

de Kooning, Willem
emulate ~ PAINT

Del ___, Tex. RIO

Del.
~ neighbor PENN
see also Delaware

___ de la Cité ILE

"___ de Lahore" LEROI

de la Hoya OSCAR

de la Mare
~ poem NOD

de la Mare, Walter POET
see also poet

___-de-lance FER

Delaney KIM

Delany DANA

___ de la Plata RIO

de la Renta OSCAR

___ de la Société ILES

De Laurentiis DINO

Delaware STATE

Delaware Water ___ GAP

delay ARREST, DEFER, HOLD, LAG, REMIT, SLOW, STALL, STAY, STOP, TABLE, WAIT
~ meetingwise TABLE
countdown ~ HOLD
legal ~ STAY
negotiations ~ SNAG
time ~ LAG
with no ~ ASAP, STAT
without ~ ANON, APACE, ASAP, NOW, SOON, STAT

delayed LATE

Delbert MANN

___ del Corso VIA

dele EDIT, ERASE
undo a ~ STET

---

delectable GOOD, SWEET

delegate AGENT

delete EDIT, EMEND, ERASE, OMIT
~ with "out" BLOT, EDIT

deleterious BAD, EVIL

delft WARE

Delhi CITY
~ locale INDIA
~ wrap SARI
city SSE of ~ AGRA
see also Indian

deli
~ draw AROMA
~ loaf RYE
~ order BLT, HAM, HERO, RYE, SALAMI, SLAW, SUB, TOGO
~ patron EATER
~ purchase BAGEL, GENOA
~ shout NEXT
~ units LBS

deliberate MEANT, MUSE, SLOW
~ act STEP

deliberation
without ~ ADLIB

Delibes LEO

delicacy TASTE, TREAT
Japanese ~ EEL
lacking ~ CRASS

delicate AERIAL, FINE, NICE, THIN
~ color TINT
~ fabric LACE

"Delicate Balance, A"
~ author ALBEE

"___ Delicate Condition" PAPAS

delicious APPLE, GOOD, SWEET

delight ELATE, GLEE, PLEASE, SEND, SUIT
~ in ADORE, BASK, LIKE, LOVE, REVEL, SAVOR
angel's ~ SRO
cries of ~ AHS
gasp of ~ AAH, OOH
show ~ GLOW, GRIN, SMILE
sounds of ~ AHS

delighted ELATED, GLAD, RAPT

delightful NICE
~ place EDEN

"Delight in Disorder" POEM

Delilah
~ in "Samson and Delilah" HEDY

delimit SET

delineate DRAW, ETCH, PAINT, TRACE

delineation MAP, TRACE

delinquent
be ~ OWE
mil. ~ AWOL

deliquesce MELT, RUN, THAW

delirious
be ~ RAVE

delirium MANIA

deli scale
~ **word** TARE

deliver DEAL, FREE, HAND, HELP, PASS, READ, REFER, SAVE, SEND, SHIP, TAKE
~ **as a blow** DEAL
~ **a tirade** RANT
~ **from** SPARE
~ **up** CEDE

deliverer
paper ~'s way ROUTE

"...deliver us from ___" EVIL

delivery
~ **extra** SETUP
~ **letters** COD
~ **truck** VAN
daily ~ MAIL, PAPER
frat-party ~ KEG
postal ~ MAIL
Santa's ~ TOY
Sun. ~ SER

dell GLEN, VALE

Della REESE
~ **in "Touched by an Angel"** TESS
creator of ~ ERLE

Delmonico ___ STEAK

Delon ALAIN

"___ De-Lovely" ITS

Delphi
~ **god** APOLLO
~ **priestess** ORACLE

___ del Plata, Argentina MAR

delta
~ **deposit** SILT
African ~ NILE

Delta
~ **competitor** TWA

Delta Center
~ **team** UTAH

"Delta of Venus"
~ **author** NIN

delts
~ **kin** ABS

delude CON, DUPE
~ **oneself** ERR

deluder LIAR

deluge GLUT, POUR, RAIN, STORM, STREAM
~ **refuge** ARK

Deluge
before the ~ OLD

DeLuise DOM

delusion DREAM, ERROR

delusive FALSE

deluxe POSH

delve CUT, DIG, PRY, ROOT

Delvecchio ALEX

Dem. POL
~ **opponent** REP
not ~ or Rep. IND

demagogue ORATOR

demand ASK, BID, CLAIM, ORDER, URGE, WANT
~ **as a price** ASK
~ **for electricity** LOAD
be in ~ SELL
bouncer's ~ OUT
ed.'s ~ SASE
heavy ~ RUN
in ~ HOT
judge's ~ ORDER
monopolist's ~ ALL

demanding LOUD, STERN

demarcate LIMIT, SET, STAKE

demarcation
line of ~ LIMIT

dematerialize MELT

demean ABASE, SHAME

demeanor AIR, CAST, MIEN, TONE

de Medici
~ **in-law** ESTE

demented DAFT, MAD

___ de mer MAL

demesne ABODE, ESTATE, HOME, LAND, MANOR, PALE

Demeter
~ **to the Romans** CERES

demi- HALF

Demi MOORE

"Demian"
~ **author** HESSE

de Mille AGNES

DeMille, Cecil B.
~ **genre** EPIC

demisemiquaver NOTE

demitasse CUP

Demme TED

demo
sitcom ~ PILOT

democracy
world's largest ~ INDIA

Democratic donkey
~ **creator** NAST

demographic
~ **datum** AGE

demoiselle CRANE, GIRL, LASS, MISS

demolish BLAST, RAZE, RUIN, SHRED, SINK, TOTAL

demolition
~ **letters** TNT

demon IMP, OGRE
~ **doing** EVIL
speed ~ RACER

demon ___ RUM

"Demon ___, The" SEED

demoniacal BAD

demonic EVIL

___ Demons (DePaul U.) BLUE

demonstrate ATTEST, CITE, SHOW
~ **literacy** READ

demonstrated SURE
which was to be ~ QED

demonstrative
~ **pronoun** THAT, THIS

demoralize ROUT

Demosthenes ORATOR
emulate ~ ORATE

Dempsey
~ **stat** KOS, TKO

demulcent BALM

demur DENY

demure PRIM, SEDATE, SHY

Demy, Jacques
~ **film of 1961** LOLA

den CAVE, HAVEN, HOLE, HOME, LAIR, ROOM
~ **din** ROAR
~ **father** LION
~ **furniture** SETTEE
~ **of iniquity** NEST
beard the lion in his ~ DARE

Den.
neighbor of ~ GER

Denali National Park
~ **locale** ALASKA

denarius COIN

Deneb STAR

Deneuve
see French

Deng
~ **predecessor** MAO

denial
Security Council ~ NYET, VETO
slangy ~ NAH

denials NOES, NOS

denigrate LIBEL, SHAME, TAINT

denigrating
~ **remark** SLUR

"___ Denim" BLUE

De Niro
~ **film, with "The"** FAN

Denise LOO

denizens
~ **of the deep** LIFE

Dennis DAY

Dennis, Patrick
~ **aunt** MAME

Dennis the Menace BRAT, IMP, PEST
~ **mother** ALICE
~ **to Mr. Wilson** PEST

"Dennis the Menace"
~ **girl** GINA

denominate LABEL

denomination SECT, TYPE

denote BODE, MEAN

denouement END, ISSUE

denounce RAIL

de novo ANEW, NEW

dense CLOSE, RANK, SLOW, SOLID
not ~ THIN

dent DING, HOLE, MAR, PIT
make a ~ MOVE

dental
~ **photo** XRAY
~ **problem** CHIP, GAP

dentist
~ **anesthetic** GAS
~ **command** RINSE
~ **deg.** DDS
~ **org.** ADA
~ **request** BITE, OPEN, RINSE
~ **supply, once** ETHER
symptom for a ~ ACHE
word to a ~ AAH

___ d'entrée CARTE

denude SKIN

denuded BARE

Denver
~ **height** MILE
~ **st.** COL
~ **zone** MDT, MST

Denver ___ BOOT, OMELET

Denver, John
~ **album** AERIE

deny BELIE, VETO
~ **use** BAN

Denys STE

deobstruct AID

deodar TREE

deodorized CLEAN

deoxyribonucleic ACID

dep. ASST
opposite of ~ ARR

depart DESERT, EXIT, FLEE, LEAVE, MOVE, SPLIT, START
~ **ender** URE

departed AWAY, GONE

department AREA, REALM

department ___ STORE

department store
~ **event** SALE

departs GOES

departure EXIT, LEAVE
~ **from the norm** BLIP
~ **from the truth** LIE, TALE
hasty ~ LAM
point of ~ BASE, GATE

Depeche ___ MODE

depend HANG, REST
~ **ender** ENCE, ENT
~ **(on)** LEAN, RELY

dependable HONEST, SAFE, SOLID, SURE, TRUE

depict DRAW, PLAY
~ **distinctly** ETCH
~ **unfairly** SKEW

depilate BARE

depilated BALD

depilatory
~ **target** HAIR

deplane ARRIVE

deplaned ALIT

deplete SAP, SPEND, USE, WASTE

depleted GONE, LOW, POOR

depletion LOSS, WASTE

deplorable SAD
~ **act** SIN
~ **fellow** LOUSE

deplore MOAN, RUE

___ de plume NOM

depone ATTEST

___ de pont TETE

deport EJECT, EXILE, OUST

deportment MIEN

depose ATTEST, OUST

deposit BED, LAY, MINE, PUT, SET, STORE
anthracite ~ COAL, SEAM
bedrock ~ ORE
bituminous ~ COAL, SEAM
carbon ~ SOOT
clayey ~ LOESS
Comstock ~ LODE, ORE
delta ~ SILT
dryer ~ LINT
dust-storm ~ SILT
make a ~ BAIL
metal ~ LODE
mineral ~ RUN, SEAM
morning ~ DEW
ore ~ LODE
river-mouth ~ DELTA, SILT
sedimentary ~ SILT
silt ~ DELTA
vein ~ ORE
windblown ~ LOESS

___-deposit box SAFE

deposition
give a ~ ATTEST, AVER

depositor
blood-bank ~ DONOR

depository SAFE, SLOT, TILL
egg ~ NEST

depot STOP
~ **abbr.** ARR, ETA
~ **(abbr.)** STA

"___ Depot" UNION

deprave ROT

depraved BAD, BASE, EVIL, LOW

depravity EVIL

deprecate CARP, SLUR

deprecation
word of ~ ONLY

depredate LOOT

depredation RAID

depress DENT

depressed BLUE, LOW

depressing BAD, SAD

depression DENT, HOLE, PIT, RUT, SINK
ridge ~ COL
slight ~ DIP

deprivation LOSS, WANT

deprive
~ **(of)** STRIP
~ **of (prefix)** DIS
~ **unjustly** ROB

deprived NEEDY
be ~ of LOSE

"De profundis" PSALM

depth
~ **charge** MINE
immeasurable ~ ABYSS
out of one's ~ ASEA, ATSEA

depths ABYSS
~ **of despair** PAIN
in the ~ of despair SAD

Dept. of Health
~ **division** FDA

depute ENABLE

deputies
~ **on horseback** POSSE

deputy AGENT, AIDE, REP

"Der ___" (Adenauer) ALTE

deranged DAFT, MAD, RABID

"Deranged"
~ **cowriter** ENO

derby HAT, RACE
~ **material** FELT
soapbox ~ RACE

Derby
~ **entrant** HORSE
~ **track** OVAL
~ **winner's flower** ROSE

deregulate FREE

Derek
~ **and others** BOS

Derek, Bo
~ **film** ORCA
number for ~ TEN

derelict ALONE, HOBO, LONE, NOMAD

deride GIBE, HOOT, SNEER, TWIT

derision
object of ~ GOAT
sound of ~ SNORT
word of ~ BAH, HAH

derisive RUDE, SNIDE, TART
~ **cry** HAH
~ **exclamation** FIE
~ **smile** SNEER
~ **sound** HISS, HOOT

derivation ROOT

derive EARN, EDUCE, ISSUE, TAKE
~ **(from)** ARISE, COME, STEM

___ de Rivoli RUE

dermal
~ **vent** PORE

dermatological
~ **concern** ACNE, PORE

dermis SKIN
~ **starter** EPI

Dern LAURA

dernier
~ **cri** FAD, MODE, RAGE

dernier ___ CRI

dernier cri FAD, MODE, RAGE

Dern, Laura
~ **mom** DIANE, LADD

derogate SHAME, SLUR

derogatory SNIDE

___ Derr Biggers EARL

derrick CRANE

derrière REAR, SEAT

"Der Ring ___ Nibelungen" DES

"Der Ring des Nibelungen" OPERA

derring-do NERVE
bit of ~ FEAT
name in ~ EVEL
tale of ~ GEST, GESTE, SAGA

derringer GUN

"Der Rosenkavalier"
Annina in ~ ALTO
Baron in ~ OCHS

Dershowitz ALAN
~ **occ.** ATT, ATTY
~ **org.** ABA
~ **specialty** LAW

"Der Spiegel"
see German

dervish
~ **religion** ISLAM
emulate a ~ SPIN

DeSario TERI

___ des Beaux-Arts ECOLE

descant ARIA, SONG

Descartes RENE
~ **conclusion** IAM
see also French

descend DIP, LAND, SLOPE
~ **ender** ENT
~ **on** MOB
~ **upon** RAID, STORM

descendant HEIR, SCION
~ **(suffix)** ITE

descendants ISSUE, SEED

descended ALIT

"___ Descending a Staircase" NUDE

descent DROP, SLIDE

describe LABEL, RELATE, TELL
~ **vividly** PAINT

descry ESPY, SEE, SPY

Desdemona
~ **enemy** IAGO
~ **handkerchief** PROP

"dese"
not ~ DOSE

desecrate TAINT

deselect DROP

Deseret
~ **today** UTAH

desert EXIT, FLEE, LEAVE, SANDS
~ **animal** CAMEL
~ **bloomers** CACTI
~ **crawler** IGUANA, SNAKE
~ **dweller** ARAB
~ **feature** DUNE
~ **fruit** DATE
~ **in Arabic** SAHARA
~ **mount** ARAB
~ **nomad's robe** ABA
~ **plant** AGAVE
~ **plants** CACTI
~ **prince** AMIR, EMEER, EMIR
~ **stopover** OASIS
~ **surface** SAND
~ **wanderer** NOMAD
African ~ SAHARA
Asian ~ GOBI
Israeli ~ NEGEV
like a ~ ARID, DRY
Mideast ~ NEGEV, SINAI
ship of the ~ CAMEL
world's largest ~ SAHARA

Desert GOBI, NEGEV, SAHARA

Desert ___ STORM

"Desert ___, The" RATS

"Desert Bloom"
~ **subject** ATEST

deserted ALONE, LONE

deserter
~ **status** AWOL
sinking-ship ~ RAT

desertlike ARID, DRY, SERE

"Desert Rats, The"
~ **director** WISE

deserts
just ~ DUE

Desert Storm
~ **locale** IRAQ
~ **target** BASRA

deserve CLAIM, EARN, MERIT, RATE

deserved DUE

deserving GOOD

desiccate DRY

desiccated ARID, DESERT, DRY, SERE

desiderate LONG

desideratum NEED, WANT

___-de-siècle FIN

design AIM, CUT, IDEA, LOGO, MODEL, PLAN
  ~ with acid ETCH
  fashion ~ ALINE
  interior ~ DECOR
  ripplelike ~ MOIRE
  stick-on ~ DECAL
  trademark ~ LOGO
  transferable ~ DECAL
  wavy ~ MOIRE

"Design ___ Living" FOR

designate ALLOT, CALL, ELECT, MAKE, NAME, PEG, SET, STYLE, TAP, TERM, TITLE

designation CLASS, TAG, TITLE
  nav. ~ USS

designer DIOR
  ~ collection LINE
  ~ item DRESS, TIE
  ~ shade ECRU

designing ARCH, DEEP, SLY

"Designing Women"
  ~ actress SMART
  ~ name ANNIE, DELTA

designs
  dizzying ~ OPART

desirable GOOD
  ~ possession ASSET
  ~ street EASY
  less ~ WORSE
  most ~ BEST, TOPS

desire ACHE, ARDOR, EROS, ITCH, LIKE, LONG, LOVE, LUST, PLEASE, URGE, WANT, YEN
  ~ earnestly ACHE
  ~ personified EROS
  feel ~ YEARN
  heart's ~ LOVE
  unquenchable ~ PANG

"___ Desire" ALLI

"Desire Under the ___" ELMS

"Desire Under the Elms"
  ~ actor IVES
  ~ actress LOREN
  ~ director MANN

desirous AVID, EAGER, HOT

desist CEASE, HALT, STOP

desk TABLE
  ~ accessory LAMP, PEN
  church ~ AMBO

___ desk CITY

"Desk ___" SET

"Desk Set"
  ~ director LANG

desktop
  ~ buy LAMP

desktop publisher
  ~ choice FONT

Des Moines
  ~ locale IOWA
  city near ~ AMES

Desmond NORMA, PAUL, TUTU

Desmond, Paul
  ~ instrument ALTO, SAX

desolate ALONE, ARID, BARE, DESERT, LONE, RAID
  ~ spot MOOR

desolation PAIN, WASTE

De Soto AUTO, CAR
  ~ contemporary NASH

despair BANE
  cry of ~ OHNO
  depths of ~ PAIN
  in the depths of ~ SAD
  utterance of ~ ALAS

desperate DIRE

"Desperate ___, The" TRAIL

despicable BAD, BASE, EVIL, LOW, MEAN, UGLY, VILE
  ~ one CAD, HEEL, SLIME, TOAD

despise ABHOR, HATE

despoil LOOT, MAR, RAID, RUIN, SACK, TAINT, WASTE

despoliation WASTE

despondent BAD, BLUE, LOW, SAD
  be ~ about RUE

despot TSAR
  ~ word LAW
  deposed ~ AMIN

desquamate PEEL, SHED

dessert CAKE, CREPE, ICE, PIE, SWEET, TART, TORTE, TREAT
  ~ trolley CART
  custard ~ FLAN
  have for ~ EAT

dessert ___ WINE

destination AIM, END, GOAL
  reach a ~ ARRIVE
  RR ~ STA

destine DOOM, FATE

destined MEANT

destiny DOOM, FATE, LOT
  individual ~ MOIRA

destitute NEEDY, POOR

destitution NEED, RUIN, WANT

destrier HORSE

destroy BLAST, DASH, END, ERASE, RAZE, RUIN, SINK, SLAY, SMASH, TOTAL, TRASH, UNDO, WASTE
  ~ documents SHRED
  ~ gradually ERODE

destroyed GONE, LOST

destroyer BOAT, SHIP
  ~ letters USS

___-destruct AUTO, SELF

destruction BANE, DOOM, HARM, LOSS, RUIN
  willful ~ ABUSE

destructive BAD, EVIL
  ~ emotion HATE
  ~ force BANE
  ~ one HUN

"Destry ___ Again" RIDES

"Destry Rides ___" AGAIN

detach CLEAR, CUT, PART

detached ALOOF, APART, COOL, ICY, LOOSE

detachment ARMY, COOL

detail FACT, ITEM, PART, RELATE
  architectural ~ DADO, OGEE
  thesaurus ~ SYN
  trivial ~ NIT

"___ Detail, The" LAST

detailed
  ~ program PLAN

details
  ~ handler AIDE

detain ARREST, HOLD, KEEP, STOP

detect ESPY, LEARN, NOSE, NOTE, SCENT, SEE, SENSE, SPOT, TRACE

detecting
  gift for ~ NOSE

detection
  ~ device RADAR, SONAR

detective AGENT, TAIL
  ~ cry AHA
  ~ discovery CLUE
  ~ duo's dog ASTA
  ~ work CASE
  do ~ work TRACE
  first name in ~ fiction ERLE
  rabbi ~ SMALL

detective story
  ~ pioneer POE

___ detector LIE, METAL, MINE

détente
  ~ result THAW

detention
  police ~ ARREST

deter STOP
  opposite of ~ ABET

deterge LAVE, RINSE, WASH

detergent SOAP
  ~ brand ALL, ERA, TIDE

deteriorate ERODE, ROT, WEAR

deterioration ROT, WEAR

determinant CAUSE

determination GRIT

determine LEARN, SEE, SET, SETTLE, TRACE

determined BENT, SET

deterrent BAR
  burglar ~ ALARM

mugger ~ MACE

detest ABHOR, HATE

detestable BAD, BASE, EVIL, UGLY, VILE

de Tirtoff, Romain
  ~ alias ERTE

___ de toilette EAU

detonating
  ~ device CAP

detonation BLAST, POP

detonator FUSE

detour AVOID, ERR

detract SLUR

detrain ARRIVE
  where to ~ DEPOT

detriment HARM

detrimental BAD, EVIL

___ de Triomphe ARC

detritus SAND, TRASH
  hillside ~ SCREE
  rock ~ SAND

Detroit
  ~ baseballer TIGER
  ~ disaster EDSEL
  ~ footballer LION
  ~ offering SEDAN
  ~ product AUTO, CAR

Detroit ___ Wings RED

Detroit River
  ~ destination ERIE

deuce CARD, TIE, TWO
  ~ beater TREY
  at ~ TIED
  point after ~ ADIN

___ deus in nobis EST

Deus Ramos, Joao de POET
  see also poet

deuterium
  ~ discoverer UREY

Deutsch
  see German

Deutschland
  see German

"Deutschland ___ Alles" UBER

deux
  ~ preceder UNE

___ deux ENTRE

De Valera, Eamon
  ~ ctry. IRE
  ~ land EIRE, ERIN

devaluation DROP

devalue SLASH, TAINT

devastate BLAST, RAID, RUIN, UNDO, WASTE

devastating BAD

devastation WASTE

de Vega LOPE

___ de Velasco LUIS

develop ARISE, EDUCE, EMERGE, GROW, MAKE, RIPEN
  ~ as a storm BREW
  ~ vigorously BOOM

developed
  fully ~ ADULT, RIPE

developer
  ~ offering LAND, LOT

development
  election-night ~ TREND
  housing ~ TRACT

de Vere, Aubrey Thomas POET
  see also poet

Devereux EARL

deviant ODD

deviate ERR, HEEL, SKEW, TURN, VEER, YAW

deviation TURN, YAW

device ART, GAME, RUSE, TRAP, WILE

___ de vie EAU

devil DEMON
  ~ ender ISH, TRY
  dust ~ EDDY
  full of the ~ BAD
  little ~ IMP
  printer's ~ PAGE
  Tasmanian ~ ANIMAL

___ devil DUST

Devil SATAN
  ~ thing EVIL

"Devil ___ Blue Dress" INA

"Devil ___ Daniel Webster, The" AND

"Devil ___ Miss Jones, The" AND

"Devil ___ Woman, The" ISA

"___-Devil" SHE

"Devil and ___ Jones, The" MISS

"Devil and Daniel Webster, The"
  ~ author BENET

"Devil in a ___ Dress" BLUE

"Devil in a Blue ___" DRESS

devilish EVIL
  ~ creature DEMON

devilkin IMP

___ de ville (city hall) HOTEL

devil-may-___ CARE

devil-may-care GAME, RASH

Devil Rays TEAM, TEN
  ~ home TAMPA

Devils SIX, TEAM
  ~ milieu ICE, RINK
  ~ org. NHL

"Devil's ___, The" BRIDE, OWN

"Devil's Doorway, The"
  ~ director MANN

devil's food CAKE

deviltry EVIL, HARM, SIN

Devine ANDY

devious DEEP, SLY, WRY
  ~ purpose ANGLE

devise BREW, COIN, MAKE, PLAN

devised MADE

devitalize SAP, TIRE

DeVito, Danny
  ~ series TAXI
  Mrs. ~ RHEA

devoid
  ~ (of) BARE
  ~ of color PALE
  ~ of dirt CLEAN
  ~ of interest BLAH
  ~ of moisture ARID, DRY, SERE
  ~ of truth FALSE

devolatilize CALM

Devonshire
  ~ drink ALE

Devonshire ___ CREAM

devote SPEND
  ~ oneself to PLY

devoted AVID, FAST, LIEGE, TRUE
  be ~ ADHERE
  be very ~ ADORE

devotedness ZEAL

devotee FAN, NUT
  ~ (suffix) IST, ITE

devotion ARDOR, LOVE, ZEAL
  letters of ~ TLC
  object of ~ ICON, IDOL

devour CRAM, EAT, ERODE, FEED, TAKE

devourer EATER

devout GOOD

dew
  bit of ~ BEAD, DROP
  fresh as the morning ~ NEW

DEW ___ LINE

de Waart EDO

Dewar SCOT, SIR

dewdrop BEAD, PEARL

Dew Drop INN

Dewey TOM

DEW line
  ~ force SAC

dewy DAMP, WET

dewy-___ EYED

Dexter, Colin
  ~ inspector MORSE

dexterity ART, EASE, TACT

dexterous ABLE, AGILE, CLEAN, DEFT, NEAT

dexterousness TACT

dextrous ABLE

Dezhnev CAPE

DFW
  ~ abbr. ARR, ETA

DH
  ~ stat RBI

___ Dhabi ABU

Dheigh, Khigh
  ~ TV series KHAN

___ d'hôte TABLE

dhow BOAT, SHIP

D.I.
  ~ rank SGT
  order from the ~ ATEASE

diabolical BAD, CRUEL, EVIL

"Diabolique"
  ~ actress STONE

diacritical
  ~ mark TILDE

diadem TIARA

Diaghilev SERGE

diagnostic
  ~ device XRAY
  ~ test EEG, SCAN

diagonal AWRY, BIAS, LINE, SLASH

diagram MAP, PLAN, PLAT, TABLE
  ~ a sentence PARSE
  architect's ~ PLAN

dial KNOB, RING
  ~ up CALL, PHONE
  dashboard ~ TACH

dial ___ TONE

dialect IDIOM

"Dial M ___ Murder" FOR

dialogue TALK
  bit of ~ LINE

"Dialogues"
  ~ author PLATO

diameters
  ~ halved RADII

diamond GEM
  ~ authority UMP
  ~ bag BASE
  ~ call OUT, SAFE
  ~ coup HOMER, STEAL
  ~ decision FAIR
  ~ feature PLATE
  ~ goof ERROR
  ~ measure CARAT
  ~ of India HOPE
  ~ once COAL
  ~ place HOME
  ~ protector TARP
  ~ source MINE
  ~ stat ERA, ERROR, HIT, HRS, RBI, RUN
  ~ stats ABS
  ~ wts. CTS
  Smithsonian ~ HOPE
  see also baseball

Diamond LEGS, NEIL, SELMA
  ~ girl LIL

DiamondBacks NINE, TEAM

Diamond Head
  ~ locale OAHU

___ Diamond Phillips LOU

"Diamond Queen, The"
  ~ actress DAHL

diamonds ICE, SUIT
  black ~ COAL
  fake ~ PASTE
  two ~ BID

"Diamonds ___ a girl's..." ARE

"Diamonds ___ Forever" ARE

Diana ROSS

"Diana"
  ~ singer ANKA

Diane ___ Furstenberg VON

diaper
  ~ holder PIN

diaphanous AIRY, CLEAR, FINE, THIN

diary LIFE, LOG
  ~ capacity YEAR
  ~ notation ENTRY
  ~ starter DEAR
  nautical ~ LOG
  put in one's ~ ENTER

"Diary ___ Chambermaid" OFA

"Diary ___ Country Priest" OFA

"Diary ___ Hitman" OFA

"Diary ___ Lost Girl" OFA

"Diary ___ Mad Housewife" OFA

"___ Diary" DEAR

"Diary of ___ Frank, The" ANNE

"Diary of a ___ Girl" LOST

"Diary of a ___ Housewife" MAD

"Diary of a Genius"
  ~ author DALI

"Diary of a Lost ___" GIRL

diastole
  systole and ~ PULSE

diatom ALGA

diatribe ABUSE
  deliver a ~ RANT

dibble DIG, TOOL

dibs
  have ~ on CLAIM

DiCaprio
  ~ familiarly LEO

dice BET, CHOP
  ~ spot PIP
  ~ throw ACES, ELEVEN, NINE, SEVEN, TEN, THREE
  ~ toss ROLL
  tamper with ~ LOAD

___ dice LIARS

dichotomous HALF

dichotomy SPLIT

"___, Dick and Harry" TOM

"Dick and Jane"
  ~ dog SPOT
  ~ verb SEE

dickens
  go like the ~ RIP, TEAR
  little ~ IMP

Dickens
  ~ character PIP, TIM
  ~ girl NELL
  ~ title start ATALE
  devour ~ READ

Dickensian
  ~ exclamation BAH

dicker DEAL, TRADE

Dickerson ERIC

dickey BIB
  ~ fastener STUD

"Dickey ___ Song, The" BIRD

Dickinson, Emily POET
  see also poet

dictate BID, FIAT, ORDER

dictation
  ~ pro STENO

dictator LORD, TSAR
  ~ aide STENO
  1970s ~ AMIN

"___ Dictator, The" GREAT

dictionary TOME
  ~ abbr. SYN
  ~ word ENTRY

dictum ACT, ADAGE, DOGMA,
  EDICT, FIAT, GNOME, LAW, SAW,
  SAYSO

"Did ___!" NOT, TOO

diddle ROB, ROOK

Diddley
  ~ and others BOS

diddly NIL

"Did not!" "Did ___!" TOO

"___ Didn't Care" IFI

dido CAPER

Dido
  ~ sister ANNA

Didrikson BABE

**"Did You ___ See a Dream
  Walking?"** EVER

die STAMP
  ~ down ABATE, EBB
  ~ high SIX
  ~ out END, FADE, PASS
  ~ partner TOOL
  ~ surface FACE, SIDE

___ die SINE

"Die ___" HARD

"Die ___ With a Vengeance"
  HARD

dieffenbachia PLANT

"Die Fledermaus" OPERA
  ~ maid ADELE

___ Diego, Calif. SAN

___ Diego Chargers SAN

___ Diego Chicken SAN

"___ Diego, I Love You" SAN

diehard MULE

___ diem PER

"Die Meistersinger" OPERA
  ~ heroine EVA

___ Diemen's Land VAN

"Die Nibelungen"
  ~ director LANG

Dieppe CITY, PORT

"Dies ___" IRAE

diet FARE, FAST
  ~ component FAT
  ~ successfully LOSE
  crash ~ FAST
  go on a ~ LOSE
  livestock ~ HAY

dietary
  ~ initials RDA
  ~ supplement IRON, ZINC

dieter
  ~ device SCALE
  ~ dread GAIN
  ~ lunch SALAD
  ~ meas. CAL
  ~ measure GRAM
  ~ no-no FAT
  ~ of rhyme SPRAT
  ~ resort SPA

dieters
  suitable for ~ LOCAL

diet food
  ~ label word LITE

dietician
  ~ recommendation BRAN

Diet-Rite COLA

"___ dieu!" MON

"Die Walküre" OPERA

differ
  ~ ender ENCE, ENT

difference
  ~ of opinion SPAT
  big ~ GAP
  split the ~ SHARE

differences
  discuss ~ ARGUE

different APART, ELSE, NEW, ODD,
  OTHER
  in a ~ way ANEW
  in ~ places APART
  make ~ ALTER, AMEND
  radically ~ POLAR

differential
  ~ part AXLE

differently ELSE

difficult HARD
  ~ journey TREK
  ~ position SPOT
  ~ situation BIND
  ~ spare SPLIT
  make less ~ EASE
  make ~ to read ENCODE
  more than ~ DIRE

difficulties
  involve in ~ MIRE

difficulty SNAG, TASK, WOE
  yarn ~ KNOT

diffident SHY

"Diff'rent Strokes"
  ~ actress PLATO, RAE

diffuse WIDE

DiFranco ANI

dig ADORE, BARB, BORE, CLAW,
  CUT, GET, GIBE, GRASP, HOE,
  JAB, LIKE, MINE, PLOW, ROOT,
  SAVOR, SCOOP, SLAP
  ~ for gold MINE
  ~ for info ASK
  ~ in EAT
  ~ out BORE, ROOT
  ~ up LEARN, ROOT, TRACE

digest CODE, LEARN, SUM, TAKE

digestion
  ~ aid BILE

digestive ___ TRACT

___ diggers CLAM

"___ Diggers of 1933" GOLD

digging
  tool for ~ SPADE

diggings PIT

"Digging the We-___" UNS

"___ diggity!" HOT

dight ADORN, DRESS

digit ONE, TOE, UNIT
  binary ~ ONE
  lower ~ TOE
  top ~ NINE

digital
  ~ adjunct NAIL
  ~ display TIME

digital watch
  ~ display LED

digitize SCAN

digits
  ~ (abbr.) NOS

Digne
  see French

dignified REGAL, SEDATE, SOBER,
  STAID

dignify EXALT, RAISE

dignitary DEAN

dignity FACE, HONOR, STATE
  ~ of manner POISE

digress ROAM

digression ASIDE

digressive LONG

digs ABODE, HOME, PAD

Dijon
  see French

dik-dik ANIMAL
  ~ relative ELAND, GNU

dike LEVEE
  ~ problem LEAK

dilapidated OLD, SEEDY, SHOT

dilate FLARE, OPEN

dilatory LATE, SLOW
  ~ tactic STALL

Dilbert
  ~ place DESK

"Dilbert" STRIP
  ~ cartoonist ADAMS

dilemma BIND, HOLE, MESS, PASS,
  POSER, SNARL
  in a ~ TORN

dilettantish ARTY

diligence LABOR, RIGOR

diligent EAGER

diligently HARD

dill ANET, HERB

Dillinger
  ~ foe GMAN
  org. that got ~ FBI

Dillon MATT

Dillon, Matt
  ~ film of 1982 TEX

dilly LULU, ONER

dillydally DRAG, IDLE, LAG, STALL,
  WAIT

dilute CUT, THIN, WATER

diluted CUT
  not ~ NEAT, PURE

dim BLUR, FADE, MIST, PALE,
  SHADE, WANE
  ~ ender WIT
  grow ~ FADE

dim ___ SUM

DiMaggio DOM, JOE
  ~ uniform number FIVE

___ Dimas, Calif. SAN

dime COIN
  ~ a dozen AMPLE
  like a ~ THIN
  word on a ~ ONE

dime ___ STORE

dimension
  fourth ~ TIME

___-dimensional THREE, TWO

dimensions SIZE, SPACE
  vert. ~ HTS

dimes
  like American ~ CLAD

diminish ABATE, ALLAY, BATE, COOL, CUT, DROP, EASE, EBB, FADE, FLAG, PARE, REMIT, SLAKE, TAPER, TRIM, WANE, WEAR

diminished
  ~ by LESS

diminution WANE, WASTE, WEAR

diminutive ELFIN, SMALL, TINY, WEE
  ~ suffix ELLE, ETTE, INE, KIN, LET, REL, ULE
  Spanish ~ suffix ITA, ITO

dimple DENT, PIT
  ~ site CHIN

dim sum
  ~ additive MSG

"Dim Sum: a Little ___ of Heart" BIT

"Dim Sum: a Little Bit of ___" HEART

dimwit CLOD, GOOSE, IDIOT, OAF

dimwitted DAFT, DENSE

din BLARE, BLAST, JAR, NOISE, ROAR, ROW
  den ~ ROAR

Dinah CAT, PET, SHORE

dinar COIN

Dinaric ALPS

dinars
  where ~ are spent IRAQ

dine EAT, FARE, FEED
  ~ at home EATIN
  ~ partner WINE
  wine and ~ FEED, FETE, WOO

___ Dine (Philo Vance creator) VAN

diner CAFE, CAR, EATER
  ~ add-on TIP
  ~ beverage JOE
  ~ choice ENTREE
  ~ fare EATS
  ~ handout MENU
  ~ offering BLT, CHILI, OMELET, PIE
  ~ order, with "the" USUAL
  ~ sandwich BLT
  ~ sign EATS, NEON
  sitcom ~ MELS

dinero MOOLA
  ~ unit PESO

Dinesen, Isak DANE

dinette NOOK

ding HIT
  parking-lot ~ DENT

ding-a-ling NUT

dingbat YOYO
  ~ of TV EDITH

ding-dong RING

dinghy BOAT
  ~ direction AFT, ASTERN
  ~ need OAR
  propel a ~ ROW

dingle DALE, DELL, GLEN

Dingle Bay
  ~ locale EIRE, ERIN

dingo ANIMAL, DOG

dingy DAFT, DRAB, GRAY, GREY

dining
  ~ area HALL
  ~ enticement AROMA
  ~ hall MESS

dining ___ CAR, ROOM

dinky MEAN, POOR, SMALL

dinner MEAL
  ~ and a movie DATE
  ~ beverage PORT, WINE
  ~ course SALAD
  ~ ender WARE
  ~ entrée CHOP, ROAST
  ~ gown DRESS
  ~ jelly ASPIC
  ~ party SOIREE
  ~ scrap ORT
  celebrity ~ ROAST
  ceremonial ~ SEDER
  dobbin's ~ OATS
  donkey ~ FEED
  get ready for ~ DRESS
  GI ~ MESS
  have ~ DINE, EAT
  have guests to ~ EATIN
  hobo's ~ STEW
  invite to ~ FEED
  Jewish holiday ~ SEDER
  one-pot ~ STEW
  order for ~ HAVE
  pig's ~ SLOP
  put out ~ SERVE
  recruit's ~ MESS
  stay home for ~ EATIN
  TV ~ MEAL

___ dinner SHORE

dinnerware
  ~ item PLATE

Dino PET
  ~ master FRED

Dino, ___ & Billy DESI

dinosaur
  ~ DNA preserver AMBER
  ~ preserver TAR

dinosaurian BIG, LARGE

dinotherian BIG, LARGE

Dinsmore ELSIE

dint DENT

diocese SEE

Diocletian CAESAR, ROMAN

Diomedes HERO

Dione MOON

Dionne MARIE

Dionysus
  ~ attendant SATYR

Dior
  ~ design ALINE

dip BAIL, BATH, BATHE, DENT, LADE, LADLE, NOD, PIT, RINSE, SAG, SCOOP, SLIP, SLOPE
  ~ in gravy SOP
  ~ into READ
  ~ out a boat BAIL
  landscape ~ DALE
  nacho ~ SALSA
  take a ~ SWIM

diploma PAPER
  ~ word ARTS

diploma ___ MILL

diplomacy TACT
  ~ alternative WAR

diplomat AGENT

diplomatic SUAVE
  ~ contract PACT

dipper BIRD, PAIL, SCOOP
  big ~ LADLE

___ Dipper BIG

dippy DAFT, MAD, OFF

dips
  place for ~ POOL

dipso SOT

dir.
  compass ~ ENE, ESE, NNE, NNW, SSE, SSW, WNW, WSW

dire ACUTE, BAD, EVIL
  in ~ straits NEEDY

dirección
  compass ~ ESTE

direct AIM, BEND, BID, HONEST, LEAD, ORDER, ORIENT, REFER, RUN, SEND, STEER, TURN
  ~ elsewhere REFER
  ~ ender ION, IVE, ORATE

directed BADE

direction LEFT, TENOR
  ~ sign ARROW
  change ~ CUT, VEER, YAW
  compass ~ EAST, ENE, ESE, NNE, NNW, SSE, SSW, WEST, WNW, WSW
  cookbook ~ ADD, BAKE, BASTE, BOIL, CHOP, DICE, FRY, HEAT, ROAST, SAUTE, SCALD, SLICE, STIR, WARM
  general ~ TREND
  haw's ~ LEFT
  in another ~ AWAY
  nautical ~ ABEAM, AFT, ALEE, ASTERN, FORE
  paint-can ~ STIR
  pendulum ~ FRO
  provide ~ STEER
  puzzle ~ ACROSS
  rainy wind ~ EAST
  script ~ FADE

stage ~ ENTER, EXIT
sunup ~ EAST

directional
  ~ marker SIGN
  ~ signal ARROW
  ~ suffix ERN

directions
  elevator ~ UPS
  needing ~ LOST

directive ORDER
  after-grace ~ EAT
  button ~ PRESS
  galley ~ STET
  stock broker's ~ SELL

directly ANON, BANG, SOON

director ARROW, BOSS, EXEC, HEAD
  ~ award OSCAR
  ~ shoot TAKE
  ~ windup WRAP
  ~ yell CUT

directory LIST, ROLL

dire straits
  in ~ NEEDY

dirge SONG
  how to play a ~ LENTO

"Dirigo"
  ~ is its motto MAINE

dirk SNEE, STEEL

dirndl DRESS

dirt EARTH, GRIT, INFO, LAND, NEWS, SOIL
  ~ path TRAIL
  ~ remover SOAP
  chunk of ~ CLOD
  devoid of ~ CLEAN
  heap ~ upon LIBEL, TAINT
  hit the ~ SLIDE
  pay ~ LODE, ORE
  powdery ~ DUST

dirt ___ BIKE

dirt-___ POOR

___ dirt PAY

dirtbag CAD

dirt-road
  ~ depression RUT

dirty BLOT, BLUE, DAUB, LEWD, LOW, MESSY, SMEAR, TAINT
  ~ clothes WASH
  ~ dog CUR
  ~ fog SMOG
  ~ linen WASH
  ~ look GLARE, SNEER
  ~ mark SMUT
  ~ place STY
  ~ word OATH
  get ~ SOIL
  give a ~ look LEER

"dirty"
  Cagney's ~ word RAT

dirty ___ LINEN, POOL, RICE

Dirty Harry COP

"___ dirty job but..." ITSA

disadvantage SNAG

___ **disadvantage** ATA

disadvantaged
  economically ~ NEEDY

disadvantageous BAD

disaffirm DENY

disagree ARGUE, DENY

disagreeable BAD, MEAN, SOUR,
  UGLY, VILE
  ~ person PILL

disagreement ROW, SCRAP, SPAT

disallow BAN, BAR, DENY, TABOO,
  TABU, VETO

disambiguate CLEAR

disappear DIE, FADE, FLEE, FLIT,
  MELT
  ~ slowly ERODE

disappear ___ thin air INTO

disappeared GONE, LOST

disappearing
  ~ act LAM
  do a ~ act ELUDE, FLEE

disappoint DASH

disappointed
  ~ reaction OHNO

disappointing BAD

disappointment
  cry of ~ OHNO, RATS

Disappointment CAPE

disapproval
  show ~ HISS, HOOT
  sound of ~ BOO, TSK, TUT

disapprove DENY

disarm MELT

disarrange UPSET

disarranged MESSY

disarray MESS
  in ~ MESSY

disassemble UNDO

disassociated APART

disaster BANE, ILL, RUIN

disastrous BAD, DIRE, EVIL

disavow DENY, DROP

disband PART, SPLIT

disbelief AWE
  sounds of ~ HAS
  word of ~ PSHAW
  words of ~ OHNO

disbelieve DENY

disbeliever
  ~ exclamation PAH, POOH

disburden EASE, RID

disburse METE, PAY, SETTLE,
  SPEND

disbursement COST

discard SCRAP, SHED, TOSS

discards TRASH

discern ESPY, READ, SEE, SENSE,
  SPOT, SPY
  try to ~ PEER

discernible CLEAR

discerning ACUTE, AWARE,
  CLEAR, DEEP, SANE, WISE

discernment EYE, TACT, TASTE

discharge ACT, AXE, BANG, BLAST,
  CAN, DROP, EGEST, EJECT, EMIT,
  ERUPT, FIRE, ISSUE, OBEY, POP,
  SHOOT, SHOT, SPEW, TEEM
  ~ as debts PAY
  electric ~ ARC

disciple
  ~ (suffix) IST, ITE

discipline RIGOR, TRAIN
  Erhard's ~ EST
  guru's ~ YOGA
  koan ~ ZEN

___**-discipline** SELF

disclaim DENY

disclaimer
  sale ~ ASIS

disclose ADMIT, BARE, SAY, STATE,
  TELL

disclosed OUT

disco DANCE, FAD
  ~ dancer GOGO
  ~ group CHIC

discolor BLOT, TAINT

discoloration SPOT

discombobulate ABASH, ADDLE,
  JAR, UPSET

discombobulated ASEA, ATSEA

discomfit ABASH, UPSET

discomfort ACHE, PAIN, PANG

discompose ABASH, IRK, PEEVE,
  TOSS, UPSET

discomposed UPSET

disconcert ABASH, ADDLE, AMAZE,
  GET, JAR, SNUB, UPSET

disconcerted UPSET

disconnect PART, UNDO, UNTIE

disconnected LOOSE

disconsolate LOW, SAD

discontent
  show ~ MOAN

discontinuance GAP

discontinue ANNUL, CEASE, CUT,
  DEFER, DROP, END, HALT,
  LAPSE, STOP
  ~ the countdown ABORT

discontinuity GAP

discord
  apple of ~ contender HERA
  Greek goddess of ~ ERIS

discordant AJAR, ATONAL

Discordia
  ~ counterpart ERIS

discount SALE, SLASH
  kind of ~ REBATE

discount ___ STORE

___ **discount** CASH, TRADE

discounted
  not ~ LIST

discountenance IRK, PEEVE, RILE,
  UPSET

discourage DETER

discouraged LOW, SAD

discouraging BAD
  ~ words NOES, NOS

discourse ESSAY, TALK, THEME,
  TREAT
  ~ with RAP

discourteous RUDE

discover ESPY, LEARN, SEE, SPY,
  TRACE

Discover
  ~ rival VISA

"Discover"
  ~ rival OMNI

discovery
  cry of ~ AHA, OHO

"Discovery"
  ~ org. NASA

discredit ABASE, BLAST, DENY,
  LIBEL, SHAME, TAINT

discredited VOID

discreet
  ~ summons PSST, PST

"Discreet Music"
  ~ composer ENO

discrete ALONE, APART

discretion TACT

discriminating ACUTE, AWARE

discrimination TACT, TASTE
  kind of ~ AGE

discursive LONG

discus EVENT
  ~ competition MEET

discuss ARGUE, CHAT, HASH, RAP,
  TALK
  ~ differences ARGUE

discussion TALK
  ~ group PANEL
  matter for ~ ISSUE
  postgame ~ RECAP

___ **discussion** PANEL

disdain ABHOR, SHUN, SNEER,
  SNUB

disdainful RUDE

disembark ARRIVE

disembarked ALIT

disembogue EMERGE, EMIT

disenact ANNUL

disencumber AID, CLEAR, FREE,
  LOOSE, RID

disengage CLEAR, FREE, PART,
  UNTIE

disentangle CLEAR, COMB, FREE,
  LOOSE, RAVEL, UNTIE

disfavor HATE

disfigure MAIM, MAR, SCAR, SPOIL

disgorge EGEST, SPEW

disgrace RUIN, SHAME, SLUR,
  SOIL, TAINT

disgraceful BAD, BASE

disguise BELIE, DRESS, FAKE,
  HIDE, MASK
  element of ~ BEARD

disgust REPEL
  cry of ~ BAH, FIE, PAH, UGH

disgusting BAD, LOW, VILE
  be ~ REPEL

dish PLATE, TRAY
  ~ alternative CABLE
  ~ ancestor AERIAL
  ~ holder TRAY
  ~ name words ALA
  ~ out DEAL, LADLE, SERVE
  ~ (out) METE
  ~ repository RACK
  baking ~ PAN
  beef ~ STEW
  cabbage ~ SLAW
  chafing ~ PAN
  cold ~ SALAD
  corned-beef ~ HASH
  crab ~ LEGS
  Easter ~ HAM
  eggs-and-cheese ~ OMELET
  frog ~ LEGS
  fruit ~ PIE, TART
  greens ~ SALAD
  Hawaiian ~ POI
  hot ~ CHILI
  lamb ~ STEW
  leftovers ~ HASH
  macaroni ~ SALAD
  main ~ ENTREE, MEAT
  meat ~ STEW
  saffron ~ RICE
  serving ~ BOAT
  side ~ SALAD
  Tahitian ~ TARO
  Texas ~ CHILI

dish ___ (serve) OUT

___ **dish** SIDE

dishcloth RAG

dishearten COW, DETER

disheartened LOW, SAD

dishes
  help with the ~ DRY
  **remove ~ from the
    table** BUS

dishevel MESS, SNARL

disheveled MESSY

dishonest BAD, FALSE
~ **one** LIAR

dishonor ABASE, RUIN, SHAME, TAINT

dishonorable BAD, BASE, FALSE
~ **one** CAD

___-dish pie DEEP

dishrag
like a ~ LIMP

dishwasher
~ **cycle** DRY, RINSE

disillusion SOUR

disillusioned SOUR

disincline DETER

disinclined AVERSE

disinfect CLEAN

disinfectant WASH
~ **target** GERM

disinfected PURE

disinformation LIE, TALE

disingenuous FALSE

disintegrate ERODE

disinterested ALOOF, FAIR, HONEST

disjoin CUT

disjointed APART

disk CHIP, PLATE
~ **contents** DATA
deejay's ~ DEMO
put on ~ CUT
rotary ~ CAM
solar ~ ATEN, ATON

___ disk HARD, LASER, SUN

disks
floppy ~ MEDIA
obsolescent ~ LPS

disk-shaped
~ **marine fish** SKATE

dislike ABHOR, HATE

dislimb HEW

dislocate EXILE

dislodge CLEAR, OUST

disloyal FALSE

dismal BAD, DIM, DRAB, SAD, VILE
the ~ sci. ECON

dismantle PART, RAZE, UNDO

dismay ALARM, AWE, COW, FEAR, UPSET
cry of ~ ALAS, OHNO

dismayed UPSET

disme COIN

dismiss AXE, CAN, DROP, EJECT, FIRE, OUST, SACK, SEND
~ **from the team** CUT

dismissal
unceremonious ~ BOOT

dismount ARRIVE

dismounted ALIT

Disney
~ **creature** DEER
~ **dog** LADY
~ **mermaid** ARIEL
~ **middle name** ELIAS
~ **network** ABC
1982 ~ film TRON

___ Disney EURO

Disneyland
~ **character** ELF

disobedient BAD

disorder MESS, RIOT
seasonal ~ FLU

disorderly MESSY, UPSET

disorganized MESSY, UPSET

disorient ADDLE, AMAZE, LOSE

disoriented ASEA, ATSEA, LOST

"___ di sortita" ARIA

disown DENY, DESERT, DROP

disparage CARP, SHAME

disparaging
~ **remark** SLUR
slyly ~ SNIDE

disparate OTHER

disparity GAP

dispassionate CALM, COOL

dispatch CLEAR, HASTE, MAIL, NEWS, NOTE, REMIT, ROUTE, SEND, SHIP, SLAY, SPEED
~ **a dragon** SLAY
PD ~ APB
with ~ APACE, FAST, SOON

dispensary
~ **stock** SERA

dispensation DOLE

dispense ALLOT, DEAL, ISSUE
~ **alms** DOLE
~ **carefully** ALLOT
~ **with** DROP, SCRAP, SPARE
what LPNs ~ TLC

dispenser
cash ~ ATM
pepper ~ MILL

dispersal
complete ~ ROUT

disperse MELT, PART, ROUT, SOW, THIN

dispersed
widely ~ SPARSE

dispirited BLUE
be ~ MOPE

displace EJECT, EXILE

display AIR, ARRAY, MODEL, PARADE, POMP
~ **case** STAND

~ **model** DEMO
~ **stand** EASEL
brilliant ~ RIOT
digital ~ TIME
gallery ~ ART, OPART
grand ~ POMP
mall ~ MAP
museum ~ ART
on ~ OPEN
put on ~ ARRAY, SHOW
showy ~ ECLAT
wall ~ ART, OPART

displays
billboard ~ ADS

displease ANGER, IRK, PEEVE, RILE

displeased IRATE, UPSET

displeasing BAD

displeasure ANGER, IRE
vocalize ~ BOO, HISS

disport AMUSE, LARK, PLAY, ROMP

dispose CLEAR, PUT
~ **of** RAZE, RID, SELL, TOSS
~ **toward** ENDEAR

disposed
~ **(to)** APT, PRONE
be ~ TEND

disposition HABIT, MOOD, TONE
~ **(suffix)** IVE

dispossess EJECT, STRIP

disprove BELIE, BLAST, DENY

Dispur
~ **state** ASSAM

disputable OPEN

dispute ARGUE, DENY, MELEE, ROW, SCRAP, SPAR, SPAT, TILT

disquiet ALARM, FEAR, TOSS, UPSET

disquieted UPSET

disquisition TRACT

Disraeli
~ **title** EARL

disregard MISS, OMIT, PASS, SKIP

disreputable BAD, BASE, SEEDY

disrepute SHAME

disrespect LIP, SASS

disrespectful PERT, RUDE
be ~ SASS

disrobe BARE, PEEL, STRIP

disrobed BARE, NUDE

disruption GAP

dissatisfaction ANGER

dissect CUT
~ **grammatically** PARSE

dissemble ACT, FAKE, LIE, MASK, POSE, SHAM

dissembler LIAR

disseminate CAST, SOW

dissent
slangy ~ NAH, NOPE

dissenters
~ **votes** NOES, NOS

dissertation ESSAY, TRACT

"Dissertation Upon Roast Pig, A"
~ **author** ELIA

disserve HARM

dissident REBEL

dissimilar ALIEN, OTHER

dissimulate ACT, LIE

dissipate MELT, THIN, WASTE

dissipated LEWD, LOOSE
~ **one** ROUE

dissipation TAINT, WASTE

dissolute BAD, BASE, LEWD, LOOSE
~ **one** RAKE

dissolve ANNUL, CUT, FADE, FUSE, MELT, RUN

dissonance NOISE

dissonant ATONAL

dissuade ARGUE, DETER

dist. ___ ATTY

distance
~ **a golf ball rolls** RUN
~ **from the equator** LAT
~ **measure** MILE, PACE, ROD
~ **(prefix)** TEL, TELE
~ **runner** MILER
at a ~ AFAR, ALOOF, APART, AWAY, FAR, OFF
at a short ~, to a poet ANEAR
Bannister's ~ MILE
go the ~ LAST
keep one's ~ AVOID, EVADE, SHUN
put ~ between SPACE
race ~ MILE
Ryun's ~ MILE
short ~ HOP, INCH, STEP

___ distance ATA, LONG

distant AFAR, ALOOF, APART, AWAY, COOL, FAR, ICY
~ **past** YORE
~ **(prefix)** TEL, TELE
not ~ NEAR

distaste
grunt of ~ UGH

distasteful BAD

distend BAG

distill DRIP

distillate ESSENCE

distillation
~ **product** ESTER

distilled CLEAN

distillery
~ **purchase** MALT

distinct APART, CLEAN, CLEAR
~ **part** UNIT
~ **period** ERA
make less ~ BLUR

distinction HONOR, NAME, NOTE, RANK, TONE
woman of ~ DAME

distinctive RARE
~ **garb** HABIT
~ **quality** AROMA, AURA

distingué REGAL

distinguish ESPY, KNOW

distinguished BIG, GREAT, NOTED

"Distinguished Gentleman, The"
~ **director** LYNN

distinguishing
~ **feature** TRAIT

distort BELIE, COLOR, LIE, SKEW, SLANT

distorted WRY

distracted LOST

distress AIL, CARE, NEED, PAIN, REND, STING, WOE
~ **signal** ACHE, FLARE, SOS
be in ~ AIL
cause of ~ BANE
cry of ~ ALARM, HELP, OHNO
sound of ~ MOAN
spasm of ~ PANG

distressed UPSET

distressing BAD, DIRE, SAD

distribute ALLOT, DEAL, ISSUE, METE, SORT

distribution DOLE

distributor
~ **part** ROTOR

district AREA, BELT, LAND, SITE, TRACT, ZONE

___ **District** LAKE

distrustful LEERY, WARY

disturb ALARM, AROUSE, FRET, IRK, JAR, MOVE, PEEVE, RILE, ROIL, ROUSE, TOSS, UPSET

disturbance ADO, DUST, MELEE, RIOT, SCENE, TODO
seismic ~ TREMOR

disturbed UPSET

disturber
~ **of the peace** WAR
princess ~ PEA
sleep ~ NOISE

disturbing BAD
~ **sound** NOISE

disunite CUT, UNTIE

disuse
fallen into ~ PASSE
fall into ~ LAPSE

dit
~ **partner** DAH

ditch CANAL, CUT, DESERT, DROP, MOAT
~ **someone** LOSE

"ditch"
De Witt Clinton ~ ERIE

___-**ditch** LAST

dither STEW

Dithers, Mr. BOSS

dithyramb SONG

dits
~ **and dahs** CODE

ditto AGAIN, ALSO, SAME
~ **rel.** ETC

ditty AIR, ARIA, SONG, TUNE
~ **bag** KIT

ditty ___ BAG

diva LEAD, STAR
~ **note** CEE
~ **performance** ARIA, OPERA
~ **song** ARIA
Met ~ ALDA

divan SOFA
~ **relative** SETTEE

divas
what ~ **do** SING

dive BAR, DROP, HOLE, SINK
~ **in** START
take a ~ LOSE

___ **dive** NOSE, SWAN

___-**dive** SKIN

diver
~ **delight** CORAL
~ **milieu** OCEAN, SEA
~ **need** AIR, TANK
~ **quest** PEARL
avian ~ AUK, LOON
Japanese pearl ~ AMA
Navy ~ SEAL
perfect score for a ~ TEN
scuba ~ **weapon** SPEAR

___ **diver** PEARL, SKIN

diverge PART, VEER

divergence
wide ~ GAP

divergent ODD, OTHER

diverse OTHER

diversify ALTER

diversion GAME, PLAY
Palm Beach ~ POLO
pre-TV ~ RADIO

divert AMUSE, AVERT, PLEASE

divertissement GAME
provide ~ AMUSE

divest BARE, EJECT, RID

divide ALLOT, CUT, PART, REND, SLICE, SPLIT
~ **up** SHARE

___ **Divide** GREAT

divided APART, HALF, TORN
~ **Asian nation** KOREA
not ~ ENTIRE

"Divided ___, The" HEART

dividend EXTRA

divider
continental ~ ATL, PAC
court ~ NET
looseleaf ~ TAB

"Divina Commedia"
~ **author** DANTE

divine ABBE
~ **archer** EROS
~ **light** HALO

"Divine Comedy, The" EPIC, EPOS, POEM
~ **author** DANTE
~ **character** ADAM, CATO, DANTE

"Divine Miss M, The" BETTE

diviner SEER

diving
~ **area** POOL
~ **bird** AUK, COOT, LOON
~ **duck** EIDER

___ **diving** SKIN

diving-bell
~ **inventor** EADS

divining ___ ROD

divisible
~ **by two** EVEN
not ~ **by two** ODD

division ARMY, CLASS, FLEET, PART, STALL, UNIT
~ **word** INTO

___ **division** LONG

___ **d'Ivoire** COTE

divorce PART, SPLIT

"Divorce American ___" STYLE

divorced APART

"___ Divorcee, The" GAY

divorcees EXES

"Divorce—Italian ___" STYLE

divot
~ **material** SOD

divulge ADMIT, BARE, BLAB, LEAK, LETON, RELATE, SAY, TELL

divulse TEAR

divvy ALLOT, PART, SHARE, SPLIT

Dixie MOUSE
~ **fighter** REB
~ **once** CSA
~ **st.** ALA

Dixon IVAN
~ **colleague** MASON

Dixon, Jeane
~ **talent, perhaps** ESP

___-**Dixon line** MASON

dizzy
feel ~ SWIM

Dizzy DEAN

"Dizzy"
~ **singer** ROE

dizzying
~ **designs** OPART

DJ
~ **albums** LPS
~ **stock-in-trade** CDS
D in ~ DISC

djellabah ROBE
~ **wearer** ARAB

Djibouti
gulf east of ~ ADEN

djinn DEMON

D.J. Jazzy Jeff
~ **song** RAP

___-**DMC** RUN

DMZ
part of ~ ZONE

DNA
~ **component** GENE
~ **ender** ASE
dinosaur ~ **preserver** AMBER
part of ~ ACID

Dnieper
city on the ~ KIEV

do ACT, BALL, BASH, EVENT, FETE, GALA, NOTE
~ **a banquet** CATER
~ **a bartending job** STIR
~ **a calculator's job** ADD
~ **a classroom chore** ERASE
~ **a CPA's job** AUDIT
~ **a crime-scene chore** DUST
~ **a double-take** REACT
~ **a fall chore** RAKE
~ **a farm job** PLOW
~ **a good turn** HELP, SERVE
~ **a grammar task** PARSE
~ **a handyman's job** RESTORE
~ **a hatchet job on** LIBEL, SLUR
~ **a homemaker's chore** SEW
~ **a horoscope** CAST
~ **a job on** HARM
~ **a kitchen chore** MASH, PARE, PEEL
~ **a landscape** PAINT
~ **a landscaping chore** MOW
~ **a laundry chore** IRON
~ **a lawn job** EDGE
~ **a legislator's job** ENACT
~ **a math task** ADD
~ **a moonlight flit** FLEE
~ **an about-face** REACT, TURN
~ **an axel** SKATE
~ **an end run** EVADE
~ **an ILGWU job** SEW
~ **an impression** APE
~ **an office job** FILE
~ **a number** SING
~ **a personnel job** HIRE
~ **a portrait** PAINT

~ a postprandial chore DRY
~ arithmetic ADD
~ a salon job COLOR, DYE, TINT
~ a scene ACT
~ a slow burn ANGER, STEAM
~ as told OBEY
~ a tailor's job ALTER
~ a takeoff APE
~ a teamster's job HAUL
~ a tire job ALINE
~ away with ANNUL, BAN
~ axels SKATE
~ basic arithmetic ADD
~ battle CLOSE
~ battle (for) VIE
~ business DEAL, TRADE
~ cameos ACT
~ columns ADD
~ community service ATONE
~ dais duty ORATE
~ detective work TRACE
~ dock work LADE
~ Easter eggs DYE
~ elementary-school homework ADD
~ Europe TOUR
~ figure eights SKATE
~ film work ACT, EDIT
~ followers RES
~ great ACE
~ handiwork TAT
~ housework DUST
~ in BEAT, RUIN, SLAY
~ lacework TAT
~ lawn work SOD, WEED
~ like APE, ECHO
~ logging SAW
~ lunch EAT, MEET
~ modeling POSE, SIT
~ needlework SEW
~ not exist ARENT
~ nothing IDLE, LOAF, LOLL, REST, SIT
~ not win LOSE
~ office work FILE
~ one's best ESSAY
~ one's duty SERVE
~ one's heart good PLEASE
~ one's part AID, HELP
~ openwork TAT
~ out of ROB
~ over MEND
~ patchwork SEW
~ penance ATONE
~ perfectly NAIL
~ petit point SEW
~ postal work SORT
~ pull-ups CHIN
~ roadwork PAVE, TAR
~ something ACT
~ summer stock ACT
~ tailoring ALTER, FIT
~ the backstroke SWIM
~ the books AUDIT
~ the butterfly SWIM
~ the crawl SWIM
~ the disappearing act ELUDE, FLEE
~ the dishes WASH
~ the trick AVAIL
~ up DRESS
~ well ACE

~ well in school LEARN
~ what one can TRY
~ without SPARE
~ woodwork SAND
~ wrong ERR, SIN
1960s ~ AFRO
beavers ~ it GNAW
bees ~ it STING
birds ~ it ROOST, SING, SOAR
brows ~ it KNIT
buttinskis ~ it PRY
can't ~ without NEED
collies ~ it HERD
dogs ~ it BITE
elaborate ~ FETE
embers ~ it GLOW
flowers ~ it OPEN
gourmets ~ it DINE
have nothing to ~ with AVOID, SHUN
have to ~ with DEAL, REFER, RELATE
henchmen ~ it ABET
just ~ it ACT
libraries ~ it LEND
make ~ ADAPT, COPE, EKE
make ~ with USE
old-fashioned ~ BEE
peacocks ~ it PREEN
satellites ~ it SCAN
some machines ~ it VEND
spellbinders ~ it ORATE
suns ~ it RISE, SET, SHINE
things to ~ AGENDA
tides ~ it EBB
time can ~ it HEAL
tongues may ~ it LASH
truckers ~ it HAUL
vampires ~ it BITE
volcanoes ~ it SPEW
what banks ~ LEND
what bookworms ~ READ
what broncs ~ REAR
what divas ~ SING
what sheepdogs ~ HERD
what spiders ~ SPIN
what tops ~ SPIN
work to ~ AGENDA

do __ T TOA

do-__ GOOD

__ do (manage somehow) MAKE

__-do (enthusiastic) CAN

"Do __ others..." UNTO

"Do __ say, not..." ASI

"D.O.A."
~ director MATE
~ star ADLER, RYAN, STERN

Doakes JOE

"__ Do Anything" ILL

"__ do anything better than you" ICAN

"Do as __, not as..." ISAY

"Do as I __!" SAY

dobbin HORSE
~ digs STALL
~ dinner OATS

~ doc VET
~ load SHAY
~ retort SNORT
~ turner GEE
color for ~ ROAN
mouthpiece for ~ BIT
see also horse

Dobbs LOU

doble
paso ~ DANCE

doc
animal ~ VET
Cabot Cove ~ SETH

"__ Doc" Duvalier PAPA

"Doc Horne"
~ humorist ADE

docile EASY, MEEK, MILD, TAME

dock BOB, CLIP, CUT, LAND, LOP, MOLE, MOOR, PARE, PIER, SNIP, STUB
~ ender YARD
~ fitting CLEAT
~ support PILE
do ~ work LADE
leave the ~ SAIL

__ dock DRY

docked
not ~ ASEA, ATSEA

docket AGENDA, BILL, LABEL, LIST
~ detail ITEM
~ doing TRIAL

dockworkers
~ org. ILA

docs MDS

doctor DRESS, HEAL, HELP, LIE, MEND, NURSE, RIG, TREAT
~ assistant NURSE
~ ender ATE
~ income FEE
~ menu DIET
~ order DOSE, STAT
~ picture XRAY
~ up FAKE
need a ~ AIL
responses to ~ AHS
word for the ~ AAH

__ doctor SPIN

__ doctor (dragonfly) SNAKE

Doctor
~ of sci-fi WHO

"Doctor __ a Wife, The" TAKES

doctoral
~ exam ORAL

doctors
~ org. AMA

"Doctor Takes a Wife, The"
~ director HALL

"Doctor Zhivago"
~ character LARA
~ director LEAN

doctrinal
~ holding TENET

doctrine CREDO, CREED, DOGMA, IDEA, ISM, RULE

docudrama
~ perhaps BIO

document ENTER, PAPER
~ addendum RIDER
auto ~ LEASE, TITLE
landlord's ~ LEASE
legal ~ DEED, LEASE, WRIT
ownership ~ DEED
travel ~ VISA

documentary DRAMA, GENRE
Fox ~ COPS

documents DATA
destroy ~ SHRED

DOD
~ division USAF
~ high-tech program SDI

doddering ANILE

dodeca
one-third of ~ TETRA

dodge AVERT, AVOID, BEG, ELUDE, EVADE, MISS, RUSE, SLIP, VEER
~ questions EVADE
artful ~ RUSE

Dodge AUTO, CAR
former ~ model ARIES, OMNI

"Dodge __" CITY

dodgeball GAME

Dodge City
~ marshal EARP

Dodgers NINE, TEAM

dodo ASS, BIRD, IDIOT

"Dodsworth"
~ actress ASTOR
~ author LEWIS

doe ANIMAL, DEER, GOAT, SHE
~ mate HART, STAG

Doe JANE

Doe, John MALE

doer ACTOR, AGENT
~ (suffix) IST
good-deed ~ HERO

does
~ not exist ISNT

"__ does it!" EASY, THAT

doesn't
~ clash GOES

"__ Doesn't Live Here Anymore" ALICE

"__ does she think she is!" WHO

"Does the Spearmint __..." LOSE

__-d'oeuvre CHEF

doff PEEL
~ opposite DON

dog ANIMAL, BAIT, CHASE, FOOT, LEMON, LOSER, PET, TAIL, TRAIL
~ bane FLEA, LICE

~ **bark** ARF
~ **biter** FLEA
~ **chain** LEASH
~ **command** BEG, COME, HEEL, SIC, SIT
~ **doc** VET
~ **ender** BANE, CART, EAR, FACE, GONE, LEG, NAP, SLED, TROT
~ **fennel** WEED
~ **in a Stephen Foster song** TRAY
~ **name** REX
~ **place** LAP
~ **reward** PAT
~ **snack** BONE
~ **star** ASTA
~ **star's first name** RIN
~ **starter** CHILI, FIRE, HANG, UNDER
~ **tags** IDS
~ **warning** GNAR
1930s movie ~ ASTA
"Beetle Bailey" ~ OTTO
big ~**, for short** LAB
comics ~ ODIE, OTTO
detectives' ~ ASTA
Dick and Jane's ~ SPOT
dirty ~ CUR
Dorothy's ~ TOTO
fictional ~ LAD
film ~ ASTA
filmdom ~ TOTO
"Frasier" ~ EDDIE
"Garfield" ~ ODIE
greet a ~ PAT
Hanna-Barbera ~ ASTRO
hot ~ HAM
incite a ~ SIC
junkyard ~ CUR
lap ~ PEKE
like a mad ~ RABID
lost ~ **in an Inge play** SHEBA
"Mutts" ~ EARL
name for a firehouse ~ SPOT
one-third of a ~**'s name** RIN
prairie ~ ANIMAL
presidential ~ FALA, HER, HIM
put on the ~ PARADE
river for which a ~ **was named** AIRE
sea ~ GOB, SALT, TAR
shaggy ~ **story** LIE, TALE
snub-nosed ~ PEKE
top ~ EXEC
TV cartoon ~ ASTRO
walk like a ~ PAD
"Wizard of Oz" ~ TOTO
work like a ~ TOIL
see also canine

dog ___ DAYS, ROSE, TAG

dog-___ EARED, TIRED

___ dog BIRD, CHILI, CORN, GUN, HOT, LAP, MOON, SEA, SLED, TOP

___-dog RED

Dog ___ (Sirius) STAR

"Dog ___" YEARS

"Dog ___ Afternoon" DAY

"___ Dog and Glory" MAD

dog-and-pony ___ SHOW

"dog ate my homework, The" ALIBI

"Dog Barking at the Moon"
~ **painter** MIRO

dog breeder
~ **org.** AKC

"Dog Day Afternoon"
~ **character** LEON

dog days
~ **forecast** HOT
~ **mo.** AUG

doge RULER

dogfaces GIS

dogfight
~ **adept** ACE

Dogg
~ **genre** RAP

doggedness GRIT

___-dogger HOT

doggerel POEM

doggie
~ **munchie** BONE

doggie ___ BAG

doggie bag
~ **bit** ORT

"Doggone it!" DARN, DRAT, RATS, SHOOT

dogie CALF
~ **call** MAA
~ **retriever** LASSO
~ **stopper** NOOSE
bring down a ~ ROPE

dogleg BEND, TURN, VEER

doglike
~ **scavenger** HYENA

dogma ISM, LAW, RULE, TENET

dogmatic SURE

___ Dog Night THREE

"Dog of Flanders, A"
~ **actor** LADD

dog owner
~ **shout** HERE

dog paddle SWIM

Dogpatch
~ **adjective** LIL
~ **creator** CAPP
~ **dad** PAW
~ **resident** ABNER

dogs
~ **do it** BITE
rain cats and ~ TEEM

dog's
~ **age** EON

dog's ___ LIFE

"___ Dogs" STRAW

"___ Dogs and Englishmen" MAD

dog show
~ **org.** AKC

dog-show
~ **winner** BEST

dogsled
~ **pullers** TEAM

"Dogs of ___, The" WAR

Dog Star
~ **neighbor** ORION

dog tag
~ **wearers** GIS

dog-tired DONE, SPENT, TIRED

dogtrot RUN

dog-walker
~ **need** LEASH

dogwood TREE
American ~ OSIER

doily
~ **material** LACE
make a ~ TAT

doing ACT
~ **business** OPEN
~ **things** ASTIR
be up and ~ STIR

"___ Do Is Dream of You" ALLI

doit COIN

"___ Do It" LETS

"___ Do It Again" LETS

do-it-yourselfer
~ **purchase** KIT

dolce ___ niente FAR

doldrums ENNUI
in the ~ BLUE, LOW, SAD

dole AID, ALMS, LOT
~ **out** ALLOT, DEAL, SHARE
~ **(out)** METE
on the ~ NEEDY

Dole BOB

doleful BAD, BLUE, LOW, SAD

Dolenz AMI

Dole, Robert
~ **org., once** SEN
~ **st.** KAN

Dolittle
~ **and others** DRS

doll TOY
~ **up** ADORN, ATTIRE, DRESS, PREEN
~ **word** DADA, MAMA
a real ~ KEN
male ~ KEN
raggedy ~ ANDY, ANN
wedding-cake ~ BRIDE

___ doll RAG

"___ Doll" SATIN

dollar
~ **bill** ONE
~ **divs.** CTS
~ **fraction** BIT, CENT
~ **fractions** CTS

~ **sign, basically** ESS
~ **slangily** CLAM
~ **starter** EURO
~ **units** CTS
~ **value** COST
bet one's bottom ~ RELY
Mexican ~ PESO

dollar ___ BILL, SIGN

dollar ___ averaging COST

___ dollar SAND, TOP

dollar bill
~ **slangily** SKIN
word on a ~ ONE, ORDO

dollars
a fistful of ~ WAD
silver ~ CACTI

dollhouse TOY

dollop DAB, GOB, PAT

dolls
popular 1980s ~ ETS

"Doll's House, A"
~ **author** IBSEN
~ **character** NORA

Dolly LEVI
~ **the clone** EWE
~ **the sheep** CLONE

"___, Dolly!" HELLO

Dollywood
~ **loc.** TENN

dolomite ORE

Dolomites RANGE

dolor BANE, PAIN, WOE

Dolores ___ Rio DEL

Dolores Del ___ RIO

___ Dolorosa VIA

dolorous SAD

dolphin ANIMAL
~ **communication** SONAR
~ **habitat** OCEAN, SEA
~ **hazard** NET
~ **relative** ORC
~ **school** POD
largest ~ ORCA

Dolphins ELEVEN, TEAM
~ **home** MIAMI
~ **org.** NFL

dolphin-safe
~ **catch** TUNA

dolt ASS, BOOR, CLOD, DOPE, GOOSE, IDIOT, LOUT, OAF

doltish SLOW

Dom TITLE

domain AREA, HOME, LAND, REALM, SPHERE
~ **(abbr.)** TERR

Dombey
~ **partner** SON

"Dombey and ___" SON

"Dombey and Son"
~ **wife** EDITH

dome HEAD, PATE, POLL, ROOF
~ **home** IGLOO
player in a ~ ASTRO

___ **dome** SALT

___ **Dome (Indianapolis arena)**
RCA

domed
~ **projection** APSE

domestic HELP, HOME, MAID
~ **bird** HEN

domesticated PET, TAME
~ **animal** PET
not ~ FERAL

domicile ABODE, HOME
~ **(abbr.)** RES
~ **in Spanish** CASA
avian ~ NEST

dominant
~ **class** ELITE
it may be ~ GENE

dominate BOSS, HOG, LEAD,
REIGN, RULE

domineer BOSS, TREAD

Domingo TENOR
~ **melody** ARIA
~ **milieu** OPERA

Domingo, Placido TENOR

___ **Domini** ANNO

Dominican Republic
~ **neighbor** HAITI

"Dominick ___ Eugene" AND

dominion LAND, REALM, REIGN,
ROD, RULE, STATE, SWAY

domino CAPE, MASK, TILE
~ **pip** ACE
~ **spot** PIP
certain ~ TREY

dominoes GAME

Domitian CAESAR

___-**domo** MAJOR

don DRESS, LORD, MAN, PEER,
WEAR
~ **attire** DRESS

Don ADAMS, OWEN, TITLE
see also Russian

"Don' ___ Go 'Way Mad" CHA

Dona ___ ANA

Doña TITLE

**"Dona Flor ___ Her Two
Husbands"** AND

**"Dona Flor and ___ Two
Husbands"** HER

**"Dona Flor and Her ___
Husbands"** TWO

Donahue PHIL, TROY

Donald
~ **and Ivana** EXES

Donald Duck
voice of ~ NASH

Donaldson ROGER, SAM
~ **network** ABC

donate DOLE, ENDOW

donation AID
blood-drive ~ PINT
charitable ~ ALMS

done ENDED, OVER, PAST
~ **for** SHOT
~ **in** SPENT, TIRED
~ **to a poet** OER
all said and ~ ENDED
have a portrait ~ POSE, SIT
things to be ~ AGENDA

done ___ turn TOA

donee HEIR

Donegal
~ **river** ERNE
from ~ IRISH

"___ Done Him Wrong" SHE

"___ Done It?" WHO

dong COIN

___-**dong** DING

"Don Giovanni" OPERA

"___ Dong School" DING

Donizetti
~ **work** OPERA

donjon KEEP

Don José
~ **in "Carmen"** TENOR

Don Juan RAKE, ROMEO, ROUE
~ **portrayer** ERROL

"Don Juan" POEM

donkey ANIMAL, BURRO, MULE
~ **cry** BRAY
~ **dinner** FEED
~ **feature** EAR
~ **in French** ANE
Democratic ~ **creator** NAST
imitate a ~ BRAY
wild ~ ASS

donkey's ___ YEARS

donna LADY
prima ~ DIVA, LEAD, STAR

Donna LOREN, REED

Donna Lucia
Charley's ~ AUNT

Donne POET
"last lamenting" thing for
~ KISS
see also poet

Donner ___ PASS

Donny
~ **sister** MARIE

donnybrook MELEE, RIOT, ROW,
SCRAP, SETTO, TODO

Donohoe AMANDA

donor
~ **campaign** ~ PAC
myrrh ~ **and others** MAGI
rib ~ ADAM

do-nothing IDLER

"Do not open ___ Christmas!"
UNTIL

"Donovan's ___" REEF

Donovan, Wild Bill
~ **agcy.** OSS

"Don Pasquale"
~ **setting** ROME

don't
~ **eat** FAST
~ **expunge** STET
~ **follow** LEAD
~ **give up** KEEP
~ **go** BIDE, STAY
~ **guess** KNOW
~ **indulge in** AVOID
~ **just sit there** ACT
~ **part with** KEEP
~ **stay fast** RUN
~ **stir** SIT

"Don't ___, It's Only Thunder"
CRY

"Don't ___ It to Heart" TAKE

"Don't ___ me!" ASK

"Don't ___ Me Why" ASK

"Don't ___ on me" TREAD

"Don't ___ Waves" MAKE

"Don't ___ With Bill" MESS

"Don't Be ___" CRUEL

"Don't bet ___!" ONIT

"Don't Bring ___" LULU

"Don't Bring Me Down"
~ **band** ELO

"Don't Cry, ___ Only Thunder"
ITS

"Don't Cry for Me, Argentina"
~ **musical** EVITA

"Don't Cry, It's ___ Thunder"
ONLY

"Don't dawdle!" ASAP

"___ Don't Eat the Daisies"
PLEASE

"___ don't fail me now!" FEET

"Don't Give Up the ___" SHIP

"Don't Go ___ the Water" NEAR

"Don't Go Breaking My Heart"
~ **name** ELTON

"Don't have a ___, man!" COW

**"Don't It Make Ya Wanna
Dance"**
~ **singer** RAITT

"___ Don't Leave" MEN

**"Don't Let the ___ Get in Your
Eyes"** STARS

"Don't look ___!" ATME, NOW

"Don't Make Me ___" OVER

"Don't Make Waves"
~ **actor** SAHL

"Don't overdo it!" EASY

"___ Don't Preach" PAPA

"Don't Rain on My ___" PARADE

"___ don't say!" YOU

"Don't Take It to ___" HEART

"Don't Take It to Heart"
~ **director** DELL

"Don't throw bouquets ___"
ATME

"Don't touch that ___!" DIAL

"Don't Worry Kyoko"
~ **singer** ONO

"Don't you ___!" DARE

"Don't You Know?"
~ **singer** REESE

donut
~ **feature** HOLE

donutlike
~ **roll** BAGEL

doodle JOT

Doolittle, Eliza
site of ~ **triumph** ASCOT

Doolittle, Hilda POET
see also poet

doom END, FATE, LOT, RUIN
till the crack of ~ EVER

doomed DIRE

do one's ___ good HEART

do one's ___ thing OWN

"Doonesbury"
~ **character** KIM

do one's heart ___ GOOD

door EXIT
~ **accessory** MAT
~ **ender** KNOB, MAN, MAT, NAIL,
POST, SILL, STEP, STOP,
YARD
~ **feature** KNOB
~ **frame** SASH
~ **handle** LEVER
~ **opener** KEY
~ **piece** SILL
~ **position** AJAR
~ **sign** ENTER
~ **sound** SLAM
~ **starter** OUT
at one's ~ CLOSE
go from door to ~ BEG
install a ~ HANG
keep the wolf from the
~ EARN
like a creaky ~,
perhaps EERIE, EERY
open ~ ENTREE
open the ~ **to** ADMIT
show the ~ OUST
trap ~ DROP

use the ~ ENTER

do or ___ DIE

___ door FIRE, OPEN, STORM, TRAP

"___ Door" STAGE

doorbell
use a ~ RING

doorkeeper USHER

doormat RUG

___-door policy OPEN

doors
like some ~ AJAR
open ~ EASE

"door's open!, The" ENTER

doorstep
~ "welcomer" MAT

doorway ENTRY
~ (abbr.) ENT
~ accessory MAT
~ part SILL
~ sign EXIT

doozy LULU, ONER, PIP

dope DATA, INFO, NEWS

dopey INANE

Dopey
~ pal DOC

doppelgänger IMAGE, TWIN

Doppler ___ RADAR

___ d'Or COTE

Dorado, El
~ treasure ORO

Dorcas
emulate ~ SEW

do-re-mi CASH, KALE, MOOLA

Doric ORDER
~ alternative IONIC

Do-Right, Dudley
~ girl NELL

Doris DAY

___ d'Orléans ILE

dorm
~ inhabitant COED
~ item BED
~ sound SNORE

dormancy REST

dormant
lie ~ SLEEP

dormer ATTIC, BAY

dormitory HALL

dormouse ANIMAL

dorms
like some ~ COED

Dorothy
~ aunt and others EMS
~ dog TOTO
~ in "The Wiz" ROSS
~ Oz adventure DREAM

~ to Em NIECE
co-panelist of ~ ARLENE

Dors DIANA

dorsal FIN

dorsal fin
~ position REAR

Dorsett TONY

Dorsey, Jimmy
~ instrumental, with "The" YAM

Dorsey, Tommy
~ theme song MARIE
~ tune MARIE, NOLA, YOU

Dortmund-___ Canal EMS

dory BOAT
~ mover OAR
use a ~ ROW

dos
~ follower TRES
~ preceder UNO

DOS
~ command ERASE
part of ~ SYST

dosage
~ (abbr.) AMT

dose CURE, PILL
~ starter MEGA
x-ray ~ REM

Dos Passos
~ trilogy USA

doss BED, COT, SLEEP

dossier DATA, FILE

Dostoevsky
~ character IDIOT
~ novel, with "The" IDIOT

dot ATOM, BEAD, BIT, IOTA, JOT, MITE, MOTE, SPOT
map ~ CAY, ISLE, ISLET, KEY

dot-dash
~ developer MORSE

dote
~ on ADORE, LOVE, SPOIL

"Do That ___ One More Time" TOME

"Do the Right Thing"
~ actress DEE
~ director LEE
~ pizzeria SALS

"___ doth protest too much, The" LADY

dottle ASH

dotty DAFT, LOCO, MAD, OFF

Douar
~ denizen ARAB

double CLONE, DUAL, DUO, GROW, HIT, IMAGE, MATE, PAIR, RAISE, TWIN
~ agent MOLE, SPY
~ curve ESS, OGEE
~ Dutch GAME
~ entendre PLAY, PUN

~ over PLEAT
~ Windsor KNOT
on the ~ ANON, APACE, ASAP, SOON, STAT

double ___ AGENT, AXEL, BASS, BILL, BIND, DATE, EAGLE, ENTRY, KNIT, PLAY, STAR, TAKE, TIME

double-___ EDGED, REED, SPACE, TEAM, TIME

double-___ sword EDGED

___ double SEE

"Double ___" DARE

"Double ___, A" LIFE

double-blind TEST

double-check TEST

double-crosser CAD, LOUSE, RAT, SNEAK

double date
half a ~ DUO, PAIR, TWO

Doubleday ABNER

double-dealer SNAKE

double-dealing FALSE

double deck
~ game CANASTA

double-decker BUS, MOTOR

double Dutch
~ need ROPE

double eagle COIN

"Double Fantasy"
~ singer ONO

double-header TRAIN

double helix
~ material DNA

double-hook
~ shape ESS

"Double Indemnity"
~ author CAIN

double-jointed AGILE

double-quick APACE, FLEET

double-reed OBOE

doublespeak CANT

doublet DUO, PAIR, TWO

double take
do a ~ REACT

___ double take DOA

double-time HIE, RACE, SPEED

double-tongued FALSE

doubloon COIN

doubt
beyond a shadow of a ~ CLEAR
have no ~ KNOW
without ~ SURE
without a ~ AYE, YES

doubter
~ exclamation HAH

"___ Doubtfire" MRS

doubtful BAD, LEERY, OPEN

Doubting Thomas
~ comment BAH

doubts IFS

douceur FEE, PAY

dough CASH, GELT, LOOT, MOOLA
~ component YEAST
~ does it RISE
Durango ~ PESO
Durban ~ RAND
lots of ~ WAD
rolling in ~ RICH
see also coin, money

doughboys
~ today GIS

doughtiness NERVE

doughty HALE

Douglas FIR, MOORE
~ locale MAN

Douglas ___ FIR

Douglas, Gordon
~ film of 1954 THEM

Douglas-Home ALEC

Douglas, Kirk
~ film of 1975 POSSE

Douglas, Lloyd C.
~ novel, with "The" ROBE

Douglas, Michael
~ to Kirk SON

Douglas, Stephen A.
emulate ~ ORATE

___ Douglas Wiggin KATE

dour SAD, STERN

douse BATHE, CLEAN, DIP

dousing BATH

___ doute SANS

dove BIRD
~ branch OLIVE
~ home COTE
~ intention PEACE
~ sound COO

Dove RITA, SOAP
~ rival DIAL

dovekie AUK

Dover CITY, PORT
~ (abbr.) STR
~ county KENT
~ fish SOLE
~ loc. DEL
~ st. DEL

dovetail AGREE, FIT, MESH, TENON

Dovzhenko, Alexander
~ film of 1930 EARTH

dowager DAME

dowdy MESSY, SEEDY

dowel PEG, PIN, RACK, ROD

___-do-well NEER

Dow Jones
  a ~ index RAILS

down BAD, EAT, HAIR, LOW, NAP, SAD
  ~ the hatch EATEN
  ~ the road LATER
  not ~ ACROSS

down ___ (Australia) UNDER

down-___ HOME

___ **down (abate)** DIE

___ **down (belittle)** CRY

___ **down (be quiet)** PIPE

___ **down (concentrate)** BEAR

___ **down (confront)** FACE

___ **down (cow)** STARE

___ **down (debunk)** SHOOT

___ **down (decimate)** MOW

___ **down (demand an answer)** PIN

___ **down (descend)** GET

___ **down (dilute)** WATER

___ **down (disappoint)** LET

___ **down (end)** RING

___ **down (erode)** WEAR

___ **down (finalize)** NAIL

___ **down (frisk)** PAT

___ **down (get married)** SETTLE

___ **down (gridiron situation)** FIRST

___ **down (hew)** CUT

___ **down (humble)** TAKE

___ **down (invoke)** CALL

___ **down (lose weight)** SLIM

___ **down (make uncomfortable, in a way)** STARE

___ **down (minimize)** PLAY

___ **down (outshout)** TALK

___ **down (raze)** TEAR

___ **down (rebuke)** DRESS

___ **down (record)** WRITE

___ **down (reduce)** BOIL, PARE, TONE

___ **down (reject)** TURN

___ **down (relax)** LIE

___ **down (resign)** STEP

___ **down (restrain)** HOLD

___ **down (review)** RUN

___ **down (scold)** DRESS

___ **down (subdue)** SLAP

___ **down (withdraw)** STAND

"___ down!" ("Quiet!") PIPE

___-down LOW, PUT, SIT

Down ___ (Maine) EAST

"___ Down" TAKE

down and ___ OUT

down-and-___ OUTER

"Down and ___ in Beverly Hills" OUT

"Down and Out in Beverly Hills"
  ~ star NOLTE

___ down a peg TAKE

"Down at ___ Joe's" PAPA

down-at-heel SEEDY

"Down by the ___" ERIE

downcast BAD, BLUE, LOW, SAD

Down East MAINE
  ~ university town ORONO

Down-Easter
  ~ state MAINE

downer BORE
  plane ~ ACE

downfall RUIN

downgrade ABASE, SLOPE

downhearted BAD, SAD

downhill
  ~ racer SLED
  ~ runner SKI
  go ~ LAPSE, SLIDE
  going ~ WORSE
  race ~ SKI

"Downhill ___" RACER

Downing Street
  ~ number TEN

"Down Memory ___" LANE

___ down on (scold) COME

downpour RAIN, SPATE, STORM

downright BALD, FLAT, HONEST, PURE, RANK, TOTAL

___ down roots PUT

downs LAND, MOOR
  ~ partner UPS
  ups and ~ LIFE

Downs
  the ~ RANGE

___ Downs EPSOM

Downs, Hugh
  ~ hometown AKRON

"Downsize ___!" THIS

downslide DROP

downstairs
  ~ worker MAID

down the ___ (throughout) LINE

down the ___ (upcoming) ROAD

___ down the curtain RING

___ down the garden path LEAD, TAKE

"Down the hatch!" TOAST

___ down the law LAY

___ down the pike COME

___ down the river SELL

down-to-earth REAL

___ down to size CUT

down to the ___ WIRE

"Down to the ___ in Ships" SEA

downtown
  ~ light NEON

___-down transformer STEP

downturn DIP, DROP, SLIP
  market ~ SLIDE

down under
  ~ bird EMU
  ~ hopper ROO
  ~ marsupial KOALA
  see also Australia

downward
  face ~ PRONE
  slope ~ DIP

downwind ALEE

down with
  ~ in French ABAS

downy
  ~ duck EIDER
  ~ surface NAP, PILE

dowry DOT

dowser
  ~ tool ROD

Dowson ERNEST

doxology PAEAN, PSALM

"Do Ya"
  ~ band ELO

doyen DEAN

doyens
  ~ (abbr.) SRS

Doyle, Arthur Conan SIR

Doyle, Popeye NARC

"Do you have two fives for ___?" ATEN

"Do You Want to ___ a Secret" KNOW

doze LOLL, NAP, NOD, REST, SLEEP

dozen
  ~ moons YEAR
  dime a ~ AMPLE

Dr. ___ (children's author) SEUSS

Dr. ___ and the Electric Mayhem TEETH

Dr. ___ Hazlitt SETH

Dr. ___ of "Battlestar Galactica" ZEE

Dr. ___ of sci-fi WHO

drab ARID, SAD, SOBER

___ drab OLIVE

drabble BLOT

drachma COIN

Dracula
  ~ outerwear CAPE
  ~ portrayer LEE
  ~ weapon BITE
  airborne ~ BAT

draft AIR, ALE, PEN, PLAN, TRACE, WRITE
  ~ animal HORSE
  ~ animals OXEN
  ~ board initials SSS
  ~ classification ONEA
  ~ horse HACK
  ~ order ALE
  allowing a ~ AJAR
  bank ~ NOTE
  second ~ REDO

draft ___ ALE

draftable ONEA

"Draft Dodger Rag"
  ~ singer OCHS

draftees GIS

drafts
  rough ~ MSS

drag ATTIRE, BORE, DRIP, HAUL, LUG, RACE, TRAIL
  ~ along LUG, PLOD, TOW
  ~ ender STER
  ~ into court HAUL
  ~ oneself along PLOD
  ~ one's feet DEFER, LAG, MOVE, STALL
  ~ out SPIN
  ~ through the mire LIBEL, SHAME, SLUR, SMEAR, TAINT
  prepare to ~ REV

drag ___ RACE, STRIP

___ drag MAIN

dragged
  ~ out LONG

dragging BEAT, SLOW

draggle BLOT, MIRE

dragnet
  part of a police ~ APB

dragon
  ~ of 1950s TV OLLIE
  ~ starter SNAP
  green ~ PLANT
  vanquish a ~ SLAY

Dragon ___ ("Terry and the Pirates" character) LADY

drag one's ___ FEET

dragonfly
  move like a ~ DART
  young ~ NAIAD

"Dragons of ___, The" EDEN

"Dragons of Eden, The"
  ~ author SAGAN

"Dragonwyck"
  ~ author SETON

Dragoti STAN

dragster AUTO, CAR, MOTOR, RACER

drain BLEED, CLEAR, DRAW, LEAK, OOZE, PIPE, RUN, SAP, TAP, TIRE
~ **cleaner** LYE
~ **ender** PIPE
~ **off resources** BLEED
~ **out** SEEP
~ **problem** CLOG
down the ~ GONE, LOST, SHOT
go down the ~ LOSE
pour down the ~ SPEND
storm ~ SEWER

___ **drain** STORM

drained SPENT
~ **of color** ASHEN, ASHY

drainpipe
~ **section** TRAP

drakar BOAT, SHIP

drake BIRD, MALE

Drake PAUL, STAN

Drake, Francis SIR

Drakensburg RANGE

drakes HES
ducks and ~ GAME

dram DROP, NIP, UNIT

drama GENRE, PLAY, TALE
~ **award** OBIE
~ **segment** ACT
courtroom ~ TRIAL
daily ~ SOAP
musical ~ OPERA
radio ~ PLAY
TV ~ PLAY

dramatic
~ **device** ASIDE, IRONY
~ **start** ACTI
~ **subdivision** ACT

dramatic ___ IRONY

dramatis personae CAST

dramatist
~ **ploy** ASIDE
British ~ SHAW

dramatize ACT, EMOTE, ENACT

Drang
Sturm und ~ DRAMA

drape ADORN, HANG, ROBE

draper
~ **measure** ELL

drapery
~ **support** ROD

drastic ACUTE, DIRE

"Drat!" DARN, NUTS, OATH, RATS

draught ALE

draughts GAME

draughty COOL

Dravidian ASIAN

draw BAIT, HAUL, LUG, TIE, TOW
~ **a bead** AIM

~ **a conclusion** EDUCE
~ **away from** GAIN
~ **back** EBB, SHY, START
~ **forth** EDUCE, EVOKE
~ **in** LURE
~ **near** COME
~ **nigh** NEAR
~ **off** AVERT, TAP
~ **on glass** ETCH
~ **out** DRAG, EDUCE, SPIN
~ **the line** BAR
~ **tight** TENSE
~ **to a close** END, PASS, STOP, WANE
~ **together** UNITE
~ **up** PEN, RAISE
~ **upon** TAP
~ **with a laser** ETCH
top ~ STAR
tournament ~ BYE

draw ___ **(elongate)** OUT

draw ___ **in the sand** ALINE

draw a ___ BATH

draw a ___ **on** BEAD

drawback SNAG

drawbacks
having no ~ IDEAL

drawer TILL
~ **attachment** KNOB
money ~ TILL
top ~ ABLE, ACE, AONE, BEST, FINE

___**-drawer** TOP

drawers
set of ~ CHEST

drawing PLAN, TRACE
~ **card** LEAD, LURE, STAR
~ **room** SALON
architectural ~ PLAN
compass ~ ARC
copy a ~ TRACE
scale ~ PLAN

drawing ___ CARD, ROOM

draw in the ___ REINS

drawl SLUR

drawn
~ **tight** TAUT, TENSE
it may be ~ BATH
lightly ~ line TRACE

___**-drawn** FINE

drawn-out LONG, SLOW
~ **fight** SIEGE

drawstring CORD

draw the ___ LINE

dray CART, SLED

Dre
~ **and others** DRS

dread AWE, DIRE, FEAR, PANIC

dreadful BAD, DIRE, VILE

dream HOPE, IDEAL, MUSE
~ **acronym** REM
~ **environment** SLEEP

~ **starter** DAY
~ **stealer** ALARM
~ **up** COIN, IDEATE

___ **dream** PIPE

"Dream ___**, The"** TEAM

"Dream ___ **With Me"** ALONG

"Dream Along With Me"
~ **singer** COMO

"Dream Children"
~ **author** ELIA

" ___ **dreaming?"** AMI

dreamland BED, NOD
in ~ ABED

dreamlike AERIAL

"Dream of Gerontius, The"
~ **composer** ELGAR

"Dream of Kings, A"
~ **director** MANN

" ___ **Dreams"** THESE

"Dreams and Projects"
~ **author** ARP

Dream Team
~ **letters** USA

dreamy AERIAL

dreary ARID, DRAB, FLAT, MEAN, SAD, SOBER

Dred ___ **Decision** SCOTT

dredge DRAG

Dre, Dr.
~ **music** RAP

dregs LEES, TRASH, WASTE
~ **of society** MOB

dreidel TOP, TOY

drench BATHE, DIP, HOSE, SOAK, SOP, STEEP, WATER, WET

drenched WET

Drescher FRAN
like ~'s speech NASAL

Dresden
~ **river** ELBE
see also German

dress ARRAY, ATTIRE, DON, DRAG, GARB, PLOW, RIG, VEST
~ **accessory** SASH
~ **bottom** HEM
~ **down** LACE, TWIT
~ **fastening** SNAP
~ **feature** SLIT
~ **in** WEAR
~ **panel** INSET
~ **splendidly** ARRAY
~ **style** ALINE, MINI, TENT
~ **up** ADORN, ARRAY, PREEN
1960s ~ MINI
beltless ~ TENT
calf-length ~ MIDI
ceremonial ~ ROBE
Ganges ~ SARI
junior ~ size NINE
loose-fitting ~ TENT
make a ~ SEW

old ~ RAG
paper-doll ~ part TAB

dress ___ CODE

dressage
~ **factor** GAIT

dress code
~ **concern** ATTIRE

dressed CLAD
be ~ in WEAR
elegantly ~ SMART

dressed to the ___ NINES

dresser CHEST
~ **feature** KNOB
flashy ~ DUDE

dresses
originator of cutout ~ ERTE

dressing
~ **gown** ROBE
hair ~ GEL
kind of ~ RANCH
place for ~ SALAD
window ~ TRIM
wood ~ tool ADZE

dressing ___ ROOM, TABLE

___ **dressing** SALAD

Dressler MARIE
~ **role** MIN

dressmaker
~ **at times** SEWER
~ **cut** BIAS

dress-up GALA

dressy CHIC
~ **event** GALA
~ **material** LAME, SATIN

Drew ELLEN

Drew, Nancy TEEN
~ **boyfriend** NED
help for ~ CLUE

Dreyer CARL

"Dr. Feelgood"
~ **of Mötley Crüe** NEIL

dribble DRIP, DROP, LEAK, SEEP, SPIT

driblet BIT, TINGE

dried
~ **herbage** HAY
~ **out** ARID, SERE, STALE
~ **up** ARID, DESERT, SERE

drift AIM, HEAP, IDLE, MASS, PILE, RANGE, ROAM, ROVE, SENSE, TENOR, TIDE, TREND, VEER, YAW
~ **(by)** SLIP
~ **material** SNOW
~ **off** NAP, NOD
~ **to leeward** SAG
get the ~ SEE

drifter HOBO, NOMAD
continental ~ PLATE

drifting ASEA, ATSEA

drill BITE, BORE, TOOL, TRAIN
~ **insert** BIT
~ **sergeant's call** HEP
~ **sgt.** NCO
civil defense ~ ALERT

___ **drill** FIRE

driller
~ **deg.** DDS
~ **org.** ADA

drink ADE, ALE, BEER, CIDER, COCOA, COLA, FLIP, MEAD, NOG, POP, PORT, RUM, SAKE, SAKI, SHOT, SIP, SNORT, SODA, TAB, TAKE, TANG, TEA, TONIC, WINE
~ **cooler** ICE
~ **in** LEARN
~ **in a way** LAP
~ **like Fido** LAP
~ **of old** MEAD
~ **opener** TAB
~ **served by the yard** ALE
~ **served with marshmallows** COCOA
~ **slowly** NURSE, SIP
~ **suffix** ADE
~ **to** TOAST
~ **topped with nutmeg** FLIP
~ **to someone's health** TOAST
~ **with straws** SODA
after-dinner ~ PORT
apple ~ CIDER
astronaut's ~ TANG
autumn ~ CIDER
bar ~ SOUR
breakfast ~ COCOA
British ~ ALE, TEA
carbonated ~ COLA, POP, SODA
ceremonied ~ TEA
citrus ~ ADE
cold ~ ADE, SODA
cold-weather ~ COCOA
curative ~ TONIC
dart-thrower's ~ ALE
draught ~ ALE
fast-food ~ COLA, SODA
fermented ~ ALE, BEER
festival ~ ALE
fit to ~ PURE
fizzy ~ COLA, POP, SODA
food and ~ DIET
fountain ~ SODA
fruit ~ ADE
give food and ~ SERVE
honey ~ MEAD
hot ~ COCOA
Japanese ~ SAKE, SAKI, TEA
lemon ~ ADE
lime ~ ADE
lo-cal ~ TAB
malt ~ ALE
mixed ~ FLIP
old sailor's ~ RUM
orange ~ ADE
picnic ~ ADE
pub ~ ALE
quick ~ SNORT
robust ~ ALE
sample a ~ SIP
short ~ TOT
small ~ DRAM

soft ~ ADE, COLA, POP, SODA, TAB
summer ~ ADE
the ~ OCEAN, SEA
Wonderland ~ TEA
XXX ~ ALE
year-end ~ NOG
see also beverage

"Drink ___ only..." TOME

drinker
hard ~ SOT
Nehi ~ RADAR

drinking
~ **aid** STRAW
~ **vessel** CUP, STEIN

"___ Drink the Water" DONT

drip BORE, LEAK, OOZE, PLOP, SEEP
~ **locale** EAVE

drip ___ PAN

drip-___ DRY

drip-dry
~ **fabric** NYLON

dripping DAMP, RAINY, WET

drippings OIL

drive GEAR, GOAD, HERD, LANE, MOTOR, PROD, RIDE, ROAD, RUN, SEND, SPIN, SPUR, STEER, URGE
~ **a Cessna** AVIATE
~ **a nail aslant** TOE
~ **a semi** HAUL
~ **at** MEAN
~ **away** OUST, REPEL, SHOO
~ **back** REPEL
~ **forward** MOVE
~ **in** ENTER, RAM
~ **into one's head** CON
~ **off** REPEL
~ **onward** IMPEL
~ **out** EJECT, EXILE, OUST, ROUT
~ **the getaway car** ABET
~ **to distraction** ENRAGE
~ **too fast** RACE, SPEED
~ **to the wall** PRESS
~ **up the wall** IRK, NAG, PEEVE, RILE, UPSET
4-wheel ~ **feature** ABS
creative ~ EGO
dangerous to ~ **on** ICY
hard, straight ~ LINER
inner ~ URGE
short ~ SPIN

drive ___ TRAIN

___ drive LINE

___-drive TEST

Drive
~ **in Beverly Hills** RODEO

drivel PAP, PRATE, ROT, TRASH

driven
like ~ **snow** PURE

___-driven software MENU

driver
~ **aid** MAP
~ **aid letters** AAA
~ **bane** FLAT, SLICE
~ **compartment** CAB
~ **org.** AAA, PGA
~ **peg** TEE
~ **purchase** GAS
~ **shout** FORE
~ **yell** FORE
be in the ~'**s seat** LEAD, PILOT
Indy ~ RACER
pile ~ RAM
plane ~ PILOT
pro ~ RACER
reindeer ~ SANTA
sleigh ~ SANTA

driver ___ ANT

___ driver CAB, PILE, SLAVE, TAXI

drivers
~ **licenses** IDS

driver's ___ SEAT

driver's license
~ **info** SEX
~ **items** IDS

"___ Drives Me Crazy" SHE

drive-through
~ **order** TOGO

drive train
~ **element** AXLE

driveway LANE
do the ~ PAVE

driving
~ **area** RANGE
~ **hazard** GLARE, ICE, MIST, SLEET
~ **need** IRON, TEE
~ **power** FIRE

"Driving ___ Daisy" MISS

driving-home
~ **stat** RBI

drizzle DRIP, MIST, RAIN, WET

drizzling WET

drizzly DAMP, RAINY

"Dr. Jekyll ___ Mr. Hyde" AND

"Dr. Jekyll and Mr. ___" HYDE

droit CLAIM

droll DRY, ODD, WRY
~ **fellow** WIT

drollery WIT

dromedary ANIMAL, CAMEL
~ **pit stop** OASIS

drone BEE, IDLER, MALE, NOISE

Drood, Edwin
~ **betrothed** ROSA

drool SPIT

droop DIE, DIP, DRAPE, FLAG, HANG, LOLL, LOP, MOPE, NOD, SAG

droopy LIMP

drop BEAD, CEASE, DELE, DRIP, END, HANG, IOTA, OMIT, PLOP, SCRAP, SINK, SLASH, TEAR, TINGE
~ **a hint** LETON
~ **a letter** MAIL, SEND, SLUR
~ **a line** WRITE
~ **anchor** LAND
~ **an easy one** ERR
~ **back** EBB
~ **cloth** SHEET
~ **clues** HINT
~ **down** DIP
~ **ender** LET
~ **from the team** CUT
~ **in a letter box** MAIL
~ **in a way** SAG
~ **in on** SEE
~ **maybe** LOSE
~ **noisily** PLOP
~ **off** ABATE, EBB, FLAG, NAP, NOD, SHED, SLEEP, SLIP, SLOPE, WANE
~ **one's jaw** GAPE
~ **out of sight** DIP, HIDE
~ **pounds** SLIM
~ **starter** DEW, EAR, EAVES, RAIN, SNOW, TEAR
~ **target** EAR, EYE
~ **the ball** ERR
a wee ~ DRAM
eye ~ TEAR
lachrymal ~ TEAR
letter ~ SLOT
ready to ~ DONE, SPENT
saline ~ TEAR

drop ___ LEAF, SHOT

drop ___ (decline) OFF

drop ___ (quit) OUT

___ drop LEMON, MAIL

___-drop NAME

drop a ___ LINE

drop-in
turnstile ~ TOKEN

"___ Drop Kid, The" LEMON

droplet BEAD, TEAR

droplets
fine ~ MIST

"drop of golden sun, A" RAY

dropped
~ **from the team** CUT
~ **pop** ERROR
with ~ **jaw** AGAPE

dropper
~ **cry** OOPS

___ dropper NAME

drops
~ **on the grass** DEW
fall in ~ DRIP

___ drop soup EGG

droshky CAB

dross SLAG, TRASH, WASTE

droughty ARID, DESERT, DRY, SERE

drove HERD, HOST, MASS, MOB

"Drove my Chevy to the ___..." LEVEE

drover
  ~ charge HERD

drowse NAP, NOD, REST, SLEEP

drowsy TIRED

"___ Dr. Ruth" ASK

Drs. MDS

drub BANG, BEAT, BLAST, LAM

drubbing ROUT

drudge DRONE, HACK, PEON, PLOD, SLAVE, TOIL
  polar ~ ELF

drudgery LABOR, TOIL

drug CURE, OPIATE
  ~ amount DOSE
  ~ cop NARC

drug-free CLEAN

druggist
  ~ container VIAL

drug-overseeing
  ~ org. FDA

druid CELT

Dru, Joanne
  ~ "Red River" role TESS

drum RAP
  ~ attachment SNARE
  ~ in the ears DIN
  ~ material STEEL
  ~ out EJECT, OUST
  ~ site EAR
  ~ sound ROLL
  beat the ~ BLARE, BRAG, CROW
  kind of ~ BASS, SNARE

drum ___ MAJOR

___ drum BASS, SNARE

"___ drummers drumming..." NINE

Drummond ACE, COP

drums
  beat the ~ for SELL

"Drums"
  ~ actor SABU

"Drums ___ the Mohawk" ALONG

drumstick LEG, MEAT

drunk LIT, REVEL

drunk ___ skunk ASA

drunkard SOT

drunken
  ~ revel SPREE
  ~ utterance HIC

Drury ALLEN, LANE

Drury ___ Theatre LANE

Drury Lane
  ~ composer ARNE

dry ARID, BAKE, BLOT, CURE, DESERT, DRAB, SERE, STALE, TAME
  ~ as wine SEC
  ~ fruit NUT
  ~ in the sun BAKE
  ~ land EARTH, SHORE
  ~ out AERATE, BLOT, SEAR
  ~ plain DESERT
  ~ riverbed WADI, WASH
  ~ run TEST, TRIAL
  ~ up SEAR
  ~ watercourse WADI
  not ~ DAMP, WET
  pat ~ BLOT
  very ~ ARID, SERE

dry ___ CELL, HOLE, ICE, ROT, RUN

dry-___ CLEAN

___-dry AIR, BONE, DRIP

dryad
  ~ dwelling TREE

dry as a ___ BONE

dry-as-dust BLAH, DRAB, TAME

Dryden KEN, POET

Dryden, John POET
  ~ work ESSAY, ODE
  see also poet

dryer
  ~ of a sort KILN
  ~ residue LINT
  hops ~ OAST

Dryer FRED

dry goods
  ~ measure YARD

drying
  ~ method DRIP
  ~ oven OAST
  spread for ~ TED

dry rot MOLD

Drysdale DON

"Dr. Zhivago"
  ~ character LARA

DST
  when ~ ends OCT

dualistic DUAL

Duane DIANE, EDDY

Duarte EVA

dub CALL, LABEL, NAME, PEG, STYLE, TAG, TERM, TITLE
  ~ in ADD
  something to ~ TAPE

Dubai
  ~ native ARAB

"DuBarry ___ a Lady" WAS

"DuBarry Was a ___" LADY

"DuBarry Was a Lady"
  ~ director RUTH

dubbed
  ~ one SIR

dubious ACUTE, LEERY

Dublin CITY
  ~ loc. IRE
  ~ locale EIRE, ERIN
  from ~ IRISH

Du Bois WEB

Dubonnet WINE

Dubos RENE

ducat
  ~ word ADMIT, ROW, SEAT

duce RULER

Duchamp
  ~ art movement DADA
  ~ subject NUDE

Duchesne PERE

duchess LADY, RANK, TITLE

Duchin EDDY, PETER

Duchovny, David
  ~ wife TEA

duchy REALM

duck AVOID, BIRD, DIP, ELUDE, EVADE, HIDE, MEAT, SHUN
  ~ cousin GOOSE
  ~ haunt POND
  cold ~ WINE
  North American ~ EIDER
  "Peter and the Wolf" ~ OBOE
  piece of ~ SAIL
  sea ~ COOT, EIDER
  sitting ~ DUPE, PREY, SAP
  type of ~ TEAL

___ duck LAME

Duck, Donald
  ~ voice NASH

duck-foot
  ~ feature WEB

ducklike
  ~ bird COOT

"___ Duckling, The" UGLY

___-duck president LAME

ducks
  ~ and drakes GAME

duck soup EASY

"Duck Soup"
  ~ actor HARPO

Ducommun ELIE

duct CANAL, MAIN, PIPE
  ~ starter VIA

duct ___ TAPE

dud DOG, LEMON, LOSER

dude BEAU, DOG
  ~ up ADORN, ATTIRE, DRESS
  cool ~ CAT
  crude ~ BOOR

dude ___ RANCH

"___, dude!" LATER

duded
  get ~ up PREEN

dudes
  place for ~ RANCH

Dudevant
  ~ pseudonym SAND

dudgeon
  high ~ ANGER, IRE, RAGE
  in high ~ MAD

___ du Diable ILE

Dudley EARL, MOORE

duds ARRAY, ATTIRE, DRESS, GARB

Dudweiler
  ~ locale SAAR

due CLAIM, DEBT, DESERT, MERIT
  ~ follower TRE
  ~ preceder UNO
  amount ~ BILL, SCORE, TOTAL
  past ~ LATE

duel
  ~ with words SPAR

dueling
  ~ weapon EPEE

"Dueling Banjos" DUET

"Duel in the ___" SUN

duelist
  ~ of 1804 BURR

"Duellists, The"
  ~ director SCOTT

dues FEE

Duesenberg AUTO, CAR

duet PAIR, TWO

duffel BAG, GEAR
  ~ bag SACK

duffel ___ BAG

duffer BOOR
  ~ cry FORE
  ~ dream ACE
  ~ goal PAR
  ~ position LIE
  ~ problem SLICE
  ~ target HOLE

dugong ANIMAL

dugout BOAT, CANOE, CAVE, DEN, HAVEN, HOLE, LAIR
  ~ bunch TEAM
  stick in the ~ BAT

___ du jour CARTE, PLAT

duke LORD, MALE, PEER, RANK, TITLE
  ~ daughter LADY
  ~ starter ARCH
  grand ~ PEER

Duke TITLE
  "Indigo" for ~ MOOD

"___ Duke" SIR

"___ Duke, The" (Wellington) IRON

"Duke of ___" EARL

Duke, Patty
  ~ real first name ANNA

"Dukes of Hazzard, The"
~ **actor** PYLE
~ **deputy** ENOS
~ **spinoff** ENOS

dulcet SWEET

___ **dulci** UTILE

"___ du lieber!" ACH

dull ABATE, ALLAY, ARID, BANAL, BLAH, DRAB, DRY, FLAT, GRAY, INERT, SAD, SLOW, SOBER, STALE, TAME
~ **brown** DRAB
~ **color** GRAY, GREY
~ **gray** DRAB
~ **noise** THUD
~ **one** BORE
~ **pain** ACHE
~ **routine** ROTE, RUT
~ **situation** DRAG
~ **surface** MAT, MATTE
~ **throb** ACHE
an épée's is ~ EDGE
grow ~ FADE
not ~ KEEN

dullard BORE, DOLT, OAF

dull-as-dishwater ARID, DRY

Dulles
~ **abbr.** ARR, ETA
~ **sight** SST

Dulles, Allen
~ **onetime org.** CIA

dullsville BLAH, BORE

dull-witted DENSE, DIM
~ **one** DODO

Dumas
~ **character** ATHOS
see also French

du Maurier, Daphne DAME

dumb DAFT, MUTE
~ **jokes** CORN
~ **move** BONER
play ~, perhaps ACT
strike ~ DAZE

dumb ___ ox ASAN

"Dumb ___" (old comic) DORA

Dumbarton
~ **denizen** SCOT

Dumbarton ___ (UN planning site) OAKS

Dumbarton Oaks ESTATE

dumbbell ASS, CLOD, DODO, DOLT, DOPE, OAF

dumbfound AMAZE, AWE, STUN, WOW

Dumbo
~ **wing** EAR

dumbstruck AGAPE

dummkopf ASS, CLOD, OAF

dummy CLOD, DODO, DOLT, DOPE, MODEL, NIT
~ **perch** KNEE

dump ABODE, AXE, SELL, STY

___ **dump** CORE

dumps
down in the ~ BLUE, LOW, SAD

Dumpster BIN
~ **locale** ALLEY
~ **material** TRASH

dun ASK, HORSE, PLY, PRESS

Dunbar, William POET, SCOT
see also poet

Duncan, King
~ **resting place** IONA

dunce ASS, CLOD, DOLT, DOPE, OAF, YOYO
~ **cap** HAT

dunce ___ CAP

dunce cap
~ **shape** CONE

"Dunciad, The" POEM
~ **poet** POPE

dun-colored DRAB

Dundee CITY, PORT
~ **denizen** SCOT
~ **miss** LASS
see also Scottish

Dundee, Crocodile
~ **girl** SUE
see also Australian

dunderhead ASS, CLOD, DODO, DOLT, DOPE, OAF

dunderheaded DAFT

dune SAND
~ **buggy** MOTOR
~ **buggy's surface** SAND

___ **dune** SAND

dungeon CAGE, HOLE, KEEP
~ **item** IRONS, RACK

"Dungeons & Dragons"
~ **beast** OGRE, ORC

dunk BATHE, DIP
~ **one** SCORE

dunk ___ SHOT

___ **dunk** SLAM

dunking BATH

Dunn NORA

Dunne IRENE

Dunninger
~ **claim** ESP

duo PAIR, TWO

dupe GOAT, HAVE, LAMB, PREY, REPRO, ROOK, SAP, SCAM, TOOL, TRAP

duped
easily ~ NAIVE

duper LIAR

Dupin, Auguste
~ **creator** POE

Dupin, Lucile
~ **pseudonym** SAND

duplex DUAL

duplicate APE, CLONE, DITTO, DUAL, IMAGE, TWIN

duplicitous FALSE
be ~ LIE

duplicity ART, WILE

DuPont
~ **HQ** DEL

durability
have ~ LAST

durable
~ **coating** ENAMEL
be ~ LAST

Durango
~ **dough** PESO
see also Spanish

Durant ARIEL
~ **Muse** CLIO

Durante
~ **trademark** NOSE

duration RUN, SPAN, TERM, TIME
datebook ~ YEAR
football-game ~ HOUR
unspecific ~ EON

Durban CITY
~ **dough** RAND
~ **locale** NATAL

Durbeyfield TESS
~ **pursuer** ALEC

Dürer
emulate ~ ETCH

during AMID, OVER
~ **office hours** DAYS

duro COIN

Durocher LEO
~ **ex** DAY
~ **moniker** LIP

Duryea DAN

___ **du Salut** PORT

Dusenberry ANN

dusk
~ **to a poet** EEN

dusky DIM, EBONY, ECRU

Düsseldorf CITY
city near ~ ESSEN
see also German

dust DIRT, GRIT
~ **bowl** DESERT
~ **collector** RAG
~ **devil** EDDY
~ **ender** BIN, PAN
~ **starter** SAW, STAR
bite the ~ LOSE
gathering ~ IDLE
leave in the ~ LOSE
throw ~ in the eyes of DUPE
valuable ~ GOLD

dust ___ STORM

dust ___ (reuse) OFF

___ **dust** GOLD

"___ Dust" RED, STAR

dustball LINT

Dust Bowl
like the ~ ARID, DRY

dustcloth RAG

dust cover
~ **item** BIO

dusted CLEAN

duster MAID, RAG

___-**duster** CROP

dusting COAT
~ **powder** TALC

___-**dusting** CROP

"Dust of Snow" POEM

"___ dust shalt thou return" UNTO

dust-storm
~ **deposit** SILT

"...___, dust to..." ASHES

dustup ADO, ROW, SCRAP, SPAT

Dutch
~ **artist** HALS
~ **cheese** EDAM
~ **city** EDAM
~ **colonist** BOER
~ **export** EDAM, TULIP
~ **royal house** ORANGE
~ **South African** BOER
~ **speaking resort island** ARUBA
~ **town** EDAM, EDE
~ **waterway** ZEE
double ~ GAME
farmer, in ~ BOER
go ~ PAY
it may be ~ TREAT
see also Holland, Netherlands

Dutch ___ DOOR, OVEN, TREAT, UNCLE

Dutch ___ India Company EAST

Dutchman's breeches PLANT

Dutch oven POT

dutiful TRUE

Dutra OLIN

Dutton, Charles
~ **TV role** ROC

duty CARE, ONUS, POST, STINT, TASK
~ **roster** ROTA
tour of ~ STINT

duty-___ FREE

Duvalier EXILE
~ **domain** HAITI

Dvina
see Russian

DVM VET

Dvorak ANN

Dvořák ANTON

dwarf ARREST, DOC, ELF, RUNT, SMALL
  ~ with spectacles DOC
  red ~ STAR
  treasure-hoarding ~ GNOME
  white ~ STAR

dwarf ___ STAR

dwarfish ELFIN

dwarflike
  ~ creature GNOME

dweeb NERD

dwell ABIDE, LIVE, STAY
  ~ on LABOR, PORE, SAVOR
  ~ (on) HARP
  ~ upon STRESS

dweller
  ~ (suffix) ITE

dwelling ABODE, HOME, NEST, ROOF
  ~ (abbr.) RES

arctic ~ IGLOO
cliff ~ AERIE
conical ~ TEPEE
cozy ~ NEST
dryad's ~ TREE
elevated ~ AERIE
hemispherical ~ IGLOO
Indian ~ TEPEE
outdoor ~ TENT
Plains ~ TEPEE
prehistoric ~ CAVE
Southwestern ~ ADOBE
stately ~ MANOR
see also home, house

Dwight
  ~ nickname IKE
  ~ opponent ADLAI

dwindle ABATE, DROP, EBB, MELT, PETER, SLOW, TAPER, WANE, WASTE

Dy ELEM
  66 for ~ ATNO

dyad ATOM, DUO, PAIR, TWO

dye COLOR, RINSE, TINGE, TINT
  ~ ingredient ALUM
  ~ plant ANIL
  ~ receptacle VAT
  blue ~ ANIL
  hair ~ HENNA

___-dye TIE

dyed-in-the-wool AVID, TOTAL

dyeing
  ~ bin VAT
  ~ instruction RINSE

dyestuff
  Egyptian ~ HENNA

dying
  ~ to know NOSY
  be ~ (for) PANT

Dykstra LEN

Dylan BOB

dynamic ALIVE, LIVE
  ~ force LIFE
  ~ starter AERO

"Dynamic ___" DUO

dynamite
  ~ cousin TNT
  use ~ on BLAST

dynamo MOTOR
  ~ part ROTOR
  human ~ DEMON, DOER

dynast LORD, RULER

dynasty CLAN, REIGN
  ancient Chinese ~ CHI

"Dynasty" SOAP
  ~ actress EVANS
  ~ network ABC

dyne-centimeter ERG

"___ d'Yvetot" LEROI

8
~ fluid ounces CUP
it's ~ hrs. behind
  Greenwich PST

"8 1/2"
~ actress AIMEE

8 1/2 x 14 LEGAL

"___ 8 3/4" AGENT

11:00
~ feature NEWS

11th grade
~ exam PSAT

18th-century
~ revolutionary MARAT

18-wheeler RIG, SEMI

"___ 80" STAR

"84 Charing Cross ___" ROAD

86 AGENT

88
~ days, for Mercury YEAR

1836
battleground of ~ ALAMO

1860s
~ govt. CSA

1881
~ shootout participant EARP

1890s
adjective for the ~ GAY

1899-1902
fighter of ~ BOER

8760
~ hours YEAR

"E"
Morse ~ DIT, DOT

E-___ MAIL

E. ___ Proulx ANNIE

each ALL, APIECE, PER

"Each Dawn I ___" DIE

"___ each life some rain..." INTO

"Each sack had ___ cats..."
SEVEN

eager AGOG, AVID, GAME, HOT,
KEEN, MAD
~ beaver DEMON
feel ~ ACHE

eagerness ARDOR, HEAT, ZEAL

eagle BIRD, COIN
~ a par-three hole ACE
~ feature CLAW, TALON
~ nest AERIE
~ on a par-3 hole ACE
~ plus two PAR
~ wearer COL
bald ~ look-alike ERN, ERNE
emulate an ~ SOAR
Muppet ~ SAM
sea ~ ERN, ERNE

eagle-___ EYED

___ eagle BALD, LEGAL, SEA

Eagle AUTO, CAR
Apollo's ~ LEM
where the ~ landed MOON

"Eagle ___ Landed, The" HAS

"Eagle ___ the Hawk, The" AND

"___ Eagle, The" (Lindbergh)
LONE

"Eagle and the Arrow, The"
~ author AESOP

eagles
like some ~ BALD

Eagles ELEVEN, TEAM
~ org. BSA, NFL

Eagle Scout RANK

eaglets
~ nursery AERIE

Eames, Emma
~ offering ARIA

EAP
part of ~ EDGAR, POE

ear ORGAN
~ area LOBE
~ cleaner SWAB
~ ender DROP, FLAP, PHONE,
RING, SHOT
~ feature CANAL
~ of corn COB
~ part CANAL, COB, LOBE

~ piercing LOUD
~ pollution DIN, NOISE
~ (prefix) OTO
bend someone's ~ BORE,
TALK
bug in one's ~ HINT
edible ~ CORN
give ~ ATTEND
lend an ~ HEED
of the ~ AURAL, OTIC
play it by ~ ADLIB
turn a deaf ~ DENY

___ ear DEAF, INNER, OUTER, TIN

___-ear DOG

"___ ear and out..." INONE

eared ___ SEAL

___-eared CROP, LOP

earful
get an ~ HEAR

Earhart
emulate ~ AVIATE

earl LORD, MALE, PEER, RANK,
TITLE

Earl TITLE

Earl ___ tea GREY

earldom
Eden's ~ AVON

Earl Grey TEA

earlier AGO, ELDER, FORE, PAST
~ in text ABOVE
~ (prefix) FORE, PRE, PRO
~ than ERE

"earlier, the better, The" ASAP,
STAT

earliest FIRST
~ letters ABC

Earl of Avon EDEN

Earl of Greystoke
~ girl JANE

early OLD, WEE

early ___ BIRD, RISER

earmark ALLOT, LABEL, SIGN,
STAMP, TAG

earmarks
have the ~ of SEEM

earn CLEAR, DRAW, GAIN, GET,
MAKE, MERIT, NET, WIN
~ a blue ribbon WIN
~ a citation SPEED
~ after taxes CLEAR
~ an Oscar ACT
~ a point SCORE
~ as profit NET
~ the crown WIN
homophone for ~ ERN,
ERNE, URN

**earned ___ average (baseball
stat)** RUN

___ earner WAGE

earnest AVID, EAGER, SOBER,
STAID, TRUE
~ money of a sort BAIL
begin in ~ SETTO
in ~ REAL

earnestly HARD

Earnhardt DALE

earnings HIRE, PAY, WAGE
CD ~ INT

ear-related OTIC

earring
~ part WIRE
~ site LOBE
kind of ~ DROP, LOOP, STUD

ears CORN
all ~ ALERT, NOSY, RAPT
animal with big ~ HARE
be all ~ HEAR
drum in the ~ DIN
of the ~ AURAL, OTIC
pin one's ~ back BEAT
prick up one's ~ PERK
rabbit ~ AERIAL
roasting ~ CORN
split the ~ DIN
up to one's ~ AWASH
wet behind the ~ NAIVE, RAW
with eyes and ~ open WARY
with ~ pricked ALERT

"ears"
CBer's ~ RADIO

___ ears (attentive) ALL

earshot
  within ~ NEAR

ear splitter DIN
  Elsa's ~ ROAR

earsplittingly ALOUD, LOUD

earth CLAY, CLOD, DIRT, DUST,
  LAND, LOAM, SOIL, TERRA
  ~ in French TERRE
  ~ in Italian TERRA
  ~ in Latin TERRA
  ~ pigment OCHER, OCHRE
  ~ tone OCHER, OCHRE
  fine ~ DUST
  rare ~ METAL
  wet ~ CLAY

earth ___ (brown) TONE

Earth
  ~ center CORE
  ~ envelope AIR, ETHER
  ~ goddess GAEA
  ~ inheritors MEEK
  ~ nearest star SOL
  ~ neighbor MARS
  ~ orbiter MIR, MOON
  ~ path ORBIT
  ~ (prefix) GEO
  ~ satellite MOON
  ~ sci. ECOL
  ~ star SUN
  ~ surface LAND
  ~ to a poet ORB
  ~ turning point AXIS
  bowels of the ~ ABYSS
  came to ~ ALIT, LIT
  end of the ~ POLE
  heaven on ~ EDEN
  in the bowels of the ~ DEEP
  most of the ~ OCEAN, SEA
  not of this ~ ALIEN
  on ~ HERE
  returned to ~ ALIT, LIT
  return to ~ LAND
  section of ~'s crust PLATE
  Teutonic ~ goddess ERDA
  walk the ~ LIVE

"Earth ___" ANGEL

"___ Earth, The" GOOD

"Earth Angel" OLDIE

earth conscious
  ~ org. EPA

___-earth element RARE

earthen
  ~ jar OLLA

earthenware CLAY
  ~ pot OLLA

"Earth Girls ___ Easy" ARE

"Earth in the Balance"
  ~ author GORE
  ~ subj. ECOL

earthling MAN

earthquake TREMOR

earthshaking LOUD

"Earth vs. the Flying Saucers"
  ~ director SEARS

Earth, Wind & ___ FIRE

earthy RAW
  ~ color ECRU
  ~ sediment SILT

ease ABATE, AID, ALLAY, HELP,
  LOOSE, SLAKE
  ~ up LAG, REST
  at ~ REST, SERENE
  epitome of ~ ABC, PIE
  put at ~ ALLAY
  take one's ~ REST

easel
  ~ display ART
  ~ part LEG

"Ease On Down the ___" ROAD

easier
  make ~ AID

easier ___ than done SAID

easier said ___ done THAN

east
  ~ ender ERN
  ~ end of a basilica APSE
  ~ in French EST
  ~ in Spanish ESTE
  ~ opposite WEST

East
  from the ~ ASIAN
  much of the ~ ASIA

East ___ (London area) END

___ East FAR, NEAR

East Asian
  ~ language LAO
  ~ river AMUR

easter
  ~ starter NOR

Easter
  ~ bloom LILY
  ~ dish HAM, LAMB
  ~ ender TIDE
  ~ event PARADE
  ~ item EGG
  ~ need DYE
  ~ preceder LENT
  ~ stamp SEAL
  color ~ eggs DYE

"Easter ___" PARADE

Eastern
  ~ bigwig AMIR, EMEER, EMIR
  ~ bishop ABBA
  ~ canal ERIE
  ~ cuisine THAI
  ~ European SERB, SLAV
  ~ garb SARI
  ~ land mass ASIA
  ~ nanny AMA, AMAH
  ~ nurse AMA, AMAH
  ~ philosophy TAO
  ~ potentate AMIR, EMEER,
    EMIR
  ~ religion ISLAM, ZEN
  ~ title AGA, AGHA

Eastern Church
  ~ title ABBA

Easter parade
  ~ attraction HAT

East Indian HINDU

"East of ___" EDEN

"East of Eden"
  ~ actor DEAN
  ~ character ARON, CAL

Eastwood, Clint
  ~ film BIRD

easy LOOSE
  ~ gait TROT
  ~ mark DUPE, LAMB, PREY,
    SAP
  ~ pace TROT
  ~ partner FREE, NICE
  ~ stride LOPE
  ~ target DUPE
  ~ task SNAP
  ~ to understand CLEAR
  ~ win ROMP, ROUT
  free and ~ LOOSE
  get an ~ A ACE
  long, ~ stride LOPE
  not ~ HARD
  take it ~ IDLE, LOAF, LOLL,
    REST, SIT, SLIDE

Easy
  ~ and others STS

"Easy ___" ACES, RIDER

"Easy ___ Hard" TOBE

"Easy ___ it!" DOES

"___ Easy, The" BIG

easy as ___ ABC, PIE

easygoing CALM, MILD

"___ Easy Pieces" FIVE

"Easy Street"
  ~ actor ELAM

"Easy to Be Hard"
  ~ musical HAIR

eat BITE, DINE, FARE, FEED, TAKE
  ~ away ERODE, FRET
  ~ away at GNAW
  ~ between meals NOSH
  ~ greedily CRAM
  ~ high off the hog DINE
  ~ in German ESSEN
  ~ into BITE, ERODE, ETCH,
    GNAW
  ~ like a horse GLUT
  ~ like an ox GLUT
  ~ more sensibly DIET
  ~ nothing FAST
  ~ out of house and
    home GLUT
  ~ up LOVE, SAVOR, SPEND,
    USE
  ~ voraciously SCARF
  bite to ~ NOSH
  get ready to ~ WASH
  mares ~ them OATS
  ready to ~ DONE
  sneak something to ~ NOSH
  what you ~ DIET

eat ___ CROW

"Eat a Bowl of ___" TEA

"Eat at Joe's" SIGN

eaten
  ~ up GONE

eater
  abalone ~ OTTER
  bamboo ~ PANDA
  big ~ HOG
  early apple ~ ADAM
  eucalyptus ~ KOALA
  finicky ~ CAT
  grass ~ COW
  insect ~ TOAD
  minnow ~ TERN
  shellfish ~ OTTER
  sweater ~ MOTH
  tin-can ~ GOAT

___-eater BEE, FIRE

___ Eaters ODOR

eatery CAFE
  ~ listing MENU
  ~ order BLT
  lure of an ~ AROMA
  NYC ~ DELI

eat humble ___ PIE

eating place TABLE
  Army ~ MESS

eat one's ___ out HEART

eats MEAL

eau WATER
  ~ de Cologne SCENT

eau de ___ VIE

eaves
  ~ locale ROOF

eavesdrop HEAR, SPY, TAP

eavesdropping NOSY
  ~ device TAP
  subject to ~ ALOUD

Eb
  ~ wife FLO

Eban ABBA

ebb ABATE, BATE, DIE, FADE, FLAG,
  LAPSE, PINE, TIDE, WANE
  ~ and flow TIDE
  lowest ~ NADIR

"Ebb ___" TIDE

Ebbets Field
  ~ great REESE

Ebenezer
  ~ exclamation BAH

Ebert ROGER
  emulate ~ RATE

ebony COLOR, INKY, JET, RAVEN,
  TREE

"Ebony and ___" IVORY

Ebro RIO

ebullience ARDOR, LIFE, PEP

ebullient AGOG

EC
  ~ member DEN, ENG, GER,
    ITAL, NOR
  part of ~ EUR

eccentric BIRD, DAFT, MAD, ODD, OUTRE
  ~ one CARD, COOT
  ~ part CAM
  ~ type NUT
  ~ wheel CAM

eccentricity TIC

ecclesiastic ABBE, ABBOT, DEAN, PADRE
  French ~ ABBE

ecclesiastical
  ~ assembly SYNOD

echelon PLANE, RANK, TIER

___ echelon REAR, TOP

echidna ANIMAL
  ~ food ANT

echo APE, PEAL, RING, ROLL
  ~ in a way APE
  Matterhorn ~ YODEL

Echo OREAD

echolocation
  ~ device SONAR

eclipse BEAT, BLUR, CAP, DIM, LEAD, SHADE, SHINE, TOP
  ~ maybe OMEN

___ eclipse LUNAR, SOLAR, TOTAL

eclogue POEM

ecology
  ~ concern AIR, OZONE, WATER
  ~ org. EPA

economic
  ~ ind. GNP
  ~ upturn BOOM

economical CLEAN

___ economics HOME

economize SAVE, SPARE, STINT

economy SIZE
  ~ size BIG, LARGE

economy ___ CLASS

___ E. Coyote WILE

ecru COLOR, TAN

ecstatic ELATED, RAPT
  make ~ ELATE
  wax ~ RAVE

ecto-
  ~ opposite ENDO, ENTO

ectomorphic SLIM

ectype IMAGE

Ecuador
  ~ neighbor PERU
  see also Spanish

Ed AMES, ASNER, OTT

edacious AVID

Edberg, Stefan SWEDE

edda SAGA

Eddie EGAN
  ~ cop character AXEL

Eddie ___ Halen VAN

___ Eddie Felson FAST

Eden
  ~ exile ADAM, EVE
  he went east of ~ CAIN
  place east of ~ NOD

Eden, Anthony EARL, SIR
  ~ earldom AVON

Eden, Barbara
  ~ character GENIE

Edenic IDEAL

Edgar AWARD, DEGAS

Edgar ___ Burroughs RICE

Edgar Allan ___ POE

edge ASSET, BIND, HEM, HONE, LACE, LIMIT, LIP, ODDS, RIM, START
  ~ (out) NOSE
  ~ (past) SIDLE
  cutting ~ LEAD
  give an ~ HONE
  improve an ~ HONE
  join at the ~ ABUT
  ocean's ~ SHORE
  on ~ TENSE, TESTY
  on the ~ of one's seat AGOG
  projecting ~ EAVE
  service ~ ADIN
  tailor's ~ HEM

edge ___ (barely defeat) OUT

"Edge of Night, The" SOAP

"Edge of the ___" CITY

edging TRIM

edgy TENSE

edible GOOD
  ~ bulb LEEK, ONION
  ~ fungus MOREL
  ~ orb PEA
  ~ pocket PITA
  ~ pulp PUREE
  ~ root BEET, OCA, TARO, YAM
  ~ seaweed AGAR
  ~ seed NUT
  ~ tuber OCA
  become ~ RIPEN
  no longer ~ STALE
  trendy ~ TOFU

edibles DIET, FARE, FEED, MEAL, MEAT

edict ACT, FIAT, LAW, ORDER

Edie ADAMS

"Edie"
  ~ author STEIN

edifice
  ~ complex MALL

edify OPEN, TRAIN

Edinburgh
  ~ resident SCOT
  see also Scottish

"Edison, the ___" MAN

Edison, Thomas
  ~ birthplace MILAN
  ~ contemporary TESLA

~ middle name ALVA
man who sneezed in ~'s first film OTT

edit ALTER, AMEND, CUT, EMEND, LOP
  ~ out DELE, ERASE, OMIT

Edith EVANS

Edith ___ (Lily Tomlin character) ANN

"___ Edith Cavell" NURSE

edition ISSUE
  newspaper's special ~ EXTRA

___ edition FIRST

editions
  like some ~ LATE

editor
  ~ compilation ERRATA
  ~ concern TEXT
  ~ doc. MSS
  ~ mark CARET, DELE
  ~ notation STET
  ~ req. SASE
  copy ~'s concern STYLE

___ editor CITY

editorial ESSAY, PROSE

Edmonton CITY
  ~ hockey player OILER
  ~ prov. ALB, ALTA

Ed, Mr. HORSE, STEED

"Edmund Fitzgerald"
  ~ cargo ORE

Edna ___ Oliver MAY

Edomites
  ~ ancestor ESAU

Edouard LALO

Édouard MANET
  see also French

Edsel AUTO, CAR, LEMON

Edsel Ford RANGE

Edsels
  start of an ~ song RAMA

"Ed Sullivan Show"
  ~ routine ACT

Eduardo
  see Spanish

educate REAR, TRAIN

educated
  ~ guess EST

"Educating ___" RITA

education
  public ~ pioneer MANN

___ education ADULT

educational
  ~ org. INST, PTA

educator
  ~ org. AFT, NEA

edulcorate CLEAN

Edward ALBEE, ELGAR, LEAR

Edward ___ Kennedy MOORE

Edwardian ___ ERA

Edwards, Blake
  ~ movie SOB

Edwin MOSES

EEC
  ~ currency ECU, EURO
  ~ member DEN, ENG, GER, ITAL, NOR
  ~ prefix EUR, EURO
  part of ~ EUR

"Eek!"
  ~ prompter MOUSE

"Eek the Cat"
  Elmo on ~ ELK

eel
  emulate an ~ SLIDE
  mud ~ SIREN

e'en
  not ~ once NEER

eensy-weensy SMALL, TINY

e'er AYE
  not quite ~ OFT

eerie
  ~ clue OMEN
  ~ loch NESS
  ~ sound MOAN

Eero
  ~ to Eliel SON

Eeyore
  ~ creator MILNE
  ~ friend OWL, POOH

ef
  ~ follower GEE

efface ANNUL

___-effacing SELF

effect CAUSE, ISSUE
  ~ one's escape ELUDE
  ~ starter AFTER
  appreciable ~ DENT
  cutting ~ BITE
  have an ~ TAKE, TELL
  lingering ~ ECHO
  not in ~ NULL
  put into ~ ENACT
  resonant ~ ECHO
  take ~ ENURE, INURE
  yodeling ~ ECHO

___ effect EDISON, LAKE, SIDE, TAKE

effective ABLE
  be ~ TAKE
  not ~ INEPT

___-effective COST

effectiveness
  ~ so to speak TEETH
  lose ~ PALL

effector DOER

effects ESTATE, GEAR

effendi SIR, TITLE
  ~ in India SAHIB

effervesce BOIL

effervescence GAS, LIFE, PEP

effervescent ALIVE, GAY
make ~ AERATE

efficacious
be ~ ACT, AVAIL, TAKE

efficiency FLAT
~ symbol, in physics ETA

efficient ABLE, ADEPT, FIT, GOOD, LEAN

effigy IMAGE

effluence AURA

effluvium ODOR, REEK

effort LABOR, STAB, TOIL, TRY
best ~ ALL
botched ~ ERROR
defensive ~ STAND
futile ~ WASTE
make an ~ ASSAY, ESSAY, EXERT, LABOR, TRY
public-relations ~ SPIN

effortless EASY

effortlessness EASE

effrontery BRASS, FACE, NERVE, SASS

effulgence SHEEN, SHINE

effuse EMERGE

effusive WARM

eft NEWT

"Egad!" DARN, DRAT, GEE, OATH, RATS
~ in German ACH

egest EMIT, SPEW

egg CELL
~ classification LARGE
~ concoction NOG, OMELET
~ ender HEAD, NOG, PLANT, SHELL
~ holder NEST
~ layer BIRD, HEN
~ on ABET, AROUSE, GOAD, IMPEL, MOVE, PRESS, PROD, ROOT, ROUSE, SPUR, URGE
~ partner DART
~ protector HEN
bad ~ CUR
golden ~ producer GOOSE
goose ~ NADA, NIL, NULL, ZERO
insect ~ NIT
lay an ~ MISS
nest ~ IRA
produce an ~ LAY
rotten ~ CAD

egg ___ CREAM, ROLL, SALAD

egg ___ soup DROP

___ egg EASTER, GOOSE, NEST

"Egg ___, The" ANDI

"Egg ___ I, The" AND

egg-and-___ DART

egghead NERD

egg hunt
~ time EASTER

eggnog
~ ingredient RUM

egg on one's ___ FACE

egg roll
~ time EASTER

eggs
~ in Latin OVA
color Easter ~ DYE
fish ~ ROE
like robins' ~ BLUE
lobster ~ ROE
produce ~ LAY
zoologist's ~ OVA

eggs ___ suisse ALA

"...eggs ___ basket" INONE

eggs-and-cheese
~ dish OMELET

egg-shaped OVAL, OVATE

eggshell COLOR, ECRU

egg timer
~ filler SAND

eggy
~ beverage NOG

ego PRIDE, SELF
alter ~ PAL
certain ~ ALTER
companions of ~ IDS

ego ___ TRIP

___ ego ALTER

egotist SNOB
~ obsession SELF

egotistical VAIN

egress EMERGE, EXIT, GATE

egret BIRD, HERON
~ cousin IBIS
emulate an ~ WADE

Egypt
~ and Syr., once UAR
capital of ~ CAIRO
city in ~ ASWAN
former president of ~ SADAT
neighbor of ~ ISR
opera set in ~ AIDA

Egyptian ARAB
~ bird IBIS
~ boy-king TUT
~ dam ASWAN
~ deity PTAH
~ dyestuff HENNA
~ god ATEN, ATON
~ goddess ISIS
~ peninsula SINAI
~ queen CLEO
~ river NILE
~ sky goddess NUT
~ solar disk ATEN, ATON
~ statesman SADAT
~ viper ASP
image in ~ art ASP
symbol of ~ royalty ASP

Egypt's Port ___ SAID

Eichhorn LISA

eider BIRD
~ cousin TEAL

eidolon IDEAL, SHADE

Eiffel Tower
~ locale PARIS

Eiger ALP

eight
~ furlongs MILE
~ in Italian OTTO
~ in Latin OCTO
~ in Spanish OCHO
~ ounces CUP
~ (prefix) OCTO
~ pts. GAL
composition for ~ OCTET
figure of ~ KNOT
group of ~ OCTET
half a figure ~ ESS
homophone for ~ AIT, ATE
piece of ~ COIN
quarter of ~ TWO

eight-___ shell OARED

"Eight ___ Out" MEN

eightball
~ requirement CUE

"Eight Days a ___" WEEK

eightfold OCTO

eighth
~ mo. AUG

eight-legged
~ creatures OCTOPI

"Eight Men ___" OUT

eights
do figure ~ SKATE

eighty-six TOSS

Eilbacher LISA

ein
~ in French UNE
~ in Italian UNO
~ in Spanish UNO

"Einsam in trüben Tagen"
~ singer ELSA

Einstein
~ birthplace GER, ULM
~ forte MATH
part of an ~ equation MASS
see also German

Eire
county in ~ CLARE

Eisenhower
~ nickname IKE
1967 ~ book ATEASE

Eisenhower, Mamie, ___ Doud NEE

Eisenhut ALP

eject CAST, EGEST, EMIT, EXILE, OUST, SPEW

ejectors
ink ~ OCTOPI

Ekberg ANITA, SWEDE

el TRAIN
~ followers EMS
~ preceder KAY
~ stop STA
where to ride the ~ CHI

"el"
cousin of ~ THE

El ___ (Heston role) CID

El ___ (Kit Carson sidekick) TORO

El ___ (Spanish hero) CID

El ___ (weather changer) NINO

"El ___ Mexico" SALON

"El ___ Presidente" SENOR

elaborate ORNATE, POSH
~ film EPIC
~ party FETE

Elaine MAY

"Elaine, the lily ___..." MAID

___ el Amarna TEL

élan DASH, FIRE, LIFE, PEP

eland ANIMAL
~ kin GNU

elapse PASS, SLIP

elapsed PAST

Elara MOON

elasticity LIFE
normal ~ TONE

elated GLAD
be ~ GLOW

elaterid DOR

elation GLEE

Elba ISLE
~ (abbr.) ISL

elbow ANGLE, JAB, PLOW, PROD
~ bender SOT
~ counterpart KNEE
~ locale ARM
~ room PLAY, SPACE

elbow ___ ROOM

elbow grease TOIL
use ~ EXERT

elbowing
like ~ RUDE

elbows PASTA
out at the ~ POOR
up to one's ~ AWASH

Elburz RANGE
~ locale IRAN

El Capitan TRAIN

"El Capitán"
~ composer SOUSA

El Cid
~ foe MOOR

"El Cid" EPIC
~ actress LOREN, PAGE
~ director MANN

El Cordobés
see Spanish

eld YORE

elder TREE
~ **statesman** DEAN
box ~ genus ACER
elver's ~ EEL

"Elder, The" CATO

elderberry WINE

Elder, Katie
~ **brood** SONS

elderly AGED, OLD

eldest FIRST
~ **son, traditionally** HEIR
Jr.'s ~, maybe III

"Eldorado"
~ **band** ELO

El Dorado
~ **treasure** ORO
see also Spanish

"El Dorado"
~ **author** POE

eldritch EERIE, EERY

Eleanor
~ **mother-in-law** SARA
~ **successor** BESS

"Eleanor and Franklin"
~ **author** LASH

___ Eleanor Roosevelt ANNA

elec.
~ **measure** AMP

elect MAKE, OPT, PLEASE, VOTE
~ **ender** ION, ORATE

elected
~ **ones** INS

election EVENT, RACE, VOTE
~ **defeat** LOSS
~ **ender** EER
~ **locale** POLL
~ **losers** OUTS
~ **mo.** NOV
~ **night abbr.** PCT
~ **selection** SLATE
~ **tactic** SMEAR
~ **winners** INS

elector
~ **ender** ATE

Electra
~ **daughter** IRIS

"Electra Glide in ___" BLUE

electric RACY
~ **bridge** ARC
~ **bulb** LAMP
~ **discharge** ARC
~ **light** LAMP
~ **power network** GRID
~ **sign** NEON
~ **stove** RANGE
~ **swimmer** EEL
~ **switch** RELAY

electric ___ EEL, EYE, METER, RAY

electrical
~ **conductor** WIRE
~ **device** RELAY

~ **storm** RAIN
~ **unit** AMP, OHM, VOLT, WATT

electrical ___ STORM

electric guitar
~ **hookup** AMP

electricity
~ **generator** EEL, RAY
demand for ~ LOAD
install ~ WIRE

electrified HOT

electrify AMAZE, AROUSE, FIRE,
MOVE, ROUSE, STIR, WIRE

electrifying
~ **fish** EEL, RAY

electrode ANODE
~ **bridge** ARC

electromagnetic
~ **storm** AURORA

electromotive force
~ **unit** VOLT

electron
~ **site** ATOM
free ~ ION
high speed ~ BETA

electronic
~ **reading** SCAN
~ **reminder** BEEP

Electronic ___ Systems DATA

electronic music
~ **pioneer** ENO

electronics
~ **giant** RCA

electron tube
~ **part** ANODE

electrum METAL

elegance CHIC, CLASS, STYLE,
TASTE, TONE

elegant CHIC, FINE, POSH, SMART
~ **accessory** BOA
~ **attire** DRESS
~ **fur** SABLE
~ **gathering** SOIREE
~ **occasion** BALL
not at all ~ CRASS

"elegant fowl"
Lear's ~ OWL

elegist POET

elegy POEM

"Elegy for Jane" POEM

**"Elegy Written in a Country
Churchyard"** POEM
~ **poet** GRAY

element METAL, PART, SPHERE,
UNIT
~ **class** METAL
~ **component** ATOM
~ **ID** ATNO
~ **in alchemy** AIR, EARTH,
FIRE, WATER
~ **of a murder mystery** ALIBI
~ **unit** ATOM
acronym ~ INIT

agenda ~ ITEM
basic ~ ROOT
common plot ~ LOVE
dance ~ STEP
metallic ~ GOLD, IRON, TIN,
ZINC
naiad's ~ WATER
natural ~ HOME
out of one's ~ ASEA, ATSEA,
LOST
stannous ~ TIN
tripod ~ LEG
TV ~ AUDIO

___ element TRACE

elemental BASIC
~ **unit** ATOM

elementary BASIC
~ **unit** ATOM

elements
basic ~ ABCS
decorative ~ ART
one of the four ~ AIR, EARTH,
FIRE, WATER

"Elements of ___, The" STYLE

"___ Elena" MARIA

elephant ANIMAL
~ **ender** INE
~ **feature** EAR
~ **group** HERD
GOP ~ creator NAST
**"Operation Dumbo Drop"
~** TAI
young ~ CALF

elephant ___ SEAL

"Elephant ___, The" MAN

"Elephant Boy" SABU

elephantine BIG, GIANT, LARGE

elephants
opera with ~ AIDA

elephant's-ear TARO

elev. ALT

elevate ELATE, EXALT, LAUD,
RAISE, REAR, RISE

elevated TALL
~ **dwelling** AERIE
~ **plain** MESA
~ **structure** ALTAR
more ~ ABOVE

elevation PEAK, RISE
land ~ MESA

elevations
~ **(abbr.)** HTS

elevator
~ **alternative** STAIR
~ **buttons** UPS
~ **compartment** CAB, CAR
~ **inventor** OTIS
~ **music** GENRE

élève
~ **locale** ECOLE

eleven SIDE

elevenses TEA

eleventh ___ HOUR

eleventh-hour LATE

elevs. HTS

elf IMP, RUNT
~ **cousin** GNOME, PERI

elfin SMALL, TINY
~ **output** TOY

El Greco
~ **adopted homeland** SPAIN
~ **birthplace** CRETE
~ **city** TOLEDO

Elia
~ **product** ESSAY
AKA ~ LAMB

Elias HOWE

elicit AROUSE, DRAW, EDUCE,
EVOKE
~ **chuckles** AMUSE

elide DROP, OMIT, SLUR

Eliel
~ **son** EERO

Elijah
~ **in the Douay** ELIAS
anathema for ~ BAAL

eliminate ANNUL, CLEAR, CUT,
DELE, DROP, ERASE, RID
~ **chaff** SIFT

Eliot NESS, POET
~ **character** BEDE
cruellest mo., to ~ APR

Eliot, George ALIAS
~ **real name** EVANS
pronoun for ~ SHE

Eliot, T.S. POET
~ **book-essay** DANTE
~ **subject** CAT
see also poet

Elisabeth
~ **in "Leaving Las
Vegas"** SERA

"___ Elise" FUR

Elisha OTIS

elite ALIST, CREAM, FONT, TYPE
~ **alternative** PICA
~ **military group** ATEAM
social ~ CREAM

elitist SNOB

elixir CURE, TONIC

Eliza
where ~ urged Dover ASCOT

Elizabeth ARDEN, DOLE, RULER

Elizabethan AGE, ERA
~ **epithet** BESS

Elizabethan ___ ERA

Elizabeth II
~ **daughter** ANNE
~ **to Edward VIII** NIECE

"Elizabeth II, Queen" BOAT,
LINER, SHIP
milieu for ~ OCEAN

elk ANIMAL, DEER
~ **cousin** MOOSE

Elk RANGE

Ella
~ **contemporary** LENA
~ **specialty** SCAT

"elle"
what ~ means SHE

Elle MODEL

"Elle" MAG

"Elle et Lui"
~ **author** SAND

___-**Ellen** VERA

___ **Ellen Ewing** SUE

Eller AUNT

Ellery
colleague of ~ ERLE, REX

Ellie
~ **to J.R.** MAMA

Elliot CASS

"___ Elliot" DOC

Elliot, Cass
~ **sobriquet** MAMA

ellipse OVAL
~ **segment** ARC

ellipsis
~ **component** DOT

ellipsoid OVAL

elliptical OVAL, OVATE, TERSE

elm TREE

Elm
~ **and others** STS

Elm City
~ **collegian** ELI

Elmer RICE
~ **mate** ELSIE
~ **to Bugs** DOC

"Elmer Gantry"
~ **author** LEWIS

Elmer's ___ GLUE

"Elmer's ___" TUNE

"Elmer the ___" GREAT

"Elmer the Great"
~ **director** LEROY

El Misti
~ **locale** ANDES, PERU

Elmo SAINT
~ **on "Eek the Cat"** ELK
~ **street** SESAME

elocutionist ORATOR

elocutionize READ

elongated LONG
~ **shape** OVAL
~ **swimmer** EEL

elongator STILT

elope FLEE

eloper
~ **of rhyme** DISH

eloquent
wax ~ ORATE

Elroy
~ **pet** ASTRO

Elroy "Crazy ___" Hirsch LEGS

els RRS

Els ERNIE

Elsa
~ **dad** LION
~ **ear-splitter** ROAR

El Salvador
see Spanish

"Elsa's Dream" ARIA

else
apart from anything
~ PERSE
before anything ~ FIRST
everything ~ REST
say something ~ ADD
something ~ NEAT, OTHER

elsewhere AWAY, OUT
direct ~ REFER

Elsie COW
~ **bull** ELMER
comment from ~ LOW, MOO

elucidate CLEAR, RAVEL

elude AVOID, EVADE, LOSE, SHUN, SLIP
~ **capture** HIDE

elusive AERIAL, EELY
~ **one** EEL

elutriate CLEAN

elver
grown-up ~ EEL

Elvis IDOL
~ **daughter** LISA
~ **recording** OLDIE
like ~' shoes SUEDE

Elvis ___ Presley ARON

"Elvis: That's the Way ___" ITIS

Ely ISLE, RON

Elysium EDEN

Elytis, Odysseus POET
see also poet

em
~ **followers** ENS
~ **preceders** ELS

"___ 'em!" SIC

Em
~ **to Dorothy** AUNT

emaciated LANK, LEAN

E-mail
~ **address ending** ORG
~ **address part** DOT
~ **command** SEND
~ **message, maybe** MEMO

emanate ARISE, COME, EMERGE, EMIT, ISSUE, OOZE, RISE, SHED, STEM, STREAM

emanation AROMA, AURA, BEAM, RAY

emancipated FREE

"___ 'em and weep!" READ

embankment LEVEE

embargo BAN

embark ENTER, LEAVE, SHIP, START
~ **on a voyage** SAIL

embarrass ABASH, ROAST, SHAME, SNUB

embarrassed
visibly ~ RED

embarrassing MESSY
~ **outbreak** SCENE

embarrassment SHAME

embassy
~ **personnel** AIDE

embattle BESET

Embden GOOSE

embed PLANT, SET

embedded
firmly ~ INSET

embedment
Hollywood Boulevard ~ STAR

embellish ADORN, BEAD, LIE, TRIM

embellishment CREST, LACE, NOTE, TRIM
add ~ ADORN
letter ~ SERIF

ember ASH

embers
~ **do it** GLOW
~ **eventually** ASHES
glowing, as ~ RED

embezzle ROB, STEAL, TAKE

embitter ANGER, SOUR

emblazon ADORN, TRIM

emblem CREST, SEAL, SIGN, TOKEN, TOTEM

embodied ALIVE

embodiment SOUL
~ **of clout** RUTH
~ **of grace** SWAN

embolden ABET, SPUR

embonpoint BIG, LARGE, OBESE

emboss STAMP

embossing
~ **tool** SEAL

embouchure LIP

embrace ADMIT, ADOPT, CARESS, CLASP, GRASP, HOLD, LOVE, PRESS, TAKE

"___ Embrace" LAST

"Embraceable ___" YOU

embrocate OIL

embrocation BALM

embroider ADORN, COLOR, LIE, SEW

embrown TAN

embryo GERM, SEED

$E = mc^2$
part of ~ MASS

emcee HOST
~ **line** INTRO
~ **platform** DAIS

"___ 'em, cowboy!" RIDE

Emden
see German

emend ALTER, AMEND, EDIT

emerald COLOR, GEM
ersatz ~ PASTE

Emerald ___ CITY, ISLE

Emerald City
~ **visitor** LION, TOTO

Emerald Isle EIRE, ERIN
from the ~ IRISH

emerge ARISE, ISSUE, LOOM, OCCUR, PEER, RISE, START
~ **victorious** WIN

emerge (from) COME

emergency
~ **CB channel** NINE
~ **road service org.** AAA
~ **signal** SOS
~ **vehicle sound** SIREN

emeritus TITLE
~ **(abbr.)** RET

Emerson ROY

Emerson, Ralph Waldo POET
~ **essay topic** ART
~ **work** ESSAY
see also poet

emery
~ **board** FILE
~ **wheel** HONE

emetic ALUM

EMF
~ **unit** VOLT

"___ 'Em High" HANG

emigrant ALIEN

emigrate LEAVE, MOVE, TREK

emigration TREK

emigré
~ **of a sort** EXILE

Émile
see French

Emilia
~ **husband** IAGO

Emily POST
~ **to Charlotte** SIS

eminence NOTE, PEAK, RANK, RISE, TITLE
  rocky ~ TOR

___ eminence GRAY

eminent BIG, GREAT, NOTED

emir ARAB

emirate
  ~ resident ARAB

emissary AGENT

emissions
  ~ watchdog EPA

emit CAST, ERUPT, ISSUE, SEND, SHED, SPEW
  ~ continuously POUR

EMK SEN
  ~ nickname TED

Emma PEEL
  ~ portrayer DIANA
  ~ successor on "The Avengers" TARA

emmet ANT

Emmy AWARD

emollient ALOE, BALM, CREAM
  ~ form CREAM

emolument FEE, PAY

Emory University
  ~ city ATLANTA

emote ACT, REACT

emoter HAM

emotion
  bigot's ~ HATE
  blusher's ~, perhaps SHAME
  burst of ~ SPASM
  feign ~ EMOTE
  Grand Canyon ~ AWE
  negative ~ HATE
  show ~ REACT
  strong ~ ANGER, FEAR, HATE, IRE, LOVE
  see also feeling

emotional
  ~ bond CORD
  ~ event DRAMA
  ~ intensity ARDOR
  ~ outburst CRY, SCENE
  ~ throe PANG
  ~ upheaval SPASM
  very ~ AGOG

empath
  ~ skill ESP

empathize BLEED

empathy
  ~ in action TACT
  have ~ CARE
  have ~ with RELATE
  lacking ~ HARD

"Empedocles on ___" ETNA

emperor LORD, MALE, TSAR
  Brazil's first ~ PEDRO
  infamous ~ NERO
  palindromic ~ OTTO
  Roman ~ CAESAR, NERO

Russian ~ TSAR

emperor ___ MOTH

"___ Emperor, The" LAST

emphasis STRESS

emphasize ASSERT, STRESS

emphatic LOUD
  ~ turndown NEVER

empire LAND, REALM
  ~ founder INCA
  former ~ USSR

___ Empire ROMAN

Empire Builder TRAIN

empiric FAKE

employ EXERT, HIRE, USE, WIELD

employed
  be ~ ACT, LABOR

___-employed SELF

employee HAND, HELP
  ~ reward RAISE
  airline ~ AGENT, PILOT
  circus ~ TAMER
  clinic ~ NURSE
  congressional ~ AIDE
  new ~ HIRE
  restaurant ~ CHEF, VALET
  theater ~ USHER
  TV diner ~ ALICE
  underpaid ~ PEON

employees HELP, LABOR

"Employees Entrance"
  ~ director RUTH

employer BOSS
  masseuse ~ SPA
  Praetorian's ~ CAESAR

employment LABOR, POST, USAGE, USE
  initiate ~ HIRE

empoison TAINT

emporium MART, STORE
  ~ event SALE
  video-game ~ ARCADE

empower ENABLE, LET

empowered ABLE

empress LADY

emptied CLEAR

emptiness GAP

empty BAIL, BARE, CLEAN, CLEAR, DRAW, FREE, IDLE, INANE, NULL, VAIN, VOID
  ~ gaze STARE
  ~ (into) RUN
  ~ (of) RID
  ~ of water BAIL
  ~ out TEEM
  ~ talk CANT, GAS, PAP, PRATE
  ~ vehicle weight TARE
  near ~ LOW

empty ___ NEST

empty-headed INANE

empyreal AERIAL

"___ 'em, Rover!" SIC

ems
  ~ followers ENS
  ~ preceders ELS

___ Ems, Germany BAD

emu BIRD
  ~ cousin RHEA
  ~ relative KIWI

emulate APE, ECHO

emulating ALA

emulator APER

emulous EAGER

___-'em-up SHOOT

en
  ~ preceders EMS

en ___ (all together) BLOC

en ___ (on the way) ROUTE

enable LET

enact MAKE, PASS, PLAY, STAGE

enacted LEGAL

enactment EDICT, LAW

enamel COAT, PAINT

enamelware TOLE

enamored
  be ~ of ADORE, LOVE

enate KIN

encapsulate SUM

Enceladus MOON

enchant LURE, TAKE

enchanted RAPT
  ~ forest inhabitant ELF
  be ~ FLIP

"Enchanted ___" APRIL

"___ Enchanted Evening" SOME

enchanting FAIR

enchantress SIREN

enchilada
  ~ filling CHILI
  ~ sauce SALSA
  the whole ~ ALL

___ enchilada BIG

"Encino Man"
  ~ actor SHORE

encircle BELT, CLASP, COIL, ORBIT, RING
  ~ to a poet ORB

encirclement SIEGE

encircling ABOUT

enclose CASE, HEM, PEN, WRAP

enclosed
  ~ patios ATRIA

enclosure AREA, CAGE, PALE, PEN, STALL
  barnyard ~ PEN
  cattle ~ YARD
  farm ~ STY

lagoon ~ ATOLL
zoo ~ CAGE

encomium HONOR

encompass BELT, SPAN

encompassed
  ~ by AMID, AMONG

encompassing ABOUT

encore AGAIN, ANEW, MORE
  give an ~
  performance RERUN
  request an ~ CLAP
  what ~ means AGAIN

"Encore!" AGAIN, MORE

encounter FACE, MEET, SEE, TASTE

encountered
  seldom ~ RARE

"___ Encounters of the Third Kind" CLOSE

encourage ABET, ASK, EGG, HELP, PROD, ROOT, SPUR, START
  ~ in evil ABET
  ~ strongly URGE

encouragement SMILE

encouraging ROSY
  ~ word GOOD, RAH, YEA, YES

encrust BAKE

encrypt CODE

encumber BIND, CLOG, LADE, LOAD

encumbered LADEN

encumbrance LIEN, ONUS, SNAG
  legal ~ LIEN

ency. REF

encyclopedia
  ~ group SET

encyclopedic LARGE

end AIM, ARREST, CEASE, CLOSE, DIE, DOOM, GOAL, HALT, LAPSE, NIB, PASS, REAR, STERN, STOP, STUB, TAG, TAIL
  ~ at ABUT
  ~ of a loaf HEEL
  ~ of a palindrome ELBA
  ~ of a series OMEGA
  ~ of the year EVE
  ~ (prefix) TEL
  bad ~ DOOM
  the unsharpened ~ ERASER

end ___ GAME, LINE, RUN, TABLE, USER, ZONE

end ___ high note ONA

___ end LOOSE, TAG, TAIL

___-end REAR, YEAR

___ End EAST, WEST

end-all
  be-all and ~ SUM

endanger RISK

endangered RARE
  ~ anthropoid ORANG

~ **layer** OZONE
~ **species' enemy** MAN

endangerment PERIL

"___ Endearing Young Charms" THOSE

endearment PAT
term of ~ ANGEL, DEAR, HON, LOVE, PET, SWEET

endeavor AIM, ASSAY, ESSAY, TRIAL, TRY

"Endeavour"
~ **org.** NASA

ended DONE, OVER, PAST
~ **to a poet** OER

___-ended OPEN

endemic LOCAL

___-ending NEVER

endive HERB

endless BIG, ETERNAL, LARGE

endlessly EVER

endo-
~ **opposite** ECTO

endocarp STONE

endodontist
~ **deg.** DDS

end of an ___, the ERA

end-of-scene
~ **direction** EXIT

end-of-semester
~ **event** EXAM, TEST

"End of the ___" ROAD

endorse ABET, ADOPT, HELP, INK, OKAY, SIGN, START

endorsement AMEN
letters of ~ OKS

endorses OKS

endorsing FOR, PRO

endow AWARD, BLESS, VEST
~ **as with talent** BLESS

endowment ASSET, AWARD
~ **beneficiary** HEIR
~ **recipient** DONEE

ends
~ **partner** ODDS
barely make ~ **meet** EKE
burn the candle at both ~ LABOR
odds and ~ REST
where ~ **meet** SEAM

___ ends LOOSE, SPLIT

___ ends meet MAKE

end table
~ **item** LAMP

endure ABIDE, BEAR, BIDE, LAST, LIVE, STAND, TAKE

enduring ETERNAL, OLD, SAME, SOLID

enduro RACE, TEST

"Endymion" POEM

ENE
~ **opposite** WSW

"___ en El Rancho Grande" ALLA

"Enemies, A ___ Story" LOVE

"Enemies, A Love Story"
~ **actress** OLIN

enemy FOE
~ **opposite** ALLY
~ **starter** ARCH
Allies' ~ AXIS
Arapaho ~ UTE
Bolshevik ~ TSAR
endangered species' ~ MAN
Iroquois ~ ERIE
Onondaga's ~ ERIE
pueblo ~ UTE
Seneca's ~ ERIE
soap's ~ DIRT
striker's ~ SCAB
the ~ THEM
see also foe

"Enemy Below, The"
~ **vessel** UBOAT

"___ Enemy Grows Older" MINE

"Enemy of the People, An"
~ **author** IBSEN

energetic ALIVE, CRISP, RACY, SPRY
~ **person** DOER

energize RESTORE, STIR

energizing TONIC

energy FIRE, LIFE, PEP, SNAP, VIM, ZAP
~ **cartel** OPEC
~ **choice** SOLAR
~ **meas.** BTU
~ **source** ATOM, SUN
burst of ~ SPASM
full of ~ ALIVE, GOGO
lose ~ SAG, TIRE
unit of food ~ CAL

___ energy SOLAR

enervate SAP, STRESS, TIRE

"___ Enfants Terribles" LES

enfant terrible BRAT

enfeeble SAP

enfold CLASP, PRESS

enforcement
~ **power** TEETH

eng.
~ **school** TECH

Eng. LANG
~ **course** LIT
~ **neighbor** IRE, SCOT
N. ~ **state** MASS

Eng. ___ LIT

engage BIND, DRAW, HIRE, MEET, MESH
~ **in** WAGE

~ **in a shouting match** SCRAP
~ **in histrionics** EMOTE
~ **in hostilities** WAR
~ **in mudslinging** SMEAR
~ **in slightly** DIP

engaged
~ **in** UPTO
become ~ MESH
one ~ **in (suffix)** EER

engage in ___ of wills ATEST

engagement DATE, TRYST
band ~ GIG

engender BREED, MAKE, PLANT, START

engine MOTOR
~ **additive** STP
~ **cover** HOOD
~ **housing** POD
~ **part** CAM, FAN
~ **sound** PURR, ROAR
race an ~ REV
rev the ~ RACE

___ engine FIRE, ION, JET, STEAM

engineer
~ **for short** TECH
American bridge ~ EADS

engineering
~ **project** DAM
~ **subj.** MATH
~ **univ.** MIT

___-engine plane TWIN

engird RING

England ISLE
~ **to America** ALLY
ctry. north of ~ SCOT
ctry. west of ~ EIRE, IRE

English ALEX
~ **assignment** ESSAY
~ **boys' school** ETON
~ **cathedral city** ELY
~ **composer** ARNE, ELGAR
~ **country festival** ALE
~ **county** KENT
~ **feast** ALE
~ **homework** ESSAY, THEME
~ **horn** REED
~ **network** BBC
~ **novelist** AMIS
~ **pianist** HESS
~ **queen** ANNE
~ **racetrack** ASCOT, EPSOM
~ **ritual** TEA
~ **river** AIRE, AVON, CAM, OUSE, TRENT
~ **scarf** ASCOT
~ **spa** BATH
see also British

English ___ HORN, LIT

English Channel
~ **feeder** ORNE, SEINE

English Derby
~ **locale** EPSOM

English horn
~ **cousin** OBOE, REED

Englishman
~ **exclamation** ISAY

"English Patient, The"
~ **award** OSCAR

___ English sheepdog OLD

engorge EAT, FEED, SATE

engrave CUT, ETCH

engraved
~ **gem** CAMEO
~ **pillar** STELE

engross AMUSE, ARREST, GRIP, HOLD, WRITE

engrossed DEEP, LOST, RAPT

engulf STEEP

enhance ADORN

enhancer
eye ~ LINER
flavor ~ HERB, SALT
reception ~ AERIAL
shoulder ~ PAD
sound ~ AMP

enigma POSER

enigmatic DEEP

"Enigma Variations"
~ **composer** ELGAR

Eniwetok ATOLL
~ **event** ATEST

enjoin BAR, BID, ORDER, PLEAD

enjoy BASK, DIG, LIKE, LOVE, SAVOR

enjoyable NICE

enjoyment BANG, PLAY, USE

enkindle FIRE

___ En-lai CHOU

enlarge ADD, FLARE, GROW
~ **a hole** REAM
~ **on** LIE
~ **upon** DRAG

enlargement
~ **maybe** INSET

enlighten CLEAR, OPEN

enlightened AWARE, SANE, WISE
be ~ KNOW

enlist ENTER

enlisted
~ **ones** GIS

enlisted ___ MAN

enlistee
~ **food** MESS

enliven AMUSE, AROUSE, FIRE

enlivening TONIC

en masse
feed ~ CATER

enmesh SNARE

enmity ANGER, HATE, SPITE

ennea-
   ~ preceder OCTO
   ~ successor DEC

ennead NINE
   one of a mythical ~ CLIO, ERATO

ennoble EXALT, HONOR, RAISE

Enoch
   ~ cousin ENOS

"Enoch ___" ARDEN

"Enoch Arden" POEM

enormity EVIL

enormous BIG, GIANT, LARGE, VAST

Enos
   ~ father SETH

enough DUE
   ~ and then some AMPLE
   ~ rope PLAY
   ~ scope ROOM
   barely ~ SCANT
   cooked ~ DONE
   give someone ~ rope LET
   hardly ~ BARE
   more than ~ AMPLE, GLUT, PLUS
   old ~ to know better ADULT

enounce STATE, TALK, UTTER

enplane LEAVE

enrage ANGER, IRE, RILE

enraged IRATE, MAD

enrapture LURE, SEND, TAKE

enrich ADORN, LARD

Enright RAY

Enright, Ray
   ~ film of 1934 DAMES

enrobed CLAD

enroll ENTER

en route
   ~ on a ship ASEA, ATSEA

ens
   ~ preceders EMS

ensconce HIDE

ensemble ATTIRE, BAND, DRESS, RIG, SUIT, TOTAL
   musical ~ OCTET, TRIO

enshrine ADORE

enshroud HIDE, SHADE, WRAP

ensign FLAG, RANK
   ~ asst. CPO
   ~ org. USN
   evil ~ IAGO

"Ensign Pulver"
   ~ actor IVES, SANDS

ensnare LURE, NAB, NET, TAKE, TRAP, WEB

ensue COME, ISSUE

ensuing AFTER, NEXT

ensure ICE

ENT
   part of ~ EAR, NOSE

entangle MAT, MESH, MIRE, RAVEL, SNARE

entanglement KNOT, NODE, WEB

Entebbe
   ~ action RAID

entendre
   double ~ PLAY, PUN

entente AXIS, PACT

enter COME
   ~ in a way TYPE
   ~ one's head OCCUR
   ~ the sweepstakes BET
   allow to ~ ADMIT

enterprise DEED, LABOR
   livestock ~ RANCH
   mom-and-pop ~ STORE

___ enterprise FREE

"Enterprise"
   ~ journey TREK
   ~ letters USS
   ~ officer DATA, SULU

"___ Enterprise" USS

enterprising EAGER

entertain AMUSE, FETE, PLEASE, TREAT

entertainer HOST
   medieval ~ BARD
   one-name ~ CHER

entertainment GAME, PLAY, TREAT
   like some ~ LIVE

"Entertainment Tonight"
   ~ cohost HART

"Enter the Dragon"
   ~ star LEE

enthrall HOLD, SEND, TAKE

enthralled AGOG, RAPT

enthuse RAVE, STIR

enthused EAGER, ELATED

enthusiasm ARDOR, ELAN, FIRE, HEAT, MANIA, PEP, VIM, ZEAL
   lack of ~ ENNUI

enthusiast FAN, NUT

enthusiastic AFIRE, AGOG, AVID, EAGER, GAME, HOT, KEEN, MAD, WARM
   ~ about INTO
   ~ cry RAH
   ~ exclamation MAN
   ~ follower FAN
   ~ sort TIGER
   hardly ~ TEPID
   overly ~ RABID

entice BAIT, DRAW, LURE, TRAP

enticement BAIT, LURE
   bakery ~ ODOR
   dining ~ AROMA

entire ALL, TOTAL
   ~ amount SUM

entirely ALL, CLEAN, CLEAR, OUT

entirety ALL, TOTAL

entitle NAME, TAG

entitled
   ~ to DUE
   be ~ to CLAIM, EARN, MERIT

entitlement
   ~ org. SSA

entity ENS, UNIT
   ~ starter NON

entourage TAIL, TRAIN

entrain LEAVE

entrance DOOR, GATE, GRIP, INLET
   ~ courts ATRIA
   ~ fee ANTE
   ~ requirement EXAM, TEST
   afford ~ to ADMIT
   curved ~ ARCH
   estate ~ GATE
   mine ~ ADIT
   thruway ~ RAMP

entranced RAPT

entrances
   open ~ ATRIA

entrancing SWEET

entrant
   Derby ~ HORSE
   Grand Prix ~ RACER

entrap GET, LURE, SNARE, WEB

entreat ASK, BEG, PLEAD, PRAY, SUE, URGE, WOO

entreaty CRY, PLEA, SUIT
   make an ~ ASK

entrechat LEAP

entrée DOOR
   ~ choice ROAST, SOLE
   ~ garnish CRESS
   ~ item MEAT
   ~ list MENU
   baked ~ HAM
   Boston ~ SCROD
   brunch ~ OMELET
   dinner ~ CHOP
   equine ~ HAY
   hearty ~ STEW

entrenched SET

entrepreneur DOER

entrust REFER

entry HALL, ITEM
   ~ fee ANTE
   ~ in red DEBT
   account ~ ITEM
   accounting ~ DEBIT, ITEM
   blue-book ~ ESSAY
   box-score ~ ATBAT
   chronicle ~ EVENT
   colliers' ~ ADIT
   forbid ~ to BAR
   job application ~ NAME
   ledger ~ ASSET, DEBIT, ITEM, LOSS

make an ~ NOTE
minus ~ DEBIT
parade ~ BAND
passport ~ STAMP, VISA
pasture ~ GATE
phrase-book ~ IDIOM
police blotter ~ ALIAS
profit and loss statement
   ~ ASSET
record-book ~ STAT
red ~ DEBIT
Sebring ~ CAR, RACER
statement ~ DEBIT
Winston Cup ~ CAR, RACER

entryway DOOR, GATE

entwine BIND, COIL, KNOT, LACE, MAT

enumerate ADD, CITE, LIST, NAME, TELL, TOTAL

enumeration LIST, POLL
   ~ shortener ETAL

enunciate SAY, TALK, UTTER

enunciated CLEAR, ORAL

envelop BATHE, CLASP, WEB, WRAP

envelope CASE
   ~ abbr. ATT, ATTN
   ~ attachment CLASP
   ~ part FLAP
   ~ requirement STAMP
   earth's ~ AIR, ETHER
   open an ~ SLIT

envenom TAINT

environ AREA, BELT

environment SPHERE, STATE
   ~ (prefix) ECO
   dream ~ SLEEP
   native ~ HOME
   sharks' ~ OCEAN, SEA
   star's ~ SPACE

environmental
   ~ org. EPA
   ~ problem SMOG
   ~ subj. ECOL

environs AREA, SITE

envisage DREAM

envision PLAN, SEE

envoy AGENT

envy SIN

enwrap DRAPE

enwreathe LOOP

enzyme
   ~ suffix ASE

Eocene EPOCH

eohippus HORSE

E.O.M.
   ~ item BILL

eon AGE

Eos
   lover of ~ ORION
   Roman ~ AURORA

eosin DYE

EPA
  ~ concern ECOL, SMOG

EPCOT
  ~ loc. FLA

Ephesus
  where ~ was IONIA

Ephron NORA

epic POEM, SAGA, TALE
  ~ reciter BARD
  Greek ~ ILIAD
  hero of a Hindu ~ RAMA
  Norse ~ EDDA, SAGA
  Scandinavian ~ EDDA
  Trojan War ~ ILIAD

___ epic (type of poem) BEAST

epicarp COAT, PEEL, RIND

epicenter MIDST

epicure EATER
  ~ morsel SNAIL

epidermis COAT, SKIN

epigram ADAGE, GNOME, MOT, SAW

epigrammatic TERSE

epilogue END, TAG
  musical ~ CODA

Epimetheus MOON

epinicion ODE

Epiphany
  ~ figures MAGI

epiphyte PLANT

episcopacy SEE

episcopate SEE

episode EVENT, FACT
  carefree ~ LARK
  histrionic ~ SCENE
  romantic ~ AMOUR

epistle
  ~ apostle PAUL

epitaph
  ~ starter HERE

epithalamion POEM

epithet LABEL, NAME, OATH, TAG
  mild ~ EGAD

epitome IDEAL

E pluribus unum LATIN

epoch AGE, DAY, ERA, TIME
  of an ~ ERAL

epode POEM

___ époque BELLE

epoxy DOPE, GLUE, RESIN

Epps OMAR

epsilon
  two after ~ ETA

Epsom SPA

Epsom ___ SALTS

Epstein ROB

equable EVEN

equal ALIKE, EVEN, LIKE, PEER, SAME
  ~ footing PAR
  ~ portion HALF
  ~ (prefix) ISO
  ~ score TIE
  ~ to the task ABLE
  without ~ ALONE

equal ___ SIGN

equality PAR

equalize EVEN

equally ALIKE, ASONE, BOTH

equanimity CALM, POISE

equator
  dist. from the ~ LAT

equerry MAN

equestrian RIDER
  ~ garb HABIT
  ~ implement CROP
  ~ sport POLO

equi-
  ~ cousin ISO

equilibrium PAR, POISE

equine HORSE, MARE, PACER
  ~ armor BARD
  ~ color GRAY, GREY
  ~ dad SIRE
  ~ entrée HAY
  ~ fodder OATS
  ~ mom MARE
  ~ restraint REIN
  ~ shade ROAN
  ~ youngster FOAL
  long-eared ~ ASS, BURRO
  loquacious ~ MRED
  ornery ~ ASS, BURRO, MULE
  small ~ ASS, BURRO
  spirited ~ STEED
  TV ~ MRED
  see also horse

equinox
  ~ mo. SEPT
  ~ sign ARIES

equip ARM, ENABLE, ENDOW, FIT, RIG

equipage TEAM

equipment GEAR, KIT, RIG
  audiophile's ~ STEREO
  backgammon ~ DICE
  concert hall ~ AMP
  fencer's ~ EPEE
  oil-drilling ~ RIG
  parrier's ~ EPEE
  roadie ~ AMP
  rocker's ~ AMP
  ski-resort ~ TBAR
  sound ~ STEREO
  Stowe ~ SKI

equipped ABLE, FIT, SET
  ~ with footwear SHOD
  ~ with tires SHOD

___ Equis DOS

equitable CLEAN, FAIR, HONEST

Equity
  ~ member ACTOR

equivalence PAR

equivalent ALIKE, LIKE, MATE, SAME
  ~ wd. SYN
  mile's ~ AMISS

equivocate EVADE, LIE

equivocator LIAR

equivoque PUN

Equus
  genus ~ member ASS, BURRO, HORSE, MULE

-er
  more than ~ EST

Er ELEM
  68 for ~ ATNO

ER
  ~ staffer EMT
  ~ supply SERA, SERUM
  ~ workers DRS, RNS

"ER"
  ~ command STAT
  ~ doc ROSS
  ~ roles DRS
  Greene's associate on ~ LEWIS

era AGE, DAY, EPOCH, TIME
  bygone ~ THEN

ERA STAT
  ~ proponent NOW

eradicate ERASE, ROOT

erase CLEAR, DELE, OMIT, UNDO, ZAP

Erato MUSE
  ~ sister CLIO

erect MAKE, RAISE, REAR, SETUP

"...ere I saw ___" ELBA

erelong ANON, SOON

eremite LONER

ergo THEN, THUS

Erhard
  ~ discipline EST

Eric IDLE, TILL

Erich SEGAL

Erich ___ Stroheim VON

Ericsson, Leif
  like ~ NORSE

Eric the ___ RED

Eric the Red
  like ~ NORSE

Erie CANAL, LAKE
  ~ st. PENN

Erie Canal
  "mule on the ~" SAL

Erikson ERIK

Erin GRAY
  ~ tongue ERSE

Eris
  brother of ~ ARES

ermine ANIMAL, FUR, STOAT

ern BIRD, EAGLE

"Ernani" OPERA

erne BIRD, EAGLE

Ernest SETON
  ~ nickname PAPA

Ernesto
  ~ nickname CHE
  see also Spanish

Ernie ELS, PYLE

Ernst & Young
  ~ staffer ACCT, CPA

erode ABRADE, EAT, GNAW, WASH, WEAR

eroded ATE

Eros AMOR, GOD, LOVE
  ~ to Aphrodite SON

erosion WEAR
  cause of beach ~ TIDE

err SIN, SLIP, TRIP

errand LABOR, TASK
  assign to an ~ SEND
  lord's ~ boy PAGE
  on an ~, maybe OUT

___ errand of mercy ONAN

"Errare humanum ___" EST

errata
  free of ~ CLEAN

erroneous BAD, FALSE

erroneously AMISS

error LAPSE, MISS, SIN, SLIP, TRIP
  ~ partner TRIAL
  ~ remover ERASER
  in ~ FALSE, OFF
  minor ~ LAPSE

ersatz FAKE, FALSE, SHAM
  ~ emerald PASTE
  ~ swing TIRE
  not ~ REAL

erstwhile AGO, PAST

Erté
  ~ forte ART
  ~ style DECO

eruct EMIT

erudite WISE

erudition LORE

erupt EMIT, FLARE, SPEW

erupter
  European ~ ETNA
  Martinique ~ PELEE

eruption BLAST, FIT, GALE, RASH, STORM
  ~ fallout ASH

Ervin SAM

Erwin STU

erythrocyte CELL

Es ELEM
   99 for ~ ATNO

Esau
   ~ father ISAAC
   ~ to Isaac SON

Esc KEY

escalade RISE, SCALE

escalate RAISE, RISE

escalator
   ~ alternative STEPS
   ~ essentially STAIR
   ~ feature TREAD
   ~ part AXLE, STEP

Escamillo
   see Spanish

escapade ANTIC, CAPER, SPREE,
   TEAR
   innocent ~ LARK

escape AVERT, AVOID, ELUDE,
   EVADE, EXIT, FLEE, LAM, OUT,
   RUN
   ~ button EJECT
   ~ clause OUT
   ~ comprehension ELUDE
   ~ from EVADE
   ~ in a way SEEP
   ~ notice PASS
   ~ one's memory ELUDE
   ~ route EXIT
   ~ vehicle POD
   make one's ~ ELUDE
   means of ~ OUT
   summer ~ CAMP

___ escape FIRE

"Escape"
   ~ director LEROY

"___ Escape, The" GREAT

escapee
   Biblical prison ~ PETER
   like an ~ LOOSE
   Sodom ~ LOT

**"Escape From the Planet of the
   ___"** APES

escargot SNAIL

escarpment CRAG

eschew AVOID, OMIT, SHUN
   ~ food FAST
   ~ humility CROW

eschewer
   fat ~ of rhyme SPRAT

Escobar
   see Spanish

Escoffier CHEF
   see also French

escort ATTEND, BEAR, BEAU, DATE,
   LEAD, SEE, SHOW, TAIL, TAKE,
   USHER
   ~ offering ARM
   ~ to a pew SEAT
   lady's ~ GENT

Escort AUTO, CAR

escritoire DESK
   ~ accessory PEN

escudo COIN

escutcheon
   ~ border ORLE
   ~ stain BLOT
   blot on the ~ TAINT

ESE
   ~ opposite WNW

___ e sempre ORA

ESG
   part of ~ ERLE

Eshkol LEVI
   ~ successor MEIR

eskers OSAR

Eskimo
   ~ home ALASKA, IGLOO
   ~ knife ULU
   ~ pole TOTEM
   ~ relative ALEUT
   ~ tongue ALEUT
   ~ vehicle SLED

Eskimo ___ DOG, PIE

ESL
   part of ~ ENG

Esmeralda
   ~ pet GOAT

esne SERF

esoteric DEEP

espalier TRAIN

espionage
   ~ org. CIA
   name in ~ HARI, MATA

esplanade MALL

ESPN
   league for ~ NBA

Esposito PHIL

espouse ADOPT, HOLD

espresso
   ~ place CAFE

___-esprit (witty one) BEL

espy SEE, SPOT

-esque
   ~ cousin INE, ISH

esquire MALE

Esquivel LAURA

ess
   ~ curve OGEE
   ~ follower TEE
   ~ preceders ARS

___ es Salaam DAR

essay AIM, ASSAY, PAPER, PROSE,
   TEST, THEME, TRACT, TRIAL, TRY

essayist
   ~ alias ELIA

"Essay on Man"
   ~ author POPE

"Essays of ___" ELIA

"Essays of Elia"
   ~ author LAMB

"esse"
   form of ~ ERAT, EST

Essen CITY
   ~ river RUHR
   see also German

essence AURA, BASIS, CORE, GIST,
   HEART, MEAT, ODOR, SOUL
   ~ of potpourri AROMA
   ~ of roses ATTAR

"Essence"
   ~ rival EBONY

Essene SECT

essential BASIC, BIG, KEY, MAIN,
   NEED
   ~ mineral IRON, ZINC
   ~ oil ATTAR
   ~ part CORE
   ~ point MEAT
   most ~ part CORE

essential ___ OIL

essentially PERSE

essentials ABCS

esses
   have trouble with ~ LISP

Essex AUTO, CAR, EARL, SHIRE

EST
   part of ~ STD

establish ARGUE, ATTEST, BASE,
   ERECT, MAKE, OPEN, PLANT,
   START
   ~ as law ENACT
   ~ deeply ROOT
   ~ oneself SETTLE, STAY

established SET
   get ~ SETTLE
   less ~ NEWER

establishment ELITE, INS, STORE
   roadside ~ INN, STAND

___ Estacado LLANO

estancia RANCH

estate ABODE, ACRES, HOME,
   LAND, MANOR, RANK
   ~ division ACRE
   ~ entrance GATE
   ~ measure ACRE
   ~ plus ASSET
   ~ staffer MAID
   country ~ MANOR
   medieval ~ MANOR
   real ~ LAND

___ estate REAL

"___ est celare artem" ARS

Esteban
   see Spanish

esteem ADORE, HONOR, LIKE
   gain ~ ENDEAR
   garner ~ RATE

___-esteem SELF

esteemed GREAT, NOTED
   highly ~ DEAR

Estefan, Gloria
   ~ home MIAMI

Estella
   ~ to Miss Havisham WARD

Esterhaus PHIL

Estes
   ~ running mate ADLAI

Esth
   ~ neighbor LETT

estimate ASSESS, CALL, DEEM,
   MAKE, PUT, RATE
   contractor's ~ BID

estimation ESTEEM

estimator
   ~ phrase ORSO

estival MILD

estivate SLEEP

estivation REST

Estonia
   ~ once SSR

estop BAR

estoppel BAR

___ est percipi ESSE

Estrada ERIK

Estrela
   Serra da ~ RANGE

estuary ARM, BAY, COVE, INLET,
   RIA, STREAM
   Amazon ~ PARA

esurient AVID

et
   ~ in English AND

et ___ ALIA, ALII

E.T. ALIEN
   ~ vehicle UFO
   TV ~ ALF

eta
   ~ follower THETA

ETA
   ~ dest. STA
   part of ~ ARR

et al.
   ~ relative ETC
   part of ~ ALIA

etc.
   ~ relative ETAL

etch DRAW

etched in ___ STONE

etcher
   ~ medium ACID

etching CUT

eternal EVER
   it springs ~ HOPE

Eternal
   the ~ LORD

"Eternal City, The" ROME

eternally EVER
~ to a poet EER

eternity AGES, EON

Ethan ALLEN

ethane GAS

Ethel
~ husband FRED
~ to John Jr. AUNT

ether AIR, GAS, SKY, SPACE

ethereal AERIAL, AIRY
~ instrument HARP

ethical HONEST, MORAL, PURE

Ethical Culture
~ originator ADLER

ethics CODE
with no sense of ~ AMORAL

ethics policing
~ org. ABA

Ethiopian
~ bishop ABBA
~ of opera AIDA
~ royal name HAILE
nomadic ~ AFAR

ethnarch RULER

ethnic
~ group RACE
~ prefix ITALO
~ (suffix) ESE

ethnobotany LORE

ethnocentric SMALL

ethos
without ~ AMORAL

ethyl GAS
~ acetate ESTER
~ ender ENE

Étienne
see French

etiolate FADE

etiquette
name in ~ AMY

"___ et lui" ELLE

Etna CONE
~ fallout ASH
~ output LAVA
emulate ~ SPEW

ETO
~ commander DDE
~ nickname IKE
part of ~ EUR

ETS
~ offering PSAT, SAT

"E.T. The ___-Terrestrial" EXTRA

"Et tu"
~ time IDES

Eu ELEM
63 for ~ ATNO

eucalyptus TREE
~ eater KOALA

Eucharist
~ table ALTAR

Eucharistic
~ rite MASS

euchre GAME

"Euclid Alone Has Looked on
Beauty Bare" POEM

Eugene DEBS
~ home OREGON
~ st. ORE

"Eugene ___" (1832 novel)
ARAM

"Eugene Onegin" OPERA
~ girl OLGA

Eulenspiegel TILL

eulogize ADORE, EXALT, HAIL,
LAUD, ORATE

eulogy HONOR

euphemize LIE

euphonium HORN

euphoria GLEE

euphoric ELATED

euphuism POSE

euphuistic ORNATE

Eur.
~ alliance NATO

Eurasian
~ bird TERN
~ range ALAI

Eurasia's ___ Mountains URAL

"Eureka!" AHA, HAH
cousin of ~ OHO

Euripides
~ drama MEDEA
~ play HELEN, ION, MEDEA
see also Greek

euro COIN

Euromoney ECU

Europa MOON
sister of ~ ASIA

Europe
~ boot ITALY
~ neighbor ASIA
do ~ TOUR
mountains between ~ and
Asia URALS
part of ~ IBERIA

European LETT
~ airline IBERIA, SAS
~ capital BERN, OSLO, PARIS,
RIGA, ROME
~ car FIAT
~ chain ALPS
~ coal region SAAR
~ country ITALY, SPAIN
~ ctry. ALB, DEN, ENG, GER,
IRE, ITAL, NOR, ROM
~ ctry., formerly USSR
~ erupter ETNA
~ flowering plant ARUM
~ high spot ALP

~ lang. GER, ITAL
~ language ERSE
~ mountain ALP
~ nation EIRE
~ nation, poetically ERIN
~ peak ALP
~ peninsula IBERIA, ITALY
~ republic EIRE
~ river EDER, ELBE, INN, ODER,
OISE
~ river valley SAAR
~ starter INDO
~ "yard" METER
north ~ LETT

___-European INDO

"Europeans, The"
~ director IVORY

Europe/Asia
~ border range URAL
~ divider URALS

Eustachian tube
~ site EAR

Euterpe MUSE
~ sister CLIO, ERATO
~ subj. MUS

Eva PERON

Eva ___ Saint MARIE

EVA
~ org. NASA

evacuate CLEAR, EGEST, EXIT,
LEAVE, MOVE, TEEM

evade AVOID, BEG, ELUDE, LOSE,
MISS, SHUN
~ the issue STALL
~ the seeker HIDE

evaluate ASSAY, ASSESS, RATE,
SET, TEST, TRY, VET
~ as a burglar CASE

evaluation TEST

Eva Marie ___ SAINT

"Evangeline" POEM

evangelist
~ command HEAL

Evans DALE

Evans, Edith DAME

Evans, Mary Ann
~ pseudonym ELIOT

Evans, Sir Arthur
~ excavation site CRETE

Evans, Walker
~ collaborator AGEE

evaporated DRY

evaporation
~ residue SALT

evasion LIE, TALE

eve.
~ preceder AFT

Eve ARDEN
~ domain EDEN
~ grandson ENOS

~ mate ADAM
~ son ABEL, CAIN
~ source RIB
~ temptation APPLE
~ youngest SETH

"___ Eve, The" LADY

"Eve Cost Adam Just One ___"
BONE

"Evelina"
~ composer ARLEN

Evelyn LEAR

even EASY, FLAT, PLANE
~ a little ANY
~ odds BET
~ once EVER
~ one ANY
~ so YET
~ the score AVENGE, PAY, TIE
~ the slightest ANY
get ~ AVENGE, PAY, REACT
make ~ PLANE
not ~ EROSE, ODD
not ~ once NEVER

evenhanded FAIR, HONEST

evening
~ affair SOIREE
~ clothes DRESS
~ hour NINE, SIX
~ in Italian SERA
~ in verse EEN
~ party BALL, ROUT
~ to a poet EEN
~ update NEWS
~ wrap STOLE
early ~ SEVEN

evening ___ DRESS, STAR

"Evening ___" SHADE

evening gown
~ material SATIN

"Evening Shade"
~ network CBS
~ st. ARK
Marilu Henner's role on
~ AVA

evening wear
~ fabric LAME

___ even keel ONAN

even-odds CLOSE

even-Steven
~ score TIE

event CASE, FACT, GALA
~ for a foxhound HUNT
Alamogordo ~ ATEST
athletic ~ GAME
baseball ~ HIT, HOMER
big ~ GALA
Bikini ~ ATEST, TEST
Breeder's Cup ~ RACE
bronco-riding ~ RODEO
bull-riding ~ RODEO
calf-roping ~ RODEO
Columbus Day ~ SALE
county ~ FAIR
department store ~ SALE
Easter ~ PARADE
emotional ~ DRAMA

__ event

end-of-semester ~ EXAM, TEST
Eniwetok ~ ATEST
figure skating ~ PAIRS
gym ~ PROM
Haymarket Square ~ RIOT
Le Mans ~ RACE
main ~ BOUT
Mardi Gras ~ PARADE
May ~, familiarly INDY
meet ~ RACE
men-only ~ STAG
merchandising ~ SALE
Olympics ~ DASH, RELAY
one-on-one ~ DUEL
pentathlon ~ EPEE
Presidents' Day ~ SALE
Red Tag ~ SALE
ring ~ BOUT
Saratoga ~ RACE
sporting ~ MEET
spring ~ THAW
taxing ~ AUDIT
track ~ DASH, RELAY
Triple Crown ~ RACE

__ event MEDIA

"__ Event, The" MAIN

even-tempered CALM, COOL, SEDATE

events
course of ~ TIDE
current ~ NEWS
tide of ~ LIFE

eventual LAST

eventuate ARRIVE, ENSUE, OCCUR

"Eve of St. __, The" AGNES

"Eve of St. Agnes, The" POEM

ever ONCE
~ and anon OFT, OFTEN
~ partner ANON
~ since ASOF
~ so much ALOT
not ~, to a poet NEER

Everage DAME, EDNA

ever and __ AGAIN, ANON

Everest
~ locale NEPAL
~ place ASIA

Everett CHAD

Everglades
~ inhabitant EGRET, IBIS
~ locale FLA

evergreen FIR, PINE, PLANT, TREE
~ shrub ERICA

Evergreen
~ St. WASH

everlasting ETERNAL

Everly Brothers DUET, DUO
one of the ~ DON, PHIL

"__ Ever Need Is You" ALLI

every ALL, EACH, PER
~ which way MESSY
each and ~ ALL

hanging on ~ word RAPT
have ~ indication of SEEM
make ~ moment count LIVE

every __ (completely) BIT

every __ and then NOW

"Every __ a Holiday" DAYS

"Every __ for Himself and God Against All" MAN

"Every __ winner!" ONEA

everybody ALL
~ opposite NOONE

"Everybody __ a Dream" HAS

"Everybody __ It" DOES

"Everybody Hurts"
~ band REM

"Everybody Loves You __" NOW

"Everybody Ought to Have a __" MAID

"Everybody's __-American" ALL

"Every Breath You Take"
~ singer STING

everyday USUAL
~ language PROSE
not ~ RARE

every now and __ THEN

everyone ALL

"Everyone Says I Love You"
~ actor ALDA
~ director ALLEN

every so __ OFTEN

everything ALL
~ else REST
~ in Spanish TODO
take ~ HOG

"Everything's Coming Up __" ROSES

everywhere
~ (prefix) OMNI
look ~ COMB

Evian SPA
see also French

evict BOOT, EJECT, OUST

evictee
paradise ~ ADAM, EVE

evidence SIGN, TRACE
court ~, sometimes DNA
creditor's ~ IOU
give ~ ATTEST
minimal ~ SHRED
trial ~ DNA
turn state's ~ SING

evident CLEAR, OPEN, OVERT

__-evident SELF

evil BAD, BANE, CRUEL, HARM, ILL, MEAN, SIN, SPITE, VILE
~ ensign IAGO
~ incarnate SATAN
~ in French MAL
~ look LEER
~ one OGRE

~ personified SATAN
~ spirit DEMON
encourage in ~ ABET

evil __ EYE

evildoer SATAN

evildoing SIN

"Evil Empire"
~ letters USSR

evil-minded BASE, MEAN

"...evil that __ do..." MEN

"Evil Woman"
~ band ELO

evince ARGUE, SHOW

Evita PERON
~ ctry. ARG

"Evita"
~ role CHE
~ subject PERON
Antonio, in ~ CHE

evoke AROUSE, EDUCE
~ affection ENDEAR
~ laughter AMUSE

evoker
groan ~, maybe PUN

evolutionary
one rung on the ~ ladder APE

evolve COME, RIPEN

ewe SHE
~ baby LAMB
~ homophone YOU
~ mate RAM
~ milieu LEA
~ sound BAA, MAA

Ewell TOM

ewer
use a ~ POUR

Ewing
~ matriarch ELLIE

Ewing, J.R.
~ concern OIL

Ewing, Patrick
~ org. NBA

Ewings
one of the ~ ELLIE, PAM

Ewok ALIEN

ex __ facto POST

"Ex-__ Bradford, The" MRS

exact ASSESS, CLAIM, LAY, TRUE
~ duplicate TWIN
~ punishment FINE
~ retribution AVENGE

exacta BET

exacting HARD, STERN

exaction TOLL

exactitude RIGOR

exactly FLAT, PAT, YES
not ~ ABOUT

exaggerate BRAG, COLOR, RANT

exaggerated TALL

exaggeration HYPE, LIE, TALE
comic ~ CAMP

exaggerator
~ suffix EST

exalt ADORE, BLESS, HAIL, HONOR, LAUD, RAISE

exalted ELATED, GREAT, RAPT

exam
~ base TEXT
~ choice FALSE, TRUE
~ format ESSAY
H.S. ~ PSAT, SAT
kind of ~ ORAL
long-answer ~ ESSAY
prepare for an ~ CRAM
take an ~ SIT

__ exam ORAL

examination TEST
~ of accounts AUDIT

examine ASK, ASSAY, AUDIT, EYE, SEE, SIFT, TRY
~ a palm READ
~ closely SCAN, SIFT, SPY
~ point by point PORE

examinee
~ F ANS
~ T ANS

examiner
future ~ SEER

example CASE, IDEAL, NOUN
for ~ SAY
imitable ~ MODEL
shining ~ HERO, IDEAL

__ example ASAN, FOR

exasperate FRET, IRE, IRK, PAIN, PEEVE, RILE, UPSET

Excalibur STEEL

excavate DIG

excavation DIG, HOLE, MINE, PIT

exceed BEAT, CAP, PASS, TOP
~ the limit SPEED

exceeding ABOVE, OVER

excel BEAT, CAP, LEAD, SHINE
~ as on an exam ACE

excellence MERIT
standard of ~ PAR

__ excellence PAR

Excellency TITLE

excellent ACE, AOK, AONE, BAD, BEST, COOL, FINE, GOOD, IDEAL, MEAN, MINT, NEAT, RARE, TOPS
~ player ACE
~ to some BAD
in ~ condition HALE

"excellent adventure"
~ participant BILL, TED

"excellent instrument"
John Adams' ~ PEN

Excelsior Springs SPA

except OMIT, ONLY, SAVE, SKIP

excepting BAR, LESS

exception
  without ~ ALL

___ exception TAKE

exceptional ODD, RARE

exceptionally EXTRA

excerpt CITE, CUT, PART
  film ~ SCENE
  movie ~ CLIP

excess FAT, GLUT
  budgetary ~ FAT
  indulge to ~ SATE
  in ~ of ABOVE, PAST
  media ~ HYPE
  swellhead's ~ EGO
  wild ~ ORGY

excessive BIG, DEAR, LARGE, ULTRA
  ~ imbiber SOT
  ~ use ABUSE

excessively TOO

exchange DEAL, SWAP, TRADE
  ~ for money SELL
  ~ ideas TALK
  ~ medium COIN
  ~ of blows BOUT
  ~ pleasantries CHAT
  ~ words on the Web CHAT
  bill of ~ NOTE
  give in ~ PAY

___ exchange ION

"___ Exchange" KEY

excise DELE, EDIT

excitable TESTY

excite ABET, AROUSE, FIRE, MOVE, ROUSE, SEND, SPUR, STIR
  ~ in slang GRAB

excited AFIRE, AGOG, ASTIR, EAGER, ELATED, HOT, MAD
  ~ about INTO
  ~ in slang APE
  get ~ FLIP
  highly ~ AGOG

excitement ADO, ARDOR, BANG, HEAT
  excessive ~ MANIA
  full of ~ AGOG
  seek ~ GAD

exciting ALIVE, RACY
  not ~ BLAH, TAME

exclaim CRY, YELL

exclamation
  ~ of annoyance TSK
  ~ of disappointment RATS
  ~ of pleasure WOW
  ~ of surprise AHA
  Brit's ~ ISAY
  derisive ~ FIE
  disbeliever's ~ PAH
  doubter's ~ HAH
  fumbler's ~ OOPS

Irish ~ AROO
  old-fashioned ~ PSHAW
  old-time ~ EGAD
  palindromic ~ AHA, HAH, OHO, WOW
  surprised ~ HELLO
  teen's ~ RAD

exclamations
  ~ of surprise AHS, OHS

exclude BAN, BAR, OMIT, OUST, SNUB, TABOO, TABU

excluding BAR
  ~ none ALL

exclusion TABOO, TABU

exclusive ELITE, SCOOP, SOLE
  ~ group ELECT, ELITE

exclusively ALL, ALONE, ONLY

excommunicate BAN, OUST

excommunication BAN

excoriate LACE, LASH, PARE, PEEL

excrescence NODE

excrete EGEST, EJECT

excruciating ACUTE, BAD

exculpate CLEAR

exculpatory
  ~ story ALIBI

excursion HIKE, RIDE, SPIN, TOUR, TRIP
  astronaut's ~ EVA

___ excursion module LUNAR

excuse ALIBI, CLEAR, FREE, OUT, PLEA, REMIT
  like a poor ~ LAME
  sick-day ~ FLU

"Excuse me!" AHEM, OOPS, SAY

excusez-___ MOI

___ exeat BENE

exec CEO
  ~ car LIMO
  ~ deg. MBA
  ~ helper STENO
  account ~ REP
  corp. ~ PRES

___ exec. ACCT

execrable BAD, BASE, EVIL, MEAN, POOR, VILE

execrate ABHOR

execute ACT, OBEY
  ~ a camel SKATE

executed DONE
  deftly ~ CLEAN

executer DOER

executes DOES

executive BOSS
  ~ extra PERK
  top ~ BARON

executives
  what ~ have SAYSO

"Executive Suite"
  ~ director WISE

executor AGENT, HEIR
  ~ responsibility ESTATE

exegesis NOTE

exemplar IDEAL, MODEL

exemplary GOOD, IDEAL, MODEL

exemplify CITE, SHOW

exempt FREE

exempted FREE

exercise EXERT, HAVE, TRAIN, USE, WIELD
  ~ accessory MAT
  ~ aftermath ACHE
  ~ as authority WIELD
  ~ center SPA
  ~ judgment DEEM
  ~ judicial power RULE
  ~ one's franchise ELECT, POLL, VOTE
  ~ place SPA
  ~ power WIELD
  ~ system YOGA
  cross-legged ~ YOGA
  deep-knee ~ BEND
  floor ~ EVENT
  meditation ~ YOGA
  piano ~ ETUDE
  written ~ THEME

exert USE
  ~ as power WIELD
  ~ oneself ASSAY, LABOR, STIR
  ~ one's will OPT
  ~ pressure LEAN

exertion TOIL

Exeter
  see British, English

exfoliate PEEL

ex-GI VET

exhalation STEAM

exhaust BLEED, BORE, CLEAR, GAS, JADE, SAP, SPEND, STRESS, TIRE, WEAR

exhaust ___ FAN, PIPE

exhausted ALLIN, BEAT, DONE, LIMP, POOR, SHOT, SPENT, TIRED

exhausting HARD
  ~ march SLOG

exhaustive BIG, LARGE, TOTAL

exhibit AIR, ARGUE, PARADE, SHOW
  MOMA ~ OPART
  on ~ OPEN
  Prado ~ ARTE

exhibition FAIR, SHOW
  ~ hall SALON
  annual ~ FAIR

exhilarate AMUSE, ELATE, MOVE, RESTORE, SEND, STIR

exhilarated ELATED

exhilaration GLEE, LIFE

exhort EGG, IMPEL, PRESS, PROD, URGE, WARN

exhortation
  host's ~ EAT
  judge's ~ ORDER

exigency NEED, PRESS, WANT

exigent DIRE

exiguous POOR, SMALL, SPARSE

exile BAN, EJECT, OUST
  ~ site ELBA
  fictional ~ NOLAN

exist ARE, LAST, LIVE
  ~ ender ENCE, ENT
  does not ~ ISNT
  do not ~ ARENT

existed BEEN, WAS, WERE

existence LIFE
  ~ in French VIE
  ~ in Latin ESSE
  come into ~ ARISE, EMERGE, LIVE
  in ~ ABOUT, ALIVE

existent ALIVE, REAL

existentialist
  ~ playwright GENET
  French ~ GIDE

existing ALIVE
  always ~ ETERNAL

exit DOOR, GATE, LEAVE, MOVE, SPLIT
  ~ quickly FLEE
  airport ~ GATE
  colliery ~ ADIT
  fast ~ LAM
  heart ~ AORTA
  make a quick ~ FLEE, HIE, RUN
  mine ~ ADIT

exit ___ POLL

exit ramp
  ~ word SLO

exits GOES

"Exit to ___" EDEN

exo-
  ~ opposite ENDO, ENTO

exodus TREK

Exodus
  ~ character AARON
  ~ idol CALF
  ~ leader MOSES
  ~ locale SINAI
  feast of the ~ SEDER

"Exodus"
  ~ author URIS
  ~ character ARI

exonerate CLEAR, FREE

exonerated CLEAR

exorbitant DEAR, STEEP

exorcism
  ~ target DEMON

exorcist
~ **adversary** DEMON

"Exorcist, The"
~ **role** REGAN

exordium ONSET

exoteric CLEAR

exotic ALIEN, ODD
~ **ender** ISM
~ **fish** TETRA

expand FLARE, GROW
~ **(abbr.)** ENL
~ **in the pan** RISE

expanse AREA, TRACT
~ **of land** ACRES, TRACT
great ~ OCEAN
land ~ AREA
rainless ~ DESERT
sandy ~ SAHARA
vast ~ OCEAN, SEA
watery ~ OCEAN, SEA
wide ~ ACRES

expansion RISE
business ~ BOOM

expansive BIG, LARGE, VAST, WIDE

expatriate EJECT, EXILE

expatriation TREK

expect ASK, AWAIT, HOPE, MEAN

expectant AGOG
~ **dad, perhaps** PACER
eagerly ~ AGOG

expectation HOPE

"___ Expectations" GREAT

expected DUE, USUAL
~ **result** NORM

expecting
be ~ AWAIT

expediency
with ~ APACE

expedient PAT

expedite AID, EASE, SPEED

expediter
return-mail ~ SASE

expedition TOUR, TREK, TRIP

expeditious FLEET, RAPID

expeditiously APACE, FAST, SOON

expeditiousness HASTE

expel EGEST, EJECT, ERUPT, EXILE, OUST

expend EXERT, PAY, USE

expenditure COST
monthly ~ RENT

expenditures
list of ~ BILL

expense COST, FEE
bear the ~ TREAT
incidental ~ TIP
office ~ RENT
overhead ~ RENT

___ expense (free) ATNO

expensive DEAR, RICH, STEEP
not as ~ LESS

experience FEEL, HAVE, KNOW, PAST, SEE, TASTE
~ **directly** KNOW
~ **REMs** SLEEP
boring ~ DRAG
gain ~ LEARN

experienced ABLE, OLD
~ **hand** VET
~ **seaman** SALT
less ~ NEWER
not ~ NAIVE, RAW

experiment TEST, TRY
~ **room** LAB
~ **with** TRY
nuclear ~ ATEST

experimental NEW, PILOT, TRIAL

experimentation TRIAL

expert ABLE, ACE, ADEPT, DAB, GOOD, GURU, PRO
~ **ender** ISE
~ **in England** DAB
harbor ~ PILOT

expertise ART, SPHERE
field of ~ AREA

expertness EASE

experts
group of ~ PANEL

expiate ATONE

expiation
make ~ ATONE

expiration END
avoid ~ RENEW

expire LAPSE

expired OUT

explain SHOW, TELL
~ **further** ADD

explanation ALIBI, CAUSE
riddle ~ KEY

___-explanatory SELF

expletive DRAT, EGAD, OATH, PSHAW
Dickensian ~ BAH
mild ~ DRAT, EGAD, PSHAW
parson's ~ AMEN
quaint ~ EGAD

explicit CLEAR, HONEST, OVERT, TOTAL

explode BANG, BLAST, ERUPT, POP, RAGE, RANT, RAVE

exploding
~ **star** NOVA

exploit ABUSE, ACT, DEED, FEAT, GEST, GESTE, USE
daring ~ GEST, GESTE
noble ~ DEED

exploitable NAIVE

exploitation ABUSE, USE

exploits
tale of heroic ~ SAGA

exploratory TRIAL

explore ROAM, ROVE, SEEK, SPY

explorer
~ **need** MAP
~ **objective** TRADE
19th-century Arctic ~ RAE
Arctic ~ ROSS
Italian ~ POLO
polar ~ SCOTT
tenth-century ~ ERIC

Explorer
~ **org.** BSA

explorers
ancient ~ NORSE

exploring
go ~ ROAM

explosion BLAST, BOOM, SHOT, STORM
outlawed ~ ATEST

explosive MINE, TNT
~ **sound** BANG, BLAST, BOOM
hidden ~ MINE

expo FAIR

Expos NINE, TEAM
~ **1990s manager** ALOU

Expo '70
~ **site** OSAKA

expose AIR, BARE, LEAK, SHOW, STRIP
~ **to a poet** OPE
~ **to the atmosphere** AERATE

exposed BALD, BARE, CLEAR, NUDE, OPEN, OUT

exposition SHOW

expostulate ARGUE, SAY

exposure RISK
~ **measure** RAD

___ exposure photo TIME

expound ORATE

express ASSERT, AVER, EMIT, FAST, PUT, RAPID, SAY, SHOW, STATE, TRAIN, UTTER
~ **alternative** LOCAL
~ **anger** SNARL
~ **a view** OPINE
~ **contempt** HISS, POOH, SNORT
~ **contentment** AAH
~ **disapproval** HOOT
~ **one's opinion** TALK
~ **one's preference** VOTE
~ **satisfaction** AAH
~ **shock** GAPE, GASP
~ **surprise** AAH
~ **vocally** UTTER
not ~ LOCAL

___ Express ORIENT

express checkout
~ **unit** ITEM

expressed ORAL

expression FACE, MIEN, TERM
pouting ~ MOUE

___-expression SELF

expressions
~ **of pleasure** AHS, OOHS

expressway BELT, PIKE, ROAD, ROUTE

expropriate GRAB, STEAL, TAKE

expulsion EXILE

expunge ANNUL, CLEAR, DELE, EDIT, ERASE, OMIT
don't ~ STET

expurgate CLEAN, CLEAR, DELE, EDIT, ERASE, LOP

exquisite ACUTE, BEAU, DUDE, FINE

ex-senior ALUM, GRAD

exsiccate DRY

ext.
opposite of ~ INT

extant ALIVE, LIVE
remain ~ ARE

extemporaneous ADLIB

extemporaneously ADLIB

extempore ADLIB

extemporize ADLIB

extend ADD, GROW, PAD
~ **across** SPAN
~ **a helping hand** AID
~ **a lease** RELET
~ **a subscription** RENEW
~ **credit** LEND
~ **in a way** RENEW

extended LONG
not ~ TERSE

extender
height ~ STILT

extension ARM, PHONE, SPAN
~ **cord** WIRE
architectural ~ ELL
collar ~ LAPEL
hilum ~ ARIL
home ~ ELL
table ~ LEAF
upward ~ RISE
wrist ~ HAND

extensive AMPLE, BIG, DEEP, GREAT, LARGE, WIDE

extent AREA, RANGE, SIZE
~ **of variation** RANGE
of great ~ VAST
to a greater ~ MORE
to a smaller ~ LESS
to some ~ ANY
to the greatest ~ MOST

extenuate THIN

exterior FACE, OUTER
~ **(prefix)** ECTO, EPI

exterminate END, RID, SLAY

exterminator
~ **target** ANT, PEST

external OUTER
~ **(prefix)** ECTO

externalize AIR

extinct OLD
~ **apteryx** MOA
~ **bird** DODO, MOA
~ **ratite** MOA

extinguish ANNUL, DAMP, END, ERASE

extinguished OUT

___ **extinguisher** FIRE

extirpate ERASE, RID, ROOT

extol ADORE, BLESS, EXALT, HAIL, HONOR, LAUD

extort BLEED

extra ADDED, ICING, MORE, NEW, OTHER, OVER, PLUS, SPARE
~ **inning** TENTH
~ **large** SIZE
~ **part** BIT
~ **poundage** FAT
~ **tire** SPARE
delivery ~ SETUP
executive's ~ PERK
give a little ~ ADD
hamburger ~ ONION
introduce something ~ ADD
margarita ~ SALT
mattress ~ PAD
omelet ~ ONION
put in something ~ ADD
uniform ~ SASH

extra ___ attraction ADDED

extra-___ hit BASE

___ **extra charge** ATNO

extract DRAW, EDUCE, ESSENCE, MINE, TAKE
~ **juice** REAM
~ **moisture from** BLOT
maple ~ SAP
pine ~ RESIN
rose ~ ATTAR

extraction KIN, RACE
~ **reminder** GAP

extraordinary ODD, RARE
not ~ USUAL

extraterrestrial ALIEN

extravagance WASTE

extravagant FREE, OUTRE
~ **advertising** HYPE
be ~ SPEND

extravaganza EVENT, GALA, PLAY
holiday ~ PARADE
mall ~ SALE
shopping ~ SPREE

extreme ACUTE, APEX, DIRE, END, FAR, GREAT, LAST, OUTRE, POLAR, ULTRA, UTTER
~ **concern** ALARM
~ **degree** NTH
~ **PR** HYPE
~ **(prefix)** ARCH
an ~ END
temperature ~ LOW

"Extreme"
~ **actor** DYER

extremely MOST, REAL, TOO
~ **(prefix)** ULTRA

"Extreme Prejudice"
~ **actor** NOLTE

extremist RABID, RAD

extremity EDGE, END, FOOT, HAND, NIB, PART, POLE, TAG, TAIL, TOE
axis ~ POLE
caudal ~ TAIL
iceberg ~ TIP
lobster ~ CLAW
pedal ~ TOE

extricate CLEAR, FREE

extrude EMIT

exuberance ARDOR, DASH, ELAN, GLEE, LIFE, PEP, ZEAL

exuberant GAY
~ **cry** YAHOO

exude BLEED, DRIP, EGEST, EJECT, EMIT, ISSUE, LEAK, OOZE, REEK, SEEP
~ **slowly** SEEP

exult CROW

exultant ELATED
~ **cry** AHA, OHO
be ~ PREEN

exultation GLEE

exuviate SHED

Exxon
~ **rival** SHELL
old name for ~ ESSO

"Exxon Valdez" OILER

Eydie
~ **husband** STEVE

eye HOLE, LEER, OGLE, OPTIC, ORB, ORGAN, SEE, STARE
~ **ailment** STY, STYE
~ **askance** LEER
~ **cover** LID
~ **drop** TEAR
~ **ender** BALL, CUP, LASH, LET, LINER, SHADE, SORE, SPOT, TOOTH
~ **enhancer** LINER
~ **irritant** MOTE
~ **lubricant** TEAR
~ **makeup** LINER
~ **nerve** OPTIC
~ **network** CBS
~ **opening** SLIT
~ **part** IRIS, LENS, UVEA
~ **pencil** LINER
~ **protector** LASH, LID
~ **sore** STY, STYE
~ **starter** SHUT
~ **suggestively** LEER
~ **the bull's eye** AIM
~ **to a poet** ORB
~ **tunic** UVEA
apple of one's ~ DEAR
black ~ TAINT
Brownie's ~ LENS
bull's ~ MIDST
catch someone's ~ DRAW
CBS ~ LOGO
give the ~ OGLE, STARE
have an ~ **to** AIM
hook and ~ CLASP
in the twinkling of an ~ ANON, SOON
it colors the ~ IRIS
it has an ~ STORM
keep an ~ **on** ATTEND, STARE, TAIL
like a needle's ~ SMALL
look straight in the ~ DARE
make a bull's ~ HIT
middle layer of the ~ UVEA
of the ~ OPTIC
private ~ TEC
with an ~ **out** ALERT

___ **eye** EVIL

eyeball ASSESS, ORB, STARE
~ **bender** OPART
meet eyeball to ~ DARE

eyebrow
~ **shape** ARC, ARCH
grammarian's ~ **raiser** AINT

___ **-eyed** CLEAR, DOE, EAGLE, MOON, SLOE, WIDE

"___-Eyed Jacks" ONE

eye-fooling
~ **pictures** OPART

eyeful LOAD
get an ~ SEE

eyeglass LENS

eyeglasses
~ **support** EAR

eyelash HAIR
within an ~ CLOSE

eyelashes
like some ~ FALSE

eyelid
~ **feature** LASH
~ **inflammation** STY, STYE

eyeliner
~ **site** LID

___ **eye movement** RAPID

eye of ___ (witch's item) NEWT

"Eye of the ___" NEEDLE

eyepiece LENS, OPTIC

eye-related OPTIC

eyes
close one's ~ **to** PASS
follow with one's ~ OGLE
keep one's ~ **peeled** SEE, STARE
lay ~ **on** ESPY, SEE
like some ~ EVIL
look at with calf's ~ OGLE
look at with sheep's ~ OGLE
make ~ LEER
make ~ **at** OGLE
pull the wool over someone's ~ LIE
throw dust in the ~ **of** DUPE
undress with the ~ LEER
with ~ **and ears open** WARY

eyes-___ ONLY

___ **eyes** MAKE, SNAKE

"___ Eyes" THESE

eyes-a-poppin' AGOG

"Eyes of ___ Mars, The" LAURA

___ **eyes on** LAY

___ **-eye steak** RIB

eyeteeth
give one's ~ **(for)** PANT

eye to eye
seeing ~ ATONE

eyewash TRASH
natural ~ TEAR

eyewitness SEER

"___ Eyre" JANE

eyrie NEST

E-Z
~ **formula** ABC

"EZ Streets"
~ **star** OLIN

1 F

.405
~ hectare ACRE

___ .45 COLT

4
game with ~ jokers CANASTA
Giant who wore ~ OTT
it's ~ hrs. behind
Greenwich EDT

"4 ___ Texas" FOR

4-F
~ org. SSS

4-H
first H in ~ HEAD

4-pointer
Scrabble ~ VEE

5
it's ~ hrs. behind
Greenwich CDT, EST

5%
~ of Europe IBERIA

5K RACE

5-pointer
Scrabble ~ KAY

5.5
~ yards ROD

14
~ pounds STONE

14-83
channels ~ UHF

15th
~ st. KEN
~ sometimes IDES

"40 ___ and a Mule" ACRES

40th
~ st. SDAK

42nd
~ st. WASH

43rd
~ st. IDA
~ state IDAHO

45 DISC, RPM

45th
~ state UTAH

"48 ___" HRS

"48 Hrs."
~ actor NOLTE

49ers ELEVEN, TEAM
~ org. NFL

49th
~ st. ALAS
~ state ALASKA

50
~ percent HALF
atomic number ~ TIN
change for a ~ TENS
one of ~ STATE

52
~ weeks YEAR
one of ~ CARD

54
~ in Rome LIV

"___ 54, Where Are You?" CAR

55
~ letters MPH
~ perhaps LIMIT
exceed ~ mph SPEED

"55 ___ at Peking" DAYS

"55 Days at Peking"
~ director RAY
~ name AVA

"400"
~ name ASTOR

"400, The" ELITE

401(k)
~ alternative IRA

500
~ sheets REAM
one of Bartholomew
Cubbins' ~ HAT

"500"
~ race INDY

___ 500 INDY

1492
~ landfall HAITI
~ ship NINA

4047
~ square meters ACRE

4077
letters before ~ MASH

4840
~ square yards ACRE

5000
game to ~ points CANASTA

5280
~ feet MILE

43,560
~ square feet ACRE

f- ___ STOP

F CLEF, ELEM, KEY
~ on some tests FALSE
9 for ~ ATNO
avoid an ~ PASS

F ___ "foxtrot" ASIN

"F ___" TROOP

F. ___ Bailey LEE

F. ___ Fitzgerald SCOTT

fa NOTE
~ follower SOL

fa ___ LALA

fab NEAT

Fab
~ rival ERA

Fabergé
~ egg glaze ENAMEL
~ object EGG

Fab Four
~ flick HELP
~ name PAUL

Fabius Maximus ROMAN

fable TALE
~ author AESOP
~ ending MORAL
~ figure ANT
underachiever of ~ HARE

fabled NOTED
~ bird ROC
~ race loser HARE

"Fables in Slang"
~ author ADE

Fabray
~ familiarly NAN

fabric ABA, CREPE, FELT, LACE,
LAME, LAWN, LENO, LINEN,
LISLE, MOIRE, NYLON, REP,
SATIN, SERGE, SILK, TOILE
~ border HEM
~ feature PILE
~ fuzz LINT
~ measure ELL
~ pattern DOTS
~ texture WALE
~ worker DYER
bit of ~ SCRAP
blouse ~ SILK
camel-hair ~ ABA
Chinese ~ SILK
coarse ~ ABA
coat ~ SERGE
corded ~ REP
cotton ~ LAWN, TOILE
crinkly ~ CREPE
curtain ~ LACE, LENO
decorative ~ LACE
delicate ~ LACE
drip-dry ~ NYLON
evening-wear ~ LAME
fancy ~ LAME, SATIN, SILK
fedora ~ FELT
flax ~ LINEN
gauzy ~ LENO
glittery ~ LAME
goat-hair ~ ABA
gold ~ LAME
hose ~ LISLE
hosiery ~ LISLE
kimono ~ SILK
linen ~ TOILE
lustrous ~ LAME, SILK
napkin ~ LINEN
open ~ LACE, NET
open-weave ~ LENO
openwork ~ MESH
parachute ~ NYLON
Pharaoh's ~ LINEN
ribbed ~ CORD, REP
sheer ~ TOILE
shiny ~ LAME, SATIN
silver ~ LAME
stocking ~ LISLE
summer ~ LINEN
synthetic ~ NYLON
tie ~ SILK
transparent ~ TOILE
wedding-dress ~ SATIN
woolen ~ FELT
worsted ~ SERGE
woven ~ KNIT, LINEN, MESH
see also material

fabricate COIN, FAKE, MAKE, SPIN

fabricated FALSE, MADE

fabrication LIE, TALE

fabricator ACTOR, LIAR

fabulist AESOP, LIAR
   American ~ ADE

fabulous EPIC, RAD

Fabulous Fifties ERA

façade ACT

face MEET, PAVE, SEE
   ~ card HONOR
   ~ courageously DARE
   ~ down PRONE
   ~ downward PRONE
   ~ in Spanish CARA
   ~ shape OVAL
   ~ starter INTER
   ~ the day ARISE, RISE
   ~ the first batter START
   ~ the music PAY
   ~ the pitcher BAT
   ~ the target AIM
   ~ value COST
   clock ~ DIAL
   come face to ~ with MEET
   do an about ~ REACT
   fall on one's ~ LOSE
   false ~ MASK
   flower with a ~ PANSY
   fly in the ~ of DARE
   grotesque ~ MASK
   have a long ~ MOPE
   laugh in someone's ~ SNEER
   loss of ~ SHAME
   make a mean ~ SNEER
   part of the ~ CHIN, EYE, LIP, NOSE
   put on a happy ~ GRIN
   show one's ~ RISE
   slap in the ~ BARB, CUT, DIG, SNUB
   slap someone's ~ BEARD
   stuff one's ~ DINE, EAT
   wear a long ~ MOPE
   wry ~ MOUE

face ___ CARD, MASK

face-___ OFF

___ face LONG, LOSE

"___ face!" ABOUT

___-face ABOUT

"___ Face" ANGEL

"Face Behind the ___, The" MASK

___-faced BALD, MOON, RED, STONE, TWO

___-faced sandwich OPEN

"___-Faced Woman" TWO

"Face in the Crowd, A"
   ~ actress NEAL

"Face of ___" FIRE

"Face/Off"
   ~ director WOO
   ~ star ALLEN, CAGE

"Face of Fire"
   ~ director BAND

"___ Faces of Eve, The" THREE

facet PHASE, SIDE

"face that launched a thousand ships, The" HELEN

facetiousness WIT

face to face
   see ~ MEET

facial
   ~ feature CHIN, EYE, LIP, NOSE, SMILE
   ~ hair BEARD

facile ABLE, EASY, GLIB, PAT

facilitate AID, EASE, ENABLE, HELP, SPEED
   ~ a felony ABET

facilitation AID

facility ART, EASE

facing ACROSS, LINER
   ~ the pitcher ATBAT

facsimile IMAGE

fact
   accessory before the ~ AID
   numerical ~ STAT
   state as ~ AVER, AVOW

___ facta BENE

faction BLOC, CABAL, CAMP, CLAN, RING, SECT, SET, SIDE
   political ~ CADRE
   religious ~ SECT

factitious SHAM

___ facto IPSO

fact of ___ LIFE

factor AGENT
   chromosome ~ SEX
   deciding ~ KEY
   genetic ~ TRAIT
   heredity ~ GENE
   inheritance ~ GENE
   interest ~ RATE
   supporting ~ BASIS

factory MILL, PLANT, SHOP
   ~ group UNION
   ~ on a stream MILL
   coin ~ MINT
   honey ~ HIVE
   steel ~ MILL

factotum AIDE, HELP

facts DATA, DOPE, INFO
   absorb ~ LEARN
   fudge the ~ LIE
   square with the ~ HOLD

"Facts of ___, The" LIFE

"Facts of Life, The"
   ~ actress RAE

factual REAL, TRUE

faculties
   mental ~ WITS
   with full ~ SOBER

faculty
   ~ head DEAN

fad MODE, RAGE, STYLE

faddish HOT

fade DIE, EBB, FLAG, MELT, PALE, PETER, WANE
   ~ away EBB, PASS, WANE
   ~ in EMERGE, RISE
   ~ out DIE

faded DRAB, OLD, PALE

fade-out
   ~ technique IRIS

fader
   fall ~ TAN

"Faerie Queene, The" EPIC, POEM
   ~ heroine UNA

fag
   ~ end LAST
   ~ out BORE

fagged
   ~ out DONE, SPENT

Fahd, King ARAB
   ~ faith ISLAM

fail DIE, FLAG, LOSE, MISS, PETER, SINK
   ~ ender URE
   ~ to attend MISS
   ~ to catch MISS
   ~ to hit MISS
   ~ to include SKIP
   ~ to keep up LAG
   ~ to mention OMIT, SKIP, SLUR
   ~ to open PASS
   ~ to see MISS
   ~ to win LOSE
   opposite of ~ ACE, PASS

"Fail-___" SAFE

failed
   ~ 27th Amendment ERA
   ~ attempt MISS

failing
   ~ that ELSE

fails
   ~ to be ISNT
   ~ to be, informally AINT

failure DUD, LOSER, MISS, RUIN
   ~ (prefix) MIS
   consistent ~ LOSER
   temporary ~ LAPSE
   utter ~, in slang DOG

Faiman PETER

fainéant DRONE

faint DIM, PALE
   become ~ FADE, WANE

"Faint heart ___ won..." NEER

fair CLEAN, CLEAR, EVEN, FINE, HONEST, MORAL, SERENE, SOSO
   ~ and square HONEST
   ~ attraction RIDE
   ~ mark CEE
   ~ offering RIDE
   ~ share HALF
   a ~ amount SOME

fair ___ PLAY, TRADE

"___ fair..." ALLS

Fair ISLE

"___ Fair" ALLS, STATE

"___ Fair, The" HORSE

Fair, A.A.
   ~ real first name ERLE

"Fair as ___, when only one..." ASTAR

Fair Deal
   ~ monogram HST

"___ fair in love..." ALLS

fairness HONOR

fair-to-middling OKAY

fairway
   ~ hazard TRAP
   ~ need IRON
   ~ position LIE
   ~ shout FORE
   trim the ~ MOW

fair weather
   ~ friend USER

fairy ELF, PERI
   ~ godmother ANGEL, DONOR
   ~ godmother's rod WAND

fairy ___ TALE

___ fairy TOOTH

"___ Fairy, The" GOOD

fairylike AERIAL, ELFIN, TINY

fairy tale LIE
   ~ baddie GIANT
   ~ beginning ONCE
   ~ character ELF
   ~ figure GNOME
   ~ last word AFTER
   ~ second word UPON
   ~ villain OGRE
   ~ word EVER
   like ~ stepmothers CRUEL

fait accompli FACT

faith ISM
   ~ (abbr.) REL
   ~ sister HOPE
   article of ~ DOGMA, TENET
   keep the ~ BEAR
   Moors' ~ ISLAM
   Muslim ~ ISLAM
   pin one's ~ on LEAN
   put ~ in RELY
   Sunni ~ ISLAM
   see also religion

faithful HONEST, LIEGE, TRUE
   ~ companion of fiction TONTO
   be ~ ADHERE

___ Faithful OLD

faithless BAD

fake ACT, FALSE, LIE, PASTE, POSE, SHAM
~ **diamonds** PASTE
~ **it** ACT
~ **someone out** DUPE
not ~ REAL, TRUE

faked SHAM
~ **contest** SETUP

faker SHAM

fakir HINDU
~ **income** ALMS
~ **religion** ISLAM

Fala DOG, PET

falafel
~ **bread** PITA

Falana LOLA

falcon BIRD
~ **feature** CLAW
~ **hunter** SPADE
~ **relative** KITE

Falcon AUTO, CAR

"Falcon ___ Over, The" TAKES

"Falcon Crest"
~ **actor** LAMAS

Falcons ELEVEN, TEAM
~ **home** ATLANTA
~ **org.** NFL

"Falcon Takes ___, The" OVER

Faldo, Nick
~ **org.** PGA

Falk PETER

fall DROP, LAPSE, PLOP, RAIN, RUIN, SINK, SLIDE, SLIP
~ **a bit** DIP
~ **apart** ROT
~ **asleep** NOD
~ **at the feet of** ADORE, KNEEL
~ **away** EBB
~ **back** EBB, LAPSE, REEL
~ **behind** LAG, TRAIL
~ **below the horizon** SET
~ **bloom** ASTER
~ **clumsily** TRIP
~ **down** DROP
~ **fader** TAN
~ **faller** LEAF
~ **flat** MISS
~ **flower** ASTER
~ **from grace** SIN
~ **from the sky** HAIL, RAIN, SLEET, SNOW
~ **gathering** CROP
~ **guy** DUPE, GOAT, SAP
~ **in drops** DRIP
~ **into disuse** LAPSE
~ **into reverie** DREAM
~ **into water** PLOP
~ **in winter** SLEET, SNOW
~ **in with** AGREE
~ **mo.** DEC, NOV, OCT, SEPT
~ **obliquely** SLOPE
~ **off** ABATE, DIE, DIP, DROP, EBB, FLAG, SLIDE
~ **off, as support** ERODE
~ **on one's face** LOSE, TRIP

~ **opposite** RISE
~ **out** SCRAP
~ **over** TIP
~ **preceder** PRIDE, TRIP
~ **slowly** DRIP
~ **to** DINE, EAT
~ **to one's knees** BOW
~ **veggie** YAM
cause to ~ TRIP
do a ~ **chore** RAKE
frozen ~ SNOW
let ~ DROP, RELATE, RUMOR, SHED
riding for a ~ SMUG

fall ___ (attack) UPON

fall ___ (collapse) APART

fall ___ (diminish) OFF

fall ___ (disagree) OUT

fall ___ (withdraw) AWAY

fall ___ backwards OVER

fall ___ line INTO

___ fall FREE

fallacious BAD, FALSE

fallacy ERROR

"___ Fall Down" ALL

fallen
~ **into disuse** PASSE
~ **tree** LOG

"Fallen ___, The" IDOL

faller
fall ~ LEAF

falling
~ **ice** SLEET
~ **sound** PLOP
like ~ **off a log** EASY

falling ___ STAR

falling-___ OUT

falling-out ROW, SPAT

"___ Fall in Love" LETS

fall into ___ LINE

fall-like CRISP

"Fall of the ___ Empire, The" ROMAN

"Fall of the Roman Empire, The"
~ **director** MANN

fall on ___ ears DEAF

fall on deaf ___ EARS

fallout
volcano ~ ASH

fallow LEA
lie ~ SIT

fallow ___ DEER

Fall River
~ **st.** MASS

___ Falls ANGEL

___ Falls, Ida. MESA

Falmouth CITY, PORT

false BAD
~ **(abbr.)** ANS
~ **appearance** ACT
~ **belief** ERROR
~ **charge** SMEAR
~ **face** MASK
~ **friend** LIAR
~ **front** ACT, POSE, SHAM
~ **god** BAAL, IDOL
~ **name** ALIAS
~ **piety** CANT
~ **report** LIBEL
~ **show** ACT
~ **statement** LIE, TALE
~ **witness** LIAR
bear ~ **witness** LIE
declare ~ DENY
give a ~ **impression** BELIE
prove ~ BELIE
sail under ~ **colors** MASK

false ___ ALARM, RIB, START, STEP

falsehood LIE, TALE
tell a ~ LIE

falsely AMISS

"___ False Move" ONE

___-false test TRUE

falsetto MALE
sing ~ YODEL

falsification LIE, TALE

falsifier LIAR

falsify BELIE, COLOR, FAKE, LIE, SKEW, SLANT
~ **accounts** PAD

falsity LIE, TALE

Falstaff SIR
~ **friend** HAL
~ **quaff** ALE
like ~ FAT, OBESE

"Falstaff" OPERA
~ **composer** ELGAR
~ **selection** ARIA
~ **soprano** ALICE
where ~ **premiered** MILAN

Falstaffian OBESE

falter LAG, LIMP, NOD, REEL

fame NAME, NOTE
attain ~ ARRIVE

"Fame"
~ **actress** ALLEN, CARA
~ **name** NIA

famed GREAT, NOTED

familia
~ **member** NINA, NINO, PADRE, TIA, TIO

familiar FREE, USUAL
~ **saying** SAW
~ **with** AWARE, ONTO, UPON
become ~ **with** ADAPT
be ~ **with** KNOW
get ~ ORIENT
less ~ NEWER
not ~ ALIEN
witch's ~ CAT

familiarity EASE

familiarize ENURE, INURE, ORIENT
~ **with** OPEN

family ILK, ISSUE, KIN
~ **man** DAD
~ **mem.** BRO, GRAM, REL, SIS
~ **member** MOM, POP
~ **members** MAS, PAS
~ **room gear** STEREO
~ **vehicle** AUTO, CAR, SEDAN
all in the ~ AKIN

"family"
~ **head** DON

family ___ MAN, NAME, ROOM, TREE

"Family ___" PLOT, TIES

"___ Family" MAMAS

"Family Ties"
~ **role** ALEX
Skippy on ~ MARC

famous BIG, GREAT, NOTED

"Famous"
~ **name** AMOS

fan NUT, STIR
~ **club focus** IDOL
~ **noise** RAH
~ **out** PART
~ **the fire** AROUSE
"American Bandstand"
~ TEEN
be a ~ ROOT
Internet ~ USER
jazz ~ CAT
like a ~ **belt** TAUT
obsessive ~ NUT
smorgasbord ~ EATER

fan ___ BELT, MAIL

fan-___ TAN

fanatic AVID, NUT
~ **ender** ISM
~ **feeling** ZEAL

fanatical AVID, MAD, RABID

fanaticism MANIA, ZEAL

fancier
flame ~ MOTH

fanciful
~ **as a story** TALL

fancy ADORE, DEEM, DREAM, IDEA, LIKE, LOVE, ORNATE, POSH, WANT
~ **affair** GALA
~ **Dan** DUDE
~ **fabric** LAME, SATIN, SILK
~ **greatly** ADORE
~ **premises** ESTATE
~ **spread** ROE
~ **wheels** LIMO
flight of ~ DREAM
have a ~ **for** LONG
passing ~ FAD
take a ~ **to** LIKE
tickle one's ~ AMUSE

fancy ___ DRESS

fancy-___ FREE

fancywork LACE

fandango DANCE

Faneuil ___ HALL

fanfare ADO, BLARE, ECLAT

fang TOOTH

fangs
   show ~ BARE

Fannie ___ MAE

"Fanny ___ Alexander" AND

fans
   like some sports ~ RABID

Fansler KATE

fan-tan GAME

"Fantasia"
   hippo's wear in ~ TUTU

fantasize DREAM, MOON

fantastic GREAT
   trip the light ~ DANCE

fantasy DREAM

Fantasy Island
   ~ wear LEI

"Fantasy Quartet for ___ and Strings" OBOE

fanzine MAG

far AWAY
   ~ down DEEP
   ~ from fore AFT
   ~ from land ASEA, ATSEA
   ~ from melodic ATONAL
   ~ from swarthy PALE
   ~ from the flock LOST
   ~ from the most LEAST
   ~ from wonderful SOSO
   ~ off AWAY
   ~ out NEAT, RAD
   ~ partner AWAY, NEAR, WIDE
   ~ point END
   ~ (prefix) TEL, TELE
   as ~ as UPTO
   few and ~ between RARE, SPARSE, THIN
   go ~ LAST, RISE
   not ~ NEAR
   not ~ off ABOUT
   not ~ off, to a poet ANEAR
   on the ~ side of ACROSS
   the ~ side of ACROSS
   thus ~ YET

far-___ GONE, OFF, OUT

___ far (yet) THUS

"...far ___ can see" ASI

Far ___ EAST, WEST

"Far ___ Place, A" OFF

far and ___ WIDE

"Far and ___" AWAY

farandole DANCE

farce PLAY, SHAM

farceur WAG, WIT

"Far Country, The"
   ~ actress ROMAN
   ~ director MANN

fare COST, DIET, EAT, MEAL, MEAT, RIDER
   ~ carrier CAB
   ~ counter METER
   ~ thee well ADIEU, ALOHA, BYE, CIAO, TATA
   bill of ~ CARD, CARTE, MEAL, MENU
   bland ~ PAP
   bridge ~ TOLL
   fast food ~ CHILI
   reduced ~ DIET
   subway ~ TOKEN

fare-___-well THEE

Far East ORIENT
   ~ land LAOS

Far Eastern
   ~ weight TAEL

___ fare-thee-well TOA

farewell
   ~ in French ADIEU
   ~ in Hawaiian ALOHA
   ~ in Italian CIAO
   ~ in Latin AVE, VALE
   ~ in Spanish ADIOS
   bid ~ LEAVE
   brief ~ BYE
   Brit's ~ TATA
   colloquial ~ LATER
   kahuna's ~ ALOHA
   slangy ~ CIAO

Farewell CAPE

"Farewell to ___, A" ARMS

far-flung BIG, LARGE, VAST, WIDE

Fargo
   ~ st. NDAK

farina MEAL

farm GROW, HOME, RAISE
   ~ animal COW, EWE, GOAT, HOG, HORSE, MARE, MULE, SOW
   ~ animals OXEN
   ~ baby CALF, FOAL, LAMB
   ~ barrier RAIL
   ~ building BARN, SILO
   ~ cackler HEN
   ~ creature ANT
   ~ enclosure PEN, STY
   ~ equipment maker DEERE
   ~ feed MASH
   ~ gate STILE
   ~ implement HOE, PLOW
   ~ male BOAR, RAM, TOM
   ~ measure ACRE
   ~ mother EWE, HEN, MARE, SOW
   ~ out LEASE, RENT
   ~ package BALE
   ~ parcel ACRE
   ~ shelter SHED
   ~ soil LOAM
   ~ sound BAA, MOO, OINK
   ~ unit ACRE, BALE
   ~ vehicle CART
   ~ worker HAND
   ~ yield CROP
   piece of the ~ ACRE

farm ___ (subcontract) OUT

___ farm ANT, FUR

"Farm ___" AID

"___ Farm" ANIMAL

farmer
   ~ addr. RFD
   ~ concern SOIL
   ~ friend RAIN
   ~ in Dutch BOER
   ~ market FAIR
   ~ measure ACRE
   ~ need HOE, PLOW, RAKE, SEED
   ~ offering CROP
   ~ org. ADA
   ~ place DELL
   ~ wake-up call CROW

___ farmer DIRT, TENANT

"Farmer in the ___, The" DELL

Farmer, James
   ~ org. CORE

"Farmers' Allminax"
   ~ humorist SHAW

farming
   ~ bureaucracy USDA

farmland LEA, SOIL
   ~ unit ACRE

farmlike RURAL

farmstead ABODE

far-out NEAT, RAD

"Far out!" WOW

farrago OLIO

Farragut
   ~ org. USN

Farrah
   ~ ex LEE

far-ranging WIDE

Farrar, Geraldine DIVA

far-reaching BIG, DEEP, LARGE, VAST, WIDE

farrier
   ~ item SHOE
   ~ tool RASP
   did a ~'s job SHOD

Farr, Jamie
   ~ outstanding feature NOSE

Farrow MIA

Farsi
   ~ speaker IRANI
   where ~ is spoken IRAN

"Far Side, The"
   ~ animal COW

farsighted WISE

farther OFF, PAST
   ~ aft AFTER
   ~ down the road LATER
   ~ from the middle OUTER

farthest LAST

farthing COIN

fascia BAND

fascicle PART

fascinate DRAW, GRIP, HOLD, LURE

fascinated AGOG, RAPT
   ~ by INTO

fascination MANIA

fashion ADAPT, CUT, MAKE, MODE, MODEL, MOLD, RAGE, SORT, STYLE, TREND, TURN
   ~ accessory BAG, SCARF, TIE
   ~ concern LABEL
   ~ design ALINE
   ~ figure MODEL
   ~ mecca PARIS
   ~ name DIOR
   ~ plate DUDE
   ~ statement DRESS
   1960s ~ MINI
   after the ~ of LIKE
   brief ~ FAD
   first name in ~ OLEG
   high ~ TON
   in ~ CHIC
   in this ~ THUS
   women's ~ ALINE

fashion ___ PLATE

fashionable CHIC, HEP, HIP, MOD, NOW, POSH, SLEEK, SMART, TONY

fashioned
   ~ like ALA

___-fashioned OLD

"___-Fashioned Garden" OLD

"___ Fashioned Love Song, An" OLD

"___-Fashioned Way, The" OLD

fashion plate
   ~ opposite SLOB

fashions
   like some ~ RETRO

fast APACE, FLEET, RAPID
   ~ car RACER
   ~ exit LAM
   ~ flyer JET, SST
   ~ food BITE
   ~ moving object BLUR
   ~ on one's feet AGILE, FLEET
   ~ on the uptake APT
   ~ partner LOOSE
   ~ time LENT
   break ~ EAT
   don't stay ~ RUN
   drive too ~ SPEED
   go ~ DASH, HIE, RACE, RUN, SPEED, TEAR
   held ~ RAPT
   make ~ BIND, LASH, RIVET, TIE
   opposite of ~ EAT
   stick ~ ADHERE

fast ___ DAY, LANE

fast-___ TALK

Fast ___ EDDIE

Fast Eddie
   ~ need CUE

fasten BELT, BIND, CLASP, CLIP, CLOSE, LACE, LASH, MOOR, NAIL, RIVET, ROOT, STRAP, TIE
~ **again** RETIE
~ **at sea** LASH
~ **on** TAG
~ **securely** RIVET
~ **shut** SEAL
~ **temporarily** PIN
~ **together** CLIP
~ **upon** GRAB

fastened SHUT

fastener BRAD, CLASP, CLIP, SNAP, STUD
beam ~ RIVET
bolt ~ NUT
collar ~ STUD
hinged door ~ HASP
jewelry ~ CLASP
metal ~ BRAD, NAIL
purse ~ CLASP
tire ~ LUG

fastening CLASP
dress ~ SNAP
string ~ KNOT

"Faster ___ a speeding bullet" THAN

"Fastest Gun ___, The" ALIVE

"Fastest Gun Alive, The"
~ **director** ROUSE

fast food
~ **drink** COLA, SODA
~ **fare** CHILI
~ **item** TACO
~ **place** DELI
~ **symbol** ARCH

fast forward
reasons to ~ ADS

fastidious NEAT, PRIM

fasting
~ **period** LENT

fastness KEEP

fast-talk DUPE, SNOW

fast-talking GLIB

fat BIG, LARD, OBESE, OIL
~ **cat** NOB
~ **eschewer of rhyme** SPRAT
~ **in French** GRAS
~ **roll of bills** WAD
animal ~ LARD, SUET
chew the ~ BLAB, CHAT, GAB, RAP, TALK, YAK
cook in ~ FRY
low in ~ LEAN

fat ___ CAT, CITY

fat ___ (resiny kindling) PINE

"Fat ___" CITY

"Fat ___ and Little Boy" MAN

"Fatagaga"
~ **collagist** ARP

fatal BAD
goddess of ~ rashness ATE

"Fatal Attraction"
~ **actress** CLOSE
~ **villain** ALEX

fatale
femme ~ SIREN

"Fat chance!" NEVER

fate LOT
Greek goddess of ~ MOIRA
tempt ~ RISK
tragic ~ DOOM

fated SURE

fateful DIRE

Fates TRIO
number of ~ THREE

___ "Fatha" Hines EARL

fathead ASS, CLOD, DOLT, OAF

father ADOPT, CAUSE, DAD, MALE, MAN, PADRE, PAPA, POP, SIRE, TITLE
~ **hermana** TIA
~ **hermano** TIO
~ **in Arabic** ABU
~ **in French** PERE
~ **in Spanish** PADRE
fille ~ PERE
fils ~ PERE
first ~ ADAM

"father"
name part meaning ~ ABU

___ father CITY

"Father ___" GOOSE

father-in-___ LAW

fatherland HOME

fatherless
~ **fellow** ADAM

"Father Murphy"
~ **actor** OLSEN

"Father of the ___" BRIDE

"Father of the Bride"
~ **role** ELLIE

fathers PAS
Jrs.' ~ SRS

Father's ___ DAY

"Fathers and ___" SONS

Father's Day
~ **gift** TIE

Father Time
~ **feature** BEARD

fathom GET, KEN, KNOW, SEE

fathomless DEEP

fatigue JADE, STRESS, TIRE, WEAR
yield to ~ SAG

fatigued ALLIN, DONE, LIMP, SPENT
become ~ SAG, TIRE

Fatima
~ **husband** ALI

"Fat Man ___ Little Boy" AND

fattening RICH

fatty OILY
~ **tissue** LARD

fatty ___ ACID

fatuous BANAL, DAFT, INANE

fatuus
ignis ~ DREAM

faucet TAP
~ **problem** DRIP, LEAK

fauld ARMOR

fault CHIP, ERROR, HOLE, LEAK, TAINT
be at ~ ERR
find ~ CARP, FRET, NAG

___ fault FOOT

faultfind CARP

faultfinder NAG, PRIG

faultily AMISS

faultless CLEAN, CLEAR

faulty AMISS, BAD, ILL, POOR

faun SATYR

fauna
~ **category** AVES
~ **counterpart** FLORA
flora and ~ LIFE

Fauntleroy, Little Lord
~ **name** ERROL

"Faust" OPERA

faux FAKE

faux ___ PAS

faux pas BONER, ERROR, SLIP, TRIP
~ **follower** OOPS
golfer's ~ SLICE
make a ~ ERR

fava BEAN

favor AEGIS, EGIS, ESTEEM
~ **one side** LIMP
curry ~ WOO
decide in ~ **of** AWARD
in ~ **of** FOR, PRO
not in ~ **of** ANTI, CON
one in ~ PRO
regard with ~ LIKE
seek ~ WOO
vote in ~ AYE, YEA, YES
win the ~ **of** ENDEAR

favorable GOOD, RIPE, ROSY
~ **notice** RAVE
~ **opinion** ESTEEM
~ **vote** AYE, YEA, YES

___-favored-nation MOST

favoring FOR, PRO
~ **(prefix)** PRO

favorite DEAR, IDOL, PET
teacher's ~ PET
tournament ~ SEED

favorite ___ SON

favorites
play ~ SIDE

"___ Favorite Sport?" MANS

favoritism BIAS
show ~ ROOT, SIDE

Fawlty Towers HOTEL

"Fawlty Towers"
~ **network** BBC

fawn ANIMAL, COLOR, DEER, DOTE, ECRU, TAN
~ **father** STAG
~ **mother** DOE
~ **over** ADORE

Fawn HALL

fawning OILY

fax REPRO, SEND
~ **button** SEND

faze JAR, UPSET

FBI
~ **agent** GMAN
~ **counterpart** CIA
~ **member** AGENT
~ **operative** AGT
British ~ CID
high-tech ~ **tool** DNA
letters in an ~ **file** AKA
part of ~ FED

"FBI Story, The"
~ **director** LEROY

FDR DEM, PRES
~ **dog** FALA
~ **follower** HST
~ **mother** SARA
~ **org.** NRA, REA, SSA, TVA
~ **Scottie** FALA
~ **successor** HST
~ **topic** FEAR
~ **veep** HST
where to see ~ DIME

Fe ELEM
~ **in chemistry** IRON
26 for ~ ATNO

___ Fe SANTA

fear ALARM, PANIC
~ **and trembling** AWE
abject ~ PANIC
ailurophobe's ~ CAT
fill with ~ ALARM, COW, SCARE
for ~ **that** LEST
gamblers' ~ RAID
respectful ~ AWE
show ~ HIE, RUN
sudden ~ ALARM
taxpayer's ~ AUDIT
xenophobe's ~ ALIEN

"Fear ___ Black Hat" OFA

"___ Fear" CAPE

fearful BAD, DIRE, LEERY, SHY
~ **creature** OGRE

"Fear in the Night"
~ **director** SHANE

fearless GAME, TAME
be ~ DARE

"Fearless"
~ **director** WEIR

Fearless Fosdick
  ~ **creator** CAPP

fearlessness DASH, GRIT, HEART

fearnought COAT

"Fear of a Black ___" HAT

fears
  lessen, as ~ ALLAY

"Fear Strikes ___" OUT

feasible SANE, UTILE

feast DINE, EAT, FARE, FEED, FETE, LUAU, MEAL, REVEL
  ~ **of the Exodus** SEDER
  ~ **on** EAT, SAVOR
  commemorative ~ SEDER
  English ~ ALE
  Hawaiian ~ LUAU
  Jewish ~ SEDER
  love ~ AGAPE
  spring ~ SEDER
  spring ~ **day** EASTER
  wahine's ~ LUAU
  Waikiki ~ LUAU

___ feast LOVE

Feast of Lots
  ~ **honoree** ESTHER

Feast of Saint ___ (January event) AGNES

feast one's ___ on EYES

feat ACT, DEED
  tumbler's ~ SPLIT

feather ILK, SORT
  ~ **stole** BOA
  light as a ~ AIRY

feather ___ BED

featherbed LOAF

featherbrain ASS, DOLT, IDIOT

featherbrained DAFT

feathered
  ~ **missile** DART
  ~ **shaft** ARROW

feather in one's ___ CAP

feather in one's ___, a CAP

featherless BARE

feather one's ___ NEST

feathers
  ~ **partner** TAR
  fuss and ~ ADO
  trim ~ PREEN
  tuft of ~ EAR

"___ Feathers" HORSE

featherweight
  ~ **weapon** JAB
  see also boxing

feathery
  ~ **scarf** BOA

feature HAVE, PHASE, STAR, TRAIT

featured
  ~ **player** LEAD

features FACE

Feb.
  ~ **follower** MAR

feckless INEPT

fecund RICH

fed
  ~ **up** MAD

fed.
  ~ **agent** GMAN, NARC, TMAN
  ~ **clean-up org.** EPA
  ~ **collection org.** IRS
  ~ **employee** AGT
  ~ **inspectors** USDA
  ~ **pension org.** SSA
  ~ **watchdog org.** EPA, FDA

___-fed CORN

Fed GMAN, TMAN

federal
  ~ **agent** GMAN, NARC, TMAN
  ~ **deficit** DEBT

federal ___ CASE

federate UNITE

federation BLOC

FedEx
  ~ **rival** UPS
  ~ **units** LBS

Fedor TSAR

fedora HAT
  ~ **fabric** FELT

"Fedora"
  ~ **highlight** ARIA

fee BILL, FARE, RATE, RENT
  entry ~ ANTE
  highway ~ TOLL
  hourly ~ RATE
  loan ~ INT
  taxi ~ FARE
  usage ~ TOLL

feeble BANAL, LAME, PALE

feeble-minded DAFT, DIM

feed DINE, EAT, FARE, HAY, KEEP, MEAL, OATS, RANGE
  ~ **a fete** CATER
  ~ **en masse** CATER
  ~ **lines to** CUE
  ~ **the kitty** ANTE
  ~ **the pigs** SLOP
  ~ **too well** SATE
  animal ~ BRAN
  basketball ~ PASS
  chicken ~ COIN, MASH
  farm ~ MASH
  foal ~ HAY
  hog ~ SLOP
  livestock ~ MASH, RYE
  off one's ~ ILL

feedback NOISE
  provide ~ REACT

feedbag
  ~ **morsel** OAT
  put on the ~ EAT

feeder STREAM

___ feeder BIRD

feel AURA, OPINE, SENSE
  ~ **achy** AIL
  ~ **in one's bones** KNOW
  ~ **pain** ACHE
  don't ~ **so good** AIL
  general ~ AURA

feeler HINT, ORGAN

feeling AURA, IDEA, LOVE, MOOD, STAND
  ~ **down** SAD
  ~ **low** SAD
  ~ **no stress** ATEASE
  ~ **of hunger** PANG
  ~ **of unworthiness** SHAME
  ~ **poorly** ILL
  ~ **sore** ACHY
  ~ **the strain** TENSE
  bad ~ ANGER, HATE
  bored ~ BLAH
  fanatic's ~ ZEAL
  fervid ~ ARDOR
  general ~ MOOD
  good ~ LOVE
  guilty ~ SHAME
  happy ~ GLEE
  have a funny ~ SENSE
  humbling ~ AWE
  ill ~ ANGER, HATE, SPITE
  impervious to ~ STOIC
  inflated ~ EGO
  inspirational ~ AWE
  intense ~ ARDOR
  intensity of ~ HEAT
  lethargic ~ ENNUI
  listless ~ ENNUI
  longing ~ ACHE, PANG
  Monday ~ BLAH
  negative ~ ANGER, HATE
  post-workout ~ ACHE
  remorseful ~ PANG
  restless ~ ITCH
  scary ~ FEAR
  sore ~ ACHE
  tickled-pink ~ GLEE
  warm ~ ARDOR, LOVE
  see also emotion

feeling no ___ PAIN

feeling one's ___ OATS

feelings
  feign ~ EMOTE
  hard ~ ANGER
  reveal one's ~ LETON
  seat of ~ SOUL
  shows ~ EMOTE

"___ Feelings" HARD

feel no ___ PAIN

feel one's ___ OATS

feet
  cold ~ FEAR
  drag one's ~ DEFER, LAG, MOVE, STALL
  fall at the ~ **of** ADORE, KNEEL
  fast on one's ~ AGILE, FLEET
  get off one's ~ LIE, SIT
  get one's ~ **wet** START, WADE
  get to one's ~ RISE, STAND
  have cold ~ FEAR
  leave one's ~ HOP, LEAP

let the grass grow under one's ~ IDLE, LOAF
light on one's ~ AGILE
on both ~ ERECT
on one's ~ ARISEN
put back on one's ~ CURE, HEAL, RESTORE
put on its ~ RAISE
put on one's ~ AID, HELP
shuffle one's ~ DANCE
three ~ YARD
throw oneself at the ~ **of** BOW
walk on bare ~ PAD

feet of ___ CLAY

feign ACT, FAKE, LIE, POSE, SEEM, SHAM

feigned FALSE

feigning ACT

Feinstein
  ~ **org.** SEN

feint RUSE

feisty
  hardly ~ TAME

Feldman, Marty
  ~ **in "Young Frankenstein"** IGOR

Felicia FARR

Félicité
  see French

___ Félicité, Que. STE

felicitous NEAT

feline CAT, PET
  ~ **sound** MEOW, MEW
  ~ **to George Herriman** KAT
  dappled ~ OCELOT
  spotted ~ GENET
  striped ~ TIGER
  tawny ~ LION, PUMA
  word to a ~ SCAT
  see also cat

Felipe ALOU
  see also Spanish

___ Felipe SAN

felis ___ LEO

Felix CAT
  ~ **roomie** OSCAR
  like ~ NEAT

Felix and Oscar
  ~ **creator** NEIL

fell AXE, CHOP, COAT, CUT, DIRE, EVIL, FERAL, HEW, HIDE, LOG, RAZE

"___ Fell" IFI

fella DUDE, MAN
  little ~ KID, LAD, TAD, TYKE
  Rose's ~ ABIE

Fell, Dr. Gideon
  ~ **creator** CARR

feller CHAP, DUDE, MALE, MAN
  tree ~ SAW

Feller BOB

Fellini
  ~ country ITALY
  ~ film ROMA
  ~ film composer ROTA

"Fellini's ___" ROMA

"___ Fell on Alabama" STARS

"___ Fell Out of Heaven" ASTAR

fellow CHAP, DOG, EGG, GENT, LAD, MALE, MAN, PEER
  ~ in Australian English MATE
  ~ in British English MATE
  ~ in German HERR
  ~ in Spanish SENOR
  clumsy ~ OAF
  deplorable ~ LOUSE
  droll ~ WIT
  fatherless ~ ADAM
  Follies ~ FLO
  fraternal ~ ELK, LION, MOOSE
  funny ~ HOOT, WAG, WIT
  ill-bred ~ BOOR
  Jamaican ~ MON
  jolly good ~ CHAP
  luckless ~ LOSER
  polite ~ GENT
  regular ~ JOE
  that ~ HIM
  underhanded ~ SNEAK
  unnamed ~ HIM
  young ~ KID, LAD, SPRIG, TAD
  see also guy

___ Fellow ODD

fellow's
  that ~ HIS

fellowship AWARD, BAND, CLAN, ORDER

___-fellow-well-met HAIL

___ fell swoop INONE

felon
  ~ deed ARSON
  aid a ~ ABET

felony
  facilitate a ~ ABET
  fiery ~ ARSON

felt
  deeply ~ INNER

felt-tip PEN

felucca BOAT, SHIP

fem.
  ~ title MRS
  not ~ MASC

female HER, LADY, SHE
  ~ antelope DOE, EWE
  ~ bear SOW
  ~ deer DOE
  ~ fowl HEN
  ~ friend, in French AMIE
  ~ goat DOE
  ~ guinea pig SOW
  ~ horse MARE
  ~ kangaroo DOE
  ~ lobster HEN
  ~ pheasant HEN
  ~ pig SOW

~ rabbit DOE
~ relative AUNT, NIECE
~ ruff REE, REEVE
~ sandpiper REE, REEVE
~ sheep EWE
~ swan PEN
~ turkey HEN
~ whale COW
campus ~ COED
first ~ Attorney
  General RENO
first ~ in Parliament ASTOR
first U.S. ~ in space RIDE
forest ~ DOE
maned ~ MARE
ovine ~ EWE
palindromic ~ ADA, ANNA, AVA
stable ~ MARE
warren ~ DOE
young ~ GIRL, LASS

females
  having males and ~ COED

feminine
  ~ ending ESS, ETTA, INA, INE
  ~ force YIN
  ~ pronoun HER, SHE

feminist
  ~ cause ERA
  ~ grp. NOW

femme
  ~ fatale SIREN
  canonized ~ STE

femur BONE
  ~ joiners ILIA
  ~ neighbor TIBIA

femur-tibia
  ~ connector KNEE

fen MIRE, MOOR, SINK, WASH

fence DUEL, EVADE, PALE, SELL
  ~ defense BARB
  ~ in LIMIT, PEN, RING
  ~ in a waterway WEIR
  ~ material WIRE
  ~ opening GATE
  ~ part POST, RAIL
  ~ picket PALE
  ~ steps STILE
  ~ support POST
  get off the ~ ACT, OPT
  porch ~ RAIL
  racetrack ~ RAIL
  steps over a ~ STILE
  sunken ~ HAHA

___ fence SNOW

fenced
  ~ area PALE, PEN
  ~ in PENT
  not ~ OPEN

fencer
  ~ choice SABER
  ~ equipment EPEE

___ fences MEND

fencing
  ~ blade EPEE
  ~ competition DUEL
  ~ leap VOLT
  art of ~ EPEE

fend
  ~ off AVERT, DETER, REPEL, STAVE

fender
  ~ bender DENT
  ~ blemish DING

Fender LEO

fenestra HOLE

___ Fe, N. Mex. SANTA

fennec ANIMAL

fennel HERB
  dog ~ WEED

Fenway Park ARENA

"fer"
  not ~ AGIN

feral
  not ~ TAME

Ferber EDNA
  ~ novel GIANT

fer-de-lance SNAKE

Ferdinand REY
  ~ land SPAIN

Ferdinand the Bull
  ~ creator LEAF

Fergie SARAH
  ~ former sister-in-law ANNE

Ferguson SARAH

Ferlinghetti
  ~ novel HER

fermata HOLD

ferment ADO, BREW, SOUR, STIR
  in a ~ ASTIR

fermented HARD
  ~ beverage ALE, BEER, CIDER, LAGER

fermenting
  ~ fungi YEAST
  ~ tank VAT

Fermi
  ~ concern ATOM

fermium METAL

fern PLANT
  future ~ SPORE

___ fern TREE

Fernando LAMAS, REY
  see also Spanish

"Fernando"
  ~ band ABBA

___ Fernando Valley SAN

"Ferngully...The ___ Rainforest" LAST

"Fern Hill" POEM

ferocious CRUEL, FERAL
  not at all ~ TAME

ferocity RAGE
  symbol of ~ TIGER

Ferrara ABEL
  ~ family name ESTE

Ferrari AUTO, CAR
  classic ~ DINO

Ferrer MEL
  ~ film LILI

ferret ANIMAL
  ~ out LEARN, ROOT, SEEK
  ~ perhaps PET

ferriferous
  ~ rock ORE

Ferrigno LOU

"Ferris Bueller's Day ___" OFF

Ferris wheel RIDE

ferrite IRON

ferrule BAND, CAP, RING

ferry BOAT, HAUL, SHIP
  operate a ~ PLY

"Ferry ___ the Mersey" ACROSS

fertile RICH
  ~ area OASIS
  ~ soil LOAM

Fertile Crescent
  ~ country IRAQ

fertility
  ~ god BAAL
  ~ goddess ISIS

fertilize DRESS

fervency ARDOR, ZEAL

fervent AVID, EAGER, HOT, WARM

fervid EAGER
  ~ feeling ARDOR

fervor ARDOR, DASH, FIRE, HEAT, LIFE, LOVE, ZEAL

fescue
  roll out the ~ SOD

fess
  ~ up ADMIT, OWN, TELL

"___ feste Burg" EIN

fester ROT

Fester UNCLE

festival GALA, REVEL
  ~ drink ALE
  ~ opener EVE
  English country ~ ALE
  spring ~ EASTER
  Vietnamese ~ TET
  winter ~ YULE

festive GALA, GAY, GLAD
  ~ occasion FETE
  ~ quaff NOG

festivity GALA

festoon ADORN, DRAPE, SWAG, TRIM

fetch COST, GET

___-fetched FAR

fete DAY, GALA, HONOR
  feed a ~ CATER
  irreverent ~ ROAST

fête champêtre MEAL

fetid BAD, RANK

fetor ODOR, REEK

___ Fe Trail SANTA

fetter BIND, TIE

fetters IRONS

fettle
  in fine ~ HALE, TRIM

fettuccine PASTA

feud
  small ~ SPAT

feudal
  ~ bigwig BARON
  ~ bondsman SERF
  ~ defense MOAT
  ~ lord LIEGE, PEER
  ~ serf ESNE
  ~ term of respect SIRE
  ~ vassal LIEGE
  ~ worker ESNE

fever HEAT
  chills and ~ AGUE
  run a ~ AIL

___ fever HAY

"Fever"
  ~ singer LEE

feverish HOT, ILL, RED
  ~ state AGUE
  feel ~ AIL

feverishness ARDOR, ZEAL

few
  ~ and far between RARE, SPARSE, THIN
  a ~ SOME
  give or take a ~ ORSO
  in a ~ minutes ANON, SOON
  of ~ words TERSE

"Few ___ Men, A" GOOD

fewer LESS
  ~ than one NONE
  score ~ points LOSE

fewest LEAST

"Few Good ___, A" MEN

___ few rounds GOA

fey ODD

fez CAP, HAT

___-fi SCI

fiancé LOVE

fiancée GIRL, LOVE

fiasco DUD, MESS, RUIN

fiat EDICT, ORDER

fib LIE, TALE

fibber LIAR

fiber HAIR
  ~ plant AGAVE
  ~ source BEAN, BRAN, OAT
  agave ~ SISAL
  artificial ~ NYLON
  cordage ~ HEMP, SISAL
  hemplike ~ SISAL
  moral ~ HONOR
  muscle ~ STRIA
  rope ~ HEMP, SISAL
  rug ~ SISAL

fiber ___ OPTIC

fiber-optics
  ~ pulse LASER

fibers
  soak ~ RET

fibster LIAR

fibula BONE
  ~ neighbor TIBIA

FICA
  ~ org. SSA

Fichtelgebirge RANGE

fichu SCARF

fiction GENRE, LIE, PROSE, TALE, YARN
  ~ antithesis FACT
  first name in detective ~ ERLE
  inferior ~ TRASH

fictitious FAKE, FALSE

fiddle
  ~ fashioner AMATI
  ~ stick BOW
  ~ with ALTER
  ~ (with) MESS, PLAY, TOY
  baritone ~ CELLO
  famous ~ AMATI
  flat-backed ~ VIOL
  kind of ~ BASS
  see also violin

___ fiddle BASS

fiddle-de-___ DEE

fiddle-de-dee POOH

fiddle-faddle POOH, TRASH

"Fiddle-faddle!" RATS

fiddlehead FERN

fiddler CRAB

fiddler ___ CRAB

fiddlers
  ~ king COLE

"Fiddlesticks!" BAH, DRAT, POOH, PSHAW, SHOOT

Fidel
  ~ country CUBA
  ~ friend CHE
  see also Spanish

"Fidelio" OPERA

fidelity
  model of ~ ENID

fidget STIR

fidgety TENSE

fido COIN

Fido DOG, PET
  ~ doc VET
  ~ find ORT
  ~ offering PAW
  ~ pal SPOT
  ~ reward BONE
  ~ tormentor FLEA
  ~ warning SNARL
  command to ~ HEEL, SIC, SIT, STAY
  greeting from ~ ARF
  see also canine, dog

"Fido Is a Hot Dog ___" NOW

"Fie!" BAH

fiefdom
  ~ possessor LORD

field ARENA, LAND, LEA, LIFE, LINE, LOT, REALM, SOD, SPHERE
  ~ day SPREE
  ~ entrance GATE
  ~ hand PEON
  ~ marshal RANK
  ~ measure ACRE
  ~ mouse VOLE
  ~ of action ARENA
  ~ of expertise AREA
  ~ unit ACRE
  ~ worker AGENT
  be part of the ~ START
  football ~ GRID
  out in left ~ FALSE, MAD
  pace the ~ LEAD
  Queens ~ SHEA
  steps in a ~ STILE
  the beasts of the ~ LIFE
  trail the ~ LOSE

field ___ CORN, DAY, EVENT, GOAL, HAND, MOUSE, TRIP

field-___ TEST

___ field LEFT, OIL

"___ Field, The" ONION

fielding
  ~ flub ERROR

field mouse
  ~ predator CAT, OWL

"Field of Dreams"
  ~ setting IOWA

field of honor
  ~ event DUEL

Field, Sally
  ~ role NORMA, NUN

Fields, W.C.
  ~ foil LEROY
  ~ "Little Chickadee" MAE
  ~ persona SOT

fiend DEMON, FAN, NUT, OGRE
  ~ ender ISH
  ~ starter ARCH
  little ~ IMP

fiendish BAD, BASE, CRUEL, EVIL, VILE

fierce ACUTE, CRUEL, FERAL, HOT
  ~ stare GLARE
  ~ whale ORCA

fiercely HARD

fieriness HEAT

fiery HOT, IRATE, RED
  ~ dance TANGO
  ~ felony ARSON
  ~ fragment EMBER
  ~ stone OPAL

"Fiesque"
  ~ composer LALO

fiesta
  ~ fare TACO

Fiesta AUTO, CAR

Fiesta Bowl
  ~ city TEMPE

"Fie, thou dishonest ___!" SATAN

fife PIPE

Fifi
  see French

fifth PART
  ~ band of a rainbow BLUE
  ~ person SETH
  ~ wheel SPARE

fifth ___ ESTATE

Fifth ___ AVE

fifth-largest
  ~ planet EARTH

fifth-rate POOR

fifty-fifty CLOSE, EVEN
  ~ chance BET
  go ~ SHARE

fig TREE
  ~ out ADORN, DRESS

fig ___ LEAF

"Figaro"
  ~ tune ARIA

fight MILL, ROW, SCRAP, SETTO
  ~ back REACT
  ~ ending TKO
  ~ endings KOS
  ~ (for) VIE
  ~ for air GASP
  ~ in a way CLAW
  ~ off REPEL
  ~ site ARENA, RING
  confused ~ MELEE
  drawn-out ~ SIEGE
  hand-to-hand ~ MELEE
  knight ~ TILT
  noisy ~ MELEE
  ready to ~ ARMED
  rigged ~ SETUP
  slight ~ SPAT
  sword ~ DUEL
  train for a ~ SPAR

fight ___ (repel) OFF

"___ Fight, The" GOOD

fighter
  Confederate ~ REB
  Dixie ~ REB
  fire ~ WATER
  turn-of-the-century ~ BOER
  Vicksburg ~ REB

"Fighter of the Century"
  ~ award-winner ALI

fighters
  germ ~ SERA

fighting ATIT

Fighting __ (Notre Dame) IRISH

Fighting Tigers
  ~ **sch.** LSU

fight tooth and __ NAIL

figment
  ~ **of the imagination** DREAM

figs. NOS

figure ADD, COST, MAKE, PLAN, RATE, SIGN
  ~ **of eight** KNOT
  ~ **of speech** IDIOM, IMAGE
  ~ **out** LEARN, SEE
  ~ **skater's maneuver** AXEL, CAMEL
  ~ **skating event** PAIRS
  ~ **up** ADD, SUM, TOTAL
  action ~ DOER
  art ~ NUDE
  bottom-line ~ SUM
  box-office ~ TAKE
  do ~ **eights** SKATE
  geometric ~ SOLID
  half a ~ **eight** ESS
  preliminary ~ EST
  public ~ LION
  sacred ~ ICON
  staff ~ NOTE

figure eight
  ~ **half** ESS
  where to do a ~ ICE, RINK

figures DATA
  track ~ ODDS

figurine IDOL, IMAGE
  ~ **material** JADE
  Mexican ~ **mineral** ONYX

Fiji
  ~ **neighbor** SAMOA

filament CORD, HAIR, LINE

filbert NUT
  ~ **cousin** PECAN

filch COP, CRIB, PALM, ROB, STEAL, TAKE

file ABRADE, EDGE, PARADE, RASP, ROW, STREAM, TOOL, TRAIN
  ~ **and forget** HIDE
  ~ **away** SAVE
  ~ **label** TAB
  ~ **partner** RANK
  ~ **subject** CASE
  coarse ~ RASP
  Indian ~ LINE
  in single ~ AROW
  rank and ~ MOB
  single ~ LINE

__ file NAIL

"__ File, The" ODESSA

filet BONE
  ~ **fish** SOLE

filet mignon STEAK

filibuster DEFER, STALL

filigree LACE

filing
  ~ **mo.** APR

filings DUST

fill GLUT, JADE, LADE
  ~ **a chair** SIT
  ~ **in** ENTER, TEMP
  ~ **one's needs** SUIT
  ~ **out** GROW, PAD
  ~ **starter** OVER
  ~ **the air** RING
  ~ **the bases** LOAD
  ~ **the bill** CATER, FIT, SERVE
  ~ **the hold** STOW
  ~ **the washer** LOAD
  ~ **too tightly** CRAM
  ~ **to overflowing** CLOG, CRAM, HEAP
  ~ **to the max** JADE, SATE
  ~ **up** LOAD, TOP
  ~ **up on** EAT
  ~ **with admiration** AWE
  ~ **with air** AERATE
  ~ **with bubbles** AERATE
  ~ **with fear** ALARM, COW, SCARE
  ~ **with happiness** ELATE
  ~ **with loathing** REPEL
  ~ **with love** ENDEAR
  ~ **with wonder** AMAZE, AWE

fille
  ~ **father** PERE
  ~ **friend** AMIE
  ~ **mother** MERE

filled
  ~ **pastry** PIE
  ~ **to the gills** LADEN
  ~ **with breezes** AIRY
  ~ **with foliage** DENSE

filler
  conversation ~ ISEE

fillers
  pause ~ ERS

fillet BAND, BONE, MEAT

fill-in
  office ~ TEMP

filling
  enchilada ~ CHILI
  lasagna ~ MEAT

filling station
  ~ **freebie** AIR
  ~ **freebie, once** MAP

fillip CLAP, SPUR

fill the __ BILL

filly ANIMAL, FOAL, GIRL, HORSE, LADY, MARE
  ~ **food** OATS
  ~ **mother** MARE
  ~ **offspring** COLT

film CINE, COAT, MIST, SHEET, SHOOT, SKIN
  ~ **container** CAN
  ~ **crew assistant** GRIP
  ~ **crew member** TECH
  ~ **developing abbr.** ENL
  ~ **fragment** CLIP

  ~ **performers' org.** SAG
  ~ **processing site** LAB
  ~ **session** SHOOT
  ~ **shot** TAKE
  ~ **specification** SPEED
  ~ **speed no.** ASA
  ~ **splicer** EDITOR
  ~ **unit** REEL
  cast-of-thousands ~ EPIC

film __ CLIP, NOIR

__ film ART

filmdom
  ~ **pooch** ASTA
  barker of ~ TOTO

film noir
  ~ **classic** DOA

filmy FINE, THIN

fils
  ~ **father** PERE
  ~ **mother** MERE

filter CLEAR, OOZE, SEEP, SIFT
  spotlight ~ GEL

__ filter (dryer feature) LINT

filth DIRT, DUST, SMUT

filthy BAD, LEWD
  ~ **stuff** DIRT

"Filthy __" RICH

__ filtration GEL

fin FIVE
  change for a ~ ONES
  turbine ~ VANE

__ fin TAIL

finagle RIG

final EXAM, LAST, NET, TEST
  ~ **bars** CODA
  ~ **bio** OBIT
  ~ **ender** IST
  ~ **point** END
  ~ **rehearsal** DRESS
  ~ **score** SUM
  ~ **word** AMEN

"Final Analysis"
  ~ **actor** GERE

finale CLOSE, CODA, END
  chess ~ MATE
  course ~ EXAM, TEST
  hymn ~ AMEN

"Final Four"
  ~ **event** SEMI
  ~ **letters** NCAA

"final frontier"
  Kirk's ~ SPACE

"Final Impact"
  ~ **actor** LAMAS

finalize SEAL

finals
  ~ **prelim** SEMI

finance ENDOW, START
  ~ **deg.** MBA

financial
  ~ **crisis** PANIC

  ~ **item** ASSET
  ~ **subj.** ECON
  ~ **transaction** LOAN
  ~ **wiz** ACCT, CPA

financial aid
  ~ **criterion** NEED

financial page
  ~ **abbr.** NYSE

financier BARON

__ financing APR, DEBT

finca RANCH

finch BIRD
  ~ **color** GOLD

Finch PETER

find SPOT
  ~ **a buyer** SELL
  ~ **a job for** HIRE, USE
  ~ **a perch** LAND
  ~ **a tenant** RENT
  ~ **attractive** LIKE
  ~ **awful** HATE
  ~ **fault** CARP, FRET, NAG
  ~ **good** LOVE
  ~ **in flagrante delicto** NAIL
  ~ **new tenants** RELET
  ~ **oneself** LAND, ORIENT
  ~ **out** HEAR, LEARN, SEE, SPY, TRACE
  ~ **repugnant** ABHOR
  ~ **revolting** ABHOR
  ~ **smashing** ADORE
  ~ **the sum** ADD, TOTAL
  archaeologist's ~ BONE, RELIC, RUIN, STELE
  beach ~ SHELL
  hard to ~ RARE
  mine ~ LODE, SEAM
  prospector's ~ LODE, ORE
  shore ~ SHELL
  sleuth's ~ CLUE
  sourdough ~ ORE
  try to ~ HUNT, SEEK
  underground ~ ORE

finder
  ~ **starter** FACT
  fish ~ SONAR
  funny-money ~ TMAN
  plane ~ RADAR
  treasure ~ MAP

__ finder RANGE

finder's __ FEE

finding FACT
  poll ~ TREND

__-finding mission FACT

findings
  proofer's ~ ERRATA

"__ Finds Andy Hardy" LOVE

fine AOK, FEE, GOOD, NICE, OKAY, RICH, THIN
  ~ **china** BONE
  ~ **cloth** SATIN
  ~ **fur** SABLE
  ~ **kettle of fish** MESS
  ~ **mount** STEED
  ~ **rain** MIST
  ~ **spray** MIST

~ **steed** ARAB
~ **steel** TOLEDO
~ **to an astronaut** AOK
~ **violin** AMATI
~ **work** ART
in ~ **fettle** HALE, TRIM
set a ~ ASSESS

fine ___ ART, ARTS

fine- ___ SPUN, TUNE

"Fine!" OKAY, SURE, YES

"___ Fine Day" ONE

fine-grained
~ **silt** LOESS

fine kettle of fish MESS

fine print
~ **type** AGATE
check the ~ READ

finery ARRAY, ATTIRE, BEST, DRESS
wedding ~ LACE

finesse ART, EASE, TACT, TASTE

finest BEST, TOP

"___ Finest Hour" THEIR

fine-tempered
~ **sword** TOLEDO

fine-tooth
~ **article** COMB
go over with a ~ **comb** HUNT

fine-toothed ___ COMB

fine-tune HONE

"Fine with me!" YES

Fingal's ___ CAVE

finger FEEL, PART, STEAL
~ **in a way** NAME, RATON
~ **opposite** TOE
~ **or two** SHOT, SNORT
~ **part** NAIL
~ **sound** SNAP
~ **starter** FORE
crook one's ~ SIGN
lift a ~ AID, STIR
not lift a ~ LOAF
put the ~ **on** NAME
shake a ~ WAG

finger- ___ PAINT

___ finger RING

fingerboard
~ **ridge** FRET

finger game
~ **cry** EVENS, ODDS

fingerling RUNT

fingernail
~ **in Spanish** UNA

finger paint
apply ~ SMEAR

finger-paint DAB, DAUB

fingerprint SIGN

fingerprinting
high-tech ~ DNA

fingers
let slip through one's ~ LOSE
like printers' ~ INKY
work one's ~ **to the**
bone LABOR, PLOD, SLAVE, TOIL

fingertip PAD

fingertips
at one's ~ NEAR
have at one's ~ KNOW, LEARN
use one's ~ FEEL

fini DONE

finial CAP, EPI

"Finian's Rainbow"
~ **composer** LANE

finicky
~ **eater** CAT

finish CAP, CEASE, CLOSE, END, STOP
~ **a course** EAT
~ **ahead of** BEAT
~ **a scene** WRAP
~ **first** BEST, WIN
~ **last** LOSE
~ **line** GOAL, WIRE
~ **off** EAT, RUIN
~ **perfectly** ACE
~ **second** LOSE
~ **the cake** ICE
~ **third** SHOW
cigar ~ STUB
coin ~ MATTE
dull ~ MAT, MATTE
glossy ~ ENAMEL
never ~ DRAG
photo ~ DRAW, MATTE, STAT

finish ___ LINE

finish'd OER

finished DONE, GONE, OVER
~ **basement feature** BAR

finisher
last-place ~ LOSER

finishing
~ **touch** HEM

finish line
~ **marker** TAPE

Finisterre CAPE

finito DONE, OVER

fink RAT, SING, TELL
be a ~ RATON

Finland
~ **native** LAPP

finless
~ **fish** EEL

Finn
certain ~ LAPP

"Finnegans Wake"
~ **wife** ANNA
last word of ~ THE

Finn, Huck TEEN
~ **craft** RAFT
~ **father** PAP

Finnish
~ **bath** SAUNA

Finsteraarhorn ALP
~ **locale** ALPS

fir TREE
~ **cousin** PINE
~ **product** CONE

fire ARDOR, AXE, BAKE, BOOT, CAN, DROP, EJECT, HEAT, LIFE, OUST, SACK, SHOOT, ZEAL
~ **aftermath** ASH
~ **crime** ARSON
~ **ender** ARM, BALL, BIRD, BOAT, DOG, MAN, SIDE, TRAP, WATER
~ **fighter** RAIN, WATER
~ **off** LOOSE
~ **of the mind** ARDOR
~ **preceder** AIM
~ **residue** ASH, SOOT
~ **sign** ARIES
~ **starter** CAMP, GUN, SPIT
~ **the pottery** BAKE
~ **up** ANGER, HEAT, MOVE, RILE, START
~ **up a motor** REV
ball of ~ STAR, SUN
breathing ~ IRATE, MAD
build a ~ **under** AROUSE, ROUSE
calm the ~ DAMP
fan the ~ AROUSE
got the ~ **going again** RELIT
hang ~ DEFER, PEND
inner ~ ARDOR, ZEAL
intentional ~ ARSON
it's sometimes in the ~ FAT
mended the ~ RELIT
open ~ SHOOT
open ~ **on** SHELL
play with ~ DARE, RISK
prepare to ~ AIM
set on ~ HEAT
set ~ **to** LIT

fire ___ ALARM, ANT, DOOR, OPAL, SALE

fire ___ **(begin)** AWAY

fire- ___ EATER

___ fire HANG, SETON, UNDER

___-fire CEASE, RAPID, SURE

"Fire ___ Time, The" NEXT

"___ Fire" SURE, UNDER

"Fire and Ice" POEM

firearm GUN, RIFLE

firearms
~ **lobby** NRA

fireball SUN

firebox
~ **innards** ALARM

firebug
~ **crime** ARSON

firecracker
~ **detonator** FUSE
~ **noise** POP

"___ Firecracker" MISS

fired
~ **up** AVID, EAGER, KEEN, LIT
~ **up again** RELIT

___-fired ALL

firedamp GAS

fire-engine ___ RED

fire escape
~ **sign** EXIT

firefighter
~ **aid** FOAM
~ **concern** ARSON
~ **need** HOSE
~ **tool** AXE

firefly
emulate a ~ GLOW

___ Fire Girl CAMP

firehouse
name for a ~ **dog** SPOT

Firenze
~ **river** ARNO
see also Italian

fireplace GRATE
~ **filler** LOG
~ **frame** GRATE
~ **remnant** ASH, EMBER

firepower
provide ~ **to** ARM

fireside
~ **activity** CHAT

"fireside is a great ___, A" OPIATE

fire station
~ **sound** ALARM

fire truck
~ **adjunct** SIREN

firewood
~ **hauler** CART
~ **quantity** CORD
make ~ CHOP, HEW
season ~ AGE, DRY

fireworks
reaction to ~ AWE, OOH

firing ___ LINE, PIN

firkin CASE, KEG, TUB

firm CRISP, FAST, HARD, IRON, SET, SOLID, SURE
~ **abbr.** INC
~ **belief** DOGMA
~ **control** GRIP
~ **grip** GRASP
~ **up** GEL, SET, TONE
make ~ SEAL, SET

___ firma TERRA

firmament BLUE, SKY, SPACE
in the ~ ABOVE

firman EDICT, FIAT

firmness TONE
lacking ~ LIMP
lose ~ SAG

firms
~ **(abbr.)** COS

Firpo LUIS

first AHEAD, AONE, BASE, BEST, EARLY, MAIN, TOPS

first ___ AID, BASE, CLASS, ESTATE, GEAR, LADY, MATE, WATER

first-___ CLASS, RATE

First
  ~ st. DEL

"First ___" LADY, LOVE

"First ___, The" NOEL, TIME

"First ___ I see tonight..." STAR

first aid
  ~ giver EMT
  ~ item TAPE
  ~ job CUT, GASH
  ~ plant ALOE

first-aid ___ KIT

first baseman
  famous ~ WHO

firstborn ELDER, ELDEST

First Cause
  the ~ LORD

first-class ACE, AONE, BAD, BEST, FINE, TOP, TOPS
  ~ stuff MAIL

first-class ___ MAIL

"First Deadly ___, The" SIN

First Dog
  1940s ~ FALA

first-down
  ~ yardage TEN

first-family
  ~ member ABEL, ADAM, CAIN, EVE, SETH

first grade
  ~ lesson ABCS

"First Knight"
  ~ actor GERE

first line
  ~ players ATEAM

first magnitude
  ~ object STAR

___ first-name basis ONA

first-of-month
  ~ payment RENT

first place
  ~ medal GOLD

first-rate ABLE, ACE, AONE, BAD, BEST, BOSS, CLASS, FINE, GOOD, GREAT, NEAT, TOP, TOPS

first-sight
  ~ phenomenon LOVE

first-string
  ~ players ATEAM

"First Wives' Club, The"
  ~ members EXES

firth ARM, BAY, COVE, INLET

fiscal
  ~ period YEAR

fiscal ___ YEAR

Fischer
  ~ specialty CHESS

fish ANGLE, BASS, CARP, CAT, COD, EEL, GAR, HAKE, OPAH, PIKE, RAY, SCROD, SHAD, SKATE, SMELT, SOLE, SPRAT, TETRA, TROUT, TUNA
  ~ bait LURE, SPRAT
  ~ balancer FIN
  ~ basket CREEL
  ~ catcher NET
  ~ delicacy ROE
  ~ eggs ROE
  ~ ender EYE, MEAL, NET, POND, TAIL
  ~ finder SONAR
  ~ food ALGA, BAIT
  ~ for PRY, SEEK
  ~ fry MEAL
  ~ haul TAKE
  ~ net SEINE
  ~ plate SCALE
  ~ pond LAKE
  ~ predator BEAR, ERN, ERNE
  ~ relish ALEC
  ~ sauce ALEC
  ~ sound PLOP
  ~ spear GIG
  ~ starter ANGEL, BLUE, CAT, FLAT, GOLD, LUNG, NEEDLE, SAIL, SHELL, STAR, SUN
  ~ story LIE, TALE, YARN
  ~ to herons PREY
  ~ trap NET, WEIR
  ~ with a charge EEL
  aquarium ~ TETRA
  Atlantic ~ COD
  blackish ~ SABLE
  bright ~ OPAH
  bright-colored ~ TETRA
  brilliant ocean ~ OPAH
  bring in a ~ LAND, NET
  canned ~ TUNA
  cave-dwelling ~ EEL
  chunk-light ~ TUNA
  clean a ~ SCALE
  cold-water ~ SMELT
  disk-shaped marine ~ SKATE
  Dover's ~ SOLE
  electrifying ~ EEL
  emulate ~ SWIM
  exotic ~ TETRA
  filet ~ SOLE
  fine kettle of ~ MESS
  finless ~ EEL
  flat ~ RAY
  food ~ BASS, COD, HAKE, SHAD, SOLE, TROUT, TUNA
  freshwater ~ BASS, CARP, GAR, PIKE, TROUT
  game ~ BASS
  ganoid ~ GAR
  gefilte ~ CARP
  Great Lakes ~ SMELT
  group of ~ SHOAL
  herringlike ~ SHAD
  kettle of ~ PASS
  lake ~ BASS, TROUT
  like a cold ~ ALOOF

long ~ EEL

long-jawed ~ GAR

migratory ~ EEL

New England ~ SCROD

North Atlantic ~ COD

ocean ~ HAKE

pond ~ CARP

rainbow ~ SMELT

sardine ~ SPRAT

scaleless ~ EEL

school of ~ SHOAL

silvery ~ SMELT

small ~ FRY

smallmouth ~ BASS

snakelike ~ EEL

soup and ~ DRESS

speckled ~ TROUT

sport ~ BASS

striped ~ BASS

sushi ~ EEL

the ~ of the sea LIFE

tiny ~ SMELT

tropical ~ OPAH, TETRA

tropical ~, perhaps PET

try for a ~ CAST

unhatched ~ ROE

vividly-colored ~ OPAH

white ~ SCROD

young ~ FRY

fish ___ CAKE, FRY, OUT

___ fish GAME, PAN, PILOT

Fish
  the ~ DANCE, SIGN

fish-and-chips
  ~ quaff ALE

fish-eater
  furry ~ OTTER

fish-eating
  ~ bird ERN, ERNE

Fisher EDDIE

fisherman
  ~ fly LURE
  ~ garment OILER
  ~ gear REEL
  ~ hangout PIER
  ~ hope BITE
  ~ lure BAIT
  ~ maneuver CAST
  ~ need BAIT, CREEL, LURE
  see also angler

fisherman's
  ~ bend KNOT

fisherman's ___ BEND

Fisher-Price
  ~ product TOY

Fishes
  the ~ SIGN

fish-eye LENS

fishhook
  ~ part BARB

fishing
  ~ boat's yield HAUL
  ~ cord LINE
  ~ device SEINE
  ~ equipment NET
  ~ fly LURE
  ~ gear BOB, LURE, NET, REEL, ROD
  ~ need BAIT
  ~ site PIER
  ~ spot LAKE, PIER, POND, STREAM
  start ~ CAST

fishing ___ POLE, ROD

___ fishing ICE

fishline
  ~ adjunct LURE

"Fish Magic"
  ~ painter KLEE

fishnet MESH

fish or ___ bait CUT

___ fish sandwich TUNA

fish story LIE, TALE
  ~ teller LIAR

fishtail PALM, SKID

fish-to-be OVA, ROE

___ fish to fry OTHER

fishwife NAG

Fisk, Carlton
  gear for ~ MITT

fission SPLIT
  ~ blast ATEST

fissionable
  ~ material ATOM

fissure ABYSS, GAP, GASH, HOLE, LEAK, RENT, SPLIT

fist HAND
  ~ material IRON

___-fisted CLOSE, HAM, TWO

fistfight ROW, SCRAP

fistful
  a ~ of dollars WAD

"Fistful of Dollars, A" OATER
  ~ director LEONE

fisticuffs MELEE, ROW

fit ABLE, ADAPT, AGREE, HALE, LEAN, SUIT, TRIM
  ~ as a fiddle TRIM
  ~ for a king REGAL
  ~ for a queen REGAL
  ~ inside NEST
  ~ of chills AGUE
  ~ of pique IRE, PET, SNIT
  ~ of temper RAGE
  ~ out ATTIRE, DRESS, RIG
  ~ sails to RIG
  ~ starter RETRO
  ~ to be tied IRATE, MAD, UPSET
  ~ to drink PURE
  ~ together MESH, NEST
  ~ up RIG
  cat ~ SPASM
  cut to ~ ADAPT, TRIM
  hissy ~ SNIT
  make ~ ADAPT
  see ~ LIKE

throw a ~ RAGE, RAMP, RANT, RAVE, STORM

fit ___ fiddle ASA

fit ___ T TOA

fit ___ tied TOBE

fitness TONE
~ **center** SPA

fitted ABLE

___ fitter PIPE

fitting APT, DUE, GOOD, MEET, NICE
conduit ~ ELL
really ~ APT

Fittipaldi RACER

fit to ___ ATEE

fit to be ___ TIED

Fitzgerald ELLA
~ **forte** SCAT

FitzGerald, Edward POET
~ **translated him** OMAR
see also poet

five SIDE
~ **o'clock shadow** BEARD
~ **(prefix)** PENT
~ **smackeroos** FIN
one of ~ SENSE
one of ~ Norse kings OLAF, OLAV
take ~ DEFER, REST

five-___ plan YEAR

"Five ___ Back" CAME

"Five ___ Final" STAR

"Five ___ Pieces" EASY

"___ Five" TAKE

five-and-___ DIME, TEN

five-and-ten STORE

five-centime
~ **piece** SOU

"Five Corners"
~ **director** BILL

five-dollar
~ **bill** FIN

five-franc
~ **coin** ECU

"Five Graves to ___" CAIRO

"Five Guys Named ___" MOE

five-in-a-row
~ **game** KENO

Five Nations
one of the ~ ONEIDA

five o'clock
~ **shadow** BEARD

fiver
change for a ~ ONES

five-spot FIN

five-star
~ **monogram** DDE
~ **name** OMAR

~ **nickname** IKE

"Five Star Final"
~ **director** LEROY

five-time
~ **Presidential candidate** DEBS
~ **Wimbledon champ** BORG

five-year ___ PLAN

fix ALTER, AMEND, CURE, EMEND, GLUE, HOLE, JAM, LIMIT, MEND, MESS, NAIL, ORIENT, PIN, PLANT, RESTORE, RIVET, ROOT, SET, SETTLE
~ **a boot** SOLE
~ **a cravat** RETIE
~ **a fight** RIG
~ **a hole** DARN
~ **a manuscript** EDIT
~ **a piano** TUNE
~ **a pump** SOLE
~ **archaeologically** DATE
~ **a seam** SEW
~ **a shoe** SOLE
~ **a shoelace** RETIE
~ **a squeak** OIL
~ **a watch** SET
~ **copy** EDIT
~ **firmly** MOOR, NAIL, RIVET, TIE
~ **fractures** SET
~ **in one's mind** LEARN
~ **in the mind** CON, ETCH
~ **in time** DATE
~ **permanently** ETCH, GLUE, NAIL, RIVET
~ **socks** DARN
~ **supper** EATIN
~ **tea** BREW
~ **the outcome** RIG
~ **the period of** DATE
~ **the potatoes** MASH
~ **the table** SET
~ **up** DRESS, REDO, RENEW, RESTORE
~ **up an old house** REHAB
~ **upon** ELECT
~ **value** ASSESS
pretty ~ MESS

"___ Fix, The" BIG

fixate DOTE

fixation MANIA
groupie's ~ IDOL

___ fixe IDEE

fixed ETERNAL, FAST, INERT, SET, STAID, SURE
~ **idea** BIAS
~ **look** STARE
~ **opinion** DOGMA
~ **procedure** ROTE
~ **quantity** UNIT
~ **routine** ROTE, RUT
firmly ~ FAST

fixed-up
~ **tire** RECAP

fizz FOAM, HISS
~ **ingredient** GIN
add ~ to AERATE
lacking ~ FLAT

fizzle HISS
~ **out** DIE

fizzler DUD

fizzy
~ **drink** COLA, SODA
make ~ AERATE

fjord BAY, COVE, INLET
~ **setting** OSLO
~ **terr.** NOR

___ Fjord OSLO

FL
see Florida

Fla.
~ **neighbor** ALA
~ **time** EDT, EST
it borders ~ ATL
see also Florida

flabbergast AMAZE, DAZE, STUN

flabbergasted AGOG

flabby FAT, LIMP

flabellum FAN

flaccid LIMP

flack
~ **concern** IMAGE

flag ALERT, FADE, GREET, IRIS, LAG, PAVE, PETER, SAG, STD, TIRE
~ **down** HAIL
~ **feature** STAR
~ **holder** POLE
~ **maker** ROSS
~ **waver** GALE
raise a red ~ WARN
wave a red ~ ENRAGE

Flag ___ DAY

flagellate BEAT, LACE

flagellum LASH, ORGAN

flagitious VILE

flagon EWER
~ **filler** ALE

flagpole MAST
~ **topper** EAGLE

flagrant BALD, OPEN

flagrante delicto
find in ~ NAIL

flagstaff POLE

flagstone SLAB

flagstones
lay ~ PAVE

"...___ flag was still there" OUR

flail BEAT, CANE, HIT, TAN

flair ART, CHIC, DASH, ELAN, NOSE, STYLE
~ **for music** EAR

flake BIT, CHIP, IOTA, PEEL, SCALE, SHED
~ **makeup** SNOW
~ **off** PEEL
~ **out** SLEEP

flakes
some ~ SOAP

___ flakes CORN

flaky DAFT, ODD, OFF
not ~ SANE

flamboyant ORNATE

flame BEAU, COLOR, FIRE, LOVE
~ **color** RED
~ **fancier** MOTH

___ flame OLD

"Flame ___ India" OVER

"Flame ___ the Arrow, The" AND

"Flame and the ___, The" ARROW

"Flame of ___ Orleans, The" NEW

"Flame Over ___" INDIA

flames
felonious ~ ARSON
in ~ AFIRE

Flames SIX, TEAM
~ **milieu** ICE, RINK
~ **org.** NHL

flaming AFIRE, HOT

"Flaming ___" STAR

flamingo BIRD

"Flamingo ___" ROAD

"Flamingo ___, The" KID

flammable
~ **gas** ETHANE

Flanders, Mr.
~ **of "The Simpsons"** NED

Flandres
Bouvier des ~ DOG, PET

flange EDGE, LIP, RIM

flank ATTEND, LOIN, MEAT, SIDE, STEAK

flap ADO, BEAT, MELEE, SPAT, STIR, TAB, TAG, TODO
~ **one's gums** GAB, YAK
gummed ~ SEAL

flapdoodle ROT

flapjack CAKE
~ **in French** CREPE

flapper GIRL

flapping LOOSE
stopped ~ ALIT, LIT

flaps
having ~ EARED

flare BLAST, LAMP
~ **up** RAGE, RAVE, RISE
send up a ~ ALARM, ALERT
solar ~ GAS

flare-___ UPS

___ flare SOLAR

flared
~ **skirt** ALINE

flash BEAM, BLAST, ELAN, FLARE, GLARE, NEWS, SHINE
~ **flood** SPATE
quicker than a ~ BANG

flash ___ CARD

___ flash INA, NEWS

flasher LAMP

flash in the ___ PAN

flashlight LAMP

flashy LOUD, ORNATE
~ **dresser** DUDE

flask VIAL

flat ABODE, ARID, BANAL, DRAB, DRY, EVEN, HOME, MAT, MATTE, NEEDY, PAD, STALE, TAME
~ **broke** POOR
~ **dweller** TENANT
~ **ender** BED, BOAT, CAR, LAND, TOP, WARE
~ **finish** MAT, MATTE
~ **fish** RAY
~ **hat** TAM
~ **hill** MESA
~ **lack** AIR
~ **payment** RENT
~ **sign** TOLET
~ **surface** PLANE
be ~ LIE
fall ~ MISS
in nothing ~ SOON
it may be ~ TIRE
leave ~ DROP
lying ~ PRONE
mud ~ MIRE
not ~ STEEP

flat ___ (car trouble) TIRE

flat-___ OUT

flat-backed
~ **fiddle** VIOL

flatboat ARK, SCOW
Mississippi ~ ARK

flat-bottomed
~ **boat** RAFT, SCOW

flatfish DAB, SOLE

flatfoot COP

Flathead TRIBE

flatland TABLE

Flatt
~ **buddy** EARL

flatten EVEN, PRESS, RAZE

flattened
~ **circle** OVAL

flattens KOS

flatter EXALT
~ **in a way** APE
~ **oneself** BRAG

flattery OIL
deceive by ~ SNOW

Flattery CAPE

flattop MESA

Flaubert
~ **character** EMMA
see also French

flaunt BRAG, CROW, PARADE

flavor AROMA, CAST, LIFE, SALT, SAVOR, TANG, TASTE
~ **enhancer** HERB, MSG, SALT
ade ~ LEMON, LIME, ORANGE
beverage ~ COLA
citrus ~ ACID, SOUR, TART
cool ~ MINT
gin-fizz ~ SLOE
juice ~ LEMON, LIME, ORANGE
liqueur ~ PEAR
pickle ~ DILL
pie ~ APPLE, LEMON
sharp ~ TANG
tangy ~ MINT

flavorful GOOD

flavoring
aromatic ~ ANISE

flavorless BLAH, FLAT

flavorsome SWEET

flaw BLOT, CHIP, DENT, ERROR, HOLE, LEAK, SCAR, SPOT, TAINT
bumper ~ DENT
can ~ DENT
clothing ~ RIP
faucet ~ LEAK
minor ~ DENT

flawless CLEAN, CLEAR, IDEAL, PURE

flax
~ **fabric** LINEN
dampen ~ RET

flaxen COLOR, TOW

flay LASH, SKIN

flea PEST
~ **in one's ear** HINT
~ **market** FAIR
~ **market stipulation** ASIS
~ **market transaction** RESALE

fleabag HOTEL
like a ~ SEEDY

flèche SPIRE

fleck BIT, DOT, IOTA, MITE, SPOT
furnace ~ ASH

Fledermaus BAT

fledgling BIRD, OWLET
~ **home** NEST

flee DESERT, EXIT, LAM, LEAVE, RUN, SCAT, SCRAM
~ **from** AVOID
~ **to a J.P.** ELOPE

fleece BLEED, CLIP, COAT, CON, HAIR, HIDE, LOOT, PELT, PILE, PREY, ROB, ROOK, SKIN, STEAL, STING, TAKE
~ **source** EWE, LLAMA

fleece-seeking
~ **ship** ARGO

fleecing CLIP
~ **activity** SCAM

fleecy
~ **animal** EWE, LLAMA, RAM

fleet AGILE, FAST, RAPID
~ **initials** USS
~ **member** BOAT, CAB, SHIP, TAXI
of the ~ NAVAL

fleet-footed AGILE

Fleet Street PRESS

Fleetwood ___ MAC

Fleischer NAT

Fleisher LEON

Fleming ART, IAN

Fleming, Alexander SIR

Fleming, Ian
~ **alma mater** ETON

flesh MEAT
~ **and blood** CLAY, KIN, LIFE
~ **starter** GOOSE
in the ~ LIVE
make one's ~ **crawl** REPEL, SCARE
the ills that ~ **is heir to** LIFE

___ flesh GOOSE

"Flesh ___ Fantasy" AND

"Flesh ___ the Devil" AND

fleshy OBESE
~ **plant** ALOE

Fletcher, Jessica
~ **doctor friend** SETH

fleur-de-___ LIS

fleur-de-lis IRIS

___-fleuve (saga) ROMAN

"___ Flew Over the Cuckoo's Nest" ONE

flex BEND

flexed
easily ~ LITHE

flexibility PLAY

flexible LITHE
~ **tube** HOSE

Flexible Flyer SLED

flexure ARC

flick FLIP

Flicka HORSE, MARE

flicker BAT, BEAM, FLARE, FLIT, GLOW, SHINE, SWAY

___-flicker FLEA

flier BET, BILL, BIRD, PILOT, RACER
Arctic ~ TERN
Atlantic ~ ERN, ERNE
Canadian ~ GOOSE, LOON
fork-tailed ~ TERN
formation ~ GOOSE
hotshot ~ ACE
lightweight ~ KITE

littoral ~ ERN, ERNE
marine ~ ERN, ERNE
mythical ~ ROC
night ~ BAT, OWL
ocean ~ ERN, ERNE, TERN
pesky ~ GNAT
piscivorous ~ ERN, ERNE
Scandinavian ~ SAS
sea ~ ERN, ERNE, TERN
shore ~ ERN, ERNE, TERN
silent ~ BAT, EAGLE, OWL
tabloid ~ UFO
take a ~ DARE, RISK
white-tailed ~ ERN, ERNE
see also airline, bird, flyer

flies
~ **to spiders** DIET, FARE, PREY
catch ~ SHAG

flight LAM, RUN
~ **abbr.** ETA
~ **agcy.** CAP
~ **approval** AOK
~ **attendant's boss** PILOT
~ **captain** PILOT
~ **dir.** ENE, ESE, NNE, NNW, SSE, SSW, WNW, WSW
~ **inducer** FEAR
~ **of fancy** DREAM
~ **part** RISER, STAIR
~ **(prefix)** AER, AERO
~ **record** LOG
~ **route** ARC
~ **starter** FLAP
~ **stat.** ARR
~ **unit** STEP
disorderly ~ ROUT
in ~ ALOFT
pertaining to ~ AERO
put to ~ REPEL, ROUT
short ~ HOP
sudden ~ LAM
take ~ FLEE, JET
top ~ ABLE, AONE

flight ___ BAG, PLAN

___ flight SPACE, TEST

"___ Flight, The" LAST

flightless
~ **bird** EMU, RHEA
~ **bird of yore** DODO, MOA

flimflam ROOK, SCAM

"Flim Flam ___, The" MAN

"___ flim-flam stories, and nothing but shams and lies" MERE

flimsy MEAN, POOR, THIN
~ **as an excuse** LAME

flinch FEAR, SHY, START

Flinders ___ RANGE

fling CAST, DANCE, DASH, HURL, LARK, LOB, ORGY, PELT, REVEL, SPREE, TEAR, TOSS, TRIAL
~ **a fly** CAST
~ **dirt** LIBEL
Highland ~ DANCE

flint STONE
~ **starter** SKIN

flintlock GUN

Flintstone FRED
 ~ boss SLATE
 ~ pet DINO

flinty COOL, CRUEL, HARD, STERN

flip PERT, SASSY, TOSS
 ~ one's lid RAGE, RAVE
 ~ over ADORE, UPEND
 ~ over pages LEAF
 ~ talk SASS
 ~ through READ, SCAN
 ~ (through) PAGE
 extremely ~ RUDE

flip ___ SIDE

flip chart
 ~ holder EASEL

flip one's ___ LID

flippancy LIP, SASS

flippant PERT, SASSY

"Flipper"
 ~ pelican PETE

flippers
 ~ user SEAL

flirt MASH, OGLE, TEASE, TOY
 ~ with EYE

flit DART, GAD, LEAVE, MOVE,
 RACE, RUN, SKIP
 ~ about GAD
 ~ by SLIP
 do a moonlight ~ FLEE

flitting
 ~ about ADO

flivver AUTO, CAR, CRATE, MOTOR

Flo
 ~ boss MEL
 ~ coworker ALICE, VERA

float BATHE, BOB, RAFT, RIDE,
 RISE, SAIL, SWIM
 ~ from TRAIL
 ~ ingredient SODA
 ~ like a butterfly FLIT
 ~ like a cork BOB
 ~ place PARADE
 ~ to the top RISE
 not ~ SINK

floater NOMAD
 flume ~ LOG
 pond ~ PAD

floating ASEA, ATSEA, AWASH

floating ___ RIB

___-floating FREE

"Float like a butterfly"
 ~ boxer ALI

flock HERD, HORDE, HOST, MOB,
 PRESS, TROOP
 ~ hangout LEA
 ~ member EWE, LAMB
 ~ sound BAA
 ~ together MASS, TROOP
 far from the ~ LOST
 leader of the ~ RAM
 of the ~ LAIC

floe
 ~ material ICE
 ice ~ BERG

___ floe ICE

flog BEAT, CANE, HIT, LAM, LASH,
 SMITE, STRAP, TAN

flogging
 ~ implement CANE

flood GLUT, LAMP, POUR, RAIN,
 SEA, SPATE, STREAM, TIDE
 ~ barrier LEVEE
 ~ control DAM
 ~ embankment LEVEE
 ~ ender GATE, TIDE
 ~ opposite EBB
 ~ point CREST
 ~ stage EBB
 ~ survivor HAM, NOAH
 ~ the market GLUT
 flash ~ SPATE

flood ___ TIDE

flood control
 ~ construction DAM
 ~ initials TVA

flooded AWASH
 be ~ SWIM

floodlight LAMP

floor AMAZE, AWE, DAZE, DROP,
 STUN
 ~ access STAIR
 ~ cover MAT, RUG
 ~ covering MAT, RUG, TILE
 ~ exercise EVENT
 ~ it RACE, SPEED
 ~ model DEMO
 ~ space AREA
 corrida ~ ARENA
 hit the ~ hard STAMP
 mop the ~ with BEAT, ROUT
 pile on the ~ RUG
 top ~ ATTIC
 truck ~ BED
 walk the ~ PACE

floor ___ LAMP, MODEL, PLAN,
 SHOW

___ floor SEA

floor model
 ~ warning ASIS

floor plan
 ~ designation DOOR

floor show
 ~ unit ACT

flop BEAT, DUD, FLAP, LOLL, LOSER
 ~ opposite HIT, SMASH
 auto ~ EDSEL

flop-___ EARED

___-flop FLIP

flophouse HOTEL

floppy LIMP, LOOSE
 ~ contents DATA

Flopsy
 ~ brother PETER

flora LEAF
 ~ and fauna LIFE

floral
 ~ garland LEI
 ~ oil ATTAR
 ~ vessel VASE

**"___ Flor and Her Two Hus-
 bands"** DONA

Florence
 ~ lang. ITAL
 ~ river ARNO
 see also Italian

Florentine
 ~ poet DANTE

floribunda ROSE

florid ORNATE, RED, ROSY

Florida STATE
 ~ acquisition TAN
 ~ bay TAMPA
 ~ city MIAMI, OCALA, TAMPA
 ~ county BAY, CLAY, DADE,
 LAKE, LEE, LEON, ORANGE
 ~ islet CAY, KEY
 ~ vacation spot KEYS

Florida's ___ National Forest
 OCALA

florin COIN

florist
 ~ need POT, VASE

"Florodora ___, The" GIRL

Florsheim
 ~ product SHOE

flossing
 ~ advocates' org. ADA

flotilla FLEET

flotsam
 ~ and jetsam TRASH

flounder DAB, SOLE

floundering ASEA, ATSEA

flour MEAL
 ~ container SACK
 ~ source OAT, RYE, SOY
 process ~ SIFT

flourish BOOM, DASH, GROW, LIVE,
 SHOW
 printing ~ SERIF

flow EMERGE, ISSUE, OOZE, ROLL,
 RUN, STREAM, TENOR, TIDE
 ~ along RUN
 ~ away EBB
 ~ forth SPEW
 ~ from ARISE, COME, RISE
 ~ opposite EBB
 ~ out BLEED, SEEP
 ~ slowly OOZE, SEEP
 ~ starter OVER
 continuous ~ STREAM
 ebb and ~ TIDE
 let ~ SHED
 stop the ~ STEM
 volcano ~ LAVA
 watch the river ~ LOAF

___ flow CASH

flower ASTER, BEAR, GLAD,
 GROW, IRIS, LILAC, LILY, OPEN,
 PANSY, PLANT, ROSE, SEGO,
 TULIP
 ~ arranging ART
 ~ bed PLOT
 ~ container URN, VASE
 ~ garland LEI
 ~ holder POT, VASE
 ~ location BED
 ~ oil ATTAR
 ~ part PETAL, SEPAL, STEM
 ~ signature ODOR
 ~ visitor BEE
 ~ with a face PANSY
 bearded ~ IRIS
 bell-shaped ~ TULIP
 bulbous ~ GLAD, TULIP
 composite ~ ASTER
 cut ~ STEM
 daisylike ~ ASTER
 floating ~ LILY
 fragrant ~ LILAC, LILY, ROSE
 full ~ ACME, PEAK
 garden ~ ASTER, GLAD, IRIS,
 ROSE, TULIP
 in full ~ RIPE
 late summer ~ ASTER
 **New Hampshire's state
 ~** LILAC
 orchidlike ~ IRIS
 perennial ~ ASTER
 pickled ~ bud CAPER
 potential ~ SEED
 rayed ~ ASTER
 showy ~ IRIS, ROSE, TULIP
 starlike ~ ASTER
 tall ~ GLAD
 Tennessee's state ~ IRIS
 thorny ~ ROSE
 trellis ~ ROSE
 US national ~ ROSE
 Utah's state ~ SEGO
 vivid-hued ~ PANSY

flower ___ GIRL

"Flower ___" (Puccini piece)
 DUET

flower bed
 ~ foundation SOIL
 smooth the ~ RAKE

flowering
 ~ shrub LILAC, ROSE
 European ~ plant ARUM
 full ~ DAY

"Flowering Peach, The"
 ~ playwright ODETS

"Flower in the Crannied Wall"
 POEM

flowerless
 ~ plant FERN, MOSS

flower petal
 ~ product ATTAR

flowerpot
 ~ locale LEDGE, SILL

flowers
 ~ do it OPEN
 ~ home BED
 goddess of ~ FLORA
 ring of ~ LEI

"Flowers in the ___" ATTIC

"Flower Song" ARIA

flowery ORNATE
~ **necklace** LEI
~ **perfume** ATTAR

flown
~ **the coop** GONE

fl. oz.
one-sixth ~ TSP

flu
~ **symptom** ACHE, AGUE
have the ~ AIL
kind of ~ ASIAN
one ~ **source** ASIA

___ **flu** ASIAN, BLUE

flub BONER, ERR, ERROR
~ **as a grounder** BOOT
fielding ~ ERROR
memory ~ LAPSE

fluctuate RANGE, SWAY, TEETER, YOYO

flue LINT, PIPE
~ **material** SOOT
~ **residue** ASH

fluent EASY, GLIB

fluff ERR, LINT, PILE
~ **up** TEASE
infielder's ~ ERROR

fluffy
~ **neckwear** BOA

Fluffy CAT, PET

fluid
~ **buildup** EDEMA
~ **container** SAC
~ **rock** LAVA
arboreal ~ SAP
body ~ SERUM
etcher's ~ ACID
life ~ SAP
pen ~ INK
plant ~ SERUM
spile ~ SAP
vital ~ SAP
writing ~ INK

fluid ___ DRAM, OUNCE

fluidity EASE

fluids
medical ~ SERA

flu-ish
feel ~ ACHE

fluke
by a ~ ONCE

flume RACE, RUN
~ **floater** LOG

flummery PAP, TRASH

flummox ADDLE

flummoxed ASEA, ATSFA

___**-flung** FAR

flunk
~ **out** LOSE
opposite of ~ ACE

flunky AIDE, PAGE, TOOL

fluorescent
~ **light** LAMP

fluoride SALT

fluorine GAS

flurry ADO, SNOW, STIR, TEAR
~ **of activity** SPASM

___ **flurry** SNOW

flush BATHE, CLEAN, COLOR, EVEN, FAT, GLOW, RICH, RINSE

flushed HOT, RED, ROSY

Flushing Meadows
~ **landmark** SHEA
~ **team** METS

fluster ABASH, ADDLE, DAZE, GET, JAR, PRESS, STEW, UPSET

flute PIPE
~ **cousin** OBOE
architectural ~ STRIA
kind of ~ ALTO

fluting STRIA

flutter ADO, BAT, BATE, BEAT, FLAP, FLIT, STIR, STREAM

flux RUN, STREAM, TIDE
magnetic ~ **unit** TESLA

fly AVIATE, EXIT, FLAP, FLIT, HIE, LURE, MOVE, PILOT, RACE, RUN, SPEED, TEAR
~ **after** CHASE
~ **alone** SOLO
~ **by** SLIP
~ **catcher** WEB
~ **ender** LEAF, PAPER
~ **high** SOAR
~ **in the face of** DARE
~ **in the ointment** SNAG
~ **off the handle** BOIL, ERUPT, RAGE, RAVE, STORM
~ **rapidly** FLIT
~ **starter** BAR, FIRE, GAD, MAY, MED, SAW, SHOO
~ **the coop** FLEE, RUN, SKIP
~ **to a spider** PREY
~ **trajectory** ARC
~ **trap** WEB
African ~ TSETSE
artificial ~ LURE
black ~ GNAT
clobber a ~ SWAT
dangerous ~ TSETSE
fishing ~ LURE
fling a ~ CAST
half a ~ TSE
hit a ~, perhaps BAT
horse ~ PEST
house ~ PEST
let ~ CAST, HURL
small ~ GNAT
they ~ **by night** BATS, OWLS

fly ___ BALL, ROD

fly ___ **the handle** OFF

fly- ___ CAST, OVER

___ **fly** CRANE, DEER, DRY, HORSE, LET, POP

"___, fly!" SHOO

"___ Fly Away" ILL

fly ball
~ **path** ARC

fly balls
retrieve, as ~ SHAG

flyboys
~ **org.** USAF

fly-by-night NOMAD

flycatcher BIRD

flyer PILOT
coastal ~ ERN, ERNE, TERN
fast ~ JET
fearless ~ ACE
formation ~ GOOSE
high ~ EAGLE, KITE
night ~ BAT, OWL
see also bird, flier

Flyers SIX, TEAM
~ **milieu** ICE, RINK
~ **org.** NHL

flying ALOFT
~ **buzzer** BEE
~ **formation** VEE
~ **machine** PLANE
~ **mammal** BAT
~ **piscivore** ERN, ERNE
~ **saucer** UFO
~ **standard** FLAG
~ **toy** KITE
go ~ AVIATE
of planes and ~ AERO

flying ___ MARE, START

"Flying ___, The" NUN

Flying Cloud
~ **in old automobiling** REO

"Flying Down to ___" RIO

"Flying Dutchman, The" BOAT, OPERA, SHIP
~ **heroine** SENTA
~ **tenor** ERIK

Flying Fortress PLANE

"Flying Leathernecks, The"
~ **director** RAY

flyleaf PAGE

"Fly Me to the ___" MOON

Flynn ERROL
~ **role** HOOD
1951 ~ **film** KIM

___ **Flynn Boyle** LARA

flyspeck DOT, IOTA, MOTE, SPOT

fly swatter
~ **material** MESH
bovine ~ TAIL

flytrap PLANT
arachnid ~ WEB

Fm ELEM
100 for ~ ATNO

FM
~ **choice** STA

f-number STOP

foal ANIMAL, BEAR, COLT, DROP, HORSE
~ **father** SIRE
~ **food** HAY, OATS
~ **mom** DAM, MARE

foam BOIL, HEAD

foaming
~ **at the mouth** IRATE, MAD, RABID, UPSET

fob ___ (foist) OFF

FOB
part of ~ FREE

focal
~ **point** NODE, POLE

Foch NINA

"fo'c'sle"
say ~ ELIDE

focus AIM, MUSE
~ **on** RIVET
~ **starter** AUTO
fan club ~ IDOL
lose ~ BLUR
main ~ THEME
panel ~ TOPIC

fodder FEED, HAY, OATS, RANGE, STRAW
mainframe ~ DATA
society-page ~ GALA

foe ENEMY
Ajax ~ DIRT
Arapaho ~ UTE
Assyrian ~ MEDE
Confederacy ~ UNION
Dillinger ~ GMAN
Gulf War ~ IRAQ
Nitti ~ NESS
Pizarro ~ INCA
Saigon ~ HANOI
Seneca ~ ERIE
WWII ~ AXIS
see also enemy

foes
pub. defender's ~ DAS

fog BLUR, DAZE, MIST, STEAM
~ **up** BLUR
dirty ~ SMOG
in a ~ ASEA, ATSEA
light ~ MIST
like ~ WET
like pea-soup ~ DENSE

"Fog" POEM

Fogelberg DAN

fogger
mirror ~ STEAM

foggy DAMP, DIM

"Foggy ___, The" DEW

fogy
old ~ DODO, ELDER

foil ARC, DASH, DETER, ELUDE, LEAF, REPEL, SHEET, STEEL, STOP
~ **alternative** EPEE, SARAN
~ **material** TIN

___ **foil** GOLD

foil-wrapped
~ **candy** KISS

___ **fois** (once: Fr.) UNE

foist
~ **(in)** DRAG

Foix
see French

fold BEND, DRAPE, PALE, PEN, PLY
~ **in** ADD
~ **inhabitant** EWE
~ **starter** BILL
cloth ~ PLEAT
coat ~ LAPEL
kilt ~ PLEAT

foldaway
~ **bed** COT

folded
~ **up** SHUT
be ~ LAP

folder FILE

folding
~ **money** ONES, TENS

folding ___ DOOR

folds
arrange in ~ DRAPE
gather into ~ PLEAT

foliage LEAF
~ **underpinning** STEM
filled with ~ DENSE

folic ACID

"Folies Bergère"
~ **city** PARIS
~ **director** RUTH

folio LEAF, PAGE, SHEET

folk
~ **dance** REEL
~ **hero from**
Kentucky BOONE
~ **history** LORE

folk ___ ART, DANCE, MASS, SONG,
TALE

folklore
~ **being** ELF
~ **meanie** OGRE
underground dweller of
~ GNOME

folks ONES
home ~ KIN
where most ~ **live** ASIA
yonder ~ THEM

"___ Folks" ("Peanuts" former
name) LIL

Follett KEN
~ **figure** SPY

follicle SAC

Follies
~ **fellow** FLO

follow DOG, ENSUE, HEED, OBEY,
SPY, TAG, TAIL, TRACE, TRAIL
~ **a circular path** ARC
~ **after** CHASE
~ **closely** APE, DOG, HEEL

~ **(from)** COME
~ **orders** OBEY
~ **suit** APE, ECHO
~ **the cookbook** ADD
~ **the leader** FILE
~ **with one's eyes** OGLE
don't ~ LEAD

follow ___ SUIT

follow- ___ UPS

follower TAIL
~ **(suffix)** IST, ITE

___ **follower** CAMP

following AFTER, LATER, NEXT,
TAIL, THEN, TRAIN
~ **(prefix)** EPI
not ~ AHEAD, LOST

follow one's ___ NOSE

"Follow the ___**"** FLEET

follow the leader
~ **player** APER

folly
curse one's ~ RUE

"___ folly to be wise" TIS

Fomalhaut STAR

foment ABET, AROUSE, FAN,
ROUSE, SOW

fond
~ **memories** PAST
~ **of mischief** SLY
be ~ **of** LIKE, LOVE
be too ~ DOTE

Fonda JANE, PETER

Fonda, Bridget
~ **film** ARIA
~ **uncle** TED

Fonda, Jane
~ **hubby** TED

Fond du ___**, Wis.** LAC

fondness ESTEEM, TASTE
have a ~ **for** LIKE

fondue DIP

font
~ **choice** AGATE, ELITE, PEARL,
PICA, ROMAN
~ **widths** EMS, ENS

Fontanne LYNN

Fonteyn, Margot DAME
~ **fulcrum** TOE
attire for ~ TUTU

food EATS, FARE, MEAL, MEAT,
MESS
~ **additive** DYE, MSG
~ **mart** DELI
~ **thickener** AGAR
~ **wrap** CELLO
fish ~ ALGA
health ~ BRAN, KELP
high-fiber ~ BRAN
ladybug ~ APHID
supply ~ CATER
unit of ~ **energy** CAL

___ **food** FAST, SOUL

___ **food cake** ANGEL

food chain
~ **bottom** ALGA

food processor
~ **setting** CHOP, PUREE

food safety
~ **org.** FDA

food storage
~ **aid** ICE

foofaraw ADO, TODO

fool ASS, CON, DOLT, DUPE, HAVE,
IDIOT, KID, LETON, SAP
~ **away** LOSE, WASTE
~ **away time** IDLE, LOAF
~ **mo.** APR
~ **month** APRIL
~ **(with)** PLAY, TOY
fortune's ~ LOSER
make a ~ **of** ROAST, SNUB
old ~ COOT
play for a ~ USE
play the ~ AMUSE

___ **fool** APRIL

Fool
the ~ TAROT

"___ Fool" IMA

fooled
not ~ **by** ONTO

foolhardy RASH

foolish DAFT, INANE, INEPT, MAD,
RASH
~ **one** ASS, SAP, YOYO
~ **talk** YAP
not ~ WISE

foolishness TRASH

"___ Foolish Things" THESE

"Fool me ___ **shame on you!..."**
ONCE

foolproof SURE

fool's ___ CAP, ERRAND, GOLD

foolscap PAPER

___ **Fools' Day** ALL

"Fool Such ___**, A"** ASI

foot UNIT
~ **covering** SHOE
~ **division** INCH
~ **ender** AGE, BALL, BATH,
GEAR, HOLD, LONG, LOOSE,
MAN, NOTE, PAD, PATH,
RACE, REST, SORE, STEP,
WEAR
~ **for a poet** IAMB
~ **it** PAD
~ **lever** PEDAL
~ **part** ARCH, HEEL, INCH, PAD,
SOLE, TOE
~ **patrol** BEAT
~ **pedal** LEVER
~ **starter** BARE, FLAT, FORE,
HOT, UNDER, WEB
~ **the bill** PAY, TREAT
~ **up** ADD
~ **width** AAA, EEE

~ **wiper** MAT
animal's ~ PAW
crow's ~ LINE
from head to ~ OVER
have a heavy ~ SPEED
hot ~ APACE
journey by ~ HIKE
metrical ~ IAMB
poetic ~ IAMB
put one's ~ **down** STAMP,
STEP
put one's ~ **in one's**
mouth ERR

___ **foot** LEAD

footage
square ~ AREA, SIZE

football GAME
~ **field** GRID
~ **filler** AIR
~ **foul** CLIP, HOLD
~ **part** LACE
~ **path** ARC
~ **play** PASS, RUN
~ **player** END
~ **score** GOAL
~ **scores** TDS
~ **setback** LOSS
~ **stand** TEE
~ **team** ELEVEN
~ **venue** ARENA
~ **yardage** GAIN
~ **yell** RAH
commit a ~ **infraction** CLIP,
HOLD
political ~ ISSUE

___ **football** ARENA

footballer
Buffalo ~ BILL
Chicago ~ BEAR
Detroit ~ LION
Indianapolis ~ COLT
New York ~ GIANT, JET
Philadelphia ~ EAGLE
Saint Louis ~ RAM

football game
~ **duration** HOUR

Football Hall of Fame
~ **state** OHIO

football's ___ **Bowl** HULA,
ORANGE, PRO, ROSE

football shaped OVATE

football-shoe
~ **part** CLEAT

football team
~ **quota** ELEVEN

Foote
~ **work** DRAMA

___**-footed** FLAT, SLOW, SURE,
WEB

footfall STEP, TREAD

"___ Foot Forward" BEST

footgear SHOE

foothold
mountaineer's ~ CRAG

footing BASE
   equal ~ PAR
   lose one's ~ TRIP

"___ Foot in Heaven" ONE

foot in the ___ DOOR

foot-leg
   ~ connector ANKLE

"Footlight ___" PARADE

footlights
   ~ locale STAGE

foot-long
   ~ object RULER

"Footloose"
   ~ director ROSS
   ~ role REN

footnote
   ~ abbr. ETAL, IBID
   ~ notation ETAL
   make a ~ CITE

footpath LANE, TRAIL

foot-pound
   ~ relative ERG

footprint SIGN, STEP

"Footprints on the ___ of time" SANDS

footrace
   ~ terminus TAPE

footrest RAIL

footstep TREAD

footwear BOOT, HOSE
   provided ~ to SHOD

___ foo yung EGG

fop BEAU, DUDE

foppery POSE

for PRO
   ~ a specific purpose ADHOC
   ~ good EVER
   ~ nothing FREE
   ~ the taking FREE

for ___ (definitely) SURE

for ___ (permanently) GOOD

for ___ measure GOOD

for ___ or money LOVE

for ___ the world ALL

___ for (approach) MAKE

___ for (attempt) SHOOT

___ for (buy) POP

___ for (endure) STAND

___ for (impersonate) PASS

___ for (request) ASK

___ for (select) OPT

___ for (summon) CALL, SEND

"...for ___ of woman born" NONE

"For ___" (Poe work) ANNIE

"For ___ a jolly good fellow" HES

"For ___ in My Life" ONCE

"For ___ know..." ALLI

"For ___ Mankind" ALL

"For ___ us a child is born" UNTO

"For ___—With Love and Squalor" ESME

for a ___ (cheaply) SONG

"For a ___ Dollars More" FEW

"___ for a Day" LADY

___ for a fall RIDE

"For a Few Dollars ___" MORE

"For a Few Dollars More"
   ~ director LEONE

forage FEED, HAY, HUNT, RAID
   ~ food HAY
   ~ plant ERS

___ for a king FIT

"___ for Alarm" CAUSE

"___ for Alibi" AIS

___-for-all FREE

"___, for all his feathers..., The" OWL

"___ for All Seasons" AMAN

"___ for All Seasons, A" MAN

foramen HOLE

"For Annie"
   ~ author POE

"___ for apple" AIS

___ for a ride TAKE

foray RAID

forbear BEAR, OMIT, REMIT

"___ for Benny, A" MEDAL

"For Better or for ___" WORSE

"For Better or for Worse"
   ~ pup EDGAR
   ~ toddler APRIL

forbid BAN, BAR, DENY, TABOO, TABU, VETO

forbidden TABOO, TABU
   ~ thing NONO

Forbidden City
   the ~ LHASA

forbidden fruit APPLE
   ~ locale EDEN

forbidding COOL, STERN

force BIND, CRAM, CREW, GIST, LEVER, MAIN, MAKE, PRY
   ~ along URGE
   ~ back REPEL
   ~ down CRAM
   ~ forward IMPEL
   ~ majeure EVENT
   ~ one's way in ENTER

   ~ open PRY
   ~ out EJECT, OUST
   ~ to go SEND
   bring ~ to bear IMPEL
   destructive ~ BANE
   driving ~ URGE
   dynamic ~ LIFE
   ground ~ ARMY
   hostile ~ ENEMY, FOE
   in ~ ALIVE
   land ~ ARMY
   Lao-Tzu's creative ~ TAO
   life ~ TAO
   marshal's ~ POSSE
   measure of ~ DYNE
   military ~ ARMY
   moving ~ AGENT
   naval ~ FLEET
   not in ~ VOID
   opposing ~ ENEMY, FOE
   remain in ~ STAND
   strike with ~ RAM
   task ~ FLEET
   tour de ~ FEAT
   unit of ~ DYNE
   vital ~ SOUL
   work ~ HELP

force ___ PLAY

___ force AIR, GALE, LIFE, TASK

Force
   dark side of the ~ EVIL

forceful
   ~ stream JET

force of ___ HABIT

"Force of ___" EVIL

force one's ___ HAND

forces
   join ~ AID, ALLY, BAND, HELP, POOL, UNITE
   muster one's ~ ARM

___ forces ARMED

"___ for Conduct" ZERO

"___ for Conquest" CITY

"For crying ___ loud!" OUT

ford WADE

Ford AUTO, CAR
   ~ contemporary EDISON
   ~ running mate DOLE
   1950s ~ EDSEL
   onetime ~ model LTD

"___ for Deadbeat" DIS

for dear ___ LIFE

Ford, Gerald
   ~ birthplace NEB, NEBR, OMAHA

Fordham
   ~ athlete RAM

Ford, Henry
   ~ son EDSEL

___ Ford Range EDSEL

fore
   ~ opposite AFT
   be at the ~ LEAD

   not ~ AFT

"fore"
   ~ site TEE

"___ for Each Other" MADE

fore and ___ AFT

fore-and-___ AFTER

forearm
   ~ bone ULNA
   ~ bones RADII

foreboding OMEN

forecast
   April ~ RAIN
   L.A. ~ SMOG
   London ~ RAIN
   weather ~ CLEAR, COOL, DAMP, DRY, FAIR, GALE, HAIL, HOT, ICY, MILD, RAIN, STORM, WARM, WET
   wintry ~ SLEET, SNOW

forecaster ORACLE
   ~ aid RADAR

forefend AVERT

forefoot PAW

forefront VAN

forego LEAD

foregoing ABOVE, OLDER

foreign ALIEN
   like some ~ wds. FEM, MASC

foreign ___ AID, CAR

foreigner ALIEN

foreign exchange
   ~ listing EURO, LIRA, LIRE, YEN

Foreign Legion
   ~ legend GESTE

foreknowledge ESP

forelimb ARM
   ~ bone ULNA

forelock BANG

foreman BOSS

Foreman
   ~ foe ALI
   ~ match BOUT
   ~ punch JAB
   ~ stat KOS, TKO
   ~ workplace ARENA, RING

foremost AONE, ARCH, BEST, BIG, FIRST, LEAD, MAIN, MAJOR, TOP, TOPS

forenoons AMS

forensic LEGAL
   ~ science tool DNA
   ~ site LAB

foreordain DOOM

foreshadow BODE, MEAN

foreshadowing HINT, OMEN

forest
   ~ clearing GLADE

~ **creature** BEAR, DEER, DOE, HARE, HART, STAG
~ **deity** PAN
~ **female** DOE
~ **flora** OAKS
~ **quaker** ASPEN
~ **sprite** ELF
~ **unit** TREE
~ **way** PATH
Shakespearean ~ ARDEN

___ **forest** RAIN

forestage APRON

forestall AVERT, BAR

forester
~ **tool** AXE

Forest of ___ ARDEN

forestry
~ **tool** AXE

foretell BODE, READ

foretoken BODE

forever AGES
~ **and a day** EON
~ **partner** ANON

"Forever ___**"** AMBER

"Forever ___ **a Day"** AND

"Forever ___ **Day"** ANDA

"Forever and a ___**"** DAY

forewarn ALERT

forewarning TIP

foreword INTRO

___ **for Fears** TEARS

forfeit FINE, LOSE
~ **ender** URE

forfeits
game with ~ LOO

forfeiture LOSS

forfend AVERT, REPEL

" ___ **for Five"** TABLE

forgather MASS, MEET

forge BEAT, FAKE, MAKE
~ **ahead** PRESS
Cyclopes' ~ ETNA

forged BAD, FAKE, FALSE, SHAM

forgery FAKE, SHAM

forget LEAVE, LOSE, MISS, OMIT, SKIP
~ **about posture** SAG
~ **it** NAY, NOPE
~ **one's place** SASS
file and ~ HIDE

"Forget ___**"** PARIS

"Forget it!" NEVER

forget-me- ___ NOT

forgive CLEAR, REMIT

forgiving BIG

forgo MISS, SHUN, SKIP, YIELD
~ **the reception** ELOPE

~ **the restaurant** EATIN

forgotten DATED, LOST
long ~ PAST

forgotten ___ MAN

___ **for granted** TAKE

" ___ **for Gumshoe"** GIS

"For heaven's ___**"** SAKE

"for here"
not ~ TOGO

"For He's a Jolly Good Fellow"
~ **end** DENY

" ___ **for Homicide"** HIS

___ **for it** ASK

fork ANGLE, PART, SPLIT
~ **out** SPEND
~ **over** HAND, PAY, REMIT
~ **prong** TINE
~ **site** ROAD
use a ~ EAT

forked
speak with ~ **tongue** LIE

forkful
~ **of food** BITE

forks
~ **and spoons** WARE

fork-tailed
~ **bird** TERN

" ___ **for Lawless"** LIS

" ___ **for Leyna"** ALL

" ___ **for Life"** LUST

forlorn ALONE, LOW, SAD

" ___ **for Love"** ALL

"For Love of ___**"** IVY

form CAST, MAKE, MODE, MOLD, RITE, USAGE
~ **a concept** IDEATE
~ **starter** UNI
cobbler's ~ LAST
foundry ~ MOLD
hollow ~ MOLD
literary ~ ODE, PROSE
qualification ~ TEST
race ~ ENTRY
shoe ~ LAST

___ **form** ART, LIFE

___-**form** FREE

___ **forma** PRO

formal ALOOF, DANCE, GALA, SOBER, STAID, STATE
~ **act** RITE
~ **address** SIR
~ **attire** DRESS
~ **dance** BALL, PROM
~ **decision** ACT
~ **forerunner** SEMI
~ **observance** RITE
~ **reception** LEVEE
~ **requirement** TIE
~ **wear of old** TOGA
stiffly ~ PRIM

" ___ **for Malice"** MIS

formalist PRIG

formality RITE

formal wear
~ **for men** TAILS

" ___ **for Man, so stealthily betrayed"** ALAS

format
instruction ~ STEPS

formation
~ **flyer** GOOSE
coral ~ ATOLL, REEF
flying ~ VEE
geological ~ DOME, MESA
goose ~ VEE
Ice Age ~ ESKER
pass in ~ FILE
volcanic ~ CONE

formative
~ **years** TEENS

" ___ **for Me"** YOU

"For Me and My ___**"** GAL

for men ___ **(stag)** ONLY

former LATE, OLD

formerly AGO, ERST, NEE, ONCE

formic ACID
~ **acid producer** ANT

formicary NEST
~ **dweller** ANT

Formicidae
~ **member** ANT

formidable STERN

Formosa
~ **(abbr.)** STR

formula RULE
~ **catcher** BIB
E-Z ~ ABC
spiritual ~ CREDO

Formula One
~ **car** RACER

formulate PUT

formulation
mental ~ IDEA

" ___ **for Night"** DAY

fornix ARCH

___ **for nothing** GOOD

" ___ **for one..."** ALL

" ___ **for One More"** ROOM

___ **for oneself** FEND

___ **for one's money, a** RUN

___ **for Peace** ATOMS

"For Pete's ___**"** SAKE

" ___ **for Red October, The"** HUNT

"Forrest Gump"
~ **locale** NAM

forsake CEDE, DESERT, DROP, EXIT, LEAVE

forsaken ALONE, LONE

for sale by ___ OWNER

"For shame!" FIE, TUT

forswear DENY

forsworn FALSE

"Forsyte ___**, The"** SAGA

"Forsyte Saga, The"
~ **novel** TOLET
~ **wife** IRENE

Forsyth BILL

fort POST
~ **ditch** MOAT
~ **opening** GATE
California ~ ORD
Niagara ~ ERIE

Fort ___**, Calif.** ORD

Fort ___**, Okla.** SILL

Fort ___**, Ont.** ERIE

Fortaleza CITY, PORT

"Fort Apache" OATER
~ **actor** AGAR

"Fort Apache, the Bronx"
~ **actor** ASNER

Fortas ABE
~ **forte** LAW

Fort Bragg
~ **cops** MPS
~ **drill leader** SGT

Fort Dix
~ **cops** MPS
~ **drill leader** SGT

forte SPHERE
psychic's ~ ESP

___ **forth (begin)** SET

___ **forth (orate)** HOLD

___ **forth (propose)** PUT

___ **forth (summon)** CALL

for the ___ **(temporarily)** NONCE

for the ___ **being** TIME

"For the ___ **of Benji"** LOVE

___ **for the books** ONE

"For the Boys"
~ **actor** CAAN, ONEAL, SEGAL
~ **name** BETTE
~ **tour grp.** USO

___ **for the course** PAR

" ___ **for the Lamps of China"** OIL

"For the Love of Benji"
~ **director** CAMP

___ **for the money** INIT

" ___ **for the money..."** ONE

for the most ___ PART

" ___ **for the poor"** ALMS

___ **for the ride** ALONG

___ **for the road** ONE

"___ for the Road"

"___ for the Road" TWO
"___ for the Seesaw" TWO
"___ for the Show" TWO
"___ for the Sun" RUN
"___ for the tears were shed to save me" TIS
"for this"
  literally ~ ADHOC
forthright HONEST, OPEN, RAW
  not ~ SLY
forthwith ANON, NOW, SOON
fortification KEEP
fortified ___ WINE
fortify ARM, LACE, MAN, STEEL
fortifying TONIC
___ for time PLAY
___ fortis AQUA
fortissimo LOUD
fortitude GRIT, HEART
Fort Knox
  ~ filler GOLD
  ~ st. KEN
  ~ unit INGOT
Fort Myers
  ~ state FLA
fortnight
  half a ~ WEEK
Fort Presque ISLE
Fortran
  ~ cousin ADA, BASIC
fortress AERIE, HAVEN, KEEP
  ~ defense MOAT
  mountain ~ AERIE
___ for trouble ASK
fortuitous ODD
fortuity EVENT
fortune CAST, DOOM, ESTATE, FATE, LOT, MINT, PILE
Fortune 500
  ~ abbr. INC
  ~ orgs. COS
fortuneteller ORACLE, SEER
  ~ deck TAROT
  ~ reading PALM
  ~ words ISEE
Fort Wayne
  ~ clock setting EDT, EST
"___ for Two" TEA
Fort Worth
  ~ st. TEX
forty
  ~ winks NAP, REST, SLEEP
  one of the back ~ ACRE
forty-niner
  ~ discovery GOLD
  ~ place MINE
  ~ stakeout CLAIM

Forty Thieves
  ~ foe ALI
Forum ARENA
  ~ attire TOGA
  ~ commissioner EDILE
  ~ language LATIN
  ~ official EDILE
  ~ site ROME
  Greek ~ AGORA
  see also Latin
"For want of a ___, the shoe..." NAIL
forward AHEAD, ALONG, GEAR, MAIL, PASS, PERT, REMIT, ROUTE, SEND
  ~ end NOSE
  ~ motion RUN
  bring ~ CITE, LAY
  drive ~ MOVE
  force ~ IMPEL
  look ~ to AWAIT, WAIT
  move ~ NOSE
  not at all ~ SHY
  press ~ SPUR
  put ~ ASSERT, LAY, POSE, RAISE
  step ~ GAIN
  urge ~ IMPEL
forward ___ PASS
___ forward FAST
forward pass
  ~ in football AERIAL
"For what ___ worth..." ITS
"For Whom the Bell Tolls"
  ~ girl MARIA
  ~ setting SPAIN
"For Your ___ Only" EYES
"For Your Eyes ___" ONLY
"For Your Eyes Only"
  ~ director GLEN
fossa HOLE, PIT
fosse MOAT
Fosse BOB
  ~ forte DANCE
Fossey, Dian
  ~ subject APE
fossil RELIC
  ~ fuel COAL, GAS, OIL
  ~ impression FERN
  ~ repository, often TAR
  ~ resin AMBER
  ~ (suffix) ITE
  ~ time PAST
fossilize AGE
fossilized OLD
foster ADOPT, FEED, NURSE, PLANT, RAISE, REAR
  ~ a felon ABET
  ~ child WARD
Foster MEG
Foster, Jodie
  ~ alma mater YALE
  ~ film NELL

Foster, Stephen
  dog in a ~ song TRAY
"Foucault's Pendulum"
  ~ author ECO
foul BAD, BASE, MEAN, TAINT, VILE
  ~ alternative FAIR
  ~ caller REF
  ~ liquid SLIME
  ~ mood SNIT
  ~ play EVIL, HARM
  ~ spot STY
  ~ up ERR, HASH, MISS, RUIN
  football ~ CLIP
  pinball ~ TILT
foul ___ BALL, LINE, PLAY, SHOT, TIP
foul-___ UPS
foulard TIE
foul-mouthed LEWD, RUDE
foulness DIRT
foul-smelling ACRID, RANK
foul-up ERROR, MESS
found BASE, ERECT, MAKE, PLANT, START
  ~ a perch ALIT, LIT
  ~ opposite LOST
  be ~ LIE, OCCUR
foundation ABCS, BASE, BASIS, BED, ROOT
  concrete ~ SLAB
  flower-bed ~ SOIL
  hair ~ SCALP
  poached-egg ~ TOAST
founded
  ~ (abbr.) EST
___-founded ILL
founder SINK
  Academy ~ PLATO
  Christian Science ~ EDDY
  Common Cause ~ NADER
  Cuzco ~ INCA
  Dadaism ~ ARP
  empire ~ INCA
  Franciscan ~'s home ASSISI
  Holy Roman Empire ~ OTTO
  Microsoft ~ GATES
  New Harmony ~ OWEN
  Pravda's ~ LENIN
  Quaker State ~ PENN
foundry MILL, PLANT
  ~ form MOLD
  ~ material METAL
  ~ product STEEL
  ~ refuse SLAG
fountain JET
  ~ coin count THREE
  ~ fare CONE
  ~ order COLA, SODA
  ~ staple STRAW
  ~ treat MALT
  coin in a ~ CENT, LIRA
  soda ~, in New England SPA
fountain ___ PEN
___ fountain SODA

Fountain PETE
fountainhead CAUSE
"Fountainhead, The"
  ~ actress NEAL
  ~ author RAND
fountain pen
  ~ filler INK
four
  ~ (prefix) TETRA
  ~ qts. GAL
  ~ roods ACRE
  ~ seasons YEAR
  ~ six-packs CASE
  ~ years, for a President TERM
  coach and ~ RIG
  one of the ~ elements AIR, EARTH, FIRE, WATER
four ___ kind OFA
four-___ (highly rated) STAR
four-___ clover LEAF
___-four TEN
Four ___ (1950s group) ACES
"Four ___" SONS
"Four ___ and a Prayer" MEN
four-bagger HOMER
Four Corners
  ~ state UTAH
four-door
  ~ model SEDAN
four-footed
  ~ companion CAT, DOG, PET
  ~ parent DAM
  ~ TV actor MRED
"Four Friends"
  ~ director PENN
fourgon VAN
four-handed
  ~ piano piece DUET
four-in-hand TIE
four-letter
  ~ word OATH
"Four Men ___ a Prayer" AND
"Four Men ___ Prayer" ANDA
four-poster BED
"Four Quartets" POEM
  ~ poet ELIOT
fours
  go on all ~ CREEP
  not on all ~ ERECT
___ fours ALL, PLUS
"Four Seasons, The"
  ~ actor ALDA
  ~ director ALDA
foursquare HONEST
four-star AONE, BEST, TOPS
  ~ review RAVE

fourth
~ **dimension** TIME
~ **in a series** DELTA
~ **man** SETH
~ **mo.** APR
~ **person** ABEL
~ **piggie's portion** NONE
~ **planet** MARS
~ **son of Aaron** ELI
~ **word of the Bible** GOD

fourth ___ ESTATE, GEAR

fourth-___ CLASS, RATE

fourth-class ___ MAIL

fourth estate PRESS

Fourth of July DATE
~ **sound** BANG

fourth-rate POOR

"Four Weddings ___ a Funeral" AND

"Four Weddings ___ Funeral" ANDA

four-wheeler
use a ~ SKATE

Fouts DAN

fowl BIRD, MEAT
~ **place** ROOST
~ **starter** PEA
barnyard ~ GOOSE
female ~ HEN
graceful ~ SWAN
wild ~ GAME

fox ANIMAL
~ **ender** TROT
~ **home** DEN, LAIR
~ **hunt** CHASE
~ **prey** HEN
baby ~ KIT
crazy like a ~ SLY

___ fox BLUE, RED

Fox BRER, TRIBE
~ **documentary** COPS
~ **shelter** TEPEE
~ **sitcom** ROC

"Fox ___ His Friends" AND

"Fox ___ the Hound, The" AND

___ Fox BRER

"___ Fox, The" DESERT

"Fox and ___ Friends" HIS

"Fox and the Hound, The"
~ **director** RICH

foxes GAME

"Foxfire"
~ **author** SETON

foxhole PIT

foxiness ART

foxtrot DANCE

"FoxTrot"
~ **pet** IGUANA

Foxx REDD

foxy ACUTE, SLY, SMART

Foy EDDIE

foyer HALL
~ **spread** RUG

___-Foy, Quebec STE

Foyt, A.J. RACER

Fozzie BEAR

Fr ELEM
87 for ~ ATNO

Fr. LANG
~ **holy woman** STE
see also French

Fra TITLE

fracas ADO, DUST, MELEE, NOISE, RIOT, ROW, SCRAP, SETTO

fraction BIT, IOTA, PART, RATIO, SCRAP, SHADE, SLICE
~ **of an inch** HAIR
decade ~ YEAR
dollar ~ BIT, CENT
horsepower ~ WATT
joule ~ ERG
loaf ~ HALF
month ~ DAY, WEEK
ounce ~ DRAM
sawbuck ~ ONE
shekel ~ AGORA
soccer-game ~ HALF
yard ~ FOOT, INCH
yen ~ SEN

fractional
~ **prefix** DEMI, HEMI, SEMI

fractions
dol. ~ CTS

fractious TESTY

fracture GAP, REND, RENT, SNAP, SPLIT
~ **detector** XRAY
glacier ~ ABYSS

___ fracture STRESS

fractures
fix ~ SET

fragile AERIAL, THIN

fragment BIT, CHIP, CHOP, IOTA, PART, RAG, SCRAP, SHRED, SNIP
fiery ~ EMBER

fragrance AROMA, ATTAR, BALM, ESSENCE, ODOR, SCENT

fragrant SWEET
~ **compound** ESTER
~ **flower** LILAC, LILY, ROSE
~ **herb** MINT
~ **oil** ATTAR
~ **resin** ELEMI
~ **tree** FIR, PINE
~ **wood** ALOE, CEDAR
make ~ CENSE, SCENT

fraidy ___ CAT

frail REEDY

"Fra Lippo Lippi" POEM

Fram
~ **rival** STP

frame DRAW, MAKE, MOLD, PLAN, PUT, RACK, REAR, RIM, SETUP, SHELL
~ **contents** LENS
~ **of film** SLIDE
~ **of mind** MOOD, STATE, TONE
bed ~ STEAD
door ~ SASH
fireplace ~ GRATE
window ~ SASH

___ frame TIME

"___ Framed Roger Rabbit" WHO

framer
~ **need** MAT
house ~ STUD

frames
~ **in a game** TEN

framework CADRE, CAGE, GRID, RACK, SASH, SHELL
metal ~ GRATE

framing
~ **need** MAT

Fran
~ **partner** OLLIE

franc COIN
~ **replacement** EURO
part of a ~ SOU

France
capital of ~ PARIS
city in ~ ALES, ARLES, CAEN, NICE, PARIS, STLO
department in ~ ISERE, ORNE
river of ~ AIRE, ISERE, LOIRE, OISE, ORNE, SEINE, YSER
site of Roman ruins in
~ ARLES
southern ~ MIDI
Tour de ~ RACE
wine valley of ~ LOIRE
see also French

___ France AIR

Frances ALDA, DEE

"Francesca da Rimini" OPERA

franchise STORE, VOTE
exercise one's ~ ELECT, POLL, VOTE

Franchot TONE

Francis ARLENE, KAY, MULE
imitate ~ BRAY

Franciscan
~ **founder's home** ASSISI

___ Francisco, Calif. SAN

___ Francisco River SAO

Francis, Dick
~ **locale** ASCOT
1988 ~ thriller, with "The" EDGE

Francis, Saint
~ **home** ASSISI

Francis Scott ___ KEY

francium METAL

Franck CESAR

Franco NERO

François
see French

Françoise SAGAN
see also French

Franco-Prussian WAR

frangipane
~ **ingredient** EGG

frangipani TREE

frank FREE, HONEST, MEAT, OPEN, RAW
~ **covering** SKIN

Frank ANNE, CAPRA
~ **daughter** TINA
~ **ex** AVA, MIA
~ **pal** DEAN
~ **partner in the comics** ERNEST

"Frank & ___" OLLIE

Frank, Anne
~ **hideout** ATTIC

Franken
~ **and others** ALS

Frankenstein
~ **assistant** IGOR
~ **milieu** LAB
~ **monster** ADAM

"Frankenstein ___ the Wolf Man" MEETS

"Frankenstein Meets the Wolf ___" MAN

Frankfort
~ **st.** KEN

Frankfurt CITY
~ **river** MAIN, ODER
see also German

frankfurter DOG, MEAT

Frankfurt on the ___ MAIN, ODER

Frankie LAINE

"Frankie ___ Johnnie" AND

Frank, Jr.
~ **sister** TINA

Franklin BEN
~ **bill** CNOTE
~ **flier** KITE
~ **invention** DST
~ **mother** SARA
~ **note** CEE
~ **opponent of 1936** ALF
like ~'s Richard POOR

Franklin Gothic FONT

Frans HALS

frantic EAGER, MAD, RABID

Franz BOAS, LEHAR
see also German

Frasier CRANE

"Frasier"
~ **dog** EDDIE

frater BRO

fraternal
~ **fellow** LION
~ **member** ELK
~ **organization** ELKS

fraternity CLAN, ORDER
~ **letter** ALPHA, BETA, CHI, DELTA, ETA, IOTA, OMEGA, PHI, PSI, RHO, TAU, THETA
~ **letters** MUS
~ **party** STAG
~ **pony** CRIB
~ **wear** PIN

"Fraternity __" ROW

fraternize BAND

frat house
~ **alternative** DORM

frat party
~ **attire** SHEET, TOGA
~ **delivery** KEG

fratricide
~ **victim** ABEL

Frau LADY, TITLE
~ **husband** HERR
see also German

fraud FAKE, LIAR, SCAM, SHAM
check for ~ AUDIT
some insurance ~ ARSON

fraudulent BAD, FALSE

fraught LADEN
~ **with meaning** DEEP

Fräulein GIRL, LASS, TITLE
see also German

fray FRET, MELEE, RAVEL, RIOT, ROW, RUN, SCRAP, WEAR
above the ~ ALOOF
ready for the ~ ARMED

Frazier JOE
~ **foe** ALI

frazzle ABRADE
worn to a ~ DONE

freak FAN, NUT
~ **out** ANGER, RAGE

freakish ODD

Freberg STAN

freckle DOT

Fred ALLEN, EBB
~ **pet** DINO
~ **sister** ADELE
~ **to Pebbles** DAD

Freddy
~ **street** ELM

Fredericksburg
~ **winner** LEE

Frederick the __ GREAT

free CLEAR, HONEST, LOOSE, OFF, SPARE, UNTIE
~ **admission** PASS
~ **and easy** LOOSE

~ **electron** ION
~ **from danger** SAFE
~ **from doubt** CLEAR
~ **from guilt** CLEAR
~ **from (prefix)** DIS
~ **from pride** MEEK
~ **from problems** EASY
~ **(of)** RID
~ **of errata** CLEAN
~ **ticket** PASS
~ **to all** OPEN
~ **up space, maybe** ERASE
~ **with words** GLIB
home ~ SAFE
remain ~ ELUDE
set ~ CLEAR, LOOSE, UNTIE

free __ AGENT, HAND, REIN, RIDE, TRADE

free __ bird ASA

__-free SCOT

Free-__ Party SOIL

free and __ CLEAR, EASY

freebie PASS
Chinese-restaurant ~ RICE, TEA
former gas-station ~ MAP
gas-station ~ AIR
hotel-desk ~ MAP
malt-shop ~ STRAW
motel ~ ICE, SOAP
office ~ PERK
restaurant ~ ROLL, WATER
supermarket ~ BAG

"Freebie and the __" BEAN

freeboot PREY, ROB

Freed ALAN, HERB

__ free delivery RURAL

freedom
~ **from care** EASE

"__ Freedom" CRY

Freedom Hall ARENA

freedom of the __ (one of Wilson's Fourteen Points) SEAS

"Freedom Road"
~ **actor** ALI

__ Free Europe RADIO

free-for-all MELEE, RIOT, ROW, SCRAP

Freeh, Louis
~ **org.** FBI

freehold LAND

freelance
~ **payment** FEE

freelancer
~ **encl.** SASE

freeload STEAL

freely ADLIB

Freeman MONA

Freer Gallery
~ **display** ART

free-throw __ LINE

Freetown
~ **money** LEONE

freeway PIKE, ROAD, ROUTE
~ **access** RAMP
~ **clogger** AUTO, CAR
~ **problem** SMOG
~ **snarl** JAM
~ **strip** LANE
see also highway

freeways
use ~ MOTOR

freewheeling OPEN

"Free Willy"
~ **whale** ORCA

freeze COOL, HALT, ICE, STUN
~ **someone out** CUT
~ **starter** ANTI

freeze-__ DRY

__ freeze DEEP

freezer
~ **name** AMANA
~ **product** ICE
~ **starter** DEEP
take out of the ~ THAW

__ freezer DEEP

freezes
when hell ~ **over** NEVER

freezing ICY
~ **temperatures** TEENS

Frehley ACE

freight LADE, LOAD
~ **amts.** LBS
~ **container** CAR
~ **hauler** SEMI
~ **weight** TON
air ~ MAIL
bearing ~ LADEN

freight __ CAR, TRAIN

freight car
~ **hopper** HOBO

freighter BOAT, SHIP
~ **destination** PORT

"__ Freischutz" DER

French
~ **adverb** ICI, MAL, TRES
~ **affirmative** OUI
~ **and Indian** WAR
~ **article** LES, UNE
~ **author** GIDE
~ **avant-garde artist** ARP
~ **cap** BERET
~ **cheese** BRIE
~ **cleric** ABBE
~ **coin** SOU
~ **color** NOIR, NOIRE, ROUGE
~ **conjunctions** ETS
~ **couturier** DIOR
~ **denial** NON
~ **direction** EST
~ **director** TATI
~ **ecclesiastic** ABBE
~ **existentialist** GIDE
~ **female** ELLE

~ **film award** CESAR
~ **flapjack** CREPE
~ **flower** LIS
~ **fries** SIDE
~ **goodbye** ADIEU
~ **hat** BERET
~ **holy woman** STE
~ **impressionist** DEGAS, MANET, MONET
~ **infinitive** ETRE
~ **lady** MME
~ **leave** LAM
~ **loaf** PAIN
~ **month** MAI
~ **Mrs.** MME
~ **narrative poem** LAI
~ **negative** NON
~ **number** SEPT, UNE
~ **Oscar** CESAR
~ **painter** ARP, DEGAS, MANET, MONET
~ **playwright** GENET
~ **possessive** SES
~ **preposition** AVEC, DANS, DES, ENTRE, SANS
~ **priest** ABBE
~ **pronoun** AMOI, ELLE, MOI, SES, UNE
~ **provincial** STYLE
~ **queen** REINE
~ **refusal** NON
~ **revolutionary** MARAT
~ **sculptor** ARP
~ **seaport** CAEN, NICE
~ **season** ETE
~ **seasoning** SEL
~ **summer** ETE
~ **title** MME
~ **turndown** NON
~ **verb** ETRE
academy, in ~ ECOLE
after, in ~ APRES
a, in ~ UNE
ait, in ~ ILE
among, in ~ ENTRE
area, in ~ AIRE
are, in ~ ETES
arm, in ~ BRAS
back, in ~ DOS
badly, in ~ MAL
be, in ~ ETRE
below, in ~ ABAS
between, in ~ ENTRE
beverage, in ~ CAFE, THE
black, in ~ NOIR, NOIRE
born, in ~ NEE
boyfriend, in ~ AMI
brainstorm, in ~ IDEE
bread, in ~ PAIN
buddy, in ~ AMI, AMIE
cabbage, in ~ CHOU
cat, in ~ CHAT
chum, in ~ AMI, AMIE
coffee in ~ CAFE
compañera, in ~ AMIE
compañero, in ~ AMI
dad, in ~ PERE
da, in ~ OUI
dance, in ~ BAL
dear, in ~ CHER
donkey, in ~ ANE
down with, in ~ ABAS
earth, in ~ TERRE
east, in ~ EST

ein, in ~ UNE
evil, in ~ MAL
father, in ~ PERE
fat, in ~ GRAS
female friend, in ~ AMIE
flapjack, in ~ CREPE
friend, in ~ AMI, AMIE
girlfriend, in ~ AMIE
golden, in ~ DOR
goodbye, in ~ ADIEU
good, in ~ BON
harm, in ~ MAL
head, in ~ TETE
"Help!" in ~ AMOI
here, in ~ ICI
hers, in ~ SES
hint, in ~ MOT
his, in ~ SES
hook, in ~ CROC
ill, in ~ MAL
in, in ~ DANS
into, in ~ DANS
island, in ~ ILE
ja, in ~ OUI
key, in ~ CLEF
kind, in ~ BON
king, in ~ ROI
land, in ~ TERRE
life, in ~ VIE
lily, in ~ LIS
love, in ~ AMOUR
low, in ~ BAS
male friend, in ~ AMI
May, in ~ MAI
me, in ~ MOI
milk, in ~ LAIT
mine, in ~ AMOI
mit, in ~ AVEC
monarch, in ~ ROI
mother, in ~ MERE
Mrs., in ~ MME
nada, in ~ RIEN
name, in ~ NOM
nein, in ~ NON
ninny, in ~ ANE
no, in ~ NON
noon, in ~ MIDI
nothing, in ~ RIEN
notice, in ~ AVIS
not, in ~ PAS
notion, in ~ IDEE
noun, in ~ NOM
nyet, in ~ NON
OK, in ~ OUI
old ~ coin ECU
one, in ~ UNE
opinion, in ~ AVIS
our, in ~ NOS
padre, in ~ ABBE
pal, in ~ AMI, AMIE
pancake, in ~ CREPE
papa, in ~ PERE
pupil, in ~ ELEVE
queen, in ~ REINE
romance, in ~ AMOUR
salt, in ~ SEL
school, in ~ ECOLE
sea, in ~ MER
seven, in ~ SEPT
she, in ~ ELLE
sí, in ~ OUI
silk, in ~ SOIE
since, in ~ DES
soft, in ~ BAS

some, in ~ DES
soul, in ~ AME
spirit, in ~ AME
spoken, in ~ DIT
spring month, in ~ MAI
sra., in ~ MME
state, in ~ ETAT
step, in ~ PAS
stocking, in ~ BAS
street, in ~ RUE
student, in ~ ELEVE
summer, in ~ ETE
take ~ leave DESERT, RUN
tea, in ~ THE
theater, in ~ CINE
the, in ~ LES
thoroughfare, in ~ RUE
to be, in ~ ETRE
upon, in ~ SUR
very, in ~ TRES
water, in ~ EAU
with, in ~ AVEC
without, in ~ SANS
word, in ~ MOT
years, in ~ ANS
yes, in ~ OUI
see also France

French ___ ALPS, DOOR, FRY, HEEL, HORN, LEAVE, SEAM, TOAST

French ___ coffee ROAST

French ___ soup ONION

"French Connection, The"
~ actor REY
~ cop NARC
~ inspiration EGAN

French door
~ component SASH

French-German
~ river SAAR

French hen
~ count THREE

French, Mr.
~ carried one CANE

French Open
~ champ BORG
1991 ~ winner SELES
seven-time ~ champ EVERT

"French Quarter"
~ director KANE

French Revolution
~ figure MARAT

French Sudan
~ today MALI

Freneau, Philip POET
see also poet

frenetic MAD, RABID

frenzied AMOK, EAGER, MAD, RABID

frenzy MANIA, RAGE

Freon GAS

frequent ATTEND
~ the library READ
~ title starter THE

frequently OFT, OFTEN
~ to a poet OFT

fresco
~ base GESSO

fresh ANEW, CLEAN, COOL, CRISP, HOT, LATE, MORE, NEW, PERT, PURE, RAW, RUDE, SASSY, SWEET
~ air OZONE
~ as a daisy NEW
~, as lettuce CRISP
~ as the morning dew NEW
~ information NEWS
~ language SASS
~ talk LIP
~ team of horses RELAY
get ~ SASS
it can be ~ AIR
less than ~ TRITE
no longer ~ OLD
not ~ STALE

fresh ___ AIR, WATER

freshen AERATE, AIR, CLEAN, PERK, RENEW
~ in a way AERATE
~ up RESTORE

freshener
breath ~ MINT

freshet SPATE, STREAM

freshly AGAIN, ANEW

freshman YEAR
~ course word INTRO
~ digs DORM
college ~, usually TEEN

freshness LIFE

"Fresh Prince of ___ Air" BEL

"Fresh Prince of Bel ___" AIR

freshwater
~ fish BASS, CARP, GAR, PIKE, TETRA, TROUT
~ mussel CLAM

___ Fresnos, Tex. LOS

fress EAT

fret CARE, MOPE, STEW

fretful TESTY

Freud
~ associate ADLER
~ daughter ANNA
~ topic EGO
see also German

Freudian
~ concepts IDS
~ stage ORAL
~ topic EGO
subject of ~ study DREAM

Freudian ___ SLIP

Frewer MATT

Fri.
~ follower SAT
girl ~ ASST
man ~ ASST

___ Fria (Arizona river) AGUA

friable CRISP
~ soil LOAM

friar ABBE, ABBOT
~ room CELL

Friars Club
~ event ROAST

fribble
~ away LOSE

fricassee MEAT, STEW

Frick
~ collection ART

friction
~ easer OIL

Friday COP, MAN, SGT
man ~ AID, AIDE

___ Friday GAL, MAN

Friday, Sgt. JOE
item for ~ FACT

"Friday the Rabbi Slept ___" LATE

"Friday the 13th"
~ prop AXE

fridge
~ door item EGG
~ maker AMANA
raid the ~ EAT, NOSH

Friedman
~ subj. ECON

Friel, Brian
~ home EIRE

friend ALLY, MATE, PAL
~ in battle ALLY
~ in French AMI, AMIE
~ in Spanish AMIGO
belle's ~ BEAU
close ~, in slang ACE

"friend in ___..., A" NEED

friendly GOOD, NICE, SWEET, WARM

___-friendly USER

Friendly FRED

"Friend or ___?" FOE

friends
~ of faunae org. SPCA
be ~ with KNOW

"Friends"
Monica's brother on ~ ROSS

friendship LOVE

"Friends of ___ Coyle, The" EDDIE

___ fries HOME

frigate BOAT, SHIP

Frigg
~ husband ODIN

fright ALARM, PANIC, SCARE
~ site STAGE
feel sudden ~ PANIC
sound of ~ GASP

___ fright STAGE

frighten ALARM, AWE, COW, UPSET
~ **off** DETER

frightened UPSET

frightening EERIE, EERY

frightful BAD, DIRE

frigid ICY

Frigid ZONE
~ **ender** AIRE

Frigidaire
~ **rival** AMANA

frijol BEAN

frill EXTRA

frilly ORNATE

fringe BANG, EDGE, HEM, LIMIT, LIP, OUTER, RIM
~ **benefit** ICING, PERK, PLUS
~ **on a golf course** APRON
add a ~ to EDGE
beyond the ~ OUTRE

Frisbee DISC, FAD, TOY

frisé
bichon ~ DOG, PET

frisk CAPER, HOP, LARK, LEAP, PLAY, ROMP, SKIP

frisky PERT, SPRY

Frito-___ LAY

frittata OMELET
~ **base** EGG

fritter CAKE
~ **away** LOSE, SPEND, WASTE
~ **away the time** IDLE, LOAF

fritz
on the ~ OUT

Fritz CAT, LANG
~ **comics brother** HANS
see also German

Fritzi
~ **to Nancy** AUNT

frivolity GLEE

frivolous GAY, IDLE
in a ~ way IDLY

frizzy CRISP
~ **top** AFRO

fro
move to and ~ FLAP, SWAY, WAG
to and ~ ABOUT

Frobisher BAY

frock DRESS

frock ___ COAT

Frodo HERO

froe TOOL

frog
~ **cousin** NEWT
~ **dish** LEGS
~ **in one's throat** RASP
~ **pad** LILY
~ **relative** TOAD

~ **starter** LEAP

___ frog TREE

"Frog and the Ox, The"
~ **author** AESOP

frog-clearing
~ **sound** AHEM

Frogner Park
~ **city** OSLO

frolic CAPER, DANCE, LARK, LEAP, PLAY, ROMP

frolicsome GAY

from ASOF
~ **in German** VON
~ **then** SINCE
~ **the top** AGAIN

from ___ one YEAR

from ___ to riches RAGS

from ___ to stern STEM

from ___ Z ATO

___ from (besides) APART

"From ___ Day Forward" THIS

"From ___ shining..." SEATO

"From ___ to Eternity" HERE

"From ___ to Mozart: Isaac Stern in China" MAO

"___ From a Mall" SCENES

"___ From a Marriage" SCENES

"___ From Brooklyn, The" KID

"___ From Childhood" SCENES

"___ From Colorado, The" MAN

"___ Frome" ETHAN

"From Here to Eternity"
~ **actress** KERR
~ **Oscar winner** REED

"___ From Ipanema, The" GIRL

"___ From Laramie, The" MAN

"From Mao to Mozart: ___ Stern in China" ISAAC

Frommer
~ **title** ITALY

"___ From Missouri, The" GIRL

"___, from New York..." LIVE

from pillar to ___ POST

"From Russia With ___" LOVE

"___ From Shanghai, The" LADY

"___ From Snowy River, The" MAN

from soup to ___ NUTS

"from soup to nuts" RANGE

"___ From Spain, The" KID

from stem to ___ STERN

"___ From 10th Avenue, The" GIRL

from the ___ one YEAR

"From the ___ World" NEW

"___ From the Alamo, The" MAN

"___ From the Hill" HOME

___ from the hip SHOOT

"___ From the Hood" TALES

"___ From the Madding Crowd" FAR

"___ From the Streets, A" CRY

"From the Terrace"
~ **author** OHARA

"___ From the Underground" NOTES

"___ From the Vienna Woods" TALES

"From This ___ Forward" DAY

"___ From U.N.C.L.E., The" MAN

___ from under OUT

"___ From Yesterday, The" MAN

"___ From Your Show of Shows" TEN

frond LEAF
~ **holder** STEM
kind of ~ PALM

fronds
plant with ~ FERN

front CHEST, FACE, SHOW
~ **ender** IER
~ **of the calf** SHIN
~ **on** FACE
~ **position** LEAD
~ **(prefix)** FORE
~ **room** SALON
be in ~ LEAD
false ~ ACT, POSE, SHAM
in ~ AHEAD, BEST, FIRST, TOPS
in ~ of ACROSS
in ~ of (prefix) ANTE, FORE, PRE, PRO
in the ~ BEST, FIRST, FORE, TOPS
neither ~ nor back SIDE
out ~ HONEST, SEEN
out in ~ AHEAD
present a bold ~ DARE
semi's ~ CAB
toward the ~ AHEAD
up ~ HONEST

front ___ LINE, PAGE

___ front DROP, POLAR, WARM

___ front (ahead) OUT

Front ___ RANGE

"Front ___, The" PAGE

frontier LIMIT
~ **transportation** STAGE

frontiersman
famous ~ BOONE

frontispiece PLATE

frontlet BAND

front page
~ **box** EAR

~ **feature** TITLE
~ **item** EVENT
~ **matter** NEWS
~ **word** EXTRA

front porch
~ **tune, perhaps** CAROL, NOEL

frosh
~ **lodgings** DORM
former ~ SOPH

frost ICE, RIME
~ **ender** BIT, BITE, LINE
~ **kin** DEW

Frost ___ BELT

Frost, David SIR

frosted ICY

frostiness NIP

frosting ICING
apply ~ ICE

Frost, Robert POET
~ **reading** POEM
see also poet

frosty ALOOF, ICED, ICY

Frosty
accessory for ~ PIPE

froth BEAT, BOIL, FOAM, HEAD, MILL, SPIT

Froward CAPE

frown FACE, GLARE, STEW

frowning STERN

frowzy MESSY

frozen ICY, SOLID
~ **dessert** ICE
~ **fall** SNOW
~ **rain** HAIL, SLEET
~ **surface** ICE
~ **water** ICE

frozen food
~ **section, perhaps** AISLE

fructify BEAR

frugal
be ~ STINT

fruit ACORN, APPLE, DATE, END, KIWI, LEMON, LIME, MELON, NUT, OLIVE, ORANGE, PEAR, SLOE, UGLI
~ **beverage** ADE, CIDER
~ **center** CORE
~ **concoction** SALAD
~ **covering** PEEL
~ **dish** PIE
~ **fancier** ADAM, EVE
~ **holder** STEM
~ **pastry** TART
~ **peel** RIND, SKIN
~ **problem** ROT
~ **producer** TREE
~ **product** CIDER, JAM
~ **skin** PEEL, RIND
autumn ~ PEAR
banned ~ spray ALAR
bear ~ GROW, RIPEN
black ~ OLIVE

breakfast ~ MELON
citrus ~ LEMON, LIME
coffee ~ BEAN
compote ~ PEAR
cupped ~ ACORN
desert ~ DATE
dry ~ NUT
fuzzy ~ KIWI
green ~ OLIVE
juicy ~ MELON, ORANGE
lumpy-shaped ~ PEAR
orchard ~ APPLE, PEAR
palm ~ DATE
prepare ~ CORE, PARE, PEEL
purple ~ SLOE
rose ~ HIP
slot-machine ~ LEMON
sour ~ LEMON, LIME
sticky ~ DATE
summer ~ MELON
tart ~ SLOE
tropical ~ DATE, MELON, UGLI
vine ~ MELON
wrinkly ~ UGLI

fruit __ BAT

fruit cup
  ~ morsel PEAR

fruitful RICH

fruiting
  ~ spike EAR

fruition
  at ~ RIPE
  come to ~ RIPEN

fruitless DRY, IDLE, VAIN
  ~ plant FERN, MOSS

Fruit of the __ LOOM

fruity BATS

frump DRAB

frumpy MESSY

frustrate AVERT, BAR, DASH,
  DETER, LIMIT, REPEL, STOP

frustrating MESSY

Frutiger FONT

fry HEAT
  ~ lightly SAUTE
  fish ~ MEAL
  small ~ KID, TAD, TOT

__ fry SMALL

__-fry DEEP, PAN, STIR

Frye, David APER

Frye, Deacon
  ~ show AMEN

frying
  ~ medium LARD

frying __ PAN

Ft.
  see Fort

"F Troop"
  ~ structure TEPEE
  the Hekawi, in ~ TRIBE

fuchsia COLOR

Fudd ELMER

fuddy-duddy DODO, PRIG

fudge DRAT, EVADE, LIE
  ~ flavoring MAPLE
  oh ~ POOH

fuel
  ~ carrier OILER
  ~ cartel OPEC
  ~ container TANK
  ~ efficiency rating org. EPA
  ~ for old locomotives COAL
  ~ gas ETHANE
  ~ measure OCTANE
  ~ source PEAT
  ~ starter SYN
  car ~ GAS
  fossil ~ COAL, GAS, OIL
  furnace ~ COAL
  heating ~ COAL, GAS, OIL
  lamp ~ OIL
  stove ~ GAS
  train ~ COAL

fuel __ OIL

Fugard
  plant in a ~ title ALOE

fugue
  ~ composer BACH

Fuji
  ~ flow LAVA
  ~ locale ASIA

Fujimori
  ~ land PERU

fulcrum
  ~ piece OAR
  it turns on a ~ LEVER

Fulda
  ~ tributary EDER

fulfill MEET

__-fulfillment SELF

fulgurate BEAM, DART

fuliginous EBONY

full ENTIRE, LADEN, TOTAL
  ~ at a theater SRO
  ~ circle LAP
  ~ complement LOAD
  ~ flower ACME, PEAK
  ~ flowering DAY
  ~ of beans FALSE
  ~ of clichés STALE
  ~ of energy ALIVE, GOGO
  ~ of excitement AGOG
  ~ of holes OPEN
  ~ of life EAGER, GAY, SPRY
  ~ of obstacles HARD
  ~ of oneself VAIN
  ~ of pep ALIVE
  ~ of (suffix) OSE
  ~ of the devil BAD
  ~ of vim and vigor HALE
  ~ of vinegar SASSY
  ~ sun DAY
  ~ supply GLUT
  ~ swing PLAY
  ~ turn COIL
  ~ wallet ROLL
  at ~ gallop APACE
  in ~ agreement ATONE
  in ~ flower RIPE

in ~ sail APACE
in ~ view OVERT, SEEN
with ~ faculties SOBER

full __ BLAST, DRESS, MOON,
  STOP

full-__ BORE, SCALE, SIZE

"Full __ ahead!" SPEED, STEAM

"Full __ and Empty Arms"
  MOON

"Full __ High" MOON

"Full __ Jacket" METAL

fullback
  ~ quest GAIN, GOAL

full-blooded PURE

full-blown AGED, RIPE

full-bodied DEEP, RICH

Fuller, Buckminster
  ~ creation DOME

full-fledged TOTAL

full-grown RIPE, TALL
  ~ sheep EWE

full house
  ~ marquee SRO

full-length
  ~ garment TOGA

"Full Metal Jacket"
  ~ land NAM

"Full of __" LIFE

full of hot __ AIR

full-size ADULT

"Full steam __!" AHEAD

full-strength NEAT, PURE

full-throated LOUD

full-time
  ~ athlete PRO

fully ALL, CLEAN, CLEAR

fulminate BOIL, ERUPT, RAGE
  ~ against LACE

fulmination BAN, BLAST

Fulton J. __ SHEEN

Fulton, Robert
  ~ power STEAM

fumble DROP, ERR, ERROR, FEEL
  ~ one's speech SLUR

fumbler BOOR, CLOD, OAF
  ~ exclamation OOPS

fumbling INEPT

fume BOIL, FRET, GAS, RAGE,
  RANT, STEAM, STEW

fuming HOT, IRATE, MAD, UPSET

fun
  ~ and games PLAY
  ~ ender STER
  ~ party BLAST
  a lot of ~ HOOT
  good clean ~ LARK
  great ~ BLAST

have ~ LARK, PLAY
have ~ at the mall SPEND
make ~ of KID, RIDE, ROAST,
  TEASE, TWIT
poke ~ at KID, RAG, RIB,
  TEASE, TWIT

fun __ FAIR

function ACT, PART, ROLE, RUN,
  USE
  ~ (as) SERVE
  ~ starter MAL
  ~ (suffix) IVE, URE
  assigned ~ ROLE
  VCR ~ ERASE

functional UTILE

functioned
  ~ as WAS

functioning ALIVE
  ~ or not ASIS
  not ~ OUT

functions GOES

fund ENDOW, MINE, STORE
  gambler's ~ STAKE
  public ~ CHEST
  ret. ~ IRA

fundamental BASIC, FIRST, KEY,
  ROOT
  ~ knowledge ABCS
  ~ origin ROOT
  ~ principle BASIS

fundamentals ABCS

fund-raiser GALA

fundraising
  ~ org. PTA

funds MOOLA, POOL
  ~ source for sculptors NEA
  borrower's ~ LOAN
  emergency ~ source ATM
  provide ~ for ENDOW

fungi
  fermenting ~ YEAST

fungus ERGOT, MOLD
  ~ pouch SAC
  edible ~ MOREL
  grain ~ SMUT

funk FEAR, SCARE
  in a ~ BLUE

funnier
  be ~ than TOP

funny ODD, RICH
  ~ bone ELBOW
  ~ business CAPER
  ~ joke RIOT
  ~ person CARD, HOOT, RIOT,
    WAG, WIT
  act ~ AMUSE
  bitingly ~ WRY
  have a ~ feeling SENSE
  too ~ for words RICH

funny __ BONE, PAPER

funny __ (dragster) CAR

"Funny __" FACE, GIRL

funny bone
~ **locale** ELBOW

funny business ANTIC

"Funny Girl"
~ **song subject** SADIE
Barbra's ~ costar OMAR

"___ funny, McGee" TAINT

funny money
~ **finder** TMAN

"___ Funny That Way" SHES

Funt ALLEN, PETER
~ **command** SMILE
~ **need** CAMERA

"Fun With Dick and Jane"
~ **actor** SEGAL

fur COAT, HAIR, HIDE, PELT, SKIN
~ **magnate** ASTOR
~ **piece** PELT, STOLE
~ **scarf** BOA
~ **source** OTTER
animal's ~ COAT
lose ~ SHED
not-so-prized ~ STOAT
royal ~ ERMINE
Russian ~ SABLE

fur ___ SEAL

___ fur FAKE

"Für ___" ELISE

fur-bearing
~ **swimmer** OTTER

furbish ADORN

Furie, Sidney J.
~ **film of 1973** HIT

Furillo CARL, COP

furious HOT, IRATE, MAD, UPSET
be ~ BOIL
make ~ ENRAGE, IRE

furl LOOP, ROLL

furlong
~ **fraction** YARD

furlongs
eight ~ MILE

furlough LEAVE, PASS

furnace
~ **button** RESET
~ **fleck** ASH
~ **fuel** COAL
~ **unit** BTU
brickmaker's ~ KILN
potter's ~ KILN

___ furnace BLAST, SOLAR

furnish CATER, FIT, LEND, PLY, YIELD

furnishing
bedside ~ LAMP
casino ~ TABLE
home ~ BED
lobby ~ SETTEE
men's ~ TIE
restaurant ~ TABLE

furnishings
room ~ DECOR

furniture BED, CRIB, DESK, SETTEE, SOFA, TABLE
~ **buildup** DUST
~ **cover** TARP
~ **finial** ACORN
~ **item** TABLE
~ **mover** VAN
~ **wood** ALDER, EBONY, MAPLE, OAK, PINE, TEAK
classroom ~ DESK
den ~ SETTEE
dining-room ~ TABLE
living-room ~ SOFA
nursery ~ CRIB
office ~ SOFA
piece of ~ BED
school ~ DESK
style of ~ ADAM

furniture designer
British ~ ADAM

furniture leg
~ **decoration** EAR

furniture shop
~ **machine** LATHE

furor ADO, FAD, RAGE, STIR, STORM, TODO

furrier
~ **offering** ERMINE, OTTER, SABLE
~ **unit** PELT

furrow CUT, ETCH, KNIT, LINE, PLOW, RUT, SEAM
narrow ~ STRIA

furrows
make ~ PLOW

furry
~ **fish-eater** OTTER
~ **foot** PAW

furs
the fur of ~ SABLE

further ABET, AGAIN, AID, ALSO, AND, HELP, MORE, NEW, OFF, PAST, SERVE, YET
~ **a felony** ABET
~ **in time** LATER
refrain from ~ action DEFER
say ~ ADD

furthermore AGAIN, ALSO, AND, MORE, PLUS, THEN, YET

furthest
~ **bound** LIMIT
~ **from the hole, in golf** AWAY
~ **point** END

furtive SLY
~ **glance** PEEP
~ **one** SNEAK
~ **org.** CIA
~ **whisper** PSST, PST

fury ANGER, IRE, RAGE
lash into a ~ ENRAGE

"Fury"
~ **director** LANG

"Fusco Brothers, The"
~ **dog** AXEL

Fusco, Paul
~ **role** ALF

fuscous ECRU

fuse HEAT, MELD, MELT, RUN, UNITE, WED
~ **metal** SMELT
~ **rating unit** AMP
~ **unit** AMP
blow a ~ RAGE

fusillade BLAST

fusilli PASTA

fusion
~ **target** ATOM

fuss ADO, CARE, FLAP, FRET, NAG, ROW, SPAT, STEW, STIR, TODO, YEAST
~ **over** DOTE
make a ~ RANT

fussbudget PRIG

fusspot PRIG

fussy ORNATE, PRIM
~ **excitement** ADO
~ **sort** PRIG

fustian RANT

fustigate BEAT

fusty CLOSE, STALE

futhark
~ **character** RUNE

futile IDLE, VAIN
~ **effort** WASTE

futon BED

Futura FONT

future LATER, TOBE
~ **examiner** SEER
~ **fern** SPORE
~ **lieutenant** CADET
~ **plant** SEED
in the ~ AFTER, AHEAD, LATER
in the near ~ ANON, SOON
sign of the ~ OMEN

futuristic NEW

futz IDLE
~ **around** LOAF

fuzz HAIR, LINT, NAP
~ **up** BLUR
fabric ~ LINT

fuzzball LINT

fuzzy DIM
~ **fruit** KIWI
~ **surface** NAP
become ~ BLUR

"Fuzzy-Wuzzy" POEM

FYI
part of ~ FOR

fyke NET

Fyodor TSAR

G CLEF, KEY
a thousand ~'s MIL

"G"
assign a ~ RATE

G ___ "gnaw" ASIN

G-___ MAN, SUIT

Ga ELEM
31 for ~ ATNO

Ga.
~ neighbor ALA, FLA, TENN
~ zone EDT, EST
see also Georgia

GA
see Georgia

gab BLAB, CHAT, PRATE, RAP, TALK, YAK

gabble CRY, PRATE

___ Gables, Fla. CORAL

Gabor EVA

Gabriel ANGEL

"Gabriel ___ the White House" OVER

___ Gabriel SAN

Gabriela
see Spanish

Gabriella
see Italian

Gabrizi ALDO

gad RANGE
~ about FLIT, MOVE, ROAM, ROVE

Gad
son of ~ ERI

"___-Gadda-Da-Vida" INA

gadfly PEST

gadget TOOL
golf ~ TEE
gridiron ~ TEE
kitchen ~ RICER
photographer's ~ CAMERA
violinist's ~ MUTE

gadolinium METAL

Gadsden Purchase
~ boundary river GILA

"Gadzooks!" EGAD

Gaea
child of ~ RHEA, TITAN
Uranus, to ~ SON

Gael CELT, SCOT
~ republic EIRE

Gaelic ERSE
~ people IRISH
son, in ~ MAC

Gaels
~ school IONA

gaff BARB, MAST, SPAR, SPUR, TRIP

gaffe ERROR, SLIP
golf ~ SLICE
make a ~ ERR
vocal ~ SLIP

gaffer
~ workplace SET

gag ___ LAW, LINE, ORDER, RULE

gaga AVID
be ~ over ADORE

gaggle MASS, MOB
~ member GOOSE

"Gag me with a spoon!" UGH

Gahagan, Helen
~ role SHE

gaiety GLEE

gain CLEAR, EARN, GET, NET, TAKE, WIN
~ a lap SIT
~ comeuppance AVENGE
~ esteem ENDEAR
~ experience LEARN
~ stature GROW
~ the upper hand BEND, BEST
~ time DEFER, STALL
~ unlawfully ROB, STEAL
~ weight GROW

gainer
place for a ~ POOL

___ gainer HALF

Gainesville
~ neighbor OCALA

Gaines, William
~ founded it MAD

gains
ill-gotten ~ LOOT

gainsay BELIE, DENY

Gainsborough
~ work OIL

gait STEP, TEMPO
bouncy ~ SKIP
easy ~ TROT
home-run ~ TROT
horse's ~ LOPE, PACE, TROT
relaxed ~ LOPE
uneven ~ LIMP

gaiter SPAT

Gaius
garment for ~ TOGA

gal
~ of song SAL
Glasgow ~ LASS
palindromic ~ ADA, AVA, EVE, LIL, NAN
see also lady

gala BASH, FETE, LEVEE, REVEL
~ gathering BASH
Western ~ RODEO

galactic
~ time period EON

Galahad HERO, MAN, SIR
~ garb ARMOR
~ mother ELAINE
~ weapon LANCE
go against ~ TILT
like ~ PURE

"___ Galahad" KID

"___ Galante" MARIE

Galápagos
~ creature IGUANA

galaxy ARMY
~ unit STAR
hot spot in the ~ SUN

Galba CAESAR, ROMAN
~ predecessor NERO
garment for ~ TOGA
see also Latin

Galbraith, John Kenneth
~ subj. ECON

gale BLAST, STORM
out of the ~ ALEE

Galeao Airport
~ locale RIO

Gale, Dorothy
~ dog TOTO

galena ORE
~ yield LEAD

Galilean
~ tetrarch HEROD

Galilee
~ port ACRE

Galileo
~ hometown PISA

gall ANGER, BILE, BRASS, FACE, FRET, IRE, NERVE, SPITE

gallant BEAU, DUDE, HERO

gallantry DASH

Gallatin ___ RANGE

galled IRATE, MAD

galleon BOAT, SHIP
~ cargo ORO
~ need MAST

gallery ARCADE, HALL, MALL, SALON, TIER
~ display ART, OPART
~ staple EASEL
London art ~ TATE

galley BOAT, SHIP
~ directive STET
~ implement OAR

galley ___ SLAVE

galleys
work on ~ EDIT

"Gallia ___ omnis divisa..." EST

Galliano
~ flavoring ANISE

galliard DANCE

Gallic
see French

Gallico PAUL

gallimaufry MESS, OLIO

Gallinas CAPE

"Gallipoli"
~ **director** WEIR

gallium METAL

gallivant GAD, RANGE, ROAM, ROVE

Gallo ERNEST

___-**gallon hat** TEN

gallop GAIT, PACE, POST, RACE, RIDE, RUN, SPEED
at full ~ APACE

___ **gallop** ATA

"Galloping Gourmet, The" KERR

Gallup
~ **activity** POLL

galoot APE, BOOR, DOLT, LOUT, LUG, OAF

galop DANCE

galore AMPLE

galosh BOOT, SHOE

Galsworthy
~ **heroine** IRENE
~ **novel** TOLET

galumph PLOD

galvanic ___ CELL

galvanization
~ **material** ZINC

galvanize AROUSE, FIRE, MOVE, ROUSE, STIR, ZINC

galvanometer
~ **measure** AMP

Galveston CITY, PORT

Galway
~ **island group** ARAN
from ~ IRISH

Galway Bay
~ **islands** ARAN
~ **location** EIRE

gam LEG

Gam RITA

Gamay WINE

gambado CAPER

gambit RUSE

gamble BET, GAME, PLAY, PUT, RISK, STAKE
~ **badly** LOSE

gambler
~ **consideration** ODDS
~ **cube** DIE
~ **cubes** DICE
~ **fund** STAKE
~ **mecca** RENO

"___ Gambles, The" LADY

gambling
~ **asset** CHIP
~ **game** FARO, KENO, LOO, MONTE

~ **stake** ANTE
~ **town** RENO

gambol CAPER, DANCE, LARK, LEAP, PLAY, ROMP, SKIP, TRIP

gambrel ROOF

game LAME, PREY
~ **aim** WIN
~ **animal** DEER, ELK, MOOSE
~ **ender** STER
~ **fish** BASS
~ **(for)** HOT
~ **from Uruguay** CANASTA
~ **item** DIE
~ **name part** TAC, TIC, TOE
~ **of chance** KENO
~ **of kings and queens** CHESS
~ **opener** ANTE
~ **overseer** REF, UMP
~ **participant** SIDE
~ **piece** MAN
~ **plan** IDEA
~ **played in chukkers** POLO
~ **played with a knife** CLUE
~ **point** SCORE
~ **to 5000 points** CANASTA
~ **unit** SET
~ **with 4 jokers** CANASTA
~ **with 12 wild cards** CANASTA
~ **with a banker** FARO
~ **with forfeits** LOO
~ **with hexagonal chips** FARO
~ **with spades laid out** FARO
bingo-like ~ KENO
board ~ CHESS, CLUE, KENO, RISK
card ~ CANASTA, FARO, GIN, LOO, MONTE, PEDRO, SKAT, STUD, UNO, WAR
casino ~ FARO
con ~ SCAM, STING
cue ~ POOL
detective ~ CLUE
double-deck ~ CANASTA
five-in-a-row ~ KENO
frames in a ~ TEN
gambling ~ FARO, KENO, LOO, MONTE
get in the ~ ANTE
go after ~ HUNT
gun ~ SKEET
kids' ~ TAG
kids' card ~ WAR
knocking ~ GIN
mallet ~ POLO
mating ~ CHESS
melding ~ CANASTA
name in ~ **shows** ALEX, MERV, PAT
numbers ~ KENO
party ~ **pin-on** TAIL
PC ~ DOOM
play a child's ~ HIDE
playground ~ TAG
Prince of Wales' ~ POLO
pub ~ DARTS, POOL
rumpus-room ~ DARTS
running ~ TAG
schoolyard ~ TAG
shooting ~ SKEET

sleuth ~ CLUE
small ~ HARE
start a tennis ~ SERVE
still in the ~ ALIVE
strategy ~ RISK
target-practice ~ SKEET
three-card ~ MONTE
traps ~ SKEET
Vegas ~ FARO, KENO
war ~ TEST
what the ~ **may be** AFOOT
whodunit board ~ CLUE

game ___ BIRD, PLAN, ROOM, SHOW

___ **game** BALL, BIG, CON, END, SHELL, WAR

"Game, ___, match" SET

"___ Game" SKIN

"___ Game, The" GIN, WAR

game board
~ **square** START

Game Boy
~ **man** MARIO

"___ Game in Town, The" ONLY

"game is ___!, The" AFOOT

gameness GRIT

games
fun and ~ PLAY
six ~ SET

___ **games** PLAY

"___Games" WAR

game show
~ **group** PANEL
~ **host** EMCEE
~ **name** ALEX, PAT
~ **prize** CAR, CASH, TRIP
~ **sound** DING
~ **VIP** EMCEE, HOST
~ **winnings** LOOT
~ **worker** MODEL

___-**game show** PRE

gamete GERM

gamin LAD

gaming
~ **cubes** DICE

gamma
~ **follower** DELTA
~ **preceder** BETA

gamma ray
~ **product** ION

gammon BEAT, HAM, TRASH, WIN

gamut RANGE, SCALE
run the ~ SPAN

gamy RANK

Gance ABEL

gander BIRD, MALE
~ **mate** GOOSE
take a ~ EYE, SEE

ganders HES

"Gandhi"
~ **setting** INDIA

Gandhi, Indira
~ **father** NEHRU

Gandhi, Mahatma HINDU
~ **associate** NEHRU
~ **home** INDIA
see also Indian

gang ARMY, BAND, CABAL, CLAN, CREW, LOT, MOB, RING, SET, TEAM, TROOP
~ **ender** STER
~ **up** MASS
one of the ~ GOON, HOOD
unruly ~ HORDE
work ~ CREW

"___ Gang" OUR

___ **gangbusters** LIKE

Ganges
~ **dress** SARI
land of the ~ INDIA

gangling LANK, LEAN, TALL, THIN

gangly LANK, THIN

gangplank RAMP

gangsta ___ RAP

gangster GOON, HOOD
George of ~ **films** RAFT

"___ Gangster, The" LAST

gangsters MOB

gangway AISLE

Gannon University
~ **locale** ERIE

ganoid
~ **fish** GAR

"___ Gantry" ELMER

Ganymede MOON

gap DALE, HOLE, LEAK, RENT, SKIP, SPACE, VOID
~ **between mountains** COL
narrow the ~ GAIN, NEAR
widen the ~ GAIN

gape OGLE, SEE, SPLIT, STARE
make ~ AMAZE

gaper CLAM, SEER

gaping OPEN
~ **hole** ABYSS
~ **maybe** AWED

garage SHED
~ **happening** SALE
~ **item** TOOL
~ **job** LUBE
~ **occupant** AUTO, CAR
bus ~ BARN
parking ~ **sign** ENTER

garage ___ SALE

garage sale
~ **warning** ASIS
sign at a ~ SOLD

Garagiola JOE

Garamond FONT

garb ARRAY, ATTIRE, COAT, DRESS, RIG, SUIT
  barbecue ~ APRON
  knight's ~ ARMOR
  priestly ~ ALB
  see also clothing, garment

garbage DIRT, LIE, SLOP, TRASH, WASTE
  ~ heap MESS

garbage disposal
  ~ button RESET

garbanzo BEAN, PEA

garbed CLAD

garble SLUR

Garbo SWEDE
  what ~ wanted to be ALONE

Garcia ANDY
  ~ film HERO

García Lorca, Federico POET
  see also poet

garçon LAD

garden YARD
  ~ access GATE
  ~ area ARBOR, BED, PLOT
  ~ bane WEED
  ~ bulb TULIP
  ~ climber IVY
  ~ container POD
  ~ dweller ADAM, EVE
  ~ entrance GATE
  ~ feature ARBOR
  ~ flower ASTER, GLAD, IRIS, LILY, ROSE, TULIP
  ~ green KALE
  ~ hose PIPE
  ~ material SOIL
  ~ path MALL
  ~ perennial LILY
  ~ pest APHID, MOLE
  ~ planting ROW
  ~ root BEET
  ~ soil LOAM
  ~ spot BED, EDEN
  ~ starter SEED
  ~ tool EDGER, HOE, HOSE, RAKE, SPADE
  ~ veggie BEET, PEA
  ~ walkway PATH
  Biblical ~ EDEN
  first ~ EDEN
  lead up the ~ path LIE
  rose ~ BED
  work in the ~ HOE, RAKE, SPADE, WEED

___ garden ROOF, TEA

"___ Garden, The" ASSAM

gardener
  ~ bane APHID
  ~ charge PLANT
  ~ concern LAWN, SOIL
  ~ device EDGER
  ~ purchase LIME, SEED
  ~ tool HOE, HOSE, RAKE, SPADE
  first ~ ADAM

"___ Gardenia, The" BLUE

Garden of ___ EDEN

"Garden of ___, The" ALLAH

"Garden of Earthly Delights, A"
  ~ author OATES

"Gardens of ___" STONE

Garden State
  ~ city LODI

garden-variety USUAL

Gardner AVA, ERLE, REA
  word in many ~ titles CASE

Gare de ___ LEST

"Gare Saint-Lazare"
  ~ painter MONET

Garfield CAT, PET
  ~ had one BEARD
  ~ hand PAW

"Garfield" STRIP
  ~ dog ODIE
  ~ girlfriend ARLENE

Garfield County
  seat of ~ ENID

Garfunkel ART

gargantuan BIG, GREAT, LARGE

gargoyle OGRE

Garibaldi
  ~ birthplace NICE

garish LOUD, ORNATE
  ~ light NEON

garland LEI, SWAG
  floral ~ LEI

Garland
  ~ costar LAHR

garlic
  ~ cousin LEEK, ONION

garment ABA, ALB, APRON, CAPE, COAT, FUR, OILER, ROBE, SACK, SARI, STOLE, TOGA, VEST
  ~ attachment TAG
  ~ cut ALINE
  ~ size LARGE, MED
  ~ tear RENT
  ~ under a chasuble ALB
  Arab ~ ABA
  armless ~ VEST
  Asian ~ SARI
  billowing ~ CAPE
  carpenter's ~ APRON
  chef's ~ APRON
  down ~ VEST
  fisherman's ~ OILER
  full-length ~ TOGA
  goat-hair ~ ABA
  Gujarat ~ SARI
  half a Polynesian ~ LAVA
  Indian ~ SARI
  kitchen ~ APRON
  loose-fitting ~ ABA, ROBE, SACK
  Middle Eastern ~ ABA
  outer ~ COAT, FUR, ROBE, STOLE
  Pakistani ~ SARI
  priest's ~ ALB
  Roman's ~ TOGA

  shorten a ~ HEM
  upper ~ VEST
  see also clothing

garment ___ BAG

garments ARRAY, ATTIRE, GARB, WEAR

garment tag
  ~ abbr. MED

garner AMASS, EARN, REAP, SAVE, STORE, TAKE
  ~ esteem RATE

garnet COLOR, GEM, RED

garnierite ORE

garnish ADORN, CAPER, DRESS, LARD, TRIM
  cocktail ~ OLIVE
  entrée ~ CRESS
  hors d'oeuvre ~ CAPER
  iced-tea ~ LEMON
  jellied ~ ASPIC
  margarita ~ LIME
  martini ~ OLIVE
  pungent ~ CRESS
  sandwich ~ CAPER
  seafood ~ LEMON

Garonne
  see French

Garr TERI

garret ATTIC

"___ Garrick, The" GREAT

garrison ARMY

Garroway DAVE, EMCEE, HOST
  ~ signoff PEACE

Garry MOORE

garter ___ SNAKE

Garvey STEVE

Gary HART
  ~ st. IND

gas ETHANE
  ~ asset OCTANE
  ~ burner LAMP
  ~ container TANK
  ~ fixture LAMP
  ~ for signs NEON
  ~ gulper AUTO, CAR
  ~ holder TANK
  ~ in a bulb NEON
  ~ in physics STATE
  ~ jet LAMP
  ~ (prefix) AER, AERO, ATM
  ~ stove RANGE
  charge with ~ AERATE
  flammable ~ ETHANE
  Geiger-counter ~ NEON
  inert ~ NEON
  knockout ~ ETHER
  natural ~ component ETHANE
  noble ~ NEON
  odorless ~ ETHANE
  old ~ brand ESSO
  out of ~ BEAT
  qty. of ~ GAL
  run out of ~ FLAG, TIRE
  tear ~ MACE

  treat with ~ AERATE

gas ___ LOG, MAIN, MASK, METER

gasbag BORE

gasconade BRAG, CROW, RANT

gases
  like some ~ INERT

gash CHIP, CUT, GAP, LEAK, MAIM, RENT, RIP, SCORE, SLASH, SLIT

gasket
  blow a ~ RAGE, RAMP, RANT

Gaslight ERA

gasline PIPE

Gaslit ___ ERA

gasoline
  ~ rating OCTANE

"Gasoline ___" ALLEY

gasp PANT
  ~ of delight OOH
  last ~ END

Gaspar
  ~ and others MAGI

gas pump
  ~ abbr. REG
  ~ datum OCTANE

gas station
  ~ offering AIR
  former ~ freebie MAP
  former ~ name ESSO

gasthaus INN

Gaston
  see French

gastronome CHEF

gat GUN, ROD

gate DOOR, EXIT
  ~ fig. ATT
  ~ receipts TAKE
  ~ starter TAIL, TOLL, WATER
  crooked ~ of nursery rhyme STILE
  farm ~ STILE
  give the ~ OUST
  starting ~ POST

"___ Gate, The" TOLL

gâteau CAKE

gateleg ___ TABLE

gateway DOOR
  ~ (abbr.) ENT
  curved ~ ARCH

Gateway ___ ARCH

Gateway 2000
  ~ rival DELL

gather AMASS, BAND, DRAW, GET, MEET, PILE, PLEAT, RAKE, SEW, TAKE, TROOP
  ~ grain REAP
  ~ into folds PLEAT
  ~ leaves RAKE
  ~ opinions POLL
  ~ roses SNIP
  ~ together MEET

gathering
~ **dust** IDLE
~ **storm** PERIL
afternoon ~ TEA
elegant ~ SOIREE
fall ~ CROP
gala ~ BASH, FETE
social ~ BEE, LEVEE, SOIREE
sophisticated ~ SALON

"Gathering of Eagles, A"
~ **director** MANN

"...gathers no ___" MOSS

Gatlin Brothers TRIO

Gatling GUN

gator
~ **cousin** CROC
~ **home, maybe** MOAT

Gator
~ **ender** ADE

Gator Bowl
~ **site** FLA

___ Gatos, Calif. LOS

Gatsby
~ **description** GREAT
~ **portrayer** LADD

"___ Gatsby, The" GREAT

Gatún LAKE

Gatwick
~ **letters** ARR, ETA

gauche RUDE
~**, in French** LEFT

gaucherie SLIP

gaucho
~ **ctry.** ARG
~ **roundup** RODEO
see also Spanish

gaudy LOUD, ORNATE
~ **sign** NEON
not ~ DRAB

gauge ASSESS, DIAL, MAKE,
METER, NORM, PUT, RATE,
SCALE
auto ~ TACH
inflation ~ PSI
pilot ~ abbr. ALT

___ gauge RAIN, WATER, WIRE

Gauls
~ **to the Romans** ENEMY, FOE

gaunt LANK, LEAN, THIN

gauntlet ARMOR
run the ~ DARE
throw down the ~ DARE

gauze LINT, MESH

gauzy FINE, THIN
~ **fabric** LENO

gavel-down
~ **word** GONE, SOLD

gavel-pounder
~ **demand** ORDER

gavel-wielder
~ **title** MADAM, SIR

gavotte DANCE

"___ Gavotte" ASCOT

Gawain HERO, SIR
~ **garb** ARMOR
~ **weapon** LANCE

gawk GAPE, OGLE, STARE
~ **at** EYE

gawky LANK, THIN

gay GALA, RIANT
~ **blade** DUDE
~ **Nineties** ERA

"Gay"
~ **city** PAREE

"___ Gay" ENOLA

Gay Nineties ERA

Gaza Strip
~ **grp.** PLO
~ **resident** ARAB

gaze
~ **at** EYE, OGLE, SEE
~ **dreamily** MOON
~ **impolitely at** LEER
~ **out the window** DREAM
~ **steadily** STARE
~ **upon** PORE
amorous ~ LEER
intent ~ STARE
riveting ~ GLARE

gazelle ANIMAL, ARIEL, GOA
~ **cousin** ELAND

gazer
crystal-ball ~ SEER

gazette NEWS, PAPER, SHEET

gazetteer
~ **abbr.** ISL, MTS, STR, TERR
~ **data** AREA

gazpacho
~ **ingredient** ONION

Gazzara BEN

G.B.
part of ~ ENG, SCOT

GBS
~ **ctry.** IRE
part of ~ SHAW

___ G. Carroll LEO

Gd ELEM
64 for ~ ATNO

Gdansk CITY, PORT
~ **resident** POLE

gds. MDSE

Ge ELEM
32 for ~ ATNO

GE
~ **acquisition** RCA
part of ~ ELEC, GEN

gear ARRAY, DRESS, KIT, RIG
~ **element** TOOTH

___ gear LOW

gears
~ **do this** MESH

gee WOW
~ **opposite** HAW
one-tenth of a ~ CEE

geek NERD

___ Gees, The BEE

"Gee whiz!" WOW

geezer COOT

Gehrig LOU

Geiger HANS

Geiger counter
set off a ~ EMIT

Geisel
~ **pen name** SEUSS

geisha
~ **accessory** FAN, OBI
~ **serving** CHA, SAKE, TEA

gel SET
lab ~ AGAR

gelatin
~ **shaper** MOLD
~ **substitute** AGAR
Chinese ~ AGAR

gelatinize SET

gelato ICE

Gelderland
~ **commune** EDE

gelding HORSE

gelid ICY

Geller URI

gelling
~ **agent** AGAR

gelt CASH, MOOLA

gem OPAL, PEARL, STONE
~ **cut** PEAR
~ **shape** OVAL
~ **unit** CARAT
~ **wts.** CTS
artificial ~ PASTE
banded ~ AGATE
black or white ~ OPAL
carved ~ CAMEO
cultured ~ PEARL
green ~ JADE
iridescent ~ OPAL
milky ~ OPAL
mount a ~ SET
orange ~ SARD
precious ~ PEARL
semiprecious ~ AGATE
unfaceted ~ OPAL, PEARL

Gem
~ **St.** IDA

Gemayel AMIN

gem-grade
~ **coal** JET

geminate DUAL

Gemini DUO, PAIR, SIGN, TWO
~ **follower** CRAB
~ **org.** NASA
mother of the ~ LEDA
when ~ starts MAY

Gem State IDAHO
~ **capital** BOISE

gemütlich SWEET

___ gen. ATTY

gender FEMALE, MALE, SEX
~ **(abbr.)** FEM, MASC
not restricted by ~ COED

gender ___ GAP

gender-changer
~ **suffix** ESS, ETTE

gene
~ **component** DNA, RNA
~ **determinant** TRAIT
locate a ~ on a
chromosome MAP

gene ___ POOL

genealogical
~ **carving** TOTEM

genealogy
~ **chart** TREE
~ **personage** AUNT

general RANK
~ **address** SIR
~ **appearance** AIR
~ **designation** STAR
~ **direction** TREND
~ **level** NORM
~ **public** MOB
~ **sense** TENOR
~ **tendency** STYLE
~ **truth** LAW, RULE
Muslim ~ AGA, AGHA

general ___ STORE

___ general MAJOR

"General Hospital" SOAP

generalissimo RULER

generally ABOUT, OFT, OFTEN

General Motors
~ **make** GEO

General Robert ___ ELEE

"General William Booth Enters
Heaven" POEM

generate BREED, CAUSE

generation AGE, DAY, ERA

generation ___ GAP

___ Generation BEAT

generis
sui ~ RARE

generous AMPLE, BIG, FREE,
LARGE, OPEN
~ **one** DONOR
~ **slice** SLAB
be ~ SHARE

generous ___ fault TOA

genesis FIRST, ONSET, RISE, START

Genesis
~ **bird** DOVE
~ **brother** ABEL
~ **fruit** APPLE
~ **landfall** ARARAT

~ **locale** EDEN
~ **name** ABEL, ADAM, ENOS, ESAU, EVE, ISAAC, NOAH
~ **shepherd** ABEL
~ **son** ABEL, CAIN, HAM, SETH
~ **to Deuteronomy** TORAH
~ **twin** ESAU
~ **vessel** ARK
~ **victim** ABEL
~ **wife** EVE, SARAH

genet ANIMAL, CAT

Genet
~ **product** DRAMA, PLAY

genetic
~ **factor** TRAIT
~ **material** DNA

genetic ___ CODE, MAP

genetic engineering
~ **product** CLONE

geneticist
~ **abbr.** DNA, RNA

Geneva LAKE

Geneviève STE

Genghis ___ KHAN

Genghis Khan
~ **follower** TATAR
~ **followers** HORDE

genial GOOD, MILD, NICE, SWEET, WARM

genie DEMON
~ **home** LAMP
TV ~ portrayer EDEN

genius FIRE
poetic ~ MUSE

"___ Genius" REAL

"___ Genius, The" MAD

___ Gennaro SAN

Genoa CITY, PORT, SALAMI

genre CLASS, ILK, ORDER, SORT, TYPE

genro ELDER, MALE

Gen. Robt. ___ ELEE

gens CLAN

gent CHAP, DUDE

genteel NICE, SEDATE

gentil
parfit ~ knight MODEL

gentility ELITE

gentle EASY, GOOD, MEEK, MELT, MILD, TAME
~ **as breezes** MILD
~ **one** LAMB
~ **slope** RISE

gentle ___ lamb ASA

"Gentle ___" BEN, GIANT

Gentle Ben BEAR
~ **doc** VET
like ~ TAME

gentleman ADULT, BARON, MALE, PEER, SIR
~ **in German** HERR
~ **in India** SRI
~ **in Spanish** SENOR
~ **of Lisbon** DOM
no ~ CAD, HEEL, RAKE, ROUE
Spanish ~ DON
that ~'s HIS

"___ Gentleman, The" LAST

gentleman's
~ **gentleman** MAN, VALET

gentlemen HES

"Gentlemen, ___ your engines" START

"___ Gentlemen From West Point" TEN

"Gentlemen Prefer Blondes"
~ **author** LOOS

gentlewoman LADY, MADAM

gentry ELITE

genu KNEE

genuflect BEND, BOW, KNEEL

genuine GOOD, HONEST, PURE, REAL, SOLID, TRUE
not ~ ACTED, FAKE, FALSE, SHAM

genus CLASS
cattle ~ BOS
heather ~ ERICA
lily ~ ALOE
macaw ~ ARA
maple ~ ACER
parrot ~ ARA

Geo AUTO, CAR

geocentric
~ **position** EARTH

geodesic ___ DOME

geoduck CLAM

geographic
~ **speck** ISLET

geographical
~ **datum** AREA

geography
~ **abbr.** ALT, ATL, ISL, LAT, MTS, PAC, STR, TER, TERR

geol. SCI

geologic
~ **formation** DOME, MESA
~ **period** EON, EPOCH, ERA

geologist
~ **sample** CORE
~ **suffix** ITE

geomancer SEER

geometer
~ **concern** AREA

geometric
~ **figure** CONE, SOLID
~ **line** ARC, AXIS, SIDE
~ **measure** AREA

geometry MATH
~ **calculation** AREA
branch of ~ PLANE, SOLID
corner, in ~ ANGLE
line in ~ AXIS

___ geometry PLANE, SOLID

geophyte PLANT

"___ Geordie" WEE

Georg OHM

George ADE, ALLEN, ELIOT, LAKE, PAL, RAFT, SAND, SEGAL
~ **brother** IRA
~ **couldn't tell it** ALIE
~ **("Grand Ole Opry" founder)** HAY
~ **of gangster films** RAFT
~ **predecessor** RON
~ **successor** BILL
~ **who was a she** ELIOT, SAND

George ___ III

George and Bill
~ **opponent** ROSS

"___ George Apley, The" LATE

George Bernard ___ SHAW

George C. ___ SCOTT

George I
~ **mother** ANNE

George, Lloyd
~ **contemporary** LENIN

"George M!"
~ **star** GREY
~ **subject** COHAN

Georges
see French

George, Saint
emulate ~ SLAY

"George Washington ___ Here" SLEPT

Georgia STATE
~ **city** ROME
~ **once** SSR
~ **plantation** TARA
city in ~ ATLANTA
it's south of ~ IRAN

Georgia ___ PINE, TECH

"___ Georgia Brown" SWEET

Georgia Dome ARENA

Georgian STYLE

georgic POEM

"Georgy ___" GIRL

Ger. LANG
~ **neighbor** POL
see also German

Geraint SIR
~ **wife** ENID

"Geraint and ___" ENID

Geraldine PAGE
~ **portrayer** FLIP

Geraldo
~ **former rival** PHIL

geranium COLOR, RED

Gerard GIL

Gerard ___ Borch TER

gerbil ANIMAL, PET

germ EGG, SEED
~ **cell** SPORE
~ **fighters** SERA
kind of ~ for short STREP

German
~ **adjective** NAH
~ **article** DAS, DER, DES, EIN, EINE
~ **art song** LIED
~ **composer** BACH
~ **denial** NEIN
~ **industrial region** RUHR, SAAR
~ **interjection** ACH, NEIN
~ **magazine** STERN
~ **mister** HERR
~ **novelist** HESSE, MANN
~ **number** DREI, ELF
~ **painter** ERNST
~ **preposition** MIT, UBER, VON
~ **pronoun** ICH, MIR, UNS
~ **refusal** NEIN
~ **sub** UBOAT
~ **surrealist** ERNST
~ **verb** ESSEN
above, in ~ UBER
ago, in ~ VON
a, in ~ EIN, EINE
avec in ~ MIT
before, in ~ VON
beyond, in ~ UBER
"Darn!" in ~ ACH
eat, in ~ ESSEN
fellow, in ~ HERR
first ~ president EBERT
from, in ~ VON
gentleman, in ~ HERR
I, in ~ ICH
in front of, in ~ VON
John, in ~ HANS
me, in ~ MIR
mister, in ~ HERR
near, in ~ NAH
no, in ~ NEIN
non, in ~ NEIN
old one, in ~ ALTE
one, in ~ EIN
over, in ~ UBER
señor, in ~ HERR
the, in ~ DAS, DER, DIE
three, in ~ DREI
us, in ~ UNS
with, in ~ MIT
see also Germany

germane APT

Germany
city in ~ BONN, ESSEN, ULM
coal-mining region in ~ SAAR
industrial region in ~ RUHR, SAAR
reservoir in ~ EDER
river in ~ EDER, ELBE, EMS, MAIN, ODER, OSTE, RHINE, RUHR
spa in ~ EMS

state in ~ HESSE
steel center in ~ ESSEN, RUHR
valley in ~ RUHR, SAAR
wine region in ~ RHINE
see also German

Germany-Poland
~ border river ODER

germfree PURE

germinal FIRST

germinate BEAR, GROW

"Gerontion"
~ poet ELIOT

Gerry ADAMS

Gershwin IRA
~ contemporary ARLEN
~ heroine BESS
~ portrayer ALDA
~ tune SOON

Gertrude STEIN
~ friend ALICE

gest ACT, DEED, FEAT, SAGA, TALE

___ **gestae** RES

"___ **Geste**" BEAU

gesticulation SIGN

gesture NOD, SIGN
~ of approval NOD
affectionate ~ KISS
affirmative ~ NOD
courteous ~ BOW
peace ~ VEE
well-wisher's ~ TOAST

get EARN, GAIN, GRASP, HAVE, IRK, MAKE, RILE, SEE, SENSE, UPSET
~ a bang out of LIKE, LOVE
~ a bead on AIM, TRAIN
~ accustomed ADAPT, ENURE, INURE
~ a charge out of LIKE
~ a check EARN
~ acquainted with MEET
~ across TALK
~ a grip on GRASP, HOLD
~ ahead ARRIVE, GAIN, RISE
~ ahead of PASS
~ a kick out of LIKE, LOVE, SAVOR
~ all worked up RANT
~ a load of EYE, SEE, SPY
~ a loan OWE
~ along AGREE, FARE, FEND, MOVE
~ along without SPARE
~ a move on HIE, RUN, STIR
~ an A on ACE
~ an earful HEAR
~ an eyeful SEE
~ an out-of-state license ELOPE
~ a paycheck EARN
~ approved SELL
~ around AVOID, EVADE
~ around to it START
~ a salary EARN
~ a serve past ACE
~ a smile out of AMUSE

~ a tan BASK, SUN
~ a taste of TRY
~ a top mark on ACE
~ away from ELUDE, EVADE, LEAVE
~ back PAY
~ beat LOSE
~ better AGE, GAIN, HEAL, MEND
~ bigger GROW
~ bored TIRE
~ brown TAN
~ bushed FLAG, TIRE
~ busy ACT
~ by PASS
~ choked up GAG
~ clear of ELUDE, EVADE
~ cracking HIE, RUN, START
~ credit OWE
~ crowned REIGN, RULE
~ dirty SOIL
~ down to business START
~ duded up PREEN
~ established SETTLE
~ even AVENGE, PAY, REACT
~ excited FLIP
~ familiar ORIENT
~ fat GAIN
~ fresh SASS
~ going IMPEL, MOVE, ROLL, START
~ here ARRIVE
~ high marks ACE
~ hitched WED
~ hitched in a hurry ELOPE
~ hold of GRASP
~ in ARRIVE
~ in line WAIT
~ in one's head CON, LEARN
~ in return REAP
~ in shape HONE, TONE, TRAIN
~ in someone's hair ANGER, IRK, PEEVE, RILE, UPSET
~ in the game ANTE
~ in the way DETER
~ into DON
~ (into) SEEP
~ into better condition RESTORE
~ it DIG, LEARN, SEE
~ licked LOSE
~ loose PART
~ lost SCAT, SCRAM, SPLIT
~ lower EBB
~ mellow AGE
~ melodramatic EMOTE
~ misty CRY
~ moldy ROT
~ moving HIE, ROLL, START
~ narrow TAPER
~ new guns REARM
~ nosy ASK, PRY
~ 100 on ACE
~ off LEAVE
~ off one's feet SIT
~ off the fence ACT, OPT
~ off the stage EXIT
~ older AGE
~ on AGE, FARE
~ on a horse RIDE
~ one's back up ANGER, IRE, IRK, PEEVE, RILE

~ one's bearings ORIENT
~ one's dander up ANGER, IRE, IRK, PEEVE, RILE
~ one's feet wet START, WADE
~ one's goat ANGER, ENRAGE, IRK, PEEVE, RILE, UPSET
~ one's hands on GRAB
~ on in years AGE
~ on one's case CARP, NAG
~ on one's feet RISE, STAND
~ on one's nerves IRK, PEEVE, RILE, UPSET
~ organized PLAN
~ out EXIT, LEAVE
~ out of bed ARISE, RISE, ROUSE
~ out of sight HIDE
~ out of the way of EVADE
~ paid EARN
~ past the goalie SCORE
~ pleasure from ADORE, LIKE
~ promoted RISE
~ prone LIE
~ ready DRESS, PREP, RIPEN
~ ready for dinner DRESS
~ ready for war ARM
~ ready to eat WASH
~ ready to fire AIM
~ rid of DROP, EJECT, END, ERASE, FIRE, LOSE, OUST, SCRAP, SELL, SHED, TOSS
~ rid of knots UNTIE
~ rid of suds RINSE
~ ripe AGE
~ ruined in the wash RUN
~ situated ORIENT, ROOST
~ sleepy NOD, TIRE
~ smart LEARN, SASS
~ soft MELT, THAW
~ somewhere ARRIVE
~ sore laughing ACHE
~ spliced WED
~ steamed up BOIL
~ support for, as an idea SELL
~ takeout, perhaps EATIN
~ taller GROW
~ tangled MAT, SNARL
~ the ball rolling OPEN, START
~ the better of BEAT, ROUT
~ the drift SEE
~ the gold WIN
~ the goods SHOP
~ the hang of LEARN, SEE
~ the idea LEARN, SEE
~ the impression FEEL, SENSE
~ the knots out COMB
~ the lead out ERASE, HIE, MOVE, RACE, RUN, TEAR
~ the lowdown HEAR, LEARN
~ the message HEAR, SEE
~ the old-fashioned way EARN
~ the picture GRASP, LEARN, SEE
~ the point SEE
~ there ARRIVE
~ the same answer AGREE
~ the scoop HEAR, LEARN
~ the show on the road START

~ the word HEAR, LEARN
~ the worst of LOSE
~ the wrinkles out IRON
~ the wrong idea MISS
~ thick GEL
~ through one's head LEARN
~ tired, with "out" PETER
~ to ANGER, ARRIVE, COME, IRK, PEEVE, RILE, UPSET
~ together AMASS, MEET, TROOP, UNITE
~ to it START
~ to know LEARN, MEET
~ to one's feet ARISE, RISE
~ too personal PRY
~ top billing STAR
~ to the bottom line ADD
~ tough ENURE, INURE
~ to work START
~ trounced LOSE
~ under someone's skin ANGER, IRE, IRK, PEEVE, RILE, UPSET
~ underway START
~ up ARISE, RISE, STAND, STIR
~ up and go EXIT, LEAVE, PART
~ upset LOSE
~ used to ADAPT, ENURE, INURE, ORIENT
~ used to change ADAPT, COPE
~ water from a well DRAW
~ well HEAL
~ wider FLARE
~ wind of HEAR, LEARN
~ wise to LEARN
hard to ~ to DENSE
out to ~ AFTER
try to ~ answers ASK

get ___ **(be active)** ABOUT

get ___ **(be compatible)** ALONG

get ___ **(escape)** AWAY

get ___ **(exact revenge)** EVEN

get ___ **(explain)** ACROSS

get ___ **(leave)** OUT

get ___ **(manage)** ALONG

get ___ **(perform with energy)** ITON

get ___ **(remind)** AFTER

get ___ **(retaliate)** EVEN

get ___ **for effort** ANA, ANE

get ___ **of (ditch)** RID

get ___ **start (sleep in)** ALATE

get ___ **the act** INTO

get ___ **the ground floor** INON

get ___ **up** ALEG

"Get ___**"** SMART

"Get ___**!"** REAL

"Get ___ **of My Cloud"** OFF

geta SHOE

get a ___ **lease on life** NEW

get a ___ of one's own medicine DOSE

get a ___ out of BANG

"Get a ___!" GRIP

"Get a ___ of that!" LOAD

"Get a ___ on!" MOVE

"Get a Job" OLDIE
    ~ syllable SHA

getaway LAM, RUN
    child's ~ CAMP
    drive the ~ car ABET
    make a ~ FLEE, RUN

"___ Get By" ILL

"Get Christie ___" LOVE

get-go ONSET, START

"Get Happy"
    ~ composer ARLEN

"___ Get It for You Wholesale" ICAN

get left holding the ___ BAG

"Get lost!" SCAT, SCRAM, SHOO, SPLIT

"___ Get Lost" LETS

"___ get me wrong!" DONT

"Get off my ___!" CASE

get one's ___ GOAT

get one's ___ together ACT

get one's ducks in ___ AROW

get on one's high ___ HORSE

"Get on the ___" BUS

"Get on the Bus"
    ~ director LEE

get-out-of-jail
    ~ money BAIL

"Get Outta My Dreams, Get Into My Car"
    ~ singer OCEAN

gets
    ~ used up GOES

"___ Gets Her Man" SHE

"Get Smart"
    ~ actor ADAMS
    99 of ~ AGENT

getter
    attention ~ AHEM, HEY, PSST, PST

getters
    alimony ~ EXES

get the ___ of BEST

get the ___ on DROP

get the ___ on the road SHOW

get the ___ out LEAD

getting
    ~ close WARM
    ~ up there AGED
    means of ~ there ROAD, ROUTE

getting ___ in years ALONG

"Getting ___ With Dad" EVEN

"Getting Even With ___" DAD

"Getting to Know You"
    ~ singer ANNA

get-together
    rural ~ BEE

Getty
    ~ product GAS, OIL

Gettysburg
    ~ addresser ABE
    ~ general LEE
    ~ soldier REB
    ~ st. PENN

Gettysburg Address
    ~ ender EARTH

get under one's ___ SKIN

getup ARRAY, ATTIRE, DRESS, GARB, SUIT
    Halloween ~ MASK

get-up ATTIRE, RIG

get-up-and-go PEP, VIM

get-well ___ CARD

"___ Get Your Gun" ANNIE

Getz STAN
    ~ instrument SAX

Gewürztraminer WINE

geyser JET

Ghana
    ~ export COCOA
    ~ neighbor TOGO
    capital of ~ ACCRA

___ ghanouj BABA

ghastly ASHEN, BAD, DIRE, EVIL, PALE

Ghats RANGE

"___ Gherardo" FRA

ghost GAME, SHADE, SOUL
    ~ costume SHEET
    white as a ~ WAN
    word for a ~ BOO

ghost ___ DANCE

ghost ___ chance OFA

"Ghost ___, The" SHIP

"Ghost ___ Mrs. Muir, The" AND

"Ghost and ___ Muir, The" MRS

"Ghost and Mrs. ___, The" MUIR

"Ghostbusters"
    ~ goo SLIME
    ~ prefix ECTO

Ghostley ALICE

ghostlike EERIE, EERY, PALE, WAN

ghost of Christmas ___, the PAST

"Ghosts"
    ~ author IBSEN

"Ghost Writer, The"
    ~ author ROTH

ghoul DEMON, OGRE
    ~ greeting BOO

GI
    ~ address APO
    ~ cops MPS
    ~ dinner MESS
    ~ garb DRAB
    ~ group UNIT
    ~ hangout USO
    ~ need AMMO
    ~ offender AWOL
    ~ source, once SSS
    order to a ~ ATEASE, HALT
    part of ~ ISSUE
    unaccounted-for ~ MIA
    see also army, military, soldier

G.I.
    ~ guy JOE
    ~ Joe TOY

Gia SCALA

Gia Lan Airport
    ~ site HANOI

giant BIG, LARGE, OGRE, TALL, TITAN
    ~ syllable FEE, FIE
    ~ to Jack FOE
    red ~ STAR

Giant
    ~ outfielder OTT

"Giant"
    ~ actor DEAN
    ~ ranch RIATA
    ~ wrestler ANDRE

giant ant
    ~ horror film THEM

Giants ELEVEN, NINE, TEAM
    ~ legend OTT
    ~ org. NFL

gib CAT

Gibb ANDY

gibber PRATE, RANT, TALK

gibbet HANG, POST

gibbon ANIMAL, APE
    Malay ~ LAR

gibbosity NODE

gibe BARB, DIG, RAG, TEASE, TWIT

giblet NECK

Gibraltar CITY, PORT
    ~ denizen APE

Gibran, Kahlil POET
    see also poet

Gibson BOB, DESERT, HOOT, MEL

Gibson ___ GIRL

gibus HAT

giddy
    be ~ REEL

Gide ANDRE

"Gidget"
    ~ actress DEE

Gielgud
    ~ title SIR
    role for ~ LEAR

gift AWARD
    ~ feature BOW
    ~ giver DONOR
    ~ receiver DONEE
    ~ topper BOW
    ~ to the needy ALMS
    ~ wrap PAPER
    aloha ~ LEI
    decorate a ~ WRAP
    engagement ~ RING
    Father's Day ~ TIE
    gossip's ~ GAB
    housewarming ~ PLANT
    medium's ~ ESP
    naughty child's Christmas ~ COAL
    Nile's ~ SILT
    prepare a ~ WRAP
    seer's ~ ESP
    small ~ TREAT
    temporary ~ LOAN

gift ___ WRAP

"___ Gift" ITSA

gift-card
    ~ word FOR

gifted ABLE, APT

gift-getter DONEE

gift-giving
    ~ time YULE

gift of ___ GAB

"Gift of the ___, The" MAGI

"Gift of the Magi, The"
    ~ device IRONY
    ~ heroine DELLA

gifts LOOT

gift-shop
    ~ item VASE

gift-wrap PAPER

gift-wrapping
    ~ need TAPE

gig ACT, BOAT, CART

gigantic BIG, GREAT, LARGE, VAST

giggle TEHEE

giggler
    ~ syllable HEE

Gigi
    see French

"Gigi"
    ~ author LOOS

"G.I. Jane"
    ~ actress DEMI, MOORE

Gilbert CASS, SARA, SIR

Gilbert & Sullivan TEAM
    ~ princess IDA

gild ADORN, COAT, DRESS, LIE, PLATE

"Gilda"
    Glenn's ~ costar RITA

"Gilded ___, The" AGE, LILY

Gildersleeve
  like ~ GREAT

gild the ___ LILY

Gilead
  balm of ~ RESIN

Gilels EMIL
  ~ **instrument** PIANO

Gilgamesh HERO

gill ORGAN
  ~ **cousin** LUNG

gill ___ NET, SLIT

Gillespie, Dizzy
  ~ **music** BOP

Gillette ANITA

Gilliam STU

gillie SHOE

Gilligan
  ~ **home** ISLE

"Gilligan's Island"
  ~ **skipper** HALE
  Ginger, in ~ TINA

gills
  four ~ PINT

gilt COLOR, GOLD

gilt-edged AONE, BEST

gimlet AWL, TOOL
  ~ **ingredient** GIN, LIME
  use a ~ BORE

gimlet-___ EYED

"Gimme Three ___" STEPS

gimmick RUSE

gin CRANE, NOOSE, SNARE, TRAP
  ~ **flavoring** SLOE
  ~ **joint** BAR
  ~ **lover** SOT
  ~ **rummy** GAME

gin ___ MILL

___ gin SLOE

Gina
  see Italian

gin and ___ TONIC

___ gin fizz SLOE

ginger ALE, BAY, COLOR, TANG

ginger ___ ALE, BEER, SNAP

Ginger
  ~ **partner** FRED
  ~ **predecessor** ADELE

gingerbread CAKE, PALM, TRIM

gingery
  ~ **cookie** SNAP

Gingrich NEWT

ginkgo TREE

Ginnie ___ MAE

"Ginny Fizz" WADE

Ginsberg ALLEN, POET, RUTH

Ginsberg, Allen POET
  see also poet

ginseng
  ~ **family member** IVY, NARD

Ginza
  ~ **coin** SEN, YEN
  ~ **light** NEON
  ~ **purchase** OBI
  see also Japanese

"___, Giorgio" YES

Giotto
  ~ **contemporary** DANTE
  place to see ~
    paintings ASSISI

Giovanni DON
  see also Italian

giraffe ANIMAL
  ~ **cousin** OKAPI
  ~ **feature** NECK

giraffelike LANK

Girardeau CAPE

girasol OPAL

gird ARM, BELT

girder BEAM
  ~ **insert** RIVET
  ~ **material** STEEL
  girth ~ BELT

girdle BAND, BELT, RING

girl LADY, LASS, MAID, MISS
  ~ **ender** ISH
  ~ **Fri.** ASST
  ~ **starter** ATTA

"___ girl!" ATTA, ITSA

"Girl ___" SHY

"Girl ___ Help It, The" CANT

"Girl ___ Likely, The" MOST

"___ Girl" CITY, THAT

"___ Girl?" NICE

"Girl Can't ___ It, The" HELP

"___ Girl Friday" HIS

girlfriend DATE, LASS, LOVE
  ~ **in French** AMIE

"___ Girl in Town" NEW

___-girl network OLD

"Girl of the Golden ___, The"
  WEST

girls
  for boys and ~ COED

girl's
  that ~ HERS

"Girls ___ Town" ABOUT

"___ Girls" LES

"___ Girls and a Sailor" TWO

"___ Girls Are Easy" EARTH

Girl Scouts
  ~ **founder** LOW

"Girl With the Hatbox, The"
  ~ **actress** STEN

girth
  ~ **girder** BELT

"Giselle"
  ~ **composer** ADAM

gist CORE, ESSENCE, IDEA, MEAT, SENSE, SUM, TENOR, THEME

"Git!" SCAT, SCRAM, SHOO

Giuseppe
  see Italian

give ALLOT, ENDOW, HAND, SAG
  ~ **a darn** CARE
  ~ **a false impression** BELIE
  ~ **a great notice** RAVE
  ~ **a hand** ABET, CLAP, ROOT
  ~ **a hang** CARE
  ~ **a helpful hint** STEER
  ~ **a high sign** ALERT
  ~ **a home to** ADOPT
  ~ **a hoot** CARE
  ~ **a lift to** ELATE, RAISE
  ~ **a little extra** ADD
  ~ **a name to** CALL
  ~ **an account** RELATE
  ~ **an audience to** HEAR
  ~ **and take** SWAP, TRADE
  ~ **an edge to** HONE
  ~ **an encore**
    performance RERUN
  ~ **a new hue to** DYE
  ~ **a new look to** REDO
  ~ **an opinion** STATE
  ~ **an R to** RATE
  ~ **a number to** PAGE
  ~ **a party for** FETE
  ~ **a PG to** RATE
  ~ **a poor review to** PAN
  ~ **a presentation** SHOW
  ~ **a rap** CARE
  ~ **as a compliment** PAY
  ~ **as an example** CITE, REFER
  ~ **as odds** LAY
  ~ **assurance** AGREE
  ~ **a thumbs-down to** PAN, RATE
  ~ **a thumbs-up to** LAUD, RATE
  ~ **autographs** SIGN
  ~ **a valedictory** ORATE
  ~ **away** BLAB, SHOW, SPARE, TELL
  ~ **a whirl** RISK
  ~ **a wide berth to** AVOID
  ~ **back** ECHO, RESTORE
  ~ **birth to** BEAR, DROP, HAVE
  ~ **ear to** ATTEND, HEED
  ~ **evidence** ATTEST
  ~ **food and drink** SERVE
  ~ **forth** EMIT, SAY, SHED, UTTER
  ~ **generously** RAIN
  ~ **guns to** ARM
  ~ **in** BEND, BOW, DEFER, YIELD
  ~ **it a whirl** ESSAY, TEST, TRY
  ~ **joy to** ELATE
  ~ **leave to** ALLOW, LET
  ~ **lessons to** TRAIN
  ~ **light** SHED
  ~ **lip to** SASS
  ~ **medicine to** DOSE

  ~ **notice to** WARN
  ~ **odds** LAY
  ~ **off** EMIT
  ~ **off steam** REEK
  ~ **on credit** LEND
  ~ **one's solemn word** ATTEST
  ~ **one's word** SAY
  ~ **one the creeps** REPEL
  ~ **orders to** BOSS
  ~ **or take a few** ORSO
  ~ **or take a little** LIKE
  ~ **out** ALLOT, DOLE, EMIT, ISSUE, METE, PETER, RUMOR, STATE
  ~ **over** CEDE
  ~ **partner** TAKE
  ~ **permission** ALLOW, LET
  ~ **pleasure to** AMUSE, ELATE
  ~ **rise to** BREED, CAUSE
  ~ **stars to** RATE
  ~ **support to** ABET, ENDOW
  ~ **surety** BAIL
  ~ **temporarily** LEND
  ~ **the boot to** AXE, CAN, FIRE
  ~ **the eye to** OGLE, STARE
  ~ **the first**
    performance OPEN
  ~ **the gate** OUST
  ~ **the go-ahead to** ALLOW, CLEAR, LET, OKAY
  ~ **the once-over** EYE, LEER, NOTE, OGLE, SCAN
  ~ **the pink slip to** AXE, CAN, FIRE
  ~ **the slip to** AVOID, ELUDE, EVADE, LOSE
  ~ **the word** ORDER
  ~ **thought to** SEE
  ~ **too much** SATE
  ~ **up** CEASE, CEDE, DROP, YIELD
  ~ **up, slangily** BAIL
  ~ **up the ship** BOW
  ~ **vent to** POUR
  ~ **walking papers** AXE, CAN, FIRE
  ~ **way** BEND, LAPSE, YIELD
  ~ **way (to)** DEFER
  ~ **zip to** SAVOR
  don't ~ up KEEP

give ___ (distribute) OUT

give ___ (donate) AWAY

give ___ (emit) OFF

give ___ (pursue) CHASE

give ___ go ITA

give ___ rein to FREE

give ___ shot ITA

give ___ to (cause) RISE

give ___ try ITA

give ___ up (assist) ALEG

"Give ___ a Chance" PEACE

"Give ___ break!" MEA, USA

"Give ___ rest!" ITA

"Give ___ Sailor" MEA

"Give ___ whirl!" ITA

give a ___ (care) HANG, HOOT

give and ___ TAKE

"___ Give a Sucker an Even Break" NEVER

giveaway
AAA ~ MAP
dead ~ SIGN

give free ___ to REIN

give it ___ AGO

give it a ___ SHOT

"Give it a ___!" REST

"Give me ___!" FIVE

"Give My Regards to Broadway"
~ composer COHAN

given APT, PRONE
~ to (suffix) OSE
be ~ LAND

given ___ NAME

give one's ___ ALL

give or take ABOUT

giver
gift ~ DONOR
party ~ HOST
shade ~ ELM, MAPLE, OAK, TREE

Giverny
~ artist MONET

gives
~ the go-ahead to OKS

give the ___ AXE

give the ___ to LIE, SLIP

give the devil ___ due HIS

"___ Give Up the Ship" DONT

giving
~ no heed DEAF
~ one DONOR
~ starter MIS

Giza
~ river NILE

gizmo
stage ~ PROP

gizzard CRAW, ORGAN

Gk.
see Greek

glabrous BALD

glacial SLOW
~ marking STRIA
~ mass BERG
~ ridge ARETE, ESKER
~ ridges OSAR

glacial ___ (Ice Age) EPOCH

glaciate COOL, ICE

glacier ICE
~ fracture ABYSS
Alaskan ~ MUIR
broken-off ~ BERG

Glacier BAY

Glacier Bay
~ sight BERG

glad ELATED
~ rags ATTIRE, DRESS, GARB
~ tidings NEWS
give the ~ eye OGLE
make ~ ELATE

glad ___ HAND, RAGS

gladden AMUSE, ELATE, PLEASE, SUIT

glades
~ starter EVER

gladiator
~ item NET
~ venue ARENA
see also Latin

Gladstone
~ prep school ETON

Gladstone ___ BAG

glamorous
~ woman SIREN
~ wrap BOA

"Glamour"
~ founder NAST
~ rival ELLE

glance KISS, PEEP, SIGN
~ from Groucho LEER
~ over READ, SCAN
impolite ~ LEER

___ glance ATA

glare BEAM, SHINE, STARE

glaring BALD, RANK

Glasgow CITY, ELLEN, PORT
~ gal LASS
see also Scottish

glasnost
~ initials USSR

glass
~ container JAR, VIAL
~ ender INE, WARE
~ imperfection STRIA
~ sheet PANE
~ source SAND
~ starter HOUR, SPY, WINE
draw on ~ ETCH
kind of ~ SLAG
like some ~ SPUN
optical ~ LENS
rocks in a ~ ICE

glass ___ EEL, SNAKE

___ glass CUT, OPAL, OPERA, PLATE, SHEET, SPUN, WATER

Glass RON

"Glass ___, The" KEY, WEB

Glass-___ Currency Act OWEN

"Glass Bead Game, The"
~ author HESSE

"Glass Bell"
~ author NIN

"Glass Bottom ___, The" BOAT

glasses
hoist ~ TOAST

"Glass Key, The"
~ star LADD

glassmaking
~ material SAND

"Glass Menagerie, The"
~ character AMANDA, LAURA

glassy CLEAR
it may be ~ STARE

Glaswegian SCOT

glaze COAT, ICE, PAINT
pottery ~ ENAMEL

glazier
~ need PANE

gleam BEAM, FLARE, GLOW, SHEEN, SHINE

gleaming LIT

glean CLEAR, DRAW, LEARN, REAP, TAKE

Gleason, Jackie
~ TV role RILEY

glee SONG
cry of ~ HAH
fill with ~ ELATE
show ~ BEAM

glee club
~ member ALTO, BASS, TENOR

gleeful ELATED, GAY, RIANT

gleeman BARD

glen DALE, VALE
wooded ~ DELL

Glen Canyon ___ DAM

Glengarry CAP, HAT

"Glengarry ___ Ross" GLEN

"Glengarry Glen ___" ROSS

Glenn CLOSE
~ "Gilda" costar RITA

Glenn, John
~ state OHIO
all right, to ~ AOK

"Glenn Miller Story, The"
~ director MANN

"___ gli amplessi" FRA

glib OILY, PAT
too ~ OILY

glide KITE, SAIL, SKATE, SKI, SKID, SLIDE, SLIP, SOAR, STEAL
~ by ELAPSE
~ on snow SKI
~ on water SKI

glider PLANE
~ wood BALSA
on a ~ ALOFT
snow ~ SLED
use a ~ SOAR

___ glider HANG

glimmer BEAM, CLUE, FLARE, GLOW, RAY, SHEEN, SHINE

glimmering IDEA

glimpse ESPY, PEEP, SEE, SPY

glint BEAM, SHEEN, SHINE

glissade SLIDE, SLIP

glisten BEAM, GLARE, GLOW, SHINE

glitch ERROR, SNAG

glitter BEAM, FLARE, GLARE, GLOW, SHEEN, SHINE

"Glitter and Be ___" GAY

glittering GALA
~ headdress TIARA
~ material LAME

___-Glo DAY

gloamin' EEN

gloaming EEN

gloat CROW

gloating SMUG

glob CLOT, DROP, MASS
~ ender ULE

global
~ area ASIA
~ band ZONE
~ speck ISLE

globe BALL, EARTH, ORB, SPHERE
a chunk of the ~ ASIA
islet, on a ~ DOT
light ~ LAMP

globetrot ROAM, TOUR

globule BALL, BEAD, DROP, SPHERE, TEAR

glogg
~ ingredient WINE

glom EYE, STEAL

glom ___ ONTO

gloom PALL, SHADE, WOE
~ partner DOOM

"...___ gloom of night..." NOR

gloomy BAD, BLUE, DIM, DOUR, GRAY, GREY, LOW, SAD, SOBER, STERN
~ atmosphere PALL
~ investor BEAR

"Gloomy Dean, The" INGE

Gloomy Gus
~ expression ALAS

glop GOO

Gloria
~ mom EDITH

"Gloria in Excelsis ___" DEO

"Gloria Patri"
~ ending AMEN

glorify ADORE, BLESS, EXALT, HAIL, HONOR, LAUD
~ oneself BRAG

gloriole HALO

glorious GREAT

glory HALO, HONOR, POMP
~ in PREEN
crowning ~ HAIR, MANE

___ **Glory** OLD

"___ Glory, The" REAL

gloss LIE, NOTE, SHEEN, SHINE
 ~ over BELIE, COAT, COLOR, ELIDE, OMIT, PASS
 nail ~ ENAMEL
 where ~ goes LIP

glossary LIST

glossy SLEEK
 ~ black RAVEN
 ~ finish ENAMEL
 ~ weave SATIN
 not ~ MAT, MATTE

glottal
 ~ noise HIC

glottal ___ STOP

glottis
 ~ starter EPI

Gloucester CITY, PORT
 ~ cape ANN
 ~ king LEAR

Gloucestershire
 ~ neighbor AVON

glove MITT
 ~ insert HAND
 ~ leather KID
 ~ part PALM
 baseball ~ MITT
 hand and ~ CLOSE
 kitchen ~ MITT

glove-compartment
 ~ item MAP

"___ Glove Killer" KID

Glover, Danny
 ~ role in "Silverado" MAL

___ **gloves** KID

glow BEAM, FLARE, SHEEN, SHINE
 ~ in the night sky AURORA
 ~ starter AFTER
 enjoy the ~ BASK
 heavenly ~ AURA

glower GLARE, STARE

glowing LIT, LIVE, RED, ROSY
 ~ ash EMBER

gloxinia PLANT

Gluck ALMA

glückliche
 ~ Reise ADIEU

glue ADHERE, BIND, DOPE, PASTE, RESIN
 first name in ~ ELMER

glum BLUE, DOUR, LOW, SAD
 not ~ GAY

Glumdalclitch GIANT

glut CRAM, EAT, JADE, SATE

glutton EATER, HOG

gluttonize DINE

gluttonous AVID

gluttony SIN

glyceride ESTER

glycerin ESTER

GM
 ~ car GEO, OLDS

G-man AGENT, AGT, FED, SPY
 ~ org. FBI

GMAT EXAM, TEST

gnar SNARL

gnarl KNOT, NODE, SNARL

gnash GRIT

gnat PEST

gnaw BITE, EAT, ERODE, FRET

gnawed
 ~ away EROSE

gnome ADAGE, ELF, IMP, MOT, RUNT, SAW

g-note THOU

GNP STAT
 ~ topic ECON

gnu ANIMAL

go BOUT, FARE, GAME, LEAVE, SHOT
 ~ across CUT, SPAN
 ~ after CHASE, SEEK, TRACE
 ~ after game HUNT
 ~ ahead LEAD, MOVE, PASS
 ~ ahead with START
 ~ along AGREE, LEAVE
 ~ along with ADMIT, ALLOW, LET, OBEY
 ~ amiss ERR
 ~ ape FLIP, RAGE, RANT, RAVE, SNAP
 ~ around AVOID, ORBIT, RING
 ~ ashore LAND
 ~ astray ERR, SIN
 ~ at a snail's pace DRAG
 ~ away EXIT, LEAVE, MOVE
 ~ away from DESERT
 ~ AWOL DESERT, FLEE
 ~ awry ERR
 ~ back on BELIE
 ~ bad ROT, SOUR, SPOIL, TURN
 ~ ballistic FLIP, RAGE, RANT, SNAP
 ~ bananas FLIP, RAGE, RANT, SNAP
 ~ before LEAD
 ~ berserk FLIP, PANIC, RAGE, RAMP, SNAP
 ~ beyond CAP, PASS, TOP
 ~ bonkers FLIP, RANT, RAVE, SNAP
 ~ by ELAPSE, LAPSE, PASS, SLIP
 ~ crazy FLIP, RAGE, RANT, SNAP
 ~ deep (into) PORE
 ~ down ABATE, EBB, LOSE, SET, SINK, WANE
 ~ downhill LAPSE, SLIDE
 ~ down the drain LOSE
 ~ Dutch SHARE
 ~ ender FER
 ~ far LAST, RISE

~ fast HIE, RACE, RUN, SPEED, TEAR
 ~ fifty-fifty SHARE
 ~ first HEAD, LEAD, OPEN
 ~ for ADORE, ELECT, LIKE, OPT
 ~ for apples BOB
 ~ for broke DARE, RISK
 ~ for it DARE, TRY
 ~ for the gold DIG, MINE, VIE
 ~ from pillar to post GAD, ROAM, ROVE
 ~ halves SHARE
 ~ head over heels FLIP, SLIP
 ~ head to head VIE
 ~ here and there ROVE
 ~ hither and yon ROVE
 ~ hungry FAST
 ~ in ENTER
 ~ in advance LEAD
 ~ in ankle-deep WADE
 ~ in search of SEEK
 ~ into a holding pattern STALL, WAIT
 ~ into a huddle MASS, MEET
 ~ into hysterics FLIP, RAGE, RAMP, RANT, SNAP
 ~ leisurely LAG
 ~ lickety-split HIE, RACE, RUN, SPEED
 ~ like a shot HIE, RACE, RUN, SPEED
 ~ like hotcakes SELL
 ~ like lightning HIE, RACE, RIP, RUN, SPEED, TEAR
 ~ nowhere STALL
 ~ off BLAST, ERUPT, RING
 ~ off-center TILT
 ~ off course ERR, VEER, YAW
 ~ on ADD, EMOTE, LAST, RANT
 ~ on a cruise SAIL
 ~ on a diet LOSE
 ~ on all fours CREEP
 ~ on and on DRAG, DRONE, RANT, RAVE, YAK
 ~ one better LEAD, TOP
 ~ (one's way) WEND
 ~ on-stage ENTER
 ~ on the lam FLEE
 ~ on the road TOUR
 ~ on the stage ACT
 ~ out EXIT, LEAVE
 ~ out with DATE, SEE
 ~ over HASH, READ
 ~ over again RECAP
 ~ over with a fine-tooth comb HUNT, PORE
 ~ past OMIT, SKIP
 ~ postal FLIP, RAGE, RANT, SNAP
 ~ public with AIR
 ~ quickly HIE, RACE, RUN, SPEED
 ~ separate ways SPLIT
 ~ "shooby-doo" SCAT
 ~ shopping SPEND
 ~ sideways EDGE
 ~ slowly CREEP, EASE, PLOD
 ~ smoothly SAIL, SLIDE
 ~ soft MELT, THAW
 ~ sour SPOIL, TURN
 ~ steady DATE, PIN
 ~ the distance LAST
 ~ through BEAR, HUNT, RIFLE, SPEND, TAKE

~ to ATTEND
 ~ to bat for AID, HELP
 ~ to bed REST, SLEEP
 ~ too fast SPEED
 ~ to pot LAPSE, SPOIL
 ~ to school LEARN
 ~ to seed DIE, LAPSE, ROT
 ~ to sleep BED, NOD
 ~ to the plate BAT
 ~ to the polls VOTE
 ~ to waste LOSE
 ~ unchallenged PASS
 ~ under CLOSE, SINK
 ~ undercover HIDE, SPY
 ~ underwater SINK
 ~ unnoticed PASS
 ~ unused SIT
 ~ up ARISE, LEAP, RISE
 ~ up against ABUT, FACE
 ~ up and down BOB
 ~ uphill RISE
 ~ up in smoke LOSE
 ~ upstairs RISE
 ~ wide of AVOID
 ~ wild (about) RAVE
 ~ wild (over) FLIP
 ~ with DATE, SEE
 ~ without AVOID, MISS, WANT
 ~ with the flow ADAPT, COPE
 come and ~ PASS
 don't ~ BIDE, STAY
 force to ~ EXILE, SEND
 get up and ~ LEAVE, PART
 give it a ~ ESSAY, TEST, TRY
 how some ~ it ALONE
 it makes the world ~ round LOVE
 let ~ AXE, FIRE, FREE, LOOSE, SACK, SPARE
 let ~ of CEDE, DROP
 one way to ~ SLOW
 order to ~ EXILE, SEND
 rarin' to ~ AVID, EAGER, KEEN
 ready to ~ SET
 really ~ for ADORE, LOVE
 way to ~ ROUTE

"go"
 the word ~ FIRST
 word before ~ SET

go ___ (become excited) APE

go ___ (cooperate) ALONG

go ___ (depart) AWAY

go ___ (exceed) OVER

go ___ (exit) OUT

go ___ (explode) OFF

go ___ (fail) UNDER

go ___ (fight) ATIT

go ___ (flip out) APE

go ___ (like) FOR

go ___ (succeed) FAR

go ___ better ONE

go ___ broke FOR

go ___ detail INTO

go ___ diet ONA

go ___ guns GREAT

go ___ it FOR
go ___ the window OUT
go-___ AHEAD, CART
___ go (axe) LET
"Go ___ Broke!" FOR
"Go ___ the Spartans" TELL
"Go ___, young man!" WEST
"Go ___ your father" ASK
"Go ___ your mother" ASK
goad ABET, AROUSE, EGG, IMPEL, MOVE, NEEDLE, PROD, ROUSE, SPUR, STING, URGE
go-ahead NOD
   gives the ~ OKS
   give the ~ ALLOW, CLEAR, LET, OKAY
"Go ahead!" SHOOT
"Go ahead...___ my day!" MAKE
goal AIM, DREAM, END, SAKE
   ~ preventer SAVE
   lacrosse ~ NET
   lofty ~ IDEAL
   soccer ~ NET
goal ___ LINE, POST
goalie
   ~ feat SAVE
   ~ milieu ICE, RINK
   ~ org. NHL
   ~ protection MASK
   get past the ~ SCORE
"Go and catch a falling star"
   ~ poet DONNE
goat ANIMAL, DUPE
   ~ feature BEARD
   ~ product FETA
   ~ sound MAA
   baby ~ KID
   billy ~ MALE
   female ~ DOE
   get one's ~ ANGER, ENRAGE, IRK, PEEVE, RILE, UPSET
   old ~ RAKE, ROUE
   Old World ~ IBEX
   smell like a ~ REEK
   wild mountain ~ IBEX
Goat
   the ~ SIGN
goatee BEARD
   ~ site CHIN
goat-footed
   ~ deity SATYR
   ~ god PAN
goat hair
   ~ garment ABA
goatish LEWD
goatsbeard WEED
goatskin KID
"Go away!" SCAT, SCRAM, SHOO
gob CLOD, HEAP, PILE, SALT, TAR
   ~ interjection AVAST
   see also nautical, sailor

gobble CRAM, NOISE
   ~ up EAT, TAKE, USE
gobbler MALE, TOM
go-between AGENT
   ~ (abbr.) AGT
Gobi DESERT
   ~ site ASIA
   like the ~ ARID, DRY
goblet CUP
   ~ part STEM
   Scottish ~ TASS
goblin DEMON, ELF, GNOME
   ~ greeting BOO
"___ go bragh!" ERIN
gobs ALOT, CREW, LOTS, MASS, OCEAN, SEA, SLEW
   where to find ~ FLEET
god
   ~ in Latin DEO
   ~ starter DEMI
   bellicose ~ ARES, MARS
   forest ~ PAN
   goat-footed ~ SATYR
   Islamic ~ ALLAH
   Koran's ~ ALLAH
   love ~ AMOR, EROS
   Phoenician ~ BAAL
   solar ~ ATEN, ATON
   sylvan ~ PAN, SATYR
   tutelary ~ LAR
   woodland ~ SATYR
"God ___" BLESS
"God ___ America" BLESS
"God ___ the Queen!" SAVE
"God ___ you!" BLESS
"God and Man at ___" YALE
god-awful BAD
"God bless us, every ___!" ONE
"___ God Created Woman" AND
goddess
   ~ in Latin DEA
"___ Goddesses, The" LOVE
go-devil SLED
godfather DON
"Godfather, The"
   ~ actor CAAN
   ~ actress SHIRE
   ~ composer ROTA
"___ Godfathers" THREE
Godfrey, Arthur EMCEE, HOST
   ~ instrument UKE
"Godfrey Daniels!" DRAT
Godiva LADY, RIDER
godmother
   ~ often AUNT
   fairy ~ ANGEL, DONOR
   fairy ~'s rod WAND
gods
   ~ in Latin DEI
God's ___ (churchyard) ACRE

"God's Little ___" ACRE
"God's Little Acre"
   ~ director MANN
Godunov BORIS
   see also Russian
Godunov, Boris TSAR
"Godzilla vs. the ___ Monster" SMOG
"___ goes!" HERE
"___ Goes My Baby" THERE
"___ Goes My Everything" THERE
"___ Goes My Heart" THERE
"___ goes nothing!" HERE
"___ goes there?" WHO
"___ Goes to Camp" ERNEST
Goethe POET
   see also German, poet
goethite ORE
gofer AIDE, PAGE
   ~ job ERRAND
Go Fish GAME
   ~ alternative WAR
"Go fly a ___!" KITE
go-getter DOER, TIGER
goggle EYE, GAPE, LEER, OGLE, STARE
goggle-___ EYED
goggles
   safety ~ MASK
going
   ~ around in circles LOST
   ~ at a snail's pace SLOW
   ~ downhill WORSE
   ~ on AFOOT, LIVE
   get ~ IMPEL, ROLL, START
   it may be ~ RATE
   keep ~ SPIN
   story ~ around RUMOR
going-___ (inspection) OVER
___-going EASY
"Going ___" HOME
"Going ___!" APE
"Going, going, ___" GONE
"Going in ___" STYLE
"Going to a ___" GOGO
"Goin' to Town"
   ~ director HALL
go it ___ ALONE
Golan Hts.
   ~ locale ISR
gold METAL
   ~ container POT
   ~ deposit DUST
   ~ fabric LAME
   ~ in Spanish ORO
   ~ item BAR, INGOT, MEDAL
   ~ measure CARAT, KARAT

   ~ record HIT
   ~ source ORE
   bar of ~ INGOT
   black ~ OIL
   coat with ~ PLATE
   dig for ~ MINE
   get the ~ WIN
   go for the ~ DIG, MINE, VIE
   old ~ COLOR
   seek ~ PAN
gold ___ DUST, LEAF, MINE
___ gold OLD
Golda MEIR
   ~ colleague ABBA
Goldberg RUBE
"Goldbergs, The"
   ~ actress BERG
"Goldberg Variations"
   ~ composer BACH
goldbrick AVOID, DRONE, EVADE, IDLER, LOAF
"Gold Bug, The"
   ~ author POE
"___ Gold Cadillac, The" SOLID
gold-chained
   ~ actor MRT
Gold Coast
   ~ capital ACCRA
"Gold Diggers of 1933"
   ~ director LEROY
golden AONE, BEST
   ~ apple bestower PARIS
   ~ calf IDOL
   ~ egg producer GOOSE
   ~ in French DOR
   ~ opportunity TIME
   man with a ~ touch MIDAS
golden ___ AGE, AGER, CALF, MEAN, OLDIE, RULE
golden ___ (century plant) ALOE
golden-___ corn EARED
Golden ___ HORDE
Golden ___ Bridge GATE
Golden ___ Warriors STATE
"Golden ___, The" ASS, BEAR, SEAL
"Golden ___ of Comedy, The" AGE
golden ager ELDER
"Golden Boy"
   ~ playwright ODETS
"Golden Cockerel, The" OPERA
goldeneye BIRD
Golden Fleece
   ~ princess MEDEA
   ~ ship ARGO
   ~ source ARIES
"Goldengirl"
   ~ actress ANTON

"Golden Girls, The"
~ **locale** MIAMI
~ **st.** FLA
Betty, in ~ ROSE
Blanche, in ~ RUE
Dorothy, on ~ BEA

Golden Globe AWARD

"Golden Hind" BOAT, SHIP

Golden Horde
~ **member** TATAR

Golden Hurricanes
~ **school** TULSA

goldenrod
~ **cousin** ASTER

golden rule
~ **word** UNTO

Golden Spike
~ **state** UTAH

gold-filled
it may be ~ TOOTH

goldfinch BIRD

"Goldfinger"
007 of ~ SEAN

goldfish CARP, PET

Goldie
~ **cohort of yore** ALAN, ARTE,
DAN, LILY, RUTH

goldilocks PLANT

Goldman EMMA

gold medal
~ **position** FIRST

gold piece
ten-dollar ~ EAGLE

gold rush
Alaskan ~ town NOME

"Goldwyn's Folly" STEN

golf GAME
~ **alert** FORE
~ **club** IRON
~ **coup** ACE
~ **gadget** TEE
~ **goof** SLICE
~ **hazard** SAND, TRAP
~ **instructor** PRO
~ **missile** BALL
~ **rarity** ACE, EAGLE
~ **score** ACE, EAGLE, PAR
~ **shot** CHIP
~ **target** CUP, HOLE, PIN
distance a ~ ball rolls RUN
furthest from the hole, in
~ AWAY
half the ~ course NINE, OUT
name in ~ TIGER

golf bag
~ **item** IRON, TEE

golf ball
~ **position** LIE

"Golf Begins at Forty"
~ **author** SNEAD

golf club
~ **end** HEAD

~ **part** SOLE, TOE
~ **VIP** PRO

golf course
~ **material** SOD

golfer
~ **benchmark** PAR
~ **dream** ACE
~ **objective** CUP, HOLE
~ **position** LIE
~ **shout** FORE
~ **vehicle** CART

golf hole
~ **edge** LIP

golfing
~ **nickname** ARNIE, SAM,
TIGER

golf shoe
~ **feature** CLEAT

Goliath GIANT
~ **to David** FOE

"Golly!" GEE

"Go, Lovely Rose" POEM

Gomer PYLE

Gomez
~ **cousin** ITT
see also Spanish

gondola BOAT
~ **alternative** TBAR
maneuver a ~ POLE

gondolier
~ **need** POLE
~ **waterway** CANAL

gone AWAY, LEFT, LOST, PAST,
SHOT
~ **by** AGO, OVER, PAST
~ **by the boards** DATED,
PASSE
~ **to seed** PASSE

___ gone ALL, FAR

"Gone ___ Finnigin" AGIN

"Gone ___ the Days" ARE

"___ Gone" SHES

"Gone Are the ___" DAYS

"___ Go Near the Water" DONT

Goneril
~ **father** LEAR
~ **sister** REGAN

"Gone With the Wind"
~ **character** OHARA
~ **locale** ATLANTA
~ **manor** TARA

gonfalon FLAG

"___ Gonna Fall in Love Again"
NEVER

**___ Gonxha Bojaxhiu (Mother
Teresa)** AGNES

Gonzales, Speedy MOUSE

Gonzalez
see Spanish

goo PASTE, SLIME
hair ~ GEL
roofer's ~ TAR

good ADEPT, SAKE
~ **buddy** BRO
~ **buy** DEAL, STEAL
~ **clean fun** LARK
~ **deal** STEAL
~ **deed** HELP
~ **for something** UTILE
~ **guy** HERO
~ **in French** BON
~ **in Italian** BENE
~ **in Latin** BENE
~ **judgment** SENSE
~ **life** EASE
~ **moods** UPS
~ **name** HONOR, REP
~ **offices** AID, HELP
~ **old days** YORE
~ **opposite** EVIL
~ **quality** ASSET
~ **sense** TACT, WIT
~ **spirits** GLEE
~ **time** BLAST
~ **times** UPS
~ **to some** BAD
~ **turn** HELP
~ **with words** GLIB
a ~ deal LOTS
as ~ as won ONICE
at a ~ clip APACE
be on ~ terms with KNOW
do a ~ turn for SERVE
do one's heart ~ PLEASE
find ~ LIKE, LOVE
have a ~ time PLAY, REVEL
hold ~ STAND
in ~ condition FIT, TRIM
in ~ order NEAT
in ~ shape FIT, SAFE, TRIM
in ~ spirits RIANT
in ~ standing SOLID
in ~ taste NICE
in ~ time EARLY
looking ~ ROSY
make ~ ATONE
make ~ as new MEND
make ~ use of AVAIL
not ~ BAD, POOR
not as ~ WORSE
not feel ~ AIL
opposite of ~ EVIL
pretty ~ FAIR, SOSO
put in a ~ word for LAUD
put in ~ repair RESTORE
showing ~ judgment SANE
something ~ to have ASSET
stand in ~ stead AID
stretch of ~ luck RUN
the ~ old days PAST
very ~ MEAN

good ___ boy OLE

good ___ days, the OLD

"good ___ was had by all, A"
TIME

good-___-nothing FOR

___ good (permanently) FOR

___ good (repay) MAKE

"Good ___" NEWS

"Good ___, The" EARTH, SON

"Good ___!" IDEA

Goodall JANE
~ **subject** APE

good as new
make ~ RESTORE

goodbye ADIEU, ADIOS, ALOHA,
CIAO, TATA
informal ~ LATER
kiss ~ LOSE
kiss ~, maybe SPEND
say ~ LEAVE, PART

"Goodbye ___" AGAIN

"Goodbye ___, The" GIRL

"Goodbye!"
~ **in French** ADIEU
~ **in Hawaiian** ALOHA
~ **in Italian** CIAO
~ **in Latin** AVE, VALE
~ **in Spanish** ADIOS

"Goodbye, Columbus"
~ **author** ROTH
Richard's ~ costar ALI

"Goodbye Girl, The"
~ **director** ROSS

"___ Good Cop" ONE

"___ Good Day" ITSA

good deed
~ **doer** HERO

___ good deed DOA

good deeds
~ **org.** BSA

"Good Earth, The"
~ **actor** MUNI
~ **wife** OLAN

Gooden
~ **nickname** DOC
~ **once** MET

___ good example SETA

"GoodFellas"
~ **boss** DON

good-for-nothing CAD, DRONE,
IDLER

"Good for what ___ you" AILS

"___ Good Friday, The" LONG

"Good golly!" EGAD

"Good grief!" EGAD

Good Hope CAPE

"Good Housekeeping"
~ **award** SEAL

goodies EATS
Christmas ~ LOOT

Gooding CUBA

"Good Intentions"
~ **author** NASH

"___ Good Lookin'" HEY

good-looking FAIR, NICE

good looks ASSET

"Good Lord!" EGAD

"Good Luck, Miss Wyckoff"
  ~ **author** INGE

goodly BIG, LARGE
  ~ **sum** PILE
  a ~ **part of** MOST

Goodman ELLEN

Goodman, Benny
  ~ **portrayer** ALLEN

"___ Good Men, A" FEW

"Good Morning, ___ Dove" MISS

"Good Morning, Miss ___" DOVE

good-natured MILD, NICE, SWEET

"Good Neighbor ___" SAM

"Goodnight"
  ~ **girl of song** IRENE

Good Queen ___ BESS

goods LINE, LOOT, WARE
  ~ **(abbr.)** MDSE
  get the ~ SHOP
  get the ~ on NAIL
  hot ~ LOOT, SWAG
  move ~ SELL, VEND
  stock of ~ LINE
  stolen ~ LOOT, SWAG
  the straight ~ FACT
  worldly ~ ESTATE

___ goods DRY, YARD

good-sized AMPLE

good-tempered EASY

**"Good, the ___, and the Ugly,
The"** BAD

**"Good, the Bad, and the ___,
The"** UGLY

**"Good, the Bad, and the Ugly,
The"** OATER
  ~ **director** LEONE
  ~ **name** ELI

___ good time ALLIN

"___ Good Time, The" LAST

"Good Times"
  ~ **actor** AMOS

___ good to be true TOO

___ good turn DOA

goodwife LADY

goody TREAT

goody ___ shoes TWO

Goodyear
  ~ **home** AKRON

goody-goody PRIG

gooey
  ~ **stuff** OOZE, SLIME

goof BONER, ERR, ERROR, SLIP,
TRIP
  ~ **off** IDLE, LOAF
  ~ **up** HASH
  diamond ~ ERROR
  golf ~ SLICE

goof-___ (idler) OFF

go off the deep ___ END

goof-off DRONE, IDLER

goofproof SURE

goofs ERRATA

goofy DAFT, LOCO, MAD, NUTS

___ goo gai pan MOO

gook DIRT

goon APE, DOLT, HOOD, OAF

goop DOPE, GEL, OOZE, SLIME

goose BIRD, MEAT
  ~ **cousin** SWAN
  ~ **down garment** VEST
  ~ **egg** NADA, NIL, NULL, ZERO
  ~ **formation** VEE
  Hawaiian ~ NENE
  use a ~ IRON

goose ___ EGG, STEP

___ goose SNOW

gooseberry
  Chinese ~ KIWI

___ gooseberry CAPE

goose bumps
  raising ~ EERIE, EERY

"Goosebumps"
  like ~ EERIE, EERY

gooseneck
  ~ **item** LAMP

GOP
  ~ **elephant creator** NAST
  ~ **member** REP
  ~ **opponent** DEM

gopher ANIMAL

gopher ___ BALL

Gorbachev
  ~ **realm** USSR
  ~ **wife** RAISA
  see also Russian

"Gorboduc" POEM

Gorcey LEO

Gordian ___ KNOT

Gordian knot POSER
  ~ **undoer's reward** ASIA

Gordie HOWE

Gordius
  problem for ~ KNOT

Gordon GALE, RUTH, SCOTT

Gordon, Dexter
  ~ **instrument** SAX

Gordon, Flash HERO
  ~ **alma mater** YALE
  ~ **milieu** SPACE
  ~ **partner** DALE

"Gordon's ___" WAR

gore PANEL, RIP, STAB

Gore
  ~ **and others** ALS

~ interest ECOL
Tipper ~, ___ Aitcheson NEE

Gore-___ TEX

Goren
  ~ **option** PASS
  ace, to ~ HONOR

gorge ABYSS, CRAM, DINE, EAT,
GAP, GLUT, SATE

Gorge of the ___ (Swiss spot)
AAR, AARE

gorget ARMOR

Gorgon HAG, OGRE

gorilla ANIMAL, APE
  ~ **cousin** ORANG

"Gorilla at ___" LARGE

"Gorillas in the ___" MIST

Goriot PERE

gormandize CRAM, DINE, EAT,
GLUT

Gosden, Freeman
  ~ **role** AMOS

"Gosh!" GEE, WOW

goshawk BIRD

gosling BIRD

Gospels
  ~ **follower** ACTS

gossamer AIRY, FINE, THIN

Gossett LOU

gossip BLAB, CHIN, DIRT, DISH,
DOPE, INFO, NEWS, NOISE,
PRATE, RAP, RUMOR, TALK,
WAG, YENTA
  ~ **gift** GAB
  ~ **tidbit** ITEM, RUMOR
  like some ~ IDLE
  piece of ~ TALE
  spread ~ YAK

gossip column
  ~ **subject** STAR
  ~ **tidbit** ITEM

gossipmonger YENTA

gossipy
  ~ **tidbit** ITEM, RUMOR

gossoon LAD

"Gösta Berlings ___" SAGA

got
  ~ **off** ALIT, LIT
  ~ **the fire going again** RELIT
  ~ **up** AROSE, ROSE

got ___ the ground floor INON

Göta CANAL

"___ Got a Brand New Bag"
PAPAS

"Got a Crush on You" IVE

"Got a Date With an ___" ANGEL

"___ Got a Name" IVE

"___ Got a Secret" IVE

"___ Got a Way" SHES

"Gotcha!" AHA, HAH, ISEE, OHO

Göteborg CITY, PORT
  ~ **resident** SWEDE

"Go Tell ___ Rhody" AUNT

"Go Tell ___ the Mountain" ITON

"Go Tell the Spartans"
  ~ **director** POST

"___ Got Five Dollars" IVE

Goth
  ~ **kin** HUN

Gothic STYLE

Gothic ___ ARCH

"___ got it!" IVE

"Got it!" ISEE

"___ Got My Eyes on You" IVE

go to ___ (deteriorate) POT,
SEED

go to ___ and ruin RACK

go to ___ for BAT

go to bat ___ FOR

go to rack and ___ RUIN

go to the ___ MAT

"___ Got Sixpence" IVE

"___ Gotta Be Me" IVE

"___ Gotta Crow" IVE

"___ Gotta Have It" SHES

___-gotten gains ILL

"Götterdämmerung" OPERA

Gottfried
  ~ **in "Lohengrin"** SWAN
  ~ **sister** ELSA

"___ Got the Whole World..."
HES

"___ Got the World on a String"
IVE

"Got to Get You ___ My Life"
INTO

"___ Got You" SHES

"___ Got You Under My Skin"
IVE

gouaches ART

Gouda
  ~ **kin** EDAM

Goudy FONT

gouge CLAW, CUT, DIG, PIT, RUT,
SCORE
  ~ **out** BORE, ROUT

goulash OLIO, STEW

Gould, Chester
  ~ **character** TESS

Gould, Jay
  ~ **railroad** ERIE

Gounod
  ~ **contemporary** LALO

gourami PET

gourd HEAD, MELON
  out of one's ~ LOCO

gourmand EATER

gourmandize DINE, EAT

gourmet EATER
  ~ **cook** CHEF

gourmets
  ~ **do it** DINE

govern HEAD, LEAD, REIGN, RULE, RUN

governable MEEK

governed
  be ~ **by** OBEY

governess NURSE
  fictional ~ ANNA, EYRE

governing
  ~ **layman** ELDER

government RULE
  ~ **agent** GMAN, NARC, TMAN
  ~ **veteran** POL

___-government SELF

governmental STATE

governor BOSS, HEAD, LORD, PAPA, RULER
  Algerian ~ DEY

"Go visit it by the ___ moonlight" PALE

govt.
  ~ **agt.** FED
  ~ **employee** AGT
  ~ **investigator** GMAN, TMAN
  ~ **org.** FBI, SSA
  ~ **program of 1933** TVA
  ~ **purchasing org.** GSA

"Go West, Young ___" MAN

go whole ___ HOG

gown DRESS, GARB
  ~ **material** LAME, SATIN, SILK
  ~ **part** TRAIN
  ~ **renters** SRS
  dressing ~ ROBE
  evening ~ DRESS

Goya
  ~ **land** SPAIN
  emulate ~ ETCH
  see also Spanish

gp. ASSN, ORG

GP
  ~ **expertise** ANAT
  ~ **org.** AMA

GPs DRS, MDS

"GQ" MAG

Gr.
  see Greek

grab CLASP, GET, GRASP, GRIP, NAB, TAKE
  ~ **a bite** EAT
  ~ **bag** OLIO
  ~ **some rays** SUN
  ~ **some shuteye** SLEEP

grab ___ BAG

grabber
  prey ~ TALON
  turf ~ CLEAT

grabby AVID

grabs
  up for ~ FREE, OPEN

grab some ___ (sunbathe) RAYS

Gracchus ROMAN

grace ADORN, EASE, ENDOW, LOVE, POISE, STYLE, TACT
  ~ **ending** AMEN
  ~ **starter** DIS
  ~ **under pressure** POISE
  ~ **word** BLESS
  embodiment of ~ SWAN
  fall from ~ SIN
  say ~ PRAY

grace ___ NOTE

grâce
  coup de ~ END

Grace MOORE

graceful AERIAL, AGILE, AIRY, CLEAN, EASY, LITHE
  ~ **fowl** SWAN
  ~ **one** PERI
  ~ **rhythm** LILT
  ~ **tree** ELM

Graceland ESTATE
  ~ **name** ARON, ELVIS
  ~ **st.** TENN

graceless
  ~ **one** OAF

Grace Van ___ ("L.A. Law" character) OWEN

Gracie ALLEN

gracile SLIM, THIN

gracious NICE, SWEET, WARM

"Gracious!" EGAD

grackle BIRD, CROW
  ~ **call** CAW

grad ALUM

grad.
  ~ **class** SRS

gradations SCALE

grade BEE, CEE, CLASS, DEE, ORDER, RAMP, RANK, RATE, RISE, SLOPE, TILT
  ~ **A** GOOD
  ~ **sch.** ELEM
  ~ **starter** RETRO
  collectible ~ MINT
  high ~ FINE
  make the ~ ARRIVE, PASS
  numismatic ~ FINE
  receive a high ~ **on** ACE

___-grade LOW

grades
  ~ **K-6** ELEM

grade-schooler KID

gradient RAMP, RISE, SLOPE, TILT

grads
  certain ~ ABS, BAS

grad school
  ~ **major** LAW, MATH

grads-to-be SRS

gradual SLOW

graduate PASS
  ~ **deg.** DDS, LLD, MBA
  ~ **for short** ALUM

"Graduate, The"
  ~ **actress** ROSS
  ~ **character** BEN, ELAINE

graduation EVENT
  ~ **gear** CAP

Graf
  ~ **rival** SELES
  see also German

"Graf ___" SPEE

graffiti
  ~ **to some** ART
  spray ~ **on** MAR

graft CUT, SCION, SHOOT
  ~ **recipient** HOST

grafting
  twig for ~ SCION

Graham KERR, NASH, OTTO

Graham, Billy REV

Graham, Bob
  ~ **st.** FLA

Grahame, Kenneth
  ~ **character** MOLE, OTTER, TOAD

grain BIT, CORN, FEED, IOTA, OAT, RICE, RYE, SHRED
  ~ **beard** AWN
  ~ **bristle** AWN
  ~ **container** BIN
  ~ **disease** ERGOT
  ~ **fungus** SMUT
  ~ **holder** CRIB
  ~ **husk** BRAN
  ~ **processor** MILL
  ~ **repository** SILO
  ~ **spike** EAR
  bread ~ RYE
  brewing ~ MALT
  cereal ~ CORN, OAT, RYE
  distiller's ~ MALT
  fiber-rich ~ OAT
  gather ~ REAP
  go against the ~ IRK, PEEVE, REPEL, RILE
  goddess of ~ CERES
  ground ~ MEAL
  Krispies ~ RICE
  pilaf ~ RICE
  pollen ~ SPORE
  whiskey ~ CORN, RYE

grains
  60 ~ DRAM
  quartz ~ SAND

gram UNIT

Gramm PHIL

grammar
  do a ~ **task** PARSE

grammarian
  ~ **concern** USAGE

grammatical
  ~ **no-no** AINT
  ~ **subject** NOUN

Grammy AWARD
  ~ **category** POP, RAP

Grammy-winning
  ~ **pianist** NERO

Grampians RANGE

grampus ORC
  ~ **family** GAM

Granada
  see Spanish

Granatelli ANDY

grand BIG, EPIC, GALA, GREAT, LARGE, PIANO, POSH, REGAL, RICH
  ~ **adventure** SAGA
  ~ **display** POMP
  ~ **duke** PEER
  ~ **ender** STAND
  ~ **occasion** GALA
  ~ **old man** DEAN, ELDER
  ~ **opera** DRAMA
  ~ **poetry** EPOS
  ~ **slam** HOMER
  ~ **slangily** THOU
  ~ **total** SUM
  a ~ THOU
  a thousand ~ MIL
  baby ~ PIANO

grand ___ OPERA, PIANO, SLAM, TOUR

Grand CANAL

Grand ___ ("Evangeline" locale) PRE

Grand ___ (Wyoming peak) TETON

Grand ___ National Park TETON

Grand ___, Nova Scotia PRE

Grand ___ Opry OLE

Grand ___ Party OLD

Grand ___ Plaza ARMY

"Grand ___" HOTEL

"Grand ___" (Schubert work) DUO

Grand Canyon
  ~ **emotion** AWE
  ~ **feature** RIM
  ~ **transport** BURRO

Grand Central STA

grandchildren
  watch the ~ SIT

Grand Coulee DAM

Granddad
  Dad, to ~ SON

grande ___ DAME

___ **Grande** RIO

___ **Grande, Ariz.** CASA

grandee LORD, PEER, RANK, TITLE
~ **title** DON

grandees ELITE

grandeur POMP, STATE

grandfather MAN

grandiloquence RANT

grandiloquent EPIC
be ~ ORATE

grandiose BIG, EPIC, LARGE, ORNATE
~ **poetry** EPOS

grandma NANA

Grandma ___ MOSES

Grandma Moses ANNA

grandmother
first ~ EVE

"___ **Grand Night for Singing**" ITSA

Grandpa
emulate ~ DOTE

___-**grandparent** GREAT

grand piano
~ **part** LEG, PEDAL

Grand Prix RACE
~ **competitor** RACER

grandson
~ **maybe** III

grandstand
~ **level** TIER
~ **sound** ROAR

grandstander HAM

"**Grand Theft** ___" AUTO

Grand Tour
~ **cont.** EUR

grange ABODE, HOME, LAND

Grange RED

Grani HORSE, STEED

granite STONE
~ **colored** GRAY, GREY
in ~ SET

granitelike HARD

granny KNOT, NANA
~ **other daughter** AUNT

Granny Smith APPLE

granola
~ **morsel** OAT

Gran Paradiso ALP

grant ADMIT, AGREE, ALLOT, ALLOW, AWARD, CEDE, ENDOW, LET, OWN
~ **a mortgage** LEND
~ **criterion** NEED
~ **recipient** DONEE
~ **temporary use of** LEASE
beggar's ~ ALMS

___ **grant** LAND

Grant AMY, LEE, LOU
~ **feature** BEARD
~ **foe** LEE

"___ **Grant**" LOU

granted
permission ~ YES

granter
wish ~ GENIE

Grantland RICE

Grant, Lou ASNER
~ **wife** EDIE
emulate ~ EDIT

grantor DONOR

granulate MILL

granule BIT, IOTA

grape BALL, COLOR, FERN, SHOT
~ **brandy** MARC
~ **plant** VINE
~ **product** WINE

grapefruit TREE
~ **league st.** FLA
~ **serving** HALF

"**Grapefruit**"
~ **author** ONO

grapes
crush ~ **old-style** TREAD

___ **grapes** SOUR

grapeshot BALL

grapevine
~ **product** RUMOR
learn through the ~ HEAR

graph MAP, TABLE
~ **ender** ITE
~ **line** AXIS
~ **starter** AUTO, ISO, ORO, PARA, TELE
connect points on a ~ PLOT
kind of ~ BAR, PIE

graph ___ PAPER

___ **graph** BAR

grapheme SIGN

graphic CLEAR
~ **starter** GEO, IDEO

graphic ___ ARTS

graphite LEAD

grapple GRASP, MEET, SCRAP
~ **with** CLOSE, FACE

gras FAT

grasp CLASP, DIG, GET, GRAB, GRIP, HAVE, HOLD, KNOW, LEARN, NAB, SEE, SWAY, TAKE
fail to ~ MISS
hard to ~ DEEP, EELY

grasping AVID

grass LAWN, PLANT, SOD
~ **eater** COW
~ **fungus** SMUT
~ **invader** WEED
~ **stalk** REED

~ **starter** BLUE, CRAB, EEL
cereal ~ OAT, RICE, RYE
cut the ~ MOW
house ~ LAWN
let the ~ **grow under one's feet** LOAF
like tall ~ REEDY
scatter, as ~ TED
swamp ~ SEDGE
tall ~ CANE

grass ___ SNAKE

___ **grass** CRAB, LEMON, RYE

"**Grass**" POEM

"**Grass** ___, **The**" HARP

grasshopper
~ **colleague** ANT

"**Grasshopper, The**"
~ **director** PARIS

"**Grass Is Always Greener Over the Septic** ___, **The**" TANK

grassland LEA, RANGE

grasslike
~ **plant** SEDGE

Grasso ELLA

grass skirt
~ **accessory** LEI
~ **dance** HULA

grassy
~ **area** LAWN
~ **plain** LLANO

___ **grata** NON

grate ABRADE, ERODE, FILE, JAR, RASP, SHRED
~ **contents** ASH, EMBER
~ **on** IRK, PEEVE, RILE
~ **upon** RASP

grated FINE

grateful
feel ~ **to** OWE

___ **gratia** DEI

"___ **Gratia Artis**" ARS

___ **gratias** DEO

gratified GLAD

gratify FEED, PLEASE, SUIT
~ **completely** SATE

gratifying NICE, SWEET

grating GRID

gratis FREE

gratuity EXTRA, FEE, PAY, TIP

grave ACUTE, BAD, DIRE, ETCH, PIT, SAD, SOBER, STAID, STERN

gravel GRIT, STONE
~ **bank** BAR

gravelly
say with a ~ **voice** RASP

graven
~ **image** IDOL

Graves PETER

Graves, Robert POET
see also poet

gravitate SETTLE
~ **(toward)** LEAN, TEND

gravity DRAW, STRESS
respond to ~ SINK
yield to ~ SAG

___ **gravity** ZERO

gravity-powered
~ **vehicle** SLED

gravy PLUS
~ **holder** BOAT
dip in ~ SOP

gravy ___ BOAT, TRAIN

gray AGE, ASHEN, COLOR, DIM, FADE
~ **matter** HEAD
become ~ AGE
dull ~ DRAB
pale ~ ASHY
shade of ~ ASH, OPAL, PEARL, SLATE, STEEL
silvery ~ ASH
soldier in ~ REB
use the ~ **matter** IDEATE

gray ___ AREA

___ **gray** IRON, PEARL, STEEL

Gray ASA, ERIN
~ **monogram** CSA
~ **subj.** ANAT
~ **work** ODE

Gray ___ LADY

graybeard ELDER

Gray, Dorian
what ~ **didn't do** AGE

gray-faced ASHEN

gray-green
~ **herb** SAGE

grayish ASHY
~ **white** ASHEN

grayish-brown ECRU

graylag BIRD, GOOSE

"___ **Gray Line, The**" LONG

Grays
~ **side** CSA

Grayson, Dick
~ **to Bruce Wayne** WARD

Gray, Thomas POET
~ **alma mater** ETON
see also poet

graze ABRADE, CARESS, EAT, FEED, KISS, RAKE, SKIN

grazer
pasture ~ EWE

grazers HERD

grazing
~ **area** LEA, RANGE

Gr. Brit.
part of ~ ENG, SCOT

grease LARD, LUBE, OIL
~ **the wheels** EASE, OIL
elbow ~ TOIL

grease ___ GUN, PAINT

___ grease AXLE, ELBOW

"Grease"
~ **prop** COMB

greasy OILY

greasy spoon
~ **patron** EATER
~ **sign** EATS

great AONE, BIG, FINE, LARGE,
MAJOR, RAD, TOPS
~ **(prefix)** MEGA
not ~ FAIR, OKAY, SOSO

great ___ APE, AUK, SEAL

great ___ heron BLUE

great-___ AUNT, UNCLE

"Great"
~ **czar** IVAN, PETER
~ **dog** DANE

Great ___ DANE

Great ___ Lake SALT, SLAVE

"Great ___, The" LIE, MAN

"Great ___ Detective, The"
MOUSE

"Great ___ in Harlem, A" DAY

"Great ___ Robbery, The" TRAIN

"Great ___ Votes, The" MAN

Great Barrier ___ REEF

Great Barrier Island OTEA

Great Barrier Reef
~ **essentially** CORAL

Great Basin DESERT

Great Bear LAKE

great blue ___ HERON

Great Britain
part of ~ WALES

"Great Compromiser, The" CLAY

"Great Day in Harlem, A"
~ **director** BACH

"Great Dictator, The"
~ **actor** OAKIE

Great Dividing ___ RANGE

greater ABOVE
~ **in seniority** ELDER
~ **part** MASS
~ **quantity** MORE
~ **than** OVER
~ **than zero** PLUS
to a ~ extent MORE

greatest AONE, BEST, FIRST, TOP,
TOPS
~ **degree** MOST

"Greatest, The" ALI

"Greatest ___ on Earth, The"
SHOW

"Greatest Show on ___, The"
EARTH

"Greatest Story ___ Told, The"
EVER

"Great Expectations"
~ **boy** PIP
~ **director** LEAN

"Great Forest, The"
~ **painter** ERNST

great horned ___ OWL

"Great Hymn to Aten" POEM

"Great idea!" AHA

"Great K&A ___ Robbery, The"
TRAIN

Great Lake ERIE
~ **canals** SOO

Great Lakes
~ **cargo** ORE
~ **fish** SMELT
~ **indigene** CREE
~ **state** OHIO
~ **tribe** ERIE

Great Leap Forward
~ **proponent** MAO

"Great Lie, The"
~ **actress** ASTOR

"Great Locomotive ___, The"
CHASE

"Great Lover, The"
~ **director** HALL

greatly ALOT

Great Mosque
~ **locale** MECCA

"Great Muppet ___, The" CAPER

Great Plains
~ **dwelling** TEPEE

Great Salt LAKE

Great Salt Lake DESERT
~ **locale** UTAH

Great Sandy DESERT

Great Seal
~ **bird** EAGLE

Great Slave LAKE

Great Smoky RANGE

Great Trek
~ **participant** BOER

Great Victoria DESERT

Great Wall
~ **locale** ASIA
~ **of China dynasty** CHIN

"Great weeds do grow ___"
APACE

great white
~ **relative** MAKO

"Great White ___, The" HOPE

greave ARMOR

grebe BIRD

Greco-___ wrestling ROMAN

Greco-Roman
~ **alternative** SUMO

Greece
ancient colony of ~ IONIA
island in ~ COS, CRETE, KOS
mountain in ~ ATHOS, OSSA
see also Greek

greed
exemplar of ~ MIDAS

greedily
eat ~ CRAM, RAVEN

greedy AVID, EAGER
~ **king** MIDAS
~ **one** HOG

Greek ATTIC
~ **architectural style** IONIC
~ **author** AESOP
~ **colonnade** STOA
~ **deity** TITAN
~ **epic** ILIAD
~ **epic poet** HOMER
~ **god** APOLLO
~ **goddess** ATE, HERA
~ **goddess of discord** ERIS
~ **goddess of fate** MOIRA
~ **goddess of peace** IRENE
~ **goddess of
wisdom** ATHENA
~ **god of love** EROS
~ **holy mountain** ATHOS
~ **letter** ALPHA, BETA, CHI,
DELTA, ETA, IOTA, OMEGA,
PHI, PSI, RHO, TAU, THETA
~ **letters** MUS
~ **marketplace** AGORA
~ **messenger of the
gods** IRIS
~ **peak** OSSA
~ **philosopher** PLATO
~ **playhouses** ODEA
~ **queen of the gods** HERA
~ **salad ingredient** FETA
~ **storyteller** AESOP
~ **strongman** ATLAS
~ **temple detail** ANTA
~ **theaters** ODEA
~ **tycoon's sobriquet** ARI
~ **vowel** ETA, IOTA, OMEGA
~ **war god** ARES
ancient ~ colony IONIA
ancient ~ dialect IONIC
ancient ~ physician GALEN
ancient ~ verse form EPOS
first ~ letter ALPHA
last ~ letter OMEGA
mainstay of ~ cuisine LAMB
next-to-last ~ letter PSI
old ~ harp LYRE
P-shaped ~ letter RHO
river of ~ myth STYX
where Greek met ~ STOA
X, in ~ CHI
see also Greece

Greek letter
~ **org.** FRAT

Greek Revival STYLE

**"Greeks ___ a Word for Them,
The"** HAD

Greek salad
~ **ingredient** FETA, OLIVE

**"Greeks Had a Word ___ Them,
The"** FOR

**"Greeks Had a Word for ___,
The"** THEM

"Greek Tycoon, The"
~ **model** ARI

Greeley EDITOR
~ **direction** WEST
emulate ~ EDIT

green NAIVE, NEW, RAW
~ **beverage** TEA
~ **dragon** PLANT
~ **feature** HOLE, PIN
~ **fruit** OLIVE
~ **gemstone** JADE
~ **light** OKAY, YES
~ **lights** OKS
~ **opposite** TEE
~ **org.** PGA
~ **sci.** ECOL
~ **shade** AQUA, JADE, LIME,
NILE, OLIVE, PEA
~ **spot** OASIS
~ **starter** EVER
~ **vegetable** KALE, PEA
~ **vegetation** LAWN
apple ~ COLOR
bluish ~ AQUA, JADE, NILE
dark ~ OLIVE
garden ~ KALE
Hooterville's were ~ ACRES
like little ~ apples TART
little ~ man ALIEN
long ~ CASH, MOOLA
not ~ RIPE
salad ~ CRESS
sea ~ AQUA
shoot for the ~ CHIP
yellowish ~ PEA

green ___ BEAN, CARD, ONION,
SNAKE, TEA

green-___ monster EYED

___ green LIME, LONG, NILE, OLIVE,
PARIS, PEA, SEA

Green RANGE
~ **and others** ALS
~ **land** EIRE, ERIN

Green ___ BERET, DAY

Green ___ Packers BAY

Green ___, Wisc. BAY

"Green ___" ACRES

"Green ___, The" DOOR

"Green ___ and Ham" EGGS

"Green ___ Danger" FOR

"Green ___ Shoes" SUEDE

"Green Acres"
~ **structure** BARN
Eddie's ~ costar EVA

Greenaway KATE, PETER

greenback BILL, NOTE, PAPER

Green Bay
former ~ quarterback STARR

Green Berets
like the ~ ELITE

green card
~ holder ALIEN, LEGAL

"Green Card"
~ director WEIR

Greene GAEL, JOE, LORNE
~ associate on "ER" LEWIS

"Green Eggs and ___" HAM

"Green Eggs and Ham"
~ author SEUSS
~ character SAM

Greene, Joe
like ~ MEAN

greenery
bit of ~ PLANT, SPRIG
sea ~ ALGA

Green Gables
~ girl ANNE

"Green Hat, The"
~ author ARLEN

greenhorn BABE, DUPE

Green Hornet, The HERO

greenish
~ blue AQUA, NILE, TEAL
~ yellow LEMON, LIME

Greenland
~ (abbr.) ISL

green light
give the ~ ALLOW, CLEAR, ENABLE, LET

"Green Man, The"
~ author AMIS

"Green Mansions"
~ hero ABEL

Green Mountain Boys
~ leader ALLEN
~ name ETHAN

greenockite ORE

Greenpeace
~ concern ATEST
~ subj. ECOL

greens KALE
mixed ~ SALAD

___ greens SALAD

Greenspan ALAN
~ org. FED
~ subj. ECON
stat for ~ GNP

Greenstreet
~ costar LORRE

greensward SOD

Greenwich ELLIE
it's 4 hrs. behind ~ EDT
it's 5 hrs. behind ~ CDT, EST
it's 6 hrs. behind ~ CST, MDT
it's 7 hrs. behind ~ MST, PDT
it's 8 hrs. behind ~ PST

Greenwich ___ Time MEAN

Greenwich Village
~ neighbor SOHO

Greenwood LEE

Greer HAL

greet ADMIT, HAIL, KISS, MEET, NOD
~ a dog PAT
~ the day ARISE, RISE
~ the moon BAY
~ the villain BOO, HISS
how to ~ a lady MAAM

greeting BOW, HELLO, HEY, NOD
~ at sea AHOY
ghostly ~ BOO
Hawaiian ~ ALOHA
Jersey ~ MOO
lion's ~ ROAR
mariner's ~ AHOY
quiet ~ NOD
telephone ~ HELLO
two-fingered ~ PEACE
warm ~ KISS

greeting ___ CARD

greeting card
~ word NOEL

"Greetings"
~ org. SSS

Gregorian
~ cycle YEAR

Gregory POPE

gremlin IMP

"Gremlins"
~ director DANTE

"Gremlins 2 The ___ Batch" NEW

"Gremlins 2 The New Batch"
~ director DANTE

grenades AMMO

Grendel OGRE

Grenoble
~ department ISERE
~ river ISERE
see also French

Gresham's ___ LAW

Gretel
see German

Gretna Green
go to ~ ELOPE

Gretzky
~ org. NHL
~ quest GOAL
~ workplace ICE, RINK
emulate ~ SKATE

grey
see gray

Grey EARL, NAN, ZANE
~ masked rider ERNE

"___ Grey Goose (Is Dead), The" OLE

greyhound RACER

Greyhound BUS

Grey, Jane LADY

Greystoke LORD
~ playmate APE

"Greystoke: The Legend of Tarzan, Lord of the ___" APES

grid NET

gridder
Miami ~ for short CANE
see also footballer

griddle PAN

gridiron NET
~ action PASS, PLAY
~ arbiter REF
~ complement ELEVEN
~ formation LINE
~ gadget TEE
~ group LINE
~ injury site KNEE
~ no-no CLIP
~ org. NFL
~ ploy FAKE
~ position END
~ quota ELEVEN
~ setback LOSS
~ stat TDS
~ unit YARD
two ~ periods HALF
see also football

gridlock JAM
~ unit AUTO, CAR

grief BANE, CARE, PAIN, STRESS, TRIAL, WOE
come to ~ LOSE

grief-stricken
be ~ SOB

Grieg
~ ctry. NOR

grievance PEEVE

grieve ACHE, FEEL, KEEN, MOAN, MOPE, RACK, RUE

grievous BAD, DIRE, EVIL, SAD, SORE

Griffey KEN

Griffin MERV

Griffith ANDY, EMILE

Griffith, D.W.
~ product EPIC

grifter
~ brainchild SCAM

grig EEL

grill ASK, GRATE, HEAT, ROAST, TEST
~ partner BAR
~ remnant EMBER
~ room BAR
~ site PATIO

grille GRATE
~ protector BRA

grillwork GRID

grim BAD, BARE, CRUEL, DIRE, DOUR, STERN

grimace FACE, GRIN, MOUE

grimalkin CAT

grime DIRT, SMUT, SOOT

Grimley
~ and others EDS

Grimm
~ bad guy OGRE
~ character GNOME
~ shoemaker ELF

grin BEAM, SMILE
~ and bear it BOW
sardonic ~ SNEER

"Grin and Bear It"
~ senator SNORT

Grinch
~ creator SEUSS
~ victim WHO

grind ABRADE, FILE, GRATE, GRIT, HONE, LABOR, MASH, MILL, PLOD, RUT, SLAVE
~ away PLOD
~ in a way HONE
daily ~ RUT

grinder HERO, MILL, MOLAR, TOOTH
~ gear ORGAN
~ grist MEAT
coffee ~ MILL

___ grinder MEAT, ORGAN

grinding
~ machine LATHE
~ substance EMERY
~ tooth MOLAR

grindstones
use ~ HONE

"___ Gringo" OLD

grip BAG, BITE, CLASP, CLIP, GRAB, GRASP, HILT, HOLD, KNOB, SWAY, TAKE
firm ~ GRASP
rider's ~ MANE, REIN
wrestler's ~ HOLD

gripe FRET, PAIN, PEEVE
~ (about) MOAN
reason to ~ ACHE

gripper
ice ~ TONG
shoe ~ CLEAT

grips
come to ~ with FACE, MEET

grisard ELDER

Grisham, John
~ profession LAW

grisly BAD, DIRE, EVIL

Gris-Nez CAPE

"Grissom ___, The" GANG

grist MEAL
grinder's ~ MEAT

grist for the ___ MILL

grit NERVE, SAND

"___ Grit" TRUE

grits
  prepare ~ BOIL

Grizabella CAT
  ~ creator ELIOT

grizzled OLD

Grizzlies FIVE, TEAM
  ~ org. NBA

grizzly BEAR, OLD
  ~ pad DEN, LAIR

Grk. LANG

groan CRY, MOAN
  ~ evoker, maybe PUN
  moan and ~ CARP

groaner PUN

groat COIN

grocer
  ~ measure CASE
  ~ need SCALE

groceries
  ~ holder BAG

grocery
  ~ buy APPLE, CAN, CHOP, EGGS, HAM, KALE, LEMON, LIME, MEAT, ORANGE, PASTA, PEAR, POP, RICE, ROAST, SALT, TEA, TIN
  ~ coupon value CENTS
  ~ section DELI

grocery ___ CART

Groening MATT
  ~ father HOMER

grog ALE
  ~ ingredient RUM

grok DIG

Grolier's
  ~ set ENC

grommet RING

groom CLIP, COMB, DRESS, MALE, MAN, MATE, PREEN
  ~ acquisition INLAW
  ~ partner BRIDE
  ~ response IDO
  Broadway ~ of 1922 ABIE

grooming
  ~ aid COMB

groove CUT, DADO, HABIT, LINE, ROTE, RUT, SCORE, SLIT, SLOT, SPLIT
  ~ on LIKE, SAVOR
  carpenter's ~ DADO
  small ~ STRIA

groovy COOL, NEAT, RAD

grope FEEL

Grosbard ULU

grosbeak BIRD

gross BAD, BIG, CRASS, EARN, FAT, GET, LARGE, LEWD, OBESE, RANK, TOTAL
  ~ deduction COST
  ~ out REPEL

not ~ NET

gross ___ (offend) OUT

"Gross!" UGH

Grosse ___, Mich. ILE

Grossglockner ALP

Gros Ventre TRIBE

grotesque ODD
  ~ face MASK

grotto ARBOR, CAVE, COVE, DEN, HOLE, LAIR

grouch BEAR, CRAB, MOPE, PILL

Groucho EMCEE, HOST, WIT
  ~ brother HARPO
  ~ cap BERET
  ~ specialty ADLIB, PUN
  glance from ~ LEER

grouchy BAD, EDGY, MEAN, RUDE, SOUR, TART, TESTY
  be ~ SNAP

ground BASE, BASIS, BED, DIRT, EARTH, FINE, LAND, SITE, SOIL
  ~ breaker HOE, SPADE
  ~ cloth SHEET
  ~ cover LAWN, PLANT, SNOW, SOD, TARP
  ~ force ARMY
  ~ grain MEAL
  ~ gripper CLEAT
  ~ (prefix) GEO
  break ~ PLOW, START
  cover ~ HIE, MOVE, RACE, RUN, SPEED, STEP
  high ~ RISE
  hit the ~ ALIT, LAND, LIT
  leave the ~ LEAP, RISE
  lose ~ SLIDE, SLIP
  near the ~ LOW
  on solid ~ SAFE
  piece of ~ AREA
  solid ~ EARTH, LAND
  stamping ~ HOME
  touch ~ LAND
  touched ~ ALIT, LIT

ground ___ BALL, CREW, RULE, WATER, ZERO

grounded ASHORE
  ~ Aussie EMU

grounder
  botched ~ ERROR

groundhog ANIMAL

"Groundhog ___" DAY

groundless IDLE

ground-level LOW

grounds AREA, BASIS, CAUSE, LAWN
  ~ for a suit LIBEL, TORT
  grunter's ~ STY
  house and ~ ABODE, ESTATE

groundsel WEED

groundwork BASE, BASIS

group ARRAY, BLOC, CLAN, CLASS, CREW, GANG, LABEL, LOT, ORDER, SET, SORT, TEAM, TROOP, UNIT
  ~ (abbr.) ASSN, ORG
  ~ on horseback POSSE

___ group PEER

grouped
  ~ merchandise LOT

groupie FAN
  ~ need IDOL

grouse BIRD, CARP, CRAB, FRET, NAG

grouter
  ~ target TILE

grove STAND
  part of a ~ TREE

groveling BASE

Grover
  ~ second vice president ADLAI

___ Grove Village, Ill. ELK

grow BOOM, BREED, PLANT, RAISE
  ~ accustomed ADAPT
  ~ better HEAL
  ~ dim FADE
  ~ like a weed RIOT
  ~ mellower AGE
  ~ older AGE
  ~ out of ARISE, EMERGE
  ~ rank RIOT
  ~ together KNIT
  ~ wearisome FLAG, PALL, TIRE
  let the grass ~ under one's feet LOAF
  where whiskers ~ CHIN

grow ___ (mature) INTO

growing
  ~ medium SOIL
  ~ out ENATE
  ~ room ACRE
  ~ vigorously RANK

growl GNAR, NOISE, ROAR, SNARL

growler
  "It's grrrreat!" ~ TONY

growly DEEP

grown ADULT, RIPE
  ~ boy MAN
  ~ up ADULT

grown-___ UPS

"___ Grows in Brooklyn, A" TREE

growth RISE
  ~ on rocks MOSS
  cypress ~ KNEE
  economic ~ BOOM
  grain ~ AWN
  new ~ SPRIG
  riverbank ~ REED
  stage of ~ ADULT
  tree ~ LEAF
  tree trunk ~ MOSS
  underground ~ ROOT
  unwelcome ~ WEED

growth ___ (annulus) RING

Groza LOU
  ~ nickname TOE

grp. ASSN, ORG

grub DIG, EATS, FARE, LABOR, MEAL, MEAT, PLOD, SLAVE
  ~ up ROOT
  barnyard ~ FEED

grubby MESSY

grudge SPITE
  carrying a ~ SORE

grudging MEAN, SMALL

gruesome BAD, DIRE, EVIL

gruff RUDE, TESTY

grumble CARP, CRAB, FRET

grumbler CRAB, NAG

Grumman LEROY

grump CRAB, MOPE

grumpy BAD, MEAN, SOUR, TESTY
  ~ mood SNIT
  be ~ MOPE

Grumpy
  ~ colleague DOC

grungy MESSY

grunt SNORT
  ~ of distaste UGH

Gruyère
  ~ coat RIND

Gstaad
  ~ gear SKI

Gt. Brit.
  part of ~ ENG, IRE, SCOT

guacamole DIP
  ~ dipper CHIP

Guadalajara
  see Spanish

Guadalupe RANGE
  see also Spanish

Guadeloupe
  ~ (abbr.) ISL

Guam TER, TERR

Guanabara BAY

guanaco ANIMAL
  ~ cousin LLAMA

Guantanamo
  ~ locale CUBA

guarantee AVOW, BAIL, ICE
  with no ~ ASIS

guaranteed ONICE, SAFE, SURE

guaranty AEGIS, EGIS

guard ATTEND, TEND
  ~ against SPARE
  ~ against (prefix) PARA
  ~ cry HALT
  be caught off ~ SLEEP
  catch off ~ AMAZE
  on one's ~ LEERY, WARY
  put on ~ ALERT, WARN

___ guard OLD, REAR

guarded ALERT, LEERY, SAFE, SHY, WARY

guarder
treasure ~ GNOME

guardian
~ charge WARD
~ spirit ANGEL

Guardian Angel
~ cap BERET

guardianship AEGIS, CARE, EGIS

"Guarding ___" TESS

Guatemala
see Spanish

Guayaquil CITY, PORT

Gucci ALDO

guck OOZE, SLIME

Gudrun
~ husband ATLI

guerdon DESERT, FEE

Guernsey COW, ISLE
~ exclamation MOO

guerre
nom de ~ ALIAS, NAME

Guerrero PEDRO

guess EDUCE, IDEA, OPINE, SHOT
~ (abbr.) EST
~ words ORSO
hazard a ~ OPINE
wild ~ SHOT

guesser
~ word ABOUT

guest
paying ~ TENANT
slumber-party ~ GIRL
unwanted ~ PEST
wedding ~ INLAW

Guest EDGAR

guesthouse INN

guest room
~ often DEN

guests
have ~ to dinner EATIN
where honored ~ sit DAIS

Guevara CHE

guff LIP, SASS

guffaw HAHA, HOOT, ROAR

guidance AID, HELP, SWAY

guide AID, HELM, HELP, KEY, LEAD, MAP, PILOT, SHOW, STEER, TAKE
~ agenda TOUR
~ for action RULE
~ to a chair SEAT
diner's ~ MENU
life ~ CREDO
Magi's ~ STAR
shopper's ~ LIST
spiritual ~ GURU
street ~ MAP
tour ~ MAP, PILOT

guide ___ DOG

"Guide ___ the Married Man, A" FOR

guided
~ by UNDER

"Guide for the Married ___, A" MAN

guideline CODE, RULE

guidepost SIGN

guiding POLAR
~ principle CREDO

"Guiding Light" SOAP

Guido
~ high note ELA
see also Italian

Guidry RON

guild CLAN, ORDER, UNION

guilder COIN

guile ART

guileful SLY

guileless HONEST, NAIVE

Guillaume
see French

guillemot
~ kin AUK

guilt SHAME

guiltless CLEAN

"Guilt of Janet ___, The" AMES

guilty
feel ~ RUE

guinea COIN
female ~ pig SOW

___ Guinea NEW

guinea pig ANIMAL, PET
~ home LAB

Guinness ALEC, SIR
~ brew ALE
~ entry FEAT

Guinness Book
~ suffix EST
~ superlative MOST

guise ATTIRE, DRESS, GARB, MASK, MIEN
~ starter DIS

guitar
~ adjunct AMP
~ ancestor LUTE
~ cousin UKE
~ ender IST
~ part FRET, NECK

___ guitar STEEL

Gujarat
~ garment SARI

gulch GAP, WADI

gules COLOR, RED

gulf ABYSS, BAY, GAP, SPACE
Arabian ~ ADEN
Arabian Sea ~ OMAN
immeasurable ~ ABYSS

Mideast ~ ADEN, OMAN
Yemen's ~ ADEN

Gulf
~ capital ADEN
~ nation YEMEN
~ st. FLA
~ sultanate OMAN
former ~ colony ADEN

Gulf ___ OIL, STREAM, WAR

Gulf Coast
~ bird EGRET
~ city TAMPA

Gulf of ___ ADEN, OMAN

Gulf of ___ (Baltic offshoot) RIGA

Gulf of Aden
~ country YEMEN
~ vessel DHOW

Gulf of Guinea
~ capital ACCRA

Gulf of Mexico
~ city TAMPA

Gulfport
~ st. MISS

"Gulf Stream, The"
~ painter HOMER

Gulf War
~ ally SYRIA
~ city BASRA
~ figure AMIR, EMEER, EMIR
~ foe IRAQ
~ missile SCUD
~ participant ARAB

gull BIRD, DUPE, MEW, STING
~ cousin TERN
small ~ MEW, TERN
where buoy meets ~ OCEAN, SEA

___ gull SEA

gullet CRAW, CROP

gullible EASY, NAIVE
~ one DUPE, SAP

"Gulliver's Travels"
~ brute YAHOO

gully GAP, WADI
form a ~ ERODE, WASH

gullywasher RAIN, STORM

gulp CRAM, GASP, PANT
~ down EAT
big ~ BELT

gulper
gas ~ AUTO, CAR

gum GLUE, RESIN, TREE
~ tree denizen BEE
~ up CLOG, HASH, SNARL
artist's ~ ERASER
sour ~ TREE

"Gumball Rally, The"
~ director BAIL

gumbo
~ ingredient FILE, OKRA

gummed
~ flap SEAL

Gump ANDY
Mrs. ~ MIN

Gump, Forrest
where ~ served NAM

gumption GRIT, NERVE

gums
beat one's ~ CHAT, YAK, YAP

gumshoe TEC

gun RIFLE, ROD
~ a motor REV
~ blast BANG
~ charge LOAD
~ filler AMMO, SHOT
~ game SKEET
~ it SPEED
~ lobby NRA
~ man COLT
big ~ LION
cap ~ TOY
carrying a ~ ARMED
discharge a ~ FIRE
gun moll's ~ GAT
light machine ~ STEN
long ~ RIFLE
point a ~ AIM
pull a ~ DRAW
squirt ~ TOY
toy ~ ammo CAP
used a ~ SHOT
WWII ~ STEN

gun ___ DOG

gun ___ (seek) FOR

gun-___ SHY

___ gun AIR, BIG, CAP, GLUE, HIRED, RAY, SPEAR, STUN, TOP, WATER

___-gun SIX

"___ Gun" TOP

gun-control
~ opponent NRA

"Gun Crazy"
~ director LEWIS

"Gunfight at the O.K. Corral" OATER

gunfighter
~ dare DRAW

"___ Gun for Hire" THIS

"Gunga ___" DIN

Gunga Din HERO

"Gunga Din" POEM
~ setting INDIA

gung-ho AVID, EAGER, HOT, INTO, KEEN
~ mood ZEAL

gunk GOO, OOZE, SLIME

gunmetal COLOR, GRAY

Gunn BEN, PETER

gunner
~ need AMMO

gunnery

gunnery
~ (abbr.) ARTY

gunning
~ for AFTER

Gunn, Peter
~ girlfriend EDIE

gunny-bag SACK

gunnysack BAG

gun owner
~ org. NRA

gunpowder TEA
~ holder KEG

Gunpowder ___ PLOT

guns
big ~ (abbr.) ARTY
get new ~ REARM
give ~ to ARM

gunshot
~ sound BANG

gunslinger
~ command DRAW

"Gunsmoke"
~ bartender SAM
~ character DOC
~ Doc ADAMS
~ network CBS
Kitty on ~ AMANDA

Guns N' ___ ROSES

Gunter
see German

Gunther, John
~ topic ASIA, USA

"___ Gun Will Travel" HAVE

guppy PET

Gurkha
~ land NEPAL

___ Gurley Brown HELEN

gurney COT

guru HINDU, LAMA, SAGE, SWAMI
~ discipline YOGA
~ title YOGI

gush EMIT, EMOTE, ERUPT, ISSUE,
JET, POUR, RACE, RAVE, RUN,
SPATE, SPEW, STREAM, TALK

gushy
~ writing SLOP

gusset PLEAT

gussy
~ up ADORN, ARRAY, ATTIRE,
DRESS, PREEN

gust BLAST, STORM

gustation TASTE

gusto ARDOR, ELAN, FIRE, LUST,
PEP, TASTE, ZEAL

Guthrie ARLO

Guthrie, Woody
~ son ARLO

guts GRIT, NERVE, SAND

gutsy GAME
~ guy HERO

gutta BEAD, DROP

Guttenberg STEVE

gutter RUN
~ site EAVE

guttural DEEP

guy CABLE, CHAP, DOG, DUDE,
GENT, LAD, MALE, MAN, ROPE,
TWIT
~ in Australian English MATE
~ in British English MATE
~ in surferese DUDE
~ partner GAL
bad ~ OGRE
courteous ~ GENT
that ~ HIM
that ~'s HIS
tough ~ HOOD
typical ~ JOE
see also fellow

___ guy WISE

"___ Guy, The" TALL

Guy Fawkes Day
~ mo. NOV

guys HES
just for ~ STAG
the bad ~ ENEMY, THEM

"Guys ___ Dolls" AND

"___ Guys" WISE

"Guys and Dolls"
~ role SARAH, SKY
~ Tony-winner ALDA

guzzle CRAM, GLUT

Guzzle, King
~ land MOO

guzzler SOT

___-guzzler GAS

"GWTW"
~ setting TARA
like Atlanta in ~ AFIRE

Gwyn NELL

Gwyneth
~ former boyfriend BRAD
role for ~ EMMA

gym ARENA
~ apparatus HORSE
~ dance HOP
~ event PROM
~ iteration REP
~ surface MAT
work out in the ~ SPAR

gymnast
~ concern TONE
~ device HORSE
~ goal TEN
~ maneuver FLIP, SPLIT
~ need MAT
like a ~ AGILE, LITHE, SPRY

gymnastics
~ competition MEET
~ equipment BEAM, HORSE
~ move SPLIT

gymnasts
like ~ AGILE

gynaeceum HAREM

gynophore STEM

___ Gynt PEER

Gynt, Peer
~ creator IBSEN
~ mother ASE

gyp ROB, ROOK, STING

"___ Gypsies, The" SEA

gypsy NOMAD
male ~ ROM

gypsy ___ CAB, MOTH

"Gypsy"
~ director LEROY
~ painter HALS

Gypsy ___ Lee ROSE

"Gypsy ___, The" BARON

Gypsy Rose ___ LEE

"Gypsys, Tramps & Thieves"
~ singer CHER

gyrate REEL, SPIN, TURN

gyration TURN

gyro
~ filler LAMB
~ need PITA
~ skewer SPIT

gyroscope
~ cousin TOP
~ essentially ROTOR
~ part AXIS
imitate a ~ SPIN

gyves IRONS

1

H ELEM
  ~ to a Greek ETA
  1 for ~ ATNO
  first ~ in 4-H HEAD

"Ha!" OHO

Haakon VI
  ~ son OLAF, OLAV

habanera DANCE

habeas corpus WRIT

haberdasher
  ~ ware HAT, TIE

habergeon MAIL

habiliment WEAR

habiliments ATTIRE, DRESS, GARB

habit ATTIRE, DRESS, GARB, ROTE, RUT, TRAIT, USAGE
  ~ wearer NUN

habitat ABODE, HOME, NEST, SPHERE
  ~ (prefix) ECO

habitation ABODE, HOME, NEST
  elevated ~ AERIE

habitual SET, USUAL
  ~ practice RULE

habitually EVER, OFT, OFTEN

habituate ADAPT, ENURE, INURE, ORIENT

habitué USER

Hachinohe CITY, PORT

hacienda ABODE, CASA, HOME
  ~ material ADOBE
  ~ room SALA

hack AXE, CAB, CHOP, CUT, GASH, HEW, HORSE, JADE, MAIM, PEN, RIP, SLASH, TAXI
  ~ it PASS
  ~ rider FARE
  not ~ it LOSE, MISS

hackberry
  ~ cousin ELM

hacker USER

hackles
  raise someone's ~ ANGER, IRK

where ~ rise NAPE

Hackman GENE
  ~ film RIOT

hackney CAB, HORSE

hackneyed BANAL, STALE, TIRED, TRITE
  ~ expression TAG
  ~ phrase ADAGE, SAW

hacksaw TOOL

"___ Had a Hammer" IFI

"___ Had a Million" IFI

haddock SCROD
  ~ cousin COD

"___ had 'em" ADAM

Hades DIS
  ~ river STYX

"___ had it!" IVE

"___ had my way..." IFI

hadn't
  wish you ~ RUE

Hadrian CAESAR, ROMAN

Hafez al-___ ASSAD

Hafiz POET
  see also poet

hafnium METAL

haft HILT

Hafun CAPE

Hagar EXILE

Hagen UTA

haggadah-reading
  ~ time SEDER

haggard DONE, PALE

Haggard MERLE
  ~ Ayesha SHE

Haggard, H. Rider
  ~ novel SHE

Haggerty DAN

haggle ARGUE, DEAL, TRADE

hagiography
  ~ subj. STE
  ~ subjs. STS

hagiologist
  ~ study SAINT

Hagman
  ~ costar EDEN

___ Hague THE

Hague, The
  see Dutch, Netherlands

hai YES

"___ Ha'i" BALI

Haida TRIBE

Haifa CITY, PORT
  ~ loc. ISR
  ~ locale ISRAEL
  port north of ~ ACRE

Haig
  ~ and others ALS
  ~ former cmd. NATO

haiku POEM

hail AVE, CALL, CRY, GREET, HONOR, ICE, LAUD, STORM
  ocean ~ AHOY
  something to ~ CAB

"___ hail!" ALL

"Hail!"
  ~ in Latin AVE

Hailey
  ~ novel HOTEL

hail-fellow-well-___ MET

hailing
  ~ call AHOY

"Hail the Conquering ___" HERO

hair SHADE, TRESS
  ~ adornment BOW
  ~ color TINT, TRAIT
  ~ coloring DYE, HENNA, RINSE
  ~ dressing GEL
  ~ ender CUT, LINE, PIN
  ~ foundation SCALP
  ~ goo GEL
  ~ hue GRAY, GREY
  ~ problem KNOT, SNARL
  ~ shop SALON
  ~ splitter PART
  ~ stylist, sometimes DYER
  ~ treatment PERM
  angel ~ PASTA

bear ~ FUR
curl one's ~ AMAZE, PERM, SCARE
facial ~ BEARD
get in someone's ~ ANGER, IRK, PEEVE, RILE, UPSET
hank of ~ TRESS
horse's ~ MANE
let down one's ~ UNDO
lock of ~ TRESS
long ~ MANE
lose ~ SHED
make one's ~ stand on end REPEL, SCARE
neaten one's ~ COMB
neither hide nor ~ NONE
ruffle, as ~ TEASE
thick ~ MANE
treat ~ DYE, RINSE, SET, TINT
win by a ~'s breadth NOSE
within a ~ CLOSE

hair ___ NET

___ hair ANGEL

"Hair"
  ~ song AIR

hair care
  ~ need COMB

hair coloring
  ~ solution RINSE

haircut TRIM

hairdo AFRO, PERM
  bountiful ~ MANE
  natural ~, informally FRO
  onetime Jesse Jackson ~ AFRO
  shaggy ~ MANE
  short ~ BOB
  type of ~ SHAG

hairdresser
  ~ at times DYER

___-haired boy FAIR

___-haired terrier WIRE

hairless BALD

hairlike FINE

hairpiece RUG

hairpin
  ~ turn BEND

hair-raiser BOO

hair-raising EERIE, EERY

hairs
 align the cross ~ AIM
 split ~ ARGUE

hairsplitting FINE

hair spray
 ~ name ADORN

hairstyle AFRO
 ~ feature PART
 sweeping ~ UPDO

hairstyles DOS

hairstyling
 ~ aid GEL

hairy
 ~ ancestor APE
 ~ Himalayan YETI

"Hairy ___, The" APE

"hairy one"
 Biblical ~ ESAU

Haiti
 see French

"Haj, The"
 ~ author URIS

___ Haji-Sheikh ALI

hajj
 ~ destination MECCA

haka DANCE

Hal LEROY

halala COIN

halberd PIKE

halcyon CALM, CLEAR, FAIR, MILD,
 SERENE

hale FIT

Hale ALAN
 ~ hero NOLAN

Hale, Jr. ALAN

___ Halen VAN

Hale, Nathan SPY
 ~ alma mater YALE

Hale, Sr. ALAN

Haley ALEX
 ~ costar LAHR

Haley, Alex
 ~ bestseller ROOTS

half PART
 ~ (prefix) DEMI, HEMI, SEMI

half-___ HOUR, LIFE, MAST, MOON,
 NOTE, PINT, SOLE, WIT

half-___ over SEAS

___ half (proletariat) OTHER

___ half bad NOT

half-baked DAFT, LAME, MAD,
 POOR

half-famished LEAN

half-gainer
 did a ~ DOVE

half-goat
 half-man, ~ PAN, SATYR

half-hearted COOL, LIMP, TEPID

half-man
 half-goat, ~ PAN, SATYR

half-moon ARC, BOW

"Half Moon" BOAT, SHIP

half-note
 ~ feature STEM

"half-off"
 ~ event SALE

halfpenny COIN

half-pike LANCE

half pint
 ~ maybe ALE

half-starved LEAN, POOR

halftime
 ~ entertainers BAND

half-truth LIE

halfway
 ~ around ABOUT

___ halfway (compromise) MEET

halfway house
 ~ program REHAB

half-wit ASS, DOLT

halibut SOLE

Halifax CITY, PORT

hall ABODE, HOME, SALON
 ~ in Spanish SALA
 dining ~ MESS
 exhibition ~ SALON

___ hall CITY, DANCE, MESS, POOL

Hall EDD
 ~ partner OATES
 cinematic ~ ANNIE

Hall & ___ OATES

"___ Hall" ANNIE, CITY

Hall, Arsenio EMCEE, HOST

"Hallelujah, ___ Bum" IMA

Hall, Jerry
 pronoun for ~ SHE

hallmark LABEL, STAMP, TRAIT

Hall, Monty EMCEE, HOST
 ~ offering DEAL

hallo CRY

Hall-of-Fame
 ~ Brave AARON
 ~ Giant OTT
 ~ Yankee RUTH

Hall-of-Famer
 NHL ~ ORR

halloo CALL, CRY, GREET, HAIL

hallow ADORE, BLESS

Hallow
 ~ ender EEN

Halloween
 ~ animal CAT
 ~ attire MASK
 ~ decoration BAT
 ~ mo. OCT
 ~ option TREAT
 ~ shout BOO
 ~ sound effect MOAN
 ~ wear SHEET

Halloween-like EERIE, EERY

halls
 central ~ ATRIA
 music ~ ODEA

hallucinate DREAM

___ Hall University SETON

hallux TOE

halo AURA, RING

halogen
 ~ suffix INE

Halsey
 ~ org. USN

halt ARREST, CEASE, END, LAME,
 REST, STALL, STAND, STAY,
 STEM, STOP, WAIT
 ~ at sea AVAST
 bring to a ~ STEM

"Halt!" AVAST, WHOA

halter ROPE

halter ___ TOP

halting LIMP

halvah
 ~ ingredient SESAME

halved SPLIT

halves
 go ~ SHARE

halyard ROPE

ham ACTOR, MEAT
 ~ alternative BLT
 ~ device RADIO
 ~ ender STER
 ~ it up ACT, EMOTE
 ~ mate EGGS, RYE
 ~ place STAGE
 ~ serving SLICE
 ~ word OVER
 make ~ CURE

Hama
 where ~ is SYRIA

Haman
 ~ nemesis ESTHER

Hambletonian
 ~ gait TROT

Hamburg CITY, PORT
 ~ river ELBE
 see also German

hamburger MEAT
 ~ extra ONION

Hamelin
 ~ menace RAT

Hamill PETE
 emulate ~ SKATE

Hamilton EDITH, EMMA, SCOTT
 ~ bill TEN
 ~ foe BURR
 ~ prov. ONT

Hamilton-Burr
 ~ meeting DUEL

Hamilton, Donald
 ~ spy HELM, MATT

Hamilton, Emma LADY

Hamilton, Scott
 ~ maneuver AXEL, CAMEL,
 SPIN
 ~ milieu ICE, RINK
 emulate ~ SKATE

"___ Hamilton Woman" THAT

Hamlet DANE
 ~ exclamation FIE
 ~ expression ALAS
 ~ infinitive TOBE
 ~ to Gertrude SON
 emulate ~ AVENGE
 what ~ smelled ARAT

"Hamlet" PLAY
 ~ extra DANE
 ~ opener ACTI
 ~ prop ARRAS
 ~ quintet ACTS
 aromatic plant in ~ RUE

Hammarskjöld DAG, SWEDE
 ~ predecessor LIE

hammer BANG, BEAT, BONE, LAM,
 MAUL, SMITE, TOOL
 ~ away STRESS
 ~ away at PEG
 ~ hurler THOR
 ~ location EAR
 ~ obliquely TOE
 ~ part CLAW, PEEN
 ~ target NAIL
 ~ throw EVENT

___ hammer CLAW

hammerhead
 ~ feature CLAW
 ~ relative MAKO

"Hammerin' Hank" AARON

Hammer, M.C.
 ~ genre RAP

Hammer, Mike TEC

hammers
 where ~ are thrown MEET

Hammerstein OSCAR

Hammett
 ~ heroine NORA
 ~ hound ASTA
 ~ private eye SPADE

hammock BED
 ~ weave NET
 use a ~ LOLL

Hammond PETER
 ~ book ATLAS
 ~ product MAP

ham on ___ RYE

hamper BIN, CLOG, LIMIT, STOP
   ~ contents WASH

hams
   what ~ try to steal SCENE

hamster PET
   ~ home CAGE

hamstring
   ~ site LEG

Han SOLO

hand HELP, MITT, UNIT
   ~ and glove CLOSE
   ~ down LEAVE
   ~ down a decision RULE
   ~ ender BAG, BILL, CAR, CART, MADE, MAID, OUT, RAIL, SAW, SOME
   ~ off RELAY
   ~ out ALLOT, DOLE, ISSUE, METE
   ~ out cards DEAL
   ~ over CEDE, PASS, REFER
   ~ part PALM
   ~ signal CLAP
   ~ starter FORE, FREE, OFF, OVER, STAGE, UNDER
   at ~ CLOSE, LOCAL, NEAR
   at ~, to a poet ANEAR
   dab ~ ACE, ADEPT
   experienced ~ VET
   extend a helping ~ AID
   field ~ PEON
   gain the upper ~ BEND, BEST
   give a ~ ABET, ROOT
   give a ~ to CLAP
   have the upper ~ LEAD
   helping ~ AID
   hold out one's ~ BEG
   issue at ~ TOPIC
   items on ~ THESE
   lay one's ~ to PLY
   lend a ~ ABET, AID, HELP, SERVE
   master ~ ACE, ADEPT
   matter at ~ TOPIC
   modest ~ PAIR
   near at ~ CLOSE
   old ~ ACE, ADEPT, PRO, VET
   on ~ SPARE
   on the other ~ AGAIN, ELSE, ONLY, YET
   open ~ PALM
   poker ~ PAIR
   start the ~ DEAL
   stick out a ~ ABET
   take by the ~ LEAD
   try one's ~ at ESSAY
   upper ~ EDGE
   whip ~ EDGE

hand ___ (distribute) OUT

hand ___ (surrender) OVER

hand ___ fist OVER

hand-___ HELD

___ hand DAB, FREE, GLAD, HIRED, HOUR, IRON, LONE, OLD, PAT

___-hand GLAD

"___ Hand" SLOW

"___ Hand, The" HIRED

handbag
   ~ part STRAP
   large ~ TOTE

handclasp GRIP

___-hand coordination EYE

hand cream
   ~ ingredient ALOE

handcuff BIND

___-handed CLEAN, HARD, LEFT, RED, TWO

handed down
   ~ stories LORE

Handel
   ~ opera NERO
   ~ oratorio SAUL

"___ Hand for the Little Lady, A" BIG

handful
   ~ maybe BRAT
   equestrian's ~ MANE

"Handful of ___, A" DUST

handhold
   commuter's ~ STRAP

handicap EDGE, ODDS

handiwork
   do ~ TAT
   spider's ~ WEB

handle CARESS, EAR, FEEL, GRIP, HOLD, KNOB, MEET, NAME, PILOT, RUN, SEETO, STRAP, TAG, TITLE, TREAT
   ~ badly ABUSE
   ~ capably WIELD
   ~ clumsily PAW
   ~ ender BAR
   ~ perfectly ACE
   ~ problems COPE
   ~ roughly MAUL, PAW
   ~ starter MIS, PAN
   ~ with care CARESS
   bucket ~ BAIL
   chest ~ KNOB
   cup ~ EAR
   dagger ~ HILT
   door ~ LEVER
   false ~ ALIAS
   fly off the ~ BOIL, ERUPT, RAGE, RAVE, STORM
   jug ~ EAR
   kettle ~ BAIL
   knife ~ GRIP
   pipe ~ STEM
   rounded ~ KNOB
   sword ~ HILT
   teacup ~ EAR
   whip ~ CROP

handles
   having ~ EARED

"Handle With ___" CARE

hand-lotion
   ~ ingredient ALOE

"___ Hand Luke" COOL

handmaid GIRL

"Handmaid's ___, The" TALE

hand-me-down RAG, USED

"___ Hand of God, The" LEFT

handout AID, ALMS, BILL, DOLE
   diner ~ MENU

handpick ELECT, TAKE

handrail
   ~ post NEWEL

hands CREW, HELP, LABOR, SWAY
   deck ~ CREW
   get one's ~ on GRAB
   hired ~ HELP
   join ~ ALLY
   lay ~ on GRAB, HARM
   like some poker ~ PAT
   shake ~ GREET
   show of ~ VOTE
   speak with one's ~ SIGN
   take one's life in one's ~ RISK
   take the law into one's own ~ AVENGE

hands-___ policy OFF

"Hands ___ the City" OVER

"Hands ___ the Table" ACROSS

"Hands Across the ___" TABLE

hands-down EASY

handshake CLASP, GRIP

handsome AMPLE, FAIR
   ~ young man APOLLO
   dark and ~ companion TALL

hands-on
   ~ class LAB

"___ hands on deck!" ALL

"Hands Over the ___" CITY

handspike BAR, LEVER

hands-up
   ~ time NOON

hand-to-hand
   ~ combat MELEE

handtruck CART

hand wringer
   ~ word ALAS

handwriting
   ~ feature SLANT
   ~ on the wall OMEN, SIGN

handy ADEPT, DEFT, NEAR, UTILE
   ~ to NEAR
   come in ~ HELP

"Handy"
   ~ man ANDY

handyman
   ~ need TOOL
   do a ~ job RESTORE

hang DRAPE
   ~ about WAIT
   ~ around LOLL, STAY, WAIT
   ~ around for AWAIT
   ~ back LAG, TRAIL, WAIT
   ~ down LOLL, PEND, SAG, TRAIL
   ~ ender DOG, NAIL, OUT, TAG

~ fire DEFER, PEND
~ in midair POISE
~ in the balance PEND
~ in the breeze DRY
~ in there LAST, TRY
~ in the sun AIR
~ limply LOP
~ loose LOLL
~ loosely DRAPE, LOP
~ on ADHERE, HOLD, LAST
~ onto HOLD, KEEP
~ out AERATE, IDLE, LOAF
~ out for AWAIT
~ out one's shingle OPEN, SETTLE
~ out to dry AIR
~ out together DATE
~ starter OVER
~ suspended POISE
~ ten RIDE
~ tough DARE
do not ~ onto LOSE
get the ~ of SEE
give a ~ CARE
have the ~ of KNOW

hang ___ FIRE, LOOSE

hang ___ (loiter) OUT

hangar SHED
   ~ bird PLANE

hanger RACK
   ~ material WIRE
   ~ support ROD

hang glide SOAR

hang gliding
   finished ~ ALIT, LIT

"Hang in ___!" THERE

hanging LOOSE
   ~ back SLOW
   ~ on every word RAPT
   classroom wall ~ MAP
   closet ~ TIE
   highway ~ SIGN
   wall ~ ARRAS

"Hanging ___, The" TREE

"Hang on a minute!" WHOA

hangout
   teen ~ MALL

hangover
   have a ~ ACHE

"___ Hangs High, The" NOOSE

hang-up SNAG

hank PART
   ~ of hair TRESS

Hank AARON, SNOW

hanker ITCH, LONG, PINE, YEARN
   ~ after LONG, WANT
   ~ for ACHE, WANT

hankering ITCH, LOVE, TASTE, URGE, YEN
   ~ (for) ACHY

Hanks TOM
   ~ film BIG

Hanna-Barbera
   ~ dog ASTRO

Hannah
like ~'s heart HARD

"Hannah ___ Her Sisters" AND

"Hannah and ___ Sisters" HER

"Hannah and Her Sisters"
~ actor CAINE
~ director ALLEN

"Hannah, Won't You Open That ___?" DOOR

Hannibal
~ crossed them ALPS

Hannigan, Miss
~ charge ANNIE

Hanoi CITY
New Year in ~ TET

Hanover CITY
see also German

Hans ARP
see also German

Hansel
see German

"Hansel and Gretel" OPERA
~ prop OVEN

hansom CAB

haole
~ greeting ALOHA
gift for a ~ LEI

"___ Hap-Hap-Happy Day" ITSA

haphazard POOR

hapless POOR, SAD

happen ARRIVE, OCCUR
~ next ENSUE
~ upon HIT, MEET
bound to ~ SURE
let ~ ALLOW
make ~ CAUSE

happening AFOOT, CASE, FACT, GALA, LIVE
~ now LIVE
important ~ EVENT
keep from ~ AVERT

___ happens (incidentally) ASIT

happenstance EVENT

happi ___ COAT

happify ELATE

"...happily ___ after" EVER

happiness GLEE, GOOD
fill with ~ ELATE
paradigm of ~ CLAM
sounds of ~ AHS

happy GAY, GLAD, RAPT
~ as a clam ELATED, RIANT
~ feeling GLEE
~ medium MEAN
~ sighs AHS
~ starter SLAP
look ~ GRIN, SMILE
make ~ ELATE, PLEASE
put on a ~ face GRIN

happy ___ HOUR

happy ___ clam ASA

Happy
~ associate DOC

"Happy ___, The" ORGAN, YEARS

"Happy ___ of Oceania, The" ISLES

"___ Happy" GIRL, LOVE

happy as a ___ CLAM, LARK

"___ Happy Breed" THIS

"Happy Days"
~ type TEEN

"Happy Days Are Here Again"
~ composer AGER

"___ Happy Feeling" THIS

"___ Happy Fella, The" MOST

happy hour
~ establishment BAR
~ order ALE, BEER, LAGER, WINE

"Happy New ___" YEAR

"Happy Trails"
~ singer DALE, EVANS, ROY

Hapsburg
see German

Harald III
city founded by ~ in 1050 OSLO

Harald, King
~ father OLAF, OLAV

harangue LACE, LASH, NAG, ORATE, RANT, RAVE, TALK

Harare CITY

harass BAIT, BESET, FRET, IRK, NAG, PEEVE, PRESS, RAG, RIDE, TEASE, UPSET

Harbach OTTO

harbinger OMEN

harbor BAY, HAVEN, HIDE, MOLE, PORT
~ alcove INLET
~ boat TUG
~ expert PILOT
~ locale COVE
~ position ALEE
~ sound TOOT
~ vessel SCOW
out of the ~ ASEA, ATSEA
safe ~ HAVEN

harbor ___ SEAL

___ Harbor, Maine BAR

___ Harbor, N.Y. SAG

___ Harbour, Fla. BAL

hard DOUR, IRON
~ approach SELL
~ by CLOSE, NEAR
~ candy DROP
~ core CADRE
~ drinker SOT
~ ender PAN, TOP, WARE
~ feelings ANGER

~ labor TOIL
~ metal IRON, STEEL
~ money CASH
~ nut to crack POSER
~ outer covering SHELL
~ question POSER
~ rain SPATE
~ roll BAGEL
~ stuff METAL
~ to believe TALL
~ to come by SPARSE
~ to find RARE
~ to get to DENSE
~ to grasp DEEP, EELY
~ up NEEDY, POOR
~ water ICE
~ work LABOR, TASK, TOIL
~ worker DEMON, DOER
bear ~ upon COST
blow ~ BRAG
breathe ~ GASP, PANT
come down ~ POUR, RAIN, TEEM
hit ~ BELT, MOVE, PASTE, SLAM
hit ~, as raindrops PELT
hit the floor ~ STAMP
laugh ~ ROAR
look ~ PEER, STARE
not ~ EASY
rain ~ POUR
ride ~ POST, SPUR
shut ~ SLAM
study ~ CRAM
take a long ~ look PORE
think ~ RACK
try ~ EXERT
work ~ LABOR, SLAVE, SLOG, TOIL

hard ___ CIDER, COAL, CORE, HAT, LENS, LINE, NEWS, PUT, SELL, WATER

hard ___ rock ASA

hard ___ to crack, a NUT

hard-___ BOIL, EDGED, HAT, LINER, NOSED, SHELL

"Hard ___ Night, A" DAYS

"___ Hard" DIE

hard-and-___ rule FAST

hard as ___ NAILS

"Hard Copy"
~ network CBS

harden ADAPT, BAKE, CAKE, DRY, GEL, SEAR, SET
~ one's heart STEEL
~ (to) ENURE, INURE

hardened
~ skin HORN

hard-fought CLOSE

hardhearted CRUEL, STERN

"Hard Hearted Hannah"
~ composer AGER

Harding ANN
~ home OHIO
~ maneuver AXEL

"Hard Lines"
~ poet NASH

hard-luck
~ case LOSER

hardly ___ (rarely) EVER

"Hardly ___ is now alive..." AMAN

hardness
~ model NAIL

hard-packed DENSE

"Hard Road to Glory, A"
~ author ASHE

hard-shell CLAM, CRAB

hardship ONUS, RIGOR, TRIAL

"Hard to ___" GET

"Hard to Kill"
~ actor SEGAL

hardtop MOTOR, SEDAN

hardware
~ item AWL, NAIL, NUT

Hardwicke
~ title SIR

"___ Hard With a Vengeance" DIE

hardwood ASH, CEDAR, EBONY, ELM, MAPLE, OAK, TEAK

hardy FIT, HALE, IRON

Hardy ANDY, OLLIE
~ character TESS
~ villain ALEC

"Hardy Boys"
~ character CHET

hare ANIMAL, HIE, RACE, RUN, SPEED
~ and hounds GAME
female ~ DOE
like a March ~ MAD
mad as a March ~ DAFT
the ~ LOSER

harebrained DAFT, MAD

harem
~ room ODA

hares
~ to hounds PREY

"___ Hari" MATA

haricot BEAN

Hari, Mata SPY

hark HEAR

harken ATTEND, HEAR

"___ Harker" SARD

"Harlan County, ___" USA

Harlem
~ theater APOLLO

harlequin ___ OPAL

"Harlequin's Carnival, The"
~ painter MIRO

Harley
~ **to some** BIKE, HOG

harm ABUSE, BANE, COST, ILL, MAIM, MAR, SIN, SPOIL, TAINT
~ **in French** MAL
out of ~'s way ALEE, SAFE
source of ~ BANE

harmful BAD, EVIL, ILL

harmfully ILL

harmless SAFE, TAME

Harmonia
~ **father** ARES

harmonica
~ **part** REED

harmonious ONE
~ **relationship** SYNC
make ~ TUNE

harmoniousness CALM

harmonium ORGAN

harmonize AGREE, FIT, MESH, PHASE, SING, SUIT, TUNE

harmony LOVE, ORDER, PEACE, SYNC, TUNE
~ **part** ALTO, BASS, TENOR
in ~ ATONE

harness GEAR, TAME
~ **part** BIT, STRAP
~ **piece** REIN
~ **sharers** TEAM
~ **strap** TRACE

harness racing
~ **gait** TROT
~ **horse** PACER

Harold ARLEN, EVANS, ROME, TEEN, UREY

"Harold ___ Maude" AND

harp CARP, NAG
~ **at** BORE
~ **cousin** LYRE
~ **on** STRESS
~ **player** ANGEL
~ **starter** AUTO
ancient ~ LYRE

harp ___ SEAL

harper BARD

Harper LEE, TESS
~ **partner** ROW

"Harper's Bazaar"
~ **illustrator** ERTE

Harpers Ferry
~ **event** RAID

"Harper's Weekly"
~ **cartoonist** NAST

Harper Valley
~ **org.** PTA

"Harper Valley ___" PTA

"Harper Valley P.T.A."
~ **actress** EDEN

harplike
~ **instrument** LYRE

harpoon LANCE, PIKE, SPEAR

"Harp Weaver, The" POEM

harpy DEMON, HAG, NAG, OGRE

harquebus GUN

harrier BIRD, RACER

Harriet AUNT, SPY
~ **to Ricky** MOM

"Harrigan"
~ **songwriter** COHAN

Harris LOU, MEL, NEIL
~ **and others** EDS
~ **title** BRER

Harrisburg
~ **st.** PENN

Harris, Ed
~ **film, with "The"** ABYSS

Harris, Joel Chandler
monicker from ~ BRER

Harris, Mrs. Phil ALICE

Harrison REX
~ **in "Star Wars"** HAN

Harrison, Rex SIR
~ **son** NOEL

harrow COMB, DIG, DRAG, PLOW, RACK, RAKE, TILL
~ **blade** DISC

Harrow
~ **rival** ETON

harrowing BAD, DIRE

"Harrumph!" AHEM

harry BAIT, FRET, RAG, RIDE, TEASE

Harry LIME
~ **successor** IKE
First Lady for ~ BESS
Light-Horse ~ LEE

"Harry ___ Tonto" AND

"Harry and ___" SON, TONTO

Harry, Prince
~ **aunt** ANNE

harsh ACID, ACRID, BAD, CRUEL, DOUR, HARD, IRON, RUDE, STERN
~ **chemical** ACID
~ **criticism** SLAM
~ **cry** CAW
~ **light** GLARE

harshness EDGE, RIGOR

harsh-sounding LOUD

hart ANIMAL, DEER, MALE, STAG

Hart CRANE, MOSS

Hartack BILL

Harte BRET

hartebeest ANIMAL
~ **kin** GNU

Hartley BOB, HAL

___-Hartley Act TAFT

Hartman LISA, PHIL

Hart, Moss
~ **book** ACTI

hart's-tongue FERN

harum-scarum LOOSE, MAD, RASH

haruspex SEER

Harvard
~ **deg.** MBA
~ **neighbor** MIT
~ **quadrangle** YARD
~ **rival** YALE

Harvarder
~ **rival** ELI

harvest CROP, CUT, REAP, TAKE, YIELD
~ **goddess** CERES, OPS
paper-company ~ TREES

harvest ___ HOME, MOON

harvester
run a ~ REAP

harvest moon
~ **mo.** OCT

Harvey PAUL

Harz RANGE

has-___ BEEN

Hasbrouck ___, N.J. HTS

hasenpfeffer MEAT, STEW

hash MESS, OLIO, STEW
~ **over** ARGUE
~ **slinger** CHEF
have some ~ EAT
make a ~ of SPOIL

hashhouse
~ **client** EATER
~ **order** EGGS
~ **sign** EATS
~ **vegetable** TATER

"___ has it..." RUMOR

Haskell EDDIE

"___ Has Landed, The" EAGLE

"Has 1001 ___!" USES

hasp CLASP

hassle IRK, PEEVE, RILE, ROW, SPAT, TRIAL, UPSET

hassock SEAT

"Hasta la vista" ADIOS

haste SPEED
~ **product** WASTE
make ~ HIE, PRESS, RACE, RUN, SPEED
wed in ~ ELOPE

"Haste makes waste" ADAGE

hasten AID, DART, DASH, HIE, RACE, RUN, SHOOT, SPEED, SPUR, TEAR, URGE
~ **off** FLEE

hastily FAST

"Hast thou ___ the Jabberwock?" SLAIN

hasty FAST, RAPID, RASH
~ **departure** LAM
~ **pudding** PAP
beat a ~ retreat FLEE, RUN

hat CAP, LID
~ **holder** HEAD
~ **material** FELT, STRAW
~ **tipper's word** MAAM
~ **tree** RACK
flat ~ TAM
French ~ BERET
jaunty ~ TAM
old ~ BANAL, DATED, PASSE, STALE, TRITE
pass the ~ BEG
soft ~ BERET
talk through one's ~ LIE

hat ___ TREE

___ hat BRASS, OLD, OPERA, SILK, STRAW, TOP

___-hat HARD

"___ Hat" TOP

hatch BEAR, BREW, COIN, DOOR, ETCH, EXIT, GATE, PLOT, SET, SIT
~ **starter** NUT

hatchback AUTO, CAR
~ **cousin** SEDAN

Hatcher TERI
~ **costar** CAIN

Hatcher, Teri
~ **TV role** LANE, LOIS

hatchery
~ **sound** PEEP
~ **unit** EGG

hatchet AXE, HACK, TOOL
do a ~ job on LIBEL, SLUR
use a ~ CHOP, CUT, HEW

hatchet ___ MAN

hatchling
~ **home** NEST

Hatch, Orrin
~ **org.** SEN
~ **state** UTAH

hatchway DOOR

hate ABHOR
~ **opposite** LOVE

hateful BAD, BASE, EVIL, MEAN
be ~ REPEL

hater
company ~ LONER

Hatfield
~ **to a McCoy** ENEMY, FOE

Hatfields CLAN

"Hatful of ___, A" RAIN

hatha-___ YOGA

Hathaway ANNE
~ **on Steve Allen's show** NYE

hat in ___ HAND

hatred SPITE
  ~ (prefix) MIS

hat room
  ~ fixture PEG

Hatter
  like Alice's ~ MAD

Hatteras CAPE

Hatterlike MAD

hat trick
  part of a ~ GOAL

hauberk ARMOR, MAIL

haughtiness AIRS, PRIDE

haughty ALOOF, REGAL, VAIN
  ~ person SNOB
  be ~ SNUB

haul BEAR, CART, DRAG, DRAW,
  LOAD, LUG, TOTE, TUG
  ~ away TOW
  ~ in ARREST, NAB
  ~ logs SKID
  ~ over the coals ROAST
  heist ~ LOOT
  long ~ TREK
  pirate's ~ SWAG
  robber's ~ LOOT

haul ___ (withdraw) OFF

___ haul LONG

hauler
  cargo ~ VAN
  coal ~ TRAM
  firewood ~ CART
  freight ~ SEMI
  trash ~ SCOW

haulm STEM

haunch HIP

haunt DEN, LAIR, NEST

haunted EERIE, EERY

"Haunted ___, The" MESA

haunted house
  ~ sound MOAN

haunting EERIE, EERY

"Haunting, The"
  ~ director WISE

hautboy OBOE, PIPE, REED

haute ___ ECOLE

haute couture
  ~ designer DIOR
  ~ magazine ELLE

___ Haute, Ind. TERRE

hauteur AIRS, PRIDE

haut monde ELITE

Havana CITY, PORT
  ~ locale CUBA
  see also Spanish

"Havana"
  ~ actress OLIN

___ Havasu City LAKE

have EAT, GET, HOLD, OWN
  ~ a ball ROMP

~ a bawl WEEP
~ a birthday AGE
~ a bug AIL
~ a crush on ADORE, LIKE
~ a hangover ACHE
~ a long face MOPE
~ a look at EYE, SEE
~ a part ACT
~ a role to play ACT
~ at one's fingertips KNOW
~ a yearning ACHE
~ bills OWE
~ coming EARN, MERIT
~ dealings with KNOW
~ dinner EAT
~ down cold KNOW
~ efficacy AVAIL
~ importance RATE
~ markers out OWE
~ no doubts KNOW
~ pain ACHE
~ relevance RELATE
~ sore muscles ACHE
~ sympathy FEEL
~ the blahs AIL
~ the hang of KNOW
~ the nerve DARE
~ the same tense AGREE
~ vitality LIVE
~ words ARGUE
~ words with SPAR

have ___ at (try) AGO

have ___ good authority ITON

have ___ in one's bonnet ABEE

have ___ of NONE

have ___ to the ground ANEAR

"Have ___ news for you!" IGOT

"Have ___ Will Travel" GUN

have a ___ BALL

have a ___ for news NOSE

have a ___ in one's bonnet BEE

have a ___ to pick BONE

"Have a ___" SEAT

"Have a ___ day!" NICE

have a go ___ (try) ATIT

"Have a nice ___!" DAY

"Have Gun Will Travel"
  ~ actor BOONE

have it ___ MADE, OUT

"___ have it, The" AYES

Havelock ELLIS

haven LAIR, OASIS, PORT, REST

have one's cake and eat it ___
  TOO

have one's heart ___ SETON

haversack BAG, KIT

haves ELITE

"___ Have to Do Is Dream" ALLI

have too many ___ in the fire
  IRONS

"Have you ___ wool?" ANY

"Have you two ___?" MET

having
  not ~ (suffix) LESS

"___ Having a Baby" SHES

"Having My Baby"
  ~ singer ANKA

havoc HARM, RUIN
  wreak ~ RAGE
  wreak ~ upon RAID, RUIN,
  UNDO, WASTE

"___ 'Havoc'" CRY

Havoline
  ~ competitor STP

Havre
  see French

haw
  ~ cousins ERS
  ~ direction LEFT
  ~ opposite GEE
  ~ partner HEM
  hem and ~ AVOID, EVADE,
  HANG, STALL

Haw.
  ~ once TER, TERR
  see also Hawaii

"___ Haw" HEE

Hawaii ISLE, STATE
  ~ (abbr.) ISL
  ~ feast LUAU
  ~ handout LEI
  ~ neckpiece LEI
  ~ once TER, TERR
  ~ port HILO
  ~ state bird NENE
  city in ~ HILO
  first governor of ~ DOLE
  hi in ~ ALOHA
  major employer in ~ DOLE
  shalom in ~ ALOHA

"Hawaii" SAGA

"Hawaii ___-O" FIVE

"___ Hawaii" BLUE

Hawaiian
  ~ carving material LAVA
  ~ cookout LUAU
  ~ dance HULA
  ~ dish POI
  ~ feast LUAU
  ~ goose NENE
  ~ instrument UKE
  ~ island LANAI, OAHU
  ~ souvenir LEI
  "Goodbye!" in ~ ALOHA
  "Hello!" in ~ ALOHA
  long, in ~ LOA

"Hawaiian ___" EYE

"Hawaiian ___ Chant" WAR

Hawaiian Punch
  ~ rival HIC

Hawaiians
  one of the ~ ISLE

Hawaii County
  ~ seat HILO

"Hawaii Five-O"
  ~ locale OAHU
  Jack of ~ LORD

hawk BIRD, CRY, SELL, VEND
  ~ home AERIE, NEST
  ~ opposite DOVE
  forked-tailed ~ KITE

hawk-___ EYED

"___ Hawk, The" SEA

Hawke ETHAN

Hawkeye
  ~ milieu MASH
  ~ portrayer ALAN, ALDA

Hawkeye State IOWA

Hawkins SADIE

Hawkins, Anthony SIR

___ Hawkins Day SADIE

hawks
  like ~ AVIAN

Hawks FIVE, TEAM
  ~ city ATLANTA
  ~ loc. ATL
  ~ org. NBA
  former home of the ~ OMNI

hawkshaw TEC

Hawkyns, John SIR

hawser CABLE, LINE, ROPE
  ~ bend KNOT

hawthorn TREE

Hawthorne
  ~ town SALEM
  ~ vehicle ESSAY

hay STRAW
  ~ bundle BALE
  ~ ender RIDE, WIRE
  ~ morsel AWN
  cut ~ MOW
  hit the ~ BED, SLEEP
  make ~ BALE

___ hay MAKE

"___ Hay" ANTIC

Hayden, Tom
  ~ 1960s org. SDS

Haydn
  ~ nickname PAPA

Hayes HELEN, ISAAC

Hayes, Rutherford B.
  ~ feature BEARD

hayfork TOOL

hayloft MOW
  ~ locale BARN

Haymarket Square
  ~ event RIOT

hayseed BOOR, OAF, RUBE

haystack
  ~ item NEEDLE

"Haystack at Giverny"
  ~ painter MONET

"Haystacks"
  ~ painter MONET

haywire AMOK

Hayworth RITA

hazard BET, DARE, GAME, PERIL, RISK, STAKE
  ~ a guess OPINE
  Arctic ~ BERG, FLOE
  boating ~ SNAG
  dolphin ~ NET
  driving ~ GLARE, ICE, MIST, SLEET
  fairway ~ TRAP
  golf ~ TRAP
  highway ~ ESS
  letter-carrier's ~ BITE
  links ~ TRAP
  marine ~ REEF
  navigational ~ BERG, FLOE, REEF, SHOAL
  road ~ ICE
  visibility ~ MIST
  winter ~ ICE, SLEET

hazardous ICY
  not ~ SAFE

haze MIST, SMOG

hazel COLOR

Hazel MAID

hazy DIM
  become ~ BLUR

HCl ACID

he MAN
  not ~ SHE

he- MAN

He ELEM
  2 for ~ ATNO

"He ___ Gets Slapped" WHO

"He ___ heavy..." AINT

"He ___ Me" NEEDS

head BOSS, DOME, FIRST, FOAM, LEAD, NOB, POLL, RULE
  ~ away EBB
  ~ covering CAP, HAIR, HAT, HOOD, SCARF, TAM
  ~ ender ACHE, BAND, DRESS, FIRST, GEAR, HUNT, LAMP, LINE, LONG, PHONE, REST, ROOM, SET, STAND
  ~ (for) AIM
  ~ for the bottom SINK
  ~ for the hills FLEE, LAM, RUN
  ~ honcho BOSS, EXEC
  ~ hurt ACHE
  ~ in French TETE
  ~ off AVERT
  ~ of state RULER
  ~ of the class BEST
  ~ opposite TAIL
  ~ out EXIT, LEAVE
  ~ part EAR, EYE, LIP, NOSE
  ~ start EDGE
  ~ starter AIR, ARROW, BONE, EGG, FORE, HARD, HOT,

MEAT, OVER, PIN, RAIL, RED, SORE, TOW
  ~ stroke PAT
  ~ support NECK
  ~ the cast STAR
  ~ up LEAD, RUN
  a ~ EACH, PER
  ale ~ FOAM
  bald ~ DOME
  be ~ and shoulders above SHINE
  beer ~ FOAM
  bend the ~ NOD
  big ~ EGO
  cathedral ~ DEAN
  chapter ~ DEAN
  comet's ~ COMA
  corporate ~ CEO
  crowned ~ LORD, RULER
  enter one's ~ OCCUR
  faculty ~ DEAN
  from ~ to foot OVER
  get in one's ~ CON, LEARN
  go head to ~ VIE
  go ~ over heels FLIP, SLIP
  had in one's ~ KNEW
  have in one's ~ LEARN
  hit someone upside the ~ BEAT
  incline the ~ NOD
  it's over your ~ HAIR, ROOF
  keep one's ~ above water TREAD
  lose one's ~ PANIC
  make one's ~ swim AWE, STUN
  meet ~ on DARE
  monastery ~ ABBE, ABBOT
  off the top of one's ~ ADLIB
  prehistoric axe ~ CELT
  roof over one's ~ ABODE, HOME
  shower ~ JET
  stick one's ~ out EMERGE
  swelled ~ EGO
  talk one's ~ off BORE
  top of one's ~ PATE
  Vatican ~ POPE

head ___ START, TRIP

head ___ (avert) OFF

head ___ heels OVER

Head EDITH

headache PEST
  pool-owner's ~ ALGAE

headband cord
  Arab ~ AGAL

headcheese MEAT

headdress
  glittering ~ TIARA
  part of pharaoh's ~ ASP

___-headed COOL

"___-Headed Woman" RED

headfirst
  reach base ~ SLIDE

headgear CAP, HAT
  artist's ~ BERET
  heavenly ~ HALO
  Highlands ~ TAM

queenly ~ TIARA
  see also hat

heading
  box-score column ~ HRS
  calendar ~ APR, AUG, DEC, FRI, MAR, MON, NOV, OCT, SAT, SEPT, SUN, WED
  list ~ TODO
  nautical ~ ALEE
  ship ~ ENE, ESE, NNE, NNW, SSE, SSW, WNW, WSW
  textbook ~ UNIT

headland CAPE, NESS

headless
  ~ statue TORSO

headlight LAMP
  ~ setting DIM

headline LEAD, STAR

headliner LEAD, STAR
  show-biz ~ STAR
  Vegas ~ ANKA

"Headlines"
  ~ comic LENO

headlong APACE, RAPID, RASH
  ~ rush RUN
  rush ~ STORM

headmost FORE

head-on
  meet ~ HIT, RAM

headpiece SCARF
  ritzy ~ TIARA

headquarters BASE, SEAT, SITE

heads
  ~ alternative TAILS
  family ~ MAS, PAS
  Hydra's ~ NINE
  make ~ or tails of LEARN
  sculpted ~ island EASTER

headset EARS, PHONE

heads or ___ TAILS

head-splitting LOUD

headstrong RASH

heads-up ALERT

head-supporting
  ~ vertebra ATLAS

"Head to ___" TOE

headway DENT, GAIN
  make ~ MOVE
  make ~ against STEM

headwear
  holy ~ HALO
  ornate ~ TIARA
  Scot's ~ TAM
  see also hat

heal CURE, KNIT, MEND, RESTORE

healer DOC
  ~ org. AMA
  horse ~ VET

Healey
  ~ and others EDS

healing
  ~ ointment BALM
  ~ plant ALOE
  ~ waters SPA
  sign of ~ SCAB

health
  ~ club SPA
  ~ food BRAN, KELP
  ~ org. FDA
  drink to someone's ~ TOAST
  good ~ ASSET
  nurse back to ~ RESTORE
  restore to ~ CURE, MEND

health ___ SPA

health care
  ~ personnel AIDE, RNS

health food
  ~ purchase TOFU
  ~ store buy KELP

healthful
  ~ intake amt. RDA
  ~ lunch SALAD

healthy CLEAN, FIT, GOOD, HALE, PERT, SANE

healthy-looking ROSY

"He and ___" SHE

heap AUTO, CAR, CRATE, MASS, MOTOR, PILE, RAFT
  ~ dirt upon LIBEL, TAINT
  ~ kudos on LAUD
  ~ on LOAD
  ~ up AMASS
  disorderly ~ MESS
  smelter's ~ SLAG
  top of the ~ ACME, AONE, BEST, ELITE

___ heap SCRAP

heaps ALOT, LOTS, OCEAN, SEA

hear SENSE
  ~ a case TRY
  ~ of ALLOW, LEARN, LET
  so all can ~ ALOUD

hearable ALOUD

hearing SENSE
  ~ organ EAR
  of ~ AURAL, OTIC

"Hear My ___" SONG

"Hear no ___..." EVIL

hearsay DIRT, NEWS, RUMOR, TALK

heart CORE, ESSENCE, EYE, GIST, GRIT, LOVE, MEAT, MIDST, ORGAN, SOUL, SUM
  ~ and soul ESSENCE
  ~ chambers ATRIA
  ~ ender ACHE, BEAT, FELT, LAND
  ~ hurt ACHE
  ~ of the matter CORE, GIST
  ~ outlet AORTA
  ~ rate PULSE
  do one's ~ good PLEASE
  harden one's ~ STEEL
  learn by ~ CON
  learned by ~ KNEW
  lose ~ MOPE

Heart

lose one's ~ to LOVE
not have the ~ HATE
set one's ~ on LONG
sick at ~ SAD
soft spot in one's ~ LOVE
take ~ HOPE
take to ~ HEED
to the ~ HOME
touch one's ~ MELT
wear one's ~ on one's
  sleeve ADORE
where the ~ is HOME

Heart
  1987 song by ~ ALONE

"Heart ___ Lonely Hunter, The"
  ISA

"___ Heart" DEAR

"___ Heart, The" EATEN

heartache CARE, WOE

"___ Heartache" ITSA

"Heart and ___" SOUL

heartbeat PULSE

"___ Heartbeats, The" FIVE

heartbreak WOE

"Heartbreak ___" HOTEL

"Heartbreak ___, The" KID

"Heartbreak House"
  ~ heroine ELLIE
  ~ playwright SHAW

heartbreaking BAD, SAD

"Heartbreak Kid, The"
  ~ director MAY

heartburn
  cause of ~ GAS

___-hearted BIG, FALSE, WARM

hearten ELATE

heartfelt DEAR, DEEP, KEEN,
  REAL, WARM

hearth GRATE
  ~ and home ABODE
  ~ residue ASH
  like an unswept ~ ASHY
  Roman ~ protector LAR

___-hearth OPEN

heartland
  ~ unit ACRE

heartless CRUEL
  ~ one BEAST, OGRE

"Heart of Dixie" ALA

heartrending BAD

hearts GAME, SUIT
  two ~ BID

heart's
  ~ desire LOVE

Hearts
  Knave of ~ booty TART
  Queen of ~ pastry TART

"Hearts ___" AFIRE

"Hearts ___ Minds" AND

"Hearts Afire"
  ~ actor ASNER

heart's-ease PANSY

heartsick LOW, SAD
  be ~ ACHE

"Hearts of the ___" WEST

heartstrings
  tug on the ~ MOVE, STIR

**"___ Hearts Were Young and
  Gay"** OUR

heartthrob LOVE

heart-to-heart CHAT, OPEN

hearty FIT, WARM
  ~ entrée STEW
  ~ laugh ROAR
  ~ meal STEAK
  ~ partner HALE
  hale and ~ FIT
  party ~ REVEL

heat ARDOR, BAKE, BOIL, FIRE,
  RACE, STRESS, WARM
  ~ conductor COIL
  ~ source COAL, SUN
  ~ unit BTU, CAL
  ~ up WARM
  ~ water BOIL
  dead ~ DRAW, TIE
  emotional ~ ANGER
  feel the ~ BASK
  join with ~ FUSE
  mind's ~ ARDOR
  prickly ~ RASH
  put the ~ on MAKE
  shriveled from ~ DRY, SERE
  source of ~ FIRE
  take the ~ off EASE

heat-___ SEAL

Heat FIVE, TEAM
  ~ home MIAMI
  ~ org. NBA

"Heat"
  ~ director MANN

"___ Heat" CITY

"___ Heat, The" BIG

heated HOT, IRATE, UPSET, WARM
  ~ tub SPA

heater GAT, GUN, ROD
  apartment ~ STEAM
  cone-shaped ~ ETNA
  gangster's ~ GAT
  lab ~ ETNA
  pack a ~ TOTE

___ heater SPACE

heath DESERT, LAND, MOOR
  ~ genus ERICA

**___ Heath (Philo Vance
  colleague)** SGT

Heathcliff CAT, PET

heather COLOR, ERICA
  where ~ grows MOOR

Heathrow
  ~ arr. SST

heating
  ~ fuel COAL, OIL

___ heating SOLAR, STEAM

"Heat of the Moment"
  ~ band ASIA

heaume ARMOR

heave CAST, GASP, HAUL, HURL,
  LOB, LUG, PANT, PELT, RAISE,
  TOSS

heave-ho BOOT, SACK
  give the ~ AXE, CAN, FIRE,
  OUST

heaven
  ~ on earth EDEN
  like ~ ABOVE
  made in ~ IDEAL
  queen of ~ HERA
  vault of ~ BLUE

heaven-___ SENT

___ heaven HOG

"Heaven ___ Us" HELP

"Heaven ___ Wait" CAN

___ heaven and earth MOVE

"Heaven Can ___" WAIT

heavenly
  ~ body, to a poet ORB

heavenly ___ (ice cream flavor)
  HASH

heavens ETHER, SKY
  the ~, to a poet ETHER

"Heavens!" EGAD

"___ Heaven's Sake" FOR

"Heavens to Betsy!" EGAD

heavenward ABOVE

heavier-than-___ AIR

heavily HARD

heaviness PALL

heavy BAD, BIG, CLOSE, DEEP,
  DENSE, FAT, LARGE, OBESE,
  RICH, SOBER
  ~ book TOME
  ~ chain ROPE
  ~ in a way DEEP
  ~ load ONUS
  ~ metal ARMOR, BRASS, IRON,
    LEAD
  ~ sound THUD
  ~ threads ARRAY, DRESS, SUIT
  ~ weight TON
  ~ winds STORM
  have a ~ foot SPEED

"heavy"
  ~ music METAL

heavy ___ CREAM, METAL, WATER

___-heavy TOP

heavy-handed
  ~ hoodlum APE

heavy-hearted BLUE, LOW, SAD

heavy hydrogen
  ~ discoverer UREY

heavy-laden SAD

heavy machinery
  ~ maker CASE

heavyset BIG, LARGE

heavyweight
  former ~ champ ALI, CLAY

hebdomad WEEK

Hebe
  brother of ~ ARES

Hebrew
  ~ dance HORA
  ~ feast SEDER
  ~ judge ELI
  ~ king SAUL
  ~ law TORAH
  ~ letter NUN, SHIN, SIN
  ~ month ADAR
  ~ months ABS
  ~ priest AARON
  ~ prophet AMOS, ELIAS, EZRA,
    HOSEA, MOSES
  ~ queen ESTHER
  ~ tribe LEVI

Hebrides
  ~ island IONA, SKYE
  ~ language ERSE
  see also Scottish

___ Hebrides INNER, OUTER

Hebron
  ~ grp. PLO

Heche ANNE

Hecht BEN

heck DRAT

heckelphone OBOE

Heckerling AMY

heckle BAIT, GIBE, HISS, NEEDLE,
  RAG, RIDE

heckler PEST
  ~ missile EGG

hectare
  ~ cousin ACRE

hectic HOT, RED

hector BAIT, FRET, NAG, RIDE,
  TEASE, TREAD

Hector HERO
  ~ home TROY
  Astyanax, to ~ SON
  when ~ was a pup PAST

Hecuba
  ~ home TROY
  Paris, to ~ SON

"Hedda Gabler"
  ~ author IBSEN

hedge EVADE
  prune the ~ SNIP, TRIM

hedged
  ~ in PENT
  thing to be ~ BET

hedgehog ANIMAL
~ **cousin** MOLE
video-game ~ SONIC

hedger LIAR

Hedin, Sven SWEDE

"He done ___ wrong..." HER

"___ he drove out of sight..." ERE

"Hee ___" HAW

heed ATTEND, CARE, OBEY
~ **the alarm** RISE
giving no ~ DEAF
pay ~ **to** TEND
take ~ HEAR

heedful ALERT

heedfulness CARE

heedless DEAF, RASH

hee-haw BRAY

"Hee Haw"
~ **humor** CORN
~ **mascot** ASS

heel CUR, END, LEAN, LIST, LOUSE, STERN, TAG
~ **attachment** TAP
~ **over** LIST
~ **partner** SOLE

___ Heel (North Carolinian) TAR

heel-and-___ TOE

heeler
ward ~ POL

___ heeler WARD

heels
at one's ~ CLOSE
cool one's ~ WAIT
down at the ~ NEEDY, SEEDY
go head over ~ SLIP, TRIP
it has two ~ LOAF
on the ~ **of** AFTER
show one's ~ FLEE, HIE, RUN
take to one's ~ DESERT, HIE, RUN
tread upon the ~ **of** TAG

Heflin VAN

Hefner, Hugh
~ **prop** PIPE

heft RAISE

hefty BIG, LARGE
~ **chunk** SLAB

Hefty
~ **rival** GLAD

hegemonic FIRST

hegira EXIT

"He Got Game"
~ **director** LEE

Heidelberg ___ MAN

Heiden ERIC

Heidi
~ **home** ALPS

heifer COW
~ **milieu** LEA

Heifetz
teacher of ~ AUER

height ACME, APEX, PEAK, TIP, TOP
~ **(abbr.)** ALT, ELEV
~ **extender** STILT
~ **of fashion** HEM, RAGE
~ **of one's power** DAY
~ **(prefix)** ALTI
~ **to a cager** ASSET
Denver's ~ MILE
rocky ~ CRAG, TOR

heighten ADORN, EXALT, RAISE, STRESS

heights ACME
reach new ~ SOAR

"Heimskringla" SAGA

Hein MEL

Heine, Heinrich POET
see also poet

heinous BAD, DIRE, EVIL, LOW, UGLY, VILE

Heinrich
see German

Heinsohn TOM

Heinz
see German

heir SCION
~ **ender** ESS
~ **homophone** AIR, ERE
~ **legacy** ESTATE
~ **perhaps** SON
the ills that flesh is ~ **to** LIFE

heirloom RELIC

heirs ISSUE
proverbial ~ MEEK

Heisler, Stuart
~ **film of 1949** TULSA

Heisman Trophy AWARD

Heiss CAROL

heist CAPER, ROB, STEAL
~ **haul** LOOT
~ **take** HAUL

Hekawi
the ~**, in "F Troop"** TRIBE

"___ He Kissed Me" THEN

held
~ **fast** RAPT
~ **up** LATE

___-held HAND

Held ANNA

"___ Heldenleben" EIN

Helen
~ **abductor** PARIS
~ **beloved** PARIS
~ **in Spanish** ELENA
~ **mother** LEDA

"Helen ___" TRENT

Helena
~ **rival** ESTEE

Hélène
see French

Helene Curtis
~ **rival** AVON

Helen of ___ TROY

helicon HORN

helicopter
~ **part** ROTOR

Helios GOD, SUN
~ **to the Romans** SOL

heliotrope COLOR

heliport
~ **site, often** ROOF

helium GAS
like ~ INERT

helix COIL, LOOP

hell
~ **denizen** DEMON
~ **feature** FIRE
~ **to Sherman** WAR
getting the ~ **out** LAM
when ~ **freezes over** NEVER

hellbent
go ~ **for leather** RIP, SPEED, TEAR

Hellenic
see Greek

Helles CAPE

hellhound DEMON, OGRE

hellion BRAT, IMP

"Hell Is ___ Heroes" FOR

hellish BAD, CRUEL, EVIL

Hellman MONTE
locale of ~**'s toys** ATTIC

hello ALOHA, CRY
say ~ GREET, NOD
sea dog's ~ AHOY

"Hello!" AHOY, ALOHA

"Hello Again"
~ **actress** LONG, NYE

"Hello, Dolly!"
~ **role** LEVI

Hell's ___ ANGEL

Hells Canyon
~ **state** IDAHO

"Hellzapoppin'"
~ **actor** OLSEN
~ **actress** RAYE
Chic's ~ **partner** OLE

helm REINS
~ **position** ALEE
take the ~ LEAD, STEER

Helm MATT

Helmer, Nora
~ **creator** IBSEN

Helmer, Torvald
~ **wife** NORA

helmet ARMOR
~ **plume** CREST
pith ~ HAT

"___ Helmet, The" STEEL

Helm, Matt SPY

Helms, Jesse
~ **org.** SEN

Helmsley LEONA

helmsman PILOT
~ **direction** ALEE

Helmut
see German

Heloise
~ **tidbit** HINT

Héloïse
see French

helot LIEGE, SERF, SLAVE
~ **cousin** ESNE

he loves
~ **in Latin** AMAT

help ABET, AID, ASSET, AVAIL, ENABLE, SERVE
~ **a borrower** LEND
~ **a waiter** BUS
~ **for the needy** ALMS
~ **in crime** ABET
~ **oneself to** ROB, TAKE
~ **with a line** CUE
~ **with the dishes** DRY
~ **with the salad** TOSS
actor's ~ CUE
ask for ~**, in a way** PRAY
be of ~ AVAIL
one of the ~ MAID, VALET
puzzle ~ HINT
wire for ~ SOS
without ~ ALONE

___-help SELF

"Help!" SOS
~ **in French** AMOI

"___ Help" ICAN

helper AIDE
~ **(abbr.)** ASST
exec's ~ STENO
holiday ~ ELF
nurse's ~ AIDE
shoemaker's ~ ELF

helpful GOOD, UTILE
~ **hint** TIP
be ~ AID
give a ~ **hint** STEER

helping DISH, PLATE
~ **hand** AID
~ **of pie** SLICE

helpless
~ **one** LAMB

"___ Help Lovin' Dat Man" CANT

helpmate LADY, LOVE

helpmeet BRIDE, MATE

help-wanted
~ **notice** SOS
~ **notices** ADS

Helsinki CITY
~ **hot spot** SAUNA

helter-skelter ABOUT, UPSET

Helvetica FONT

hem EDGE, SEW
~ **and haw** AVOID, EVADE, HANG, STALL
~ **cousins** ERS
~ **in** BESET, CAGE, LIMIT, RING
~ **partner** HAW
make a ~ SEW
raise the ~**, maybe** ALTER
tack up a ~ BASTE

hematite ORE

hemi- HALF

hemidemisemiquaver NOTE

hemimorphite ORE

Hemingway ERNEST
~ **locale** SPAIN
~ **medium** PROSE
~ **setting** SEA
~ **sobriquet** PAPA

Hemingway, Mariel
~ **grandfather** ERNEST

hemline
change a ~ ALTER

hemlock TREE

hemmed
~ **in** PENT

hemp ROPE
~ **product** OPIATE, ROPE
moisten ~ RET

hemp-like
~ **fiber** SISAL

Hemsley, Sherman
~ **sitcom** AMEN

hen BIRD, SHE
~ **lack** TEETH
~ **product** EGG
like a wet ~ IRATE, MAD
scarcer than ~**'s teeth** RARE

___ **hen** SAGE

henbit WEED

hence ERGO, THEN, THUS

henchman AIDE
play the ~ ABET

Henderson, Rickey
~ **theft** BASE

henhouse ROOST

Henie, Sonja
~ **home** OSLO
emulate ~ SKATE

Henley
one of a pair at ~ OAR

henna COLOR, DYE, RINSE
~ **user** DYER

Henner, Marilu
~ **role on "Evening Shade"** AVA

henpeck NAG

Henri
see French

Henry CLAY, MOORE
~ **son** EDSEL

Henry ___ **Commager** STEELE

"Henry Aldrich, __" EDITOR

Henry, John
~ **drove it** STEEL

"Henry & June"
~ **author** NIN
~ **role** ANAIS, NIN
June, in ~ UMA

Henry, O.
~ **device** IRONY

Henry, Patrick ORATOR

Henry V
~ **nickname** HAL

Henry VI
~ **founded it** ETON

Henry VIII
~ **Catherine** PARR
~ **desire** SON
~ **second wife** ANNE
~ **sixth wife** PARR
~ **wife count** SIX
like ~ OBESE

Henson
~ **creation** ERNIE

hen's teeth
like ~ RARE

Hentoff NAT

hep ONTO

Hepburn
~ **Holiday** ROMAN
~ **nickname** KATE

Hepburn, Audrey
~ **real first name** EDDA

Hephaestus
mother of ~ HERA

Hepplewhite STYLE

heptad SEVEN

heptarch RULER

her SHE
~ **ender** SELF
his and ~ THEIR
not ~ HIM

Her
~ **predecessor** FALA

Her ___ **Highness** SERENE

"Her ___" Georgia Gibbs NIBS

Hera
~ **mother** RHEA
~ **son** ARES
rival of ~ LEDA

"___ Her About It" TELL

Heracles
~ **ship** ARGO

herald RING

heraldic
~ **band** ORLE

herb ANISE, DILL, MINT, PLANT, RUE, SAGE
~ **ender** OSE
aromatic ~ ANISE, DILL, MINT, SAGE
carrot family ~ ANISE
fragrant ~ MINT
gray-green ~ SAGE
kitchen ~ SAGE
medicinal ~ SAGE
onetime medicinal ~ RUE
parsley family ~ ANISE
soup ~ DILL
stuffing ~ SAGE
tea ~ MINT

Herb CAEN

herbage LAWN
dried ~ HAY

herbal
~ **beverage** TEA
~ **soother** ALOE

Herber ARNIE

Herbert AGAR, ROSS

Herbert ___ **Karajan** VON

Herbert, Frank
~ **opus** DUNE

Herbert, George POET
see also poet

Herbert, Victor
org. cofounded by ~ ASCAP

herbicide
~ **target** WEED

Herbie MANN
~ **in film** AUTO, CAR

herculean BIG, HARD, LARGE

Hercules GIANT, HERO
one of twelve for ~ LABOR

herd CREW, HOST, MASS, MOB, RUN, TROOP
~ **sheep** TEND
~ **sound** LOW
~ **together** BAND
it's heard in a ~ BAA
one of the ~ STEER
ride ~ **on** BOSS, RUN, TEND

herder
reindeer ~ LAPP

___ **herd on** RIDE

herdsman
first ~ ABEL

here
~ **and there** ABOUT
~ **in French** ICI
~ **in Latin** HIC
~ **partner** NOW
get ~ ARRIVE
go ~ **and there** ROVE
not ~ GONE, THERE
out of ~ AWAY
the ones ~ THESE

here ___ **now** AND

"Here ___" AMI

"Here ___!" GOES

"Here ___ nothing!" GOES

"Here ___ the Waves" COME

hereabout
~ **to a poet** ANEAR

hereafter LATER

here and ___ NOW, THERE

"Here Comes Mr. Jordan"
~ **director** HALL

"Here Comes the ___" SUN

"Here Comes the Groom"
~ **director** CAPRA

"Here Come the Warm Jets"
~ **artist** ENO

heredity
~ **factor** GENE
~ **letters** DNA, RNA

herein ENC

"Here Is Your War"
~ **author** PYLE

"___ Here, Private Hargrove" SEE

"Here's looking at you!" TOAST

"Here's mud in your eye!" TOAST

"Here's to ___!" YOU

"Here's to you!" TOAST

heretic REBEL

heretofore AGO
~ **mentioned** ABOVE

hereupon ANON, SOON

"___ Her Go" ILET

hermana
father's ~ TIA
madre's ~ TIA
mother's ~ TIA
padre's ~ TIA

Herman, Jerry
~ **musical** MAME

Hermann HESSE

hermano
father's ~ TIO
madre's ~ TIO
mother's ~ TIO
padre's ~ TIO

Herman, Pee Wee
~ **persona** NERD

Herman's Hermits
~ **leader** NOONE

Hermes
~ **invention** LYRE
half brother of ~ ARES

hermit CRAB, LONER
like a ~ ALONE

hermitage CELL, COT, HAVEN, HOME, NEST

Hermosillo
   see Spanish

Hernando
   see Spanish

"Hernani"
   ~ **author** HUGO

"Herne's ___, The" EGG

hero IDOL, LEAD, MAN, SUB
   ~ **ender** INE, ISM
   ~ **starter** ANTI
   ~ **work** DEED

"___ Hero" LOCAL

Herod
   Salome, to ~ NIECE

heroes
   where ~ are made DELI

"Heroes ___ Sale" FOR

"Heroes for ___" SALE

heroic BIG, GAME, GREAT
   ~ **account** SAGA
   ~ **achievement** FEAT
   ~ **poetry** EPOS
   ~ **story** GEST, GESTE
   ~ **tale** EDDA, EPIC, SAGA
   ~ **work** EPOS

"Heroides"
   ~ **author** OVID

heroine LEAD, STAR

heroism GRIT

heron BIRD
   ~ **cousin** CRANE, IBIS
   white-plumed ~ EGRET

"___ Her on Monday" IMET

Herr MAN, TITLE
   see also German

Herrick, Robert POET
   see also poet

Herriman
   ~ **feline** KAT

herring SPRAT
   red ~ RUSE

___ herring RED

herringlike
   ~ **fish** SHAD

Herriot, James SCOT, VET

hers
   ~ **in French** SES
   not ~ HIS

Herschel, William SIR

Hersey
   ~ **locale** ADANO

Hershey
   ~ **product** KISS
   ~ **rival** MARS
   ~ **st.** PENN
   ~ **unit** BAR

Hershfield
   ~ **cartoon character** ABIE

Hershiser OREL
   ~ **stat** ERA

"___ Her to Heaven" LEAVE

hertz
   ~ **starter** MEGA

Hertz
   ~ **rival** ALAMO, AVIS

Hervey ALLEN, IRENE

"He's a ___" REBEL

"___, He's Crazy" MAMA

Hesiod POET
   see also poet

hesitant LEERY, SLOW
   ~ **sounds** ERS

hesitate HANG, WAIT

hesitater
   ~ **syllables** ERS

"He's making ___ and checking it twice..." ALIST

Hesse
   river in ~ EDER
   see also German

Hess, Myra DAME

"He's So ___" FINE, SHY

"Hester Street"
   ~ **actress** KANE

Heston
   ~ **adversary** APE
   ~ **role** CID, HUR, MOSES

heterophyte PLANT

"He that would ___ would pick a pocket" PUN

het up AFIRE, AGOG, RILED

hew AXE, CHIP, CHOP, CUT, HACK, LOG, SLASH, SPLIT

he was
   ~ **in Latin** ERAT

hewer AXE

"He Who ___ Slapped" GETS

Hewitt DON

hex ___ SIGN

hex-
   ~ **halved** TRI
   ~ **predecessor** PENT

hexad SIX
   half a ~ TRIAD, TRIO

hex-sign
   ~ **locale** BARN

"Hey!" AHOY, CRY, PSST, PST
   say ~ YELL

heyday ACME, PEAK

Heyerdahl THOR
   ~ **island destination** EASTER
   ~ **transport** RAFT

"___ Hey Hey Kiss Him Goodbye" NANA

"Hey, kids! What time ___?" ISIT

"Hey there!" AHOY

"Hey you!" AHOY, PSST, PST

Hf ELEM
   72 for ~ ATNO

Hg ELEM
   80 for ~ ATNO

hgt. ALT, ELEV

hgts. MTS

HHH
   org. cofounded by ~ ADA

HHS
   ~ **org.** SSA

"hi"
   say ~ to GREET

hi-___ RES

Hi
   ~ **comic-strip wife** LOIS

"Hi" ALOHA, CRY

"Hi ___!" MOM

"Hi-___, Hi-Lo" LILI

HI
   see Hawaii

"Hi and Lois"
   ~ **kid** CHIP, DITTO, DOT

hiatus GAP, LAPSE, SPACE, WAIT

Hiawatha HERO
   ~ **boat** CANOE

hibachi
   ~ **feature** GRATE
   ~ **residue** ASH

hibernate REST, SLEEP
   place to ~ DEN, LAIR

hibernation REST, SLEEP
   ~ **home** DEN, LAIR

Hibernia ERIN

Hibernian CELT, IRISH

hibiscus
   ~ **cousin** OKRA

hiccup SPASM

hick BOOR, OAF, RUBE

hickory TREE

"___ Hickory" OLD

hidalgo LORD, MAN, PEER

Hidalgo
   see Spanish

hidden DEEP, INNER
   ~ **explosive** MINE
   ~ **snag** TRAP
   ~ **supply** STASH
   not ~ OVERT

hide BLUR, COAT, MASK, PELT, SKIN, STASH
   ~ **away** STASH, STORE
   ~ **nor hair** NONE
   ~ **partner** HAIR, SEEK
   ~ **the gray** DYE
   animal ~ PELT
   brushed ~ SUEDE
   it can ~ a bed SOFA
   neither ~ nor hair NONE
   tan someone's ~ BEAT, CANE

hide ___ hair NOR

hide-and-___ SEEK

hide-and-seek GAME
   ~ **spot** BASE

hideaway DEN, HAVEN, HOME, LAIR, NEST, NOOK
   mountain ~ CAVE

hidebound PRIM, SET

"Hide in Plain Sight"
   ~ **director** CAAN

hideous BAD, EVIL

hideout DEN, LAIR, NEST

hides
   cure ~ TAN

hiding
   ~ **place** DEN, LAIR
   come out of ~ EMERGE

hie DART, RUN, SHOOT, SPEED, TEAR

hierarch RULER

hierarchy
   place in the ~ RANK

hierodule SLAVE

hieroglyph SIGN

hi-fi
   ~ **buys** LPS
   ~ **component** AMP
   ~ **upgrade** STEREO

Higgins, Henry
   ~ **creator** SHAW

higgle DEAL

high ALOFT, BIG, LARGE, TALL
   ~ **abode** AERIE
   ~ **ball** LOB
   ~ **birth** RANK
   ~ **card** ACE
   ~ **command** BRASS
   ~ **country** TIBET
   ~ **dudgeon** ANGER, IRE, RAGE
   ~ **ender** BALL, LAND, RISE, TAIL
   ~ **fashion** TON
   ~ **flyer** KITE
   ~ **grade** FINE, MINT
   ~ **ground** RISE
   ~ **home** AERIE
   ~ **in alcohol** HARD
   ~ **in music** ALT
   ~ **in place names** ALTA
   ~ **isolated rock** SCAR
   ~ **jinks** LARK, PLAY
   ~ **jump** EVENT, LEAP
   ~ **kingdom** NEPAL
   ~ **land** MESA, NEPAL
   ~ **mountain** ALP
   ~ **muckamuck** PASHA
   ~ **musically** ALT
   ~ **nest** AERIE
   ~ **note** ELA
   ~ **old time** LARK
   ~ **opinion** ESTEEM
   ~ **partner** DRY, LOW
   ~ **point** ACME, APEX, CREST, PEAK, TOP
   ~ **point of a Swiss tour** ALP
   ~ **power** NTH

high ___

~ (prefix) ALTI
~ rating AONE, ONEA
~ regard ESTEEM
~ seas MAIN
~ sign HINT
~ society ELITE
~ speed electron BETA
~ spirits ELAN, GLEE
~ spot ATTIC
~ tea MEAL
~ time NOON
~ trump ACE
~ up ABOVE, ALOFT
~ wind BLAST
blow sky ~ BLAST
eat ~ off the hog DINE
European ~ spot ALP
fly ~ SOAR
get ~ marks on ACE
give a ~ sign ALERT
hold ~ HONOR
home up ~ AERIE
in ~ dudgeon IRATE, MAD
in ~ gear APACE
in ~ spirits ELATED, GAY
in ~ style CHIC
look ~ and low RAKE, ROOT
low to ~ RANGE
not ~ LOW
of ~ rank GREAT
on ~ ABOVE, ALOFT
rate ~ DIG, LIKE, LOVE
receive a ~ grade on ACE
the ~ and mighty ELITE
up ~ ALOFT

high ___ BEAM, GEAR, HAT, HORSE, MASS, NOON, SEAS, SIGN, STYLE, TEA, TIDE, TIME, WIRE

high ___ kite ASA

high-___ CLASS, END, OCTANE, RISE, TECH, TEST, TONED

high-___ (cool greeting) FIVE

high-___ (snub) HAT

high-___ mark WATER

___ high (elated) ONA

___-high KNEE, SKY

"High ___" NOON, TOR

"High ___ of Loving, The" COST

"High ___ the Mighty, The" AND

"___ High" ACES, SKY

high and ___ DRY

highball
~ ingredient RYE

highbrow SNOB

high-ceiling
~ lobbies ATRIA

highchair
~ part TRAY

high-class ELITE

___ High Dam ASWAN

higher
~ in rank ABOVE
~ than bass TENOR

~ up OVER
pile it ~ and deeper BRAG

higher-___ UPS

highest AONE, BEST, FIRST, TOP, TOPS
~ point ACME, PEAK
~ (prefix) ARCH

highest-quality AONE, BEST, FIRST, TOPS

___-High-Everything-Else (Pooh-Bah) LORD

highfalutin
~ manner AIRS
~ type SNOB

high fashion
~ magazine ELLE
~ model IMAN

high fiber
~ food BRAN

high-five
~ slapper PALM
~ sound SLAP

high-flown EPIC, ORNATE

high-grade AONE, TOPS

high-hat ALOOF, SNOB, SNUB
~ look SNEER

"High Hopes"
~ animal ANT, RAM

Highland
~ dance REEL
~ family CLAN
~ fling DANCE
~ girl LASS
~ headgear TAM
~ hollow GLEN
~ slope BRAE
~ tongue ERSE
~ youth LAD
see also Scottish

Highlander CELT, GAEL, SCOT
~ tongue ERSE
see also Scottish

Highlands
see Scottish

highlight PEAK, STRESS

highlights RECAP

high-minded BIG, GOOD, GREAT, HONEST, MORAL, PURE

high-muck-a-muck BOSS, NABOB, NOB

Highness TITLE

"High Noon" OATER
~ singer LAINE

high on the ___ HOG

high-pH
~ substance LYE

high-pitched REEDY
~ bark YELP

"High Plains Drifter" OATER

"High Pressure"
~ director LEROY

high-priced DEAR, STEEP

high-priority MAIN

"High Rollers"
~ props DICE

high school
~ class ART, MATH, SCI, SHOP, TRIG
~ dance HOP, PROM
~ student TEEN
~ subj. ALG, BIO, ENG, MATH, MUS, SCI

high seas
~ greeting AHOY

"High Sierra"
Humphrey's ~ costar IDA

"High Society"
~ name COLE

___ High Stadium MILE

___ high standard SETA

highstrung EDGY, TAUT, TENSE

hightail
~ it FLEE, HIE, LAM, LEAVE, RACE, RUN, SCAT, SCRAM, SPEED, TEAR

high tea
~ food SCONE

high-tech
~ banking serv. ATM
~ FBI tool DNA
~ light LASER
~ memo EMAIL
~ recordings CDS
~ scanner CAT
~ surgical device LASER

high-tension HOT

high-test GAS

high-toned CHIC

highway PATH, PIKE, ROAD, ROUTE
~ agcy. DOT
~ alert FLARE
~ covering TAR
~ crosser, maybe DEER
~ feature RAMP
~ fee TOLL
~ hanging SIGN
~ hauler SEMI
~ hazard ESS
~ marker CONE
~ material TAR
~ noisemaker HORN
~ segment LANE
~ sight AUTO, CAR
~ sign EATS, EXIT, SLO, SLOW
ancient ~ VIA
see also freeway

"highway"
liner's ~ OCEAN, SEA

"Highwayman, The" POEM
~ heroine BESS

hijack ROB, STEAL, TAKE

hike CAMP, MOVE, RAISE, TREK
pay ~ RAISE
ready for a ~ SHOD

Hiken NAT

hiker
~ need MAP

hiking
~ path TRAIL

Hilaire Germain Edgar ___ DEGAS

hilarious RICH
~ person PANIC, RIOT

hilarity GLEE

"Hi-Lili, ___" HILO

hill HEAP, RISE, SLOPE, TOR
~ bottom FOOT
~ builder ANT
~ companion DALE
~ resident ANT
~ slope SIDE
flat-topped ~ MESA
isolated ~ MESA
rounded ~ KNOB
sand ~ DUNE
Scottish ~ BRAE

___ hill ANT

Hill ANITA, JOE, SAM

"Hill, The"
~ group SENATE

___ Hill BOOT

___ hill and dale OER

Hillary, Edmund SIR
~ hangout NEPAL

hilliness ROLL

hillock RISE

hills
city of seven ~ ROME
head for the ~ RUN
like the ~ OLD
number of Rome's ~ SEVEN
old as the ~ AGED

___ Hill, San Francisco NOB

hillside SLOPE
~ detritus SCREE

"Hills of ___, The" HOME

"Hill Street Blues"
~ actor OLIN
~ character COP

hilltop CREST

Hilo CITY, PORT
see also Hawaii

Hilton HOTEL

"___ Hilton, The" HANOI

hilum
~ extension ARIL

him
~ ender SELF
July was named for ~ CAESAR
not ~ HER

Himalayan CAT
~ animal YAK
~ city LHASA

~ country NEPAL, TIBET
aromatic ~ plant NARD
hairy ~ YETI

Himalayas
  ~ home ASIA

Himalia MOON

"__ Him in Paris" IMET

hind AFTER, ANIMAL, DEER, DOE, ROE
  ~ foot PAW
  ~ mate STAG
  on one's ~ legs ERECT
  rise on the ~ legs RAMP, REAR

hinder ARREST, AVERT, BAR, CLOG, DETER, LIMIT, STOP

Hindi
  ~ cousin URDU

hindmost LAST
  ~ part REAR

hindquarters END, HIP, REAR

hindrance BAR, SNAG

Hindu
  ~ ascetic YOGI
  ~ class CASTE
  ~ discipline YOGA
  ~ leader NEHRU
  ~ lute SITAR
  ~ melody RAGA
  ~ monarchy NEPAL
  ~ mystic SWAMI, YOGI
  ~ philosophy YOGA
  ~ practicer YOGI
  ~ princess RANEE, RANI
  ~ teacher GURU, SWAMI
  ~ title SRI
  ~ woman's attire SARI
  hero of a ~ epic RAMA

Hinduism REL

Hindu Kush RANGE

Hindustani
  ~ derivative URDU

Hines EARL

Hines, Gregory
  ~ film TAP
  ~ milieu TAP

Hines, Jerome BASS, BASSO

hinge AXIS, REST
  ~ on HANG
  anatomical ~ KNEE

hinged
  ~ fastener HASP

hinny ANIMAL
  ~ mother ASS
  ~ opposite MULE

hint BIT, CAST, CLUE, CUE, DAB, DASH, LEAD, NOTE, SHADE, TASTE, TINGE, TRACE
  ~ at ANGLE, MEAN
  ~ in French MOT
  drop a ~ LETON
  give a helpful ~ STEER
  helpful ~ TIP
  not a ~ NONE

prompter's ~ CUE

Hinton, S.E.
  ~ novel TEX

hip AWARE, CHIC, COOL, MOD, NEW, SMART, WISE
  ~ about ONTO
  ~ bones ILIA
  ~ ender STER
  ~ swiveler ELVIS

hip __ BOOT, ROOF

hip-__ HOP

hipbones ILIA

hip-hop RAP

hippety-hop LEAP

hippie
  ~ home PAD

hippocras WINE

Hippocrates
  ~ wrote one OATH

Hippocratic __ OATH

hippodrome ARENA

Hippolyte
  ~ father ARES

hippopotamic BIG, LARGE

hippopotamus ANIMAL

Hippo Regius CITY, PORT

hippy BIG, LARGE
  ~ dance HULA

__ hips ROSE

hipster CAT

Hiram, King
  ~ home TYRE

hircine LEWD

hire RENT
  ~ a crew MAN
  ~ a lawyer SUE
  ~ out LEASE, LET, RENT

hired
  ~ car CAB, TAXI
  ~ hands HELP
  ~ muscle GOON

hired __ HAND

"Hired __, The" HAND

hireling HACK, HELP, TOOL

Hires
  ~ rival DADS

Hiroshima CITY, PORT

"Hiroshima, __ Amour" MON

"Hiroshima, Mon __" AMOUR

Hirschfeld
  ~ and others ALS
  ~ daughter NINA

Hirsch, Judd
  ~ sitcom TAXI

hirsute
  ~ adornment BEARD

Hirt
  ~ and others ALS

Hirt, Al
  ~ instrument HORN
  ~ tune JAVA

his
  ~ and her THEIR
  ~ in French SES

his __ (the boss) NIBS

"His __ Friday" GIRL

"Hi, sailor!" AHOY

his and __ HERS

"His Master's Voice"
  ~ co. RCA

Hispanic
  see Spanish

Hispaniola
  ~ part HAITI

"Hispaniola" BOAT, SHIP

hiss GIBE, HOOT, NOISE, SPIT
  ~ cousin BOO

Hiss ALGER

hisser SNAKE

hissy
  ~ fit SNIT

historian
  ~ word AGO

historic
  ~ event FIRST
  ~ org. DAR
  ~ period AGE
  ~ starter PRE

historical
  ~ period AGE, ERA
  ~ piece BIO
  ~ souvenir RELIC
  of an ~ time ERAL

history AGO, GENRE, PAST
  ~ homework ESSAY
  ~ segment ERA
  bit of ~ RELIC
  chapter of ~ ERA
  folk ~ LORE
  Muse of ~ CLIO
  personal ~ BIO

__ history CASE, ORAL

history book
  ~ verb WAS

"History Is __ at Night" MADE

histrion ACTOR

histrionic
  ~ episode SCENE

histrionics DRAMA, RANT

hit BANG, BASH, BAT, BEAT, BELT, BOP, CHOP, CLAP, CLIP, LASH, OCCUR, PASTE, PELT, RAM, SLAM, SLAP, SMASH, SMITE, SWAT
  ~ abbr. SRO
  ~ a fly, perhaps BAT
  ~ aloft LOB

~ and rebound CAROM
~ bottom SINK
~ broadside RAM
~ hard MOVE, PASTE, PELT, SLAM
~ it off AGREE
~ like a ton of bricks STUN
~ someone upside the head BEAT
~ starter MEGA
~ the bell RING
~ the boards TREAD
~ the books CRAM, READ
~ the ceiling ERUPT, RAGE, RANT, SNAP
~ the deck ARISE, RISE
~ the dirt SLIDE
~ the floor hard STAMP
~ the ground ALIT, LAND, LIT
~ the hay BED, SLEEP
~ the jackpot WIN
~ the + key ADD
~ the mall SHOP
~ the road LEAVE, PART, ROVE, SCAT, SCRAM, START, TOUR
~ the roof RAGE, RANT, SNAP
~ the runway LAND
~ the sack BED, REST, SLEEP
~ the slopes SKI
~ the spot PLEASE, SUIT
~ the tarmac LAND
~ the trail START
~ town COME
~ upon LEARN
~ with a laser ZAP
base-clearing ~ HOMER
big ~ SMASH
fail to ~ MISS
make a ~ SCORE
ready to ~ ATBAT
solid ~, in baseball LINER

hit __ PARADE

hit __ (discover) UPON

__ hit BASE

hit a __ SNAG

hit-and-__ MISS

hitch BIND, KNOT, LIMP, MOOR, NOOSE, RIDE, ROPE, SNAG, SNARL, STAKE
  ~ on TAG
  ~ one's wagon to a star AIM
  ~ up HIKE
  ~ up with MATE
  clove ~ KNOT
  half ~ KNOT
  timber ~ KNOT
  weaver's ~ KNOT

Hitchcock, Alfred SIR
  ~ favorite designer HEAD
  ~ film of 1948 ROPE
  many a ~ performance CAMEO
  Mrs. ~ ALMA

hitched
  get ~ WED
  get ~ in a hurry ELOPE

hitching __ POST

"Hitch your wagon to ___" ASTAR

hither
~ **and thither** ABOUT
~ **partner** YON
draw ~ LURE
move ~ **and thither** GAD,
ROAM, ROVE

hither and ___ YON

___-hither look COME

hit it ___ BIG, OFF

hit-or-___ MISS

hit-or-miss LOOSE

hitter
~ **chance** ATBAT
~ **stat** RBI
bull's-eye ~ DART
home-run ~ **run** TROT
pinch ~ SUB

hit the ___ HAY, ROAD, ROOF,
SACK, SPOT

hit the ___ on the head NAIL

"Hit the road!" SCAT, SCRAM,
SHOO

hit the roof
~ **as Santa** ALIT, LIT

hitting ATBAT

___-hitting HARD

hive
~ **resident** BEE, DRONE

"Hi-yo Silver, ___!" AWAY

HMO
~ **employee** DOC
~ **workers** DRS, MDS, RNS

HMS
part of ~ HER, HIS, SHIP

ho CRY

Ho DON, ELEM
~ **home, once** HANOI
67 for ~ ATNO

Hoad LEW

hoagie HERO, SUB
~ **ingredient** ONION
where to get a ~ DELI

hoagy HERO, SUB

hoar RIME

hoard AMASS, ARMY, SAVE, STASH,
STORE

hoarder
~ **cry** MINE, MORE
~ **goal** ALL

hoarfrost ICE, RIME

hoarse
yell oneself ~ ROOT

hoary AGED, OLD, PASSE

hoax FAKE, LIE, SHAM

hob LEDGE
~ **ender** NOB

Hobbit
~ **community** SHIRE
~ **foe** ORC

hobble BIND, CLOG, LIMP, STEP

hobbledehoy LAD, OAF

hobbler
~ **support** CANE

hobbling LAME

hobby BAG
~ **ender** IST

hobbyhorse TOY

hobbyist
~ **wood** BALSA

hobby shop
~ **buy** KIT

hobgoblin DEMON, ELF, GNOME,
IMP

hobo NOMAD
~ **dinner** STEW

Hoboken CITY, PORT

hobos
what ~ **ride** RAILS

Hobson LAURA

Hobson's
~ **choice** BIND, HORSE

"Hoc ___ in votis" ERAT

Hoccleve, Thomas POET
see also poet

Ho Chi Minh City CITY, PORT

Ho Chi Minh Trail
~ **locale** LAOS

hock ANKLE
be in ~ OWE
horse's ~ ANKLE

hockey GAME
~ **arena** RINK
~ **great** ORR
~ **infraction** ICING
~ **prize** CUP
~ **puck** DISC
~ **structure** CAGE
~ **surface** ICE
~ **target** GOAL
~ **team** SIX
Alberta ~ **player** OILER
Edmonton ~ **player** OILER
ice ~ GAME
ice ~ **locale** ARENA
Winnipeg ~ **player** JET

hockey player
~ **protection** PAD

hockey rink
~ **surface** ICE

hockey sportscaster
~ **cry** SCORE

hodgepodge MESS, OLIO

Hodges EDDIE, GIL

Ho, Don
~ **dish** POI
~ **do** LUAU
~ **greeting** ALOHA

~ **island** OAHU
~ **neckwear** LEI

hoe DIG, TOOL, WEED
~ **cousin** RAKE
~ **target** CLOD

hoedown DANCE
~ **date** GAL
~ **prop** BALE, HAY

Hoffer ERIC

Hoffman
~ **film** HERO

Hoffman ___, Ill. ESTATES

Hoffman, W.
~ **play of 1985** ASIS

hog ANIMAL, EATER
~ **feed** SLOP
~ **fodder** MAST
~ **home** PEN, STY
eat high off the ~ DINE
wild ~ BOAR

hog-___ TIE

___ hog ROAD

Hogan BEN, PAUL
~ **rival** SNEAD

Hogan, Hulk
surface for ~ MAT
victory for ~ PIN

"Hogan's ___" GOAT

"Hogan's Heroes"
~ **actor** CRANE

Hogarth
~ **subject** RAKE

hogback CREST

Hogg IMA

hoggish AVID

hognose ___ SNAKE

hognose snake ADDER

hogshead CASE, UNIT

hogwash LIE, ROT, SLOP, TRASH

hog-wild RABID

Hohe Tauern RANGE

ho-hum BLAH, DRAB, SOSO
~ **feeling** ENNUI
same old ~ RUT

hoi polloi MOB

hoist CRANE, LEVER, RAISE, REAR
~ **anchor** LEAVE
~ **glasses** TOAST
~ **the blue peter** SAIL

hoisting
~ **device** CRANE

hoity-toity
~ **group** ELITE
~ **one** SNOB

___ Ho Kelly CHIN

hokey FAKE, FALSE, SHAM

Hokkaido
~ **locale** ASIA

~ **native** AINU
see also Japanese

hokum ROT, TRASH

Holbein HANS

Holbrook HAL

hold ADHERE, ARGUE, AVER,
AVOW, BIN, BITE, CARESS,
CLAIM, CLASP, DEEM, ESTEEM,
GRASP, GRIP, HAVE, KEEP,
OPINE, OWN, TAKE
~ **a position** POSE
~ **as a car** SEAT
~ **as an opinion** DEEM
~ **as attention** RIVET
~ **a session** MEET
~ **back** ARREST, DETER, HANG,
LEASH, REIN, SAVE, SPARE,
STAY, STEM
~ **captive** TAKE
~ **close** PRESS
~ **dear** ADORE, DOTE, LIKE,
LOVE
~ **down** PIN
~ **down a job** EARN
~ **fast** BIND
~ **forth** ORATE, RANT, TALK
~ **good** STAND
~ **high** HONOR
~ **in** LEASH, LIMIT
~ **in abeyance** DEFER
~ **in reserve** SAVE
~ **in respect** ESTEEM
~ **in view** SEE
~ **it** CEASE, STOP
~ **like a sword** WIELD
~ **off** DEFER, REPEL, STALL,
STEM, TABLE, WAIT
~ **off for** AWAIT
~ **office** SERVE
~ **on** LIVE, WAIT
~ **one's horses** REIN, WAIT
~ **one's own** COPE
~ **on to** KEEP
~ **out against** STAND
~ **out one's hand** BEG
~ **precious** ADORE
~ **starter** TOE
~ **sway** RULE
~ **the attention of** ARREST
~ **the deed to** OWN
~ **the phone** STOP
~ **the reins** LEAD
~ **the scepter** REIGN
~ **tight** CLASP
~ **to firmly** ADHERE
~ **up** BEAR, DEFER, DETER,
HALT, LAST, PROP, RAISE,
ROB, TABLE
~ **water** WASH
~ **your horses** REIN
can ~ TAKE
catch ~ **of** GRAB
fill the ~ STOW
hard to ~ EELY
it'll ~ **water** CUP, VASE
lay ~ **of** GET, GRAB, GRASP,
NAB
place in a ~ STOW
place in the ~ LADE
put on ~ DEFER
quit one's ~ **on** CEDE

hold ___ (be logical) WATER

hold ___ (keep) OVER

hold ___ (last) OUT

hold ___ (resist) OFF

hold ___ (rule) SWAY

"Hold ___ Co-ed" THAT

"Hold ___ Ghost" THAT

Holden, William
  ~ last film SOB

holder CASE

holders
  book ~ ENDS

holding ASSET, CLAIM
  bank ~ LIEN
  go into a ~ pattern STALL,
    WAIT
  land ~ ESTATE
  lord's ~ LAND
  poker ~ HAND
  put in a ~ pattern DEFER

holding ___ TANK

holdings ESTATE

"Hold it!" HEY, STOP, WHOA

"Hold Me Thrill Me ___ Me" KISS

"Hold on!" HEY, STOP, WHOA

"Hold on a ___!" SEC

hold one's ___ OWN

"Hold On Tight"
  ~ band ELO

holds
  it ~ the line REEL

"Hold That ___" COED

hold the ___ LINE, PHONE

"Hold the Line"
  ~ band TOTO

holdup WAIT

"Hold Your ___" MAN

hole DENT, GAP, LAIR, LEAK, SINK,
  SPACE
  ~ card ACE
  ~ in one ACE
  ~ maker AWL, MOTH
  ~ up HIDE
  air ~ NOSE
  be in the ~ OWE
  black ~, once STAR
  blow ~ NOSE
  deep ~ PIT
  enlarge a ~ REAM
  fix a ~ DARN
  furthest from the ~, in
    golf AWAY
  gaping ~ ABYSS
  it's sometimes in the ~ ACE
  make a ~ DIG
  needle ~ EYE
  pipe ~ LEAK
  put a ~ in STAVE
  put someone in the ~ COST
  repair a ~ DARN
  roll with a ~ BAGEL

swimming ~ POND, POOL
Swiss-cheese ~ EYE
water ~ LAKE, POND, POOL
watering ~ BAR, OASIS, POND
wear a ~ in the rug PACE
widen a ~ REAM

hole ___ CARD, INONE

___ hole AIR, DRY, WATER

hole-in-one ACE

holes
  full of ~ OPEN

holiday GALA, LEAVE, REST
  ~ cheer NOG
  ~ extravaganza PARADE
  ~ helper ELF
  ~ mo. DEC
  ~ period YULE
  ~ preceder EVE
  ~ purchase FIR
  ~ season NOEL, YULE
  ~ song CAROL, NOEL
  ~ visitor SANTA
  Asian ~ TET
  Jewish ~ dinner SEDER
  spring ~ EASTER

___ holiday LEGAL, ROMAN

"Holiday ___" INN, ONICE

"___ Holiday" ROMAN

holidayless
  ~ mo. AUG

Holiday, Polly
  ~ role FLO

holier-___-thou THAN

holier-than-___ THOU

Holiness
  his ~ POPE

Holland TOM
  ~ export EDAM, TULIP
  ~ seaport EDAM
  Hook of ~ PORT
  see also Dutch, Netherlands

holler BAWL, BLARE, CALL, CRY,
  HOOT, RANT, ROAR, YELL
  hoot and ~ RANT

Holliday DOC
  ~ pal EARP

Holliday, Polly
  ~ role FLO

Holliman EARL

Hollings ERNEST

hollow CAVE, COVE, DEN, HOLE,
  LAIR, PAN, PIT, SINK, VAIN, VALE
  ~ form MOLD
  ~ out DIG, SCOOP
  ~ place HOLE
  ~ stone GEODE
  highland ~ GLEN
  secluded ~ DELL
  small ~ DENT

hollow-cheeked LEAN

hollowed
  not ~ out SOLID

"Hollow Men, The"
  ~ monogram TSE
  ~ poet ELIOT

holly TREE

Hollywood
  ~ clashers EGOS
  ~ figure AGENT, REP
  ~ luminary STAR
  ~ profession ACTOR
  ~ terrier ASTA
  ~ type ACTOR
  ~ walk-on EXTRA
  ~ workplace SET

Hollywood ___ BED

"___ Hollywood" DOC

Hollywood Boulevard
  ~ crosser VINE
  ~ embedment STAR

"Hollywood Squares"
  ~ answer choice AGREE
  number of ~ NINE
  opening in ~ TIC

holm
  ~ oak TREE

Holm IAN

Holman NAT

Holmes
  ~ carriage SHAY
  ~ clue ASH
  ~ girl ELSIE
  ~ quest CLUE
  adverb for ~ AFOOT
  prop for ~ PIPE
  task for ~ CASE
  vehicle in a ~ poem SHAY

hologram
  ~ maker LASER

holography
  ~ tool LASER

Holstein COW
  ~ comment MOO
  ~ home BARN

holster
  ~ item GUN

Holt TIM

Holt, Laura
  ~ partner STEELE

Holtz LOU

holy PURE
  ~ terror IMP

holy ___ DAY, OIL, WAR, WATER

Holy ___ ARK, LAND, SEE, WEEK,
  WRIT

"Holy ___!" COW, TOLEDO

"Holy cow!" EGAD, EGADS, GEE

Holyfield
  ~ feat TKO
  ~ hit JAB
  ~ stat KOS
  see also boxer

"Holy mackerel!" EGAD, EGADS,
  GEE, WOW

"Holy moly!" EGAD, EGADS, GEE,
  WOW

Holy One LORD

Holy Roman Empire
  ~ founder OTTO

"Holy smoke!" EGAD, EGADS,
  GEE, WOW

"Holy Sonnets"
  ~ poet DONNE

"Holy Toledo!" EGAD, EGADS,
  GEE, WOW

holy water
  ~ basin FONT

Holy Week
  ~ wraps it up LENT

Holzman RED

homage ESTEEM, HONOR
  pay ~ to ADORE, LAUD, SERVE
  poetic ~ ODE

"Homage to the Square" OPART

homburg HAT

___ Homburg, Germany BAD

home ABODE, BASE, NEST, PAD,
  ROOF
  ~ base, in sci-fi EARTH
  ~ ender STEAD
  ~ in Spanish CASA
  ~ on the range RANCH
  ~ site PLOT
  large ~ ESTATE
  lofty ~ AERIE
  opposite of ~ AWAY
  Southwest ~ ADOBE
  see also house

home ___ BASE, FREE, PAGE,
  PLATE, PORT, RULE, RUN

home- ___ BREW, STYLE

___ home MOTOR

"Home ___" ALONE

"Home Before Dark"
  ~ director LEROY

homecoming
  ~ celebrant ALUM, GRAD

"Homecoming, The"
  ~ director HALL

home delivery
  ~ terr. RTE

home entertainment
  ~ name ATARI

home equity ___ LOAN

home heating
  ~ need GAS, OIL

Homeier SKIP

"Home Improvement"
  ~ actor ALLEN
  ~ name TIM
  ~ network ABC
  ~ prop TOOL

homeless
  make ~ OUST

homemaker
  ~ **nemesis** DUST
  do a ~ chore SEW

"home of the brave" USA

"Home on the ___" RANGE

homeowner
  ~ **paper** DEED
  ~ **pride** LAWN

___-home pay TAKE

homer HIT, RUN
  ~ **king** AARON
  trying for a ~ ATBAT

Homer POET
  ~ **instrument** LYRE
  ~ **mart** AGORA
  ~ **opus** EPIC, ILIAD
  see also Greek, poet

Homeric EPIC
  ~ **genre** EPOS
  ~ **tale** ILIAD

home run
  ~ **descriptor** GONE
  ~ **hitter's run** TROT
  four-time N.L. ~
    leader AARON

home runs
  hitter of 511 ~ OTT
  hitter of 714 ~ RUTH
  hitter of 755 ~ AARON

Homer, Winslow
  ~ **home** MAINE

HOMES
  part of ~ ERIE

home-school
  ~ **org.** PTA

home security
  ~ **device** ALARM

homesite LOT

homespun MEAN
  first name in ~ humor ERMA

homestead ABODE, SETTLE
  large ~ ESTATE

Homestead ___ ACT

Homestead Act
  ~ **measure** ACRE
  ~ **offering** LAND

homesteader TENANT
  ~ **tract** CLAIM

___ home to roost COME

home video
  ~ **format** BETA

homework
  do elementary-school ~ ADD
  English ~ ESSAY, THEME
  history ~ ESSAY

homily TRACT
  ~ **(abbr.)** SER

___ homo ECCE

homogenize MELD

homogenous ALIKE

Homolka OSCAR

homologous ALIKE, LIKE

Homo sapiens MAN

Homs
  where ~ is SYRIA

hon DEAR

honcho BOSS
  company ~ CEO

Honda AUTO, CAR

"Hondo" OATER

Honduras
  see Spanish

hone EDGE

honed KEEN

honest CLEAN, FAIR, GOOD, OPEN,
  REAL, TRUE
  ~ **president** ABE

"Honest ___/ My Desdemona
  must I leave to thee" IAGO

honest-to-goodness REAL

honesty HONOR
  exemplar of ~ ABE

honey BEAR, DEAR, LOVE, SWEET
  ~ **bunch** BEES
  ~ **drink** MEAD
  ~ **factory** HIVE
  ~ **maker** BEE
  ~ **repository** COMB
  color of ~ AMBER, GOLD
  fermented ~ MEAD
  like ~ SWEET

honey ___ BEAR

honeybunch DEAR

honeycomb PIT
  ~ **unit** CELL

honeycreeper BIRD

honeydew MELON

Honey Fitz
  ~ **daughter** ROSE

"Honey, I Blew Up the ___" KID

"___ Honey in the Rock" SWEET

honeymoon
  ~ **island** ARUBA

"Honeymooners, The"
  ~ **role** ALICE
  Jackie's ~ costar ART

"Honeymoon in ___" BALI

"Honeymoon in Vegas"
  ~ **actor** CAAN, CAGE

"Honeysuckle ___" ROSE

honey-tongued GLIB

Hong Kong CITY, FLU, PORT
  ~ **locale** ASIA
  ~ **native** ASIAN

Hong Kong ___ FLU

"Honi soit qui ___ y pense" MAL

honk BLARE, BLAST, NOISE, TOOT

honker GOOSE, HORN

honky-tonk BAR

"Honky Tonk ___ Blues" TRAIN

Honolulu CITY, PORT
  ~ **greeting** ALOHA
  ~ **locale** OAHU
  ~ **shindig** LUAU
  see also Hawaii

Honolulu's ___ Bowl ALOHA,
  HULA

honor ADORE, AWARD, ESTEEM,
  EXALT, FETE, HAIL, LAUD, PAY
  ~ **card** ACE, TEN
  ~ **greatly** ADORE
  ~ **with insults** ROAST
  badge of ~ MEDAL
  battle of ~ DUEL
  in ~ of AFTER, FOR
  place of ~ DAIS, HEAD
  top ~ ACE
  word of ~ OATH

honorable CLEAN, GOOD, GREAT,
  HONEST, MORAL, PURE

honorarium AWARD, FEE

honorary
  ~ **deg.** LLD

honored DEAR
  where ~ guests sit DAIS

___-honored TIME

honoree
  ~ **spot** DAIS

honorific TAG
  female ~ MAAM, MADAM
  Japanese ~ SAN

honors
  confer ~ AWARD

honor society
  ~ **letter** BETA, PHI

honor student
  ~ **blemish** CEE

Honshu
  ~ **aperitif** SAKE, SAKI
  ~ **port** OSAKA
  ~ **resort port** ITO
  ~ **wraparound** OBI
  hailing from ~ ASIAN
  see also Japanese

hoo-___ HAH

hooch
  slug of ~ BELT

hood APE, GOON
  ~ **piece** GAT

'hood AREA

Hood
  ~ **and others** MTS

hooded
  ~ **snake** COBRA

hoodlum APE, GOON

hoodlums MOB

Hood, Robin
  ~ **Marian** MAID

  ~ **portrayer** ERROL
  ~ **quaff** ALE
  ~ **weapon** ARROW, BOW

Hood, Thomas POET
  see also poet

hoodwink CON, DUPE, HAVE,
  SNARE

hooey BLAH, TRASH

hoof FOOT
  ~ **it** DANCE, HIKE, PAD, STEP
  steak on the ~ STEER

hoofbeat STEP

hoofed
  ~ **animal** TAPIR

hoo-ha ADO, TODO

hook BARB, CLAW, LURE, STEAL
  ~ **and eye** CLASP
  ~ **attachment** BAIT
  ~ **cousin** CLASP
  ~ **in French** CROC
  ~ **opposite** SLICE
  ~ **up with** MEET
  alternative to a ~ JAB
  opposite of ~ SLICE
  prepare a ~ BAIT

hook ___ SHOT

hook, ___, and sinker LINE

___ hook MEAT

"Hook"
  ~ **character** NANA, PAN,
    PETER, SMEE

hookah PIPE

hook and ___ EYE

Hook, Captain
  ~ **alma mater** ETON
  ~ **nemesis** CROC, PAN, PETER
  ~ **sidekick** SMEE

hooked
  ~ **on** INTO

"Hooked ___ Feeling" ONA

Hook of Holland PORT

hoop BAND, RING, TOY
  ~ **edge** RIM
  ~ **ender** STER
  ~ **site** EAR
  basketball ~ RIM

hoop ___ SNAKE

___-Hoop HULA

Hooper TOBE

hoopla ADO, HYPE

Hoople MAJOR
  ~ **cry** EGAD

hoopoe BIRD

hoops
  ~ **maneuver** STEAL
  ~ **org.** NBA
  ~ **venue** ARENA
  bygone ~ org. ABA
  jump through ~ OBEY
  see also basketball

hoopster
Boston ~ CELT
Indiana ~ PACER
Miami ~ HEAT
New Jersey ~ NET
Phoenix ~ SUN
San Antonio ~ SPUR
Seattle ~ SONIC
see also basketball

"Hooray ___ Love" FOR

"Hooray for ___" LOVE

"Hooray for Love"
~ director LANG

hoosegow CAN, PEN, STIR
~ cubicle CELL

Hoosier
~ humorist ADE
~ poet RILEY
~ St. IND

hoot CRY, GIBE, HISS, NOISE, YELL
~ and holler RANT, RAVE
~ maker OWL
give a ~ CARE

hoot ___ OWL

hootchy-kootchy DANCE

hootenanny SING

Hooterville
~ had green ones ACRES

Hoover DAM

Hoover Dam
~ lake MEAD

Hoover, Herbert
~ birthplace IOWA
~ missus LOU

Hoover, J. Edgar
~ employee GMAN
~ org. FBI

hooves
like some horses' ~ SHOD

hop BALL, CAPER, DANCE, LEAP,
LOPE, SKIP
~ ender SACK
~ into the tub BATHE
~ out of bed ARISE
~ over CLEAR
~ starter BAR
~ to it ACT, HIE, MOVE, RUN
playful ~ CAPER
sock ~ DANCE

hop, ___, and a jump SKIP

___-hop HIP, TABLE

Hop ___ ("Bonanza" cook) SING

hope AIM, DREAM
angler's ~ BITE

hope (for) LONG

hope (to) MEAN

hope ___ CHEST

Hope BOB, LANGE

"Hope ___ Glory" AND

Hope, Bob
~ sponsor USO

Hope/Crosby
~ destination BALI, RIO
~ locale ROAD

Hope Diamond
~ units CTS

hopeful EAGER, ROSY

**"Hope Is the Thing With
Feathers"** POEM

hopeless BAD, INEPT, LOST

Hopi TRIBE

"___ hoping!" HERES

Hopkins
~ and others BOS

Hopkins, Anthony SIR

Hopkins, Gerard Manley POET
see also poet

hop-o'-my-thumb RUNT

Hoppe
~ game POOL

hopped up AVID
all ~ about MAD

hopper BIN, FLEA, TOAD
~ filler COAL
down-under ~ ROO
freight-car ~ HOBO
little ~ TOAD

Hopper, Hedda
~ trademark HAT

hopping
~ animal HARE

hopping ___ MAD

hopping mad
be ~ BOIL

hops
~ beverage ALE
~ kiln OAST

hopscotch GAME

hora DANCE

Horace MANN, POET, ROMAN
~ contemporary OVID
~ work ODE
see also poet

Horae
one of the ~ IRENE

Horatian ___ ODE

Horatio ALGER, DANE

horde ARMY, BAND, CREW, HERD,
HOST, MOB, PRESS, TROOP
~ member HUN

hordeolum STY

horizon
fall below the ~ SET
on the ~ AFAR, AHEAD

"___ Horizon" LOST

horizontal EVEN, FLAT, PRONE
~ bar EVENT, RAIL
~ supporter BEAM

horizontally ACROSS

Hormuz
~ (abbr.) STR
**nation on the Strait of
~** IRAN

horn SIREN
~ accessory MUTE
~ in NOSE, PRY
~ sound BEEP
~ starter TIN
big ~ TUBA
blow one's ~ BLARE
English ~ REED
man with a ~ HARPO
orchestra ~ ALTO
play the ~ TOOT
toot one's own ~ BRAG,
CROW

___ horn (shofar) RAMS

Horn CAPE

hornbeam TREE

hornbill BIRD
~ home NEST

horn-blower
~ sound TOOT

Hornblower
~ wife MARIA

Hornblower, Horatio HERO
~ milieu OCEAN, SEA

Horne LENA
~ solo ARIA

"___ Horne" DOC

horned
~ goddess ISIS

horned ___ TOAD

___ horned owl GREAT

Horne, Marilyn DIVA
~ solo ARIA

Horner, Jack EATER
~ last words AMI
~ treat PIE
emulate ~ EAT

hornet PEST
~ home NEST

hornet's
~ nest ADO

Hornets FIVE, TEAM
~ org. NBA

hornpipe DANCE

horns
lock ~ ARGUE, CLOSE
**take the bull by the
~** BEARD, DARE
the ~ of a dilemma MESS

Hornsby
~ nickname RAJAH

hornswoggle CON, HAVE, SNOW

Hornung PAUL

horologe DIAL

horoscope
do a ~ CAST

Horowitz
~ instrument PIANO

horrendous BAD

horrible BAD, DIRE, EVIL, UGLY,
VILE

horrid BAD, VILE

horrific DIRE

horrify SCARE

horripilating EERIE, EERY

horror FEAR
~ film, with "The" OMEN
giant-ant ~ film THEM
stark ~ PANIC
view with ~ ABHOR, HATE

horror film
~ aide IGOR
~ prop BAT
~ sound GASP, MOAN

"Horrors!" EEK, OHNO, UGH

hors d'oeuvre
~ garnish CAPER
~ spread PATE

horse ANIMAL, ARAB, BAY, MARE,
PET, PINTO, RACER, ROAN,
STEED
~ and carriage RIG
~ around LARK, PLAY
~ brake REIN
~ color BAY
~ command GEE, HAW, WHOA
~ cousin ASS
~ ender HAIR, HIDE, PLAY,
RACE, SHOE
~ fly PEST
~ gait LOPE, PACE, TROT
~ hair MANE
~ healer VET
~ hock ANKLE
~ home BARN
~ meal HAY, OATS
~ mouthpiece BIT
~ noise SNORT
~ opera DRAMA, OATER
~ pace GAIT, TROT
~ preceder CART
~ show FAIR
~ show locale ARENA
~ stopper WHOA
~ trade DEAL
back the wrong ~ LOSE
carriage ~ HACK
charley ~ SPASM
draft ~ HACK
eat like a ~ GLUT
father ~ SIRE, STUD
female ~ MARE
get on a ~ RIDE
harness-racing ~ PACER
left, to a ~ HAW
mother ~ MARE
multicolored ~ ROAN
old ~ NAG
pack ~ HACK
pommel ~ EVENT
reddish-brown ~ ROAN
right, to a ~ GEE
rocking ~ TOY
saddle ~ HACK

horse ___

speckled ~ ROAN
spotted ~ PAINT
stocky ~ COB
the Phantom's ~ HERO
TV's talking ~ MRED
where ~ races start GATE
work ~ HACK
young ~ COLT, FOAL

horse ___ OPERA, RACE, SENSE, TRADE

___ horse IRON, SEA

___-horse WAR

"___ Horse, The" IRON

horse-and-buggy PASSE
~ users AMISH

horseback
~ rider outfit HABIT
deputies on ~ POSSE
go by ~ RIDE

horsefeathers TRASH

horse-height
~ measure HAND

horsehide BALL

"Horse in the ___ Flannel Suit, The" GRAY

"Horse in the Gray Flannel ___, The" SUIT

horseless
~ carriage AUTO, CAR

Horse of the Year
1947 ~ ARMED

horseplay GAME

horsepower
~ coiner WATT
~ fraction WATT

horses
fresh team of ~ RELAY
group of ~ SPAN, TEAM
hold one's ~ REIN, WAIT
like some ~' hooves SHOD

horseshoe ARCH, BOW, CRAB

horseshoes GAME
play ~ TOSS

horsetail PLANT

horse-to-be FOAL

___-horse town ONE

horse-trade SWAP

horsewhip BEAT, LACE, LASH, TAN

"Horse Without a ___, The" HEAD

horsey
~ sport POLO

Horsley LEE

Horton
~ creator SEUSS

"Horton Hears a ___!" WHO

Horus GOD
~ to Osiris SON
mother of ~ ISIS

hose
~ down WET
~ filler LEG
~ material NYLON
~ mishap RUN, SNAG
~ part HEEL, TOE
garden ~ PIPE

hosiery
~ fabric LISLE
~ material NYLON
~ shade ECRU, NUDE, TAUPE

Hoskins BOB
~ role SMEE

hosp.
~ chart EEG
~ employee EMT
~ employees DRS, MDS, RNS
~ facilities ERS, ORS
~ supply MED

hospice HAVEN, HOTEL, INN

hospitable
be ~ to HOST, TREAT
not ~ ICY

hospital
~ capacity BEDS
~ furniture BED
~ supply SERA, SERUM
~ unit WARD
~ worker NURSE

"___ Hospitality" OUR

Hoss
~ brother ADAM, JOE
~ father BEN
~ to Ben SON

host ARMY, BAND, CATER, CREW, HERD, HORDE, MOB, OCEAN, PILE, PRESS, RAFT, SEA, SLEW
~ ender ESS
~ request RSVP
former Miss America ~ ELY
game-show ~ EMCEE
play ~ EMCEE, TREAT
roast ~ EMCEE
Valhalla ~ ODIN

hostel INN

hostess
former Washington ~ MESTA

"Hostess with the Mostes'" MESTA

hostile ALIEN, ENEMY, ILL, UGLY

hostilities WAR
suspension of ~ PEACE

hostility ANGER, HATE, IRE, SPITE

hot EAGER, LIVE, NEW, RED
~ air GAS, STEAM, TALK, TRASH
~ beverage COCOA, TEA
~ chip dip SALSA
~ chocolate COCOA
~ coal EMBER
~ crime ARSON
~ dish CHILI
~ ender BED, HEAD, SHOT
~ foot APACE
~ goods LOOT
~ item FAD, NEWS, RAGE

~ lead CLUE
~ mo. AUG
~ off the press FAD, NEW
~ pants FAD, RAGE
~ pepper CHILI
~ rocks ICE, LAVA
~ rod AUTO, CAR, RACER
~ sauce MOLE
~ spot DESERT, KILN, OVEN, SAUNA, SPA
~ spot in the galaxy SUN
~ spring SPA
~ stuff ANGER, FIRE, LAVA
~ temper ANGER
~ topic ISSUE
~ to trot EAGER
~ trend RAGE
~ tub SPA
~ under the collar IRATE, RILED, SORE, UPSET
~ water HOLE
blow ~ and cold HANG
it can be ~ AIR
jalapeño ~ stuff SALSA
not ~ WARM
not so ~ COOL, MILD, SOSO, TEPID

hot ___ AIR, CAKE, DOG, LINE, PLATE, POT, ROD, SEAT, SPOT, TUB, WATER

hot ___ the collar UNDER

hot-___ (start without a key) WIRE

hot-___ bottle WATER

___-hot RED

"Hot ___" WATER

"Hot ___ and Cold Feet" LEAD

"Hot ___" Houlihan LIPS

hot-air
~ bath SAUNA

hotbed NEST

hotcakes
go like ~ SELL

hot cross
~ bun time LENT

"Hot cross buns, ___ penny, two..." ONEA

hot dog HAM
~ covering SKIN
~ length, perhaps FOOT
~ topping CHILI
place to buy a ~ STAND

hotel ABODE, INN
~ convenience SAFE
~ employee VALET
~ ender IER
~ housekeeper MAID
~ lobby locale DESK
~ offering BED
~ price RATE
~ sign EXIT, ICE
~ supply LINEN
~ visit STAY
country ~ INN
floating ~ LINER
imposing ~ lobbies ATRIA

"Hotel ___ Hampshire, The" NEW

hôtelier HOST

hotfoot
~ it DASH, HIE, RACE, RUN, SPEED

hotheaded IRATE, RASH

"Hot Lead ___ Cold Feet" AND

"Hot Lead and Cold ___" FEET

"Hot Lips" NURSE
TV series featuring ~ MASH

hot on the ___ TRAIL

Hotpoint
~ rival AMANA

hot rod AUTO, CAR, MOTOR

hotshot
~ flier ACE

"Hot Shots"
~ actor SHEEN

Hot Springs SPA
~ st. ARK

Hotspur
~ slayer HAL

"___ Hot Summer, The" LONG

"___ Hot Ta Trot" TOO

hot to ___ TROT

"___ Hot to Handle" TOO

hot weather
~ quencher ADE

Houlihan MAJOR, NURSE

Houlihan, "Hot Lips"
~ show MASH

hound ANIMAL, BAIT, BESET, CHASE, DOG, TAG
~ quarry HARE
~ trail SCENT

___ hound MEDIA

"Hound ___" DOG

"Hound-___ Man" DOG

"Hound-Dog ___" MAN

"Hound of Heaven, The" POEM

hounds
chase ~ RIDE
hare and ~ GAME
ride to ~ HUNT

hound's-___ check TOOTH

hour TIME
~ in Spanish HORA
at the eleventh ~ LATE
evening ~ NINE, SIX, TEN
man of the ~ HERO, LION
prime-time ~ NINE, TEN
wee ~ ONE, TWO

___ hour ZERO

___-hour HALF, OFF

hourglass
~ filler SAND

hours
~ from now LATER
after ~ LATE
in the wee ~ EARLY
like some ~ WEE
until the wee ~ LATE
while away the ~ IDLE, LOAF, TOY

___-hours AFTER

"___ Hours" AFTER

"___ Hours to Kill" THREE

"___ Hour With You" ONE

house ABODE, BED, CLAN, ROOF
~ and grounds ABODE, ESTATE
~ and lot HOME
~ beverage WINE
~ cleaner, in England CHAR
~ covering PAINT
~ drawing PLAN
~ ender BOAT, COAT, HOLD, MAID, MATE, PLANT, SIT, TOP, WARE
~ fly PEST
~ framer STUD
~ grass LAWN
~ in Spanish CASA
~ lot YARD
~ organ PAPER
~ paper DEED
~ part DOOR
~ pet CAT, DOG
~ publication ORGAN
~ shader ELM, OAK, TREE
~ site LOT
~ starter ALE, BATH, BIRD, BOAT, FIRE, HOT, ICE, MAD, PLAY, ROAD, TEA, WARE
~ style RANCH
~ top ATTIC
~ wing ELL
big ~ MANOR
bird ~ NEST
bring down the ~ RAZE, WOW
coat for a ~ PAINT
eat out of ~ and home GLUT
fix up an old ~ REHAB
great ~ ESTATE
high ~ AERIE
ice ~ IGLOO
large ~ ESTATE
manor ~ ABODE
Netherlands royal ~ ORANGE
not a new ~ RESALE
one-story ~ RANCH
on the ~ FREE
Parisian ~ of design DIOR
public ~ BAR, INN
tree ~ NEST
upper ~ SENATE
see also home

house ___ ARREST, CALL, MOUSE, ORGAN, SEAT

___ house BIG, CLEAN, HASH, MANOR, OPEN, OPERA, RANCH, ROW, SAFE, SOLAR, TRACT, TREE

House
~ counterpart SENATE

~ divider AISLE
~ mem. REP

"___ House" ANIMAL, OUR, ROAD, THIS

"___ House, The" BIG, RED

"House at ___ Corner, The" POOH

"House Beautiful"
~ topic DECOR

"Houseboat"
~ actress LOREN

housebreak TRAIN

housebroken TAME

"House by the River, The"
~ director LANG

housecat PET

housecoat ROBE

___ House cookies TOLL

housefly PEST

houseguest TENANT

household
~ animal CAT, DOG, PET
~ appliance IRON
~ chore WASH
~ member CAT, DAD, DOG, MOM, PET, SIS
~ worker MAID
Scottish ~ CLAN

household god
Roman ~ LAR

housekeeper
hotel ~ MAID

housemaid's ___ KNEE

House of ___ DIOR

"House of ___" USHER

"House of ___, The" FEAR

"House of ___ the Gables, The" SEVEN

House of Lancaster
~ symbol ROSE

House of Lords
~ member BARON, PEER, SIR

House of Stuart
~ monarch ANNE

"House of the Rising ___" SUN

"House of the Seven Gables, The"
~ director MAY
~ site SALEM

House of York
~ symbol ROSE

houseplant FERN
spiny ~ ALOE

houseplants
tend the ~ WATER

house-sitter TENANT

housetop ROOF
~ sight VANE

housewarming
~ gift PLANT

housework
do ~ DUST

housing CASE
~ development TRACT
engine ~ POD
missile ~ SILO
tractor ~ BARN

Housman, A.E. POET
see also poet

Houston CITY, MATT, PORT, SAM
~ agcy. NASA
~ athlete ASTRO
~ athlete of yore AERO
~ st. TEX
~ university RICE

"___ Houston" MATT

Houyhnhnms
~ subject YAHOO

hovel ABODE, CRIB, HOLE, HOME, SHED, STY

hover HANG, POISE, SOAR, STAY, WAIT

hovering ABOVE

Hovhaness ALAN

how
~ ender EVER
~ in Spanish COMO
~ others see us IMAGE
~ starter ANY, SOME
~ you feel MOOD
knows ~ CAN

"___ how!" AND

___-how KNOW

"How ___?" COME

"How ___, brown cow" NOW

"How ___ doing?" AMI

"How ___ I Am" DRY

"How ___ that grab you?" DOES

"How ___ you!" DARE

"How about ___!" THAT

"How about that!" GEE

Howard KEEL, KEN, MOE, RON, STERN

Howard, Leslie
~ role ROMEO

Howard, Ron
~ role OPIE

"Howards ___" END

"Howards End"
~ director IVORY

"How awful!" ALAS

"How Can I Be ___" SURE

"How Can I Be Sure"
~ singer EDDIE

"How Deep Is the ___?" OCEAN

"How disgusting!" UGH

"How does that ___ you?" GRAB

"How do I love ___?" THEE

"How do I love thee?" POEM

"How Do You Speak to an ___" ANGEL

"How Dry ___" IAM

"Howdy!"
say ~ to GREET

"___ Howdy Doody time!" ITS

Howe ELIAS
~ on "Cheers" ALLEY

however YET

"How Green ___ My Valley" WAS

"How High the ___" MOON

howitzer GUN
~ need AMMO

howitzers
~ (abbr.) ARTY

howl BAWL, BAY, CRY, KEEN, NOISE, RAVE, ROAR, STORM
~ at the moon BAY
like a wolf's ~ EERIE, EERY

"Howling, The"
~ director DANTE

"Howling ___" Murdock of "The A-Team" MAD

howls
like ~ in the night EERIE, EERY

"How now! ___?" ARAT

"How soothing!" AAH

"How sweet ___!" ITIS

"How the ___ Was Won" WEST

"How the Grinch ___ Christmas" STOLE

"How the Other Half Lives"
~ author RIIS

"How the West ___ Won" WAS

"How the West Was ___" WON

"How the West Was Won" OATER

how-to
~ part STEP

"How to ___ a Million" STEAL

"How to Get ___ in Advertising" AHEAD

"How U ___ Me Now" LIKE

"How U Like Me ___" NOW

"How was ___ know?" ITO

hoyden BRAT, GIRL, KID, LASS, SNIP

Hoyle FRED

hr.
~ part MIN, SEC

H&R Block
~ staffer CPA

HRH
  part of ~ HER, HIS

H.S.
  ~ **course** ALG, BIO, ENG, MATH, MUS, SCI
  ~ **exam** PSAT, SAT
  ~ **organization** PTA
  ~ **science** BIO
  ~ **VIPs** SRS
  certain ~ student SEN
  see also high school

Hsing-Hsing PANDA

HST DEM, PRES
  ~ **successor** DDE
  ~ **would-be successor** AES

ht. ALT, ELEV

hub CORE, MECCA, MIDST
  ~ **of old Athens** AGORA
  wheel ~ NAVE

"Hubba-hubba!" WOW

Hubbard CAL

Hubbard, Mother DRESS
  ~ **pet** DOG
  ~ **quest** BONE
  like ~ OLD
  like ~'s cupboard BARE

Hubbell CARL
  ~ **teammate** OTT

Hubble
  ~ **component** LENS

hubble-bubble PIPE

hubbub ADO, CRY, DIN, FLAP, NOISE, STIR, TODO, YEAST

hubby MATE

hubris PRIDE
  ~ **source** EGO

huck
  ~ **ender** STER

"Hud"
  ~ **cinematographer** HOWE
  ~ **Oscar-winner** NEAL

huddle HEAP, MEET, PRESS
  ~ **count** ELEVEN
  go into a ~ MASS

Hudson AUTO, BAY, CAR
  ~ **contemporary** REO
  city on the ~ TROY

Hudson Bay
  ~ **tribe** CREE

Hudson River
  ~ **canal** ERIE

hue COLOR, DYE, SHADE, TINGE, TINT, TONE
  ~ **and cry** ALARM, NOISE
  ~ **changer** DYE
  ~ **partner** CRY
  blue ~ TEAL
  green ~ LIME
  hair ~ GRAY, GREY
  sunset ~ RED
  yellow ~ LEMON
  see also color

hue and cry ADO

huemul DEER

Huey LONG

Huey, Dewey, and Louie TRIO

huff ANGER, GASP, PET, SNIT, SNORT
  ~ **and puff** GASP, PANT
  in a ~ IRATE, MAD, UPSET

huffy IRATE, SOUR, TESTY, UPSET

hug CARESS, CLASP, GREET, HOLD, LOVE, PRESS

___ hug BEAR

huge AMPLE, BIG, EPIC, GIANT, GREAT, LARGE, VAST
  ~ **amount** SLEW
  ~ **(prefix)** MEGA

___-huggers HIP

hugging CLOSE

Hughes TED

Hugo AWARD
  see also French

"___ Huguenots" LES

huit
  ~ **preceder** SEPT

hula DANCE
  ~ **accessory** LEI
  ~ **strings** UKE
  where to see a ~ LUAU

Hula-Hoops FAD

hulking BIG, LARGE

Hulk, The HERO

hulky BIG, LARGE

hull CASE, COAT, PEEL, POD, SHELL, SKIN
  ~ **appendage** FIN
  ~ **backbone** KEEL
  ~ **interior** HOLD
  ~ **piece** RIB
  ~ **plank** WALE
  bean ~ POD
  outer ~ of a trimaran AMA

Hull
  ~ **workplace** ICE, RINK
  "Constitution" commander
  ~ ISAAC

hullabaloo ADO, DIN, FLAP, NOISE, STIR

Hulme
  ~ **heroine** NUN

Hulot
  ~ **portrayer** TATI

hum DRONE, NOISE, STIR
  ~ **of business** PRESS

human
  ~ **being** SELF, SOUL
  ~ **body** CLAY
  ~ **dynamo** DEMON, DOER
  act ~ ERR
  the ~ condition LIFE
  the ~ race EARTH, MAN

human ___ RACE

"Human Concretion"
  ~ **artist** ARP

humane BIG, GOOD, GREAT
  ~ **org.** SPCA

humanitarian
  ~ **concern** NEEDY

humanities ARTS

humanity EARTH

"Humanoids From the ___" DEEP

Humbard REX

Humber
  ~ **tributary** TRENT

humble ABASE, LOW, MEAN, MEEK, POOR, SMALL
  ~ **oneself to** BOW
  not ~ VAIN
  take a ~ position KNEEL

humble ___ PIE

humbled
  meal for the ~ CROW

___ humble pie EAT

Humboldt BAY

humbug BLAH, POOH, PRATE, ROT, TRASH

"___ humbug!" BAH

"Humbug!" BAH, PAH, PSHAW

humdinger LULU, ONER, PIP

humdrum ARID, BANAL, BLAH, DRAB, SLOW, STALE, TAME

humerus BONE
  ~ **neighbor** ULNA
  ~ **site** ARM

humid CLOSE, DAMP

humidify DAMP

humidity DAMP

humiliate ABASE, ROAST, SHAME, SNUB

humiliated SMALL

humiliation SHAME

humility
  eschew ~ BRAG, CROW

hummer BIRD

hummingbird
  move like a ~ DART

humongous BIG, GIANT, LARGE, VAST
  ~ **(prefix)** MEGA
  ~ **quantity** OCEAN, RAFT, SCAD, SEA

humor MOOD, PLEASE, WIT
  ~ **response** HAHA
  bad ~ ANGER
  black ~ GENRE
  bodily ~ BILE
  country ~ CORN

first name in homespun
  ~ ERMA

"Hee Haw" ~ CORN

overwhelm, as with ~ SLAY

sardonic ~ IRONY

sense of ~ WIT

some ~ CAMP

unsophisticated ~ CORN

humorous DRY, RICH
  dryly ~ WRY

hump NODE
  ~ **it** HIE, RACE, RUN

humpback
  ~ **home** OCEAN, SEA

humped
  ~ **animal** CAMEL

Humpty Dumpty EGG
  like ~ OVAL, OVATE

"Humpty Dumpty sat ___ wall" ONA

humus EARTH, LAND, SOIL

Hun
  ~ **king** ATLI

hunch BEND
  have a ~ FEEL, OPINE, SENSE

___ hunch ONA

"Hunchback of Notre ___, The" DAME

"Hunchback of Notre Dame, The"
  ~ **director** WISE

hundred
  DC ~ SENATE
  one in a ~ CENT
  one ~ percent FINE

"___ Hundred and One Dalmatians" ONE

hundred dollar
  ~ **bill** CNOTE

"___ Hundred Men and a Girl" ONE

"Hundred Secret Senses, The"
  ~ **author** TAN

hundredth
  ~ **part (abbr.)** PCT

Hundred Years' ___ WAR

Hungarian
  ~ **composer** LEHAR
  ~ **violinist** AUER

hunger ITCH, LONG, YEARN
  ~ **for** DIE, NEED, PINE, WANT
  end one's ~ EAT
  feeling of ~ PANG

hunger strike
  go on a ~ FAST

hungry AVID
  go ~ FAST

hungry ___ bear ASA

"___ Hungry" STAY

hung up LATE

hunk CLOD, MASS, PART, SLAB, SLICE, STUD
~ of junk LEMON
Olympian ~ APOLLO

hunker
~ down SIT

Hunkpapa TRIBE

hunky-dory AOK, FINE, GOOD, ROSY

hunt SEEK, TRAIL
~ and peck TYPE
fox ~ CHASE
goddess of the ~ DIANA
scavenger ~ GAME
treasure ~ GAME

Hunt HELEN

"Hunt ___ Red October, The" FOR

"___ Hunt" MAN

hunted
the ~ PREY

hunter HORSE
~ mark PREY
~ need AMMO
~ org. NRA
~ post STAND
~ prey GAME
~ weapon RIFLE
Biblical ~ ESAU
cartoon ~ ELMER
celestial ~ ORION
falcon ~ SPADE
mythical ~ ORION
treasure ~'s aid SONAR
wildebeest ~ LION

Hunter EVAN, IAN, KIM, TAB, TIM

"___ Hunter, The" DEER

Hunter, Holly
~ film, with "The" PIANO

hunter's ___ MOON

Hunter, Tim
~ film of 1982 TEX

"Hunt for ___ October, The" RED

hunting CHASE

Hunt, Leigh
see poet

Huntley CHET

Huntsville
~ st. ALA

Huntz HALL

Hupmobile AUTO, CAR
~ contemporary REO

"___-Hur" BEN

hurdle BAR, LEAP, SNAG
lawyer's ~ BAR
student's ~ ORAL

hurdy-gurdy ORGAN

hurl CAST, DASH, LOB, PASS, PELT,
SLAM, TOSS
~ defiance at DARE
~ forth ERUPT

hurler
~ stat. ERA
mythic hammer ~ THOR

hurly-burly ADO, MELEE

Hurok SOL

Huron LAKE, TRIBE
~ neighbor ERIE
~ st. SDAK

"Hurrah!" CRY
~ in Spanish OLE

"___ Hurrah, The" LAST

hurray
~ preceder HIP

hurricane STORM
~ center EYE
~ track PATH
1964 ~ DORA
1972 ~ AGNES
every other ~ HER
like a ~ center CALM

hurricane ___ LAMP

Hurricanes SIX, TEAM
~ milieu ICE, RINK
~ org. NHL
~ school MIAMI

hurried RAPID

hurriedly APACE

hurry ADO, DART, DASH, HASTE,
HIE, RACE, RUN, SPEED, TEAR
~ along TROT
~ off FLIT
great ~ PRESS
leave in a ~ FLEE, HIE, RUN

"Hurry!" ASAP, STAT
~ in a hospital STAT

hurrying ADO

hurry-scurry ADO

hurry-up
~ letters ASAP
~ word STAT

"Hurry up and ___" WAIT

hurt ACHE, AIL, COST, HARM, MAIM,
MAR, PAIN, SCAR, SMART
~ a toe STUB
dull ~ ACHE

hurtful BAD, EVIL, ILL

hurting ACHY, SORE

hurtle PLOW

husband MALE, MAN, MATE, SAVE,
SPARE, STORE
~ and wife DUO, PAIR
first ~ ADAM
Frau's ~ HERR

___ husbandry ANIMAL

husbands
former ~ EXES

"Husbands ___ Wives" AND

"Husbands and Wives"
~ director ALLEN

hush ALLAY, CALM, MUTE, PEACE

hushed LOW

hush-hush
~ org. CIA

"Hush...Hush, ___ Charlotte" SWEET

Husing TED

husk CASE, COAT, PARE, PEEL,
POD, SHELL, SKIN
grain ~ BRAN

husker
~ unit EAR

husking ___ BEE

husky BIG, HALE, LARGE
~ group TEAM
~ load SLED

hussar
~ blade SABER

Hussein, King ARAB

hustle ADO, HASTE, HIE, PRESS,
RACE, RUN, SCAM, SELL, SPEED,
STIR

"Hustler, The"
~ prop CUE, RACK

hut ABODE, CAMP, COT, HOLE,
HOME, SHED
dome-shaped ~ IGLOO

"hut"
~ follower ONE

hutch ABODE, CHEST, HOME, PEN

Hutch
TV's ~ SOUL

Huxley, Julian SIR
book by ~ ANTS

Huxtable ADA

Huxtable, Cliff
~ portrayer, familiarly COS

"Huzzah!" CRY
~ in Spanish OLE

hwy. RTE
~ sign abbr. ALT

hwys. RDS

hyacinth COLOR
~ home BED

hyaline CLEAR

hyalite OPAL

Hyams PETER

Hyannis
~ course COD, SCROD

hybrid MULE, PLANT

Hyde, Mr.
like ~ EVIL

Hyde Park
~ carrier PRAM
pad off ~ FLAT
see also British, English

Hyderabad CITY
~ dress SARI
see also Indian

Hydra
constellation near ~ LEO
number of ~'s heads NINE

hydrant
~ hookup HOSE

___ hydrant FIRE

hydraulic ___ PRESS, RAM

hydrocarbon
~ suffix ANE, ENE
simple ~ ETHANE

hydrochloric ACID

hydroelectric
~ org. TVA
~ project DAM

hydrofoil BOAT, SHIP

hydrogen GAS
~ sulfide GAS

hydromassage
~ facility SPA

hydrophobic RABID

hydrophyte
tiny ~ ALGA

hydroplane BOAT

Hydrox
~ rival OREO

hydroxide
~ solution LYE

hydroxyl
~ compound ENOL

hyena ANIMAL
Capp's ~ LENA

hyetal RAINY

___ hygiene ORAL

Hyman MAC

___ Hyman Award FLO

hymenopteran BEE

hymn LAUD, POEM, PSALM, SING,
SONG, TUNE
~ accompaniment ORGAN
~ finale AMEN
~ of praise ODE, PAEAN

"Hymn to Apollo" POEM

"Hymn to Intellectual Beauty" POEM

"Hymn to Proserpine" POEM

"Hymn to the Night" POEM

hype
~ up AROUSE

hyper
hardly ~ SEDATE, STAID

hyperbola ARC, BOW

hyperbolize BRAG, RANT

Hyperion MOON, TITAN
daughter of ~ EOS

hypertrophic BIG, LARGE

hyperventilate PANT

hyphen
~ **kin** DASH

hypnosis
~ **starter** SELF

hypnotic OPIATE

hypnotist
~ **word** SLEEP

hypnotized UNDER

hypo NEEDLE

hypochondriac
~ **complaint** ACHE

hypocrisy CANT, POSE

hypocrite LIAR, SHAM

hypocritical FALSE
act ~ LIE, MASK

hypos
~ **contents** SERA

hypostasis ESSENCE

hypotenuse SIDE

hypothesis IDEA, ISM

hypothetical PURE

hypotheticals IFS

hyrax ANIMAL

hyson TEA

hysteria MANIA, PANIC

hysterical
something ~ RIOT

hysterics
go into ~ RAGE, RAMP, RANT

Hyundai AUTO, CAR
~ **headquarters** KOREA

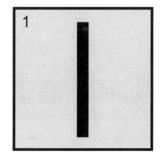

1

i
~ before e except after
   c RULE

"¡"
complete an ~ DOT

I ELEM
~ in German ICH
~ in Latin EGO
~ to a Roman ONE
53 for ~ ATNO
Greek ~ IOTA

"I"
~ in "The King and I" ANNA
~ trouble EGO

"I __" SPY

"I __!" SAY

"I __ a Male War Bride" WAS

"I __ America Singing" HEAR

"I __ a Parade" LOVE

"I __ a Symphony" HEAR

"I __ a Teenage Werewolf" WAS

"I __ at the Stars" AIM

"I __ a Zombie for the FBI" WAS

"I __ Camera" AMA

"I __ Dancer" AMA

"I __ Fine" FEEL

"I __ Fugitive From a Chain
Gang" AMA

"I __ Get It for You Wholesale"
CAN

"I __ Get No Satisfaction" CANT

"I __ Get Started" CANT

"I __ Good" FEEL

"I __ Got Nobody" AINT

"I __ Have Eyes for You" ONLY

"I __ Letter to My Love" SENTA

"I __ Lucy" LOVE

"I __ Made to Love Her" WAS

"I __ My Sugar in Salt Lake
City" LOST

"I __ no kick from cham-
pagne..." GET

"I __ Plenty o' Nuttin'" GOT

"I __ Promised You a Rose
Garden" NEVER

"I __ Rhythm" GOT

"I __ Rock" AMA

"I __ Russia $1200" OWE

"I __ Sang for My Father"
NEVER

"I __ See for Miles" CAN

"I __ Stop Loving You" CANT

"I __ thee late a rosy" SENT

"I __ the Sheriff" SHOT

"I __ Thief" AMA

"I __ Three Lives" LED

"I __ to Cook Book" HATE

"I __ to Hold Your Hand" WANT

"I __ to Live!" WANT

"I __ Trouble" LOVE

"I __ what I see..." EAT

"I __ What You Did" SAW

"I __ You" LOVE, NEED, WANT

"I __ You, Alice B. Toklas" LOVE

"I __ You Babe" GOT

"I __ you one!" OWE

"I __ you so!" TOLD

"I, __" TINA

I-__ BEAM

__ I (communications satellite)
ECHO

Ia.
   see Iowa

I-70 RTE

I-79
~ terminus ERIE

I-80 RTE

I-95 RTE

Iacocca LEE

"Iacta alea __" EST

IAD
~ abbr. ARR, ETA
~ posting ETA

Iago
emulate ~ LIE

"I agree!" AMEN

"I Aim at the __" STARS

"I Ain't __ Nobody" GOT

"I Ain't Marching Anymore"
~ singer OCHS

__ I Am SAM

"I Am a __" CAMERA

"I Am a Fugitive From a Chain
__" GANG

"I Am a Fugitive From a Chain
Gang"
~ actor MUNI
~ director LEROY

iamb FOOT

"I am the __ of the sphere..."
OWNER

-ian
~ cousin IST, ITE, STER

Iapetus MOON, TITAN

"__ I a stinker?" AINT

Ibarguren, Eva
née ~ PERON

"__ Ibbetson" PETER

I-beam PILE
~ material STEEL

"I beg your pardon!" AHEM

I believe
~ in Latin CREDO

"I Believe"
~ singer LAINE

Iberia
most of ~ SPAIN

Iberian
~ river EBRO

ibex ANIMAL, GOAT

ibid. SAME

ibis BIRD

IBM
~ and others COS
~ rival APPLE, DEC
part of ~ BUS, INT

IBM-compatible
not ~ MAC

Ibn Saud ARAB

Ibsen NORSE
~ character ASE, NORA
~ home OSLO
~ specialty DRAMA

ibuprofen
~ target ACHE

Icahn CARL

"I Can __ It for You Wholesale"
GET

"I Can Get It __ You Wholesale"
FOR

"I Can Get It for __ Wholesale"
YOU

"I cannot tell __" ALIE

"I Can See Clearly Now"
~ singer NASH

"I Can't __" WAIT

Icarus
~ to Daedalus SON
emulate ~ SOAR

ICBM
1950s ~ ATLAS
part of ~ INTER

ice COOL, GEM, STONE
~ chunk FLOE
~ field FLOE
~ floe BERG
~ gripper TONG
~ hockey GAME
~ hockey locale ARENA
~ house IGLOO
~ mass BERG, CALF, FLOE
~ melter RAIN, SALT, TEA
~ palace RINK
~ pellets HAIL, SLEET
~ pick AWL, TOOL

ice ___

~ **rink** ARENA
~ **skater's move** AXEL
block of ~ FLOE
break the ~ OPEN, START
falling ~ SLEET
liquor over cracked ~ MIST
move on ~ SKATE
oceanic ~ FLOE
on ~ SURE
put on ~ DEFER, TABLE
skate on thin ~ BEARD, RISK
travel on ~ SKATE
wayward ~ BERG
without ~ NEAT
work out on ~ SKATE

ice ___ BAG, BLUE, CREAM, FLOE, SHEET, SHOW, SKATE, STORM, WATER

___ ice DRY

Ice AGE

Ice ___ AGE

Ice Age
~ **formation** ESKER

iceberg
~ **extremity** TIP

iceboat
~ **necessity** SAIL

icebox
~ **visit** RAID
raid the ~ NOSH

icebreaker BOAT, SHIP

___ ice cap POLAR

Ice Capades
~ **jump** AXEL
~ **workplace** ARENA, RINK

ice cream TREAT
~ **holder** CONE
~ **ingredient** AGAR
~ **server** SCOOP
~ **serving** DIP
~ **thickener** AGAR
~ **treat** CONE, MALT, SODA

ice cream ___ CONE, SODA

Ice Cube
~ **music** RAP

iced
~ **beverage** TEA
~ **dessert** CAKE

iced ___ TEA

iced tea
~ **addition** LEMON, MINT

Ice Follies
~ **venue** RINK

ice-free OPEN

ice hockey
~ **team** SIX

Icel. ISL

Iceland
~ **(abbr.)** ISL

Icelandic
~ **prose** SAGA
~ **tale** EDDA

"Ice Maiden, The" EVERT

Iceni TRIBE

"Ice Palace"
~ **residence** IGLOO

___ Ice Shelf ROSS

ice-show
~ **venue** ARENA, RINK

Ice-T
~ **specialty** RAP

"Ich ___ ein Berliner" BIN

Ichabod CRANE

"Ichabod" POEM

"Ich bin ___ Berliner" EIN

"___ ich liebte" ACH

ichthyoid EEL

icicle
~ **site** EAVE

icing
~ **design** ROSE
~ **on the cake** PLUS
add ~ **to** TOP

"Ick!" UGH

icky
~ **stuff** GOO, SLIME

"I, Claudius"
~ **attire** TOGA
~ **character** NERO

icon IDOL, IMAGE, TOTEM
corporate ~ LOGO

iconoclast REBEL

iconoclastic
~ **art movement** DADA

icosahedron
one of an ~**'s twenty** FACE

"I could ___ unfold..." ATALE

"I couldn't care ___!" LESS

ICU
part of ~ CARE, UNIT

icy ALOOF, BAD
treat an ~ **road** SALT, SAND

id
~ **counterpart** EGO
ATM ~ PIN

id ___ EST

ID CARD, LABEL
~ **data** AGE
ask for an ~ CARD
auto ~ PLATE
means of ~ DNA
provide ~ TAG
see also Idaho

Ida
~ **and others** MTS

Ida ___ ("Kudzu" character) MAE

"Ida, ___ as Apple Cider" SWEET

Ida.
~ **neighbor** NEV
see also Idaho

Idaho STATE
~ **city** BOISE
~ **county** ADA
~ **neighbor** OREGON, UTAH
~ **river** BOISE, SNAKE

___-Ida potatoes ORE

"Ida, Sweet as ___ Cider" APPLE

"I'd be happy to!" YES

"I'd Be Surprisingly Good for You"
~ **musical** EVITA

idea HINT, IMAGE
~ **giver** MUSE
~ **source** GERM
fixed ~ BIAS
get the ~ LEARN, SEE
get the wrong ~ MISS
main ~ GIST, SUM, THEME, TOPIC
vague ~ CLUE

ideal MODEL
~ **ender** ISM, IST
beau ~ MODEL

___ ideal BEAU

idealist
~ **need** CAUSE

idealistic AERIAL

idealize DREAM, EXALT

ideas
exchange ~ TALK
watered-down ~ PAP

"___ Ideas" IGET

identical EVEN, SAME, TWIN
not ~ OTHER

identically ALIKE

identification LABEL

identify LABEL, NAME, PEG, SPOT, TAG
~ **a caller** TRACE

identifying
~ **melody** THEME

identity EGO, PAR, SELF
a question of ~ WHO

ideogram SIGN

ideology CREDO, ISM, TENET

"id est"
the id in ~ THAT

Idi AMIN

idiom ARGOT

idiomatic
~ **language** SLANG

idiosyncrasy HABIT, TIC, TRAIT

idiosyncratic ODD

idiot ASS, DODO, DOLT, DOPE
~ **box** SET

idiotic DAFT, INANE, MAD

Iditarod RACE
~ **conveyance** SLED
~ **destination** NOME

~ **locale** ALASKA
~ **puller** DOG

idle FREE, INERT, LAG, LOAF, OFF, REST, SIT, STOP, VAIN
~ **away** WEAR
~ **talk** GAB, GAS, NEWS, PRATE, TRASH, YAP
make ~ **conversation** CHAT, CHIN, GAB, YAK
remain ~ SIT

Idle ERIC

idler DRONE
~ **antithesis** DOER

idling SLOW

"I'd Love You to Want Me"
~ **singer** LOBO

"I do"
~ **pledger** BRIDE
~ **site** ALTAR
say ~ MATE, WED

"I Do, I Do, I Do, I Do, I Do"
~ **band** ABBA

idol HERO
Biblical ~ BAAL, CALF
matinée ~ MALE

idolize ADORE, DOTE, EXALT, LOVE

"I do not ___ for any crown..." ASK

"___ I Don't Have You" SINCE

"I don't think so!" NAH, NOPE

"I Don't Want ___ Right" TOBE

"I don't want to!" NAH, NOPE

"I Dreamed ___ Hill-Billy Heaven" OFA

"I Dream of Jeannie"
~ **actress** EDEN
~ **role** ROGER, TONY

idyll POEM
~ **setting** LEA

idyllic
~ **locale** EDEN

idyllist POET

"Idylls of the King" POEM
~ **lady** ELAINE, ENID

i.e. IDEST
part of ~ EST

"I eat what ___" ISEE

Ieoh Ming ___ PEI

if
~ **not** ELSE
look as ~ SEEM

"If" POEM
last word of Kipling's ~ SON

"If ___ Could Only Cook" YOU

"If ___ I See You Again" EVER

"If ___ I Would Leave You" EVER

"If ___ make it there..." ICAN

"If ___ the Circus" IRAN

"If ___ the Zoo" IRAN

"If ___ Tuesday, This Must Be Belgium" ITS

"If all ___ fails..." ELSE

"I Feel ___" FINE

"I Feel the Earth ___" MOVE

"___ I Fell for You" SINCE

"If Ever I ___ You Again" SEE

"If I ___ a Million" HAD

"If I ___ King" WERE

"If I ___ you..." WERE

"___ if I can help it!" NOT

"If I Could Turn Back Time"
 ~ singer CHER

"If I Had a Hammer"
 ~ singer TRINI

"If I Only Had the Nerve"
 ~ singer LAHR

"If It Die..."
 ~ autobiographer GIDE

"If It's Tuesday, ___ Must Be Belgium" THIS

"If I've told you ___,..." ONCE

"If I Were King of the Forest"
 ~ singer LAHR

"If looks could kill"
 ~ look GLARE

I forbid
 ~ in Latin VETO

"I Fought the ___" LAW

"If the ___ fits..." SHOE

"If This ___" ISIT

"If Winter comes, can Spring be ___ behind?" FAR

"If you ___" PLEASE

"If you ___ Susie..." KNEW

"If You Could ___ Cook" ONLY

"I Get ___" IDEAS

"I get it!" AHA

"___ I Get It Right" TIL

"I give up!" UNCLE

igloo ABODE
 ~ shape DOME

igloo-shaped
 onetime ~ auto PACER

igneous
 ~ rock LAVA

ignis
 ~ fatuus DREAM

ignite FIRE, HEAT, START
 ~ the spark AROUSE

ignited LIT
 ~ again RELIT

ignition
 ~ component COIL

awaiting ~ UNLIT

ignition system
 ~ part CAM

ignoble BASE, EVIL, LOW, MEAN, SMALL, UGLY, VILE

ignominy SHAME

ignore CUT, ELIDE, OMIT, SHUN, SKIP, SNUB
 ~ the limit SPEED
 ~ the script ADLIB
 word alphabetizers ~ THE

ignorer
 strike ~ SCAB

Igor
 ~ to Frankenstein AIDE

"I Got ___" ANAME

"I Got Rhythm"
 last word of ~ MORE

"I Got You Babe"
 ~ singer CHER

"___ I had heard of Lucy Gray" OFT

"I Hate ___" MEN

"I hope to see London once ___ die" EREI

"___ II" (DeLillo novel) MAO

II Chronicles
 book after ~ EZRA

"I intended ___" ANODE

Ijsselmeer LAKE

IJsselmeer
 town on the ~ EDAM

Ike GEN
 ~ alma mater ARMY
 ~ ex TINA
 ~ former address APO
 ~ monogram DDE
 ~ opponent ADLAI
 ~ WWII command ETO
 like ~ BALD
 when ~'s invasion started DDAY

"___ Ike" ALIBI

ikebana ART

"I Kid You Not"
 ~ author PAAR

"I kissed thee ___ kill'd thee" EREI

"___ I Kissed You" TIL

"I Knew a Woman" POEM

"I knew it!" AHA

IL
 see Illinois

Ile-de-France
 ~ river OISE

Ile de la ___ CITE

Ile de la Cité
 ~ site SEINE

"I Left My Heart at the Stage ___ Canteen" DOOR

___-Iles, Quebec SEPT

ILGWU
 do an ~ job SEW

"Iliad" EPIC, EPOS, POEM
 ~ author HOMER
 ~ deity HERA
 ~ figure APOLLO, ARES, ATHENA, HELEN, HERA, PARIS
 ~ locale TROY
 messenger, in the ~ IRIS

Iliamna LAKE

Iliescu ION

"I Like ___" BEER, IKE

"I Like It Like ___" THAT

"I Like Your ___" STYLE

Ilium TROY

ilk CUT, GENRE, LIKE, LOT, MOLD, ORDER, RACE, SORT, TYPE

ill AMISS, EVIL, HARM, WOE
 ~ in French MAL
 ~ (prefix) MAL, MIS
 ~ repute SHAME
 ~ temper BILE, IRE, PET
 ~ treatment ABUSE
 ~ will ANGER, HATE, IRE, SPITE
 feel ~ AIL
 looking ~ ASHEN, ASHY, PALE, WAN
 speak ~ of ABASE, LIBEL, SLUR

ill- BRED

Ill.
 ~ neighbor IND, KEN
 see also Illinois

"I'll ___ at Your Wedding" DANCE

"I'll ___ Forget What's 'is Name" NEVER

"I'll ___ Manhattan" TAKE

"I'll ___ my hat!" EAT

"I'll ___ Tomorrow" CRY

ill-advised MAD, RASH

ill at ___ EASE

"I'll Be ___ for Christmas" HOME

"I'll Be With You in ___ Blossom Time" APPLE

ill-boding DIRE

ill-bred CRASS, LOUD, RAW
 ~ fellow BOOR

"I'll Cry Tomorrow"
 ~ director MANN

ill-defined DIM

ill-disposed ACRID, AVERSE

ill-done BAD

illegal
 make ~ BAN

illegible
 render ~ SMEAR

ill-fated BAD, DIRE
 ~ sibling rival ABEL

"I'll get right ___, chief!" ONIT

ill-humored DOUR, RUDE, SOUR, TESTY

illiberal MEAN

illimitable BIG, ETERNAL, LARGE, VAST

Illinois STATE
 ~ Benedictine College site LISLE
 ~ city CAIRO
 ~ neighbor IOWA
 city in ~ CAIRO

"I'll leave it ___ you!" UPTO

ill-looking ASHEN, ASHY, PALE, WAN

ill-mannered CRASS, RUDE
 ~ one BOOR, OAF

ill-natured BAD, MEAN

"I'll Never ___ Again" SMILE

"I'll Never Forget What's 'is ___" NAME

illogical DAFT, FALSE, MAD

ill-omened BAD, DIRE

ills
 the ~ that flesh is heir to LIFE

"I'll say!" AMEN

ill-starred BAD, DIRE

"I'll String ___ With You" ALONG

ill-tempered ACID, MEAN, TART, TESTY
 ~ goddess ERIS
 ~ person OGRE

ill-time MISS

ill-treat ABUSE, MAUL

illuminate GLOW, SHINE

illuminated CLEAR, LIT

illumination LAMP

illumined LIT

ill-use ABUSE, MAUL

illusion DREAM, ERROR

illusional
 ~ painting OPART

illusionist
 ~ org. SAM

illustrate DRAW, SHOW
 ~ by CITE

illustration ART, CASE, PLATE
 book ~ PLATE
 letterhead ~ LOGO
 user-friendly ~ ICON

illustrative
 ~ of LIKE

illustrator
Russian-born ~ ERTE

illustrious BIG, GREAT, NOTED

"ill wind nobody blows good, An" OBOE

ill-wisher ENEMY, FOE

ilmenite ORE

"Il nome della ___" ROSA

Iloilo CITY, PORT

"I Lost My Sugar in ___ Lake City" SALT

"I Lost My Sugar in Salt Lake ___" CITY

I love
~ in Latin AMO

"I Love ___" PARIS

"I Love ___ Again" YOU

"I Love ___, Alice B. Toklas" YOU

"___ I Love" THEE

"___ I Love, The" MAN

"I Love a Parade"
~ composer ARLEN

"I loved you ___" EVER

"___ I Love Her" AND

"I Love Lucy"
~ character ETHEL, FRED
~ name DESI
~ network CBS

"I Love Trouble"
~ actor NOLTE

"I Love You ___" AGAIN

"I Love You, ___ B. Toklas" ALICE

"Il Trovatore" OPERA

Ilyich
Tolstoy's ~ IVAN

"I'm ___" AMAN

"I'm ___" ("Nashville" song) EASY

"I'm ___!" ("Ta-ta!") OFF

"I'm ___ it!" AGIN

"I'm ___ Lisa" NOT

"I'm ___ your tricks!" ONTO

I.M. PEI

"I'm a ___" LOSER

"___, I'm Adam" MADAM

image
~ maker CAMERA
ancestral ~ TOTEM
computer-screen ~ ICON
graven ~ IDOL
holy ~ ICON
indistinct ~ BLUR
Kirlian ~ AURA
mental ~ IDEA
radar ~ BLIP
Rorschach ~ BLOT
temple ~ IDOL

the very ~ of LIKE

"___ Image" SPLIT

imaginary AERIAL
~ line AXIS
not ~ REAL

imagination
product of the ~ DREAM, IDEA

imaginative NEW

imagine DREAM, IDEATE, SEE

"Imagine"
woman in ~ ONO

imagist POET

imago ADULT

imam MALE, TITLE
~ deity ALLAH

Iman MODEL

imaret INN

"___ I Married, The" MAN

imbecile ASS, CLOD, DODO, DOLT, GOOSE

imbecilic DAFT, INANE, MAD

imbed PLANT

imbibe LAP

imbiber
excessive ~ SOT

imbroglio MELEE, ROW, SNARL

imbrue SOAK, STEEP

imbue DYE, SOAK, STEEP

"I'm Dancing as Fast ___ Can" ASI

Imelda
~ obsession SHOE

"I met ___ with..." AMAN

"___ I Met You" UNTIL

"I'm game!" LETS

"I'm Gonna ___ You Sucka" GIT

"I'm Gonna Git ___ Sucka" YOU

imitable
~ example MODEL

imitate APE, ECHO

imitation FAKE, FALSE, PASTE, SHAM
~ (suffix) EEN, ETTE, INE
in ~ of AFTER, ALA

"Imitation of ___" LIFE

imitative
~ words ALA

imitator APE, APER
nature's ~ ART

immaculate CLEAN, PURE

Immanuel KANT, LORD

immaterial AIRY

immature NAIVE

immeasurable DEEP, RICH, VAST
~ gulf ABYSS
~ time EON

immediate
~ to a poet ANEAR

immediately ANON, ASAP, NOW, SOON, STAT, THEN

immemorial OLD, PAST

___ immemorial TIME

immense BIG, GREAT, LARGE, VAST

immensely ALOT

immerse BATHE, DIP, SOAK, STEEP, WASH

immersed RAPT

immersion BATH

immigrant ALIEN
~ island ELLIS

"Immigrants, The"
~ author FAST

imminent NEAR
~ to a poet ANEAR
appear ~ LOOM

immobile INERT
be ~ LIE

immobility REST

immobilize PIN

immoderately TOO

immodest LEWD, RACY

immoral BAD
~ sort RAKE

"Immoralist, The"
~ author GIDE

immortal ETERNAL

"Immortal ___" HATE

"Immortal Beloved"
~ director ROSE

immovable FAST, SET, STERN
be ~ ABIDE

immunizing
~ agents SERA

immunology
~ name SABIN, SALK

immure CAGE

immured PENT

immutable ETERNAL
be ~ ABIDE

"I'm No ___" ANGEL

"I'm not ___ complain" ONETO

"I'm Not ___" LISA

Imogene COCA
~ cohort SID

"I'm outta here!" ADIEU, BYE, CIAO, LATER, TATA

imp BRAT, DEMON, ELF

impact HIT, SMASH
~ harshly JAR

impair HARM, MAIM, MAR, SPOIL, WEAR

impala ANIMAL
~ kin ELAND, GNU

Impala AUTO, CAR

impale GORE, SPEAR

impart LEND, RELATE, SAY

impartial BIG, EVEN, FAIR, HONEST

impassable DENSE

impasse BIND

impassion AROUSE, HEAT, MOVE, ROUSE, STIR

impassioned DEEP, EAGER, MAD

impassive CALM, COOL, SEDATE, STOIC

impatience HASTE

impatient BAD, EAGER, EDGY, TESTY

impeccable CLEAN, PURE

impecuniosity NEED

impecunious NEEDY, POOR

impecuniousness WANT

impede BAR, CLOG, DETER, LIMIT, STOP
~ legally ESTOP

impediment BAR, SNAG

impedimenta GEAR, TRAPS

impel AROUSE, BEND, BIND, MAKE, MOVE, PRESS, PROD, URGE

impend AWAIT, LOOM

impending NEAR

impenetrable DEEP, DENSE

imperative MAIN, ORDER

imperceptible SLOW

imperfect POOR

imperfection CHIP, DENT, MAR, MOLE, SPOT, TAINT

imperial BEARD, REGAL

imperil RISK

imperishable ETERNAL

impersonal DRY
~ pronoun ONE

impersonate APE, PLAY

impersonates DOES

impersonator ACTOR, APER

impertinence NERVE, SASS

impertinent FLIP, RUDE, SASSY
~ one SNIP

imperturbability POISE

imperturbable CALM, COOL, EVEN, SEDATE, SERENE, STOIC

impervious SET
   ~ to feeling STOIC

impetrate ASK, PRAY, URGE

impetuous EAGER, HOT, RASH

impetuousness ELAN

impetus SPUR, URGE

impiety SIN

impious BAD

impish ELFIN
   ~ one ELF

implacable CRUEL, IRON, STERN

implant ROOT, SET

implement START, TOOL, USE
   baker's ~ PEEL
   bricklayer's ~ HOD
   casino ~ RAKE
   farm ~ HOE, PLOW, RAKE
   galley ~ OAR
   lawn ~ EDGER
   manicure ~ FILE
   pizzeria ~ PEEL
   rider's ~ CROP
   sculler's ~ OAR
   wherry ~ OAR
   woodsman's ~ AXE, SAW
   see also tool

implements GEAR

implicate RATON

implication SENSE

implicit TACIT

implied
   ~ as approval TACIT

implore ASK, BEG, CRY, PLEAD, PRAY, SUE, URGE

imply HINT, MEAN, SAY

impolite CRASS, PERT, RUDE, SASSY
   ~ look LEER, OGLE, SNEER, STARE
   ~ one BOOR, LOUT
   ~ sound HIC

import MEAN, SENSE, STRESS

importance NOTE, RANK, STRESS
   self-~ EGO

important BIG, DEAR, GREAT, KEY, MAJOR
   ~ happening EVENT
   ~ one LION
   ~ period EPOCH
   ~ time AGE, ERA
   ~ work OPUS
   be ~ RATE
   most ~ MAIN
   most ~ part GIST
   most ~ (prefix) ARCH

__-important ALL, SELF

importune ASK, BEG, PLEAD, PLY, PRAY, SUE, URGE, WOO

impose ASK, ASSESS, LAY, PUT
   ~ upon ABUSE, USE

imposed
   easily ~ upon MEEK

imposing BIG, LARGE, REGAL
   ~ hotel lobbies ATRIA
   ~ residence ESTATE, MANOR

impossible
   ~ to miss OVERT
   make ~ BAN

"__ Impossible" ITS

impost TOLL

impostor FAKE, SHAM

imposture SHAM

impound CAGE, HOLD, TAKE

impoverish RUIN

impoverished NEEDY, POOR

impoverishment LOSS

impractical MAD

imprecate BLAST

imprecation BAN, OATH

imprecise
   ~ ordinal NTH

impregnable SAFE

impress ETCH, ROB, SET, STEAL, SWAY
   ~ deeply AWE, ETCH
   ~ in a way DENT

impressed
   more than ~ AWED

impression AIR, DENT, IDEA, IMAGE, SENSE, STAMP
   fossil ~ FERN
   get the ~ FEEL, SENSE
   give a false ~ BELIE
   have the ~ OPINE
   lasting ~ SCAR
   make an ~ MOVE, STAMP

impressionist APER
   French ~ DEGAS, MONET

Impressionist
   ~ forerunner MANET

impressive REGAL
   ~ grouping ARRAY

imprest LOAN

imprimatur SEAL

imprint ETCH, SEAL, STAMP
   letterhead ~ LOGO

imprison CAGE, HOLD

improbable TALL

impromptu ADHOC, ADLIB
   ~ decision-maker FLIP
   ~ music session JAM
   ~ screwdriver DIME

improper AMISS, BAD, BLUE, RAW
   slightly ~ RACY

improv
   ~ bit ADLIB, GAG, SKIT

improve AMEND, EDIT, EMEND, GAIN, HEAL, HELP, HONE, MEND
   ~ an edge HONE

   ~ as skills HONE
   ~ as wine AGE
   ~ in a way REDO
   ~ manuscripts EDIT

improved
   ~ partner NEW

"__ Improvement" HOME

improvements
   make ~ in AMEND, EMEND

improvise ADLIB, RIG
   ~ in a way FAKE

improvised ADHOC
   ~ line ADLIB

impudence FACE, LIP, NERVE, SASS

impudent FLIP, PERT, RUDE, SASSY
   ~ one SNIP
   be ~ SASS

impugn CARP

impulse URGE, YEN

__ impulse ONAN

impulsive EAGER, RASH

impure BAD

impute LAY, TAINT

"I'm Sorry"
   ~ singer LEE

"I'm so sorry!" ALAS

"...__ I'm told" ORSO

Imus DON
   ~ brother FRED
   ~ medium RADIO

"I'm working __!" ONIT

in CHIC, ENTREE, HOME, NOW
   ~ a dead heat EVEN
   ~ a foul mood SORE
   ~ agreement ASONE, ATONE
   ~ a huff IRATE, UPSET
   ~ alignment EVEN
   ~ any way EVER
   ~ a while LATER
   ~ broad daylight OVERT
   ~ case LEST
   ~ concert ASONE, ATONE
   ~ disarray MESSY
   ~ front AHEAD, FIRST
   ~ good health FIT, HALE
   ~ in French DANS
   ~ neutral IDLE
   ~ on HEP, HIP
   ~ one piece ENTIRE
   ~ one's birthday suit BARE, NUDE
   ~ one's right mind SANE
   ~ payment of FOR
   ~ perpetuity EVER
   ~ plain view OVERT
   ~ play, as a ball LIVE
   ~ position SET
   ~ readiness ONICE
   ~ reserve APART
   ~ short supply SCANT
   ~ tatters SHOT
   ~ the ball park CLOSE, NEAR

   ~ the center AMID, AMONG
   ~ the wee hours EARLY
   ~ with AMID, AMONG
   ~ years past ONCE

in __ (actually) ESSE

in __ (attuned) SYNC

in __ (bored) ARUT

in __ (completely) TOTO

in __ (following) TOW

in __ (lined up) AROW

in __ (secretly) CAMERA

in __ (stuck) ARUT

in __ (synchronized) PHASE

in __ (under control) HAND

in __ (waiting) STORE

in __ (wholly) TOTO

in __ condition MINT

in __ course DUE

in __ event ANY

in __ for (awaiting) LINE

in __ land (spacy) LALA

in __ of (rather than) LIEU

in __ parentis LOCO

in __ time (soon) GOOD

__ in (admit) TAKE

__ in (approach) CLOSE

__ in (arrest) RUN

__ in (barricade) SHUT

__ in (beat) ALL

__ in (be aware) TUNE

__ in (capture) ROPE

__ in (contribute) CHIP

__ in (enter) COME

__ in (enter en masse) PILE

__ in (exhausted) ALL, DONE

__ in (get up late) SLEEP

__ in (interrupt) CUT

__ in (intervene) STEP

__ in (introduce gradually) PHASE

__ in (intrude) HORN

__ in (liquidate) CASH

__ in (provide info) CLUE

__ in (relate) TIE

__ in (retire) TURN

__ in (slayed) DID

__ in (start) DIG

__ in (store away) LAY

__ in (sub) STAND

__ in (substitute) SIT

__ in (trap) HEM

___ in

___ in (yield) CAVE

___-in (argument) RUN

___-in (cinch) SHOO

___-in (gradual appearance) IRIS

___-in (protest) SIT

___-in (very short putt) TAP

In ELEM
   49 for ~ ATNO

"In ___" (Elton John tune) NEON

"In ___ Chicago" OLD

"In ___ is truth" WINE

"In ___ Only" NAME

"In ___ Our Life" THIS

"In ___ Virginia" OLE

"In-___, The" LAWS

"___-In" STAND

IN
   see Indiana

in a ___ (agitated) SNIT

in a ___ (excited) STATE

in a ___ (strapped) BIND

"In a beautiful ___-green boat" PEA

___ in a blue moon ONCE

"___ in a Cage" LADY

inaccessible ALOOF, COOL

inaccuracy ERROR, LIE, TALE

inaccurate BAD, FALSE, OFF
   be ~ ERR

in a coon's ___ AGE

"In a cowslip's bell ___" ILIE

inactive IDLE, INERT, SLOW
   ~ (abbr.) RET
   be ~ LIE
   not ~ ASTIR

inactivity PEACE, REST

___ in a day's work ALL

inadequacy WANT

inadequate BARE, LAME, POOR, SCANT, SMALL, THIN

inadvertence MISS, SKIP

"___ in a Green Jacket" LADY

in-a-hurry
   ~ letters ASAP
   ~ word STAT

"___ in a Lifetime" ONCE

"In a Little Gypsy ___ Room" TEA

in all ___ conscience GOOD

"In a Lonely Place"
   ~ director RAY

"___ in a manger..." AWAY

"___ in America" LOST, MADE, ONLY

"___ in a Million" ONE

inamorata GIRL, LOVE

inamorato BEAU, LOVE

inane BANAL, DAFT

inanity CAMP

in any ___ EVENT

in any ___ (regardless) CASE

"In a pig's ___!" EYE

___ in "apple" AAS

in apple-pie ___ ORDER

inappreciable MERE, SMALL, TINY

inappropriate AMISS, INEPT

inappropriately AMISS

Inari LAKE

"___ in Arms" BABES

inasmuch
   ~ as SINCE

"___ in a Taxi" LOVE

"___ in a Teacup" STORM

inattentive DEAF
   become ~ NOD

inaugurate OPEN, START, USHER

inauguration ONSET
   ~ highlight OATH

inauspicious BAD, DIRE, ILL

___ in "aviary" AAS

in-between AMID, AMONG

"___ in Black" MEN

"___ in Black, The" SPY

"___ in B Minor" MASS

inboard-outboard
   ~ engine MOTOR

inc.
   ~ cousin LTD

"Inc."
   ~ listings COS

Inca RULER
   ~ territory PERU

Inca Empire
   ~ locale ANDES

incalculable VAST

"___ in Calico" AGAL

incandesce BEAM, GLOW, SHINE

incandescence GLOW

incandescent CLEAR
   ~ light LAMP

incarcerate CAGE

incarnadine RED

incarnate LIVE
   evil ~ SATAN

incautious RASH

Incaviglia PETE

"___ in Cell Block 11" RIOT

incense ANGER, BALM, ENRAGE, IRE, IRK, PEEVE, RILE

incensed IRATE, MAD, UPSET

incentive BAIT, CAUSE, SPUR
   sale ~ REBATE

inception FIRST, ONSET, ROOT, START

incessant ETERNAL

incessantly AWAY, EVER

inch CREEP, EASE, UNIT
   ~ along EDGE, LAG
   ~ multiple FOOT
   ~ sideways SIDLE
   fraction of an ~ HAIR, MIL

inches
   nine ~ SPAN

___ in chief EDITOR

inchmeal SLOW

Inchon CITY, PORT
   ~ country KOREA

incident EVENT, FACT

incidental EXTRA, SIDE
   ~ expense TIP

incinerate ASH, CHAR, HEAT

incinerator
   ~ debris ASH

incise CUT, ETCH, OPEN, SCORE, SLASH

incision CUT, GAP, GASH, SLIT

incisive KEEN

incisor TOOTH

Incitatus HORSE, STEED

incite ABET, AROUSE, EGG, FAN, FIRE, GOAD, IMPEL, MOVE, PROD, ROUSE, SPUR, STING, URGE
   ~ a dog SIC

"___ in Clear River" EVIL

inclemency RIGOR

inclement BAD, RAINY, RAW
   ~ weather SLEET

inclination AIM, BENT, BIAS, CAST, HABIT, SLANT, SLOPE, TASTE, TILT, TREND, TURN
   ~ to anger BILE
   natural ~ BENT
   strong ~ URGE, YEN

incline BEND, BIAS, DROP, HEEL, LEAD, LEAN, LIST, RAMP, RISE, SLANT, SLOPE, TEND, TILT, TREND
   ~ the head NOD

inclined ATILT, BENT, PRONE
   ~ at sea ALIST
   ~ plane RAMP
   ~ (to) APT
   ~ to (suffix) ISH
   be ~ LEAN, SLOPE, TEND
   feel ~ LIKE
   highly ~ STEEP
   not ~ AVERSE

include ADD, HAVE
   opposite of ~ DROP, OMIT

included
   ~ with AMID, AMONG
   not ~ APART, OUT

including ALSO, AND, PLUS
   not ~ SANS

inclusive TOTAL
   ~ abbr. ETC
   ~ pronoun OUR, OURS

___-inclusive ALL

___ incognita TERRA

incognito
   go ~ MASK

incognizant DEAF

income ALMS, FARE, FEE, RENT, TAKE
   ~ (abbr.) REV
   investor ~ INT

incoming
   ~ plane ARR
   ~ plane datum ETA

incommensurate SMALL

incomparable ALONE, GREAT, RARE
   ~ ender EST

incompetent INEPT

incompletely HALF, PART

incomprehensible DEEP, HARD

incongruity IRONY

incongruousness IRONY

inconsequential SMALL, TINY

inconsiderate CRASS, RUDE

inconsistency
   story ~ HOLE

inconsolable SAD

incontestable CLEAR, SURE

incontrovertible SOLID, SURE

incorporate MELD, UNITE

incorporeal AERIAL

incorrect BAD, FALSE, OFF
   ~ (prefix) PARA
   be ~ ERR

incorruptible HONEST

incr. ENL
   ~ in benefits COLA

increase ADD, BOOM, GAIN, GROW, HIKE, PAD, RAISE, RISE
   ~ the volume BLARE
   price ~ HIKE
   salary ~ RAISE

increased
   ~ by AND, PLUS

increases UPS

incredible TALL

"Incredible Shrinking ___, The" MAN

increment RISE
    inflation-related ~ COLA

incriminate RATON

in crowd CLAN, ELITE

incrustation RIND

incubate SIT

incubus DEMON, DREAM

inculcate PLANT, TRAIN
    ~ as suspicion SOW

incumbency POST

incumbents INS

incursion RAID

"___ in D" TANGO

Ind.
    ~ neighbor ILL, KEN
    see also Indiana

indecency DIRT

indecent BAD, BASE, BLUE, LEWD

indecision
    ~ sounds ERS

indecisive
    be ~ HEM, TEETER

indeed AMEN, AYE, EVEN, NAY, YEA, YES

"___, indeed!" YES

indefinite OPEN
    ~ amount ANY, FEW, SOME

"___ Indefinite" TIME

indelible INK, SET

indelicate CRASS, RACY

indemnify PAY

indentation BAY, RUT

indentured
    ~ toiler ESNE, SERF

Independence
    ~ initials HST

"Independence Day"
    ~ attackers ETS

Independence Hall
    ~ st. PENN

independent FREE
    ~ one LONER

independently ALONE, APART

indestructible ETERNAL
    be ~ ABIDE

indeterminate GRAY, GREY
    ~ amount ANY

index KEY, LIST

indexing
    word ignored in ~ THE

India INK
    ~ invader ARYAN
    ~ location ASIA
    ~ native HINDU
    ~ neighbor NEPAL
    actor from ~ SABU

board game from ~ CHESS
bwana, in ~ SAHIB
city in ~ AGRA
diamond of ~ HOPE
district of ~ GOA
effendi, in ~ SAHIB
former title in ~ SAHIB
Mogul capital of ~ AGRA
princess of ~ RANEE, RANI
sir, in ~ SAHIB
social stratum, in ~ CASTE
song of ~ RAGA
state in ~ ASSAM
stringed instrument of
    ~ SITAR
wood from ~ EBONY
    see also Indian

India ___ INK, PAPER

___ India AIR

Indian ASIAN, OCEAN
    ~ address SAHIB, SRI
    ~ boat CANOE
    ~ carving TOTEM
    ~ coin ANNA
    ~ dwelling TEPEE
    ~ export TEA
    ~ file LINE
    ~ garment SARI
    ~ instrument SITAR
    ~ music RAGA
    ~ nursemaid AMA, AMAH
    ~ pipe PLANT
    ~ prince RAJAH
    ~ princess RANEE, RANI
    ~ state ASSAM
    ~ statesman NEHRU
    ~ subdivision TRIBE
    ~ tea source ASSAM
    ~ tribe CREE, ERIE, HOPI
    ~ weight SER
    French and ~ WAR
    on the ~ ASEA, ATSEA
    palindromic ~ OTO
    see also India

Indian ___ CORN, FILE

Indiana STATE
    ~ basketballer PACER
    ~ humorist ADE

"Indiana ___" MOON

"___, Indiana" EERIE

Indiana Jones HERO
    ~ quest ARK

"Indiana Jones and the Temple of ___" DOOM

Indianapolis
    ~ footballer COLT

Indiana, Robert
    ~ painting LOVE

Indian Head CENT

Indian Ocean
    ~ vessel DHOW

Indianola
    ~ location IOWA

"Indian Runner, The"
    ~ actor MORSE
    ~ director PENN

Indians TEAM, TEN

Indic
    ~ language URDU

indicate ARGUE, BODE, HINT, MEAN, NAME, SHOW
    ~ approval NOD
    ~ a preference OPT
    ~ by signs BODE

indication CLUE, CUE, NOD, SIGN, TOKEN, TRACE
    advance ~ OMEN
    chart ~ TREND
    have every ~ of SEEM
    map ~ ROAD, ROUTE
    subtle ~ HINT

indicative
    ~ of LIKE

indicator ARROW, DIAL, NEEDLE

indicium TOKEN

indict NAME, SUE

indiction EDICT

___ Indies EAST, WEST

indifference
    total ~ ENNUI

indifferent ALOOF, COOL, DEAF, DRY, SOSO, STOIC
    ~ to right or wrong AMORAL

indigence NEED, WANT

indigenous LOCAL

indigent NEEDY, POOR

indigestion GAS

indignant IRATE, SORE, UPSET

indignation ANGER, IRE

indigo ANIL, BLUE, COLOR, DYE

indigo ___ SNAKE

"___ Indigo" MOOD

Indira
    ~ father NEHRU
    attire for ~ SARI
    see also Indian

indiscreet RASH

indiscretion SLIP

indispensable BASIC, MAIN

indisposed AVERSE, ILL
    be ~ AIL

indisposition ILL

indisputable CLEAR, SOLID, SURE

indistinct DIM, PALE
    ~ image BLUR
    ~ noise THUD
    become ~ BLUR, FADE

indistinguishably ASONE

indite WRITE

indium METAL

individual ALONE, LONE, MAN, ONE, ONLY, SELF, SOLE, SOUL
    ~ destiny MOIRA

~ item UNIT
~ performance SOLO
unique ~ ONER

individualist LONER

individually ALONE, APIECE, EACH

indivisible ONE
    literally, ~ ATOM

Indo-___ ARYAN

Indo-___ languages ARYAN

Indochina
    ~ native TAI, THAI
    part of ~ LAOS

Indochinese
    ~ language LAO

indoctrinate PLANT, TRAIN

Indo-European ARYAN

Indo-Iranian ARYAN

indolence REST

indolent IDLE

indomitability NERVE

indomitable IRON

Indonesia
    ~ division ISLE
    ~ et al. OPEC
    ~ until 1949 TER, TERR

Indonesian
    ~ coin SEN
    ~ export TEA
    ~ island BALI, JAVA
    ~ ox ANOA
    ~ tribe ATA

indoor
    ~ bazaar MALL
    ~ design DECOR

indoor-outdoor
    ~ rooms ATRIA

indubitable SURE

indubitably AYE, YES

induce LURE, SWAY, URGE

inducement BAIT, SPUR
    offer an ~ LURE

induction
    ~ org. SSS

induction ___ COIL

induction motor
    ~ pioneer TESLA

indulge DOTE, PET, SPOIL
    ~ in reverie MOON
    ~ one's curiosity ASK
    ~ to excess SATE
    ~ wanderlust ROAM
    don't ~ in AVOID, SHUN

indulgence LEAVE

indulgent EASY, LOOSE
    be ~ CATER

___-indulgent SELF

indurate CAKE

industrial
~ **center** MILL
~ **tub** VAT

industrial ___ ARTS

industrialist
powerful ~ BARON

industrious
~ **insect** ANT, BEE

industriously HARD

industriousness TOIL

industry LABOR, TOIL
~ **watchdog org.** OSHA
captain of ~ BARON
capt. of ~ CEO

"Industry"
~ **is its motto** UTAH

Indy 500 RACE
~ **advertiser** STP
~ **driver** RACER
~ **letters** STP
~ **prop** FLAG
~ **time** MAY
~ **unit** LAP

inebriate SOT

inebriated LIT

inedible BAD

ineffective VAIN, VOID

ineffectual LAME, VOID

inefficient INEPT

"___ in E flat major" OCTET

"___ in Egypt" ISRAEL

inelastic IRON, TENSE

ineluctable SURE

inept
~ **one** CLOD, OAF, YOYO
~ **opponent** SETUP
socially ~ **one** NERD

inert IDLE
~ **gas** NEON

inertia REST

inescapable SURE

"___ in Europa" ONCE

"I Never ___ for My Father" SANG

"I Never Promised ___ a Rose Garden" YOU

"I Never Promised You ___ Garden" AROSE

"I Never Promised You a ___ Garden" ROSE

"I Never Promised You a Rose Garden"
~ **director** PAGE

"I Never Sang ___ My Father" FOR

"I never saw a Moor—" POEM

inevitable SURE
the ~ FATE

inexact LOOSE
~ **phrase** ORSO
be ~ LIE

in excelsis ___ DEO

inexhaustible RICH, VAST

inexorable STERN, SURE

inexperienced NAIVE, NEW, RAW

inexplicable DEEP

infallible SURE

infamous EVIL
~ **emperor** NERO

infamy EVIL, SHAME

infancy START

infant BABE, KID, TOT
~ **attention-getter** BAWL
~ **sound** GOO
~ **word** DADA, MAMA
range ~ CALF

infantry ARMY
~ **weapon** RIFLE

infatuated MAD
be ~ FLIP

in favor
not ~ ANTI

infect TAINT

infection TAINT
throat ~ STREP

infer DRAW, EDUCE
~ **ender** ENCE

inferior LESS, MEAN, OFF, POOR, WORSE
~ **fiction** TRASH
~ **product** DOG
~ **to** UNDER

"inferiority complex"
~ **coiner** ADLER

infernal BAD, CRUEL, EVIL
~ **pit** ABYSS
~ **river** STYX

"Inferno, The"
~ **poet** DANTE

inferred TACIT

infertile ARID, DESERT, DRY, SERE

infested RIFE

infield
~ **corner** BASE, HOME
~ **covering** TARP

infielder
~ **fluff** ERROR

infiltrate ENTER

infiltrator MOLE, SPY

infinite BIG, ETERNAL, GREAT, LARGE, VAST

infinitesimal TINY, WEE

infinitive
misuse an ~ SPLIT

infirm ANILE

infirmity ILL, LIMP

inflame ANGER, AROUSE, ENRAGE, FIRE, HEAT, RILE, ROUSE, SPUR, STING

inflamed EAGER, MAD, RED, SORE

inflammation
~ **(suffix)** ITIS
eyelid ~ STY, STYE

inflate PAD

inflated
~ **feeling** EGO
~ **language** RANT

inflation RISE
~ **gauge** PSI

inflection NOTE, TONE

inflexibility RIGOR

inflexible IRON, SET, STERN, TENSE

inflict
~ **pain** HARM

in-flight
~ **announcement** ETA
~ **offering** MEAL

inflow TIDE

influence BEND, DRAG, DRAW, ENTREE, HOLD, LEAD, MOLD, STEER, SWAY
astral ~ FATE
range of ~ SPHERE
sphere of ~ AREA, ORBIT
try to ~ PLEAD, PRESS, URGE

influential BIG, GREAT
~ **one** NABOB
~ **people** ELITE

info DOPE, NEWS
~ **request encl.** SASE
unconfirmed ~ RUMOR

info-gathering
~ **org.** CIA, FBI

infomercials ADS

inform POST, SAY, SING, TELL, WARN
~ **on** BLAB, RAT

informal EASY, FREE, LOOSE
~ **conversation** CHAT
~ **eatery** CAFE
~ **goodbye** CIAO, LATER, TATA
~ **usage** SLANG

informality EASE

informant SPY

information DATA, FACT, NEWS
~ **source, with "the"** NET, WEB
bit of ~ FACT
fresh ~ NEWS
inside ~ DOPE
point of ~ ITEM
solicit ~ ASK

"Information, The"
~ **author** AMIS

Information ___ AGE

"Information ___" PLEASE

informative
~ **book** TEXT

informed AWARE, HEP, HIP, ONTO, WISE
~ **about** HEP, HIP, UPON
be ~ **of** HEAR, LEARN

informer RAT

infra ___ DIG

infra-
~ **opposite** ULTRA

infraction
arcade ~ TILT
hockey ~ ICING

infrared
~ **light** LAMP
~ **radiation** HEAT

infrastructure BASIS

infrequent FEW, RARE, THIN

in front of
~ **in German** VON

infuriate ANGER, ENRAGE, IRE, RILE

infuriated IRATE, MAD, UPSET

infuriating BAD

infuriation ANGER, IRE

infuse LACE, PLANT, SOAK, STEEP
~ **with oxygen** AERATE

Ingalls LAURA

Inge
~ **dog** SHEBA
~ **forte** DRAMA

ingenious ABLE, NEAT, SMART

ingénue LAMB

ingenuity ART, WITS

ingenuous FREE, HONEST, NAIVE

ingenuousness EASE

ingest EAT, TAKE

inglorious MEAN

ingloriousness SHAME

Ingmar
~ **protégé** LIV

in good ___ TIME

ingot BAR

ingrain ETCH, PLANT

ingrained SET
~ **activity** HABIT

ingratiate ENDEAR

ingredient PART

Ingres
artist influenced by ~ DEGAS

ingress DOOR, ENTREE, ENTRY, GATE, ROAD

Ingrid
~ **daughter** PIA
~ **role** ILSA

inhabit SETTLE

inhabitant TENANT
   ~ **of (suffix)** ESE
   ~ **place** ABODE
   ~ **(suffix)** ITE

inhabitants
   pants ~ ANTS

inhalation
   pleasant ~ AROMA

inhale DRAW
   ~ **suddenly** GASP

___ in hand CAP, HAT

"___ in Heaven" MADE, TEARS

"In Heaven There Is No ___"
   BEER

inherently PERSE

inherit GET

inheritance ESTATE
   ~ **factor** GENE

inheritors
   Earth ~ MEEK

inhibit ARREST, BIND, DETER

"___ in hoary winter's night" ASI

inhospitable COOL, ICY

___-in housekeeper LIVE, SLEEP

inhuman ANIMAL, BAD, CRUEL, MEAN

inhumane BAD, CRUEL, MEAN

inhumanity
   man's ~ **to man** LIFE

"___ inhumanity to..." MANS

inimical ALIEN, AVERSE, EVIL

inimitable ALONE

"___ in Indiana" HOME

inion BONE

iniquitous BAD, EVIL, VILE

iniquity EVIL, SIN
   den of ~ NEST
   place of ~ DEN

initial EARLY, FIRST, NEW, SIGN
   ~ **stage** ONSET

initiate CAUSE, OPEN, START

initiation ONSET, START

injected
   not ~ ORAL

injection SHOT

injudicious RASH

injunction BAR, EDICT, FIAT, LAW, ORDER

injure ABUSE, COST, CUT, HARM, MAIM, MAR, MAUL, SCAR

injured CUT, LAME, SORE

injurious BAD, EVIL

injury ABUSE, ILL
   ~ **result** SCAB
   muscle ~ TEAR

ink SIGN
   ~ **ejectors** OCTOPI
   ~ **ender** BLOT, HORN, STAND
   ~ **sac** ORGAN
   ~ **smear** BLOT
   ~ **source** PEN, SOY
   big ~ **user** PRESS
   black as ~ RAVEN, SABLE
   debit ~ RED
   red ~ DEBT, LOSS

ink-___ printer JET

___ ink INDIA, RED

"Ink"
   Mary's ~ **costar** TED

inkblot ___ TEST

inkling CLUE, HINT, IDEA, NOTE, TRACE

inkwell
   ~ **site of old** DESK

inky EBONY, JET, RAVEN, SABLE
   ~ **to a poet** EBON

inky ___ CAP

Inland SEA

___-in-law SON

inlay ENAMEL
   ~ **material** NACRE

inlet ARM, BAY, COVE, HAVEN, RIA

in-line
   ~ **device** SKATE

___ in line NEXT

"In Living Color"
   ~ **segment** SKIT

"___ in Love?" AMI

"___ in Love With Amy" ONCE

inmate
   Spandau's last ~ HESS

in medias ___ RES

"In Memorium" POEM

___ in mind BEAR, KEEP

inmost DEEP

"___ in my backyard!" NOT

"___ in My Crown" STARS

"___ in My Heart" YOURE

"___ in my memory lock'd" TIS

"___ in My Shoes" SAND

inn HOTEL, REST

___ inn MOTOR

in name ___ ONLY

innards
   inner tube ~ AIR
   PC ~ ROM
   scarecrow's ~ STRAW
   walnut's ~ MEAT

"___ in Needle Park, The" PANIC

inner
   ~ **circle** CADRE, ELITE
   ~ **contentment** PEACE

   ~ **core** SOUL
   ~ **drive** URGE
   ~ **fire** ARDOR
   ~ **(prefix)** ENDO, ENTO
   ~ **self** SOUL
   ~ **shrine** ALTAR
   ~ **workings** CORE
   refresh the ~ **man** DINE, EAT

inner ___ CITY, EAR

innermost
   ~ **part** CORE

inner-tube
   ~ **innards** AIR
   ~ **outsides** TIRE

"___ in New York, The" SAINT

inning BOUT
   ~ **unit** OUT
   extra ~ TENTH
   outs in an ~ SIX

Innis ROY
   ~ **org.** CORE

Innisfail EIRE, ERIN, ISLE

Innisfree EIRE, ERIN, ISLE

innkeeper HOST
   ~ **in Italian** OSTE

in no ___ (soon) TIME

innocent BABE, CLEAN, LAMB, NAIVE, PURE
   ~ **escapade** LARK
   prove ~ CLEAR

Innocent POPE

innocuous MILD, SAFE

Innsbruck
   ~ **range** ALPS
   see also German

innuendo HINT, SLUR

"___ in October, A" DAY

inoculants SERA

inoculation SHOT

inoffensive CLEAN

"In Old Monterey" OATER

___ in on (aim) ZERO

in one ___ and out the other EAR

___ in one's belfry BATS

___ in one's bones FEEL

___ in one's ear FLEA

___ in one's own juice STEW

___ in one's pants ANTS

___ in one's ways SET

inoperative NOGO, NULL, OUT, VOID

inordinate GREAT

inordinately TOO

inornate BALD

in other words
   ~ **in Latin** IDEST

"___ in our time" PEACE

Inouye, Daniel
   ~ **org.** SEN

"___ in Paris" APRIL

"___ in Paris..." ONCE

___ in Peoria PLAY

"___ in Plain Sight" HIDE

___ in point CASE

input DATA, ENTER, TYPE
   pluviometer ~ RAIN

inquire ASK, PRY, SEEK

inquiry HUNT
   make an ~ ASK

inquisitive NOSY
   be ~ ASK

"___ in Red, The" LADY

inroad RAID

ins and ___ OUTS

insane DAFT, MAD

insatiable AVID
   ~ **desire** LUST

insatiate AVID

inscribe ENTER, ETCH, SIGN, WRITE

inscribed
   ~ **rock** STELE

inscription
   cover ~ TITLE

insect FLEA, GNAT
   ~ **eater** TOAD
   ~ **egg** NIT
   ~ **wings** ALAE
   busy ~ ANT, BEE
   night ~ MOTH
   parasitic ~ LOUSE
   pesky ~ GNAT
   social ~ ANT, BEE
   stinging ~ BEE

insecticide DDT

insects
   parasitic ~ LICE

insecurity RISK

insensible
   make ~ BLUR

insensitive CRASS, DEAF
   ~ **one** BOOR, CLOD

inseparable CLOSE, ONE

insert ADD, EDIT, LEAF, PANEL
   ~ **mark** CARET
   ltr. ~ ENC, SASE
   protective ~ LINER

"in seventh heaven" IDIOM

in short ___ ORDER

inside
   ~ **(prefix)** ENDO, ENTO
   ~ **the foul line** FAIR
   cover the ~ LINE

inside ___ OUT

"Inside ___" ASIA

"___ Inside, The" FEAR

insider
~ **talk** ARGOT

insidious BAD, EVIL

insightful SMART, WISE
~ **response** AHA

insignia SEAL
brigadier general's ~ STAR
captain's ~ BAR
colonel's ~ EAGLE

insignificant MEAN, MERE, NULL, SMALL, TINY, VAIN
~ **one** SNIP, TWIT
most ~ LEAST

insincere FALSE
~ **talk** CANT

insincerity ACT, CANT

insinuate HINT, MEAN, SAY

insinuation DIG, SLUR, SMEAR

insinuative SNIDE

insipid ARID, BANAL, BLAH, FLAT, INANE, LIMP, STALE, TAME
~ **one** DRIP
become ~ PALL

insist ARGUE, AVER, AVOW, PLY, PRESS, STATE
~ **ender** ENCE, ENT
~ **upon** ASSERT, AVER, MAKE, STRESS

insolence LIP, NERVE

insolent RUDE, SASSY
be ~ SASS

insoluble HARD, SOLID

insolvent NEEDY, POOR

insouciance EASE

"___ in Space" LOST

inspect ASSAY, EYE, NOTE, SCAN, SEE, TEST
~ **carefully** SIFT
~ **the joint** CASE

inspection AUDIT, TEST

Inspector ___ (John Creasey detective) WEST

___ Inspector ("The Katzenjammer Kids" character) DER

inspiration AWE, CAUSE, IDEA, LAMP
~ **for a poet** ERATO, MUSE
romantic ~ MOON, ROSE, STARS
source of ~ MUSE

inspirational
~ **feeling** AWE

inspire AROUSE, EGG, EXALT, FIRE, HELP, MOVE, STIR
~ **awe** AMAZE
~ **reverence** AWE

inspired AVID, EAGER

inst. SEC

install PUT, SEAT
~ **a door** HANG
~ **cable** LAY
~ **carpeting** LAY
~ **electricity** WIRE
~ **in office** SEAT
~ **tile** LAY

installment PART

instance CASE
for ~ SAY, THUS

instant RAPID, SEC, TIME
this ~ NOW

___ instant INAN

instantaneously SOON

instead ELSE
~ **of** FOR

instigate ABET, AROUSE, CAUSE, EGG, FAN, LEAD, ROUSE, SOW, SPUR, START, URGE

instill PLANT

instinct URGE

"___ Instinct" BASIC

instinctive ANIMAL

instinctual ANIMAL

institute MAKE, OPEN, START, USHER

___ in stride TAKE

instruct SHOW, TRAIN

instruction
~ **format** STEPS
~ **starter** FIRST
assembly ~ STEP

instructor
country-club ~ PRO

instrument AGENT, DUPE, TOOL

instrument ___ PANEL

instruments GEAR
int.-bearing ~ CDS

insubstantial AIRY, THIN, TRITE

insufferable BAD
~ **sort** PILL

insufficiency NEED, WANT

insufficient LAME, SMALL, THIN

___ in "sugar" SAS

insular SMALL

insult ABASE, ANGER, BARB, CUT, DIG, SLAP, SLUR, SNUB
~ **slangily** DIS

insulter
kettle's ~ POT

insulting RUDE, SMART, SNIDE
~ **look** SNEER

insults
honor with ~ ROAST

insupportable HARD

insurance
~ **addendum** RIDER
~ **center** OMAHA
~ **claim** LOSS
~ **factor** RISK
~ **paperwork** CLAIM
~ **worker** AGENT
aerialist's ~ NET
kind of ~ AUTO, CAR, HOME, LIFE, TERM

insured
~ **person** RISK

insurgent REBEL

insurrection RIOT

insurrectionist REBEL

intact ENTIRE, PURE, SAFE

intaglio STAMP
~ **counterpart** CAMEO
~ **stone** ONYX

___ in "tango" TAS

"...in tears amid the ___ corn" ALIEN

integers
~ **(abbr.)** NOS
like half the ~ EVEN, ODD

integrity ASSET, HONOR

integument ARIL, COAT, PEEL, SKIN

intellect HEAD, SENSE

intellection IDEA

intellectual
~ **to some** NERD

___-intellectual ANTI

intelligence HEAD, NEWS, SENSE, WIT
~ **agent** SPY
~ **org.** CIA
person of ~ AGENT

intelligent ABLE, ACUTE, AWARE, KEEN, SMART

intelligible CLEAR

Intellivision
former ~ **rival** ATARI

intend AIM, MEAN, PLAN

intended LOVE

intense ACUTE, AVID, DEEP, DENSE, GREAT, HOT, KEEN, LOUD, RICH
~ **beam** LASER
~ **look** STARE

intensely HARD

intensify STRESS

intensity ARDOR, FIRE, HEAT, LIFE, ZEAL

___-intensive LABOR

intent AIM, DEEP, HOT, KEEN, RAPT, SENSE
~ **gaze** STARE
malicious ~ SPITE

intention AIM, END, GOAL

intentional MEANT
~ **fire** ARSON

"___ Intentions, The" BEST

inter ___ ALIA, ALII

interact BAND, RELATE

interbuilding
~ **passage** ALLEY

intercede AID, HELP

intercept GET, STOP

interchange SWAP, TRADE

interchangeable ALIKE, SAME

intercom
~ **call** PAGE

interdict BAN, BAR, TABOO, TABU, VETO

interdiction BAN, BAR, TABOO, TABU, VETO

interest AMUSE, CLAIM, DRAW, GAIN, SAKE, STAKE
~ **amt.** PCT
~ **calculation** YIELD
~ **factor** RATE
~ **starter** SELF
devoid of ~ BLAH
have an ~ **in** OWN
in the ~ **of** FOR
lose ~ NOD, PALL, TIRE
major ~ BAG
personal ~ STAKE
provide at ~ LEND, LOAN
show sudden ~ PERK

___-interest SELF

interested GAME
be ~ CARE
intensely ~ AFIRE
unduly ~ NOSY

interesting
not ~ BANAL, BLAH, DRY

interfere CLOG, PRY
~ **(with)** MESS

interference NOISE
reception ~ SNOW
run ~ **for** AID, HELP

interim GAP, LAPSE

interior
~ **(prefix)** ENDO, ENTO

"Interiors"
~ **actress** PAGE
~ **director** ALLEN

interject ADD, PLANT

interjection AAH, AHA, BAH, DARN, DRAT, FIE, GEE, OHO, OOPS, POOH, PSHAW, UGH, WOW
archaic ~ FIE
German ~ ACH
palindromic ~ AHA, HAH, OHO, WOW

interjections AHS, OHS

Interlaken
~ **river** AAR, AARE

interlock BIND, KNIT, MESH

interlude LAPSE, REST

intermediary AGENT, REP

interminable ETERNAL, LARGE, LONG, SLOW, VAST

interminably EVER

intermingle MELD, WED

intermission LAPSE, REST

intermit DEFER

intermix WED

intern CAGE
~ **beat** WARD

internal
~ **(prefix)** ENDO, ENTO

"Internal Affairs"
~ **actor** GERE

internal-combustion
~ **engine** MOTOR

internalize
~ **anger** STEW

international
~ **treaty** PACT

International ___ Line DATE

Internet
~ **fan** USER
~ **messages** EMAIL
~ **programming**
language JAVA
~ **separator** DOT
~ **suffix** ORG
~ **"surfer"** USER
the ~ WEB

internists
~ **(abbr.)** MDS
~ **org.** AMA

interoffice
~ **communiqué** MEMO

interpellate ASK

interpret MAKE, PUT, READ
~ **omens** CAST

interpretation SPIN

interpreter
omen ~ SEER

interregnum GAP, LAPSE

interrogate ASK, PRY

interrogative
~ **pronoun** WHO

interrupt ARREST

interruption GAP, LAPSE
polite ~ AHEM

interruptions
program ~ ADS

intersect CUT

intersection ANGLE
kind of ~ TEE

Interstate PIKE, ROAD, ROUTE
~ **(abbr.)** RTE
~ **access** RAMP
~ **hauler** SEMI
~ **sight** AUTO, CAR

~ **sign** EXIT, GAS
see also freeway, highway

Interstates
~ **(abbr.)** RDS

interstice GAP, SPACE

intertwine LACE, MESH

interval EPOCH, ERA, LAG, LAPSE, SPACE, TERM

intervals
place at ~ SPACE

intervene PRY

interview ASK, SEE

___ interview EXIT

interviewer
be the ~ ASK

"Interview With the Vampire"
~ **actor** REA
~ **author** RICE

interweave LACE, MAT, PLAT

in the ___ (active) SWIM

in the ___ (assured) BAG

in the ___ (at a loss) RED

in the ___ (aware) KNOW

in the ___ (current) AIR

in the ___ (finally) END

in the ___ (informed) LOOP

in the ___ (playing well) ZONE

in the ___ (safe) CLEAR

in the ___ boat SAME

in the ___ of luxury LAP

in the ___ of Morpheus ARMS

in the ___ of the moment HEAT

"In the ___" (Nixon book) ARENA

"In the ___ of Fire" LINE

"In the ___ of the Father" NAME

"In the ___ of the Night" HEAT

"In the ___ Old Summertime"
GOOD

"___ in the Afternoon" LOVE

"___ in the arm SHOT

"___ in the Attic" TOYS

"___ in the bag!" ITS

"___ in the Balance" EARTH

___-in-the-bone BRED

___ in the bucket, a DROP

___ in the bud NIP

"___ in the Clowns" SEND

___ in the cold OUT

"___ in the Country, A" DAY

"___ in the Crowd, A" FACE

___ in the dark LEAP, SHOT

"___ in the Dark, A" CRY, SHOT

"in the doghouse" IDIOM

___ in the door FOOT

"___ in the Family" ALL

___ in the fire (undertakings)
IRONS

"In the Good ___ Summertime"
OLD

___ in the grass SNAKE

"___ in the Gray Flannel Suit, The" HORSE, MAN

"___ in the Gutter" MOON

"___ in the Hat, The" CAT

"___ in the Head, A" HOLE

"___ in the Heart of Texas" DEEP

___ in the hole ACE

"___ in the Iron Mask, The" MAN

"___ in the Life, A" DAY

"In the Line of ___" FIRE

"In the Line of Fire"
Clint's ~ costar RENE

in the long ___ RUN

___ in the manger DOG

"___ in the Money" WERE

"___ in the Moon, The" MAN

"In the name of ___" ALLAH

"___! In the Name of Love"
STOP

___ in the neck PAIN

___ in the new RING

in the nick of ___ TIME

"___ in the Night" FEAR

"...in the pot, ___ days old" NINE

"___ in there!" HANG

"___ in the Saddle" TALL

in the same ___ BOAT

in the same place
~ **in Latin** IBID

___ in the shade MADE

"In the Shadows of the ___"
STARS

___ in the sky PIE

"___ in the Stars" LOST

"___ in the Streets" PANIC

"___ in the Sun" DUEL

"___ in the Wall Gang, The"
HOLE

"___ in the White Suit, The" MAN

"___ in the Wilderness" MAN

___ in the woods BABE

___-in-the-wool DYED

"In This ___ Life" OUR

in this day and ___ AGE

"In This Our ___" LIFE

intimacy LOVE

intimate BODE, CLOSE, HINT, INNER, MEAN, NEAR, PAL, RUMOR, WARM

intimation CLUE, LEAD, TRACE

"___ in Time" (Astaire autobiog-raphy) STEPS

"___ in Time of Hesitation"
ANODE

intimidate ALARM, AWE, COW, DETER, SCARE, TREAD

intimidation AWE

___ in "Timothy" TAS

into
~ **in French** DANS
___ into (assail) LAY
___ into (attack) LACE, RIP, SAIL, TEAR
___ into (discuss) GET
___ into (meet) RUN
___ into (reduce, as resources)
EAT
___ into (scolded) LIT
___ into account TAKE

"Into each ___ some rain..." LIFE

intolerable BAD, HARD

Intolerable ___ (pre-Revolution enactment) ACTS

intolerance BIAS

intone SING

intoned ORAL

___ into one's own COME

___ into question CALL

"Into the ___" WEST

___ into the ground RUN

___ into the hands of PLAY

"Into the Night"
~ **host** DEES

"Into Thin ___" AIR

intoxicated LIT
not ~ SOBER

"___ in Toyland" BABES

intrepid GAME
~ **warrior** LION
be ~ DARE

"Intrepid" BOAT, SHIP

intrigue CABAL, LURE, PLOT
~ **metaphorically** WEB

intrinsic BASIC

intrinsically PERSE

introduce START
~ **in court** ENTER
~ **something extra** ADD

introduced
be ~ to MEET

introducer
act ~ EMCEE, HOST

introductory NEW
~ material ABCS

introit PSALM

introvert LONER

introverted SHY

intrude ENTER, NOSE, PRY

"Intruder in the ___" DUST

intrusion RAID

intrusive NOSY

intuit FEEL, SENSE

intuition SENSE
~ plus ESP

intuitive
~ step LEAP

in two shakes of a lamb's ___
TAIL

Inuit TRIBE

inundate GLUT

inundated
be ~ SWIM

inundation SPATE

inure ADAPT, STEEL

invade ENTER, RAID

invader
~ of a kind GERM
barbarian ~ HUN
eighth-century ~ of
Spain MOOR
Mongol ~ TATAR

"Invaders From ___" MARS

invalid NULL

invalidate ANNUL, UNDO, VOID

invaluable RICH

invariable ETERNAL

invasion RAID
when Ike's ~ started DDAY
WWII ~ site STLO

"Invasion of the ___ Girls" BEE

**"Invasion of the Body Snatch-
ers"**
~ prop POD

invective ABUSE, OATH
bit of ~ BARB

inveigh
~ (against) RAIL

inveigle EGG, LURE, SNARE, TRAP

invent COIN, MAKE

invention LIE, TALE
mother of ~ IDEA

"Inventions of the Monsters"
~ artist DALI

inventive ABLE

inventor
~ cry AHA
~ monogram TAE
~ need IDEA
code ~ MORSE
diving-bell ~ EADS
elevator ~ OTIS
kinetoscope ~ EDISON
light-bulb ~ EDISON
megaphone ~ EDISON
mimeograph ~ EDISON
phonograph ~ EDISON
Polaroid ~ LAND
rope-a-dope ~ ALI
Scottish ~ WATT
steel plow ~ DEERE
stock-ticker ~ EDISON
telegraph ~ MORSE

inventory ASSET, LIST, ROLL,
STORE
~ abbr. ETC
~ unit ITEM

Inverness
~ inhabitant SCOT
see also Scottish

inversion
temperature ~
problem SMOG

invert SWAP, UPEND, UPSET

inverted UPSET

invest ENDOW, PUT, ROBE, SEAT

investigate DIG, PRY, SEEK, SPY
~ in a way SIFT

investigation AUDIT, HUNT

investigator AGENT
~ job CASE
govt. ~ GMAN, TMAN

investment ASSET, STAKE
~ choices CDS
~ inc. INT
~ letters IRA
~ options CDS
~ return YIELD

investor
~ bane LOSS
~ concern RISK, YIELD
pessimistic ~ BEAR

inveterate AVID

invidious MEAN

invidiousness SPITE

invigorant TONIC

invigorating CRISP, TONIC

invigoration LIFE

invigorative TONIC

invisible ___ INK

"Invisible ___, The" MAN

"Invisible Man, The"
~ actor RAINS

"Invisible Man Returns, The"
~ director MAY

invitation BID
~ addendum RSVP

~ word COME

invite ASK, BID, CALL, DRAW,
EVOKE, WOO
~ a citation SPEED
~ to dinner FEED

invitees
top ~ ALIST

invocation CALL

invoice BILL, TAB
~ abbr. AMT
~ stamp PAID
~ word NET, PAY, REMIT

invoke ADORE, PRAY

involucre CASE, COAT

involuntary
~ movement START, TIC
~ return REPO
~ sound HIC

involve REFER
~ in difficulties MIRE

involved
~ in UPTO
~ with INTO

___-in vote WRITE

invulnerable SAFE

___-in-waiting LADY, MAID

"___ in war..." FIRST

"In Which We ___" SERVE

"In Which We Serve"
~ director LEAN

"___ in White" LADY

"___ in Winter, The" LION

"___ in Wonderland" ALEX, ALICE

"___ in Yonkers" LOST

"___ in Your Eyes" LOST

Io MOON, MOTH

Io.
see Iowa

iodate SALT

iodine
~ source KELP

Iolani Palace
~ locale OAHU

"Iolanthe" OPERA

**"Iolanthe, or the Peer and the
___"** PERI

Iolcos
ship from ~ ARGO

ion
~ source ATOM

Iona College
~ athlete GAEL

Ione SKYE

Ionesco
~ soprano BALD

Ionia
sage born in ~ BIAS

Ionian SEA

Ionian Sea
view from the ~ ETNA

Ionic ORDER

"I Only Have ___ for You" EYES

"I Only Have Eyes for You"
~ musical DAMES

iota ATOM, BIT, DOT, JOT, MITE,
SCRAP, SHADE, SHRED, TAD,
TRACE
~ preceder THETA
not an ~ NONE
two before ~ ETA

IOU DEBT, NOTE
receive an ~ for LEND

IOUs
have ~ OWE

Iowa STATE
~ campus site AMES
~ college COE
~ commune AMANA
~ crop CORN

Iowa's ___ Society AMANA

Iowa State
~ city AMES

Ipanema
~ locale RIO

___ ipsa loquitur RES

Ir ELEM
77 for ~ ATNO

IRA
~ accrual INT
~ investments CDS
part of ~ ACCT, ARMY, IND,
IRISH, RET

Iráklion
~ locale CRETE

Iran
~ coin RIAL
~ et al. OPEC
~ neighbor IRAQ
~ potentate of yore SHAH
~ title IMAM
ancient part of ~ ELAM

Irani
ancient ~ MEDE

"I ran out of gas" ALIBI

Iraq
~ city BASRA
~ et al. OPEC
~ neighbor IRAN, SYRIA
~ province BASRA

Iraqi ARAB, ASIAN
~ export DATE
~ port BASRA

irascibility BILE

irascible BAD, EDGY, IRATE, MEAN,
SOUR, TART, TESTY, UGLY

irate MAD, WARM

ire ANGER, RAGE

Ire.
~ (abbr.) ISL

"I read you!" ROGER

Ireland EIRE, ERIN
~ coastal islands ARAN
~ county CLARE, TARA
~ symbol HARP
~ to a poet ERIN
river of ~ ERNE
see also Irish

"I Remember ___" MAMA

Irene CARA, PAPAS, RYAN

Irene ___ (Sherlock Holmes' love)
ADLER

iridescent
~ gem OPAL
~ reptile BOA

iridium METAL

Irina
see Russian

iris FLAG
~ locale EYE
~ place UVEA

"Irises" OIL

Irish
~ county CLARE
~ dramatist SHAW
~ exclamation AROO
~ isles ARAN
~ language ERSE
~ national symbol HARP
~ product LINEN
~ river ERNE
~ sea god LER
John, in ~ SEAN
part of many ~ names MAC
seat of ancient ~ kings TARA
word on ~ coins EIRE
see also Ireland

Irish ___ SEA, STEW

Irish ___ (seaweed) MOSS

Irishman CELT

Irish Republic EIRE

Irish Rose
~ lover ABIE

Irish Sea
~ feeder DEE
~ island MAN

irk ANGER, FRET, PEEVE, RILE,
STEAM, UPSET

irked SORE
easily ~ TESTY

irksome BAD
~ one PEST

Irkutsk CITY
see also Russian

iron METAL, PRESS
~ alloy STEEL
~ beginner AND, FLAT, GRID
~ clothes ARMOR, MAIL
~ ender CLAD, STONE, WARE,
WEED
~ holder BAG

~ pumper's unit REP
~ source ORE
~ starter FLAT, GRID
make pig ~ SMELT
shooting ~ GUN, RIFLE, ROD
use a branding ~ SEAR

iron ___ BLUE, GRAY, HAND,
HORSE, MAN

iron ___ (settle) OUT

___ iron ANGLE, CAST, STEAM

Iron AGE

"Iron & ___" SILK

Iron ___ AGE

"Iron ___, The" HORSE, MASK

"___ iron bars a cage" NOR

ironclad BOAT, SHIP

"___: Iron Eagle III" ACES

ironfisted STERN

"Iron Horse, The" OATER

ironic ACRID, ARCH, WRY

iron in the ___ FIRE

iron-on
~ picture DECAL

iron oxide
~ pigment OCHER, OCHRE

"Ironside"
~ actor BURR

"___ Ironsides" OLD

"Iron & Silk"
~ director SUN

iron-willed STERN

Iroquoian ONEIDA

Iroquois TRIBE
~ enemy ERIE
~ language ERIE, ONEIDA
~ tribe ONEIDA
certain ~ ERIE

irrational DAFT, MAD, RABID

Irrawaddy
ruined city on the ~ AVA

irrefragable CLEAR, SOLID, SURE

irrefutable CLEAR, SOLID, SURE

irreg.
not ~ STD

irregular ODD
not ~ EVEN

irresponsible RASH
~ one CAD, HEEL

irretrievable LOST

irreverent
~ fete ROAST

irrevocable SURE
~ damage RUIN

irrigate BATHE, RINSE, WASH,
WATER

irrigation
~ need HOSE, WATER

~ project DAM
needing ~ ARID, DRY

irritable EDGY, TESTY
~ one CRAB

irritant MACE, PEST, TRIAL
eye ~ MOTE

irritate ANGER, FRET, GET, GRATE,
IRE, IRK, PEEVE, RAG, RILE,
ROIL, STING, TEASE, UPSET

irritated SORE, WARM
~ state SNIT

irritating
~ to the nose ACRID

irritation ITCH
cause ~ GRATE
throat ~ RASP

IRS
~ action AUDIT
~ agent TMAN
~ collection time APR
~ employee ACCT, CPA
busy mo. for the ~ APR
part of ~ INT, REV

IRS form
~ item IRA

Irving AMY, STONE
~ snoozer RIP

Irving, Henry SIR

Irwin ALLEN, HALE, SHAW

is
~ in Spanish ESTA
~ not, to some AINT
~ plurally ARE
all there ~ SUM
no longer ~ WAS

"Is ___ Burning?" PARIS

"Is ___ Necessary?" SEX

"Is ___ so?" THAT

Isaac STERN
~ mother SARAH
son of ~ ESAU

Isabel
see Spanish

Isabella d'___ ESTE

"Isabella: or The Pot of Basil"
POEM

"___ is a great wild country"
OURS

"___ Is a Harsh Mistress, The"
MOON

"___ is a jealous mistress" ART

"___ Is a Lonely Number" ONE

**"___ Is a Many Splendored
Thing"** LOVE

"___ Is a Tramp, The" LADY

"...___ I saw Elba" ERE

"I Saw What ___ Did" YOU

"I Saw What You ___" DID

"___ I say more?" NEED

"___ is back, The" PRIDE

"___ Is Born" ASTAR

"___ Is Born, A" STAR

"___ is but a dream" LIFE

"___ is cast, The" DIE

Ischl SPA

"___ Is Down, The" MOON

"I second that!" AMEN

"I see!" AHA

Isère
see French

Isfahan
~ country IRAN
~ native IRANI

"___ is forgiven" ALL

"___ Is Green, The" CORN

"I Shall Not Care" POEM

"___ Is High, The" TIDE

Ishmael EXILE
~ captain AHAB
descendant of ~ ARAB

"I should say ___!" NOT

"Ishtar"
~ beast CAMEL

isinglass MICA

"...___ is in Heaven" ASIT

Isis
animal sacred to ~ COW

"___ Is It" THIS

"Is it a boy ___ girl?" ORA

"Is it soup ___?" YET

**"___ Is Killing the Great Chefs of
Europe?"** WHO

Islam REL
God of ~ ALLAH

Islamic
~ center MECCA
~ deity ALLAH
~ leader IMAM
~ republic IRAN
~ ruler AMIR, EMEER, EMIR

island ATOLL
~ feast LUAU
~ greeting ALOHA
~ in French ILE
~ nation MALTA
~ near Borneo JAVA
~ near Java BALI
~ near Naples CAPRI
~ near Venezuela ARUBA
~ near Venice LIDO
~ off Italy ELBA, LIDO
~ off Manhattan ELLIS
~ off Scotland IONA
~ of large statues EASTER
~ south of Sicily MALTA
~ welcome ALOHA, LEI
Adriatic ~ LIDO
Aegean ~ COS, CRETE, KOS
Alaskan ~ ATTU

"___ Island"

Aleutian ~ ATTU
Antilles ~ ARUBA
Asian ~ JAVA
Austral. ~ TAS
barrier ~ CAY, KEY
Bay of Naples ~ CAPRI
Blue Grotto ~ CAPRI
Caribbean resort ~ ARUBA
Chilean ~ EASTER
coral ~ CAY, KEY
Diamond Head ~ OAHU
Dutch-speaking resort
   ~ ARUBA
English ~ ELY
exile ~ ELBA
Galway ~ group ARAN
Greek ~ COS, CRETE, KOS
Hawaiian ~ LANAI, OAHU
Hebrides ~ IONA, SKYE
honeymoon ~ ARUBA
immigration ~ ELLIS
Indonesian ~ BALI, JAVA
Irish Sea ~ MAN
Jakarta's ~ JAVA
Lesser Sunda ~ BALI
Mediterranean ~ CAPRI,
   CRETE, ELBA, MALTA
Micronesian ~ YAP
Minoan ~ CRETE
New York ~ ELLIS, FIRE
offshore ~ CAY, KEY
Pacific ~ EASTER
pineapple ~ LANAI
river ~ AIT
romantic ~ BALI, CAPRI
Scottish ~ SKYE
sculpted heads ~ EASTER
shamrock ~ EIRE
small ~ CAY, KEY
South Pacific ~ EASTER
Valletta's ~ MALTA
Waikiki's ~ OAHU
West Indies ~ ARUBA

"___ Island" ONAN

___ Island (immigrants' spot)
   ELLIS

___ Island (Niagara Falls divider)
   GOAT

"___ Island Earth" THIS

Islanders SIX, TEAM
   ~ milieu ICE, RINK
   ~ org. NHL

"Island of ___ Souls" LOST

"Island of the Day Before, The"
   ~ author ECO

islands
   Ireland's coastal ~ ARAN
   Pacific ~ SAMOA

___ Islands, Alaska FAR, NEAR

"Islands in the ___" STREAM

___ Islands of Galway Bay ARAN

"___ Island With You" ONAN

Isle of ___ CAPRI, MAN

Isle of Man
   ~ man GAEL

Isle of Mull
   ~ neighbor IONA

islet AIT, CAY, KEY, LAND
   ~ on a globe DOT
   Florida ~ CAY, KEY
   sandy ~ ATOLL
   West Indies ~ CAY, KEY

ism TENET

"___ is me!" WOE

"I smell ___!" ARAT

"___ is more" LESS

"___ Is My Affair" THIS

"___ Is My Country" THIS

"___ is my shepherd..., The"
   LORD

"___ Is Not Enough" ONCE

isn't
   ~ able to CANT
   ~ on the street AINT
   say it ~ so DENY

isobar
   ~ locale MAP

Isocrates ORATOR

isolate EXILE, PART

isolated ALONE, APART, LONE,
   SOLE
   ~ hill MESA
   high ~ rock SCAR

isomeric
   ~ (prefix) PARA

isotope
   oxygen ~ OZONE

Isr.
   ~ neighbor SYR

Israel
   ~ ender ITE
   ~ neighbor SYRIA
   first king of ~ SAUL
   king of ~ AHAB
   tribe of ~ GAD
   where ~ is ASIA

Israeli
   ~ airline ELAL
   ~ coin AGORA
   ~ dance HORA
   ~ desert NEGEV
   ~ diplomat EBAN
   ~ port ACRE
   former ~ leader MEIR
   former ~ Prime
      Minister MEIR

"Israel in the World"
   ~ author EBAN

Israelite
   ~ leader MOSES

"Israfel"
   ~ author POE

Israfil ANGEL

Issa POET
   see also poet

issei
   ~ child NISEI

"___ Is Silence, The" REST

"___ Is Sleeping" ENID

"Is so!"
   ~ rebuttal AINT

"___ Is Spinal Tap" THIS

issue COME, EMERGE, EMIT,
   EVENT, HEIR, OOZE, POUR, RISE,
   SCION, SEEP, SPEW, STREAM
   ~ a caveat WARN
   ~ at hand TOPIC
   ~ forth EMERGE, RUN, SEND
   ~ (from) ARISE
   ~ side BEAT, CON, COOL, PRO
   campaign ~ ECON
   contract ~ RAISE
   evade the ~ STALL

___ issue TAKE

Issy
   see French

-ist
   ~ cousin ITE, STER

Istanbul CITY, PORT

"___ Is the Army" THIS

"___ Is the Black Dahlia?" WHO

"___ is the time..." NOW

"___ Is the Time" THIS

"___ is the winter..." NOW

"Is this a dagger ___..." ISEE

isthmus LAND, NECK, PASS

"___ is to say..." THAT

ISU
   ~ site AMES

Isuzu AUTO, CAR

"___ is well" ALL

"___ Is Willing, The" LADY

"___ is yet to be, The" BEST

"___ Is Your Life" THIS

"it ___ far far better thing..." ISA

___ it (leave) BEAT

___ it (loaf) DOG

___ it (succeed) MAKE

___ it (walk) LEG

"___ it!" CAN, COOL, DARN, HIT,
   STOW

"It"
   ~ game TAG

"It ___ a Thief" TAKES

"It ___ a Very Good Year" WAS

"It ___ Fair" ISNT

"It ___ From Beneath the Sea"
   CAME

"It ___ From Outer Space" CAME

"It ___ laugh" ISTO

"It ___ Necessarily So" AINT

"It ___ Right" ISNT

"It ___ to Be You" HAD

"It'$ ___ Money" ONLY

It.
   see Italian

"___ It" (Michael Jackson tune)
   BEAT

"___ It" (Yankovic parody) EAT

___ it a day CALL

"___ It Again, Sam" PLAY

**"It ain't a fit night out for man
   or ___"** BEAST

Ital. LANG
   see also Italian

Italia
   see Italian

Italian
   ~ art patron ESTE
   ~ capital ROME
   ~ car FIAT
   ~ city GENOA, LODI, MILAN,
      ROME, TRENT
   ~ commune ASTI, ESTE
   ~ currency LIRA, LIRE
   ~ explorer POLO
   ~ farewell CIAO
   ~ food PASTA
   ~ lake COMO
   ~ magistrate DOGE
   ~ monk FRA
   ~ noble house ESTE
   ~ novelist ECO
   ~ number DUE, OTTO, SEI,
      TRE, UNO
   ~ peak MONTE
   ~ poet DANTE
   ~ port GENOA
   ~ pronoun MIA
   ~ Renaissance surname ESTE
   ~ resort LIDO
   ~ river ARNO
   ~ sports car, informally ALFA
   ~ town ASSISI
   ~ violinmaker AMATI
   ~ volcano ETNA
   art, in ~ ARTE
   asset, in ~ BENE
   away, in ~ VIA
   be, in ~ SER
   dear, in ~ CARA
   earth, in ~ TERRA
   eight, in ~ OTTO
   ein, in ~ UNO
   evening, in ~ SERA
   "Goodbye!" in ~ CIAO
   good, in ~ BENE
   innkeeper, in ~ OSTE
   ladder, in ~ SCALA
   land, in ~ TERRA
   love, in ~ AMORE
   moon, in ~ LUNA
   my, in ~ MIA
   off, in ~ VIA
   one, in ~ UNO
   road, in ~ VIA
   six, in ~ SEI
   skill, in ~ ARTE

street, in ~ VIA
they, in ~ ESSE, ESSO
three, in ~ TRE
to be, in ~ SER
two, in ~ DUE
way, in ~ VIA
see also Italy

Italian ___ ALPS, ICES

italic TYPE

italics TYPE
what ~ show STRESS

"I Talk to the ___" TREES

___ it all ABOVE

___-it-all KNOW

"___ it all now!" ISEE

Italy
~ shape BOOT
island off ~ ELBA, LIDO
last queen of ~ ELENA
republic near ~ MALTA
see also Italian

"___ It a Pity" ISNT

Itar-___ TASS

Itasca LAKE

"I taut I ___ a puddy tat!" TAW

"I taut I taw a putty ___!" TAT

"___ It Be" LET

___ it big HIT

___ it by ear PLAY

"It Came From ___ Space" OUTER

"It Came From Beneath the ___" SEA

"It Came From Outer ___" SPACE

"___ It Can Be Told" NOW

"It Can't Happen Here"
~ author LEWIS

itch SMART, STING, URGE, YEN
~ for LUST
have an ~ for WANT
scratch an ~ REACT

itching EAGER
~ to know NOSY

"It Could Happen to ___" YOU

"It Could Happen to You"
~ actor CAGE

-ite
~ cousin ESE, IST, STER

item FACT, PART
clickable ~ ICON

itemization
~ of a sort MENU

itemize LIST

items
~ on hand THESE

___-item veto LINE

iterate ECHO

iteration ECHO
bodybuilder's ~ REP

"___ It Funky Now" AINT

"It Girl, The" BOW

"It Had to Be ___" YOU

"It Happened ___ Night" ONE

"It Happened at the World's ___" FAIR

"It Happened One Night"
~ director CAPRA

"I thought so!" AHA

itinerant NOMAD

itinerary ROUTE, RTE
~ planner AAA
~ word VIA

itinerate ROVE

"___ It Is" YES

"___! it is an ever-fixed mark" ONO

"___ It Kinda Fun" ISNT

___ it like it is TELL

"___ It Make My Brown Eyes Blue" DONT

"It might have ___" BEEN

"It Must Be ___" HIM

"It Must Be Him"
~ singer CARR

"It never ___ but it pours!" RAINS

Ito LANCE

___ it off HIT

"I told you so!" SEE

Ito, Midori
~ maneuver AXEL, CAMEL, SPIN
~ milieu ICE, RINK
emulate ~ SKATE

___ it on POUR

___ it on the chin TAKE

___ it on thick LAY

"___ it or leave it!" TAKE

"It Pays ___ Ignorant" TOBE

___ it quits CALL

"___ It Rain?" WAS

"___ it rich...?" ISNT

"___ It Romantic?" ISNT

"It's ___ cry..." AFAR

"It's ___ for Me to Say" NOT

"It's ___ I'm After" LOVE

"It's ___ Late" TOO

"It's ___ Love" ONLY

"It's ___ Make Believe" ONLY

"It's ___ of cake!" APIECE

"It's ___ than you think" LATER

"It's ___ time!" ABOUT

"It's ___ to Tell a Lie" ASIN

"It's ___ True" ALL

"It's ___ Unusual" NOT

"It's ___-win situation!" ANO

"It's ___ you!" UPTO

"It's a ___!" DEAL, GIRL

"It's a ___ Unusual Day" MOST

"It's a bird! It's a ___!" PLANE

"It's about ___!" TIME

"It's All ___" TRUE

"It's All in the ___" GAME

"It's all the ___ to me!" SAME

"It's Always ___ Weather" FAIR

"It's a Sin to Tell ___" ALIE

"It's a whole new ___ game!" BALL

"It's a Wonderful ___" LIFE

"It's a Wonderful Life"
~ actress REED
~ director CAPRA

"It's been ___!" AGES

"It's clear now!" AHA, ISEE

itself
by ~ APART, PERSE
in a class by ~ RARE
present ~ EMERGE, OCCUR

"It's grrrreat!"
~ growler TONY

"It Should Happen to ___" YOU

"It's Howdy Doody ___" TIME

"It's Impossible"
~ singer COMO

"It's in the ___!" BAG

"It's just ___ thought!" ASI

"It's Love I'm ___" AFTER

"It's My ___" TURN

"It's My Party"
~ singer GORE

"It's no ___!" USE

"It's not the ___ moon..." PALE

"___ It Snow" LET

"It's okay with me!" FINE

"It's Only a ___ Moon" PAPER

"It's Only a Paper ___" MOON

"It's Only a Paper Moon"
~ composer ARLEN
~ lyricist ROSE

"It's still the same ___ story..." OLD

"It Started With ___" EVE

"It's the ___ old shillelagh..." SAME

"It's the ___ Old Song" SAME

"It's the ___ old story" SAME

"It's the Same Old ___" SONG

"It's Tough ___ Famous" TOBE

itsy-bitsy SMALL, TEENY, TINY, WEE

ITT
~ and others COS
part of ~ INT, TEL, TELE

"___ it the truth?" AINT

___ it to (compliment) HAND

"___ it to the Marines!" TELL

itty-bitty SMALL, TEENY, TINY, WEE

___ it up (overact) HAM

___ it up (retire) HANG

___ it up (revel) LIVE

"___ It Up" RIP

it was
~ in Latin ERAT

"It was ___ joke!" ALLA

"It was ___ mistake!" ALLA

"It was the ___ I could do" LEAST

Ivan TSAR
see also Russian

Ivana
see Russian

Ivanhoe HERO
~ weapon LANCE

"Ivanhoe"
~ author SCOTT
~ contest TILT

Ivanovna ANNA

Ivan the Terrible TSAR

"I've ___ a Secret" GOT

"I've ___ had!" BEEN

"I've ___ it!" HAD

"I've ___ Lonely Too Long" BEEN

"I've ___ to London to..." BEEN

"I've ___ Working on the Railroad" BEEN

"I've Always Loved ___" YOU

"I've been ___!" HAD

"I've Got ___ in Kalamazoo" AGAL

"I've Got a ___ in Kalamazoo" GAL

"I've Got a Secret"
~ host ALLEN, MOORE

"I've gotcha now!" AHA

"I've Gotta ___" CROW

"I've Got You ___" BABE

"I've had it ___ here!" UPTO

"I've Just ___ a Face" SEEN

"___! I've Said It Again" THERE

"I Vespri Siciliani"

"I Vespri Siciliani"
~ **heroine** ELENA

"I've Told Every Little ___" STAR

ivories KEYS, PIANO
tickle the ~ PLAY

ivory BONE, COLOR, KEY

Ivory SOAP

Ivory Coast
~ **neighbor** MALI

ivory-nut PALM

ivory tower
~ **figure** DEAN

ivy VINE
emulate ~ CREEP

Ivy League
~ **team** PENN, YALE

Ivy Leaguer ELI, TIGER

I.W. ABEL

"I Walk the ___" LINE

"I Walk the Line"
~ **singer** CASH

"I Wandered Lonely as a Cloud"
POEM

"I Wanna ___ Your Hand" HOLD

"I Wanna Hold Your ___" HAND

"I Want ___" AMAN, YOU

"I Want ___ Happy" TOBE

"I want it ___!" ALL

"I Want to ___!" LIVE

"I Want to Live!"
~ **director** WISE

"I want you, I ___..." NEED

"I Was a ___ War Bride" MALE

"I Was a Male ___ Bride" WAR

"I Was a Male War ___" BRIDE

"I was at my girlfriend's" ALIBI

"I Was the ___" ONE

"___ I Went Mad" ERE

"I Whistle a Happy ___" TUNE

"I Will Follow ___" HIM

"I win"
~ **in chess** MATE

Iwo Jima
~ **terrain** SAND

"I Won't ___" DANCE

IX
~ **opposite number** III

Izmir CITY, PORT

"Izzy and ___" MOE

"j"
  complete a ~ DOT

J
  ~ **and others** DRS
  position of ~ TENTH

J-___ BAR

J. ___ Hoover EDGAR

ja YES
  ~ **in French** OUI

jab DIG, PROD, SLAP, STAB
  boxing ~ LEFT

Jabalpur CITY

Jabba the Hutt ALIEN
  like ~ OBESE

jabber BLAB, GAB, PRATE, TALK,
  YAK, YAP

jabbering NOISE

"Jabberwocky"
  start of ~ TWAS

jacana BIRD

jacaranda TREE

___ jacet HIC

___ Jacinto Day SAN

jack CARD, FLAG, TOOL
  ~ **ender** POT
  ~ **predecessor** TEN
  ~ **up** HIKE, RAISE
  a ~ **in cribbage** NIBS, NOB

jack ___ PINE

Jack ELAM, LORD, OAKIE, PAAR,
  SOO, SPRAT
  ~ **adversary** GIANT
  ~ **tool** AXE

"Jack ___ could eat no fat..."
  SPRAT

___ Jack UNION

"___ Jack" SAINT

jack-a-dandy BEAU, DUDE

jackal ANIMAL, DOG

"Jackal, The" ALIAS

jackanapes BRAT

Jack and Jill
  ~ **prop** PAIL

"Jack and the Beanstalk"
  ~ **syllable** FIE

Jack-be-nimble
  like ~ AGILE, SPRY

"___ Jack City" NEW

jackdaw BIRD, CROW

jacket CASE, COAT, ETON, LINER,
  SHELL, SKIN, WRAP
  ~ **fastener** SNAP
  ~ **material** SUEDE
  ~ **part** ARM, LAPEL
  ~ **style** ETON, MAO, NEHRU
  1960s ~ MAO, NEHRU
  flak ~ VEST
  pants and ~ SUIT
  pea ~ WRAP
  sleeveless ~ VEST
  yellow ~ PEST

___ jacket DUST, ETON, IKE, LIFE,
  MAO, PEA, SHELL

Jack Frost RIME

Jackie MASON
  ~ **second** ARI
  ~ **sister** LEE
  ~ **to Roseanne** SIS

jack-in-the-box TOY
  ~ **part** LID

jack-in-the-pulpit ARUM

jackknife
  did a ~ DOVE

jack-of-___-trades ALL

jack-o'-lantern LAMP
  ~ **feature** GRIN

jackpot POOL, STAKE
  hit the ~ WIN

jackrabbit HARE

"Jack Robinson"
  before one can say ~ SOON

jacks GAME

Jackson ALAN, ANNE, KATE,
  PETER, STU
  ~ **and others** BOS
  ~ **predecessor** ADAMS

~ **st.** MISS
  loser to ~ **in 1832** CLAY

Jackson ___, Wyo. HOLE

Jackson, Anne
  ~ **spouse** ELI

Jackson 5
  ~ **member** TITO
  ~ **song** ABC

Jackson Hole
  ~ **county** TETON
  ~ **river** SNAKE

Jackson, Jesse
  onetime ~ **hairdo** AFRO

Jackson, Michael IDOL
  ~ **album** BAD
  ~ **onetime do** AFRO
  ~ **song** BAD, BEN

Jackson, Stonewall
  ~ **biographer** TATE

Jacksonville CITY, PORT

jackstraws GAME

"Jack the ___ Killer" GIANT

Jacob RIIS
  ~ **to Esau** TWIN
  brother of ~ ESAU
  daughter of ~ DINAH
  father of ~ ISAAC
  son of ~ DAN, GAD, LEVI
  twin of ~ ESAU
  wife of ~ LEAH

Jacquard
  ~ **invention** LOOM

Jacqueline du ___ PRE

Jacques TATI
  see also French

Jacques ___ Cousteau YVES

Jacuzzi SPA
  enjoy the ~ SOAK

jade BORE, COLOR, GEM, GLUT,
  HACK, HORSE, NAG, PALL, SATE,
  TIRE

jaded DONE, SPENT, TIRED

jaeger BIRD

Jafar GENIE

Jaffe RONA, SAM

jag GASH, SLASH, SPREE, TEAR

jagged
  ~ **as a leaf** EROSE
  ~ **rock** CRAG

"Jagged ___" EDGE

"Jagged Edge"
  ~ **actress** CLOSE

Jagger DEAN

Jagger, Mick STONE
  Mrs. ~ HALL

jaguar ANIMAL, CAT
  ~ **cousin** OCELOT

Jaguar AUTO, CAR

Jaguars ELEVEN, TEAM
  ~ **org.** NFL

Jahan SHAH

Jahan, Shah
  ~ **built here** AGRA

jai ___ ALAI

jai alai GAME

jail ARREST, BARS, CAGE
  ~ **unit** CELL

jailbird CON

jailbreak LAM, RUN

jailer
  ~ **need** KEY

j'aime
  ~ **in Latin** AMO

Jaime
  see Spanish

Jainism REL

Jaipur
  see Indian

Jakarta
  ~ **island** JAVA

"Jake's Thing"
  ~ **author** AMIS

"Jake's Women"
  ~ **actor** ALDA

jalapeño
  ~ **hot stuff** SALSA

Jalisco
see Spanish

jalopy AUTO, CAR, CRATE, HEAP, MOTOR

jalousie
~ feature SLAT

jam CLOG, CRAM, LOAD, MESS, MOB, PLAY, PRESS
~ holder JAR
~ ingredient AUTO, CAR
~ starter LOG
traffic ~ SNARL

___ jam INA, LOG

___ Jam PEARL

JAMA
~ readers DRS, MDS

"Jamaica ___" INN

Jamaican
~ citrus UGLI
~ export RUM
~ fellow MON

jambeau ARMOR

jamboree
~ org. BSA
~ participant TROOP
~ shelter TENT

James AGEE, BEARD, CAAN, ETTA, HORNE, IVORY, MASON, OLGA, ORR, STEVE

James ___ Carter EARL

James ___ Jones EARL

"James ___ the Giant Peach" AND

"___ James" BEAU

"___, James!" HOME

"James and the ___ Peach" GIANT

"James and the Giant Peach"
~ author DAHL

James Buchanan ___ EADS

James II
~ daughter ANNE

James W. ___ HORNE

James Whitcomb ___ RILEY

Jamie FARR

Jamie ___ Curtis LEE

Jamie Lee
~ father TONY

jammed
~ together DENSE

jam-packed CLOSE, SOLID

Jan.
~ predecessor DEC

Janáček LEOS

Jan and ___ DEAN

Jane DOE, EYRE, ROE
~ creator EDGAR
~ to Peter SIS

"Jane ___" EYRE

"___ Jane" LADY

Janeiro
Rio de ~ CITY, PORT

Janet EVANS, RENO
Attorney General ~ RENO

Janeway ELIOT

jangle DIN, JAR, NOISE, RING

Janis ELSIE, IAN

Jannings EMIL

"Janos the Hero" POEM

___ Janszoon Tasman ABEL

January
~ event SALE
~ in Spanish ENERO
~ to December YEAR
~ warming THAW

Janus GOD, MOON

Janzen LEE

japan ENAMEL

Japan
~ ender ESE
~ location ASIA
city of ~ USA
where ~ is ORIENT

Japanese ASIAN
~ aborigine AINU
~ admiral ITO
~ affirmative HAI
~ airline ANA
~ ancient capital EDO
~ bed MAT
~ beetle PEST
~ beverage SAKE, SAKI
~ coin SEN
~ currency YEN
~ delicacy EEL
~ diver AMA
~ drink TEA
~ first prime minister ITO
~ gelatin AGAR
~ honorific SAN
~ lantern LAMP
~ legislature DIET
~ metropolis OSAKA
~ red snapper TAI
~ sash OBI
~ statesman ITO
~ wine SAKE, SAKI
~ wrestling SUMO
bread, in ~ PAN
rain, in ~ AME
yes, in ~ HAI
see also Japan

Japanese-American NISEI

jar GRATE, HIT, POT, STUN, VASE
~ top LID
earthen ~ OLLA

___ jar MASON

jardiniere POT, URN

jargon ARGOT, CANT, IDIOM, SLANG
~ suffix ESE

jargonelle PEAR

Jarreau
~ and others ALS

jarring LOUD

jasmine VINE

___ jasmine CAPE

Jason HERO
~ ship ARGO
~ wife MEDEA

jasper GEM

jaunt HIKE, RIDE, ROAM, ROVE, SPIN, TOUR, TRIP
short ~ HOP

jaunty PERT, SASSY, SMART
~ hat BERET, TAM

java JOE
~ brewer URN
~ locale CAFE

Java SEA
~ coin SEN
~ neighbor BALI

Java ___ MAN

Java Sea
~ locale BALI

javelin EVENT, LANCE, PIKE, SPEAR

jaw BONE, CHIN, GAB, TALK
drop one's ~ GAPE
lower ~ CHIN
with dropped ~ AGAPE

Jawaharlal NEHRU

jawbone
~ source ASS

Jaworski LEON

"Jaws"
~ boat ORCA
~ sighting FIN

___ Jaw, Saskatchewan MOOSE

Jaws of ___ LIFE

jay BIRD
~ adjective AVIAN
~ follower KAY

___ jay BLUE

___-jay VEE

Jay LENO

Jayhawker
~ St. KAN

___ Jay Lerner ALAN

jazz GENRE
~ fan CAT
~ genre SCAT
~ instrument AXE, SAX
~ job GIG
~ performance SET
~ session JAM
~ singing name ELLA
~ style BOP
~ up PERK
appreciate ~ DIG
like some ~ COOL

Jazz FIVE, TEAM
~ home UTAH
~ org. NBA

"Jazz ___ Summer's Day" ONA

"Jazz on a Summer's ___" DAY

"Jazz on a Summer's Day"
~ director STERN

jazz rock
~ singer STING

jazz/rock
Latin ~ SALSA

jazzy LOUD

JC
~ degrees AAS

J.C. SNEAD

J, Dr.
~ league NBA

jealous
~ wife of myth HERA

"jealous mistress"
Emerson's ~ ART

Jean ARP, BACH, GENET, KERR
see also French

___ Jean Baker NORMA

Jeanne ABEL
~ d'Arc STE
see also French

Jeanne d'___ ARC

Jeanne d'Arc STE
see also French

Jean Paul ___ MARAT

jeans
~ name LEE, LEVI
~ partner TEE
cut of some ~ SLIM

___ jeans BLUE

jeep MOTOR

jeer DIG, GIBE, HISS, HOOT, SNEER

Jeeves VALET

Jeff
~ brother BEAU
~ to Beau BRO

Jefferson
~ bill TWO
~ predecessor ADAMS
~ VP BURR

"Jefferson in Paris"
~ actor NOLTE

"Jeffersons, The"
~ producer LEAR

Jeffers, Robinson POET
like ~ stallion ROAN
see also poet

Jeffreys ANNE

Jehoshaphat
~ father ASA

Jehovah LORD

jejune ARID, BANAL, DRY, FLAT, INANE

Jekyll
  ~ alter ego HYDE
  ~ hangout LAB

Jekyll and Hyde
  like ~ DUAL

jell CLOT, SET

jelled SOLID
  ~ garnish ASPIC

"Jellicle Ball"
  ~ musical CATS

jellied
  ~ delicacy EEL

Jell-O
  ~ shaper MOLD

jelly
  ~ container JAR
  ~ roll CAKE
  dinner ~ ASPIC
  petroleum ~ OIL

"Jelly's ___ Jam" LAST

Jellystone Park
  ~ bear YOGI

Jemima AUNT

Jemison MAE

jennet ANIMAL, ASS, MARE

Jennifer GREY
  ~ on "WKRP" LONI

Jennifer ___ Hewitt LOVE

"Jennifer ___ Here" SLEPT

Jennings PETER
  ~ forte NEWS
  ~ network ABC

jenny ASS, MARE, MULE

"Jennyanydots"
  ~ (Eliot character) CAT

"Jenufa" OPERA

jeopardize BET, STAKE

jeopardy PERIL, RISK
  put in ~ RISK

"Jeopardy!"
  ~ name ALEX
  ~ ques. ANS
  emulate a ~ contestant ASK

jerboa ANIMAL
  ~ cousin RAT

jereed LANCE

Jeremy IRONS
  ~ singing partner CHAD

Jergens ADELE

jerk ASS, BOB, CAD, CLOD, DOLT, DOPE, HEEL, IDIOT, LOUT, OAF, SHY, SPASM, START, TIC, TOSS, TUG, YOYO
  ~ companion CLEAN

___ jerk KNEE, SODA

___-jerker TEAR

jerkin VEST

jerky MEAT
  ~ motion BOB

jerry ___ CAN

Jerry HALL, LEWIS, MOUSE, PARIS, REES, RICE, VALE, WEST
  ~ ex-partner DEAN
  ~ friend ELAINE
  ~ partner BEN
  Tom and ~ ingredient RUM

"Jerry"
  he was "Tom" to Paul's
  ~ ART

jerry-built MEAN, POOR
  ~ structure SHED

Jerry Lee ___ LEWIS

"Jerry Maguire"
  Jerry, in ~ TOM

Jersey COW, ISLE
  ~ comment MOO

Jerseys
  bunch of ~ HERD

Jerusalem
  ~ is its cap. ISR

"Jerusalem Delivered" EPIC, POEM

___ Jesse Jackson REV

"___ Jesse James" ALIAS

Jessel, George EMCEE, HOST

Jessica LANGE

___ Jessica Parker SARAH

Jessie AMES

jest GAG, KID, PLAY
  ~ with TEASE

"Jest 'Fore Christmas" POEM

Jesús ALOU

jet COAL, COLOR, EBON, ERUPT, PLANE, POUR, SABLE, SST
  ~ black EBONY, ONYX
  ~ jockey PILOT
  ~ route LANE
  ~ set ELITE
  ~ to a poet EBON
  gas ~ LAMP
  speedy ~ SST

jet ___ LAG, SET, STREAM

___ jet GAS

Jet ___ SKI

___ Jet LEAR

jet-black EBONY, RAVEN

jeté LEAP

Jets ELEVEN, GANG, SIX, TEAM
  ~ milieu ICE, RINK
  ~ org. NFL, NHL

jetsam
  ~ of 1773 TEA
  Boston Harbor ~ TEA
  flotsam and ~ TRASH

jet set
  ~ city NICE
  ~ need VISA

Jetson, George
  ~ dog ASTRO
  ~ wife JANE

Jetson, Judy
  ~ high school ORBIT

jettison DROP, EJECT, SCRAP, SHED

jetty INKY, MOLE, PIER, SABLE

jeu
  ~ de mots PUN

jewel GEM, PEARL, PIN, STONE
  ~ from the sea PEARL
  ~ thief's term ICE

jeweler
  ~ measure CARAT, KARAT

jewelfish PET

"Jewel of the ___, The" NILE

jewelry
  ~ case SAFE
  ~ fastener CLASP
  ~ holder CHEST
  ~ material AMBER
  ~ piece PIN
  cheap ~ PASTE
  costume ~ PASTE
  piece of ~ RING
  royal ~ TIARA

jewelry box
  ~ opener HASP

"Jewels"
  ~ author STEEL

"Jewel Song" ARIA

Jewish
  ~ holiday dinner SEDER
  ~ month ADAR
  ~ mystic ESSENE
  ~ prophet EZRA

Jewish ___ RYE

Jezebel
  ~ deity BAAL
  ~ hometown TYRE
  ~ husband AHAB
  ~ portrayer BETTE

"Jezebel"
  ~ singer LAINE

JFK DEM, PRES
  ~ abbr. ARR, ETA
  ~ arrival SST
  ~ imperative ASK
  ~ predecessor DDE
  ~ quote starter ASK
  ~ successor ARI
  ~ to RFK BRO
  ~ UN ambassador AES
  start of a ~ quote ICH

"JFK"
  ~ actor ASNER
  ~ director STONE

Jiang Qing
  ~ husband MAO

jib SAIL, SHEET
  ~ support MAST

jibe AGREE, FIT, MESH
  ~ at CARP, SNEER

Jicarilla TRIBE

jiff SEC

jiffy SEC
  in a ~ ANON, SOON

___ jiffy INA

jig DANCE, LURE
  in ~ time NOW

___ jig IRISH

jigger SAIL, SHOT, SNORT, TOT

jiggerful NIP, SNORT

jiggle JAR, MOVE, TEETER

jihad WAR

Jihan SADAT

Jillian ANN

jillions ALOT, SCAD

jilt DESERT, DROP

jilter CAD

"___ Jim" (Joseph Conrad novel) LORD

___ Jima IWO

jim-dandy NEAT

Jimenez
  ~ portrayer DANA

Jiménez, Juan Ramón POET
  see also poet

Jimmie NOONE

jimmy BAR, LEVER, OPEN, PRY

Jimmy ARIAS, ELLIS, KEY
  ~ daughter AMY
  ~ successor RON

Jimmy Carter Library
  ~ site ATLANTA

jingle NOISE, POEM, RING, SONG
  ~ writer ADMAN

"Jingle Bells" CAROL, NOEL
  ~ preposition OER

jingler COIN

jingles
  where ~ are heard ADS

jinks
  high ~ PLAY

jinn DEMON

jinni DEMON

jipijapa HAT, PLANT

jitney BUS, CAB, MOTOR
  ~ relative CAB

jitterbug DANCE

jittery EDGY, TENSE
  not at all ~ COOL

jive DANCE, DUPE, IDIOM, KID, RAG

jiver CAT

JKL
  telephone's ~ FIVE

Jo
  ~ sister AMY, MEG
  Alcott's ~ AUNT

___-Jo FLO

Joad TOM

Joan MIRO

Joanie
  she played ~ ERIN

Joanne DRU

Joan of ___ ARC

"Joan of ___" PARIS

Joan Van ___ ARK

___ Joaquin Valley SAN

job LABOR, LINE, POST, STINT, TASK
  ~ figuratively HAT
  nose ~ BOB

job ___ LOT

job-___ HOP, HUNT

___ job DESK, ODD, SNOW

___ job (service station specialty) LUBE

Job
  ~ lot WOE
  book before ~ ESTHER

Jobs
  ~ company APPLE

job safety
  ~ org. OSHA

Jocasta
  Oedipus, to ~ SON

jockey RIDER
  ~ controller REIN
  ~ item CROP
  ~ often LOSER
  jet ~ PILOT

___ jockey DISC

jocosity WIT

jocular
  ~ sounds HAHA
  ~ suffix AROO, EROO

jocularity GLEE, WIT

joe JAVA

Joe DANTE, MAY
  G.I. ~ TOY
  Mauldin's ~ and others GIS

Joe ___ (NFL cofounder) CARR

Joel GREY
  book after ~ AMOS

joe-pye WEED

jocy ANIMAL, ROO

Joey DEE

Joey ___ and the Starliters DEE

"___ Joey" PAL

jog GAIT, RUN, STIR, TROT
  ~ the memory CUE, PROD

jog ___ TROT

jogger
  ~ woe ACHE
  memory ~ NOTE

Johannesburg CITY
  ~ bread RAND

Johann Sebastian ___ BACH

john
  ~ starter DEMI

John ADAMS, AGAR, ALDEN, AMOS, DAHL, DEERE, DOE, DONNE, ELTON, GAY, GLEN, HAY, KERR, LAHR, MUIR, POPE, RAITT, WOO
  ~ in German HANS
  ~ in Irish SEAN
  ~ in Russian IVAN
  ~ in Scottish IAN
  ~ in Welsh EVAN
  ~ (Kunta Kinte portrayer) AMOS
  book after ~ ACTS

John ___ (tractor name) DEERE

John ___ Jones PAUL

John ___ Passos DOS

"John ___ Green" DEERE

"John Anderson My Jo" POEM

John and Yoko
  ~ son SEAN

"___ John B." SLOOP

"John Barleycorn" POEM

John Boyd ___ ORR

"John Brown's Body"
  ~ poet BENET

John Dickson ___ CARR

"___ John Doe" MEET

John, Elton SIR

John Hancock Building
  ~ architect PEI

John Jacob ___ ASTOR

John L. ___ LEWIS

Johnny CASH
  bandleader for ~ DOC

Johnny ___ (Dixie soldier) REB

"Johnny ___" ANGEL, APOLLO, COOL, EAGER, SUEDE

Johnny ___ Note" ONE

Johnny-___-lately COME

"___ Johnny!" HERES

"Johnny Angel"
  ~ star RAFT

johnnycake PONE

"Johnny Eager"
  ~ director LEROY

"Johnny Guitar"
  ~ director RAY

Johnny-jump-___ UPS

"Johnny One ___" NOTE

Johnny-on-the-___ SPOT

Johnny Reb
  ~ org. CSA

"Johnny's Theme"
  ~ songwriter ANKA

John Paul POPE

John Paul II POLE, POPE

John Philip ___ SOUSA

John Quincy ___ ADAMS

___ johns LONG

Johns Hopkins
  ~ subj. ANAT

___ John Silver LONG

Johnson ARTE, DON, TOM, VAN

Johnson, Lady Bird
  ~ middle name ALTA

Johnson, Randy
  face ~ BAT
  like ~ pitches FAST
  nickname ~ UNIT

Johnston JOE

John Stuart ___ MILL

Joie LEE

joie de vivre ELAN

join ABUT, ADD, BAND, BIND, CLOSE, ENTER, FIT, MEET, MELD, PASTE, SEW, SIDE, TIE
  ~ a jury SIT
  ~ as hands CLASP
  ~ at the edge ABUT
  ~ at the seams SEW
  ~ combat CLOSE
  ~ forces AID, ALLY, BAND, HELP, POOL, UNITE
  ~ hands ALLY
  ~ securely TENON
  ~ the army SERVE
  ~ the chorus SING
  ~ together ALLY, MELD, POOL, TIE, WED
  ~ up TEAM
  ~ with heat FUSE

joined ONE
  ~ with PLUS

joiner
  common ~ AND

joiners
  femur ~ ILIA

joining
  ~ point SEAM

joint ELBOW
  ~ problem ACHE
  ~ tenant CON
  after-hours ~ BAR
  corporeal ~ KNEE
  gin ~ BAR
  half a ~ TENON
  inspect the ~ CASE
  large ~ of beef BARON
  leg ~ ANKLE, KNEE

pelvic ~ HIP
plumber's ~ ELL, TEE
snack ~ DELI
stem ~ NODE
tarsal ~ ANKLE
the ~ STIR
workout ~ SPA

___ joint CLIP, GIN

Joint Chiefs
  ~ off. GEN

joist BEAM, PROP

joke GAG, KID
  ~ ender STER
  ~ response HAHA
  funny ~ RIOT
  knock-knock ~ PUN
  practical ~ CAPER, DIDO, GAG
  trite ~ CORN

joker CARD, WIT
  practical ~ WAG

jokes
  dumb ~ CORN
  tell ~ AMUSE

jokester CARD, WAG, WIT
  ~ prop ACT

Jolie
  ~ daughter EVA

Joliet
  ~ discovery ERIE

Joliot-Curie IRENE

jolly GAY
  ~ days YULE
  ~ good fellow CHAP

Jolly ___ ROGER

"Jolly ___" (Hals painting) TRIO

Jolly Green ___, The GIANT

Jolly Roger FLAG

"Jolly Roger"
  ~ crewman SMEE

"Jolly Toper, The"
  ~ painter HALS

"Jolly Trio"
  ~ painter HALS

Jolson
  ~ and others ALS
  ~ real first name ASA

jolt HIT, JAR, MOVE, RAM, ROUSE, STIR, STUN, TREMOR, ZAP

Joltin' Joe
  brother of ~ DOM

Jon AGEE

Jon ___ Jovi BON

Jonas SALK

Jonathan APPLE, LYNN

"Jonathan Livingston Seagull"
  ~ author BACH

Jones AMOS, LEROI, TOM
  ~ nickname INDY
  ~ of jazz ETTA

"___ Jones" TOM

Jones, Barnaby
~ portrayer EBSEN

Jones, Buck
~ special OATER

Jones, Casey
~ vehicle TRAIN

Jones, Davy
~ locker OCEAN, SEA

Jones, Parnelli RACER

Jones, Tom
~ country WALES

Jong ERICA

jongleur BARD

Jonson BEN, POET
~ work ODE

Jonson, Ben
see poet

Joplin SCOTT
~ genre RAG

Joplin, Janis
~ nickname PEARL

Jord.
~ neighbor SYR

Jordan NEIL
~ neighbor IRAQ, SYRIA
former queen of ~ ALIA
where ~ is ASIA

___ Jordan AIR

Jordanian ARAB

Jordan, Michael
~ org. NBA
~ target NET

Jor-El
~ wife LARA

Jorge
see Spanish

___ Jorge (one of the Azores)
SAO

José
see Spanish

___ José SAN

Joseph KANE
~ mantle COAT

"Joseph and His Brothers"
~ author MANN

Joseph H. ___ LEWIS

josh KID, PLAY, RAG, RIB, TEASE

Joshua ___ National Park TREE

joskin BOOR

joss IDOL, IMAGE
burn a ~ stick CENSE

jostle ELBOW, JAR, PLOW, TOSS

jot ATOM, BIT, DOT, IOTA, MITE, TAD,
TRACE, WRITE
~ down ENTER, LOG, NOTE,
PEN, WRITE
not a ~ NONE

jotting
classroom ~ NOTE

joule
~ fraction ERG

joules
1055 ~ BTU

jounce BOB

"Jour de Fête"
~ actor TATI

journal LIFE, LOG, MAG, ORGAN,
PAPER
~ boss EDITOR
~ ender ESE
~ note ENTRY
~ page DAY
~ VIPs EDS
Kirk's ~ LOG
ship's ~ LOG
trade ~ ORGAN

journalism
yellow ~ LIBEL

journalist
~ approach ANGLE, SLANT
WWII ~ PYLE

journalists PRESS

journey RIDE, ROAM, ROVE, TOUR,
TRIP
~ by foot HIKE
~ end HOME
~ in Latin ITER
~ segment LEG
difficult ~ TREK

"Journey ___ Fear" INTO

"Journey ___ Margaret" FOR

journeyer NOMAD

"Journey Into ___" FEAR

journeys GOES

**"Journey to the Center of the
___"** EARTH

"Journey-work of the ___"
STARS

joust BOUT, MEET, SPAR, TILT
ready to ~ ATILT

jouster
~ protection ARMOR

jousting ATILT
~ arena LISTS
~ weapon LANCE
like a ~ knight ATILT

___ Jovi BON

jovial GAY

jowl
cheek by ~ NEAR

joy GLEE
~ ender RIDE
~ partner PRIDE
~ ride SPIN
express ~ AAH
fill with ~ ELATE
sign of ~, maybe TEAR
song of ~ PAEAN
sounds of ~ AHS

Joyce ELLA

Joyce ___ Oates CAROL

Joyce Carol ___ OATES

Joyce, James
~ homeland EIRE, ERIN
Mrs. ~ NORA

"Joyeux ___" NOEL

joyful ELATED
~ cry AAH

joyless SAD

"Joy Luck Club, The"
~ author TAN

joyous GALA, GAY, GLAD, RAPT

joyride RUN, SPIN

joystick
use a ~ AVIATE

J.P.
flee to a ~ ELOPE

jr.
next year's ~ SOPH

Jr.
~ eldest, maybe III

J.R.
~ mother ELLIE
~ to Ellie SON

jrs.
~ exam PSAT
former ~ SRS

J. Thaddeus ___ TOAD

Juan PERON
wife of ~ EVA, EVITA
see also Spanish

"___ Juan" DON

Juana
see Spanish

___ Juan Capistrano SAN

Juan Carlos REY
~ country SPAIN
daughter of ~ ELENA

"___ Juan DeMarco" DON

___ Juan Hill SAN

Juanita
see Spanish

Juárez
see Spanish

juba DANCE

Jubal EARLY

jubilant ELATED, GAY, GLAD
make ~ ELATE

jubilation GLEE

jubilee DAY, GALA

Judah
king of ~ ASA
mother of ~ LEAH

Judah Ben-___ HUR

Judaic
~ literature TORAH

Judaism REL

Judd NAOMI

Judd, Wynonna
~ mother NAOMI

"___ Jude" HEY

Judea
king of ~ HEROD

judge ASSESS, CALL, DEEM,
ESTEEM, HOLD, MAKE, RATE
~ addr. HON
~ demand ORDER
~ exhortation ORDER
~ expertise LAW
~ garb ROBE
~ job TRIAL
~ order STAY
Old Testament ~ ELI
sports ~ REF
tell the ~ PLEAD

Judge Roy ___ BEAN

Judges
book after ~ RUTH

judgment ACT, DOOM
artistic ~ TASTE
await ~ PEND
bad ~ ERROR
breach of ~ LAPSE
exercise ~ DEEM
good ~ SENSE
make a ~ RULE
of sound ~ SANE
pass ~ on ASSAY
use poor ~ ERR

___ judgment SNAP

judgments
make ~ ASSESS

___ judicata RES

judicial
~ contest SUIT
~ garment ROBE
~ order STAY
make a ~ decision RULE

judicious SAGE, SANE, SOBER,
WISE

judiciousness TACT

Judith
~ husband ESAU

"Judith"
~ composer ARNE

judo
~ attire GIS
~ award BELT
~ level DAN

Judy CARNE

jug
~ handle EAR
juice in a ~ CIDER
wide-mouthed ~ EWER

jug ___ BAND

juggernaut IDOL

juggle RIG

Juggler
　the ~ TAROT

Jughead TEEN

"jug of ___, a loaf..., A" WINE

"jug of wine..., A"
　~ poet OMAR

juice SAP
　~ container CAN
　~ drink ADE
　~ in a jug CIDER
　~ source APPLE, LEMON, LIME, ORANGE
　digestive ~ BILE
　extract ~ REAM
　fermented ~ CIDER

___ juice (milk) MOO

juiceless DRY, SERE

juices
　seal in the ~ SEAR

juicy
　~ fruit MELON, ORANGE

Juilliard
　~ subj. MUS

juin
　~ preceder MAI

jujube DATE

jukebox
　~ part SLOT

"Juke Box Baby"
　~ singer COMO

Jul.
　~ follower AUG

julep
　~ flavoring MINT

Jules BASS
　see also French

"Jules ___ Jim" AND

Julia
　~ brother ERIC

Julian ROMAN
　~ to John SON

Julianne MOORE

Julia, Raul
　~ musical NINE

Julia Ward ___ HOWE

"___ Julie" MISS

Juliet
　~ beloved ROMEO
　~ betrothed PARIS

Juliette LOW

Julio
　see Spanish

Julio ___ Chavez CESAR

Julius CAESAR, POPE

"Julius ___" CAESAR

"Julius Caesar" PLAY
　~ locale SENATE
　~ name MARC

~ quintet ACTS
~ role CATO

Julius La ___ ROSA

July
　~ clock setting DST
　~ sign CRAB
　~ was named for him CAESAR

July 3 EVE

jumble HASH, MELD, MELEE, MESS, OLIO, PILE, SNARL, UPSET

jumbled MESSY, UPSET

"Jumblies, The"
　~ poet LEAR

jumbo BIG, GIANT, LARGE, SIZE

Jumna
　city on the ~ AGRA

jump CAPER, HOP, LEAP, SKIP, START
　~ about DANCE, PLAY
　~ all over LACE
　~ as a spark ARC
　~ down someone's throat LACE
　~ over CLEAR, SKIP
　~ rope GAME, SKIP
　~ through hoops OBEY
　~ up RAISE
　broad ~ LEAP
　high ~ EVENT, LEAP
　long ~ EVENT, LEAP
　skating ~ AXEL

jump ___ BAIL, BALL, CUT, ROPE, SEAT, SHOT

jump-___ OFF, START

___ jump LONG, SKI

jumper HORSE, SLED
　Aussie ~ ROO

jumper ___ CABLE

jumper cable
　~ connection ANODE

jumping ___ BEAN

jumping-___ place OFF

"Jumpin' Jack Flash, it's ___" AGAS

jump the ___ GUN

jumpy EDGY

junco BIRD

junction SEAM

juncture NODE, SEAM, TIME

June
　~ bug DOR
　~ dance PROM
　~ honoree DAD, GRAD
　~ phrase IDO

"June ___" BRIDE

June 6, 1944 DDAY

Juneau
　~ state ALASKA

"June Brought the ___" ROSES

jung
　~ opposite ALT

Jung CARL
　~ topic EGO

Jungfrau ALP
　~ locale ALPS

jungle
　~ creature APE, BOA, HYENA, LION, TAPIR
　~ crusher BOA
　~ home DEN, LAIR
　~ king LION
　~ pig TAPIR
　~ snake BOA
　~ sound ROAR
　~ swinger APE
　~ vine LIANA
　~ woman JANE
　asphalt ~ CITY

"Jungle Book, The"
　~ actor SABU
　~ setting INDIA

"Jungle Fever"
　~ actress DEE
　~ director LEE

Jungle Jim HERO

junglelike RANK

jungly RANK

junior SIZE, SON, YEAR
　~ college degs. AAS
　~ dress size NINE
　~ miss KID
　~ officer CADET
　~ sibling SIS

Junior
　watch ~ SIT

Junior League
　~ wannabe DEB

juniors
　H.S. ~' exam PSAT

juniper TREE
　~ product GIN

junk BOAT, GEAR, SCRAP, SHIP, TRASH
　~ ender YARD
　~ mail ADS
　~ up TAINT
　piece of ~ DOG, LEMON

junk ___ ART, DNA, MAIL

junket RUN, SPIN, TOUR, TRIP

junky MEAN, POOR

junkyard dog
　like a ~ MEAN

Juno DEA
　~ counterpart HERA
　~ messenger IRIS
　~ offered him a kingdom PARIS

junta BLOC, CABAL, GANG
　~ act EDICT

junto BAND, BLOC, CABAL, RING

Jupiter DEO, GOD
　~ domain SKY
　~ mother OPS
　~ neighbor MARS
　moon of ~ LEDA

Jura RANGE

"Jurassic Park"
　~ actress DERN
　~ letters DNA
　~ material AMBER
　~ role ELLIE
　~ T. Rex CLONE

___ jure IPSO

juridical LEGAL

juris
　corpus ~ CODE, LAW

jurisdiction PALE, REALM, SPHERE

jurisprudence LAW

juristic LEGAL

jurors PANEL

jury PANEL
　~ member PEER
　join a ~ SIT

jury-___ RIG

just CLEAN, EVEN, FAIR, HONEST, MERE, MORAL, ONLY
　~ a bit NIP
　~ a bite TASTE
　~ about CLOSE, NEAR
　~ a little NIP
　~ as LIKE
　~ beat EDGE, NOSE
　~ bought NEW
　~ deserts DUE
　~ for guys STAG
　~ in NEW
　~ miss sinking, as a putt LIP
　~ OK SOSO
　~ once EVER
　~ out HOT, NEW
　~ published NEW
　~ purchased NEW
　~ reward DESERT
　~ right IDEAL
　~ so PAT
　~ the same ALIKE
　~ washed CLEAN

just ___ (almost) ABOUT

"Just ___ Am" ASI

"Just ___ Look" ONE

"Just ___ of the Guys" ONE

"Just ___ of Those Things" ONE

"Just ___ suspected!" ASI

"Just ___ thought!" ASI

"Just ___ You" FOR

just a ___ TAD

"Just a ___!" SEC

"Just a minute!" WHOA

"Just Do It"
　~ company NIKE

___ juste MOT

"Just for ___" YOU

justice
  bring to ~ SUE, TRY

Justice Dept.
  ~ div. FBI
  ~ employee ATTY

"___ justice for all" AND

justice of the ___ PEACE

justification ALIBI, CAUSE, PLEA
  means ~ ENDS

___-justification SELF

___-justify COST

"Justine"
  ~ actress AIMEE

"Just kidding!" NOT

"Just One of ___ Things" THOSE

"Just Shoot Me"
  ~ actor SEGAL

just the ___ SAME

"Just the facts, ___" MAAM

"Just the Way ___ Are" YOU

"Just the Way You ___" ARE

"Just this ___..." ONCE

"Just Walking in the Rain"
  ~ singer RAY

jute
  ~ cousin HEMP

Jutland
  ~ resident DANE

Juvenal ROMAN
  see also Latin

juvenile KID, TEEN

juxtapose ABUT

juxtaposed NEAR

K ELEM
   ~ follower MART
   19 for ~ ATNO

___-K (toddlers' school) PRE

K-6
   grades ~ ELEM

Kaaba
   ~ dedicatee ALLAH

Kabibble ISH

kabob
   ~ skewer SPIT

"Kaboom!" BANG

kabuki DRAMA
   ~ performer MALE

Kabul CITY
   ~ continent ASIA

kachina
   ~ creator HOPI

Kadiddlehopper CLEM

kaffiyeh
   ~ cord AGAL

Kafka
   ~ novel, with "The" TRIAL

Kagoshima CITY, PORT

Kahn OTTO

kaiser LORD, ROLL, RULER, TITLE
   ~ counterpart TSAR

Kaiser AUTO, CAR

kakapo BIRD

Kal ___ KAN

Kalahari DESERT
   like the ~ ARID, DRY

kale CASH

"Kaleidoscope"
   ~ author STEEL

"Kalevala" EPIC

Kalin TOM

Kaline
   ~ and others ALS

kalpa AGE, ERA

Kama LOVE
   see also Russian

"Kama Sutra"
   ~ subject SEX

Kamehameha Highway
   ~ locale OAHU

Kaminska IDA

Kampala
   former ~ kingpin AMIN

Kampuchea
   ~ continent ASIA

Kan.
   ~ neighbor NEB, NEBR
   see also Kansas

Kananga CITY

Kandinsky
   ~ colleague KLEE
   ~ output ART

Kane CAROL, ERICA
   ~ last memory SLED
   ~ Xanadu ESTATE

"Kane and ___" ABEL

Kanga
   ~ creator MILNE
   ~ offspring ROO

kangaroo ANIMAL
   female ~ DOE
   large ~ EURO

kangaroo ___ RAT

Kans.
   see Kansas

Kansa TRIBE

Kansas BAND, STATE
   ~ politician DOLE
   ~ pooch TOTO
   ~ river OSAGE

"Kansas ___ Confidential" CITY

"Kansas ___ Kitty" CITY

Kansas City
   ~ newspaper STAR

Kant
   see German

Kantor SETH

kaolin CLAY

"___ Kapital" DAS

Kapitän
   ~ command UBOAT

"Kapow!" BOOM, SLAM

kappa
   ~ preceder IOTA

Kappelhoff
   Doris née ~ DAY

kaput OUT, OVER, SHOT

Kara SEA

Karachi CITY, PORT
   ~ language URDU

Karakorum RANGE

Kara Kum DESERT

Karamazov IVAN

karate
   ~ attire GIS
   ~ blow CHOP
   ~ level DAN
   ~ wear BELT

"Karate ___, The" KID

Kareem
   ~ alma mater UCLA
   ~ formerly LEW
   ~ God ALLAH

Karen ALLEN

Karenin
   ~ wife ANNA

"___ Karenina" ANNA

Karim
   ~ of the Khans AGA

___ Karim al-Husainy (Aga Khan IV) SHAH

Karlfeldt, Erik POET
   see also poet

Karloff BORIS

Karlovy Vary SPA

Karlson PHIL

karma DOOM, FATE

Karnak
   ~ river NILE

Karolyi BELA

Karpov
   ~ castle ROOK
   ~ forte CHESS
   see also chess

Karras ALEX

Kashmir
   ~ feature VALE

Kasparov
   ~ castle ROOK
   ~ coup de grâce MATE
   ~ game CHESS
   clobber ~ MATE
   see also chess

Kassebaum, Nancy
   former ~ org. SEN

Kassel
   ~ river EDER

___ Kat Club KIT

Kate MOSS
   ~ companion ALLIE
   like ~, when the curtain falls TAME

"Kate & ___" ALLIE

"Kate & Allie"
   ~ role EMMA
   Emma in ~ ARI

Katharine ROSS

Katharine ___ Bates LEE

Kathleen NOONE

"Katie Went to ___" HAITI

Katmandu
   ~ land NEPAL

Kato
   ~ to the Green Hornet AIDE

"___ K&A Train Robbery, The" GREAT

Katzenjammer KID
   ~ kid HANS

Kauai
   ~ (abbr.) ISL
   ~ greeting ALOHA
   ~ keepsake LEI
   ~ neighbor OAHU
   see also Hawaiian

Kaufman BEL

Kaufman, Andy
~ sitcom TAXI

Kavafian ANI

kay
~ follower ELL
~ followers ELS

Kay STARR
title for ~ SIR

kayak BOAT
~ cousin CANOE

kayaker
~ need OAR

Kaye Lani ___ Rafko RAE

Kazakh
~ river URAL

Kazakhstan
~ lake ARAL
~ once SSR
~ sea ARAL

Kazan ELIA
~ republic TATAR

Kazurinsky TIM

k.d. LANG

kea BIRD

Keaton DIANE

Keaton, Elyse
~ son ALEX
~ to Alex MOM

Keaton, Mallory
~ brother ALEX

Keaton, Michael
~ role MOM

Keats POET
~ work ODE, POEM
Muse for ~ ERATO
subject for ~ URN
"Sylvan historian," to ~ URN
see also poet

Keatsian
~ saint AGNES

kebab
~ meat LAMB
shish ~ MEAT

Keebler
~ worker ELF

Keefe TIM

keel
~ over LIST, TIP
~ pole MAST

keel ___ (capsize) OVER

Keeler, Ruby
~ dance style TAP

keen ACID, ACUTE, AVID, BAWL,
CLEAR, CRY, EAGER, FINE,
MOAN, NEAT, RACY, RAW,
SMART, SOB
~ perception WIT

"Keen!" NEAT

Keene
~ sleuth DREW

Keenen ___ Wayans IVORY

keenness EDGE

keen-sighted ACUTE

keep CAN, HAVE, HAVEN, HOLD,
LAST, OWN, SAVE, STORE
~ after NAG
~ a low profile HIDE
~ an account LOG
~ an eye on ATTEND, STARE,
TAIL, TEND
~ at bay REPEL, STEM
~ at it GOON, PLOD
~ away from SHUN
~ clear of ELUDE, EVADE
~ company with DATE
~ dark HIDE
~ for oneself HOG
~ from happening AVERT,
AVOID, DETER
~ going SPIN
~ in stitches AMUSE
~ in the pantry STORE
~ minutes ENTER
~ occupied AMUSE
~ on LAST
~ one's chin up BEAR
~ one's distance AVOID,
EVADE, SHUN
~ one's eyes peeled SEE
~ one's head above
water TREAD
~ one's shirt on WAIT
~ out BAN, BAR, TABOO, TABU
~ out of sight HIDE
~ score ENTER
~ smiling AMUSE
~ someone company ATTEND
~ subscribing RENEW
~ the engine running IDLE
~ the faith BEAR
~ the pot boiling EARN
~ the wolf from the
door EARN
~ time TAP, TIME
~ time manually CLAP
~ trying LABOR
~ under control LEASH
~ under wraps HIDE
~ up STAY
~ up with the times ADAPT
fail to ~ a poker face REACT
fail to ~ up LAG
not ~ a secret BLAB, TELL

keep ___ (persist) ATIT

keep ___ on TABS

keep ___ to the ground ANEAR

keep an ___ out EYE

keep an ___ to the ground EAR

keep a straight ___ FACE

keeper
~ starter BAR, BEE, DOOR,
GAME, GATE, GOAL, INN,
SCORE, SHOP, STORE, TIME
cookie ~ JAR

keeping CARE
in ~ (with) ALONG

keep one's ___ HEAD

keep one's ___ clean NOSE

keep one's ___ peeled EYES

keep one's ___ up CHIN

keeps
for ~ EVER
it ~ the doc away APPLE
Santa ~ one ALIST

___ keeps (permanently) FOR

keepsake RELIC, TOKEN
Kauai ~ LEI

keepsakes
place for ~ ATTIC

keep the ___ PEACE

"Keep your ___ shut!" TRAP, YAP

Kefauver ESTES
~ home TENN
~ title SEN

keg CASE
~ adjunct TAP
~ contents ALE, BEER
~ cousin VAT

kegler
~ button RESET
~ locale ALLEY
~ milieu LANE
~ target PIN
see also bowling

keg party
~ locale FRAT

Keith MOON

kelek RAFT

kelep ANT

Keller HELEN

Kelley, Kitty
~ creation BIO

Kelljan BOB

Kellogg-Briand PACT

kelly COLOR

Kelly GENE, MOIRA, RENO

"___ Kelly" NED

Kelly, Emmett
~ persona HOBO

Kelly, Walt
~ cartoon POGO

kelp ALGA, ALGAE
~ concoction AGAR

Kelvin SCALE

Kemo Sabe
~ companion TONTO
~ trademark MASK

Kemper
~ in Kansas City ARENA

kempt NEAT
not ~ SEEDY

Ken.
~ neighbor IND
see also Kentucky

Kendall KAY

"Kenilworth"
~ author SCOTT
~ heroine AMY

Kennedy CLAN, ETHEL, TED, TOM
~ coin HALF
~ matriarch ROSE
~ quote starter ASK
start of a ~
proclamation ICH

Kennedy, Carolyn, ___ Bessette
NEE

Kennedy Center
~ focus ART

Kennedy, Jacqueline, ___
Bouvier NEE

Kennedy Library
~ architect PEI

Kennedy, Ted
~ middle name MOORE
~ org. SEN

kennel
~ confinement CAGE
~ feature RUN
~ sound ARF, YELP

Kenneth MARS

Kenny G
~ instrument SAX

Kenobi, Obi-Wan HERO

Kensington ___ Stone RUNE

Kent
~ colleague LANE, OLSEN

Kenton ERLE, STAN

Kentucky STATE
~ county BOONE
~ pioneer BOONE
~ statesman CLAY

Kentucky Derby RACE
~ month MAY
~ winner ___ E. Tee
(1992) LIL

Kenworthy, Jr. PAUL

Kenyon, Kathleen DAME

Keogh PLAN
~ relative IRA

kepi CAP, HAT

kept
~ under wraps PENT

kerchief SCARF

Kerensky
~ successor LENIN

Kerman
~ country IRAN

Kermit
~ cousin TOAD
~ street SESAME

Kern
~ contemporary ARLEN

kernel CORE, ESSENCE, GIST,
HEART, MEAT, NUT, PIT, SEED,
SOUL, STONE, SUM
~ holder COB, EAR

kernite ORE

Kern, Jerome
~ **song** WHO

kerosene OIL

Kerouac BEAT
~ **character** SAL

Kerr ANITA
~ **role** ANNA

Kerr, Graham CHEF

Kerrigan, Nancy
~ **footwear** SKATE
~ **maneuver** AXEL, CAMEL,
SPIN
~ **milieu** ICE, RINK

Kesey KEN

kestrel BIRD

ketch BOAT, SHIP

Ketchikan CITY, PORT
~ **locale** ALASKA

Ketchum HAL

ketchup
~ **noise** PLOP

Kett ETTA

kettle
~ **handle** BAIL
~ **insulter** POT
~ **of fish** MESS, PASS
~ **starter** TEA

Kettle
~ **and others** MAS, PAS

Keuka LAKE

Kevin
~ **costar in "Tin Cup"** RENE

key ISLE, ISLET, LEAD, MAIN, NOTE,
PASS, POLAR
~ **ender** CARD, HOLE, NOTE,
PAD, STONE
~ **group** CADRE
~ **in** ENTER
~ **in French** CLEF
~ **letter** BETA, PHI
~ **loc.** FLA
~ **material** IVORY
~ **note** TONIC
~ **officers group** CADRE
~ **personnel** CADRE
~ **point** GIST
~ **starter** PASS, TURN
~ **word** CUE
ATM ~ ENTER
calculator ~ SIN, SINE
computer ~ ALT, DEL, ENTER,
HOME, INS, TAB
hit the + ~ ADD
lacking a ~ ATONAL
phone ~ STAR
piano ~ NOTE
typewriter ~ TAB
under lock and ~ SAFE

key ___ CARD, RING

___-key LOW, OFF

Key TED

Key ___ pie LIME

keyboard PIANO
~ **instrument** ORGAN
~ **setting** TAB
~ **stroke** TAP
use a ~ ENTER, TYPE

keyed
~ **up** EDGY, TENSE
not ~ ATONAL

keyhole SLOT
look through a ~ PEEP

keyless ATONAL

Key lime ___ PIE

Keynes
~ **subj.** ECON

keynote THEME, TOPIC

keys
like some ~ MAJOR

keystone
~ **site** ARCH

Keystone
~ **missile** PIE
~ **St.** PENN

Keystone State
~ **port** ERIE

keystroke
long ~ DAH
short ~ DIT

Key West CITY, PORT

KFC
~ **piece** LEG

kg. AMT

KGB
~ **counterpart** CIA

Khachaturian ARAM

khaki COLOR
like ~ DRAB

Khali
Rub al ~ DESERT

khan HOTEL, INN, LORD, RULER
~ **relative** AGA, AGHA

Khan AGA

Khan, Jasmine
~ **grandfather** AGA

Khans
Karim of the ~ AGA

Khartoum
~ **river** NILE

Khayyám OMAR
~ **product** TENT
see also poet

khedive RULER

Khirghiz
~ **range** ALAI

Khmer ___ ROUGE

Khomeini IRANI
~ **land** IRAN

Khrushchev
~ **ctry.** USSR

Khyber ___ PASS

kibbutz
~ **dance** HORA

kibosh
put the ~ **on** BAN, END, STEM,
STOP, VETO

kick BANG, LIFE, TANG
~ **around** ABUSE, ARGUE,
HASH, MAUL
~ **back** LOLL
~ **in** ANTE
~ **off** OPEN, START
~ **oneself** RUE
~ **out** BAN, BOOT, EJECT, OUST
~ **over the traces** REBEL
~ **starter** SIDE
get a ~ **out of** LIKE, LOVE,
SAVOR
with a ~ RACY

kick ___ (begin) OFF

kick ___ (oust) OUT

___ kick DROP, FREE, TOP

Kickapoo TRIBE

kickback CUT, PAY

kicker
~ **asset** TOE
~ **target** SHIN

kicking
~ **partner** ALIVE
still ~ SPRY

**Kicking ___ ("Dances With
Wolves" shaman)** BIRD

kickoff ONSET, START
~ **prop** TEE
Rose Bowl ~ PARADE

kid ANIMAL, BRAT, GOAT, LAD, RAG,
RIB, SON, SUEDE, TEASE, TOT,
TWIT, TYKE
~ **ammo** PEA
~ **in Spanish** NINA, NINO
~ **stickum** PASTE
~ **transport** BIKE
fresh ~ BRAT
nasty ~ BRAT
obnoxious ~ BRAT
rotten ~ IMP

"Kid Brother, The"
~ **director** HOWE

Kidder
role for ~ LANE

kiddie
use the ~ **pool** WADE

kiddie ___ (children's books) LIT

kiddie lit
~ **doctor** SEUSS
~ **sleuth** DREW

kiddies
not for ~ ADULT

kidding
wasn't ~ MEANT

"___ kidding!" YOURE

"Kid From ___, The" SPAIN

"___ Kid in Town" NEW

"Kid Millions"
~ **director** RUTH

kidnap STEAL
legendary ~ **victim** HELEN

"Kidnapped"
~ **monogram** RLS

kidney BEAN, ILK, MOLD, ORDER,
ORGAN, SORT, STAMP

kids
~ **card game** WAR
~ **computer language** LOGO
~ **game** TAG
~ **sch.** ELEM
one with ~ GOAT
tend the ~ SIT

"Kids ___ Alright, The" ARE

"___ Kids" RICH

"Kids Are Alright, The"
~ **band, with "The"** WHO
~ **director** STEIN

___ Kids on the Block NEW

Kiefer
~ **to Donald** SON

kieffer ___ PEAR

Kiel CANAL
see also German

kielbasa MEAT

Kierkegaard, Sören DANE

Kieron MOORE

Kiev CITY

Kiki DEE

Kilauea
~ **output** LAVA
city near ~ HILO

Kildare
~ **and others** DRS
~ **org.** AMA

Kiley, Steven
~ **org.** AMA

kill PREY
~ **a bill** VETO
~ **time** IDLE, LOAF, WAIT

killer
~ **whale** ORC, ORCA
bug ~ DDT
weed ~ HOE

"killer"
Belushi's ~ **character** BEE

"___ Killer" LADY

"Killers, The"
Burt's ~ **costar** AVA

Killy
~ **runner** SKI

Kilmer POET
~ **opus** TREES
~ **subject** TREE
see also poet

Kilmer, Val
~ **role** SAINT

kiln BAKE, HEAT, OAST, OVEN
  put in a ~ DRY
  use a ~ BAKE

kilograms
  907 ~ TON

kilowatt-hour
  ~ fraction ERG

"Kilroy ___ here" WAS

kilt
  ~ cousin ALINE
  ~ fold PLEAT
  ~ wearer GAEL, SCOT

kilter
  out of ~ AMISS, ATILT, AWRY

kiltie
  ~ kin CLAN

Kim
  Kipling's ~ OHARA

kimchi
  ~ country KOREA

kimono ROBE
  ~ fabric SILK
  ~ tie OBI

kin
  ~ (abbr.) REL

-kin
  kin of ~ ULE

kind CAST, CLASS, GENRE, GOOD, ILK, LIKE, LOT, MAKE, MILD, MOLD, NICE, ORDER, SORT, STAMP, STYLE, TYPE
  ~ in French BON
  ~ in Latin ALMA
  ~ of (prefix) SEMI
  ~ of (suffix) ISH
  of a ~ LIKE
  two of a ~ ALIKE

"Kind ___" LADY

kindergarten
  ~ adhesive PASTE
  ~ break NAP
  ~ denizen TOT
  ~ fare ABCS
  ~ song opening ABC

"Kindergarten ___" COP

kindergartener TOT, TYKE

kindest
  ~ regards BEST

kindhearted BIG, GOOD, GREAT, NICE, SWEET

"Kind Hearts ___ Coronets" AND

kindle AROUSE, EVOKE, FIRE, HEAT, RAISE, ROUSE, STIR

kindled LIT
  ~ anew RELIT

kindly NICE, PLEASE

___ kindly to TAKE

kindness LOVE

"___ Kind of Hero" SOME

"___ Kind of Woman" HIS, THAT

kindred LIKE

kinetic ___ ART

kinetoscope
  ~ inventor EDISON
  ~ inventor's monogram TAE

kinfolk CLAN

king BED, CARD, LORD, MALE, RULER, TITLE
  ~ address SIRE
  ~ beater ACE
  ~ beater, in pinochle TEN
  ~ before David SAUL
  ~ in French ROI
  ~ in Latin REX
  ~ in Spanish REY
  ~ of beasts LION
  ~ of Israel AHAB, SAUL
  ~ of Judah ASA
  ~ of Judea HEROD
  ~ of the road HOBO
  ~ order EDICT
  ~ superior ACE
  "A Midsummer Night's Dream" ~ OBERON
  Bard's ~ LEAR
  Biblical ~ ABNER, AHAB, ASA, HEROD, REBA, SAUL
  college founded by a ~ ETON
  fiddlers' ~ COLE
  first ~ of Israel SAUL
  fit for a ~ REGAL
  former Bulgarian ~ BORIS
  former ring ~ ALI
  Gloucester's ~ LEAR
  greedy ~ MIDAS
  homer ~ AARON
  Hun ~ ATLI
  jungle ~ LION
  land of Anna's ~ SIAM
  merry ~ of nursery rhymes COLE
  Midianite ~ REBA
  New Testament ~ HEROD
  Norse mythical ~ ATLI
  nursery-rhyme ~ COLE
  Phrygian ~ MIDAS
  Shakespearean ~ LEAR
  strikeout ~ RYAN
  Thailand ~ RAMA
  "The King and I" ~ YUL
  third ~ of Judah ASA
  "Volsunga Saga" ~ ATLI

king ___ COBRA, CRAB, SNAKE

king-___ SIZE

___ king ALA

King ALAN, BENE, DON, RANCH
  ~ had one DREAM
  ~ in a Steve Martin tune TUT
  ~ of Phrygia MIDAS
  Jack Kent's comic-strip ~ AROO
  like a ~ novel EERIE, EERY

"King, The" ELVIS
  ~ daughter LISA
  ~ middle name ARON
  ~ portrayer YUL

King ___-Saud IBN

King ___ Trio COLE

"King ___" LEAR, RAT, TUT

"King ___" (old comic) AROO

"King ___, The" ANDI

"King ___ Country" AND

"King ___ I, The" AND

"King ___ Out, The" STEPS

"___ King" SKY

"___ King, The" LION

___ King (Louis XIV) SUN

"King and I, The"
  ~ actress KERR
  ~ director LANG
  ~ locale SIAM
  ~ role ANNA
  Deborah's ~ costar YUL
  Deborah's role in ~ ANNA
  "I" in ~ ANNA

King Arthur
  ~ foster brother KAY
  ~ sister ANNE
  ~ time YORE

King, Billie Jean, ___ Moffitt NEE

___ King Cole NAT, OLD

"King Cotton"
  ~ composer SOUSA

"King David"
  ~ actor GERE

kingdom LAND, REALM, STATE
  ~ east of Babylonia ELAM
  ~ east of the Tigris ELAM
  Alley Oop's ~ MOO
  ancient ~ ELAM
  Anna's ~ SIAM
  Asian ~ NEPAL
  Biblical ~ ELAM
  Brynner's ~ SIAM
  former French ~ ARLES
  high ~ NEPAL
  Himalayan ~ NEPAL
  Juno offered him a ~ PARIS
  Mesopotamian ~ ELAM
  Old Testament ~ SHEBA
  Persian Gulf ~ ELAM
  Susa's ~ ELAM

___ kingdom ANIMAL

Kingdome ARENA

"kingdom of heaven is like unto ___..., The" ANET

"Kingfish, The" LONG

kingfisher BIRD
  ~ coif CREST

King James
  ~ pronoun THEE

King Kong APE, GIANT

"King Kong"
  ~ actress LANGE
  Fay, in ~ ANN

King Lear
  ~ daughter REGAN

"King Lear"
  Kurosawa's ~ RAN

kingly REGAL

"kingly"
  ~ name REX

King, Martin Luther
  ~ addr. REV

"King of Kings"
  ~ director RAY

"King of the ___" ROAD

"King Olaf"
  ~ composer ELGAR

kingpin TSAR
  former Kampala ~ AMIN
  office ~ BOSS
  social ~ LION

"King Ralph"
  ~ actor OTOOLE

King Ranch
  ~ unit ACRE

"King Rat"
  ~ actor SEGAL

kings
  game of ~ and queens CHESS
  name for Danish ~ ERIC
  one of five Norse ~ OLAF, OLAV
  seat of ancient Irish ~ TARA

Kings FIVE, SIX, TEAM
  ~ milieu ICE, RINK
  ~ org. NBA, NHL

"Kings ___" ROW

Kingsfield
  ~ profession LAW

King's Head, The
  ~ order ALE

"King's Henchmen, The" OPERA

kingship REIGN, RULE

king-size BIG, GIANT, LARGE

king-sized ___ BED

Kingsley AMIS, BEN

King, Stephen
  ~ home MAINE
  ~ topic EVIL
  enjoy ~ READ
  like a ~ novel EERIE, EERY

"King Steps ___, The" OUT

Kingston ___, The TRIO

King Tut's ___ TOMB

kink COIL, LOOP, PANG, ROLL, SNARL

kinkajou ANIMAL

Kinks
  ~ song LOLA

kinky ODD

Kinsey
  ~ concern SEX

Kinshasa CITY

kinship TIE
  ~ group CLAN

Kinski, Nastassja
~ **role** TESS

kiosk STALL, STAND
~ **buy** ELLE, OMNI, TIME

Kiowa TRIBE

kip BED

Kipling
~ **biographer** AMIS
~ **character** DIN, KIM
~ **homeland** INDIA
~ **Kim** OHARA
~ **setting** INDIA
~ **villain** COBRA

kipper CURE, SALT

kips
where ~ are spent LAOS

kir WINE

Kirghiz
~ **once** SSR
~ **range** ALAI

Kirk LISA, WISE
~ **"final frontier"** SPACE
Michael Douglas, to ~ SON

Kirk, Captain
~ **birthplace** IOWA
~ **helmsman** SULU
~ **journal** LOG

Kirkland LANE

Kirlian
~ **image** AURA

Kirstie ALLEY
~ **costar** TED
~ **role** HOWE

Kiska
~ **locale** ALASKA
~ **native** ALEUT

kismet DOOM, FATE, LOT

"Kismet"
~ **setting** IRAQ

kiss ABUT, CARESS, GREET, NECK
~ **good-bye** LOSE, SPEND
~ **off** END
~ **partner** TELL

"Kiss an ___ Good Mornin'"
ANGEL

"Kiss an Angel Good Mornin'"
~ **singer** PRIDE

kiss and ___ TELL

Kissel AUTO, CAR

kisser FACE, LIPS, PAN, TRAP
baby ~ POL

kisses
~ **symbolically** EXES

"Kisses Sweeter Than ___" WINE

kissing ___ KIN

"Kiss, Kiss"
~ **author** DAHL

"Kiss Me ___" KATE

"Kiss my grits"
~ **diner** MELS

~ **sayer** FLO

kit GEAR, RIG
~ **and caboodle** ALL, ENTIRE, LOT
sewing ~ ETUI

___ kit MESS, PRESS

Kit ___ Club KAT

kitchen ROOM
~ **appliance** OVEN, RANGE
~ **attraction** AROMA
~ **denizen of song** DINAH
~ **ender** ETTE
~ **gadget** RICER
~ **garment** APRON
~ **glove** MITT
~ **herb** SAGE
~ **meas.** TBS, TSP
~ **pro** CHEF
~ **refuse** SLOP
~ **spice** MACE
~ **staple** OIL, OLEO, SALT, YEAST
~ **staple, once** LARD
~ **tear-jerker** ONION
~ **topper** LID
~ **utensil** LADLE, PAN, POT, RICER
~ **wrap** SARAN
do a ~ **chore** DICE, MASH, PARE, PEEL, RICE
kind of ~ EATIN
one in the ~ CHEF

"Kitchen ___, The" TOTO

KitchenAid
~ **rival** AMANA

Kitchener EARL
~ **foe** BOER

"Kitchen God's Wife, The"
~ **author** TAN

kite BIRD, SOAR, TOY
~ **appendage** TAIL
~ **cousin** STILT
~ **end** TAIL
~ **nemesis** TREE

Kite TOM
~ **org.** PGA

kith and ___ KIN

kithara LYRE

KITT AUTO, CAR

kitten BEAR, CAT, PET
~ **cry** MEOW, MEW

kittiwake BIRD

kitty CAT, PET, POOL, POT, STAKE, TILL
~ **comment** MEOW, MEW
~ **contribution** ANTE
command to ~ SCAT
retiree's ~ IRA
start the ~ ANTE

Kitty, Miss
~ **establishment** BAR
~ **favorite** MATT
~ **portrayer in "Gunsmoke"** AMANDA

Kivu LAKE

Kiwanian
~ **colleague** LION

kiwi BIRD
~ **extinct cousin** MOA
~ **kin** EMU

"kiwi"
language from which ~ **comes** MAORI

Kjellin ALF

KJV
~ **opener** GEN

klaxon HORN

Klee
~ **colleague** ARP
~ **work** ART

Klein ANNE
~ **style** ALINE

"___ kleine Nachtmusik" EINE

Klein's Obsession SCENT

Klemperer OTTO

Klensch ELSA

klieg
~ **light** LAMP

Kline, Kevin
~ **movie** DAVE

Klinger
~ **hometown** TOLEDO
~ **portrayer** FARR

Klingon ALIEN

Klink
~ **rank** COL

KLM
~ **destination** EUR, NOR
~ **rival** SAS

Klondike
~ **strike** GOLD

"Klondike ___" ANNIE

Klondike Annie
~ **portrayer** MAE

Klugman, Jack
~ **"Odd Couple" role** OSCAR

klutz BOOR, LOUT, OAF
~ **comment** OOPS

klutzy INEPT

knack ART, FEEL, HANG
~ **for music** EAR

"Knack, ___ How to Get It, The"
AND

"Knack, and How to ___ It, The"
GET

knapsack BAG, KIT
~ **part** STRAP

knave CAD, CARD, DOG

Knave of Hearts
~ **booty** TART

knavish BAD, BASE, MEAN

knead MOLD

knee
~ **concealer** MIDI
~ **counterpart** ELBOW
~ **neighbor** CALF, SHIN, TIBIA
~ **saver** RUG
bend the ~ **to** OBEY
go on bended ~ PLEAD
scrape, as the ~ SKIN

knee-___ DEEP

knee bend
Nureyev's ~ PLIE

"Knee-Deep in June" POEM

knee-high LOW

kneehole DESK

knee jerk
do a ~ REACT

kneel BEND
~ **before** ADORE, BOW

kneeling
~ **site** ALTAR

knees
ask on one's ~ PLEAD
bring to one's ~ BEND
fall to one's ~ BOW
go down on one's ~ KNEEL

"___ knees, The" BEES

knell PEAL, RING, TOLL
death ~ DOOM

knew
~ **homophone** GNU

"___ Knew" IFI

Knickerbockers FIVE, TEAM
~ **org.** NBA

knickknack TOY

Knicks FIVE, TEAM
~ **loc.** MSG
~ **org.** NBA

Knievel EVEL

Knievel, Robbie
~ **father** EVEL

knife LANCE, SNEE, STAB, STEEL, TOOL
~ **handle** GRIP
~ **handle material** NACRE
~ **part** HILT
~ **wound** GASH
Eskimo ~ ULU
game played with a ~ CLUE
surgical ~ LANCE
use a ~ SLIT

___ knife STEAK

"___ Knife, The" BIG

knife-edged KEEN

"Knife in the ___" WATER

knife-sharp KEEN

knight HERO, MALE, RANK, SIR, TITLE
~ **attire** ARMOR, MAIL
~ **consort** LADY
~ **feat** DEED
~ **fight** TILT

~ **garb** ARMOR, MAIL
~ **lady** DAME
~ **weapon** LANCE
~ **wife** DAME
address for a ~ SIR
Arthurian ~ KAY
like a jousting ~ ATILT
mail for a ~ ARMOR
Round Table ~ KAY
white ~ HERO

Knight BOB, ERIC, TED

"___ Knight" FIRST

knighted
prepare to be ~ KNEEL

Knight, Gladys
~ **backup** PIP

knighthood ORDER

knightly
place for ~ **combat** LISTS

knights of ___ YORE

knight-to-be PAGE

knish
where to nosh on a ~ DELI

knit HEAL, MEND, UNITE

___-knit CLOSE

knitter
~ **need** NEEDLE, YARN

knives
like ~ EDGED

knob DIAL, NODE
ornamental ~ BOSS
stereo ~ BASS
TV ~ DIAL, TINT
violin ~ PEG

knobby
~ **item** KNEE

knock BANG, BAT, DIS, GIBE, HIT,
RAP, SLAP, TAP
~ **about** ABUSE, BEAT, MAUL,
RANGE, ROAM, ROVE
~ **down** EARN, RAZE, SMITE
~ **down a peg** ABASE
~ **for a loop** AMAZE, DAZE,
STUN
~ **off** CEASE, END, STOP
~ **one's socks off** AWE, WOW
~ **out** AWE, SLAY, TIRE, WOW
~ **over** ROB, UPSET
~ **senseless** STUN
~ **someone's block off** BEAT
~ **starter** ANTI
~ **stopper** OCTANE
~ **the socks off** AWE, WOW
~ **to pieces** RAZE
reply to a ~ ENTER

"Knock ___ Kiss" MEA

knockabout SLOOP

knocked for a loop
be ~ REEL

knocking
~ **game** GIN

"Knockin' on Heaven's ___"
DOOR

"Knock it off!" STOP, WHOA

knock-knock
~ **joke** PUN

knockoff CLONE

"Knock on ___ Door" ANY

knockout HIT
~ **gas** ETHER
~ **in boxing slang** ERASER

knock the socks ___ OFF

knoll RING, RISE

knop NODE

Knossos
~ **site** CRETE

knot CLAN, MASS, MAT, NODE,
SNARL, TIE, UNITE
~ **again** RETIE
~ **detail** LOOP
~ **ender** HOLE
~ **starter** BOW, SLIP, TOP
~ **up** RAVEL
make a new ~ RETIE
rope ~ NOOSE
tie the ~ MATE, UNITE, WED

___ knot LOVE, REEF

knots
be in ~ ACHE
get rid of ~ COMB, UNTIE
in ~ TENSE
where ~ **get tied** ALTAR

"Knots Landing"
~ **actress** NOONE

knotted FAST
~ **up** TENSE

Knotts DON

knotty HARD
~ **point** POSER
~ **wood** PINE

knotty ___ PINE

knot-tying
~ **org.** BSA
~ **words** IDO

knout LASH, ROD

know
~ **how to** CAN
~ **instinctively** FEEL
~ **to Scotty** KEN
before you ~ **it** ANON, SOON
get to ~ LEARN, MEET
in the ~ AWARE, HEP, HIP,
ONTO, WISE
itching to ~ NOSY
just ~ FEEL, SENSE
let people ~ AIR
old enough to ~
better ADULT
want to ~ ASK

"___ Know" ALLI

know-how ART

knowing AWARE, HEP, HIP, INON,
SAGE, SLY, SMART, WISE
~ **about** ONTO
~ **look** LEER

"___ know is what..." ALLI

know-it-___ ALL

knowledge KEN
anecdotal ~ LORE
basic ~ ABCS
body of ~ LORE
fundamental ~ ABCS
gain ~ LEARN
having ~ AWARE
having private ~ INON
seek ~ ASK
traditional ~ LORE

knowledgeable ABLE, AWARE,
GOOD, HEP, HIP, SMART, WISE
~ **about** UPON
~ **one** ORACLE

known
also ~ **as** ALIAS
become ~ EMERGE
make ~ ADMIT, AIR, BARE,
LEAK, OUT, POST, RELATE,
RUMOR, SAY, STATE, TELL
once ~ **as** NEE

know the ___ SCORE

Knox, John SCOT

Knoxville
~ **st.** TENN
its HQ is ~ TVA

knuckle
~ **down** ATTEND
~ **under** OBEY

knucklehead CLOD, DODO, DOLT,
DOPE, IDIOT, OAF

knuckles
~ **material** BRASS

knur KNOB, KNOT, NODE

knurl KNOB, KNOT, NODE

Knute
one of ~**'s successors** ARA

"Knute Rockne, ___ American"
ALL

KO
~ **count** TEN
~ **counter** REF

koala ANIMAL

koan
~ **discipline** ZEN

Kobe CITY, PORT

Koblenz
see German

Kobo ABE

kobold GNOME

Koch
~ **and others** EDS

Kodiak BEAR
~ **state** ALASKA

Kofi ___ Annan ATTA

Kohl
see German

Kojak
like ~ BALD

Ko-Ko
~ **weapon** SNEE

Koko Nor LAKE

kola NUT

Köln
see German

Konstantin
see Russian

Kon-Tiki
~ **Museum city** OSLO

"Kon-Tiki" RAFT
~ **builder** THOR
~ **embarkation point** PERU
~ **material** BALSA

kook NUT

kookaburra BIRD

___ "Kookie" Byrnes EDD

kooky DAFT, LOCO, MAD, ODD

Kool-Aid
~ **flavor** LIME

Koontz, Dean
like a ~ **novel** EERIE, EERY

Koppel TED
~ **network** ABC

Koran
~ **deity** ALLAH

Korbut OLGA

Korda, Zoltan
~ **film of 1943** SAHARA

Korea
~ **continent** ASIA
TV series set in ~ MASH

Korean ASIAN

kosher GOOD, LEGAL

Kostelanetz ANDRE

Kotcheff TED

Kottke LEO

Koufax
~ **stat** ERA

Koussevitzky SERGE

Kovacs ERNIE
Mrs. ~ EDIE

Kovic RON

Kowloon CITY, PORT

kowtow BEND, BOW, KNEEL

KP
~ **word** PEEL

Kr ELEM
36 for ~ ATNO

kraal PALE, STAD

kraft PAPER

krait ADDER, SNAKE
~ **kin** ASP

Krakatoa
~ **output** ASH

Kramden, Ralph
~ collection FARE
~ vehicle BUS
~ wife ALICE
Norton, to ~ PAL

Krasner LEE

Krasny PAUL

K-ration MEAL

Krazy
~ stuff GLUE

"Krazy ___" KAT

Kremlin
~ name LENIN

Kreskin
~ claim ESP

Krishna SHAH
~ devotee HINDU
~ home INDIA

___ Krishna HARE

Krispies
~ grain RICE

Kriss Kringle SANTA

Kristi
emulate ~ SKATE

Kristin OTTO

Kristofferson KRIS

Kroft STEVE

Krohn BILL

krona COIN

krone COIN

Krueger, Freddy
~ street ELM

Kruger OTTO
~ ender RAND

Krugerrand COIN

Krull, Felix
~ creator MANN

Krupa GENE

Krupp
~ home ESSEN, RUHR

krypton GAS
like ~ INERT

KS
see Kansas

Kuala Lumpur CITY

Kubla Khan
~ continent ASIA

"Kubla Khan" POEM

kuchen CAKE

Kuda Bux, "the man with the ___ eyes" XRAY

kudos ECLAT, HONOR
heap ~ on LAUD

Kudrow LISA

kudu ANIMAL
~ cousin ELAND

kudzu VINE

Kukla
~ creator BURR
~ friend FRAN
~ partner OLLIE

"Kukla, ___, and Ollie" FRAN

"Kukla, Fran, and ___" OLLIE

Kuklapolitan
~ player OLLIE

kulak
see Russian

kumquat TREE
~ cover RIND
~ shape OVAL

Kun BELA

kundalini LIFE

kung fu
~ star LEE

Kunlun RANGE

Kunstler, William
~ forte LAW
~ occ. ATT, ATTY
~ org. ABA

Kunta Kinte
~ portrayer AMOS

Kurd ASIAN

Kurdish
~ home IRAN

Kure CITY, PORT

Kuril Islands
~ aborigine AINU

Kurosawa
~ film RAN
~ film of 1985 RAN
~ "King Lear" RAN

kurrajong TREE

Kurt ADLER

kurus
100 ~ LIRA

Kuryakin
~ partner SOLO

Kurys DIANE

Kuwait
~ et al. OPEC
~ location ARABIA
~ neighbor IRAQ
~ peninsula ARABIA
~ ruler AMIR, EMEER, EMIR

Kuwaiti ARAB

kvass
~ ingredient RYE
~ relative BEER

kvetch CARP, CRAB, NAG

Kwan, Michelle
~ milieu ICE, RINK

___ kwon do TAE

Ky.
~ neighbor TENN
see also Kentucky

Kyle ROTE

Kyoga LAKE

kyoodle YAP

Kyoto CITY
~ coin SEN, YEN
see also Japanese

Kyrgyz
~ mountains ALAI

Kyrgyzstan
~ locale ASIA

Kyser KAY

Kyushu
see Japanese

1

L SIZE

"L'___, c'est moi" ETAT

"L'___-midi d'un Faune" APRES

L. ___ Hubbard RON

la NOTE
   ~ preceder SOL

La ELEM
   57 for ~ ATNO

La ___ (Milan opera house)
SCALA

"La ___" (Debussy work) MER

"La ___ aux Folles" CAGE

"La ___ en Rose" VIE

"La ___ Trema" TERRA

La.
   ~ neighbor ARK, MISS, TEX
   see also Louisiana

LA
   see Louisiana

L.A.
   ~ forecast SMOG
   ~ Olympics boycotter USSR
   ~ Union STA
   ~ zone PDT, PST
   part of ~ LOS

"L.A. ___" LAW

L-1011 JET

lab
   ~ animal MOUSE, RAT
   ~ assistant of film IGOR
   ~ charge FEE
   ~ container VIAL
   ~ culture AGAR
   ~ heater ETNA
   ~ liquid ACID
   ~ project TEST
   ~ runner MOUSE
   ~ shout AHA

Laban
   ~ daughter LEAH

lab-culture
   ~ medium AGAR

label DECAL, LIST, MAKE, NAME,
PEG, RATE, SIGN, STYLE, TAB,
TAG, TERM, TITLE
   ~ info SIZE
   diet-food ~ word LITE
   file ~ TAB

LaBelle PATTI

"La Belle ___" PAREE

"La Belle Dame ___ Merci" SANS

"La Belle Dame sans Merci"
POEM

Labine CLEM

"La Bohème" OPERA
   musical based on ~ RENT

labor PLOD, SLAVE, TASK, TUG
   ~ group UNION
   hard ~ TOIL

labor ___ UNION

___ labor HARD

Labor
   ~ ender ITE

Labor Day MON
   ~ mo. SEPT

Labor Dept.
   ~ org. OSHA

laborer HAND, HELP, PEON
   medieval ~ ESNE
   unskilled ~ PEON

___ laborer DAY

laborious HARD

laboriousness TOIL

Labrador SEA

La Brea ___ pits TAR

labyrinth
   ~ ender INE
   ~ locale CRETE

labyrinthine HARD

lac RESIN

lace BEAT, BIND, CORD, HIT
   ~ feature KNOT
   ~ heavily LARD
   ~ into PELT
   ~ starter INTER

~ up TIE
apply ~ TRIM
make ~ TAT

lacerate CLAW, MAIM, RACK, RIP,
TEAR

laceration BITE, CUT, GASH, RIP,
TEAR

laces
   fix your ~ RETIE

lacework MESH, NET

Lacey COP

lachrymal
   ~ drop TEAR
   be ~ CRY, SOB, WEEP

lachrymose LOW, SAD
   become ~ CRY, SOB, WEEP

lack NEED, WANT
   ~ of enthusiasm ENNUI
   ~ of subtlety CAMP
   ~ (prefix) MIS
   apod ~ FOOT
   flatfoot's ~ ARCH
   flat's ~ AIR
   hen's ~ TEETH
   lioness' ~ MANE
   Manx cat's ~ TAIL
   matzoh's ~ YEAST
   opposite of ~ HAVE, OWN
   skim milk's ~ FAT
   standee's ~ LAP

lackadaisical LOOSE

"Lackaday!" ALAS

___-Lackawanna Railroad ERIE

lackey PAGE, TOOL

lacking BARE, NEEDY, POOR,
SANS, SHY
   ~ a key ATONAL
   ~ brightness DIM
   ~ color WAN
   ~ delicacy CRASS
   ~ empathy HARD
   ~ firmness LIMP
   ~ fresh air CLOSE
   ~ moisture ARID, SERE
   ~ nothing ENTIRE
   ~ pitch ATONAL
   ~ pizazz DRAB

~ principles AMORAL
~ substance INANE, THIN
~ (suffix) LESS
~ volume THIN

lackluster DRAB

lackwit DOPE

"La classe de danse"
   ~ painter DEGAS

"La Clemenza di ___" TITO

laconic BALD, TERSE

Lacoste RENE

lacquer COAT, ENAMEL, PAINT
   ~ component ELEMI, RESIN

lacquerware TOLE

lacrosse GAME
   ~ area GOAL
   ~ goal NET
   ~ team TEN

___ Lactea (Milky Way, to Galba)
VIA

lactic ACID

lacuna GAP, SPACE

lacy OPEN

lad KID, MALE, SON
   ~ date LASS
   Dad's ~ SON

Ladd ALAN, DIANE

Ladd, Alan
   ~ film of 1946 OSS
   ~ western SHANE

ladder RUN
   ~ base HEEL
   ~ cousin STAIR
   ~ in Italian SCALA
   ~ part STEP
   **one rung on the evolution-
   ary ~** APE

___ ladder AERIAL

ladder-back
   ~ part SLAT

"Ladders to Fire"
   ~ author NIN

laddie SON

lade BAIL

"La Dee ___" DAH

ladies
one of the ~ HER, SHE

ladies'
~ **man** CAD, DUDE, RAKE, ROUE
~ **room** HAREM, ODA

"Ladies' ___, The" MAN

"Ladies' Man, The"
~ **director** LEWIS

lading LOAD

ladino HORSE

ladle BAIL, DIP, DISH, LADE, SCOOP

Ladoga LAKE

"La Dolce Vita"
~ **actress** AIMEE
~ **composer** ROTA

"La donna è mobile" ARIA

"___ la Douce" IRMA

lady ADULT, TITLE
~ **alternative** TIGER
~ **in an apron** MAID
~ **in Spanish** SRA
~ **love** GIRL
baronet's ~ DAME
belonging to the ~ HERS
bonny ~ LASS
cleaning ~ CHAR
deep-voiced ~ ALTO
first ~ EVE
first ~'s home EDEN
first ~'s mate ADAM
former Soviet first ~ RAISA
knight's ~ DAME
lea ~ EWE
little ~ GIRL
lord's ~ DAME
old ~ LOVE, MATE
old ~'s habitat SHOE
palindromic ~ ADA, AVA, EVE, MAAM, MADAM, NAN
Portuguese ~ DONA
slangy ~ DAME, GAL
Spanish ~ DONA
that ~ HER, SHE
what to call a ~ MAAM
young ~ GIRL, LASS, MAID, MISS

Lady TITLE

Lady ___ (blues singer) DAY

Lady ___ (Girl Guides founder) AGNES

Lady ___ Spencer DIANA

"Lady ___" JANE

"Lady ___" (Trollope work) ANNA

"Lady ___, The" EVE

"Lady ___ a Chance, A" TAKES

"Lady ___ a Day" FOR

"Lady ___ Cage" INA

"Lady ___ the Tramp" AND

"Lady ___ Train" ONA

"Lady ___ Tramp, The" ISA

"___ Lady" FIRST

"Lady Be ___" COOL, GOOD

Lady Bird
~ **follower** PAT
~ **middle name** ALTA

ladybug
~ **food** APHID

"Lady Chatterley's Lover"
like ~ RACY

"___ Lady Down" GRAY

ladyfinger CAKE

"Lady for a ___" DAY

"Lady for a Day"
~ **director** CAPRA

"Lady in ___, The" RED

"Lady in a ___" CAGE

Lady Jane ___ GREY

lady-killer DUDE, RAKE

"Lady Killer"
~ **director** RUTH

"Lady L"
~ **actress** LOREN

ladylove DEAR

Lady Luck FATE

"Lady of ___" SPAIN

"Lady of Spain, I ___ you" ADORE

"Lady on a ___" TRAIN

"Lady or the ___?, The" TIGER

lady's
~ **escort** GENT
~ **man** SIR
~ **mate** LORD
~ **shoe** FLAT
~ **term of address** MAAM
~ **title** MADAM
that ~ HERS

"Lady Sings the Blues"
~ **actress** ROSS

"Lady Windermere's ___" FAN

Laertes DANE
~ **to Polonius** SON

"la femme" ELLE

Lafitte
see French

La Fontaine
model for the writer
~ AESOP

"La forza ___ destino" DEL

lag
~ **behind** DRAG, TRAIL

___ lag JET, TIME

"L'Age ___" DOR

lager BEER
~ **cousin** ALE

~ **holder** KEG

Lagerlöf SELMA, SWEDE

laggard DRONE

lagging SLOW

"La Gioconda" OPERA
~ **highlight** ARIA
~ **name** LISA, MONA

lagniappe EXTRA, TIP

lagomorph HARE

lagoon BAY, LAKE, POOL
~ **relative** POND
~ **site** ATOLL

"___ Lagoon, The" BLUE

Lagos CITY

LaGuardia
~ **abbr.** ARR, ETA

"La Guerre ___ Finie" EST

La Hague CAPE

lah-di-___ DAH

Lahontan LAKE

Lahr, Bert
~ **role** LION

laid
~ **off** IDLE
~ **up** ABED, ILL

Laine CLEO

lair DEN, HAVEN, HOLE, HOME
hawk's ~ AERIE

laird LORD, PEER

laissez-faire LOOSE

laity
~ **place** PEW

Lajoie NAP

lake MERE
~ **bird** LOON
~ **boat** CANOE
~ **dweller** ALGAE, SWAN
~ **fish** BASS, TROUT
~ **maker** DAM
~ **near Carson City** TAHOE
~ **near Syracuse** ONEIDA
~ **relative** POND
African ~ CHAD
Boulder Dam's ~ MEAD
Buffalo's ~ ERIE
California-Nevada ~ TAHOE
Cleveland's ~ ERIE
Hoover Dam's ~ MEAD
Italian ~ COMO
Lombardy ~ COMO
mountain ~ TARN
Nevada ~ MEAD
New York ~ ONEIDA
salt ~ **of Australia** EYRE
saltwater ~ ARAL
Scottish ~ AWE
small ~ POOL
Toledo's ~ ERIE

lake ___ TROUT

"Lake ___ of Innisfree, The" ISLE

"___ Lake" SWAN

"___ Lake" (Doctorow novel) LOON

Lake Baikal
~ **continent** ASIA
river flowing from ~ LENA

Lake Erie
city on ~ TOLEDO

Lake Mich.
city on ~ CHI

Lake Nasser
~ **dam** ASWAN
~ **site** NILE

Lake of Brienz
~ **river** AAR, AARE

Lake Placid SPA
~ **gear** SKI

Lakers FIVE, TEAM
~ **org.** NBA

___ Lakes GREAT

Lake Tahoe
city near ~ RENO

Lake Titicaca
~ **locale** ANDES

Lake Victoria
~ **outlet** NILE

"Lake Wobegon ___" DAYS

"Lakmé" OPERA
~ **highlight** ARIA

Lakota TRIBE

"___ la la!" OOH

___-la-la TRA

"___ La La" SHA

"___ La La La Suzy" TRA

LaLanne
~ **place** SPA

"L.A. Law" DRAMA
~ **actress** DEY
~ **business** CASE
~ **character** ARNIE, ELI
~ **characters** DAS
~ **figure** ATT, ATTY
Corbin played him on
~ ARNIE
Van Owen player on ~ DEY

Lalique RENE

lallygag LOAF

lam RUN
~ **it for love** ELOPE
go on the ~ FLEE
on the ~ LOOSE

lama
~ **land** TIBET

"___ Lama Ding Dong" RAMA

Lamarr HEDY

Lamartine, Alphonse Marie de POET
see also poet

lamb ANIMAL, BEAR, DROP, MEAT
~ **cry** BAA, MAA
~ **dad** RAM

~ **dish** STEW
~ **lament** BAA, MAA
~ **mother** DAM, EWE
~ **place** COTE
~ **seasoning** MINT
~ **source** EWE
cut of ~ CHOP
in two shakes of a ~'s tail ANON, SOON
like a ~ OVINE

Lamb
~ **pen name** ELIA
~ **work** ESSAY

lambada DANCE, FAD, STEP

lambaste BEAT, CREAM, HIT, LASH, SMITE, TAN, TRIM

Lamb, Charles ELIA

Lamb Chop
~ **puppeteer** LEWIS, SHARI
like ~ OVINE

lambda
~ **followers** MUS

Lambeau Field ARENA

lambent AGILE, CLEAR

lamblike MEEK

lame MAIM

lamebrain CLOD, DODO, DOLT, OAF

lamebrained INANE

lamella SCALE

lament ALAS, BAWL, CRY, KEEN, MOAN, REACT, RUE, SOB, WEEP

lamentable BAD, SAD

"la mer"
land in ~ ILE

"Lamia" POEM

lamina COAT, LEAF, SCALE, SHEET

laminate COAT

Lammermoor, Lucia di
like ~ MAD

Lamont
~ **portrayer** ALEC

lamp
~ **cover** SHADE
~ **dweller** GENIE
~ **fuel** OIL
~ **part** HARP

___ **lamp** ARC, LAVA, POLE, SUN

"...lamp ___ my feet" UNTO

"___ Lamp, The" BLUE

lampblack SOOT

lampoon IRONY, SKIT, TWIT

lampoonist WIT

lamppost-sign
~ **abbr.** AVE

lamprey EEL

lampshade
~ **support** HARP

LAN
part of ~ AREA

Lanai ISLE
~ **(abbr.)** ISL

Lancaster
~ **symbol** ROSE

Lancaster, Burt
~ **role** ELMER, MOSES

Lancaster County
~ **group** AMISH

lance CUT, OPEN, PIKE, SLIT, SPEAR, STAB
carrying a ~ ATILT

Lance BIRD, ITO

Lancelot HERO, SIR
colleague of ~ KAY
lover of ~ ELAINE

"Lancer ___" SPY

Lanchester ELSA

land ARRIVE, BAG, ESTATE, SOIL, SPACE, STATE, TERRA
~ **elevation** MESA
~ **expanse** AREA
~ **force** ARMY
~ **holding** ESTATE
~ **in a boat** NET
~ **in French** TERRE
~ **in Italian** TERRA
~ **in Latin** TERRA
~ **measure** ACRE, ARE
~ **parcel** LOT
~ **rover** MOTOR
bit of ~ ISLET
boggy ~ FEN
builder's ~ LOT
dry ~ EARTH, SHORE
expanse of ~ ACRES, TRACT
high ~ MESA, NEPAL, TIBET
large ~ holding ESTATE
largest ~ mass ASIA
lots of ~ ACRES
low ~ FEN
narrow ~ SPIT
native ~ HOME, SOD
no man's ~ DESERT
not on ~ ASEA, ATSEA
on ~ ASHORE
piece of ~ ACRE, LOT
seagirt ~ ISLE
small ~ mass, in French ILE
unimproved ~ LOT
work the ~ DRESS, PLOW

land ___ MASS

land-___ POOR

___ **land (Los Angeles)** LALA

___ **Land (Verne harpooner)** NED

landau AUTO, CAR, MOTOR

landed ALIT, LIT
~ **lord** BARON
~ **property** ESTATE

Landers ANN, LEW

Landers, Ann TWIN

landfall
1492 ~ HAITI

ark ~ ARARAT

landfill
~ **fodder** TRASH

landgrave LORD, PEER

landing
~ **area** STRIP
~ **place** LEVEE, PIER
~ **site** STAIR
~ **site of 1969** MOON
ark's ~ site ARARAT
made a ~ ALIT, LIT

landing ___ GEAR, STRIP

___ **landing** LUNAR

landing time
~ **(abbr.)** ARR

landlady OWNER

landlocked
~ **country** LAOS

landlord OWNER
~ **document** LEASE
~ **income** RENT
~ **need** TENANT
~ **notice** TOLET

"Landlord of New York" ASTOR

landlubber
~ **locale** ASHORE

landmark EVENT
~ **miniseries** ROOTS
Flushing Meadows ~ SHEA
Paris ~ ARCH
Saint Louis ~ ARCH
San Antonio ~ ALAMO

land of Nod
in the ~ ABED, OUT

"Land of the ___" LOST

"land of the free" USA

Landon ALF

landowner
Scottish ~ LAIRD

Landry TOM

Land's ___ END

"Land sakes!" EGAD

landscape ART, SCENE
~ **dip** DALE
do a ~ PAINT

landscaper
~ **shrub** ROSE

landscaping
~ **tool** EDGER

landscapist
Seine ~ MONET

Land's End CAPE

landslide ROUT
~ **result** SCREE

lane ALLEY, PATH, ROAD, ROUTE
~ **button** RESET
~ **conversion** SPARE
~ **marker** CONE
bike ~ PATH

___ **lane** AIR, FAST

Lane ABBE, DIANE, LOIS
~ **coworker** KENT, OLSEN

"___-Lane Blacktop" TWO

lang
auld ~ syne PAST

lang. ENG, GER, ITAL, LAT, PORT, SPAN

Lang
~ **of Smallville** LANA

Lang, Clubber
~ **portrayer** MRT

Lange HOPE, TED

Langland, William POET
see also poet

Langley
~ **org.** CIA

language IDIOM
~ **suffix** ESE
anc. ~ LAT
coarse ~ ABUSE
Eur. ~ GER, ITAL
written ~ PROSE

___ **language** SIGN

languid WAN

languish AIL, DIE, FADE, FLAG, LAPSE

languor ENNUI

Lanier, Sidney POET
see also poet

lank THIN

___ **Lanka** SRI

lanky LEAN, SLIM, SPARE, TALL, THIN

Lanny ROSS

lanolin OIL

Lansbury
~ **Broadway role** MAME

lantern LAMP

lantern-jawed
~ **host** LENO

lanthanum METAL

lanyard CORD, LINE, ROPE

Lanza MARIO, TENOR

Lao
~ **neighbor** TAI, THAI

Lao-___ TSE

Laos
~ **locale** ASIA

Laotian ASIAN
~ **monetary unit** ATT
~ **neighbor** TAI, THAI

Lao-tzu SAGE
way of ~ TAO

lap LAVE
~ **dog** PEKE
form a ~ SIT
lose a ~ ARISE
planetary ~ YEAR

lap ___ DOG, ROBE

___ lap PACE

La Paz
  see Spanish

lapidarist
  ~ concern GEM
  ~ measure CARAT

lapidate STONE

lapillus STONE

lapin HARE

lapis lazuli AZURE, BLUE, GEM

La Plata CITY, PORT

Lapp NOMAD

lapped
  ~ by the tide AWASH

lapsang TEA

lapse DIE, ERR, PASS, SIN, SLIDE, STOP, TRIP

___-lapse TIME

Laptev SEA

Laptev Sea
  ~ feeder LENA

laptop
  ~ fare DATA

lapwing BIRD

Laraine DAY
  ~ ex LEO

larboard LEFT, PORT

"Larceny, ___" INC

larch TREE

lard FAT, OIL
  ~ substitute OLEO

lardlike OILY

Lardner RING

"La Repasseuse"
  ~ painter DEGAS

lares MANES

large AMPLE, BIG, GOOD, SIZE
  ~ (prefix) MEGA

large-headed
  ~ rivet STUD

largemouth ___ BASS

largeness SIZE

Largent STEVE

larger MAJOR
  make ~ PAD

larger-than-life EPIC

large-scale MASS

largess ALMS

largo TEMPO

Largo KEY

"___ Largo" KEY

lariat LASSO, RIATA, ROPE
  ~ loop NOOSE

lark ANTIC, BIRD, CAPER, PLAY, SPREE
  ~ forte SONG

larrup HIT, SWAT, TAN

Larry ADLER, BIRD, FINE
  ~ partner MOE

Larry, Moe and Curly TRIO

"Larry Sanders Show, The"
  ~ actor TORN

Larsen DON

LaRue LASH

Lary YALE

laryngologist
  word for the ~ AAH

lasagna PASTA
  ~ filling MEAT
  land of ~ ITALY

La Salle AUTO, CAR

La Scala
  ~ highlight ARIA
  ~ home MILAN
  ~ production OPERA

"La Scala di ___" SETA

Lascaux CAVE

lascivious LEWD
  ~ look LEER, OGLE

"la señorita" ELLA

laser
  ~ output RAY
  ~ sound ZAP
  hit with a ~ ZAP

laser ___ BEAM, DISC

La Serena CITY, PORT

lash BEAT, BIND, CUT, LACE, LAM, MOVE, ROD, STRAP, TAN
  ~ down STRAP
  ~ holder LID
  ~ into a fury ENRAGE
  ~ out HIT

"Lasher"
  ~ author RICE

Lash La___ RUE

Las Palmas CITY, PORT

lass GAL, MAID, MISS
  ~ counterpart LAD

Lassen ___, Calif. PEAK

lassie GIRL, KID, MAID

"Lassie"
  Corey Stuart on ~ BRAY

"Lassie ___ Home" COME

"Lassie Come ___" HOME

lassitude ENNUI

lasso RIATA, ROPE
  ~ loop NOOSE

last ABIDE, HOLD, KEEP, LIVE, NEW, STAND, WEAR
  ~ mo. DEC
  ~ of a series OMEGA

last ___ STRAW

"Last ___, The" MILE, PANDA

"Last ___ From Gun Hill" TRAIN

"Last ___ From Madrid, The" TRAIN

"Last ___ in Paris" TANGO

"Last ___ I Saw Paris, The" TIME

"Last ___ of Pompeii, The" DAYS

"Last ___ Time, The" GOOD

"Last Action ___" HERO

"Last American ___, The" HERO

"Last Angry ___, The" MAN

"Last Angry Man, The"
  ~ director MANN
  ~ star MUNI

last but ___ least NOT

last, but not ___ LEAST

"Last Command, The"
  ~ locale ALAMO

"Last Days of Pompeii, The"
  ~ heroine IONE

"Last Emperor, The"
  ~ actor LONE, OTOOLE

"Last Frontier, The" ALASKA

"Last Good ___, The" TIME

lasting ETERNAL, OLD, SAME
  ~ impression SCAR
  ~ starter EVER

"last lamenting"
  Donne's ~ thing KISS

last-minute
  ~ book insertion ERRATA

"___ Last Night..." ABOUT

"Last Night at the ___" ALAMO

"Last of ___ Cheyney, The" MRS

"Last of Sheila, The"
  ~ director ROSS

"Last of the ___ Bums" SKI

"Last of the Mohicans, The"
  ~ director MANN

"Last of the Red Hot ___" MAMAS

"Last one in ___ rotten egg!" ISA

"Last Picture ___, The" SHOW

last-place
  ~ finisher LOSER

"Last Seduction, The"
  ~ director DAHL

"Last Supper, The"
  ~ city MILAN

"Last Tango in ___" PARIS

"Last Time I ___ Paris, The" SAW

"Last Time I Saw ___, The" PARIS

"Last Train From ___ Hill" GUN

"Last Voyage, The"
  ~ director STONE

Las Vegas
  ~ area STRIP
  ~ bullet ACE
  ~ machine SLOT
  ~ st. NEV

Laszlo, Victor
  ~ wife ILSA

Lat. LANG
  see also Latin

Latakia
  ~ locale SYRIA

latch BAR, CLASP, CLOSE, SHUT
  ~ onto GRAB, GRASP, GRIP, HOLD
  door ~ HASP

latch ___ (grab) ONTO

latchet LACE

late
  ~ bloomer ASTER
  ~ for work ABED
  ~ morning ELEVEN
  ~ (prefix) NEO

"Late ___, The" SHOW

"___ Late" ITS

lateen SAIL

lateen-rigged
  ~ craft DHOW

late-model NEW

latency SLEEP

late-news
  ~ hour ELEVEN

late-night
  ~ host DAVE, LENO

late-October
  ~ suffix EEN

later AFTER, ANON, THEN
  ~ than PAST
  at a ~ time AFTER
  not ~ NOW
  sooner or ~ ANON

"Later!" BYE, TATA
  ~ in French ADIEU
  ~ in Hawaiian ALOHA
  ~ in Italian CIAO
  ~ in Latin AVE, VALE
  ~ in Spanish ADIOS

lateral
  ~ part SIDE
  ~ starter TRI, UNI

laterally
  ~ nautically ABEAM

"Late Show"
  ~ feature RERUN

latest HOT, LAST, NEW, RAGE
  ~ thing FAD, MODE, NEW, RAGE, STYLE
  the ~ NEWS

"___ Late the Hero" TOO

"___ late to turn back now!" TOO

latex
~ **product** PAINT

lath SLAT

Lathan STAN

Lathen EMMA

lather CLEAN, FOAM, HEAD
~ **source** SOAP

Latin
~ **abbr.** ETAL, ETC
~ **animal** URSA
~ **article** LAS, LOS, UNA, UNO
~ **dance** SAMBA, TANGO
~ **greeting** AVE
~ **infinitive** ESSE
~ **jazz/rock** SALSA
~ **number** OCTO
~ **preposition** SINE
~ **salutation** AVE, VALE
~ **speaker** ROMAN
~ **trio** III
~ **verb** AMAS, AMAT, AMO, ERAT
art, in ~ ARS
bear, in ~ URSA
behold, in ~ ECCE
be, in ~ ESSE
being, in ~ ESSE
bird, in ~ AVIS
birds, in ~ AVES
bones, in ~ OSSA
breakfast items, in ~ OVA
day, in ~ DIEM
earth, in ~ TERRA
eggs, in ~ OVA
eight, in ~ OCTO
existence, in ~ ESSE
goddess, in ~ DEA
god, in ~ DEO
gods, in ~ DEI
good, in ~ BENE
Helios, in ~ SOL
he loves, in ~ AMAT
here, in ~ HIC
he was, in ~ ERAT
I believe, in ~ CREDO
I forbid, in ~ VETO
I, in ~ EGO
I love, in ~ AMO
in other words, in ~ IDEST
in the same place, in ~ IBID
it was, in ~ ERAT
j'aime, in ~ AMO
journey, in ~ ITER
kind, in ~ ALMA
king, in ~ REX
land, in ~ TERRA
life, in ~ ESSE
look, in ~ ECCE
love, in ~ AMOR
monarch, in ~ REX
moon, in ~ LUNA
mouths, in ~ ORA
no, in ~ NON
often bracketed bit of ~ SIC
one, in ~ UNA
others, in ~ ALIA
passage, in ~ ITER
pray, in ~ ORA
road, in ~ ITER, VIA
room, in ~ CAMERA

route, in ~ VIA
Selene, in ~ LUNA
she loves, in ~ AMAT
so, in ~ SIC
"So long!" in ~ AVE, VALE
sun, in ~ SOL
that is, in ~ IDEST
therefore, in ~ ERGO
thing, in ~ RES
this, in ~ HIC
thus, in ~ ERGO, SIC
to be, in ~ ESSE
uncommon, in ~ RARA
useful ~ **abbr.** ETAL
water, in ~ AQUA
way, in ~ ITER
wings, in ~ ALAE
without, in ~ SINE
you love, in ~ AMAS

Latina
see Spanish

Latin America
see Spanish

Latino
see Spanish

latitude PLAY, ROOM, RUN, SPACE
~ **segment** ARC

___ latitudes HORSE

"La Traviata" OPERA
~ **piece** ARIA

lats
~ **neighbors** ABS

latte
place for a ~ CAFE

Latter-___ Saint DAY

lattice ARBOR, GRATE
~ **piece** LATH

latticework ARBOR

"La Tulipe ___" NOIRE

Latvia
~ **capital** RIGA
~ **once** SSR

Latvian LETT

laud ADORE, CITE, EXALT, HAIL, HONOR

laudable GOOD

laudanum OPIATE

Lauder ESTEE

lauds HOUR

laugh HAHA, REACT, ROAR
~ **a minute** PANIC
~ **derisively** HOOT, SNEER, SNORT
~ **syllable** HEE
hearty ~ ROAR
make ~ AMUSE
silly ~ TEHEE
villain's ~ HAH

laugh ___ RIOT

laugh ___ (dismiss) AWAY, OFF

___ laugh HORSE, LAST

laughable INANE, MAD

"Laugh-In"
~ **bit** SKIT
~ **name** ARTE, DAN, LILY, RUTH

laughing RIANT
~ **carnivore** HYENA
~ **sounds** HAHA

laughing ___ GAS, HYENA

"___ Laughing" ENTER, EXIT

"Laughing Cavalier, The"
~ **painter** HALS

laughingstock ASS, GOAT

laughs
barrel of ~ RIOT

laughter HAHA, HAS
burst of ~ GALE, PEAL
evoke ~ AMUSE
loud ~ ROAR

"Laughter in the ___" RAIN

Laughton, Charles
~ **wife** ELSA

laugh-track
~ **syllables** HAHA

launch HURL, OPEN, SHOOT, START, USHER
~ **area** PAD
~ **compartment** POD
~ **org.** NASA
cancel a ~ ABORT

launder CLEAN, LAVE, WASH

laundry WASH
~ **cycle** RINSE, SPIN
~ **fixture** SINK
~ **need** SOAP
~ **quantity** LOAD
do a ~ **chore** IRON

laundry ___ LIST

laundry-room
~ **brand** ALL, ERA, TIDE
~ **collection** LINT

Laura DERN

Laura ___ Giacomo SAN

___ laureate POET

laurel BAY, TREE
~ **wreath substitute** MEDAL
wear the ~ WIN
wreathe with ~ HONOR

Laurel STAN

Laurel and Hardy DUO, PAIR, TEAM

Laurel/Hardy
~ **link** AND

laurels AWARD, HONOR, PALM

Laurentians RANGE

"___ Laurie" ANNIE

Lautenberg, Frank
~ **org.** SEN

Lauter
~ **and others** EDS

lava STONE
~ **particles** ASH

~ **spouter** ETNA
~ **variety** SLAG
let out ~ ERUPT, SPEW

lavabo BATH

lavage BATH

lava lamps FAD

lavatory BATH
Brit's ~ LOO

lave BATHE, CLEAN, DIP, RINSE, WASH

"___ Laveau" MARIE

Lavelli DANTE

lavender COLOR
pale ~ LILAC

___ lavender SEA

"Lavender Hill ___, The" MOB

"Lavender Hill Mob, The"
~ **comedian** BASS

Laver ROD
~ **contemporary** ASHE

"La Vie en ___" ROSE

Lavin, Linda
~ **sitcom** ALICE

lavish AMPLE, FREE, ORNATE, POSH, RAIN, RICH, SPEND
~ **affection** DOTE

"___ la vista, baby!" HASTA

"La vita nuova"
~ **author** DANTE

law ACT, CODE, EDICT, FIAT, RULE, TENET
~ **and order** PEACE
~ **deg.** LLD
~ **partner** ORDER
~ **passed by Congress** ACT
action at ~ SUIT
body of ~ CODE
establish as ~ ENACT
Hebrew ~ TORAH
lay down the ~ LEAD, ORDER
make into ~ ENACT
permitted by ~ LEGAL
prohibit by ~ ESTOP
take the ~ **into one's own hands** AVENGE
within the ~ LEGAL
wrongful act, in ~ TORT

law ___ oneself, a UNTO

___ law BLUE, LEASH, LEMON

"Law & ___" ORDER

"Law ___ Disorder" AND

"Law ___ Jake Wade, The" AND

"Law ___ Order" AND

___ Law (i=v/r) OHMS

law-abiding HONEST, SOLID

"Law and ___" ORDER

"Law and Jake ___, The" WADE

Lawford PAT, PETER

lawful

lawful LEGAL
  ~ claim DUE

"law is a ___, a idiot, The" ASS

lawless EVIL

"Lawless ___, The" BREED

lawmaker
  ~ org. SEN

lawmaking
  ~ body SENATE

lawman
  legendary ~ EARP

lawn LAND, YARD
  ~ bowling GAME
  ~ chemical LIME
  ~ implement EDGER
  ~ material SOD
  ~ pest MOLE
  do ~ work WEED
  repair the ~ SOD
  start a ~ SEED
  tend the ~ MOW

lawn-care
  ~ product LIME
  ~ tool EDGER

lawnmower
  ~ brand DEERE

lawnwork
  do ~ SOD

"Law & Order"
  ~ characters DAS

Lawrence CAROL, STEVE
  ~ locale ARABIA

___ Lawrence College SARAH

Lawrence, D.H.
  start of a ~ title LADY

Lawrence, Gertrude
  ~ film bio STAR
  ~ role ANNA

"Lawrence of ___" ARABIA

"Lawrence of Arabia"
  ~ actor OTOOLE, RAINS
  ~ director LEAN
  ~ locale DESERT
  ~ name ALEC, OMAR

Lawrence, Vicki
  ~ role MAMA

laws
  set of ~ CODE

lawsuits
  cause of some ~ LIBEL, TORT

"law, the"
  ~ to Mr. Bumble ASS

"Law West of the Pecos, The" BEAN

lawyer
  ~ (abbr.) ATT, ATTY
  ~ concern CASE
  ~ deg. LLD
  ~ hurdle BAR
  ~ org. ABA
  ~ thing RES
  hire a ~ SUE

"Lawyer ___" MAN

lawyers
  ~ group BAR

lawyer's ___ exam BAR

lax LIMP, LOOSE

LAX
  ~ abbr. ARR, ETA
  ~ client TWA

lay AIR, ARIA, ODE, POEM, PUT, SET, SONG
  ~ an egg MISS
  ~ aside SAVE, TABLE
  ~ a sidewalk PAVE
  ~ at anchor RIDE
  ~ a wager BET, PLAY
  ~ away SAVE
  ~ bare SHOW, SKIN
  ~ by AMASS, SAVE, STORE
  ~ concrete PAVE, POUR
  ~ dormant SLEEP
  ~ down SET
  ~ down the law LEAD, ORDER
  ~ down the lawn SOD
  ~ eyes on ESPY, SEE, SPOT
  ~ flagstones PAVE
  ~ hands on GRAB, HARM
  ~ hold of GET, GRAB, GRASP, NAB
  ~ in AMASS, STORE
  ~ into BEAT, HIT, LACE, SMITE, TAN
  ~ it on thick BRAG, LIE
  ~ low HIDE
  ~ off IDLE, STOP
  ~ one's hand to PLY
  ~ on the line RISK
  ~ out MAP, PAY, SPEND
  ~ out in advance PLAN
  ~ over TABLE
  ~ stones PAVE
  ~ the cornerstone START
  ~ up AMASS, STORE
  ~ waste BLAST, RAID, RAZE, RUIN, SACK

lay ___ (knock down) LOW

lay ___ (quit) OFF

lay ___ (reject) ASIDE

lay ___ (save) AWAY

lay ___ the line ITON

lay ___ thick ITON

lay ___ to CLAIM

lay-___ UPS

"Lay, ___, Lay" LADY

layabout IDLER

Layamon POET
  see also poet

lay an ___ EGG

lay down the ___ LAW

"___ Lay Dying" ASI

layer BED, HEN, LEAF, PLY, SHEET, TIER
  ~ deposit EGG
  ~ of paint COAT

atmospheric ~ OZONE
egg ~ BIRD, HEN
endangered ~ OZONE
lettuce ~ BED
mining ~ LEDGE, STRIP
ocular ~ UVEA
ore ~ SEAM
outer ~ RIND
paper ~ PLY
protective ~ OZONE
stratosphere ~ OZONE
surface ~ SKIN
thin ~ SHEET
unwanted ~ DUST
wedding-cake ~ TIER

___ layer OZONE

layered
  ~ rock ONYX, SHALE

"Layla"
  ~ singer ERIC

layman
  governing ~ ELDER

lay of the ___ LAND

layout PLAN, SETUP

layover STAY, STOP

Lazar, Swifty AGENT

Lazarus EMMA

laze IDLE, LIE, LOAF, LOLL, REST

LaZonga MME

lazy IDLE
  ~ one IDLER
  ~ Susan TRAY
  be ~ LOAF
  in a ~ way IDLY

lazybones DRONE

LBJ DEM, PRES
  ~ beagle HER, HIM

LCD
  part of ~ LEAST

"L'chayim!" TOAST

Le ___ Soleil (Louis XIV) ROI

"Le ___" MANS

"Le ___" (Massenet work) CID

"Le ___ de Lahore" ROI

"Le ___ d'Ys" ROI

"Le ___ Goriot" PERE

lea LAND, RANGE
  ~ cry BAA, MAA
  ~ lady EWE
  ~ sound LOW, MOO

leach CLEAR, OOZE, SEEP

lead AMMO, LEASH, METAL, SHOW, STAR, STEER
  ~ balloon DUD, LOSER
  ~ down the aisle USHER
  ~ down the primrose path LURE
  ~ off OPEN, START
  ~ on ABET, DUPE
  ~ part HERO
  ~ pellets SHOT

~ pumper GAT
~ source ORE
~ starter MIS
~ to the altar WED
~ up the garden path LIE
get the ~ out HIE, RACE, RUN
hot ~ CLUE
in the ~ AHEAD
male ~ HERO
opera ~, often TENOR
slight ~ EDGE
take the ~ HEAD

lead ___ TIME

lead ___ ("Clue" weapon) PIPE

___ lead (minium) RED

"___ Lead and Cold Feet" HOT

lead down the garden ___ PATH

leader BOSS, CORD, HEAD, PILOT, ROPE
  ~ (suffix) ARCH
  org. ~ PRES

___ leader LOSS

leaders
  ~ set it PACE
  Army ~ BRASS

leadership
  ~ group CADRE
  ~ position HELM

lead-in INTRO

leading AHEAD, BEST, BIG, FIRST, KEY, MAIN, TOP
  ~ man ACTOR, HERO, STAR

leading ___ EDGE, LADY, MAN, TONE

leading lady STAR

lead to the ___ ALTAR

leaf ORGAN, PAGE, PLY, SHEET
  ~ adjective EROSE
  ~ for brewing PEKOE, TEA
  ~ holder STEM
  ~ opening PORE
  ~ part LOBE
  ~ starting point NODE
  ~ through READ, SCAN
  ~ vein RIB
  calyx ~ SEPAL
  like a maple ~ EROSE
  palm ~ FAN
  walking ~ FERN
  water lily ~ PAD

___ leaf BAY, DROP, GOLD

___-leaf LOOSE

"___ Leaf" ANEW

"___ Leaf, A" NEW

___-leaf binder LOOSE

___-leaf cluster OAK

leafless BARE

leaflet BILL, TRACT

"___ Leaf Rag" MAPLE

Leafs SIX, TEAM
  ~ milieu ICE, RINK

~ org. NHL

___-leaf table DROP

leaf-to-stem
~ mark SCAR

leafy
~ green vegetable KALE
~ shelter ARBOR

league AXIS, BLOC, CABAL, CLAN, PACT, RING
~ (abbr.) ASSN
~ together BAND

___ league BIG

___ League ARAB, IVY

"___ League" MAJOR

"League of ___ Own, A" THEIR

"League of Their ___, A" OWN

Leah
son of ~ LEVI

leak BLAB, DRIP, DROP, EMIT, OOZE, RUMOR, RUN, SEEP, SING
~ sound HISS
stop the ~ STEM

"Leakin' ___" LENA

leaking
work in a ~ boat BAIL

lean HEEL, LANK, LIST, PROP, RELY, SLANT, SLIM, SPARE, THIN, TILT, TIP, TRIM
~ backward ARCH
~ eater SPRAT
~ on ABUT, PROP
~ over BEND, DRAPE
~ to one side CANT, HEEL, LIST
~ toward TEND
~ upon ABUT

Leander
~ beloved HERO

leaning ALIST, ATILT, BIAS, CAST, HABIT, SLANT
~ to one side ALIST

Leaning Tower
~ site PISA
like the ~ ATILT

lean-to SHED

leap CAPER, DART, HOP, SKIP, START
~ over CLEAR
~ up RISE
fencing ~ VOLT
skater's ~ AXEL

leap ___ YEAR

leaper
lunar ~ COW

leapfrog GAME, HOP

Lear POET
~ daughter REGAN
~ product JET, POEM
"elegant fowl", to ~ OWL
loyal companion to ~ KENT
see also poet

learn GET, HEAR, KNOW
~ by heart CON
~ in a hurry CRAM
~ the ropes ADAPT, TRAIN
~ through the grapevine HEAR
one way to ~ ROTE
quick to ~ APT, SMART
try to ~ ASK

learned ABLE, READ, WISE
~ about UPON
~ book TOME
~ one SAGE

learning LORE
~ method ROTE
early ~ method ABCS

Leary, Denis
~ comedy, with "The" REF

lease HIRE, LET, RENT
~ holder TENANT
extend a ~ RELET, RENEW

___-Lease Act LEND

leaseholder TENANT

___ lease on life ANEW

___ lease on life, a NEW

leash BIND, LEAD, STRAP

leash ___ LAW

least
~ (abbr.) MIN

leather HIDE, SKIN
~ accessory BELT
~ band STRAP
~ ender ETTE
~ essentially HIDE
~ strap REIN
~ tool AWL
bookbinder's ~ ROAN
decorate, as ~ TOOL
glove ~ KID
go hellbent for ~ RIP
make ~ TAN
sheepskin ~ ROAN
tan ~ CURE
type of ~ ELK, SUEDE
work with ~ TOOL

"Leatherstocking"
~ piece TALE

"Leatherstocking ___" TALES

leather-to-be PELT

leathery HARD

leave DESERT, ENDOW, EXIT, MOVE, SPLIT
~ agape AWE, WOW
~ behind LEAD
~ dock SAIL
~ flat DROP
~ hastily SKIP
~ home MOVE
~ in STET
~ in a hurry FLEE, HIE, RUN
~ in awe AMAZE, WOW
~ in the dust LOSE
~ in the lurch DESERT
~ no choice IMPEL
~ no stone unturned DIG,

HUNT, RAKE, SEEK
~ no trace DIE, FADE
~ no vestige of RAZE
~ off CEASE, END, OMIT, STOP
~ one's feet LEAP
~ one's seat ARISE, RISE
~ open-mouthed AMAZE, AWE, STUN, WOW
~ out DROP, ELIDE, OMIT, SKIP, TABOO, TABU
~ port SAIL
~ secretly ELOPE
~ shore SAIL
~ slack-jawed AMAZE, AWE, STUN, WOW
~ the cocoon EMERGE
~ the dock SAIL
~ the ground LEAP, RISE
~ the path ROVE
~ the plane suddenly EJECT
~ the water EMERGE
~ undone OMIT, SKIP
~ uninjured SPARE
~ wide-eyed AMAZE, AWE, STUN, WOW
French ~ LAM
give ~ to ALLOW, LET
on ~ ASHORE
take ~ PART
take French ~ DESERT, RUN
take sick ~ AIL
takes one's ~ GOES

leave ___ (stop) OFF

___ leave SHORE

"Leave ___ to Heaven" HER

"Leave It to Beaver"
~ pal EDDIE

"Leave me ___!" ALONE

leaven YEAST

leaves GOES
gather ~ RAKE
like autumn ~ SERE
lose ~ SHED
notched, as ~ EROSE

"Leaves of Grass" POEM

leave well enough ___ ALONE

leaving
~ out BAR, SAVE

"Leaving ___ Jet Plane" ONA

"Leaving ___ Vegas" LAS

"___ Leaving Home" SHES

"Leaving Las Vegas"
Elisabeth, in ~ SERA

leavings REST, SLOP, TRASH, WASTE

Leb.
~ neighbor ISR, SYR

Lebanese ARAB, ASIAN
~ port TYRE
~ symbol CEDAR

Lebanon
~ locale ASIA
~ neighbor SYRIA
tree of ~ CEDAR

LeBlanc MATT

Le Bourget
~ alternative ORLY

Lebowitz FRAN

Le Cain ERROL

Le Carré
~ figure AGENT, SPY

lecher GOAT, RAKE, ROUE

lecherous LEWD
~ look LEER, OGLE

lechwe
~ cousin ELAND

"Le Coq ___" DOR

"Le Coq d'Or" OPERA

Lecter-like EVIL

lectern AMBO, DESK, STAND
~ locale DAIS

lecture CLASS, ORATE, RAG, TALK
~ (abbr.) SER
place for a ~ DAIS

lecturer ORATOR
~ place DAIS

Leda MOON
daughter of ~ HELEN

ledge BAR, LIP, REST, SILL, TABLE
rocky ~ CRAG

ledger
~ abbr. AMT
~ check AUDIT
~ div. ACCT
~ entry ASSET, DEBIT, ITEM, LOSS
~ expert CPA
put in the ~ ENTER

___-le-duc BAR

Led Zeppelin
~ gear AMP

Lee ANN, ELDER, SARA, STAN
~ to Grant ENEMY, FOE

Lee ___ Cleef VAN

Lee ___ Meriwether ANN

"___ Lee" AURA

___-Lee (Klinger's bride) SOON

leech DRONE

Leeds
~ river AIRE
see also British

leek
~ relative ONION

Lee, Lorelei
~ creator LOOS

___ Lee Masters EDGAR

Lee, Pamela, ___ Anderson NEE

leer EYE, OGLE

Lee, R.E.
~ nation CSA
~ rank GEN

leery SHY, WARY

lees WASTE

leeward
  drift to ~ SAG

leeway PLAY, ROOM, SPACE

left GONE, OVER, RED
  ~ ender IST
  ~ on a ship PORT
  ~ over SPARE
  ~ the chair AROSE
  ~ the plane ALIT
  ~ the sack AROSE
  ~ to a horse HAW
  be ~ with NET
  in the time ~ YET
  out in ~ field FALSE, MAD
  to the ~ ASIDE
  what's ~ REST

"Left ___ of God, The" HAND

Left Bank
  ~ cap BERET
  ~ river SEINE
  see also French

"Left Hand of ___, The" GOD

leftover EXTRA, ODD, ORT, PLUS,
SCRAP, TAIL
  apple ~ CORE
  barbecue ~ ASH, EMBER
  cherry ~ STEM
  fire ~ SMUT
  smelting ~ SLAG
  ticket ~ STUB

leftovers HASH, REST, TRASH
  ~ dish HASH

left ventricle
  ~ outlet AORTA

leg GAM, PART
  ~ bone SHIN, TIBIA
  ~ ender FOOT
  ~ joint ANKLE, KNEE
  ~ part CALF
  ~ puller LIAR
  ~ starter BOOT, DOG, FORE
  ~ up EDGE, HAND
  plant ~ STEM
  pull someone's ~ KID, PLAY,
TEASE
  shake a ~ HIE, MOVE, RUN,
STIR
  wooden ~ PEG

legacy
  ~ recipient HEIR
  heir's ~ ESTATE

legal
  ~ action SUIT
  ~ claim LIEN
  ~ code LAW
  ~ defense ALIBI
  ~ delay STAY
  ~ document DEED, TITLE,
WRIT
  ~ encumbrance LIEN
  ~ ender ESE
  ~ matter RES
  ~ memo starter INRE
  ~ move PLEA
  ~ offs. DAS
  ~ org. ABA

  ~ posting BAIL
  ~ profession BAR, LAW
  ~ rep ATT, ATTY
  ~ restraint ARREST, LIEN
  ~ starter PARA
  ~ suit CASE
  ~ tender BILL, CASH, NOTE,
PAPER
  ~ unknown DOE
  ~ wrongdoing TORT
  bring ~ action SUE
  make ~ SIGN
  the ~ profession BAR

legal ___ AGE, AID, EAGLE, FEE,
PAD

legal-___ SIZE

legalese
  ~ phrase ASTO, INRE
  prevent, in ~ ESTOP

legalize CLEAR, ENACT

Le Gallienne EVA

legatee HEIR

legato
  ~ symbol SLUR

legend KEY, TALE

"Legend of the ___ Flower, The"
STONE

legends LORE

___-legged race THREE

leggy LANK
  ~ bird EGRET

leghorn BIRD, HAT

Leghorn HEN
  see also Italian

legible CLEAN, CLEAR

legion HEAP, HORDE, HOST, MASS,
MOB, OCEAN, PILE, SEA
  Roman ~ ARMY

"___ Legion, The" FIRST

legiron
  place for a ~ ANKLE

legis.
  ~ sitting SESS

legislate ENACT, PASS

legislation ACT

legislative
  ~ appendage RIDER
  ~ body SENATE
  ~ matter ACT

legislators
  ~ mtg. SESS

legislature
  Japanese ~ DIET

legit LEGAL

legitimate FAIR, LEGAL, TRUE

leg-puller LIAR

legs
  go on hind ~ RAMP, REAR
  on one's hind ~ ERECT

  on one's last ~ DONE
  stretch one's ~ PACE

___ legs CRAB, SEA

leg to ___ on, a STAND

legume BEAN, PEA
  ~ holder POD

legwear HOSE

Le Havre CITY, PORT
  city near ~ CAEN
  see also French

Lehman ERNEST

Lehmann LOTTE

Lehr LEW

Lehrer TOM

lehua TREE

Leia
  ~ rescuer HAN

Leibman RON

Leibovitz ANNIE

Leicester EARL

Leif
  ~ father ERIC
  ~ to Eric SON

Leigh
  role for ~ OHARA

Leilani
  ~ greeting ALOHA
  see also Hawaiian

"___ Leilani" SWEET

Leipzig CITY
  see also German

leis
  occasion for ~ LUAU

leisure EASE, REST, TIME
  ~ companion ARTS
  ~ pursuit PLAY
  at ~ FREE, IDLE

leisurely EASY, IDLY, SLOW

leitmotif THEME

Lejeune CAMP

lek COIN

"L'Elisir d'___" AMORE

LEM
  ~ locale MOON
  ~ org. NASA
  Apollo 11 ~ EAGLE
  part of ~ LUNAR

___ Leman LAC

Le Mans RACE
  see also French

LeMay
  ~ command SAC

Lemieux MARIO
  ~ org. NHL

lemming ANIMAL

Lemmon, Jack
  ~ film of 1989 DAD

lemon COLOR, DOG, DUD, LOSER,
TREE
  ~ candy DROP
  ~ cooler ADE
  ~ cousin DOG
  ~ drink ADE
  ~ ender ADE
  ~ meringue PIE
  ~ partner LIME
  ~ sometimes AUTO, CAR
  famous ~ EDSEL

lemon ___ DROP, LAW, OIL

"Lemon ___ Kid, The" DROP

lemonade
  ~ location STAND

"Le Monde"
  see French

"Lemon Drop ___, The" KID

lemon-lime
  ~ drink ADE

lemony ACID, SOUR, TART

lemur ANIMAL
  ~ cousin APE

lemures MANES

Lena HORNE, OLIN
  ~ locale ASIA
  see also Russian

Lena the ___ HYENA

lend LOAN
  ~ a hand ABET, AID, HELP,
SERVE
  ~ an ear HEED
  ~ moral support ROOT

lend ___ (listen) ANEAR

Lend-___ Act LEASE

lend an ___ EAR

"...___ lender be" NORA

Lendl IVAN
  ~ pointmaker ACE
  like ~ lobs ARCED
  see also tennis

length
  ~ of a pool LAP
  ~ of cloth YARD
  ~ of office TERM
  ~ times width AREA
  at arm's ~ ALOOF
  course ~ TERM
  old unit of ~ ROOD
  on the ~ of ALONG
  relay ~ MILE
  skirt ~ MIDI, MINI
  speak at ~ DRAG, ORATE
  unit of ~ FOOT, INCH, MILE,
ROD

lengthen DRAG, GROW, SPIN

lengths
  dash ~ EMS, ENS

lengthwise ALONG

lengthy LONG

Leni PAUL

lenient EASY, LOOSE, MILD

Lenin RED
  ~ **ctry.** USSR
  ~ **deposee** TSAR
  ~ **loyalist** RED

Leningrad CITY, PORT
  Battle of ~ SIEGE
  see also Russian

Lennon, John
  ~ **middle name** ONO
  ~ **spouse** ONO

Lennon, Julian
  ~ **stepmother** ONO

Lennon, Sean
  ~ **mom** ONO

Lennox ANNIE

Lenny MOORE

Leno, Jay EMCEE, HOST
  ~ **predecessor** ALLEN, PAAR
  ~ **prominent feature** CHIN

"Lenore"
  ~ **poet** POE

lens OPTIC
  ~ **holder** RIM
  ~ **opening** IRIS

lent
  it may be ~ ANEAR, EAR

Lent
  ~ **follower** EASTER
  observe ~ FAST

Lenten
  ~ **symbol** ASH

lento TEMPO

Lenya LOTTE

Leo LION, POPE, SIGN
  ~ **constituent** STAR
  ~ **locution** ROAR
  ~ **mo.** AUG
  ~ **neckpiece** MANE
  ~ **predecessor** CRAB

Leon AMES, ERROL, HESS, URIS

León
  see Spanish

Léon
  see French

Leonardo
  see Italian

Leonhard EULER

Leonid
  see Russian

Leonides HERO

leonine
  ~ **group** PRIDE
  ~ **ruff** MANE

Leonowens ANNA

Leonowens, Anna
  where ~ **taught** SIAM

leopard ANIMAL, CAT
  ~ **sound** SNARL
  snow ~ OUNCE

leopard ___ MOTH

"Leopard, The"
  ~ **composer** ROTA

leopardlike
  ~ **animal** OCELOT

Leopold ALDO, AUER

lepidolite ORE

lepidopterist
  ~ **gear** NET

leprechaun GNOME, IMP
  ~ **country** EIRE, ERIN
  ~ **cousin** ELF, GNOME
  like a ~ ELFIN

leprechauns
  like ~ WEE

Leptis Magna CITY, PORT

lepton COIN

___ lepton TAU

Lepus
  constellation ~ HARE

Lerner CARL

"___ le roi!" ABAS

"Le Roi d'Ys"
  ~ **composer** LALO

"Le Rouge et le ___" NOIR

"les"
  cousin of ~ THE

Lesage ALAIN

"Les Bergeries"
  ~ **author** ANET

"Les Fleurs du ___" MAL

lesion SORE

Lesley GORE

Lesley ___ Warren ANN

"Les Misérables"
  ~ **author** HUGO
  ~ **setting** SEWER

"Les nuits d'___" ETE

Lesotho
  ~ **river** ORANGE

less
  ~ **than all** SOME
  ~ **than one** NIL
  feel ~ **than perfect** AIL
  make ~ ALLAY
  more or ~ ABOUT, NEAR
  more or ~ **the same** LIKE
  salary ~ **deductions** NET

"Less ___ Zero" THAN

"___ Less Bell to Answer" ONE

lessee TENANT
  ~ **payment** RENT

lessen ABATE, ALLAY, AMEND,
BATE, COOL, DROP, EASE, FADE,
FLAG, PARE, REMIT, SAG, SLAKE,
THIN, WANE

lesser
  ~ **(prefix)** DEMI

lesser ___ APE, PANDA

Lesser Sunda
  ~ **island** BALI

lesson CLASS, MORAL
  ballet ~ STEP
  first-grade ~ ABCS

"Lesson From ___, A" ALOES

lessons
  give ~ TRAIN

"Less Than Zero"
  ~ **author** ELLIS

Lestat
  ~ **creator** RICE

Lester ___ Rey DEL

Lester, Richard
  ~ **film of 1965** HELP
  ~ **film of 1979** CUBA

"Lest we lose our ___" EDENS

let ADMIT, ALLOW, HIRE, LEASE,
RENT
  ~ **down one's hair** UNDO
  ~ **fall** DROP, RELATE, RUMOR,
SHED
  ~ **flow** SHED
  ~ **fly** CAST, HURL
  ~ **go** AXE, FIRE, FREE, LOOSE,
SACK, SPARE
  ~ **go of** CEDE, DROP
  ~ **happen** ALLOW
  ~ **in** ADMIT
  ~ **it out** BLAB, TELL
  ~ **it stand** STET
  ~ **loose** FREE
  ~ **off** CLEAR, EMIT
  ~ **off steam** YELL
  ~ **on** ADMIT, OWN
  ~ **one's mind wander** MISS,
SLEEP
  ~ **out** ALTER, FREE, LOAN,
LOOSE, SAY, TELL
  ~ **out lava** ERUPT, SPEW
  ~ **pass** ALLOW
  ~ **people know** AIR
  ~ **slide** OMIT
  ~ **slip** BLAB, LEAK, MISS, TELL
  ~ **slip through one's
    fingers** LOSE
  ~ **someone have it** BEAT,
HARM, LACE
  ~ **the cat out of the
    bag** LEAK, TELL
  ~ **the grass grow under
    one's feet** LOAF
  ~ **up** ABATE, CEASE, EASE,
EBB, FLAG
  ~ **use** LEND
  ~ **well enough alone** AVOID

let ___ (divulge) OUT, SLIP

"Let a ___ Be..." SMILE

"L'état c'est ___" MOI

"Let 'Em Eat ___" CAKE

"Let 'Em Eat Cake"
  ~ **song** MINE

"Let 'er ___!" RIP

"Lethal Weapon"
  Danny's ~ **costar** MEL

lethargic INERT, LIMP
  ~ **feeling** ENNUI
  ~ **one** SNAIL

lethargize TIRE

lethargy ENNUI
  causing ~ OPIATE

"___ Let Me Be Misunderstood"
DONT

"Let Me Be the ___" ONE

"(Let Me Be Your) Teddy ___"
BEAR

**"Let me not to the marriage of
true minds"** POEM

"Let No ___ Write My Epitaph"
MAN

"Let one's ___ down HAIR

"Let's ___ Lost" GET

"Let's ___ Love" MAKE

"Let's ___ the Music and Dance"
FACE

"Let's call ___ day!" ITA

"Let's Do It ___" AGAIN

"Let's Do It Again"
  ~ **director** HALL

"Let's Face the Music and ___"
DANCE

"Let's Fall in Love"
  ~ **composer** ARLEN

"Let's Get ___" ITON, LOST

let sleeping dogs ___ LIE

"Let sleeping dogs lie" ADAGE

"Let's Make ___" LOVE

"Let's Make a Deal"
  ~ **choice** DOOR
  ~ **host** HALL

"Let's shake on it!" DEAL

letter SIGN
  ~ **abbr.** ATT, ATTN
  ~ **closer** SEAL
  ~ **drop** SLOT
  ~ **starter** DEAR
  first ~ **(abbr.)** INIT

___-letter day RED

letterhead PAPER
  ~ **abbr.** INC
  ~ **illustration** LOGO

Letterman DAVE, EMCEE, HOST
  ~ **network** CBS
  ~ **rival** LENO
  first item on a ~ **list** TEN

Letterman, David EMCEE, HOST

Lettermen, The TRIO

letters MAIL
  ~ **companions** ARTS
  earliest ~ ABC

___ letters CALL

"___ Letters" LOVE

"Letter to ___ Wives, A" THREE

"Let the ___ Times Roll" GOOD

"Let the Good Times ___" ROLL

"Let the Good Times Roll"
~ **director** ABEL

"Let them eat ___" CAKE

"Let the Sunshine In"
~ **musical** HAIR

"Letting Go"
~ **author** ROTH

lettuce CASH, KALE, MOOLA
~ **cousin** KALE
~ **layer** BED
~ **piece** LEAF
~ **unit** HEAD
big piece of ~ CNOTE
fresh, as ~ CRISP
kind of ~ COS

letup PEACE, REST, STOP

"Let us ___" PRAY

"Let Us Now Praise Famous Men"
~ **author** AGEE

leu COIN

Levant OSCAR

Levantine
~ **state** SYRIA

"Le veau ___" DOR

level AIM, CLASS, ESTATE, EVEN, FLAT, LOG, PLANE, RANK, RAZE, STAGE, STEP, TABLE, TIER
general ~ NORM
grandstand ~ TIER
highest ~ PEAK
make ~ TRUE
management ~ TIER
not on the ~ ATILT
on the ~ HONEST, TRUE
theater ~ TIER
top ~ ACME, PEAK

___ level SEA, WATER

___-level LOW, SPLIT, TOP

levelheaded SANE, SOBER

levelheadedness SENSE

___-level job ENTRY

Leven LAKE

Levenson SAM

lever BAR, OAR, PRY
foot ~ PEDAL
organ ~ PEDAL, STOP
piano ~ PEDAL
pull the ~ VOTE
use a ~ PRY

leverage HOLD

leveret ANIMAL, HARE

Lévesque RENE

Levi
~ **rival** LEE
mother of ~ LEAH

leviathan BIG, GIANT, LARGE, VAST

levigate ABRADE

Levin IRA, MARC, SID

"___ Levine, The" ANGEL

levitate RISE

levitated AROSE

Levon ___-Petrosyan TER

levy ASSESS, PRESS, PUT, TOLL

lewd
~ **look** LEER

Lewis ALLEN, CARL, SHARI, TED

Lewis and Clark
~ **explored it** IDAHO

Lewis, Carl
~ **event** DASH
challenge ~ RACE

Lewis, Huey
~ **band, with "the"** NEWS

Lewis, Jerry EMCEE, HOST

Lewis, Sinclair
~ **alma mater** YALE
~ **character** ELMER
~ **street** MAIN

Lex. ___ AVE

lexicography
first name in ~ NOAH

lexicon
J.A.H. Murray's ~ OED
multivol. ~ OED

Leyden ___ JAR

LGA
~ **abbr.** ARR, ETA

lge.
smaller than ~ MED

Lhasa
~ **leader** LAMA
~ **locale** ASIA, TIBET

Lhasa ___ APSO

Li ELEM
3 for ~ ATNO

liability BILL, DEBT, RISK
opposite of ~ ASSET

liable APT, PRONE
not ~ **to** ABOVE

liaison AMOUR, LOVE

liana PLANT, VINE

libation
London ~ ALE
seaman's ~ RUM
see also beverage, drink

libel ABUSE, SHAME, SLUR, SMEAR, TAINT, TORT

"Libeled ___" LADY

libeler LIAR

liberal AMPLE, FREE, LEFT

liberal ___ ARTS

liberals LEFT

liberate CLEAR, FREE, LOOSE, RID, SAVE, STEAL, TAKE

liberated FREE

Liberia's
~ **flag has one** STAR

libertine RAKE, ROUE, SATYR

liberty PLAY
at ~ CLEAR, LOOSE

libidinous LEWD

Libra SIGN
~ **mo.** OCT
~ **stone** OPAL

libraries
~ **do it** LEND

library ROOM
~ **item** TOME
~ **no-no** NOISE
~ **sect.** REF
~ **sound** PSST, PST
~ **transaction** LOAN
frequent the ~ READ

library ___ CARD, PASTE

libretto TEXT
~ **feature** ARIA

Libya
~ **neighbor** CHAD, NIGER
~ **org.** OPEC
most of ~ SAHARA

Libyan DESERT

"Licence to Kill"
~ **director** GLEN

license ENABLE, LEAVE, LET, PAPER, PASS, PLAY, RUN
~ **bureau sight** LINE
~ **charge** FEE
~ **plate** TAG

license ___ FEE, PLATE

licensed LEGAL

license plate
~ **sticker** DECAL

licenses
driver's ~ IDS

licentious LEWD, LOOSE

lichen MOSS, PLANT

Lichtenfield TED

Lichtenstein ROY

licit LEGAL

lick BEAT, TAN
~ **and stick** SEAL
not a ~ NONE

lick (up) LAP

lick ___ promise ANDA

___ lick SALT

lickerish LEWD

lickety-split APACE, FAST, SOON
go ~ HIE, RACE, RUN, SPEED

licking
it takes a ~ STAMP

licorice PLANT
~ **flavoring** ANISE

lid CAP, HAT, TOP
blow the ~ **off** LEAK
flip one's ~ RAGE, RAVE
Lyons ~ BERET
see also hat

"Lida ___" ROSE

Liddy
~ **radio nickname** GMAN

lidless OPEN

lido
what to do in a ~ SWIM

lie MASK, TALE
~ **adjacent to** ABUT
~ **around** LOAF, LOLL
~ **dormant** SLEEP
~ **down** REST
~ **fallow** SIT
~ **in store for** AWAIT
~ **in the sun** BAKE, BASK, BATHE, TAN
~ **in the tub** SOAK
~ **low** DROP, HIDE, WAIT
~ **next to** ABUT
~ **on the beach** SUN
~ **poolside** BASK
~ **prone** BOW
~ **still** REST
~ **to** HALT, STOP
give the ~ **to** BLAST
tell a ~ FAKE

___ lie BIG

"___ Lie, The" GREAT

Liebfraumilch WINE

Lieblich AMIA

Liechtenstein
~ **loc.** EUR
~ **locale** ALPS

lie-down NAP

"___ Lied von der Erde" DAS

liege MAN

Liege
town near ~ SPA

"___ Lies" TRUE

"___, lies, and videotape" SEX

"Lies My Father ___ Me" TOLD

Lie, Trygve
~ **home** OSLO

lieu STEAD

lieut.
~ **right arm** SGT

lieutenant AIDE, RANK
future ~ CADET

lieutenant-to-be CADET

life ELAN, FIRE, TERM, VIM
~ **fluid** SAP
~ **force** TAO
~ **guide** CREDO, CREED
~ **in French** VIE
~ **in Latin** ESSE
~ **lot** FATE

          "...like a big pizza pie, that's ___"

~ of Riley EASE
~ of the party WIT
~ (prefix) BIO
~ saver HERO
~ story BIO
bigger than ~ EPIC
breathe ~ into FIRE
breathe new ~ into RENEW
condition of ~ ESTATE
former ~ PAST
full of ~ EAGER, GAY, SPRY
good ~ EASE
marine ~ ALGA, ALGAE
not on your ~ NAY, NEVER, NOPE
plant ~ FLORA
put new ~ into RESTORE
rudimentary ~ GERM
sea ~ ALGAE
sign of ~ PULSE
stage of ~ AGE
take one's ~ in one's hands RISK
walk of ~ LINE, SPHERE

life ___ RAFT, SPAN
life-___ SIZE
___-life HALF
"Life ___ Death of Colonel Blimp, The" AND
"Life ___ Pogo Stick" ONA
"Life and Times of Judge Roy ___, The" BEAN
"Life Begins ___ Andy Hardy" FOR
"Life Begins for ___ Hardy" ANDY
lifeblood ESSENCE
life force
~ in acupuncture CHI
"Life Goes On"
~ network ABC
lifeguard
~ beat POOL
"Life is but a ___" DREAM
life-jacket
~ name MAE
lifeless ARID, BANAL, BLAH, DRAB, DRY, FLAT
lifeline
~ locale PALM
"Life of ___, The" RILEY
"Life of ___ Zola, The" EMILE
lifer CON
lifesaver HERO
"___ Life Strange" ISNT
lifetime AGE
lifetimes
many ~ EON
"___ Life to Live" ONE
life vests
name in ~ MAE, WEST

"Life With Father"
~ actor AMES
~ author DAY
~ family DAYS
lifework LINE, TRADE
Liffey
~ locale EIRE, ERIN
lift COP, CRANE, RAISE, RIDE, ROB, STEAL, TAKE
~ a finger AID, STIR
~ anchor SAIL
~ as oysters TONG
~ buttons UPS
~ the spirits of ELATE
~ up ELATE, EXALT
~ upright REAR
give a ~ RAISE
give a ~ to CART
he gave us a ~ OTIS
kind of ~ TRAM
kind of ski ~ TBAR
not ~ a finger LOAF
schusser's ~ TBAR
___ lift SKI
lifter
mythical ~ ATLAS
wallet ~ DIP
lifting
~ device LEVER
"Liftoff!"
last number before ~ ONE
"Lift that ___!" BALE
ligament CORD
ligate TIE
ligature CORD, TIE
light AIRY, DAY, EASY, FIRE
~ as a feather AERIAL, AIRY
~ beam LASER
~ bedstead COT
~ bulb inventor EDISON
~ bulb, symbolically IDEA
~ bulb unit WATT
~ carom KISS
~ fixture LAMP
~ for serenaders MOON
~ globe LAMP
~ in a tube NEON
~ into HIT, LACE
~ meal SALAD
~ on one's feet AGILE, SPRY
~ out HIE, LEAVE, RACE, RUN
~ punishment SLAP
~ rain MIST
~ regulator IRIS
~ shaft BEAM, RAY
~ show AURORA
~ snack BITE
~ source LAMP
~ starter DAY, FAN, FIRE, GAS, HEAD, LAMP, LIME, MOON, PEN, SIDE, SKY, SPOT, STAR, STOP, SUN, TAIL
~ subj. OPT
~ tap PAT
~ touch KISS, TAP
~ tune AIR, LILT
~ upon HIT
~ vessel LAMP

~ weight OUNCE
~ wine ROSE
~ wood BALSA
blinding ~ GLARE
bright night ~ NEON
bring to ~ BARE, LEAK, TELL
brought to ~ OUT
come to ~ ARISE, ARISEN, EMERGE
day ~ SUN
dazzling ~ GLARE
divine ~ HALO
downtown ~ NEON
electric ~ LAMP
garish ~ NEON
Ginza ~ NEON
give ~ SHED
give the green ~ ALLOW, CLEAR, ENABLE, LET
green ~ OKAY, YES
harsh ~ GLARE
high-tech ~ LASER
incandescent ~ LAMP
infra-red ~ LAMP
klieg ~ LAMP
marquee ~ NEON
navigation ~ LAMP
neon ~ LAMP
night ~ LAMP, STAR
pilot ~ LAMP
plight ~ FLARE
polar ~ AURORA
ray of ~ BEAM
reading ~ LAMP
red ~ ALARM, ALERT
ring of ~ HALO
see the ~ LEARN
shed ~ SHINE
shed ~ on CLEAR, RAVEL
signal ~ LAMP
sky ~ MOON, STAR, SUN
soft ~ GLOW
source of ~ SUN
store-window ~ NEON
theater ~ NEON
throw ~ on SHOW
traffic ~ LAMP
trip the ~ fantastic DANCE
tungsten ~ LAMP
warning ~ FLARE
light ___ METER, OPERA, PEN, SHOW
___ light PILOT
Light ALLIE
"Light ___, The" AHEAD
"Light ___ Failed, The" THAT
Light-___ Harry Lee HORSE
light a ___ under FIRE
light-dawning
~ cry AHA
lighted CLEAR
~ up LIT
lighten EASE
~ one's menu DIET
~ the load AID, HELP
lightener
coffee ~ CREAM
lighter-than-___ AIR

light-fingered DEFT
light-footed AGILE, FAST, FLEET, SPRY
light-headed
feel ~ SWIM
lighthearted GAY, GLAD
lightheartedness GLEE
"Light-Horse Harry" LEE
lighthouse LAMP
lighting
~ device LAMP
"Light in the ___, A" ATTIC
lightning BEAM
~ by-product OZONE
ball ~ GAS
go like ~ HIE, RACE, RIP, RUN, SPEED, TEAR
like ~ FAST
thunder and ~ STORM
lightning ___ ROD
___ lightning BALL, SHEET
Lightning SIX, TEAM
~ home TAMPA
~ milieu ICE, RINK
~ org. NHL
home of the NHL's ~ TAMPA
lights
arctic ~ AURORA
green ~ OKS
put up in ~ BILL
lights ___ OUT
"___ Lights" CITY
"lights out" TAPS
light switch
~ positions ONS
"Light That Failed, The" POEM
"___ Light Up My Life" YOU
lightweight FINE
~ flier KITE
lignite COAL
lignum
~ vitae TREE
Ligurian Sea
~ feeder ARNO
~ port GENOA
likable NICE
like AKIN, ALA, DIG, PLEASE, SAVOR
~ (suffix) INE, ISH, OSE
like ___ (candidly) ITIS
like ___ (impulsively) MAD
like ___ in a pod PEAS
like ___ of bricks ATON
"Like ___ not..." ITOR
like a ___ (quickly) SHOT
like a ___ balloon LEAD
"...like a big pizza pie, that's ___" AMORE

___ **like a bird** EAT

likeable NICE, SWEET

like a fish out of ___ WATER

like a house ___ AFIRE

like father, like ___ SON

___ **like hotcakes** SELL

"___ Like It Hot" SOME

like it or ___ NOT

likelihood ODDS

likely PRONE, ROSY

"likely story!, A" HAH

like-minded ONE

likeness ECHO, ICON, IDOL, IMAGE

"Like Niobe, ___ tears" ALL

"___ Like Old Times" SEEMS

like peas in a ___ POD

"___ Like the Wind" SHES

likewise ALSO, DITTO, TOO
~ **not** NOR

liking ESTEEM, LOVE, TASTE, TOOTH
have a ~ for LEAN
to one's ~ SWEET

"Li'l ___" ABNER

"Li'l Abner"
~ **cartoonist** CAPP

lilac COLOR

liliaceous
~ **plant** ALOE

Liliuokalani
~ **greeting** ALOHA
see also Hawaiian

Lille CITY
see also French

Lillehammer
~ **loc.** NOR
city near ~ OSLO

Lillian ROTH

Lillie BEA

Lilliputian ELFIN, RUNT, SMALL, TEENY, TINY, WEE

Lilly ELI

lilt SING, TUNE

lily
~ **cousin** ONION
~ **genus** ALOE
~ **in French** LIS
~ **maid of Astolat** ELAINE
~ **pad** LEAF
African ~ ALOE
calla ~ ARUM
member of the ~ family LEEK
water ~ leaf PAD

lily ___ PAD

___ **lily** DAY, EASTER, POND, SEGO, TIGER, WATER

Lily
~ **cohort** ARTE

___ **Lily** TIGER

lily-livered BASE

lily-pad
~ **locale** POND

lily-white CLEAN

lima BEAN

Lima CITY
~ **locale** OHIO, PERU
see also Spanish

limb ARM, LEG, PART
anterior ~ ARM
it may be out on a ~ NEST
lower ~ GAM, LEG
out on a ~ TREED

Limbaugh
~ **medium** RADIO

limber AGILE, LITHE, SPRY
~ **with language** GLIB

limbo DANCE

lime COLOR, TREE
~ **drink** ADE
~ **ender** ADE

limekiln OVEN

limelight LAMP

limelike ACID, SOUR, TART

limen EVE

___ **lime pie** KEY

limerick POEM
~ **man** LEAR
~ **opener** THERE

Limerick
~ **land** EIRE, ERIN
county north of ~ CLARE

limes
like ~ ACID, SOUR, TART

limey SALT

limit EDGE, END, LID, RANGE, SET, STINT, TIE
~ **to daydreamers** SKY
beyond the ~ ULTRA
budget ~ CAP
exceed the ~ SPEED
outer ~ EDGE, RIM
over the ~ LONG
salary ~ CAP
spending ~ CAP

___ **limit** SPEED, TIME

limited LOCAL, SCANT, TRAIN
~ **in scope** SMALL
~ **time** TERM

limiting CLOSE

limitless BIG, LARGE, VAST

limits PALE
outer ~ EDGE, ETHER

___ **-limits** OFF

"___ Limits, The" OUTER

"Limit 10 ___" ITEMS

limn DRAW

limo MOTOR
take a ~ RIDE

Limoges
see French

limonite ORE

Limón, José
~ **milieu** DANCE

limousine AUTO, CAR, MOTOR, SEDAN

limp STALE
~ **along** DRAG
~ **as hair** LANK

limpid CLEAR

limping LAME

limp-watch
~ **painter** DALI

linchpin
~ **locale** AXLE

Lincoln ABE, AUTO, CAR, CITY, ELMO
~ **bill** FIVE
~ **coin** CENT
~ **feature** BEARD
~ **son** TAD
~ **st.** NEB, NEBR
like ~ TALL

Lincoln Center
~ **attraction** MET
~ **focus** ART

"___ Lincoln in Illinois" ABE

Linda EVANS, GRAY, HUNT

Lindbergh ANNE
emulate ~ AVIATE

linden TREE

Linden HAL

Lind, Jenny SWEDE

Lindros ERIC

Lindsay, Vachel POET
see also poet

Lindstrom PIA

lindy DANCE, HOP

Lindy
how ~ flew ALONE, SOLO

line ALIBI, CABLE, CLAN, CORD, FILE, GAME, ROPE, ROW, TAIL, TRADE
~ **in geometry** AXIS
~ **of cars** MAKE
~ **of demarcation** LIMIT
~ **of stitches** SEAM
~ **of symmetry** AXIS
~ **of work** TRADE
~ **starter** AIR, DATE, HEAD, LIFE, SKY
~ **to the audience** ASIDE
~ **up** ARRAY, DRESS, ORDER, ORIENT, RANGE, RANK, SPACE
actor's ~ ASIDE
atlas ~ ROAD, ROUTE
at the end of the ~ LAST

bad bottom ~ LOSS
be out of ~ ERR
border ~ METE
bottom ~ TAKE, TOTAL
boundary ~ METE
Cartesian ~ AXIS
central ~ AXIS
clothes ~ HEM, SEAM
commuter ~ RAIL
curtain ~ TAG
curved ~ ARC
customary ~ of travel BEAT, ROUTE
down the ~ ALONG, ANON
draw the ~ BAR
drop a ~ WRITE
drop a ~ to WRITE
finish ~ END, GOAL, TAPE, WIRE
first in ~ ELDEST, NEXT
geometric ~ AXIS
get to the bottom ~ ADD
graph ~ AXIS
help with a ~ CUE
imaginary ~ AXIS
improvised ~ ADLIB
in a ~ AROW
in ~ (with) ALONG
it holds the ~ REEL
lay on the ~ RISK
lightly drawn ~ TRACE
map ~ ROAD, ROUTE
next in ~ HEIR
oblique ~ BIAS
oil ~ PIPE
out of ~ AWRY
phone ~ CORD
put on the ~ BET
revolution ~ AXIS
rotation ~ AXIS
stand in ~ WAIT
story ~ PLOT
straight ~ ROW
telephone ~ CORD, WIRE
the bottom ~ COST
toe the ~ OBEY
top of the ~ AONE, BEST
unscripted ~ ADLIB
wait in ~ STAND

line-___ UPS

line-___ veto ITEM

___ **line** DEW, GAG, GOAL, HOT, SNOW, STAG, TAG, TREE, WATER

___ **-line** OFF

lineage CASTE, CLAN, KIN, SEED, STEM

linear EVEN
~ **measure** ROD, YARD
~ **unit** FOOT

lined
~ **up** AROW

line-item ___ VETO

lineman
~ **challenge** POLE
pass-catching ~ END

linen LAWN
~ **fabric** TOILE
~ **marking** HERS, HIS
~ **robe** ALB

~ shade ECRU
~ vestment ALB
bed ~ SHEET
color of ~ ECRU
dirty ~ WASH

___ linen IRISH, TABLE

liner BOAT, SHIP
~ place PIER

___-liner HARD, ONE

"Liner ___ a Lady, The" SHES

___ Line Railroad SOO

"Liner She's a Lady, The" POEM

lines PART
along the ~ of LIKE
Chicago ~ ELS
feed ~ CUE
make straight ~ RULE
train ~ RRS

"Lines Composed a Few Miles
Above Tintern Abbey" POEM

"Lines on the Mermaid Tavern"
POEM

lineup AGENDA, ARRAY, CARD,
LIST, SLATE

line up
~ in the crosshairs AIM

___ Ling NAN

linger BIDE, DRAG, HANG, LAG,
STAY, WAIT
~ behind TRAIL

lingerie
~ item BRA, SLIP

Ling-Ling PANDA

lingo ARGOT, CANT, IDIOM, SLANG

linguine PASTA

___ Lingus AER

liniment BALM, CREAM, OIL
~ target ACHE

lining
closet ~ CEDAR
shell ~ NACRE

link CLASP, CORD, RELATE, SPAN,
TIE, UNITE
~ firmly FUSE, KNIT
~ up UNITE
clause ~ NOR

linking
~ word AND

Linkletter ART, EMCEE, HOST

links
~ achievement ACE
~ area TEE
~ feature HOLE
~ goal PAR
~ hazard TRAP
~ org. PGA
~ platform TEE
~ position LIE
~ shout FORE
~ transport CART
see also golf

Linnaeus SWEDE

linnet BIRD

linoleic ACID

linoleum
~ alternative TILE
~ measurement AREA
~ unit TILE

linseed ___ OIL

lint DUST
~ collector SERGE, TRAP

lintel BEAM

Linus YALE

Linus Van ___ PELT

Linzer ___ TORTE

lion ANIMAL, BEAST, CAT
~ ender ESS
~ fare MEAT
~ greeting ROAR
~ home DEN, LAIR
~ pack PRIDE
~ pride MANE
~ share MASS, MOST
~ trainer TAMER
MGM ~ LEO, LOGO
mountain ~ PUMA
name for a ~ LEO
sea ~ ANIMAL
twist the ~'s tail DARE

___ lion ANT, SEA

Lion
the ~ SIGN

"___ Lion" PAPER

lioness ELSA

lionhearted GAME

lionize EXALT, HONOR

"Lion King, The"
~ heavy HYENA
~ villain SCAR
Mufasa's brother in ~ SCAR

"Lion of God, The" ALI

lion's ___ SHARE

Lions ELEVEN, TEAM
~ colleagues ELKS, MOOSE
~ org. NFL

lip EDGE, RIM, SASS
~ application BALM
~ service CANT
curl a ~ SNEER
give ~ to SASS
having a stiff upper ~ STOIC
something 'twixt cup and
~ SLIP

lip-___ SYNC

lip-balm
~ target CHAP

Lipinski TARA

Lipinski, Tara
~ feat AXEL
~ milieu ICE, RINK

Lipizzaner HORSE, STEED
~ feature MANE

Li Po POET
see also poet

liposuction
~ target FAT

___ Lippo Lippi FRA

lippy
~ one SNIP

lips
like some ~ FAT

"___ Lips Are Sealed" OUR

___ Lips Houlihan HOT

Lipstadt AARON

"___ Lips, Those Eyes" THOSE

lipstick PAINT, TREE
~ shade RED

liquefy FUSE, MELT, RUN, THAW

liqueur
~ flavor PEAR
~ flavoring ANISE

liquid
~ container VIAL
~ holder EWER
~ in physics STATE
~ meas. GAL
~ measure LITER, OUNCE,
PINT
burn with ~ SCALD
etching ~ ACID
foul ~ SLIME
lab ~ ACID
viscous ~ TAR

liquid ___ ASSET

"Liquid ___" SKY

liquidate CLEAR, PAY, SELL,
SETTLE

liquids
transfusion ~ SERA

liquor GIN
~ flavoring SLOE
~ over cracked ice MIST
add ~ to LACE
Caribbean ~ RUM
malt ~ ALE
spot of ~ DRAM
sugar-cane ~ RUM

liquor-free DRY

"Liquor is quicker"
~ author NASH

lira
~ replacement EURO

Lisa
~ to Bart SIS

Lisa ___ Presley MARIE

"___ Lisa" MONA

Lisa Lisa & Cult ___ JAM

Lisa Marie
~ dad ELVIS

Lisbon CITY
gentleman of ~ DOM

Lisette REESE

lisp SLUR

lisper
problem letter for a ~ ESS

lissome AGILE, LITHE

list AGENDA, BILL, ENTER, HEEL,
LEAN, ROLL, SLANT, TABLE, TILT,
TIP
~ component ITEM
~ heading TODO
~ item ENTRY
~ of choices MENU
~ of expenditures BILL
~ of mistakes ERRATA
~ shortener ETAL, ETC
activities ~ AGENDA
be on the sick ~ AIL
computer ~ MENU
members ~ ROLL
restaurant ~ MENU
typo ~ ERRATA
voting ~ POLL
wine ~ CARTE, MENU

___ list TODO, WANT, WINE

listen ATTEND, HEAR, HEED
~ attentively PERK
~ in AUDIT
~ up HEED
unwilling to ~ DEAF
willing to ~ OPEN

listener EAR

listening
~ device EAR

___ listening EASY

"Listen to the ___" WARM

"Listen to the Mocking ___"
BIRD

lister PLOW

Listerine
~ target GERM

listing ATILT
eatery ~ MENU
menu ~ ENTREE, ITEM
nominee ~ SLATE
NYSE ~ ITT
playbill ~ CAST
prandial ~ MENU

listless DAMP, INERT
~ feeling ENNUI

listlessness ENNUI

Liszt
~ piece ETUDE

lit AFIRE, CLEAR
poorly ~ DIM

litchi NUT, TREE

lite LOCAL

literacy
demonstrate ~ READ

literary
~ bell town ADANO
~ category DRAMA, GENRE
~ collie LAD
~ device IRONY
~ drudge HACK

~ **form** ODE, PROSE
~ **initials** RLS, TSE
~ **miscellany** ANA
~ **mistakes** ERRATA
~ **monogram** RLS, TSE
~ **pseudonym** ELIA, SAKI
~ **rep.** AGT
~ **sketch** CAMEO
~ **style (suffix)** ESE
~ **VIP** LION
~ **work** ESSAY, OPUS
thirteenth-century ~
  work EDDA

literary ___ LION

literature
Judaic ~ TORAH

lithe AGILE, SLIM, SPRY

lithium METAL

litho-
meaning of ~ STONE

lithograph PLATE

lithographer
famous ~ IVES

lithophyte PLANT

Lithuania
~ once SSR

Lithuanian
~ neighbor LETT

litigate SUE

litigation SUIT

litigious
be ~ SUE

litmus DYE
~ bluer BASE
~ reddener ACID
use ~ TEST

litmus ___ PAPER

litter BEAR, BED, DROP, MESS,
TRASH
~ member RUNT
pick of the ~ CREAM

litterbug SLOB

little APER, ELFIN, SMALL, TINY,
WEE
~ bit DAB, IOTA, JOT
~ boy KID, TAD, TYKE
~ devil IMP
~ dickens IMP
~ girl KID
~ green man ALIEN
~ lizard NEWT
~ more than MERE
~ one ELF, TOT
~ piggy TOE
~ (prefix) MINI
~ shaver LAD, TOT, TYKE
~ (suffix) ETTE, ULE
~ terror BRAT
~ while BIT
a ~ PART, SOME
a ~ bit TAD
give a ~ extra ADD
give or take a ~ LIKE
in a ~ while ANON, SOON
just a ~ NIP

quite a ~ PILE

"little ___ told me, A" BIRD

Little RICH

Little ___ EVA, NELL

"Little ___" CAESAR, LULU, NEMO,
ODESSA

"Little ___, The" ARK, GIANT

"Little ___ Book" ORGAN, RED

"Little ___ Echo" SIR

"Little ___ Fauntleroy" LORD

"Little ___ Flowers" IDAS

"Little ___ Man" BIG

"Little ___ Marker" MISS

"Little ___ of Horrors, The"
SHOP

"Little ___ Rooney" ANNIE

"Little ___ Tate" MAN

"Little ___, What Now?" MAN

"Little Annie Rooney"
~ pooch ZERO

"Little Big ___" MAN

"Little Big Man"
~ director PENN

"little bird ___ me, A" TOLD

"Little Birds"
~ author NIN

"Little Bit of ___, A" SOAP

"Little Bitty Tear, A"
~ singer IVES

"Little Boy ___" BLUE, LOST

little by little
move ~ EDGE

"Little Caesar"
~ director LEROY

"Little Colonel, The" REESE

"Little Darlings"
~ actress ONEAL

"Little Drummer ___, The" GIRL

"Little Engine, The"
verb from ~ CAN

"Little Eyolf"
~ author IBSEN

"___ Little Fishes" THREE

"___ Little Fool" POOR

"___ Little Foys, The" SEVEN

"Little Giant, The"
~ director RUTH

"Little Gidding"
~ author ELIOT

"___ Little Girls in Blue" THREE

"Little House on the Prairie"
~ girl LAURA

"___ Little Indians" TEN

"Little Jeannie"
~ name ELTON

Little Joe
~ brother ADAM

Little League
~ coach, usually DAD

"Little Man ___" TATE

"Little Man, What ___?" NOW

"Little Mermaid, The"
~ character ARIEL, ERIC
Sebastian, in ~ CRAB

"Little Miss Marker"
~ director HALL

Little Miss Muffet EATER

littleneck CLAM

"Little Orphan ___" ANNIE

Little Orphan Annie
like ~ ELEVEN

"Little Orphan Annie"
~ cartoonist GRAY
~ henchman ASP

"Little Orphant Annie" POEM
~ poet RILEY

"little piggy" TOE

"___ little piggy..." THIS

Little Pigs
~ building material STRAW

"Little pitchers have big ___"
EARS

"Little Princess, The"
~ director LANG

Littler GENE

"Little Red ___, The" HEN

"Little Red Book"
~ author MAO

Little Red Riding ___ HOOD

Little, Rich APER
act like ~ APE

"___ Little Rich Girl" POOR

Little Rock
~ st. ARK

"Little Sir ___" ECHO

"___ Little Sister" DANCE

"Littlest ___, The" REBEL

"Littlest ___ Thieves, The"
HORSE

"___ Little Street in Singapore"
ONA

"___ Little Teapot" IMA

"Little Things Mean ___" ALOT

"___ little white lies" THOSE

"Little Women"
~ girl AMY, MEG
Meg, of the ~ ELDEST

"___ Little Words" THREE

littoral
~ phenomenon TIDE
~ region SHORE

liturgical
~ language LATIN
~ poem PSALM
~ robe ALB

liturgy RITE

Liu Pang
~ dynasty HAN

Liv
Broadway role for ~ MAMA

live ABIDE, LAST, ROOM, STAY
~ and breathe ARE
~ it up REVEL
~ on air FAST
~ partner LEARN
~ up to HONOR
place to ~ ABODE, HOME
where most people ~ ASIA
words to ~ by ADAGE,
CREDO, CREED

live ___ OAK, WIRE

live and ___ LEARN

"___ live and breathe!" ASI

"Live and Let ___" DIE

live by one's ___ WITS

lived BEEN, WAS

___-lived LONG

"...lived happily ___ after" EVER

"Live From the ___" MET

livelihood KEEP, TRADE

liveliness FIRE, LIFE, PEP, SNAP,
VIM

lively AGILE, ALERT, ASTIR, CRISP,
PERT, RACY, SASSY, SMART,
SPRY, WARM

"___ lively!" STEP

liven
~ up PERK

liver MEAT, ORGAN
~ output BILE
~ paste PATE

___-livered LILY

___ liver oil COD

Liverpool CITY, PORT
see also British

liverwort
~ cousin MOSS

livery ATTIRE, DRESS, GARB,
GEAR, SUIT

lives
cat's ~ NINE

"Lives ___ Bengal Lancer, The"
OFA

"___ Lives of Thomasina, The"
THREE

livestock
~ enterprise RANCH

~ feed MASH, RYE
~ shelter BARN
~ show FAIR
~ sustenance FEED
"___ Live With Me" COME

livid IRATE, PALE, UPSET

living
~ daylights SENSE
~ quarters ABODE
~ room SALON
~ space AREA
scratch out a ~ EKE

living ___ END, ROOM, WAGE

"Living ___, The" DESERT, END

"___ Living" EASY

"Living and Loving"
~ author LOREN

"Living Daylights, The"
~ band AHA
~ instrument CELLO

"Living in the ___" PAST

living room
~ appliance of old RADIO
~ furniture SOFA
~ piece SETTEE

Livingstone, David SCOT

Livorno CITY, PORT
island S of ~ ELBA
see also Italian

livre COIN

Livy ROMAN
~ contemporary OVID
~ togs TOGA
see also Latin

lixivium LYE

Liz
~ ex EDDIE
role for ~ CLEO

"___ Liza Jane" LIL

lizard
little ~ NEWT
lounge ~ IDLER
Mexican ~ IGUANA
southwestern ~ UTA
young ~ EFT

Lizard Head CAPE

lizardlike
~ amphibian EFT

Lizette REESE

lizzie
tin ~ AUTO, CAR

___ lizzie TIN

"Lizzie Borden took an ___..." AXE

___ Lizzy THIN

L.L. ___ BEAN

L.L. ___ J COOL

llama ANIMAL
~ milieu ANDES, PERU

llano LEA

LL.B.
~ holder ATT, ATTY
~ org. ABA

L.L. Cool J
~ genre RAP

LL.D.
~ holder ATT, ATTY
~ org. ABA

Lloyd NOLAN

Lloyd Webber
~ score CATS, EVITA

lo-___ CAL

load HEAP, LADE, LOT, MASS, ONUS, PILE, SCAD, STOW, TASK
~ cargo STOW
~ starter CASE
~ up AMASS, STORE
~ with freight LADE
Comstock ~ ORE
get a ~ of EYE, SEE, SPY
heavy ~ ONUS
lighten the ~ AID, HELP
share the ~ HELP
take a ~ off SIT

___-load OFF

loaded LADEN, RICH, RIFE
~ question TRAP
~ with calories RICH
~ with curry HOT
they may be ~ BASES

loaded for ___ BEAR

loading
~ site PIER

loads ALOT
~ of fun GAS

loaf IDLE, LOLL
~ fraction HALF
bakery ~ RYE
part of a ~ SLICE

___ loaf MEAT

loafer DRONE, IDLER, SHOE

loafers
wearing ~ SHOD

loam DIRT, EARTH, LAND, SOIL

loamy
~ soil LOESS

loan DEBT, LEND
~ abbr. APR
~ fee INT
get a ~ OWE
variable-interest ~ ARM

loan-ad
~ initials APR

loath AVERSE
nothing ~ GLAD

loathe ABHOR, HATE

loathesome VILE

loathing HATE
fill with ~ REPEL

loathsome BAD, BASE, EVIL, UGLY, VILE
~ one TOAD

lob ARC, PASS, SHOT, TOSS
~ path ARC

lobbies
high-ceiling ~ ATRIA

lobby HALL, URGE
~ ender IST
~ furnishing SETTEE
DC gun ~ NRA
health-care ~ org. AMA
liberal ~ org. ADA

lobbying
~ org. ASSN

lobe
~ adornment STUD
~ locale EAR

loblolly PINE, TREE

"___ Lobo" RIO

___ Lobos LOS

lobscouse STEW

lobster
~ eater's wear BIB
~ eggs ROE
~ extremity CLAW
~ home SHELL
~ locale MAINE
~ pot TRAP
~ roe CORAL
~ sauce ingredient EGG
~ serving CLAW
~ trap POT
female ~ HEN

lobster ___ Diavolo FRA

local BAR, TRAIN
~ language IDIOM
~ plants FLORA
it may be ~ COLOR

local ___ COLOR

lo-cal LITE
~ drink TAB

"Local ___" HERO

locale AREA, SCENE, SITE, STAGE

locality AREA, SITE, SPOT

Locarno PACT

locate BASE, ORIENT, PLANT, PUT, SETTLE, SITE, SPOT

located
be ~ LIE, SIT
centrally ~ AMID, AMONG

location AREA, SCENE, SITE, SPOT, STEAD

loch LAKE
eerie ~ NESS

Loch ___ monster NESS

Lochinvar HERO

lock CLASP, CLOSE, SEAL, TIE
~ companion KEY
~ horns ARGUE, CLOSE
~ maker YALE

~ of hair TRESS
~ out BAR
~ part HASP
~ starter ANTI, FORE, GRID, HEAD, HEM, LOVE, OAR, PAD, WED
under ~ and key SAFE

___ lock AIR

Locke
~ work ESSAY

locked SHUT
~ up SAFE

locker CHEST, SAFE
Davy Jones' ~ OCEAN, SEA

locker-room
~ supply TALC

locket
~ shape HEART
item in a ~ CAMEO

Lockheed
~ product PLANE

Lockheed ___-Star TRI

locks HAIR
~ locale CANAL
alter ~ DYE

___ Locks SOO

"Locksmith"
~ painter KLEE

locksmithing TRADE

lock, stock, and barrel ALL

lockup CELL, STIR

loco AMOK, BATS, DAFT, MAD
not ~ SANE

Loco, Antonio
~ genre RAP

locomotion RUN
organ of ~ FOOT

"Locomotion"
~ girl EVA

locomotive
~ part CAB, CAM

"___ Locomotive Chase, The" GREAT

locust TREE

locution TERM, USAGE

lode MINE, ORE, RUN
mother ~ ORE

lodge ABIDE, BED, CAMP, CLAN, HOME, HOTEL, INN, LIVE, PLANT, ROOM, STAY
~ member ELK, LION, MASON, MOOSE
bear ~ DEN, LAIR

___ lodge MOTOR

lodgepole ___ PINE

lodger TENANT

lodging ABODE, HOTEL, INN
~ place HOTEL, REST, ROOM
tor ~ AERIE

lodgings HOME
  frosh ~ DORM
  take ~ RENT
  temporary ~ CAMP

Lódz CITY
  ~ resident POLE

lo-fat LITE

loft ATTIC
  ~ contents BALE, HAY

lofty AERIAL, GREAT, TALL
  ~ abode AERIE
  ~ capital LHASA, LIMA
  ~ goal IDEAL
  ~ place BARN
  ~ spaces ATRIA
  make ~ EXALT

log ENTER
  ~ a few z's NAP, REST, SLEEP
  ~ cabin ABODE, HOME
  ~ ender JAM, ROLL
  ~ notation ENTRY
  ~ starter ANA, EPI
  bump on a ~ NODE
  concealed ~ SNAG
  like falling off a ~ EASY
  shift a ~ TONG

___ log GAS, YULE

Logan ELLA
  ~ abbr. ARR, ETA
  ~ locale UTAH

Logan Airport
  ~ on baggage tags BOS

"Logan's Run"
  ~ android REM

logger
  ~ tool AXE, SAW

loggia ARCADE

logging
  do ~ AXE, HEW, SAW

logic SENSE

logical SANE
  ~ starter ECO, IDEO

logician
  ~ abbr. QED
  ~ transition ERGO

logo LABEL, SIGN
  CBS ~ EYE
  Pinkerton ~ EYE

logs
  haul ~ SKID
  saw ~ SLEEP, SNORE
  sawing ~ ABED

logwood TREE

-logy
  ~ cousin ISM

Lohengrin
  ~ transport SWAN

"Lohengrin" OPERA
  ~ role ELSA
  Gottfried, in ~ SWAN

loin
  ~ cut TBONE

Loire
  see French

Lois LANE

"Lois & Clark"
  ~ network ABC
  ~ star CAIN
  Dean's ~ costar TERI
  Lois, in ~ TERI

loiter DRAG, IDLE, LAG, LOLL, STAY, WAIT
  ~ about LOAF

"Lolita"
  ~ actor MASON

loll IDLE, LIE, REST
  ~ around LOAF
  ~ in the sun BASK

lollapalooza LULU, ONER

"Lollipop" BOAT, SHIP

"Lollipops and ___" ROSES

Lollobrigida GINA

Loman, Willie
  ~ goal SALE
  emulate ~ SELL

Lombard ALAIN

Lombardy
  ~ capital MILAN
  ~ lake COMO
  ~ land ITALY

Lomé
  its capital is ~ TOGO

Lomond LAKE

Lomond, Loch
  see Scottish

___-Lon BAN

London ROY
  ~ apartment FLAT
  ~ art gallery TATE
  ~ biscuit SCONE
  ~ district SOHO
  ~ drink TEA
  ~ exclamation ISAY
  ~ forecast RAIN
  ~ libation ALE
  ~ network BBC
  ~ park HYDE
  ~ streetcar TRAM
  ~ stroller PRAM
  ~ thanks TAS
  car trunk, in ~ BOOT
  like ~ in 1666 AFIRE
  spruce, in ~ TRIG
  street in ~ FLEET
  see also British

Londonderry CITY, PORT
  from ~ IRISH

"Londonderry ___" AIR

"London Fields"
  ~ author AMIS

London, Jack ALIAS

London's ___ End EAST

London's Big ___ BEN

lone ONE, ONLY, SOLE

"Lone ___, The" (Lindbergh) EAGLE

"Loneliness of the ___ Distance Runner, The" LONG

"Lonely ___, The" MAN

"Lonely ___ the Brave" ARE

"Lonely Boy"
  ~ singer ANKA

"___ Lonely Place" INA

Lone Ranger HERO
  ~ attire MASK
  ~ companion TONTO

"Lone Ranger, The" OATER
  ~ actor MOORE

Lone Ranger and Tonto DUO, PAIR

"___ Lonesome" RIDE

Lone Star
  ~ shrine ALAMO
  ~ St. TEX

"Lone Star Trail, The" OATER

"Lone Wolf ___ Hunt, The" SPY

"Lone Wolf Spy ___, The" HUNT

long LANK
  ~ account SAGA
  ~ ago EARLY, OLD, ONCE, PAST, YORE
  ~ bath SOAK
  ~ bout SIEGE
  ~ car LIMO
  ~ curl TRESS
  ~ easy stride LOPE
  ~ fish EEL
  ~ for LOVE, MISS, WANT
  ~ (for) ACHE, ITCH, PINE, YEARN
  ~ gone PAST
  ~ green MOOLA
  ~ gun RIFLE
  ~ hair MANE
  ~ haul TREK
  ~ in Hawaiian LOA
  ~ in the tooth AGED, OLD
  ~ jump EVENT, LEAP
  ~ lead-in ERE
  ~ look STARE
  ~ nail CLAW
  ~ past YORE
  ~ period AGE, EON
  ~ poem EPIC
  ~ shoal SPIT
  ~ shot BET, RISK
  ~ starter ERE, PRO
  ~ story EPIC, SAGA
  ~ struggle SIEGE
  ~ time AGE, EON, YEARS
  ~ walk HIKE
  a ~ time EON, YEARS
  a ~ way off AFAR, FAR
  before ~ ANON, LATER, SOON
  ere ~ ANON, SOON
  look too ~ OGLE, STARE
  of ~ standing OLD
  take a ~ hard look PORE
  walk a ~ way TREK
  wear a ~ face MOPE

long ___ AGO, HAUL, SHOT, SUIT, TON

long ___ of the law ARM

long-___ RANGE, TERM, TIME

long-___ dog EARED

long-___ owl EARED

long.
  opposite of ~ LAT

Long NIA
  ~ successor on "Cheers" ALLEY

"Long ___ and Far Away" AGO

"Long ___ Friday, The" GOOD

"Long ___ Journey Into Night" DAYS

"Long ___ Line, The" GRAY

"Long ___ no see!" TIME

"Long ___ Sally" TALL

"Long ___ Summer, The" HOT

"Long and Winding ___" ROAD

long-answer
  ~ exam ESSAY

long-armed
  ~ entity LAW

"___ longa, vita brevis" ARS

Long Beach CITY, PORT

long-billed
  ~ bird HERON, SNIPE

longbow
  ~ ammo ARROW

"Long Day's Journey ___ Night" INTO

long-distance
  ~ cost TOLL
  ~ runner RACER

long-drawn-___ OUT

longe ROPE

long-eared
  ~ beast ASS, BURRO
  ~ rodent HARE

longer MORE
  no ~ a minor ADULT
  no ~ chic OUT, PASSE
  no ~ edible STALE
  no ~ fresh OLD
  no ~ in style OUT
  no ~ is WAS
  no ~ novel STALE
  no ~ trendy PASSE
  no ~ used DATED
  of ~ standing ELDER

"Longest ___, The" DAY, YARD

"Longest Day, The"
  ~ actor ANKA
  ~ author RYAN

longevity LEGS, LIFE

long-faced LOW, SAD

Longfellow POET
  ~ character ALDEN
  see also poet

"Long Gray ___, The" LINE

longhair CAT

longhorn STEER

longing ACHE, EAGER, HOPE, ITCH, YEN
  ~ feeling ACHE, PANG

longings
  have ~ ACHE, PINE

Long Island Sound
  ~ city RYE

longleaf PINE

long-legged LANK, TALL
  ~ bird HERON

long-lived OLD

"Long, Long ___" AGO

"long, long way to run, A" FAR

Long March
  ~ leader MAO

long-necked
  ~ bird SWAN
  ~ lute SITAR

long-plumed
  ~ bird EGRET

long-running
  ~ show HIT

Longs ___, Colo. PEAK

longshoremen
  ~ org. ILA

longstanding OLD

Longstreet, Mike
  ~ carried one CANE

long-suffering
  ~ one SAINT

long-tailed
  ~ rodent RAT

long-term
  ~ acct. IRA

long time ago, a ONCE

"Longtime Companion"
  ~ director RENE

"Long Voyage ___, The" HOME

"Long Walk ___, The" HOME

___ long way GOA

"___ Long Way to Tipperary" ITSA

long-winded
  ~ one BORE

looby BOOR

look CAST, EYE, HUNT, MIEN, MODE, SEE
  ~ after ATTEND, KEEP, SEETO, SIT, TEND
  ~ ahead PLAN
  ~ amused GRIN
  ~ as if SEEM

~ at EYE, FACE, OGLE, SEE
~ closely PEER, STARE
~ daggers GLARE
~ dejected MOPE
~ down one's nose SNEER
~ down upon ABHOR
~ everywhere COMB
~ favorably (on) SMILE
~ fixedly STARE
~ for AWAIT, SEEK
~ for fingerprints DUST
~ forward to AWAIT, WAIT
~ furtively PEEP
~ good on SUIT
~ happy SMILE
~ hard PEER, STARE
~ high and low RAKE, ROOT
~ in Latin ECCE
~ like SEEM
~ listlessly MOON
~ narrowly PEER
~ on the bright side HOPE
~ over CASE, READ, SCAN
~ right through
  someone CUT
~ straight in the eye DARE
~ the joint over CASE
~ through a keyhole PEEP
~ too long OGLE, STARE
~ toward FACE
~ up and down OGLE
~ upon DEEM
~ up to ESTEEM, HONOR
amiable ~ GRIN, SMILE
angry ~ GLARE
blank ~ STARE
bold ~ LEER
come-hither ~ PASS
dirty ~ GLARE, SNEER
evil ~ LEER
fierce ~ GLARE
fixed ~ STARE
furtive ~ PEEP
have a ~ at READ, SCAN
healthy ~ GLOW
high-hat's ~ SNEER
impolite ~ OGLE, SNEER, STARE
intense ~ STARE
lascivious ~ LEER, OGLE
long ~ STARE
Lothario's ~ OGLE
lovely to ~ at FAIR
malicious ~ LEER
menacing ~ GLARE
ogler's ~ STARE
quick ~ PEEP
radiant ~ BEAM
rude ~ LEER, STARE
sheepish ~ GRIN
sinister ~ LEER
sly ~ LEER
sneak a ~ PEEP
take a long hard ~ PORE
take a quick ~ SCAN
wanton ~ LEER

look ___ (be wary) OUT

look ___ (explore) INTO

look ___ (seek) FOR

look ___ (tend) AFTER

look ___ (visit) INON

look-___ ALIKE, SEE

"Look ___!" ALIVE, ATME

"Look ___, I'm as helpless..." ATME

"Look ___ (I'm in Love)" ATME

"Look ___ this way..." ATIT

"Look ___ ye leap" ERE

look-alike CLONE
  bald eagle's ~ ERN, ERNE

look and ___ FEEL

"Look at Me, I'm Sandra ___" DEE

"___ Look Back" DONT

"Look Back in ___" ANGER

look before you ___ LEAP

"___ Look Down, The" STARS

"Looker"
  ~ actress DEY

looker-on SEER

looking
  ~ good ROSY
  ~ ill PALE
  ~ peaked ILL

"___ looking at you, kid" HERES

"Looking for Mr. Goodbar"
  ~ actor GERE
  ~ name DIANE

Looking Glass
  ~ girl ALICE

"...look into the ___ of time..." SEEDS

"___! Look Me Over!" HEY

"___ Look Now" DONT

lookout
  ~ point AERIE
  be a ~ ABET
  on the ~ ALERT, WARY

Lookout CAPE

Lookout Mtn.
  state seen from ~ ALA

looks
  good ~ ASSET

look-see
  have a ~ SCAN

"Look what I found!" AHA

loom EMERGE, ISSUE, NEAR, REAR, RISE, SOAR
  ~ up SHOW

looming NEAR

loon BIRD

loony BATS, DAFT, LOCO, MAD

loop ARC, BEND, NOOSE, RING, TAG
  adjustable ~ NOOSE
  knock for a ~ AMAZE, AWE, STUN, WOW
  needlework ~ BRIDE
  rope ~ NOOSE

saddle ~ LUG

Loop
  ~ trains ELS

loophole OUT

loops
  form ~ COIL

loopy
  not ~ SANE

Loos ANITA

loose EASY, FREE, LEWD, UNDO
  ~ article END
  ~ garment ROBE
  ~ partner FAST
  ~ robe ABA
  ~ rock SCREE
  ~ soil DIRT
  cut ~ REVEL
  get ~ PART
  having a few ~ screws MAD
  let ~ FREE, UNTIE
  they may be ~ ENDS

loose ___ ENDS

___ loose CUT, HANG

loose-fitting
  ~ dress TENT
  ~ garment ABA, SACK

looseleaf
  ~ divider TAB

loose-limbed AGILE, LITHE

loosen EASE, UNDO, UNTIE
  ~ the pursestrings SPEND
  ~ up CALM, DIG

loosey-goosey ATEASE

loot CASH, HAUL, RAID, RIFLE, ROB, SACK, STAKE, STEAL, SWAG

lop BOB, CHOP, CROP, HEW, NIP, PARE
  ~ off CUT, HACK, SNIP

lop-___ EARED

lope RUN, TROT

Lopez TRINI

Lopez, Vincent
  ~ theme NOLA

Lop Nur LAKE

lopsided ATILT
  ~ win ROUT

loquacious LONG
  ~ equine MRED
  be ~ PRATE, TALK

loquat TREE

lord BARON, MALE, PEER, TITLE
  ~ and master MATE
  ~ errand boy PAGE
  ~ holding LAND
  ~ over RULE
  feudal ~ LIEGE, PEER
  landed ~ BARON
  Valkyries' ~ ODIN

Lord TITLE

Lord ___ Wimsey PETER

"Lord ___ a Duck" LOVE

"___ Lord, The" WAR

"Lord God Made ___ All, The" THEM

Lord High Everything ___ ELSE

"Lord Jim"
~ **actor** OTOOLE

"Lord knows ___ tried!" IVE

lordling PEER

lordly REGAL

"Lord of the Rings"
~ **creature** ENT

lord's
~ **home** MANOR
~ **lady** DAME
~ **mate** LADY
~ **servant** SERF

Lords
House of ~ **member** PEER

"lords a-leaping"
~ **day** TENTH

lords-and-ladies PLANT

lordship TITLE

"Lordy!" EGAD

Lorelei LEE, SIREN
river of the ~ RHINE

Loren, Sophia
~ **birthplace** ROME
~ **role of 1953** AIDA

Lorenz HART

Lorenzo LAMAS
see also Spanish

___ Lorenzo, Calif. SAN

"Lorenzo's ___" OIL

"Lorenzo's Oil"
~ **actor** NOLTE

Loretta LYNN

lorgnette
~ **part** LENS

lorica ARMOR, COAT, MAIL, SKIN

"___ Lorraine" SWEET

Lorre PETER

lorry MOTOR, VAN

lory BIRD

Los ___, Calif. ALTOS

Los ___ Rio DEL

Los Angeles CITY, PORT
~ **suburb** ORANGE
City of ~ TRAIN

Los Del ___ RIO

lose
~ **appeal** PALL
~ **brightness** FADE, PALE
~ **buoyancy** SINK
~ **color** BLEED, FADE, PALE
~ **control** PANIC, RAVE, SKID, SNAP

~ **effectiveness** PALL
~ **energy** SAG, TIRE
~ **firmness** SAG
~ **focus** BLUR
~ **fur** SHED
~ **ground** SLIDE
~ **hair** SHED
~ **heart** MOPE
~ **interest** NOD, PALL, TIRE
~ **it** RAGE, SNAP
~ **luster** FADE
~ **no time** FLEE, HIE, RACE, RUN, SPEED
~ **one's balance** SLIP
~ **one's coat** SHED
~ **one's cool** BOIL, RAGE
~ **one's footing** TRIP
~ **one's head** PANIC
~ **one's heart to** LOVE
~ **one's temper** BOIL, RAVE, SNARL, STORM
~ **on purpose** DIET
~ **out on** MISS
~ **pep** FLAG, TIRE
~ **resilience** SAG
~ **rigidity** SAG
~ **solidity** MELT
~ **someone** ELUDE
~ **strength** DIE, FLAG
~ **tautness** SAG
~ **tension** SAG
~ **(to)** BOW
~ **traction** SKID, SLIDE
~ **vigor** FADE
~ **weight** DIET, SLIM

loser DUD
~ **cry** UNCLE
~ **of 1917** TSAR
storied ~ HARE
two-time ~ **of the 1950s** AES

___ loser SORE

"___ Loser" IMA

losers
election ~ OUTS
like some ~ SORE

Losey, Joseph
~ **film of 1962** EVA

losing
~ **proposition** DIET

"Losing My Religion"
~ **band** REM

loss COST
~ **of face** SHAME
at a ~ ASEA, ATSEA
business ~ BATH
feel the ~ **of** MISS
profit and ~ **statement entry** ASSET
take a ~ **in** EAT

___ loss for words ATA

lost ASEA, ATSEA
~ **dog in an Inge play** SHEBA
~ **(in)** DEEP
~ **in thought** RAPT
be ~ **in thought** DREAM, MUSE

"___ lost!" GET

"___ Lost and Time Remembered" TIME

Lost Dutchman MINE

"lost generation"
~ **coiner** STEIN

"Lost Horizon"
~ **character** LAMA
~ **director** CAPRA
~ **locale** TIBET

"Lost in a ___" HAREM

"Lost in the ___" STARS

"Lost in the Stars"
~ **director** MANN

Lost River RANGE

"___ Lost You" IVE

lot CAST, CROP, FATE, HORDE, LAND, PLAT, RAFT, SHARE, SITE, SORT, TRACT
~ **filler** AUTO, CAR
~ **map** PLAT
~ **measure** ACRE, AREA
~ **of money** PILE
a ~ OFT, OFTEN, SCAD, TON
a ~ **of fun** HOOT
house and ~ HOME
house's ~ YARD
life's ~ FATE
not a ~ FEW
poor ~ DOOM
the whole ~ ALL

___ lot ODD

___ lot (few) NOTA

Lothario RAKE, ROMEO, ROUE, SATYR
~ **look** OGLE

Loti
see French

lotion BALM, CREAM, OIL, WASH
~ **ingredient** ALOE
healing ~ BALM

lots ATON, HEAP, MASS, OCEAN, PILE, SCAD, SEA, SLEW, WADS
~ **of land** ACRES
~ **of money** WAD
lots of ~ ACRES

Lott TRENT

lottery
~ **org., once** SSS
play the ~ BET

"Lottery, The"
~ **projectile** STONE

lotto
~ **cousin** KENO

lotus-___ EATER

Lou
he broke ~'s **record** CAL

loud
~ **laughter** ROAR
~ **noise** BANG, BOOM, CLAP, DIN, POP, SLAM, THUD
~ **sound** BLARE, BOOM
not ~ LOW

loudspeaker HORN

Louella
modern-day ~ RONA

lough LAKE

"Lou Grant"
~ **actor** ASNER

Louis NYE, ROI
see also French

"Louisa"
~ **director** HALL

louis d'or COIN

Louis-Dreyfus, Julia
~ **TV role** ELAINE

Louise ANITA, LAKE, TINA

"Louise" OPERA
~ **soprano** IRMA

___ Louise Huxtable ADA

Louisiana STATE
~ **politician** LONG

Louis IV LEROI, ROI

Louis L'___ AMOUR

Louis Quatorze LEROI, ROI, STYLE
see also French

Louisville
~ **river** OHIO
~ **st.** KEN

Louis XIV LEROI, ROI
see also French

Louis XVI LEROI, ROI
~ **wife** MARIE

lounge BAR, IDLE, LIE, LOLL, SALON, SOFA
~ **around** LOAF, LOLL
~ **lizard** IDLER
cocktail ~ BAR

loupe LENS

loup-garou DEMON

louse
~ **up** HASH, SPOIL
son of a ~ NIT
tomato ~ APHID

lousy BAD, MEAN, POOR

lout APE, BOOR, CAD, CLOD, OAF, YAHOO

loutish CRASS, RUDE

louver
~ **part** SLAT

l'Ouverture
~ **country** HAITI

Louvre
~ **annex architect** PEI
~ **display** ART, OILS
~ **locale** PARIS
~ **statue** NIKE
first name in the ~ MONA
see also French

lovable
become ~ ENDEAR

love ADORE, ARDOR, BEAU, DEAR,

DIG, LIKE, ZERO
~ **feast** AGAPE
~ **god** AMOR, EROS
~ **handles** FAT
~ **in French** AMOUR
~ **in Italian** AMORE
~ **in Latin** AMOR
~ **in Spanish** AMOR
~ **seat** SOFA
~ **too much** DOTE
be in ~ **with** ADORE
fill with ~ ENDEAR
lady ~ GIRL
lam it for ~ ELOPE
lyric ~ **poem** LAI
shower with ~ ADORE
symbol of ~ HEART, RING
what ~ **may mean** ZERO

love ___ APPLE, KNOT, NEST, SEAT

love- ___ **relationship** HATE

"___ love!" IMIN

"Love ___" ZONE

"Love ___, The" BOAT, PARADE

"Love ___ Battlefield" ISA

"Love ___ Death" AND

"Love ___ Many Faces" HAS

"Love ___ Many Splendored Thing" ISA

"Love ___ of J. Alfred Prufrock, The" SONG

"Love ___ Taxi" INA

"Love ___ the Ruins" AMONG

"Love ___ Wonderful Thing" ISA

"Love, ___" (Kaufman work) ETC

"___ Love" FIRST, ISIT, MAD, OUR, TRUE

"___ Love a Duck" LORD

"Love and Death"
~ **director** ALLEN

"___ Love a Stranger" NEVER

"Love at ___ Bite" FIRST

"Love at First ___" BITE

lovebird PET

Love Boat
enjoying the ~ ASEA, ATSEA

"Love Boat, The" LINER
~ **bartender** ISAAC

Love, Courtney
~ **band** HOLE

Lovecraft, H.P.
like ~ **stories** EERIE, EERY

loved
~ **one** DEAR, IDOL, LIFE
much ~ SWEET

"Loved ___, The" ONES

"___ Loved You" IFI

"Love Finds ___ Hardy" ANDY

"___ Love Her" ANDI

"___ Love I'm After" ITS

love-in-a- ___ MIST

"Love in a ___" TAXI

"Love in the First Degree"
~ **actor** OWEN

"Love Is Not All: It Is Not Meat nor Drink" POEM

Lovelace, Richard POET
see also poet

"Love Letters in the ___" SAND

lovelier
make ~ ADORN

lovely FAIR

"...lovely ___ tree" ASA

"Lovely ___, meter maid..." RITA

"___ Lovely Day Today" ITSA

"Love Me or ___ Me" LEAVE

"Love Me Tender"
~ **actor** EGAN

"Love of Life" SOAP

"___ Love or Money" FOR

"Love Potion Number ___" NINE

lover BEAU, ROMEO
lure a ~ WOO

"Lover ___ Back" COME

"___ Lover" DREAM

"___ Lover, The" GREAT

"Loverboy"
~ **singer** OCEAN

"Lover Come Back"
~ **director** MANN

lovers PAIR

lovers' ___ KNOT, LANE

"Lovers and ___ Strangers" OTHER

"Lovers and Other Strangers"
~ **actress** MEARA

"___ Loves Angela" AARON

loveseat SETTEE

"___ Loves Mambo" PAPA

"___ loves me..." SHE

"___ Loves Me Not" SHE

"Love Song of J. Alfred Prufrock, The" POEM

"Love Story"
~ **actor** ONEAL
~ **author** SEGAL
~ **composer** LAI
Ryan's ~ **costar** ALI

"___ Loves You" SHE

"Love the World ___" AWAY

"Love thy neighbor" ADAGE

"___ Love You" PSI

"___ Love You So" ANDI

loving CUP
~ **touch** CARESS

"Loving" SOAP

loving cup
~ **feature** EAR

low BASE, BASS, EVIL, GEAR, MEAN, MOO, NOISE, SAD
~ **blow** DIG
~ **card** TREY, TWO
~ **card in skat** SEVEN
~ **character** SNAKE
~ **down** DEEP
~ **in fat** LEAN
~ **in French** BAS
~ **in pitch** BASS
~ **island** CAY, KEY
~ **joint** ANKLE
~ **land** FEN
~ **mark** DEE
~ **point** NADIR
~ **tide** EBB
~ **to high** RANGE
~ **voice** ALTO, BASS, BASSO
~ **water** EBB
feeling ~ BLUE, SAD
keep a ~ **profile** HIDE
lay ~ HIDE
lie ~ DROP, HIDE, WAIT
look high and ~ RAKE, ROOT
morally ~ BASE
run at a ~ **speed** IDLE

low ___ BEAM, ROAD, TIDE, WATER

low- ___ CAL, END, KEY, RES, RISE, TECH

___ **low** LAY, LIE

lowborn MEAN

lowbrow YAHOO

lowdown BASE, DOPE, INFO, MEAN, NEWS, RUMOR, SCOOP
get the ~ HEAR, LEARN

Lowe CHAD, ROB

Lowell AMY

Lowell, Amy POET
see also poet

Lowell, James Russell EDITOR, POET
see also poet

lower ABASE, CUT, DIM, GLARE, LESS, PARE, SLASH
~ **class** MOB
~ **digit** TOE
~ **in rank** ABASE
~ **jaw** CHIN
~ **limb** GAM, LEG
~ **oneself** KNEEL
~ **part** ROOT
~ **prices** SLASH
~ **than** UNDER
~ **than, to a poet** NEATH
get ~ EBB

lower ___ CLASS

Lower California BAJA

lowercase SMALL

lowering DIM

Lowe, Rob
~ **brother** CHAD

lowest
~ **ante** CENT
~ **pinochle card** NINE
~ **point** EBB, NADIR

"lowest form of wit" PUN

low-grade MEAN, POOR

lowlife CAD, CREEP, CUR, HEEL, SLIME, TOAD, YAHOO

lowly MEAN

low-lying
~ **area** DALE, VALE

low man
~ **at the opera** BASSO

low-pH
~ **compound** ACID

low-pitched BASS, DEEP

low-quality POOR
~ **publication** TRASH

low-tech
~ **navigation aid** OAR

lox
~ **companion** BAGEL

Loy
~ **costar** ASTA

loyal FAST, LIEGE, SURE, TRUE
~ **ender** IST
be ~ **to** OBEY
remain ~ ADHERE

loyalist
colonial ~ TORY

Loyal Order of ___ MOOSE

loyalty ARDOR
maintain ~ ADHERE
model of ~ ENID

lozenge DROP, PILL

LP DISC
~ **device** STEREO
~ **holder** LINER
~ **problem** SKIP
~ **speed** RPM
~ **successors** CDS
make an ~ PRESS

LPNs
what ~ **dispense** TLC

LPs
today's ~ CDS

"L-Shaped ___, The" ROOM

LST
part of ~ SHIP, TANK

lt.
~ **right hand** SGT
~ **saluter** NCO
~ **trainer** ROTC
rank above ~ CAP
rank below ~ SGT

ltd.
~ **kin** INC

LTJG
~ **subordinate** ENS

Lu ELEM
71 for ~ ATNO

Luanda
~ tongue BANTU

Luang Prabang
~ land LAOS

luau
~ accompaniment UKE
~ entertainment HULA
~ fare POI
~ neckwear LEI
~ spread TARO

lubber
~ place ASHORE

lube OIL

Lübeck CITY, PORT

Lubitsch ERNST

Lubovitch LAR

lubricant OIL
eye ~ TEAR

lubricate OIL

lubricated OILY

lubricious LEWD

Lucan POET, ROMAN
see also poet

Lucci, Susan
~ role ERICA

Luce CLARE
~ publication TIME

lucent CLEAR

___ Lucia SANTA

"Lucia di Lammermoor" OPERA

lucid CLEAR, SANE

Lucie's
~ brother DESI
~ dad DESI

Lucifer ANGEL, SATAN
~ forte EVIL

Lucifer and Pansy
~ boy ABNER

luciferous CLEAR

"___ Lucille" LALA

Lucite RESIN

luck LADY
press one's ~ DARE
stretch of good ~ RUN
try one's ~ GAME, PLAY

"Luck ___ Lady" BEA

"___ Luck" LADY, PURE

"Luck and Pluck"
~ author ALGER

"Luck Be a ___" LADY

"Luckiest ___ in the World, The"
MAN

Luckman SID

Lucknow CITY

"Luck of Roaring Camp, The"
~ author HARTE

luck of the ___ IRISH

lucky
~ number SEVEN
be ~ WIN

"Lucky Jim"
~ author AMIS

lucrative FAT

lucre CASH, CENTS

Lucretius POET, ROMAN
see also poet

lucubrate WRITE

luculent CLEAR

Lucy STONE
~ friend ETHEL
~ husband DESI
~ landlord FRED
he loved ~ DESI
role for ~ MAME

"Lucy"
~ telecast RERUN

"Lucy Gray" POEM

"Lucy in the ___ With Dia-monds" SKY

Ludden ALLEN

ludicrous DAFT, INANE, MAD, RICH

Ludwig EMIL

Ludwig ___ Beethoven VON

Ludwig ___ Drake VON

"___ luego!" HASTA

Luftwaffe
~ foe RAF

lug APE, BOOR, CART, DRAG,
DRAW, HAUL, LOUT, MOVE, OAF,
TOTE

lug ___ NUT

lug-___ SOLED

Lugar, Richard
~ org. SEN

luge SLED

luggage BAG, CASE, GEAR, TRAPS
collect, as ~ CLAIM

lugger BOAT, SHIP

Lugosi BELA
~ role IGOR

lugubrious SAD

Luigi ALVA
see also Italian

Luis
see Spanish

___ Luis, Brazil SAO

___ Luis Obispo, Calif. SAN

___ Luis Potosí, Mexico SAN

Luke
book by ~ ACTS

lukewarm COOL, DAMP, LIMP,
MILD, SOSO, TEPID

lull ALLAY, CALM, PEACE, REST

lullaby SONG, TUNE

lulu ONER, PIP

"Lulu" OPERA
~ composer BERG

Lum
~ partner ABNER

"Lum and Abner"
~ setting STORE

lumbago ACHE

lumbar
~ region HIP

lumber PLOD
~ source ASH, MAPLE, OAK,
PINE
process ~ SAW
stadium ~ BAT

lumberjack
~ need AXE, SAW

luminary LAMP, LION, SAGE,
SPHERE, STAR, SUN

luminesce SHINE

luminosity FIRE, GLOW

luminous CLEAR, LIT
~ bands AURORA
~ cloud HALO

luminousness SHEEN

lummox APE, BOOR, CLOD, LOUT,
OAF, YAHOO
~ cry OOPS
like a ~ INEPT

lummoxlike DENSE

lump CLOD, CLOT, GOB, KNOB,
KNOT, MASS, NODE, WAD
~ together MASS

lump ___ SUM

lumpish DENSE

lumpy-shaped
~ fruit PEAR

luna ___ MOTH

Luna MOON

lunar
~ leaper COW
~ phenomenon TIDE
~ plain MARE, SEA
~ pull TIDE
~ sea MARE
~ valley RILL

lunar ___ YEAR

___ Lunas, N. Mex. LOS

lunatic DAFT, MAD, NUT

lunch BITE, DINE, EAT, FARE, MEAL
~ counter BAR
~ ender EON
~ hour NOON
~ order BLT, HERO
~ period, often HOUR
at ~, maybe OUT

dieter's ~ SALAD
do ~ EAT, MEET
have ~ DINE, EAT
healthful ~ SALAD
how some order ~ TOGO

___ lunch FREE

"Lunch ___" (Jean Kerr book)
HOUR

luncheon MEAL
~ ender ETTE

luncheonette
~ lure AROMA
~ order BLT

"Luncheon on the Grass"
~ artist MANET

"Lunch Poems"
~ poet OHARA

lunchroom
~ lure AROMA

lunchtime
~ for some NOON, ONE
~ reading MENU
~ stop DELI

___ Lund ("Casablanca
character) ILSA

Lundy ISLE

lung ORGAN

___-Lung AQUA

lunge PLOW
~ (at) SNAP

lungful AIR

lungs
at the top of one's ~ ALOUD

lunkhead APE, ASS, CLOD, DOLT,
OAF, SAP

Lunts
~ milieu STAGE

lunula ARC

lupine FERAL

Lupino IDA

LuPone PATTI
~ role EVITA

Lupus PETER

Luraschi TONY

lurch REEL, ROLL, TEETER, TOSS
leave in the ~ DESERT

lure BAIT, DRAW, EGG
~ a lover WOO
culinary ~ AROMA
fisherman's ~ BAIT
shopper's ~ SALE

lures
consumer ~ ADS

lurk STEAL

lush RANK, RICH, SOT

"Lusitania" BOAT, LINER, SHIP
~ sinker UBOAT

lust SIN

"Lust ___ Life" FOR

Lustbader ERIC

luster GLOW, SHEEN, SHINE
  lose ~ FADE

lusterless DRAB, MAT, MATTE
  ~ finish MAT, MATTE

"Lust for ___" LIFE

"Lust for Life"
  ~ author STONE

lustful LEWD

lustily ALOUD, HARD

lustrate CLEAN

lustrous SLEEK
  ~ black EBON, RAVEN
  ~ fabric LAME, SATIN, SILK

lusty HALE

"Lusty ___, The" MEN

"Lusty Men, The"
  ~ director RAY

lute
  ~ cousin LYRE, VIOL

~ feature FRET
Hindu ~ SITAR

lutefisk COD
  ~ tenderizer LYE

Luther ADLER

Luthor
  ~ to Superman ENEMY, FOE

Luthor, Lex
  like ~ EVIL

Lutz LEAP
  ~ alternative AXEL
  where to do a ~ ICE, RINK

"___ Luv U" PSI

Lux.
  ~ neighbor GER

Luxor
  ~ stream NILE
  city south of ~ ASWAN

luxuriant RANK

luxuriate BASK
  ~ in SAVOR

luxurious POSH, RICH
  ~ fur SABLE
  hardly ~ SEEDY

luxury EASE
  ~ car LIMO

Lw ELEM
  103 for ~ ATNO

lwyr. ATT

lycanthrope DEMON

lycopodium MOSS

Lycra
  ~ cousin NYLON

Lydgate, John POET
  see also poet

"Lydia the Tattooed ___" LADY

"Lyin' ___" EYES

lying FALSE, SIN
  ~ down FLAT
  ~ flat PRONE
  ~ still INERT

lymph ___ NODE

Lynde PAUL

Lynley CAROL

Lynn VERA

Lynne, Jeff
  ~ rock band ELO

lynx ANIMAL, CAT

Lyon SUE
  see also French

lyonnaise
  ~ ingredient ONION

Lyons CITY
  ~ lid BERET
  see also French

lyre
  ~ cousin HARP
  goddess with a ~ ERATO

lyric POEM, SONG
  ~ love poem LAI
  ~ poem ODE

lyricist POET

Lysithea MOON

m
~ to Einstein MASS

M SIZE
McDonald's giant ~ LOGO

"M"
~ **actor** LORRE
~ **director** LANG
~ **portrayer** LEE

M ___ "Mary" ASIN

"___ M?" NOR

___ Ma YOYO

MA
~ **zone** EDT, EST
see also Massachusetts

M.A.
part of ~ ARTS

ma'am
~ **companion** SIR

"___, ma'am" YES

Ma and Pa
~ **operation** STORE

"Ma and Pa Kettle at ___" HOME

Mab
~ **mate** OBERON

"Ma Belle ___" AMIE

Mac
~ **producer** APPLE

macabre EERIE, EERY
master of the ~ POE

macadam
~ **ingredient** TAR
put down ~ PAVE

macadamia NUT, TREE

macadamize PAVE

Macao CITY, PORT

macaque ANIMAL

macaroni DUDE, PASTA
~ **dish** SALAD
~ **shape** ELBOW

MacArthur
onetime ~ command KOREA

Macaulay, Rose DAME

macaw ARA, BIRD

Macbeth LADY, SCOT
~ **resting place** IONA

"Macbeth" DRAMA, PLAY
~ **recipe ingredient** NEWT

"Macbeth shall ___ no more!"
SLEEP

MacDonald ROSS
~ **costar** EDDY
like ~ OLD

Macduff SCOT

mace WAND
~ **source** ARIL

Macedonian
~ **neighbor** SERB

macerate RET

MacGraw ALI

MacGregor CLAN, SCOT

Mach ERNST

Machiavellian BAD, FALSE, SLY
~ **concern** END

machinate CABAL

machination GAME, PLOT, RUSE

machine BLOC, GANG
~ **part** CAM, COG, GEAR
~ **pattern** DIE
~ **stitch** SEW
~ **tool** LATHE
carpentry ~ LATHE
construction ~ CRANE
cotton-processing ~ GIN
flying ~ PLANE
grinding ~ LATHE
Las Vegas ~ SLOT
light ~ gun STEN
printing ~ PRESS
shaping ~ LATHE
ski-slope ~ TOW
stamping ~ DIE
textile ~ LOOM
Vail ~ TBAR

machine ___ SHOP

machine-___ WASH

___ machine SLOT, TIME

"___ Machine, The" TIME

machinery GEAR

machines
some ~ do it VEND

machine-shop
~ **wear** APRON

macho
~ **guy** STUD

Machree, Mother
~ **milieu** ERIN

Mach 2
~ **traveler** SST

Machu Picchu
~ **locale** PERU
~ **resident** INCA

Macintosh APPLE

Mack TED

Mackenzies RANGE

mackerel ___ SKY

___ mackerel HORSE

mackinaw COAT, WRAP

mackintosh COAT

Mack, Ted EMCEE, HOST

MacLaine, Shirley
~ **role of 1963** IRMA
~ **role of 1994** TESS

MacLeish, Archibald POET
see also poet

MacMahon ALINE

Macmillan
~ **predecessor** EDEN

MacMurray FRED

Macnee
~ **TV role** STEED

MacNeice, Louis POET
see also poet

MacNelly, Jeff
~ **comic strip** SHOE

MacNicol PETER

Macpherson ELLE

macrocosm ALL, SPACE

macroeconomic
~ **stat** GNP

macromolecular
~ **letters** DNA

maculate TAINT

maculation TAINT

mad IRATE, RABID, UPSET
~ **as a hatter** DAFT, LOCO
~ **as a wet hen** IRATE, UPSET
~ **mood** RAGE
~ **rush** DASH
be ~ about ADORE, LOVE
make ~ ANGER, ENRAGE, IRE,
IRK, PEEVE, RILE, UPSET
run like ~ TEAR

mad ___ hatter ASA

mad ___ hornet ASA

___ mad (impulsively) LIKE

"Mad" MAG

"Mad ___" LOVE

"Mad ___ and Glory" DOG

"Mad ___ Music" ABOUT

Mad. ___ AVE

"Mad About You"
~ **actress** HUNT
~ **cousin** IRA

Madagascar
~ **(abbr.)** ISL

madam LADY
~ **mate** SIR

Madam TITLE

"Madam ___" SATAN

"Madama Butterfly"
~ **piece** ARIA

madame LADY, MADAM

Madame TITLE
see also French

"Madame ___" ROSA

"Madame Butterfly" OPERA

"Madame Curie"
~ **director** LEROY

"Madame X"
~ **name** LANA

"Madam, I'm ___" ADAM

"mad as a hatter" IDIOM

madcap RASH

madden ANGER, ENRAGE, IRE, IRK, PEEVE, RILE

maddog
~ skullcap PLANT

"Mad Dog ___ Glory" AND

"Mad Dog and Glory"
Glory, in ~ UMA

Maddow BEN

Maddux, Greg ACE
~ stat ERA

made
~ a landing ALIT, LIT
~ in heaven IDEAL
~ known OUT
~ of money RICH
~ of (suffix) INE
~ to last SOLID
where vows are ~ ALTAR

___-made (artificial) MAN

"Made ___ Each Other" FOR

"Made for ___ Other" EACH

"Made for Each ___" OTHER

"Made for Each Other"
~ director BEAN

made in the ___ USA

Madeira WINE

madeleine CAKE

Madeleine
see French

mademoiselle GIRL, LADY, LASS

Mademoiselle TITLE
see also French

"Mademoiselle"
~ rival ELLE

made-to-___ ORDER

Madigan AMY

Madison CITY

Madison ___ AVE

Madison Avenue
~ output ADS
~ worker ADMAN

Madison, Oscar SLOB
like ~ MESSY
unlike ~ NEAT

Madison Square Garden ARENA

"___ Mad Mad Mad Mad World"
ITSA

Mad Max HERO
~ portrayer MEL

madness MANIA

"___ Madness, A" FINE

Madonna
~ book SEX
~ ex PENN, SEAN
~ role EVA, EVITA
famous ~ PIETA

Madras CITY
~ country INDIA
~ language URDU
see also Indian

madre's
~ brother TIO
~ hermana TIA
~ hermano TIO
~ sister TIA

Madrid CITY
~ neighbor AVILA
city NW of ~ LEON
see also Spanish

madrigal LAY, SONG

madrona TREE

Mae WEST

___ Mae Brown RITA

Maecenas ANGEL

"Maelzel's Chess-Player"
~ author POE

maestro ACE

Maeterlinck, Maurice POET
see also poet

Mafia MOB
~ boss DON

magazine EBONY, ISSUE, ORGAN
~ contents AMMO
~ execs EDS
~ fillers ADS
~ piece ESSAY, ITEM
~ section ROTO
~ stand RACK
~ VIPs EDS
fashion ~ ELLE
German ~ STERN
news ~ TIME
picture ~ LIFE
satire ~ MAD
science ~ OMNI
small-business ~ INC
Sun. ~ section ROTO
"What, me worry?" ~ MAD
women's ~ SELF

Magaziner IRA

magazines MEDIA, PRESS

Magda
~ sister EVA
~ to Zsa Zsa SIS

Magdeburg
~ river ELBE

Magellan
~ (abbr.) STR

magenta COLOR

Maggie NAG

"Maggie ___" MAY

Maggiore LAKE

Magi TRIO
~ carrier CAMEL
~ guide STAR
emulate the ~ ADORE

magic
~ lantern LAMP

~ spirit GENIE
~ word PLEASE

Magic FIVE, TEAM
~ org. NBA

"___ Magic" ITS

"Magical Mystery ___" TOUR

"___ Magic Christmas" ONE

"Magic Flute, The" OPERA

magician
~ baton WAND
~ tool SAW

Magic Marker PEN

"___ Magic Moment" THIS

"Magic Mountain, The"
~ author MANN

"Magic Theater"
~ painter KLEE

Maginot LINE

magistrate
Roman ~ EDILE

Maglie SAL

magma LAVA

Magnani ANNA

magnanimity HEART

magnanimous BIG, GREAT

magnate BARON, LION

Magnavox
~ rival RCA

magnesium METAL
~ silicate TALC

magnet LURE
tourist ~ MECCA

"Magnet and ___" STEEL

"Magnet and Steel"
~ singer EGAN

magnetic
~ induction unit TESLA

magnetic ___ POLE, STORM

magnetism DRAW
have ~ LURE

___ magnetism ANIMAL

magnetite ORE

magnets
~ attract it IRON

Magnificat SONG

magnificence POMP, STATE

magnificent FINE, GALA, GREAT, REGAL, RICH

"Magnificent ___, The" DOPE, SEVEN

"Magnificent Dope, The"
~ director LANG

"___ Magnificent Men in Their Flying Machines" THOSE

"Magnificent Seven, The"
~ gunslinger LEE

~ name ELI, YUL

magnifico PEER, RANK

magnifier LENS

magnify ADORE, EXALT, HAIL, HONOR, LAUD, LIE, RAISE

magnifying
~ glass LENS

magniloquize ORATE

Magnitogorsk
~ river URAL

magnitude SIZE

magnolia TREE

Magnolia
~ St. MISS

"___ Magnolias" STEEL

___-Magnon CRO

magnum
~ opus TOME

magnum ___ OPUS

Magnum
~ greeting ALOHA
~ venue OAHU
where ~ served, for short NAM

Magnus EDIE

Magnuson ANN

magpie BIRD

Magritte RENE
~ contemporary DALI

magueys CACTI

Maguire, Jerry AGENT, REP

magus SAGE, SEER

Magwitch ABEL

"Mahabharata" EPIC, POEM

maharajah LORD, RULER, TITLE

maharani LADY, TITLE
~ cover SARI

maharishi TITLE

mahatma SAGE

Mahatma TITLE

Mahayana
~ teacher LAMA

"Ma, he's making eyes ___"
ATME

mah-jongg GAME
~ counter TILE

Mahler, Mrs. ALMA

mahogany TREE

Mahogany Row
~ denizen EXEC

mahout
~ master SAHIB

Mahre
emulate ~ SKI

mai ___ TAI

Maia STAR

maid GIRL, HELP, LASS
~ **target** DUST
British ~ CHAR
lily ~ **of Astolat** ELAINE

___ **maid** METER

___ **maid (card game)** OLD

maiden GIRL, LASS, MISS
~ **lack** WIN
yon ~ HER, SHE

___ **Maiden** IRON

maidenhair FERN, TREE

maiden name
~ **indicator** NEE

maidens
like certain ~ FAIR

"M'aidez!" ALARM, ALERT, HELP, SOS

maid of ___ HONOR

"Maid of ___**"** SALEM

"Maid of Athens, ___ **we part"** ERE

maids HELP
pretty ~ **place** AROW

"Maids, The"
~ **author** GENET

Maidstone
~ **county** KENT

Maidu TRIBE

Maigret
see French

mail ARMOR, POST, SEND
~ **a payment** REMIT
~ **carrier abbr.** RTE
~ **drop service** APO
~ **motto word** NOR
~ **pouch** BAG, SACK
~ **receptacle** SLOT
~ **starter** AIR
Army ~ **addr.** APO
birthday ~ CARD
by return ~ SOON
junk ~ ADS
knight's ~ ARMOR
purchase by ~ ORDER

mail ___ CALL, DROP, ORDER

___ **mail** FAN, HATE

mail chute
~ **feature** SLOT

mailer
return ~ SASE

mailing
prepare for ~ SEAL

mail order
~ **request** COD

"Mail Order Bride"
~ **actor** EBSEN, OATES

mailroom
work in the ~ SORT

maim HARM

maimed LAME

main ARCH, BIG, FIRST, HEAD, KEY, OCEAN, SEA
~ **body** MASS, TEXT
~ **character** HERO
~ **course** ENTREE, MEAT
~ **course of study** MAJOR
~ **event** BOUT
~ **idea** SUM, THEME, TOPIC
~ **ingredient** BASE
~ **meaning** ESSENCE
~ **player** STAR
~ **point** GIST
~ **role** LEAD
~ **story** PLOT
bounding ~ OCEAN, SEA
on the ~ ASEA, ATSEA
ride the bounding ~ SAIL
water ~ PIPE
with might and ~ HARD

main ___ DRAG, LINE, STEM

___ **main** GAS, WATER

Main
~ **and others** STS

"Main ___**, The"** EVENT

Maine STATE
~ **animal** MOOSE
~ **state tree** PINE
University of ~ **locale** ORONO

"Maine" BOAT, SHIP

Maine coon ___ CAT

"Main Event, The"
~ **actor** ONEAL

mainsail SHEET

mainspring CAUSE, ROOT

mainstay PROP

mainstream
not ~ OUTRE
out of the ~ APART

"Main Street"
~ **author** LEWIS

maintain ARGUE, ASSERT, AVER, AVOW, CLAIM, FEED, HAVE, HOLD, KEEP, STATE
~ **loyalty** ADHERE

Mainz
see German

"Mais ___**!"** OUI

___ **maison** ALA

maisonette ABODE, HOME

mai tai
~ **ingredient** RUM

maître d'
~ **offering** MENU

maize COLOR, CORN

maj.
~ **subordinate** CAP
~ **superior** COL, GEN

Majerle DAN

___ **majesté** LESE

majestic BIG, EPIC, GALA, GREAT, LARGE, REGAL
~ **address** SIRE
~ **tale** EPIC
~ **wader** EGRET

majesty LORD, RULER

___ **majesty** LESE

Majesty TITLE

majeure
force ~ EVENT

majolica
~ **glaze** TIN

major FIRST, KEY, MAIN, RANK
~ **ender** ETTE
~ **interest** BAG
~ **work** OPUS
coll. ~ BIO, ECO, ECON, ENG, MATH, MUS
college ~ ART, BIO, DRAMA, MATH
grad-school ~ LAW

Major ___ ANDRE

Major ___ **Hoople** AMOS

"Major ___**"** DAD

"Major ___ **the Minor, The"** AND

___ **Major** URSA

"Major Barbara"
~ **author** SHAW

Majorca
see Spanish

"Major Dad"
~ **actress** REED
~ **network** CBS

majority MASS, MOST, PART

majority of ___**, a** ONE

___ **Majority, The** MORAL

Major, John TORY

major league
~ **transaction** TRADE

major leaguer PRO

Majors LEE

make CAUSE, EARN, IMPEL, NET, SORT
~ **a backup** SAVE
~ **a basket** SINK
~ **a bet** GAME, PLAY
~ **a blooper** ERR
~ **a blouse** SEW
~ **a boner** ERR
~ **a boo-boo** ERR
~ **a bootee** KNIT
~ **a bow** TIE
~ **a breeze** FAN
~ **a buck** EARN
~ **a bull's-eye** HIT
~ **a bundle** BALE
~ **a cardigan** KNIT
~ **a casserole** BAKE
~ **a choice of** DRAW
~ **a claim** ASSERT
~ **a clean slate** ERASE
~ **a close study of** PORE

~ **a comment** SAY
~ **a connection** TIE
~ **a copy of** CLONE
~ **acquaintance with** MEET
~ **a cryptogram** ENCODE
~ **a decision** ACT, DEEM, RULE
~ **a dent** MOVE
~ **a deposit** BAIL, SAVE
~ **adjustments** ADAPT
~ **a doily** TAT
~ **a dress** SEW
~ **a fool of** ROAST, SNUB
~ **a footnote** CITE
~ **after** CHASE
~ **a fuss** RANT
~ **a gaffe** ERR
~ **a getaway** FLEE, LOSE, RUN
~ **a hash of** SPOIL
~ **a hem** SEW
~ **a hit** SCORE
~ **a hole** DIG
~ **airtight** SEAL
~ **a judgment** RULE
~ **a lap** SIT
~ **a law** ENACT
~ **a long story short** EDIT
~ **a match** WED
~ **a mean face** SNEER
~ **amends** ATONE, REMIT
~ **a misstatement** LIE
~ **a mistake** ERR, TRIP
~ **a motion** MOVE
~ **a move** ACT
~ **an address** ORATE, TALK
~ **an afghan** KNIT
~ **an appeal** ASK, PRAY
~ **an appearance** ARISE, ATTEND, COME, ENTER
~ **an appointment** NAME
~ **an appointment with** DATE
~ **an aquatint** ETCH
~ **an effort** ASSAY, ESSAY, EXERT, LABOR, TRY
~ **an entreaty** ASK
~ **an entry** NOTE
~ **a new knot** RETIE
~ **an excuse** ALIBI
~ **angry** ENRAGE, IRE, RILE
~ **an impression** DENT, MOVE, STAMP
~ **an inquiry** ASK
~ **an LP** PRESS
~ **a note** JOT
~ **a note of** LOG
~ **an outburst** ERUPT
~ **an outline** TRACE
~ **antimacassars** TAT
~ **a parabola** ARC
~ **a petition** PRAY
~ **a phrase** COIN
~ **a play for** GRAB
~ **a point** SCORE
~ **a pretty penny** EARN
~ **a profit** CLEAR
~ **a quick exit** FLEE, HIE, RUN
~ **a record** PRESS
~ **a remark** STATE, UTTER
~ **arrangements** PLAN
~ **a run** SCORE
~ **a run for it** LAM
~ **a scarf** KNIT
~ **a scene** ACT, RAGE, RANT
~ **a seam** SEW

~ a secret message ENCODE
~ a shambles of RUIN
~ ashamed ABASH
~ a sharp turn VEER
~ a sheepshank TIE
~ a sign NOD
~ a solecism ERR
~ a special point of STRESS
~ a speech ORATE, TALK
~ a splash RATE
~ a statement AVER, AVOW, SAY
~ a sweater KNIT
~ a temporary stitch BASTE
~ a touchdown SCORE
~ a tunnel BORE, DIG
~ available OPEN
~ a video TAPE
~ aware of ALERT
~ a web SPIN
~ a wish HOPE
~ a wrong move ERR
~ batik DYE
~ beam ELATE
~ beer BREW
~ believe ACT
~ beloved ENDEAR
~ better AMEND, EMEND, MEND
~ bigger (abbr.) ENL
~ binding SIGN
~ bisque PUREE
~ blank ERASE
~ blush ABASH
~ boo-boos ERR
~ bread BAKE, EARN
~ brownies BAKE
~ bubbly AERATE
~ cake BAKE
~ candles DIP
~ capital out of AVAIL
~ certain SETTLE
~ changes to ADAPT, ALTER, AMEND, EMEND, REDO
~ cherished ENDEAR
~ chips FRY
~ clear OPEN, SHOW, STATE
~ clothing SEW
~ cloudy ROIL
~ coffee BREW, PERK
~ coins MINT
~ coleslaw SHRED
~ complicated RAVEL
~ confetti SHRED
~ confused ADDLE
~ contact HIT
~ conversation CHAT, CHIN, GAB, RAP, TALK, YAK
~ cookies BAKE
~ corrections to AMEND, EMEND
~ current RENEW
~ different ADAPT, ALTER, AMEND, EMEND
~ difficult to read ENCODE
~ do ADAPT, COPE, EKE
~ doilies TAT
~ do with USE
~ easier AID
~ ecstatic ELATE
~ effervescent AERATE
~ enemies ENRAGE
~ even PLANE

~ every moment count LIVE
~ expiation ATONE
~ eyes at LEER, OGLE
~ fast BIND, LASH, RIVET, TIE
~ firewood CHOP, HEW
~ firm SEAL, SET
~ fit ADAPT, ALTER
~ fizzy AERATE
~ (for) HEAD
~ fragrant CENSE, SCENT
~ fun of KID, RAG, RIB, RIDE, ROAST, TEASE, TWIT
~ furious ENRAGE, IRE
~ furrows PLOW
~ gape AMAZE, AWE, STUN, WOW
~ glad ELATE, PLEASE
~ good ATONE
~ good as new CURE, HEAL, MEND
~ good use of AVAIL
~ gussets SEW
~ ham CURE
~ happen CAUSE
~ happy ELATE, PLEASE
~ harmonious TUNE
~ haste HIE, PRESS, RACE, RUN, SPEED
~ hay BALE
~ heads or tails of LEARN
~ headway MOVE
~ headway against STEM
~ holy BLESS
~ homeless OUST
~ humble AWE
~ illegal BAN
~ impossible BAN
~ improvements in EMEND
~ indistinct BLUR
~ inoperative ANNUL
~ insensible BLUR
~ into law ENACT
~ it ARRIVE, COME
~ it big ARRIVE
~ it snappy DASH, HIE, RACE, RUN, SPEED, TEAR
~ jubilant ELATE
~ judgments ASSESS, DEEM
~ known ADMIT, AIR, BARE, LEAK, POST, RELATE, RUMOR, SAY, STATE, TELL
~ lace TAT
~ larger PAD
~ laugh AMUSE
~ leather TAN
~ legal SIGN
~ leg warmers KNIT
~ less ALLAY
~ less difficult EASE
~ less distinct BLUR
~ less wild TAME
~ level EVEN, TRUE
~ like APE
~ like a snake COIL
~ lofty EXALT
~ lovelier ADORN
~ mad ANGER, ENRAGE, IRE, IRK, PEEVE, RILE, UPSET
~ mention of CITE, REFER
~ merry AMUSE, REVEL
~ mischief LARK
~ mistakes ERR
~ modifications to ADAPT, ALTER, AMEND, EMEND

~ money COIN, EARN, MINT
~ more beautiful ADORN
~ more effective HONE
~ much of EXALT, LAUD
~ muddy ROIL
~ muffins BAKE
~ new RESTORE
~ nice to PAT
~ no bones about ADMIT, AVER, AVOW, LETON, SAY, STATE
~ obeisance KNEEL
~ off DESERT, LEAVE, MOVE
~ official ENACT
~ off limits BAR
~ off with NIP, ROB, STEAL
~ one UNITE, WED
~ one's blood run cold SCARE
~ one's day ELATE
~ oneself LABOR
~ oneself scarce AVOID, ELUDE, EVADE, FLEE
~ oneself useful HELP
~ one's escape ELUDE
~ one's hair stand on end REPEL, SCARE
~ one's head swim STUN
~ one shudder REPEL
~ one's jaw drop AMAZE, AWE, STUN, WOW
~ one's mark SIGN
~ one's own ADOPT
~ one's way WEND
~ orange juice REAM
~ out CARESS, ESPY, FARE, KISS, NECK, SEE, SPOT, SPY
~ out of whole cloth LIE
~ over REDO, RESTORE
~ pay FINE
~ pictures DRAW
~ pig iron SMELT
~ plain CLEAR, RAVEL, SHOW
~ possible ENABLE, SETUP
~ preparations PLAN
~ pretty ADORN
~ progress GAIN, MOVE
~ proud ELATE
~ provisions (for) ALLOW
~ public AIR, BARE
~ quake SCARE
~ rapid strides MOVE, RUN
~ raw CHAP
~ ready PREP
~ reminisce EVOKE
~ repairs to MEND
~ reparation ATONE
~ restitution ATONE, REMIT
~ rhapsodic ELATE
~ right ATONE
~ secret ENCODE
~ self-conscious ABASH
~ seltzer AERATE
~ serious SOBER
~ sharp HONE
~ shore LAND
~ shorter CLIP, CUT, TRIM
~ shy ABASH
~ simmer HEAT
~ slippery OIL
~ smooth EVEN, OIL, SAND
~ socks KNIT
~ soda water AERATE
~ someone's blood

boil ANGER, IRK, PEEVE, RILE, UPSET
~ someone see red ANGER, IRE, IRK, PEEVE, RILE, UPSET
~ sore ANGER, IRE, IRK, PEEVE, RILE, UPSET
~ sound CURE, HEAL, MEND
~ sparkling AERATE
~ start SCARE
~ straight lines RULE
~ strips TEAR
~ suitable ADAPT
~ taboo BAN, BAR
~ tea BREW, STEEP
~ tears CRY
~ the acquaintance of MEET
~ the grade ARRIVE, PASS
~ the most of AVAIL, USE
~ the scene ARRIVE, COME, ENTER
~ time HIE, RACE, SPEED
~ tolerable EASE
~ tracks FLEE, HIE, RACE, RUN, SPEED, TEAR
~ tractable TAME
~ typos ERR
~ unclean TAINT
~ uniform EVEN
~ unsteady TIP
~ untrue BELIE
~ up ATONE, LIE
~ up for AMEND
~ up one's mind ACT, ELECT, OPT, SET
~ up on the spot ADLIB
~ up-to-date RENEW
~ usable ADAPT
~ useless SPOIL
~ use of AVAIL, TAKE, WIELD
~ vacant CLEAR
~ vertical RAISE
~ void ANNUL
~ vows WED
~ waterproof SEAL
~ well CURE, MEND
~ well-liked ENDEAR
~ whole CURE, HEAL, HELP, MEND
~ whoopee REVEL
~ worthy of EARN
~ yarn SPIN
~ yawn BORE
~ z's SNORE
barely ~ ends meet EKE
not ~ it LOSE

make ___ (rush) HASTE

make ___ for oneself ANAME

make ___ meet ENDS

make ___ of it AGO

make ___ while the sun shines HAY

make ___ with OFF

"Make ___ double!" ITA

"Make ___ for Daddy" ROOM

"Make ___ Miracle" MEA

make a ___ in one HOLE

make a ___ of faith LEAP

"Make a ___ on Me" MOVE

"___ Make a Deal"

"___ Make a Deal" LETS

make-believe FAKE, FALSE, PLAY, SHAM

"___ Make Believe" ONLY

"make do"
~ amount LESS

"Make it ___ for my baby..." ONE

"Make it snappy!" ASAP, STAT

"Make like a ___ and leave" TREE

"___ Make Love" LETS

make love, not ___ WAR

"___ Make Loving Fun" YOU

"___ make me laugh!" DONT

"Make my day" DARE

maker
~ (suffix) IST

"___ makes two of us!" THAT

make the ___ (attend) SCENE

make the ___ fly FUR

make the ___ of MOST

"Make the ___ of it" MOST

"Make thee ___ of greatness" ANAME

makeup LINER, PAINT, ROUGE
~ name ESTEE
apply ~ DAB
eye ~ LINER

"___ Make Waves" DONT

"Make Way ___ Tomorrow" FOR

___-making (historic) EPOCH

"___ Making Sense" STOP

Malabar Coast
~ district GOA

Malacca CANE
~ (abbr.) STR

malachite ORE

maladroit INEPT

malady EVIL, ILL
chronic ~ (suffix) ITIS
cold-weather ~ FLU
root ~ ROT

Malaga WINE

Málaga CITY, PORT
see also Spanish

malagueña DANCE

malamute DOG
~ burden SLED

Malaprop MRS

malaria
~ symptom AGUE

malarkey ROT, TRASH

Malay
~ dagger KRIS
~ gibbon LAR

~ mammal TAPIR

Malaysian
~ export TIN
~ neighbor TAI, THAI

"Malcolm X"
~ director LEE

malcontent CRAB, REBEL

mal de ___ MER, TETE

Maldives
~ capital MALE

male HIM, MAN
~ bee DRONE
~ cat TOM
~ deer HART, STAG
~ doll KEN
~ friend, in French AMI
~ gypsy ROM
~ lead HERO
~ offspring SON
~ parent SIRE
~ raccoon BOAR
~ swan COB
~ turkey TOM
~ voice BASS, TENOR
ardent ~ ROMEO
unattached ~ STAG

"Male ___, The" ANIMAL

"Male and Female"
~ author MEAD

malediction BAN, OATH

malefic EVIL

maleficent CRUEL, EVIL

males HES
having ~ and females COED

malevolence EVIL, HATE, SIN, SPITE

malevolent BAD, CRUEL, EVIL

malfunction
memory ~ LAPSE

Malherbe, François de POET
see also poet

Mali
~ desert SAHARA
~ neighbor NIGER

malic ACID

malice HATE, SPITE

malicious BAD, EVIL, MEAN, SNIDE
~ burning ARSON
~ intent SPITE
~ look LEER
slyly ~ SNIDE

maliciousness EVIL, SIN

malign SLUR
~ in street lingo DIS

malignant EVIL

malinger AVOID, EVADE, LOAF

malkin HARE

mall
~ area ARCADE
~ binge SPREE
~ component STORE

~ display MAP
~ extravaganza SALE
~ forerunner AGORA
~ frequenter TEEN
~ tenant SHOP, STORE
have fun at the ~ SHOP, SPEND
hit the ~ SHOP

___ Mall PALL

mallard BIRD
~ cousin TEAL

Mallarmé, Stéphane POET
see also poet

malleable
~ metal TIN

mallet BAT, TOOL
~ game POLO

malleus BONE

Mallon MEG

Mallorca
see Spanish

Malmö CITY, PORT
~ native SWEDE

malmsey WINE

malodorous BAD, RANK

Malone MOSES, SAM

Malone, Moses
~ org. NBA

Malraux ANDRE

malt
~ beverage ALE, BEER, LAGER
~ dryer OAST
~ ender ASE, OSE

Malta
~ (abbr.) ISL
~ currency LIRA, LIRE

Maltese CAT
~ remark MEOW, MEW

"Maltese Falcon, The"
~ actor LORRE
~ actress ASTOR
Lorre, in ~ CAIRO

Malthus
~ subj. ECON
~ work ESSAY

maltreat ABUSE, HARM, MAUL

maltreatment ABUSE

malt-shop
~ freebie STRAW
~ order SODA

mama MATE

Mama
~ warning DONT, NONO

Mama ___ Elliot CASS

"Mama ___" SAID

"Mama ___ Knock You Out" SAID

Mamas and the ___, The PAPAS

"Mama Teach Me to ___" DANCE

mamba SNAKE

mambo DANCE

Mame
~ to Patrick AUNT

Mamie
~ predecessor BESS
~ spouse IKE

"Mamma ___!" MIA

mammal ANIMAL, APE, BAT, BEAST, CAT, COATI, COW, DEER, DOG, GOAT, HARE, HORSE, LION, MOLE, MULE, OTTER, PANDA, SEAL, TAPIR, TIGER, YAK
aquatic ~ OTTER, SEAL
bearlike ~ PANDA
burrowing ~ MOLE
Chinese ~ PANDA
flying ~ BAT
hoofed ~ TAPIR
large tropical ~ TAPIR
Malay ~ TAPIR
nocturnal ~ BAT
piglike ~ TAPIR
river ~ OTTER
shaggy ~ YAK
tailless ~ APE
Tibetan ~ PANDA
tropical American ~ COATI
web-footed ~ OTTER

mammalian
~ characteristic HAIR

"Mamma Mia"
~ group ABBA

mammoth ANIMAL, BIG, GIANT, LARGE, VAST

Mammoth ___ National Park CAVE

Mammoth Cave
~ st. KEN

man ADULT, MALE
~ Fri. ASST
~ starter FORE
family ~ DAD
Lady's ~ EARL, LORD, PEER
traveling ~ NOMAD

man ___ town ABOUT

man-___ DAY, HOUR, MADE, YEAR

___ man BEST, CON, JAVA, STRAW, YES

___ man (unanimously) TOA

___-man APE, PAC, YES

Man ISLE, RAY
~ (abbr.) ISL

"Man, The" STAN

"Man ___" HUNT

"Man ___ All Seasons, A" FOR

"Man ___ Came to Dinner, The" WHO

"Man ___ Fell to Earth, The" WHO

"Man ___ Knew Too Much, The" WHO

"Man ___ Loved Cat Dancing, The" WHO

"Man ___ Shot Liberty Valance, The" WHO

"Man ___ social animal" ISA

"Man ___ String" ONA

"Man ___ Thousand Faces" OFA

"Man ___ Tightrope" ONA

"Man ___ Woman, A" ANDA

"Man ___ Would Be King, The" WHO

Man.
  ~ neighbor ONT

"___ Man" IMA, NOONE, PIANO, RAIN, REPO, SOUL

"___ Man, The" BEST, GREAT, NEXT, OMEGA, THIN

"___ Man" (Kinks tune) APE

___ Man ("The Wizard of Oz" character) TIN

___-Man PAC

"man, a ___, a canal..., A" PLAN

manacle BIND

manacles IRONS

manage BOSS, COPE, FARE, LEAD, RUN
  ~ without SPARE

manageable EASY, TAME

management
  ~ level TIER
  ~ opposite LABOR

manager BOSS, EXEC, HEAD

Managua LAKE
  see also Spanish

"___ mañana!" HASTA

mañana LATER
  ~ marking TILDE

"Man and a Woman, A"
  ~ actress AIMEE

"___ Man and Little Boy" FAT

"Man and Superman"
  ~ author SHAW

"___ Man and the Sea, The" OLD

Manannan
  ~ father LER

man-at-___ ARMS

manatee ANIMAL, SIREN

Manaus CITY, PORT

___-man band ONE

"Man Called ___, A" HORSE, PETER

Manche
  ~ capital STLO

Manchester
  see British

Manchurian
  ~ boundary river AMUR

Mancini RAY

mandala ICON

"Mandalay" POEM

mandarin RULER

mandarin ___ ORANGE

mandate ACT, EDICT, FIAT, LAW, ORDER

mandated LEGAL

Mandeville, John SIR

Mandoki LUIS

mandolin
  ~ ancestor LUTE
  ~ part PEG

mandrake PLANT

mandrel AXIS

Mandrells TRIO

mandrill ANIMAL

mane CREST, HAIR
  ~ site NAPE

maned
  ~ animal LION
  ~ female MARE
  ~ grouping PRIDE

Manet
  ~ medium OIL

maneuver EASE, RUSE, STALL, WILE
  acrobatic ~ SPLIT
  aerial ~ SPIN
  dance ~ DIP

"___-Man Fever" PAC

"___ Man Flint" OUR

"Man for ___ Seasons, A" ALL

"man for all seasons," The MORE

Manfred MANN

"Manfred" POEM

"Man From ___, The" UNCLE

"Man From Laramie, The"
  ~ director MANN

"Man From the ___, The" ALAMO

"Man From U.N.C.L.E., The"
  ~ role SOLO

manganese METAL

manger CRIB
  ~ locale BARN
  ~ visitors MAGI

mangle MAIM, MAUL, PRESS, TEAR
  use a ~ IRON

mango TREE

"___ Man Goes Home, The" THIN

mangosteen TREE

mangrove TREE

mangy MEAN, SEEDY
  ~ mutt CUR

manhandle ABUSE, MAUL, PAW

Manhattan
  ~ (abbr.) ISL
  ~ district SOHO
  ~ ender ITE
  ~ ingredient RYE
  ~ Project participant UREY
  island off ~ ELLIS

"Manhattan"
  ~ director ALLEN

"Manhattan Murder Mystery"
  ~ actor ALDA
  ~ director ALLEN

manhunt
  ~ letters APB

"Man Hunt"
  ~ director LANG

"Manhunter"
  ~ director MANN

"Man I ___, The" LOVE

mania FAD

maniacal RABID

manicotti PASTA

manicurist
  ~ concern NAIL
  ~ implement FILE
  ~ item EMERY, ENAMEL

manifest ARGUE, ATTEST, CLEAR, OPEN, OVERT, RISE, SHOW, STATE

manifestation SIGN, TOKEN

manifesto EDICT, LAW

manifold GREAT

manikin MODEL

manila PAPER

Manila CITY

Manila ___ HEMP

Manilow
  ~ instrument PIANO

"Man in a Slouch Hat"
  ~ painter HALS

"Man in Black, The" CASH

"Man in the ___, The" MOON

"Man in the ___ Flannel Suit, The" GRAY

"Man in the ___ Mask, The" IRON

"Man in the Gray Flannel ___, The" SUIT

"Man in the Iron ___, The" MASK

"Man in the White ___, The" SUIT

maniple BAND

manipulate ANGLE, RIG, USE, WIELD

manipulation GAME, USAGE, USE

manipulative
  ~ often SLY
  ~ type USER

Manitoba
  ~ tribe CREE

mankind EARTH, LIFE, RACE

manlike MALE

Mann AIMEE, RON

manna
  Mormon ~ SEGO

Mann, Anthony
  ~ film of 1947 TMEN

Mann, Daniel
  ~ film of 1961 ADA

mannequin MODEL
  ~ part ARM

manner AIR, CUT, MIEN, MODE, SORT, STYLE, TYPE
  ~ of speaking IDIOM, TONE, USAGE
  ~ of walking STEP
  affected ~ AIRS
  dignity of ~ POISE
  in the ~ of ALA
  in this ~ THUS
  leisurely ~ EASE

___-mannered ILL

mannerism TIC, TRAIT

mannerless
  ~ one BOOR, CAD, OAF

___ manner of speaking INA

___ manners TABLE

___ Manners MISS

Manners, Miss
  ~ subject TACT

Mann, Michael
  ~ film of 1995 HEAT

Man of ___, The (Superman) STEEL

"Man of ___" ARAN, IRON, STEEL

___ Man of Alcatraz BIRD

"Man of a Thousand Faces, The" LON

Man of Steel
  ~ monogram ESS

man of the ___ HOUR, YEAR

"Man of the ___" WEST

"Man of the West"
  ~ director MANN

"Man of the Year"
  ~ magazine TIME

man-of-war BOAT, SHIP

Manolete
  ~ foe TORO
  see also Spanish

"Manon" OPERA
  ~ piece ARIA

man-on-the-moon
  ~ org. NASA

manor ESTATE, HOME
  ~ **house** ABODE
  ~ **master** LORD
  ~ **worker** SERF
  "Gone With the Wind"
    ~ TARA

manor house
  ~ **locale** ESTATE

___ man out ODD

"___ Man Out" ODD

Man O'War
  only horse to beat ~ UPSET

Man Ray
  ~ **art** DADA

man's
  no ~ land DESERT
  that ~ HIS

mansard ATTIC, ROOF
  ~ **part** EAVE

manservant VALET

Mansfield, Peter
  ~ **book, with "The"** ARABS

___-man show ONE

mansion ABODE, HOME, MANOR
  ~ **and grounds** ESTATE

man-size BIG, LARGE

"___ Man's Navy" THIS

"___ Man's Way" ONE

manta CAPE, RAY, WRAP

manteau CAPE

mantel LEDGE

mantelet CAPE

mantelpiece LEDGE

"Mantis"
  ~ **actor** REES

mantle CAPE, DRAPE, PALL, WRAP
  priest's ~ COPE

Mantle
  ~ **forte** RBI
  ~ **number** SEVEN

mantrap SIREN

___ Man Triathlon IRON

mantua WRAP

manual TEXT

manual arts
  ~ **workroom** SHOP

Manuel
  see Spanish

manufacture FAKE, LIE, MAKE

manufacturer
  ~ **come-on** REBATE
  ~ **tag** LABEL

manumit FREE, LOOSE

manus HAND

manuscript
  ~ **encl.** SASE
  ~ **notation** STET

~ polisher EDITOR
correct a ~ EMEND
fix a ~ EDIT

"___ Man Votes, The" GREAT

"Man Who ___ Liberty Valance, The" SHOT

"Man Who ___ to Dinner, The" CAME

"Man Who ___ Too Much, The" KNEW

"Man Who Fell to ___, The" EARTH

"Man Who Knew ___ Much, The" TOO

"Man Who Loved ___ Dancing, The" CAT

"Man Who Loved Cat Dancing, The" OATER

"Man Who Never ___, The" WAS

"Man Who Shot Liberty Valance, The" OATER
  ~ **actress** NOLAN

"Man With ___ Brains, The" TWO

"Man With ___ Red Shoe, The" ONE

"Man Without ___, The" ASTAR

"Man Without a ___, The" FACE, STAR

"Man Without a Country, The"
  ~ **author** HALE
  ~ **man** NOLAN

"Man With the ___, The" HOE

"Man With the Golden ___, The" ARM, GUN

"Man With the Hoe, The" POEM

"Man, Woman ___ Child" AND

Manx CAT
  ~ **cat's lack** TAIL
  ~ **language** ERSE

many ALOT, LOTS
  ~ **a millennium** EON
  ~ **times** OFT, OFTEN
  great ~ GOB, LOT, LOTS, SCAD
  not ~ FEW
  not too ~ SOME
  with ~ of AMID, AMONG

many-armed
  ~ **animals** OCTOPI

many-colored GAY
  ~ **stone** OPAL

"___ Many Crooks" TOO

"___ Many Girls" TOO

"___ Many Husbands" TOO

many moons ___ AGO

many-petaled
  ~ **flower** ROSE

"many splendored thing, A" LOVE

Mao ___-tung TSE

Maoris
  bird ~ once hunted MOA

map PLAN, PLAT
  ~ **abbr.** ALT, ATL, ISL, LAT, MTS, PAC, STR, TER, TERR
  ~ **book** ATLAS
  ~ **close-up** INSET
  ~ **dir.** ENE, ESE, NNE, NNW, SSE, SSW, WNW, WSW
  ~ **dot** ISLET
  ~ **line** ROAD, ROUTE, RTE
  ~ **out** DRAW, PLAN, PLOT, ROUTE
  blue spot on a ~ LAKE
  city ~ PLAT
  city ~ abbr. AVE
  city ~ features STS
  former ~ abbr. USSR
  right on the ~ EAST
  surveyor's ~ PLAT
  topographic ~ info ELEV
  word on a mall ~ HERE

___ map ROAD

maple TREE
  ~ **extract** SAP
  ~ **genus** ACER
  like a ~ leaf EROSE
  like ~ seeds ALAR

"Maple ___ Rag" LEAF

Maple Leaf COIN

"Maple Leaf ___" RAG

Maple Leafs SIX, TEAM
  ~ **milieu** ICE, RINK
  ~ **org.** NHL

mapmaker
  ~ **aid** GRID

mapping
  ~ **target** GENE

___ mapping GENE

mar BLOT, CHIP, DENT, HARM, SCAR, SPOIL, TAINT

Mar ___ Plata, Argentina DEL

Mar.
  ~ **follower** APR

Mara ADELE, TIM

marabou BIRD

Maracaibo CITY, LAKE, PORT

Marat
  see French

"Marat/___" SADE

marathon EVENT, RACE
  ~ **contender** RACER
  ~ **handout** WATER
  ~ **terminus** TAPE
  ~ **unit** MILE

"Marathon ___" MAN

maraud RIFLE, ROB, SACK

marauder HUN

Maravich PETE

marble AGATE, BALL, CAKE
  ~ **block** SLAB
  kind of ~ AGATE
  shooting ~ TAW

marble ___ CAKE

marbles GAME

Marc
  ~ **beloved** CLEO

Marcel CARNE
  see also French

march HIKE, MOVE, PARADE, TREK, TROOP
  ~ **along** TREAD
  ~ **ender** HALT
  ~ **on** MOB, PRESS
  ~ **up to the cannon's mouth** BEARD
  1965 ~ site SELMA
  exhausting ~ SLOG
  steal a ~ on LEAD

March ALEX, HAL
  ~ **date** IDES
  ~ **follower** APRIL
  ~ **sign** ARIES
  like a ~ hare DAFT, MAD
  one of the ~ sisters MEG
  youngest ~ daughter AMY

March ___ HARE

___ marche PAS

"Marche ___" SLAVE

Marchello, Peppi
  ~ **prop** BAT

marchers
  univ. ~ ROTC

marchesa RANK, TITLE

marchese RANK, TITLE

Marchese d'___ ESTE

March 15 IDES
  ~ **question** ETTU

marching
  ~ **order** HALT

"Marching Along"
  ~ **autobiographer** SOUSA

marching band
  ~ **member** TUBA

marchioness LADY, RANK, TITLE

"March King, The" SOUSA

"March Madness"
  ~ **org.** NCAA

"March of the ___, The" TOYS

March 17
  ~ **celebrants** IRISH

Marciano
  ~ **stat** KOS, TKO

Marco POLO
  see also Italian

Marconi
  ~ **invention** RADIO

___ Marcos, Tex. SAN

Marcus ALLEN

Marcus Aurelius CAESAR, ROMAN, STOIC
  physician of ~ GALEN
  see also Latin

Marcus Porcius ___ CATO

"Marcus Welby, M.D."
  Consuelo on ~ ELENA

Mardi ___ GRAS

Mardi Gras GALA
  ~ event PARADE
  ~ follower LENT
  ~ VIP REX

mare ANIMAL, HORSE, SHE
  ~ at times DAM
  ~ nest MESS
  ~ offspring FOAL
  by shank's ~ AFOOT
  shank's ~ LEG

Marengo HORSE, STEED

mares
  ~ eat them OATS

mare's ___ (hoax) NEST

mare's-___ cloud TAIL

mare's-nest MESS

Margaret MEAD
  ~ dad's monogram HST
  ~ mother BESS
  ~ nickname MEG, PEG

margarine OLEO
  ~ serving PAT

margarita
  ~ extra SALT
  ~ garnish LIME

Margaux
  ~ grandfather ERNEST

margin EDGE, END, HEM, LIMIT, LIP, PLAY, RIM, ROOM, SIDE, SPACE
  defeat by a narrow ~ NOSE
  narrow ~ HAIR, INCH

marginal
  ~ notation DELE, STET

marginalia NOTE

margin for ___ ERROR

Margot
  role for ~ LOIS

margrave LORD, PEER, TITLE

margravine LADY

___-Margret ANN

Margrethe II DANE

Marguerite
  see French

Maria
  see Spanish

"Maria ___" ELENA

___ Maria SANTA, TIA

"___ Maria" AVE

mariachi
  ~ wear SERAPE

Marian MAID

Mariana Trench
  like the ~ DEEP

Marianne MOORE

Marie STE
  see also French

"___ Marie" ROSE

Marie Antoinette REINE

Mariel CITY, PORT
  ~ grandpa ERNEST
  site of ~ CUBA

Marienbad SPA

___ Marie Saint EVA

Marilyn HORNE
  ~ real first name NORMA

marina
  ~ place COVE
  ~ rental SLIP
  ~ sight MAST, SPAR
  ~ site, often INLET
  ~ tenant BOAT

Marina
  see Russian

Marina del ___, Calif. REY

Marinaro
  ~ and others EDS

marinate SOAK, STEEP

marine NAVAL
  ~ fish SKATE
  ~ life ALGA, ALGAE
  ~ shelter COVE
  ~ starter AQUA, SUB, ULTRA

marine ___ ALGA

mariner GOB, SALT, TAR
  ~ heading ENE, ESE, NNE, NNW, SSE, SSW, WNW, WSW
  ancient ~ NOAH
  Norse ~ ERIC

mariners CREW

Mariners TEAM, TEN

Marino DAN

___ Marino SAN

Mario PEI
  see also Italian

Marion LORNE, ROSS

marionette TOY

Maris ADA, ROGER

maritime NAVAL
  ~ saint ELMO

Maritime ALPS

___ Maritime SEINE

marjoram HERB

mark AIM, ATTEND, BLOT, COIN, DOT, HEED, LABEL, SCAR, SEAL, SIGN, SPOT, TAG, TRAIT
  ~ down NOTE, REBATE, SLASH
  ~ ender UPS
  ~ off evenly RULE
  ~ of repetition DITTO
  ~ on one's character BLOT

  ~ replacement EURO
  ~ starter EAR, HALL, LAND, POST, TRADE, WATER
  ~ through ERASE
  ~ time SIT, WAIT
  ~ up EDIT
  auto-mishap ~ DENT
  be wide of the ~ ERR
  black ~ LIBEL, SMUT, TAINT
  Braille ~ DOT
  bumper ~ DENT
  diacritical ~ TILDE
  dirty ~ SMUT
  distinguishing ~ TRAIT
  easy ~ DUPE, LAMB, PREY, SAP, SETUP
  editor's ~ CARET, DELE, STET
  fair ~ CEE
  hunter's ~ PREY
  insert ~ CARET
  leaf-to-stem ~ SCAR
  leave a ~ SCAR
  low ~ DEE
  mediocre ~ CEE
  mind-changing ~ STET
  miss the ~ ERR
  near-failing ~ DEE
  off the ~ AMISS, AWRY, BAD
  on the ~ APT, TRUE
  pointillist ~ DOT
  printer's ~ CARET, DELE
  proofer's ~ CARET
  punctuation ~ DASH
  put a ~ on LABEL
  staccato ~ DOT
  time-saving ~ DITTO
  wide of the ~ FALSE
  x may ~ it SPOT

mark ___ TIME

Mark LANE, ROTH
  ~ to Tristan UNCLE

markdown SALE

marked CLEAR
  ~ down CUT

markedly EXTRA

marker CHIP, DEBT, IOU, PEN, SIGN, STELE, STONE, TAG
  boundary ~ RAIL, STAKE
  cribbage ~ PEG
  directional ~ SIGN
  finish-line ~ TAPE
  golf-hole ~ PIN
  highway ~ CONE
  meter ~ NEEDLE
  permanent ~ PEN
  slalom ~ GATE
  stickball ~ SEWER

market SELL, STORE, VEND
  ~ aid CART
  ~ downturn SLIDE
  ~ figure COST
  ~ order SELL
  ~ rise GAIN
  ~ value COST
  Attic ~ AGORA
  be in the ~ for SHOP
  farmer's ~ FAIR
  flea ~ FAIR
  flood the ~ GLUT
  off the ~ SOLD

  open-air ~ FAIR
  play the ~ TRADE
  visit the ~ SHOP

___ market FLEA

___-market MASS

marketable HOT

marketing
  ~ starter TELE

marketing budget
  ~ items ADS

marketplace
  Greek ~ AGORA

Market Square ARENA

Markey ENID

Markham MONTE
  ~ subject's tool HOE

Markham, Edwin POET
  see also poet

markhor GOAT

marking
  glacial ~ STRIA
  Mars ~ CANAL
  Morgan ~ STAR
  raccoon ~ MASK
  ruler ~ INCH
  Spanish ~ TILDE

Markle PETER

marks
  ballot ~ EXES
  get high ~ ACE

marksman SHOT
  ~ forte AIM
  ~ order FIRE

markup
  ~ basis COST

marl SOIL

"___ Marlene" LILI

Marley BOB

Marlins NINE, TEAM
  ~ home MIAMI
  ~ locale FLA

Marlo
  ~ man PHIL

Marlowe, Christopher POET
  see also poet

Marmaduke DOG, PET

marmalade CAT, JAM
  ~ ingredient PEEL, RIND

marmoset ANIMAL

marmot ANIMAL

Marne
  see French

maroon COLOR, RED

marooned ALONE

"Marouf"
  baritone in ~ ALI

Marple MISS

Marple, Miss JANE

marquee
  ~ **light** NEON
  full-house ~ SRO

marquess PEER

Marquette PERE

marquis LORD, MALE, PEER, RANK, TITLE
  rank below ~ EARL

Marquis DON

Marquis de ___ SADE

marquise GEM

marriage RITE, UNION
  ~ **locale** ALTAR
  ~ **symbol** RING
  before ~ NEE
  it's given in ~ HAND
  perform a ~ UNITE
  relative by ~ INLAW

"Marriage ___ Private Affair" ISA

"___ Marriage" SPITE

marriageable
  ~ **one** MISS

"Marriage Italian Style"
  ~ **actress** LOREN

"Marriage of Figaro, The" OPERA

marriage vow
  ~ **word** WORSE

married ONE

"Married to the ___" MOB

marrow CORE, ESSENCE, HEART, MEAT, SOUL

___ marrow BONE

marry ALLY, MELD, UNITE, WED
  ~ **off** PAIR
  ~ **on the run** ELOPE
  persuade to ~ WIN

Marryin' ___ ("Li'l Abner" character) SAM

Mars ARES, BAR, DEO, GOD, ORB
  ~ **marking** CANAL
  ~ **neighbor** EARTH
  from ~ ALIEN
  Remus, to ~ SON
  Romulus, to ~ SON

Marsala WINE
  ~ **meat** VEAL

Marsalis
  ~ **instrument** HORN

Marseille
  see French

Marseilles CITY, PORT
  see also French

marsh FEN, MIRE, MOOR, SINK, WASH
  ~ **bird** EGRET, HERON, RAIL, SNIPE
  ~ **plant** REED, SEDGE

marsh ___ GAS

___ marsh SALT

Marsh MAE

marshal ARRAY, LEAD, ORDER
  ~ **force** POSSE
  field ~ RANK

Marshal ___ TITO

Marshall ___ PLAN

"___ Marshall, Counselor at Law" OWEN

Marshall, Frank
  ~ **film of 1993** ALIVE

Marshall, Penny
  ~ **ex** ROB
  ~ **film of 1988** BIG

"Marshes of Glynn, The" POEM

marshmallow PLANT

"Marshmallow ___" MOON

marshy DAMP

Marston ___ (1644 battle site) MOOR

marsupial ANIMAL, EURO, KOALA
  ~ **for short** ROO

marsupium BAG, SAC

mart SHOP, STORE
  food ~ DELI

marten ANIMAL, FUR
  ~ **kin** SABLE

Martha RAYE

"Martha" OPERA

"Martha & ___" ETHEL

Martha's Vineyard ISLE
  ~ **(abbr.)** ISL

martial
  ~ **god** ARES

martial ___ ARTS, LAW

Martial POET, ROMAN
  see also poet

martial arts
  ~ **attire** BELT, GIS
  ~ **blow** CHOP
  ~ **legend** LEE

Martian ALIEN
  ~ **craft, maybe** UFO

Martians ETS

Martí, José POET
  ~ **homeland** CUBA
  see also poet

martin BIRD

Martin AMIS, DEAN, POPE, SHEEN, STEVE, TONY

"Martin ___" (Jack London book) EDEN

___ Martín SAN

Martin, Dean
  ~ **film of 1961** ADA
  ~ **nickname** DINO
  ~ **onetime partner** LEWIS
  ~ **role** HELM
  ~ **song topic** AMORE

~ specialty ROAST

Martinelli ELSA

martini
  ~ **garnish** OLIVE
  ~ **ingredient** GIN
  ~ **preference** DRY

Martinique ILE
  ~ **(abbr.)** ISL
  ~ **erupter** PELEE
  ~ **Mrs.** MME
  see also French

martinis
  like some ~ DRY

Martin Luther King ___ DAY

Martino
  ~ **and others** ALS

Martin, Steve
  ~ **birthplace** WACO
  King in a ~ **tune** TUT

Marton EVA

Marty
  ~ **portrayer** ERNEST

"Marty"
  ~ **director** MANN

martyr
  Roman ~ AGNES

marvel AWE

Marvell, Andrew POET
  see also poet

marvelous GOOD, RARE

Marvin LEE

marvy NEAT

Marx HARPO, RED
  ~ **ender** ISM, IST
  ~ **exhortation** UNITE
  ~ **instrument** HARP

Marx, Arthur HARPO

Marx, Groucho EMCEE, HOST, WIT
  ~ **brother** HARPO
  ~ **cap** BERET
  ~ **specialty** ADLIB
  glance from ~ LEER

Marxist LENIN, RED

Mary ASTOR, HART, URE
  ~ **boss at WJM** LOU
  follower of ~ LAMB
  like ~'s little lamb OVINE
  sound from ~'s pet BAA

Mary ___ (cosmetics name) KAY

Mary ___ Retton LOU

"Mary ___ a little lamb" HAD

___ Mary HAIL

Maryam d'___ ABO

Mary Baker ___ EDDY

Mary Kay ASH
  ~ **competitor** ESTEE
  ~ **rival** AVON

Maryland STATE
  ~ **state bird** ORIOLE

~ state tree OAK

Mary Montagu LADY

Mary Tyler ___ MOORE

"Mary Tyler Moore Show, The"
  ~ **actor** ASNER
  ~ **anchorman** TED

Mascagni
  ~ **flirt** LOLA
  ~ **opera** IRIS

mascara LINER
  ~ **applicator** WAND
  ~ **site** LASH

mascot
  Army ~ MULE
  Baylor ~ BEAR
  MGM ~ LEO, LION
  Navy ~ GOAT
  Princeton ~ TIGER
  West Point ~ MULE

masculine MALE

Masefield, John POET
  see also poet

mash PAP
  ~ **thoroughly** PUREE

___ mash SOUR

"M*A*S*H"
  ~ **actor** ALDA, FARR
  ~ **clerk** RADAR
  ~ **dwelling** TENT
  ~ **extra** NURSE
  ~ **extras** GIS, MPS
  ~ **meal** MESS
  ~ **network** CBS
  ~ **nurse** ABLE
  ~ **setting** KOREA
  O'Reilly of ~ RADAR

masher
  ~ **comeuppance** SLAP
  ~ **expression** LEER

M*A*S*H 4077 UNIT

mashie IRON

mask BLUR
  ~ **part** SLIT

___ mask FACE, GAS, SKI

"Mask"
  ~ **actress** CHER

"___ Mask, The" IRON

masked ___ BALL

Masked Man
  ~ **companion** TONTO

masking ___ TAPE

"Mask of Dimitrios, The"
  ~ **actor** LORRE

masochistic CRUEL

mason
  ~ **tool** HOD

mason ___ BEE

Mason-Dixon ___ LINE

Mason, James
  ~ **role** NEMO

Mason jar
~ **topper** LID

Mason, Perry
~ **assistant** DELLA
~ **occ.** ATT, ATTY
~ **org.** ABA
~ **profession** LAW
~ **title word** CASE
job for ~ CASE

___ **masqué** BAL

"Masque of Alfred, The"
~ **composer** ARNE

masquerade ACT, BALL, POSE

mass BAND, CAKE, CLOT, GOB, HEAP, HORDE, PILE, RITE, SIZE
~ **conclusion** AMEN
~ **of Mongols** HORDE
~ **place** ALTAR
~ **seating** PEW
~ **vestment** ALB
compact ~ WAD
ice ~ BERG
largest land ~ ASIA
small ~ WAD

mass ___ MEDIA

___ **mass** AIR

Mass
see Latin

Mass.
~ **ocean** ATL
see also Massachusetts

Massachusetts STATE
~ **cape** ANN, COD
~ **state tree** ELM
~ **town** SALEM

massage
~ **milieu** SPA
~ **need** OIL
in need of a ~,
  perhaps TENSE
need a ~ ACHE
needing a ~ ACHY

Massari LEA

masse
feed en ~ CATER

Massenet
~ **melody** ARIA
~ **work** OPERA

masses
vulgar ~ MOB

masseur
~ **employer** SPA
~ **need** OIL
~ **target** ACHE

Massey ILONA

massif RANGE

"Mass in B Minor"
~ **composer** BACH

massive BIG, FAT, GREAT, LARGE, VAST
~ **ref.** OED

mass transit
~ **unit** BUS, TRAIN

mast POLE, SPAR
~ **support** STAY

___ **-mast** HALF

master ACE, BEND, BOSS, GET, LEARN, LORD, OWNER, TAME
~ **hand** ACE, ADEPT
~ **in Arabic** SAHIB
~ **of ceremonies** EMCEE, HOST
~ **of counterpoint** BACH
~ **of the macabre** POE
~ **starter** POST
~ **stroke** FEAT
be ~ of KNOW
lord and ~ MATE
manor ~ LORD
past ~ ACE
PC ~ program DOS
shogi ~ DAN

master ___ KEY, PLAN

___ **master** OLD, PAST, TASK

masterful ADEPT

masterly ABLE

"Master Melvin" OTT

mastermind PLAN, PLOT, RUN

masterpiece GEM

masters
like some ~ OLD

Masters
~ **org.** PGA
three-time ~ champ SNEAD

Masters, Edgar Lee POET
see also poet

Masterson BAT, PETER, SKY
~ **colleague** EARP
~ **prop** CANE

Masterson, Mrs. Sky SARAH

"___ Master's Voice" HIS

mastery GRASP, GRIP, SWAY

masthead SIGN
~ **figs.** EDS
~ **listing** EDITOR

mastic RESIN

masticate BITE, EAT, GNAW

mastodon ANIMAL, GIANT

Mastroianni
~ **costar** LOREN

mat RAVEL, RUG
~ **starter** BATH
~ **victory** PIN

Mata ___ HARI

Matabele BANTU

matador
~ **foe, in Spanish** TORO

Matamoros CITY, PORT
see also Spanish

Matanzas
site of ~ CUBA

Matapan CAPE

match AGREE, BOOT, FIT, GAME, MATE, MEET, SUIT
~ **(against)** PIT
~ **division** SET
~ **end, often** TKO
~ **job** ARSON
~ **race runner-up** LOSER
~ **stopper** TKO
~ **the last raise** CALL
~ **up** PAIR
boxing ~ BOUT, MELEE
engage in a shouting
  ~ SCRAP
make a ~ WED
prepare for a ~ SPAR
put another ~ to RELIT
put a ~ to FIRE
start a ~ SERVE
struck a ~ LIT
wrestling ~ BOUT

___ **match** TEST

matched DUAL
~ **group** SET
~ **pair** TEAM
~ **set** PAIR

matching LIKE, SAME, TWIN
~ **outfit** SUIT
~ **piece** MATE
not ~ ODD

matchless ALONE, FIRST, GREAT, RARE

matchlock GUN

matchmaker
~ **from Olympus** EROS

mate BREED, BRIDE, LADY, PAIR, PAL

___ **mate** FIRST, SOUL

mateless LONE, ODD

matelot GOB, SALT, TAR

matelots CREW

___ **Mateo, Calif.** SAN

___ **mater** ALMA, PIA, TERRA

material
~ **holdings** ESTATE
~ **(suffix)** INE
abrasive ~ EMERY
assayed ~ ORE
atoll ~ CORAL
badge ~ TIN
barbell ~ IRON
basket-weaver's ~ OSIER
bead ~ NACRE
bed ~ BRASS
bog ~ PEAT
bonanza ~ ORE
building ~ STEEL
burlap ~ HEMP
button ~ NACRE
casa ~ ADOBE
cellular ~ DNA, RNA
chalkboard ~ SLATE
chest ~ CEDAR
chromosome ~ DNA
curtain ~ IRON
cutlass ~ STEEL
divot ~ SOD
doily ~ LACE

dressy ~ LAME, SATIN
drift ~ SNOW
drum ~ STEEL
evening-gown ~ SATIN
figurine ~ JADE
fissionable ~ ATOM
fist ~ IRON
floe ~ ICE
flue ~ SOOT
foil ~ TIN
foundry ~ METAL
galvanization ~ ZINC
garden ~ SOIL
genetic ~ DNA
girder ~ STEEL
glassmaking ~ SAND
glittery ~ LAME
golf-course ~ SOD
gown ~ SATIN
hacienda ~ ADOBE
hat ~ FELT, STRAW
Hawaiian carving ~ LAVA
highway ~ TAR
hosiery ~ NYLON
I-beam ~ STEEL
jacket ~ SUEDE
jewelry ~ AMBER
key ~ IVORY
knuckles' ~ BRASS
lawn ~ SOD
Little Pigs building ~ STRAW
loft ~ HAY
lustrous ~ SATIN
mawkish ~ CORN
mine ~ COAL, GOLD, ORE
model ~ BALSA
modeling ~ CLAY
nugget ~ GOLD
outfield ~ SOD
packaging ~ SARAN
paving ~ TAR
peat-bog ~ MOSS
pigeon ~ CLAY
pipemaker's ~ COB
potter's ~ CLAY
printed ~ TEXT
pueblo ~ ADOBE
raw ~ ORE
recyclable ~ SCRAP
reef ~ CORAL
reworking of ~ HASH
roofing ~ SLATE
scrimshaw ~ IVORY
sculptor's ~ CLAY
sheet ~ SATIN
shoe ~ SUEDE
sock ~ LISLE
Southwestern building
  ~ ADOBE
splicer's ~ GENE
sticky ~ GOO
stocking ~ LISLE, SILK
stole ~ SABLE
suit ~ SERGE
swatch of ~ SNIP
tablecloth ~ LINEN
thatching ~ REED
thread ~ LISLE
tie ~ REP
tole ~ TIN
tooth ~ ENAMEL
tower ~ IVORY
trap ~ SAND
trimming ~ LACE

__ material

turf ~ PEAT
tusk ~ IVORY
twine ~ SISAL
wash-and-wear ~ NYLON
waste ~ SCRAP
wicker ~ OSIER
see also fabric

__ material RAW

"Material __" GIRL

materialize EMERGE, LOOM, OCCUR

__ materials RAW

matériel GEAR
issue ~ ARM

maternal
~ **kin** ENATE

"__ maternelle" ECOLE

Maté, Rudolph
~ **film of 1950** DOA

mates
former ~ EXES
pas' ~ MAS

math
~ **calc.** PCT
~ **concept** SET
~ **course** ALG, TRIG
~ **expression** ISTO
~ **proof abbr.** QED
~ **pupil, at times** ADDER
~ **relation** RATIO
~ **rule** LAW
~ **starter** AFTER
~ **work** AREA
do a ~ **task** ADD

__ math NEW

mathematician
~ **letters** QED
x and y, to a ~ AXES

Matheson TIM

Mathewson GIANT
~ **stat** ERA

matinée SHOW
~ **hero** IDOL
~ **idol** MALE

"Matinee"
~ **director** DANTE

mating
~ **game** CHESS

"Mating __, The" GAME

matins HOUR

Matisse
~ **piece** ART
medium for ~ OIL

Matlock BEN
~ **matter** CASE
~ **occ.** ATT, ATTY
~ **org.** ABA
~ **profession** LAW

matriarch DAME
Biblical ~ LEAH, SARAH

matriculate ENTER

matrimony
commit ~ WED

matrix ARRAY, BED, MOLD

__-matrix printer DOT

matron DAME, LADY
~ **title** MRS

matron of __ HONOR

Matson OLLIE

Matt __ (Dean Martin role) HELM

matter CARE, CASE, ISSUE
~ **at hand** TOPIC
~ **for discussion** ISSUE
~ **of course** HABIT
~ **of retribution** TAT
~ **starter** ANTI
bit of ~ ATOM
front-page ~ NEWS
gray ~ HEAD
heart of the ~ CORE, GIST
in the ~ **of** ASTO
legal ~ RES
legislative ~ ACT
Mauna Loa ~ LAVA
particulate ~ DIRT, GRIT
printed ~ TEXT
state of ~ GAS, SOLID
subject ~ TOPIC
use the gray ~ IDEATE
viscous ~ SLIME
volcanic ~ SLAG

__ matter (intellect) GRAY

Matterhorn ALP
~ **echo** YODEL

matter-of-fact HONEST

"__ matter of fact..." ASA

Matthew
~ **original name** LEVI

Mattingly DON

mattock AXE, HACK, TOOL
use a ~ DIG

mattress BED, PAD
~ **covering** SHEET
~ **extra** PAD
~ **filler** AIR
~ **part** COIL
~ **preference** HARD
~ **support** SLAT
on the ~ ABED

__ mattress AIR

Matty ALOU

maturate RIPEN

mature ADULT, AGE, AGED, GROW, RIPE, RIPEN
~ **in a way** DUE
like ~ **cornstalks** EARED

matured RIPE

maturing
~ **agent** AGER

maturity
reach ~ RIPEN

matutinally EARLY

matzoh
~ **lack** YEAST
meal with ~ SEDER

Maud ADAMS

Maude
~ **portrayer** BEA

"Maude"
~ **producer** LEAR

Maugham
~ **novel, with "The"** HERO
~ **opus** RAIN

Maui ISLE
~ **(abbr.)** ISL
~ **greeting** ALOHA
~ **memento** LEI
~ **music maker** UKE
neighbor of ~ LANAI
see also Hawaiian

maul ABUSE, BEAT, HARM, MAIM, PAW

Mauna __ KEA, LOA

Mauna Loa
~ **locale** HILO
~ **matter** LAVA

maunder PRATE, RAVE

maundy
~ **money** ALMS

Maureen OHARA
~ **O'Sullivan's daughter** MIA

Maurice EVANS
see also French

Mauritania
~ **desert** SAHARA
~ **neighbor** MALI

Mauritanian ARAB

Mauritius
bird of ~, **once** DODO

Maurois ANDRE
Shelley biography by ~ ARIEL

mauve COLOR

maven GURU, PRO

Maverick BRET

"Maverick"
Mel, in ~ BRET

Mavericks FIVE, TEAM
~ **org.** NBA

mavin ACE

mavourneen
~ **home** EIRE, ERIN

Mavs FIVE, TEAM
~ **org.** NBA

maw CRAW, CROP, PIT

mawkish
~ **material** CORN

max.
~ **opposite** MIN

Max BAER, ERNST

Max __ Sydow VON

"__ Max" MAD

"__ Max Beyond Thunderdome" MAD

"Max Dugan Returns"
~ **actress** MASON
~ **director** ROSS

maxi
~ **terminus** ANKLE

maxim ADAGE, GNOME, MORAL, MOT, SAW

Maxim
see French

maximal TOP

Maximilian von __ SPEE

maximum ACME, CAP, LID, LIMIT, MOST, PEAK, TOP
reach a ~ PEAK

Maximus
Circus ~ ARENA

max out PEAK

Maxwell AUTO, CAR, ELSA, LOIS, SHANE, SMART
~ **contemporary** REO
~ **nanny** FRAN
Don Adams' ~ SMART

__ Maxwell (Dabney Coleman role) SLAP

may
be that as it ~ YET

May CAPE, ELAINE, JOE
~ **birthstone** AGATE
~ **ender** POLE
~ **event, familiarly** INDY
~ **honoree** MOM
~ **in French** MAI
~ **preceder** APR, APRIL

May __ APPLE, DAY, WINE

"Maybe __ ragged and funny..." WERE

Mayberry
~ **aunt** BEE
~ **druggist** ELLIE
~ **sheriff** ANDY
~ **tippler** OTIS
~ **youngster** OPIE

"Mayberry __" RFD

maybes IFS

"Mayday!" ALARM, ALERT, HELP, SOS

"Mayflower"
~ **pole** MAST

Mayflower Compact
~ **signer** ALDEN

"May I help you?" YES

"May I interrupt?" AHEM

"May it not be an __!" OMEN

__ May Lester ("Tobacco Road" character) ELLIE

Maynard KEN

Maynard, Ken
~ **film** OATER

___ **May, N.J.** CAPE

mayo
~ **holder** JAR

___ **May Oliver** EDNA

mayonnaise
~ **cover** LID

mayor
~ **bailiwick** CITY
former Palm Springs ~ BONO

Ma, Yo-Yo
~ **birthplace** PARIS
~ **instrument** CELLO

Mays, Willie GIANT

Maytag
~ **rival** AMANA

___ **May Wong** ANNA

Mazatlán CITY, PORT
see also Spanish

maze
~ **word** ENTER, START

Mazo ___ **Roche** DELA

mazuma GELT, MOOLA

mazurka DANCE

Mazursky PAUL

MB
part of ~ MEGA

MBA
~ **course** ECON

Mboya TOM

M.C. HOST

McAnuff DES

McArdle, Andrea
~ **role** ANNIE

MCAT
~ **passer, in time** DOC

McBain
~ **and others** EDS

"McCabe & ___ Miller" MRS

McCarey LEO

McCarthy PETER
~ **trunkmate** SNERD

McCartney PAUL
~ **album** RAM
~ **colleague** STARR
~ **instrument** BASS
~ **tune** JET

McCartney, Paul SIR

McCarver TIM

McClanahan RUE

McClellan
~ **adversary** LEE

McCloud SAM
~ **hometown** TAOS

McClurg EDIE

McCormack, John TENOR

McCowen ALEC

McCoy AMOS
a ~, to a Hatfield ENEMY, FOE

McCoys CLAN

"___ McCoys, The" REAL

"___ McCoy, the" REAL

McCrae, John POET
see also poet

McDaniel MEL

McDonald's
~ **giant M** LOGO

McDowall, Roddy
~ **character** APE

McElwee ROSS

McEnroe
~ **ex** ONEAL
~ **rival** BORG

McEntire REBA

McEveety, Vincent
~ **film of 1981** AMY

McFerrin, Bobby
sing like ~ SCAT

McGee, Fibber
~ **closet** MESS
~ **medium** RADIO

McGehee SCOTT

"___ McGinty, The" GREAT

McGovern, George
~ **st.** SDAK

McGrew DAN
~ **lady** LOU

McGuire DON
~ **and others** ALS

McGuire Sisters TRIO

McGwire, Mark
stat for ~ HOMER, RBI

MCI
~ **rival** ATT

McIntosh APPLE

McIntyre HAL

"___ McKee" SADIE

McKellen IAN

McKern LEO

McKinley
~ **and others** MTS
~ **birthplace** OHIO

McKinley, Mrs. William IDA

McKinney, Tamara
emulate ~ SKI

McKuen ROD

McLean, Va.
~ **org.** CIA

McMahon
~ **and others** EDS
~ **word** HERES

"McMillan ___ Wife" AND

McNally
~ **partner** RAND

McNaughton IAN

McNichols ARENA

McPherson AIMEE

McQueen STEVE

McShane IAN

McTavish
see Scottish

Md ELEM
101 for ~ ATNO

Md.
~ **institution** USNA
~ **neighbor** DEL
see also Maryland

MD
~ **assistants** RNS
~ **command** STAT
~ **org.** AMA
~ **request** EEG
~ **specialty** ENT
~ **zone** EDT, EST
future ~ **course** ANAT
see also Maryland

MDs DRS
~ **places** ERS, ORS

me SELF
~ **in French** MOI
~ **in German** MIR
belonging to ~ MINE
excuse ~ AHEM, OOPS
gag ~ **with a spoon** UGH
not ~ YOU
woe is ~ OHNO

"Me ___ My Shadow" AND

"Me, ___ I call myself" ANAME

Me.
see Maine

"___ Me" SUE, USE

"___ Me" (Rolling Stones tune)
TELL

ME
see Maine

Mead LAKE
~ **locale** SAMOA

meadow LAND, LEA, RANGE
~ **bird** LARK
~ **call** MOO
~ **ender** LARK
~ **mom** EWE
~ **mouse** VOLE
~ **remark** BAA, MAA, MOO

meadow ___ MOUSE, RUE

Meadowlands ARENA

meadowlark
~ **cousin** WREN

Meadowlark LEMON

Meadows, Jayne
~ **husband** ALLEN, STEVE

meager BARE, FEW, LEAN, MEAN,
POOR, SCANT, SLIM, SMALL,
SPARE, SPARSE, THIN

meal MESS
~ **choice** DISH
~ **counter** BAR
~ **feature** ENTREE
~ **for the humbled** CROW
~ **ingredient** CORN, OAT
~ **starter** OAT, SALAD
~ **with matzoh** SEDER
Army ~ MESS
clam ~ BAKE
group ~ MESS
have a ~ EAT
hearty ~ STEAK
horse ~ HAY
light ~ SALAD
"M*A*S*H" ~ MESS
mess-hall ~ HASH
morning ~ EGGS
Passover ~ SEDER
porcine ~ SLOP
quick ~ BITE

___ **meal** BONE, CORN

meals FARE
eat between ~ NOSH
place for alfresco ~ PATIO

mean BAD, BASE, CRUEL, EVIL,
NORM, POOR, SMALL, SNIDE,
UGLY
~ **kid** IMP
~ **partner** LEAN
~ **person** CUR, OGRE
make a ~ **face** SNEER
take to ~ READ

"Me and ___ Jones" MRS

meander BEND, RANGE, ROAM,
ROVE, RUN

"___ Me and My Gal" FOR

"Me and My Shadow"
~ **composer** ROSE

**"Me and You ___ Dog Named
Boo"** ANDA

**"Me and You and a Dog Named
___"** BOO

"Meanest ___ in the World, The"
MAN

meanie OGRE

meaning GIST, SENSE, TENOR
fraught with ~ DEEP
main ~ ESSENCE

meaningful DEEP
~ **relationship** LOVE

meaningless INANE

meanness HARM, SIN, SPITE

means AGENT, DOOR, KEY, MODE,
ORGAN, PATH, ROAD
~ **justifiers** ENDS
~ **of access** ENTREE, RAMP
~ **of escape** OUT
~ **of getting there** ROAD
~ **of ID** DNA
~ **of support** LABOR, LEG
~ **of transportation** AUTO,
BUS, CAB, CAR, TRAIN
by all ~ AMEN, YES
by ~ of VIA
having the ~ ABLE

mean-spirited LOW

meant
~ to be heard ALOUD

mean-tempered SOUR

meantime
in the ~ UNTIL

"Meanwhile, back at the ___..." RANCH

Meara ANNE

"___ Me a River" CRY

measly MEAN, MERE, POOR, SMALL

measure ACT, ASSESS, DOSE, LAW, METER, PACE, RATE, STEP, TIME, UNIT
~ marker BAR
distance ~ FOOT, INCH, METER, MILE, ROD, YARD
field ~ ACRE
surface ~ AREA
tailor's ~ TAPE

___ measure DRY, TAPE

measured EVEN, SLOW
~ amount DOSE
~ step PACE

measureless BIG, LARGE, VAST

measurements SIZE

measures
circle ~ RADII
printers' ~ EMS
take ~ ACT
type ~ EMS, ENS

measuring
~ device DIAL, RULE, RULER

meat GIST, SOUL
~ alternative TOFU
~ cut LOIN, TBONE
~ dish STEW
~ in Spanish CARNE
~ jelly ASPIC
~ serving CHOP
calf ~ VEAL
deli ~ HAM, SALAMI
exotic ~ EMU
kebab ~ LAMB
Marsala ~ VEAL
moisten ~ BASTE
piece of dark ~ LEG
red ~ STEAK
treat ~ CORN, CURE

___ meat RED

Meat ___ LOAF

meat-and-potatoes BASIC
~ concoction HASH

meatball DOLT, OAF

meathead DOLT, OAF

Meathead
~ mother-in-law EDITH

mecca
fashion ~ PARIS
gamblers' ~ RENO
Mormons' ~ UTAH
skiing ~ ASPEN, TAHOE

Mecca
~ country ARABIA

mech.
~ guru TECH

Mecham EVAN

mechanic
~ job LUBE
specialty ~ AUTO, CAR

mechanical
~ procedure ROTE

mechanism GEAR, TOOL

Med.
country on the ~ ISR, SYR

Medak PETER

medal AWARD
~ attachment CLASP
~ color GOLD
~ shape STAR
~ winner BEST, HERO
first-place ~ GOLD

"Medal ___ Benny, A" FOR

medallion MEAT, MEDAL, SEAL

meddle NOSE, PRY

meddler YENTA

meddlesome NOSY

Medea
~ sailed on it ARGO

"Medea" DRAMA

"___ Me Deadly" KISS

Medford DON

Medgar EVERS

media PRESS
~ excess HYPE
~ messages ADS
music ~ CDS

media ___ EVENT

___ media MASS

Media
modern ~ IRAN

median
~ strip MALL

mediate CALM, SETTLE

mediators
goal of some ~ PEACE

medic EMT
~ starter PARA

medical
~ beam LASER
~ charge FEE
~ deg. DDS
~ discovery CURE
~ exam EEG
~ fluids SERA
~ org. AMA
~ personnel DRS, MDS, RNS
~ specialty ENT
~ suffix ITIS
~ test XRAY
~ worker NURSE

medicalese CANT

medical school
~ subj. ANAT

Medicare
~ org. SSA

medicate DOSE, TREAT

medication PILL

Medici
~ in-law ESTE

medicinal HERB
~ amount DOSE
~ herb SAGE
~ medium PILL
~ plant ALOE
onetime ~ herb RUE

medicine CURE, TONIC
~ bottle VIAL
~ portion DOSE
folk ~ LORE
give ~ to DOSE
practice ~ TREAT
take one's ~ PAY

medicine ___ BALL, MAN, SHOW

Medicine ___, Alberta HAT

Medicine Bow RANGE

medicine testing
~ org. FDA

medico DOC

medieval
~ ballad LAY
~ blade SNEE
~ bondsman ESNE
~ defense MOAT
~ entertainer BARD
~ estate MANOR
~ instrument LUTE
~ laborer ESNE, SERF
~ quaff MEAD
~ shield ECU
~ strings LUTE
~ tale GEST, GESTE
~ title SIR
~ weapon AXE, MACE

Medina
~ country ARABIA
person from ~ ARAB

mediocre BLAH, FAIR, POOR, SOSO
~ mark CEE
~ writer HACK

meditate MUSE, PRAY

meditating RAPT

meditation
~ exercise YOGA

meditative
~ sect ZEN

Mediterranean SEA
~ country ITALY, SYRIA
~ feeder EBRO
~ island CAPRI, CRETE, ELBA, MALTA
~ N shore EUR
~ port ORAN
~ resort NICE
~ shipping center MALTA

~ staple OLIVE

medium AGENT, SEER, SIZE
~ skill ESP

"Medium ___" COOL

medium-dry SEC

medium-sized
~ sofa SETTEE

medley OLIO

Médoc WINE

___-me-downs HAND

___-med student PRE

Medusa
~ bearer AEGIS, EGIS
~ home OCEAN, SEA
~ tress SNAKE
she holds ~'s head ATHENA

meed DESERT, FEE

meek MILD, SHY, TAME
~ one LAMB
inheritance of the ~ EARTH

Meek
~ comic-strip partner EEK

meerkat
~ milieu DESERT

meerschaum PIPE
~ part STEM

Meese
~ and others EDS

meet ABUT, APT, DUE, FACE, FIT, GOOD, GREET, PAY, SEE
~ a raise CALL, SEE
~ defiantly DARE
~ event RACE
~ eyeball to eyeball DARE
~ head-on HIT
~ one's Waterloo LOSE
~ participant RACER
~ segment EVENT
~ the challenge COPE
~ the dawn ARISE
~ the requirements PASS
~ with SEE
barely make ends ~ EKE
broncobusters' ~ RODEO
orthographic ~ BEE
where ends ~ SEAM

___ meet SWAP

meeting DATE, DIET, TRYST
~ (abbr.) SESS
~ plan AGENDA
attend a ~ SIT
conduct a ~ HOLD
secret ~ TRYST

___ meeting CAMP

meetinghouse HALL

meeting place
Greek ~ AGORA

"Meet John ___" DOE

"Meet John Doe"
~ director CAPRA

"Meet Me ___ Louis" INST

Mefistofele
~ singer BASS, BASSO

"Mefistofele" OPERA
~ soprano ELENA

Meg RYAN
~ sister AMY

megacorporation GIANT

megalopolis CITY

megaphone HORN
~ inventor EDISON

megastar IDOL, LION

megatherian BIG, LARGE

megilla TALE, YARN

"___ Me Go, Lover" LET

Megrez STAR

mehitabel CAT
~ prey MOUSE
comment from ~ MEOW, MEW

"___ me in!" DEAL

"___ Me in St. Louis" MEET

"___ Me Irresponsible" CALL

"___ Me Kangaroo Down, Sport" TIE

"___ Me Kate" KISS

Mekong ___ DELTA

Mekong River
~ country LAOS
~ dweller LAO

Mel ALLEN, OTT

Melampus SEER

melancholy BAD, BLUE, ENNUI, LOW, PALL, SAD

mélange OLIO

Melanie
~ to Pittypat NIECE

Melba MOORE

Melba ___ TOAST

Melba, Nellie DAME, DIVA

Melbourne CITY
see also Australian

Melchior
~ and others MAGI
like ~ WISE

Melchior, Lauritz TENOR

melding
~ game CANASTA

melee ADO, RIOT, ROW, SCRAP, SETTO

Melendez BILL

Melete MUSE

mellifluous RICH, SWEET

mellow AGE, LOOSE, MELT, MILD, RIPE, RIPEN

Melmac
visitor from ~ ALF

melodeon ORGAN
~ part REED

melodic
far from ~ ATONAL

melodious SWEET
~ syllable TRA
not ~ ATONAL

melodrama GENRE, PLAY
~ man HERO
TV ~ SOAP

melodramatic
~ cry ALAS, OHO
~ one HAM
get ~ EMOTE

melody AIR, SONG, TUNE
bouncy ~ LILT
cantata ~ ARIA
Hindu ~ RAGA
identifying ~ THEME
oratorio ~ ARIA

melon COLOR
~ throwaway RIND

Melpomene MUSE
~ sister CLIO, ERATO

"Melrose Place"
~ role AMANDA

Mel's Diner
~ waitress ALICE, FLO, VERA

melt FUSE, HEAT, MOVE, RUN, THAW
~ away FADE

meltdown
~ site CORE

melter
ice ~ SALT

melting ___ POT

melting watch
~ artist DALI

Melville
~ captain AHAB
~ novel OMOO
~ setting OCEAN, SEA

Melvin LAIRD

"Melvin ___ Howard" AND

"___ Me Madam" CALL

member LEG, PART, UNIT
familia ~ NINA, NINO, PADRE, TIA, TIO

members
~ list ROLL

membrane SKIN

memento RELIC, TOKEN
Maui ~ LEI
opening-night ~ STUB
skiing ~, perhaps CAST

Memling HANS

Memnon
~ mother EOS

memo NOTE
~ abbr. ASAP, ATTN
~ starter INRE
debt ~ IOU
high-tech ~ EMAIL

___-mémoire AIDE

memorabilia ANA

memorable
~ period EPOCH, ERA

memoranda DATA

memorandum NOTE

Memorial Day
~ race INDY

memories
fond ~ PAST

"Memories of ___" ELD

memorization
~ process ROTE

memorize CON, KNOW, LEARN

memorized
have ~ KNOW

memory
~ flub LAPSE
~ jogger NOTE
~ unit BIT
commit to ~ LEARN
computer ~ CORE, RAM
jog the ~ CUE, PROD
plant in ~ ETCH

memory ___ LANE, TRACE

"Memory"
~ musical CATS

memos
prepare ~ TYPE

Memphis
~ river NILE
~ st. TENN

"Memphis ___" BELLE

memsahib LADY, MADAM

men
admitting ~ and women COED
for ~ only STAG
org. for tall ~ NBA
pert. to ~ MASC
where ~ are from MARS

"Men ___ Leave" DONT

"___ Men" TIN

"___ Men, The" TALL

___ Men (super-robots of comic books) METAL

menace LOOM, PERIL, RISK, SCARE
African ~ CROC, TSETSE
Hamelin ~ RAT
North Atlantic ~ FLOE
ranch ~ PUMA
red ~ FIRE

menacing BAD, EVIL
be vaguely ~ LOOM

menagerie
~ member ANIMAL, BEAST

mend ALTER, DARN, HEAL, KNIT, RESTORE, TAPE

mendacious FALSE

mendacity LIE, TALE

mended
~ the fire RELIT

Mendel's ___ LAW

mender
~ target HOLE

mendicant NEEDY
~ cry ALMS

"Mending Wall" POEM

Mendocino CAPE

"Men Don't ___" LEAVE

"Men Don't Leave"
~ actress LANGE

Menelaus
wife of ~ HELEN

"___ Men From Now" SEVEN

menhaden
~ cousin SHAD

menial HACK, HELP
~ work LABOR
~ worker PEON, SLAVE
~ workers HELP
medieval ~ SERF

"___ men in a tub..." THREE

"Men in Black"
~ concern ETS
~ menace ALIEN

meniscus ARC, BOW, LENS

Menlo Park
~ initials TAE
~ middle name ALVA
~ wizard EDISON

Mennonite SECT
~ sect AMISH

Mennonites SECT

"___ Me No Flowers" SEND

"___ Men of Missouri" BAD

"Men of the Fighting ___" LADY

"___ Men on a Horse" THREE

"___ me no questions..." ASK

mens HEAD

mens ___ in corpore sano SANA

men's
~ club FRAT
~ furnishing TIE

mensch MAN

"...___ men's souls" TRY

mental DAFT, MAD
~ discipline YOGA
~ faculties WITS
~ perception KEN
~ picture IDEA, IMAGE

mentalist (cont.)
~ **strain** STRESS
~ **suffering** PAIN
~ **telepathy** ESP
~ **turmoil** PANIC

mentalist
~ **asset** ESP

mention CITE, NAME, NOTE, RELATE, SAY
fail to ~ OMIT, SKIP, SLUR
make ~ **of** REFER
not to ~ ALONG, ALSO, AND, PLUS

mentioned
heretofore ~ ABOVE

mentis
compos ~ FIT, SANE
non compos ~ DAFT, MAD

mentor GURU, LAMP, SAGE

menu CARD, CARTE, FARE, MEAL
~ **listing** ENTREE, ITEM, SALAD
~ **phrase** ALA
~ **selection** ORDER
~ **symbol** ICON
lighten one's ~ DIET

Menuhin
~ **contemporary** STERN

"Men Working"
~ **indicator** CONE

"___ Me or Leave Me" LOVE

"___ me out" HEAR

"___ Me Out to the Ball Game" TAKE

meow CRY, MEW, NOISE

___ meow, the CATS

Mephistopheles SATAN
~ **forte** EVIL

Mephistophelian BAD

mephitic RANK

mephitis GAS, REEK

mercantilism TRADE

Mercator
~ **projection** MAP
~ **tome** ATLAS

merchandise LINE, SELL
~ **warning** ASIS
grouped ~ LOT
piece of ~ WARE

Merchandise ___ MART

merchandising
~ **event** SALE

merchantman BOAT, SHIP

merciful MILD
be ~ SPARE

merciless CRUEL, HARD, IRON

Merckx EDDY

mercury METAL

Mercury AUTO, CAR, DEO, GOD, ORB
~ **model** SABLE
~ **sun** SOL

number of ~
astronauts SEVEN

Mercury-___ 6 ATLAS

Mercury Theatre
~ **name** ORSON

Mercutio
~ **friend** ROMEO

mere BARE, LAKE, PURE

Meredith DON, LEE

merely ONLY

merengue DANCE

meretricious FALSE

merganser BIRD

merge BAND, CLOSE, FUSE, MELD, UNITE, WED
gradually ~ MELT

"Merge" SIGN

merger DEAL, UNION

"Merger ___" MANIA

"___ Me, Rhonda" HELP

meridian NOON

___ meridiem ANTE, POST

meringue
~ **ingredient** EGG
lemon ~ PIE

merino
~ **mama** EWE

merit DESERT, EARN, RATE

merit badge
~ **holder** SASH
~ **org.** BSA

merited DUE

meritocracy ELITE

meritorious GOOD

merits
weigh the ~ **of** ASSESS

Meriwether LEE

Merkel UNA

Merle OBERON

merlin BIRD

Merlin OLSEN, SEER

merlot WINE

mermaid
~ **feature** TAIL
~ **habitat** OCEAN, SEA

"Mermaids"
~ **actress** CHER

Merman ETHEL
~ **role** ANNIE, MESTA

Merriam EVE
~ **ex** ERNEST

merrie ___ England OLDE

"Merrily We ___" LIVE

"Merrimac" BOAT, SHIP

merriment GLEE

Merrivale, Henry SIR

merry GALA, GAY, GLAD
~ **king of nursery rhymes** COLE
~ **melody** LILT
~ **month** MAY
~ **sound** HAHA
make ~ AMUSE, REVEL

merrymaking GAME, RIOT

"Merry Widow, The"
~ **actor** LAMAS
~ **composer** LEHAR

Mertz ETHEL, FRED

Mervyn LEROY

mesa
~ **dweller** HOPI

Mesabi
~ **product** IRON, ORE
~ **workplace** MINE

Mesabi ___ RANGE

Mesa Verde
~ **sight** RUIN

mescal
~ **source** AGAVE

Mescalero TRIBE

mescals CACTI

mesh FIT, LACE, NET, SUIT, WEB
cotton ~ LENO

Meshed
~ **native** IRANI

meshes SNARE

meshuga MAD

meshwork LACE

mesmerize GRIP

mesmerized RAPT, UNDER

meson
~ **place** ATOM

___ meson ETA

mesophyte PLANT

Mesopotamia
~ **today** IRAQ

Mesopotamian
~ **kingdom** ELAM

Mesozoic ERA

mess HEAP, MEAL, SNARL
~ **around** LAG
~ **location** HALL
~ **up** ERR, HASH, MAR, SPOIL

mess ___ HALL, KIT

message CABLE, MEMO, NEWS, NOTE, THEME, WIRE
~ **bearer** PAGE
~ **concealer** CODE
~ **taker** AIDE
~ **via modem** EMAIL
AOL ~ MAIL
CompuServe ~ MAIL
E-mail ~, **maybe** MEMO
get the ~ HEAR, SEE
make a secret ~ ENCODE

postcard ~ NOTE
post-it ~ MEMO
Prodigy ~ MAIL
radio ~ SOS
secret ~ CODE
send a ~ **to** WIRE
Sun. ~ SER

"Message From ___" NAM

"Message received" ROGER

messages
media ~ ADS
modern ~ EMAIL

Messalina ROMAN

messenger AGENT, PAGE
~ **vehicle** BIKE
Greek ~ **of the gods** IRIS

messenger ___ RNA

mess hall
~ **amenity** TRAY
~ **meal** HASH

"Messiah"
~ **piece** ARIA

Messick DALE

Messina CITY, PORT

messuage ABODE, HOME

messy
~ **person** SLOB
~ **place** STY

Mestrovic IVAN

met
seldom ~ **with** RARE

Met
~ **diva** ALDA, HORNE
~ **man** BASS, BASSO, TENOR
~ **performance** OPERA
~ **production** AIDA, TOSCA
~ **role** AIDA, NORMA, TOSCA
~ **show-stopper** ARIA, SOLO
~ **singer** ALTO, BASS, BASSO, TENOR
~ **song** ARIA
~ **VIP** DIVA

metal BRASS, GOLD, IRON, STEEL, TIN, ZINC
~ **bar** INGOT
~ **clasp** CLIP
~ **deposit** LODE, ORE
~ **fastener** BRAD, NAIL
~ **framework** GRATE
~ **receptacle** CAN, PAN, POT, TIN
~ **refuse** SLAG
~ **rod** BAR
~ **thread** WIRE
~ **used in alloys** TIN, ZINC
car ~ STEEL
cast ~ INGOT
coat with ~ PLATE
crude ~ ORE
cutlery ~ STEEL
fuse ~ SMELT
heavy ~ ARMOR, BRASS, IRON, LEAD
lacquered ~ TOLE
malleable ~ TIN
painted ~ TOLE

precious ~ GOLD
pyrite ~ IRON
raw ~ ORE
refine ~ SMELT
rustproof ~ GOLD
sheathed with ~ CLAD
sheet of ~ PLATE
soft ~ TIN
thin ~ overlay WASH
write on ~ ETCH

___ metal SHEET

metallic
~ cloth LAME
~ element GOLD, IRON, TIN, ZINC
~ sound DING

metalware TOLE

metalworker
~ pin RIVET

metalworking
~ tool LATHE

metamorphose ADAPT, ALTER

"Metamorphosis"
~ poet OVID

metaphysical
~ poet DONNE

"Metaphysics of Morals"
~ author KANT

mete ALLOT
~ out DEAL, DOLE, SHARE

meteor
~ ender ITE
~ path ARC

meteoric FLEET

meteorological
~ adjective TIDAL
~ datum LOW
~ info TEMP
~ prefix AER, AERO

meter RATE, TEMPO, TIME
~ marker NEEDLE
~ money COIN
~ reading FARE
~ relative YARD
~ starter ALTI, NANO
~ user POET
cubic ~ STERE

meter ___ MAID

metered
~ transport CAB

meter maid
Beatles' ~ RITA

methane GAS

"___ Me That You Love Me, Junie Moon" TELL

"___ Me the Pillow You Dream On" SEND

method LINE, MODE, PATH, PLAN, RULE, STYLE
~ (abbr.) SYST
drying ~ DRIP
learning ~ ROTE

methodical EVEN, SLOW

methodize ORDER

methodology MODE

"___ Me Thrill Me Kiss Me" HOLD

Methuselah
~ to Enoch SON
grandson of ~ NOAH
like ~ AGED, OLD

meticulousness CARE, RIGOR

Metis MOON

"___ Me Tonight" LOVE

"Me, too!" DITTO

metric
~ composition ODE, POEM
~ quart LITER
~ starter ISO
~ surface measure ARE
~ syllable FOOT
~ unit ARE, GRAM, LITER, METER, STERE
~ weight TON

metric ___ (1,000 kilos) TON

metrical
~ foot IAMB
~ tribute ODE

metro CITY
~ alternative CAB

Metro GEO

Metrodome ARENA

metronome
~ setting TEMPO

"___ Metropole" CAFE

metropolis CITY

"Metropolis"
~ director LANG

metropolitan
~ area CITY
~ problem SMOG

Mets NINE, TEAM
~ stadium SHEA
~ star of 1969 AGEE

Metter ALAN

mettle DASH, GRIT, HEART, METAL, NERVE, SAND

Metz
see French

"___ Me Up" START

"___ me up, Scotty!" BEAM

Meuse
city on the ~ LIEGE, SEDAN

mew CAGE, CRY, LAIR, NOISE

"___ me with a spoon!" GAG

mewl CRY

mews ALLEY

Mex.
~ neighbor CAL, TEX

___-Mex TEX

Mexicali
~ locale BAJA
see also Spanish

"Mexicali ___" ROSE

"Mexicali Rose" OATER

Mexican
~ blanket SERAPE
~ city LEON
~ condiment SALSA
~ dollar PESO
~ export OPAL
~ figurine mineral ONYX
~ lizard IGUANA
~ peninsula BAJA
~ raccoon COATI
~ region BAJA
~ sauce MOLE
see also Spanish

"Mexican ___ Dance" HAT

"Mexican Hat ___" DANCE

"Mexican Spitfire"
~ actor ERROL

Mexico
see Spanish

Mexico City
~ newspaper, with "El" SOL
see also Spanish

Meyer RAY

Meyers ANN, ARI

mezza-mezza SOSO

mezzanine LOGE, TIER

"___ M for Murder" DIAL

Mg ELEM
12 for ~ ATNO

MGM
~ lion LOGO
~ mascot LEO, LION
~ motto start ARS
~ sound effect ROAR
~ workplace LOT
part of ~ METRO

mgmt.
~ VIP CEO

mgr. EXEC

mi NOTE
it's two past ~ SOL

"Mi ___ es su..." CASA

MI
see Michigan

Mia SARA
emulate ~ ADOPT

"___ Mia" CARA

"___ Mia!" MAMA

Miami CITY, PORT
~ basketballers HEAT
~ county DADE
~ gridder, for short CANE
~ state OHIO
summer hrs. in ~ EDT
winter hrs. in ~ EST

Miami's ___ Bowl ORANGE

miaow MEW, NOISE

miasma GAS

miasmal RANK

mice
~ to cats PREY

Mich.
~ neighbor IND, OHIO, ONT
see also Michigan

Michael ANGEL, CAINE, MANN, MOORE

"Michael"
~ character ANGEL

"Michael Collins"
~ actor REA

Michaelmas
~ daisy ASTER

"Michael, Row the Boat ___" ASHORE

Michaels LORNE
~ and others ALS

Michael's
~ "Disclosure" star DEMI

Michelangelo
~ sculpture PIETA
~ work ARTE
see also Italian

Michele LEE

Michelin
~ product TIRE

Michelle MAMA

___ Michelle Gellar SARAH

Michener
~ genre SAGA
~ novel ALASKA, IBERIA, SPACE

"Mi chiamano Mimi" ARIA

Michigan LAKE, STATE
~ canals SOO
~ city TROY
~ college ALMA

Michigan/Ontario
~ region SOO

Mick MARS

Mickey MOUSE
one of ~'s wives AVA

Mickey ___ MOUSE

mickey-mouse SMALL

mickle BIG, LARGE

Micmac TRIBE

micraner ANT

microbe GERM

microbiologist
~ gel AGAR
Russian-born ~ SABIN

microbrewery
~ product ALE

Micronesian
~ island YAP

micronutrient IRON, ZINC

microorganism GERM

microscope
~ **accessory** SLIDE
~ **part** LENS

___ microscope ION

microscopic SMALL, TEENY, TINY, WEE
~ **amount** TRACE
~ **animal** AMEBA
~ **organism** ALGA

Microsoft
~ **magnate** GATES
~ **product** DOS
~ **rival** APPLE

microwave HEAT, OVEN
~ **brand** AMANA
~ **maybe** BAKE
use the ~ ZAP

mid-___ car SIZE

midafternoon THREE

midair
hang in ~ POISE

Midas
~ **touch** GOLD

midday NOON
~ **break** NAP

middie
~ **counterpart** CADET

middies
~ **sch.** USNA

middle EYE, MIDST
~ **layer of the eye** UVEA
~ **of a sleeve** ELBOW
~ **way** MEAN
~ **X or O** TAC
bend in the ~ SAG
farther from the ~ OUTER
in the ~ of AMID, AMONG

middle ___ AGE, CLASS, EAR

middle-___ AGED

Middle ___ AGES, EAST

"Middle Age Crazy"
~ **actress** DERN

Middle Earth
~ **beast** ORC

Middle East
~ **airline** ELAL
~ **bread** PITA
~ **garment** ABA
~ **nation** IRAN, IRAQ, ISRAEL, OMAN, YEMEN
~ **resident** ARAB, IRANI, OMANI
~ **ruler** AMIR, EMEER, EMIR
former ~ **leader** SADAT
see also Mideast

middleman AGENT, REP
colonial ~ ALDEN

"Middlemarch"
~ **author** ELIOT

middle-of-the-___ ROAD

middling FAIR, SOSO
~ **grade** CEE

middy
~ **opponent** CADET

Mideast
~ **belief** ISLAM
~ **capital** ADEN, SANA
~ **carrier** ELAL
~ **country** IRAN, IRAQ, ISRAEL, OMAN, YEMEN
~ **ctry.** ISR, SYR
~ **dam** ASWAN
~ **desert** NEGEV, SINAI
~ **export** OIL
~ **flier** ELAL
~ **grp.** PLO
~ **gulf** ADEN, OMAN
~ **habitant** ARAB
~ **head of state** AMIR, EMEER, EMIR
~ **leader** ASSAD
~ **missile** SCUD
~ **money** RIAL
~ **name** ALI
~ **native** ARAB, IRANI, OMANI
~ **palace area** HAREM
~ **peninsula** SINAI
~ **port** ADEN
~ **potentate** AGA, AGHA
~ **theocracy** IRAN
~ **title** AGA, AGHA, IMAM
former ~ **alliance** UAR
see also Middle East

midevening TEN

midge GNAT

midget RUNT, SMALL

___-midi APRES

Midianite
~ **king** REBA

Midler BETTE

midmonth
~ **day** IDES

midmorning NINE, TEN

midnight
~ **opposite** NOON
~ **or beyond** LATE
burn the ~ **oil** CRAM, LABOR, SLAVE, TOIL

midnight ___ SUN

"Midnight ___" LACE, RUN

"Midnight ___, A" CLEAR

"Midnight ___ to Georgia" TRAIN

"___ Midnight" AFTER

"Midnight at the ___" OASIS

"Midnight Lace"
~ **actress** DAY

Midnight Sun
~ **dweller** LAPP

midocean
in ~ ASEA, ATSEA

Midori ITO

midpoint MEAN, MIDST

midsection CORE

midshipman
~ **counterpart** CADET

midst DEEP, EYE
in the ~ of AMONG
in the ~ of (prefix) INTER

Midsummer ___ (June 23) EVE

"Midsummer Night's ___, A" DREAM

"Midsummer Night's ___ Comedy, A" SEX

"Midsummer Night's Dream, A"
fairy king of ~ OBERON

"Midsummer Night's Sex Comedy, A"
~ **director** ALLEN

midterm EXAM, TEST

midway
~ **attraction** RIDE

Midway ISLES
~ **alternative** OHARE
~ **loc.** CHI
~ **stat** ARR, ETA

Midwest
~ **city** OMAHA
~ **Indian** OSAGE, UTE
~ **sight** SILO
~ **st.** ILL, IND, KAN, NDAK, NEB, NEBR, SDAK
~ **state** IOWA

midyear EXAM, TEST

mien AIR, CAST

Mies van ___ Rohe DER

miff ANGER, IRK, PEEVE, RILE, UPSET

miffed SORE, WARM
more than ~ MAD

might ARM, MAIN, MAY, SINEW
~ **partner** MAIN
with ~ **and main** HARD

mightier
~ **than** ABOVE, OVER
it's ~ than the sword PEN

"Might I interrupt?" AHEM

mighty BIG, LARGE
~ **mite** ATOM
~ **one of myth** TITAN
~ **predator** LION
~ **tree** OAK
the high and ~ ELITE

mighty ___ oak ASAN

Mighty ___ MOUSE

"Mighty ___ Young" JOE

"Mighty Aphrodite"
~ **director** ALLEN

"Mighty Barnum, The"
~ **director** LANG

Mighty Ducks SIX, TEAM
~ **milieu** ICE, RINK
~ **org.** NHL

Mighty Joe Young APE

"Mighty Lak' ___" AROSE

"Mighty Lak' a ___" ROSE

"Mighty Morphin Power Rangers: The Movie"
~ **villain** OOZE

Mighty Mouse HERO
~ **garb** CAPE

mignon
~ **ender** ETTE

"Mignon" OPERA

migraine ACHE

migrant HOBO
~ **worker** NOMAD

migrate LEAVE, MOVE, TREK

migration TREK

migrator NOMAD

migratory
~ **bird** GOOSE, LOON, TERN

___ Miguel (largest of the Azores) SAO

mikado RULER

"Mikado"
one of a ~ **trio** MAID

mike
~ **adjunct** AMP
~ **problem** ECHO
place for a ~ LAPEL

"___ Mike" Tyson IRON

Mikhail TSAR
~ **spouse** RAISA
~ **successor** BORIS
see also Russian

Mikita STAN

mil.
~ **address** APO
~ **boat** LST
~ **folks** GIS
~ **group** REG
~ **offender** AWOL
~ **program** ROTC
~ **rank** COL, ENS, GEN, SGT
~ **rank category** NCO
~ **vehicle** LST

"Mila 18"
~ **author** URIS

"Milagro Beanfield ___, The" WAR

Milan CITY
~ **ender** ESE
~ **site** ITALY
city near ~ LODI
see also Italian

Milano
see Italian

Milan's La ___ SCALA

mild EASY, GOOD, MEEK, TAME
~ **disagreement** SPAT
~ **expletive** DRAT, EGAD, GAD, PSHAW
~ **spice** MACE

mildew MOLD, PLANT, ROT, SPOIL

mildewed BAD

mildewy DAMP

mild-mannered MEEK, TAME

"Mildred Pierce"
  ~ actress ARDEN
  ~ author CAIN

mile
  ~ ender POST, STONE
  ~ equivalent AMISS

___ mile SEA

"___ Mile, The" LAST

Mile High Center
  ~ architect PEI

Mile High Stadium ARENA

___-mile limit THREE

milepost SIGN

miler RACER
  ~ concern PACE

miles
  ~ away AFAR
  ~ per hour RATE

Miles SARAH, VERA

milestone EVENT, SIGN
  pilot's ~ SOLO

Milestone LEWIS

milieu AREA, SCENE, SITE, STAGE
  cop's ~ BEAT

___ Militaire ECOLE

militant
  ~ campus org. SDS
  ~ god MARS
  ~ Olympian ARES

militarize ARM

military
  ~ addr. APO
  ~ address SIR
  ~ base POST
  ~ bed COT
  ~ boat LST
  ~ command ATEASE, FIRE
  ~ commando SEAL
  ~ decoration MEDAL
  ~ defense STAND
  ~ facility BASE
  ~ group ARMY, CADRE
  ~ grp. REG
  ~ headquarters BASE
  ~ installation SILO
  ~ melody TAPS
  ~ need AMMO
  ~ offender AWOL
  ~ officers BRASS
  ~ org. SAC, USAF, USN
  ~ prog. ROTC
  ~ quarters CAMP
  ~ rank COL, ENS, GEN, SGT
  ~ rank category NCO
  ~ signal TAPS
  ~ student CADET
  ~ subdivision UNIT
  ~ tactic SIEGE
  ~ training group CADRE

~ tyro CADET
~ vacation LEAVE
~ vehicle LST
~ VIPs BRASS
campus ~ org. ROTC
elite ~ group ATEAM
see also army, GI

militia ARMY

milk TAP
  ~ alternative CREAM
  ~ a scene HAM
  ~ component FAT
  ~ grader USDA
  ~ in French LAIT
  ~ in prescriptions LAC
  ~ quantity PINT
  ~ snake ADDER
  ~ source COW, EWE, GOAT
  ~ train LOCAL
  like supermarket ~ DATED
  skim ~ lack FAT

milk ___ RUN, SNAKE, TOAST, TOOTH

___ milk ICE

milk carton
  ~ info DATE

milksop PANSY

"___ Milk Wood" UNDER

milky
  ~ gemstone OPAL

Milky Way BAR
  ~ unit STAR

mill PLANT
  ~ about STIR
  ~ ender DAM, STONE
  ~ input IRON
  ~ output STEEL
  ~ pond LAKE
  ~ to a cent TENTH
  go through the ~ BEAR

___ mill GIN, STEEL

Milland RAY

Millay EDNA

___ Millay ("Red River" woman) TESS

Millay, Edna St. Vincent POET
  see also poet

millennia AGES

millennium AGE
  ~ unit YEAR
  many a ~ EON

Miller ANN, BEER, MERLE, ROGER, STEVE

Miller, George
  ~ film of 1994 ANDRE

millerite ORE

Miller, Joaquin POET
  see also poet

Miller, Joe
  ~ stock-in-trade CORN

Millett KATE

Millie AUNT, DOG, PET
  Bushes' ~ DOG, PET

millinery
  ~ item HAT

million
  ~ ender AIRE
  ~ (prefix) MEGA
  cool ~ PILE
  not in a ~ years NEVER
  one in a ~ GEM, PEARL, RARE

millionaire
  ~ digs ESTATE
  ~ home MANOR

"Millionaire ___ Christy, A" FOR

"Millionairess, The"
  ~ actress LOREN

"___ Million B.C." ONE

"Million Dollar ___" LEGS

"___ Million Dollar Man, The" SIX

millions MINT

"___ Millions" KID

million-selling GOLD

millipede
  ~ mover FOOT

Mill, James SCOT

Millo DIVA

"Mill on the Floss, The"
  ~ author ELIOT

mills
  ten ~ CENT

Mills ENOS, ERIE

millstone LOAD, ONUS

millstream RACE

Milne, A.A.
  ~ character OWL, POOH, ROO
  ~ first name ALAN

Milo O'___ SHEA

Milosevic SERB

milquetoast PANSY
  like a ~ MEEK

Milstein
  teacher of ~ AUER

Miltie, Uncle BERLE
  ~ contemporary SID

Milton AGER, BERLE

Milton, John POET
  ~ nutbrown brew ALE
  see also poet

Milwaukee
  ~ beverage BEER

Mimas MOON

mime APE, APER

mimeograph
  ~ inventor EDISON

Mimi
  see French

mimic APE, APER, ECHO
  natural ~ MYNA

mimosa TREE

min. INST
  ~ division SEC
  many ~ HRS

minacity PERIL

minatory BAD

mince CHOP, DICE, HASH, PIE

minced FINE
  ~ oath DARN, DRAT

mincemeat PIE

mind ATTEND, CARE, HEAD, HEED, OBEY, SELF, SIT, TEND
  ~ other people's business PRY
  ~ picture IMAGE
  ~ reader SEER
  ~ reader's talent ESP
  ~ the baby SIT
  ~ the phone MAN
  ~ the plants WATER
  bear in ~ HEED
  be of one ~ AGREE
  blow one's ~ AMAZE, AWE, DAZE, STUN
  bring to ~ EVOKE
  come to ~ ARISE
  cross one's ~ OCCUR
  fire of the ~ ARDOR
  fix in one's ~ CON, ETCH, LEARN
  frame of ~ MOOD, STATE, TONE
  have a ~ to LIKE
  have in ~ AIM, KNOW, MEAN, PLAN
  in one's right ~ SANE
  let one's ~ wander SLEEP
  make up one's ~ ACT, ELECT, SET
  of a ~ (to) APT, PRONE
  of sound ~ ABLE, SANE
  of unsound ~ MAD
  out of ~ ASIDE
  out of one's ~ DAFT, LOCO, MAD
  peace of ~ EASE
  presence of ~ POISE
  rational ~ EGO
  revolve in the ~ PORE
  set one's ~ to BEND
  state of ~ MOOD, TONE
  strength of ~ METAL

mind-___ SET

"___ mind!" NEVER

Mindanao
  ~ volcano APO

mind-changing
  ~ mark STET

___-minded CLOSE, EVIL, FAIR, LIKE, LOW, OPEN, SMALL

mindful ALERT, AWARE, WARY
  ~ of ONTO

mindfulness CARE, HEED

mindless INANE

mind reader
~ **gift** ESP

minds
of two ~ TORN

mind's ___ EYE

mind-set HABIT, MOOD

mind's-eye
~ **view** IMAGE

Mindy
~ **portrayer** PAM

mine BORE, DIG, HOLE, PIT
~ **car** TRAM
~ **detector** SONAR
~ **entrance** ADIT
~ **find** COAL, LODE, ORE, SEAM
~ **in French** AMOI
~ **in part** OURS
~ **shaft** PIT
~ **vapor** DAMP
coal ~ PIT
not ~ HERS, HIS
yours and ~ OUR, OURS

___ mine GOLD

"___ Mine" ENEMY, HES

"___ Mine" (Dorsey tune) NOT

"Mine eyes have ___..." SEEN

Mineo SAL

miner
~ **discovery** ORE
~ **land** CLAIM

Miner STEVE

mineral METAL, OIL, ORE
~ **deposit** RUN, SEAM
~ **in seawater** SALT
~ **nutrient** IRON, ZINC
~ **springs** SPA
~ **suffix** ITE
~ **vein** LODE
Australian ~ OPAL
green ~ JADE
lustrous ~ SPAR
Mexican figurine ~ ONYX
nutritive ~ IRON, ZINC
orange-red ~ SARD
rare ~ GEM
shiny ~ MICA
silicate ~ MICA
soft ~ TALC
translucent ~ MICA, OPAL

mineral ___ OIL, WATER

___ minérale EAU

mineralogist
~ **suffix** ITE

"___ Miner's Daughter" COAL

Minerva DEA
~ **symbol** OWL
Greek counterpart of
~ ATHENA

minestrone
~ **follower, maybe** PASTA

minesweeper
fictional ~ CAINE

miney
~ **follower** MOE

Ming
~ **thing** VASE

mingle MELD, STIR, WED

mingling
~ **with** AMID, AMONG
averse to ~ SHY

Mingo
~ **portrayer** AMES

Ming the Merciless
daughter of ~ AURA

Mingus
~ **instrument** BASS

mini SMALL

miniature SMALL, TINY, TOY, WEE

miniaturizing
~ **suffix** ETTE

minibike MOTOR

mini-craze FAD

mini-explosion POP

mini-feud SPAT

minikin SMALL

minim DROP, NOTE

minimal LEAST, SCANT, TOKEN
~ **amount** BIT, HOOT, IOTA, TAD
~ **evidence** SHRED
~ **money** CENT, SONG

minimum LEAST, LIMIT

minimum ___ WAGE

mining
~ **layer** STRIP
~ **tool** GAD

minion TOOL

miniseries
~ **maybe** EPIC
landmark ~ ROOTS

minister ABBE, AGENT, ATTEND, HELP, PADRE, TREAT
~ **(abbr.)** REV
~ **home** MANSE
~ **to** HEAL, NURSE, RESTORE, SERVE, TEND
~ **(to)** CATER
Japan's first prime ~ ITO
prime ~ HEAD

"Ministry of ___" FEAR

"Ministry of Fear"
~ **director** LANG

"___ Miniver" MRS

"Miniver Cheevy" POEM

mink ANIMAL, COAT, FUR
~ **alternative** ERMINE
~ **home** RANCH
~ **relative** OTTER

___ mink RANCH

Minkoff ROB

Minn.
~ **neighbor** MAN, NDAK, ONT, SDAK
see also Minnesota

minnesinger BARD

Minnesota STATE
~ **baseball player** TWIN

Minnesota Fats
~ **game** POOL
~ **need** CUE
~ **shot** CAROM

Minnie MOUSE, PEARL

"Minnie ___ Moskowitz" AND

"Minnie the Moocher"
~ **name** CAB

minnow
~ **eater** TERN
~ **family member** CARP

minnows BAIT

Minoan
~ **island** CRETE

minor SMALL, TEEN
~ **business part** COG
~ **damage** DENT
~ **mistake** SLIP
~ **player** COG, EXTRA
~ **prophet** HOSEA
~ **quake** TREMOR
~ **task** ERRAND
no longer a ~ ADULT

___ Minor ASIA, URSA

minor-league MEAN, SMALL

Minos
~ **home** CRETE

Minot
~ **st.** NDAK

Minotaur OGRE
~ **home** CRETE

Minsk CITY
see also Russian

minstrel BARD, POET
~ **instrument** LUTE
~ **poem** LAY

minstrel ___ SHOW

mint COIN, HERB, MAKE, NEW, PILE
~ **family member** SAGE
~ **jelly** ASPIC
~ **jelly accompaniment** LAMB
~ **output** CENT, COIN, DIME
in ~ **condition** NEW
not ~ USED

mintage CASH

minty
~ **taste** TANG

minuet DANCE
~ **movement** TRIO

minus BAR, LESS, SANS, SAVE
~ **entry** DEBIT

minus ___ SIGN

minuscule SMALL, TEENY, TINY, WEE

minute SMALL, TEENY, TINY, WEE
~ **div.** SEC
~ **hands, essentially** RADII
~ **(prefix)** NANO
any ~ ANON, SOON
at the last ~ LATE
laugh a ~ PANIC
this ~ NOW, STAT

minute ___ HAND, STEAK

___ minute LAST

___ minute (soon) INA

Minute ___ RICE

minutes
in a few ~ ANON, SOON
keep ~ ENTER, NOTE
sixty ~ HOUR

"___ Minutes More" FIVE

"___ Minutes With Andy Rooney, A" FEW

minx BRAT, GIRL, LASS, SNIP

Miocene ___ EPOCH

Mir
~ **milieu** SPACE

Mira STAR

miracle SIGN

"Miracle ___" MILE

"___ Miracle" ITSA

"Miracle Mile"
~ **actor** AGAR

"Miracle of ___ Lady of Fatima, The" OUR

"Miracle of Our ___ of Fatima, The" LADY

"Miracle on 34th Street"
~ **actress** OHARA

"Miracle Woman, The"
~ **director** CAPRA

"Miracle Worker, The"
~ **director** PENN
~ **role** ANNIE, HELEN

mirage DREAM, ERROR
~ **perhaps** OASIS

Miranda MOON

mire CLAY, DIRT, FEN, OOZE, SINK, SLOP, SOIL
drag through the ~ LIBEL, SHAME, SLUR, SMEAR

Miriam
~ **brother** AARON, MOSES

Mirren, Helen
~ **film of 1984** CAL

mirror APE, ECHO
~ **fogger** STEAM
~ **in a way** ECHO
~ **product** IMAGE

mirror ___ IMAGE

mirth GLEE

mirthful GAY, RIANT
~ **sound** HAHA

miry DAMP

misadd ERR

misapplication WASTE

misapply WASTE

misappropriate STEAL, TAKE

misbehave SIN

misbehaver IMP

"__ Misbehavin'" AINT

misbehaving BAD
~ **child** BRAT, IMP, TYKE

miscalculate ERR

miscalculation ERROR

miscellaneous ODD
~ **info** ANA

miscellany HASH, OLIO
literary ~ ANA

Mischa AUER

mischief ANTIC, HARM
~ **maker** DEMON, IMP
fond of ~ SLY
make ~ LARK

mischief-maker ELF

mischievous ARCH, BAD, ELFIN, SLY
~ **child** IMP, TYKE
~ **creature** ELF

misconception ERROR

misconstruction ERROR

miscreant CAD, DOG

miscue ERR, ERROR, TRIP

misdeal ERR

misdeed SIN

misdemeanor ERROR

misdo ERR

mise
~ **en scène** SET

misemploy WASTE

misemployment WASTE

miserable BAD, MEAN, POOR, SAD, VILE

"__ Misérables" LES

"Miserere" PSALM

miserly CLOSE, MEAN, NEAR, SMALL

misery ACHE, BANE, EVIL, ILL, PAIN, WOE

"Misery"
~ **actor** CAAN

misfit LOSER
social ~ NERD

misfortune EVIL, ILL, RUIN, WOE

misgiving FEAR, PANG

misgivings
have ~ **about** RUE

misguess ERR

misguided OFF

mishandle ABUSE

mishap
banana-peel ~ SLIP
hose ~ RUN, SNAG
parking ~ DENT

mishmash HASH, MESS, OLIO

misinform LIE

misjudge ERR

mislay LOSE

mislead BELIE, CON, DUPE, LIE

misleader LIAR

misleading FALSE
~ **move** RUSE

misled OFF

mislike HATE

miso
~ **ingredient** SOY

mispickel ORE

misplace LOSE

misplay ERR, ERROR

misprint ERROR

mispronounce LISP

mispronunciation ERROR

misread
~ **lines** ERR

"Misreadings"
~ **author** ECO

misreckon ERR

misrepresent BELIE, COLOR, LIBEL, LIE

misrepresentation LIE, TALE

misrepresented BAD

miss GIRL, LADY, LASS, MAID, OMIT, TITLE
~ **a syllable** ELIDE
~ **at a ball** DEB
~ **out on** LOSE
~ **partner** HIT
~ **the mark** ERR
any ~ HER, SHE
impossible to ~ OVERT
junior ~ KID
Scottish ~ LASS
sophisticated ~ DEB

__ miss NEAR

Miss
~ **in Japanese** SAN
~ **in Spanish** SRTA

Miss __ (Dora Jessie Saint)
READ

"Miss __ at the Cirque Fernando" LOLA

"Miss __ Regrets" OTIS

"Miss __ Thompson" SADIE

Miss.
neighbor of ~ ALA, ARK, TENN, TEX
see also Mississippi

__ Miss OLE

Miss America
~ **attire** SASH
~ **wear** TIARA
former ~ **host** ELY

"Miss America"
~ **author** STERN

"__ Miss Brooks" OUR

missed
~ **item** BOAT

"__ Miss Gibbs" OUR

missile ARROW, NIKE, SHOT
~ **housing** SILO
~ **limitation acronym** START
~ **of yore** ARROW, SPEAR, STONE
~ **part** CONE
~ **path** ARC
~ **storage site** SILO
ballistic ~ THOR
blowgun ~ DART
bow ~ ARROW
catapult ~ STONE
certain ~ SAM
classroom ~ ERASER
Cupid's ~ DART
feathered ~ DART
golf ~ BALL
Gulf War ~ SCUD
heckler's ~ EGG
Keystone ~ PIE
Olympic Games ~ SHOT
US ~ TITAN

missing GONE, LOST
search for a ~ **person** TRACE

"Missing"
~ **actor** SHEA

mission TASK
NASA ~ APOLLO
scrap a ~ ABORT
Texas ~ ALAMO

Mississippi STATE
~ **feeder** RED
~ **flatboat** ARK
~ **mud** SILT
~ **river vessel** STR

Mississippi __ DELTA

Mississippi River
~ **state** IOWA

missive NOTE

missives MAIL

"Miss Mama __" AIMEE

Missouri STATE
~ **neighbor** IOWA
~ **tributary** OSAGE
lead-in for ~ USS

Missouri River
~ **city** OMAHA
~ **tribe** OTO, OTOE

misspeak ERR

misspell ERR

misspend WASTE

misspent LOST
~ **youth** PAST

"Miss Saigon"
~ **setting** NAM

misstatement
make a ~ LIE

misstep ERR, ERROR, SLIP, TRIP

Miss Universe
~ **prize** TIARA

missus BRIDE

mist BATHE, RAIN, STEAM

mistake BONER, ERROR, LAPSE, TRIP
~ **remover** ERASER
make a ~ ERR, TRIP
minor ~ SLIP

mistake maker
~ **cry** OOPS

mistaken FALSE, OFF
be ~ ERR

mistakenly AMISS

mistakes
list of ~ ERRATA
make ~ ERR

mister MALE
~ **in German** HERR
~ **in India** SAHIB, SRI
~ **in Spanish** SENOR

Mister SIR

Mister Ed HORSE
~ **locks** MANE

"Mister Roberts"
~ **director** LEROY
Pulver in ~ ENS

Misti, El
~ **fallout** ASH

mistletoe PLANT
~ **mo.** DEC
~ **ritual** KISS
~ **unit** SPRIG

Mistral, Gabriela POET
see also poet

mistreat ABUSE, MAUL

mistreatment ABUSE

mistress GIRL, LADY, OWNER
past ~ ACE

mistrust FEAR

mistrustful LEERY

misty DAMP, DIM, WET

misty-__ EYED

"__ Misty for Me" PLAY

misunderstand ERR

misunderstanding ERROR

misuse ABUSE, HARM, WASTE
~ **an infinitive** SPLIT

mit
~ **in French** AVEC
~ **in Spanish** CON

MIT
~ **grad** ENG
part of ~ INST, MASS, TECH

Mitchell DIVA, ERIC, LEONA
~ **heroine** OHARA
~ **mansion** TARA

mite ATOM, BIT, DAB, DOT, IOTA, JOT, PEST, SCRAP
mighty ~ ATOM

miter HAT

Mithras SUN

mitigate ABATE, ALLAY, CUT, EASE, HELP, SLAKE

"Mitla Pass"
~ **author** URIS

mitt HAND

Mitterrand
see French

mittimus EDICT, ORDER

Mitty, Mrs. NAG

___ **mitzvah** BAR, BAS, BAT

"Mi Vida Loca (My Crazy ___)" LIFE

mix BEAT, MELD, STIR
~ **up** ADDLE
moonshine ~ MASH
potter's ~ PASTE

mix-___ UPS

___ **mix (hiker's snack)** TRAIL

Mix TOM

mixed
~ **bag** OLIO, STEW
~ **breed** MULE
~ **drink** FLIP
~ **greens** SALAD
they may be ~ NUTS

mixer DANCE
~ **for rum** COLA
bar ~ SODA, TONIC, WATER

mixologist
~ **measure** SHOT
~ **milieu** BAR

Mix, Tom
~ **film** OATER
~ **horse** TONY

mixture HASH, OLIO
brickmaking ~ LOAM

"___ Miz" LES

Mizar STAR

mizzen MAST, SAIL

mizzen-royal MAST

mizzle MIST, RAIN

mizzling RAINY

MLB
~ **stat** ABS, ERA, HRS, RBI
~ **stats** BAS

"M'Liss"
~ **author** HARTE

MLK
title for ~ REV

Mlle.
~ **in Spanish** SRTA
canonized ~ STE
married ~ MME

Mme.
~ **in Spanish** SRA
~ **in the US** MRS

Mn ELEM
25 for ~ ATNO

MN
see Minnesota

Mneme MUSE

mnemonic
~ **device** CUE

Mnemosyne
~ **daughter** CLIO, ERATO

MNO
~ **on a phone** SIX
telephone's ~ SIX

___-**mo** SLO

Mo ELEM
42 for ~ ATNO

Mo.
~ **neighbor** ARK, ILL, IOWA, KAN, KEN, TENN
president from ~ HST
see also Missouri

MO
see Missouri

moa BIRD
~ **cousin** KIWI

moan CRY, NOISE
~ **and groan** CARP

mob ARMY, BAND, CREW, GANG, HOST, MASS, PRESS, RING, ROUT
~ **ender** STER
~ **scene** RIOT

Mobil
~ **product** GAS, OIL

mobile ART
~ **home** ABODE, TENT, TEPEE
~ **starter** AUTO, SNOW

mobile ___ HOME, PHONE

Mobile
~ **st.** ALA

"___-Mobile, The" GNOME

mobilize BAND, RAISE
~ **again** REARM

Möbius
~ **creation** STRIP

Möbius strip
a ~ has only one SIDE

mobs
like some ~ UGLY

mobster HOOD
~ **weapon** GAT

Moby Dick
~ **domain** OCEAN, SEA

"Moby Dick"
~ **captain** AHAB
The Crossed Harpoons, in ~ INN

moccasin PAC, SHOE
water ~ SNAKE

mocha COLOR

Mocha
~ **land** YEMEN

___ **Mochis** LOS

mock APE, FALSE, GIBE, HOOT, RAG, SHAM, TEASE, TWIT
~ **modesty** POSE

mock ___ ORANGE

mock-___ UPS

"Mocker Mocked, The"
~ **artist** KLEE

mockery IRONY

mocking TART

mockingbird APER

mod NEW
~ **ender** ULE

mode CUT, STYLE
~ **of travel** AUTO, BUS, CAR, JET, LIMO, PLANE, RAIL, SST, TRAIN
à la ~ NEW
in the ~ of ALA

___ **mode** ALA

model CAST, IDEAL, MAKE, MOLD, TYPE, WEAR
~ **airplane** TOY
~ **asset** POISE, SMILE
~ **before assembly** KIT
~ **binder** GLUE
~ **material** BALSA
~ **maybe** SIT
~ **need** AGENT, REP
~ **of fidelity** ENID
~ **often** POSER
~ **of virtue** SAINT
be a ~ POSE
beefcake ~ STUD
display ~ DEMO
four-door ~ SEDAN
hardness ~ NAIL
high-fashion ~ IMAN
live ~ POSER
role ~ HERO, IDEAL, IDOL
small ~ MINI
worn-out ~ CRATE

___ **model** ROLE, SCALE

"Model ___ the Marriage Broker, The" AND

model airplanes
wood for ~ BALSA

model builder
~ **need** GLUE

modeling
~ **buy** KIT
~ **material** CLAY

~ **wood** BALSA
do ~ POSE

Model T
~ **contemporary** REO

modem
messages via ~ EMAIL

moderate ABATE, ALLAY, BATE, COOL, EASE, EASY, FAIR, HELP, MILD, SLAKE, SLOW, SOBER, SOSO, TAME

moderato TEMPO

modern NEW
~ **agora** MALL
~ **ailment** STRESS
~ **arena** DOME
~ **art form** DADA
~ **courtyard** PATIO
~ **messages** EMAIL
~ **(prefix)** NEO
~ **starter** ULTRA
~ **surgical tool** LASER
~ **wall display** OPART
like some ~ music ATONAL
not ~ OLD

modern ___ DANCE

"Modern Fables"
~ **author** ADE

modernistic NEW

modernize REDO

"___ Modern Maidens" OUR

"Modern Times"
~ **tune** SMILE

modest POOR, SHY, SMALL, SOSO
~ **hand** PAIR

"Modest Proposal, A" TRACT

modesty
mock ~ POSE

modicum ATOM, BIT, DAB, DROP, IOTA, MITE, PART, SCRAP, SHRED
~ **commodity** SENSE

modification
without ~ ASIS

modifications
make ~ to ADAPT, ALTER, AMEND, EDIT, EMEND

modified
it's often ~ NOUN

modify ADAPT, ALTER, AMEND, EDIT, FIT, SUIT

Modigliani
~ **specialty** ART

modish CHIC, SMART

Modoc TRIBE

modulation TONE

module UNIT

modus operandi LINE

Moe BERG

Moe, Tommy
emulate ~ SKI

Moffo ANNA, DIVA
　~ solo ARIA

Mogadishu
　model from ~ IMAN

"Mogambo"
　Clark's ~ costar AVA

Mogollon RANGE

mogul NABOB, RULER, TSAR
　business ~ TITAN

Mogul ERA
　~ capital of India AGRA

mohair
　~ maker GOAT

Mohammed
　~ religion ISLAM
　~ son-in-law ALI
　birthplace of ~ MECCA

Mohave TRIBE

Mohawk TRIBE
　~ craft CANOE
　city on the ~ UTICA
　noted ~ sporter MRT

Mohawk River Valley
　~ tribe ONEIDA

Mohican TRIBE

Mohs scale
　1 on the ~ TALC

mohur COIN

moidore COIN

moiety HALF, PART

moil LABOR, PLOD

"__ moi le déluge" APRES

__ Moines, Iowa DES

Moises ALOU

moist DAMP, RAINY
　~ ender URE

moisten BASTE, BATHE, DIP,
　WATER, WET
　~ hemp RET
　~ meat BASTE
　~ with water WASH

moistened WET

moisture DAMP, STEAM, WATER
　extract ~ from BLOT
　lacking ~ ARID, DRY, SERE
　lose ~ SEEP
　morning ~ DEW

moistureless ARID, DESERT, DRY,
　SERE

moisturizer
　skin ~ ALOE

Mojave DESERT, TRIBE
　~ plant AGAVE
　~ scenery CACTI
　like the ~ ARID, DRY

molar TOOTH
　~ malady ACHE

molasses
　~ product RUM
　like ~ SLOW

move like ~ LAG, OOZE

mold CAST, CUT, ILK, LAST, MAKE,
　ORDER, PLANT, ROT, SORT,
　SPOIL, STAMP, TURN
　casting ~ DIE
　cast in the same ~ LIKE
　plaster ~ CAST
　printing ~ MAT
　rye ~ ERGOT
　shoemaker's ~ LAST

Moldavia
　~ once SSR

molder DIE, FADE, ROT

molding
　~ profile ESS
　decorative ~ TRIM
　s-shaped ~ OGEE
　window ~ LEDGE

moldy BAD, STALE
　get ~ ROT

mole AGENT, ANIMAL, SPY

molecular
　~ biology topic DNA, GENE,
　RNA
　~ component ATOM

molecule IOTA, MITE
　~ part ATOM
　genetic ~ RNA

"Mole People, The"
　~ actor AGAR

moleskin
　~ color TAUPE

molest ABUSE

Molière
　~ girl ELISE
　~ milieu DRAMA

Molinaro
　~ and others ALS

Moline, III.
　~ manufacturer DEERE

__ moll GUN

mollify ALLAY, CALM, EASE,
　PLEASE, TAME

mollusk SNAIL
　bivalve ~ CLAM

mollusks
　tentacled ~ OCTOPI

molly PET

Molly BERG, YARD

"Molly __ Me" AND

mollycoddle SPOIL

Molokai
　~ banquet LUAU
　~ greeting ALOHA
　~ neighbor OAHU
　see also Hawaiian

molt CAST, SHED

molten
　~ rock LAVA

molybdenite ORE

molybdenum METAL

mom
　dad's ~ GRAM, NANA

Mom
　~ month MAY
　on ~'s side ENATE

MOMA
　~ artist DALI, KLEE
　~ exhibit OPART
　part of ~ ART
　some ~ works DADA

mom-and-pop SMALL

Mombasa CITY, PORT

moment TIME
　~ of truth TEST
　at the ~ NOW, YET
　in a ~ ANON, SOON
　make every ~ count LIVE
　momentous ~ DDAY

"__ Moment, The" LOST

momentarily ANON, SOON

"Momentary __ of Reason, A"
　LAPSE

momentous GREAT
　~ moment DDAY

__ moment's notice ATA, ONA

"__ moment too soon!" NOTA

momentum
　~ component SPEED

mommy
　mommy's ~ GRAM, NANA

mon __ AMI

"Mona __" LISA

Monaco
　city near ~ NICE

monad ATOM

Mona Lisa
　~ attribute SMILE

"Mona Lisa"
　~ singer COLE, NAT

monarch LORD, RULER
　~ in French ROI
　~ in Latin REX
　~ in Spanish REY
　absolute ~ TSAR
　Mardi Gras ~ REX
　Mideast ~ AMIR, EMEER, EMIR
　Saint Petersburg ~ TSAR
　tragic ~ LEAR

"...monarch of __ survey" ALLI

monarchy REIGN
　Hindu ~ NEPAL

monarque ROI

monastery
　~ head ABBE, ABBOT

Monastery of __ IONA

monastic ABBE, ABBOT
　~ chamber CELL
　~ leader ABBOT
　~ title DOM, FRA

monaural
　not ~ STEREO

monazite ORE

Monday
　~ feeling BLAH

"Monday, Monday"
　~ half MAMAS, PAPAS

monde
　~ starter DEMI

__ monde BEAU

"Mondo __" CANE

"Mondo Cane"
　~ song MORE

Monet
　~ contemporary DEGAS
　~ mastery ART

monetary
　~ punishment FINE
　it may be ~ GAIN

money BILL, CASH, COIN, GELT,
　GOLD, LOOT, MOOLA, PAPER
　~ back REBATE
　~ dispenser ATM
　~ drawer TILL
　~ for an AARP member IRA
　~ for a poor box ALMS
　~ in the bank ACCT, ASSET
　~ maker DIE, MINT
　~ medium PAPER
　~ owed DEBT
　~ source LOAN
　~ to burn PILE
　~ unit COIN
　Chilean ~ PESO
　Common Market ~ ECU,
　EURO
　earnest ~ of a sort BAIL
　exchange for ~ SELL
　folding ~ ONES, TENS
　get-out-of-jail ~ BAIL
　hard ~ CASH
　Italian ~ LIRA, LIRE
　lots of ~ PILE, WAD
　made of ~ RICH
　make ~ COIN, EARN, MINT
　maundy ~ ALMS
　meter ~ COIN
　Mideast ~ RIAL
　minimal ~ CENT, SONG
　Omani ~ RIAL
　paper ~ BILL, NOTE
　Philippines ~ PESO
　pin ~ COIN
　place ~ BET
　pocket ~ COIN
　provide ~ at interest LOAN
　put ~ in ANTE, BET
　right on the ~ AOK
　risk ~ BET
　San Marino ~ LIRA, LIRE
　spend ~ PAY
　take the ~ and run FLEE
　throw ~ around SPEND
　throw ~ away WASTE
　throw good ~ after
　bad WASTE
　Turkish ~ LIRA
　up-front ~ ANTE
　Vatican City ~ LIRA, LIRE

money ___

money ___
Zurich ~ **maven** GNOME
see also coin

money ___ ORDER, PLANT

___ money BIG, HOT, MAD, OLD, PAPER, PIN, SEED, SMART

"Money ___, The" PIT

"Money ___ everything!" ISNT

moneybox CHEST, SAFE

money clip
~ **contents** ONES, TENS, WAD

moneyed FAT, RICH

money-grubbing CRASS

moneyless NEEDY

"Money, Money, Money"
~ **band** ABBA

Mongibello ETNA

Mongkut, King
~ **domain** SIAM
~ **nanny** ANNA
~ **portrayer** YUL

Mongol ASIAN
~ **invader** TATAR
~ **monk** LAMA
~ **ruler** KHAN
~ **turf** ASIA
ancient ~ HUN
nomadic ~ **tribe** HORDE

Mongolia
~ **location** ASIA
like ~ ARID, DRY

___ Mongolia INNER, OUTER

Mongolian
~ **desert** GOBI
ancient ~ TATAR

Mongols
mass of ~ HORDE

mongoose ANIMAL
~ **foe** COBRA

"Mongoose"
boxing's ~ MOORE

mongrel CUR, DOG

Monica SELES
~ **brother on "Friends"** ROSS

___ Monica, Calif. SANTA

Monicelli MARIO

moniker NAME, TAG

Monique
see French

monitor ATTEND, NOTE, SEETO

"Monitor" SHIP

monk ABBE, ABBOT
~ **garb** HABIT
~ **of yore** ESSENE
~ **quarters** CELL
~ **superior** ABBOT
~ **title** DOM, FRA
Asian ~ LAMA

Monkees
~ **movie** HEAD

~ **song of 1967** SHE

monkey ANIMAL, APE
~ **business** LARK, PLAY
~ **cousin** ORANG
~ **pot** TREE
~ **puzzle** TREE
~ **suit** DRESS, TAILS

monkey ___ BARS

Monkey
the ~ DANCE

"Monkey ___, monkey do" SEE

monkey-see-monkey-do
~ **practitioner** APER

monkeyshine ANTIC, DIDO

monkfish LOTTE

Monk, Thelonious
~ **music** BOP

mono
~ **successor** STEREO

mono-
~ **cousin** UNI

monocle LENS

monogram
~ **unit** INIT
1952 election ~ AES, DDE

monograph THEME, TRACT

monolith STONE

monomachy DUEL

"Mon Oncle"
~ **actor** TATI
~ **director** TATI

monopolist
~ **demand** ALL

monopolize HOG

Monopoly GAME
~ **card** DEED
~ **cube** DIE
~ **need** DICE
~ **piece** DEED, HOTEL
~ **player's collection** RENT
~ **prop** HOTEL
~ **properties** RRS
~ **token** IRON

monosaccharide
~ **suffix** OSE

monotone
~ **maybe** BORE

monotonous ARID, DRY, FLAT, SLOW

monoxide
carbon ~ GAS

Monroe EARL
~ **successor** ADAMS

monsieur
~ **in German** HERR
~ **in Spanish** SENOR

Monsieur MAN, TITLE
see also French

"Monsieur Verdoux"
~ **actress** RAYE

Monsignor TITLE

monsoon RAIN

monsoonal WET

monster BEAST, DEMON, GIANT, OGRE

___ monster GILA

"Monster"
~ **band** REM

"Monster ___" MASH

"Monster ___ Box" INA

monsters
bug-eyed ~ ETS

monstrance CASE

monstrous BIG, GREAT, LARGE

Mont.
~ **neighbor** ALB, ALTA, IDA, NDAK, SDAK
see also Montana

Montague
~ **heir** ROMEO

Montaigne
~ **work** ESSAY

Montale, Eugenio POET
see also poet

Montana JOE, STATE
~ **motto starter** ORO
~ **neighbor** IDAHO
~ **tribe** CROW

Montana Indian CREE

Montand YVES

Mont Blanc ALP
see also French

monte
three-card ~ GAME

Monte ___ (second highest Alpine peak) ROSA

___ Monte DEL

Monte Carlo
~ **action** BET

Montego ___ BAY

Montego Bay CITY, PORT

Montemezzi ITALO

"Monterey ___" POP

montero CAP, HAT

Monte Rosa ALP

Monterrey
see Spanish

Montevideo CITY
see also Spanish

Montez LOLA

Montgomery WARD, WES
~ **milieu** ETO
~ **sch.** ASU
~ **st.** ALA

month MOON
~ **for showers** APRIL
~ **fraction** WEEK

Aries ~ APRIL
fool's ~ APRIL
Hebrew ~ ADAR
Kentucky Derby ~ MAY
kind of ~ LUNAR
merry ~ MAY
Purim ~ ADAR
Ram's ~ APRIL
showery ~ APRIL
Spanish ~ ENERO
spring ~ APRIL, MAY

monthly ORGAN, PAPER, SHEET

months
twelve ~ YEAR

Monticello ESTATE
~ **nickname** TOM

Montmartre
see French

Montreal CITY, PORT
~ **baseballer** EXPO
~ **subway** METRO
see also French

Montréal
see French

Montreal's ___ '67 EXPO

Montrose SCOT

Monty HALL

Monty Python
~ **opener** ITS

"Monty Python"
~ **member** IDLE

"Monty Python's The Meaning of ___" LIFE

monument STELE, STONE

monumental BIG, EPIC, LARGE, VAST

moo CRY, LOW, NOISE
~ **relative** BAA, OINK

moo ___ gai pan GOO

mooch STEAL
~ **off** BEG

mood AURA, CAST, STYLE, TONE
~ **rings** FAD
foul ~ PET, SNIT
gung-ho ~ ZEAL
in a foul ~ IRATE, MAD, RILED, SORE, UPSET
in a high-fiving ~ ELATED, GLAD
mad ~ RAGE

moods
good ~ UPS

moody DOUR

Moody RON

Moody's
~ **best rating** AAA

moolah CASH, GELT, KALE, LOOT, WAD

moon ORB, SPHERE
~ **appearance** PHASE
~ **dweller** MAN

~ ender BEAM, CALF, LIT, RISE, SET, SHINE, STONE
~ goddess DIANA, LUNA
~ in Italian LUNA
~ in Latin LUNA
~ lander LEM
~ landing program APOLLO
~ of Jupiter LEDA
~ of Saturn RHEA, TITAN
~ of Uranus ARIEL, OBERON
~ phenomenon HALO
~ plain MARE
~ pull TIDE
~ ring HALO
~ track ORBIT
howl at the ~ BAY
of the ~ LUNAR
Tranquillity, on the ~ SEA

___ moon NEW

___-moon HALF

Moon ___ Zappa UNIT

"Moon ___" PILOT

"Moon ___ Miami" OVER

"Moon ___ Parador" OVER

"Moon ___ Sixpence, The" AND

"___ Moon" PAPER

moon-based LUNAR

moonbeam RAY

mooncraft
first manned ~ EAGLE

moonfish OPAH

"Moon Is ___, The" BLUE

moonlight
do a ~ flit FLEE

"Moonlight ___ Valentino" AND

"Moonlight and ___" ROSES

"Moonlight Gambler"
~ singer LAINE

"Moonlighting"
~ plot CASE

"Moon Over ___" MIAMI

"Moon Over Miami"
~ director LANG

moons
dozen ~ YEAR
many ~ EON

moonscape
~ feature RILL

moonshine LIE, PRATE, TALE
~ ingredient CORN, MASH

moonshot
~ mission APOLLO
~ org. NASA

moonstone GEM

"___ Moon Street" HALF

moonstruck DAFT

"Moonstruck"
~ actor CAGE
~ Oscar-winner CHER
~ song AMORE

Moon Unit
~ to Dweezil SIS

moonwort FERN

moor DESERT, LAND, ROPE, STAKE, TIE

Moor
~ betrayer IAGO

moorage HAVEN

Moore DEMI, DIVA, POET, ROGER
~ costar ASNER

Moore, Clement POET
~ character SANTA
~ first word TWAS
see also poet

Moorehead AGNES

Moore, Marianne POET
see also poet

Moore, Roger
~ TV role SAINT

Moore, Thomas
~ subject ERIN

mooring CABLE
~ site COVE, INLET

Moorish STYLE

Moors
~ faith ISLAM

moose ANIMAL, DEER
~ cousin DEER, ELK

Moose
like Archie's pal ~ DENSE

Moosehead LAKE

moot OPEN
~ point ISSUE

mop CLEAN, HAIR, SWAB, WASH
~ the floor with ROUT

___ mop DRY, DUST

mope FRET, STEW

moped
~ user RIDER

moppet KID, TOT, TYKE

Mopsus SEER

moral GOOD, PURE
~ fiber HONOR
~ lapse SIN
~ precept ETHIC
~ principle HONOR
~ slip LAPSE
~ standard ETHIC
lend ~ support ROOT

moral code
~ element ETHIC

Morales
see Spanish

moralist
ancient ~ AESOP
Roman ~ CATO

morality
~ play DRAMA

moralizer AESOP

morals
of doubtful ~ LOOSE

Moran ERIN

morass MIRE, WASH

Morath INGE

moratorium WAIT

Moravian SLAV

moray EEL
like a ~ EELY

mordant ACID, ACRID, TART

more ELSE, EXTRA, NEW
~ in Spanish MAS
~ or less ABOUT, NEAR
~ or less the same LIKE
~ than ABOVE, OVER
~ than enough AMPLE, GLUT, PLUS
~ than half MOST
~ than none ANY
~ than occasionally OFT, OFTEN
~ than odd EERIE, EERY
~ than one SOME
~ than that ALSO
~ than willing AVID, EAGER, KEEN
~ to minimalists LESS
~ willingly FIRST
no ~ ONCE, STOP
nothing ~ than MERE, ONLY
once ~ AGAIN, ANEW
one or ~ ANY
one ~ time AGAIN, ANEW, OVER
say ~ ADD
what's ~ ALSO, AND, PLUS

more ___ meets the eye THAN

"More ___ a Feeling" THAN

"More ___ You, The" ISEE

"More ___ You Know" THAN

"More deadly than a ___ dog's tooth" MAD

Moreno RITA

more or ___ LESS

moreover AGAIN, ALSO, AND, TOO, YET

"___ More River" ONE

mores ETHOS, ORDER

More, Thomas SIR
~ work ESSAY

"___ More, With Feeling" ONCE

Morgan HORSE
~ marking STAR

Morgan, Dr. REX

Morgenstern, Mrs. IDA

morion ARMOR

Morita PAT

___ Moritz SAINT

Mork ALIEN
~ and others ETS

~ leader ORSON
~ spaceship EGG

"Mork and Mindy"
Robin's ~ costar PAM

Morley SAFER

Mormon
~ manna SEGO
~ predecessor UTE
~ state UTAH
senior ~ ELDER

morn
~ opposite EVE

morning
~ follower NOON
~ hrs. AMS
~ meal EGGS
~ moisture DEW
~ sound ALARM
~ wear ROBE
fresh as the ~ dew NEW
greet the ~ ARISE
late ~ ELEVEN

morning ___ STAR

"Morning ___, The" AFTER

"Morning ___ (Nine to Five)" TRAIN

"___ Morning, Miss Dove" GOOD

mornings
~ briefly AMS

"___ Morning, Vietnam" GOOD

"Morning Watch, The"
~ author AGEE

"___ Mornin' Rain" EARLY

morns AMS

Moro ALDO

Morocco
~ capital RABAT
~ mount CAMEL
mountains of ~ ATLAS

Moroni ANGEL

morose BLUE, DOUR, SAD, SOUR

morph
~ starter ECTO, ENDO

Morpheus
arms of ~ SLEEP

Morphy
~ game CHESS

morris DANCE

Morris ANITA, CAT, ERROL, PET, WEST
~ doc VET
make like ~ PURR

Morris, Jack
~ stat ERA

Morris Jesup CAPE

Morrison JANE, TONI, VAN

Morrison, Jim DOOR

Morrissey PAUL

Morrissey, Paul
~ film of 1972 HEAT

Morris, William
~ employee AGENT, REP

Morrow ROB

___ **Morrow Lindbergh** ANNE

Morse
~ code word DAH, DIT
~ invention CODE
~ symbol DASH, DOT
e, to ~ DIT, DOT
t, to ~ DAH, DASH

Morse ___ CODE

Morse code
~ message SOS
send ~ TAP

morsel ATOM, BIT, BITE, CHIP, PART, SCRAP, SNIP, TASTE
~ of wisdom PEARL
feedbag ~ OAT
food ~ ORT

Mort SAHL

"Mortal ___, The" STORM

mortar
~ trough HOD

mortarboard CAP, HAT

"Morte d'Arthur" POEM

mortgage DEBT, IOU, LIEN, LOAN
~ datum RATE
grant a ~ LEND
take out a ~ OWE

Morticia
~ cousin ITT

mortify SHAME, SNUB

Mortimer ADLER
Bergen's dummy ~ SNERD
voice of ~ EDGAR

mortise
~ partner TENON

Morton LEVI
~ product SALT

mosaic
~ detail INSET
~ piece TILE

Mosconi
~ game POOL
~ prop RACK
~ stick CUE

Moscow CITY
~ news acronym TASS
~ ruler, once TSAR
~ state IDAHO
city south of ~ OREL
see also Russian

Moselle WINE
~ tributary SAAR

Moses
~ attire ROBE
~ brother AARON
~ mountain SINAI
five books of ~ TORAH
number for ~ TEN

Moses, Grandma ANNA
emulate ~ PAINT

"Moses und ___" ARON

mosey DRAG, LAG, MOVE

Moslem
~ Almighty ALLAH
~ chief AGA, AGHA
~ cleric IMAM
~ household HAREM
~ prince AMIR, EMEER, EMIR
~ religion ISLAM

mosque
~ leader IMAM
~ roof DOME

Mosque of ___ (Jerusalem landmark) OMAR

mosquito FERN, PEST
~ barrier NET

mosquito ___ NET

"Mosquito Coast, The"
~ director WEIR

moss COLOR, PLANT
~ source PEAT

moss ___ ROSE

___ moss PEAT

Moss HART, KATE

"Mosses From an Old ___" MANSE

moss-grown PASSE

most BEST
~ in Spanish MAS
~ opposite LEAST

mostaccioli PASTA

"Most Dangerous ___, The" GAME

Mostel ZERO

Most High LORD

"___ Most Likely, The" GIRL

"___ Most Unusual Day" ITSA

Most Valuable Player AWARD

"Most Wanted"
~ org. FBI

mot ADAGE, SAW
bon ~ PUN

___ mot BON

mote ATOM, DOT, IOTA

motel HOTEL, INN, REST
~ amenity POOL, SAUNA
~ approver AAA
~ freebie ICE, SOAP
~ vacancy ROOM

motes DUST

moth
~ detractor CEDAR
pale-green ~ LUNA

moth-___ EATEN

___ moth LUNA, TIGER

mothballs
put in ~ STORE, TABLE

moth-eaten STALE

mother ADOPT, MAMA, MOM, NUN, SHE
~ in French MERE
~ of Col. Tibbets ENOLA
~ starter STEP
man without a ~ ADAM

mother ___ LODE, WIT

mother ___ (fusser) HEN

mother-___ INLAW

___ mother DEN, EARTH

Mother ___ GOOSE, TERESA

Mother ___ (US saint) SETON

"Mother ___ Tights" WORE

"Mother, ___ I?" MAY

Mother Goose
~ dwelling SHOE

"Mother Goose Suite"
~ composer RAVEL

mother-in-___ LAW

"Mother-in-___" LAW

"Mother, Jugs & ___" SPEED

motherland HOME

mother-of-___ PEARL

mother-of-pearl NACRE

mother of the ___ BRIDE

mother's
~ directive EAT
~ hermana TIA
~ hermano TIO
~ relative ENATE
~ sibling AUNT, UNCLE

Mother's ___ DAY

mother superior
~ counterpart ABBOT

"Mother Wore Tights"
~ director LANG

moth repellent
~ wood CEDAR

motif THEME

motile LIVE

motion ACT, FLAG, NOD, SIGN
~ picture CINE
forward ~ RUN
in ~ AFOOT, ASTIR
make a ~ MOVE
ocean ~ TIDE
quivering ~ TIC, TREMOR
set in ~ START
sudden ~ DART
sweeping ~ SLASH

___ motion SLOW

"___-Motion, The" LOCO

motionless CALM, INERT
not ~ ASTIR

motionlessness PEACE

motion picture
~ (prefix) CINE

motivate AROUSE, FIRE, MOVE, PROD, STIR
~ to action IMPEL

motivation
lack of ~ ENNUI

motive CAUSE
secret ~ ANGLE

mot juste
like a ~ APT

motley PIED

motocross RACE

Moto, Mr.
~ portrayer LORRE

motor RIDE
~ court INN
~ inn HOTEL
~ part CAM
~ trip SPIN
gun a ~ REV

motor ___ HOME

motorcade LINE, PARADE

motorcycle
~ hero EVEL
large ~ HOG

"Motorcycle ___" MAMA

motorcyclist RIDER
daring ~ EVEL

motorist
~ choice RTE
~ org. AAA

Motown
~ megastar ROSS
~ sound SOUL

mots
jeu de ~ PUN

mottle SPOT

motto
"Dirigo" is its ~ MAINE
start of MGM's ~ ARS
start of North Carolina's ~ ESSE
start of Oregon's ~ ALIS
start of the Musketeers' ~ ALL

moue FACE

moujik BOOR

moulin MILL

"Moulin ___" ROUGE

mound CLOD, DUNE, HEAP, PILE
~ star ACE
~ stat ERA
pitcher's ~ SLAB

Mound Builders TRIBE

mount ARISE, HORSE, MARE, PACER, RIDE, RISE, SCALE, SOAR, STEED
~ a gemstone SET
~ a picture HANG
~ as a gem SET

~ **a soapbox** ORATE
~ **the barricades** REBEL
~ **up** RIDE
~ **up to** RUN, TOTAL
~ **with "on"** HOP
Biblical ~ ARARAT
desert ~ ARAB, CAMEL
hero's ~ STEED
knight's ~ STEED
Palm Sunday ~ ASS
rodeo ~ STEER
Sahara ~ CAMEL

Mount ___, N.C. AIRY

Mount ___, Oreg. HOOD

mountain HEAP, MASS, OCEAN, PEAK, PILE, SEA
~ **air** YODEL
~ **chain** RANGE
~ **crest** ARETE
~ **curve** ESS
~ **denizen** GOAT, IBEX
~ **ender** EER
~ **feature** CRAG
~ **fortress** AERIE
~ **hideaway** CAVE
~ **home** AERIE
~ **in Crete** IDA
~ **in Sicily** ETNA
~ **lake** TARN
~ **lion** PUMA
~ **near Troy** IDA
~ **nymph** OREAD
~ **pass** COL, GAP
~ **pool** TARN
~ **(prefix)** ORO
~ **road abbr.** ALT, ELEV
~ **route** PASS
~ **sacred to Buddhism** OMEI
~ **sound** ECHO
~ **top** CREST
~ **transport** BURRO, MULE
European ~ ALP
Greek ~ ATHOS, OSSA
high ~ ALP
Moses' ~ SINAI
round ~ **peak** DOME
Swiss ~ ALP
Tasmanian ~ OSSA
Thessaly ~ OSSA
top of the ~ ACME
Turkish ~ ARARAT

mountain ___ ASH, DEW, GOAT, LION, RANGE

Mountain ___
~ **st.** COL, IDA, NEV

Mountain Dew SODA

mountaineer
~ **foothold** CRAG
~ **goal** ACME
~ **refrain** YODEL

mountain goat
~ **spot** CRAG
like a ~ AGILE

mountainous BIG, LARGE, STEEP

mountains
~ **between Europe and Asia** URALS
gap between ~ COL
Kirghiz ~ ALAI

Matterhorn's ~ ALPS
North African ~ ATLAS
Old World ~ URAL
South American ~ ANDES
Utah ~ UINTA

mountainside
~ **debris** SCREE

"Mountains of the ___" MOON

mountaintop ACME, APEX, PEAK

Mount Blackburn
~ **locale** ALASKA

Mount Bona
~ **state** ALASKA

Mount Carmel
~ **loc.** ISR

mountebank FAKE

mounter
soapbox ~ ORATOR

Mount Hood
~ **setting** PDT, PST
~ **state** OREGON

Mount Ida
locale of ~ CRETE

Mounties
~ **org.** RCMP

Mount Katahdin
~ **locale** MAINE

Mount McKinley
~ **locale** ALASKA

Mount Narodnaya
~ **range** URALS

Mount Rainier
~ **st.** WASH

Mount Rushmore
~ **st.** SDAK

Mount Saint Helens
~ **output** ASH, LAVA
~ **st.** WASH
emulate ~ ERUPT, SPEW

Mount Vernon ESTATE

mourn ACHE, CRY, KEEN, RUE, SOB

mournful LOW, SAD

mourning ___ DOVE

mouse ANIMAL, DANCE, PEST
~ **appendage** TAIL
~ **catcher** CAT, TRAP
~ **locale, in pugilism** EYE
~ **spotter reaction** EEK
~ **target** ICON
~ **to an owl** PREY
field ~ VOLE
move like a ~ DART
poor as a church ~ NEEDY
use a ~ DRAG
white ~ PET

mouse ___ DEER

"mouse!, A" EEK

___ mouse DEER, PINE

"Mouse ___ Roared, The" THAT

"___ Mouse" TOA

mouse-colored DRAB

"___ Mouse Detective, The" GREAT

mouselike
~ **rodent** VOLE

"Mouse on the ___, The" MOON

mouser CAT

mouse-tail PLANT

"___ Mouse That Roared" THE

Mouskouri NANA

moussaka
~ **ingredient** LAMB

mousse
~ **alternative** GEL

mousseline de ___ SOIE

mousy DRAB

mouth SAY, TRAP, YAP
~ **off** DIS, SASS, YAP
~ **part** LIP, ROOF
~ **(prefix)** ORO
down in the ~ LOW, SAD
foaming at the ~ IRATE, MAD, RABID, UPSET
it has a big ~ JAR
march up to the cannon's ~ BEARD
of the ~ ORAL
open one's ~ TALK
open one's big ~ BLAB
put one's foot in one's ~ ERR
run off at the ~ TALK, YAK
shoot off one's ~ BRAG, RANT, YAK

mouth ___ ORGAN

mouth ___ (sass) OFF

___ mouth MOTOR

___-mouth BAD

___-mouthed CLOSE, OPEN

mouthful BITE, GOB, TASTE

mouthing
~ **off** LIP

mouthpiece AGENT, REP
~ **(abbr.)** ATT, ATTY
~ **org.** ABA
horse's ~ BIT
instrument ~ REED

mouths
~ **in Latin** ORA

mouth-to-mouth ORAL
~ **recitation** RUMOR

mouthwash approving
~ **org.** ADA

mouth-watering RICH

move ACT, AROUSE, GET, IMPEL, PROD, ROLL, ROUSE, SELL, STEP, STIR
~ **about** GAD, ROVE
~ **ahead slowly** NOSE
~ **a muscle** STIR

~ **(around)** MILL
~ **at a snail's pace** INCH, LAG
~ **back and forth** BOB, SWAY, WAG
~ **blithely** SKIP
~ **by degrees** INCH
~ **carefully** EASE
~ **cautiously** EDGE
~ **close to the ground** CREEP
~ **edgewise** SIDLE
~ **effortlessly** SAIL
~ **erratically** DART, FLIT
~ **fast** HIE, RACE, RUN, SPEED
~ **forward** NOSE
~ **furtively** SIDLE, SNEAK
~ **gingerly** EASE
~ **goods** SELL
~ **hither and thither** ROVE
~ **into position** SET
~ **laboriously** PLOD
~ **laterally** SIDLE
~ **like a crab** SIDLE
~ **listlessly** MOPE
~ **obliquely** SKEW
~ **on** LEAVE
~ **on hands and knees** CREEP
~ **on ice** SKATE
~ **on the runway** TAXI
~ **quickly** HIE, RACE, RUN, SPEED, TEAR
~ **rapidly** DART, FLIT
~ **rhythmically** SWAY
~ **secretly** STEAL
~ **sideways** EDGE
~ **slightly** STIR
~ **slowly** CREEP, INCH
~ **smoothly** SLIDE
~ **softly** PAD
~ **stealthily** SNEAK
~ **suddenly** DART, SHOOT
~ **swiftly** CLIP, FLIT, HIE, RACE, RUN, SPEED, TEAR
~ **swiftly, as clouds** SCUD
~ **to and fro** FLAP, SWAY, WAG
~ **to tears** GET
~ **to the music** DANCE
~ **toward** NEAR
~ **(toward)** COME, HEAD, TEND
~ **unsteadily** LIMP, TEETER
~ **unsteadily, at sea** YAW
~ **up** ARISE, RAISE, RISE
~ **up and down** BOB, TEETER
~ **with a fulcrum** LEVER
~ **with the wind** SAIL
dumb ~ BONER
get a ~ **on** HIE, RUN, STIR
make a ~ ACT
make a wrong ~ ERR
not ~ STAY
not ~ **a muscle** LOAF
one on the ~ NOMAD
on the ~ AFOOT, ASTIR
put a ~ **on** CHASE
wrong ~ ERROR

moved
be ~ CRY, REACT, SOB

move heaven and ___ EARTH

"Move it!"
Shakespeare's ~ HIE

movement CAUSE, TENOR
  involuntary ~ SPASM, START, TIC
  quick ~ DART
  quicker-than-the-eye ~ BLUR
  sonata ~ TRIO

mover CAUSE
  ~ and shaker DOER
  canoe ~ OAR
  cattle ~ PROD
  furniture ~ VAN
  prime ~ ACTOR, CAUSE
  rubber-tree ~ of song ANT
  slow ~ SNAIL

movie CINE
  ~ excerpt CLIP
  ~ lot locale SET
  ~ prefix CINE
  ~ union SAG
  be in a ~ ACT

moviegoer
  NC-17 ~ ADULT

movies
  review ~ RATE

moving ASTIR
  ~ around ABOUT
  ~ force AGENT
  ~ piece CAM
  ~ quickly and freely AGILE
  ~ vehicle VAN
  company of ~ vans FLEET
  get ~ HIE, ROLL, RUN
  not ~ INERT

moving ___ VAN

mow CROP, CUT, LOP

Mowbray ALAN

mower
  place for a ~ SHED
  ___ mower LAWN

Mowgli HERO

mowing
  ~ site LAWN

moxie GRIT, NERVE

Moyers BILL

Mozart
  ~ beat TEMPO
  ~ offering OPERA
  Trojan princess of a ~ opera ILIA

mozzetta CAPE

MP
  ~ quest AWOL

MPAA
  work for the ~ RATE

MPG
  ~ monitor EPA
  part of ~ GAL, PER

MPH
  part of ~ HOUR, PER

Mr. MAN, TITLE
  ~ in Japanese SAN
  ~ in Spanish SENOR

Mr. ___ (man of integrity) CLEAN

Mr. ___ (VIP) BIG

"Mr. ___" (Keaton film) MOM

"Mr. ___ Goes to Town" DEEDS

"Mr. ___ Mrs. Smith" AND

"Mr. and ___ Smith" MRS

Mr. Big LION

"Mr. Blandings Builds ___ Dream House" HIS

"Mr. Blandings Builds His ___ House" DREAM

"Mr. Deeds ___ to Town" GOES

"Mr. Deeds Goes to Town"
  ~ director CAPRA

M.R.E.
  ~ eaters GIS

Mr. Fix-it
  play ~ MEND

"Mr. Flood's Party" POEM

"Mr. Holland's ___" OPUS

"Mr. Hulot's Holiday"
  ~ director TATI
  ~ star TATI

MRI
  ~ exam SCAN

"Mr. Moto's ___ Warning" LAST

Mr. Potato ___ HEAD

"Mr. Republican" TAFT

"Mr. Roboto"
  ~ band STYX

Mrs. LADY, MADAM, TITLE
  ~ in French MME
  ~ in Japanese SAN
  ~ in Spanish SRA
  new ~ BRIDE

Mrs. ___ (Folger's spokesperson) OLSEN

"Mrs. ___" (Maugham play) DOT

"Mrs. Battle's Opinions on Whist"
  ~ author LAMB

"___ Mrs. Carrolls, The" TWO

"___ Mrs. Leslie" ABOUT

"Mrs. Miniver"
  ~ actor OWEN

"Mr. Smith ___ to Washington" GOES

"Mr. Smith Goes to Washington"
  ~ director CAPRA

"Mr. Television" BERLE

Ms. LADY, MADAM, TITLE
  ~ alternative MRS
  ~ in Japanese SAN
  ~ in Spanish SRTA

"Ms."
  ~ rival ELLE

MS
  ~ accompaniment SASE
  ~ readers EDS
  see also Mississippi

MS-___ DOS

M.S.
  part of ~ SCI

M-16 RIFLE

"Ms. Found ___ Bottle" INA

M.Sgt. NCO

MST
  part of ~ STD

Mt.
  see Mount

MT
  see Montana

mtg. APPT

MTV
  ~ prize AVA
  ~ viewer TEEN
  part of ~ TELE

Mubarak ARAB
  ~ capital CAIRO
  ~ predecessor SADAT

much ALOT
  ~ going on PRESS
  ~ loved SWEET
  ~ taken by INTO
  ~ the same ALIKE, CLOSE, LIKE
  ~ used TRITE
  as ~ as UPTO
  give too ~ SATE
  love too ~ DOTE
  make ~ of EXALT, LAUD
  not as ~ LESS
  very ~ ALOT
  without ~ thought IDLY

"Much ___ About Nothing" ADO

muchacha
  see Spanish

"___ Muchachos" ADIOS

"Much Ado"
  ~ daughter HERO

"Much Ado ___ Nothing" ABOUT

much-bruised
  ~ item EGO

much-heard BANAL

"___ Much Is Not Enough" TOO

mucho LOTS

much-touted NOTED

mucilage GLUE, PASTE

muck DIRT, GOO, MIRE, OOZE, SLIME, SLOP, SOIL
  ~ up TAINT

muck ___ (loiter) ABOUT

muckamuck
  high ~ LION, PASHA

mucker BOOR

muckrake LIBEL

mud CLAY, DIRT, EARTH, MIRE, OOZE, SLIME, SOIL
  ~ eel SIREN
  ~ flat MIRE
  ~ product PIE
  drag through the ~ LIBEL, SMEAR, TAINT
  here's ~ in your eye TOAST
  Mississippi ~ SILT
  sink in ~ MIRE
  sling ~ SLUR
  stick in the ~ MIRE
  sticky ~ SLIME
  throw ~ on LIBEL, SLUR
  wet ~ SLOP

mud ___ BATH, CAT, EEL, FLAT, HEN, PIE

Mudd ROGER

mudder HORSE, RACER

muddle ADDLE, DAZE, HASH, MESS, SNARL, STIR, UPSET
  ~ one's words SLUR

muddled ASEA, ATSEA, MESSY, UPSET

muddleheaded ASEA, ATSEA, DAFT, DENSE

muddy DAUB, DIM, MIRE, SPOT
  ~ spot STY
  ~ track RUT
  make ~ ROIL

Mud Hens
  where the ~ play TOLEDO

mudhole PIT

"___ mud in your eye!" HERES

mudslinger
  ~ statement SLUR

mudslinging
  engage in ~ SMEAR

muezzin
  ~ God ALLAH

Mufasa
  ~ pride MANE
  Disney ~ LION
  emulate ~ ROAR

muff ERR, ERROR, HASH, MISS
  ~ it ERR
  ~ locale EAR

muffed
  ~ grounder ERROR

Muffet, Miss
  what ~ did SAT

muffin GEM
  ~ starter RAGA

___ muffin BRAN, CORN

muffins
  make ~ BAKE

muffle GAG, MUTE

muffled DIM

muffler SCARF
  ~ of a sort MUTE

muffling
~ **device** MUTE

mug CUP, FACE, HARM, PAN, ROB, STEIN, TRAP
~ **filler** ALE, BEER
~ **for the camera** POSE

mug ___ SHOT

mugger
~ **deterrent** MACE

Muggs, J. Fred APE

muggy CLOSE, DAMP, WET

mugho ___ PINE

Muhammad ALI
~ **birthplace** MECCA
~ **faith** ISLAM

mukluk BOOT

mulberry COLOR, TREE

___ mulberry PAPER

mulct FINE, ROB, ROOK, STEAL

Mulder
~ **org.** FBI

Muldoon COP

mule ANIMAL, SHOE
~ **cousin** BURRO
~ **father** ASS
~ **follower** PLOW
~ **mother** MARE
~ **of folk song** SAL
~ **talk** BRAY
command to a ~ GEE, HAW
its mascot is a ~ ARMY

mule ___ DEER

"Mule ___" TRAIN

mules
sporting ~ SHOD

mule Sal's canal ERIE

"___ Mules for Sister Sara" TWO

muleta CAPE
~ **color** RED

"Mule Train"
~ **singer** LAINE

Mulgrew KATE

"Mulholland Falls"
~ **actor** NOLTE

mull HEAT
~ **over** MUSE, PORE, ROLL, SEE

mullah MALE

Mullens, Miss
caller on ~ in Longfellow ALDEN

mulligan STEW

Mulligan, Richard
~ **show** SOAP

Mullins MOON

mullion POST

multicolored PIED, SHOT
~ **horse** ROAN

~ parrot MACAW
~ quartz AGATE

multiflora ROSE

multi-person
~ **race** RELAY

multiple
~ **of two** EVEN

multiple-choice
~ **answer** FALSE, TRUE
~ **word** ANY
not ~ ESSAY

multiplication
~ **symbol** DOT

multiplication ___ TABLE

multiply BREED, GROW, RISE

multitude ARMY, BAND, CREW, HEAP, HERD, HORDE, HOST, LOT, MASS, MOB, OCEAN, PILE, SEA, TROOP
clamorous ~ ROUT

mum BEER, MUTE, TACIT

mumble SLUR, STALL, TALK

mumblety-peg GAME

mummer ACTOR

mummy
famous ~ TUT

"Mummy's ___, The" HAND

"Mum's ___ word!" THE

munch BITE, EAT, GNAW
~ **out** CRAM

Munchausen BARON, LIAR
like ~'s tales TALL

Munch, Edvard
~ **home** OSLO

München
see German

munchies
one with the ~ EATER

munchkin
~ **kin** ELF

munchy NOSH

Muncie
~ **st.** IND

mundane LAY

mundify CLEAN

mung BEAN

Muni PAUL
role for ~ EMILE

Munich PACT
see also German

municipality CITY

munificent FREE

munitions AMMO, ARMS

Munro ALICE
~ **pseudonym** SAKI

Munro, H.H. SAKI

Munson ONA

Munster
~ **county** CLARE
~ **kid** EDDIE
~ **pet** IGOR, SPOT

Münster
see German

Munster, Mrs. LILY

muntjac ANIMAL, DEER

Muppet ELMO, ERNIE, OSCAR
~ **drummer** ANIMAL
~ **eagle** SAM

"___ Muppet Caper, The" GREAT

"Muppet Christmas ___, The" CAROL

"Muppets ___ Manhattan, The" TAKE

mural ART
~ **starter** INTER

"Murder ___" ONE

"Murder ___" (Miss Marple movie) AHOY

"Murder ___, The" MAN

"Murder ___ Foul" MOST

"Murder ___ Honeymoon" ONA

"Murder, ___" INC

"Murder, ___ Said" SHE

"Murder, ___ Wrote" SHE

"___ Murder at St. Trinian's" BLUE

"Murder at the ___" ABA

"Murder by Death"
~ **director** MOORE

"Murder, He ___" SAYS

"Murder in the Cathedral"
~ **author** ELIOT
~ **monogram** TSE

"Murder, My ___" SWEET

"Murder on the ___ Express" ORIENT

"___ Murders, The" ABC

"Murder, She ___" SAID, WROTE

"Murders in the ___ Morgue, The" RUE

Murdoch IRIS

muriatic ACID

murid MOUSE

murine MOUSE

murky DIM

Murmansk CITY, PORT
see also Russian

murmur COO, DRONE, LAP
~ **of admiration** OOH
~ **of approval** AAH
cat's ~ PURR
surf's ~ ROTE

murmurs
~ **of appreciation** AHS, OHS

Murnau, F.W.
~ **film of 1931** TABU

Murphy BED, BEN, DALE, EDDIE

"Murphy Brown"
~ **network** CBS
~ **tavern owner** PHIL

Murphy, Eddie
~ **movie** RAW

Murphy, Rose Mary
~ **hubby** ABIE

Murphy's ___ LAW

"Murphy's War"
~ **actor** OTOOLE

Murray ANNE, MAE

Murray, Arthur
~ **lesson** STEP, TANGO

Murray, J.A.H.
~ **lexicon** OED

murrey COLOR, RED

Murrow
~ **and others** EDS
~ **milieu** NEWS
~ **network** CBS

mus.
~ **adaptation** ARR

muscat WINE

Muscat
~ **is its capital** OMAN
~ **native** ARAB

muscle SINEW
~ **cramp** KNOT
~ **fiber** STRIA
~ **injury** TEAR
~ **strain** ACHE
~ **tension** TONE
~ **twitch** SPASM
back ~, in the gym LAT
hired ~ GOON
move a ~ STIR
not move a ~ LOAF
show some ~ EXERT

muscleman
mythical ~ ATLAS

muscles
belly ~ ABS
work one's ~ EXERT

muscovite MICA

muscular BIG, FIT, HALE, LARGE

muse DREAM, PORE
~ **count** NINE

Muse
~ **complement** NINE
~ **domain** ARTS
~ **instrument** LYRE
~ **of history** CLIO
~ **of poetry** ERATO
gift from a ~ IDEA

museum
~ **artifact** RELIC
~ **display** ART
~ **piece** TORSO
~ **vessel** URN
NY art ~ MET

mush PAP, PASTE

musher
~ **conveyance** SLED

mushroom BOOM, GROW, MOREL, PLANT, RISE

mushroom-to-be SPORE

Musial STAN

music ART
~ **copyright org.** ASCAP
~ **enhancer** AMP
~ **holder** STAND
~ **media** CDS
~ **org.** ASCAP
~ **whose name means "color"** RAGA
1950s ~ BOP
1990s ~ RAP
knack for ~ EAR
like modern ~ ATONAL
sheet ~ **abbr.** ARR
student's ~ ETUDE

music ___ HALL

___ music SHEET, SOUL

"Music ___, The" MAN

musical
~ **ability** EAR
~ **based on "La Bohème"** RENT
~ **beginning** INTRO
~ **chairs** GAME
~ **chime** TONE
~ **chord** TRIAD
~ **combo** TRIO
~ **comedy** GENRE
~ **composition** DUET, ETUDE, OCTET, OPUS, SONG, TRIO, TUNE
~ **conclusion** CODA
~ **drama** OPERA
~ **ending** CODA, FINE
~ **ensemble** BAND, TRIO
~ **epilogue** CODA
~ **instrument** HARP, HORN, LUTE, LYRE, OBOE, ORGAN, PIANO, UKE
~ **measure** BAR
~ **notation** CLEF, REST, SLUR
~ **note** SOL
~ **notes** LAS, RES
~ **quality** TONE
~ **sample** DEMO
~ **set in Argentina** EVITA
~ **study** ETUDE
~ **symbol** FLAT, NOTE
~ **tempo** TIME
Broadway ~ CATS
Broadway ~ **set in Argentina** EVITA
classical ~ OPERA
music for a ~ SCORE
one of the ~ **B's** BACH
rock ~ HAIR
Tony-winning ~ CATS, RENT

musical chairs
~ **quest** SEAT

musical instrument
ancient ~ LYRE

"Music Box"
~ **actress** LANGE

"Music for Airports"
~ **composer** ENO

music hall
~ **tune** RAG

music halls ODEA

musician
~ **job** GIG
rock ~ **elec. gear** AMP

"Music in the ___" AIR

"Music in the Air"
~ **director** MAY

"Music Man, The"
~ **locale** IOWA

"Music of the Night, The" ARIA

musk
~ **ender** MELON

musk ___ DEER, OXEN, ROSE

muskeg FEN

muskellunge PIKE

musket GUN
~ **ender** EER

Musketeers
one of the ~ ATHOS
start of the ~ **motto** ALL

"___ Musketeers, The" THREE

Muskie, Ed
~ **state** MAINE

muskrat ANIMAL

Muslim ERA
~ **faith** ISLAM
~ **god** ALLAH
~ **holy place** MECCA
~ **official** AGA, AGHA, AMIR, EMEER, EMIR
~ **ruler** AGA, AGHA
~ **scholar** IMAM
~ **state** IRAN
~ **world** ISLAM

muss MESS

mussel
~ **cousin** CLAM

mussels
prepare ~ STEAM

Musset, Alfred de POET
see also poet

must MOLD
novelist's ~ IDEA

must-___ READ, SEE

mustache HAIR
~ **site** LIP

mustachioed
~ **surrealist** DALI

mustang ANIMAL, HORSE

Mustang AUTO, CAR

Mustangs
~ **sch.** SMU

mustard COLOR, HERB, SEED
~ **family plant** COLE, CRESS, KALE
like some ~ MILD

Mustard, Colonel
~ **game** CLUE

Mustard, Mr.
like the Beatles' ~ MEAN

"___ Must Be Joking!" YOU

"___ Must Die, The" BEAST

muster BAND, CALL, RAISE, ROLL
~ **one's forces** ARM

___ muster PASS

mustiness MOLD

musty CLOSE, STALE

mutate ALTER

mutation
~ **undergoer** GENE

mute TACIT
piano ~ PEDAL

mute ___ SWAN

muted LOW, THIN

mutilate HACK, MAIM, MAR

mutineer REBEL

mutiny REBEL, RISE, STORM

"___ Mutiny, The" CAINE

mutt CUR, DOG
~ **remark** ARF

Mutt and Jeff DUO, PAIR

mutter TALK

mutton MEAT
~ **chops** BEARD

muttonhead ASS

"Mutts"
~ **dog** EARL

mutual SAME
~ **attraction** LOVE
~ **(prefix)** INTER

"___ Mutual Friend" OUR

mutual fund
~ **acct.** IRA
~ **charge** LOAD

mutually AMONG
~ **(prefix)** INTER

Mutual of ___ OMAHA

muumuu
~ **accessory** LEI

muzhik
see Russian

"___ Muzik" POP

muzjik BOOR

muzzle NOSE, STOP

MVP
part of ~ MOST

my
~ **in Italian** MIA

be ~ **guest** YES

My ___ perfume SIN

My ___, Vietnam LAI

"My ___" IDEAL

"My ___" (Nancy Reagan book) TURN

"My ___!" EYE

"My ___ and Only" ONE

"My ___ are sealed!" LIPS

"My ___ Foot" LEFT

"My ___ Godfrey" MAN

"My ___ Heaven" BLUE

"My ___ is as a lusty winter..." AGE

"My ___ Is Julia Ross" NAME

"My ___ Lady" FAIR

"My ___ Private Idaho" OWN

"My ___ Sal" GAL

"My ___ Sons" THREE

"My ___ Story" OWN

"My ___ Trigger" PAL

Myanmar
~ **continent** ASIA
~ **export** TEAK
~ **neighbor** LAOS

"___ My Baby Comes Home" TIL

"My Blue Heaven"
~ **director** ROSS

"My Bonnie ___ over..." LIES

"My Bonnie Lies Over the ___" OCEAN

"___ my brother's keeper?" AMI

Mycenaean ERA

"My Cherie ___" AMOUR

"___ My Children" ALL

"My country ___ of thee..." TIS

___ my cup of tea NOT

"My Cup Runneth Over"
~ **singer** AMES

"...my dainty ___! I shall miss thee" ARIEL

"My dame has lost her ___" SHOE

"My Darling Clementine"
Fonda in ~ EARP

"My Dinner With ___" ANDRE

"My dog ___ fleas" HAS

"___ my drift?" GET

Myerson ALAN, BESS

"___ My Ex's Live in Texas" ALL

"My Eyes ___ You" ADORED

"___ My Eyes" CLOSE

"My Fair ___" LADY

"My Fair Lady"
  ~ **racetrack** ASCOT
  Audrey's ~ costar REX

"My father moved through dooms of love" POEM

"My Father, The ___" HERO

"___ My Father Told Me" LIES

"My Favorite ___" SPY, YEAR

"My Favorite Year"
  ~ **actor** OTOOLE

"My Foolish ___" HEART

"My Friend ___" IRMA

"My Friend Flicka"
  ~ **author** OHARA

"My Gal ___" SAL

"___ My Girl" SHES, YOURE

"My goodness!" GEE, WOW

"___ My Guy" HES

"My Heart Leaps Up When I Behold" POEM

"My Heart's in the Highlands" POEM

"My Heroes Have Always ___ Cowboys" BEEN

"My Home Town"
  ~ **singer** ANKA

"___ My Jamaica" YOURE

"My Last Duchess" POEM

"My Left ___" FOOT

"My Life"
  ~ **autobiographer** MEIR

"___ my lips!" READ

"My Little ___" GIRL

"My Little Girl"
  ~ **actress** MEARA

"My Lost Youth" POEM

"___ My Love" SLEEP

"My Love Is Like a Red, Red ___" ROSE

"___, my Love! ye do me wrong" ALAS

"My man!" BRO

"My Mother the ___" CAR

"My, my!" TSK

myna BIRD, PET

"My Name Is ___" ARAM

"My Name Is Julia ___" ROSS

"My Name Is Julia Ross"
  ~ **director** LEWIS

"___ My Neck in High Muddy Water" UPTO

Mynheer TITLE

"My Old ___ Sally" AUNT

"My One and ___" ONLY

"My Own Private ___" IDAHO

"My Pal Trigger" OATER

"___ My Party" ITS

"My People"
  ~ **author** EBAN

Myra HESS

Myrdal ALVA

Myrdal, Gunnar SWEDE

myrmecologist
  ~ **subject** ANT

Myrna
  role for ~ NORA

myrrh
  ~ **donor and others** MAGI

___ myrtle CREPE

Myshkin, Prince IDIOT

"My Sister ___" SAM

"___ My Song" HEAR

"___ My Sons" ALL

"___ my soul!" BLESS

"___! My Soul!" OOH

"___ My Souvenirs" AMONG

mysteries
  first name in ~ ERLE

mysterious DEEP, EERIE, EERY
  ~ **aphorism** RUNE
  ~ **Norse character** RUNE
  ~ **sighting** UFO

"___ Mysterious Night" ONE

mystery GENRE, POSER
  ~ **board game** CLUE
  ~ **element** CLUE
  ~ **writers' award** EDGAR

mystery ___ PLAY

"Mystery ___" TRAIN

"Mystery of the White ___" ROOM

mystic SEER
  ~ **letter** RUNE
  ancient ~ ESSENE
  Hindu ~ SWAMI, YOGI

mystical DEEP
  ~ **cards** TAROT
  ~ **emanation** AURA

mystified LOST

mystify DAZE, POSE

mystique AURA

"My Sweet ___" LORD

myth TALE

mythology
  branch of ~ NORSE, ROMAN

mythomaniac LIAR

"My Three ___" SONS

"My Three Sons"
  ~ **role** CHIP, ERNIE, STEVE

"___ My Turn" ITS

"My Two ___" DADS

"___ My Voice Broke, The" YEAR

"My Way"
  ~ **songwriter** ANKA

"My Wild ___ Rose" IRISH

"My Wild Irish ___" ROSE

"___ my word!" UPON

"My word!" EGAD, EGADS

"___ My World" COLOR

"___ 9 From Outer Space" PLAN

9 to 5
~ **in the classifieds** DAYS

19
~ **of 26** ESS

19th
~ **st.** IND

1920s
~ **craze** YOYO
~ **look** DECO

1930s
~ **auto** AERO
~ **dance** SHAG
~ **legislation** NRA

90
less than ~ degrees ACUTE

90 degree
~ **shape** ELL

90 degrees EAST
~ **from fore-and-aft** ABEAM
~ **from north** EAST

"92 in the ___" SHADE

94th ___ Squadron AERO

99 AGENT

"99 and 44/100% ___" PURE

907
~ **kilograms** TON

911
~ **responder** EMS, EMT

1900
one at war in ~ BOER

1905
~ **song girl** SAL

1914
~ **battle site** YSER

1917
loser of ~ TSAR
winner of ~ LENIN

"1919"
~ **trilogy** USA

1933
govt. program estab. in
~ NRA, TVA

1940s
~ **music** BOP
~ **song** OLDIE

1945
~ **meeting site** YALTA

1949
pact since ~ NATO

1950s
~ **dance** HOP
~ **music** BOP
~ **pres.** DDE, HST
~ **record** OLDIE
chairman of the ~ MAO
first name in ~ politics ADLAI,
IKE

1955
~ **pact** SEATO

1960
grp. founded in ~ OPEC

1960s
~ **catchword** PEACE
~ **dress** MINI
~ **hairdo** AFRO
~ **jacket** NEHRU
~ **musical** HAIR
~ **protest org.** SDS
~ **style** MOD
~ **tune** OLDIE
~ **war zone** NAM

1965
~ **march site** SELMA

1969
~ **landing site** MOON

1990s
~ **interjection** NOT

"90125"
~ **band** YES

N ELEM
7 for ~ ATNO

N ___ "Nancy" ASIN

Na ELEM
11 for ~ ATNO

N.A.
part of ~ AMER

NAACP
part of ~ ASSN

nab ARREST, BAG, GRAB, GRASP,
GRIP, NAIL, SNARE

Nabisco
~ **brand** OREO

nabob NOB
~ **residence** ESTATE

Nabokov
~ **novel** ADA

Nabors
~ **role** PYLE

nacho
~ **dip** SALSA

NaCl SALT

nada NIL, ZERO
~ **in French** RIEN

Nadelman ELIE

Nadia
~ **predecessor** OLGA

nadir EBB

nae
~ **sayer** SCOT

N. Afr.
~ **country** ALG, TUN

NAFTA
~ **signatory** USA
part of ~ AMER, FREE, TRADE

nag CARP, FRET, HACK, HARP,
HORSE, JADE, RIDE

Nagano
see Japanese

Nagano Olympics
~ **network** CBS

Nagasaki CITY, PORT

nagging
~ **pain** ACHE

Nagoya
see Japanese

nah NAY, NOPE

Naha CITY, PORT

Nahum TATE

naiad
~ **element** WATER

Naidu, Sarojini POET
see also poet

naif BABE

nail ARREST, BRAD, CLAW, LAND,
NAB
~ **container** KEG
~ **down** PEG, SET
~ **gloss** ENAMEL
~ **groomer** EMERY
~ **locale** TOE
~ **partner** TOOTH
~ **polish** ENAMEL
~ **set** TOOL
~ **shaper** FILE
curved ~ CLAW
drive a ~ aslant TOE
kind of ~ BRAD
like some ~ polish CLEAR
long ~ CLAW

nail ___ FILE

nail file
~ **abrasive** EMERY

nails
decorate ~ PAINT

Naina
~ **predecessor** RAISA

Nairn
see Scottish

Nairobi CITY

"Nairobi ___, The" TRIO

naive
~ **one** BABE

naked BALD, BARE, NUDE, POOR
~ **truth** FACT
not ~ CLAD

naked ___ EYE

naked ___ jaybird ASA

"Naked ___, The" APE, CITY, GUN,
KISS, PREY, SPUR

"Naked ___ the Dead, The" AND

"Naked Spur, The"
~ **director** MANN

"___-Naked Truth, The" HALF

Nala LION

Naldi NITA

Namath JOE
~ once JET, RAM

namaycush TROUT

namby-pamby PANSY

name CALL, CITE, LABEL, MAKE, REFER, SAY, STYLE, TAG, TERM, TITLE
~ in French NOM
fake ~ ALIAS
ind. of another ~ AKA

name-___ DROP

___ name BIG, CODE, FIRST, PEN, TRADE

___-name BIG

named
originally ~ NEE

namedropper SNOB

"Name Game, The"
~ singer ELLIS

"Name of the ___, The" GAME

"Name of the Rose, The"
~ author ECO
~ setting ITALY

nameplate SIGN

names
name ~ BARE, BLAB, LEAK, RAT, SING

nametag SIGN
~ site LAPEL

"Name That ___" TUNE

"Name That Tune"
~ clue NOTE

Namib DESERT

Namibia
~ native BANTU

"Namouna"
~ composer LALO

"Nana"
~ actress STEN
~ name ANNA

___ Na Na SHA

"Na Na Hey Hey Kiss Him Goodbye"
~ band STEAM

Nancy AMES, DREW
see also French

"___ 'n Andy" AMOS

Nanette
words to ~ NONO

Nanking CITY
~ native ASIAN

Nan Ling RANGE

nanny GOAT, NURSE
~ offspring KID
a ~ pushes it PRAM
Asian ~ AMA, AMAH

Nanook
~ home IGLOO
~ vehicle SLED

Nantes CITY, PORT
~ river LOIRE
see also French

Nantucket
~ (abbr.) ISL

Nantucket Island
~ loc. ATL

NaOH BASE
~ solution LYE

Naomi
~ daughter-in-law RUTH
colleague of ~ ELLE

nap NOD, PILE, REST, SLEEP
~ inducer BORE
~ loudly SNORE
~ starter CAT

Napa Valley
~ product WINE

nape NECK

napery LINEN

Napier, John SCOT

napkin BIB
~ fabric LINEN
~ place LAP, TABLE

Naples CITY, PORT
island near ~ CAPRI
see also Italian

napless BARE

napoleon COIN, GAME

Napoleon EXILE, SOLO
~ emblem EAGLE
~ fate EXILE
~ island ELBA
~ victory site LODI
river ~ navigated NILE
word in a ~
palindrome ABLE, ELBA, ERE, SAW, WAS
see also French

Napoleon ___ SOLO

Napoleonic ___ CODE, ERA

Napoli
see Italian

napping
~ place SOFA

narc
~ org. DEA

narcissistic VAIN

Narcissus
like ~ VAIN
nymph who loved ~ ECHO
play ~ PREEN
what ~ fell in love with EGO, IMAGE, SELF

narghile PIPE

Narnia
~ creator LEWIS

Narragansett BAY

narrate RELATE, SPIN, TELL

narration TALE

narrative EPIC, TALE
~ (abbr.) ACCT
French ~ poem LAI
legendary ~ SAGA

narrow CLOSE, MEAN, SMALL, TAPER, THIN
~ aperture SLIT
~ band STRAP
~ board LATH
~ boat CANOE
~ connector NECK
~ cut SLIT
~ furrow STRIA
~ land SPIT
~ margin HAIR, NOSE
~ opening SLOT
~ passage INLET
~ passageway LANE
~ piece STRIP
~ platform RISER
~ route PASS
~ shelf LEDGE
~ street ALLEY
~ strip SHRED
~ the gap GAIN, NEAR
get ~ TAPER
not ~ WIDE

narrower LESS

narrow-minded MEAN

narrow-mindedness BIAS

narrows INLET, NECK, PASS

narthex
~ neighbor APSE, NAVE

narwhal ANIMAL

nary
~ a soul NONE, NOONE

NASA
~ affirmative AOK
~ chimp ENOS
~ decision NOGO
~ destination MARS, MIR, MOON, ORBIT
~ mission APOLLO
~ name ALAN, NEIL, RIDE
~ rocket ATLAS
~ spacewalk EVA
~ vehicle LEM
part of ~ SPACE

nasal
~ expression SNORE, SNORT
~ input AROMA, ODOR
~ passage NOSE

NASCAR
~ sponsor STP
part of ~ ASSN, AUTO

nascence START

Nascimento, Edson Arantes do PELE

NASDAQ
~ orgs. COS
~ rival NYSE
~ transaction TRADE

Nash AUTO, CAR, OGDEN, POET
~ two-L beast LLAMA
one-L ~ priest LAMA

Nash, Ogden
~ output POEM
see also poet

Nashville
~ st. TENN

Nashville ___ (1960s pop group) TEENS

"Nashville ___" CATS

Nassau CITY, PORT

Nasser LAKE
~ org. UAR
~ successor SADAT

Nastase ILIE

nastiness SPITE

nasty ACRID, BAD, CRUEL, LOW, MEAN, MESSY, SNIDE, SOUR, UGLY, VILE
~ as a comment ACID
~ glance LEER
~ mood SNIT
~ name SADE
~ pup CUR
~ smile SNEER

"Nasty"
~ on the courts ILIE

Nat COLE

natal
~ starter NEO

Natalia
see Italian

Natalie COLE
~ father NAT
~ played her MARIA

Natasha
~ aunt LYNN
see also Russian

natatorium POOL

Natchez
~ st. MISS

Natchez ___ TRACE

Nathan HALE, LANE

Nathanael WEST

nation LAND, STATE

national
~ spirit ETHOS
~ starter INTER
~ symbol FLAG
not ~ LOCAL

national ___ DEBT

"National Enquirer"
~ rival STAR

"National Geographic"
~ insert MAP

nationalist
~ org. IRA

nationality
~ suffix ESE, ISH

National League
~ division EAST, WEST
~ stadium SHEA

National Leaguer ASTRO, EXPO, GIANT, MET

Nation, Carry DRY
  ~ weapon AXE
  like ~ SOBER

"___ nation indivisible..." ONE

nations
  allied ~ BLOC

nationwide RIFE

native LOCAL
  ~ (suffix) ESE, ITE

"Native ___" SON

Native American
  ~ group TRIBE

nativity
  ~ figures MAGI

Nat King ___ COLE

NATO PACT
  ~ cousin OAS
  ~ nation CAN, DEN, ENG, GER, ITAL, ITALY, NOR, PORT, SPAIN, USA
  ~ organizer DDE
  former ~ commander HAIG
  part of ~ ATL, ORG

natter CHAT, GAB, TALK, YAK

natterjack TOAD

natty CHIC, NEAT, SMART, TRIM

natural EASY, FREE, PURE, RAW, REAL
  ~ crystals SNOW
  ~ element HOME
  ~ eyewash TEAR
  ~ mimic MYNA
  ~ pigment OCHER, OCHRE
  ~ pouch SAC
  ~ resource OIL, ORE, WATER
  ~ right DUE
  it may be ~ GAS
  Vegas ~ ELEVEN, SEVEN

"natural" AFRO

natural ___ GAS, LAW

natural food
  ~ additive HERB

natural gas
  ~ constituent ETHANE

naturalists
  ~ study FLORA

"Naturally!" YES

"___ Naturally" ACT

naturalness EASE

nature ESSENCE, ILK, LIFE, ORDER, SORT
  ~ imitator ART
  ~ outing HIKE
  ~ (prefix) ECO
  ~ walk TRAIL
  basic ~ ESSENCE
  building block of ~ ATOM
  by its very ~ PERSE
  of the ~ of (suffix) INE
  second ~ HABIT

nature ___ TRAIL

___-natured GOOD, ILL

naturel
  au ~ BARE, NUDE

naught NIL, NONE, ZERO
  bring to ~ DASH, UNDO

naughty BAD
  ~ child's Christmas gift COAL
  ~ youngster BRAT

"Naughty ___ of Shady Lane, The" LADY

"Naughty, naughty!" TSK

nautical
  ~ assent AYE
  ~ command AVAST
  ~ diary LOG
  ~ dir. ENE, ESE, NNE, NNW, SSE, SSW, WNW, WSW
  ~ direction ABEAM, AFT, ALEE, ASTERN, FORE
  ~ gear RIG
  ~ greeting AHOY
  ~ group CREW
  ~ hdg. ENE, ESE, NNE, NNW, SSE, SSW, WNW, WSW
  ~ speed KNOT
  ~ starter AERO, ASTRO

___ nautilus PAPER

Nautilus
  ~ locale SPA

"Nautilus"
  ~ branch USN
  ~ captain NEMO

Navajo TRIBE

naval
  ~ alert SOS
  ~ arena OCEAN, SEA
  ~ call AVAST
  ~ designation USS
  ~ force FLEET
  ~ monogram USN
  ~ rank CPO, ENS
  ~ response AYE
  ~ second-in-command EXEC

naval maneuvers
  on ~ ASEA, ATSEA

Navarre
  see Spanish

nave
  ~ bisector AISLE
  ~ neighbor APSE

navel
  ~ filler LINT

navel ___ ORANGE

navigable OPEN

navigate BOAT, PILOT, PLY, RUN, SAIL, STEER
  ~ in air AVIATE
  ~ on snow SKI

navigation
  ~ light LAMP
  low-tech ~ aid OAR

navigational
  ~ aid MAP
  ~ device RADAR, SONAR
  ~ hazard BERG, REEF, SHOAL

navigator PILOT
  ~ concern ROUTE
  ~ need MAP

Navigator Islands SAMOA

navy BEAN, BLUE, COLOR, FLEET

navy ___ BEAN, BLUE

Navy
  ~ diver SEAL
  ~ man GOB
  ~ NCO CPO
  ~ position RANK
  ~ reply AYE
  ~ rival ARMY

"Navy ___" SEALS

navy yard
  ~ area PIER

naw NAY, NOPE

nay
  ~ opposite AYE
  ~ sayer ANTI

nays
  yeas and ~ VOTE

naysay DENY

naysayer ANTI

Nazarenes SECT

Nazimova ALLA

Nb ELEM
  41 for ~ ATNO

N.B.
  part of ~ BENE, NOTA

NBA
  ~ locale UTAH
  ~ official REF
  ~ player CELT, HEAT, NET, PACER, PRO, SPUR, SUN
  former ~ venue OMNI
  like most ~ players TALL
  part of ~ ASSN

NBC
  ~ peacock LOGO
  ~ rival ABC, CBS
  ~ soap, to fans DAYS
  former ~ owner RCA

N.C.
  ~ neighbor TENN
  ~ zone EDT, EST
  water off ~ ATL
  see also North Carolina

NCAA
  ~ regional EAST, WEST
  ~ rival NIT
  part of ~ ASSN

NCO SGT
  ~ for short SARGE
  Navy ~ CPO
  part of ~ NON

NCOs
  boot camp ~ DIS

NC-17
  ~ moviegoer ADULT

Nd ELEM
  60 for ~ ATNO

ND
  see North Dakota

N. Dak.
  ~ neighbor MAN
  see also North Dakota

ne ___ ultra PLUS

Ne ELEM
  10 for ~ ATNO

NE
  ~ city BOS
  ~ state PENN
  see also Nebraska

NEA
  ~ rival AFT
  part of ~ ARTS, ASSN

Neanderthal
  ~ home CAVE

Neanderthal ___ MAN

neap TIDE

near ABOUT, CLOSE, COME, LOCAL
  ~ in German NAH
  ~ (prefix) EPI, PARA
  ~ (suffix) ISH

near ___ BEER, MISS

Near ___ EAST

nearby ABOUT, CLOSE, LOCAL
  not ~ AFAR
  objects ~ THESE

"Nearer, My God, to ___" THEE

nearest NEXT
  ~ one THIS
  Earth's ~ star SOL

near-failing
  ~ mark DEE

Near Island ATTU

nearly ABOUT, CLOSE

near-rapture GLEE

___ 'n' Easy NICE

neat CLEAN, PURE, TAUT, TRIM
  ~ in Liverpool TRIG
  not ~ MESSY
  stiffly ~ PRIM

neat ___ pin ASA

neat as a ___ PIN

neaten CLEAN, TRIM
  ~ as a bed MAKE
  ~ one's hair COMB
  ~ the shrubbery CLIP

neath UNDER
  opposite of ~ OER

neatness ORDER

neatnik
  ~ bane DIRT, DUST

~ nemesis SLOB
"Neato!" COOL
neat's-___ oil FOOT
neat's-foot ___ OIL
neb BILL, NIB, NOSE
Neb.
   see Nebraska
nebbish DRIP, NERD
Nebr.
   ~ neighbor IOWA, KAN, SDAK
   see also Nebraska
Nebraska STATE
   ~ county OTOE
   ~ metropolis OMAHA
   ~ neighbor IOWA
   ~ tribe OMAHA
   mil. group headquartered in
    ~ SAC
nebula
   ~ in Taurus CRAB
nebulous DIM
   ~ emanation AURA
necessary BASIC
   ~ part COG
necessitate IMPEL, MAKE
___ necessities BARE
necessity NEED
neck CAPE, CARESS, KISS, PET
   ~ and neck CLOSE, EVEN,
    TIED
   ~ nicety BOA
   ~ of the woods AREA
   ~ warmer SCARF
   back of the ~ NAPE
   neck and ~ TIED
   pain in the ~ ACHE, BORE,
    PEEVE, PEST
   stick one's ~ out BET, CRANE,
    RISK
   stretch the ~ CRANE
___ neck CREW, SCOOP
___-necked LOW
___-necked pheasant RING
necklace
   ~ part BEAD, CLASP
   flowery ~ LEI
   place for a ~ clasp NAPE
neckline
   ~ shape VEE
neckpiece BOA, LEI
necktie ASCOT
   like an orange ~ LOUD
neckwear ASCOT, TIE
   fluffy ~ BOA
   luau ~ LEI
necromancer ORACLE, SEER
nectar
   ~ collector BEE, HIVE
   ~ ender INE
   ~ source PEAR
nectarous SWEET

neddy HORSE
need CALL, USE, WANT
   ~ a scratch ITCH
   ~ aspirin ACHE
"___ Need" ALLI
Needham HAL
neediness WANT
"___ Need Is the Girl" ALLI
needle BAIT, DIG, EGG, GOAD,
   LEAF, PEAK, PROD, RIB, RIDE,
   TEASE, TWIT
   ~ case ETUI
   ~ feature HOLE
   ~ hole EYE
   ~ point ENE, ESE, NNE, NNW,
    SSE, SSW, WNW, WSW
   ~ producer PINE
   like a ~'s eye SMALL
   pine ~ LEAF
   ply a ~ SEW
___ needle PINE
needlefish GAR
needlepoint
   ~ need MESH
needles
   on pins and ~ EDGY, TENSE
needle-shaped ACUTE
needlework LACE
   ~ loop BRIDE
   do ~ SEW
needs
   check-cashing ~ IDS
   fill one's ~ SUIT
Neely CAM
ne'er-do-well CAD, DRONE, IDLER,
   LOSER
nefarious BAD, BASE, EVIL, LOW,
   VILE
nefariousness HARM
Nefertiti
   ~ god ATEN, ATON
   ~ river NILE
   ~ to Tut AUNT
Nefud DESERT
negate ANNUL, DENY, ERASE,
   UNDO, VOID
negative NAY, NOT
   ~ contraction AINT, CANT,
    DONT, ISNT
   ~ emotion ANGER, HATE
   ~ prefix DIS, NON
   ~ reply NAY, NOPE
   ~ suffix LESS
   ~ votes NOES, NOS
   no-no ~ AINT
   slangy ~ NAH, NOPE
Negev DESERT
   ~ loc. ISR
   like the ~ ARID, DRY
neglect OMIT, SKIP, WASTE
   show ~ ROT
neglectful LOOSE

negligence LAPSE
negligible MEAN, SMALL
negotiate DEAL, SELL, SETTLE
   ~ the slopes SLED
negotiation DEAL
negotiations
   ~ delay SNAG
   conclude ~ AGREE
negotiator AGENT, REP
   ~ asset TACT
___ Negro RIO
negus
   ~ ingredient WINE
Nehemiah
   book after ~ ESTHER
   book before ~ EZRA
Nehi
   ~ drinker RADAR
Nehru
   see Indian
neigh CRY, NOISE
   ~ cousin BRAY
   ~ homophone NAY, NEE
neighbor ABUT
"...___ 'neighbor' and 'weigh'"
   ASIN
neighborhood AREA, BEAT, SPOT,
   ZONE
   ~ sign LOST
   in the ~ LOCAL, NEAR
   in the ~ of ABOUT
   in the ~, to a poet ANEAR
neighboring CLOSE, NEXT
neighborly SWEET
"___ Neighbor Sam" GOOD
Neiman LEROY
nein
   ~ in French NON
   ~ in Latin NON
   ~ in Russian NYET
   ~ in Scottish NAE
___-Neisse Line ODER
neither
   partner of ~ NOR
neither fish ___ fowl NOR
neither here ___ there NOR
neither here nor ___ THERE
"Neither snow, ___ rain,..." NOR
Nejd
   where ~ is ARABIA
"___ Nell" OUR
Nellie ROSS
   ~ man EMILE
"___, Nellie!" WHOA
Nelligan KATE
___ nelly NICE
Nels
   ~ to Marta SON

nelson HOLD
___ nelson HALF
Nelson EDDY, GENE
"Nelson"
   Haydn's ~ MASS
Nelson, Tony
   ~ servant GENIE
nemesis ENEMY, FOE, RUIN
Nemesis
   play ~ AVENGE
neoclassical STYLE
   ~ architect ADAM
Neolithic
   ~ chisel CELT
neologize COIN, MINT
neon GAS
   ~ light LAMP
   ~ tetra PET
   like ~ INERT
neon ___ TETRA
neonate BABE, KID
neophyte BABE
neoteric NEW
Nepal
   ~ ender ESE
   ~ locale ASIA
   ~ neighbor INDIA
nephew MALE
   ~ sister NIECE
nephrite JADE
Nephthys
   sister of ~ ISIS
ne plus ___ ULTRA
ne plus ultra ACME, AONE, APEX,
   BEST, FIRST, IDEAL, MODEL,
   PEAK, TOP, TOPS
Neptune DEO, GOD, OCEAN, ORB,
   SEA
   ~ domain OCEAN, SEA
   Celtic ~ LER
neptunium METAL
nerd DRIP, SAP
Nereid MOON
Nereids
   one of the ~ IONE
Nero CAESAR, PETER, ROMAN
   ~ city ROME
   ~ instrument PIANO
   ~ to Agrippina SON
   outfit for ~ TOGA
   start of ~'s reign LIV
   see also Latin
neroli ___ OIL
Neruda PABLO
Neruda, Pablo POET
   see also poet
nerve FACE, GRIT, SAND, STEEL
   eye's ~ OPTIC
   have the ~ DARE

___ nerve OPTIC

nerve-racking TENSE

nerves
  a bundle of ~ EDGY, TENSE
  get on one's ~ IRK, UPSET

nerves of ___ STEEL

nervous EDGY, SHY, TENSE
  ~ tension STRESS

nervousness FEAR

nervy GAME, SASSY

ness CAPE

Ness ELIOT, FED, LAKE
  ~ colleague TMAN
  ~ to Capone ENEMY, FOE

Nessen RON

Ness, Loch
  see Scottish

Nessman
  ~ of WKRP LES

nest ABODE, AERIE, DEN, HAVEN, HOME, LAIR, NOOK
  ~ sound PEEP
  eagle's ~ AERIE
  hornet's ~ ADO
  mare's ~ MESS

nest ___ EGG

"N'est-ce ___?" PAS

nest egg
  ~ initials IRA

nesting
  ~ place TREE

nestle CARESS, PET

nestling
  certain ~ OWLET

"nest of robins..., A"
  ~ poem TREES

Nestor SAGE
  like ~ WISE

net CLEAR, EARN, GAIN, GET, HAUL, MESH, SNARE, TAKE
  ~ holder RIM
  ~ surfer USER
  fish ~ SEINE
  work without a ~ DARE

net ___ value ASSET

Netanyahu
  ~ predecessor PERES

Neth.
  ~ neighbor GER

nether LOW

Netherlands
  ~ commune EDE
  ~ royal house ORANGE
  see also Dutch, Holland

netherworld ABYSS

net judge
  ~ call LET

netman
  Swedish ~ BORG

Nets FIVE, TEAM
  ~ org. NBA

netting LACE, MESH, WEB

nettle ANGER, FRET, GRATE, IRE, IRK, PEEVE, RILE, STING, UPSET, WEED

nettled IRATE, MAD, UPSET

Nettleton LOIS

network MESH, WEB
  ~ (abbr.) SYST
  ~ transmission FEED
  electrical ~ GRID
  English ~ BBC
  TV ~ ABC, CBS

networks
  TV ~ MEDIA

net worth
  ~ component ASSET

Neuchâtel LAKE

Neuilly-sur-___ SEINE

Neuman, Alfred E.
  ~ mag MAD

Neumann, Kurt
  ~ film of 1952, with "The" RING

neural
  ~ network RETE

neurological
  ~ exam. EEG

neutral
  ~ color ECRU, GRAY, GREY, TAN, TAUPE
  ethically ~ AMORAL
  race in ~ REV
  run in ~ IDLE

neutralize ANNUL, UNDO

neutralizer
  base ~ ACID

neutralizing
  ~ (prefix) ANTI

neutron ___ STAR

"Neutron ___" DANCE

Nev.
  ~ neighbor CAL, IDA, ORE, OREGON, UTAH
  see also Nevada

Nevada STATE
  ~ casino SAHARA, SANDS
  ~ county NYE
  ~ county seat ELY
  ~ lake MEAD
  ~ neighbor OREGON, UTAH
  ~ town ELY, RENO
  University of ~ site RENO

"___ ne va plus" RIEN

never
  ~ to a poet NEER
  ~ to return PAST

"Never ___ Die" SAY

"Never ___ Diet" SAY

"Never ___ Wolf" CRY

"___ Never Can Tell" YOU

never-ending ETERNAL, SLOW, VAST

never-failing SURE

"___ Never Forget What's 'is Name" ILL

"Never Give a Sucker an ___ Break" EVEN

"Nevermore"
  ~ sayer RAVEN

Nevers
  see French

"Never Say ___" DIE, DIET

"Never Say Never ___" AGAIN

"___ Never Seen Those Eyes" MAMAS

"___ Never Smile Again" ILL

nevertheless YET

"___ never too late..." ITS

"___ Never Too Young" YOURE

Neville AARON

Nevski, Alexander HERO

nevus MOLE

new LATE
  ~ growth SPRIG
  ~ Mrs. BRIDE
  ~ (prefix) NEO
  ~ singles EXES
  breathe ~ life into RENEW
  build ~ tissue HEAL
  fashionably ~ MOD
  homophone of ~ GNU, KNEW
  like ~ MINT
  make good as ~ MEND
  not ~ USED
  put ~ life into RESTORE
  reach ~ heights SOAR

new ___ MATH, MEDIA, MOON, YEAR

new ___ on life, a LEASE

New ___ AGE, DEAL, LEFT, STYLE

New ___ (holistic medicine practicer) AGER

New ___, Conn. HAVEN

New ___ Day YEARS

New ___, La. IBERIA

"New ___, A" LEAF

New Age
  ~ glow AURA

Newark CITY, PORT
  ~ st. DEL

New Baskerville FONT

New Bedford CITY, PORT

newborn KID, NEW

Newbrook PETER

New Brunswick
  ~ neighbor MAINE

Newcastle CITY, PORT
  ~ product COAL

Newcastle ___ Tyne UPON

Newcastle upon ___ TYNE

Newcombe
  foe of ~ ASHE

newcomer ALIEN
  paddock ~ FOAL
  ranch ~ DUDE

New Deal
  ~ org. NRA, REA, SSA, TVA

New Delhi
  see Indian

newel POST

New England
  ~ campus MIT, YALE
  ~ cape ANN, COD
  ~ fish SCROD
  ~ soda fountain SPA
  ~ st. MASS
  ~ state MAINE

newest LAST

Newf. ISL

New Hampshire HEN, STATE
  ~ neighbor MAINE
  ~ state flower LILAC

"___ New Hampshire, The" HOTEL

New Harmony
  ~ founder OWEN

Newhart BOB

"Newhart"
  ~ setting INN

New Haven
  ~ school YALE
  ~ student ELI
  ~ tree ELM

New Jersey STATE
  ~ cager NET
  ~ cape MAY
  ~ city LODI
  ~ ender ITE
  ~ university DREW

"New Leaf, A"
  ~ director MAY

new lease on ___, a LIFE

New Left
  ~ org. SDS

"New Life, A"
  ~ actor ALDA

"New Look"
  ~ designer DIOR

newlywed BRIDE

Newman PAUL

New Mexico STATE
  ~ Amerind UTE
  ~ county EDDY, LEA, LUNA, OTERO, TAOS
  ~ lake UTE
  ~ resort TAOS

Newmeyer FRED

New Orleans CITY, PORT
~ **gridder** SAINT
City of ~ TRAIN

"New Republic"
~ **piece** ESSAY

New Riders of the Purple ___, The SAGE

New Rochelle
~ **college** IONA

news DIRT, DOPE, INFO
~ **article** ITEM
~ **exclusive** SCOOP
~ **item** CLIP, OBIT
~ **magazine** TIME
~ **maker** STAR
~ **media** PRESS
~ **medium** RADIO
~ **perspective** SLANT
~ **source** LEAK, PAPER, RADIO
~ **summary** RECAP
~ **time** ELEVEN, SEVEN
bad ~ on Wall Street SLIDE
break the ~ LEAK, TELL
former ~ org. UPI
Moscow ~ acronym TASS
piece of ~ EVENT
reaction to bad ~ OHNO
receive, as ~ HEAR

___ **news** HARD

"___ News" GOOD

"___ News Bears, The" BAD

newsboy
~ **cry** EXTRA

news bureau
USSR ~ TASS

news conference
~ **attendees** MEDIA, PRESS

newshawk
~ **goal** SCOOP

newsletter PAPER

New South ___ WALES

newspaper ORGAN, SHEET
~ **bigwig** EDITOR
~ **business** PRESS
~ **execs** EDS
~ **feature** COL
~ **items** ADS
~ **notice** OBIT
~ **page part** COL
~ **part** SECT
~ **pictorial section** ROTO
~ **piece** ITEM
~ **scoop** BEAT
~ **section** DESK, METRO
~ **special edition** EXTRA
~ **type size** AGATE
third-rate ~ RAG

newspapers MEDIA, PRESS

newsreel
~ **segment** EVENT

newsroom
~ **figure** EDITOR
~ **post** DESK

"Newsweek" MAG
~ **items** ADS

~ **rival** TIME

newt EFT
~ **immature** EFT

New Testament
~ **book** ACTS
~ **king** HEROD
~ **sages** MAGI
~ **villain** HEROD

newton
~ **cousin** DYNE

Newton ISAAC

Newton, Isaac SIR

"New Woman"
~ **rival** SELF

New World
~ **abbr.** AMER
~ **alliance** OAS

New Year
~ **in Hanoi** TET
~ **noise** TOOT
~ **resolution, often** DIET
lunar ~ TET

New Year's ___ DAY, EVE

New Year's Day
word sung on ~ LANG, SYNE

New York CITY, PORT, STATE
~ **ballpark** SHEA
~ **baseball player** MET
~ **canal** ERIE
~ **city** ROME, TROY, UTICA
~ **college** IONA
~ **county** ERIE
~ **footballer** GIANT, JET
~ **island** ELLIS, FIRE
~ **lake** ONEIDA
~ **river** EAST
~ **state flower** ROSE
~ **suburb** RYE
~ **university** PACE

"New York ___ of Mind" STATE

New York City
~ **area** SOHO
~ **river** EAST
~ **suburb** RYE

New York Cosmos
~ **star** PELE

New York cut STEAK

"New York Enquirer"
~ **boss** KANE

"New Yorker, The"
~ **cartoonist** ARNO, REA
~ **founder** ROSS

___ **New York minute** INA

New York Times
onetime ~ publisher OCHS

New Zealand
~ **aborigine** MAORI
~ **bird** KIWI
~ **export** LAMB
~ **extinct bird** MOA
~ **parrot** KEA

New Zealander KIWI

next AFTER, LATER, THEN
~ **in line** HEIR
be ~ to ABUT
column ~ to ones TENS
coming ~ AFTER
happen ~ ENSUE
lie ~ to ABUT

"Next ___, The" MAN

"Next ___, Greenwich Village" STOP

"Next ___ We Love" TIME

next-door NEAR

"___ Next Spring" COME

"Next Time We ___" LOVE

nexus CORD, TIE

Nez Percé TRIBE

NFC
~ **division** EAST, WEST

NFL
~ **city** TAMPA
~ **conference** EAST, WEST
~ **player** BEAR, BILL, CARD, COLT, EAGLE, GIANT, JET, LION, OILER, PRO, RAM, SAINT
~ **scores** TDS
~ **unit** ELEVEN

Nfld. ISL

Ngami LAKE

Ngo Dinh ___ DIEM

N.H.
~ **neighbor** MASS
see also New Hampshire

NHL
~ **city** OTTAWA
~ **Hall-of-Famer** HOWE, ORR
~ **player** CAP, JET, LEAF, OILER, PRO, STAR
~ **player at times** ICER
~ **team, in headlines** ISLES
~ **venue** ICE, RINK
play for the ~ SKATE

Ni ELEM
28 for ~ ATNO

niacin ACID

Niagara
~ **fort** ERIE

Niagara Falls
~ **prov.** ONT

Niamey
~ **country** NIGER

nib BILL, END, NOSE, PEN

nibble BITE, EAT, GNAW, NIP, NOSH
have a ~ NOSH

nibbler EATER

"___ Nibelungen" DIE

"Nibelungenlied" EPIC, SAGA

Nibelungs
~ **hoard** GOLD

niblick IRON

Niblo FRED

___ **nibs** HER, HIS

Nicaragua
see Spanish

Nicaraguan
~ **city** LEON

niccolite ORE

nice FINE, SWEET
~ **expression** SMILE
~ **request** PLEASE
insincerely ~ OILY
make ~ to PAT
not ~ MEAN

Nice
see French

"Nice ___?" GIRL

"Nice guys finish ___" LAST

Nice 'N' ___ EASY

Nicene ___ CREED

"___ nice place to visit..." ITSA

niche BAY, COVE, HOLE, NOOK
artist's ~ GENRE
church ~ APSE
cozy ~ NEST

Nicholas RAY, SAINT, TSAR

___ **Nicholas** SAINT

"Nicholas Nickleby"
~ **actor** REES

Nichols ANNE, RED
~ **partner** MAY

Nichols, Anne
~ **hero** ABIE

nick CHIP, CUT, DENT, DING, GASH, HOLE, MAR, NIP, PIT, SCORE, SNIP
fender ~ DENT

Nick ADAMS, NOLTE
~ **dog** ASTA
~ **name** SANTA
~ **wife** NORA

___ **Nick** OLD, SAINT

"___ Nick Beal" ALIAS

nickel COIN, METAL
~ **partner** DIME
wooden ~ FAKE, SHAM
word on a ~ CENTS, GOD

nickel-and-___ DIME

nickelodeon
~ **opening** SLOT

nickels
two ~ DIME

Nicklaus, Jack
~ **alma mater** OSU
~ **org.** PGA
see also golf

Nickleby
~ **portrayer** REES

nickname LABEL, TAG
~ **in Spanish** MOTE

"Nick of Time"
~ Grammy-winner RAITT

Nicolaou TED

Nicolas CAGE
see also French

___ **Nicole Smith** ANNA

Nicolo AMATI

Nicolson ADELA

nictitate BAT

Nidal ABU

nidus NEST

Nielsen
~ letters ABC, CBS

Nietzsche
see German

nifty FINE, NEAT

Niger
~ native IBO
~ neighbor CHAD, MALI

Nigeria
~ et al. OPEC
~ neighbor CHAD

Nigerian EDO
~ city ABA, EDE, ILA
~ native IBO
~ singer SADE

niggardly MEAN, NEAR

niggling MERE

nigh ABOUT, ANEAR, CLOSE, NEAR

night
~ attire ROBE
~ before EVE
~ ender CAP, JAR, LIFE, MARE, SHADE, SPOT, STAND, TIME
~ flyer BAT, OWL
~ insect MOTH
~ light LAMP, NEON, STAR
~ shade EBON, SABLE
~ sound SNORE
~ spot BED
~ starter OVER, WEEK
place to spend the ~ BED, HOTEL, INN, PAD, ROOM
work day and ~ LABOR, TOIL

night ___ OWL, TABLE

___-**night** ALL

"Night ___**"** NURSE, TRAIN

"Night ___ **a Thousand Eyes, The"** HAS

"Night ___**" Lane** TRAIN

"Night ___ **Morning"** INTO

"Night ___ **Night"** UNTO

" ___ **Night"** PROM

"Night at the ___**, A"** OPERA

" ___ **Night at the Alamo"** LAST

"Night at the Opera, A"
~ role OTIS
~ song ALONE

nightcap GAME, HAT

nightclub BAR
~ number SONG
~ routine ACT

"Night Court"
~ actress POST
~ clerk MAC
~ name SELMA

night crawler BAIT

___-**nighter** ALL

Nightingale NURSE
~ prop LAMP

nightjar BIRD

"Nightline"
~ name TED
~ network ABC

" ___ **Night Long"** ALL

nightmare BANE, DREAM
~ street ELM
Congressman's ~ LOSS
have a ~ DREAM
taxpayer's ~ AUDIT

"Nightmare ___**"** ALLEY

"Nightmare on ___ **Street, A"** ELM

"Nightmare on Elm Street 3: ___ **Warriors, A"** DREAM

"Night Moves"
~ director PENN

"Night Music"
~ playwright ODETS

"Night My Number ___ **Up, The"** CAME

" ___ **Night of Love"** ONE

"Night of the ___**, The"** IGUANA

"Night of the Grizzly, The"
~ actor ELY

"Night of the Hunter, The"
~ screenwriter AGEE

"Night of the Iguana, The"
~ actress KERR

"Night on ___**"** EARTH

"Night on ___ **Mountain"** BALD

nights
stay awake ~ STEW

nightshade WEED

night shift
~ worker ELF

night sky
~ sight STAR

" ___ **Nights on a Slow-Moving Train"** WARM

nightspot CAFE

nighttime EVE
~ to a poet EEN

"Night Train"
~ of the gridiron LANE

nigrescent RAVEN

nigritudinous RAVEN

Niigata CITY, PORT

Nike
~ swoosh LOGO

Nikita
see Russian

"Nikki, Wild ___ **of the North"** DOG

Nikola TESLA

Nikolai
see Russian

Nikolaidi ELENA

nil NADA, ZERO
~ in Spanish NADA

Nile
~ city ASWAN, CAIRO
~ dam ASWAN
~ denizen CROC
~ feature DELTA
~ gift SILT
~ queen, for short CLEO
~ reptile ASP
~ wader IBIS
desert bordering the ~ SAHARA
opera set near the ~ AIDA

Nile ___ DELTA

___ **Nile** BLUE

Nilsson, Birgit SWEDE

nimble ADEPT, AGILE, ALERT, DEFT, FAST, FLEET, LITHE, SPRY

nimbus AURA, HALO, RING

NIMBY
part of ~ NOT, YARD

Nîmes
~ neighbor ALES

nimiety GLUT

Nimitz
~ org. USN

" ___ **Nimitz"** USS

Nimzowitsch
~ of chess ARON

Nin ANAIS

"Niña" BOAT, SHIP

nincompoop ASS, DODO, DOLT, DOPE, GOOSE, OAF, TWIT

nine SIDE
~ inches SPAN
one of ~ CLIO, ERATO, MUSE

nine ___ **wonder** DAYS

ninepins GAME

___-**nine-tails** CATO

nineteenth ___ HOLE

"Nine, ten, a big fat ___**"** HEN

___ **Nineties** GAY

Nineveh
~ locale, today IRAQ

nine yards
the whole ~ ALL

ninja
~ move CHOP

Ninja Turtles
~ home SEWER

ninny ASS, DOLT, GOOSE, IDIOT, OAF, SAP
~ in French ANE

Ninotchka
see Russian

Nintendo GAME
~ hero MARIO
~ predecessor ATARI

Niobe
~ output TEAR
emulate ~ WEEP

niobium METAL

nip BITE, DAB, SHOT, SIP, SNAP, SNORT
~ and tuck CLOSE
~ in sports EDGE
~ in the bud ARREST, STAY, STOP
~ starter CAT

nipa PALM

Nipigon LAKE

nipper CLAW, DOG

nippy COOL, RAW

nirvana EDEN, HOME

Nirvana
~ seeker HINDU

Nisan
~ preceder ADAR

"N Is for ___**" (Grafton novel)** NOOSE

Nissan AUTO, CAR

nit LOUSE
~ ender WIT

NIT
~ rival NCAA

nitid CLEAR

nitpick ARGUE, CARP, NAG

nitpicker PRIG

nitrate ESTER, SALT

nitric ACID

nitrite ESTER, SALT

nitrogen GAS
it's mostly ~ AIR

nitrous oxide GAS

nits
adult ~ LICE

Nittany ___ LIONS

Nitti
~ nabber TMAN
~ nemesis NESS

nitty-gritty BASIC, CORE, ESSENCE, GIST

nitwit ASS, CLOD, DOPE, OAF

nix BAN, DENY, VETO

Nixon
~ '72 org. CREEP

"Nixon"
~ actress ALLEN
~ director STONE

"Nixon in China" OPERA

Nixon, Mrs. PAT

Nixon, Pat, née ___ RYAN

N.J.
~ neighbor DEL, PENN
~ ocean ATL
see also New Jersey

NL
~ stat HRS, RBI
~ team METS, REDS

NLRB
L in ~ LABOR

N.M.
see New Mexico

N. Mex.
see New Mexico

NNE
~ opposite SSW

NNW
~ opposite SSE

no NAY, NOPE
~ big thing BLIP
~ brain surgeon DENSE
~ contest, maybe PLEA
~ ender SIREE
~ friend ENEMY, FOE
~ gentleman CAD, HEEL, RAKE, ROUE
~ good POOR
~ great shakes MEAN, SOSO
~ in French NON
~ in German NEIN
~ in Latin NON
~ in Russian NYET
~ in Scottish NAE
~ longer a minor ADULT
~ longer available TAKEN
~ longer chic OUT, PASSE
~ longer crisp STALE
~ longer edible STALE
~ longer fresh OLD
~ longer in style OUT
~ longer in vogue PASSE
~ longer is WAS
~ longer novel STALE
~ longer popular OUT
~ longer sleeping ASTIR
~ longer trendy PASSE
~ longer used DATED
~ man's land DESERT
~ more ONCE, STOP
~ more than MERE, ONLY
~ picnic HARD
~ Prince Charming CAD
~ problem EASY
~ rocket scientist DENSE, DIM
~ sweat EASY
~ voter ANTI
~ walk in the park HARD
at ~ time NEVER
for ~ reason IDLY
giving ~ heed DEAF
have ~ doubt KNOW

have ~ stomach for HATE
have ~ use for HATE
having ~ deferments ONEA
having ~ slack TAUT
in ~ time ANON, SOON
it waits for ~ man TIDE, TIME
leave ~ choice IMPEL
leave ~ stone unturned DIG, HUNT, RAKE, SEEK
leave ~ vestige of RAZE
lose ~ time FLEE, HIE, RACE, RUN, SPEED
make ~ bones about ADMIT
point of ~ return, tennis-wise ACE
President's ~ VETO
say ~ to DENY
strong ~ NEVER
take ~ note of CUT
take ~ notice of SNUB
unable to say ~ MEEK
under ~ circumstances NEVER
waste ~ time FLEE, HIE, RUN
with ~ delay STAT
with ~ guarantee ASIS
with ~ sense of ethics AMORAL

no ___ (interminably) END

no ___ (register button) SALE

no ___ lost LOVE

no ___ shakes GREAT

no ___ ways about it TWO

no-___ CAL, HIT, LOAD, LOSE, PAR, SHOW, WIN

no-___ clause TRADE

no-___ fund LOAD

no-___-um SEE

No DRAMA, ELEM, LAKE
~ and others DRS
102 for ~ ATNO

"No ___" (Duran quote) MAS

"No ___" (menu phrase) MSG

"No ___" (Sartre work) EXIT

"No ___!" DICE, SIREE

"No ___, ands, or buts!" IFS

"No ___ Bob!" SIREE

"No ___ for Sergeants" TIME

"No ___ Love" OTHER

"No ___, no gain" PAIN

"No ___ on the Bullet" NAME

"No ___ Please, We're British" SEX

"No ___ Songs for Me" SAD

"No ___ talk to" ONETO

"No ___ Women" MORE

"No, ___ Much!" NOT

no-account IDLER

Noachian OLD

Noah
~ count TWO
~ craft ARK
~ landing place ARARAT
~ passengers PAIRS
~ son HAM

"___ No Angels" WERE

nob GENT, HEAD

Nobel SWEDE
~ invention TNT
~ poet's monogram TSE

Nobel, Alfred SWEDE

Nobelist
Chemistry ~ 1934 UREY
Chemistry ~ 1991 ERNST
Literature ~ 1925 SHAW
Literature ~ 1929 MANN
Literature ~ 1930 LEWIS
Literature ~ 1946 HESSE
Literature ~ 1947 GIDE
Literature ~ 1948 ELIOT
Literature ~ 1960 PERSE
Peace ~ 1912 ROOT
Peace ~ 1969 ILO
Peace ~ 1978 SADAT
Peace ~ 1979 TERESA
Peace ~ 1984 TUTU
Peace ~ 1987 ARIAS
Peace ~ 1994 PERES
Physics ~ 1943 STERN

Nobel Prize AWARD
~ category ECON
~ city OSLO

nobility ELITE, RANK
~ title DAME, SIR

___ nobis pacem DONA

noble BARON, BIG, DAME, EARL, GOOD, GREAT, LORD, PURE, REGAL
~ exploit DEED
~ gas NEON
~ Italian name ESTE
Arab ~ AGA, AGHA

noble ___ GAS, METAL

"Noble ___, The" SLAV

nobleman BARON, EARL, LORD, PEER
Arabian ~ AMIR, EMEER, EMIR
British ~ PEER

"noblest ___ of them all, The" ROMAN

noblewoman DAME, LADY

nobody NOONE, ZERO

"Nobody ___ It Better" DOES

"___ No Crime" AINT

nocturnal
~ mammal BAT
~ noise SNORE
~ predator OWL
~ sound HOOT

nocuous BAD, EVIL, ILL

nod BOB, BOW, REST, SIGN, SLEEP
~ ender ULE
gives the ~ to OKS

Nod
land of ~ SLEEP
land west of ~ EDEN

noddle DOME, HEAD

noddy TERN

node KNOT

nods OKS

noel CAROL, SONG

Noel YULE
~ name SANTA
~ trio MAGI

Noël PERE

"___ no evil..." HEAR

"___ No Evil" SEE

"No fooling!" HONEST

nog
~ ingredient EGG

Nogales
see Spanish

noggin BEAN, DOME, HEAD, PATE
conk on the ~ BOP

no-good MEAN

___ no good UPTO

"___ No Good" YOURE

no-goodnik CAD, LOUSE, OGRE, RAT

"no guarantees"
~ phrase ASIS

Noh DRAMA
~ prop FAN

"No Highway in the ___" SKY

no-holds-barred FREE, LOOSE, OPEN

"___ No Hooks" USE

___ no ice CUT

no ifs, ___, or buts ANDS

noir BET
film ~ GENRE
pinot ~ WINE
rouge et ~ GAME

___ noir CAFE

noire
bête ~ BANE, FEAR

noise BLAST, DIN
~ about RUMOR
~ abroad POST, SAY
background ~ DIN
crowd ~ RAH, ROAR
dull ~ THUD
firecracker ~ POP
glottal ~ HIC
horse's ~ SNORT
incubator ~ PEEP
indistinct ~ THUD
ketchup ~ PLOP
loud ~ BANG, BOOM, CLAP, DIN, POP, SLAM, THUD
nasal ~ SNORT
New Year's ~ TOOT
nose ~ SNORE

pet-shop ~ ARF
phone-machine ~ BEEP
street ~ SIREN
traffic-jam ~ BLARE
wake-up ~ ALARM

noiseless MUTE

"Noiseless Patient Spider, A" POEM

noisemaker HORN

"Noises Off"
~ actor CAINE, REEVE

noisette MEAT

noisily ALOUD

noisome BAD, RANK

noisy LOUD
~ bird MACAW, PIE
be ~ at night SNORE

"___ no kick from champagne" IGET

"No kidding!" HONEST

___ Nol LON

Nolan RYAN

Nolan, Philip
~ fate EXILE

no love ___ LOST

nol-pros ANNUL

Nolte
~ film, with "The" DEEP

nom
~ de guerre ALIAS, NAME
~ de plume ALIAS, NAME

nomad
~ home TENT
be a ~ ROAM
desert ~ robe ABA
Northern ~ LAPP

nomadic
~ Mongol tribe HORDE

nomads
emulate ~ ROVE

"No man is an island"
~ poet DONNE

"No Man of Her ___" OWN

no man's ___ LAND

Nome
~ home ALASKA, IGLOO

no mean ___ FEAT

nominal MEAN, SMALL

nominate NAME

nominee
~ listing SLATE
Oscar ~ ACTOR

nomologist
~ forte LAW

"No more Mr. ___ Guy!" NICE

"___ no more, my lady" WEEP

"No more seats"
~ letters SRO

"___ No Mountain High Enough" AINT

non
~ in German NEIN
~ in Russian NYET
~ in Scottish NAE
sine qua ~ GIST, NEED

nonagenarian ELDER

nonce
for the ~ NOW

nonchalance EASE

nonchalant COOL

noncitizen ALIEN

nonclerical LAIC, LAY

noncom NCO, SGT
~ nickname SARGE

noncommittal
~ response ISEE

non compos mentis DAFT, MAD

nonconformist LONER, REBEL

nonconformists
~ swim against it TIDE

nondiscriminatory OPEN

none NARY, NIL, ZERO
~ too bright DENSE
~ too promising DIRE
excluding ~ ALL
second to ~ AONE, BEST, FIRST, TOP, TOPS

___ none (without exception) BAR

non-earthling ALIEN

non-earthlings ETS

"None But the Lonely Heart"
~ role ADA

nonecclesiastical LAIC, LAY

nonentity ZERO

none of the ___ ABOVE

"none of the above"
~ alternative OTHER

nones HOUR
~ plus eight IDES

nonessential EXTRA

nonet
~ number NINE

nonetheless YET

non-ethical AMORAL

non-exclusive OPEN

nonexistent NULL

nonextant LATE

nonfeasance LAPSE

nonfictional REAL

nonflowering
~ plant FERN, MOSS

nonitalicized ROMAN

nonministerial LAIC, LAY

non-motorized
~ vehicle BIKE

no-no DONT, TABOO, TABU
dieter's ~ FAT
football ~ CLIP
George Washington ~ LIE, TALE
grammatical ~ AINT
gridiron ~ CLIP
library ~ NOISE
PBS ~ ADS
statistician's ~ BIAS
vegetarian's ~ MEAT

"No, No, Nanette"
~ lyricist CAESAR

nonpareil ACE, ALONE, AONE, BEST, FIRST, GEM, IDEAL, MODEL, ONER, RARE, TOP

nonpastoral LAIC

nonpayment
~ result REPO

nonpermanent
~ staffer TEMP

nonperson EXILE

"Non più andrai" ARIA

nonplus ADDLE, DAZE, GET, POSE, SHAME

nonplussed ASEA, ATSEA, LOST

nonpoisonous SAFE

nonproductive ARID

nonprofessional LAY

nonproliferation
~ treaty SALT

nonreactive INERT

nonsense BLAH, PAP, POOH, ROT, TRASH

"Nonsense!" BAH, POOH, TUT

nonsensical DAFT, INANE, MAD

nonsocial
~ one NERD

nonspecific LOOSE
~ adjective ANY

nonstandard
~ contraction AINT

nonstop ETERNAL

nonsupporter ANTI

nonterrestrial ALIEN

nontransparent DENSE

nonverbal
~ OK NOD

nonviolent MILD

nonwinner LOSER

noodle BEAN, DOLT, HEAD, NOB, NUT
like a wet ~ LIMP

noodlehead DOLT, SAP

noodles PASTA

nook BAY, COVE

noon
~ in French MIDI
~ starter AFTER, FORE

Noonan FRED, TOM

Noonan, Chris
~ film of 1995 BABE

Noonan, Fred
emulate ~ AVIATE

"No Ordinary Love"
~ singer SADE

noose LOOP, RING, ROPE, SNARE
~ essentially LOOP

"No pain, no ___" GAIN

nopals CACTI

"No Particular Place ___" TOGO

nope NAH, NAY
~ opposite YEP

"No problemo!" EASY

nor'___ EASTER

Nor.
~ neighbor DEN, FIN

Nora
~ dog ASTA

Nordenskjöld SWEDE

Nordic ARYAN
~ name ERIK

Nordiques SIX, TEAM
~ milieu ICE, RINK
~ org. NHL

Nordkyn CAPE

Nordstrom ELMER

"No, really!" HONEST

Norfolk
~ ale NOG

Norfolk Island ___ PINE

___ nor hair HIDE

norm MEAN, MODEL, PAR, USUAL

Norm
~ occupation on "Cheers" CPA
~ wife on "Cheers" VERA

"Norma" OPERA
~ piece ARIA

"Norma ___" RAE

"Norma ___" (Glaspell novel) ASHE

normal PAR, SANE
~ (abbr.) REG, STD
~ elasticity TONE

Norman DIVA, LEAR, RENE, STONE
~ city CAEN

Norman ___ Geddes BEL

___ Normandes ILES

Normandy
~ battle site STLO
~ beach UTAH
~ event DDAY
~ river ORNE

~ **town** CAEN
see also French

Norman, Greg
~ **org.** PGA
see also golf

Norman, Jessye DIVA
~ **forte** OPERA
~ **specialty** ARIA

Norman Vincent ___ PEALE

Norris Division
~ **org.** NHL

Norris, Frank
~ **novel, with "The"** PIT

Norse
~ **epic** EDDA, SAGA
~ **god** ODIN
~ **god of war** THOR
~ **mariner** ERIC
~ **mythical king** ATLI
~ **royal name** OLAF, OLAV
~ **symbol** RUNE

___ Norte DEL

north
~ **ender** ERN

___ north TRUE

North OLLIE, SEA
The ~ UNION

North ___ POLE, STAR

North African
~ **mountains** ATLAS
~ **official** PASHA
~ **port** ORAN
~ **range** ATLAS
~ **ruler** DEY

North American
~ **capital** OTTAWA

Northamptonshire
~ **river** OUSE

North Atlantic
~ **fish** COD
~ **menace** FLOE
~ **sighting** BERG, FLOE

"North by Northwest"
~ **actress** SAINT
Cary's ~ costar EVA

North Carolina STATE
~ **county** ASHE, EDEN, SELMA
start of ~ motto ESSE

North Dakota STATE

"North Dallas Forty"
~ **actor** NOLTE
~ **author** GENT

northeaster GALE, STORM

Northeastern U.
~ **neighbor** MIT

Northern ___ apple SPY

Northern European LAPP

"Northern Exposure"
~ **animal** BEAR, MOOSE
~ **network** CBS
~ **setting** ALASKA
~ **wild man** ADAM

Northern Native American ERIE

north forty
~ **unit** ACRE

"___ North Frederick" TEN

North, Oliver
~ **rank** COL

North Pole
~ **denizen** SANTA
~ **worker** ELF

North Sea
~ **arm** ELBE
~ **feeder** ELBE, EMS, ODER, RHINE, TEES, TYNE, YSER
~ **floater** BERG
~ **hazard** FLOE

"___ Northside 777" CALL

North Slope
~ **quest** OIL
~ **state** ALASKA

"North to ___" ALASKA

"North to the Future"
~ **state** ALASKA

Northumberland
~ **river** TYNE

Northumbrian
~ **neighbor** SCOT

northwards ABOVE

Northwest
~ **competitor** TWA
~ **peak** HOOD
~ **river** SNAKE
~ **state** OREGON

Northwestern
~ **capital** SALEM

Norton
~ **and others** EDS
~ **foe** ALI

Norton, Ed
~ **to Kramden** PAL
~ **wear** HAT, VEST
~ **workplace** SEWER

Norway
~ **capital** OSLO
~ **native** LAPP
patron saint of ~ OLAF, OLAV

Norway ___ MAPLE, PINE, RAT

Norwegian
~ **playwright** IBSEN
certain ~ LAPP

"Norwegian Wood"
~ **instrument** SITAR

"No Sad Songs ___ Me" FOR

"No Sad Songs for Me"
~ **director** MATE

nose ORGAN
~ **around** PRY
~ **count** POLL
~ **job** BOB
~ **noise** SNORE
~ **out** EDGE, SEEK
~ **stimulus** ODOR
~ **to nose** CLOSE

by a ~ CLOSE
like a hound's ~ KEEN
look down one's ~ SNEER
offend the ~ REEK
of the ~ NASAL
say through the ~ SNORT
stick one's ~ in PRY
turn up one's ~ SNEER
turn up one's ~ at SNUB

nose ___ CONE

nose ___ (just beat) OUT

___ nose ROMAN

nosebag
~ **bit** OAT
~ **fill** FEED

___-nosed HARD, SNUB

no-see-um GNAT

nosegay
~ **holder** VASE

noseguard
sports car's ~ BRA

nose-in-the-air
~ **type** SNOB

nosepiece ARMOR

noses
like some ~ ROMAN

Nosferatu
~ **garb** CAPE

nosh BITE, EAT
party ~ CHIP, DIP, NUT

no-show
military ~ AWOL

nostalgic
~ **clothes style** RETRO
~ **song** OLDIE
~ **song ending** SYNE
~ **time** YORE
feel ~ for MISS

"Nostalgic ___" ECHO

nostoc ALGA

Nostradamus SEER

nostrils NOSE
assault the ~ REEK

no-strings-attached FREE, LOOSE

nostrum CURE

"___ nostrum" MARE

"___ No Sunshine" AINT

nosy
~ **one** YENTA
get ~ ASK, PRY

not
~ **abed** ASTIR
~ **a blabbermouth** CLAM
~ **absent** HERE
~ **adventurous** STAID
~ **a gentleman** CAD
~ **agin** FER
~ **allowed** TABOO, TABU
~ **an ordinary novel** EPIC
~ **a problem** EASY

~ **as** LESS
~ **a success** DUD
~ **at work** IDLE, OFF
~ **bad** OKAY, SOSO
~ **be perfect** ERR
~ **budge** STAY
~ **canned** ONTAP
~ **carrying a piece** CLEAN
~ **colorful** DRAB
~ **dawdle** HIE, RACE, RUN, SPEED
~ **decided** OPEN
~ **distant** NEAR
~ **early** LATE
~ **elsewhere** HERE
~ **enunciate** ELIDE
~ **even** EROSE
~ **exciting** BLAH, TAME
~ **excluded** INON
~ **ferocious** TAME
~ **found** LOST
~ **friendly** COOL
~ **genuine** FAKE
~ **glum** GAY
~ **great** OKAY
~ **green** RIPE
~ **his** HERS
~ **home** OUT
~ **imagined** REAL
~ **in** OUT
~ **inactive** ASTIR
~ **in French** PAS
~ **in operation** IDLE, OFF
~ **in port** ASEA, ATSEA
~ **in Scottish** NAE
~ **in use** FREE
~ **keyed** ATONAL
~ **motionless** ASTIR
~ **move** STAY
~ **Mr. Right** CAD
~ **naughty** NICE
~ **nude** CLAD
~ **odd** EVEN
~ **on the rocks** NEAT
~ **plentiful** SPARSE
~ **(prefix)** DIS, NON
~ **prerecorded** LIVE
~ **prompt** LATE
~ **quite soggy** DAMP
~ **real** SHAM
~ **relaxed** TAUT
~ **scintillating** BANAL
~ **smart** DIM, SLOW
~ **spicy** MILD
~ **stiff** LIMP
~ **straight** ATILT, AWRY
~ **sure** LEERY
~ **sweet** DRY
~ **swift** DENSE
~ **taped** LIVE
~ **thrilling** BLAH
~ **to be persuaded** DEAF
~ **upright** ATILT
~ **urban** RURAL
~ **windy** CALM
~ **yet resolved** OPEN

not ___ a trick MISS

not ___ bad HALF

___-not HAVE

"...not ___ do" ASI

"Not ___!" AGAIN

"Not ___ bet!"

"Not ___ bet!" ONA
"Not ___ can help it!" IFI
"Not ___ Stranger" ASA
nota ___ BENE
notable LION, NAME
  ~ **time** ERA
notables ELITE
notably EXTRA
"...not always what they ___" SEEM
notarize SIGN
notary
  ~ **need** SEAL, STAMP
notation ENTRY
  datebk. ~ APPT
notch CHIP, CUT, DENT, GAP, HOLE, PEG, PIT, SCORE, SLASH, SLOT
notched
  ~ **as leaves** EROSE
"___ Not Dressing" WERE
note ATTEND, ENTER, MEMO, PAPER, SEE
  ~ **ender** PAD, PAPER
  ~ **starter** KEY
  bank ~ CASH
  debtor's ~ IOU
  high ~ ALT, CEE, ELA
  journal ~ ENTRY
  key ~ TONIC
  make a ~ JOT
  make a ~ **of** LOG
  office ~ MEMO
  promissory ~ IOU
  scale ~ SOL
  take no ~ **of** CUT, SNUB
  take ~ **of** HEED, SEE
___ note HALF
notebook
  ~ **contents** PAPER
  ~ **unit** LEAF
  small ~ PAD
noted GREAT
notes DATA
  ~ **of the scale** DOS, LAS, MIS, RES, TIS
  compare ~ RAP
  on-line ~ EMAIL
"___ Note Samba" ONE
"Notes of a Native ___" SON
noteworthy BIG
"___ Not for Me to Say" ITS
"Not from where ___!" ISIT
"not guilty" PLEA
  say ~ PLEAD
not half ___ BAD
"Nothin' doin'!" NAH, NOPE
nothing NIL, NONE, ZERO
  ~ **but** ALL, MERE, ONLY
  ~ **in French** RIEN
  ~ **in Spanish** NADA

~ **opposite** ALL
~ **special** USUAL
~ **to a tennis player** LOVE
~ **to brag about** SOSO
do ~ IDLE, LOAF, LOLL, REST
eat ~ FAST
have ~ **to do with** AVOID, SHUN
in ~ **flat** ANON, SOON
it's ~ LOVE
lacking ~ ENTIRE
reduce to ~ ANNUL, RAZE
with ~ **on** BARE, NUDE
___-nothing KNOW
"Nothing but ___" (perfect shot) NET
"Nothing But ___" AMAN
"Nothing But a ___" MAN
"Nothing but blue skies do ___" ISEE
"Nothing But the ___" BEST
"Nothing Gold Can Stay" POEM
___-Nothings (1840s political group) KNOW
"Nothing to it!" EASY
notice ATTEND, BILL, ESPY, EYE, HEED, SEE, SPOT
  ~ (abbr.) ATT, ATTN
  ~ **in French** AVIS
  B'way ~ SRO
  dismiss without ~ AXE
  escape ~ PASS
  favorable ~ RAVE
  give a great ~ RAVE
  help-wanted ~ SOS
  landlord's ~ TOLET
  newspaper ~ OBIT
  public ~ SIGN
  put on ~ ALERT, WARN
  put up a ~ POST
  take no ~ **of** SNUB
  take ~ **of** HEED
noticeable
  ~ **reduction** DENT
  hardly ~ DIM
notices
  correction ~ ERRATA
  help-wanted ~ ADS
  sale ~ ADS
  sandwich-board ~ ADS
"Not if ___ help it!" ICAN
notification NEWS
notify TELL, WARN
"No Time ___ Sergeants" FOR
"No Time for Sergeants"
  ~ **director** LEROY
"Not interested!" NAH, NOPE
not in the ___ LEAST
notion IDEA
  ~ **in French** IDEE
  ~ (prefix) IDEO
  have a ~ IDEATE
  preconceived ~ BIAS

notions
  ~ **case** ETUI
not know from ___ ADAM
"___ Not Married" WERE
not my ___ TYPE
not my cup of ___ TEA
"Not on ___!" ABET
"...not one ___ for tribute" CENT
not one red ___ CENT
"Not on your life!" NAY, NEVER, NOPE
Notre ___ DAME
Notre Dame
  ~ **river** SEINE
  ~ **sight** ILE
  ~ **team** IRISH
  former ~ **name** ARA
  see also French
not-so-hot
  ~ **grade** DEE
"Not So Stories"
  ~ **author** SAKI
"___ Not There" SHES
Nottingham
  ~ **river** TRENT
"___ not to reason why..." OURS
"___ Not Unusual" ITS
"___ not what your country..." ASK
notwithstanding ASIDE, YET
not worth a ___ SOU
"Not worth his ___" SALT
"Not you ___!" AGAIN
"___ Not You" SHES
NO U ___ TURN
nought ZERO
  bring to ~ RUIN
noun
  ~ **in French** NOM
  ~ **starter** PRO
  ~ **suffix** EER, ENCE, ENT, INE, ION, ISM, IST, SHIP, URE
nouns
  like some ~ (abbr.) FEM
  like some foreign ~ MASC
nourish FEED, HELP, SERVE
nourished
  was ~ ATE
nourishment DIET, FARE, MEAL, MEAT
  take in ~ EAT
___ nous ENTRE
"___ no use!" ITS
nouveau
  art ~ STYLE
___ nouveau ART

Nov.
  ~ **event** ELEC
  ~ **follower** DEC
  ~ **predecessor** OCT
nova STAR
  ~ **anagram** AVON
  bossa ~ DANCE
___ Nova ARS
Novak KIM
  ~ **colleague** EVANS
nòve
  ~ **preceder** OTTO
novel GENRE, NEW, PROSE, TALE
  ~ **ender** ETTE, IST
___ novel DIME
novelist
  ~ **forte** PLOT
novelty FAD
November
  ~ **honoree** VET
  ~ **line-up** SLATE
  ~ **victors** INS
November 1
  ~ **honoree** SAINT
November 11
  ~ **marcher** VET
Novgorod
  see Russian
novice BABE, NUN
Novi Sad
  ~ **native** SERB
novo
  de ~ ANEW, NEW
Novus ___ Seclorum ORDO
now ANON, ASAP, HERE, STAT, YET
  ~ **and forever** ETERNAL
  ~ **on "ER"** STAT
  ~ **partner** HERE, THEN
  ~ **starter** ERE
  any time ~ ANON, SOON
  before ~ AGO, ONCE
  between then and ~ SINCE
  happening ~ LIVE
  not ~ LATER, THEN
  up to ~ YET
___ now (from this point) ASOF
___ now (previously) UNTIL
___ now (until this moment) UPTO
"___ now!" ACT
"Now ___ here!" SEE
"Now ___ seen everything!" IVE
"Now ___ theater near you!" ATA
"Now ___ this!" HEAR
"___ Now" TIL
NOW
  ~ **cause** ERA
now and ___ THEN

"No Way ___" OUT

"___ No Way" AINT

"No Way to ___ a Lady" TREAT

"No Way to Treat a ___" LADY

"___ No Way to Treat a Lady" AINT

"___ Now for Something Completely Different" AND

nowhere
  ~ near AFAR
  go ~ STALL

"Nowhere ___" MAN

"Now I get it!" AHA

no-win
  ~ situation TIE

"Now It Can Be ___" TOLD

"Now I understand!" AHA

"Now I've ___ everything!" SEEN

"___ Now Miguel" AND

"___ No Woman" AINT

"___ no wonder!" ITS

now or ___ NEVER

"___ Now or Never" ITS

"Now see ___!" HERE

"Now We Are Six"
  ~ author MILNE

noxious BAD, EVIL
  ~ plant WEED

Noyes, Alfred POET
  see also poet

nozzle JET

Np ELEM
  93 for ~ ATNO

NPR
  part of ~ RADIO

NRA
  ~ symbol EAGLE
  part of ~ ASSN

NSA ORG

NSC
  org. that advises the ~ CIA

N.T.
  ~ book COL, GAL, MATT, REV, ROM

nu
  ~ preceders MUS

nuance SHADE, TINGE

nub CORE, HEART, KNOT, NODE

nubble NODE

Nubian ___ DESERT

nucha NAPE
  ~ site NECK

nuclear
  ~ energy source ATOM
  ~ experiment ATEST
  ~ reactor PILE

  ~ reactor part CORE

nucleic ACID
  ~ compound RNA

nucleus CADRE, CORE, HEART, MIDST

nude BARE
  not ~ CLAD

"Nude Lying on a ___" SOFA

nudge ELBOW, IMPEL, JAB, PROD
  ~ ahead SPEED

nudnik PEST, PILL, TWIT

nueve
  ~ preceder OCHO

nugatory MERE, NULL, VAIN, VOID

nugget
  ~ material GOLD
  cookie ~ CHIP

Nuggets FIVE, TEAM
  ~ org. NBA

nuisance BANE, PAIN, PEEVE, PEST, TRIAL

nuke ZAP

null
  declare ~ and void ANNUL

null and ___ VOID

nullify ABORT, DENY, ERASE, REMIT, UNDO, VOID

numb BLUR, INERT

numbat
  ~ tidbit ANT

number ADD, FIVE, NINE, ONE, SEVEN, SIX, SONG, SUM, TEN, THREE, TOTAL, TUNE, TWO
  ~ cruncher ACCT, CPA
  antiknock ~ OCTANE
  a ~ of SOME
  birthday ~ AGE
  cabaret ~ SONG, TUNE
  chosen ~ FEW
  commandment ~ TEN
  countdown ~ FIVE, NINE, ONE, SEVEN, SIX, TEN, THREE, TWO, ZERO
  do a ~ SING
  Downing Street ~ TEN
  entire ~ ALL
  give a ~ to PAGE
  great ~ HOST, SCAD
  have someone's ~ PEG
  indeterminate ~ ANY, SOME
  large ~ RAFT, RASH, SLEW, SPATE, TON
  limited ~ FEW
  lucky ~ SEVEN
  nonet ~ NINE
  Sha Na Na ~ OLDIE
  small ~ FEW

___ number REAL

___ number can play ANY

numbered
  ~ composition OPUS

___ number on DOA

number one BEST, FIRST, TOP, TOPS

numbers
  ~ game KENO
  combine ~ ADD
  like left-hand page ~ EVEN
  study of ~ MATH
  Vegas ~ ODDS

numbers ___ GAME

___ numeral ROMAN

numerical
  ~ correspondence RATIO
  ~ fact STAT
  ~ prefix OCTO, TER, TETRA, TRI
  ~ suffix ETH, TEEN

numerous AMPLE, RIFE

numismatic
  ~ grade FINE

numskull ASS, DODO, DOLT, DOPE, IDIOT, OAF

nun
  ~ room CELL
  ~ wear HABIT
  Albanian-born ~ TERESA

nuncupative ORAL

Nunn SAM

nuptial
  ~ party member BRIDE
  ~ phrase IDO
  ~ starter PRE

nuptials
  ~ site ALTAR

Nuremberg CITY
  see also German

Nureyev
  ~ knee bend PLIE
  ~ specialty LEAP
  ~ step PAS
  see also ballet

Nürnberg CITY
  see also German

nurse ATTEND, CURE, HEAL, HELP, RAISE, REAR, TEND
  ~ a drink SIP
  ~ back to health RESTORE
  ~ helper AIDE
  ~ org. ANA
  ~ portion DOSE
  ~ specialty TLC
  Eastern ~ AMA, AMAH

"Nurse ___ Cavell" EDITH

nursemaid
  Bombay ~ AMA, AMAH

nursery ROOM
  ~ cry DADA, MAMA
  ~ furniture CRIB
  ~ medium PEAT
  ~ packet SEED
  ~ playmate TOT
  ~ purchase PLANT, SOIL

___ nursery DAY

nursery rhyme
  ~ trio MICE
  crooked gate of ~ STILE
  home of ~ SHOE
  merry king of ~ COLE

nursery school
  ~ item CLAY
  ~ ritual NAP

nursery schooler TOT

nurse's ___ AIDE

nursing
  ~ subj. ANAT
  name in ~ CLARA

nurture BREED, FEED, HELP, NURSE, RAISE, REAR, TEND

nut FAN, PIT
  ~ cake TORTE
  ~ case SHELL
  ~ essentially SEED
  ~ part MEAT
  ~ source TREE
  hard ~ to crack POSER
  kind of ~ ACORN, PECAN
  oak ~ ACORN
  off one's ~ LOCO
  tire ~ LUG

___ nut PINE

Nut
  ~ daughter ISIS

nuthatch BIRD
  ~ home NEST

nutmeg TREE
  ~ cousin MACE
  ~ cover ARIL
  drink topped with ~ FLIP

nutria FUR

nutrient
  mineral ~ IRON, ZINC

nutriment FARE

nutrition
  ~ abbr. RDA
  ~ watchdog FDA

nutritional
  ~ concern DIET
  ~ need IRON, ZINC
  ~ supplement YEAST
  ~ unit GRAM

nutritious
  ~ bean SOY

nutritive
  ~ mineral IRON, ZINC

nuts BATS, DAFT, LOCO, MAD

"Nuts!" DARN, DRAT, RATS

nutshell
  ~ contents MEAT
  put in a ~ SUM

___ nutshell INA

nutty BATS, DAFT, INANE, LOCO, MAD, OFF, RICH

nutty ___ fruitcake ASA

"Nutty Professor, The"
  ~ director LEWIS

nuzzle CARESS, NOSE, PET, PRESS

NV
> *see* Nevada

NW
> **~ state** IDA, ORE, WASH

NWT
> **part of ~** TER, TERR

N.Y.
> **~ baseballer** MET
> **~ neighbor** MASS, ONT, PENN
> **~ nine** METS
> **~ summer time** EDT
> **~ zone** EST
> *see also* New York

nyanza LAKE

Nyasa LAKE

NYC
> **~ borough** MAN
> **~ clock setting** EDT, EST
> **~ dwelling** APT
> **~ opera house** MET
> **~ sports venue** MSG

NY Central
> **~ and others** RRS

Nye, Bill
> **~ subj.** SCI

nyet NAY
> **~ in French** NON
> **~ in Latin** NON
> **~ in Scottish** NAE

nylon
> **ruin a ~** SNAG

nylons HOSE

Nyman LENA

nymph GIRL
> **~ chaser** SATYR
> **mountain ~** OREAD
> **sea ~** IONE, SIREN
> **water ~** NAIAD

NYPD
> **~ call** APB

"NYPD Blue"
> **~ character** COP
> **~ network** ABC
> **Dennis' ~ role** ANDY

Nyro LAURA

NYSE
> **~ listing** ITT
> **~ membership** SEAT
> **~ regulator** SEC

N.Z.
> *see* New Zealand

1/640
  ~ square mile ACRE

1/8
  ~ ounce DRAM

1/48
  ~ c. TSP

1.0
  ~ grade DEE

1
  ~ on the Mohs scale TALC
  ~ 2, and 3 NOS
  score a ~ on ACE

1-A
  ~ org. SSS
  postpone a ~ DEFER

1-pointer
  Scrabble ~ ESS, TEE

1-pointers
  Scrabble ~ ARS, ELS, ENS

1.77
  ~ grams DRAM

100% ALL, PURE

$100
  ~ bill CNOTE

100
  ~ centavos PESO
  ~ centesimi LIRA
  ~ dinars RIAL
  ~ kurus LIRA
  ~ sawbucks THOU
  ~ smackers CNOTE
  ~ square meters ARE

100%
  be less than ~ AIL

100
  get ~ on ACE
  one of Argus' ~ EYE

100-meter ___ DASH

100-yard
  ~ race DASH

102
  Roman ~ CII

"___ 110th Street" ACROSS

128
  ~ cu. ft. of wood CORD

~ fl. oz. GAL

160
  ~ square rods ACRE

180°
  ~ from ENE WSW
  ~ from ESE WNW
  ~ from NNE SSW
  ~ from NNW SSE
  ~ from SSE NNW
  ~ from SSW NNE
  ~ from WNW ESE
  ~ from WSW ENE

$1,000
  ~ slangily GEE

"1000 Faces"
  ~ actor LON

"1,001 ___" USES

"1,001 Arabian Nights"
  ~ hero ALI

100,000
  ~ rupees LAC

$1,000,000
  ~ for short MIL

123-45-6789
  ~ org. SSA

O ELEM, TYPE
  ~ preceders ENS
  8 for ~ ATNO
  first ~, maybe TIC

"O"
  code word for ~ OBOE, OSCAR
  Jackie's ~ ARI

"O, ___ fortune's fool!" IAM

O-___ RING

"___-O" (Belafonte tune) DAY

oaf BOOR, CLOD, DOLT, LOUT, LUG, SAP

oafish CRASS

Oahu
  ~ (abbr.) ISL
  ~ cookout LUAU
  ~ greeting ALOHA
  ~ souvenir LEI
  see also Hawaiian

oak TREE
  ~ nut ACORN
  like an ~ leaf EROSE

oak ___ cluster LEAF

___ oak LIVE

Oakland CITY, PORT

Oakley ANNIE

Oakley, Annie PASS
  emulate ~ AIM

Oak Ridge
  ~ st. TENN

oar
  ~ wood ASH

oars
  ply the ~ ROW

oarsmen CREW

OAS
  ~ member ARG, CAN, COL, CUBA, HAITI, PAN, PERU, USA
  part of ~ AMER, ORG

oasis
  ~ of a sort BAR
  ~ view PALM, SAND

oast KILN, OVEN

oat
  ~ beard AWN
  ~ eater of song MARE

oater
  ~ backdrop MESA
  ~ command DRAW
  ~ extras POSSE
  ~ name HOOT
  ~ prop GUN
  ~ scenery RANCH

Oates
  ~ partner HALL

Oates, Joyce Carol
  ~ novel THEM

oath
  common ~ IDO
  mild ~ DARN, DRAT, GAD
  old ~ EGAD, EGADS, FIE
  say under ~ ATTEST

oats FEED
  sow wild ~ REVEL

Oaxaca CITY
  see also Spanish

Ob
  see Russian

obdurate IRON

obedience class
  ~ command BEG, HEEL, SIT, STAY

obedient GOOD, MEEK

obeisance NOD
  pay ~ KNEEL

obelisk STONE

Oberammergau
  see German

Oberlin
  ~ locale OHIO

Oberon MERLE, MOON

obey ADHERE, HEED, KEEP, SERVE
  ~ a coxswain OAR, ROW
  ~ the alarm ARISE
  ~ the bailiff RISE

obfuscate ADDLE, BLUR, DIM

obi SASH

Obi-___ Kenobi WAN

Obie AWARD
  ~ contender ACTOR

Obi-Wan HERO
  ~ portrayer ALEC
  AKA ~ BEN

object AIM, CARE, DENY, END, GOAL, ITEM, NOUN
  ~ from the past RELIC
  ~ of value ASSET
  ~ of worship GOD, ICON, IDOL
  celestial ~ MOON, ORB, SUN

objectionable BAD, ILL, UGLY, VILE

objective AIM, CASE, END, FAIR, GOAL, HONEST, LENS
  Apollo ~ MOON
  armistice ~ PEACE
  auditioner's ~ ROLE
  explorer's ~ TRADE
  golfer's ~ HOLE
  promotion ~ SALE
  slider's ~ BASE

ultimate ~ END

objects
nearby ~ THESE
remote ~ THOSE

objet d'___ ART

objurgate LACE

obligate BIND, TIE

obligated
be ~ to OWE

obligation DEBT, ONUS, TASK, TIE
charge an ~ DEBIT

obligations
have ~ OWE

oblige BIND, HELP, HOLD, IMPEL, MAKE, SERVE, TIE

obliged
be ~ OWE

obliging MEEK

oblique SIDE
~ direction SLANT
~ line BIAS, CANT

obliquely AWRY

obliqueness SLANT

obliterate ANNUL, ERASE, RAZE, UNDO

obliterated GONE, LOST

oblivion
sunk in ~ LOST

oblivious DEAF

obloquy ABUSE, SHAME

obnoxious BAD, MEAN, RUDE, VILE
~ one CREEP

oboe PIPE, REED
like an ~'s sound REEDY

obol COIN

Oboler ARCH

Oboler, Arch
~ film of 1951 FIVE

obols
place to spend ~ AGORA

Obote
~ foe AMIN

O'Brian, Hugh
~ role EARP

O'Brien DAN, EDNA, PAT

O'Brien, Edmond
~ film of 1949 DOA

Obringa
~ today AAR, AARE

___ obscura CAMERA

obscure BLUR, DEEP, DIM, HIDE, MASK, SHADE

obsecrate URGE

observance HABIT
formal ~ RITE
soothsayer's ~ OMEN

spring ~ EASTER

observant ALERT, AWARE, WARY

observation
pithy ~ MOT

___ Observatory NAVAL

observe ADHERE, ESPY, EYE, HEED, NOTE, OBEY, SEE, SPOT, SPY
~ Lent FAST
~ Yom Kippur ATONE

observer SEER

___ Observer (1992 mission) MARS

obsessed
~ by INTO

obsession LIFE, MANIA
egotist's ~ SELF
pyromaniac's ~ ARSON

Obsession SCENT

obsessive
~ fan NUT

obsidian
~ origin LAVA

obsolesce AGE, FADE

obsolescent DATED, OLD, OUT

obsolete DATED, OLD, PASSE
~ geog. term SSR
become ~ DATE

obstacle BAR, SNAG

obstacles
teamwork ~ EGOS

obstinate SET
~ equine ASS, MULE

obstreperous LOUD

obstruct BAR, CLOG, DAM, DETER, STOP
~ in a way HIDE

obstruction DAM, SNAG

obtain GAIN, GET, HAVE, TAKE, WIN
~ in Dogpatch GIT
~ justly EARN
~ the title WIN

obtainable OPEN

obtest ASK, CRY, URGE

obtrude START

obtrusive LOUD

obtuse CRASS, DENSE, SLOW
not ~ ACUTE

obtuse ___ ANGLE

obviate AVERT, BAR

obvious CLEAR, EASY, OVERT

"O Captain! My Captain!" POEM

Ocasek, Ric
~ band CARS

O'Casey SEAN
~ home EIRE, ERIN
~ work DRAMA, PLAY

occasion CASE, CAUSE, EVENT, GALA, PEG, TIME, USE
elegant ~ BALL
festive ~ FETE, GALA
have ~ for NEED
on any ~ EVER
on no ~ NEVER
particular ~ NONCE

occasional FEW, ODD

Occident WEST

occipital BONE

occipital ___ LOBE

occlude BAR, SHUT

occult DEEP

occupant TENANT
~ agreement LEASE

occupation LIFE, LINE, TRADE

occupational
~ suffix EER, IER, IST, STER

occupied
~ with INTO, UPTO

occupier TENANT

occupy AMUSE, ARREST, HOLD, TAKE, USE
~ an ottoman SIT
~ as a post MAN
~ temporarily LEASE, RENT
~ the throne REIGN

occur ARRIVE, COME
~ subsequently ENSUE

occurrence CASE, EVENT, FACT

occurring
~ twice (prefix) SEMI

occurs
as it ~ LIVE

ocean DEEP, HEAP, MAIN, MASS, PILE, SEA, TON
~ (abbr.) ATL, PAC
~ area DEEP
~ contents WATER
~ depths ABYSS
~ edge SHORE
~ fish COD, HAKE, OPAH
~ flier TERN
~ hail AHOY
~ ingredient SALT
~ liner BOAT, SHIP
~ motion TIDE
~ plant ALGA
~ predator MAKO
~ route LANE
~ sound ROAR
~ surge TIDE
~ vessel BOAT, LINER, SHIP
back, on the ~ AFT
enjoy the ~ BATHE
like an ~ trench DEEP
on the ~ ASEA, ATSEA
ring in the ~ ATOLL
spot in the ~ ISLE
traverse the ~ SAIL

oceanic
~ ice FLOE

Oceanides
one of the ~ ASIA

ocean liner
~ (abbr.) STR
on an ~ ASEA, ATSEA

oceans ALOT

"Ocean's ___" ELEVEN

Oceanus TITAN
daughter of ~ ASIA

ocelot ANIMAL, CAT

ocher COLOR
yellow ~ SIL

Ocho ___, Jamaica RIOS

"___ O'Clock Jump" ONE

"___ o'clock scholar, A" TEN

"O come, let us ___ Him" ADORE

O'Connor DES, PAT, UNA

O'Connor, Pat
~ film of 1984 CAL

Oct.
~ follower NOV
~ predecessor SEPT
it ends in ~ DST

octagon
~ word STOP

octave
first ~ above treble clef ALT

Octavia
~ husband NERO

Octavian ROMAN
see also Latin

octet
~ in Spanish OCHO
octopus' ~ ARMS
one of a milking ~ MAID

October
~ birthstone OPAL
position of ~ TENTH

October 31
~ option TREAT
~ prop MASK

October Revolution
~ name LENIN

octogenarian ELDER

octopus
~ appendage ARM
~ defense INK
~ home OCEAN, SEA
~ octet ARMS
female ~ HEN

"Octopussy"
~ actress ADAMS
~ director GLEN

ocular LENS
~ layer UVEA

oculist
~ concern EYE

Oda ___ Brown MAE

odalisque SLAVE
  ~ **residence** HAREM

O'Day ANITA

odd EERIE, EERY, NEW
  ~ **job** LABOR, TASK
  ~ **one** NUT
  not ~ EVEN

odd ___ LOT

"Odd ___ **Out"** MAN

"Odd Couple, The"
  ~ **role** OSCAR, SPEED

oddity TIC

Oddjob
  ~ **creator** IAN

"Odd Man ___ **"** OUT

"Odd Man Out"
  ~ **actor** MASON
  ~ **director** REED

odds
  ~ **and ends** REST
  ~ **companion** ENDS
  ~ **essentially** RATIO
  at ~ CON, OUT
  give, as ~ LAY
  set at ~ PIT
  take the ~ BET
  unlikely, as ~ SLIM

"Odds ___ **..."** ARE

"Odds Against Tomorrow"
  ~ **director** WISE

ode POEM
  ~ **subject** URN

"Ode ___ **Nightingale"** TOA

"Ode: Intimations of Immortality" POEM

Odense
  ~ **native** DANE

"Ode on a Grecian ___ **"** URN

"Ode on a Grecian Urn" POEM

"Ode on Melancholy" POEM

Odessa CITY, PORT

"Odessa ___ **, The"** FILE

"Ode to a Nightingale" POEM

"Ode to Billy ___ **"** JOE

"Ode to the West Wind" POEM

Odin GOD
  ~ **son** THOR
  re ~ NORSE
  Tyr, to ~ SON

odious BAD, MEAN, VILE
  ~ **one** TOAD

odist
  ~ **Muse** ERATO

odium HATE, SPITE

odometer
  ~ **abbr.** MPH
  ~ **unit** MILE

odometers
  tamper with ~ RESET

odor SCENT
  ~ **detector** NOSE
  pleasant ~ AROMA
  unpleasant ~ REEK

odoriferous RANK

odorless
  ~ **gas** ETHANE

odorous
  ~ **starter** MAL

Odysseus HERO
  ~ **advisor** ATHENA
  emulate ~ ROAM

odyssey TREK, TRIP

"Odyssey, The" EPIC, EPOS, POEM
  ~ **author** HOMER
  ~ **character** ARETE, ATHENA, HELEN
  ~ **peak** OSSA

" ___ **Oe"** ALOHA

Oedipus
  ~ **to Jocasta** SON
  Polynices, to ~ SON

"Oedipus ___ **"** REX

oenochoe EWER

oenologist
  ~ **business** WINE

oenology
  ~ **topic** AROMA

Oenone
  ~ **husband** PARIS

o'er
  ~ **opposite** NEATH

Oerter
  ~ **and others** ALS

oeuvre OPUS

of ___ **(eminent)** NOTE

of ___ **(recently)** LATE

of ___ **proportions** EPIC

___ **of (before)** AHEAD

___ **of (learn)** HEAR

___ **of (onto)** AWARE

"Of ___ **and Men"** MICE

"Of ___ **I Sing"** THEE

" ___ **of a Black Hat"** FEAR

___ **of absence** LEAVE

" ___ **of Aces"** PAIR

" ___ **of a Clown"** TEARS

" ___ **of a Dog, The"** HEART

" ___ **of Adrian Messenger, The"** LIST

___ **of affairs** STATE

" ___ **of Africa"** OUT

___ **of a gun** SON

___ **of a kind** ONE, TWO

___ **of ale** YARD

___ **of allegiance** OATH

" ___ **of All Fears, The"** SUM

" ___ **of America"** MEN

" ___ **of Angels"** CITY

" ___ **of Angels"** RAGE

" ___ **of Anxiety, The"** AGE

O'Faolain SEAN

___ **of approval** SEAL, STAMP

" ___ **of a Preacher Man"** SON

" ___ **of Aquarius, The"** AGE

" ___ **of Aran"** MAN

___ **of arms** COAT

" ___ **of a Sailor"** SON

___ **of a sudden** ALL

" ___ **of a Thousand Faces"** MAN

___ **of attack** PLAN

___ **of attainder** BILL

" ___ **of a Tub, The"** TALE

___ **of averages** LAW

" ___ **of a Woman"** SCENT

___ **of Azov** SEA

___ **of Base** ACE

___ **of beef** SIDE

" ___ **of Bernadette, The"** SONG

___ **-of-Bethlehem** STAR

___ **of Biscay** BAY

___ **of bounds** OUT

___ **of breath** OUT

" ___ **of Bright Water"** RING

___ **of burden** BEAST

" ___ **of Burlesque"** LADY

" ___ **of Call"** PORT

___ **of Capri** ISLE

___ **of Cassini** OVAL

___ **of chance** GAME

___ **of character** OUT

___ **of china** SET

___ **of clay** FEET

___ **of Cleves** ANNE

___ **of color** RIOT

___ **of commission** OUT

" ___ **of Concord, The"** **(Emerson)** SAGE

___ **of consciousness** STREAM

___ **of consent** AGE

___ **of contention** BONE

"Of course!" AYE, ISEE, SURE, YES

___ **-of-court** OUT

___ **of Court** INNS

___ **of credit** LINE

" ___ **of Darkness"** EDGE

___ **-of-date** OUT

___ **of David** STAR

" ___ **of Death"** DANCE, KISS

" ___ **of Death, The"** PEARL

" ___ **of Decision"** YEARS

" ___ **of Destruction"** EVE

" ___ **of Dimitrios, The"** MASK

" ___ **of Divorcement, A"** BILL

___ **-of-doors** OUT

" ___ **of Dracula"** SON

___ **of drawers** CHEST

" ___ **of Duty"** TOUR

___ **of 1812** WAR

" ___ **of Eden"** EAST

" ___ **of Emile Zola, The"** LIFE

" ___ **of Endearment"** TERMS

" ___ **of Enemies, The"** BEST

___ **of ethics** CODE

" ___ **of Everything, The"** BEST

___ **of exchange** RATE

off AMISS, AWAY, SOUR
  ~ **in Italian** VIA
  ~ **opposites** ONS
  ~ **plumb** ATILT
  ~ **the beam** LOCO
  ~ **the deep end** APE
  ~ **the hook** FREE
  ~ **the mark** WIDE
  ~ **the wall** INANE

off ___ **tangent** ONA

off- ___ KEY, LINE, LOAD, PEAK, SITE

off- ___ **vehicle** ROAD

off.
  Army ~ COL, GEN, SGT

___ **off** BEG, CALL, CAST, CUT, EASE, FAIR, FEND, HEAD, HOLD, KEEP, KISS, LAY, LOG, LOP, MAKE, PALM, PUT, REEL, RIP, ROPE, RUN, SEAL, SEE, SELL, SET, SHOW, SHUT, SIGN, STAVE, STEP, TAKE, TEAR, TEE, TELL, TOP, TOSS, WARD, WEAR, WRITE

___ **off (alienate)** TURN

___ **off (annoy)** TEE

___ **off (axe)** LAY

___ **off (cancel)** WRITE

___ off

___ off (decamp) TAKE
___ off (decrease) DROP, TAIL
___ off (do quickly) TOSS
___ off (explode) SET
___ off (foist) PASS
___ off (forestall) STAVE
___ off (give up on) WRITE
___ off (go first) LEAD
___ off (make angry) TEE
___ off (measure) STEP
___ off (partition) ROPE
___ off (prevent) STAVE
___ off (rant) POP
___ off (recite) REEL
___ off (reduce gradually) TAPER
___ off (repel) FEND, STAVE
___ off (reserve) ROPE
___ off (scold) TELL
___ off (set sail) CAST
___ off (slacken) EASE
___ off (steal) RIP
___ off (succeed) COME
___ off (truncate) LOP
___ off (write quickly) FIRE
___-off BAKE, FAR, RIP, SPIN, TIP, TRADE, WRITE
"Off ___ Comet" ONA
"Off ___, on..." AGAIN
___ of faith LEAP
___ of Fame HALL
___ of fare BILL
"___ of Father Mouret, The" SIN
offbeat ODD
Off-Broadway
  ~ trophy OBIE
off-camera
  ~ comment ASIDE
off-center ATILT, AWRY
  go ~ TILT
off-color LEWD, RACY
off-course AWRY, LOST
  go ~ YAW
off-duty FREE, IDLE
Offenbach
  see German
offend ANGER, CUT, SNUB
  ~ the nose REEK
offended SORE
offender
  mil. ~ AWOL

offense SIN
  beat the ~ REPEL
  civil ~ TORT
  show ~, perhaps SLAP
offensive BAD, RANK, RUDE, VILE
  take the ~ LEAD
offensive ___ END, LINE
offer BID, SAY
  ~ a chair to SEAT
  ~ an inducement LURE
  ~ a position HIRE
  ~ as a farewell BID
  ~ assurance ATTEST, AVER, AVOW
  ~ for a price SELL, VEND
  ~ one's thoughts OPINE
  ~ temporarily LEND
  auto-dealership ~ LEASE
  businessman's ~ CARD
  cash-back ~ REBATE
  tender an ~ BID
offered BADE
___ offering PEACE
off guard
  be ~ SLEEP
offhand ADLIB
office SHOP
  ~ accessory ERASER
  ~ acronym ASAP
  ~ communication MEMO
  ~ expense RENT
  ~ fill-in TEMP
  ~ freebie PERK
  ~ furniture DESK, SOFA
  ~ kingpin BOSS
  ~ note MEMO
  ~ plant FERN
  ~ seeker POL
  ~ skill STENO
  ~ stamp PAID
  ~ (suffix) SHIP
  ~ wear SUIT, TIE
  ~ worker PAGE, STENO
  ~ writer PEN
  do an ~ job FILE
  hold ~ SERVE
  home ~ DEN
  install in ~ SEAT
  length of ~ TERM
  post ~ GAME
  put in ~ ELECT
  remove from ~ OUST
  seek ~ RUN
  symbol of ~ MACE
  work in an ~ TYPE
___ office LAND, POST
___ Office OVAL
office-communication
  ~ system EMAIL
officeholders INS
officer
  ~ command ATEASE, HALT
  antidrug ~ NARC
  Army ~ MAJOR
  church ~ ELDER
  DEA ~ NARC
  junior ~ CADET

Ottoman ~ AGA, AGHA
petty ~ RANK
police ~ COP
ship's ~ MATE
staff ~ AIDE
warrant ~ RANK
"Officer and a Gentleman, An"
  ~ actor GERE
officers
  military ~ BRASS
officer-to-be CADET
offices
  good ~ AID, HELP
___ offices GOOD
official DEAN, STATE
  ~ order WRIT
  ~ proceedings ACTA
  ~ proclamation EDICT
  ~ seal STAMP
  ~ standing RANK
  ballpark ~ UMP
  banquet ~ EMCEE, HOST
  Canadian town-council
    ~ REEVE
  college ~ DEAN
  court ~ REF
  Muslim ~ AGA, AGHA, AMIR, EMEER, EMIR
  Ottoman ~ AGA, AGHA
  Roman ~ EDILE
  sports ~ REF, UMP
  Venetian ~ DOGE
officialese CANT
"___ of Fire" BALL, FACE, RING
offish ALOOF, COOL
"___ off it!" COME
off-key FLAT
off-limits TABOO, TABU
  ~ activity NONO
"___ of Flubber" SON
off one's ___ FEED
"___ of Fools" SHIP
___ of Four GANG
"___ of Four, The" SIGN
"___ Off Place" AFAR
"___ Off Place, A" FAR
off-ramp EXIT
"___ of Frankenstein" BRIDE, SON
___ of Freedom MEDAL
offscourings SLOP
offset ATONE
offshoot SCION, SPRIG, SPUR
  church ~ SECT
offshore ASEA, ATSEA
  ~ structure RIG
offspring HEIR, ISSUE, SCION, SEED
  bossy's ~ CALF

filly's ~ COLT
male ~ SON
nanny's ~ KID
vixen's ~ KIT
off the ___ (immediately) BAT
off-the-___ RACK
"Off the Court"
  ~ author ASHE
off-the-cuff ADLIB
___ off the old block CHIP
off-the-wall ODD, OUTRE
"___ off to see the Wizard..." WERE
off-track LOST
"___ of Fu Manchu, The" FACE
"___ of Fury" SON
"___ of Fury, A" DAY
off-white BONE, CREAM, PEARL
___ off with (steal) MAKE
___ of Galilee SEA
___ of Gilead BALM
___ of God ACT
"___ of God" AGNES
"___ of Godzilla" SON
___ of Good Feeling ERA
___ of goods BILL
"___ of Gravity" LAWS
"___ of Green Gables" ANNE
"___ of Greenwich Village, The" POPE
___ of Greystoke (Tarzan) EARL
___ of Hadrian STOA
___ of hand OUT
___ of health BILL
"___ of Heaven" DAYS, GATES
"___ of Hiawatha, The" SONG
"___ of Hoffman, The" TALES
"___ of Honey, A" TASTE
___ of honor MAID
___ of Honor MEDAL
___ of hope RAY
"___ of Hope" CITY
___ of humor SENSE
___ of influence SPHERE
"___ of Innocence, The" AGE
___ of Iran SHAH
"___ of Iron" MAN
"___ of Iwo Jima" SANDS
___ of Japan SEA
"___ of Jezebel" SINS

"___ of Jimmy Dolan, The" LIFE
"___ of Katie Elder, The" SONS
"___ of Kin" NEXT
"___ of Kings, A" DREAM
___ of lading BILL
"___ of La Mancha" MAN
___ of lamb RACK
"___ of Laura Mars" EYES
___ of learning SEAT
___ of least resistance PATH
___ of Lebanon CEDAR
___ of life FACT, SLICE
___ of line OUT
"___ of Living Dangerously, The" YEAR
___-of-living increase COST
"___ of Livin' to Do" ALOT
"___ of Loss, A" SENSE
"___ of Love" SEA
"___ of Love, The" DESERT
___ of lovebirds PAIR
___ of luxury, the LAP
"___ of Madelon Claudet, The" SIN
___ of mandamus WRIT
"___ of Manhattan" TALES
"___ of Marble" MAN
___ of Marmara SEA
"___ of Me" ALL
"___ of means by no means..." AMAN
___ of measure UNIT
"Of Mice ___ Men" AND
"Of Mice and ___" MEN
"Of Mice and Men" ~ actor STEELE
___ of Misrule LORD
"___ of Money, The" COLOR
"___ of Monte Cristo, The" SON
"___ of Mrs. Cheyney, The" LAST
"___ of Murder, An" ACT
"___ of My Love" BEST
"___ of Myself" SONG
___ of Nantes EDICT
___ of nerves WAR
"___ of New Orleans" CITY
"___ of New York, The" TOAST
"___ of Night, The" EDGE
___ of nowhere OUT
___ of office OATH

___ of Okhotsk SEA
___ of one'e eye APPLE
___ of one's existence BANE
___ of one's eye APPLE
"___ of One's Own, A" ROOM
___ of Orléans MAID
"___ of Our Lives" DAYS
"___ of Ours" ONE
"___ of Our Teeth, The" SKIN
"___ of Our Time, A" HERO
"___ of Paleface" SON
___ of paradise BIRD
"___ of Paris, The" RAGE
___ of passage RITE
___ of Pigs BAY
___ of Pines ISLE
___ of plenty HORN
___-of-pocket expenses OUT
"___ of Pooh, The" TAO
___ of pottage MESS
"___ of prevention is..., An" OUNCE
___ of prey BIRD
___ of print OUT
"___ of Ranchipur, The" RAINS
"___ of Reason, The" AGE
___ of Rights BILL
"___ of Riley, The" LIFE
"___ of robins in her hair..." ANEST
___ of roses ATTAR, BED
___ of sale BILL
"___ of Salem" MAID
"___ of Samothrace" NIKE
"___ of San Antone" ROSE
"___ of Sand" ROPE
___ of Sandwich EARL
"___ of Scotland Yard, The" CODE
___ of scrimmage LINE
___ of Sharon ROSE
"___ of Sheila, The" LAST
___ of sight LINE, OUT
"___ of Silence" CODE
"___ of Solomon" ODES, SONG
___ of sorts OUT
"___ of Spain" LADY
___ of Spain, Trinidad PORT
___ of spending, an ORGY

"___ of Spring, The" RITE
"___ of St. Agnes, The" EVE
"___ of Steel" ABS
___ of step OUT
"___ of St. Mark, The" EVE
___ of stock OUT
"___ of Summer" END
___ of sunlight RAY
___ of tears VALE
often-inflated ~ item EGO
"___ of Terror" REIGN, TALES
of the ___ (crucial) ESSENCE
___ of the above NONE
___ of the action APIECE
___ of the American Revolution SONS
___ of the Americas AVE
"___ of the Ancient Mariner, The" RIME
"___ of the Apostles" ACTS
___ of the art STATE
"___ of the Ball" BELLE
"___ of the Bigtime Spenders" LAST
___ of the blue OUT
"___ of the Brave" HOME
"___ of the Cat" YEAR
"___ of the Cave Bear, The" CLAN
"___ of the Century" SALE
"___ of the City" EDGE
"___ of the City, The" BEAST
___ of the cloth MAN
___ of the Covenant ARK
___ of the crime SCENE
___ of the crop CREAM
___ of the cross SIGN
"___ of the Dead" ISLE
"___ of the Deal, The" ART
of the deepest ___ DYE
"___ of the Desert" SONS
"___ of the Divide" WEST
"___ of the D'Urbervilles" TESS
"...___ of thee" TIS
"___ of the Earth" SALT
"___ of the Fighting Lady" MEN
"___ of the Flies, The" LORD
"___ of the Fog" OUT
"___ of the Fugue, The" ART

"___ of the Spider Woman"

"___ of the Game" NAME
___ of the Garter ORDER
"___ of the Greasepaint, the Smell of the Crowd, The" ROAR
"___ of the Heart, The" ACT
___ of the house LADY, MAN
___ of the iceberg TIP
"___ of Their Lives, The" TIME
"___ of the Islands" SONG
"___ of the Jackal, The" DAY
"___ of the Kingdom, The" KEYS
"___ of the Lake, The" LADY
___ of the land, the FAT
___ of the line END
"___ of the Locust, The" DAY
"___ of the Lonesome Pine, The" TRAIL
"___ of the Marines" PRIDE
___-of-the-mill RUN
"___ of the Mind" ALIE
"___ of the Mohicans, The" LAST
___-of-the-moment SPUR
"___ of the Morning" ANGEL
"___ of the Needle" EYE
"___ of the Nineties" BELLE
___ of the party LIFE
"___ of the Past" OUT
"___ of the People, An" ENEMY
"___ of the Perverse, The" IMP
___ of the Pioneers SONS
___ of the question OUT
"___ of the Rings, The" LORD
"___ of the River" BEND
"___ of the Road" END
"___ of the Rose, The" NAME
"___ of the Roses, The" WAR
___ of the running OUT
"___ of the Screw, The" TURN
"___ of These Days" SOME
"___ of these days, Alice..." ONE
"___ of These Nights" ONE
"___ of the Sheik" SON
"___ of the Shirt, The" SONG
"___ of the Sixth Happiness, The" INN
"___ of the Ski Bums" LAST
"___ of the Snake" UNION
"___ of the South" SONG
"___ of the Spider Woman" KISS

"___ of the Story, The" REST
"___ of the Sun" EAST
"___ of the Thousand Days" ANNE
"___ of the Tiger" EYE
___ of the tongue SLIP
"___ of the Town, The" TALK
"___ of the Triffids" DAY
"___ of the Union" STATE
___ of the Unknown Soldier TOMB
___ of the valley LILY
___ of the way OUT
"___ of the West" MAN
"___ of the Wild, The" CALL
___ of the woods NECK, OUT
___ of the Woods LAKE
___ of the woodwork OUT
"___ of the World, The" EDGE
"___ of the Worlds, The" WAR
"___ of the Yankees, The" PRIDE
"...___ of thieves" ADEN
"___ of This Earth" NOT
___ of this world OUT
___ of thumb RULE
___ of thunder CLAP
___ of Titus (Roman landmark) ARCH
___-of-town OUT
"...___ of traitors" ANEST
"___ of Tralee, The" ROSE
___ of Tranquility SEA
"___ of Triumph" ARCH
"... ___ of troubles" ASEA
___ of Troy HELEN
___ of turn OUT
"___ of Two Cities" ATALE
"___ of Two Cities, A" TALE
"___ of Violence" ACT
___ of voice TONE
___ of war ACT, TUG
___ of wax BALL
___ of whack OUT
___ of Wight ISLE
"___ of Wine and Roses" DAYS
___ of wintergreen OIL
___ of wisdom PEARL
___ of woe TALE
"___ of Wooden Clogs, The" TREE

___ of worms CAN
___ of Worms DIET
"___ of Wrath" DAY
"___ of your beeswax!" NONE
___ of your business NONE
"___ of Zanzibar" WEST
"___ of Zorro, The" SIGN
Ogden NASH
~ state UTAH
ogee ARCH
~ shape ESS
Oglala TRIBE
ogle EYE, GAPE, LEER, SEE, STARE
ogler
~ look STARE
ogre BEAST, DEMON, GIANT
ogress HAG
ogrish MEAN
oh
~ fudge POOH
"oh!"
cockney for ~ COO
"Oh ___ Golden Slippers" DEM
"Oh!" ISEE
~ in German ACH
"Oh! ___ can you see..." SAY
"Oh, ___!" DEAR, GOD, MAMA
"Oh, ___ in England..." TOBE
Oh.
~ neighbor IND, KEN, PENN
see also Ohio
O'Hara
~ estate TARA
~ Joey PAL
O'Hare
~ abbr. ARR, ETA
~ loc. CHI
~ on luggage tags ORD
"Oh, boy!" WOW
"Oh, But ___" IDO
"Oh, dear!" ALAS
"O Henry, ___ thine eyes!" OPE
O. Henry ALIAS
"Oh, give ___ home" MEA
"Oh, heck!" DARN, DRAT, RATS
"Oh, How I ___ to Get Up in the Morning" HATE
Ohio STATE
~ city AKRON, AVON, LIMA, TOLEDO
~ college town KENT
~ county ERIE
~ Indian ERIE
~ political name TAFT
~ town ADA
river to the ~ MIAMI

University of ~ site MIAMI
"Oh, Look ___ Now" ATME
"Oh, my!" ALAS, EGAD
"Oh! My ___" PAPA
"Oh, no!" DARN, DRAT, RATS
"Oh, no! Not ___!" AGAIN
___-o-Honey BIT
"Oh! Susanna"
~ star STORM
"Oh, what a relief ___!" ITIS
"Oh what fun ___..." ITIS
"Oh, woe!" ALAS
-oid
~ cousin ISH
oil
~ additive STP
~ alternative GAS
~ cartel OPEC
~ company's former name ESSO
~ exporter IRAN
~ from petals ATTAR
~ job LUBE
~ line PIPE
~ source COD, CORN, PALM, SESAME, SOY
aromatic ~ ANISE
banana ~ ESTER
boil in ~ FRY
burn the midnight ~ CRAM, LABOR, SLAVE, TOIL
cook lightly in ~ SAUTE
essential ~ ATTAR
oil ___ CAN, LAMP, PAINT, PAN
___ oil CORN, LAMP, MOTOR, OLIVE, SALAD, SHALE, SNAKE
"Oil ___ the Lamps of China" FOR
oil-bearing
~ rock SHALE
"Oil Capital of the World" TULSA
oil drilling
~ equipment RIG
oiler BOAT, SHIP
Oilers ELEVEN, SIX, TEAM
~ milieu ICE, RINK
~ org. NFL, NHL
"Oil for the Lamps of China"
~ director LEROY
oils ART, MEDIA, PAINT
oil spill
~ barrier BOOM
oilstone HONE
oily FAT, GLIB, SLEEK
oink CRY, NOISE, SNORT
oinker HOG
~ home PEN, STY
ointment BALM, CREAM, OIL
ancient ~ NARD

bit of ~ DAB
fly in the ~ SNAG
soothing ~ ALOE
Oise
see French
Ojibwa TRIBE
language akin to ~ CREE
OK ALLOW, ENABLE, FAIR, NICE, ROGER, SIGN, YEAH, YEP, YES
~ at sea AYE
~ in French OUI
better than ~ FINE
just ~ SOSO
non-verbal ~ NOD
say ~ to ALLOW
see also Oklahoma
Oka
see Russian
okapi ANIMAL
Oka River
city on the ~ OREL
okay AMEN, GOOD, SAFE, YEAH, YEP, YES
skipper's ~ AYE
Okayama CITY
O.K. Corral
~ name EARP
Okeechobee LAKE
Okhotsk SEA
~ feeder AMUR
Okla.
~ campus OSU
~ neighbor ARK, KAN, TEX
~ once TER, TERR
see also Oklahoma
Oklahoma STATE
~ city ADA, ENID, TULSA
~ fort SILL
~ tribe OSAGE, OTO, OTOE
"Oklahoma ___, The" KID
"Oklahoma!"
~ prop BALE
~ villain FRY
Oksana
see Russian
Oktoberfest
~ basic BEER
~ need KEG, STEIN
~ sight TENT
"Ol' ___ River" MAN
Olaf
~ capital OSLO
~ ctry. NOR
~ subjects NORSE
___ O'Lakes butter LAND
___ ol' boy GOOD
old DATED, PASSE, STALE
~ ender STER
~ hat OUT
old ___ GIRL, GOLD, HAND, HAT, ROSE, TALE

old ___ (out-of-date) HAT

old-___ LINE, TIME

old-___ network BOY, GIRL

___-old AGE

Old ___ LATIN, MAID, NORSE

Old ___ (Satan) NED

Old ___, The SOD

"Old ___, The" MAID

"Old ___ and the Sea, The" MAN

"Old ___ Bucket, The" OAKEN

"Old ___ Cod" CAPE

Old Blue ___ EYES

___ old boy GOOD

Old Castile
~ **province** AVILA

"___, old chap..." ISAY

old college ___, the TRY

Old Colony
~ **St.** MASS

"___ Old Cowhand" IMAN

"Old Creole ___" DAYS

"Old Curiosity ___, The" SHOP

"Old Curiosity Shop, The"
~ **heroine** NELL

"Old Devil ___" MOON

"Old Devils, The"
~ **author** AMIS

olden
~ **times** YORE
in ~ days AGO

Oldenburg CITY
see also German

Old English
~ **laborer** ESNE
~ **letter** ETH

older
~ **mems.** SRS
grow ~ AGE

oldest FIRST

old-fashioned DATED, PASSE
~ **albums** LPS
~ **bag** GRIP
~ **do** BEE
~ **exclamation** PSHAW
~ **ingredient** RYE
~ **remedy** TONIC
~ **suffix** EST, ETH
~ **wedding word** OBEY
get the ~ way EARN

Oldfield, Barney RACER

"Old Fuss and Feathers" SCOTT

Old Glory FLAG

"Old Gray ___, The" MARE

___ old grind, the SAME

Old Harry SATAN

"___ Old House" THIS

oldie SONG

"___ Oldies but Goodies" THOSE

"Old Ironsides" BOAT, SHIP

Old King ___ COLE

"Old MacDonald ___..." HAD

old maid GAME

"Old Man ___ the Sea, The" AND

"Old Man and the ___, The" SEA

"Old Man, Woman and Flower"
~ **painter** ERNST

"___ Old Moon, The" SAME

Old Nick SATAN

Old Norse
~ **inscription** RUNE

old one
~ **in German** ALTE

Olds
old ~ REO

Old Scratch SATAN
~ **specialty** EVIL

"Old Second Inning"
~ **McCarver** TIM

Old Smokey
~ **topper** SNOW

Old Sod
from the ~ IRISH

Old Sod, The EIRE, ERIN

"Old Soft ___, The" SHOE

Olds, Ransom
~ **middle name** ELI

oldster ELDER

___ old story, the SAME

"Old Swimmin' Hole, The" POEM

Old Testament
~ **book** AMOS, ESTHER, EZRA, HOSEA
~ **country** ARAM
~ **heroine** ESTHER
~ **judge** ELI
~ **kingdom** SHEBA
~ **name** RUTH
~ **patriarch** ENOS
see also Bible, Biblical

old-timer ELDER, VET

"Old Uncle ___" NED

Old West
~ **conveyance** STAGE
weapon of the ~ COLT

old wives' ___ TALE

Old World
~ **cont.** EUR

olé
~ **accompaniment** CLAP

Ole OLSEN

Ole ___ MISS

"Olé ___" (1976 album) ELO

"Olé!" CRY, RAH

oleaceous
~ **tree** ASH

O'Leary, Hazel
~ **org.** DOE

oleate ESTER

"Ole Buttermilk ___" SKY

Ole Miss
~ **student** REBEL

oleo
~ **holder** TUB
~ **serving** PAT

oleoresin ELEMI

Olestra
~ **lack** FAT
org. that approved ~ FDA

olfaction SCENT

olfactory
~ **attack** REEK
~ **input** ODOR
~ **organ** NOSE
~ **stimulus** AROMA

Olin KEN, LENA

olio STEW

olive COLOR, TREE
~ **product** OIL

olive ___ DRAB, OIL

Olive OYL

Oliver STONE
~ **partner** STAN

"Oliver!"
~ **director** REED
Oliver in ~ REED

"Oliver's Story"
~ **author** SEGAL

"Oliver Twist"
~ **director** LEAN

olive tree
~ **cousin** ASH

Olivia d'___ ABO

Olivier
~ **title** LORD, SIR
emulate ~ ACT

olla STEW

olla podrida STEW

Ollie
~ **friend** FRAN
~ **partner** STAN

"Olly, olly ___ free!" OXEN

Olsen MRS, OLE
~ **coworker** KENT, LANE

"O Lucky ___!" MAN

Olympia
~ **st.** WASH

"Olympia"
~ **painter** MANET

Manet's ~ NUDE

Olympian ALOOF
~ **award** MEDAL
~ **hunk** APOLLO
~ **queen** HERA
~ **quest** GOLD
~ **skier** MOE
militant ~ ARES

Olympics GAME
~ **award** GOLD
~ **chant** USA
~ **contest** EVENT
~ **event** DASH, EPEE, RELAY
~ **missile** SHOT
~ **perfection** TEN
~ **prize** MEDAL
~ **race unit** METER
~ **weapon** EPEE, SABER
1900 Summer ~ site PARIS
1904 Summer ~ site USA
1924 Summer ~ site PARIS
1932 Summer ~ site USA
1932 Winter ~ site USA
1952 Winter ~ site OSLO
1956 Winter ~ site ITALY
1960 Summer ~ site ITALY, ROME
1960 Winter ~ site USA
1980 Summer ~ site USSR
1980 Winter ~ site USA
1984 Summer ~ site USA
1988 Summer ~ site KOREA
1992 Summer ~ site SPAIN
1996 Summer ~
site ATLANTA, USA
2002 Winter ~ site USA
first ~ site ELIS
item of ~ gear DISC, EPEE
L.A. ~ boycotter USSR
site of the first ~ ELIS

Olympic Stadium
~ **player** EXPO

Olympus
~ **inhabitant** APOLLO, ARES, HERA
~ **matchmaker** EROS
~ **neighbor** OSSA
~ **resident** GOD
~ **troublemaker** ERIS

Omaha TRIBE
~ **home** TEPEE
~ **st.** NEB, NEBR

Oman
~ **neighbor** YEMEN
~ **title** AMIR, EMEER, EMIR

Omani ARAB
~ **land** ARABIA
~ **money** RIAL

Omar Khayyám POET

omega END
~ **counterpart** ZEE
~ **in physics** OHM
~ **opposite** ALPHA
~ **preceder** PSI
alpha and ~ TOTAL

"O Mein ___" PAPA

omelet
~ **cooker** PAN

omen
~ extra HAM, ONION
~ ingredient EGG

omen SIGN
~ interpreter SEER
be an ~ of BODE

omens
interpret ~ CAST

ominous BAD, DIRE, UGLY

omission CUT, ERROR, LAPSE, SKIP

omit DROP, SKIP
~ in fast-food lingo HOLD
~ in pronunciation ELIDE

omitting
~ none ALL

omni
~ ender BUS

Omni ARENA

omnia vincit ___ AMOR

omnibus MOTOR

Omni, The
~ locale ATLANTA

omnivore BEAR, GOAT

omphaloskepsis
~ find LINT

Omri
son of ~ AHAB

Omsk CITY, PORT

___-o'-mutton LEG

"___ o' My Heart" PEG

on ABOVE, ASOF, ATOP, LIT
~ a date OUT
~ an ocean liner ASEA, ATSEA
~ a winning streak HOT
~ (prefix) EPI
~ the bounding main ASEA, ATSEA
~ the crest ATOP
~ the double FAST
~ the lam LOOSE

on ___ (anxious) EDGE

on ___ (available) CALL, HAND, TAP

on ___ (blazing) FIRE

on ___ (in reserve) ICE

on ___ (in theory) PAPER

on ___ (punctual) TIME

on ___ (stored away) FILE

on ___ (tense) EDGE

on ___ (upright) END

on ___ (waiting) HOLD

on ___ ear ITS

on ___ fours ALL

on ___ of the world TOP

on-___ AIR, LINE, SITE, STAGE

on-___ (gossip) DIT

___ on (assume) TAKE

___ on (belabor) HARP

___ on (be patient) HOLD

___ on (betray) RAT

___ on (check for fit) TRY

___ on (convinced) SOLD

___ on (discover) HIT

___ on (encourage) EGG

___ on (endure) HANG

___ on (enthusiastic about) BIG

___ on (fuss over) DOTE

___ on (pretend) LET, PUT

___ on (prod) EGG

___ on (repressed) TROD

___ on (shadow) SPY

___ on (spoil) DOTE

___ on (spur) EGG

___ on (squelch) SIT

___ on (talk too much) RUN

___ on (trample) STEP

___ on (trust) RELY

___ on (wear) HAVE

___-on ADD, HEAD, ODDS, SLIP

"On ___ Blindness" HIS

"On ___ Majesty's Secret Service" HER

"On ___ of Old Smoky" TOP

"On ___ Sunday" ANY

"___ On" (Buddy Holly tune) RAVE

"___ On" (HBO sitcom) DREAM

ON ___ (studio sign) AIR

on a ___ (lucky) ROLL

on a ___-to-know basis NEED

"On a ___ Day..." CLEAR

"___ on a bet!" NOT

on a fool's ___ ERRAND

onager ASS

"___ on a Grecian Urn" ODE

"___ on a Hot Tin Roof" CAT

___ on a limb OUT

"___ on a Match" THREE

on an ___ keel EVEN

on an even ___ KEEL

Onassis
~ nickname ARI

"___ on a String" MAN

"___ on a Swing" MAN

"___ on a Train" LADY

"___ on a tuffet..." SAT

"...on a wing ___ prayer" ANDA

on bended ___ KNEE

"On Borrowed ___" TIME

"On Boxing"
~ author OATES

once ERST
~ called NEE
not even ~, to a poet NEER

once ___ blue moon INA

once ___ while INA

"Once ___ a midnight..." UPON

"Once ___ a time..." UPON

"Once ___ Lifetime" INA

"Once in ___..." PARIS

once in a blue ___ MOON

"Once in Love With ___" AMY

once more AGAIN, ANEW

once-over
give the ~ EYE, LEER, NOTE, OGLE, SCAN

"Once Upon a ___ in America" TIME

"Once Upon a ___ in the West" TIME

once upon a time AGO

"Once Upon a Time in America"
~ director LEONE

"Once Upon a Time in the ___" WEST

"Once Upon a Time in the West"
~ director LEONE

"___ Oncle" MON

oncoming AHEAD

"On Dangerous Ground"
~ director RAY

"___ on Down the Road" EASE

one ACE, UNIT
~ and only LONE
~ concerned with (suffix) EER
~ engaged in (suffix) EER
~ in a wool coat EWE
~ in French UNE
~ in German EIN
~ in Italian UNO
~ in Latin UNA
~ in Scottish ANE
~ in Spanish UNA, UNO
~ (prefix) MON, UNI
~ starter ANY, SOME
at least ~ ANY, SOME

one ___ at a time DAY, STEP

one ___ customer TOA

one ___ fits all SIZE

one ___ kind OFA

one ___ the books FOR

one ___ time ATA

one-___ LINER, SHOT, STEP, TIME

one-___ bandit ARMED

one-___ car OWNER

one-___ hit BASE

one-___ punch TWO

one-___ show MAN

one-___ town HORSE

___ one ADMIT

___ one (nobody) NOTA

___ one (the beginning) DAY

"...one ___ two!" (Welk intro) ANDA

"One ___ Bell to Answer" LESS

"One ___ Beyond" STEP

"One ___ Day" FINE

"One ___ fits all" SIZE

"One ___ in Heaven" FOOT

"One ___ Lonely Number" ISA

"One ___ Million" INA

"One ___ Move" FALSE

"One ___ River" MORE

"One ___ to Live" LIFE

"One ___ Way" MANS

"One ___ With You" HOUR

"One, ___, Three" TWO

"One-___ Jacks" EYED

"___ One, The" OTHER

O'Neal RYAN

one and ___ ALL, ONLY

one-armed bandit
~ feature SLOT

one-billionth
~ (prefix) NANO

one by one
taken ~ EACH

one-celled
~ animal AMEBA
~ plant ALGA

"One Day ___ Time" ATA

___ one-eighty DOA

"One False ___" MOVE

"One Flew ___ the Cuckoo's Nest" OVER

"One Flew Over the Cuckoo's ___" NEST

"One for My Baby"
~ singer HORNE

one-for-one
~ deal SWAP, TRADE

"...___ one for the Gipper" WIN

Onega LAKE

one-horse MEAN, SMALL
~ carriage GIG

one-hoss
~ vehicle SHAY

"One Hour With ___" YOU

"One Hundred ___ and a Girl" MEN

"One Hundred ___ One Dalmatians" AND

"One Hundred and ___ Dalmatians" ONE

"One Hundred Men ___ a Girl" AND

"One Hundred Men ___ Girl" ANDA

"One Hundred Men and a ___" GIRL

Oneida LAKE, TRIBE
~ cousin ERIE

O'Neill TIP
~ and others EDS

O'Neill, Eugene
~ daughter OONA
~ forte DRAMA
~ hairy one APE
~ opus PLAY
~ play ILE
~ tree ELM

"One I Love, The"
~ band REM

one-in-a-million RARE

oneiromancy
~ subject DREAM

one-L
~ Nash subject LAMA

"One Life to Live" SOAP

one-liner GAG
~ response HAHA

"One-L lama"
~ poet NASH

one-man
~ band SOLO

one-man ___ SHOW

"One Minute to ___" ZERO

one-name
~ entertainer CHER

oneness PEACE

"One Night of ___" LOVE

"One Note ___" SAMBA

"One of ___" (Cather book) OURS

"One of ___ days, Alice..." THESE

___ one on TIE

one-on-one
~ event DUEL

one or the ___ OTHER

one-pot
~ dinner STEW

"One Potato, ___ Potato" TWO

one-quarter
~ acre ROOD

oner LULU

___ one right SERVE

ones
column next to ~ TENS
the ~ here THESE
the ~ over there THOSE

___ one's ballot CAST

oneself
all by ~ ALONE

"___ One's for You" THIS

___ one's hair TEAR

one-sidedness BIAS, SLANT

___ one's pockets LINE

one-spot ACE

"One's-Self I Sing" POEM

___ one's shirt LOSE

one-step DANCE

___ one's time BIDE

one-striper ENS

___ one's wheels SPIN

___ one's words EAT

one-tenth
~ of a gee CEE

one-term
first ~ president ADAMS

one that got ___, the AWAY

one thing ___ time ATA

one-third
~ of a dog's name RIN
~ of dodeca- TETRA

onetime LATE

"___ one to grow on" AND

"One Touch of Venus"
Venus in ~ AVA

one-two
start of a ~ JAB

"One, Two, ___" THREE

one-way
~ symbol ARROW

one way or the ___ OTHER

"One with Nineveh and ___" TYRE

one-woman ___ SHOW

"___ on Film" AGEE

___ on fire (ignite) SET

"On Golden ___" POND

"On Golden Pond"
~ bird LOON

"On Her Majesty's Secret Service"
~ director HUNT

ONI
part of ~ NAVAL

"___ on Ice" SOUL

"___ on Indolence" ODE

___-o'-nine-tails CAT

onion
~ cousin LEEK
~ cover SKIN
~ product RING

___ onion PEARL

onions
cook ~, perhaps SAUTE
react to ~ CRY

onionskin PAPER

___ on it SLEEP, STEP

"___ on it!" (Fonzie remark) SIT

on its ___ (topsy-turvy) EAR

"On Liberty"
~ author MILL

on-line
~ conversation CHAT
~ notes EMAIL
one ~ USER

only ALL, ALONE, LONE, MERE, ONE, SOLE

"___ only" EYES

___-only (secret) EYES

"Only ___" AROSE, YOU

"Only ___ in Town, The" GAME

"Only Angels ___ Wings" HAVE

"only animal that blushes" MAN

___ only as directed USE

"___ Only Had a Brain" IFI

"___ Only Live Once" YOU

"___ Only Live Twice" YOU

"___ Only Make Believe" ITS

___-only memory READ

"___ Only Money" ITS

"Only You"
~ actor ZANE

"___ on Main Street, The" SHOP

"___ on Me" LEAN

"On Moonlight ___" BAY

"On My ___" (Patti LaBelle tune) OWN

"___ on My Pillow" TEARS

"___ on My Shoulder" ANGEL

Onondaga
~ enemy ERIE

on one's ___ OWN, TOES

___ on one's hands SIT

"___ on parle français" ICI

onrush STREAM

"On seeing the Elgin Marbles" POEM

onset START

onslaught ONSET, RAID, STORM

"___ on Solitude" ODE

onstage
~ phone PROP
walk ~ ENTER

"___ on Sunday" NEVER

Ont.
~ neighbor MAN

Ontario LAKE
~ city OTTAWA
~ Indian CREE
~ neighbor ERIE
~ river TRENT

Ontario's ___ Point PELEE

on the ___ DOLE, ROAD

on the ___ (active) MOVE

on the ___ (alert) BALL

on the ___ (at large) LOOSE

on the ___ (at odds) OUTS

on the ___ (corrupt) TAKE

on the ___ (ebbing) WANE

on the ___ (exact) BEAM

on the ___ (exactly) DOT, NOSE

on the ___ (extracurricularly) SIDE

on the ___ (fleeing) LAM, RUN

on the ___ (healing) MEND

on the ___ (in jeopardy) LINE

on the ___ (instantly) SPOT

on the ___ (precariously) EDGE

on the ___ (surreptitiously) SLY

on the ___ (wary) ALERT

on the ___ wavelength SAME

on-the-___ reporter SCENE

"On the ___" (Kerouac book) ROAD

"On the ___ hand..." OTHER

"On the ___ With Charles Kuralt" ROAD

"On the Avenue"
~ director RUTH

___ on the back PAT

___ on the barrelhead CASH

"On the Beach"
Gregory's ~ costar AVA

"___ on the Bus" GET

___ on the cake ICING

on-the-cob
   ~ treat CORN

___ on the cob CORN

___ on the dog PUT

on the double ASAP, STAT

"___ on the Eiffel Tower, The" MAN

"___ on the Floss, The" MILL

"___ on the Flying Trapeze, The" MAN

___ on the gas STEP

"On the Good ___ Lollipop" SHIP

"___ on the Moon, The" MOUSE

"___ on the Range" HOME

on the right ___ FOOT

"On the Riviera"
   ~ director LANG

"On the Road ___" AGAIN

"___ on the Run" BAND, NUNS

"On the Third Day"
   ~ band ELO

"On the Waterfront"
   ~ actress SAINT

___ on the wrist SLAP

on the wrong ___ FOOT

___-on tie CLIP

onto AWARE

___ on to (keep) HANG

"___ on Truckin'" KEEP

onus LOAD

onward AHEAD, ALONG
   drive ~ IMPEL

___ on words PLAY

"___ on you!" SHAME

"On Your ___" TOES

"___ on your life!" NOT

"___ on yourself!" RELY

onyx GEM
   ~ decoration CAMEO

"Oo ___ Baby, I Love You" WEE

oodles ALOT, HEAP, LOTS, MASS, OCEAN, PILE, RAFT, SEA, TON, WADS

"Ooh ___!" LALA

ooh and ___ AAH

"Ooh Poo ___ Doo" PAH

oology
   ~ subject EGGS

oolong TEA

oom-___ PAH

oom-pah
   ~ instrument TUBA

oomph DASH, ELAN, PEP, SNAP, VIM

___-oop ALLEY

Oop, Alley
   ~ kingdom MOO

ooze BLEED, DIRT, DRIP, DROP, EMIT, ISSUE, LEAK, MIRE, SEEP, SLIME, SLOP

op ___ ART

___-op PRE

opal GEM
   ~ ender INE
   ~ mo. OCT

___ opal FIRE

opaque DENSE

op art
   ~ pattern MOIRE

"O patria mia" ARIA
   ~ singer AIDA

op. cit.
   cousin of ~ IBID

OPEC BLOC, PACT
   ~ concern OIL
   ~ leader AMIR, EMEER, EMIR
   ~ member ARAB, IRAN, IRAQ
   ~ representative IRANI
   ~ vessel OILER
   part of ~ ORG

op-ed PAGE
   ~ piece ESSAY

Opel AUTO, CAR

open AIRY, AJAR, CLEAN, CLEAR, EASY, FREE, HONEST, LOOSE, RAISE, RAW, START
   ~ a barrel TAP
   ~ an envelope SLIT
   ~ a package UNDO
   ~ as sneakers UNTIE
   ~ carriage SHAY
   ~ country MOOR, SPACE
   ~ door ENTREE
   ~ doors EASE
   ~ entrances ATRIA
   ~ fabric LACE, NET
   ~ fire SHOOT
   ~ fire on SHELL
   ~ hand PALM
   ~ one's mouth BLAB, TALK
   ~ pit MINE
   ~ slightly AJAR
   ~ space ROOM
   ~ space in a forest GLADE
   ~ the door to ADMIT
   ~ the throttle GUN
   ~ tract LLANO
   ~ up ADMIT
   ~ wide GAPE
   ~ (with) LEAD
   bring out in the ~ AIR
   burst ~ ERUPT
   come ~ UNDO
   cut ~ LANCE
   fail to ~ PASS
   force ~ PRY
   in the ~ OUT, OVERT
   not ~ SHUT, SLY

not ~ to ABOVE
wide ~ AGAPE
with eyes and ears ~ WARY

open-___ ENDED

___-open WIDE

"Open" SIGN

"Open ___" CITY, SESAME

"Open ___" (dentist's order) WIDE

open a ___ of worms CAN

open-air
   ~ lobbies ATRIA
   ~ market FAIR
   ~ pool LIDO

open-and-___ case SHUT

Open Door Policy
   ~ proponent HAY

opened
   ~ a crack AJAR

opener KEY

open-handed
   ~ move SLAP

open-hearted NAIVE, WARM

opening CUT, DOOR, EXIT, GAP, GATE, HOLE, LEAK, PEEP, RENT, SLIT, SPACE, SPLIT, START, VOID
   ~ part of a play ACTI
   ~ word HELLO
   ~ words INTRO
   dermal ~ PORE
   eye ~ SLIT
   fort ~ GATE
   job ~ SLOT
   leaf ~ PORE
   lens ~ IRIS
   narrow ~ SLOT
   piggy bank ~ SLOT

opening night
   ~ memento STUB

open-mouthed AGAPE, AGOG
   leave ~ AMAZE, AWE, STUN, WOW

open 9 ___ 5 TIL

"Open sesame!"
   ~ speaker ALI, BABA

"Open the ___, Richard" DOOR

open-weave
   ~ fabric LENO

"Open wide!"
   ~ response AAH

"Open Window, The"
   ~ author SAKI

openwork LACE
   ~ fabric MESH
   do ~ TAT

opera ART, GENRE, OPUS
   ~ box LOGE
   ~ division ACT
   ~ hero, often TENOR
   ~ highlight ARIA
   ~ opener ACTI

~ prince IGOR
~ princess AIDA
~ prop SPEAR
~ set in Egypt AIDA
~ singer DIVA
~ slave AIDA
~ solo ARIA
~ villainess, often ALTO
~ villain, often BASS, BASSO
~ written for the opening of the Suez Canal AIDA
American ~ role BESS
grand ~ DRAMA
horse ~ DRAMA, OATER
NYC ~ house MET
perform in an ~ SING
soap ~ DRAMA

opera ___ HAT

___ opera HORSE, SOAP, SPACE

opera house
   ~ section TIER
   New York City ~ MET

operate ACT, MAN, RUN, STEER, USE

operating
   not ~ IDLE, OFF
   standard ~ procedure MODE

operation USE
   ~ locs. ERS, ORS
   in ~ ALIVE
   police ~ RAID, STING
   sting ~ CON, SETUP, TRAP
   undercover ~ STING

Operation Desert ___ STORM

"Operation Dumbo Drop"
   ~ elephant TAI

Operation Overlord
   when ~ began DDAY

operative AGENT, ALIVE, SPY
   White House ~ AIDE

operator USER
   amateur-radio ~ HAM
   big-time ~ DOER

___-operator OWNER

operetta
   ~ composer LEHAR

operoseness LABOR

Ophelia DANE

ophidian ASP, SNAKE

ophthalmic OPTIC

opiate DOPE

Opie ALAN
   ~ aunt BEE
   ~ father ANDY
   ~ portrayer RON

opine AVER, DEEM, EDUCE, HOLD, IDEATE, SAY

opinion IDEA, SAY, SLANT, STAND
   ~ in French AVIS
   ~ piece ESSAY
   difference of ~ SPAT
   express one's ~ TALK
   favorable ~ ESTEEM

fixed ~ DOGMA
give an ~ STATE
high ~ ESTEEM
voice an ~ SAY
voice an ~, perhaps ARGUE

opinionated SMALL
~ work ESSAY

opinions
gather ~ POLL

opossum ANIMAL

opp. ANT

oppidan LOCAL

opponent ANTI, CON, ENEMY, FOE

opportune PAT, RIPE

opportunist USER

opportunity SHOT, START, TIME, TURN
at the first ~ ANON, SOON
golden ~ TIME

oppose BEARD, BELIE, DARE, DENY, FACE, MEET, PIT, PLAY, REACT
~ authority REBEL

opposed AGIN, ALIEN, ANTI, AVERSE
~ to, informally AGIN
diametrically ~ POLAR

opposer ANTI
Brady Bill ~ NRA

opposing ANTI
~ force ENEMY, FOE
~ (prefix) ANTI
~ vote NAY

opposite POLAR
~ (prefix) ANTI, DIS

"Opposite ___, The" SEX

opposition ENEMY, FOE
in ~ to ANTI, CON
put in ~ PIT

oppositionist ANTI

oppress TREAD

oppression ROD

oppressive BAD, CLOSE, HARD

opprobrious BAD, VILE

opprobrium SHAME

Oprah
~ daily need TOPIC
~ former rival PHIL
~ production
company HARPO
~ stock-in-trade TALK
emulate ~ DIET

Opry
~ st. TENN

opt
~ for ELECT, TAKE

optical
~ device LENS

optimal BEST, FIRST, IDEAL

optimism HOPE

optimistic ROSY
~ phrase ICAN

optimum BEST, FIRST

optional EXTRA

options
list of ~ MENU

opulence EASE

opulent POSH, RICH

opuntias CACTI

opus ESSAY, PLAY
magnum ~ TOME

"Or ___!" ELSE

OR
~ workers DRS, RNS
see also Oregon

oracle SAGE, SEER
~ words ISEE

oral EXAM, TEST
~ history LORE
~ report TALK

orally ALOUD

oral surgeon
~ deg. DDS

Oran CITY, PORT

orang ANIMAL, APE

orange SODA, TREE
~ container CRATE
~ cover PEEL, RIND
~ drink ADE
~ ender ADE
~ gemstone SARD
~ pekoe TEA
~ seed PIP
~ vegetable YAM
kind of ~ OSAGE
make ~ juice REAM

orange ___ PEKOE

orange blossom
~ ingredient GIN

Orange Blossom Special TRAIN

Orange Bowl
~ locale MIAMI
~ st. FLA

orange-red
~ mineral SARD

orange-yellow
dark ~ AMBER

orangutan ANIMAL, APE

Oranjestad
~ island ARUBA

orarion STOLE

orate RANT, SAY, TALK

oration TALK

orator
~ perch DAIS
~ ploy IRONY
Roman ~ CATO

oratorio
~ melody ARIA

orb BALL, EYE, SPHERE, STAR, SUN
edible ~ PEA

Orbison ROY

Orbison, Roy TENOR
~ tune LEAH

orbit AREA, PATH
~ segment ARC
~ shape OVAL

___ orbit LUNAR, POLAR

orbital
~ period YEAR
~ point APSE
~ segment ARC

orbiter
~ locale SPACE
earth ~ MIR

___ orbiter LUNAR

Orbiter
~ org. NASA

___-or-break MAKE

orchard STAND
~ component TREE
~ fruit APPLE, PEAR
~ product NUT
former ~ spray ALAR

orchestra BAND
~ locale PIT
~ member CELLO, HARP, HORN, OBOE, PIANO, REED, TUBA
~ sect. STR
~ section BRASS
arrange for an ~ SCORE
high in the ~ ALT

orchestra ___ PIT

orchidlike
~ flower IRIS

ORD
~ abbr. ARR, ETA
~ locale CHI

ordain ENACT, FATE, ORDER

ordained SET

ordeal FIRE, TRIAL
student's ~ EXAM, TEST

order ACT, ARRAY, ASK, BID, BOSS, CALL, CASTE, CLASS, FIAT, LAW, LEAD, LOT, RANK, RULE, SORT, SPACE, TELL
~ (abbr.) SYST
~ around BOSS
~ for dinner EAT, HAVE
~ partner LAW
~ to a GI ATEASE, HALT
~ to go EATIN, SEND
apple-pie ~ TRIM
authoritative ~ EDICT
bakery ~ RYE
bar ~ ALE, BEER, LAGER, NEAT, RYE, SHOT
batting ~ CARD
breakfast ~ EGG, HAM, OMELET, ROLL, TOAST

court ~ LAW, WRIT
deli ~ BLT, HERO, SALAMI, TOGO
doctor's ~ DOSE, STAT
drive-through ~ TOGO
fountain ~ COLA, SODA
hashhouse ~ EGGS
in ~ TAUT
in apple-pie ~ NEAT
in short ~ ANON, SOON
judicial ~ STAY, WRIT
king's ~ EDICT
law and ~ PEACE
malt-shop ~ SODA
mom's pre-dinner ~ WASH
on the ~ of LIKE
out of ~ AMISS
photographer's ~ SMILE
pizza ~ PIE
pork ~ CHOP
public ~ PEACE
put in ~ FILE, MEND, RANGE, SORT
rathskeller ~ STEIN
religious ~ SECT
rib ~ RACK
sandwich ~ BLT, TUNA
seafood ~ COD
sentry's ~ HALT
soda ~ DIET
soda-fountain ~ MALT
south-of-the-border ~ TACO
steak ~ RARE, TBONE
trader's ~ SELL
Wall Street ~ PUT

___ order GAG, MAIL, TALL

ordered BADE

orderliness TRIM

orderly AIDE, CLEAN, NEAT, TAUT, TRIM

Order of ___ LENIN

orders
follow ~ OBEY

ordinal
~ suffix ETH
imprecise ~ NTH

ordinals
~ (abbr.) NOS

ordinance ACT, EDICT, LAW, ORDER, RULE

ordinary BANAL, FAIR, MERE, SOSO, TRITE, USUAL
~ sz. REG
~ talk PROSE
out of the ~ ODD, RARE

"___ Ordinary Man" IMAN

ordnance ARMS

ore
~ bed RUN
~ carrier SCOW
~ layer SEAM
~ material METAL
~ source LODE, MINE
~ suffix ITE
~ test ASSAY
~ truck TRAM
analyze ~ ASSAY

process ~ SMELT

öre COIN

Ore.
~ **campus** OSU
~ **neighbor** CAL, IDA, NEV, WASH
~ **zone** PDT, PST
see also Oregon

Oreg.
see Oregon

oregano HERB

Oregon STATE, TRAIL
~ **campus** OSU
~ **capital** SALEM
~ **county** COOS
~ **neighbor** CAL, IDA, IDAHO, NEV, WASH
~ **zone** PDT, PST
start of ~'s motto ALIS

Oregon ___ FIR, TRAIL

Oregon Trail
~ **city** BOISE

O'Reilly
~ **of "M*A*S*H"** RADAR

Orem
~ **state** UTAH

Orenburg CITY
~ **river** URAL
see also Russian

Orestes
~ **to Agamemnon** SON

"Orfeo" OPERA

"Orfeo ed Euridice"
~ **soprano** AMOR

Orff CARL

org. ASSN

organ
~ **ender** ISM
~ **lever** PEDAL, STOP
~ **of circulation** HEART
~ **of locomotion** FOOT
~ **part** KEY, PEDAL, PIPE
~ **voice** OBOE
acoustic ~ EAR
breathing ~ LUNG
hearing ~ EAR
house ~ PAPER
largest ~ SKIN
lendable ~ EAR
olfactory ~ NOSE
respiratory ~ LUNG
sense ~ EAR, EYE, NOSE, SKIN
tin ~ EAR

organ-___ cactus PIPE

___ organ PIPE, SENSE

organic
~ **compound** ENOL, ESTER
~ **compound suffix** ENE, INE
~ **unit** CELL

organism
~ **(prefix)** BIO

organization SETUP

organize ORDER, SETUP, SORT, START

organized
~ **crime** MOB
~ **group** TEAM
get ~ PLAN

organizer FILE

organ-pipes CACTI

oribi ANIMAL

oriel BAY

Orient ASIA, EAST

orienteer
~ **need** MAP

"Orient Express" TRAIN
~ **unit** CAR

orifice GAP, HOLE, PORE

oriflamme FLAG

origami
~ **need** PAPER

origin BASE, FONT, GERM, HEAD, ONSET, ROOT, SEED, START
~ **to a poet** FONT
phoenix ~ ASHES

original EARLY, FIRST, MODEL, NEW

original ___ SIN

originally FIRST

originate ARISE, CAUSE, COIN, COME, ISSUE, MAKE, RISE, STEM

Orinoco RIO

oriole BIRD

Orioles TEAM, TEN

Orion
~ **has one** BELT
~ **lover** EOS

orison CRY
~ **ending** AMEN

Orkin RUTH
~ **target** ANT

Orlando CITY, TONY

"Orlando Furioso" EPIC

Orleans
river at ~ LOIRE

___ Orleans NEW

Orléans
see French

___ Orleans Saints NEW

Orly
see French

___ or miss HIT

ormolu METAL

ornament ADORN, BEAD, DRESS, GEM, PEARL, PIN, TRIM
~ **silverware** CHASE
Christmas ~ ANGEL, BALL, TREE

place for an ~ HOOD
pump ~ CLIP
top ~ EPI
tree ~ ANGEL

ornamental PLANT
~ **band** SASH
~ **border** DADO
~ **button** STUD
~ **knob** BOSS
~ **stamp** SEAL
~ **vine** IVY
wreath ~ CONE

ornamentation DECOR, LACE, TRIM

Orne
city on the ~ CAEN

___ Orne Jewett SARAH

ornery
~ **equine** ASS
~ **mood** SNIT

ornithological AVIAN

___-or-nothing ALL

"___ or Not to Be" TOBE

orotund BIG

O'Rourke SGT

Oroville DAM

orphan
comics ~ ANNIE

Orphan Annie
~ **protector** ASP

"Orphans of the ___" STORM

Orpheus POET
~ **instrument** LYRE
see also poet

orphrey HEM

Orr, Bobby
~ **milieu** ICE, RINK
~ **org.** NHL
emulate ~ SKATE

___ or shine RAIN

Orsk
~ **river** URAL

Orson BEAN
one of ~'s exes RITA

___ or swim SINK

ort SCRAP

Ortegal CAPE

"___ or the Tiger?, The" LADY

orthodontist
~ **concern** BITE
~ **deg.** DDS
~ **org.** ADA

orthopedist
~ **tool** XRAY

ortolan BIRD

Orton, Joe
~ **play** LOOT

"Or to take ___ against a sea..." ARMS

Orwell, George ALIAS
~ **alma mater** ETON
~ **birthplace** INDIA
~ **real first name** ERIC

Ory KID

oryx ANIMAL

orzo PASTA

Os ELEM
76 for ~ ATNO

Osage ORANGE, TRIBE

Osage ___ ORANGE

Osaka CITY
~ **beverage** SAKE, SAKI
see also Japanese

Osbiston ALAN

Oscar AWARD
~ **but not Felix** SLOB
~ **cousin** OBIE, TONY
~ **nominee** ACTOR
earn an ~ ACT
French equivalent of the ~ CESAR

Oscar ___ Hoya DELA

Oscar ___ Renta DELA

Oscar ___ Sanchez ARIAS

Oscar night
~ **sight** STAR

Oscar the Grouch CRAB

oscillate SWAY

oscillation PULSE, TREMOR

osculate KISS

___-o'-shanter TAM

Osiris GOD
Anubis, to ~ SON
Horus, to ~ SON
sister of ~ ISIS
wife of ~ ISIS

Oslo CITY
from ~ NORSE
rock trio from ~ AHA

Osman AMIR, EMEER, EMIR

osmium METAL

Osmond ALAN, MARIE

Osmonds
~ **home** UTAH
~ **tune** YOYO

osmose SEEP

osmunda FERN

osprey BIRD
~ **cousin** ERN, ERNE

OSS
~ **successor** CIA

Ossa
~ **and others** MTS

ossicle BONE

ostensorium CASE

ostentation PARADE, POMP, SHOW

ostentatious ORNATE

osteoporosis
~ **site** BONE

Ostia
~ **neighbor** ROMA
see also Italian

ostracize BAR, EXILE, OUST, TABOO, TABU

ostrich BIRD, FERN
~ **cousin** EMU, RHEA
~ **look-alike** MOA

O'Sullivan, Maureen
~ **role** JANE

Oswald the ___ REEVE

Oswego LAKE

O.T.
~ **book** BAR, EZRA, GEN, HOSEA, ISA, LAM, MAC, NAH
~ **heroine** ESTHER
part of ~ OLD

O3 OZONE

"O Tannenbaum" CAROL
~ **subject** FIR, TREE

otary
like an ~ EARED

OTB
~ **part of** OFF
~ **posting** ODDS

"Otello" OPERA
~ **role** IAGO

Othello MOOR

"Othello" PLAY
~ **character** IAGO
~ **opener** ACTI

"___ o' the mornin'" TOP

other ELSE, MORE, NEW
~ **in Spanish** OTRA
~ **people** THEM
~ **than** ELSE

other fish to ___ FRY

others
~ **in Latin** ALIA
avoiding ~ SHY
how ~ see us IMAGE
so ~ may hear ALOUD

others' THEIR

otherwise ELSE
~ **called** AKA, ALIAS

"otherwise"
~ **literally** ALIAS

otherworldly EERIE, EERY

"___ o' the Times" SIGN

otic AURAL

otiose IDLE

Otis AMOS, MISS

Oto TRIBE
~ **prey** BISON

otolaryngology
~ **(abbr.)** ENT
~ **focus** EAR

otologist
~ **concern** EAR

O'Toole PETER

Otranto
~ **(abbr.)** STR

Ott MEL

Ottawa CITY
~ **prov.** ONT
inc. in ~ LTD

otter ANIMAL
~ **milieu** OCEAN, SEA

Otto
see German

Otto ___ Bismarck VON

ottoman SOFA
occupy an ~ SIT

Ottoman
~ **VIP** AGA, AGHA, PASHA

Ottumwa
~ **state** IOWA

Ouachita RANGE

oui YES
~ **opposite** NON

Ouija GAME
~ **board answer** YES

"Oui, oui"
~ **in Spanish** SISI

ounce UNIT
~ **cousin** GRAM
~ **fraction** DRAM
~ **of whiskey** SHOT
not an ~ NONE

ounces
eight fluid ~ CUP

ouphe ELF

our
~ **in French** NOS
not ~ THEIR

"Our ___" GANG

"Our Gang"
~ **author** ROTH
~ **pooch** PETE

"Our Hearts ___ Young and Gay" WERE

"Our Hearts Were Young ___ Gay" AND

"Our Hearts Were Young and ___" GAY

"Our Hearts Were Young and Gay"
~ **director** ALLEN

"Our Love Is on the Fault ___" LINE

"Our Man in Havana"
~ **actor** IVES

"Our Miss Brooks"
~ **actress** ARDEN

"Our righteousnesses are as filthy ___..." RAGS

ourselves
~ **in Spanish** NOS

"Our Vines ___ Tender Grapes" HAVE

Ouse
~ **feeder** AIRE, CAM

oust EJECT, EXILE, FIRE

ouster BOOT

out ALIBI, AWAY, GONE, OLD, PASSE
~ **for the night** ABED
~ **of bed** ASTIR
~ **of fashion** DATED, PASSE
~ **of kilter** AWRY
~ **of one's gourd** LOCO
~ **of place** AMISS
~ **of the harbor** ASEA, ATSEA
~ **of the sack** RISEN
~ **of whack** AMISS, ATILT

out ___ (audibly) LOUD

out ___ limb ONA

___ out ASK, BAIL, BAWL, COP, DOPE, EASE, EDGE, EKE, FAKE, GET, HASH, IRON, LASH, LAY, LOG, MAP, METE, NOSE, OPT, PAN, PETER, PHASE, REAM, RIDE, SELL, SEND, SHELL, SHUT, SIT, SPACE, SPIN, STORM, TROT, TUNE, WEAR, WEED

___ out (allot) METE

___ out (barely beat) EDGE, NOSE

___ out (barely manage) EKE

___ out (become) TURN

___ out (become dazed) SPACE

___ out (begin) SET

___ out (be gone) RUN

___ out (be prominent) STAND

___ out (betray) SELL

___ out (date) ASK

___ out (deceive) FAKE

___ out (decline) OPT

___ out (defeat) BEAT

___ out (delete) TAKE

___ out (diminish) PETER

___ out (disburse) PAY

___ out (discontinue) PHASE

___ out (discuss) HASH

___ out (distribute) DISH, HAND, METE, PASS

___ out (eliminate) RULE, WEED

___ out (endure) HOLD, RIDE

___ out (escape) BAIL

___ out (exhaust) WEAR

___ out (exile) CAST

___ out (finish) CLOSE, PLAY

___ out (get rid of tactfully) EASE

___ out (ignore) TUNE

___ out (just get by) EKE

___ out (knock cold) LAY

___ out (lambaste) REAM

___ out (leave) CLEAR, GET, SHIP

___ out (leave in a huff) STORM

___ out (loiter) HANG

___ out (lose control) SPIN

___ out (miss) SIT

___ out (pay) SHELL

___ out (phone for a pizza) SEND

___ out (plan) MAP

___ out (prevent from scoring) SHUT

___ out (prove) BEAR

___ out (quit) BOW, DROP

___ out (renege) COP

___ out (resolve) IRON

___ out (scold) BAWL

___ out (show off) TROT

___ out (sleep) SACK

___ out (solve) DOPE

___ out (stop) CUT

___ out (strike suddenly) LASH

___ out (succeed) PAN

___ out (surveil) STAKE

___ out (terminate a session) LOG

___ out (test) TRY

___ out (upbraid) BAWL

___ out (withdraw) OPT

"___ out!" FAR

___-out FAR, READ, SHOOT, SOLD

"Out!" CALL, SCAT, SCRAM, SHOO

___ out a living EKE

out-and-out BALD, CLEAR, FLAT, RANK, TOTAL, UTTER

outback
~ **bird** EMU
~ **denizen** ROO
~ **mineral** OPAL

outboard MOTOR

outbrazen DARE

outbreak FIT, ONSET, RASH, RIOT, START
   embarrassing ~ SCENE

outbuilding SHED

outburst FIT, FLARE, GALE, SCENE, SPASM, STORM
   emotional ~ CRY, SCENE
   make an ~ ERUPT
   solar ~ FLARE
   sudden ~ FLARE

outcast EXILE, LEPER, LONER
   high-school ~ NERD

"Outcast of the Islands"
   ~ director REED

"Outcasts of Poker Flat, The"
   ~ author HARTE

outcome END, EVENT, FATE, ISSUE
   fix the ~ RIG

outcropping CRAG, LEDGE

outcry NOISE, ROAR, ROW, YELL

outdated OLD, PASSE, STALE

outdistance LEAD

outdo BEAT, BEST, CAP, LEAD, TOP

outdoor
   ~ area PATIO
   ~ dwelling TENT
   ~ residence CAMP

outer
   ~ coat SKIN
   ~ covering DRESS
   ~ edge RIM
   ~ garment FUR, ROBE
   ~ layer RIND
   ~ limit EDGE, RIM
   ~ limits EDGE, ETHER
   ~ (prefix) ECTO, EPI
   ~ space SKY
   hard ~ covering SHELL
   in ~ space MAD

outer ___ EAR, SPACE

outer space
   ~ (prefix) ASTRO

outfield
   ~ material SOD

outfielder
   ~ pride ARM

outfit ARM, ATTIRE, BAND, DRESS, GANG, GARB, GEAR, LOT, RIG, SUIT
   Army ~ UNIT
   coordinated ~ SET
   horseback rider's ~ HABIT
   matching ~ SUIT

outfitted CLAD

outflow ISSUE, TIDE

outgoing
   not ~ SHY

out in ___ field LEFT

outing HIKE, RIDE, SPIN, TRIP
   nature ~ HIKE
   romantic ~ DATE

shopping ~ SPREE

"Outland"
   ~ penguin OPUS

outlander ALIEN

outlandish EERIE, EERY, ODD, OUTRE
   not ~ SANE

outlaw BAN, BAR

"Outlaw, The"
   Jane Russell, in ~ RIO

"___ Outlaw, The" LAST

"Outlaw—Josey Wales, The" OATER

outlawry BAN

outlay COST, RATE, SPEND

outlet EXIT, PORE, STORE

outline AGENDA, DRAW, ETCH, MAP, PLAN, PLOT
   ~ sharply ETCH
   make an ~ TRACE

outlook MOOD

outmoded DATED, OLD, PASSE
   ~ title MRS

out of ___ DATE, GAS, HAND, LINE, SORTS, STEP, STYLE, SYNC, TURN

out of ___ (antiquated) DATE

out of ___ (awry) SYNC

out of ___ (cutting in) TURN

out of ___ (exhausted) GAS

out of ___ (forthwith) HAND

out of ___ (grumpy) SORTS

out of ___ (passé) STYLE

out of ___ (unruly) LINE

out of ___ world THIS

___ out of (reject) OPT

"...out of a sow's ___" EAR

out-of-date OLD, PASSE, STALE

out of line PERT

___ out of mind TIME

"Out of my dreams and ___ your arms..." INTO

out of sight NEAT

out of style DATED, PASSE

out of the ___ BLUE

"Out of the ___" PAST

"Out of the Blue"
   ~ band ELO

"Out of the Cradle Endlessly Rocking" POEM

"Out of the frying pan, ___ the fire" INTO

out of the way
   not ~ USUAL

"Out of Time"
   ~ band REM

"Out of Towners, The"
   ~ actress MEARA

___ out one's welcome WEAR

outperform LEAD

outplay BEST, LEAD

outpost
   Army ~ BASE, CAMP

"___ Outpost, The" LAST

outpouring
   sudden ~ SPATE

output YIELD
   brewer's ~ ALE

outrage IRE, SIN

outraged IRATE, UPSET

outrageous MAD

"Outrageous Fortune"
   ~ actress LONG

outrank LEAD

outranking OVER

outrigger CANOE

outright BALD, HONEST, PURE, TOTAL, UTTER

outrival LEAD

outrun BEAT, LEAD

outs
   ~ in an inning SIX

outscore BEST, WIN

outset TOP
   at the ~ FIRST

outshine CAP, LEAD, TOP

outside FACE
   ~ (prefix) ECTO
   burn the ~ of SEAR

"Outside ___, The" MAN

outsider ALIEN, LONER

"Outsider, The"
   ~ director MANN

outsides
   inner-tube ~ TIRE

outsized BIG, LARGE

outspoken FREE, HONEST, ORAL

outspread BIG, LARGE, LONG

outstanding ACE, AONE, BEST, BIG, DUE, GREAT, MAIN, RARE, TOPS
   ~ amount DEBT
   ~ person ONER

outstretched WIDE

outstrip BEAT, CAP, LEAD, LOSE, PASS, TOP
   ~ the wind RACE, RUN, SPEED

"Outta here!" SCAT, SCRAM, SHOO

___ out the red carpet ROLL

"Out to ___" SEA

___ out to pasture PUT

outwear LAST

outwit GET, HAVE

outwrestle PIN

ouzel BIRD

ouzo
   ~ flavoring ANISE

ova ROE

ovate OVAL

oven RANGE
   ~ accessory MITT
   ~ emanation AROMA
   ~ name AMANA
   brewer's ~ OAST
   brickmaker's ~ KILN
   use the ~ BAKE, HEAT, ROAST

oven ___ MITT

ovenlike HOT

over ABOVE, ACROSS, AGAIN, ANEW, ATOP, DONE, ENDED, PAST, UPON
   ~ and above ELSE
   ~ and done PAST
   ~ in German UBER
   ~ (prefix) EPI, SUR
   ~ there, to a poet YON
   ~ to a poet OER
   not ~ UNDER

___ over (accomplish) PUT

___ over (affect) COME

___ over (anew) ALL

___ over (carry through) TIDE

___ over (discuss) TALK

___ over (exceed) RUN

___ over (faint) KEEL

___ over (ignore) PASS

___ over (ponder) TURN

___ over (postpone) HOLD, LAY

___ over (read) PORE

___ over (redo) MAKE

___ over (relinquish) HAND

___-over ONCE

"Over ___" THERE

overabundance FAT, GLUT

overact EMOTE, HAM

overage PLUS

overalls
   ~ part BIB

over and ___ ABOVE, OUT

___ over a new leaf TURN

overanxious EAGER

overawe COW

__ **over backward** BEND, LEAN

overbearing STERN
not ~ MEEK

overblown TALL

"__ overboard!" MAN

overbold RASH

overburden LABOR, LADE, LOAD

overcast BLUR, DIM, GRAY, GREY, SHADE
gloomy ~ PALL

overcharge BLEED, CLIP, LOAD, ROOK, SOAK, STING
~ for tickets SCALP

overcome AWE, BEAT, LEAD, TAME
~ adversity COPE, WIN

overconfidence PRIDE

overconfident RASH, SMUG

overconsumption WASTE

overcook CHAR

overcrowd CLOG, CRAM, JAM

overcrowded DENSE

overdo LABOR
~ a role EMOTE
~ TLC DOTE

overdone ARTY, BANAL, ORNATE, TALL, TRITE

overdramatize EMOTE, HAM

overdub ADD

overdue LATE

overeagerness ZEAL

overeat CRAM, GLUT

overestimate ERR

overexert
~ oneself LABOR

overexertion
~ result ACHE

overfeed GLUT, SATE

overfill CLOG, CRAM, JAM, LOAD

overflow RUN, TEEM

overflowing AMPLE, AWASH, RICH, RIFE
fill to ~ CLOG, CRAM, HEAP

overfond
be ~ DOTE

overgrown BIG, LARGE, RANK, REEDY

overhand __ KNOT

overhang EAVE, LEDGE

overhaul REDO, RENEW

overhead ABOVE, ALOFT, ATOP, COST
~ curve ARCH
~ expense RENT
~ railways ELS
circle ~ HALO

overhead-__ engine CAM

__ over heels HEAD

"Over hill, over __..." DALE

overindulge CRAM, DOTE, GLUT, SATE

overindulgence ORGY

overinquisitive
~ one YENTA
be ~ NOSE, PEER, PRY

overjoy ELATE

Overland TRAIL

overlay COAT, ENAMEL, PLATE, TOP
thin metal ~ WASH

overleap LEAD

__ over lightly ONCE

overload TASK
~ protector FUSE

overlook MISS, OMIT, SKIP

overlord RULER

overly TOO

"__ Over Miami" MOON

overmuch DEAR, TOO

overnight SOON
~ routine SLEEP
~ success HIT
~ temperature, usually LOW

overnight __ BAG

overpack CRAM

overpamper SPOIL

"__ Over Parador" MOON

overpower AWE, BEAT, STOP

overpriced STEEP

overprotect SPOIL

overproud SMUG

overreact PANIC

override ANNUL

overripen ROT

overrule ANNUL, VETO

overrun RIFE, TEEM

oversatisfy SATE

oversee BOSS, LEAD, RUN, TEND

overseer BOSS
game ~ REF, UMP

overshadow BLUR, LEAD, TOP

overshoe BOOT

overshoot
~ the puck ICE

oversight ERROR, LAPSE, MISS, SKIP

oversize BIG, LARGE

overspending WASTE

__ over spilled milk CRY

overspread DRAPE, LAY

overstate BRAG

overstatement LIE, TALE

overstrung TENSE

overstuff CRAM, LOAD

oversupply GLUT, SATE

overt OPEN

overtake GAIN, PASS

overtax LOAD, STRESS, TASK, TIRE

"Over the __" EDGE, GOAL

"Over the __-dark sea" WINE

__ over the coals HAUL, RAKE

"Over the Rainbow"
~ composer ARLEN

"Over There"
~ composer COHAN

overthrow BEAT, RISE
~ first ERR

overtime
~ situation TIE

overtrustful NAIVE

overture INTRO, PASS
~ follower ACTI

overturn KEEL, UPEND, UPSET

overused STALE, TRITE

overwary LEERY

overweener
~ forte EGO

overweeningness PRIDE

overweight BIG, LARGE, OBESE

overwhelm AMAZE, AWE, BEAT, LOAD, ROUT, SNOW, STUN, WOW
~ as with humor SLAY

overwhelming
~ victory ROUT

overwork STRESS, TIRE

overworked TRITE

overwrought EDGY

overzealous RABID

Ovett
~ rival COE

Ovid POET, ROMAN
~ work ODE
see also Latin, poet

oviform OVAL

ovine
~ female EWE
~ sound BAA, MAA

ovo
ab ~ NEW

ovule SEED

ovum EGG

owed DUE
money ~ DEBT

Owen DON

Owens
~ forte DASH

Owen Stanley __ RANGE

Owen, Wilfred POET
see also poet

owing DUE

owl BIRD
~ claws PLANT
~ hangout BARN
~ sound HOOT, WHO
mouse, to an ~ PREY

__ owl BARN, HOOT

"Owl __ the Pussycat, The" AND

"Owl and the Pussycat, The" POEM
~ director ROSS

"Owl and the Pussy-Cat, The"
~ author LEAR

owllike WISE

owl/pussycat
~ destination SEA

owls
like some ~ EARED

Owls, The RICE

own ASSERT, AVOW, CLAIM, HAVE, HOLD
~ up to ADMIT
call one's ~ HAVE
hold one's ~ COPE
make one's ~ ADOPT
not ~ RENT
on one's ~ ALONE
sing one's ~ praises BRAG
take the law into one's ~ hands AVENGE
toot one's ~ horn BRAG, CROW
under one's ~ steam ALONE

owned
previously ~ USED

owner
~ certificate DEED

"Owner of a Lonely Heart"
~ band YES

ownership
proof of ~ DEED, TITLE

ox ANIMAL, BOOR, LOUT, MALE, OAF, STEER
Asian ~ ANOA, YAK
big ~ OAF
Celebes ~ ANOA
eat like an ~ GLUT
Paul Bunyan's blue ~ BABE

"Ox-__ Incident, The" BOW

oxalate ESTER, SALT

oxalic ACID

oxblood COLOR

Oxbridge
~ **prep school** ETON

oxen
team of ~ SPAN

oxford SHOE

Oxford
~ **outerwear** MAC
~ **teacher** DON
see also British, English

oxide
~ **component** METAL
nitrous ~ GAS

___ **oxide (rust)** IRON

___ **oxide ointment** ZINC

oxlike
~ **ruminant** GNU

Oxydol
~ **rival** ALL, ERA, TIDE

oxygen GAS
~ **isotope** OZONE
~ **producer** LEAF, PLANT, TREE
~ **source** AIR
add ~ **to** AERATE
it's 21% ~ AIR

oxygenate AERATE, AIR

"Oy!" ALAS, OHNO

Oyl OLIVE

oyster COLOR
~ **cousin** CLAM
~ **home** BED
~ **largesse** PEARL
young ~ SPAT

oyster ___ BED, CRAB, PLANT

___ **oyster** SEED

___ **Oyster Cult** BLUE

oysters
lift, as ~ TONG

"Oysters ___ **season"** RIN

oz.
many ~ LBS

Oz AMOS, SCOTT
~ **actor** LAHR
~ **role** LION
canine in ~ TOTO

ozone AIR, GAS

"Ozymandias" POEM

1

p ___ "Peter" ASIN

p ___ "pfennig" ASIN

p ___ "phony" ASIN

p ___ "pneumatic" ASIN

p ___ "puzzle" ASIN

P ELEM
   15 for ~ ATNO

___ P. (Dickens character) AGED

Pa ELEM
   91 for ~ ATNO

Pa.
   ~ neighbor DEL, OHIO
   ~ zone EDT, EST
   see also Pennsylvania

PA
   see Pennsylvania

P.A.
   ~ system component AMP

Paar
   ~ follower LENO
   ~ preceder ALLEN

Paar, Jack EMCEE, HOST

PABA
   part of ~ ACID, AMINO, PARA

Pablo
   see Spanish

"___ Pablo" AKA

Pablum PAP

Pabst BEER

pabulum MEAL

Pac-___ conference TEN

Pac.
   from Atl. to ~ USA

PAC
   ~ donee REP, SEN

paca ANIMAL

pace CLIP, GAIT, MOVE, RATE,
   SPEED, STEP, TEMPO
   easy ~ LOPE, TROT
   fast ~ CLIP
   go at a snail's ~ DRAG, LAG
   going at a snail's ~ SLOW

horse's ~ GAIT
its ~ is slow SNAIL
pick up the ~ DASH, HIE,
   RACE, RUN, SPEED, TEAR
set the ~ LEAD
tortoise ~ SLOW

pace ___ CAR

pacer HORSE

Pacers FIVE, TEAM
   ~ org. NBA
   former org. of the ~ ABA

paces
   put through the ~ TEST

pachinko GAME

pachisi GAME

pachyderm ANIMAL

pacific MILD, SERENE

Pacific OCEAN
   ~ greeting ALOHA
   ~ island EASTER
   ~ islands SAMOA
   ~ sea CORAL
   former ~ alliance SEATO
   land west of the ~ ASIA
   on the ~ ASEA, ATSEA
   toward the ~ WEST

Pacific ___ OCEAN, RIM, TIME

"___ Pacific" UNION

Pacific Coast
   ~ range ANDES
   ~ st. CAL, ORE, WASH

"Pacific Princess" BOAT, LINER,
   SHIP

Pacific Rim
   ~ locale ASIA

pacifier SOP

pacifist DOVE

pacify ABATE, ALLAY, CALM, EASE,
   SETTLE, TAME

Pacino
   ~ and others ALS

___ Pacis ARA

pack BAND, CREW, GANG, HEAP,
   HOST, JAM, LOT, MASS, MOB,

RING, STOW
~ a heater TOTE
~ animal ASS, BURRO, LLAMA,
   MULE
~ away EAT, STORE, STOW
~ down TAMP
~ horse HACK
~ in LOAD
~ it in EAT
~ member HYENA
~ tightly CRAM, JAM
~ unit DEN
~ up CASE
lion ~ PRIDE

pack ___ ANIMAL, ICE, RAT, TRAIN

___ pack ICE, SIX

___ Pack BRAT, RAT

package BALE, CASE, WRAP
   ~ binder CORD
   ~ delivery serv. UPS
   ~ letters COD
   ~ of paper REAM
   ~ sealer TAPE
   CARE ~ AID
   farm ~ BALE
   open a ~ UNDO
   secure a ~ TIE
   send a ~ MAIL, SHIP

package ___ DEAL, STORE, TOUR

packages MAIL

package store
   ~ buy ALE, BEER, RUM, RYE,
   WINE

packaging
   ~ material SARAN

Packard AUTO, CAR

packed SOLID
   ~ like sardines CLOSE
   tightly ~ DENSE

___-packed JAM

Packers ELEVEN, TEAM
   ~ org. NFL
   former ~ quarterback STARR

packet BALE, BOAT, SHIP
   nursery ~ SEED

packing
   ~ a pistol ARMED
   ~ cement LUTE

~ container CRATE
send ~ EXILE, OUST

___ packing SEND

Pac-Man
   ~ home ARCADE
   ~ morsel DOT
   blue ghost, in ~ INKY
   emulate ~ EAT

PAC money
   ~ recipient REP, SEN

Paco
   see Spanish

pact DEAL
   ~ since 1949 NATO
   defunct ~ SEATO
   party to a defense ~ ALLY
   tenant's ~ LEASE
   US-USSR ~ SALT

Pac-10
   ~ sch. ASU, CAL, ORE,
   OREGON, OSU, UCLA, WASH

pad ABODE, FLAT, HOME, MAT,
   SNEAK, STEP, TREAD
   ~ off Hyde Park FLAT
   ~ purpose STENO
   brake ~ SHOE
   frog's ~ LILY
   hair ~ RAT
   lily ~ LEAF
   nomad's ~ TENT
   peer's ~ ESTATE
   tumbler's ~ MAT

___ pad KNEE, LEGAL, LILY, STENO

Padang CITY, PORT

Paddington BEAR
   ~ in London STA

paddle OAR, ROW

___ paddle DOG

paddleball GAME

paddlewheeler BOAT, SHIP

paddock PALE, PEN, TOAD
   ~ adjunct HASP
   ~ newcomer FOAL
   ~ occupant MARE
   ~ papa SIRE

paddy
   ~ crop RICE

padlock BAR, CLOSE, SHUT
~ **partner** HASP

padre ABBE
~ **in French** ABBE

Padre Island
~ **st.** TEX

padre's
~ **brother** TIO
~ **hermana** TIA
~ **hermano** TIO
~ **sister** TIA

Padres NINE, TEAM

Padua
town near ~ ESTE

Paducah
~ **st.** KEN

paean LAUD, PSALM, SONG

paella STEW
~ **base** RICE
~ **cooker** OLLA

___ **paese** BEL

pagan
~ **ender** ISM

"Paganini"
~ **composer** LEHAR

"Pagan Love ___" SONG

page AIDE, BEEP, CALL, LEAF,
SHEET
~ **at times** USHER
atlas ~ MAP
book ~ LEAF
cal. ~ APR, AUG, DEC, MAR,
NOV, OCT, SEPT
journal ~ DAY
like left-hand ~
numbers EVEN
like right-hand ~
numbers ODD
turn to a ~ OPEN

___ **page** HOME, TITLE, WEB

Page PATTI

pageant GALA, PLAY
~ **figures** MAGI
~ **prop** TIARA
Christmas ~ **figures** MAGI

pageantry PARADE, POMP, SHOW
display of ~ ECLAT

pageboy
~ **relative** BOB

pager
~ **signal** BEEP

pages
flip over ~ LEAF
turn ~ FLIP

"Pagliacci" OPERA
Canio, in ~ TENOR

Pagnol, Marcel
~ **film of 1936** CESAR

Pago Pago CITY, PORT
~ **locale** SAMOA

pah POOH

pahlavi COIN

Pahlavi IRANI
~ **realm, once** IRAN
~ **title** SHAH

pahoehoe LAVA

paid
~ **notices** ADS
~ **performer** PRO
get ~ EARN
to be ~ DUE

"Paid"
~ **marker** STAMP

Paige, Satchel
~ **real first name** LEROY

pail CAN

pain ACHE, AIL, BANE, COST
~ **in the neck** ACHE, BORE,
PEEVE, PEST
~ **reliever** OPIATE
cry of ~ YELP
dull ~ ACHE
hunger ~ PANG
shooting ~ STAB

Paine, Thomas
~ **piece** ESSAY

painful ACHY, BAD, HARD, SAD,
SORE
~ **sensation** ACHE

painkiller OPIATE

painless EASY

pains
~ **partner** ACHES
aches and ~ WOE
great ~ CARE
great ~, **for short** TLC

painstakingness CARE

paint COLOR, DYE, ENAMEL,
HORSE, PINTO
~ **a rosy picture** FAKE
~ **container** CAN
~ **crudely** DAUB
~ **layer** COAT
~ **roughly** SMEAR
~ **the town red** REVEL
apply ~ COAT
kind of ~ ENAMEL
remove ~ STRIP

___ **paint** OIL, WAR

paintbrush
~ **material** NYLON

painted
~ **metal** TOLE
freshly ~ WET

painted ___ (butterfly) LADY

Painted ___ DESERT

"Painted ___, The" MESA

Painted Desert
~ **feature** MESA

painter LINE, ROPE
~ **stand** EASEL

painting ART, IMAGE
~ **family name** PEALE

~ **medium** OIL
~ **subject** NUDE
~ **surface** GESSO
illusional ~ OPART
work on an old ~,
perhaps RESTORE

___ **painting** OIL, SAND

paintings ART

paint-store
~ **purchase** ENAMEL

paint the town ___ RED

pair DUO, TWO
~ **connector** AND
~ **up** MATE
au ~ MAID
board-game ~ DICE
matched ~ TEAM
one of a ~ HALF, MATE, TWIN
show a clean ~ **of heels** FLEE

paired DUAL

pairs
~ **skating** EVENT

Paisley IAN

Paiute TRIBE

pajama
~ **coverer** ROBE
~ **material** SILK

"Pajama ___, The" GAME

"Pajama Game, The"
~ **actor** RAITT
~ **actress** DAY
~ **composer** ADLER
~ **lyricist** ROSS

Pakistan
~ **location** ASIA
~ **neighbor** INDIA, IRAN
language of ~ URDU

Pakistani ASIAN
~ **garment** SARI

Pakula ALAN

pal BRO, MATE
~ **in French** AMI, AMIE
~ **in Spanish** AMIGO

___ **pal** GAL, PEN

palace ABODE, HOME
~ **protection** MOAT
ice ~ ARENA, RINK
Mideast ~ **area** HAREM
pinball ~ ARCADE

paladin HERO, MAN

Paladin
~ **portrayer** BOONE

palaestra ARENA

palatability TASTE

palate TASTE

palatinate REALM

palatine CAPE

Palatine
~ **garb** TOGA

Palatine Hill
~ **site** ROME

Palatino FONT

palaver CHAT, PRATE, TALK, YAK

palazzo ABODE, HOME

pale ASHEN, ASHY, DIM, FADE,
REALM, STAKE, WAN
~ **color** TINT
~ **gray** ASHY
~ **lavender** LILAC
~ **potable** ALE
~ **yellow** LEMON
beyond the ~ TABOO, TABU

pale-___ DRY

"Pale"
~ **brew** ALE

"Pale ___, The" (Christie book)
HORSE

"pale blue dot"
Sagan's ~ EARTH

"Paleface, The"
~ **actor** HOPE

pale-faced ASHY

pale green
~ **moth** LUNA

paleo-
opposite of ~ NEO

paleontologist
~ **discovery** BONE

Paleozoic ERA

Palestine
city of ancient ~ DAN

Palestinian
ancient ~ ESSENE

paletot COAT

palette
~ **partner** EASEL
~ **pigment** OCHER, OCHRE
~ **shape** OVAL

Paley, William
~ **presided here** CBS

palfrey HORSE

palindrome
~ **part** EREI
~ **place** ELBA
~ **start** ABLE, AMANA, MADAM
man in a ~ ADAM

palindromic
~ **address** MAAM, MADAM
~ **animal** EWE
~ **city** ADA, EDE
~ **computer language** ADA
~ **constellation** ARA
~ **emperor** OTTO
~ **exclamation** AHA, HAH,
OHO, TUT, WOW
~ **female** ADA, ANNA, AVA, EVE,
LIL, NAN
~ **Indian** OTO
~ **lady** MADAM
~ **name** ADA, ANNA, AVA, BOB,
EVE, LIL, NAN
~ **periodical** ELLE

~ pop group AHA
~ potentate AGA
~ principle TENET
~ rock group ABBA
~ time NOON
~ title DAD, MADAM, MOM, POP
~ verb TAT

palinode POEM

palisade CRAG, PALE, POST

"Pal Joey"
~ author OHARA

pall JADE

Pall ___ MALL

palla WRAP

palladium METAL

Palladium
~ portrayal ATHENA

Pallas ___ ATHENA

pallet BED, COT
shipping ~ SKID

palliate ABATE, ALLAY, EASE, HELP

palliative BALM
~ plant ALOE

pallid ASHEN, ASHY, PALE, WAN

pall-mall GAME

palm HAND, NIP, STEAL, TREE
~ fruit DATE
~ leaf FAN
~ reader SEER
cat's ~ PAD
examine a ~ READ
grease someone's ~ OIL
kind of ~ SEGO

palm ___ (foist) OFF

___ palm DATE

Palma
see Spanish

___ Palmas LAS

Palm Beach
~ diversion POLO
~ residence ESTATE
~ st. FLA

Palmer ARNIE
~ followers ARMY

Palmer, Arnold
~ org. PGA
see also golf

Palmer, Jim ORIOLE

palmist SEER

palm reader
~ phrase ISEE

palms-down
~ call SAFE

Palm Springs
former ~ mayor BONO

Palm Sunday
~ mount ASS
~ period LENT

palo
~ verde TREE

Palo ___, Calif. ALTO

palomino HORSE
~ pride MANE

palooka LOUT, OAF

Palooka JOE
~ bride ANN

Palos
see Spanish

palpable REAL

palpate FEEL

palpitate BEAT, PANT

palsy-walsy CLOSE

palter DEAL, LIE

palterer LIAR

Paltrow, Gwyneth
~ role EMMA

paltry MEAN, MERE, SCANT, THIN, TINY

Pamela MASON

pampas LEA
~ bird RHEA
~ cousin LLANO

pamper DOTE, PET, SPOIL

pampering
~ for short TLC

pamphlet TRACT

Pamplona
~ runner TORO
see also Spanish

pan DISH, FACE, POT, SIFT
~ ender CAKE
~ opposite RAVE
~ starter DISH, DUST, HARD
baking ~ SHEET, TIN
expand in the ~ RISE

pan ___ (succeed) OUT

pan-___ FRY

Pan PETER, SATYR

Pan-___ makeup CAKE

"___ Pan" PETER

"___-Pan" TAI

panacea BALM, CURE

panache CHIC, DASH, ELAN, STYLE
lacking ~ BLAH

___ Pan Alley TIN

Panama CANAL, HAT
see also Spanish

Panama Canal
~ ocean ATL, PAC

Panama City
~ st. FLA

"Panama Deception, The"
~ director TRENT

"Panama Hattie"
~ name COLE, ETHEL

Pan American Union
~ successor OAS

Panamint ___ RANGE

Panasonic
~ rival RCA

pan-broil FRY

pancake LAND
~ in French CREPE
like a ~ FLAT
thin ~ CREPE

pancakes
prepare ~ FRY

Panchen ___ LAMA

Pancho
see Spanish

panda ANIMAL

pandemonium DIN, MELEE, NOISE, RIOT, ROW

Pandora
what ~ unleashed ILLS

pane PLATE, SHEET
~ holder SASH

panegyrize ADORE, EXALT

panel SHEET
~ focus TOPIC
dress ~ INSET

___ panel SOLAR

Panetta LEON

pan-fry SAUTE

pang ACHE, PAIN, STAB

pangolin ANIMAL
~ snack ANT

pangs
feel ~ ACHE

panhandle BEG

Panhandle
~ site ALASKA, TEX

panhandler
~ request ALMS

panic FEAR, SCARE
~ button ALARM

panic button
push the ~ ALERT

panned
it's often ~ GOLD

panoply ARMOR, ARRAY, MAIL

panorama SCENE

panoramic BIG, LARGE

Pan, Peter
imitate ~ CROW

pant GASP

Pantagruel GIANT

panther ANIMAL, CAT
~ perch TREE

"___ Panther" JOE

Panthers ELEVEN, SIX, TEAM
~ home MIAMI

~ milieu ICE, RINK
~ org. NFL, NHL

___ Panthers GRAY

pantomime APE
~ dance HULA

pantomimist APER
~ French TATI

pantothenic ACID

pantry
~ item CAN, TIN
keep in the ~ STORE
old ~ supply LARD

pants
~ and jacket SUIT
~ cut SLIM
~ feature PLEAT, SEAM
~ inhabitants ANTS
~ part KNEE, LEG, SEAT
~ specification LONG
~ unit PAIR
hot ~ FAD, RAGE
wear the ~ LEAD

___ pants CAPRI, HAREM, HOT, KNEE

"pants on fire"
~ person LIAR

pantyhose
~ color ECRU, TAN, TAUPE
~ part LEG

pantywaist PANSY

panzer TANK

Paolo
see Italian

papa DAD, MATE
~ in French PERE
~ partner MAMA
paddock ~ SIRE

"Papa"
~ real name ERNEST

Papa ___ DOC

"Papa ___ a Rollin' Stone" WAS

___ Papa Bell COOL

Papa Doc
~ country HAITI

Papago TRIBE

papal
~ headdress TIARA
~ name LEO, PAUL, PIUS

Papas IRENE

papaw TREE

papaya TREE

Papeete CITY, PORT

paper ESSAY, NEWS, SHEET
~ airplane part FLAP
~ chief EDITOR
~ covering EMERY
~ deliverer's way ROUTE
~ holder CLIP, PAD
~ lantern LAMP
~ layer PLY
~ measure REAM

paper ___

~ money BILL, NOTE
~ size LEGAL
~ starter NEWS, SAND, TAR
Baltimore ~ SUN
business owner's ~ LEASE
decorative ~ CREPE
Denver ~ POST
Federalist ~ ESSAY
house ~ DEED
Indianapolis ~ STAR
Kansas City ~ STAR
package of ~ REAM
party ~ CREPE
piece of ~ LEAF, SHEET
promissory ~ NOTE
put on ~ PEN, WRITE
renter's ~ LEASE
Sacramento ~ BEE
school ~ ESSAY, THEME
term ~ THEME
today's ~ NEWS
Washington ~ POST

paper ___ BAG, CLIP, MILL, TIGER, TRAIL

paper-___ THIN

___ paper CREPE, END, LAID, RICE, TERM, TRADE

"Paper, The"
~ actress CLOSE

"Paper ___" LION, MOON

"Paper ___, The" CHASE

paperback
~ publisher AVON
name in ~ publishing DELL

paper company
~ harvest TREES

paper doll TOY
~ dress part SLOT, TAB

"Paper Lion"
~ actor ALDA

"Paper Moon"
~ Oscar winner ONEAL

"Paper or plastic?"
~ item BAG

papers DATA
the ~ PRESS
walking ~ SACK

paperwork
insurance ~ CLAIM

papoose KID

Pappas IKE

pappy PAPA

papule NODE

papyrus REED, SEDGE

Paquin ANNA

par
~ (abbr.) STD
~ for the course NORM
below ~ LESS, POOR
feel below ~ AIL
neither under nor over
~ EVEN
not up to ~ OFF

on a ~ EVEN
two under ~ EAGLE
up to ~ FIT

Par.
~ neighbor ARG

parable TALE

parabola ARC, BOW
make a ~ ARC

parabolic
~ path ARC

parachute DROP
~ material NYLON
~ part CORD
~ strap RISER

parade AIR, ARRAY, BRAG, CROW, FILE, LINE, MODEL, SHOW, STREAM, TROOP
~ command HALT
~ day EASTER
~ feature BAND
~ honoree HERO
~ stopper RAIN
Pasadena ~ posy ROSE

___ parade HIT

"___ Parade" EASTER

"___ Parade, The" BIG, LOVE

paradigm IDEAL, MODEL, TYPE
~ of happiness CLAM

paradise EDEN
~ evictee ADAM, EVE
in ~ ELATED

Paradise
Kerouac's ~ SAL

"Paradise ___" LOST

"___-Paradise, The" DEMI

"Paradise is where ___" IAM

"Paradise Lost" EPIC, POEM
~ angel ARIEL
~ character ADAM, EVE, SATAN, SIN
~ playwright ODETS
~ setting EDEN

paradisiacal
~ locale EDEN

paragon HERO, IDEAL, MODEL

paragraph PART

Paraguay
see Spanish

parakeet BIRD, PET
~ home CAGE
~ treat SEED

parallel AGREE, ALIKE, CLOSE, EVEN
~ to ALONG, LIKE

parallel ___ BARS

Paramaribo CITY, PORT

paramedic
~ letters EMT
~ org. EMS

paramedics
~ purpose AID

paramount BEST, BIG, FIRST, LEAD, MAIN, MAJOR, TOP, TOPS

Paramount
~ workplace LOT, SET

paramour BEAU, LOVE

Paraná CITY, PORT

Paraná River
~ ctry. ARG

paranormal EERIE, EERY
~ ability ESP

paraphernalia GEAR, ITEMS, KIT, RIG

parapsychology
~ acronym PSI
~ pioneer RHINE
~ subj. ESP

parasailing
finished ~ ALIT, LIT

parasite DRONE, LOUSE
~ need HOST
plant ~ APHID
tiny ~ MITE

parasites LICE

parasol SHADE

parboil HEAT, SCALD

parcel AREA, DOLE, LAND, LOT, MAIL, PLAT
~ letters COD
~ of land ACRE
~ out ALLOT, SHARE
~ (out) DEAL, METE
~ partner PART
~ post MAIL
auction ~ LOT
farm ~ ACRE
land ~ LOT
send a ~ SHIP

parcel ___ POST

Parcells BILL
~ nickname TUNA

parcels
how some ~ arrive COD

parch BAKE, DRY, HEAT, ROAST, SEAR

parched ARID, DESERT, DRY, SERE

Parcheesi GAME
~ piece DIE

parching HOT

parchment PAPER

pardner PAL

Pardo DON

pardon CLEAR, REMIT

"Pardon me" AHEM

"Pardon My ___" PAST

"Pardonnez-___!" MOI

pare CLIP, CUT, LOP, PEEL, SKIN, TRIM

___ Paree GAY

parent DAD, MAMA, MOM, PAPA, RAISE, REAR
~ (abbr.) REL
~ admonition DONT, EAT, STOP
barnyard ~ EWE, GOOSE, HEN, MARE, RAM, SIRE, SOW
cub's ~ LION
male ~ SIRE
mule's ~ ASS, MARE
porcine ~ BOAR, SOW
quadruped's ~ SIRE
Sansei ~ NISEI

"Parent ___, The" TRAP

parentage LINE

parental
~ nickname DAD, MOM, POP

parenthesis
~ shape ARC

parents MAS, PAS
new ~ decision NAME

Paretsky SARA

par excellence AONE

parfit
~ gentil knight MODEL

parget COAT

pariah EXILE, LONER
social ~ CREEP
treat like a ~ SHUN

parimutuel
~ listing ODDS
~ transaction BET

parings WASTE

Paris CITY
~ abductee HELEN
~ airport ORLY
~ home TROY
~ landmark ARCH
~ river SEINE
~ subway METRO
~ to Hecuba SON
~ to Ulysses ENEMY, FOE
a pittance in ~ SOU
fast way to ~ SST
see also French

"Paris ___" TROUT

Parisian
~ house of design DIOR
see also French

parity PAR

park LAND, PET, PLANT, PUT
~ alcove ARBOR
~ carefully EASE
~ path TRAIL
London ~ HYDE
place to ~ LOT

___ park THEME

Park ___ AVE, RANGE

"Park ___" ROW

___ Park HYDE

"___ Park, The" DEER

parka COAT, WRAP
~ **part** HOOD

Park Chung ___ HEE

___ Park, Colo. ESTES

parker
car ~ VALET

Parker ALAN, FESS, NOSY, WIT
~ **fluid** INK

Parker, Charlie
~ **instrument** ALTO, SAX
~ **music** BOP
~ **nickname** BIRD

Parker, Dorothy WIT

Parker, Fess
~ **role** BOONE

Parker House HOTEL, ROLL

___ Park, Ill. OAK

parking
~ **attendant** VALET
~ **garage sign** ENTER
~ **lot sight** AUTO, CAR
~ **mishap** DENT
~ **space** STALL
airport ~ **area** APRON
railroad's ~ **space** YARD

parking ___ LOT, METER, SPACE

___ parking VALET

"parking lot"
airfield ~ APRON

parking scofflaw
~ **stopper** BOOT

"___ Parkington" MRS

Park, Mungo SCOT

___ Park, N.Y. HYDE

Parks ROSA

Parks, Bert
~ **successor** ELY

parkway ROAD, ROUTE

parlance ARGOT, IDIOM, USAGE

parlay BET
~ **a bet** RIDE

parley MEET, TALK

parliament
Japan's ~ DIET

Parliament
~ **member** LORD, PEER
~ **vote** AYE
first female in ~ ASTOR

parlor ROOM, SALON
~ **piece** SETTEE, SOFA
beauty ~ SALON

parlor ___ CAR, GAME

___ parmigiana VEAL

parochial LOCAL, SMALL

parodist WIT

parody APE, GENRE, IRONY, SKIT

parol ORAL

parole FREE

paronomasia PUN

paroxysm FIT, SPASM

parquetry
~ **wood** OAK

parrier
~ **equipment** EPEE

parrot APE, APER, BIRD, ECHO, PET
~ **genus** ARA
~ **home** CAGE
~ **word** HELLO
emulate a ~ APE
large ~ KEA, MACAW

parry AVERT, AVOID, EVADE, FEND, REPEL

Parsees SECT

Parseghian ARA

"Parsifal" OPERA
~ **opener** ACTI

parsimonious CLOSE, MEAN, NEAR
be ~ STINT

parsley HERB
~ **family herb** ANISE
~ **piece** SPRIG
~ **relative** DILL

"Parsley, ___, Rosemary and Thyme" SAGE

parsnip ROOT

parson PADRE
~ **expletive** AMEN
~ **home** MANSE

parsonage MANSE

Parsons ___ TABLE

part GAPE, ROLE, SHARE, SLICE
~ **(prefix)** DEMI

part-___ SONG, TIME

___ part ACTA, BIT, TAKE

par-3
eagle on a ~ **hole** ACE

partake FARE
~ **of** EAT, HAVE, TASTE, TRY, USE

parted SPLIT

Parthenon
~ **goddess** ATHENA

Parthenope SIREN

partial
~ **(prefix)** DEMI, HEMI, SEMI
~ **refund** REBATE
be ~ **to** LIKE

partiality BIAS

participant ACTOR

participate ATTEND, ENTER
~ **in** ENTER, TASTE
~ **in a regatta, perhaps** ROW
chance to ~ TURN

participating INON
not ~ INERT

participation
price of ~ ANTE

particle ATOM, DOT, IOTA, MOTE, SCRAP
atomic ~ BETA
burning ~ EMBER
charged ~ ION
soot ~ SMUT

___ particle ALPHA, BETA, PSI

particles
lava ~ ASH

particular FACT, ITEM
~ **occasion** NONCE

particularity TRAIT

particularization BILL

particulate
~ **matter** ASH, DIRT, GRIT

partiers
closing-night ~ CAST

parties DOS
it may be broken at ~ ICE

parting
~ **shot** TAG
~ **word** BYE, CIAO, EXIT, LATER
~ **words** TATA

parting ___ SHOT

partisan FAN
~ **starter** NON
~ **(suffix)** IST, ITE
be ~ ROOT, SIDE

"Partita ___ Minor" INE

partition ALLOT, PANEL, SHARE
Ping-Pong ~ NET

partly HALF
~ **(prefix)** DEMI, HEMI, SEMI

partner BRIDE, LADY, MATE

partnerless ALONE

partnership
~ **word** AND, SON

partridge BIRD
~ **tree** PEAR

"...partridge ___ pear tree" INA

Partridge ERIC
~ **concern** SLANG

"Partridge Family, The"
~ **actress** DEY

"...___ partridge in a pear tree" ANDA

parts
having two ~ DUAL

part-time ODD

parturition LABOR

party CLAN, CREW, GALA, GANG, LEVEE, LOT, POSSE, REVEL, SIDE
~ **divider on the Hill** AISLE
~ **food** CHIP, DIP, NUT, PATE, SALSA

~ **giver** HOST
~ **hearty** REVEL
~ **honoree** DEB
~ **mem.** DEM, REP
~ **paper** CREPE
~ **pick** SLATE
~ **pooper** BORE
~ **spread** BRIE, PATE
~ **staple** KEG
~ **to** INON
~ **to a treaty** ALLY
bachelor ~ STAG
be a ~ **to** ABET
big ~ BASH, BLAST, FETE, GALA
debutante's ~ BALL
dinner ~ SOIREE
evening ~ BALL, ROUT
frat ~ STAG
give a ~ **for** FETE, HONOR
hostile ~ ENEMY, FOE
life of the ~ CARD, WIT
old-fashioned ~ BEE
poi ~ LUAU
political ~ **offering** SLATE
Polynesian ~ LUAU
quilting ~ BEE
search ~ POSSE
supply a ~ CATER
wild ~ BLAST

party ___ ANIMAL, LINE

___ party HEN, TEA, WAR

"Party ___" GIRL, WIRE

"___ Party" DONS

"___ Party, The" LAST

"Party Girl"
~ **director** RAY

party thrower
~ **plea** RSVP

Parvati
~ **devotee** HINDU

parvenu YAHOO

pas
~ **mates** MAS

Pasadena
~ **happening** PARADE
~ **parade posy** ROSE

Pascagoula
~ **st.** MISS

Pascal
see French

Pasch EASTER

pas de ___ CHAT

pas de deux DANCE
~ **ending** CODA

pasha RULER
Tunis ~ DEY

Pasha ALI

Pasiphaë MOON

paso doble DANCE

pass AERIAL, BYE, COVE, ELAPSE, END, GAP, HAND, LAPSE, SLIDE, STAB
~ **a bill** ADOPT, ENACT

~ along RELAY, SEND
~ around TURN
~ as time SPEND
~ catcher END
~ easily ACE
~ ender IVE
~ in formation FILE
~ judgment on ASSAY
~ out AWARD, DEAL, SLEEP
~ out refreshments SERVE
~ over CLEAR, ELIDE, LEAP, MISS, OMIT, SKIP, SLUR
~ slowly DRAG
~ starter OVER, SUR, UNDER
~ the buck REFER
~ the hat BEG
~ the time of day CHAT
~ the word TELL
~ through BEAR
~ through a sieve SIFT
~ time idly LOAF
~ up OMIT, SKIP
bring to ~ CAUSE
come to ~ ARRIVE, OCCUR
it will ~ TIME
let ~ ALLOW
mountain ~ COL, GAP
tournament ~ BYE

pass ___ (distribute) OUT

pass ___ (foist) OFF

pass ___ (ignore) OVER

pass ___ (impersonate) FOR

___ Pass (near Pikes Peak) UTE

passable FAIR, OKAY, OPEN, SOSO

passage AISLE, ALLEY, CUT, FARE, HALL, LANE, PIPE, TRAIL
~ in Latin ITER
~ out EXIT
~ to the sea INLET
bird of ~ HOBO, NOMAD
brain ~ ITER
horizontal ~ ADIT
interbuilding ~ ALLEY
musical ~ CODA
theater ~ AISLE
trolley ~ FARE
underground ~ SEWER
yield ~ to ADMIT

"Passage to ___, A" INDIA

"Passage to India, A"
~ director LEAN
~ woman ADELA

passageway AISLE, ALLEY, ARCADE, CANAL, HALL, LANE, PATH
covered ~ ARCADE
narrow ~ LANE

passbook
~ abbr. ACCT, INT
~ info BAL

passé DATED, OLD, OUT, STALE

passed
it's ~ by Congress ACT, BILL, LAW

passel LOT, RAFT, SLEW

passenger FARE, RIDER
~ car SEDAN
~ payment FARE
~ ship LINER
~ vehicle AUTO, BUS, CAR
~ vessel LINER, SHIP
ark ~ HAM, NOAH
pea-green boat ~ OWL
stroller ~ TOT
taxi ~ FARE

passengers
where ~ wait DEPOT

passe-partout KEY

Passepartout
~ to Phileas Fogg VALET

passer
baton ~ race RELAY

Passer IVAN

passes
~ on OKS

___ passim SIC

passing
~ fancy FAD
~ grade CEE
mention in ~ NOTE

passion ARDOR, EROS, FIRE, HEAT, LIFE, LOVE, MANIA, RAGE, ZEAL
aesthete's ~ ARTS
feel ~ for ADORE
god of ~ AMOR, EROS
tender ~ LOVE

passionate AVID, HOT, KEEN, MAD

passionless COOL

"Passion of ___, The" ANNA

"Passion of Joan of ___, The" ARC

passive COOL, INERT, MEEK

Passover
~ beverage WINE
~ meal SEDER

passport
~ department STATE
~ entry STAMP
~ stamp VISA

passports IDS

pass the ___ HAT, TIME

pass the ___ of day TIME

password SIGN

past AFTER, OLD, OVER
~ due LATE
~ its prime PASSE
~ master ACE
~ mistress ACE
~ (prefix) PARA
~ the deadline LATE
be ~ ELAPSE
edge ~ SIDLE
from ages ~ OLD
get a serve ~ ACE
get ~ the goalie SCORE
go ~ OMIT, SKIP
in the ~ AGO, ONCE, THEN
it may be ~ TENSE

object from the ~ RELIC
skip ~ commercials ZAP
the ~ ELD
times ~ YORE

past ___ (late) DUE

pasta
~ alternative RICE
~ shape ELBOW

paste BANG, BEAT, BIND, GEM, GLUE, HIT, LAM, MASH, SMITE
artist's ~ GESSO
liver ~ PATE

pasteboard PAPER

pastel
~ color AQUA, LILAC

Pasternak BORIS
~ heroine LARA

Pasteur
Oscar-winner as ~ MUNI

pasteurized
not ~ RAW

pastiche OLIO

pastime BAG, GAME, PLAY

pastor ABBE, PADRE

pastoral RURAL
~ god PAN
~ spot LEA

pastrami MEAT
~ partner RYE
~ place DELI

pastry CAKE, PIE, ROLL, TART, TORTE
~ chef, at times ICER
Queen of Hearts' ~ TART
tartlike ~ FLAN

pasturage HAY, LAND

pasture FEED, LAND, LEA, RANGE, SOD
~ entry GATE
~ in poetry MEAD
~ lands ACRES
~ mom EWE
~ plaint BAA, MAA, MOO

pasty ASHY, PALE

pasty-faced ASHEN, ASHY, WAN

pat CARESS, CLAP, DAB, PET, TAP
~ down TAMP
~ dry BLOT
~ gently DAB
~ oneself on the back BRAG, PREEN
stand ~ STAY

pat. ___ PEND

Pat BOONE, CASH, EMCEE, HOST
~ boss MERV
~ to Sigourney DAD

"Pat ___ Mike" AND

Patagonia
~ loc. ARG

patch MEND, RESTORE, SEW, SPOT
~ site HOLE

~ up HEAL, RESTORE
item in a ~ MELON, PEA
place for a ~ KNEE
reason for a ~ RIP

Patch DAN

"Patch of ___, A" BLUE

patchwork OLIO

patchy PIED

pate DOME, HEAD, NOB, POLL

pâté MEAT

pâté de foie ___ GRAS

patella BONE, KNEE

paten DISH, PLATE

patent CLEAR, OPEN, OVERT

pater DAD, PAPA

paternal MALE

path ALLEY, BEAT, LANE, ORBIT, ROAD, ROUTE, TRACE
~ of virtuous conduct TAO
~ starter OSTEO, TELE, WAR
~ to the altar AISLE
ball's ~ ARC
beat a ~ TREAD
beaten ~ RUT, TRAIL
bike ~ LANE
bridal ~ AISLE
bridle ~ TRAIL
car's ~ ROAD
Chinese ~ TAO
comet's ~ ARC
dirt ~ TRAIL
Earth's ~ ORBIT
follow a circular ~ ARC
garden ~ MALL
hiking ~ TRAIL
lead down the primrose ~ LURE
lead up the garden ~ LIE
leave the ~ ROVE
meteor's ~ ARC
missile ~ ARC
parabolic ~ ARC
park ~ TRAIL
pendulum's ~ ARC
planetary ~ ARC, ORBIT, OVAL
revolutionary ~ ORBIT
satellite's ~ ORBIT
sprinter's ~ LANE
stray from the ~ SIN
wilderness ~ TRACE

Pathet ___ LAO

pathetic BAD, LAME, POOR, SAD

Pathfinder
~ destination MARS
~ launcher NASA

pathogen GERM

pathos DRAMA
sign of ~ TEAR

pathway LANE, TRAIL
sloped ~ RAMP
supermarket ~ AISLE

patience GAME
cultivate ~ WAIT
show ~ AWAIT

tax someone's ~ BORE
test the ~ of TRY
try someone's ~ IRK, PEEVE

patient CASE, MEEK
~ attendants RNS
~ response AAH
be ~ AWAIT, SIT, WAIT
transplant ~ DONEE
vet ~ CAT, COW, DOG, EWE, HORSE, PET, SOW

patina SHEET

patio
~ (abbr.) TER, TERR
~ cousin LANAI
~ server CART
~ site YARD

patios
enclosed ~ ATRIA
Roman ~ ATRIA

patisserie
~ offering TART

Patmore, Coventry POET
see also poet

Patna CITY

patois ARGOT, CANT, IDIOM, SLANG

Paton ALAN

___ patriae AMOR

patriarch ELDER, MALE, RANK, RULER, TITLE
Biblical ~ ENOS, ISAAC

Patricia NEAL

patrician BARON, PEER

Patrick ONEAL, SAINT

___ Patrick Harris NEIL

Patrick, Saint
~ land EIRE, ERIN
~ people IRISH
~ service MASS

___ Patrick's Day SAINT

patriot
~ ender ISM

"Patriot Games"
~ character RYAN

patriotic
~ org. DAR

Patriot missile
~ target SCUD

Patriots ELEVEN, TEAM
~ org. NFL

patrol
police ~ BEAT
what a ~ car might get APB

patrol ___ CAR

___ patrol SHORE

"___ Patrol" RAT

"___ Patrol, The" LOST

patrolman COP

patron ANGEL, USER
~ ender ESS

diner ~ EATER

patron ___ SAINT

patronage AEGIS, EGIS, HELP

patronize USE
~ a restaurant EAT

patron of the ___ ARTS

patron saint
~ of lawyers IVES
~ of young girls AGNES

Pats ELEVEN, TEAM
~ org. NFL

patsy DUPE, GOAT, LAMB, PREY, SAP

patten BOOT, SHOE

patter CANT, GAB, TALK
~ provider EMCEE, HOST
sports commentator's ~ COLOR

pattern HABIT, IDEAL, MODEL, MOLD, NORM
behavior ~ HABIT
fabric ~ DOTS
go into a holding ~ STALL
machine ~ DIE
Op Art ~ MOIRE
put in a holding ~ DEFER
rhythmic ~ for a poet METER
speech ~ TONE
statistical ~ TREND
wavelike ~ MOIRE

Patti PAGE

Patton
~ rank GEN
~ superior DDE
~ vehicle TANK

"Patton"
~ actor SCOTT

Patty BERG

paucity WANT

Paul ANKA, KLEE, LES, MUNI, POPE, SAINT, TSAR
~ ex-singing partner ART

Paul ___ Hindenburg VON

pauldron ARMOR

Pauley JANE

Pauline
~ adventure PERIL

Paul, Les
~ tune NOLA

___ Paulo, Brazil SAO

"Paul Revere's ___" RIDE

___ Paul's MRS

Paulsen AXEL, PAT

Pauly SHORE

pause CEASE, GAP, HALT, HOLD, LAPSE, REST, SPACE, STOP, WAIT
~ fillers ERS
~ that refreshes NAP

pavane DANCE
~ accompaniment LUTE

Pavarotti TENOR
~ milieu OPERA
~ piece ARIA
see also Italian

pave
~ the way AID, EASE, ENABLE, HELP

pavement ROAD
~ letters SLO

paver
~ need TAR

pavilion TENT

"___ Pavilions, The" FAR

paving
~ material TAR

Pavlov IVAN

Pavlova ANNA

Pavo
neighbor of ~ ARA

paw CARESS, CLAW, FEEL, FOOT, HAND, MITT
bottom of a ~ PAD
cat's ~ DUPE

pawn DUPE, TOOL

Pawnee TRIBE
~ cousin ERIE
~ home TEPEE

Pax
~ counterpart IRENE

pay ATONE, HIRE, REMIT, SETTLE
~ as a bill FOOT
~ attention to HEAR, HEED, NOTE
~ back AVENGE, REBATE
~ by mail REMIT
~ court to SUE, WOO
~ dirt LODE, ORE
~ ender LOAD, OLA, ROLL
~ for OWN
~ for room and board TENANT
~ for services HIRE
~ heed to TEND
~ hike RAISE
~ homage to ADORE, KNEEL, LAUD, SERVE
~ incr. COLA
~ into the pot ANTE
~ no attention to SLUR, SNUB
~ off CLEAR, OIL
~ one's share ANTE
~ out SPEND
~ the bill TREAT
~ the penalty ATONE
~ to play ANTE
~ to use LEASE, RENT
~ tribute to CITE, HAIL, HONOR, LAUD
~ up SETTLE
~ with plastic OWE
~ with "up" ANTE
must ~ OWE
one way to ~ CASH

promise to ~ IOU

pay ___ DIRT

pay ___ (disburse) OUT

___ pay BASE, MERIT, NET

payable DUE
account ~ BILL

paycheck
~ abbr. HRS
~ amount NET
~ remainder STUB
get a ~ EARN

payee
Apr. ~ IRS

payer
rent ~ TENANT

paying
~ attention ALERT
~ guest TENANT

payment COST, FEE, RATE, RENT
~ details TERMS
~ means CASH
first-of-month ~ RENT
freelance ~ FEE
mail a ~ REMIT
passenger's ~ FARE
poker ~ ANTE
rider's ~ FARE

payoff
pitchman's ~ SALE

payola SOP

payout
~ ratio ODDS

pay period
common ~ WEEK

pay phone
~ feature SLOT

payroll
put on the ~ HIRE

pay stub
~ word NET

pay through the ___ NOSE

pay TV CABLE
~ letters HBO

Pb ELEM, LEAD
82 for ~ ATNO

PBJ
~ alternative BLT

PBS
~ benefactor NEA
~ no-no's ADS
~ science program NOVA
~ supplier BBC
~ topic ART

PC
~ alternative MAC
~ button RESET
~ capacity RAM
~ clicker MOUSE
~ command EDIT, SAVE, SORT
~ communication EMAIL
~ component ROM
~ enthusiast USER
~ food DATA

~ **game** DOOM
~ **innards** ROM
~ **key** ALT, ENTER, INS, TAB
~ **master program** DOS
~ **media** CDS
~ **memory unit** MEG
~ **menu selection** HELP
~ **screen** CRT
~ **screen image** ICON
~ **system** DOS

PCB
~ **regulator** EPA

PCs
name in ~ DELL

Pd ELEM
46 for ~ ATNO

PD
~ **broadcast** APB
~ **rank** SGT

PDQ APACE, ASAP, STAT

P.D.Q. ___ BACH

pea
~ **container** POD
~ **jacket** WRAP

___ **pea** SNOW, SWEET

peace CALM, REST
~ **and quiet** ORDER
~ **gesture** VEE
~ **goddess** IRENE
~ **in Russian** MIR
~ **of mind** EASE
~ **symbol** DOVE
at ~ SERENE
disturber of the ~ WAR

peace ___ PIPE

"Peace ___" TRAIN

peaceable MEEK

peaceful CALM, MILD, SERENE

"Peaceful ___ Feeling" EASY

peacefulness CALM, EASE

Peace Garden
~ **St.** NDAK

peacenik DOVE

peach COLOR, PIE, RAT, SING, TREE
~ **center** PIT

peaches and ___ CREAM

Peaches and ___ HERB

peachy ___ KEEN

peacoat WRAP

peacock BIRD, DUDE, MALE
~ **feather spot** EYE
~ **pride** TRAIN
like a ~ VAIN
NBC ~ LOGO

peacock ___ BLUE, ORE

peacocks
~ **do it** PREEN

Peacock Throne
~ **country** IRAN

pea-green
~ **boat passenger** OWL

peahen BIRD

peak ACME, ALP, APEX, CAP, CREST, NIB, SPIRE, TIP, TOP, TOR
~ **covering** SNOW
~ **fig.** ALT, ELEV
at the ~ **of** ATOP
bare ~ TOR
Biblical ~ ARARAT, SINAI
Greek ~ ATHOS, OSSA
Italian ~ MONTE
Oregon ~ HOOD
rocky ~ SPIRE
round mountain ~ DOME
Swiss ~ ALP
tall ~ SPIRE
Wyoming ~ TETON

___**-peak** OFF

peaked ACUTE, WAN

peaks
~ **(abbr.)** MTS
Peruvian ~ ANDES

"___ Peaks" TWIN

peal CLAP, NOISE, RING, ROLL, TOLL
~ **of laughter** GALE

peanut
~ **product** OIL

"Peanuts" STRIP
~ **expletive** RATS

pear TREE
kind of ~ BOSC

pearl COLOR, GEM
~ **starter** SAND
~ **weight** CARAT
Japanese ~ **diver** AMA

pearl ___ GRAY

___ **pearl** SEED

Pearl ___ JAM

Pearl ___ Bailey MAE

"Pearl Fishers, The" OPERA

Pearl Harbor
~ **locale** OAHU

Pearl Mosque
~ **city** AGRA
~ **country** INDIA

pears
prickly ~ CACTI

pear-shaped
~ **instrument** LUTE
~ **sounds** OHS

Pearson DREW

Pears, Peter TENOR
~ **piece** ARIA

Peary
of interest to ~ POLAR

peas
~ **purchase** CAN

peasant BOOR, PEON, SERF

peashooter TOY

peat ___ MOSS

peat bog MOOR
~ **material** MOSS

peau de ___ SOIE

pebble STONE

Pebble Beach
~ **peg** TEE
~ **warning** FORE
see also golf

Pebbles
~ **pet** DINO
~ **pop** FRED

"___ Pebbles, The" SAND

pecan NUT, TREE

peccadillo ERROR, SIN

peccancy SIN

peccant BAD

peccary ANIMAL

peck HEAP, MASS
~ **away at** PEG
~ **partner** HUNT
hunt and ~ TYPE

Peck, Gregory
~ **film, with "The"** OMEN
~ **role** AHAB

pecking ___ ORDER

Peckinpah SAM

"Peck's ___ Boy" BAD

Pecksniff SETH

pecs
~ **partners** ABS

pectin
react to ~ GEL

pectoral FIN

peculate ROB, STEAL

peculiar DAFT, EERIE, EERY, ODD, OFF

peculiarity TRAIT

pedagogues
~ **org.** AFT, NEA

pedal BIKE
~ **extremity** FOOT, TOE
~ **pusher** FOOT
foot ~ LEVER
put the ~ **to the metal** SPEED

pedal ___ guitar STEEL

pedant PRIG

peddle SELL, VEND

peddler
~ **goal** SALE

pedestal FOOT
~ **figure** IDOL
~ **part** BASE, DADO
put on a ~ ADORE, ESTEEM, EXALT

pedestrian BANAL, SOSO, TRITE

pedicel STEM

pedicurist
~ **coat** ENAMEL
~ **target** TOE

pedigree CLAN, CLASS
~ **org.** AKC

pedigreed PURE

Pedro
see Spanish

Pedro Alonzo ___ NINO

"___ Pedro Bums, The" SAN

peduncle STEM

Pee ___ Reese WEE

Pee ___ River DEE

Pee ___ Russell WEE

peek SEE
~ **at** EYE, SEE
sneak a ~ PRY

peekaboo GAME

"Peekaboo, ___ you!" ISEE

peel BARE, CASE, COAT, PARE, SHED, SHELL, SKIN, STRIP
fruit ~ RIND

Peel EMMA
~ **partner** STEED

"Peel ___ grape" MEA

peeled
keep one's eyes ~ SEE

peeling RIND

___**-peen hammer** BALL

peep CRY, NOISE, PIPE, SEE

Peep
~ **and others** BOS

peeper EYE, SPY

peepers
use one's ~ EYE, SEE, STARE

peephole SLIT

Peeples NIA

peer BARON, EARL, LIKE, LORD, OGLE, STARE
~ **at** EYE
~ **ender** ESS
~ **pad** ESTATE
~ **recognition** HONOR
sheik's ~ AMIR, EMEER, EMIR
without ~ ALONE

peerage
~ **member** BARON, EARL, LORD

Peerce, Jan TENOR

peeress DAME, LADY

"Peer Gynt"
~ **author** IBSEN
~ **character** ASE

peerless ALONE, AONE, BEST, FIRST, RARE, TOP, TOPS

peeve ANGER, FRET, IRK, RILE, ROIL, UPSET

___ **peeve** PET

peeved IRATE, MAD, SORE, UPSET

peevish EDGY, IRATE, RUDE, SOUR, TART, TESTY, UPSET
~ **mood** SNIT

peevishness BILE

peewee RUNT, SMALL

Pee Wee
~ **first baseman** GIL

Pee Wee ___ REESE

peg AIM, LABEL, STAKE, STOP
~ **away at** LABOR, PLOD
driver's ~ TEE
take down a ~ ABASE

Pegasus HORSE, STEED
like ~ ALATE

Peggy CASS, LEE, REA

"Peggy ___" SUE

"Peggy ___ Got Married" SUE

"Peg o' My ___" HEART

"Peg Woffington"
~ **author** READE

peignoir ROBE

peke DOG, PET, TOY

Peking
~ **ender** ESE

Peking ___ MAN

Pekingese DOG, PET, TOY

pekoe TEA

___ pekoe ORANGE

pelage COAT

Pelée
~ **flow** LAVA

pelerine CAPE

pelican BIRD

Pelion
~ **base** OSSA

pelisse CAPE, WRAP

pellet BALL, BEAD, PILL, SHOT

pellets BBS, HAIL
ice ~ HAIL, SLEET
lead ~ SHOT
pistol ~ AMMO

pellicle COAT, SKIN

pell mell APACE

pellucid CLEAR

Peloponnesian WAR

Peloponnesus
~ **region** ELIS

pelt COAT, FUR, HAIL, HAIR, HIDE, HIE, HIT, PLY, RACE, RUN, SKIN, STONE

pelvic
~ **bones** ILIA
~ **joint** HIP

pelvis BONE, HIP

pemmican MEAT

pen BIRD, CAGE, PALE, SHE, STIR, STY, SWAN, WRITE, YARD
~ **dweller** SOW
~ **fluid** INK
~ **in** LIMIT
~ **mate** COB
~ **name** ALIAS
~ **problem** LEAK
~ **starter** PLAY
pig ~ MESS
put ~ to paper WRITE
slip of the ~ ERROR

pen ___ NAME, PAL

Peña
see Spanish

penal ___ CODE

penalize FINE

penalty COST, FINE
~ **caller** REF
non-payer's ~ REPO
pay the ~ ATONE
speeder's ~ FINE

penance
do ~ ATONE

penchant BENT, HABIT

pencil BEAM, NOTE, RAY
~ **end** ERASER
~ **filler** LEAD
~ **holder, maybe** EAR
~ **partner** PAD
~ **wood** CEDAR
eye ~ LINER
use a ~ WRITE
worn-down ~ STUB

___-pencil BLUE

pencil box
~ **item** RULER

pencils
like some ~ HARD

pend DRAPE, HANG

pendant BOB, DROP

pending
be ~ AWAIT

Pendleton CAMP

Pend Oreille LAKE

pendulum
~ **direction** FRO
~ **path** ARC

Penelope
Telemachus, to ~ SON

Penelope ___ Miller ANN

penetrate BORE, ENTER, SEE, SOAK, STAB, TAP
~ **slowly** SEEP

penetrating ACUTE, DEEP, INTO, KEEN, LOUD, RAW
~ **beam** LASER, XRAY

penguin BIRD
"Outland" ~ OPUS

"Penguin ___ Murder, The" POOL

penguins
like ~ AVIAN

Penguins SIX, TEAM
~ **milieu** ICE, RINK
~ **org.** NHL

penicillin
~ **source** MOLD
~ **target, for short** STREP

peninsula CAPE, LAND, NECK
~ **of southern Arabia** ADEN
Asian ~ ARABIA
Egyptian ~ SINAI
European ~ IBERIA, ITALY
Mexican ~ BAJA
Red Sea ~ ARABIA, SINAI
small ~ SPIT
two-nation ~ IBERIA

penitent
be ~ ATONE, RUE

penitential
~ **period** LENT

penmanship HAND

Penn SEAN, STA
~ **pronoun** THEE, THOU

Penn.
~ **neighbor** DEL, OHIO
~ **zone** EDT, EST
see also Pennsylvania

Penn. ___ AVE, STA

Penna.
see Pennsylvania

pennant FLAG

penne PASTA

Pennell EAGLE

Penney, J.C.
~ **middle name** CASH

pennies
~ **abbr.** CTS
pinch ~ SAVE, STINT

"Pennies From Heaven"
~ **director** ROSS

penniless NEEDY, POOR

Pennines ALPS, RANGE

Pennock HERB

pennon FLAG

Penn, Sean
~ **film debut** TAPS

Pennsylvania STATE
~ **people** AMISH
~ **port** ERIE

Pennsylvania Dutch SECT, STYLE

penny CENT, COIN
~ **ante** GAME
~ **black** STAMP
~ **often** ANTE
make a pretty ~ EARN
word on a ~ CENT, GOD, ONE
worth a pretty ~ RICH

penny ___ ANTE, ARCADE

"Penny ___" LANE

penny-ante MEAN

pennycress WEED

penny-pinching MEAN, NEAR

"Penny wise, pound foolish" ADAGE

Penobscot
town on the ~ ORONO

penpoint NEB, NIB

Penrod
~ **friend** SAM

Pensacola CITY, PORT

pension HOTEL, INN
fed. ~ org. SSA
on a ~ (abbr.) RET
self-made ~ plan IRA

pension law
~ **verb** VEST

Pentagon
~ **bigwigs** BRASS
~ **VIP** GEN

pentagram STAR

pentameter
~ **unit** FOOT

Pentateuch TORAH
~ **author** MOSES

pentathlon
modern ~ event EPEE

penthouse ABODE, HOME
~ **of a sort** AERIE
in the ~ ATOP
like a ~ POSH

pentlandite ORE

penultimate
~ **day** EVE
~ **fairy-tale word** EVER
~ **mo.** NOV
~ **round** SEMI

penurious CLOSE, MEAN, POOR

penury NEED, WANT

Penzias ARNO

peon BOOR, SERF
~ **of yore** ESNE

peons MOB

people SETTLE
beautiful ~ CREAM
bunch of ~ TROOP
crush of ~ MOB
influential ~ ELITE
let ~ know AIR
mind other ~'s business PRY
values of a ~ ETHOS
where most ~ live ASIA
zero ~ NOONE

"People" MAG
~ **people** STARS

"People ___ Funny" ARE

"People ___ Strange" ARE

"People, ___, The" YES

"___ People" CAT, SHOW

"___ People, The"

"___ People, The" RAIN

"___ People of Paris, The" POOR

"People's Choice, The"
~ author AGAR
~ hound CLEO

"___ People's Money" OTHER

"People Will ___" TALK

"People, Yes, The" POEM

Peoria
~ st. ILL

pep FIRE, LIFE, SNAP, VIM
full of ~ AGILE, ALIVE, SPRY
lose ~ FLAG, TIRE

pep ___ TALK

Pepe Le ___ PEW

Pepe Le Pew
~ defense ODOR

pepo MELON

Peppard, George
~ show, with "The" ATEAM

pepper DOT, HAIL, PELT, PLY,
SHELL
~ companion SALT
~ dispenser MILL
~ picker PETER
~ pot STEW
hot ~ CHILI

pepper ___ MILL, POT

___ pepper CHILI, HOT, RED

Pepper ART, SGT
~ and others DRS
Dr. ~ relative COLA

pepper-and-___ SALT

peppermint HERB

Peppermint Patty
~ to Marcie SIR

"Peppermint Twist"
Joey of ~ DEE

pepper pot
~ ingredient MEAT, OKRA

peppery HOT

peppy ALIVE, RACY, SPRY

pep rally
~ cry RAH

Pepsi COLA, POP, SODA

Pepsico
~ product COLA

Pepys
~ destination BED

"Pequod" BOAT, SHIP
~ captain AHAB

per APIECE, EACH

per ___ CENT, DIEM

perambulate MOVE, ROAM, ROVE,
STEP, TREAD

per capita EACH

perceive ESPY, FEEL, GRASP,
KNOW, LEARN, SEE, SENSE,
TASTE
~ sound HEAR

percent
~ ender AGE, ILE
fifty ~ HALF
one hundred ~ FINE

percentage CUT, PART, RATE,
RATIO, SHARE

"___-Per-Cent Solution, The"
SEVEN

perceptible CLEAR, REAL

perception GRASP, IDEA, IMAGE,
KEN, TACT, TASTE
keen ~ WIT

perceptive ACUTE, CLEAR, KEEN,
SMART, WISE

perch ABODE, REST, ROOST, SEAT,
SETTLE, SIT
crane operator's ~ CAB
find a ~ LAND
high ~ AERIE
returned to the ~ ALIT, LIT
Santa's ~ LAP

perched
~ upon ATOP
be precariously ~ TEETER

Percheron ANIMAL, HORSE
~ cousin ARAB
~ repast OATS

perciatelli PASTA

percipient AWARE

percolate CLEAR, DRIP, DROP,
ISSUE, OOZE, RUN, SEEP

percussion CLAP
~ instrument TRAP

percussion ___ CAP

Percy, Thomas POET
see also poet

perdition RUIN
act of ~ RIOT

"___ Père" BEAU

Père David's ___ DEER

peregrinate ROAM, ROVE, TOUR

peregrine BIRD
~ home AERIE

perennial PLANT
garden ~ ASTER, LILY, ROSE
woody ~ used in
medicine RUE

Peretti ELSA

perfect AOK, AONE, BEST, CLEAN,
HONE, IDEAL, PURE, TOPS
~ condition MINT
~ place EDEN
~ rating TEN
~ serve ACE
feel less than ~ AIL
in ~ harmony ATONE
it can be ~ TENSE

"Perfect ___, The" (Le Carré
novel) SPY

perfection IDEAL, PEAK
Olympic ~ TEN

perfectly PAT

"Perfect World, A"
~ actress DERN

perfidious BAD, BASE, FALSE

perfidy EVIL

perforate BORE, CLAW

perforated OPEN

perforation HOLE, LEAK

perforator NEEDLE

perform ACT, EMOTE, ENACT,
STAGE
~ alone SOLO
~ a marriage UNITE
~ in an opera SING
~ well SHINE

performance ACT, DEED, PLAY,
SHOW
~ site DAIS, STAGE
acknowledge a ~ CLAP
diva's ~ ARIA
give an encore ~ RERUN
give the first ~ OPEN
individual ~ SOLO
jazz ~ GIG, SET
Met ~ OPERA
short ~ ACT, SKIT
virtuoso ~ ECLAT

performer ACTOR, DOER
~ platform STAGE
~ (suffix) IST
bit-part ~ EXTRA
circus ~ FLEA, SEAL
coffeehouse ~ POET
kabuki ~ MALE
operatic ~ BASSO
paid ~ PRO
solo ~ DIVA
stage ~ ACTOR
top ~ ACE
unbilled ~ EXTRA

performers CAST

performing LIVE

performing ___ ARTS, SEAL

performs DOES

perfume AROMA, BALM, ESSENCE,
ODOR, SCENT
~ amount DAB
~ base ATTAR
~ holder VIAL
~ ingredient ATTAR, ESTER
~ measure DRAM
~ scent LILAC
spread ~ CENSE

perfumed SWEET

perfumery
~ bit PETAL

perfunctory RAPID, TOKEN

pergola ARBOR

pericarp ARIL

Pericles ORATOR

peridot GEM
~ mo. AUG

Perignon
~ title DOM

perigynous
~ flower ROSE

peril RISK

perimeter EDGE, LIMIT
~ surroundings AREA

period AGE, BOUT, DAY, DOT,
PHASE, STAGE
~ before EVE
~ of decline EBB
~ of office TERM
~ of rule REIGN
~ of time SPACE
appropriate ~ TIME
calendar ~ YEAR
coming-of-age ~ TEENS
distinct ~ ERA
fasting ~ LENT
fiscal ~ YEAR
fix the ~ of DATE
galactic time ~ EON
geologic ~ ERA
historical ~ AGE, EPOCH, ERA
holiday ~ YULE
long ~ AGE, EON
lunch ~, often HOUR
memorable ~ EPOCH, ERA
orbital ~ YEAR
Palm Sunday's ~ LENT
part of a ~ EPOCH
penitential ~ LENT
preceding ~ EVE
probationary ~ TRIAL
prolonged ~ of
trouble SIEGE
prosperous ~ BOOM
school ~ TERM
set ~ of time TERM
time ~ SPAN
within a short ~ ANON, SOON
work ~ WEEK

periodic ERAL

periodical MAG, ORGAN, PAPER,
SHEET
palindromic ~ ELLE

periodically OFT, OFTEN

periodicals MEDIA, PRESS

periodic table
~ category GAS, METAL
~ fig. ATNO
~ mem. ELEM

periodontist
~ deg. DDS
~ org. ADA

periods
two gridiron ~ HALF
two or more ~ ERA

peripheral OUTER

periphery EDGE, LIMIT, RIM

peristyle ARCADE, PATIO

peristyles
kin of ~ ATRIA

perjure
~ oneself LIE

perjured FALSE

perjurer LIAR

perk PLUS
~ up ELATE

Perkins CARL, TONY

Perkins, Maxwell EDITOR
emulate ~ EDIT

perky CUTE, PERT

Perle MESTA

Perlman RHEA, RON

perm
~ follow-up SET

perm.
not ~ TEMP

permanent ETERNAL, FAST, SET
~ marker PEN
~ place SALON
be ~ ABIDE, LAST

permanent ___ PRESS, TOOTH

permeate SEEP, SOAK

permissible LEGAL

permission LEAVE
~ granted YES
give ~ to ALLOW, LET
has ~ MAY
written ~ PASS

permissive
~ word MAY

permit ADMIT, ALLOW, BEAR, CLEAR, ENABLE, LET, PASS
travel ~ VISA

"Permit Me Voyage"
~ author AGEE

permitted ABLE, LEGAL

pernicious BAD, EVIL

perniciousness HARM

Pernod
~ ingredient ANISE

Perón EVA, EVITA

perorate DRAG, ORATE

Perot ROSS

perp
pick up a ~ ARREST, NAB

perpendicular ERECT, STEEP
~ surface SIDE
~ to the keel ABEAM
off the ~ ALIST

perpetual ETERNAL

perpetually EVER

"Perpetual Peace"
~ author KANT

perplex AMAZE, DAZE, GET, POSE

perplexed ASEA, ATSEA, LOST

perquisite FEE, PLUS

Perrine, Valerie
~ "Superman" role EVE

Perrins
~ partner LEA

Perry COMO, ELLIS
~ assistant DELLA
~ creator ERLE
~ victory site ERIE

"Perry Mason"
~ actor BURR, HALE

persecute RAG

Persepolis
where ~ is IRAN

Perseus HERO
~ to Danaë SON
neighbor of ~ ARIES

persevere ABIDE, LIVE, PEG, PLOD, TOIL

persevering ATIT

Persia
~ today IRAN

Persian CAT, IRANI, MELON
~ poet OMAR
~ remark MEOW, MEW
~ ruler SHAH
~ sprite PERI
ancient ~ MEDE

Persian Gulf
~ city BASRA
~ vessel OILER
ancient ~ kingdom ELAM

persiflage TALK

persimmon TREE

persist ABIDE, HOLD, LAST, LIVE, PEG
~ ender ENCE, ENT

"Persistence of Memory"
~ artist DALI

persistent ETERNAL

Persky BILL

persnickety NICE

person SELF, SORT, SOUL
a ~ EACH, ONE
annoying ~ PAIN, PEST
busy ~ DOER
canonized ~ SAINT
charitable ~ DONOR
clever ~ WIT
coarse ~ YAHOO
condescending ~ SNOB
disagreeable ~ PILL
energetic ~ DOER
fifth ~ SETH
first ~ ADAM
fourth ~ ABEL
from person to ~ ALONG
funny ~ CARD, RIOT, WAG, WIT
haughty ~ SNOB
hilarious ~ PANIC, RIOT
holy ~ SAINT
in ~ LIVE
inept ~ CLOD, OAF
insured ~ RISK
mean ~ OGRE

messy ~ SLOB
nose-in-the-air ~ SNOB
outstanding ~ ONER
per ~ APIECE, EACH
policy ~ AGENT
powerful ~ TITAN, TSAR
remarkable ~ ONER
right-hand ~ AIDE
search for a missing
~ TRACE
second ~ EVE, YOU
self-righteous ~ PRIG
stubborn ~ MULE
stuck-up ~ SNOB
third ~ CAIN, SHE
tiresome ~ BORE, PILL
undocumented ~ ALIEN
which ~ WHO

___ person (unanimously)
ASONE

persona
cast ~ ROLE
public ~ IMAGE

persona ___ grata NON

personage NAME, STAR

personages ELITE

personal SOLE
~ attendant VALET
~ care worker AIDE
~ history BIO
~ interest STAKE
~ quirk TIC
~ viewpoint SLANT
get too ~ PRY
some are ~ ADS

personal ___ ADS

"Personal ___" BEST

personality SELF
~ part EGO

personality clash
~ cause EGO

personnel HELP
~ datum AGE
embassy ~ AIDE
enlisted ~ GIS
health-care ~ AIDE
key ~ CADRE
ship's ~ CREW

"Person to Person"
~ network CBS

perspective ANGLE, SLANT

perspicacious ACUTE, CLEAR, DEEP, KEEN, WISE

perspicacity SENSE

perspicuous CLEAR

perspire EGEST, EMIT, OOZE, STEW

persuade ARGUE, EGG, IMPEL, LEAD, MOVE, PLEAD, SELL, SWAY, URGE
~ to marry WIN

persuaded SURE

persuasion CAMP, CREED, TYPE

pert CUTE, FLIP, RUDE, SASSY

pertain REFER, RELATE

pertaining
~ to INRE
~ to (suffix) ILE, INE, ISH

Perth CITY
see also Australian

pertinent APT
~ words ASTO

perturb AIL, ANGER, IRK, JAR, PEEVE, UPSET

perturbed UPSET

Peru
~ capital LIMA
~ mountains ANDES
see also Peruvian, Spanish

Perugia
town in ~ ASSISI

peruse CON, PORE, READ, SCAN
~ carefully CON
~ casually LEAF

Peruvian
~ beast LLAMA
~ coin SOL
~ of old INCA
~ peaks ANDES
~ town AMBO
see also Peru, Spanish

pervade SOAK

pervasive
~ quality AURA, ODOR

perverse WRY

perversity EVIL

___-per-view PAY

pes FOOT

Pesci JOE

pesky
~ bug GNAT
~ plant WEED

peso COIN

pessimistic
~ investor BEAR

pest ANT, PAIN, TRIAL
animal ~ FLEA
biting ~ GNAT
closet ~ MOTH
cornfield ~ CROW
garden ~ APHID, MOLE
picnic ~ ANT
rose ~ APHID
tiny ~ MITE

pester FRET, IRK, NAG, NEEDLE, PEEVE, RAG, TEASE

pesthole STY

pesticide
banned ~ DDT

pestilential DIRE, EVIL

pestle
use a ~ STAMP

pests
plant ~ LICE

pet CARESS, LOVE, NECK
~ **name** DEAR, HON
~ **of rhyme** LAMB
~ **owner's need** LEASH
~ **pest** FLEA
~ **rocks** FAD
chatty ~ MYNA
house ~ CAT, DOG
in a ~ IRATE, UPSET

"pet"
~ **complaint** PEEVE

pet ___ PEEVE

petal LEAF
~ **base** SEPAL
~ **oil** ATTAR

petasus HAT

Pete BEST, DOG, ROSE

peter
~ **out** DIE, EBB, END, PASS,
STOP, WANE
blue ~ FLAG
hoist the blue ~ SAIL

___ peter BLUE

Peter ARNO, HALL, HUNT, LORRE,
NERO, NOONE, OTOOLE, PAN,
SAINT, TSAR, WEIR

Peter ___ Rubens PAUL

"Peter ___" PAN

"Peter and the Wolf"
~ **duck** OBOE

"Peter Grimes" OPERA

Peter Mark ___ ROGET

Peter Pan
~ **kin** ETON

"Peter Pan"
~ **beast** CROC
~ **dog** NANA
~ **pirate** SMEE
like the boys in ~ LOST

Peter, Paul, and Mary TRIO

"Peter, Peter, pumpkin ___..."
EATER

"Peter Quince at the Clavier"
POEM

"Peter Rabbit" TALE

**"Peter Rabbit and ___ of Beatrix
Potter"** TALES

Peterson OSCAR

Peters, Roberta
~ **piece** ARIA

Peter the Great TSAR

"___ Pete's sake!" FOR

petiole STEM

petit chou LOVE

petite SIZE, SMALL, TINY, WEE
~ **opposite** LARGE

petition ASK, BEG, PLEA, PLEAD,
SUE, SUIT, WOO
make a ~ PRAY

pet lover
~ **org.** SPCA

Petrarch
~ **beloved** LAURA

Petrarch, Francesco POET
see also poet

petrel BIRD
~ **lair** AERIE

petri dish
~ **contents** AGAR

Petrie ANN

___ Petrie (Dick Van Dyke role)
ROB

Petrie, Laura
~ **husband** ROB

petrified
~ **sap** AMBER

petrify COW

Pet Rocks FAD

petrol GAS

petroleum OIL
~ **byproduct** ETHANE, TAR
name in ~ HESS

Petrozavodsk CITY
see also Russian

Petruchio TAMER
~ **intended** KATE
emulate ~ TAME

pet shop
~ **buy** CAGE
~ **noise** ARF
~ **purchase** LEASH

petticoat SLIP

pettifogger PRIG

petting zoo
like ~ animals TAME

Pettit BOB

Pettitte ANDY

petty MEAN, SMALL
~ **cash** COIN
~ **officer** RANK
~ **quarrel** SPAT

petty ___ CASH

petulant RUDE, TART, TESTY
~ **mood** SNIT
~ **one** CRAB

Petunia Pig SOW

peut-___ ETRE

pew SEAT
~ **cousin** SETTEE
~ **locale** NAVE
~ **separator** AISLE
escort to a ~ SEAT
use a ~ SIT

pewit BIRD

pewter
~ **component** LEAD, TIN

peyotes CACTI

"Peyton Place" SOAP
~ **actor** NOLAN, ONEAL
Allison on ~ MIA
Rodney on ~ RYAN
street in ~ ELM

PFC
~ **address** APO
~ **boss** SGT
like a ~ ENL

PFCs GIS

pfennig COIN

PG
give a ~ RATE

PGA
~ **legend** SNEAD
~ **member** PRO
~ **platform** TEE
part of ~ ASSN

pH
~ **less than 7** ACID
~ **more than 7** BASE

phaeton AUTO, CAR, MOTOR

phalanx ARMY, BONE

phantasm SHADE

phantasmagorical EERIE, EERY

phantom SHADE, SOUL
~ **milieu** OPERA

"Phantom ___" LADY

"Phantom of the ___" OPERA

"Phantom of the Opera"
~ **instrument** ORGAN
~ **prop** MASK

phantoms MANES

Phantom, The HERO
~ **horse** HERO

"Phar ___" LAP

pharaoh RULER, TITLE

Pharaoh
~ **fabric** LINEN
~ **god** ATEN, ATON, PTAH
famous ~ TUT
snake on ~'s headdress ASP

Pharisees SECT

pharmaceutical PILL

pharmaceuticals
~ **watchdog** FDA

pharmacist
~ **container** VIAL
~ **measure** DRAM
~ **quantity** DOSE
NaCl, to a ~ SAL

"Pharsalia" EPIC

phase STAGE, STEP

phase constant
~ **in physics** BETA

"Phase IV"
~ **foe** ANT

phaser
~ **setting** STUN

Ph.D.
~ **exam** ORALS
~ **hurdle** ORAL

pheasant BIRD
female ~ HEN

"Phenix ___ Story, The" CITY

phenol
~ **compound** ESTER

___ phenomena (ESP, etc.) PSI

phenomenal RARE

phenomenon FACT

phi
~ **follower** CHI

Phi ___ Kappa BETA

Phil OCHS

Philadelphia
~ **clock setting** EDT, EST
~ **footballer** EAGLE
~ **st.** PENN
~ **suburb** MEDIA

"Philadelphia Freedom"
~ **name** ELTON

Philae
her temple was at ~ ISIS

philanderer CAD, SATYR

"Philanderer, The"
~ **author** SHAW

philanthropic
~ **one** DONOR

philanthropy AID, HELP

philatelist
~ **concern** STAMP

philately
~ **offering** ISSUE

Philbin, Regis EMCEE, HOST

Philby, Kim MOLE, SPY

philematologist
~ **study** KISS

Philip HALE, ROTH

Philippe
see French

philippic
deliver a ~ RANT

Philippines
~ **money** PESO
~ **peak** APO

___ Philip Randolph ASA

Philips EMO

Philips, Ambrose POET
see also poet

Philistine YAHOO

Phillies NINE, TEAM

Phillips LOUD, STONE

Phillips, Michelle
~ **once** MAMA

Phillips 66
~ **rival** ESSO

Phillips University
home of ~ ENID

Phillpotts EDEN

philodendron
~ family ARUM

philosopher SAGE
~ universal TAO
Greek ~ PLATO

philosophical CALM, DEEP

philosophy ART, CREDO, CREED,
ISM, STAND
Eastern ~ TAO
Hindu ~ YOGA

phi-psi
~ link CHI

phiz FACE, PAN

phlegmatic COOL, INERT, SLOW,
STOIC

Phnom Penh CITY

phobia FEAR
~ starter AGORA

Phobos MOON
~ orbits it MARS
father of ~ ARES

Phoebe MOON, TITAN

"___ Phoebe" DEAR

Phoebus SOL, SUN

Phoenician
~ deity BAAL
ancient ~ city TYRE

phoenix BIRD
~ origin ASHES
emulated the ~ ROSE

Phoenix
~ hoopster SUN
~ suburb MESA
city near ~ TEMPE
town north of ~ ADOBE

phone CALL, DIAL, RING
~ bug TAP
~ button HOLD
~ call beginning HELLO
~ co. ITT
~ cord shape COIL
~ key STAR
~ line CORD
~ machine noise BEEP
~ sound TONE
~ starter EAR, HEAD, MEGA,
TELE
ABC, on a ~ TWO
DEF, on a ~ THREE
former ~ feature DIAL
hold the ~ STOP
JKL, on a ~ FIVE
mind the ~ MAN
MNO, on a ~ SIX
onstage ~ PROP
PRS, on a ~ SEVEN
WXY, on a ~ NINE
see also telephone

___ phone CELL

"Phone ___ From a Stranger"
CALL

phone book
home, in the ~ RES
put in a ~ LIST

phonic
~ starter STEREO

phonogram SIGN

phonograph STEREO
~ inventor EDISON
~ inventor's monogram TAE
~ part ARM
~ record DISC

phony BAD, FAKE, FALSE, PASTE,
SHAM
~ gems PASTE
~ handle ALIAS

"Phooey!" BAH, DARN, DRAT, FIE,
NUTS, RATS

phosphate SALT

phosphorescence GLOW

photo IMAGE, SHOT
~ ender STAT
~ finish MAT, MATTE
~ session SHOOT
~ snapper CAMERA
~ starter TELE
~ tint SEPIA
~ transparency SLIDE
blow up a ~ (abbr.) ENL
physician's ~ XRAY
take a ~ of SHOOT, SNAP
trim a ~ CROP

photo-___ ESSAY, OPS

___ photo AERIAL

photocopy REPRO, STAT

photographer
~ buy LENS
~ gadget CAMERA
~ order SMILE
~ woe BLUR
far-side-of-the-moon ~ LUNA

photographers
news ~ MEDIA, PRESS

photogravure
~ process, for short ROTO

photoplay DRAMA

Photostat REPRO

Phouma, Souvanna
~ country LAOS

phrase PART, PUT, SAY
descriptive ~ LABEL

phrase book
~ entry IDIOM

phraseology STYLE, USAGE

phrenitis MANIA

Phrygia
King of ~ MIDAS

phylum
~ subdivision CLASS

phys. SCI

physic CURE, PILL

physical ANIMAL, EXAM, REAL
~ discipline YOGA

physician
~ org. AMA
~ photo XRAY
~ turned wordsmith ROGET
ancient Greek ~ GALEN

"Physician, ___ thyself" HEAL

physicist
~ concern ATOM
~ particle ION
~ workplace LAB

physics
~ calculation MASS
~ starter ASTRO, GEO
~ unit DYNE, ERG, RAD
gas, in ~ STATE
liquid, in ~ STATE
solid, in ~ STATE

physiognomy FACE

pi
~ follower RHO

P.I. TEC
~ job CASE
see also detective, Philippines

Piaf EDITH
see also French

pianist
English ~ HESS
Grammy-winning ~ NERO

piano
~ exercise ETUDE, SCALE
~ hammer material FELT
~ key NOTE
~ key material EBONY, IVORY
~ lever PEDAL
~ part KEY, LEG
~ piece NOLA, RAG
fix a ~ TUNE
four-handed ~ piece DUET

piano ___ BAR, ROLL

"Piano, The"
~ heroine ADA

"Piano ___" (Billy Joel tune) MAN

piano/violin
~ piece DUET

piassava PALM

piaster COIN

piazza ARCADE, PATIO

pica FONT, TYPE
~ alternative ELITE
~ widths EMS

picador
~ opponent TORO
~ weapon LANCE

Picasso PABLO
~ cap BERET
~ contemporary MIRO
~ mastery ART
~ sister LOLA

picayune MEAN, SMALL

Piccadilly
~ statue EROS

~ trolley TRAM

___ piccata VEAL

piccolo PIPE

Piccolo ___ PETE

Pichel, Irving
~ film of 1935 SHE
~ film of 1946 OSS

pick DRAW, ELECT, HACK, OPT,
TAKE, TOOL
~ at CARP, NAG
~ of the litter CREAM
~ on BAIT, NAG, RIB, TEASE
~ one's way FEEL
~ out ELECT
~ up ARREST, EARN, GAIN,
GET, HEAR, LEARN, NAB
~ up a lease RENEW
~ up a perp ARREST, NAB
~ up a stitch KNIT
~ up furtively PALM
~ up on SEE
~ up the check PAY, TREAT
~ up the pace HIE, RACE,
RUN, SPEED
ice ~ TOOL
party ~ SLATE
work ~ and shovel DIG

pick ___ (examine) OVER

pick ___ (select) OUT

___ pick ICE

pickaxe HACK
~ cousin ADZE

picked
it may be ~ BONE

Pickens SLIM

picker
~ starter NIT

___ picker RAG

picker-upper TONIC

picket POST, STAKE
fence ~ PALE

picket ___ LINE

"Picket Fences"
~ character ADAM

picket line
~ crosser SCAB

picking
prime for the ~ RIPE
quibbler's ~ NIT

pickings HAUL
slim ~ FEW

pickle BIND, CURE, HOLE, JAM,
MESS, PASS, SALT, SPOT, STATE,
STEEP
~ flavor DILL
~ piece SPEAR

___ pickle DILL, INA

pickled
~ flower bud CAPER
~ veggie BEET

pickling
~ ingredient ALUM

pick-me-___

pick-me-___ UPS

pick-me-up TONIC

pickpocket DIP

pickup TONIC
~ enclosure CAB
~ truck MOTOR

pick-up
for ~ TOGO

picnic EAT, MEAL
~ drink ADE
~ fare SLAW
~ loaf RYE
~ pest ANT
~ spoiler RAIN
~ spread EATS
~ umbrella TREE

"Picnic"
~ writer INGE

___-Picone EVAN

pictograph
computer ~ ICON

pictorial
newspaper ~ section ROTO

picture DRAW, MAP, PAINT, SCENE, SEE
~ backing MAT
~ holder NAIL
~ magazine LIFE
~ of oneself EGO
~ on a rural road sign DEER
~ puzzle REBUS
~ within a picture INSET
25-cent ~ EAGLE
CAT ~ SCAN
doctor's ~ XRAY
get the ~ GRASP, LEARN, SEE
iron-on ~ DECAL
mental ~ IDEA, IMAGE
motion ~ CINE
mount a ~ HANG
paint a rosy ~ FAKE
posse ~ OATER
snap, as a ~ TAKE
take a ~ SHOOT

picture ___ HAT

"Picture ___!" THIS

"Picture of Dorian ___, The"
GRAY

pictures
eye-fooling ~ OPART

"___ Picture Show, The" LAST

piddling MEAN, POOR, SMALL, THIN

pie TREAT
~ crust SHELL
~ ingredient APPLE, LEMON, LIME, PECAN
~ plate PAN
helping of ~ SLICE
piece of the ~ SHARE
small ~ TART

pie ___ PAN, PLANT, TIN

pie ___ mode ALA

pie à la ___ MODE

piebald HORSE
~ pony PINTO

piece ESSAY, GAT, GUN, PART, RAG, ROD, SLICE
playing ~ MAN

___ piece (consistent) OFA

pièce de résistance DISH

piece of ___ (something simple)
CAKE

piece of cake EASY

pieces
~ partner BITS
blow to ~ BLAST, RUIN
in ~ APART
knock to ~ RAZE
pull to ~ TEAR
tear to ~ REND

"Pieces of Eight"
~ band STYX

pie chart
~ lines RADII

pie-cooling
~ place SILL

pie crust
~ ingredient LARD

pied-à-___ TERRE

Piedmont
~ city ASTI

Pied Piper
~ follower RAT
emulate the ~ RID

___ Piedras, P.R. RIO

Piegan TRIBE

pie in the ___ SKY

pielike EASY

pier ANTA, PILE, POST
~ foundation PILE
architectural ~ ANTA

pierce BORE, CLAW, GORE, REND, SPEAR, STAB, STING, TAP

Pierce AUTO, CAR, EGAN
~ on "M*A*S*H" ALDA
where ~ served KOREA

Pierce ___ (old auto) ARROW

Pierce Arrow
~ contemporary REO

pierced
~ object EAR, LOBE

piercing ACUTE, KEEN, LOUD
~ stare GLARE
~ tool AWL

Pierette
see French

Pierre
~ loc. SDAK
~ tube METRO
see also French

Piers Paul ___ READ

pie-throwing
~ comic SALES

piety
false ~ CANT

"Piffle!" BAH

pig ANIMAL, EATER, HOG, METAL
~ digs PEN, STY
~ dinner SLOP
~ in a poke BET
~ out CRAM, DINE, EAT, GLUT
~ share ALL
~ talk OINK
~ thief of rhyme TOM
female ~ SOW
female guinea ~ SOW
guinea ~ ANIMAL, PET
jungle ~ TAPIR
make ~ iron SMELT
male ~ BOAR
movie ~ BABE
wild ~ BOAR

pig ___ IRON, LATIN

pig ___ (overeat) OUT

pig ___ blanket INA

pig ___ poke INA

pigeon BIRD, DUPE, GOAT, LAMB, PREY, TOOL
~ cousin DOVE
~ home COTE
~ material CLAY
~ sound COO
~ undoing SCAM
clay ~ BIRD
stool ~ RAT
walk like a ~ BOB

pigeon-___ TOED

pigeonhole DEFER, FILE, RATE, SLOT, SORT, TABLE
~ locale DESK

"Pigeons in the grass, ___" ALAS

piggie
fourth ~'s portion NONE

piggish AVID

piggy
little ~ TOE

Piggy MISS

piggy-bank
~ opening SLOT

Piggy, Miss SOW
~ pronoun MOI
see also French

piglet
~ mom SOW
~ pop BOAR

Piglet
~ creator MILNE
pal of ~ OWL, POOH

piglike
~ mammal TAPIR

pigment COLOR, DYE, PAINT, TINT
cuttlefish ~ SEPIA
natural ~ OCHER, OCHRE

pignus LIEN

pignut TREE

pigpen MESS, STY

pigs LAW
feed the ~ SLOP

"___ pig's eye!" INA

pigskin BALL
~ prop TEE

"Pigskin ___" PARADE

pigstick HUNT

pigsty MESS, PEN

Pig & Whistle
~ order ALE

pika ANIMAL
~ kin HARE

pike LANCE, ROAD, ROUTE, SPEAR

pike ___ EEL

Pikes ___ (Colorado landmark)
PEAK

pikestaff STAVE

pilaf
~ grain RICE

Pilar
see Spanish

pilaster ANTA

Pilatus ALP

pile AMASS, BEAM, HEAP, MASS, NAP, OCEAN, PIER, POST, RAFT, SEA
~ driver RAM
~ it higher and deeper BRAG
~ it on LIE
~ on LADE, LOAD
~ on the floor RUG
~ up AMASS, SAVE, STORE
put on the ~ ADD
thick ~ SHAG

pile-___ UPS

piles ALOT
put in ~ SORT

pileus CAP

pilfer CRIB, ROB, STEAL, TAKE

pilgrim
~ destination MECCA
Chaucer ~ NUN, REEVE

Pilgrim
~ pronoun THEE, THOU
memorable ~ ALDEN

pilgrimage TRIP
~ end MECCA

pilgrims
Biblical ~ MAGI

piling PIER

pill BALL, BORE, CREEP, DOSE, DRAG
~ allotment DOSE

pillage LOOT, PREY, RAID, RIFLE, ROB, SACK, WASTE

pillar PIER, PILE, POST
~ of heaven, to Pindar ETNA
engraved ~ STELE

go from ~ to post ROAM, ROVE

pillbox HAT

pillow
  ~ candy MINT
  ~ cover SHAM
  ~ filler FOAM

pillow ___ SHAM

"Pillow ___" TALK

pillowcase SLIP

pillowcases LINEN

"___ Pillows" SATIN

"Pillow Talk"
  ~ actress DAY

pilot AVIATE, LEAD, RUN, SAIL, STEER
  ~ affirmative ROGER
  ~ button EJECT
  ~ concern DRAG
  ~ light LAMP
  ~ milestone SOLO
  ~ place HELM, PLANE
  ~ starter AUTO
  ~ the shuttle ORBIT
  expert ~ ACE
  fine, to a ~ AOK
  like a UFO ~ ALIEN
  sky ~ PADRE

___ pilot SKY, TEST

"___ Pilot" MOON

pilotless
  ~ plane DRONE

pilots
  UFO ~ ETS

pilsner BEER, LAGER

Piltdown ___ MAN

pilus HAIR

Pima TRIBE

pimiento
  ~ holder OLIVE

Pimlico
  ~ event RACE
  ~ racer HORSE

Pim, Mr.
  ~ creator MILNE

pin
  ~ down PRESS
  ~ holder ETUI
  ~ money COIN
  ~ one's ears back BEAT
  ~ one's faith on LEAN
  ~ relative NAIL
  bowling ~ MAPLE
  hard to ~ down EELY
  kind of ~ CAMEO
  like a ~ NEAT
  metalworker's ~ RIVET
  part of a ~ HEAD
  place for a ~ LAPEL
  wooden ~ PEG

pin ___ OAK

PIN
  ~ prompter ATM

piña colada
  ~ ingredient RUM

pinafore APRON, BIB

"Pinafore" BOAT, SHIP

Pinatubo
  ~ output LAVA
  ~ residue ASH
  emulate ~ ERUPT

pinball GAME
  ~ foul TILT
  ~ palace ARCADE
  ~ path ARC

"Pinball Wizard"
  ~ band WHO

pince-nez
  ~ part LENS

pincer CLAW

pincers ORGAN

pinch ARREST, DAB, DASH, DROP, HOLE, IOTA, MESS, NAB, NIP, PAIN, PASS, ROB, STEAL, TAKE
  ~ hitter SUB
  ~ pennies SAVE, STINT

pinch-___ HIT

pinchbeck BASE, FAKE, SHAM

pinched NEEDY, POOR, THIN

Pindar POET
  ~ work ODE
  pillar of heaven, to ~ ETNA
  see also Greek, poet

Pindaric ___ ODE

Pindus RANGE

pine ACHE, FRET, LONG, MOPE, TREE, YEARN
  ~ extract RESIN
  ~ family member FIR
  ~ for LOVE, MISS, NEED, WANT
  ~ (for) ACHE, DIE
  ~ needle LEAF
  ~ product CONE, NEEDLE, NUT, TAR

pine ___ CONE, NEEDLE, NUT, TAR

___ pine SLASH

pineapple
  ~ name DOLE

"Pineapple King, The" DOLE

Pine Bluff
  ~ st. ARK

Pine Tree State MAINE

Ping-Pong GAME
  ~ need BALL, NET
  ~ surface TABLE

pinguid OILY

pinhead ASS, CLOD, GOOSE, IDIOT, OAF

Piniella LOU

pinion BIND
  ~ partner RACK

pink ROSY
  ~ flower ASTER
  ~ shade CORAL
  ~ slip SACK
  deep ~ MELON, ROSE
  in the ~ HALE
  not in the ~ ILL
  tickle ~ SUIT
  tickled ~ ELATED, GLAD

pink ___ (cocktail) LADY

Pinkerton
  ~ logo EYE

pinkish
  ~ yellow CORAL

pink lady
  ~ ingredient GIN

pinko LEFT, RED

"Pink Panther Strikes ___, The" AGAIN

pink-slip AXE, BOOT, CAN

Pinky LEE

pinna
  ~ locale EAR

pinnace BOAT, SAIL, SHIP

pinnacle ACME, APEX, CAP, CREST, PEAK, SPIRE, TIP, TOP, TOR

Pinocchio
  ~ at times LIAR
  ~ polygraph NOSE
  ~ undoing LIE

"Pinocchio"
  ~ goldfish CLEO

pinochle GAME
  ~ card TEN
  ~ holding MELD
  lowest ~ card NINE

pinole MEAL

piñon NUT, TREE

pinot WINE

pinprick DOT

pins
  on ~ and needles EDGY, TENSE

pinsetter
  ~ place ALLEY, LANE

Pinsk CITY
  see also Russian

pint ALE, UNIT

"Pinta" BOAT, SHIP
  ~ companion NINA

pintail
  ~ cousin TEAL

pinto BEAN, HORSE

Pinto AUTO, CAR

pint-sized ELFIN, SMALL, TEENY, TINY

pinwheel TOY

Pinza, Ezio BASS, BASSO

pion
  ~ place ATOM

pioneer LEAD, OPEN
  automobile ~ OLDS
  broadcast ~ RCA
  calculus ~ EULER
  detective-story ~ POE
  ESP ~ RHINE
  induction-motor ~ TESLA
  Kentucky ~ BOONE
  pistol ~ COLT
  polio vaccine ~ SALK
  public education ~ MANN
  Sierra Club ~ MUIR
  video-game ~ ATARI

pious GOOD
  ~ ending AMEN

pip DOT, LULU, PIT, SEED, STONE
  domino ~ ACE

pipe
  ~ bowl, maybe COB
  ~ cleaner LYE, SNAKE
  ~ cutter SAW
  ~ handle STEM
  ~ hole LEAK
  ~ instrument ORGAN
  ~ joint ELL
  ~ material COB
  ~ problem DRIP
  ~ up SAY, TALK
  clean a ~ REAM
  curved ~ TRAP
  Indian ~ PLANT
  kind of ~ BRIAR, ELBOW
  put down ~ LAY
  water ~ MAIN

pipe ___ DREAM, ORGAN

___ pipe PEACE

___-pipe cactus ORGAN

pipeline MAIN

piper
  mythical ~ PAN
  the ~'s son TOM

"___ Piper, The" PIED

"___ pipers piping..." TEN

piping REEDY

piping ___ HOT

pipistrelle BAT

pipit BIRD
  ~ cousin LARK

"Pippa Passes" POEM

Pippen, Scottie
  ~ org. NBA

Pippig UTA

pippin APPLE, SEED

pipsqueak RUNT

piquancy NIP, SALT, SAVOR, TANG

piquant HOT, RACY, TART
  not ~ BLAH, MILD

pique ANGER, AROUSE, FRET, IRK, MOVE, PEEVE, PET, RILE, TEASE, UPSET
  fit of ~ IRE, SNIT

piqued IRATE, MAD, UPSET, WARM

piquet GAME

Piraeus CITY, PORT

"Piranha"
  ~ director DANTE

pirate CRIB, ROB, SACK, STEAL, TAKE
  ~ drink RUM
  ~ haul SWAG
  ~ quest LOOT
  ~ trunk CHEST
  fictional ~ SMEE

Pirates NINE, TEAM

Pirelli
  ~ product TIRE

pirogue CANOE

pirouette DANCE, REEL, SPIN

Pisa
  ~ river ARNO

Pisces SIGN
  ~ follower ARIES
  part of ~ STAR

piscivore
  flying ~ ERN, ERNE

pismire ANT

pismo ___ CLAM

pistachio COLOR, NUT, TREE

piste TRAIL

pistol COLT, GAT, GUN, ROD
  ~ pellets AMMO
  packing a ~ ARMED
  water ~ TOY

___ pistol CAP, WATER

pistole COIN

"Pistol Packin' ___" MAMA

pistol-packing ARMED

piston RAM

Pistons FIVE, TEAM
  ~ org. NBA

pit ABYSS, DENT, HOLE, SEED, STONE
  ~ oneself (against) PLAY
  bottomless ~ ABYSS
  cherry ~ STONE
  open ~ MINE

pit ___ BOSS, STOP

"Pit ___ the Pendulum, The" AND

"___ Pit, The" SNAKE

pitbull DOG
  ~ sound GNAR

pitch CAST, ERECT, GAME, HURL, KEY, LABOR, LEAN, LOB, REEL, ROLL, SELL, SLANT, SLOPE, TONE, TOSS
  ~ a tent ABIDE, CAMP, STAY

~ black UNLIT
~ detector EAR
~ in AID, HELP
~ indicator CLEF
~ path ARC
~ sensitivity EAR
~ source PINE, TAR
~ water BAIL
high in ~ ALT
lacking ~ ATONAL
low in ~ BASS
sales ~ LINE, TALK
slow ~ LOB
what suitors ~ WOO

pitch ___ PINE, PIPE, WOO

pitch ___-hitter ANO

pitch-black RAVEN

pitchblende ORE

pitch-dark JET, SABLE

pitched
  it may be ~ TENT, WOO

pitcher
  ~ achievement SAVE
  ~ asset ARM
  ~ dread HIT, HOMER
  ~ goal OUT, WIN
  ~ mound SLAB
  ~ of a sort ADMAN
  ~ part EAR, LIP
  ~ stat ERA
  ~ target MITT, PLATE
  ~ to the batter FOE
  big-mouthed ~ EWER
  face the ~ BAT
  facing the ~ ATBAT
  water ~ EWER

pitcher ___ PLANT

pitchers
  ~ want it low ERA
  like some ~ EARED

pitches
  sales ~ ADS

pitchfork
  ~ tooth TINE

pitchman
  ~ payoff SALE

___-pitch softball SLO

piteous SAD

pitfall SNAG, TRAP

pith CORE, ESSENCE, GIST, HEART, MEAT, SOUL
  ~ helmet HAT

Pithecanthropus
  ~ relative APE

pithecologist
  ~ study APE

pithy CRISP, TERSE
  ~ remark MOT
  ~ saying ADAGE
  short ~ expression GNOME

pitiful POOR, SAD

pitiless CRUEL, HARD, STERN

Pitman ISAAC
  ~ pupil STENO

Pitney, Gene
  ~ song of 1963 MECCA

pits
  in the ~ SAD
  the ~ NADIR

pit stop
  ~ item AIR, GAS, OIL, TIRE
  dromedary ~ OASIS

Pitt BRAD
  emulate ~ ORATE

pittance BIT, DOLE, MITE, PART, SOU
  a ~ in Paris SOU
  like a ~ MERE

Pittsburgh
  ~ product COAL, STEEL
  ~ river OHIO
  ~ st. PENN
  city north of ~ ERIE

Pittypat AUNT

pity ACHE, FEEL
  cry of ~ ALAS
  feel ~ ACHE

"pity this busy monster, manunkind" POEM

Pius POPE

pivot SLEW, SLUE, SPIN, TURN
  ballet ~ TOE
  turn on a ~ SLEW, SLUE

pivotal KEY, MAIN, POLAR
  ~ point TOE

pixel DOT

pixie ELF, GNOME, IMP

Pixie MOUSE

pixielike ELFIN

pixilated DAFT

Pizarro
  ~ capital LIMA
  ~ conquest PERU
  ~ foe INCA
  see also Spanish

pizazz CHIC, CLASS, DASH, ELAN, STYLE, VIM
  lacking ~ BLAH, DRAB

Piz Bernina ALP

pizza PIE
  ~ portion SLICE
  ~ topper ONION
  have a ~ EAT

pizzeria
  ~ appliance OVEN
  ~ implement PEEL
  ~ patron EATER
  "Do the Right Thing" ~ SALS

pizzicato NOTE

placard BILL, SIGN

placate CALM, PLEASE

place ESTATE, LAY, LIE, LIEU, ORIENT, PLANT, PUT, ROLE,

SCENE, SET, SITE, SPOT, STAGE, STEAD
  ~ on a pedestal ADORE
  ~ starter ANY, DIS, SOME
  at that ~, to a poet YON

place ___ CARD, MAT

place ___ (gamble) ABET

___ place (happen) TAKE

___ Place (Sundance's girlfriend) ETTA

"Place in the ___, A" SUN

placekicker
  ~ pride TOE
  ~ prop TEE

placement SITE

"___, Place or Steal" WIN

places
  change ~ MOVE
  in different ~ APART

place setting
  ~ base MAT
  ~ piece DISH, PLATE

"Places in the ___" HEART

Place Vendôme
  ~ city, in song PAREE

placid CALM, EVEN, MEEK, SERENE, STAID, TAME

Placid LAKE

Placido TENOR
  ~ piece ARIA

plagiarist FAKE

plagiarize CRIB, ROB, STEAL, TAKE

plague BAIT, BANE, FRET, IRK, PEEVE, RAG

"Plague, The"
  ~ locale ORAN

plagued
  ~ (by) BESET

plaid
  ~ wearers CLAN

___ plaid GLEN

plain BALD, BARE, CLEAR, DRY, HONEST, LEA, OPEN, RAW, SOBER
  ~ sailing EASY
  ~ speaking PROSE
  alluvial ~ DELTA
  dry ~ DESERT
  elevated ~ MESA
  grassy ~ LLANO
  in ~ view OPEN, OVERT
  lunar ~ MARE, SEA
  make ~ CLEAR, RAVEL, SHOW
  put in ~ sight SHOW
  treeless ~ LLANO

"___, Plain and Tall" SARAH

plainchant SONG

plain-dealing HONEST

___ Plaines, Ill. DES

Plain People AMISH

Plains
~ **animal** BISON
~ **dweller** UTE
~ **dwelling** TEPEE
~ **Indian** CREE, CROW, TETON
~ **roamers** BISON
~ **state** IOWA

___ **Plains** GREAT

plain-spoken CLEAR

plaint
pasture ~ MOO
pound ~ ARF
puss's ~ MEOW, MEW
Shakespearean ~ ALAS

plaintiff
be a ~ SUE

plaintive SAD

"___ plaisir!" AVEC

plait BIND, PLAT, TRESS

plan AGENDA, DREAM, IDEA, MAP, PATH
~ **(for)** ALLOW
~ **of action** AGENDA, SETUP
~ **portion** STEP
~ **secretly** PLOT
~ **staller** SNAG
come up with a ~ IDEATE
food ~ DIET
game ~ IDEA
meeting ~ AGENDA
not according to ~ AMISS
retirement ~ IRA
secret ~ PLOT
weight-reduction ~ DIET

___ **plan** GAME

"___ plan, a canal..." AMANA

plane EVEN, FILE, FLAT, LINER, TOOL, TREE
~ **alternative** TRAIN
~ **downer** ACE
~ **driver** PILOT
~ **locale** SKY
~ **reservation** SEAT
~ **seating choice** AISLE
~ **stabilizer** FIN
~ **starter** AERO, AIR, AQUA, TRI
Air France ~ SST
bring the ~ **in** LAND
British Airways ~ SST
crystal ~ FACE
fast ~ JET, SST
inclined ~ RAMP
incoming ~ **datum** ARR, ETA
kind of ~ PROP
left the ~ ALIT, LIT
on a ~ EVEN
pilotless ~ DRONE
rear of a ~ TAIL
remote-controlled ~ DRONE
WWII ~ ZERO

plane crash
~ **movie of 1993** ALIVE

planes
group of ~ FLEET
of ~ **and flying** AERO
using ~ AERIAL
word on many ~ AIR

planet EARTH, SPHERE
~ **to a poet** ORB
fifth-largest ~ EARTH
fourth ~ MARS
once around the ~ ORBIT
red ~ MARS
third ~ **from the sun** EARTH

planetarium
Chicago ~ ADLER

planetary
~ **lap** YEAR
~ **path** ARC, ORBIT

"Planet of the ___" APES

"Planet of the Apes"
~ **setting** EARTH

plangent LOUD

planimeter
~ **measurement** AREA

plank BEAM, SLAB
~ **starter** GANG
Aspen ~ SKI
ship ~ WALE
Stowe ~ SKI

planks
polish ~ SAND

plankton
~ **component** ALGA

"Plan 9 From Outer Space"
~ **alien** EROS

___ **planning** ESTATE

plans
have ~ MEAN
without ~ FREE

plant LAY, MILL, PUT, SEED, SET, SHOP, SOW
~ **anchor** ROOT
~ **firmly** SEAT
~ **fluid** SERUM
~ **in memory** ETCH
~ **leg** STEM
~ **life** FLORA
~ **malady** EDEMA
~ **oneself** ABIDE, STAY
~ **parasite** APHID
~ **part** AWN
~ **pests** LICE
~ **shoot** SPIRE
~ **sprout** SPEAR
~ **starter** EGG, SEED
~ **used in beer-making** HOP
~ **used in cosmetics** ALOE
~ **with fronds** FERN
amaryllis family ~ ALOE
aquatic ~ ALGA
aromatic ~ NARD, RUE
century ~ AGAVE, ALOE
chlorophyll ~ ALGA
climbing ~ IVY, LIANA, VINE
desert ~ AGAVE
dye-yielding ~ ANIL, HENNA
European flowering ~ ARUM
fiber ~ AGAVE
first-aid ~ ALOE
fleshy ~ ALOE
flowerless ~ FERN, MOSS
forage ~ ERS
future ~ SEED

grape ~ VINE
grasslike ~ SEDGE
healing ~ ALOE
heath ~ ERICA
licorice ~ ANISE
liliaceous ~ ALOE
marsh ~ REED, SEDGE
medicinal ~ ALOE
Mojave ~ AGAVE
mustard family ~ COLE, CRESS, KALE
nonflowering ~ MOSS
noxious ~ WEED
ocean ~ ALGA
office ~ FERN
one-celled ~ ALGA
palliative ~ ALOE
pesky ~ WEED
place to ~ BED
pod ~ PEA
poison ~ IVY
prickly ~ BRIAR, ROSE
primitive ~ ALGAE
pungent ~ ONION
purgative-yielding ~ ALOE
riverbank ~ SEDGE
rootless ~ ALGA
rushlike ~ SEDGE
salad ~ CRESS
salt-water ~ ALGA
seedless ~ FERN
sesame ~ TIL
soothing ~ ALOE
spiny ~ AGAVE, ALOE
tequila ~ AGAVE
terrarium ~ FERN
therapeutic ~ ALOE
twining ~ HOP
umbel family ~ ANISE
unwanted ~ WEED
water ~ ALGA
woodland ~ MOSS, TREE

plantain WEED

plantation ABODE, ESTATE, HOME, MANOR
fictional ~ TARA

planter's punch
~ **ingredient** RUM
~ **juice** LIME

planting BED
~ **medium** SOIL
~ **tool** HOE, RAKE, SPADE
garden ~ ROW

plants FLORA
carbonized ~ PEAT
care for ~ WATER
desert ~ CACTI
Polynesian ~ TIS
prickly ~ CACTI

plant-to-be SEED

plaque AWARD, PLATE

plash LAP

plasm
~ **starter** ECTO, ENDO

plaster COAT, DAUB
~ **mold** CAST
~ **of Paris** GESSO
~ **support** LATH

plastic FAKE, SHAM
~ **substitute** CASH
clear ~ SARAN
use ~ OWE

Plastic ___ Band ONO

plastics
~ **component** RESIN

plastron ARMOR, MAIL

plat LOT, MAP
~ **portion** ACRE

plate ARMOR, DISH, TRAY
~ **cleaner, often** UMP
~ **of glass** PANE
~ **scraping** ORT
come to the ~ BAT
cross the ~ SCORE
fashion ~ DUDE
fish ~ SCALE
home ~ BASE
license ~ TAG
pass the ~ BEG
pie ~ PAN

___ **plate** HOME, HOT, TIN

plateau TABLE
~ **cousin** MESA

___**-plate special** BLUE

platform REST, SHOE, STAND, TABLE
links ~ TEE
narrow ~ RISER
performer's ~ STAGE
raised ~ ALTAR, DAIS
stage ~ RISER
warehouse ~ SKID

platform ___ BED

Plath, Sylvia POET
~ **title** ARIEL
see also poet

plating SHEET

platinum COLOR, METAL

"Platinum Blonde"
~ **director** CAPRA

platitude ADAGE, MORAL, SAW, TAG

platitudinous BANAL, STALE, TIRED, TRITE

Plato
~ **dialogue** ION
~ **hangout** STOA
subject of ~'s Symposium EROS
see also Greek

platoon UNIT
~ **mems.** GIS

"Platoon"
~ **actor** SHEEN
~ **director** STONE
~ **locale** NAM
~ **studio** ORION

platter DISC, DISH, PLATE, TRAY

Platte River
~ **tribe, once** OTO, OTOE

platters LPS
  ~ **now** CDS

platy PET

plaudits ECLAT

plausible SANE

Plautus ROMAN
  ~ **work** PLAY

play ACT, GAME, ROOM, SPACE, TOY
  ~ **a child's game** HIDE
  ~ **again** RERUN
  ~ **a part** ACT, ENACT
  ~ **area** STAGE, YARD
  ~ **at full volume** BLAST
  ~ **by ear** ADLIB
  ~ **caller** UMP
  ~ **division** ACT, SCENE
  ~ **dumb, perhaps** ACT
  ~ **ender** BILL, GIRL, LET, LIST, MATE, OFF, PEN, ROOM, SUIT, TIME
  ~ **favorites** SIDE
  ~ **for a fool** USE
  ~ **for the NHL** SKATE
  ~ **for time** STALL
  ~ **hero** SAVE
  ~ **horseshoes** TOSS
  ~ **host** EMCEE, TREAT
  ~ **interlocutor** ASK
  ~ **in the sandbox** DIG
  ~ **in the water** BATHE, WADE
  ~ **it by ear** ADLIB
  ~ **it for all it's worth** HAM
  ~ **matchmaker** SETUP
  ~ **on the heartstrings** MOVE
  ~ **on words** PUN
  ~ **part** ACT, ACTI
  ~ **place** SET
  ~ **poker** BET
  ~ **quoits** TOSS
  ~ **reveille** ROUSE
  ~ **roster** CAST
  ~ **start** ACTI
  ~ **starter** END, GUN, HORSE, INTER, OUT, UNDER
  ~ **stoolie** BLAB, RATON, SING
  ~ **the fool** AMUSE
  ~ **the ham** EMOTE
  ~ **the horn** TOOT
  ~ **the lottery** BET
  ~ **the market** TRADE
  ~ **the ponies** BET, GAME
  ~ **the siren** LURE
  ~ **the slots** BET
  ~ **the wheel** GAME
  ~ **thing** PROP
  ~ **truant** EVADE
  ~ **up** STRESS
  ~ **with fire** RISK
  ~ **written in Czech** RUR
  be in a ~ ACT
  bring into ~ EXERT, USE
  canasta ~ MELD
  chance to ~ TURN
  child's ~ EASY
  football ~ PASS, RUN
  foul ~ EVIL, HARM
  how to ~ **solitaire** ALONE
  in ~**, as a ball** LIVE
  kind of ~ DRAMA, SKIT
  make a ~ **for** GRAB

morality ~ DRAMA
pay to ~ ANTE
put in ~ SERVE
robot ~ RUR
serious ~ DRAMA
short ~ ACT, SKIT
still in ~ ALIVE
where the deer and the antelope ~ RANGE

play ___ (cooperate) ALONG, BALL

play ___ (finish) OUT

play ___ and loose FAST

___ play FAIR, MEDAL

___-play ROLE

"Play ___" TIME

playact EMOTE

playacting POSE

playbill
  ~ **listing** CAST, ROLE
  ~ **paragraph** BIO

playboy CAD, RAKE, ROUE

play by ___ EAR

played
  ~ **out** ALLIN, DONE, SPENT, TIRED

player ACTOR
  ~ **intermediary** AGENT, REP
  excellent ~ ACE
  featured ~ LEAD
  football ~ END
  jazz ~ CAT
  main ~ STAR
  minor ~ COG, EXTRA
  paid ~ PRO
  record ~ STEREO
  role ~ ACTOR
  seeded ~**'s perk** BYE

player ___ PIANO

___ player TAPE, TEAM

players CAST
  first-string ~ ATEAM
  set of ~ TEAM

play fast and ___ LOOSE

play for ___ TIME

playful GAY
  ~ **animal** OTTER, SEAL
  ~ **trick** ANTIC

playground
  ~ **apparatus** SLIDE
  ~ **game** TAG

playhouses
  Greek ~ ODEA

playing ___ CARD

playing card ACE, HEART, SPADE, TREY

___-playing record LONG

"Play It ___ Lays" ASIT

"Play It ___, Sam" AGAIN

"Play It Again, ___" SAM

"Play It Again, Sam"
  ~ **director** ROSS
  ~ **star** ALLEN

play it by ___ EAR

play it close to the ___ VEST

"Play it, Sam!"
  ~ **speaker** ILSA

playmate PAL
  antelope's ~ DEER
  nursery ~ TOT

"Play Misty ___ Me" FOR

playoff
  ~ **setting** ARENA

playoffs
  spring ~ **org.** NBA

playpen
  ~ **amusement** TOY

plaything TOY

"Play Time"
  ~ **actor** TATI
  ~ **author** TATI
  ~ **director** TATI

playwright
  ~ **award** OBIE, TONY
  ~ **device** ASIDE
  ~ **offering** DRAMA
  American ~ ODETS
  existentialist ~ GENET
  French ~ GENET
  Norwegian ~ IBSEN
  start for a ~ ACTI

plaza AREA, MALL

Plaza
  the ~ HOTEL

plea CRY, SUIT
  feline ~ MEOW, MEW
  party thrower's ~ RSVP
  sea ~ SOS

plead ASK, BEG, CRY, PRAY
  ~ **(with)** ARGUE

pleasant GOOD, MILD, NICE, SUAVE, SWEET
  ~ **odor** AROMA
  ~ **song** AIR, LILT
  ~ **surprise** TREAT

pleasantries
  exchange ~ CHAT

pleasantry MOT

please AMUSE, ELATE, LIKE, SUIT
  ~ **refrain** DONT

"Please ___ Eat the Daisies" DONT

pleased GLAD
  ~ **as Punch** ELATED
  ~ **expression** GRIN
  ~ **sounds** AHS
  not ~ SORE

"Please Don't ___ the Daisies" EAT

"Pleased to ___ you" MEET

pleaser
  child ~ TOY

crowd ~ PARADE

pleasing NICE, SWEET

pleasure PLAY
  ~ **craft** SLOOP
  exclamation of ~ WOW
  express ~ AAH
  expressions of ~ AHS
  give ~ **to** AMUSE
  show ~ GRIN, SMILE
  sigh of ~ AAH
  special ~ TREAT
  take ~ **in** ADORE, BASK, LIKE, SAVOR

"Pleasure of ___ Company, The" HIS

pleat
  ~ **alternative** SLIT

plebe CADET
  ~ **sch.** USNA
  last year's ~ SOPH

plebeian MEAN

plebes
  important word for ~ SIR

plebiscite VOTE

pledge ASSERT, ATTEST, AVOW, OATH, SAY, TOAST
  ~ **one's word** AGREE

Pledge of Allegiance
  ~ **last word** ALL

Pleiades
  ~ **father** ATLAS
  ~ **number** SEVEN
  ~ **pursuer** ORION
  one of the ~ STAR

Pleistocene EPOCH
  ~ **feature** ICE

plenary TOTAL

plenitude STORE

plentiful AMPLE, RICH
  more than ~ RIFE
  not ~ SPARSE

plenty ALOT, AMPLE, DUE, EASE, HEAP, LOTS, PILE, TONS
  ~ **old-style** ENOW
  in ~ **of time** EARLY
  Roman goddess of ~ OPS

"Plenty"
  ~ **playwright** HARE

"___ Plenty o' Nuthin'" IGOT

plenum DIET

plethora GLUT, OCEAN, SEA, STORE

plexus RETE

___ plexus SOLAR

pliant LITHE

___-plié DEMI

pliers TOOL

plight CASE, HOLE, JAM, LOT, MESS, OATH
  ~ **light** FLARE

plimsoll SHOE

plinth BASE, FOOT, REST

Pliny ROMAN
   see also Latin

Pliny the ___ ELDER

Pliny the Younger ORATOR
   where ~ served SENATE

plod DRAG, MOVE, STEP, TREAD, TREK
   ~ along LABOR, SLOG

plodding SLOW

plop DROP, SIT, THUD

plot ANGLE, BED, CABAL, LOT, MAP, PLAN, PLAT, RUSE
   ~ measure ACRE
   ~ twist IRONY
   common ~ element LOVE
   garden ~ BED

plot ___ LINE

Plotinus ROMAN

plottage ACRES, AREA

plotter
   literary ~ IAGO

plotters CABAL

plover BIRD

plow DRESS, TILL
   ~ part SOLE
   ~ puller MULE
   ~ pullers OXEN
   ~ the waves SAIL
   ~ (through) SLOG, WADE
   steel ~ inventor DEERE

plow ___ (overwhelm) UNDER

plow ___ (ram) INTO

plowhorses
   like ~ SHOD

ploy ART, MOVE, RUSE, TRAP
   advertising ~ HYPE
   legal ~ ALIBI

pluck GRIT, HEART, METAL, NERVE, SAND
   ~ up courage DARE

plucky GAME

plug HACK, HORSE, JADE, JAM, LID, LURE, NAG, SEAL, TAP, WAD
   ~ away at LABOR, PEG, PLOD
   ~ ender OLA
   ~ partner PLAY
   ~ place EAR
   ~ up CLOG, STEM
   kind of electrical ~ MALE
   pull the ~ on STOP

plug ___ (connect) INTO

___ plug EAR

plugs ADS

plum COLOR, TREE
   wild ~ SLOE

plumage DRESS

plumb ERECT, LEAD, TRUE
   ~ bob LEAD

~ crazy LOCO
   off ~ ATILT

plumb ___ BOB, LINE

Plumb EVE

plumbago LEAD

plumber
   ~ concern DRIP, LEAK
   ~ connection ELL
   ~ joint TEE
   ~ supply PIPE
   ~ tool SNAKE

plumbum LEAD

plume CREST, PEN
   ~ oneself BRAG
   ~ source EGRET
   helmet ~ CREST
   nom de ~ ALIAS, NAME

Plummer AMANDA

plummet DROP, LEAD, SINK

plump BIG, FAT, LARGE, OBESE, PLOP

Plum, Professor
   ~ game CLUE

plum pudding
   ~ ingredient SUET

plunder HAUL, LOOT, RAID, RIFLE, ROB, SACK, STEAL, STRIP, SWAG, TAKE, WASTE

plunge DIP, DROP, PLOW
   take the ~ DARE, START, WED

plunk PLOP

plural
   ~ pronoun THESE, THOSE
   ~ verb ARE, HAVE

plurality
   not quite a ~ HALF

pluralizer ESS

plus ALSO, AND, ASSET, EXTRA, TOO
   ~ in Spanish MAS
   ~ starter NON

plus ___ SIGN

plush ORNATE, PILE, POSH

Plutarch
   ~ biographical subject CATO
   see also Greek

Pluto ORB

plutocrat NABOB, NOB
   ~ acres ESTATE

plutocrats
   like ~ RICH

plutonium METAL

pluvial RAINY

pluviometer
   ~ input RAIN

pluviometers
   what ~ measure RAIN

pluvious RAINY

ply RUN
   ~ a needle SEW
   ~ one's trade LABOR
   ~ the oars ROW

___-ply BIAS, THREE, TWO

plying
   ~ away ATIT

Plymouth CITY, PORT

Plymouth Rock HEN

Plympton BILL

plywood
   ~ sheet PANEL

Pm ELEM
   61 for ~ ATNO

PM
   early ~ AFT
   when AM meets ~ NOON

pneuma LIFE, SOUL

"Pnin"
   ~ shelf mate ADA

Po ELEM
   ~ basin city MILAN
   ~ locale ITALY
   84 for ~ ATNO

PO
   ~ competitor UPS
   ~ designation RFD
   ~ directive COD
   ~ itinerary RTE
   branch ~ STA
   busy mo. at the ~ DEC

poach BOIL, STEAL

poached egg
   ~ foundation TOAST

Pocahontas
   ~ shelter TEPEE
   ~ transport CANOE

Pocatello
   ~ locale IDAHO
   ~ st. IDA

pocket EARN, GET, MAKE, NET, NIP, ROB, STEAL, TAKE
   ~ billiards POOL
   ~ contents LINT
   ~ money CENT, COIN, DIME
   ~ protector FLAP
   ~ watch repository VEST
   bread with a ~ PITA
   out of ~ NEEDY

pocket ___ MOUSE, VETO

___ pocket AIR, SIDE

___-pocket VEST

pocketbook BAG

"pocket full of ___, A" RYE

"Pocketful of Miracles"
   ~ director CAPRA
   Glenn's ~ costar BETTE

Pocono Mountains
   ~ st. PENN

Poconos RANGE

poculiform
   ~ item CUP

pod CASE, SHELL, SKIN
   ~ contents SEED
   ~ dweller PEA
   ~ member SEAL
   ~ starter MEGA, OCTO, TRI
   stew ~ OKRA

podiatrist
   ~ concern ARCH, FOOT, TOE

podium DAIS, FOOT, STAND
   take the ~ ORATE

___ podrida OLLA

Poe POET
   ~ family name USHER
   ~ Morgue RUE
   ~ night visitor RAVEN
   emulate ~'s raven RAP
   like a ~ tale EERIE, EERY
   see also poet

poem ODE, PSALM
   ~ part LINE, STAVE
   Christmas ~ opener TWAS
   French narrative ~ LAI
   liturgical ~ PSALM
   long ~ EPIC
   lyric ~ ODE
   medieval ~ LAI
   minstrel's ~ LAY

___ poem TONE

"Poema del Cid" EPIC

poet BARD, BENET, CRANE, DANTE, DONNE, ELIOT, GRAY, HOMER, HOOD, HUNT, LEAR, MOORE, NASH, OMAR, OVID, POE, POPE, READ, RILEY, TATE
   ~ concern METER
   ~ ender ASTER, ESS
   ~ inspiration MUSE
   ~ Muse ERATO
   above, to a ~ OER
   accentual rhythm for a
     ~ METER
   adverb for a ~ ANEAR, EEN, EER, ENOW, NEER, OER, OFT, YON
   again and again, to a ~ OFT
   air, to a ~ ETHER
   ajar, to a ~ OPE
   all the time, to a ~ EER
   almost, to a ~ ANEAR
   always, to a ~ EER
   American ~ TATE
   around, to a ~ ANEAR
   at hand, to a ~ ANEAR
   at no time, to a ~ NEER
   atop, to a ~ OER
   at that place, to a ~ YON
   beat for a ~ METER
   before, to a ~ ERE
   below, to a ~ NEATH
   black, to a ~ EBON
   circle, to a ~ ORB
   close by, to a ~ ANEAR
   completed, to a ~ OER
   concealed by, to a ~ NEATH
   concern for a ~ METER
   concluded, to a ~ OER
   constantly, to a ~ EER

contraction for a ~ EEN, EER, NEATH, NEER, OER, TIS, TWAS
covered by, to a ~ NEATH
dark, to a ~ EBON
done, to a ~ OER
dusk, to a ~ EEN
Earth, to a ~ ORB
encircle, to a ~ ORB
enclose, to a ~ ORB
ended, to a ~ OER
eternally, to a ~ EER
evening, to a ~ EEN
expose, to a ~ OPE
eye, to a ~ ORB
foot for a ~ IAMB
frequently, to a ~ OFT
heavenly body, to a ~ ORB
hereabout, to a ~ ANEAR
Hoosier ~ RILEY
humorous ~ NASH
immediate, to a ~ ANEAR
imminent, to a ~ ANEAR
inky, to a ~ EBON
in proximity, to a ~ ANEAR
inspiration for a ~ ERATO, MUSE
in the vicinity, to a ~ ANEAR
Ireland, to a ~ ERIN
jet, to a ~ EBON
lower than, to a ~ NEATH
many times, to a ~ OFT
never, to a ~ NEER
nighttime, to a ~ EEN
not at all, to a ~ NEER
not ever, to a ~ NEER
not far off, to a ~ ANEAR
not shut, to a ~ OPE
on top of, to a ~ OER
origin, to a ~ FONT
over there, to a ~ YON
over, to a ~ OER
Persian ~ OMAR
plaint for a ~ ALAS
planet, to a ~ ORB
preposition for a ~ ERE, NEATH, OER
pugilistic ~ ALI
range of activity, to a ~ ORB
repeatedly, to a ~ OFT
reveal, to a ~ OPE
rhythmic pattern for a ~ METER
Roman ~ OVID
ship, to a ~ KEEL
sky, to a ~ ETHER
source, to a ~ FONT
space, to a ~ ETHER
spring, to a ~ FONT
sufficient to a ~ ENOW
the heavens, to a ~ ETHER
time after time, to a ~ OFT
twilight, to a ~ EEN
unclose, to a ~ OPE
uncover, to a ~ OPE
under, to a ~ NEATH
unfold, to a ~ OPE
unit for a ~ FOOT, IAMB
unlock, to a ~ OPE
verb for a ~ OPE
wellspring, to a ~ FONT
yet, to a ~ EEN

"___ Poetica" ARS

poetry ART
classic ~ EPOS
not ~ PROSE
piece of ~ LINE
rhythmic pattern in ~ METER

___ Poets LAKE

pogo stick TOY

pogs FAD

poi
~ base TARO
~ party LUAU

poignant ACUTE, DEEP, KEEN

point AIM, APEX, BARB, CAPE, DOT, REFER
~ at the target AIM
~ in the right direction ORIENT
~ in time DATE, DAY
~ of concern ISSUE
~ of departure BASE, GATE
~ of information ITEM
~ of no return, tennis-wise ACE
~ of perfection ACME
~ of view ANGLE, SIDE
~ out CITE, NOTE, REFER, SHOW
~ to ARGUE, BODE
~ up STRESS
at any ~ EVER
at that ~ THEN
at this ~ HERE
belabor a ~ ARGUE
blue ~ CAT
cardinal ~ EAST, WEST
center ~ MEAN
centering ~ NODE
come to a ~ TAPER
compass ~ ENE, ESE, NNE, NNW, SSE, SSW, WNW, WSW
decimal ~ DOT
earth's turning ~ AXIS
essential ~ MEAT
examine point by ~ PORE
final ~ END
focal ~ NODE, POLE
furthest ~ END
game ~ SCORE
get the ~ SEE
high ~ ACME, APEX, CREST, PEAK, TOP
improve a ~ HONE
joining ~ SEAM
knotty ~ POSER
leaf's starting ~ NODE
lowest ~ EBB, NADIR
main ~ GIST
make a ~ SCORE
make a great ~ ACE
make a special ~ of STRESS
moot ~ ISSUE
needle ~ ENE, ESE, NNE, NNW, SSE, SSW, WNW, WSW
pivotal ~ TOE
remotest ~ DEEP
seal ~ CAT
starting ~ BASE, BASIS
sticking ~ CRAW
stopping ~ LIMIT
strong ~ ASSET
to the ~ APT, CRISP, TERSE

to this ~ YET
turning ~ AXIS, AXLE, HEAD
utensil ~ TINE
writer's ~ NIB
WWII turning ~ DDAY

point ___ MAN

___ point DEW, SET, SORE

___ Point WEST

pointed ACUTE, TART
~ as wit ACID
~ part BARB
~ roof SPIRE
~ tool AWL
~ weapon DART

pointedness EDGE

pointer ARROW, CLUE, DOG, LEAD, NEEDLE, SIGN, TIP
compass ~ NEEDLE
vane ~ ARROW

Pointer Sisters
one of the ~ ANITA

pointillism
~ detail DOT

___-point landing THREE

pointless IDLE, INANE, MAD

points
connect ~ on a graph PLOT
score fewer ~ LOSE
six ~ in tennis SET

pointy shoes
~ wearer ELF

Poirot
~ whodunit locale NILE

poise ASSET, CALM, EASE, TACT

poised CALM, SEDATE, SERENE

poison BANE, TAINT
~ plant IVY
another's ~ MEAT

poison ___ IVY, OAK, PEN, PILL

poison ivy
~ symptom ITCH, RASH

poisonous BAD, EVIL
~ letters DDT
~ snake ADDER, ASP, COBRA

Poitiers
~ padre ABBE
see also French

poke AROUSE, DIG, GOAD, JAB, LAG, MOVE, PROD, SACK
~ along DRAG
~ around ROOT
~ around for SEEK
~ fun at KID, RAG, RIB, TEASE, TWIT
~ in a way ELBOW
~ one's nose where it doesn't belong PRY
~ sharply JAB
~ starter COW, SLOW
pig in a ~ BET

"Poke ___ Annie" SALAD

poker GAME
~ action CALL, RAISE
~ bullet ACE
~ card ACE, NINE, TREY
~ coin CHIP
~ command DEAL
~ declaration IMIN
~ hand PAIR
~ holding HAND
~ payment ANTE, STAKE
~ stake BET
~ unit CARD, HAND
~ winnings POT
kind of ~ DRAW, STUD
like some ~ hands PAT
meet a ~ bet SEE

poker ___ FACE

___ poker DRAW, LIARS, STUD

poker chip
~ maybe ANTE

poker face
fail to keep a ~ REACT

poker-faced STOIC

Poker Flat
~ chronicler HARTE

pokey PEN, SLOW, STIR

pol
~ concern IMAGE, VOTE
~ often ORATOR

pol.
~ contributor PAC
~ party DEM, REP

Pol ___ POT

Pol.
neighbor of ~ GER

Poland
~ export COAL

Poland China HOG
~ comment OINK
~ home PEN, STY

Poland/Germany
~ divider ODER

Polanski ROMAN

Polanski, Roman
~ film of 1979 TESS
~ film, with "The" TENANT

polar
~ cap ICE
~ light AURORA
~ man SANTA

polar ___ AXIS, BEAR, CAP

polar bear
~ country ALASKA

Polaris STAR

Polaroid
~ inventor LAND
~ product CAMERA, LENS

pole AXIS, BAR, BEAM, BEAN, END, MAST, POST, ROD, STAVE
~ along SKI
~ ender AXE, CAT, STAR
~ starter BEAN, TAD
~ vault EVENT, LEAP

angler's ~ ROD
antenna ~ MAST
clothes ~ TREE
Eskimo's ~ TOTEM
fishing ~ ROD
kind of ~ TOTEM
ship's ~ BOOM, MAST, SPAR

pole ___ BEAN, LAMP

___ pole SKI, TOTEM

Pole SLAV

poleax HACK, PIKE

poles
  ~ connector AXIS

poleyn ARMOR

poli ___ SCI

police LAW
  ~ blotter entry AKA, ALIAS
  ~ bulletin ALERT, APB
  ~ detention ARREST
  ~ hdqrs. STA
  ~ officer COP
  ~ operation RAID, STING
  ~ patrol BEAT
  ~ slangily HEAT
  ~ target GANG
  ~ team SWAT
  ecol. ~ EPA
  name on a ~ blotter DOE

police ___ DOG, STATE

police car
  ~ device SIREN

police drama
  ~ with "The" FBI

police movie
  ~ highlight CHASE

policy LINE, STAND
  ~ person AGENT
  ~ postscript RIDER
  determined ~ STAND

polio vaccine
  ~ developer SABIN, SALK

polish AMEND, CHIC, CLEAN, EDIT, EMEND, POISE, SHEEN, SHINE, STYLE, TACT, TASTE
  ~ off EAT
  ~ partner SPIT
  ~ planks SAND
  ~ prose EDIT
  like some nail ~ CLEAR
  nail ~ ENAMEL

polish ___ (finish) OFF

___ polish NAIL

___-polish APPLE

polished ADEPT, FINE, SLEEK, SUAVE

polisher
  manuscript ~ EDITOR

Polish/German
  ~ border river ODER

polishing
  ~ agent EMERY

polite SUAVE, SWEET
  ~ address MAAM, MADAM
  ~ word PLEASE, SIR

politeness TACT, TASTE

politesse TASTE

politic
  body ~ STATE

political
  ~ abbr. DEM, REP, SEN
  ~ alliance BLOC
  ~ battlefield ARENA
  ~ bloc LABOR
  ~ body UNION
  ~ campaign RACE
  ~ division LAND, STATE, WARD
  ~ faction CADRE
  ~ football ISSUE
  ~ party offering SLATE
  ~ ploy SMEAR
  ~ position STAND
  ~ principles DOGMA
  ~ scandal suffix GATE

politics
  ~ starter GEO

polka DANCE

polka ___ DOT

poll DOME, ELECT, VOTE
  ~ ender STER
  ~ finding TREND

___ poll EXIT

pollack
  ~ cousin COD

Pollack
  ~ pieces ART

polled BALD

pollen
  ~ grain SPORE
  ~ spreader BEE

Pollin ABE

pollinator BEE

pollock
  ~ kin COD

polloi
  hoi ~ MOB

pollute HARM, TAINT

polluted BAD
  not ~ PURE

pollution BANE, DIRT, TAINT
  ~ control org. EPA
  air ~ SMOG
  ear ~ BLARE, NOISE

Pollux STAR
  ~ mother LEDA
  ~ to Castor TWIN
  ~ to Leda SON

Polly ADLER, AUNT
  ~ pad CAGE
  ~ to Tom AUNT

polo GAME
  ~ participant HORSE
  water ~ GAME

___ polo WATER

Polo Grounds
  ~ star OTT

Polo, Marco
  where ~ traveled ASIA, ORIENT

polonaise DANCE

polonium METAL

Polonius
  ~ hiding place ARRAS

poltergeists
  like ~ EERIE, EERY

poly
  ~ ender ESTER, MATH

poly ___ SCI

polybasite ORE

polychrome
  ~ parrot MACAW

polygon
  ~ corner ANGLE

polygraph
  ~ flunker LIAR
  challenge the ~ LIE

Polyhymnia MUSE
  ~ domain SONG
  ~ sister CLIO, ERATO

polymeric
  ~ (prefix) PARA

polymerization
  ~ candidate ESTER

Polynesia
  part of ~ ISLE

Polynesian MAORI
  ~ dance HULA
  ~ farewell ALOHA
  ~ food POI
  ~ party LUAU
  ~ plants TIS
  ~ porch LANAI
  ~ tongue MAORI
  ~ tuber TARO
  see also Hawaiian

Polynices
  ~ to Oedipus SON

___ Polytechnique ECOLE

pomade CREAM, OIL

pomatum CREAM

pomegranate TREE

Pomeranian DOG, PET, TOY

pomme de ___ TERRE

pommel BANG, BEAT, PELT, SMITE
  ~ horse EVENT

pommel ___ HORSE

pomp ECLAT, SHOW

Pompadour MME

"Pomp and Circumstance"
  ~ composer ELGAR

Pompeii
  ~ courts ATRIA

~ covering ASH
~ heroine IONE
~ undoing LAVA

Pompey ROMAN
  ~ to Caesar ENEMY, FOE

pompom
  place for a ~ TAM

pompous BIG, VAIN
  ~ one ASS

Ponce de ___ LEON

Ponch
  ~ on "CHiPs" ERIK

poncho CAPE, WRAP
  ~ relative SERAPE

pond LAKE, MERE, POOL
  ~ covering ALGAE
  ~ denizen EFT
  ~ fish CARP
  ~ floater PAD
  ~ maker DAM
  ~ organism ALGA
  ~ sight LILY
  big ~ OCEAN, SEA

___ pond LILY, SOLAR

ponder IDEATE, MUSE, PORE

ponderosa PINE

Ponderosa RANCH
  ~ brother ADAM, JOE
  ~ pop BEN
  Ben of the ~ LORNE

ponderous BIG, FAT, LARGE, SLOW, SOBER

___ pone CORN

Pong
  ~ producer ATARI

pongid APE

ponies
  play the ~ BET, GAME

Pons LILY
  ~ specialty ARIA, OPERA

Ponselle ROSA
  ~ role AIDA

Pontchartrain LAKE

Ponte Vecchio
  ~ river ARNO

Pontiac AUTO, CAR
  former ~ GTO

Pontiac Silverdome
  ~ player LION

Ponti, Carlo
  ~ spouse LOREN

pontificate ORATE, RANT, TALK

pontoon RAFT

pony ANIMAL, CRIB, DANCE, HORSE, NAG, PET, RACER, TROT
  ~ reply SNORT
  ~ up ANTE, PAY
  cow ~ NAG
  frat ~ CRIB
  piebald ~ PINTO
  Shetland ~ HORSE

___ pony
spotted ~ PAINT
see also horse

___ pony COW, POLO

"___ Pony, The" RED

Pony Express
~ load MAIL

"Pony Express ___" RIDER

Ponzi
~ scheme SCAM

pooch DOG
see also dog

poodle DOG
~ size TOY

Pooh BEAR
~ creator MILNE
pal of ~ OWL, ROO

Pooh-___ BAH

pool GAME, LAKE, MELD, MERE, POND, UNITE
~ accessory RACK, SLIDE
~ adjunct CUE
~ battle MEET
~ chemical ACID
~ distance LAP
~ division LANE
~ maneuver CAROM
~ place HALL
~ problem ALGAE
~ shot CAROM
~ worker STENO
enjoy a ~ SWIM
item in a ~ GENE
length of a ~ LAP
mountain ~ TARN
open-air ~ LIDO
use the ~ SWIM

pool ___ TABLE

___ pool CAR, GENE, MOTOR, TIDAL

poolside
~ area PATIO
lie ~ BASK

pool table
~ covering FELT

poop DATA, DOPE, INFO, SCOOP, STERN
~ out TIRE

"___ Poo Pah Doo" OOH

pooped ALLIN, BEAT, SPENT, TIRED

___ pooped to pop TOO

pooper
party ~ BORE

poor BAD, MEAN, NEEDY, VILE
~ as a church mouse NEEDY
~ boy HERO
~ grade DEE
~ lot DOOM
use ~ judgment ERR

poor box
~ contents ALMS

Poor Clare NUN

"poor dog"
what the ~ had NONE

___ poor example SETA

poorhouse
in the ~ NEEDY

"Poor Little ___ Girl" RICH

"Poor Little Rich ___" GIRL

poorly BAD, ILL

"Poor Richard's Almanack"
~ feature ADAGE

"___ poor Yorick!" ALAS

pop BANG, COLA, DAD, PAPA, SNAP, SODA
~ a question ASK
~ container CAN
~ ender CORN, GUN, OVER, TOP
~ hero IDOL
~ partner MOM, SNAP
~ the cork OPEN
~ tune SONG
~ up ARISE, EMERGE, RISE
a ~ APIECE, EACH, PER
dropped ~ ERROR
soda ~ COLA

pop ___ ART, WINE

pop-___ TOP

___ pop SODA

Pop-___ TART

popcorn
~ holder TUB
~ topper SALT

pope MALE, RANK
WWII ~ PIUS

Pope
~ calendar ORDO
~ medium ESSAY
~ rite MASS
~ teachings DOGMA
~ topper TIARA
~ who crowned Charlemagne LEO
~ work ESSAY

Pope, Alexander POET
see also poet

popes
name of six ~ PAUL
name of thirteen ~ LEO
name of twelve ~ PIUS

Popeye GOB, SALT, TAR
~ affirmative AYE
~ after eating spinach HERO
~ girlfriend OLIVE
~ greeting AHOY
~ prop PIPE
~ to Pipeye UNCLE
~ verb YAM

pop fly
~ path ARC

popgun TOY

popinjay BEAU, DUDE

Popish Plot
~ fabricator OATES

Popkin LEO

poplar TREE
~ cousin ASPEN
Southwestern ~ ALAMO

"Poplars"
~ painter MONET

Popocatepetl
~ flow LAVA

Poppaea
~ husband NERO

___-popping EYE

poppy COLOR, SEED

poppycock POOH, ROT, TRASH

pops DAD, PAPA, PAS

Popsicle ICE

pop-top
~ beverage COLA

populace MOB

popular HOT
~ classic OLDIE
be ~ REIGN

populate SETTLE

populated
thinly ~ SPARSE

population SIZE
like a city's ~ DENSE

___ population growth ZERO

"Populus"
~ tree ALAMO

porcelain CLAY

porch
~ adjunct STEP
~ fence RAIL
Hellenic ~ STOA
Polynesian ~ LANAI

porcine
~ home PEN, STY
~ meal SLOP
~ parent BOAR, SOW
~ sound OINK

porcupine ANIMAL

pore HOLE
~ over CON, EYE, READ

Porgy
~ love BESS

"Porgy and ___" BESS

"Porgy and Bess" OPERA

Porgy/Bess
~ link AND

pork MEAT
~ cut LOIN
~ fat LARD
~ order CHOP

"Pork ___ Hill" CHOP

porker HOG
~ hangout PEN, STY

porkpie HAT
~ material FELT

Porky Pig BOAR
~ word OINK

porous OPEN

porpoise ANIMAL

porridge PAP
~ portion MESS

porringer DISH

port HAVEN, LEFT, WINE
~ ender ABLE, AGE, HOLE, SIDE
~ in a storm HOME
~ near Casablanca RABAT
~ on the Ijsselmeer EDAM
~ on the Shatt-al-Arab BASRA
~ side LEFT
~ starter AIR, CAR, JET, PASS, RAP, SEA, SPACE, TELE
~ when sailing north WEST
~ when sailing south EAST
Algerian ~ ORAN
ancient Rome's ~ OSTIA
Arabian Peninsula ~ ADEN
Baltic ~ RIGA
Black Sea ~ ODESSA
Brazilian ~ NATAL, RIO
come into ~ LAND
Crimean ~ YALTA
cruise ~ RIO
Galilee ~ ACRE
home ~ BASE
Honshu ~ ITO, OSAKA
Israeli ~ ACRE
Italian ~ GENOA
leave ~ SAIL
Ligurian Sea ~ GENOA
Mediterranean ~ NICE, ORAN
Mideast ~ ADEN
North African ~ ORAN
not in ~ ASEA, ATSEA
Skagerrak ~ OSLO
South American ~ RIO
South Pacific ~ APIA
Ukrainian ~ ODESSA
Upolu ~ APIA
West African ~ DAKAR

Port ___ SAID

Port. LANG

portable
~ bed COT
~ dwelling TENT, TEPEE

portage CART, LUG, TOTE
~ item CANOE

portal DOOR, GATE

Port-au-Prince
~ location HAITI

portend BODE, MEAN

portent OMEN, SIGN

portentous DIRE, UGLY

porter
~ cousin ALE, BEER

Porter COLE

Porter, Cole
~ alma mater YALE
~ hometown PERU

~ in college ELI
~ musical heroine KATE
~ regretful miss OTIS
~ song PAREE

porterhouse STEAK
~ alternative TBONE

portfolio
~ item ASSET
~ option IRA

Porthos
~ partner ATHOS
~ weapon EPEE

portico ARCADE, STOA

Portinari, Beatrice
~ admirer DANTE

"___ port in a storm" ANY

portion CUT, FATE, LOT, SHARE,
SLICE, SOME
equitable ~ SHARE

Portland
~ st. ORE
~ state MAINE
~ time zone EST, PDT, PST

Portland ___ Blazers TRAIL

Portland cement
~ ingredient SHALE

portly BIG, FAT, LARGE, OBESE

portmanteau BAG

"Portnoy's Complaint"
~ author ROTH

port of ___ CALL, ENTRY

Port-of-___, Trinidad SPAIN

Portoferraio
~ island ELBA

portrait ART, IMAGE
~ medium OIL
~ starter SELF
do a ~ PAINT
have a ~ done POSE, SIT

___-portrait SELF

portraitist
Dutch ~ HALS

**"Portrait of the Artist ___ Young
Man, A"** ASA

**"Portrait of the Artist as a
Young ___, A"** MAN

portray DRAW, ENACT, PLAY

portrayal IMAGE, ROLE

ports
between ~ ASEA, ATSEA

Portugal
~ locale IBERIA
~ neighbor SPAIN

Portuguese
~ title DOM, DONA
former ~ colony GOA

Portuguese ___ dog WATER

posada INN

pose ASK, MODEL, SIT
~ a question ASK
rattlesnake's ~ COIL
strike a ~ MODEL

Poseidon
~ domain OCEAN, SEA
~ mother RHEA
Celtic ~ LER
Triton, to ~ SON

poser MODEL

poseur FAKE

posies
place for ~ VASE

posit PUT

position CASTE, CLASS, ESTATE,
POSE, POST, PUT, RANK, SEAT,
SET, SITE, SLANT, SLOT, SPOT,
STEAD, TENET
~ as bricks LAY
light-switch ~ OFF

positions
change ~ RESET, STIR
light-switch ~ ONS

positive CLEAR, FLAT, PLUS, ROSY,
SURE
~ sign PLUS
~ thinker PEALE
~ vote AYE, YEA, YES

"Positively ___!" NOT

"Positive Thinking"
~ proponent PEALE

posse GANG
~ picture OATER

possess HAVE, HOLD, OWN

possessed MAD
like one ~ RABID

___-possessed SELF

possessing
~ (suffix) OSE
~ talent ABLE

possession
prized ~ GEM
valuable ~ ASSET
yield ~ of CEDE

possessions ESTATE, GEAR

possessive AVID
~ pronoun HERS, HIS, ITS,
MINE, OUR, OURS, THEIR

possessor OWNER

posset
~ ingredient WINE

possibilities IFS

possibility BET

possible
make ~ ENABLE, SETUP

possum
comic-strip ~ POGO

___ possum PLAY

post AFTER, BASE, BILL, MAIL,

MAST, PALE, PIER, PILE, PLANT,
RACE, SEND, STAKE
~ ender AGE, CARD, DATE,
HASTE, HOLE, MAN, PONE
~ office GAME
~ opposite PRE
~ starter BED, GATE, LAMP,
MILE, OUT, SIGN
banister ~ NEWEL
Cabinet ~ LABOR, STATE
go from pillar to ~ ROAM,
ROVE
handrail ~ NEWEL
hunter's ~ STAND
masthead ~ EDITOR
newsroom ~ DESK
ostiary ~ DOOR
parcel ~ MAIL
sleep at one's ~ LOAF
tout's ~ RAIL
wooden ~ STAKE

post-___ (surgical follow-ups)
OPS

___ post GOAL

Post TED

postage
roll of ~ stamps COIL

postage ___ DUE, METER, STAMP

postal
~ abbr. APO, RFD
~ delivery MAIL

Postal Creed
~ word NOR, RAIN, SLEET,
SNOW

Postal Service
~ symbol EAGLE

postaxial
~ bone ULNA

postcard
~ message NOTE

"Postcards From the ___" EDGE

posted AWARE
it may be ~ BAIL

poster BILL, SIGN

poster ___ PAINT

posterior AFTER, HIP, LAST, REAR

posterity ISSUE, SEED

postern DOOR, EXIT, GATE

"Postern of ___" FATE

postfix ADD, TAG

postgame
~ discussion RECAP

postgraduate ADULT
~ deg. MBA

posthaste APACE, ASAP, FAST,
STAT

postilion RIDER

postindustrial ERA

posting
airport ~ ARR, ETA

bank ~ RATE
racetrack ~ ODDS
storm ~ ALERT
street ~ SIGN

Post-It
~ message MEMO

postlude TAG

postman
~ assignment ROUTE
~ challenge DOG, ICE, RAIN,
SLEET, SNOW

**"Postman Always Rings Twice,
The"**
~ author CAIN
Cora in ~ LANA

post office
~ buy STAMP
~ machine SCALE
~ poster datum ALIAS
~ unit OUNCE
do ~ work SORT

Poston TOM

postpone DEFER, REMIT, STAY,
STOP, TABLE

postponed LATE

postponement STAY, WAIT

postproduction
do ~ work EDIT

post-Reformation
~ council TRENT

postscript TAG
musical ~ CODA
policy ~ RIDER
write a ~ ADD

postulant NUN

postulate ASSERT

posture POSE
forget about ~ SAG

posturing CAMP

Post, Wilbur
~ pal MRED

postworkout
~ feeling ACHE

post-WWII
~ alliance NATO

posy
~ portion LEAF, PETAL, STEM

pot PILE, POOL, STAKE
~ booster ANTE
~ contents TEA
~ cousin PAN
~ ender SHOT
~ item CHIP
~ protector ENAMEL
~ top LID
cooking ~ OLLA
go to ~ LAPSE, SPOIL
keep the ~ boiling EARN
lobster ~ TRAP
monkey ~ TREE
pepper ~ STEW
take the ~ WIN

pot ___

pot ___ ROAST

___ pot HOT

potable
nonpotent ~ ADE
pale ~ ALE
potent ~ ALE, BEER, LAGER, MEAD, PORT, RUM, RYE, WINE
Tokyo ~ SAKE, SAKI

potash LYE

potassium METAL
~ hydroxide LYE

potassium ___ (astringent) ALUM

potato
~ alternative RICE
~ covering SKIN
~ in Spanish PAPA
~ part EYE, SKIN
~ preparer RICER
baking ~ IDAHO
sweet ~ PIE, YAM

potato ___ CHIP, SALAD, SKIN

___ potato HOT, IDAHO, SWEET

potato chip
~ partner DIP
Brit's ~ CRISP

"Potato Eaters, The" OIL

potatoes
~ partner MEAT
~ portion SCOOP
like some ~ SMALL
prepare ~ GRATE, MASH, PARE, PEEL

___ potatoes SMALL

Potato Head, Mr.
~ add-on EAR

"___ Potato, Two Potato" ONE

pot-au-feu MEAT, STEW

potboiler
~ author HACK

"Potemkin"
~ mutiny site ODESSA

potent ABLE, RICH
~ potable ALE, BEER, LAGER, MEAD, PORT, RUM, RYE, SAKE, SAKI
~ starter OMNI

potentate AMIR, EMEER, EMIR, LORD, RULER
~ of yore TSAR
Iran ~ of yore SHAH
Mideast ~ AGA, AGHA
Punjab ~ RAJAH

potential
~ flower SEED
has the ~ to MAY

pother ADO, STEW, STIR, TODO

potherb PLANT

pothole PIT
~ locale ROAD

pothook
~ shape ESS

___ potion LOVE

potpourri OLIO
essence of ~ AROMA

pots
mind the ~ WATER

Potsdam
see German

potshot BARB
take a ~ SNIPE

pottage
~ buyer ESAU

potter
~ furnace KILN
~ material CLAY
~ mix PASTE

Potter
Melville's ~ ISRAEL

Potter, Colonel
~ aide RADAR
~ program MASH

potters
noted ~ HOPI

potter's ___ CLAY

Potter, Sherman
~ rank COL

potter's wheel
~ kin LATHE

pottery ART, CLAY, WARE
~ glaze ENAMEL
~ producer OVEN
bake ~ FIRE
fire the ~ BAKE
kind of ~ WARE

potting
~ soil LOAM

Potts ANNIE

potty DAFT, MAD

pouch BAG, SAC, SACK

pouilly-fuissé WINE

poulard HEN

poultry MEAT
~ buy HEN
~ product EGG
~ seasoning SAGE

pounce CLAW, LEAP
~ on NAB
~ upon GRAB, RAID

pound BANG, BEAT, CAGE, CAKE, CLAP, HIT, LAM, MASH, NAIL, PELT, PEN, SMITE, STAMP, UNIT
~ down TAMP
~ fraction OUNCE
~ in RAM
~ portion OUNCE
~ sound ARF, YELP
Brit. ~ STER

pound ___ CAKE

___-pound FOOT

Pound EZRA

poundage
extra ~ FAT

Pound, Ezra POET
~ birthplace IDAHO
see also poet

pounds
~ shillings, and pence LSD
take off ~ DIET, LOSE, SLIM

Poundstone PAULA

pour ISSUE, RAIN, STORM, TEEM
~ down the drain SPEND
~ forth EMIT, ERUPT, OOZE, RELATE, SHED
~ out EMERGE, SPEW, TEEM

pour ___ (exert oneself) ITON

pourboire FEE, PAY, TIP

pouring WET

pout FRET, MOPE, MOUE, STEW

pouter BIRD
~ mood SNIT

poverty NEED, RUIN

poverty-stricken NEEDY, POOR

pow BANG

powder DUST, MEAL, MILL
~ blue COLOR
~ container HORN
bath ~ TALC
take a ~ LEAVE
takes a ~ GOES
xerography ~ TONER

powder ___ BLUE, KEG

___ powder CHILI, ONION

powdered FINE
~ chocolate COCOA

powder puff
use a ~ DAB

powdery FINE
~ dirt DUST
~ residue ASH

Powell ADAM, PAUL

Powell, Colin
~ org. USA
~ rank GEN

Powell/Keeler
~ film of 1934 DAMES

power ARM, REIGN, SINEW
~ cable LINE
~ hunger LUST
~ metaphorically REINS
~ org. REA
~ source ATOM, ELEC, GAS, MOTOR, OIL, STEAM, SUN
~ starter FIRE, HORSE, MAN, WATER
~ unit WATT
come to ~ ARISE
decision-making ~ SAYSO
driving ~ FIRE
enforcement ~ TEETH
exercise ~ RULE, WIELD
friendly ~ ALLY
height of one's ~ DAY
high ~ NTH
onetime colonial ~ SPAIN
paranormal ~ ESP

possessing ~ ABLE
subway ~ source RAIL
those in ~ INS
will ~ GRIT
without ~ INERT, NULL

power ___ BASE, ELITE, LINE, PLANT, PLAY, TRAIN

___ power AIR, SOLAR

"Power"
~ actor GERE

"Power ___ the Glory, The" AND

"Power, ___ and Politics" PASTA

PowerBook
~ maker APPLE

powerful ABLE, BIG, DEEP
~ beam LASER
~ blow SWAT
~ industrialist BARON
~ person TITAN
more ~ than ABOVE

powerhouse DEMON

Powers
TV role for ~ HART

Powers, Austin AGENT, SPY

powers that be INS

power train
~ part GEAR

Powhatan TRIBE

powwow CHAT

Pozzuoli CITY, PORT

Pr ELEM
59 for ~ ATNO

PR
~ concern IMAGE, REP
~ job HYPE
~ man AGT

practical SANE, SOBER, UTILE
~ joke CAPER, DIDO, GAG
~ joker WAG
having no ~ value INANE
having ~ value UTILE

practical ___ NURSE

practice HABIT, MODE, PLY, USAGE, USE
~ diligently PLY
~ in the ring SPAR
~ medicine TREAT
~ stoicism ENURE, INURE
~ (suffix) ISM
customary ~ RITE, RULE
Dr.'s ~ MED
piano ~ SCALE
piano ~ piece ETUDE

practiced ABLE, ADEPT

practitioner
~ (suffix) IST, ITE
solo ~ LONER

Prado
~ display ART

praetor
~ superior EDILE

Praetorian
  ~ **employer** CAESAR

Prague CITY
  ~ **resident** SLAV

prairie LEA, LLANO, RANGE
  ~ **dog** ANIMAL

Prairie
  ~ **St.** ILL

praise CITE, EXALT, HAIL, HONOR, LAUD
  ~ **crazily** HYPE
  ~ **highly** RAVE
  hymn of ~ ODE, PAEAN
  song of ~ LAUD
  word of ~ GOOD

praises
  sing one's own ~ BRAG, CROW
  sing the ~ **of** LAUD

praiseworthy GOOD

praline
  ~ **ingredient** PECAN

pram BOAT
  ~ **pusher** NANA

prance CAPER, DANCE, LEAP, SKIP

prandial
  ~ **listing** MENU

prank ANTIC, CAPER, DIDO, GAG, LARK
  ~ **ender** STER

prankster BRAT, IMP, WAG
  assist a ~ ABET
  Shakespearean ~ ARIEL

prate BLAB, CARP, NOISE, TALK

pratfall ERROR
  take a ~ MISS

prattle BLAB, CHAT, GAB, NOISE, PRATE, TALK, YAK, YAP

"Pravda"
  ~ **founder** LENIN
  ~ **source** TASS

praxis USAGE

pray BEG, CRY
  ~ **in Latin** ORA
  ~ **to** ASK

prayer
  ~ **ending** AMEN
  ~ **shawl** SCARF
  rosary ~ AVE

"Prayer for ___ Meany, A" OWEN

prayer wheel
  ~ **user** LAMA

pre-
  ~ **cousin** ANTE

preach ORATE, RANT, TALK

preacher ORATOR, PADRE
  ~ **spot** ALTAR
  ~ **word** AMEN

Preacher ROE

preadamic EARLY

Preakness RACE

prearrange PLAN, RIG, SETUP

prearranged SET

pre-cable
  ~ **need** AERIAL

Precambrian ERA

precariousness PERIL, RISK

___ precaution ASA

precede LEAD

precedence
  take ~ RANK

precedent CASE

___ precedent SETA

preceding ABOVE
  ~ **night** EVE
  ~ **(prefix)** FORE

precept DOGMA, FIAT, ISM, LAW, RULE, TENET

preceptor GURU

precepts
  cultural ~ ETHIC, ETHOS

precinct AREA, WARD
  ~ **worker** COP

precious CUTE, DEAR, PET, RARE, RICH, SWEET
  ~ **gem** OPAL, PEARL
  ~ **metal** GOLD
  ~ **resource** TIME
  ~ **stone** GEM, JADE

precipice DROP, EDGE

precipitate RAIN, RAPID, RASH
  ~ **heavily** POUR, TEEM

precipitation RAIN
  icy ~ HAIL
  winter ~ SLEET, SNOW

precipitous RASH, STEEP
  ~ **cliff** SCAR

précis RECAP

precise NEAT, NICE, TRUE

precisely AMEN, BANG, FLAT, YES

precision CARE, RIGOR

preclude AVERT, BAN, BAR

precocious EARLY

precognition ESP

pre-Columbian OLD

preconception BIAS

preconditions IFS

precook HEAT

pre-crime
  ~ **activity** PLOT

precursor
  holiday ~ EVE
  trial's ~ ARREST

predator EATER
  ~ **quarry** PREY
  field-mouse ~ OWL
  fish ~ ERN, ERNE

  nocturnal ~ OWL
  ocean ~ MAKO
  Southwest ~ PUMA
  veldt ~ HYENA, LION

predatory FERAL

predestination FATE

predestine DOOM, FATE

predestined SURE

predetermine DOOM, RIG

predicament BIND, HOLE, JAM, MESS, NODE, PASS, SNARL, SPOT, STEW

predicate ASSERT, SAY

predict READ

prediction
  ~ **maker** SEER
  weather ~ CLEAR, DRY, FAIR, GALE, HAIL, RAIN, SLEET, SNOW, STORM

predictive
  ~ **power** ESP

predilection BENT, BIAS, TASTE

pre-dinner
  mom's ~ **order** WASH

predispose BIAS, LEAD

predisposed PRONE

predisposition BENT, BIAS, TASTE

predominance REIGN

predominant BEST, FIRST, MAIN, MAJOR

predominate LEAD

preeminent AONE, BEST, FIRST, GREAT, MAIN, MAJOR, NOTED, STAR, TOP, TOPS
  be ~ RULE

preening
  prone to ~ VAIN

pre-entrée
  ~ **course** SALAD

preface
  ~ **for short** INTRO

prefer LEAN, LIKE, PLEASE
  ~ **charges** SUE
  ~ **ender** ENCE

preference TASTE

preferred
  ~ **group** ALIST, ELITE

preglacial EARLY

pregraduation
  ~ **dance** PROM

prehistoric EARLY, OLD, PAST
  ~ **axe head** CELT
  ~ **discovery** FIRE
  ~ **dwelling** CAVE
  ~ **tool** ADZE, AXE

pre-holiday
  ~ **night** EVE

pre-intermission
  ~ **period** ACTI

prejudice BIAS, SLANT

prejudiced SMALL

prelate
  ~ **tribunal** ROTA

prelect ORATE

prelector ORATOR

pre-Lenin
  ~ **ruler** TSAR

prelim EVENT, INTRO
  finals ~ SEMI
  sports ~ TRIAL

preliminary
  ~ **race** HEAT

prelude
  ~ **follower** ACTI
  bowl-game ~ PARADE

"Prelude ___ Kiss" TOA

"___ Preludes" LES

pre-lunch
  ~ **times** AMS

premature EARLY, RASH

premed
  ~ **class** ANAT

premeditate PLAN, PLOT

premier FIRST, HEAD, LEAD, MAIN

premiere FIRST, LEAD, SHOW

Preminger OTTO
  ~ **film of 1944** LAURA

premise TOPIC

premises
  fancy ~ ESTATE

premium AWARD, EXTRA, GAS
  at a ~ DEAR, RARE

___ premium (scarce) ATA

premonitory DIRE

pre-noon
  ~ **times** AMS

Prentiss PAULA

___ Prentiss (Ann Sheridan role) NORA

preoccupation MANIA

preoccupied LOST
  be ~ DREAM

preordain FATE

pre-owned USED

prep
  ~ **for finals** CRAM
  British ~ **school** ETON

prepaid
  not ~ COD

preparations
  make ~ PLAN

prepare ARM, FIT, MAKE, SETUP, TRAIN
  ~ **a gift** WRAP
  ~ **a hook** BAIT
  ~ **a press** INK

prepared
~ a steak SEAR
~ a turkey DRESS
~ avocado for
  guacamole MASH
~ bacon FRY
~ brandy AGE
~ champagne ICE
~ cheese GRATE
~ cherries STEM
~ chestnuts ROAST
~ clams STEAM
~ coconut GRATE
~ copy EDIT
~ for a match SPAR
~ for an exam CRAM
~ for battle ARM
~ for mailing SEAL
~ for publication EDIT
~ for shipment WRAP
~ for the future PLAN
~ for war ARM
~ for work DRESS
~ fruit CORE, PARE, PEEL, PIT, PUREE, SLICE, WASH
~ grits BOIL
~ memos TYPE
~ mushrooms SAUTE
~ pancakes FRY
~ Parmesan GRATE
~ potatoes BAKE, BOIL, GRATE, MASH, PARE, PEEL, RICE
~ the table SET
~ to be knighted KNEEL
~ to be shot POSE
~ to drag REV
~ to fire AIM
~ to propose KNEEL
~ to publish EDIT
~ to shoot DRAW
~ to take off TAXI
~ veggies BOIL, CREAM, SAUTE, STEAM
~ wine AGE

prepared SET

preparer
food ~ CHEF
potato ~ RICER

preponderance MASS

preposition ABOUT, ABOVE, ACROSS, AFTER, ALA, ALOFT, ALONG, AMID, AMONG, APRES, ASOF, ASTO, ATOP, BAR, ERE, FOR, FORE, FRO, INRE, INTO, LESS, LIKE, MIDST, NEAR, NEATH, OER, OFF, ONTO, OUT, OVER, PACE, PAST, PER, SANS, SAVE, SINCE, THAN, TIL, TILL, UNDER, UNTIL, UNTO, UPON, VIA
~ for a poet ERE, NEATH, OER

preposterous INANE, TALL

prerecord TAPE

pre-release
~ software version BETA

prerequisite NEED, WANT

prerogative
presidential ~ VETO

Pres. EXEC

presage BODE, OMEN

presbyter ELDER

preschooler KID, TOT

prescribe ORDER

prescribed
~ amount DOSE

prescript EDICT

prescription
~ data DOSE
~ org. FDA

presence MIEN
~ of mind POISE

present AWARD, CITE, NONCE, NOW, SHOW, STAGE
~ a bold front DARE
~ a case ARGUE
~ an affidavit ATTEST
~ itself EMERGE, OCCUR
~ oneself ARRIVE
~ starter OMNI
~ topper BOW
at the ~ time NOW, YET
be ~ at ATTEND
before the ~ AGO
be the ~ trend REIGN
in its ~ state ASIS
it may be ~ TENSE
not ~ AWAY, OUT

present-___ DAY

"Present!" HERE

presentation
give a ~ SHOW
SRO ~ HIT

present-day NEW

presentee
social ~ DEB

presently ANON, SOON

Preservation ___ HALL

preservative AGAR

preserve CAN, CURE, DRY, KEEP, SALT, SAVE, TIN
~ on video TAPE
~ with salt CORN

preserver
dinosaur ~ TAR
dinosaur DNA ~ AMBER
shoe ~ TREE

___ preserver LIFE

preserves JAM
~ container JAR

preside
~ at tea POUR
~ over BOSS, HEAD, LEAD, RULE

president HEAD
~ often CEO
Federalist ~ ADAMS
first one-term ~ ADAMS
former German ~ EBERT
former ~ of Egypt SADAT
former Vietnamese ~ DIEM
four years, for a ~ TERM

honest ~ ABE
second ~ ADAMS
sixteenth ~, familiarly ABE
sixth ~ ADAMS
Syria's ~ ASSAD
terse ~ CAL
twenty-seventh ~ TAFT

presidential
~ candidate of 1996 DOLE
~ initials DDE, HST
~ instrument SAX
~ nickname ABE, BILL, CAL, IKE
~ no VETO
~ pooch FALA, HER, HIM
~ prerogative VETO
five-time ~ candidate DEBS

president pro ___ TEM

presidents
name of two ~ ADAMS

"President's ___, The" LADY

Presidents' Day
~ event SALE

Presley ELVIS, LISA
~ middle name ARON

Presley, Elvis
~ tune DONT

pre-Soviet
~ ruler TSAR

Presque ISLE

Presque ___, Me. ISLE

Presque Isle
~ lake ERIE
~ st. PENN

press ARMY, AROUSE, ASK, BEAR, BEG, CLASP, IRON, JAM, MOB, PLY, URGE
~ card PASS
~ coverage INK
~ down TAMP
~ ender ROOM, RUN, URE
~ for URGE
~ forward SPUR
~ home STRESS
~ in DENT
~ into service ENROL, USE
~ on IMPEL, MOVE
~ one's luck DARE
~ release NEWS
~ secretary AIDE
~ staffers EDS
~ starter WINE
former Soviet ~ arm TASS
hot off the ~ NEW
prepare a ~ INK
the ~ MEDIA

press ___ AGENT, KIT, RUN, TIME

___ press HAND, WEB

pressed
closely ~ package BALE

___-pressed HARD

pressing ACUTE, DIRE

press release
~ addressees MEDIA

pressure HEAT, IMPEL, MAKE, STRESS, URGE
~ meas. ATM, PSI
~ unit BAR
apply ~ IMPEL, MAKE
decrease ~ EASE
exert ~ LEAN, URGE
grace under ~ POISE

___ pressure AIR, PEER

___-pressure LOW

prestige FACE, HONOR, NOTE, RANK
have ~ RATE

presto FAST, TEMPO

Preston SGT

Preston, Sergeant
~ horse REX
~ org. RCMP
~ vehicle SLED

presume DEEM, OPINE
~ upon USE

presumption NERVE, PRIDE

___ presumptive HEIR

presumptuous
~ one SNIP

pre-taped
not ~ LIVE

preteen KID, LAD
~ sch. ELEM

pretend ACT, FAKE, LETON, LIE, SHAM

pretended FAKE, FALSE

pretense ACT, AIRS, CANT, MASK, POSE, RUSE, SHAM, SHOW

___ pretenses FALSE

pretension ART

pretensions AIRS

pretentious ARTY, BIG, ORNATE

preterit TENSE

preternatural EERIE, EERY, ODD

pretext ALIBI, PEG, PLEA, STALL

Pretoria CITY
~ coin RAND

pretty CUTE, FAIR
~ fix MESS
~ good FAIR
~ much the same LIKE
~ near CLOSE
~ up ADORN
make a ~ penny EARN
worth a ~ penny RICH

pretty ___, a PASS

pretty ___ picture ASA

"Pretty Boy" Floyd
emulate ~ ROB

"Pretty Maids ___ a Row" ALLIN

"Pretty Maids ___ in a Row" ALL

"Pretty Maids All ___ Row" INA

"Pretty Maids All in __" AROW

"Pretty Maids All in a __" ROW

"pretty please"
  say ~ BEG

"Pretty Woman"
  ~ actor GERE

pre-TV
  ~ diversion RADIO

pretzel
  ~ topping SALT

prevail REIGN, WIN
  ~ over BEAT, TOP, WIN
  ~ upon MAKE, MOVE, URGE

prevailing MAIN, RIFE, USUAL

prevalent ABOUT, RIFE, USUAL
  be ~ REIGN, RULE

prevaricate EVADE, LIE

prevarication LIE, TALE

prevaricator LIAR

pre-Velcro
  ~ item SNAP

prevent AVERT, BAR, DETER, FEND, STAY, STOP
  ~ in legalese ESTOP

preventer
  goal ~ SAVE

prevention
  ~ unit OUNCE

__ preview SNEAK

Previn ANDRE
  ~ ex MIA

previous FORE, LAST, PAST

previously ONCE

Prévost ABBE

prexy
  ~ often CEO

prey CHASE, GAME
  ~ grabber TALON
  angler's ~ BASS
  bird of ~ EAGLE, ERN, ERNE
  cat's ~ MOUSE
  fox's ~ HEN
  hound's ~ HARE
  hunter's ~ GAME
  lion's ~ GNU
  mongoose ~ RAT, SNAKE
  Oto ~ BISON

preyer
  cornfield ~ CROW

prez EXEC

Priam
  ~ home TROY
  ~ son PARIS
  Troilus, to ~ SON

price COST, FEE, RATE, TAB
  ~ break DISC
  ~ ceiling CAP
  ~ cut SLASH
  ~ of admission FARE, FEE
  ~ of participation ANTE
  ~ rise HIKE

~ ticket TAG
~ word EACH, PER
offer for a ~ SELL, VEND
set a ~ ASK
ticket ~ FARE

price __ TAG, WAR

__ price ATA, LIST

Price MARC
  ~ selection ARIA

price-earnings __ RATIO

Price, Leontyne
  ~ forte ARIA, OPERA
  ~ role AIDA

priceless RARE, RICH
  ~ individual GEM

prices
  decline, as stock ~ SAG
  lower ~ SLASH, TRIM
  raise ~ HIKE

pricey DEAR, STEEP

__ pricing UNIT

pricked
  with ears ~ ALERT

prickle BARB, ITCH, NEEDLE, SMART, STING

prickly EDGY
  ~ plant BRIAR

prickly __ HEAT, PEAR

prickly pear
  ~ home DESERT

pride EGO, SIN
  ~ member LION
  ~ oneself PREEN
  a matter of ~ EGO
  brewer's ~ ALE, BEER, LAGER
  fill with ~ ELATE
  free from ~ MEEK
  homeowner's ~ LAWN
  lion's ~ MANE
  outfielder's ~ ARM
  palomino's ~ MANE
  peacock's ~ TAIL, TRAIN
  placekicker's ~ TOE
  pumper's ~ ABS
  rooster's ~ COMB, CREST
  sailor's ~ KNOT
  self ~ EGO
  take ~ PREEN
  trucker's ~ RIG
  veteran's ~ MEDAL
  weightlifter's ~ TORSO

"Pride __ Prejudice" AND

prie-dieu
  use a ~ KNEEL

priest ABBOT, PADRE, RANK
  ~ calendar ORDO
  ~ ender ESS
  ~ garment ALB
  ~ in a Nash verse LAMA
  ~ mantle COPE
  ~ robe ALB
  ~ title ABBE
  ~ vestment ALB
  Asian ~ LAMA
  Biblical ~ ELI

French ~ ABBE
Muslim ~ IMAM
one-L ~ LAMA

"Priest"
  ~ director BIRD

priestess
  Delphi ~ ORACLE

priestly
  ~ garb ALB
  not ~ LAIC

"Priest of __" LOVE

priggish PRIM, STAID

prim SEDATE, STAID

prima
  ~ ballerina LEAD

primacy LEAD, STRESS

prima donna DIVA, LEAD, STAR
  ~ problem EGO

primal EARLY, FIRST
  ~ chaos ABYSS
  ~ quality ESSENCE

"Primal __" FEAR

"Primal Fear"
  ~ actor GERE

primary BASIC, BIG, FIRST, LEAD, MAIN, MAJOR
  ~ color BLUE, RED
  ~ sch. ELEM

primary __ CARE, COLOR

primate APE, ORANG

primatologist
  ~ subject APE, ORANG

__ primavera PASTA

prime AONE, BEST, DAY, FINE, FIRST, GOOD, HOUR, LEAD, MAIN, MAJOR, PAINT, PEAK, TOPS
  ~ for the picking RIPE
  ~ minister HEAD
  ~ mover ACTOR, CAUSE
  ~ social category ALIST, ELITE
  ~ the pot ANTE
  fifth ~ ELEVEN
  first ~ TWO
  fourth ~ SEVEN
  in one's ~ RIPE
  it may be ~ RATE
  Japan's first ~ minister ITO
  like ~ steak AGED
  past its ~ PASSE
  second ~ THREE
  third ~ FIVE

prime __ RATE, TIME

"Prime __" CUT

primed SET

prime minister
  1950s British ~ EDEN
  India's first ~ NEHRU

"Prime of __ Jean Brodie, The" MISS

primer PAINT, TEXT
  ~ lessons ABCS

  ~ perhaps COAT

prime time
  ~ hour TEN

primeval EARLY, OLD

primitive EARLY, OLD
  ~ plant ALGAE
  ~ (prefix) PRO
  ~ urges IDS

primo AONE, BEST, FINE, GOOD, GREAT, TOPS

Primo LEVI

primogenital FIRST

primogenitary ELDEST

primordial EARLY, OLD

primp PREEN

primrose COLOR
  lead down the ~ path LURE

primrose __ PATH

__ primrose CAPE

prince LORD, MALE, RULER, TITLE
  Bard's ~ HAL
  Indian ~ RAJAH
  Islamic ~ AMIR, EMEER, EMIR
  operatic ~ IGOR
  Trojan ~ PARIS

Prince HAL
  ~ of Darkness SATAN
  ~ of Wales HEIR
  ~ of Wales' game POLO

"Prince __" ("Aladdin" song) ALI

"Prince __" (Borodin opera) IGOR

"Prince __ the Pauper, The" AND

Prince Charming
  no ~ CAD, DRIP

"Prince Igor" OPERA

princeling PEER

princely BIG, REGAL

"Prince of the __" CITY

"Prince of Tides, The"
  ~ actor NOLTE

Prince Rupert CITY, PORT

prince's __ (woodland plant) PINE

princess LADY, TITLE
  ~ adornment TIARA
  ~ disturber PEA
  ~ of India RANEE, RANI
  English ~ ANNE
  Golden Fleece ~ MEDEA
  opera ~ AIDA

Princess __ (Sleeping Beauty) AURORA

"Princess __" IDA

"Princess __ the Pirate, The" AND

"Princess Caraboo"
~ **actor** REA

"Princess Comes ___, The"
ACROSS

Princess Margaret ___ ROSE

Princeton
~ **mascot** TIGER

"Prince Valiant"
Arn's domain, in ~ ORR

principal ARCH, BASIC, BIG, FIRST, HEAD, HERO, KEY, MAIN, MAJOR, STAR
~ **character** LEAD

principality LAND

principle BASIS, CAUSE, DOGMA, ESSENCE, IDEAL, ISM, LAW, RULE
~ **of good conduct** ETHIC
animating ~ LIFE, SOUL
Chinese ~ YIN
Confucian ~ TAO
fundamental ~ BASIS
group ~ TENET
guiding ~ CREDO
mathematical ~ LAW
moral ~ HONOR
palindromic ~ TENET
religious ~ TENET
scientific ~ LAW

Principle
man with a ~ PETER

principled MORAL

principles
body of ~ ETHIC
lacking ~ AMORAL
political ~ DOGMA
set of ~ CREDO

print ISSUE
~ **indelibly** ETCH
block ~ CUT
smear in ~ LIBEL

___ print FINE, SMALL

printed
~ **material** TEXT

printemps
~ **follower** ETE

printer
~ **goofs** ERRATA
~ **mark** CARET, DELE, STET
~ **measure** PICA
~ **measures** EMS, ENS
~ **option** FONT
~ **proof** REPRO
~ **purchase** INK
~ **stroke** SERIF
~ **tray** FONT

___ printer COLOR, LASER

printer's
~ **devil** AIDE, PAGE

printing ISSUE, RUN
~ **fluid** INK
~ **goofs** ERRATA
~ **machine** PRESS
~ **mark** CARET, DELE, STET

~ **mold** MAT
~ **process** ROTO
~ **style** ITAL
compose for ~ SET

printing ___ PRESS

prior ABBE, FORE, OLD, PAST
~ **boss** ABBOT
~ **(prefix)** ANTE, PRE
~ **superior** ABBOT
give ~ notice ALERT, WARN

prioress NUN

prioritize RANK, RATE

prison BARS, CAN, STIR
~ **unit** CELL
~ **yard** PALE
Biblical ~ escapee PETER

prisoner
~ **wear** IRONS

"Prisoner of Chillon, The" POEM

prissy PRIM

pristine EARLY, NEW

private INNER, RANK
~ **lingo** ARGOT
~ **source** STASH
~ **word** SIR
having ~ knowledge INON
in ~ ASIDE

private ___ EYE

"Private ___ of Henry VIII, The"
LIFE

"Private ___ of Sherlock Holmes, The" LIFE

"Private Affairs of ___ Ami, The"
BEL

"Private Affairs of Bel ___, The"
AMI

private eye TEC
~ **at times** TAIL

private jet
~ **maker** LEAR

"Private Lives of Elizabeth ___ Essex, The" AND

privately APART

private school
~ **teacher** NUN

privation LOSS, NEED, WANT

privilege HONOR

privileged ELITE

privy to INON

prix fixe MEAL

prize ADORE, AWARD, ESTEEM, LIKE, LOVE, PEARL
~ **of the Nibelung** RING
athlete's ~ MEDAL
game-show ~ CAR, CASH, TRIP
Olympics ~ GOLD, MEDAL
take the ~ WIN
winner's ~ CUP

___ prize DOOR

"Prize, The"
~ **name** ELKE

prized DEAR, PET
~ **possession** GEM

prizefight BOUT
~ **venue** ARENA

prizefighter
~ **wear** ROBE

"Prizefighter ___ the Lady, The"
AND

"Prizefighter and the ___, The"
LADY

"Prize of ___, A" GOLD

___ Prizm GEO

"Prizzi's ___" HONOR

pro ACE, ADEPT, FOR
~ **bono** FREE
~ **opposite** ANTI, CON
~ **vote** AYE, YEA, YES
campaign ~ POL
dictation ~ STENO
kitchen ~ CHEF

pro ___ BONO, RATA, TEM

___ pro (give up amateur status)
TURN

proactive
~ **one** DOER

pro-am EVENT

probability ODDS

probable ___ CAUSE

___ probandi ONUS

probate
~ **concern** ESTATE

probation TRIAL

probationary
~ **period** TRIAL

probe ASK, ASSAY, DIG, ENTER, PRY, SCAN, TAP, TEST
~ **for** SEEK

___ probe SPACE

problem ISSUE, POSER, WOE

problems
free from ~ EASY
publishing ~ ERRATA
series of ~ SIEGE

proboscis NOSE

procedure
~ **part** STEP
mechanical ~ ROTE
standard operating ~ MODE

proceed ISSUE, MOVE, RUN, WEND
~ **briskly** TROT
~ **(from)** ARISE

proceeding ACT, LAW

proceedings
official ~ ACTA

proceeds GOES, TAKE
concert ~ GATE

process
~ **flour** SIFT
~ **lumber** SAW
~ **ore** SMELT
~ **(suffix)** ENCE, ISM, URE
in ~ AFOOT
memorization ~ ROTE
part of a ~ STEP
printing ~ ROTO

___ process DUE

processed
not ~ RAW

___ processing DATA

procession LINE, PARADE, TRAIN

processor
grain ~ MILL
vegetable ~ RICER
wood ~ SAW

proclaim AVER, AVOW, CRY, ORATE, RING, STATE, TELL
~ **noisily** BLARE

___-proclaimed SELF

proclamation ACT, BAN, FIAT, LAW
official ~ EDICT

proclivity BENT, BIAS, CAST, HABIT, TASTE, TURN
have a ~ LEAN

procrastinate DEFER, STALL

procrastinating SLOW
stop ~ ACT

procrastinative LATE

procrastinator
~ **opposite** DOER
like a ~ LATE

procrastinatory LATE

Procrustean
~ **prop** BED

Procter & Gamble
~ **detergent** ERA
~ **soap** IVORY, LAVA
~ **toothpaste** CREST

proctor
~ **cry** TIME

procure EARN, GAIN, GET, HAVE, TAKE, WIN

procurement TAKE

Procyon STAR

prod ABET, AROUSE, DIG, EGG, GOAD, IMPEL, JAB, MOVE, NEEDLE, PRESS, ROUSE, SPUR, STING, URGE
~ **to activity** STIR
cattle ~ GOAD

prodigal ___ SON

prodigality WASTE

prodigious BIG, GREAT, LARGE

prodigy ACE

Prodigy
~ **patron** USER

produce BEAR, BREED, CAUSE, MAKE, STAGE, YIELD
~ **a show** STAGE
~ **as written** CITE
~ **dividends** EARN
~ **eggs** LAY

product
~ **(suffix)** ITE

___ **product** END

production
La Scala ~ OPERA
stage ~ DRAMA

___ **production** MASS

productive FAT, RICH
~ **activity** LABOR

prof
~ **aides** TAS
~ **concoction** EXAM, TEST
~ **degree** PHD

___ **prof.** ASST

profane LAIC, LAY, TAINT

profess ASSERT, AVER, AVOW, CLAIM, SAY, STATE

profession GAME, LINE, TRADE

"Professional, The"
~ **actor** RENO

professor RANK
~ **perhaps** SAGE

proffer BID

proficiency EASE

proficient ABLE, ADEPT, GOOD, UPON

profile BIO, FACE
~ **projection** NOSE
keep a low ~ HIDE

profit AVAIL, EARN, GAIN, NET, PAY
~ **and loss statement entry** ASSET
~ **counterpart** LOSS
~ **ender** EER
~ **from** USE
realize a ~ CLEAR, NET

___-**profit** FOR

profits TAKE

profligacy WASTE

profligate BAD, LEWD
~ **one** RAKE, ROUE

profound DEEP, GREAT, HARD, WISE

profs
~ **usually** DRS

profundity ABYSS, DEEP

___ **profundo** BASSO

profuse AMPLE, RICH

profusion MASS, PILE, SEA
~ **of colors** RIOT

progenitor SIRE

progeny ISSUE, SCION, SEED, SONS

prognosticate READ

prognosticator ORACLE, SEER

program AGENDA, CARD, PLAN, SHOW
~ **a smart card** ENCODE
~ **choices** MENU
~ **interruptions** ADS
business ~ AGENDA
detailed ~ PLAN
gone from the ~ ERASED
halfway-house ~ REHAB
PC master ~ DOS
radio ~ NEWS

"Program, The"
~ **actor** CAAN

programming language ADA, BASIC
Internet ~ JAVA

progress BOOM, GAIN, GROW, MOVE
in ~ AFOOT
make ~ GAIN, MOVE
slight ~ DENT
small ~ STEP

"___ Progress, The" RAKES

progression RISE, SCALE, TRAIN

progressive LEFT

prohibit BAN, BAR, DENY, TABOO, TABU, VETO
~ **by law** ESTOP

prohibited TABOO, TABU
~ **act** NONO

prohibition BAN, BAR, DONT, LAW, TABOO, TABU, VETO
~ **word** DONT, NOT

Prohibitionist DRY
~ **foe** WET

project HANG, HURL, PLAN

projectile ARROW, BALL, SHELL, SHOT
~ **path** ARC
Olympic ~ DISC
pub ~ DART

projecting
~ **rock** CRAG
~ **window** ORIEL

projection KNOB, LEDGE, LOBE, NODE, NOSE, SNAG, SPUR, TOOTH
~ **on a wheel** CAM
bireme ~ RAM
domed ~ APSE
profile ~ NOSE
roof ~ EAVE
rough ~ SNAG
rounded ~ LOBE
shelflike ~ LEDGE
small ~ TAB

projection room
~ **unit** REEL

Project Mercury
~ **org.** NASA

projector
~ **insert** SLIDE
~ **part** LENS

Prokofiev
~ **hero** PETER

proletariat LABOR, MOB

prolific
be ~ TEEM

prolix LONG
not ~ CRISP, TERSE

prologue INTRO

prolong DRAG, SPIN, TRAIL

prolonge ___ KNOT

prolonged
~ **period of trouble** SIEGE

prom BALL, DANCE, HOP
~ **attendee** TEEN
~ **goers** SRS
~ **partner** DATE
~ **transport** LIMO

promenade DANCE, MALL, PARADE
sheltered ~ **for Socrates** STOA

Prometheus TITAN
brother of ~ ATLAS

"Prometheus Unbound" DRAMA

prominence CRAG, PEAK, RISE

prominent BIG, CLEAR, GREAT, LARGE, NOTED

promise AGREE, AVOW, OATH, SAY
~ **to pay** IOU
~ **word** SOON
campaign ~, **often** LIE

promising APT, ROSY
none too ~ DIRE

promissory
~ **note** IOU
~ **paper** NOTE

promo
~ **maker** ADMAN
~ **recording** DEMO

promontory CAPE, CREST, HEAD, LAND, NESS, SPIT

promos ADS

promote ABET, BOOM, EXALT, HELP, RAISE

promoted
got ~ ROSE

promoter AGENT, ANGEL
~ **concern** GATE
insurance ~ AGENT

promotion
~ **basis** MERIT
~ **objective** SALE

prompt ABET, AROUSE, CUE, EARLY, HINT, LEAD, MOVE, RAPID, SPUR, START, URGE
more than ~ EARLY
not ~ LATE

promptly ANON, SOON

promptness HASTE

promulgate SOW, STATE

prone FLAT
~ **(to)** APT
~ **to preening** VAIN
~ **to snoop** NOSY
be ~ LIE
be ~ **(to)** LEAN
lie ~ BOW

proneness BIAS, CAST

prong BARB, TINE

pronghorn ANIMAL

___ **pro nobis** ORA

pronoun ALL, ANY, BOTH, FEW, HER, HERS, HIM, HIS, ITS, MINE, NONE, NOONE, ONE, OUR, OURS, SAME, SHE, SOME, THAT, THEE, THEIR, THEM, THERE, THESE, THIS, THOSE, THOU, WHO, YOU
~ **in a wedding vow** THEE
~ **type** REL
Biblical ~ THEE, THOU
Brooklynese ~ DEM, DOSE
couple's ~ OUR, OURS
demonstrative ~ THAT, THESE, THIS, THOSE
feminine ~ HER, HERS, SHE
group ~ OUR, OURS, THEIR
hoarder's ~ MINE
impersonal ~ ONE
inclusive ~ OUR, OURS
interrogative ~ WHO
masculine ~ HIM, HIS
plural ~ THESE, THOSE
possessive ~ HER, HERS, HIS, ITS, OUR, OURS, THEIR
Quaker ~ THEE, THOU
relative ~ THAT
sharer's ~ OUR, OURS
towel ~ HERS, HIS
woman's ~ HER, HERS

pronounce SAY, STATE, UTTER
~ **carelessly** SLUR

pronounced CLEAR, GREAT, ORAL

pronouncement DOOM, EDICT
authoritative ~ FIAT

pronouns
like some ~ **(abbr.)** FEM, MASC

pronto ANON, ASAP, NOW, SOON, STAT
~ **to a doctor** STAT

pronunciation
omit in ~ ELIDE

proof TRIAL
~ **of ownership** DEED, TITLE
~ **of purchase, briefly** REC
~ **word** ERGO
math ~ **abbr.** QED
printer's ~ REPRO

___-**proof** IDIOT

proofread EDIT

proofreader
~ **findings** ERRATA

~ mark CARET, DELE, STET

proofs
~ of age IDS

prop BEAM, CANE, HOLD, LEG, POST, REST, SHORE, STAKE, STAY

propaganda
~ often LIE

propagate BEAR, BREED, GROW, PLANT, SOW
~ in a way CLONE

propane GAS

propel CAST, EJECT, GOAD, HURL, MOVE, PROD, SHOOT, SPUR
~ a dinghy ROW
~ a raft POLE
~ a shell OAR

___-propelled JET, SELF

propeller
kind of ~ OAR

propeller-head NERD

propensity BENT, BIAS, CAST, HABIT, TASTE
have a ~ LEAN

proper DUE, FIT, GOOD, MEET, NICE, SEDATE, STAID
~ partner PRIM
it may be ~ NOUN
not ~ AMISS
right and ~ DUE

proper ___ NOUN

property ESTATE, LAND, LOT, TRAIT
~ attachment LIEN
~ holder OWNER
govt. ~ overseer GSA
landed ~ ACRES, ESTATE
piece of ~ ASSET, LAND
prospector's ~ CLAIM
stolen ~ SWAG
title to ~ DEED

___ property REAL

prophet ORACLE, SEER
Biblical ~ AMOS, ELIAS, EZRA, HOSEA, MOSES

propitiate ALLAY, ATONE, CALM

propitious GOOD, RIPE

proportion ALLOT, RATIO
~ (abbr.) PCT
~ words ISTO

proportions SIZE
of grand ~ EPIC

proposal BID, PLAN
~ reply YES

propose AIM, ASK, MOVE, PUT, SAY
prepare to ~ KNEEL

proposed
where toasts are ~ DAIS

proposer
~ support KNEE

proposition ASK, TOPIC
losing ~ DIET

propound ASSERT, POSE

propre
amour ~ EGO

___-propre AMOUR

proprietor OWNER

___ proprietorship SOLE

propriety TASTE
violating ~ OUTRE, RUDE

props
set the stage with ~ DRESS

___ propulsion ION, JET

prorate ALLOT

prorogue DEFER

pros. ___ ATTY

prosaic ARID, BANAL, DRY, FI AT, STALE, TRITE

prosaicism TAG

proscenium APRON

prosciutto HAM, MEAT
~ purveyor DELI

proscribe BAN, DENY, TABOO, TABU

proscribed TABOO, TABU
~ action NONO

proscription BAN, BAR, TABOO, TABU

prose
improve ~ EMEND
lively, as ~ CRISP
piece of ~ ESSAY
polish ~ EDIT
twist of ~ IRONY

prosecute SUE, TRY

prosecutors
~ (abbr.) DAS

"Prosit!" TOAST

prospect HOPE, SCENE

prospector
~ aid MAP
~ find LODE, ORE
~ place MINE
~ property CLAIM
~ test ASSAY
~ tool PAN

prosper ARRIVE, BOOM, LIVE, RISE

prosperity EASE

Prospero
~ servant ARIEL

prosperous FAT, RICH
~ period BOOM

Prost ALAIN

prostrate FLAT, LOW, PRONE, SMITE, TIRE
~ oneself BOW, KNEEL
be ~ LIE

prosy ARID, BANAL, DRY, FLAT

protagonist HERO, LEAD

Protagoras ORATOR

protect ATTEND, SAVE

protected ALEE, SAFE
~ place HAVEN

protection AEGIS, ARMOR, CARE, EGIS, HELP, LEE, SHADE
~ from cold WRAP
~ in a purse MACE
~ money ICE
catcher's ~ MASK, PAD
goalie's ~ MASK, PAD
government ~ agency FDA
hockey player's ~ PAD
jouster's ~ ARMOR
palace ~ MOAT

protective
~ coating ENAMEL
~ covering ARMOR, TARP
~ insert LINER
~ layer OZONE

protector
auto-grille ~ BRA
ballfield ~ TARP
chest ~ BIB, VEST
clothing ~ APRON
desert ~ ABA
eye ~ LASH
pocket ~ FLAP
sole ~ TAP

protectorate
former British ~ ADEN

protein
~ acid AMINO
~ source EGG, MEAT, SOY
~ synthesis need RNA

protest DENY
~ figuratively STORM

proton
~ place ATOM

protoprogenitor ADAM

prototype MODEL

protozoan AMEBA

protract DRAG, TRAIL

protracted LONG, SLOW

protractor
what a ~ measures ANGLE

protrusion LEDGE, NODE

protuberance KNOB, KNOT, LOBE, NODE

proud VAIN
make ~ ELATE

"Proud ___, The" ONES, REBEL

proustite ORE

prov.
Canadian ~ ALB, ALTA, MAN, ONT, PEI

prove ARGUE, ATTEST, SETTLE, SHOW, TEST
~ false BELIE
~ innocent CLEAR
~ otherwise ARENT
~ useful AVAIL

proven SURE
~ otherwise ISNT
something ~ FACT

Provence
city in ~ ARLES
see also French

provender FEED, HAY, MEAL
~ preparer CHEF
provide ~ to CATER

proverb ADAGE, GNOME, MORAL, MOT, SAW

provide FIT
~ an excuse ALIBI
~ assistance AID
~ direction STEER
~ divertissement AMUSE
~ feedback REACT
~ food CATER
~ for FEED, KEEP
~ funds for ENDOW
~ ID TAG
~ money at interest LEND, LOAN
~ oxygen to AERATE
~ pro tem LEND
~ provender to CATER, FEED
~ something more ADD
~ staffing MAN
~ temporarily LEND, LOAN
~ weapons ARM
~ with new weapons REARM

provided
~ footwear to SHOD

Providence CITY, PORT
sch. south of ~ URI

province AREA, PALE, REALM, SITE, SPHERE, ZONE
~ Can. ALB, ALTA, MAN, ONT, PEI

Provincetown
~ cape COD

provincial LOCAL, RURAL, SMALL
French ~ STYLE

provisional TRIAL
~ worker TEMP

provisions DIET, FARE, FEED, MEAL
make ~ (for) ALLOW

proviso
contract ~ TERM
sales ~ ASIS

Provo CITY
~ state UTAH

___ provocateur AGENT

provocation DARE

provoke ABET, ANGER, AROUSE, ASK, DARE, EGG, ENRAGE, FRET, GOAD, IRE, IRK, LEAD, PEEVE, RILE, ROIL, ROUSE, TEASE, UPSET, URGE

provoked IRATE, UPSET

provost HEAD

prow NOSE
~ opposite STERN

prowl NOSE, ROAM, ROVE, SLIP, SNEAK, STEAL
~ car AUTO, MOTOR
on the ~ LOOSE

prowl ___ CAR

proximate CLOSE, LOCAL, NEAR, NEXT

proximity
in ~ NEAR
in ~, to a poet ANEAR

proxy AGENT, AGT, REP

Proyas ALEX

PRS
telephone's ~ SEVEN

prudence CARE, HEED, TACT

"___ Prudence" DEAR

prudent SAGE, SANE, SMART, SOBER, WARY, WISE

Prudhoe BAY

Prudhoe Bay
~ craft OILER
~ product OIL
~ state ALASKA

Prudhomme, Paul CHEF
~ ingredient OKRA

prudish BLUE, NICE, PRIM

"Prufrock"
~ monogram TSE

Prufrock, J. Alfred
~ creator ELIOT

prune BOB, CHOP, CLIP, CUT, HEW, LOP, PARE, SNIP, THIN, TRIM

prurient LEWD

Prussian ___ BLUE

prussic ACID

prutah COIN

pry BAR, LEVER, NOSE, ROOT
~ bar LEVER
~ up RAISE

pry ___ BAR

pryer
~ need LEVER

prying NOSY
~ tool LEVER

Prynne, Hester
~ daughter PEARL

Pryor, Richard
~ film of 1982, with "The" TOY

Pry, Paul
like ~ NOSY

Przewalski's ___ HORSE

psalm LAUD, SONG
~ adverb YEA

PSAT EXAM, TEST
~ provider ETS

pseudo BASE, FAKE, FALSE, SHAM

pseudoaesthetic ARTY

pseudologist LIAR

pseudonym ALIAS, MASK, NAME
~ letters AKA
children's-book ~ SEUSS
literary ~ ELIA
Munro's ~ SAKI

pseudopod
~ possessor AMEBA

P-shaped
~ Greek letter RHO

pshaw POOH

psi
~ follower OMEGA
~ preceder CHI

psilomelane ORE

"Psst!" HEY
~ cousin AHEM

PST
part of ~ PAC, STD

psych
~ out SCARE
~ up ABET

psyche SELF, SOUL
~ component EGO
~ components IDS
~ up AROUSE

Psyche
~ beloved EROS
see also Latin

Psyche ___ KNOT

psyched AGOG, AVID, EAGER, KEEN

psychiatrist
Austrian ~ ADLER

psychic SEER
~ power ESP
~ sight AURA

psychology
~ starter PARA

Pt ELEM
78 for ~ ATNO

PT ___ BOAT

PTA
~ member DAD, MOM
part of ~ ASSN

Ptah GOD

ptarmigan BIRD

pteridophyte PLANT

"Ptui!" FIE

Pu ELEM
94 for ~ ATNO

pub BAR, INN
~ brew ALE, BEER, LAGER
~ expression ONTAP
~ game DARTS, POOL
~ projectile DART
~ serving PINT

pub-crawl SPREE

pub-crawler SOT

puberty
past ~ ADULT

public OPEN, OVERT
~ assembly DIET
~ education pioneer MANN
~ figure LION
~ fund CHEST
~ house BAR, INN
~ notice SIGN
~ notices ADS
~ order PEACE
~ persona IMAGE
~ sentiment PULSE
~ spat SCENE
~ speaker ORATOR
~ transport BUS, CAB, PLANE, TAXI, TRAIN
~ walk MALL
become ~ OUT
general ~ MOB
make ~ AIR, BARE
use ~ transportation RIDE

"Public ___" ENEMY

___ publica RES

publican
~ offering ALE

publication ISSUE, ORGAN, PAPER
bks. before ~ MSS
house ~ ORGAN
low-quality ~ TRASH
Luce ~ TIME
prepare for ~ EDIT
slick ~ MAG
unprestigious ~ RAG

Public Citizen, Inc.
~ founder NADER

public defender ATT, ATTY

publicity HYPE, INK
~ info BIO

publicize AIR, BARE, POST

public relations
~ matter IMAGE

publish ISSUE, STATE, WRITE

published
just ~ NEW

publisher
~ crime LIBEL
~ org. ABA
onetime New York Times ~ OCHS

publishing
~ execs EDS
~ problems ERRATA

Puccini
~ opera EDGAR, TOSCA
~ piece ARIA
~ work OPERA

puce COLOR

puck ELF, IMP
hockey ~ DISC

Puck
~ master OBERON

puckish ELFIN
~ expression GRIN

pudding TREAT
hasty ~ PAP
thickened, as ~ SET

puddle POOL
~ relative POND

pudu DEER

pueblo
~ enemy UTE
~ material ADOBE
~ resident HOPI

Pueblo TRIBE
~ people HOPI

Puente TITO

Puento
~ music SALSA

Puenzo LUIS

puerile INANE

Puerto Rico
~ (abbr.) ISL

puff EXALT, GASP
~ out PAD
~ up ELATE
huff and ~ GASP, PANT
long ~ DRAG

puff ___ ADDER

___ puff CREAM

puffin AUK, BIRD

puffiness EDEMA

___ Puffs COCOA

puffy LARGE

pug DOG, TOY
~ place RING
~ punch JAB
it may be ~ NOSE

Puget Sound INLET

pugilist
~ garb ROBE
~ milieu RING
~ stat KOS, TKO
~ weapon JAB

pugmark TRAIL

pug-nosed SNUB

pulchritudinous FAIR

pule CRY

Pulitzer AWARD
~ category DRAMA
~ contemporary OCHS

pull DRAG, ENTREE, HAUL, LUG, TOW, TUG
~ a boner ERR
~ a bowstring DRAW
~ a gun DRAW
~ ahead of PASS
~ along TRAIL
~ an all-nighter CRAM
~ apart REND, SPLIT, TEAR
~ a scam CON
~ down EARN, GET, MAKE, NET, RAZE
~ in ARRIVE, COME, DRAW, NAB, ROPE

~ off a coup OUST
~ one's leg KID, TEASE
~ out DRAW, FLEE, MOVE
~ out of DROP
~ over HALT, STOP
~ someone's leg PLAY, TEASE
~ the lever VOTE
~ the plug on END, STOP
~ the trigger FIRE
~ the wool over someone's eyes CON, DUPE, LIE, SCAM
~ through HEAL, MEND
~ together AMASS, BAND, UNITE
~ to pieces REND, TEAR
~ tricks LARK
~ up HALT, HIKE, RAISE, REST, STOP
~ up stakes LEAVE, MOVE
~ up to the bar CHIN
bar ~ TAP
moon's ~ TIDE

pull ___ RANK

pull ___ (accomplish) OFF

pull ___ (grocery stat) DATE

pull ___ (leave) OUT

pull ___ (withdraw) AWAY

pull-___ TAB, UPS

___-pull LEG

pull a fast ___ ONE

pulled
it may be ~ LEG

puller
leg ~ LIAR
plow ~ MULE
stagecoach ~ TEAM

___-puller LEG

pullers
dogsled ~ TEAM
plow ~ OXEN

pullet BIRD, HEN

pulley CRANE

Pullman CAR, TRAIN

pull out ___ the stops ALL

pullover TEE

pullulate TEEM

pull-ups
do ~ CHIN

pulmonary
~ organ LUNG

pulp MASH, PASTE, PUREE

"Pulp Fiction"
John's ~ costar UMA
Uma in ~ MIA

pulpit AMBO, STAND
~ addr. SER

pulsate BEAT

pulse BEAT, PLANT
fiber-optics ~ LASER

Pulver
~ rank ENS

pulverize BEAT, MASH, MILL, RAZE, ROUT, SMASH

pulverized FINE

puma ANIMAL, CAT

Puma
~ rival NIKE

pumice
~ feature PORE
~ source LAVA
use ~ ABRADE

pummel BANG, BEAT, HARM, HIT, LAM, MAUL, PELT, SMITE

pump SHOE
~ abbr. GAL
~ detail OCTANE
~ in a way ASK
~ off DRAW
~ ornament CLIP
~ purchase GAS
circulatory ~ HEART
fix a ~ SOLE
what bodybuilders ~ IRON
word on a ~ AIR

pump ___ (work out) IRON

___ pump AIR, GAS, HEAT

pumped
it may be ~ IRON

pumper
~ pride ABS

pumpernickel
~ relative RYE

"Pumping ___" IRON

pumpkin COLOR, PIE

pumpkin ___ PIE

"Pumpkin ___, The" EATER

pumpkin eater
~ of rhyme PETER

pumps
wearing ~ SHOD

pun GAG, PLAY
~ ender STER

punch AWL, BANG, BEAT, BELT, CHOP, DIG, FIRE, HIT, JAB, LIFE, PASTE, PELT, SALT, SMITE, TANG, TOOL
~ cattle HERD
~ in ARRIVE, COME, ENTER
~ kin ADE
~ server LADLE
boxer's ~ CHOP, JAB
planter's ~ ingredient RUM
punchless ~ ADE
spike the ~ LACE
zombie's ~ RUM

punch ___ CARD, LINE

punch ___ (leave) OUT

Punch
pleased as ~ ELATED

punchbowl
~ partner LADLE

puncheon LOG, SLAB

puncher
cowhide ~ AWL

punches
roll with the ~ ADAPT, COPE

punching
~ tool AWL

punching ___ BAG

punchless
~ punch ADE

punchline END
~ reaction HAHA

punctilious PRIM
~ one PRIG

punctual
not ~ LATE

punctuate DOT, STRESS

punctuation
~ mark DASH

puncture BITE, CLAW, HOLE, LEAK, STAB, STING
~ result FLAT

punctured FLAT

puncturing
~ tool AWL

pundit GURU, SAGE, SWAMI

pung SLED

pungency BITE, SALT, TANG

pungent ACRID, HOT, RACY
~ garnish CRESS
~ plant ONION
very ~ ACRID

Punic WAR

Punic War
~ city UTICA

punish AVENGE, FINE
~ severely CANE, TAR

punishing BAD

punishment RAP, ROD
light ~ SLAP
monetary ~ FINE

Punjab
~ cohort ASP
~ friend ANNIE
~ potentate RAJAH
~ royal woman RANEE, RANI

punk BLAH, HOOD, KID

punkah FAN

punkie GNAT

punster CARD, WAG, WIT

punt BET, BOAT, PLAY

Punta ___ ARENAS

Punta Arenas CITY, PORT

Punta del ___, Uruguay ESTE

punter
~ org. NFL

Punxsutawney ___ PHIL

puny MEAN, POOR, SMALL
~ pup RUNT

pup BEAR, DOG, PET
~ protest YELP
nasty ~ CUR
smallest ~ RUNT
when Hector was a ~ PAST, YORE

pup ___ TENT

pupil
~ companion LENS
~ covering UVEA
~ gift APPLE
~ in French ELEVE
~ locale EYE, IRIS
~ place DESK, EYE
math ~, at times ADDER

puppet DUPE, TOOL, TOY

___ puppet HAND

"Puppet ___ String" ONA

puppy BRAT, DOG, PET

puppy ___ LOVE

"Puppy ___" LOVE

"Puppy Love"
~ singer ANKA

___ pura AQUA

Purcell SARAH

purchase GET, HOLD
~ alternative LEASE
~ offer BID

purchased
just ~ NEW

purchaser
software ~ USER

purchasing
govt. ~ org. GSA

pure CLEAN, CLEAR, MERE, NEAT, SOLID, SWEET, UTTER

purée PASTE

purely ALL, ONLY

Pure Reason
~ exponent KANT

"Pure Woman, A"
~ of an 1891 novel TESS

purfle ADORN, EDGE

"Purgatorio"
~ author DANTE

purge CLEAN

purify CLEAN

Purim
~ month ADAR
~ queen ESTHER

purist PRIG

puritan PRIG

puritanical BLUE, PRIM, SOBER, STERN

purity
rate for ~ ASSAY

purl EDGE, KNIT, LAP

purlieu AREA, SITE

purloin CRIB, NIP, ROB, STEAL, TAKE

"Purloined Letter, The"
  ~ author POE

purple
  dark ~ fruit SLOE
  it may be ~ PROSE
  shade of ~ LILAC

"Purple ___" RAIN

"Purple ___, The" HEART

"Purple ___ of Cairo, The" ROSE

"___ Purple" DEEP

"___ Purple, The" COLOR

Purple Heart AWARD, MEDAL

"Purple People ___" EATER

"Purple Rose of ___, The" CAIRO

"Purple Rose of Cairo, The"
  ~ director ALLEN

purplish
  ~ blue AZURE
  ~ flower ASTER

purport ESSENCE
  general ~ TENOR

purpose AIM, CAUSE, END, GOAL, PLAN, SAKE, SENSE, USE
  devious ~ ANGLE
  serve the ~ AVAIL
  serving a ~ UTILE
  suited to its ~ APT
  suit the ~ SERVE
  ultimate ~ END
  without ~ IDLY

___-purpose ALL, DUAL

purposeful
  ~ one DOER

purr CRY, DRONE, NOISE

purrer CAT

purse BAG, POOL, STAKE
  ~ carrier STRAP
  ~ fastener CLASP, SNAP
  ~ item COMB
  big ~ TOTE
  change ~ BAG
  loosen the ~ strings SPEND
  protection in a ~ MACE
  shepherd's ~ WEED
  tighten the ~ strings STINT

___ purse COIN

purslane WEED

pursue CHASE, HUNT, SEEK, TAG, TRAIL, WOO
  ~ one's course WEND
  ~ relentlessly DOG
  ~ romantically WOO

pursuer BEAU
  Pleiades ~ ORION

pursuers
  outlaw's ~ POSSE

pursuing AFTER, INTO

pursuit CHASE, HUNT
  cultural ~ ARTS
  in ~ of AFTER
  leisure ~ PLAY
  thespian's ~ ROLE

"Pursuit of the Graf ___" SPEE

purvey CATER, FEED

Purviance EDNA

purview KEN, PALE
  ump's ~ BASE, PLATE

Pusan CITY, PORT
  ~ country KOREA

push BEAR, ELBOW, EXERT, GOAD, IMPEL, JAM, MOVE, PRESS, PROD, SELL
  ~ ahead NOSE
  ~ around BOSS
  ~ back REPEL
  ~ button predecessor DIAL
  ~ down DENT, TAMP
  ~ for URGE
  ~ forward IMPEL
  ~ in DENT
  ~ off LEAVE, PART, SPLIT, START
  ~ oneself LABOR
  ~ rudely ELBOW
  ~ (through) SLOG
  ~ to the limit TEST

push ___ (depart) OFF

pushcart
  ~ purchase ICE

pushed
  ~ together DENSE

pusher
  pram ~ NANA

___ pushers PEDAL

pushes
  a nanny ~ it PRAM

Pushkin
  ~ hero BORIS

pushover DUPE, SAP, SNAP
  like a ~ EASY

pushy EAGER
  be ~ ELBOW

puss FACE, PAN

Puss-in-Boots CAT

pussycat
  ~ suitor OWL

"Pussy cat, pussy cat, where have you ___?" BEEN

pussyfoot SNEAK, STEAL

put LAY, PLANT
  ~ aboard LADE
  ~ across SHOW
  ~ a damper on SLAKE
  ~ a hole in STAVE
  ~ a mark on LABEL
  ~ a match to FIRE, LIT
  ~ ammo in LOAD
  ~ a move on CHASE

~ an end to ANNUL, CEASE, STOP
~ another match to RELIT
~ a question ASK, POSE
~ aside ALLOW, DEFER, ONICE, SAVE, STORE, TABLE
~ a spell on ZAP
~ asunder TEAR
~ at ease ALLAY
~ at risk BET
~ a value on ASSESS, RATE
~ away CRAM, EAT, FILE, SAVE, STASH, STORE, STOW
~ away alphabetically FILE, SORT
~ back RESTORE
~ back on one's feet CURE
~ back to zero RESET
~ belowdecks STOW
~ by STASH
~ distance between SPACE
~ down ABASE, DIS, END, LAY, NOTE, PEN, SLAM, SLUR, TWIT, WRITE
~ down, as track LAY
~ down pipe LAY
~ down roots SETTLE
~ down stakes ABIDE, STAY
~ faith in RELY
~ forcibly CLAP
~ forward ASSERT, EXERT, ISSUE, LAY, POSE, RAISE, SAY
~ in a box CASE, CRATE
~ in a call DIAL, PHONE, RING
~ in a good word for LAUD
~ in a holding pattern DEFER
~ in an appearance COME
~ in a nutshell RECAP, SUM
~ in a row ALINE, RANK
~ in a snit ANGER, IRK, PEEVE, RILE, UPSET
~ in cold storage DEFER, TABLE
~ in fizz AERATE
~ in good repair RESTORE
~ in groups SORT
~ in jeopardy RISK
~ in mothballs STORE, TABLE
~ in office ELECT
~ in one's diary ENTER
~ in opposition PIT
~ in order FILE, MEND, RANGE, SORT
~ in piles SORT
~ in plain sight SHOW
~ in play SERVE
~ in position SET
~ in something extra ADD
~ in sync PHASE
~ in the closet HANG
~ in the hold LADE
~ in the hole COST
~ in the ledger ENTER
~ into action EXERT
~ into cipher ENCODE
~ into circulation ISSUE
~ into effect ENACT
~ into folders FILE
~ into service USE
~ into shape RENEW
~ into the pot ANTE

~ into words RELATE, SAY, STATE, TALK, UTTER
~ it to ASK
~ money in ANTE
~ money on BET
~ new life into RESTORE
~ off DEFER, DETER, REMIT, STALL
~ on ADD, DON, DRESS, GAIN, HIRE, KID, SLIP, STAGE, WEAR
~ on a back burner DEFER, TABLE
~ on a happy face GRIN, SMILE
~ on airs POSE
~ on an act FAKE
~ on a pedestal ADORE, ESTEEM, EXALT
~ on a play ENACT, STAGE
~ on apparel DRESS
~ on a show ACT, AMUSE, STAGE
~ on board LADE, LOAD
~ on CD ENCODE
~ on disk CUT
~ on display ARRAY, SHOW
~ one over on CON, GET, HAVE
~ one past ACE
~ one's foot down STAMP, STEP
~ one's foot in one's mouth ERR
~ one's two cents in ADD
~ on guard ALERT, WARN
~ on hold DEFER, TABLE
~ on notice ALERT, WARN
~ on one's feet AID, RAISE
~ on one's tab BILL
~ on paper PEN, WRITE
~ on radio AIR
~ on tape CUT
~ on the air RADIO
~ on the alert ALARM, WARN
~ on the books ENACT, ENTER
~ on the brakes SLOW
~ on the dog PARADE
~ on the feedbag EAT
~ on the line BET, RISK
~ on the payroll HIRE
~ on the pile ADD
~ on the shelf DEFER, TABLE
~ on the street BAIL
~ on TV AIR
~ on weight GAIN
~ on years AGE
~ out ANGER, EMIT, EXERT, IRK, ISSUE, OUST, PEEVE, RILE
~ out a runner TAG
~ out dinner SERVE
~ pen to paper WRITE
~ right AMEND, REMIT
~ someone on PLAY, TEASE
~ the collar on ARREST, NAB
~ the finger on NAME
~ the heat on MAKE
~ the kibosh on BAN, END, HALT, STEM, STOP, VETO
~ the pedal to the metal SPEED

put ___

~ the screws to IMPEL, MAKE, MOVE
~ through the paces TEST
~ to ASK, POSE
~ to advantage USE
~ to flight REPEL, ROUT
~ together ADD, AMASS, MAKE
~ to rest ALLAY
~ to rights ORDER
~ to sea SAIL
~ to sleep BORE
~ to the blush SHAME
~ to the proof ASSAY, TEST, TRY
~ to use EXERT, PLY
~ to work HIRE, USE
~ two and two together ADD
~ under SEDATE
~ under observation EYE
~ up ANTE, BED, BET, ERECT, MAKE, RAISE, REAR
~ up a notice POST
~ up curtains HANG
~ up in lights BILL
~ up wallpaper PASTE
~ up with ABIDE, ALLOW, BEAR, LET, STAND, TAKE
~ words to music SET
shot ~ EVENT
stay ~ HOLD
what some ~ on AIRS

put ___ (accomplish) OVER
put ___ (delay) OFF
put ___ (explain) ACROSS
put ___ (extinguish) OUT
put ___ (save) AWAY
put ___ (save up) ASIDE

put ___ act ONAN
put ___ disadvantage ATA
put ___ good word for INA
put ___ show ONA
put-___ UPON
___ put HARD, SHOT, STAY
"Put ___ Happy Face" ONA
"Put a ___ on it!" LID
"Put a lid ___!" ONIT
putdown SLAM, SLUR, SNUB
sharp ~ SLAP
put down ___ ROOTS
Put-in-Bay
~ lake ERIE
Putnam ISRAEL
put-off LATE
put on ___ AIRS
put-on FAKE, FALSE, RUSE, SHAM
snob's ~ AIRS
put on an ___ ACT
put one's ___ in OAR
put one's foot ___ INIT
put on the ___ DOG, MAP
putrid BAD, RANK
putt
first to ~ AWAY
putter PLAY
~ org. PGA

put the ___ before the horse CART
put the ___ on ARM, BITE
putting
~ on aesthetic airs ARTY
___-putting OFF
"Puttin' on the Ritz"
~ singer TACO
put to ___ REST, SHAME
put to the ___ TEST
"Put up or ___ up!" SHUT
"Put Your Head on My Shoulder"
~ singer ANKA
Puzo MARIO
~ character DON
puzzle DAZE, GET, KNOT
~ direction ACROSS
~ element CLUE
~ help HINT
~ over MUSE
Chinese ~ POSER
kind of ~ REBUS
puzzled ASEA, ATSEA, LOST
puzzler
~ need ERASER
puzzling HARD
pvt.
~ superior NCO
like a ~ ENL
pwr.
~ source ELEC

Pygmalion
sister of ~ DIDO
"Pygmalion"
~ author SHAW
~ opener ACTI
pygmy RUNT, SMALL
Pyle ERNIE
pylon POST
traffic ~ CONE
Pym MRS
pyramid PILE
~ actually TOMB
~ part BASE
~ tip APEX
glass ~ architect PEI
Pyrenees RANGE
region south of the ~ IBERIA
pyrite ORE
___ pyrite IRON
pyrolusite ORE
pyromania ARSON
pyromaniac
~ crime ARSON
Pythias
~ to Damon PAL
python BOA, SNAKE
pyx CASE
"Pyx, The"
~ director HART

Q
~ **neighbor** TAB
~ **successors** RST

Q ___ "queen" ASIN

Q-___ TIP

"Q & A"
~ **actor** NOLTE

Q&A
part of ~ ANS

Qabus bin Said, Sultan OMANI

Qatar
~ **et al.** OPEC
~ **leader** AMIR, EMEER, EMIR
~ **locale** ARABIA, ASIA
~ **neighbor** OMAN

Qatari ARAB

Qattara Depression DESERT

QB
~ **objectives** TDS
~ **org.** NFL

"QB VII"
~ **author** URIS

QED
~ **part** ERAT

QE2 BOAT, LINER, SHIP
aboard the ~ ASEA, ATSEA

Qinghai LAKE

qintar COIN

Qom
~ **country** IRAN
~ **resident** IRANI

Q-Tip SWAB

qty. AMT
least ~ MIN
liquid ~ GAL

Q-U
~ **link** RST

qua
sine ~ non GIST, NEED

qua ___ (here and there) ELA

quack CRY, FAKE
~ **grass** WEED

"Quackser Fortune ___ a Cousin
in the Bronx" HAS

quad PATIO, YARD
~ **building** DORM

quadr-
~ **predecessor** TRI
~ **successor** PENT

quadrangle PATIO
Harvard ~ YARD

quadrille DANCE

quadrumane APE

quadruped BEAST
~ **parent** SIRE
sprightly ~ COLT

quadruple GROW

quads
~ **kin** ABS

quaestor
~ **subordinate** EDILE

quaff ALE, BEER, RUM
~ **quantity** PINT
citrus ~ ADE
medieval ~ MEAD
Yuletide ~ NOG
see also beverage, drink

quag MIRE

quagga
~ **cousin** HORSE

quaggy LIMP

quagmire FEN

quahog CLAM

Quaid, Dennis
~ **film of 1988** DOA

Quai d'Orsay
view from the ~ SEINE

quail BIRD, FEAR, SHY, START
~ **from** HATE

quaint ODD

quake
make ~ SCARE
minor ~ TREMOR

quaker
forest ~ ASPEN

Quaker
~ **pronoun** THEE, THOU

~ **verb** ART

Quakers SECT

Quaker State
~ **city** ERIE
~ **founder** PENN

quaking
~ **tree** ASPEN

qualification ASSET
~ **form** TEST

qualified ABLE, APT, FIT, GOOD

qualifiers IFS

qualify ENABLE, PASS
~ **for** EARN

quality AROMA, AURA, FINE,
ODOR, STYLE, TONE
~ **(suffix)** ISM, NESS, SHIP
characteristic ~ AROMA,
SAVOR
cheerleader's ~ PEP
musical ~ TONE
pervasive ~ AURA, ODOR
primal ~ ESSENCE
sophisticated ~ CLASS
useful ~ ASSET
vivid ~ COLOR
winter-air ~ NIP

qualm FEAR, PANG

"___ quam videri" ESSE

quandary BIND, HOLE, MESS,
PASS, SNARL

Quang ___ TRI

Quangtri
~ **locale** NAM

___ qua non SINE

Quantico
org. that trains at ~ FBI

quantity DEAL, DOSE, MASS, SIZE,
STORE, SUM
blood-bank ~ UNIT
cook's ~ DASH
firewood ~ CORD
fixed ~ UNIT
greater ~ MORE
humungous ~ SCAD
large ~ ACRE, GOB, LOT, MASS,
OCEAN, RAFT, SEA, TON,
YARD

liquid ~ LITER, PINT
medicine ~ DOSE
not in ~ APIECE
small ~ DASH, DRAM, DROP,
IOTA
tea ~ SPOT

Quant, Mary
~ **design** MINI
~ **look** MOD

"Quantum ___" LEAP

"Quantum Leap"
~ **role** SAM

quarantine
in ~ ALONE

quark
~ **container** ATOM

___ quark TOP

quarrel ROW, SCRAP, SETTO, SPAT,
TILT

quarrelsome TESTY

quarry GAME, MINE, PIT, PREY
~ **cousin** MINE
~ **yield** STONE
cat's ~ RAT
dogcatcher's ~ CUR
hound's ~ HARE
predator's ~ PREY
sniggler's ~ EEL

quart UNIT
~ **ender** ILE
half a ~ PINT
metric ~ LITER
quarter of a ~ CUP

quarter AREA, BED, COIN, CUT,
PART, REALM, ROOM, SPOT,
ZONE
~ **of a quart** CUP
~ **of eight** TWO
half of a ~ BIT
less than a ~ TENTH

quarter ___ HORSE, NOTE

___ Quarter LATIN

quarterback
~ **move** FADE
~ **resource** ARM
~ **signal** HIKE
~ **target** END
~ **throw** PASS

quarterly
- former Packers ~ STARR
- tackle the ~ SACK
- the ~ takes it SNAP

quarterly ORGAN, PAPER

quarters ABODE, HOME, STALL
- ~ in a sultan's palace HAREM
- at close ~ NEAR
- bivouac ~ TENT
- campus ~ DORM
- cardinal's ~ NEST
- cramped ~ CELL
- living ~ ABODE
- military ~ CAMP
- monk's ~ CELL
- Scout ~ TENT
- seraglio ~ ODA
- sow's ~ PEN, STY
- squalid ~ STY
- take up ~ ABIDE
- two ~ HALF
- winter ~ DEN

quartet
- ~ member ALTO, BASS, BASSO, TENOR
- ~ minus one TRIO
- deck ~ ACES, TENS
- half a ~ DUO, PAIR, TWO
- square's ~ SIDES

"___ Quartet" (Beethoven piece) HARP

quartz
- ~ color ROSE
- ~ grains SAND
- deep-orange ~ SARD
- like ~ HARD
- multicolored ~ AGATE
- smoky ~ GEM

___ quartz ROSE

quash ANNUL, END, HALT, ROUT, STEM, STOP
- ~ legally ESTOP

quasi NEAR

Quasimodo
- ~ creator HUGO
- ~ portrayer LON

Quasimodo, Salvatore POET
- see also poet

Quatermain, Allan HERO

quatrainist
- famous ~ OMAR

quattro
- ~ preceder TRE

quaver NOTE, SING, TREMOR

quavering REEDY

quay HAVEN, LEVEE, MOLE, PIER

Quayle DAN

Quayle, Dan
- ~ st. IND
- ~ successor GORE

"Que ___..." SERA

Que.
- ~ neighbor ONT

Quebec
- ~ neighbor MAINE
- see also French

Quechua INCA

Queeg
- ~ ship CAINE

queen ANT, CARD, LADY, TITLE
- ~ address MAAM
- ~ beater ACE
- ~ home HIVE
- ~ in French REINE
- ~ mate DRONE
- ~ of Carthage DIDO
- ~ of heaven HERA
- ~ subject BEE
- English ~ ANNE
- former ~ of Spain ENA
- Greek ~ of the gods HERA
- legendary ~ DIDO
- Nile ~, for short CLEO
- Old Testament ~ ESTHER
- Olympian ~ HERA
- scat ~ ELLA

queen-___ SIZE

Queen
- ~ fliers RAF
- ~ of Hearts' pastry TART

Queen ___ ANNE

"Queen ___" BEE

"___ Queen, The" BEET, MAY

Queen Anne STYLE

Queen Anne's ___ LACE

"Queen-Anne's-Lace" POEM

"Queen Elizabeth" BOAT, LINER, SHIP

Queen, Ellery
- co-creator of ~ LEE

queenly REGAL

"Queen Mary" BOAT, LINER, SHIP

Queen Maud RANGE

Queen of ___ SHEBA

"Queen of the West, The" DALE, EVANS

queens
- game of kings and ~ CHESS

Queens
- ~ field SHEA
- ~ team METS
- ~ tennis stadium ASHE

queen-sized ___ BED

Queequeg
- ~ captain AHAB

queer ODD

Queler EVE

quell ALLAY, END, HALT, STAY, STEM, STOP

"___ Que Nada" MAS

quench ALLAY, SLAKE
- ~ completely SATE

quencher
- thirst ~ ADE, ALE, BEER, TEA, WATER

quenelle MEAT

Quentin CRISP

___ Quentin SAN

"Que pasa?"
- reply to ~ NADA

quercus OAK

quern MILL

querulous TESTY

query ASK
- ~ encl. SASE

ques.
- ~ response ANS

"Que Sera, Sera"
- ~ singer DAY

quest HUNT, SEEK
- actor's ~ OSCAR
- boxer's ~ TITLE
- carnivore ~ MEAT
- commuter's ~ EXIT
- dove's ~ PEACE
- open-season ~ DEER
- pirate's ~ LOOT
- researcher's ~ CURE
- sourdough's ~ CLAIM, GOLD
- thespian's ~ ROLE

"Quest ___ Fire" FOR

"Questa notte" ARIA

"Quest for ___" FIRE

question ASK, ISSUE, POLL, POSER, PRY, SEEK
- ~ to Brutus ETTU
- anticipatory ~ AND
- a ~ of identity WHO
- ask a ~ POSE
- baffling ~ POSER
- beyond ~ CLEAR, SURE, TRUE
- Caesar's ~ ETTU
- kind of ~ ESSAY
- loaded ~ TRAP
- pose a ~ ASK
- reporter's ~ WHO
- word in a sentry's ~ FOE

questionable BAD, OPEN

questionables IFS

questioners
- conference ~ MEDIA, PRESS

questionnaire
- ~ datum SEX
- ~ info AGE

"___ questions?" ANY

quetzal BIRD

queue FILE, LINE, ROW, TAIL, TRAIL, TRAIN
- ~ after Q RST
- airport ~ CABS

queued
- ~ up AROW

quibble ARGUE, EVADE

quibbler
- ~ picking NIT

quiche PIE
- ~ alternative OMELET
- ~ ingredient EGG

quick AGILE, ALIVE, AWARE, FAST, FLEET, RAPID, SMART, SPRY
- ~ change LEAP
- ~ drink SNORT
- ~ look PEEP
- ~ meal BITE, NOSH
- ~ movement DART
- ~ on one's feet AGILE
- ~ snake RACER
- ~ step TROT
- ~ to learn APT, SMART
- ~ trip HOP, RUN, SPIN
- ~ with a reply GLIB
- make a ~ exit FLEE, HIE, RUN
- mentally ~ AGILE
- pretty ~ ANON, SOON
- reach a ~ conclusion LEAP
- take a ~ look at SCAN
- too ~ RASH
- to the ~ HOME
- unduly ~ RASH

quick ___ wink ASA

quicken FIRE, RESTORE, SPUR, STIR

quicker
- ~ than a flash BANG

quicker-than-the-eye
- ~ movement BLUR

quickly APACE, ASAP, FAST, SOON, STAT

quickness HASTE, SPEED

quick on the ___ DRAW

quicksilver METAL

quick-witted AGILE, ALERT, KEEN

quid ___ quo PRO

quiddity ESSENCE, SOUL

quidnunc YENTA
- like a ~ NOSY

quid pro quo SWAP, TRADE

quiescence PEACE, REST

quiet ABATE, ALLAY, CALM, EASE, GAG, MUTE, PEACE, SEDATE, SERENE, SETTLE, SLAKE, SLOW, TACIT
- ~ down ABATE
- ~ greeting NOD
- ~ one CLAM
- ~ partner PEACE
- ~ street LANE
- ~ type MOUSE
- be ~ REST
- peace and ~ ORDER
- remain ~ LIE, SIT

quiet ___ mouse ASA

Quiet ___ (rock group) RIOT

"Quiet ___, The" MAN

"Quiet Man, The"
- ~ star OHARA

"___ Quiet on the Western Front" ALL

quietus END, REST

"Quigley Down ___" UNDER

quill BARB, PEN
~ **end** NIB

quilt SEW
~ **stuffing** EIDER
crazy ~ OLIO

quilting
~ **party** BEE

quince TREE

"Quincy"
~ **actor** ITO

Quindlen ANNA

quinine
~ **water** TONIC

Quintana Roo
see Spanish

Quint, Capt.
~ **boat** ORCA

quintessence CORE, CREAM, GIST, HEART, MEAT, PEARL, SOUL, SUM

quintet
one of a wet ~ ERIE

quip GAG, GIBE, MOT

quipster CARD, WAG, WIT

quipu
~ **maker** INCA

quirk TRAIT
behavioral ~ TIC
language ~ IDIOM

quirky ODD

quirt LASH, ROD

quit CEASE, CLEAR, END, EXIT, HALT, LEAVE
~ **a course** DROP
~ **one's hold on** CEDE
~ **stalling** ACT
~ **the scene** FLEE, RUN

quitclaim DEED

quite
~ **a while** DAYS, EON

Quito CITY
see also Spanish

quits
call it ~ END, HALT, STOP

quitter
~ **cry** UNCLE
~ **word** CANT

quitting time
~ **for some** FIVE

quiver BEAT, BOIL, FEAR, STIR, TREMOR
~ **item** ARROW

quivering
~ **motion** TIC, TREMOR
~ **tree** ASPEN

qui vive
on the ~ ALERT, AWARE, WARY

"___ Quixote" DON

Quixote, Don HERO

quiz ASK, EXAM, PRY, TEST
~ **answer** FALSE, TRUE
~ **resp.** ANS

___ quiz POP

"Quiz ___" SHOW

quiz show
~ **host** EMCEE

Qum
~ **country** IRAN

native of ~ IRANI

Qumran
~ **inhabitant** ESSENE

quod ___ demonstrandum ERAT

quod ___ faciendum ERAT

quoits GAME
play ~ TOSS

quondam AGO, ERST, OLD

quota DOLE, LIMIT, SHARE, STINT

quotation COST, CUT, RATE
~ **attribution** ANON
commercial ~ COST

quote CITE, CLIP, REFER
betting ~ ODDS

quotes
source of ~ NYSE

"Quoth the ___..." RAVEN

"Quo Vadis?"
~ **actress** KERR
~ **character** NERO, PETER
~ **director** LEROY
~ **garb** TOGA

R
  ~ followers STU
  give an ~ RATE

___-ra AMEN

Ra ELEM, SUN
  88 for ~ ATNO
  symbol of ~ ATEN, ATON

"Ra" BOAT, SHIP

Rabat CITY

rabbi
  ~ detective SMALL

"Rabbi Ben ___" EZRA

rabbit ANIMAL
  ~ cousin HARE
  ~ ears AERIAL
  ~ feature EAR
  ~ foot PAW
  female ~ DOE
  fictional ~ BRER, PETER, ROGER
  toon ~ ROGER

rabbit ___ EARS

Rabbit AUTO, BRER, CAR, PETER, ROGER

"Rabbit ___" TEST

"Rabbit, ___" RUN

___ Rabbit BRER

"___ Rabbit and Tales of Beatrix Potter" PETER

"rabbit food" SALAD

Rabbitt EDDIE

rabble MOB, ROUT

rabblement ADO

rabid AVID, IRATE, MAD

Rabin
  ~ predecessor MEIR
  ~ successor PERES

"___-Ra-Boom-De-Re" TARA

raccoon ANIMAL, FUR
  ~ cousin COATI, PANDA
  ~ marking MASK
  male ~ BOAR

race DART, DASH, EVENT, HIE, RUN,

SPEED, TEAR
  ~ an engine REV
  ~ competitor ENTRY
  ~ course OVAL
  ~ distance MILE
  ~ downhill SKI
  ~ form ENTRY
  ~ place GATE
  ~ portion LAP
  ~ starter GUN
  ~ unit METER, MILE, YARD
  ~ winner barrier TAPE
  auto ~ INDY
  baton passer's ~ RELAY
  Epsom ~, with "the" OAKS
  fabled ~ loser HARE
  letters on some ~ cars STP
  match ~ runner-up LOSER
  Olympic ~ unit METER
  preliminary ~ HEAT
  the human ~ EARTH, MAN

___ race DRAG, FOOT, HORSE, RAT, RELAY, ROAD

Race CAPE

"___ Race, The" RAT

racecar
  ~ sponsor STP

racecourse
  British ~ ASCOT, EPSOM

racehorse NAG, PACER
  certain ~ MARE

racer HORSE, SNAKE
  ~ gauge TACH
  Aesop ~ HARE
  cocky ~ HARE
  downhill ~ SKI, SLED
  kind of ~ MILER

"racer's edge, The" STP

races
  where horse ~ start GATE

racetrack OVAL
  ~ boundary RAIL
  ~ circuit LAP
  ~ figures ODDS
  ~ margin NOSE
  ~ prop GATE
  English ~ ASCOT, EPSOM
  painter of ~ scenes DEGAS

Rachel
  ~ sister LEAH

"Rachel ___ the Stranger" AND

Rachins ALAN

Racine
  ~ play ESTHER
  see also French

racing
  ~ boat SHELL
  ~ circuit LAP

racing-car
  ~ letters GTO

"Racing With the ___" MOON

rack CRIB, GAIT, LAMB, STAND
  ~ and ruin DOOM
  ~ for fodder CRIB
  ~ partner RUIN
  ~ starter COAT, HAT, HAY
  coat ~ TREE
  hay ~ CRIB

racket ADO, BAT, BLARE, BLAST, DIN, GAME, JAR, LINE, NOISE, ROW, SCAM
  ~ ender EER
  sleeper's ~ SNORE

rackety LOUD

racking BAD

___-racking NERVE

Rackstraw, Ralph GOB, TAR

racquetball GAME

racy
  hardly ~ TAME

Radames
  ~ love AIDA

radar
  ~ blip ECHO
  ~ image BLIP
  ~ measure MPH
  ~ sweep SCAN

Radar
  ~ home IOWA
  ~ milieu MASH

Radarange
  ~ maker AMANA

Radcliffe ANN

radial TIRE
  ~ feature TREAD
  ~ filler AIR
  British ~ TYRE

radiance FIRE, GLOW, SHEEN, SHINE

radiant CLEAR
  be ~ GLOW, SHINE

radiate BEAM, CAST, EMIT, GLOW, SHED, SHINE

radiation AURA
  ~ monitoring org. EPA
  ~ unit REM
  infrared ~ HEAT

radiator
  ~ output HEAT, STEAM
  ~ part COIL, VANE
  ~ sound SSS

radical BASIC, LEFT, ULTRA
  1960s ~ org. SDS

radicle ROOT

radio CABLE, SEND
  ~ bands AMS
  ~ drama PLAY
  ~ format NEWS, TALK
  ~ hobbyist HAM
  ~ message SOS
  ~ part DIAL
  ~ receiver SET
  ~ response OUT, OVER, ROGER
  ~ spots ADS
  ~ stations MEDIA
  ~ stns. AMS
  ~ studio sign ONAIR
  ~ tuner KNOB
  ~ wire AERIAL
  London ~ BBC
  put on the ~ AIR

"Radio ___" DAYS

radioactive HOT
  ~ particle BETA

"Radio Days"
  ~ director ALLEN

"Radio Free Europe"
  ~ band REM

radiograph XRAY

radios
truckers' ~ CBS

radish ROOT

radium METAL

"Radium ___" CITY

radius BONE
~ **companion** ULNA
~ **location** ARM

radix ROOT

radon GAS
like ~ INERT

Radziwill LEE

"___ Rae" NORMA

Rae, Norma
~ **concern** UNION

___ Rafael, Calif. SAN

Rafelson BOB

Rafelson, Bob
~ **film of 1968** HEAD

raffia PALM

Rafsanjani IRANI
~ **country** IRAN

raft HEAP, MASS, MOB, OCEAN,
PILE, SEA, STORE
~ **wood** BALSA
propel a ~ POLE

___ raft LIFE

rafter BEAM, PROP
~ **locale** ROOF

rafts ALOT

rag BAIT, GIBE, ORGAN, PAPER,
RIDE, SHEET, SHRED, TEASE
~ **ender** TAG
chew the ~ BLAB, CHAT, GAB,
RAP, TALK, YAK
like a wet ~ LIMP

rag ___ TRADE

raga
first name in ~ RAVI

rag doll ANDY, ANN

rage ANGER, BOIL, FAD, IRE,
MANIA, MODE, RAMP, RAVE,
RIOT, STORM, STYLE
all the ~ CHIC, HOT, NEW
current ~ FAD

"Rage of ___, The" PARIS

"Rage to Live, A"
~ **author** OHARA

ragged EROSE, SEEDY, TORN
~ **robin** PLANT

"Ragged Dick"
~ **author** ALGER

"Raggedy ___" ANDY, ANN, MAN

raggedy-edged EROSE

"Raggedy Man, The" POEM
~ **poet** RILEY

raging IRATE, MAD, RABID, UPSET

ragout HASH, MEAT, OLIO, STEW
~ **ingredient** ONION

rags
glad ~ ATTIRE, DRESS, GARB
in ~ NEEDY, POOR

___ rags GLAD

rags-to-riches
~ **author** ALGER

ragtag
~ **and bobtail** MOB, ROUT

Rahal, Bobby RACER

rah-rah AVID, KEEN

raid LOOT, ROB, SACK
~ **the fridge** EAT, NOSH

___ raid AIR

Raid
~ **target** ANT

raider
~ **of old** HUN

Raiders ELEVEN, TEAM
~ **org.** NFL

"Raiders of the ___ Ark" LOST

"Raiders of the Lost ___" ARK

"Raiders of the Lost Ark"
~ **snake** ASP

rail BAR, BIRD, TRAIN
~ **against** LACE
~ **connection** TIE
~ **crossing sign** STOP
~ **relative** COOT
~ **rider** HOBO
go by ~ TRAIN
like a ~ THIN
strike a ~ CAROM

railing BAR, HOLD

raillery GIBE, TALK

raillike THIN

railroad
~ **beam** TIE
~ **cars** TRAIN
~ **lantern** LAMP
~ **parking space** YARD
~ **station** STOP
~ **terminal** DEPOT
~ **unit** CAR
Jay Gould ~ ERIE
Lackawanna ~ partner ERIE
mine ~ TRAM

"Railroaded!"
~ **director** MANN

railsplitter
famous ~ ABE

railway TRAIN

___ railway COG

railways
overhead ~ ELS

railyard
~ **denizen** HOBO

raiment ARRAY, ATTIRE, DRESS,
GARB, GEAR, WEAR
in ~ CLAD

Raimi SAM

rain POUR, STORM, WATER
~ **cats and dogs** TEEM
~ **check** STUB
~ **collector** EAVE, POND
~ **component** ACID
~ **dancer** HOPI
~ **gear** MAC
~ **hard** POUR
~ **in Japanese** AME
~ **without** DRY
anti-acid ~ org. EPA
bit of ~ DROP
fine ~ MIST
frozen ~ HAIL, SLEET
hard ~ SPATE
without ~ ARID, DESERT, DRY,
SERE

rain ___ and dogs CATS

___ rain ACID

"...rain ___ sleet..." NOR

"Rain"
~ **role** SADIE

"Rain ___" MAN

"Rain, ___, and Speed" STEAM

rainbow ARC, IRIS
~ **color** BLUE, ORANGE, RED
~ **end** POT
~ **fish** SMELT, TROUT
~ **goddess** IRIS
~ **segment** HUE
shaped like a ~ ARCED

rainbow ___ TROUT

"Rainbow ___, The" TRAIL

"___ Rainbow" NEON

Rainbow Falls
~ **site** HILO

raincheck
take a ~ MISS, WAIT

raincoat WRAP
Brit's ~ MAC
winterize a ~ LINE

rain delay
~ **coverup** TARP

raindrop
~ **sound** PLOP

raindrops
hit hard, as ~ PELT

**"Raindrops ___ Fallin' on My
Head"** KEEP

**"Raindrops Keep Fallin' on My
___"** HEAD

Rainer IRIS

Rainer, Luise
~ **Oscar-winning role** OLAN

Raines ELLA, TIM

Rainey
~ **and others** MAS

rainfall
~ **measure** INCH

Rainier
~ **and others** MTS

"___ Raining Men" ITS

"Rain in Spain, The" TANGO

rainless ARID, DESERT, DRY, SERE

"Rains ___, The" CAME

"Raintree County"
~ **actor** ABEL

rainwear MAC

rainy BAD, DAMP, WET
~ **wind direction** EAST
it's saved for a ~ day TARP
not ~ ARID, DRY

rainy ___ DAY

Rainy LAKE

rainy day
~ **rarity** CAB
prepare for a ~ PLAN, SAVE

"Rainy Night in ___, A" RIO

Raisa
see Russian

raise BREED, ERECT, GROW, HIKE,
REAR
~ **a red flag** ALERT, WARN
~ **a ruckus** RAVE, RIOT
~ **as a question** ASK, POSE
~ **as prices** HIKE
~ **cattle** RANCH
~ **hackles** ANGER, IRK, PEEVE,
RILE, UPSET
~ **high** EXALT
~ **in status** EXALT
~ **one's voice** YELL
~ **reason** MERIT
~ **the hem, maybe** ALTER
~ **the roof** REVEL
~ **the spirits of** ELATE
~ **the temperature** WARM
meet a ~ CALL, SEE
something to ~ CAIN

raise ___ CAIN

___ raise MERIT, PAY

raised
~ **platform** DAIS

raiser
curtain ~ ACT, EVENT, INTRO

raises UPS

raise the ___ ROOF

"Raise the ___ Lantern" RED

___-raising HAIR

"Raising Arizona"
~ **actor** CAGE

"Raisin in the ___, A" SUN

"Raisin in the Sun, A"
~ **actress** DEE

raison d'___ ETAT, ETRE

raison d'être BASIS, CAUSE, END

raj REIGN, RULE

Raj
~ **servant** AMA, AMAH

rajah RULER
~ **land** INDIA

Rajiv
~ **wife** RANEE, RANI

Rajiv
see Indian

Rajput
~ **wrap** SARI
see also Indian

"Raj Quartet, The"
~ **title** SAHIB

rake CAD, COMB, ROUE, SATYR, TOOL
~ **cousin** HOE
~ **part** TINE

rake-off CUT, PAY

"Rake's Progress, The" OPERA

rakish FAST, GAY, LEWD, SMART

Raleigh, Walter SIR

rally AROUSE, GAIN, MASS, MEET, ROUSE, STIR
road ~ RACE

___ **rally** PEP, ROAD

Ralph NADER, SMART

ram ANIMAL, JAM, MALE, PRESS, SLAM
~ **down** CRAM, LOAD
~ **mate** EWE
~ **remark** BAA
sign of the ~ ARIES
young ~ LAMB

Ram ARIES
~ **month** APRIL
the ~ SIGN

RAM
~ **counterpart** ROM

Rama HERO

"Rama ___ Ding Dong" LAMA

ramada ARBOR

Ramadan
~ **observance** FAST

"Ramayana" EPIC, POEM, SAGA

ramble DOTE, GAD, HIKE, PRATE, RAVE, ROAM, TALK
~ **around** ROVE
~ **on** YAK

rambler NOMAD, ROSE

rambling LONG, MAD
~ **sort** NOMAD

"Rambling ___" ROSE

"Rambling Rose"
~ **actress** DERN, LADD

"___ ramblin' wreck..." IMA

"Rambo"
~ **setting** NAM

"Ramcaritmanas" POEM

ramekin PAN

Ramiz ALIA

Ramón
see Spanish

ramp RISE, SLANT, SLOPE, TILT
~ **alternative** STAIR

highway ~ EXIT

___ **ramp** EXIT

rampage RIOT, TEAR
go on a ~ RIOT
on a ~ AMOK
on the ~ LOOSE

___ **rampage** ONA

rampaging AMOK

rampant ERECT, RIFE
be ~ REIGN
run ~ RAGE

ramparts
~ **surrounder** MOAT
assail the ~ STORM
storm the ~ ARISE

ramrod IMPEL

"Ramrod"
~ **guitarist** EDDY

Rams ELEVEN, TEAM
~ **org.** NFL

___ **Ramsay ("The Black Stallion" hero)** ALEC

Ramses
~ **river** NILE

ramshackle OLD

___ **-ran** ALSO

Rancagua CITY
see also Spanish

ranch ABODE, HOME
~ **menace** PUMA
~ **ruminant** CALF, HORSE, STEER
~ **unit** ACRE
~ **vacationer** DUDE
~ **worker** HAND

___ **ranch** DUDE

rancher
~ **need** HAY, LASSO, WATER
~ **responsibility** HERD
~ **tool** PROD

rancheria ABODE, HOME

ranchero
~ **wrap** SERAPE

rancho ABODE, HOME

"Rancho Notorious"
~ **director** LANG

rancid BAD, RANK, SOUR

rancor EVIL, HATE, SIN, SPITE

Randall TONY

Rand McNally
~ **product** ATLAS, MAP

Randolph SCOTT

"Random Harvest"
~ **director** LEROY

Rand, Sally
gear for ~ FAN

Randy OWEN
~ **skating partner** TAI

range ARRAY, BAND, HIKE, RANK, ROAM, ROVE, RUN, SCALE, SIZE, SPHERE
~ **(abbr.)** MTS
~ **animal** STEER
~ **infant** CALF
~ **of activity, to a poet** ORB
~ **of awareness** KEN
~ **of influence** SPHERE
~ **piece** RIFLE
~ **roamer** BISON
~ **rope** LASSO
Aconcagua's ~ ANDES
Asian ~ ALAI
at close ~ NEAR
Caspian Sea ~ URAL
Chilean ~ ANDES
Europe/Asia border ~ URAL
home on the ~ TENT, TEPEE
Innsbruck ~ ALPS
Moroccan ~ ATLAS
Mount Narodnaya's ~ URALS
out of ~ AFAR
part of the ~ OVEN
Rocky Mountain ~ TETON, UINTA
Russian ~ ALAI
sax ~ ALTO, TENOR
voice ~ ALTO, BASS, TENOR

___ **-range** LONG

Rangeley LAKE

Rangers SIX, TEAM, TEN
~ **milieu** ICE, RINK
~ **org.** NHL

___ **Ranger, The** LONE

___ **-ranging** WIDE

rangy LANK, LEAN, SLIM, TALL, THIN

rani
~ **servant** AMA, AMAH
~ **spouse** RAJAH
~ **wear** SARI

rank BAD, CASTE, CLASS, FILE, ORDER, RANGE, RATE, SORT, TIER, TOTAL
~ **and file** MOB
~ **contestants** SEED
~ **partner** FILE
~ **sensation** ODOR
~ **(suffix)** SHIP
Boy Scout ~ EAGLE, LIFE, STAR
elevate in ~ EXALT
grow ~ ROT
higher in ~ ABOVE
lower in ~ ABASE
of high ~ GREAT

rank and ___ FILE

ranking FIRST

rankle ANGER, IRK, PEEVE, RILE, SMART, UPSET

ranks
in ~ AROW

ransack COMB, HUNT, LOOT, RAID, RIFLE, ROB, SACK, SEEK

ransom FREE

Ransom ___ Olds ELI

Ransom Eli ___ OLDS

Ransom, John POET
see also poet

"Ransom of ___ Chief, The" RED

rant RAGE, RAVE, STORM

rant and ___ RAVE

"___ Ran the Circus" IFI

"___ Ran the Zoo" IFI

ranting IRATE, MAD, UPSET

rap BANG, BAT, CHAT, CLAP, GENRE, HIT, IDIOM, TALK
~ **enthusiast, maybe** TEEN
~ **session** TALK
give a ~ CARE

rap ___ SHEET

rapacious AVID, FERAL

rapacity LUST

"Rape of the Lock, The" POEM
~ **author** POPE

Raphael ANGEL

rapid FAST, FLEET
~ **pace** CLIP
make ~ **strides** DASH, HIE, MOVE, RACE, RUN, SPEED, TEAR

rapid-___ FIRE

Rapid City
~ **st.** SDAK

rapidity HASTE, PACE, SPEED

rapidly APACE, FAST

rapids STREAM
~ **conveyance** RAFT

___ **Rapids, Iowa** CEDAR

rapier STEEL
~ **cousin** EPEE

rapierlike KEEN

rapper
knock a ~ DIS

rapport LOVE, PEACE

rapscallion CAD, DOG, IMP

rap sheet
~ **word** AKA, ALIAS

rap speak
friend, in ~ BRO

rapt DEEP, LOST
~ **ender** URE

raptor EAGLE, OWL
~ **nest** AERIE
~ **victim** PREY

Raptors FIVE, TEAM
~ **org.** NBA

rapture ARDOR, LOVE

rapturous
~ **verse** ODE

Rapunzel
~ **ladder** HAIR
~ **pride** TRESS

rara ___ AVIS

rara avis ONER

rarae ___ AVES

rare ODD
~ bird ONER
~ earth METAL
~ mineral GEM
rarer than ~ RAW

rare-___ element EARTH

rarefied AERIAL, THIN

rarefy THIN

rarer
~ than rare RAW

rarin'
~ to go AVID, EAGER, KEEN

rascal BRAT, CAD, DOG, IMP

rascally BAD

rash ITCH, MAD
not ~ SANE

Rash STEVE

rasher SLICE

rashness
goddess of ~ ATE

rasp ABRADE, ERODE, FILE, GRATE

raspberry BOO, COLOR, GIBE, HISS
~ bit SEED
~ cousin HOOT
~ stem CANE

"Raspberry ___" BERET

"Rasputin ___ the Empress" AND

rat ANIMAL, SING, TELL
~ domain SEWER
~ ender ATAT
~ milieu LAB
~ of film BEN
~ out on DESERT
~ undoing TRAP
rug ~ TOT

rat ___ RACE

rat-___ ATAT

___ rata PRO

ratafia
~ ingredient WINE

ratatouille STEW

ratchet COG

rate ASSESS, EARN, FEE, MERIT,
RANK, TEMPO
~ (abbr.) PCT
~ for purity ASSAY
~ highly DIG, EXALT, LIKE,
LOVE
~ of speed CLIP, PACE
~ poorly PAN
~ starter PRO
heart ~ PULSE

___-rate CUT, FIRST

rated
highly ~ AAA, AONE, BEST,
ONEA, TOPS

rater
film ~ unit STAR

rathe EARLY

rather
~ (suffix) ISH

Rather DAN
~ bailiwick NEWS
~ network CBS

"___ Rather Be With Me" SHED

"Rather you ___ me" THAN

rathole MESS

rathskeller
~ order ALE, BEER, LAGER,
STEIN

ratify ADOPT, ENACT, PASS, SEAL

rating RANK
~ a D POOR
~ unit STAR
bond ~ AAA, BAA
gasoline ~ OCTANE
perfect ~ TEN
superior ~ AONE, ONEA
Wimbledon ~ SEED

ratio
~ phrase ISTO
math ~ SINE
payout ~ ODDS

___ ratio GEAR

ratiocinate ARGUE

ration ALLOT, DOLE, LIMIT, LOT,
PART, SHARE, STINT
~ (out) METE

rational SAGE, SANE, SOLID
~ ender ISM
~ mind EGO

rationale CASE, PEG

rationality SENSE

rations DIET, FARE, KEEP, MEAL

ratite EMU, KIWI, RHEA
extinct ~ MOA

ratline ROPE

Rat Pack
~ member DEAN, DINO, PETER

rat race
~ result STRESS

rats
~ to cats PREY

"Rats!" DARN, DRAT

"___ Rats, The" DESERT

rattan CANE, PALM, ROD

rattle GET, JAR, NOISE, TOY, UPSET
~ on PRATE, TALK
chest ~ RALE

rattlebrained DAFT

rattled
it may get ~ SABER

rattler SNAKE
~ position COIL

rattletrap AUTO, CAR, CRATE,
HEAP, MOTOR

___-rattling SABER

raucous LOUD
~ cry CAW
~ sound BLARE

Raul
see Spanish

rauwolfia TREE

ravage ERODE, SACK, WASTE

ravager HUN

rave RAGE, STORM
~ partner RANT

ravel SNARL

raven BIRD, EBONY, INKY, JET,
SABLE
~ cousin CROW
emulate Poe's ~ RAP

"Raven, The" POEM
~ author POE
first word of ~ ONCE

ravening AVID

ravenous FERAL

Ravens ELEVEN, TEAM
~ org. NFL

"Raven's Wing"
~ author OATES

ravine ABYSS, DALE, GAP, WADI

raving IRATE, MAD, UPSET
stark ~ mad RABID

ravioli PASTA

ravished RAPT

raw NEW, RED, SORE
~ information DATA
~ metal ORE
~ sienna COLOR
it may be ~ DATA, DEAL
make ~ CHAP

"Raw ___" DEAL

rawboned LANK, LEAN, POOR,
SPARE, THIN

"Raw Deal"
~ director MANN

rawhide LASH

"Rawhide"
~ prop LASSO, RIATA
~ singer LAINE

Rawls LOU

raw silk
color of ~ ECRU

ray BEAM, SKATE, STREAM
kind of ~ BETA

ray ___ GUN

___ ray ALPHA, BETA, DELTA

Ray ALDO, MAN

Rayburn GENE, SAM

rayed
~ flower ASTER

ray gun
use a ~ ZAP

___ Ray Hutton INA

Ray, Johnnie
~ tune CRY

Raymond BURR

**___ Raymond ("Flash Gordon"
creator)** ALEX

Raymond B. ___ WEST

rays RADII
catch some ~ BASK, SUN, TAN

raze RUIN

razor
~ asset EDGE
ready a ~ HONE

razor ___ CLAM

razorback BOAR, HOG

Razorbacks
~ st. ARK

razor-billed
~ bird AUK

"Razor's ___, The" EDGE

razz GIBE, HISS, HOOT, NEEDLE,
RIB, TEASE, TWIT

razzle-dazzle ECLAT

Rb ELEM
37 for ~ ATNO

RBI STAT

RC COLA

RCA Dome ARENA

RCMP
~ rank SGT

rd. AVE, RTE

rds. STS

re ABOUT, ASTO, NOTE

Re ELEM
75 for ~ ATNO

reach ABUT, AREA, COME, GET, HIT,
MAKE, RANGE, TOTAL, WIN
~ accord AGREE
~ across SPAN
~ a decision ACT
~ a destination ARRIVE
~ a maximum PEAK
~ a quick conclusion LEAP
~ base headfirst SLIDE
~ into TAP
~ maturity RIPEN
~ new heights GROW, SOAR
~ the top SCALE
out of ~ FAR, SAFE
within ~ CLOSE, NEAR

reached
~ the tarmac ALIT, LIT

___-reaching FAR

react
~ to a compliment BEAM
~ to an uppercut REEL
~ to a sneeze BLESS
~ to onions CRY

reaction

~ with surprise LEAP, START
unlikely to ~ CALM, COOL, INERT, SERENE

reaction
~ to a rodent EEK
~ to bad news ALAS, OHNO
~ to fireworks AAH, OOH, WOW
~ to rudeness SLAP
~ to Stonehenge AWE
amused ~ HAHA
angry ~ RISE
astonished ~ WOW
critical ~ PAN, RAVE
disappointed ~ DARN, DRAT, OHNO, RATS
flu ~ AGUE

reactor
~ part ROD
nuclear ~ PILE

read PORE, SCAN, SEE
~ bar codes SCAN
~ closely PORE
~ the riot act to WARN
~ the signs CAST
it may be ~ PALM
make difficult to ~ ENCODE
one way to ~ ALOUD
something to ~ LIPS

read-___ memory ONLY

___-read LIP, SPEED

readable CLEAN

"Read all ___ it" ABOUT

"Read 'em and ___!" WEEP

reader
~ need LAMP
"Barron's" ~ EXEC
manuscript ~ EDITOR
mind ~ SEER
mind ~ talent ESP

___ reader (fortuneteller) PALM

"Reader's Digest"
~ lack, until 1955 ADS

"Reader's Encyclopedia"
~ editor BENET

Read, Herbert POET
see also poet

readiness
state of ~ ALERT

reading
~ light LAMP
~ position, often ABED
~ room DEN
basement ~ METER
compass ~ ENE, ESE, NNE, NNW, SSE, SSW, WNW, WSW
course ~ TEXT
electronic ~ SCAN
epic ~ SAGA
fortuneteller's ~ PALM
lunchtime ~ MENU
oracle's ~ FATE
radar gun ~ MPH
seismograph ~ TREMOR
speedometer ~ MPH
tach ~ REV

taximeter ~ FARE
waiting-room ~ MAG
weighty ~ TOME

___ reading LIP

Reading
~ and others RRS

"Read my ___!" LIPS

Read, Piers Paul
~ thriller ALIVE

read the ___ act RIOT

read the riot ___ ACT

ready DONE, RIPE
~ a crossbow AIM
~ and willing EAGER, GAME, KEEN
~ a printing press INK
~ a razor HONE
~ a rifle AIM
~ companion ABLE
~ follower SET
~ for action ALERT, ARM, EAGER, FIT, GAME
~ for a hike SHOD
~ for battle ARMED
~ to brag VAIN
~ to burst IRATE, MAD, UPSET
~ to drop ALLIN, BEAT, SPENT, TIRED
~ to fight ARMED
~ to go ONTAP, SET
~ to hit ATBAT
~ to joust ATILT
~ to sell, as brandy AGED
~ to spit IRATE, UPSET
~ to swing ATBAT
~ to try GAME
~ wine AGE
at the ~ HERE, ONTAP
be ~ WAIT
be ~ for AWAIT
get ~ RIPEN
get ~ for dinner DRESS
get ~ informally PREP
get ~ to eat WASH

___ ready MAKE

___-ready CAMERA

"Ready, ___, fire!" AIM

"Ready or ___, here I come!" NOT

"Ready to Wear"
~ actor REA
~ actress LOREN

ready, willing, and ___ ABLE

Reagan RON
~ advisor MEESE
~ and Wyman EXES
~ appointee REGAN
~ attorney general MEESE
~ prog. SDI
~ secretary of state HAIG
~ was its pres. SAG

reagent
chemist's ~ ACID

real COIN, HONEST, SOLID, TRUE
~ ender ISM, IST
for ~ TRUE

it may be ~ ESTATE

real ___ ESTATE, TIME

"___ real!" GET

real estate ASSET, LAND
~ document DEED, LEASE
~ notice TOLET
~ unit ACRE, LOT

real estate ___ AGENT

realgar ORE

realistic SOBER, TRUE

reality FACT

realization
cry of ~ AHA

___-realization SELF

realize ARRIVE, GAIN, GET, GRASP, KNOW, LEARN, NET, REAP, SEE
~ a profit CLEAR
~ in a way SENSE

"really big"
Sullivan had a ~ one SHOW

"___ Really Want" ALLI

"___ Really Want to Do" ALLI

realm AREA, LAND, SPHERE, STATE
~ of beauty ART

Realtor
~ chart PLAT
~ offering HOME, LOT
~ sticker SOLD
~ transaction RESALE

realty
~ abbr. GAR
~ unit ACRE, LOT

ream BORE
~ unit SHEET

reanimate AROUSE

reap CUT, EARN, GET
~ what one has sown PAY

rear BREED, ERECT, RAISE, RISE, STERN
~ end LAST
~ of a plane TAIL
~ up RAMP
bringing up the ~ LAST
bring up the ~ LAG, TRAIL
in the ~ LAST
toward the ~ AFT, ASTERN

reared
~ up ERECT

rearmost AFTER, END, LAST

rearrange ALTER

rearview mirror
~ decoration DICE

rearward AFT

reason AIM, ARGUE, CALL, CAUSE, EDUCE, END, SAKE, SENSE
~ for being CAUSE
~ out EDUCE
~ (with) PLEAD
for no ~ IDLY
for that ~ ERGO, THEN, THUS
rhyme or ~ SENSE

reasonable FAIR, SAGE, SANE, SOLID

reasons
~ to fast forward ADS

reassure CALM
~ Rover PAT

Reb
~ general LEE
~ letters CSA
Yank, to a ~ ENEMY, FOE

Rebecca WEST

Rebekah
husband of ~ ISAAC
son of ~ ESAU

rebel ARISE, RISE
~ org. CSA

rebel ___ YELL

"Rebel, The"
~ singer CASH

"Rebel ___" YELL

rebellion RIOT

"Rebel-Rouser"
~ guitarist EDDY

"Rebel Without a ___" CAUSE

"Rebel Without a Cause"
~ actor DEAN
~ director RAY
Plato in ~ SAL

"Rebel Yell"
~ singer IDOL

reboant LOUD

rebound CAROM, ECHO

rebozo SCARF

rebuff CUT, SHUN, SLAP, SNUB

rebuffs NOES, NOS

rebuke SLAP, TRIM, TWIT

rec ___ ROOM

recalcitrant AVERSE

recall CITE, EVOKE
beyond ~ LOST

"___ recall..." ASI

"___ Recall" TOTAL

recant DENY, DROP

recap TIRE

recapitulate HASH, SUM

recast ALTER

recede EBB, LAPSE, WANE

receipt PAPER, STUB
~ word PAID

receipts SUM
gate ~ TAKE
total ~ GATE

receivable DUE
account ~ IOU

receive ADMIT, GET, GREET, HAVE, TAKE

"received"
   pilot's ~ ROGER

receiver DONEE, HEIR, RADIO
   audio ~ EAR
   gift ~ DONEE
   letter ~ SLOT
   radio-wave ~ SET
   television ~ SET
   TV signal ~ DISH
   wide ~ END

__ receiver WIDE

receiving __ LINE

recent LATE, NEW, PAST
   ~ (prefix) NEO
   most ~ LAST

receptacle BAG, BIN, CAN, CASE, CHEST, CRATE, CUP, DISH, FILE, JAR, PAIL, POT, TANK
   dye ~ VAT
   mail ~ SLOT
   metal ~ CAN
   shallow ~ TRAY
   water ~ SINK

reception LEVEE, SALON
   ~ aid DISH
   ~ enhancer AERIAL
   ~ interference SNOW
   ~ room SALON
   formal ~ LEVEE

receptive OPEN

recess ARBOR, BAY, COVE, DEFER, HALT, HOLE, NOOK, REST, WAIT
   church ~ APSE
   coastal ~ COVE
   flowered ~ ARBOR
   shady ~ ARBOR
   shore ~ INLET

recession EBB, WANE

recessive
   it may be ~ GENE

rechannel TURN

recherché RARE

recidivism LAPSE

Recife CITY
   city near ~ NATAL

recipe
   ~ amount DASH
   ~ amt. TBS, TSP
   ~ direction ADD, BAKE, BEAT, BOIL, CHOP, DICE, HEAT, SAUTE, SCALD, STIR
   ~ measure CUP
   ~ part STEP
   ~ phrase ALA
   crockpot ~ STEW

recipient
   endowment ~ DONEE
   legacy ~ HEIR
   Ten Commandments ~ MOSES

reciprocal
   cosecant's ~ SINE

reciprocally
   ~ (prefix) INTER

reciprocity TRADE

recital
   ~ instrument HARP, ORGAN, PIANO
   ~ piece DUET, SOLO

recitation TALK
   child's ~ ABCS
   mouth-to-mouth ~ RUMOR

recite READ, SAY, TELL
   ~ dramatically EMOTE
   ~ pompously ORATE
   ~ the rosary PRAY

reciter ORATOR
   epic ~ BARD

reckless MAD, RASH
   ~ Olympian ATE

recklessly
   spend ~ WASTE

reckon ADD, DEEM, ESTEEM, HOLD, MAKE, OPINE, RATE, TOTAL
   ~ (with) COPE, DEAL

reckoning BILL

recline LIE, REST
   ~ idly LOLL

reclining FLAT, PRONE

"Reclining __" (Modigliani work) NUDE

recluse LONER, NUN

recognition AWARD, HONOR, MEDAL
   Olympiad ~ MEDAL
   peer ~ HONOR
   sounds of ~ OHS
   words of ~ ISEE

recognizable CLEAR

recognize ADMIT, CITE, HONOR, KNOW, NOD, NOTE, OWN, SEE, SENSE, SPOT
   ~ as an undercover cop MAKE

recognized
   widely ~ NOTED

recoil FEAR, REACT, REBEL, SHY, START

recollect CITE

recolor DYE

recombinant __ DNA

recommend CITE

recompense ATONE, DESERT, HIRE, PAY, TOLL

reconcile AGREE, ATONE, HEAL, SETTLE

reconciliation PEACE

recondite DEEP

reconnoiter SPY

reconsideration
   ~ word YET

reconstruct ALTER

record ENTER, ENTRY, LOG, NOTE, POST, TAPE
   ~ company LABEL
   ~ holder FILE
   ~ player STEREO
   ~ speed RPM
   1950s ~ OLDIE
   baseball ~ STAT
   gold ~ HIT
   make a ~ PRESS
   phonograph ~ DISC
   sample ~ DEMO
   trip ~ LOG
   Watergate ~ TAPE
   without a ~ CLEAN

record book
   ~ entry STAT
   ~ suffix EST

recorder PIPE
   ~ fodder TAPE

__ recorder TAPE

recording
   ~ company LABEL
   ~ medium DISC, TAPE
   spec ~ DEMO

recordings
   high-tech ~ CDS

record label
   longtime ~ RCA

records
   certain ~ LPS
   check of business ~ AUDIT
   modern ~ CDS

recount SPIN, TELL

recoup RESTORE

recover HEAL, MEND

recovered
   ~ from OVER

recovery CURE
   ~ regiment REHAB

recreate ENACT

recreation GAME, PLAY
   ~ area CAMP

recreational
   ~ vehicle CANOE

rec room DEN

recruit
   ~ dinner MESS

recruiting poster
   ~ verb WANT

recruits GIS

recruit-to-be ONEA

rectangular
   ~ groove DADO

rectify AMEND, MEND, REMIT

recto LEAF, PAGE, SHEET

rector DEAN, PADRE

rectory MANSE

recumbent FLAT, PRONE
   be ~ LIE

recuperate HEAL

recuperation CURE
   rest and ~ LEAVE

recurrently AGAIN

recurring
   ~ idea THEME

recyclable
   ~ item CAN
   ~ material SCRAP

recycled USED

red COLOR, RARE, ROSY, WINE
   ~ chalcedony SARD
   ~ dwarf STAR
   ~ dye HENNA
   ~ entry DEBIT
   ~ giant STAR
   ~ herring RUSE
   ~ ink DEBT, LOSS
   ~ letters USSR
   ~ light ALARM, ALERT
   ~ meat STEAK
   ~ menace FIRE
   ~ on the inside RARE
   ~ planet MARS
   ~ preceder AMBER
   ~ snapper, in Japan TAI
   ~ tag event SALE
   ~ vegetable BEET
   be in the ~ OWE
   cause to see ~ ANGER, IRK, PEEVE, RILE, UPSET
   cut through ~ tape AID
   entry in ~ DEBIT, DEBT
   it makes a bull see ~ CAPE
   it turns litmus ~ ACID
   man in ~ SANTA
   name meaning ~ ROY
   paint the town ~ REVEL
   raise a ~ flag ALERT, WARN
   roll out the ~ carpet GREET
   see ~ BOIL
   seeing ~ IRATE, MAD, UPSET
   shade of ~ ROSE
   wave a ~ flag ENRAGE
   what ~ means STOP
   yellowish ~ CORAL

red __ ALERT, ANT, CEDAR, CENT, CORAL, DEER, GIANT, HEAT, INK, MAPLE, MEAT, OAK, OCHER, OCHRE, OSIER, PINE, TAPE, TIDE, WINE

red __ (cardinal) HAT

red-__ EYE, HOT

__ red SEE

Red SEA
   ~ leader MAO
   role for ~ CLEM

Red __ SEA

Red __, The BARON

"Red __" ALERT, DUST

"Red __ at Morning" SKY

"Red __ Express" BALL

"Red __ for a Blue Lady" ROSES

"Red __ in the Sunset" SAILS

"___ Red" BIG

redact EDIT, EMEND

redactor EDITOR
~ **word** DELE, STET

"Red and White"
~ **painter** KLEE

red as a ___ BEET

"Red Badge of Courage, The"
~ **author** CRANE
~ **topic** WAR

"Red Balloon"
~ **painter** KLEE

Red Baron, The ACE

redbreast BIRD

redbud TREE

redcap
~ **burden** BAG
~ **domain** DEPOT

Red Cloud
~ **residence** TEPEE

Redcoat
~ **general** HOWE
Continental, to a ~ ENEMY, FOE

redcoats
~ **to the north** RCMP

Red Cross
~ **supply** SERA, SERUM
~ **volunteer** DONOR

redden CHAP, GLOW
crack and ~ CHAP

reddener
litmus ~ ACID

Redding OTIS

reddish-brown BAY, COCOA, HENNA
~ **gem** SARD
~ **horse** ROAN

Reddy HELEN

redeem ATONE, CASH, SAVE

redeye gravy
~ **source** HAM

Redford, Robert
~ **movie of 1966, with "The"** CHASE

Redgrave LYNN

redhanded
catch ~ NAIL

redhead
~ **dye** HENNA
become a ~ DYE
historic ~ ERIC

red-hot LIVE

"Red House Mystery, The"
~ **author** MILNE

redingote COAT

red ink
~ **amount** LOSS

redirect ALTER, DETER

red-letter
~ **sign** EXIT

redness
exemplar of ~ BEET

redo EDIT

"Red October" SUB
~ **device** SONAR

redolence AROMA, ODOR, SCENT

"___ Red One, The" BIG

redoubtable DIRE

red-pencil DELE

"Red Planet" MARS

redpoll BIRD

redress AMEND, REMIT
seek ~ SUE

Red River
~ **capital** HANOI

"Red River"
~ **actress** DRU
Joanne Dru's ~ role TESS

"Red Rock ___" WEST

"Red Rock West"
~ **director** DAHL

"Red Roses for a Blue ___" LADY

Red Ryder HERO

Reds NINE, TEAM

"Reds"
~ **role** REED

Red Sea
~ **country** YEMEN
~ **peninsula** ARABIA, SINAI
~ **vessel** DHOW

Redskins ELEVEN, TEAM
~ **org.** NFL

Red Sox TEAM, TEN

Red Square
~ **figure** LENIN

redstart BIRD

redtop HAY

reduce ABATE, ALLAY, BATE, COOL, CUT, DIET, EASE, FILE, LOP, PARE, SLAKE, SLASH, SLIM, TRIM
~ **as expenses** PARE
~ **sail** REEF
~ **speed** SLOW
~ **tension** EASE
~ **to charcoal** CHAR
~ **to nothing** ANNUL, RAZE, UNDO

reduced LESS, LOW
in ~ circumstances NEEDY

reduction CUT, DROP, REBATE, SALE, SLASH
noticeable ~ DENT

"Red Wheelbarrow, The" POEM

Red Wings SIX, TEAM
~ **milieu** ICE, RINK
~ **org.** NHL

redwood TREE

redwoods
like ~ TALL

Reebok
~ **rival** NIKE

reechoing LOUD

reed ARROW, CANE, OBOE, PIPE, PLANT, STRAW

Reed CAROL, LOU, REX
~ **and others** MDS

Reed, Donna
~ **TV surname** STONE

Reed, John
movie about ~ REDS

reedlike SLIM

reef BAR, LAND, LEDGE, SHOAL
~ **material** CORAL
coral ~ CAY, KEY, LEDGE

reef ___ KNOT

___ reef CORAL

reeking BAD, RANK

reel COIL, DANCE, SPIN, SWAY, TEETER
~ **in** LAND
film ~ holder CAN
Virginia ~ DANCE

reel ___ (say easily) OFF

re-election
~ **runners** INS

Reese DELLA, MASON

Reeve, Christopher
~ **role** KENT

Reeves, George
~ **role** KENT

Reeves, Keanu
~ **movie** SPEED

ref
~ **call** TIME, TKO
~ **relative** UMP
~ **signal** TEE

refection MEAL

refer
~ **ender** ENCE, ENT
~ **to** CITE

referee
~ **count** TEN

reference
~ **work** ENC, OED
use as a ~ CITE

reference book ATLAS
~ **direction** SEE
~ **name** ROGET

referendum VOTE
~ **choice** YES

refinable
~ **rock** ORE

refine HONE
~ **metal** SMELT

refined NICE, SEDATE
it's ~ OIL, ORE
not ~ CRASS, RAW

refinement CLASS, STYLE, TACT, TASTE

refinery
~ **output** METAL
~ **residue** SLAG

refinish RESTORE

reflect ECHO, MUSE, PORE
~ **upon** SEE

reflection IMAGE, SLUR, SMEAR
sound ~ ECHO

___ reflection UPON

reflective DEEP

reflex
~ **ender** IVE
~ **testing site** KNEE

___ reflex GAG

reflux EBB

reform ALTER, AMEND

reformer
school ~ MANN

refrain AVOID, HOLD
~ **from** CEASE, DEFER
~ **syllables** FALA, LALA
mountaineer's ~ YODEL
part of a ~ TRA
please ~ DONT

refresh AIR, SLAKE
~ **a stamp pad** INK
~ **oneself** REST, SLEEP
~ **the inner man** DINE, EAT
~ **the memory** CUE

refreshes
pause that ~ NAP

refreshing COOL
cool and ~ ICY

refreshment ADE

refreshments EATS
pass out ~ SERVE

refried BEAN

refrigerant ETHANE

refrigerate COOL, ICE

refrigerator
~ **name** AMANA

refuel
~ **the body** EAT

refueling
~ **area** PIT

refuge HAVEN, HOME, LAIR, NEST, OASIS, REST
~ **seeker** ALIEN
leafy ~ ARBOR
place of ~ ARK, HAVEN, LAIR
wayfarer's ~ INN

refulgence FLARE, SHEEN

refund PAY
partial ~ REBATE

refurbish RENEW

refusal VETO
informal ~ NAH, NOPE

refusals NOES, NOS

refuse BAR, DENY, DIRT, TRASH, WASTE
  ~ admission BAR
  ~ assent DENY
  ~ to approve VETO
  ~ to commit HEM
  foundry ~ SLAG
  kitchen ~ SLOP

refusenik
  ~ word NYET

refusing
  ~ to listen DEAF

refute BELIE, DENY

reg. STD

regal
  ~ headwear TIARA

regale AMUSE, CATER, DINE

regalia ARRAY, GARB, GEAR, SEAL
  ~ item ORB
  bit of ~ TIARA

Regan
  ~ father LEAR

regard DEEM, ESTEEM, EYE, HEED, HOLD, HONOR, NOTE, RATE, SEE
  ~ with awe GAPE
  ~ with favor LIKE
  high ~ ESTEEM
  in high ~ ADORED
  in ~ to ABOUT, INRE

regardful AWARE

regarding AFTER, ASTO, OVER

regardless DEAF, YET

regards
  as ~ ABOUT, INRE
  kindest ~ BEST

regatta RACE
  ~ team CREW
  ~ vessel SHELL
  participate in a ~ ROW

regency REIGN

regenerate HEAL

regent DEAN, RULER

___ regia AQUA

regime DIET, REIGN

regimen DIET, FARE
  recovery ~ REHAB

regiment ARMY, TROOP

Reginald OWEN

"Reginald"
  ~ author SAKI

Reginald Van Gleason ___ III

region AREA, BELT, LAND, SITE, SPOT, TRACT, ZONE
  geog. ~ TER, TERR

regional LOCAL

regions
  upper ~ of space ETHER

register ENROL, ENTER, LIST, POLL, READ, ROLL, SHOW
  ~ ringer SALE

cash ~ TILL
social ~ LIST

___ register CASH

registered ___ MAIL, NURSE

___ regni ANNO

regress EBB, SINK
  ~ ender IVE

regression LAPSE

regret RUE
  word of ~ ALAS

regretful BAD

regrettable SAD

regular EVEN, GAS, USUAL
  ~ fellow JOE

regularly OFT, OFTEN

regulate ORDER, PHASE, SET

regulation ACT, CODE, EDICT, LAW, RULE

regulations
  building ~ CODE
  rules and ~ LAW

regulatory
  ~ org. EPA, FDA, SEC

Regulus STAR
  ~ constellation LEO

rehabilitate HEAL, HELP, RESTORE

Rehan ADA

rehearsal TRIAL
  final ~ DRESS

___ rehearsal DRESS

"Rehearsal of a Ballet"
  ~ painter DEGAS

rehearse
  ~ boxing SPAR

rehearsing
  without ~ ADLIB

reheat WARM

Reid KATE, TIM

Reid, Thomas SCOT

reign LEAD, RULE

"Reign of Terror"
  ~ director MANN

reimburse PAY, REMIT, RESTORE

rein LEASH

___ rein FREE

reindeer
  ~ driver SANTA
  ~ herder LAPP
  Santa's ~ before Rudolph OCTET

Reiner CARL, ROB

Reiner, Carl
  ~ kid ROB

Reiner, Rob
  ~ father CARL

reinforce
  ~ in a way LINE

reinforcement STAY

Reinking ANN

reins HELM
  hold the ~ LEAD
  take the ~ STEER

Reiser PAUL
  ~ costar HUNT

REIT
  part of ~ REAL

reiterate ECHO

Reitman IVAN

Reitman, Ivan
  ~ film of 1993 DAVE

reject BAN, DENY, DESERT, DROP, VETO

rejection SNUB, VETO
  word of ~ UGH

rejections NOES, NOS

rejoice
  ~ in LIKE

rejoicing ELATED

rejoin SAY

rejoinder
  ~ (abbr.) ANS
  sharp ~ NIP

rejuvenate RENEW

rekindle EVOKE

relate SPIN, TELL

related AKIN
  maternally ~ ENATE

relating
  ~ to (suffix) ILE, INE

relation KIN
  mathematical ~ RATIO

relations KIN

"___ Relations" OUR

relationship TIE
  end a ~ PART
  meaningful ~ LOVE

relative AUNT, BRO, DAD, MOM, POP, SIS, SON, UNCLE
  ~ through marriage INLAW

relatives KIN

relax BEND, CALM, EASE, IDLE, LIE, LOAF, LOLL, REST, SIT, SLOW
  ~ as rules BEND
  place to ~ DEN

"Relax!" ATEASE

relaxation EASE

relaxed ATEASE, CALM, FREE, LOOSE
  not ~ EDGY, TAUT, TENSE

relaxing EASY

relay RACE, SEND

relay ___ RACE

relay race
  ~ length MILE
  ~ portion LEG

release CLEAR, DROP, EMIT, FREE, LOOSE, REMIT, UNTIE
  press ~ NEWS

___ release NEWS, PRESS

___-release TIME

released
  just ~ NEW

relegate REFER

relent BEND, THAW, YIELD

relentless CRUEL, ETERNAL, IRON, STERN

relentlessly EVER, HARD

relevant APT

reliable HONEST, SAFE, SANE, SOLID, SURE, TRUE

___-reliance SELF

relic SIGN
  cathedral ~ ICON

relief AID, DOLE, HELP
  ~ of a sort ALMS
  ~ org. ARC, CARE
  express ~ AAH
  on ~ NEEDY
  sigh of ~ AAH, PHEW
  sounds of ~ AHS
  source of ~ BALM

relief ___ MAP

___-relief BAS

relief pitcher
  ~ feat SAVE

relieve ABATE, ALLAY, CURE, EASE, FREE, RID

relieved EASY
  ~ murmur AAH, PHEW

reliever
  ~ goal SAVE
  pain ~ OPIATE

___-relievo ALTO, BASSO

religion
  Eastern ~ HINDU, ISLAM, ZEN
  follower of an Eastern ~ HINDU

religious
  ~ belief CREED
  ~ ceremony MASS, RITE
  ~ counter BEAD
  ~ deg. STD
  ~ doctrine DOGMA
  ~ faction SECT
  ~ painting touch AURA
  ~ principle TENET
  ~ scroll TORAH
  ~ song PSALM
  ~ symbol ICON
  ~ title REV, STE
  Apennines ~ center ASSISI

relinquish CEDE, LOSE, YIELD

relinquisher
  rib ~ ADAM

reliquary ALTAR, CASE, CHEST, TOMB

relish ADORE, LIKE, LOVE, SAVOR, TANG, TASTE
  fish ~ ALEC

relish tray
  ~ item OLIVE

relocate MOVE

reluctant AVERSE
  be ~ HATE

rely
  ~ (on) LEAN

REM
  experience ~ DREAM, SLEEP
  part of ~ EYE, RAPID

REM ___ SLEEP

remain ABIDE, BIDE, LAST, STAY
  ~ behind WAIT
  ~ extant ARE
  ~ free ELUDE
  ~ idle SIT
  ~ in force STAND
  ~ in place STAY
  ~ in residence ABIDE
  ~ loyal ADHERE
  ~ quiet LIE, SIT
  ~ undecided PEND
  ~ undone WAIT
  ~ unused SIT
  ~ upright STAND
  ~ valid HOLD

remainder PLUS, REST, TAIL
  check ~ STUB

remaining LEFT, ODD, OVER

remains ASHES, REST

"Remains ___ Seen" TOBE

"Remains of the ___, The" DAY

"Remains of the Day, The"
  ~ director IVORY

"Remains to Be ___" SEEN

remand HOLD

remark DIG, HEED, NOTE, SAY
  ~ to an audience ASIDE
  butterfingers' ~ OOPS
  critical ~ JAB
  libelous ~ SLUR
  parenthetical ~ ASIDE
  pithy ~ MOT
  pointed ~ BARB
  spontaneous ~ ADLIB

remarkable RARE
  ~ person ONER
  ~ thing LULU

remarkably EXTRA

Rembrandt PEALE
  ~ painting OIL

remedial
  ~ treatment CURE

remedy AMEND, CURE, HEAL, HELP, MEND, PILL
  burn ~ ALOE
  old-fashioned ~ TONIC

remember CITE
  a time to ~ ERA
  craft to ~ MAINE

not ~ LOSE
place to ~ ALAMO
time to ~ EPOCH, ERA

"Remember"
  one to ~ MAMA

"Remember My ___" NAME

"Remember the ___" DAY

"Remember the ___!" ALAMO, MAINE

remembrance RELIC, TOKEN

Remick LEE

remind EVOKE
  ~ too often CARP, NAG

reminder CUE, NOTE
  electronic ~ BEEP
  kind of ~ IOU
  written ~ MEMO

"___ reminds me..." THAT

"Remington ___" STEELE

remiss LOOSE

remit MAIL, PAY, SEND

remnant END, PART, RAG, SCRAP, SHRED, TAG, TAIL
  ~ of the past RELIC
  fireplace ~ ASH
  smoldering ~ EMBER

remnants WASTE

remodel ADAPT, ALTER, REDO, RESTORE

remodeling
  ~ project ELL

___ Remo, Italy SAN

remonstrate ARGUE

remorse SHAME
  be stung with ~ SMART
  feel ~ RUE
  feeling of ~ PANG
  sign of ~ TEAR

remorseless CRUEL, MEAN

remote ALIEN, ALOOF, AWAY, COOL, DRY, FAR, ICY, OLD
  ~ button MUTE, REC
  a ~ distance AFAR

remote control
  TV ~ button MUTE, REC

remotest
  ~ point DEEP

remove CLEAR, DELE, EJECT, ERASE, RID, SNIP, TAKE
  ~ as a knot UNDO
  ~ as branches LOP
  ~ dishes from the table BUS
  ~ forcibly OUST
  ~ from a manuscript DELE
  ~ from office OUST
  ~ illegally STEAL
  ~ paint STRIP
  ~ (prefix) DIS
  ~ rind PARE, PEEL
  ~ soap RINSE
  ~ trees CLEAR
  ~ water BAIL

~ wrinkles IRON

removed ALOOF

remover
  dirt ~ SOAP
  mistake ~ ERASER
  snow ~ PLOW

Remsen IRA

remunerate PAY, REMIT

remuneration FEE, HIRE, PAY

Remus ROMAN, TWIN, UNCLE
  ~ mother ILIA

Remus, Uncle
  ~ character BRER
  ~ term of address BRER

Ren DOG

Renaissance STYLE
  ~ instrument LUTE

Renaissance ___ MAN

Ren and Stimpy DUO, PAIR

rend CHOP, CLAW, RIP, SPLIT, TEAR

Rendell RUTH

render MAKE, PUT, SAY, SING, YIELD
  ~ a decision RULE
  ~ illegible SMEAR
  ~ speechless AMAZE, AWE, STUN, WOW

"Render ___ Caesar..." UNTO

renders DOES

rendezvous DATE, LOVE
  ~ with MEET
  romantic ~ TRYST

"Rendezvous With ___" RAMA

René
  see French

Renée
  see French

renege DESERT, DROP

renewed
  not get ~ LAPSE

Renfrew
  ~ resident SCOT

Reno
  ~ opening ANTE
  ~ rollers DICE
  ~ st. NEV
  ~ zone PDT, PST

Renoir
  ~ associate DEGAS, MONET
  ~ subject NUDE

Renoir, Jean
  ~ film NANA
  ~ film heroine ELENA

renounce DESERT, DROP

renovate REDO, RENEW

renown NOTE

renowned BIG, GREAT, NOTED

rent COST, GAP, GASH, HIRE,

LEASE, LET, RATE, RIP, SPLIT, TEAR, TORN
  ~ out LEASE
  ~ out again RELET
  ~ payer TENANT
  for ~ TOLET
  place to ~ a room INN

rent-a-___ CAR

rentable OPEN

rental
  ~ agreement LEASE
  ~ sign TOLET
  boardinghouse ~ ROOM
  lake ~ CANOE
  marina ~ SLIP
  metered ~ CAB
  prom-night ~ LIMO

renter
  ~ paper LEASE

renters
  gown ~ SRS

REO AUTO, CAR
  ~ maker OLDS
  part of ~ ELI, OLDS

rep AGENT, AGT
  state ~ SEN

Rep. POL
  ~ colleague DEM
  ~ counterpart SEN
  not ~ or Dem. IND

repair AMEND, EXIT, MEND, MOVE
  ~ chairs CANE
  ~ socks DARN
  ~ the lawn SOD
  beyond ~ SHOT
  put in good ~ RESTORE

repair bill
  ~ part LABOR

repairs
  make ~ to MEND
  without ~ ASIS

reparation
  make ~ ATONE

repartee MOT, WIT

repast FEED, MEAL

repay AVENGE
  must ~ OWE

repeal ANNUL, UNDO

repeat ECHO, RELATE, SAY, STRESS
  ~ oneself, in a way CLONE
  without ~ ONCE

repeatedly AGAIN, AWAY, EVER, OFT, OFTEN
  ~ to a poet OFT

repeater GUN

repellent BAD, VILE

___-repellent WATER

repent ATONE
  ~ of RUE

repetition ECHO, ROTE
  mark of ~ DITTO

rephrase AMEND, EDIT

replace
  ~ a button SEW

replacement SUB, TEMP

replete RIFE

replica CAST, CLONE, IMAGE, MODEL

reply NOTE, REACT, SAY
  ~ (abbr.) ANS
  ~ to a knock ENTER
  ~ to "Que pasa?" NADA
  affirmative ~ ROGER
  enc. for ~ SASE
  Navy ~ AYE
  negative ~ NAH, NAY, NOPE
  pony's ~ SNORT
  proposal ~ AYE, NAY, YEA, YES
  roll-call ~ AYE, HERE, NAY, YEA, YES
  rude ~ SASS

report BANG, BLAST, BOOM, LEAK, LOG, NEWS, NOISE, POP, RUMOR, SAY, SHOT, TELL
  ~ maker GUN
  daily ~ NEWS
  distort a ~ SLANT
  false ~ LIBEL
  oral ~ TALK
  startling ~ BANG
  unfounded ~ RUMOR
  weather ~ CLEAR, DRY, FAIR, HAIL, HOT, MILD, RAIN, SLEET, SNOW, STORM, WARM, WET

report ___ CARD

reporter
  ~ angle SLANT
  ~ boss EDITOR
  ~ coup SCOOP
  ~ question WHO

reporters PRESS

reporting
  ~ to UNDER

repose CALM, EASE, LIE, PEACE, REST, SLEEP

repository CASE, CHEST, FILE, MINE, SAFE
  fossil ~ often TAR
  grain ~ SILO
  honey ~ COMB
  pocket-watch ~ VEST
  Torah ~ ARK

reprehensible BAD, BASE, EVIL, LOW, VILE

represent DRAW

representation ICON, IMAGE, MAP, TOKEN, TOTEM
  symbolic ~ REBUS

representative AGENT
  ~ (abbr.) AGT
  ~ of LIKE
  OPEC ~ IRANI

repress GAG, HOLD

reprieve DEFER, STAY

reprimand SLAP, TRIM

repro STAT

reproach CARP, SHAME, TRIM, TWIT
  word of ~ SHAME, TSK

___-reproach SELF

reproachful VILE

reproduce APE, BREED

reproduction CAST, IMAGE, MODEL

reproof
  sound of ~ TSK, TUT

reprove TRIM

reptile ASP, BOA, CROC, SNAKE
  Cleopatra ~ ASP

republic LAND, STATE

"Republic, The"
  ~ author PLATO

Republican
  ~ of note DOLE

"Republican, Mr." TAFT

repudiate BELIE, DENY, DESERT, DROP

repugnance HATE

repugnant BAD, VILE

reputable CLEAN, GOOD, HONEST, SAFE

reputation NAME, ODOR
  ruin a ~ SMEAR

repute FACE, HONOR, ODOR
  ill ~ SHAME

request ASK, CALL, ORDER, PLEA, PLEAD, SEEK
  ~ an encore CLAP
  ~ fervently BEG
  ~ sweetener PLEASE
  barbershop ~ TRIM
  beggar's ~ ALMS
  dentist's ~ OPEN
  host's ~ RSVP
  nice ~ PLEASE
  roast-beef ~ RARE
  salon ~ RINSE, SET
  seating ~ AISLE
  shooter's ~ SMILE
  waiter's ~ ORDER

"Requiem ___ a Heavyweight" FOR

"Requiem for ___" EVITA

"Requiescat in ___" PACE

require ASK, MAKE, NEED, ORDER, TAKE, WANT
  ~ a rubdown ACHE

required DUE
  beyond what's ~ EXTRA

requirement NEED, WANT
  entrance ~ EXAM, TEST

requirements
  meet the ~ PASS

requisite MAIN, NEED, WANT

requital DESERT

requite AVENGE, REACT

rescind ANNUL, UNDO, VOID

rescript EDICT

rescue FREE, HELP, SAVE

"Rescue 911"
  ~ network CBS

rescuer
  ~ maybe HERO

"Rescuers Down ___, The" UNDER

research DIG, SEEK
  ~ place LAB
  ~ thoroughly DIG

resembling ALA, LIKE
  ~ (prefix) PARA
  ~ (suffix) INE

resentful SORE

resentment ANGER

reserve AMASS, EXTRA, HOLD, SAVE, SPARE, STORE
  hold in ~ SAVE
  in ~ APART, ASIDE, ONICE, ONTAP, SPARE

reserved ALOOF, ICY, SHY, SOBER, STAID, TAKEN
  ~ seat SPACE
  be ~ for AWAIT

reservoir LAKE, MINE, POND, POOL, STORE, TANK
  ~ filler RAIN

res gestae ACTS, DEEDS

reside ABIDE, LIVE, ROOM, STAY

residence ABODE, ESTATE, HOME, PAD
  bluebird's ~ NEST
  change of ~ MOVE
  outdoor ~ CAMP
  Palm Beach ~ ESTATE
  remain in ~ ABIDE
  reverend's ~ MANSE
  vicar's ~ MANSE

residency ABODE, HOME

resident LOCAL, TENANT
  ~ (suffix) ITE
  temporary ~ TENANT

residue REST
  evaporation ~ SALT
  fire ~ ASH, SOOT
  powdery ~ ASH
  refinery ~ SLAG
  river ~ SILT
  wood ~ ASH

residuum REST

resign LEAVE, YIELD
  ~ oneself BOW

resilience LIFE, SINEW

resiliency TONE

resin LAC
  fossil ~ AMBER
  fragrant ~ ELEMI

resist REBEL

resistance STAND
  ~ symbol OMEGA
  ~ unit OHM
  air ~ DRAG

resistant AVERSE
  ~ to fading FAST

___-resistant WATER

Resnais ALAIN

resolute SET, SETON

resoluteness GRIT, NERVE

resolution ACT, HEART

resolve AIM, GRIT, SETTLE, STEEL

resonant DEEP, RICH
  ~ effect ECHO

resonate PEAL, RING, ROLL

resort CAMP, SPA
  ~ place ISLE
  ~ spot CAPRI
  ~ to REFER, USE
  beach ~ LIDO
  Belgian ~ SPA
  Black Sea ~ YALTA
  British ~ BATH
  Caribbean ~ ARUBA
  Colorado ski ~ ASPEN
  dieter's ~ SPA
  Dutch-speaking ~ island ARUBA
  Honshu ~ port ITO
  Italian ~ LIDO
  New Mexico ~ TAOS
  Riviera ~ NICE
  Rockies ~ ASPEN
  Sierra Nevada ~ TAHOE
  skiers' ~ ASPEN
  Utah ski ~ ALTA
  Venetian ~ LIDO

___ resort LAST

resound BLARE, BOOM, ECHO, PEAL, RING, ROLL

resounding DEEP, LOUD

resource ASSET
  natural ~ COAL, OIL, ORE, WATER
  pecuniary ~ ASSET
  precious ~ TIME
  quarterback's ~ ARM
  shared ~ POOL

resourceful ABLE

resources ESTATE
  having the ~ ABLE

resp. ANS

respect ESTEEM, HEED, HONOR
  deep ~ AWE
  feudal term of ~ SIRE
  in ~ to OVER
  show ~ BOW, KNEEL
  term of ~ ABBA, MAAM, MADAM, MISS, SIR, SIRE
  with ~ to ABOUT, INRE

___-respect SELF

respectable FAIR, GOOD, HONEST, NICE, SOSO

respected
~ one, maybe ELDER

respectful
~ address ABBA, MAAM, MADAM, SIR
~ fear AWE

respecting ASTO

respectively APIECE, EACH

respiratory
~ organ LUNG
~ sound RALE

respire DRAW, LIVE

respiring ALIVE

respite DEFER, REST, STOP, WAIT

resplendent CLEAR, REGAL, RICH

respond SAY
~ ender ENT
~ to a stimulus ACT, REACT
~ to gravity SAG, SINK
~ to reveille RISE

response
~ time LAG
~ to a revelation AHA
~ to danger FEAR
attendee's ~ HERE
bride's ~ IDO
church ~ AMEN
groom's ~ IDO
humor ~ HAHA
insight ~ AHA
naval ~ AYE
negative ~ NAH, NAY, NOPE
oath ~ IDO
patient ~ AAH
positive ~ AYE, YEA, YES
quiz ~ FALSE, TRUE
radioer's ~ ROGER
roll-call ~ AYE, NAY, YEA, YES
SOS ~ AID, HELP
uncompromising ~ NEVER

responses
~ to doctor AHS

responsibility CARE, DEBT, LOAD, ONUS

responsible HONEST, SAFE, SANE
be ~ for OWN, SEETO

responsive KEEN
become more ~ THAW

responsiveness HEART

rest ABIDE, CEASE, EASE, LAY, LEAVE, LIE, NAP, SIT, SLEEP, STOP
~ against LEAN, PROP
~ and recuperation LEAVE
~ area STOP
~ assured HOPE
~ (on) HANG, RELY
~ stop INN
at ~ IDLE
came to ~ ALIT, LIT
climber's ~ LEDGE
put to ~ ALLAY

rest ___ AREA, STOP

restaurant CAFE
~ bill TAB

~ choice ORDER
~ employee CHEF, VALET
~ freebie ROLL, WATER
~ furnishing TABLE
~ list MENU
~ order TOGO
~ patron EATER
forgo the ~ EATIN
patronize a ~ DINE

restaurateur
~ of cinema ALICE

restful CALM, SERENE

restfulness EASE, PEACE

resting ATEASE, IDLE
~ on ATOP
~ place BED, INN, SEAT, SETTEE

restitution
make ~ ATONE, REMIT

restive EDGY

restless EDGY
~ feeling ITCH
be ~ TOSS

rest on one's ___ OARS

restorative CURE, HELP, TONIC

restore CURE, HEAL, HELP, MEND, RENEW, UNDO

restrain BAR, BATE, CAGE, DAMP, DETER, GAG, HOLD, LEASH, LIMIT, REIN, STOP, TIE

restrained STAID

restraint
canine ~ LEASH, STRAP
equine ~ BIT, REIN
legal ~ ARREST, LIEN

restrict BAN, BIND, LIMIT, STINT

restricted LOCAL
not ~ OPEN
not ~ by gender COED

restricted ___ AREA

restricting CLOSE

restriction LAW, LIMIT, RULE
property ~ LIEN

result END, ENSUE, EVENT, ISSUE
~ (from) ARISE
as a ~ ERGO, THEN, THUS
bull-market ~ RISE
collision ~ DENT
detente ~ THAW
end ~ SUM
expected ~ NORM
injury ~ SCAB
landslide ~ SCREE
overexertion ~ ACHE
rat-race ~ STRESS
rumor ~ maybe SCARE
stress ~ maybe ULCER
workout ~ ACHE
wrestling ~ DRAW

resultingly ERGO, THEN, THUS

resume RENEW

resurface
~ a road PAVE, TAR

resurgently ANEW

resurrection FERN

resuscitate RENEW, RESTORE

ret SOAK, STEEP

Reta SHAW

retail SELL, VEND
~ establishment MART, SHOP, STORE
~ grouping LINE

retailer
~ concern SALE

retain HAVE, HIRE, HOLD, KEEP, OWN

retainer FEE

retaliate AVENGE, GET, REACT

retard SLOW

retardant
apple-ripening ~ ALAR

rete MESH

reticent ALOOF, CLOSE, SHY

reticle NET

reticule BAG

reticulum NET

retina
~ cell CONE, ROD
~ neighbor LENS

retinue TAIL, TRAIN

retire EXIT, REST, SLEEP
~ from DROP
signal to ~ TAPS

retired ABED
~ soldier VET

retiree ELDER
~ benefits' org. SSA

retirement
~ plan IRA

retiring SHY

retort MOT, SAY
~ (abbr.) ANS

retouch RESTORE

retract ANNUL, DENY

retread TIRE

retreading
in need of ~ BALD

retreat AVOID, DEN, EXIT, HAVEN, HOME, LAIR, NEST, NOOK, OASIS, REST
beat a hasty ~ FLEE, HIE, RUN
calorie counters' ~ SPA
hasty ~ LAM
jungle ~ DEN
leafy ~ ARBOR
snug ~ NEST
summer ~ CAMP, SHADE

retrench PARE

retribution
exact ~ AVENGE
goddess of ~ ATE
matter of ~ TAT

retrieve GET

retriever
~ for short LAB
~ trace SCENT
dogie ~ LASSO

retrocede EBB

retrograde DIE, LAPSE

retrogress LAPSE

retsina WINE

return ARRIVE
~ swing FRO
~ the compliment PAY
~ to earth LAND
bond ~ YIELD
by ~ mail SOON
get in ~ REAP
investment ~ YIELD
involuntary ~ REPO
never to ~ GONE, PAST
point of no ~ tennis-wise ACE
without option of ~ ASIS

"Return ___ Man Called Horse, The" OFA

returnable
it's not ~ ACE

returned
~ to earth ALIT, LIT

"Return From the ___" ASHES

"Return of Frank James, The"
~ director LANG

"Return of the Secaucus ___" SEVEN

returns
~ expert CPA
~ org. IRS

Reuben
~ bread RYE

reuner ALUM, GRAD

reunion
~ attendee ALUM, AUNT, GRAD, NIECE
~ group CLAN, CLASS, KIN
fam. ~ attendee REL

Reunion
~ in Dallas ARENA

Réunion
see French

rev
~ the engine GUN, RACE

Rev.
~ address SER

revamp RENEW

reveal ADMIT, AIR, BARE, LEAK, LETON, SAY, SHOW, STAMP, STATE, TELL
~ oneself EMERGE
~ one's feelings LETON
~ to a poet OPE

revealed OUT

reveille
~ opposite TAPS

respond to ~ RISE
sound ~ AROUSE, ROUSE

"___ Reveille" TIL

revel BASK, SPREE, TEAR
~ **in** LIKE, LOVE, SAVOR

revelation DIRT, ORACLE
response to a ~ AHA

revelry ORGY, PLAY, RIOT, TEAR

revenge
movie ~ **seeker** NERD
take ~ **on** GET

"Revenge of the ___" NERDS

revenue TAKE
~ **source** SALE
deduction from ~ DEBIT
source of TV ~ ADS

revenuer TMAN

reverberate BLARE, ECHO, PEAL,
RING, ROLL

reverberating LOUD

revere ADORE, ESTEEM, EXALT,
HONOR, LAUD

revered
~ **object** ICON
~ **one** IDOL

reverence ADORE, AWE, ESTEEM
show ~ KNEEL

reverend PADRE
~ **mother** NUN
~ **residence** MANSE

Reverend TITLE

reverent
~ **fear** AWE

Revere, Paul
emulate ~ AROUSE, RIDE

reverie DREAM
indulge in ~ MOON, MUSE

reversal RUIN

"Reversal of Fortune"
~ **actor** IRONS
~ **actress** CLOSE

reverse ALTER, ANNUL, DENY,
GEAR, UNDO

reversible
~ **exclamation** AHA, HAH,
OHO, TUT, WOW

reversion LAPSE

revet PAVE

review AUDIT, HASH, PARADE,
READ, SCAN, TRIAL
~ **as damage** ASSESS
~ **board** PANEL
~ **movies** RATE
~ **with "up"** BONE
bad ~ PAN
four-star ~ RAVE

reviewer
text ~ EDITOR
thumbs-up ~ EBERT

revile ABUSE, LACE, SLUR

revise ALTER, AMEND, EDIT,
EMEND, MEND

reviser EDITOR

revisionist
~ **starter** NEO

revitalize RENEW

revival
~ **setting** TENT

revival meeting
~ **shout** AMEN

revived
~ **(prefix)** NEO

Revlon
~ **rival** AVON

revoke ANNUL, VOID

revolt RIOT, RISE

revolting BAD, LOW, RANK, VILE
find ~ ABHOR, HATE

"Revolting!" UGH

revolution LAP, ORBIT
~ **line** AXIS
~ **site of 1979** IRAN
time for one ~ YEAR

revolutionary NEW, REBEL
~ **core** CADRE
~ **path** ORBIT
Chinese ~ MAO
French ~ MARAT
Russian ~ LENIN

Revolutionary WAR

Revolutionary War
~ **general** GATES
~ **hero** ALLEN
~ **name** ETHAN
~ **spy** HALE

revolve SPIN, TURN
~ **around** ORBIT
~ **in the mind** PORE

revolver ARM, GUN, ROD
~ **inventor** COLT

revolving DOOR
~ **part** ROTOR

revolving ___ DOOR

revue SHOW
~ **segment** SKIT

revulsion HATE

reward DUE, MEDAL, PAY, STAKE
dog's ~ PAT
employee's ~ RAISE
Gordian Knot undoer's
~ ASIA
gymnast's ~ TEN
just ~ DESERT
waiter's ~ TIP

rework EDIT

reworking
~ **of material** HASH

rewrite EDIT, EMEND

rex LORD, RULER

Rex CAT, REED

Rexroth, Kenneth POET
see also poet

Reynard
like ~ SLY

"Reynard the Fox" EPIC

Reynolds ALLIE, LYNN

Reynolds, Burt
~ **film, with "The"** END

Reynolds, Debbie
~ **musical revival** IRENE

Reynosa
see Spanish

RFD
part of ~ FREE, RURAL

RFK, Mrs. ETHEL

Rh ELEM
45 for ~ ATNO

rhapsodize DREAM, TALK

"___ Rhapsody" ALTO

"Rhapsody in ___" BLUE

rhea BIRD
~ **cousin** EMU

Rhea MOON, TITAN
~ **to the Romans** OPS

rhebok ANIMAL

Rheims
see French

"___ Rheingold" DAS

rhenium METAL

rhesus ANIMAL

rhetoric RANT

rhetorician ORATOR

Rhine WINE
~ **feeder** AAR, AARE, RUHR
city on the ~ BONN

Rhine, J.B.
~ **field** ESP

Rhineland
~ **product** WINE

rhinestone GEM

rhino
~ **cousin** TAPIR
~ **feature** HORN

rhinoceros ANIMAL

rhizome ROOT

"Rhoda"
~ **mother** IDA

Rhode Island STATE
~ **motto** HOPE

Rhode Island Red HEN

Rhodes CITY, HARI, PORT
see also Greek

rhodium METAL

rhodochrosite ORE

Rhodope RANGE

rhonchus SNORE

Rhone
~ **feeder** ISERE
city on the ~ ARLES
see also French

rhubarb PIE, ROW, SCRAP, SETTO

rhum
~ **cake** BABA

rhyme
~ **maker** BARD, POET
~ **or reason** SENSE
~ **scheme** ABBA
crooked gate of ~ STILE
dieter of ~ SPRAT
eloper of ~ DISH
merry king of ~ COLE
nursery ~ **trio** MICE
pet of ~ LAMB
pig thief of ~ TOM
spoon's companion, in
~ DISH

rhymer BARD, POET

rhymester BARD, POET

rhyolite LAVA

rhythm BEAT, LILT, METER, PULSE,
STRESS, TEMPO
accentual ~ **for a**
poet METER
body ~ PULSE
graceful ~ LILT

___ rhythm ALPHA, BETA

"___ Rhythm" IGOT

rhythmic
~ **pattern in poetry** METER

rhythmical
~ **movement** DANCE

R.I.
~ **neighbor** MASS
part of ~ ISL
see also Rhode Island

ria INLET

rials
where ~ **are spent** IRAN

rialto
~ **eye-catcher** NEON

riant GAY

riata LASSO, ROPE
~ **end** NOOSE

rib BONE, GIBE, KID, NEEDLE, RAG,
TEASE
~ **order** RACK
~ **relinquisher** ADAM
~ **slangily** SLAT

rib ___ CAGE, ROAST

rib-___ steak EYE

___ rib FALSE, TRUE

"___ Rib" ADAMS

ribald LEWD, RACY

ribaldry DIRT

ribbed
~ **fabric** REP

ribbit NOISE

ribbon BAND, CORD, LACE, MEDAL, SHRED, STRIP, TAPE
  blue ~ AWARD, FIRST
  earn a blue ~ WIN

ribbon ___ SNAKE

___ ribbon BLUE, RED

rib-eye STEAK

ribonucleic ACID

ribs MEAT

rib-tickler HOOT

Ricardo
  see Spanish

Ricardo, Ricky
  ~ portrayer DESI

Ricci NINA

rice
  ~ wine SAKE, SAKI

rice ___ PAPER

Rice ANNE, ELMER, TIM
  ~ University athlete OWL

___ Rice Burroughs EDGAR

Rice Krispies
  ~ sound POP, SNAP

Rice, Tim
  ~ musical CHESS

rich AMPLE, DEEP, FAT
  ~ biscuit SCONE
  ~ cake TORTE
  ~ fur SABLE
  ~ person HAVE
  ~ soil LOAM
  ~ supply LODE
  niche for the ~ SAFE

Richard BOONE, EGAN, GERE, LEWIS, ROE, STEELE
  like Franklin's ~ POOR

"Richard ___" III

"Richard Cory" POEM

Richard Henry ___ DANA

Richard III
  ~ need HORSE

"Richard III" PLAY

Richards ANN, RENEE

"___ Richard's Almanack" POOR

Richards, Keith STONE

Richards, Mary
  ~ player MOORE

Richardson IAN, TONY

riches GOLD, LOOT

"Richest ___ in the World, The" GIRL

Richie
  ~ portrayer RON

Richie, Lionel
  ~ tune EASY

"Rich Man, Poor Man"
  ~ actor NOLTE
  ~ author SHAW

~ Emmy-winner ASNER

Richmond
  ~ was its cap. CSA

Richter
  ~ concern TREMOR

Richthofen ACE

rick
  ~ starter HAY

Rick DEES
  end of ~'s toast KID

Rickenbacker ACE, EDDIE

rickety LOOSE
  ~ auto CRATE
  ~ ship TUB
  not as ~ SAFER

rickey
  ~ ingredient GIN, LIME

Ricki LAKE

Rickles DON

rickrack TRIM

Rick's
  ~ pianist SAM

Ricky
  ~ landlady ETHEL
  ~ landlord FRED
  ~ portrayer DESI

ricochet CAROM, SKIP

rid CLEAR, FREE
  get ~ of DROP, EJECT, ERASE, FIRE, OUST, SCRAP, SELL, SHED
  get ~ of knots UNTIE
  get ~ of the suds RINSE

riddle KNOT, POSER
  ~ explanation KEY
  answer to the Sphinx's ~ MAN

ride BAIT, TEASE
  ~ a bike PEDAL
  ~ at anchor REST
  ~ hard POST, SPUR
  ~ herd on BOSS, RUN, TEND
  ~ roughshod over BOSS, TREAD
  ~ starter HAY
  ~ the bench SIT
  ~ the rapids RAFT
  ~ the ump BOO
  ~ the waves SAIL
  ~ to hounds HUNT
  allow to ~ LETON
  bride's ~ LIMO
  go for a ~ BIKE, MOTOR
  short ~ SPIN
  take for a ~ DUPE
  there for the ~ ALONG
  what hobos ~ RAILS

ride ___ a fall FOR

ride ___ on HERD

___ ride FREE

Rideau CANAL

Rideau Canal
  ~ terminus OTTAWA

rider FARE, TAG
  ~ command WHOA
  ~ goad SPUR
  ~ implement CROP
  ~ payment FARE
  ~ stance SEAT
  ~ strap REIN
  boxcar ~ HOBO
  hack ~ FARE
  horseback ~'s outfit HABIT
  rail ~ HOBO
  UFO ~ ALIEN

"___ Rider" EASY, PALE

"___ Rider, The" RANGE

ride roughshod ___ OVER

"___ Riders" SKY

"___ Riders, The" LONG

"Riders of the Purple ___" SAGE

"Riders of the Purple Sage"
  ~ author GREY

"Ride the High Country"
  ~ actor SCOTT

"Ride the Pink ___" HORSE

ridge CREST, LEDGE, REEF, SEAM, STRIA
  ~ depression COL
  corduroy ~ RIB, WALE
  fingerboard ~ FRET
  glacial ~ ARETE, ESKER
  sandy ~ DUNE

___ Ridge Boys, The OAK

___ Ridge Mountains BLUE

ridges
  glacial ~ OSAR

___ Ridge, Tenn. OAK

ridicule GIBE, KID, RAG, RIDE, ROAST, SNEER, TWIT

ridiculous INANE, MAD

riding
  ~ attire HABIT
  ~ for a fall SMUG
  ~ stick CROP
  ~ the waves ASEA, ATSEA

riding ___ HABIT

Ridley SCOTT

Rieger ALEX

Riesling WINE

Riesner DEAN

rife AWASH, RICH

riffle LEAF, PAGE

riffraff MOB, ROUT

rifle ARM, GUN, RAID, ROB
  ~ peephole BEAD
  ~ through RAKE
  carrying a ~ ARMED
  ready a ~ AIM

___ rifle AIR

rifleman SHOT

rift CUT, GAP, RENT, SPLIT

"rift within the ___" LUTE

rig ARM, FIT, GARB, GEAR, KIT, MOTOR, SEMI, SETUP, SUIT
  ~ out ARRAY, ATTIRE
  big ~ SEMI

Riga CITY, PORT
  ~ resident LETT

rigadoon DANCE

rigatoni PASTA

Rigel STAR
  ~ constellation ORION

Rigg DIANA
  role for ~ EMMA, PEEL

rigging GEAR, ROPE
  ~ support MAST, SPAR

right ERECT, MORAL
  ~ and proper DUE
  ~ angle ELBOW, ELL
  ~ away ASAP, STAT
  ~ ender IST
  ~ off the bat FIRST
  ~ off the stove HOT
  ~ on AMEN
  ~ on the button BANG
  ~ on the map EAST
  ~ on the money AOK
  all ~ AYE, GOOD, OKAY, SAFE, YES
  at ~ angles to the keel ABEAM
  be ~ for FIT, SUIT
  give one's ~ arm for PANT
  have a ~ to EARN, MERIT
  it may be ~ ANGLE
  just ~ IDEAL
  look ~ through someone CUT
  natural ~ DUE
  not ~ AMISS, AWRY, LEFT, OFF
  set ~ AMEND, ATONE, CURE, MEND, REMIT
  to the ~ ASIDE, GEE

right ___ ANGLE

right ___ and there THEN

right ___ the bat OFF

right ___ up SIDE

"___ right!" EYES

"___, right" YEAH

"Right!" AYE, YES

right and wrong
  uncaring of ~ AMORAL

right angle
  less than a ~ ACUTE

right-angle
  ~ shape ELL
  ~ shapes ELS

right as ___ RAIN

right away ANON, ASAP, NOW, SOON, STAT

"Right Bank"
  ~ author NEAL

righteous CLEAN, MORAL, SMUG
  ~ indignation ANGER

Righteous Brothers
   one of the ~ BILL

rightful DUE, LEGAL, TRUE

Right Guard
   ~ rival BAN

right-hand
   ~ person AIDE, ASST

right-minded SANE

rightmost
   ~ column UNITS

Right, Mr.
   not ~ CAD, HEEL

"___ Right Now" ALL

righto AYE, YES

right off the ___ BAT

"Right on!" AMEN

rights
   have ~ to CLAIM, OWN
   put to ~ ORDER

"Right Stuff, The"
   ~ org. NASA

"___ right up!" STEP

"___ right with the world!" ALLS

"Right you ___!" ARE

rigid CRUEL, DOUR, HARD, IRON,
   PRIM, SET, STAID, STERN, TAUT,
   TENSE

rigidity
   lose ~ SAG

rigidness RIGOR

rigmarole PRATE

"Rigoletto" OPERA
   ~ piece ARIA

rigorous HARD, STERN

___ rigueur ALA

Riis, Jacob DANE

Rijksmuseum
   ~ artist HALS

rile ANGER, FRET, IRK, PEEVE,
   UPSET
   ~ up AROUSE

riled IRATE, MAD, UPSET, WARM

Riley PAT
   life of ~ EASE

Riley, James Whitcomb POET
   see also poet

Riley, Mrs. Chester PEG

Rilke, Rainer Maria POET
   see also poet

rill RUN, STREAM

rim EDGE, LIMIT, LIP

Rimbaud, Arthur POET
   see also poet

rime ICE

**"Rime of the Ancient Mariner,
The"** POEM

rin
   ten ~ SEN

"Rinaldo" OPERA

rind CASE, COAT, PEEL, SKIN
   remove ~ PARE, PEEL

ring ARENA, BAND, BELT, BLARE,
   BLOC, CABAL, CALL, CLAN,
   HALO, LOOP, NOISE, PEAL, SEAL,
   TOLL
   ~ a warning bell ALARM,
     ALERT
   ~ boundary ROPE
   ~ decision DRAW, TKO
   ~ ender LET, SIDE, TAIL, TOSS
   ~ event BOUT
   ~ in OPEN, START
   ~ in the ocean ATOLL
   ~ legend ALI
   ~ of flowers LEI
   ~ of light HALO
   ~ of water MOAT
   ~ part GEM
   ~ site, perhaps EAR
   ~ starter EAR
   ~ surface MAT
   ~ up ADD, CALL, DIAL, GET,
     PHONE, SUM, TOTAL
   ~ victories KOS
   athletic ~ ARENA
   moon ~ HALO
   practice in the ~ SPAR
   rodeo ~ ARENA
   thing on a ~ KEY
   third man in the ~ REF

___ ring BRASS, MOOD

"Ring"
   ~ goddess ERDA
   Wagner's ~ EPIC

ring-a-levio GAME

___-ring circus THREE

"___ Ring des Nibelungen" DER

ringer
   register ~ SALE

ringhals SNAKE

ringing
   ~ sound DING, PEAL

ringlet TRESS

ringlets HAIR

Ringling Brothers
   one of the ~ OTTO

ringmaster EMCEE

"Ring My Bell"
   ~ singer Anita WARD

Ringo STARR
   ~ colleague PAUL

"Ring of ___" FIRE

"Ring of Bright ___" WATER

"Ring of Bright Water"
   ~ character OTTER

ring of fire
   ~ output LAVA

rings COIL
   mood ~ FAD
   run ~ around BEAT, BEST,
     LEAD, TOP

___ rings around RUN

ring-tailed
   ~ animal COATI
   ~ cat GENET

ringtoss GAME
   ~ target PEG

rink ARENA
   ~ jump AXEL
   ~ surface ICE
   ~ wear SKATE

rinky-dink SMALL

rinse BATHE, CLEAN, LAVE, WASH
   salon ~ HENNA

rinsing BATH

Rin Tin ___ TIN

"Rin Tin Tin"
   ~ network ABC

Rinzai ___ ZEN

"Rio ___" LOBO, RITA

Rio Branco
   ~ state ACRE

"Rio Bravo" OATER

Rio de ___ ORO

Rio de Janeiro CITY, PORT
   ~ dance SAMBA

Rio Grande
   ~ feeder PECOS

"Rio Grande" OATER

Rioja WINE

"Rio Lobo" OATER
   ~ actor ELAM

___ Rios, Jamaica OCHO

riot MELEE, REBEL, STORM
   ~ spray MACE
   read the ~ act WARN

riot ___ ACT

___ Rio, Tex. DEL

"Riot in ___ Block 11" CELL

riotous
   ~ group MOB

rip CLAW, RACE, RENT, SLASH,
   SNAG, SPLIT, TEAR, TIDE
   ~ apart REND
   ~ into LACE
   ~ off ROB, ROOK, STEAL, TAKE
   ~ up SHRED

rip ___ TIDE

rip ___ (steal) OFF

Rip TORN

ripe
   get ~ AGE

ripen AGE, GROW

ripened ADULT

ripener AGER

Ripken CAL, ORIOLE
   stat for ~ ATBAT, GAME, RBI

"Ripley's Believe It or ___" NOT

rip-off SCAM

riposte HIT, MOT

ripped RENT, TORN

ripping FINE
   ~ good time GAS

ripple BATHE, LAP

ripplelike
   ~ design MOIRE

rip-roaring LOUD

ripsnorter LULU

"Riptide"
   ~ actor BRAY

rise CREST, EMERGE, GAIN, GROW,
   HIKE, LOOM, RAMP, SLOPE,
   SOAR, STAND, START
   ~ on the hind legs RAMP,
     REAR
   ~ over TOP
   ~ to the occasion COPE
   ~ up REAR, REBEL, RIOT
   give ~ to BREED, CAUSE
   market ~ GAIN
   price ~ HIKE
   where hackles ~ NAPE

___-rise LOW

"Rise and ___!" SHINE

risen
   not ~ ABED

riser STEP
   ~ cousin TREAD
   ~ plus tread STAIR
   early ~ SUN

___ riser EARLY

rises
   it ~ to the top CREAM

rishi SAGE

"Rising ___" SUN

___-rising flour SELF

risk DARE, PERIL, STAKE
   ~ a ticket SPEED
   ~ money BET
   not at ~ SAFE
   worrier's ~ ULCER

risk coverage
   ~ (abbr.) INS

risk-free SAFE

risky
   ~ business DARE

risqué RACY
   beyond ~ LEWD

rissole MEAT

ristorante
   ~ course PASTA

Rita GAM
   see also Spanish

Rita ___ Brown MAE

"Rita, ___ and Bob Too" SUE

"___ Rita" RIO

"Rita, Sue ___ Bob Too" AND

"Rita, Sue and ___ Too" BOB

"Rita, Sue and Bob ___" TOO

Ritchie, Michael
~ film of 1975 SMILE

rite
~ site ALTAR
religious ~ MASS

rite of passage
teen ~ PROM

"Ritorna vincitor"
~ singer AIDA

Ritter TEX

Ritter, John
~ dad TEX

Ritt, Martin
~ film of 1987 NUTS

ritual POMP
afternoon ~ NAP
champagne ~ TOAST
courtroom ~ OATH, PLEA
English ~ TEA
Japanese ~ TEA
Saturday night ~ BATH
trial ~ PLEA

Ritz, The HOTEL
home of ~ PARIS

ritzy CHIC, POSH
~ auto LIMO
~ group ELITE
~ headpiece TIARA
~ home ESTATE
~ rock GEM
~ shop SALON
hardly ~ SEEDY

rival ENEMY, FOE, VIE
~ of (prefix) ANTI

rivalry
victim of sibling ~ ABEL

"Rivals, The"
~ character ACRES

rive CUT, HACK, REND

river
~ at Thebes NILE
~ barrier DAM
~ bend ELBOW
~ bottom BED
~ curve BEND
~ feature DELTA
~ feeder STREAM
~ flowing from Lake
    Baikal LENA
~ for which a dog was
    named AIRE
~ in Hesse EDER
~ in Scotland DEE
~ in Spanish RIO
~ island AIT
~ mammal OTTER
~ near Stonehenge AVON
~ of Greek myth STYX
~ of Ireland ERNE

~ of Tours LOIRE
~ region DELTA
~ residue SILT
~ source HEAD
~ structure LEVEE
~ to Donegal Bay ERNE
~ to the Colorado GILA
~ to the Humber OUSE
~ to the North Sea EMS
~ transport RAFT
~ valley DALE
~ vessel CANOE
Aberdeen's ~ DEE
African ~ NIGER, NILE
Alpine ~ AAR, AARE, ISERE
Arizona ~ GILA, SALT
Bard's ~ AVON
Bedfordshire ~ OUSE
Belgian ~ OISE, YSER
Berne's ~ AARE
Bern's ~ AAR
Bonn's ~ RHINE
Brazilian border ~ ACRE
Caen's ~ ORNE
Canadian ~ OTTAWA
Carpathian ~ ODER
Catalonian ~ EBRO
Charon's ~ STYX
Chinese ~ HAN
Cincinnati's ~ OHIO
Cologne's ~ RHINE
Czech ~ ELBE, ODER
East Asian ~ AMUR
Egyptian ~ NILE
English ~ AVON, CAM, OUSE,
    TRENT
Essen's ~ RUHR
European ~ EDER, ELBE,
    ODER, OISE
European ~ valley SAAR
Firenze's ~ ARNO
Florence's ~ ARNO
Frankfurt's ~ ODER
French ~ ISERE, LOIRE, OISE,
    ORNE, SEINE, YSER
French/German ~ SAAR
Gadsden Purchase boundary
    ~ GILA
German ~ EDER, ELBE, EMS,
    ODER, OSTE, RHINE, RUHR
German/French ~ SAAR
German/Polish border
    ~ ODER
Grenoble's ~ ISERE
Hades ~ STYX
Hamburg's ~ ELBE
Hessian ~ EDER
Iberian ~ EBRO
Idaho ~ SNAKE
Ile-de-France ~ OISE
infernal ~ STYX
Interlaken's ~ AAR, AARE
Irish ~ ERNE
Italian ~ ARNO
Jackson Hole's ~ SNAKE
Kansas ~ OSAGE
Kassel's ~ EDER
Kazakh ~ URAL
Khartoum's ~ NILE
Leeds' ~ AIRE
Left Bank ~ SEINE
Louisville's ~ OHIO
Magnitogorsk's ~ URAL

Manchurian ~ AMUR
Nantes' ~ LOIRE
New York ~ EAST
Normandy ~ ORNE
Northumberland ~ TYNE
Northwest ~ SNAKE
Notre Dame's ~ SEINE
Nottingham's ~ TRENT
Ontario ~ TRENT
Orenburg's ~ URAL
Orsk's ~ URAL
Paris' ~ SEINE
Pisa's ~ ARNO
Pittsburgh ~ OHIO
Polish/German border
    ~ ODER
Rouen's ~ SEINE
Russian ~ DON, LENA
Salisbury Plain ~ AVON
Saragossa's ~ EBRO
Scottish ~ DEE
sell down the ~ DESERT
Siberian ~ LENA
Silesian ~ ODER
Sino-Russian ~ AMUR
Solothurn's ~ AAR, AARE
South African ~ ORANGE
Spain's longest ~ EBRO
Stratford's ~ AVON
Swiss ~ AAR, AARE
Tempe's ~ SALT
Texas ~ PECOS
Tuscany ~ ARNO
underworld ~ STYX
watch the ~ flow LOAF
Welsh ~ DEE
Wheeling's ~ OHIO
White or Blue ~ NILE
world's longest ~ NILE
Yakutsk's ~ LENA
Yorkshire ~ AIRE, OUSE, URE
Zaragoza's ~ EBRO

river ___ HORSE, OTTER

"River ___, The" NIGER, RAT,
SEINE

"___ River" MOON, RED

riverbank SHORE
~ growth REED
~ plant SEDGE

riverbed
~ item STONE
dry ~ WADI, WASH

riverboat
kind of ~ TUG

River City
~ state IOWA

Riverfront Stadium
~ player RED

river mouth
~ deposit DELTA, SILT

"River Niger, The"
~ director SHAH

___ River, N.J. TOMS

"River's ___" EDGE

"River's ___, The" EDGE

Rivers, Joan EMCEE, HOST

"River, Stay 'Way From My ___"
DOOR

rivet ARREST, GRIP, NAIL, PEG
large-headed ~ STUD

riveted SET

riveting
~ gaze GLARE

Riviera
~ acquisition TAN
~ resort NICE
see also French

rivulet RIA, RILL, STREAM

Riyadh
~ resident ARAB

riyal COIN

Rizzo
~ of the Muppets RAT

Rizzuto PHIL
~ rival REESE

RMN PRES
~ first VP STA
~ was his Vice President DDE

Rn ELEM
86 for ~ ATNO

RN
~ asset TLC
~ org. ANA
~ stations ERS, ORS

RNA
~ ender ASE
part of ~ ACID

RNs
places for ~ ERS, ORS
workers with ~ DRS, MDS

roach PEST

Roach HAL

road PASS, PATH, ROUTE
~ charge TOLL
~ covering TAR
~ curve ESS
~ ender BED, SIDE, STER
~ guide MAP
~ hazard ICE
~ in French RUE
~ in Italian VIA
~ in Latin ITER, VIA
~ rescue org. AAA
~ service TOW
~ sign GAS, SLO, SLOW, STOP,
    YIELD
~ signal FLARE
~ starter RAIL
~ warning SLO, SLOW
bend in the ~ TURN
build a ~ PAVE
burn up the ~ RACE, SPEED,
    TEAR
country ~ LANE
country ~ feature RUT
do ~ work PAVE, TAR
emergency ~ service
    org. AAA
farther down the ~ LATER
get the show on the
    ~ START

go by ~ MOTOR
go on the ~ TOUR
hit the ~ LEAVE, PART, ROVE, SCAT, SCRAM, START
king of the ~ HOBO
mountain ~ ESS
mountain ~ abbr. ELEV
one for the ~ CAR
on the ~ AWAY
resurface a ~ PAVE, TAR
Roman ~ ITER
side ~ LANE
take the wrong ~ ERR
toll ~ PIKE
treat an icy ~ SALT, SAND

road ___ ATLAS, HOG, MAP, SHOW, TEST

___ road LOW

"Road"
~ film destination BALI, RIO
name in ~ pictures HOPE

roadhouse INN

roadie
~ equipment AMP

road map
~ abbr. RTE
~ feature INSET
~ org. AAA

"Road Not ___, The" TAKEN

"Road Not Taken, The" POEM

road rally RACE
~ need MAP

Road Runner
~ cartoon backdrop MESA
~ sound BEEP

roads
like winter ~ ICY
take the back ~ MOTOR

road show
~ grp. USO

roadside
~ establishment INN, STAND
~ sign EATS
~ warning FLARE

road sign GAS, SLO, SLOW, STOP, YIELD
~ shape ARROW
~ warning DIP
~ word AHEAD

roadster AUTO, CAR, MOTOR

road to ___, the RUIN

"Road to ___" BALI, RIO

"Road to ___, The" OMAHA

"Road to Morocco"
~ talker CAMEL

___-road vehicle OFF

roadway
~ sign EATS

Roald DAHL

roam GAD, HIKE, RANGE, ROVE

roamer NOMAD
range ~ BISON, STEER

roaming
~ freely LOOSE

"Roaming far and wide until ___ hour" ALATE

roan BAY, HORSE

roar BAWL, BLARE, BLAST, BOOM, DIN, NOISE, PEAL, RAVE, STORM, YELL
cannon ~ BOOM
stadium ~ RAH

___-roaring RIP

Roaring Fork River
town on the ~ ASPEN

Roaring Twenties ERA

roast BAKE, HEAT, MEAT, TEASE
~ host EMCEE
~ seasoning SAGE
~ table DAIS
have ~ beef EAT
kind of ~ LOIN

___ roast POT, RIB

roaster PAN

roasting HOT
~ device SPIT
~ ears CORN
~ place OVEN

rob LOOT, RIFLE, STEAL, TAKE

Rob ___ ROY

Robbe-Grillet ALAIN

robber
~ chaser COP
bank ~ nemesis ALARM

robber ___ BARON

robbery CAPER

Robbins TIM

robe DON, DRESS, GARB, VEST
~ starter BATH
altar ~ ALB
Arab ~ ABA

___ robe LAP

"Robe, The"
~ role PETER

robed CLAD

robe de ___ BAL

Robert ALDA, DOLE, MOORE, MORSE, OWEN, PEEL, SHAW, WISE

Robert ___ ELEE

Robert ___ Warren PENN

Robert B. ___ BEAN

Robert E. ___ LEE

"___ Robert" Feller RAPID

Roberto
see Spanish

Roberts ERIC, ORAL

"___ Roberts" BOB

Roberts, Julia
~ brother ERIC

Robertson DALE, OSCAR, PAT

Roberts, Oral
~ city TULSA

___ Roberts University ORAL

Robert the Bruce SCOT
where ~ was crowned SCONE

Robeson PAUL

robin BIRD
~ class AVES
a ~'s is blue EGG
ragged ~ PLANT

Robin HERO
~ portrayer in 1938 ERROL
accessory for ~ CAPE

Robin ___ HOOD

"Robin ___: Prince of Thieves" HOOD

"Robin ___ the Seven Hoods" AND

"Robin and the ___ Hoods" SEVEN

Robin, Christopher
~ creator MILNE

Robin Hood
~ beneficiaries POOR
~ quarry RICH

"Robin Hood" OPERA

robin's-egg BLUE, COLOR

"___ Robinson" MRS

Robinson, Brooks ORIOLE

Robinson, Edwin Arlington POET
see also poet

Robinson, Frank ORIOLE, RED

roble TREE

robot TOOL

robots
play about ~ RUR

Rob Roy SCOT

"Rob Roy"
~ author SCOTT
~ girl LASS

Robson, Mark
~ film of 1955 TRIAL

robust ALIVE, BIG, FIT, HALE, IRON, LARGE
~ drink ALE

robustness VIM

roc BIRD

Roca CAPE

Rocco ALEX

Rochat ERIC

Rochester
~ love EYRE
~ to Benny VALET
~ ward ADELE

rock DANCE, GEM, GEMS, GENRE, JAR, MOVE, REEL, STONE, TOSS
~ accumulation SCREE
~ and roll GENRE
~ bottom NADIR
~ crystal GEM
~ detritus SAND
~ formed from shale SLATE
~ genre ACID, HARD, METAL, RAP
~ gently SWAY
~ group ABBA, AHA, KISS, ORES
~ musician's elec. gear AMP
~ music, to some NOISE
~ partner ROLL
~ ridge ARETE
~ scratch STRIA
~ shelf LEDGE
~ (suffix) ITE
built like a ~ SOLID
clay ~ SHALE
colorful ~ AGATE
crystal-filled ~ GEODE
crystalline ~ SPAR
easily split ~ SHALE
ferriferous ~ ORE
fluid ~ LAVA
high isolated ~ SCAR
hot ~ LAVA
igneous ~ LAVA
inscribed ~ STELE
jagged ~ CRAG
layered ~ SHALE
like a ~ HARD
loose ~ SCREE
molten ~ LAVA
oil-bearing ~ SHALE
overhanging ~ LEDGE
projecting ~ CRAG
refinable ~ ORE
ritzy ~ GEM
rugged ~ CRAG
soft ~ TALC
valuable ~ ORE
volcanic ~ LAVA

"rock"
Biblical ~ PETER

rock ___ BASS, CRAB, SALT, WREN

___ rock ACID, HARD, PET

Rock-___ OLA

"___ Rock" COP

"___ Rock, The" HOT

"Rock-a-___ Baby" BYE

rock and ___ ROLL, RYE

rock and roll
~ classic OLDIE
~ genre METAL

"Rock and Roll All Nite"
~ band KISS

"Rock and Roll Is ___ to Stay" HERE

rock band
~ gear AMP

___ Rock Cafe HARD

rock concert
  ~ **need** AMP

Rock Cornish HEN

Rockefeller
  ~ **handout** DIME
  co. founded by ~ ESSO

rocker
  ~ **equipment** AMP
  ~ **part** ARM
  off one's ~ DAFT, LOCO, MAD

rocket SOAR
  ~ **deviation** YAW
  ~ **ender** EER
  ~ **housing** SILO
  ~ **org.** NASA
  ~ **path** ARC
  ~ **section** STAGE
  ~ **top** NOSE
  booster ~ ATLAS
  dame's ~ PLANT
  kind of ~ RETRO
  NASA ~ ATLAS
  US ~ THOR

rocket ___ SHIP

___ rocket ION

Rockets FIVE, TEAM
  ~ **org.** NBA

Rockies NINE, TEAM
  ~ **(abbr.)** MTS
  ~ **range** UINTA
  ~ **resort** ASPEN
  ~ **ruminant** ELK
  ~ **zone** MDT, MST

rocking ___ HORSE

"Rocking ___ Winner, The"
  HORSE

rocking horse TOY

"Rock Island ___, The" LINE

"Rock 'n' ___ High School" ROLL

"Rock of ___" AGES

rocks ICE
  barbecue ~ LAVA
  growth on ~ MOSS
  hot ~ LAVA
  not on the ~ NEAT
  on the ~ ICED, POOR
  pet ~ FAD

rock video
  ~ **award** AVA

Rockwell KENT

"___ Rock West" RED

rocky HARD
  ~ **eminence** TOR
  ~ **ledge** CRAG
  ~ **peak** SPIRE
  ~ **spur** ARETE
  bare ~ slope SCAR

Rocky
  ~ **opponent** APOLLO, CREED
  ~ **to Bullwinkle** PAL
  enemy of ~ BORIS

"Rocky"
  ~ **actress** SHIRE

"Rocky ___" III

"Rocky ___ to Dublin, The"
  ROAD

"Rocky Horror Picture ___, The"
  SHOW

"Rocky Horror Picture Show, The"
  ~ **hero** BRAD

"Rocky III"
  ~ **actor** MRT

Rocky Mountain
  ~ **hrs.** MDT, MST
  ~ **range** TETON
  ~ **town** ASPEN
  ~ **tribe** UTE

Rocky Road
  ~ **serving** SCOOP

rococo ORNATE, STYLE
  too ~ ARTY

rocs
  like ~ AVIAN

rod AXIS, BAR, CANE, GAT, GUN,
  POLE, STAKE, STAVE, WAND
  auto ~ AXLE
  barbecue ~ SPIT
  fairy godmother's ~ WAND
  hot ~ AUTO, CAR, RACER
  metal ~ BAR
  wheel ~ AXLE

___ rod HOT, TIE

rod and ___ REEL

Roddenberry GENE

rodent ANIMAL, MOUSE
  long-eared ~ HARE
  long-tailed ~ RAT
  mouselike ~ VOLE
  reaction to a ~ EEK
  underground ~ MOLE

rodeo
  ~ **gear** LASSO
  ~ **mount** STEER
  ~ **prop** NOOSE, RIATA
  ~ **ring** ARENA
  compete in a ~ ROPE

Rodgers BILL
  ~ **collaborator** HART

Rodgers and Hart
  ~ **song** SOON

Rodin
  ~ **sculpture** ADAM
  ~ **sculpture, with "The"** KISS
  ~ **subject** NUDE

Rodman, Dennis
  ~ **org.** NBA

rodomontade BRAG, RANT

rods
  many square ~ ACRES

roe ANIMAL, DEER, EGGS, OVA,
  STAG
  ~ **source** SHAD
  lobster ~ CORAL

roe ___ DEER

roebuck DEER, MALE

Roebuck
  ~ **partner** SEARS

Roentgen
  ~ **discovery** XRAY

roentgenogram XRAY

Roethke, Theodore POET
  see also poet

Roe vs. ___ WADE

roger YES

Roger EBERT, MOORE, REES
  ~ **co-reviewer** GENE

"Roger & Me"
  ~ **director** MOORE

Rogers FRED, ROY
  ~ **partner** EVANS

Rogers/Astaire
  ~ **locale** RIO

Rogers, Buck HERO

Rogers, Kenny
  ~ **song** LADY

Rogers, Mrs. DALE

Rogers St. Johns ADELA

Rogers, Will
  prop for ~ LASSO, ROPE

Roget
  ~ **entry** SYN

rogue CAD, DOG

"Rogue ___" COP

roguish ARCH, BAD, SLY
  ~ **wit** WAG

Rohmer ERIC, SAX

Rohmer, Sax ALIAS

roi LORD

roil MOVE

roister BRAG, CROW, PLAY, REVEL

roistering LOUD

Roker
  ~ **and others** ALS

Rolaids
  ~ **target** ACID

Roland HERO

role PART
  assign a ~ CAST
  brief ~ CAMEO

role models
  jrs.' ~ SRS

Rolfe, Rebecca, ___ Pocahontas
  NEE

roll BAGEL, COIL, LIST, ROAR, ROB,
  RUN, SAIL
  ~ **along** ELAPSE
  ~ **call** VOTE
  ~ **down the street** SKATE
  ~ **ender** AWAY, OUT, OVER
  ~ **in** COME
  ~ **of stamps** COIL
  ~ **on the tarmac** TAXI
  ~ **out** ARISE, RISE, SHOW
  ~ **out the fescue** SOD

  ~ **out the red carpet** GREET
  ~ **snake eyes** LOSE
  ~ **starter** BED, LOG, PAY,
    STEAM
  ~ **topping** SESAME
  ~ **up** AMASS
  ~ **up one's sleeves** START
  ~ **with a hole** BAGEL
  ~ **with the punches** ADAPT,
    COPE
  donutlike ~ BAGEL
  fat ~ of bills WAD
  hard ~ BAGEL
  jelly ~ CAKE
  on a ~ HOT
  rock and ~ GENRE

roll ___ BAR, CALL

roll ___ (introduce) OUT

___ roll EGG, HONOR, ONA

"Roll ___ bones!" DEM

rollback REBATE

roll call
  ~ **response** AYE, HERE, NAY,
    YEA, YES

Rolle ESTHER

roller
  ~ **ender** SKATE
  ~ **starter** STEAM

"Rollerball"
  ~ **actor** CAAN

rollerblade SKATE

roller coaster RIDE
  ~ **feature** DIP

roller derby GAME
  ~ **track** OVAL

rollers
  Reno ~ DICE
  use ~ SET

roller skate
  ~ **accessory** KEY

roller skater
  ~ **hangout** RINK

rollick LARK, PLAY, ROMP

rollicking GAY

rolling
  ~ **in dough** RICH
  ~ **stone** HOBO, NOMAD
  get the ball ~ OPEN, START
  over the ~ main ASEA, ATSEA

rolling ___ MILL, PIN, STOP

rolling stock
  ~ **repository** YARD

rolling stone
  ~ **lack** MOSS

Rollins, Sonny
  ~ **instrument** SAX

roll out the ___ carpet RED

rollover
  ~ **subj.** IRA

rolls
  distance a golf ball ~ RUN
  tax ~ POLL

Rolls AUTO, CAR

Rolls Royce AUTO, CAR
~ **trunk** BOOT

rolltop DESK

Rölvaag OLE

ROM
~ **medium** DISC
part of ONLY, READ
part of ~ ONLY, READ

Roma
see Italian

romaine COS

Roman RUTH, TYPE
~ **3** III
~ **52** LII
~ **54** LIV
~ **102** CII
~ **bronze** AES
~ **calendar date** IDES
~ **censor** CATO
~ **coin** AES
~ **consul** CATO
~ **council** SENATE
~ **domestic deity** LAR
~ **emperor** CAESAR, NERO
~ **ethicist** CATO
~ **games official** EDILE
~ **garment** TOGA
~ **historian** CATO
~ **I** EGO, ONE
~ **II** TWO
~ **III** THREE
~ **IX** NINE
~ **language** LATIN
~ **legion** ARMY
~ **magistrate** EDILE
~ **official** EDILE
~ **orator** CATO
~ **patios** ATRIA
~ **poet** OVID
~ **port** OSTIA
~ **road** ITER
~ **rooms** ATRIA
~ **theaters** ODEA
~ **trio** III
~ **V** FIVE
~ **VI** SIX
~ **VII** SEVEN
~ **X** TEN
~ **XI** ELEVEN
French site of ~ ruins ARLES
it may be ~ NOSE
not ~ ITAL
see also Latin

Roman ___ NOSE

roman à ___ CLEF

Roman candle
~ **path** ARC

romance DREAM, GENRE, LOVE,
TALE, WOO
~ **in French** AMOUR
~ **of yore** GEST, GESTE

Romance
~ **lang.** ITAL

"___ Romance" TRUE

"Romance of ___ Ridge, The"
ROSY

"Romance on the High ___"
SEAS

romances
big name in ~ STEEL

"Romancing the ___" STONE

Romanesque STYLE

roman-fleuve SAGA

Romanian
~ **dance** HORA

Romano
~ **cheese milk source** EWE

"Romanoff ___ Juliet" AND

Romanov
~ **title** TSAR
see also Russian

Roman ruins
~ **site in France** ARLES

Romans
book before ~ ACTS

**"Roman Spring of ___ Stone,
The"** MRS

"Roman Spring of Mrs. ___, The"
STONE

romantic
~ **ender** IST
~ **episode** AMOUR
~ **inspiration** MOON
~ **isle** CAPRI
~ **offering** ROSE
~ **outing** DATE
~ **rendezvous** TRYST
~ **work** POEM

"___ Romantic" TOO

romanticize EXALT

Rombauer IRMA

Rome APPLE, CITY
bishop of ~ POPE
home of ~ ITALY
like ~ ETERNAL
number of ~'s hills SEVEN
see also Italian, Latin

Rome Beauty APPLE

Romeo BEAU
~ **rendezvous** TRYST
~ **rival** PARIS

"Romeo ___ Juliet" AND

___ Romeo ALFA

Romeo and Juliet
emulate ~ ELOPE

"Romeo and Juliet" OPERA, PLAY
~ **event** TRYST
~ **role** NURSE

"Romeo Is Bleeding"
~ **actress** OLIN

Romero CESAR

romp CAPER, HOP, LARK, LEAP,
PLAY, REVEL, SKIP, SPREE
blithe ~ LARK

Romulan ALIEN

Romulus ROMAN, TWIN
~ **to Mars** SON
~ **to Remus** TWIN
mother of ~ ILIA

Ron ELY, MANN

rondeau POEM, SONG

rondel POEM

Ronny and the Daytonas
~ **tune** GTO

Ronsard, Pierre de POET
see also poet

Roo
~ **creator** MILNE

roods
four ~ ACRE

roof TOP
~ **over one's head** ABODE,
HOME
~ **problem** DRIP
~ **projection** EAVE
~ **runoff** RAIN
~ **topper** AERIAL, EPI, VANE
curved ~ DOME
hit the ~ RAGE, RANT, RAVE,
ROAR, SNAP, STORM
mosque ~ DOME
on the ~ **of** ATOP
pointed ~ SPIRE
raise the ~ REVEL

___ roof HIP

roofed-in
~ **gallery** ARCADE

roofing
~ **material** SLATE, TILE
~ **sealant** TAR

roofless OPEN

"roof of the world"
~ **locale** ASIA, TIBET

rooftop
~ **gadget** AERIAL

rook CROW, DUPE, HAVE, ROB

rookie
~ **socialite** DEB

"Rookie, The"
~ **actor** SHEEN

"Rookie of the ___" YEAR

Rookie of the Year AWARD

"Rookie of the Year"
~ **director** STERN

room DEN, SPACE
~ **and board** KEEP
~ **at the top** ATTIC
~ **connector** HALL
~ **cooler** FAN
~ **ender** ETTE, MATE
~ **extension** ELL
~ **furnishings** DECOR
~ **in Latin** CAMERA
~ **in Spanish** SALA
~ **scheme** DECOR
~ **starter** ANTE, BALL, BAR,
BATH, BED, CLASS, COAT,
ELBOW, HEAD, HOME, LEG,
NEWS, PLAY, POOL, STATE,

SUN, TAP, TEA, WASH
~ **to spare** PLAY
book-lined ~ DEN
chem ~ LAB
Clue ~ HALL
college ~ DORM
convent ~ CELL
Dad's ~ DEN
decorate a ~ PAPER
drawing ~ SALON
elbow ~ PLAY, SPACE
experiment ~ LAB
family ~ DEN
friar's ~ CELL
front ~ SALON
grill ~ BAR
growing ~ ACRE, SPACE
hacienda ~ SALA
harem ~ ODA
have ~ for SEAT, SIT
home ~ DEN
ladies' ~ of a sort HAREM,
ODA
living ~ SALON
nun's ~ CELL
pay for ~ and board TENANT
place to rent a ~ INN
reading ~ DEN
rec ~ DEN
reception ~ SALON
semicircular ~ APSE
spare ~ PLAY
teen's ~ often MESS
tiny ~ CELL
trophy ~ DEN
TV ~ DEN
unfinished ~ ATTIC
video ~ DEN
visitor's ~ SALON
White House ~ EAST
with ~ to spare AMPLE
zenana ~ ODA

___ room CHAT, DAY, GAME, REC

"Room ___ One More" FOR

"___ Room, The" WAR

"Room at ___" ARLES

"Room at the ___" TOP

roomer TENANT

"Room for ___ More" ONE

"Room for One ___" MORE

roommate
Kate's TV ~ ALLIE

rooms ABODE, FLAT, HOME
like many teens' ~ MESSY
Roman ~ ATRIA

room-service
~ **prop** TRAY

room to ___ SPARE

"Room With a View, A"
~ **director** IVORY
~ **view** ARNO

roomy AMPLE, BIG, EASY, LARGE,
LOOSE, OPEN, WIDE

Rooney ANDY, ART

Rooney, Mickey
~ **first wife** AVA

Roosevelt
~ role of 1940 EDISON

Roosevelt DAM
~ matriarch SARA
~ successor TAFT

Roosevelt, Teddy
daughter of ~ ALICE
wife of ~ ALICE

roost ABODE, REST, SETTLE, SIT
~ sitter HEN
rule the ~ LEAD

rooster MALE
~ mate HEN
~ pride COMB, CREST
~ replacement ALARM
~ sound CROW

root BASE, BASIS, BEER, CAUSE,
GERM, PLANT
~ cause SEED
~ crop YAM
~ malady ROT
edible ~ BEET, OCA, TARO,
YAM

root ___ BEER, CROP

root beer
~ alternative COLA, SODA
~ brand DADS

rooted SET

___-rooted DEEP

rooter FAN
~ word RAH

___-rooter ROTO

rootless
~ plant ALGA

roots
put down ~ SETTLE

"Roots" SAGA
~ Emmy-winner ASNER

rootstock TARO

rope CABLE, CORD, LASH, LINE,
NOOSE
~ feature KNOT
~ fiber HEMP, SISAL
~ in LASSO, LURE, TRAP
~ loop NOOSE
~ someone in DUPE
cowboy's ~ LASSO, RIATA
enough ~ PLAY
jump ~ GAME, SKIP
strong ~ CABLE
use ~ BIND

rope ___ TOW

"Rope-a-dope"
~ boxer ALI

"Rope of ___" SAND

Roper ELMO
~ report POLL

ropes
learn the ~ ADAPT

Rorem NED

rorqual ANIMAL, SEI

Rorschach TEST
~ image BLOT

~ medium INK

___ rosa SUB

Rosa
see Spanish

___ Rosa, Calif. SANTA

Rosalind
role for ~ MAME

Rosalynn
~ youngest AMY

"Rosamond"
~ composer ARNE

"Rosanna"
~ band TOTO

Rosa Parks Day
~ mo. DEC

Rosario CITY, PORT

rosary
~ bead AVE
~ part BEAD
~ prayer AVE
recite the ~ PRAY

roscoe GAT, ROD

rose COLOR, RED
~ clinger APHID
~ extract ATTAR
~ fruit HIP
~ holder STEM
~ locale BED
~ pest APHID
old ~ COLOR
tea ~ COLOR

rose ___ HIP, WATER

___ rose TEA

rosé WINE

Rose PETE
~ forte HITS
~ lover ABIE
like Abie's ~ IRISH

"Rose ___" MARIE

"Rose ___, The" NUDE

"Rose ___ rose..." ISA

Roseanne
~ TV husband DAN
like ~'s speech NASAL

"Roseanne"
~ network ABC
Darlene, on ~ SARA

Rose Bowl
~ kickoff PARADE
~ org. NCAA

Rosebud SLED
~ owner KANE

"Rose for ___ Maria, A" ANA

"Rose is a rose is a rose"
~ author STEIN

"Roseland"
~ director IVORY

"Rose Marie"
~ actor LAMAS
~ org. RCMP

rosemary HERB

Rosemary
~ portrayer MIA

Rosen
~ and others ALS

Rosenberg ALAN

"___ Rosenkavalier" DER

roses
bed of ~ EASE
essence of ~ ATTAR
gather ~ SNIP

"Roses ___ red..." ARE

"Rose Tattoo, The"
~ director MANN

Rosetta ___ STONE

Rosewall KEN

rosewood TREE

Rosie
~ fastener RIVET

"Rosie!"
~ director RICH

rosin
~ source PINE

Rosinante HORSE, NAG

Ross DIANA, SEA
~ product FLAG

Ross ___ Shelf ICE

Ross, Betsy SEWER
~ requirement NEEDLE
emulate ~ SEW

Rossetti DANTE

Rossetti, Dante POET
see also poet

"Rosshalde"
~ author HESSE

Rossini
~ subject TELL
~ work OPERA

Rossiya
see Russian

___ Ross Trophy ART

Rosten LEO

roster BILL, LIST, POLL, ROLL
~ of the best ALIST
candidate ~ SLATE
duty ~ ROTA
play ~ CAST

Rostov CITY, PORT

Rostropovich
~ instrument CELLO

rostrum DAIS, NOSE, STAND

rosy RED
hardly ~ ASHEN, ASHY, PALE,
WAN
paint a ~ picture FAKE

rosy-fingered
~ godess AURORA

rot ADDLE, SPOIL, TRASH

rota ROLL

Rota NINO

rotary
~ disk CAM

rotate EDDY, SPIN, TURN
~ to an astronaut YAW

rotating
~ piece CAM

rotation
~ line AXIS

___ rotation CROP

rote
learn by ~ CON

rotelle PASTA

Roth
~ plan IRA

rotini PASTA

rotisserie SPIT

rotten BAD, MEAN, POOR, VILE
~ kid IMP

rotten to the ___ CORE

rotter CAD, HEEL, ROUE

Rotterdam CITY, PORT
see also Dutch, Netherlands

rotund BIG, LARGE, OBESE

rotunda DOME

roué RAKE, SATYR

Rouen
~ river SEINE
see also French

"Rouen Cathedral"
~ painter MONET

rouge BET, PAINT
~ et noir GAME

rouge et ___ NOIR

rough HARD, RUDE
~ ender SHOD
~ it CAMP
~ projection SNAG
~ up BEAT, LAM, MAUL
having a ~ surface MAT,
MATTE
metal in the ~ ORE

rough ___ CUT

roughage BRAN

roughen ABRADE, CHAP
~ from cold CHAP

roughhewn RUDE

roughhouse PLAY

roughly ABOUT, NEAR, ORSO

roughneck GOON

roughrider TAMER

roughshod
ride ~ over BOSS, TREAD

roulade MEAT

roulette GAME
~ bet EVEN, NOIR, ODD, RED

round BOUT, ORBIT
  ~ dance HORA
  ~ mountain peak DOME
  ~ of applause HAND
  ~ thing ORB
  ~ top DOME
  ~ trip LAP
  ~ up AMASS, BEAD, HERD
  ~ up crops REAP
  bring ~ RESTORE
  buy a ~ TREAT
  it makes the world go
    ~ LOVE
  one ~ LAP
  tournament ~ SEMI, SEMIS
  turn round and ~ REEL

round ___ DANCE, STEAK, TRIP

___ round TOP

___-round YEAR

"Round ___, The" TABLE

"Roundabout"
  ~ band YES

"Round and Round"
  ~ singer COMO

rounded
  ~ hill KNOB
  ~ projection LOBE

roundelay SONG

roundish OVAL

rounds
  go a few ~ SPAR
  the ~ TOUR

Round Table
  ~ knight KAY
  ~ title SIR

roundup
  ~ device PROD
  ~ group HERD
  ~ need LASSO
  ~ site RANGE

"Round up the ___ suspects"
  USUAL

rouse GOAD, MOVE, PROD, STING,
  STIR, URGE
  ~ to EGG

Roush EDD

rousing
  ~ cheer YEA

Rousseau
  ~ novel EMILE

rout BEAT, REPEL

route BEAT, LINE, PATH, ROAD,
  SEND
  ~ in Latin VIA
  ~ in Spanish VIA
  ~ recommender AAA
  air ~ LANE
  cop's ~ BEAT
  en ~ in a way ASEA, ATSEA
  flight ~ ARC
  Hannibal's ~ ALPS
  mountain ~ PASS
  ocean ~ LANE
  rural ~ LANE
  usher's ~ AISLE

___ route RURAL, TRADE

router TOOL

routine ACT, HABIT, USUAL
  cheerleaders' ~ YELL
  comedy ~ SKIT
  daily ~ HABIT
  dull ~ ROTE, RUT
  nightclub ~ ACT
  overnight ~ SLEEP
  vaudeville ~ ACT, OLIO

rove GAD, HIKE, RANGE, ROAM

rover HOBO, NOMAD
  land ~ MOTOR, NOMAD

___ rover SEA

Rover
  ~ doc VET
  ~ remark ARF
  scrap for ~ ORT

row FILE, LINE, MELEE, OAR, RANK,
  SCRAP, SETTO, SPAT, TODO
  ~ of seats TIER
  calendar ~ WEEK
  put in a ~ ALINE, RANK

___ row CORN, SKID

rowan ASH

Rowan CARL, DAN

rowboat GIG
  ~ need OAR
  ~ problem LEAK

rowdy LOUD
  ~ party ORGY

rowdydow ADO, FLAP, MELEE,
  TODO

rowel SPUR

rowing
  ~ team CREW
  ~ team member OAR

Rowland EVANS, ROY

Rowlands GENA

Rowland V. ___ LEE

Rowlf
  ~ of the Muppets DOG

rows
  series of ~ TIER

"Roxanne"
  Daryl's ~ costar STEVE

Roxy Music
  ~ co-founder ENO

___ Roy ROB

royal FERN, PALM, REGAL
  ~ address SIRE
  ~ decree EDICT, FIAT
  ~ ender IST
  ~ fur ERMINE
  ~ jewelry TIARA
  ~ personage RULER
  ~ school ETON
  ~ sport POLO
  ~ symbol ORB
  British ~ informally ANDY
  Netherlands ~
    house ORANGE

  Norse ~ name OLAF, OLAV
  Punjab ~ woman RANEE,
    RANI
  Thailand ~ name RAMA

royal ___ BLUE, PALM

Royal ___, Mich. OAK

"Royal ___ of the Sun" HUNT

___ Royale National Park ISLE

___ Royal Highness HER, HIS

"Royal Hunt of the ___" SUN

royal jelly
  ~ producer BEE

Royals TEAM, TEN

royalties
  ~ org. ASCAP

___ Royce ("Car Wash" band)
  ROSE

Roy G. Biv
  part of ~ BLUE, HUE, ORANGE,
    RED

Roy's
  ~ wife DALE

Rozelle PETE

RPI
  ~ rival MIT
  part of ~ INST

RPM
  ~ indicator TACH
  part of ~ MIN, PER, REV

RPMs
  step up the ~ REV

RPS
  part of ~ PER, REV, SEC

RR
  ~ destination STA
  ~ info ETA

R&R LEAVE
  ~ grp. USO
  part of ~ REST

R-rated
  ~ or higher ADULT

R-rating
  ~ cause GORE

RSVP ANS
  ~ insert SASE
  part of ~ SIL

rtes. RDS, STS

Ru ELEM
  44 for ~ ATNO

rub ABRADE, WEAR
  ~ away ERODE
  ~ out ERASE, OMIT
  ~ the wrong way FRET, IRE,
    IRK, PEEVE, RILE

"rub-a-dub-dub"
  ~ craft TUB

"Rubáiyát, The" POEM
  ~ poet OMAR
  ~ word ENOW

Rub al Khali DESERT

rubber BOOT, ERASER, TREE
  ~ ball TOY
  ~ city AKRON
  ~ product ERASER
  ~ tree ULE
  pitcher's ~ SLAB
  spongy ~ FOAM
  tire ~ TREAD

rubber ___ BALL, BAND, PLANT,
  STAMP, TREE

___ rubber CREPE, FOAM, HARD,
  INDIA

"Rubber Ball"
  ~ singer VEE

"Rubber Duckie"
  ~ singer ERNIE

rubberized
  ~ canvas TARP

rubberneck EYE, GAPE, OGLE,
  SEER, STARE

rubber stamp OKAY
  ~ word PAID, VOID

rubber-stamps OKS

rubber tree
  ~ mover of song ANT

rubbish DIRT, DUST, POOH, ROT,
  SLOP, TRASH

rubble DUST

rubdown
  require a ~ ACHE

rube BOOR, CLOD, OAF, YAHOO

Rubens
  ~ subject NUDE

Rubicon
  ~ crosser CAESAR

rubicund RED, ROSY

rubidium METAL

Rubinstein ANTON

rubric LAW, RULE

ruby COLOR, GEM, RED

Ruby DEE
  ~ hubby OSSIE

rucksack BAG, KIT

ruckus ADO, DIN, MELEE, NOISE,
  RIOT, ROW, SCRAP, STIR, TODO
  raise a ~ RAVE, RIOT

rudder HELM
  ~ locale AFT, STERN
  toward the ~ ASTERN
  use the ~ STEER

ruddiness COLOR

ruddle ORE

ruddy RED, ROSY
  opposite of ~ ASHEN, ASHY,
    PALE, WAN

rude CRASS, PERT, SMART
  ~ look LEER, SNEER, STARE
  ~ one BOOR, CAD
  ~ reply SASS
  be ~ to DIS

rudeness LIP
  reaction to ~ SLAP

rudiment ROOT

rudimentary FIRST
  ~ life GERM
  ~ (prefix) PRO

rudiments ABCS

Rudner RITA

Rudolf ABEL, HESS

Rudolph ALAN, MATE
  ~ master SANTA

"Rudolph the Red-___ Reindeer"
NOSED

rue
  ~ one's run ACHE
  wall ~ FERN

Rue
  costar of ~ BEA

rueful BAD, SAD, WRY

"Rue Morgue"
  ~ author POE
  ~ culprit APE

ruer
  ~ word ALAS

ruff BIRD
  female ~ REE, REEVE
  leonine ~ MANE

ruffian HOOD, YAHOO

ruffle ABASH, ANGER, FRET, GET, IRK, JAR, MOVE, PEEVE, RILE, ROIL, UPSET
  ~ as hair TEASE

ruffled IRATE, UPSET

rufiyaa COIN

rufous RED

rug MAT, SHAG
  ~ cover CAP, HAT
  ~ coverage AREA
  ~ exporter IRAN
  ~ feature PILE
  ~ fiber SISAL
  ~ rat TOT
  ~ texture NAP
  cut a ~ DANCE
  wear a hole in the ~ PACE

___ rug AREA

rugby
  ~ score TRY

rugged BIG, HALE, HARD, LARGE
  ~ rock CRAG

"Ruggles of ___ Gap" RED

"Ruggles of Red ___" GAP

rug rat TOT

rugs
  clean ~ BEAT
  like some ~ OVAL

Ruhr
  ~ city ESSEN
  see also German

ruin BANE, DASH, DOOM, EVIL, HARM, LOSS, MAR, SINK, SMASH, SPOIL, WASTE
  ~ a nylon SNAG
  ~ a reputation SMEAR
  ~ partner RACK
  bring to ~ UNDO
  cause of ~ BANE
  rack and ~ DOOM

ruinate UNDO

ruination BANE, DOOM

ruined LOST, POOR, SHOT
  get ~ in the wash RUN

ruiner
  report-card ~ DEE

ruining
  ~ thing BANE

ruinous BAD

ruins
  ancient ~ RELIC

Rukeyser, Muriel POET
  see also poet

rule CODE, DOGMA, FIAT, HEAD, LAW, LINE, NORM, ORDER, REIGN, ROD, SWAY
  ~ (abbr.) REG
  ~ of conduct LAW
  ~ out BAR, TABOO, TABU, VETO
  ~ the roost LEAD
  mathematical ~ LAW
  period of ~ REIGN

rule ___ (eliminate) OUT

___ rule ASA, GAG, HOME, MOB, SLIDE

Rule ANN

"Rule, Britannia"
  ~ composer ARNE

ruled
  it may be ~ ROOST

"___ Ruled the World" IFI

ruler LORD, SCALE
  ~ marking INCH
  ~ of Venice DOGE
  ~ part INCH
  ~ (suffix) ARCH
  absolute ~ TSAR
  Mideast ~ AMIR, EMEER, EMIR
  Mongol ~ KHAN
  Muslim ~ AGA, AGHA
  North African ~ DEY
  Persian ~ SHAH
  pre-Soviet ~ TSAR
  underworld ~ DIS

ruler's
  ~ length FOOT

rules
  ~ and regulations LAW
  not against the ~ LEGAL

"Rules of the ___" GAME

"___ rules the gods..." LOVE

rule the ___ ROOST

ruling ACT
  ~ class ELITE

umpire's ~ FAIR

"Ruling ___, The" CLASS

"Ruling Voice, The"
  ~ director LEE

rum
  ~ cake BABA
  mixer for ~ COLA

___ rum BAY

rumba DANCE, STEP

rumble BOOM, MELEE, NOISE, PEAL, RIOT, ROAR, ROLL

rumble ___ SEAT

"Rumble in the Jungle"
  ~ boxer ALI

rumbling DEEP

ruminant ANIMAL, DEER
  African ~ OKAPI
  Andes ~ LLAMA
  large ~ MOOSE
  oxlike ~ GNU
  ranch ~ STEER
  Rockies ~ ELK
  untamed ~ DEER

ruminate MUSE, PORE, SEE

rummage HUNT, RAKE, SEEK
  ~ around ROOT
  ~ through RIFLE

rummage ___ SALE

rummy GAME, SOT
  ~ group MELD
  ~ variety CANASTA, GIN

rumor DIRT, LIE, NEWS, NOISE, TALE
  ~ result, maybe SCARE
  ~ source, often LEAK

rumor ___ MILL

rumormonger YENTA

rumors NOISE, TALK

rump HIP, REAR, SEAT

Rumpelteazer
  ~ creator ELIOT

rumpus DIN, DUST, MELEE, NOISE, RIOT, ROW, SCRAP

rumpus ___ ROOM

run BLEED, DART, DASH, HEAD, HIE, MOVE, NORM, POUR, RACE, RASH, SPEED, STREAM, TEAR
  ~ across MEET
  ~ a fever AIL
  ~ afoul of someone ANGER, IRK, PEEVE, RILE
  ~ after CHASE, HUNT, SEEK
  ~ a harvester REAP
  ~ ahead LEAD
  ~ amok RAGE, RIOT, STORM
  ~ around GAD, ROAM, ROVE
  ~ as dye BLEED
  ~ a store SELL, VEND
  ~ at a low speed IDLE
  ~ away FLEE
  ~ away to marry ELOPE
  ~ circles around BEAT, BEST, LEAD, TOP

~ counter to BELIE
~ down ABASE, CHASE, SEEDY
~ easily LOPE
~ fast DASH, HARE
~ fast, clockwise GAIN
~ for it FLEE
~ from bachelorhood ELOPE
~ in ARREST, NAB
~ in neutral IDLE
~ interference for AID, HELP
~ in the wash BLEED
~ into HIT, MEET, RAM
~ its course END, PASS, STOP
~ last LOSE
~ lightly TROT
~ like the wind HIE, RACE, SPEED, TEAR
~ off FLEE, HIE, REPEL, SKIP
~ off at the mouth BLAB, GAB, TALK, YAK
~ off the page BLEED
~ on PRATE
~ on TV AIR
~ out ELAPSE, LAPSE, SKIP
~ out of gas DIE, PETER, TIRE
~ out on DESERT, DROP
~ over SCAN, TREAD
~ rampant RAGE
~ second LOSE
~ swiftly SCUD
~ the gamut SPAN
~ the gauntlet DARE
~ the show RULE
~ the stereo PLAY
~ through READ, SPEND
~ to the JP ELOPE
~ up RAISE, SEW
~ up a tab OWE
~ up the phone bill GAB
~ wild RIOT
~ words together SLUR
cut and ~ AVOID, DESERT, FLEE
do an end ~ EVADE
dry ~ TEST, TRIAL
home-run hitter's ~ TROT
leisurely ~ LOPE
make a ~ SCORE
make a ~ for it LAM
make one's blood ~ cold SCARE
marry on the ~ ELOPE
one way to ~ AMOK, RIOT
rue one's ~ ACHE
short ~ DASH
ski ~ TRAIL
slalom ~ ESS
slow ~ TROT
take the money and ~ FLEE
trial ~ TEST
where ships ~ aground REEF

run ___ AMOK, RIOT

run ___ (chase) AFTER

run ___ (find) ACROSS

run ___ (leave) ALONG, OFF

run ___ (meet) INTO

___ run DRY, END, HOME, LONG, PRESS, SKI, TRIAL

"Run ___ the Sun" FOR

"Run, __, run!" SPOT

runabout AUTO, BOAT, CAR

"Runaround __" SUE

runaway
~ **of rhyme** DISH

"Runaway __" TRAIN

runcible spoon
~ **feature** TINE

rundle STEP

Run-D.M.C.
~ **genre** RAP

rundown RECAP
~ **car** HEAP

run-down MEAN, OLD, SEEDY

"Run for the __" SUN

rung PEG, STAVE, STEP
**one ~ on the evolutionary
ladder** APE

run-in ROW, SCRAP, SPAT

runnel RILL, STREAM

runner PAGE, RUG, SCARF, SKI,
STEM
~ **concern** PACE
~ **distance** MILE
~ **goal** TAPE
~ **starter** FORE, ROAD, RUM
~ **unit** LAP
cross-country ~ RACER
distance ~ MILER
downhill ~ SKI
errand ~ PAGE
lab ~ MOUSE, RAT
long-distance ~ RACER
Pamplona ~ TORO
put out a ~ TAG
scarlet ~ BEAN
Senate ~ PAGE
snow ~ SKI

__ Runner ROAD

runners
~ **carry it** SLED
~ **of song** MICE
re-election ~ INS
travel on wooden ~ SKI

runner-up LOSER

running
~ **around** ADO
~ **away** LAM
~ **behind** LATE
~ **game** TAG
~ **knot** NOOSE
~ **over** AMPLE
~ **partner** OFF
~ **track** OVAL
~ **wild** AMOK
still in the ~ ALIVE

running __ HEAD, KNOT, MATE,
SHOE

"Running __" BEAR

"Running __, The" MAN

"Running Man, The"
~ **director** REED

"Running on __" ICE

"__ Runnings" COOL

running shoe
~ **name** NIKE

runny THIN

Runnymede
~ **raincoat** MAC
see also British, English

runoff
~ **site** EAVE
roof ~ RAIN

run-of-the-mill BANAL, SOSO,
TAME, USUAL

"Run Silent, Run __" DEEP

"Run Silent, Run Deep"
~ **director** WISE

run-through TEST

run to __ SEED

runty SMALL

runway LANE, PATH, STRIP
boat ~ RAMP
hit the ~ ALIT, LAND, LIT
move on the ~ TAXI
redo the ~ PAVE

"Run with the __ and hunt..."
HARE

rupee COIN

rural
~ **addr.** RFD
~ **agcy.** TVA
~ **crossing** STILE
~ **districts** LAND
~ **rd.** RTE
~ **route** LANE
~ **stopover** INN
~ **structure** BARN, PEN, SHED,
SILO, STY
~ **tune** LAY

rural __ delivery FREE

"Rusalka" OPERA

ruse ART, FAKE, MOVE, PLOT,
STALL, TRAP

rush DART, DASH, HASTE, HIE,
LEAP, PRESS, RACE, REED, RIP,
RUN, SPATE, SPEED, TEAR
~ **at** MOB
~ **headlong** STORM
~ **letters** ASAP
~ **to the altar** ELOPE
~ **word** STAT
give the bum's ~ to OUST
headlong ~ RUN
mad ~ DASH
the bum's ~ SACK

rush __ HOUR

__ rush GOLD, INA

"__ Rush, The" GOLD

Rush, Geoffrey
~ **film of 1996** SHINE

rush hour
~ **component** AUTO, CAR
~ **feature** JAM

rushing RAPID

rushlight LAMP

rushlike
~ **plant** SEDGE

Rushmore
~ **and others** MTS

Rusk DEAN

Russ. LANG
neighbor of ~ EST, FIN
see also Russian

russe
charlotte ~ CAKE

Russell ANDY, BILL, JANE, KEN,
LEON, ROUSE
~ **role** MAME

Russell __ College SAGE

Russell, Andy
1944 ~ song AMOR

Russell, Jane
~ **in "The Outlaw"** RIO

Russell, Kurt
~ **role** EARP

Russell, Mark
~ **instrument** PIANO

Russell, Rosalind
~ **role** MAME

russet APPLE, BAY, COLOR, RED

Russia
~ **once** SSR
see also Russian

Russian
~ **affirmatives** DAS
~ **city** OREL
~ **color** RED
~ **commune** MIR
~ **czar** IVAN
~ **emperor** TSAR
~ **epic hero** IGOR
~ **fur** SABLE
~ **mountains** ALAI
~ **place-name suffix** GRAD
~ **revolutionary** LENIN, RED
~ **river** DON, LENA
~ **sea** ARAL
~ **symbol** BEAR
~ **village** MIR
John, in ~ IVAN
no, in ~ NYET
peace, in ~ MIR
typical ~ IVAN

Russian Blue CAT

Russian-born
~ **illustrator** ERTE
~ **microbiologist** SABIN

"Russians __ Coming..., The"
ARE

Russo RENE

rust COLOR, EAT, FRET, MOLD
~ **away** ERODE

rust __ BELT

"Rust __ Sleeps" NEVER

rust-colored BAY

rustic BOOR, RUBE, RURAL
~ **stopover** CAMP
~ **structure** BARN
~ **way** LANE

rustle MOAN, RAID, STIR

rustproof
~ **coating** ZINC

rusty RED

rut HABIT

__ rut INA

Ruth BABE, ROMAN
~ **and others** DRS
~ **mother-in-law** NAOMI

Ruth, Babe
~ **number** THREE
~ **specialty** HOMER
~ **stat** HRS, RBI
~ **sultanate** SWAT
~ **topper** AARON

Ruth, Dr.
~ **specialty** SEX

ruthenium METAL

Rutherford ANN, ERNEST
~ **concern** ATOM

Ruthian
~ **blast** HOMER, SWAT

ruthless CRUEL, HARD, STERN

rutile ORE

Rutledge ANN

ruttish LEWD

Ruwenzori RANGE

Ruy Díaz de Bivar CID

RV
part of ~ REC

R-V
~ **connectors** STU

Rx
~ **amount** DOSE
~ **giver** DOC
~ **givers** DRS, MDS
~ **writers org.** AMA

rya RUG, SHAG

Ryan IRENE, MEG, NOLAN, ONEAL
emulate ~ HURL

"Ryan Express, The" NOLAN

Ryan, Nolan
~ **once** ASTRO, MET

"__ Ryan's Express" VON

"Ryan's Hope" SOAP

Ryder Cup
~ **shout** FORE

rye
~ **mold** ERGOT
~ **partner** HAM
rocks with ~ ICE

Ryokan POET
see also poet

Ryun MILER
~ **distance** MILE

2nd
~ **st.** PENN

6th
~ **st.** MASS

6
it's ~ **hrs. behind**
Greenwich CST, MDT

7
it's ~ **hrs. behind**
Greenwich MST, PDT
pH less than ~ ACID
pH more than ~ BASE, BASIC

"7 Faces of Dr. ___" LAO

"7 Faces of Dr. Lao"
~ **director** PAL

16
~ **drams** OUNCE

16
~ **tablespoons** CUP

16th
~ **st.** TENN

"16 ___ of Glory" DAYS

16.5
~ **feet** ROD

17th
~ **state** OHIO

60
~ **secs.** MIN

___ 60 (acceleration standard)
OTO

60 minutes
~ **in Spanish** HORA

"60 Minutes"
~ **regular** SAFER
~ **name** ANDY
~ **network** CBS

65
~ **perhaps** LIMIT

66 RTE

"___ 66" ROUTE

70%
it's ~ **nitrogen** AIR

72
~ **often** PAR

76ers FIVE, TEAM
~ **org.** NBA

"77 Sunset ___" STRIP

"77 Sunset Strip"
Byrnes of ~ EDD
Jeff's ~ partner STU

78 DISC, RPM

666
its number is ~ BEAST

707 JET, PLANE

727 JET, PLANE

737 JET, PLANE

747 JET, PLANE
control a ~ AVIATE
one of two on a ~ AISLE

755
hitter of ~ home runs AARON

767 JET, PLANE

768
~ **tsps.** GAL

777 JET, PLANE

1666
like London in ~ AFIRE

1692
~ **trial site** SALEM

1773
jetsam of ~ TEA

"1776"
~ **director** HUNT
~ **role** ADAMS, LEE

7,926
ball ~ miles in
diameter EARTH

17,000,000
about ~ square miles ASIA

"s"
mispronounce ~ LISP

S ELEM, SIZE
16 for ~ ATNO

S ___ "sugar" ASIN

S.A.
~ **country** ARG, COL, PAR

Saab
~ **model** AERO

Saar
see German

Saarinen ALINE, EERO

Saatchi
~ **product** ADS

sabaton ARMOR

Sabbath
~ **activity** REST

sabbatical LEAVE

saber STEEL
~ **handle** HILT
~ **set-to** DUEL
alternative to a ~ EPEE

Saberhagen BRET

sabertooth CAT, TIGER

sable ANIMAL, COLOR, EBON,
EBONY, FUR, INKY, JET, RAVEN

Sable CAPE

sabot CLOG, SHOE

Sabres SIX, TEAM
~ **milieu** ICE, RINK
~ **org.** NHL

Sabrina the Witch TEEN
~ **portrayer** HART

sac CASE
ink ~ ORGAN

___ sac AIR

SAC
~ **headquarters** OMAHA

saccharin
~ **discoverer Remsen** IRA

saccharine SWEET

sachem LORD, RULER

Sacher
~ **torte** CAKE

Sacher ___ TORTE

sachet
~ **feature** AROMA
~ **item** PETAL

Sachs, Hans POET
see also poet

sack BAG, BED, CAN, DROP, EJECT,
FIRE, LOOT, OUST, PREY, RAID,
RIFLE, ROB, STEAL, WASTE,
WINE
~ **designer** DIOR
~ **in football** LOSS
~ **out** BED, REST, SLEEP
diamond ~ BASE
hit the ~ BED, REST, SLEEP
in the ~ ABED
leave the ~ ARISE, RISE
sad ~ LOSER

sack ___ (sleep) OUT

___ sack SAD

sackcloth and ___ ASHES

sacked
~ **out** ABED

sacrament RITE

Sacramento RANGE
~ **newspaper** BEE
~ **st.** CAL

sacred
~ **ceremony** RITE
~ **chest** ARK
~ **image** ICON, IDOL
~ **music** PSALM
~ **spot** ALTAR
Egyptian ~ bird IBIS
mountain ~ to
Buddhism OMEI

sacred ___ COW, IBIS

"Sacred Wood, The"
~ **author** ELIOT

sacrifice COST
~ **site** ALTAR

sacrificial ___ LAMB

sacrum BONE

sad BAD, BLUE, LOW, SOBER
~ **sack** LOSER
~ **sound** SOB
make ~ work of HASH

sad ___ SACK

Sadat ARAB

sadden PAIN

saddle LOIN, MEAT, SEAT
  ~ **bag** BAG
  ~ **horse** HACK
  ~ **loop** LUG
  ~ **part** HORN
  ~ **up** RIDE
  ~ **with** LOAD

saddle ___ SHOE, SOAP

saddlemaker
  ~ **tool** AWL

"___/Sade" MARAT

Sadie Hawkins Day
  ~ **creator** CAPP

"___ Sadie Thompson" MISS

sadist OGRE

sadistic CRUEL

sadly ALAS

sadness
  show ~ CRY, SOB, WEEP

Sad Sack
  ~ **girlfriend** SADIE

"___ sae weary..." ANDI

safari TREK, TRIP
  ~ **camp** BASE
  ~ **sighting** GNU, OKAPI

safe
  ~ **harbor** HAVEN
  not ~ OUT
  on the ~ side ALEE

"Safe!" CALL

safe-conduct PASS

safeguard AEGIS, ARMOR, CARE,
  EGIS
  aerialist's ~ NET
  splatter ~ APRON

safekeeping CARE

Safer, Morley
  ~ **network** CBS

safety
  ~ **device** NET
  ~ **goggles** MASK
  ~ **specifications** CODE

safety ___ BELT, LAMP, NET, PIN

"Safety ___" FIRST, LAST

safflower OIL

saffron COLOR
  ~ **dish** RICE
  ~ **family** IRIS

Safire, William
  ~ **concern** USAGE

sag FLAG, HANG, LOLL, NOD,
  SETTLE, SINK

SAG
  ~ **member** ACTOR
  former ~ president ASNER

saga EPIC, TALE, YARN
  Icelandic ~ EDDA

poetic ~ EPOS

sagacious ABLE, DEEP, WISE

sagacity TACT

Sagami SEA

Sagan CARL

sage HERB, ORACLE, WISE
  Roman ~ CATO

sage ___ HEN

Sagebrush
  ~ **St.** NEV

Sagebrush State
  ~ **city** RENO

sages
  New Testament ~ MAGI

sagging LOOSE

Sagitta ARROW

Sagittarius SIGN
  ~ **projectile** ARROW

sago PALM

saguaro
  ~ **locale** DESERT

saguaros CACTI

Sahara DESERT
  ~ **beast** CAMEL
  ~ **mountains** ATLAS
  ~ **nation** MALI, NIGER
  ~ **rarity** RAIN
  ~ **robe** ABA
  ~ **scarcity** WATER
  ~ **sight** DUNE
  ~ **stop-off** OASIS
  ~ **wanderer** NOMAD
  like the ~ ARID, DRY, SERE,
  VAST

Saharan DRY

Sahel DESERT

sahib MAN
  ~ **address** SRI

sahibs
  land of ~ INDIA

said ORAL, PUT
  all ~ and done ENDED
  ewe ~ it BAA

"___ said..." ASI

___ Said PORT

"___ Said" MAMA

"___ Said a Mouthful" YOU

"___ said it!" YOU

**"___ said there'd be days like
  this"** MAMA

saiga ANIMAL

Saigon CITY, PORT

sail BOAT, FLIT, KITE, PLY, SHEET,
  STEAM
  ~ **before the wind** SCUD
  ~ **holder** MAST
  ~ **(into)** LACE

~ into each other SCRAP
~ (over) LEAP
~ support SPAR
~ through ACE
~ under false colors MASK
in full ~ APACE
reduce ~ REEF
set ~ LEAVE, SHIP, START
under ~ ASEA, ATSEA

___ sail LUG, SET

"Sail ___ Ship of State!" ONO

sailboat
  ~ **stabilizer** KEEL
  kind of ~ CAT

sailing ASEA, ATSEA
  ~ **vessel** BOAT, SHIP, SLOOP
  smooth ~ EASY

**"Sailing, sailing, over the
  bounding ___"** MAIN

sailor GOB, HAT, SWAB, TAR
  ~ **affirmative** AYE
  ~ **cry** AHOY, AVAST
  ~ **direction** ALEE
  ~ **pride** KNOT
  ~ **sighting** LAND
  old ~ SALT
  old ~ drink RUM
  wooden-shoe ~ NOD

sailoring ATSEA

sailors CREW
  patron of ~ ELMO

sailplane SOAR

sails
  adjust the ~ TRIM
  fit ~ to RIG

"___ Sails in the Sunset" RED

"...sail the ___ blue" OCEAN

sail the seven ___ SEAS

Saimaa LAKE

saint
  ~ **image** ICON
  Avila's ~ TERESA
  first American-born ~ SETON
  patron ~ of Norway OLAF,
  OLAV
  sailors' ~ ELMO

Saint
  see St.

Saint ___ College of Minnesota
  OLAF

Saint ___, Fla. PETE

Saint Agnes' ___ (January 20)
  EVE

Saint Andrews
  ~ **shout** FORE
  ~ **starting point** TEE

Saint Augustine
  ~ **st.** FLA

Saint Bernard
  ~ **beat** ALPS
  fictional ~ NEIL

Saint Elmo's ___ FIRE

Saint Helena
  ~ **(abbr.)** ISL

"Saint in ___ York, The" NEW

"Saint Joan"
  ~ **author** SHAW

Saint-John PERSE

"Saint John Passion"
  ~ **composer** BACH

Saint John's CITY, PORT

Saint Kitts ISLE
  ~ **(abbr.)** ISL

Saint Kitts ___ Nevis AND

Saint Laurent YVES
  ~ **birthplace** ORAN

Saint-Léger, Alexis POET
  see also poet

Saint-Lô
  see French

Saint Louis CITY, PORT
  ~ **attraction** ARCH
  ~ **bridge** EADS
  ~ **football player** RAM
  ~ **hockey player** BLUE
  ~ **landmark** ARCH

Saint Mark
  symbol of ~ LION

Saint Nick
  ~ **accessory** PIPE
  ~ **mo.** DEC
  see also Santa

Saint Patrick's Day
  ~ **event** PARADE

Saint Paul
  ~ **feature** DOME
  ~ **once** SAUL
  architect of ~ WREN
  book with ~'s story ACTS
  longtime dean of ~ INGE

Saint Pete
  ~ **neighbor** TAMPA
  ~ **setting** EDT, EST
  ~ **st.** FLA

Saint Peter
  music to ~'s ears HARP

Saint Peter's
  ~ **service** MASS
  feature of ~ DOME

Saint Petersburg CITY, PORT
  ~ **monarch** TSAR
  ~ **neighbor** TAMPA
  see also Russian

saint's ___ DAY

Saints ELEVEN, TEAM
  ~ **org.** NFL

___ Saints' Day ALL

Saint Teresa of ___ AVILA

Saint-Tropez
  see French

Saint Valentine's ___ DAY

Saint Vincent CAPE

saison ETE

Sajak EMCEE, HOST, PAT
purchase from ~
perhaps ANA, ANE, ANI, ANO

Sakakawea LAKE

sake WINE
~ base RICE

"___ sakes alive!" LAND

saki WINE
~ base RICE

Saki ALIAS

Saks GENE

Sal GAL, MULE
mule ~'s canal ERIE

sala
~ site CASA

salaam BEND, BOW, GREET

salacious LEWD

salaciousness LUST

salad
~ base EGG, PASTA, TUNA
~ choice CAESAR
~ follower ENTREE
~ green CRESS
~ ingredient ONION
complete a ~ DRESS
deli ~ SLAW
help with the ~ TOSS
molded ~ ASPIC

salad ___ BAR, DAYS, OIL

___ salad CAESAR, EGG, TUNA

salad bowl
~ wood TEAK

salad dressing
~ ingredient OIL

Saladin
~ citadel site CAIRO

salamander EFT, NEWT

salami
~ seller DELI

___ salami GENOA

salary FEE, HIRE, PAY, WAGE
~ increase RAISE
~ less deductions NET
~ limit CAP
get a ~ EARN

Salchow
~ relative AXEL
where to do a ~ ICE, RINK

sale
~ disclaimer ASIS
~ incentive REBATE
~ notices ADS
~ word LIMIT, ONLY
bill of ~ PAPER
item for ~ WARE

offer for ~ VEND

___ sale FIRE, TAG, YARD

Salem
~ st. MASS, ORE

"Salem's ___" LOT

Salerno
see Italian

sales
~ condition ASIS
~ pitch LINE, TALK
~ pitches ADS
~ sample DEMO
~ unit EACH

sales ___ REP, SLIP

salesperson AGENT, REP

salicyclic ___ ACID

salicylate ESTER

salient CLEAR

saline SALT
~ drop TEAR

Salinger
~ character ESME

Salisbury ___ STEAK

Salisbury Plain
~ river AVON

Salk
~ contemporary SABIN
~ product SERUM

sallet ARMOR

sallies
~ forth GOES

sallow ASHEN, PALE, WAN

Sallust ROMAN

sally RAID
~ forth MOVE, START
~ lunn CAKE

Sally RAND, RIDE

"Sally Go Round the ___" ROSES

sally lunn CAKE

salmagundi HASH, OLIO, SALAD, STEW

salmi STEW

salmon COLOR, RED
~ serving STEAK
smoked ~ NOVA
young ~ PARR

Salmon P. ___ CHASE

Salmon River RANGE

Salome
~ to Herod NIECE

"Salome" OPERA
~ character HEROD
~ solo ARIA

salon
~ color HENNA
~ concern HAIR

~ job DYE, PERM, RINSE, SET, TINT
~ solution DYE
~ sound SNIP
~ supply GEL

Salonga LEA

saloon BAR, INN
~ order ALE, BEER

salsa DANCE, DIP
~ holder CHIP
like some ~ HOT, MILD

salt CURE, GOB, TAR
~ away KEEP, SAVE, STORE, STOW
~ in French SEL
~ lake of Australia EYRE
~ meas. TSP
~ response AYE
~ shout AHOY, AVAST
~ source SEA
~ water OCEAN
~ word AHOY
acid ~ ESTER
his wife turned to ~ LOT
preserve with ~ CORN

salt ___ DOME

salt ___ (save) AWAY

___ salt SEA, TABLE

SALT PACT
~ participant USSR
~ talks subject ARMS
part of ~ ARMS

saltation LEAP

saltbox
~ topper ROOF

___ Salt Lake GREAT

Salt Lake City
~ athlete UTE
~ locale UTAH

Salt-N-Pepa TRIO
~ music RAP

"Salt of the ___" EARTH

Salton SEA

Salton Sea LAKE

___ salts BATH, EPSOM

salt water
~ plant ALGA
~ spawner EEL

salty
~ drop TEAR
~ spread ROE

salubrious GOOD

"Salud!" TOAST

saluki DOG

salutary GOOD

salutation BOW, HELLO, NOD
~ word DEAR, SIRS
islands ~ ALOHA
street ~ BRO
swab ~ AHOY

salute GREET, HAIL, TOAST

Salvador DALI

___ Salvador SAN

Salvation Army
~ temp SANTA
~ trainee CADET

salve BALM, CREAM, HELP, OIL
~ ingredient ALOE

salver DISH, TRAY

salvia
~ cousin SAGE

salvo FIRE

Salwen HAL

Salzburg
~ environs ALPS

Sam ADAMS, BASS, SNEAD, SPADE, UNCLE
~ love on "Cheers" DIANE

Sam ___ (Seuss character) IAM

Sam Adams
~ product ALE

Samantha
~ dotty aunt CLARA

Samaritan
~ offering HELP
be a ~ AID

___ Samaritan GOOD

samarium METAL

samba DANCE, STEP

sambar DEER

same ALIKE, DITTO, EVEN
~ (prefix) ISO, SYN
all the ~ YET
chipped off the ~ block AKIN
get the ~ answer AGREE
in the ~ way as LIKE
just the ~ ALIKE
much the ~ ALIKE, CLOSE, LIKE
not the ~ OTHER
on the ~ wavelength ALIKE
the ~ old grind RUT

"Same ___ Me" OLE

"Same ___, Next Year" TIME

"Same here!" DITTO

sameness PAR

same-old-same-old RUT

"Same Time, ___ Year" NEXT

"Same Time, Next ___" YEAR

"Same Time, Next Year"
~ actor ALDA

Samms EMMA

Samoa
studier of ~ MEAD

Samoan
~ staple POI

Samos
  site of ancient ~ IONIA
  storyteller of ~ AESOP

samovar POT, URN
  ~ serving TEA

Samoyed DOG, PET
  ~ burden SLED

sample BIT, EAT, TASTE, TEST, TRY
  ~ a drink SIP
  assayer's ~ ORE
  geologist's ~ CORE
  sales ~ DEMO

Sampras PETE
  ~ serve ACE
  ~ unit SET
  see also tennis

"Samson ___ Delilah" AND

"Samson and Delilah"
  Delilah, in ~ HEDY

"Samson et Dalila" OPERA

Sam the ___ SHAM

Samuel ADAMS, MORSE
  ~ teacher ELI

Samuel F.B. ___ MORSE

Samuelson, Paul
  ~ subj. ECON

"___ Samurai, The" SEVEN

"___ s'amuse" LEROI

San ___, Calif. PEDRO

San ___ Channel PEDRO

San ___, Italy REMO

San ___ Obispo, Calif. LUIS

San ___, Philippines PABLO

San ___ Potosí, Mexico LUIS

Sana
  ~ locale YEMEN

San Antonio
  ~ basketball player SPUR
  ~ landmark ALAMO
  ~ st. TEX

San Bernardino RANGE

sanctify ADORE, BLESS, EXALT

sanctimony CANT, POSE

sanction ADOPT, ALLOW, BLESS, CLEAR, ENABLE, LEAVE, LET, OKAY, PASS
  ~ misdeeds ABET

"___ Sanction, The" LOO

sanctions OKS

sanctity
  sign of ~ HALO

___ sanctorum ACTA

sanctuary AERIE, ALTAR, HAVEN, LAIR, OASIS

___ sanctum INNER

sand ABRADE, DIRT, FACE, GRIT, NERVE, RASP
  ~ bar LAND, LEDGE, REEF, SHOAL
  ~ ender BAG, HOG, PAPER, STONE, STORM
  ~ hill DUNE
  fine ~ SILT
  kind of ~ SLAG

sand ___ BAR, DAB, EEL, TRAP

sandal SHOE
  ~ part STRAP

sandals
  wearing ~ SHOD

sandalwood TREE

sandarac TREE

sandbag BEAT, HIT, LAM, SMITE

sandbank BAR, LAND, LEDGE, REEF, SHOAL

sandbox
  ~ need PAIL
  ~ patron KID, TOT, TYKE

"Sandbox, The"
  ~ author ALBEE

Sandburg CARL, POET
  see also poet

Sanders, Deion
  ~ nickname NEON

Sanders, George
  ~ persona CAD

Sanders, Harland
  ~ title COL

Sand, George ALIAS

sandhill CRANE

San Diego CITY, PORT
  ~ baseball player PADRE

"San Diego, I ___ You" LOVE

"San Diego, I Love ___" YOU

Sandler ADAM

sandpaper
  ~ covering GRIT
  use ~ ABRADE

"Sand Pebbles, The"
  ~ director WISE

sandpiper SNIPE
  female ~ REE, REEVE

Sandra DEE

Sandra ___ O'Connor DAY

Sands DIANA

"Sands of ___, The" DEE

"Sands of ___ Jima" IWO

"Sands of Iwo Jima"
  ~ actor AGAR

Sandusky
  ~ lake ERIE
  ~ locale OHIO

sandwich HERO, JAM, SUB
  ~ base RYE
  ~ filler HAM, TUNA
  ~ garnish CAPER
  ~ order BLT, MELT
  ~ pocket PITA
  ~ shop DELI
  ~ wrapper SARAN
  big ~ HERO, SUB
  big ~ name MAC
  grilled ~ MELT
  submarine ~ HERO

sandwich board
  ~ notices ADS

Sandwich Islands
  ~ greeting ALOHA

sandy
  ~ color ECRU, TAN
  ~ deposit SILT
  ~ expanse ERG, SAHARA
  ~ islet ATOLL
  ~ ridge DUNE
  ~ soil LOAM

Sandy
  ~ owner ANNIE
  ~ shakes with it PAW
  ~ sound ARF

___ Sandy Desert GREAT

sane FIT, SOBER

"Sanford ___ Son" AND

"Sanford and ___" SON

"Sanford and Son"
  ~ producer LEAR
  Fred on ~ REDD
  Redd, in ~ FRED

San Francisco CITY, PORT
  ~ baseballer GIANT
  ~ water BAY

San Gabriel RANGE

sang-froid CALM, POISE

San Giacomo LAURA

Sangre de Cristo RANGE

sangria
  ~ ingredient WINE

sanguine ROSY
  not ~ ASHEN, ASHY, PALE, WAN

sanitary PURE

sanitize CLEAN

sanitized CLEAN

San José
  see Spanish

San Juan RANGE
  see also Spanish

San Juan Hill
  ~ locale CUBA

San Lucas CAPE

San Marino
  ~ currency LIRA, LIRE

San Remo CITY, PORT
  ~ currency LIRA, LIRE

sans
  ~ opposite AVEC

sans ___ SERIF

San Salvador
  see Spanish

Sansei
  ~ parent NISEI

sansevieria PLANT

Santa
  ~ bane SOOT
  ~ delivery TOY
  ~ helper ELF
  ~ jingle REINS
  ~ makes one LIST
  ~ reindeer, before Rudolph OCTET
  ~ vehicle SLED
  letter to ~ LIST
  prop for ~ PIPE

Santa ___ (Alamo figure) ANNA

Santa ___, Calif. ANA, ANITA, CLARA, ROSA

Santa ___ racetrack ANITA

Santa ___ winds ANA

Santa Anna
  ~ battleground ALAMO

"Santa Barbara" SOAP

Santa Claus
  ~ artist NAST

Santa Fe TRAIL
  ~ brick ADOBE
  town near ~ TAOS

Santa Fe Trail
  ~ stop TAOS

"Santa Maria" BOAT, SHIP
  ~ companion NINA

Santee TRIBE

Santha ___ Rau RAMA

Santiago CITY
  ~ milieu SEA
  see also Spanish

Santo RON

Santo Domingo
  see Spanish

Santos CITY, PORT

Saône
  see French

Sao Paulo CITY

sap BLEED, ERODE, TIRE
  ~ source MAPLE
  ~ sucker APHID
  collect ~ TAP
  petrified ~ AMBER

Saperstein ABE

sapidity TASTE

sapiens
  homo ~ MAN, RACE

sapient SAGE, WISE

sapless ARID, DRY, LIMP

sapling TREE

sapodilla TREE

sapor TASTE

Sapphic ___ ODE

sapphire BLUE, COLOR, GEM
  ~ mo. SEPT

___ sapphire STAR

Sappho POET
  see also Greek, poet

Sapporo CITY
  ~ sport SUMO
  see also Japanese

"Saps ___" ATSEA

"Saps at ___" SEA

Sara LEE, MIA

saraband DANCE, STEP

Saracen ARAB
  ~ to a Crusader ENEMY, FOE

Sarafian, Richard C.
  ~ film of 1965 ANDY

Saragossa
  ~ river EBRO

Sarah
  son of ~ ISAAC

Sarah ___ Jewett ORNE

Sarajevo
  ~ citizen SERB

Sarandon, Susan
  **~ in "Dead Man
    Walking"** NUN

Saratoga
  ~ event RACE

Saratoga Springs SPA

Sarazen GENE

sarcasm ACID, IRONY

sarcastic ACID, ACRID, EDGED,
  RUDE, SNIDE, TART, WRY
  ~ comment SLAP
  ~ remark GIBE

sard GEM

sardine SPRAT
  ~ holder TIN

sardines
  packed like ~ CLOSE, SOLID

Sardinia
  ~ (abbr.) ISL

sardonic ACID, TART, WRY
  ~ grin SNEER
  ~ style IRONY

saree
  ~ wearer RANEE

Sarek ALIEN

Sargasso SEA
  ~ swimmer EEL

Sargasso ___ SEA

Sarge
  ~ status NCO

sari DRESS
  ~ wearer RANEE, RANI
  use a ~ DRAPE

saris
  land of ~ INDIA

Sarnoff
  ~ org. RCA

sarong
  ~ relative SARI

Sarouk RUG

Saroyan
  ~ character ARAM

Sartre
  see French

Sasdy PETER

SASE ENC
  part of ~ SELF

sash BAND, BELT
  ~ filler PANE
  ~ stopper SILL
  Japanese ~ OBI

sashimi
  ~ fare EEL
  like ~ RAW

Sask.
  ~ neighbor ALB, ALTA, MAN,
    NDAK

Saskatchewan
  ~ tribe CREE

Sasquatch
  ~ cousin YETI

sass LIP

sassafras TREE

Sassanid ERA

sassy FLIP, PERT
  ~ one SNIP

"...sat ___ tuffet..." ONA

Sat.
  ~ preceder FRI

SAT EXAM, TEST
  ~ fill-in ANS
  ~ preparers ETS
  ~ provider ETS
  ~ section MATH
  ~ subj. ENG
  ~ taker TEEN
  ~ takers SRS

Satan
  like ~ EVIL

"___ Satan" MADAM

satanic BAD, EVIL

satchel BAG, GRIP
  ~ binder STRAP

Satchel
  ~ mom MIA

Satchmo
  ~ instrument HORN
  sing like ~ RASP

"...sat down beside ___..." HER

sate FEED, GLUT, JADE, PALL

satellite MOON
  ~ broadcast FEED
  ~ path ORBIT
  **communications ~ of the
    1960s** ECHO
  see also moon

satellite ___ DISH

satellites
  ~ do it SCAN

Satie ERIK
  see also French

satiety GLUT

satinwood TREE

satiny SLEEK

satire GENRE
  ~ magazine MAD

satiric
  ~ device IRONY

satirical ACID, ACRID

satirize TWIT

satisfaction
  exact ~ for AVENGE
  express ~ AAH
  seek ~ in a way SUE
  sounds of ~ AHS

satisfactory FAIR, GOOD, NICE
  ~ grade CEE
  better than ~ FINE

satisfied EASY, GLAD
  ~ sound PURR
  ~ sounds AHS

___-satisfied SELF

satisfy MEET, OBEY, PASS, PAY,
  PLEASE, SLAKE, SUIT

satrap RULER

saturate BATHE, GLUT, SOAK, SOP,
  STEEP, WET

saturated WET

saturated ___ FAT

Saturday
  ~ night ritual BATH

"Saturday Night ___" LIVE

saturn
  ~ ender INE

Saturn AUTO, CAR, GOD, ORB
  ~ daughter CERES
  ~ ender ALIA
  ~ wife OPS
  largest moon of ~ TITAN
  moon of ~ RHEA

saturnalia BLAST, ORGY, TEAR

Satyajit RAY

satyr RAKE
  ~ in part GOAT

satyric
  ~ trait LUST

satyrlike LEWD

sauce FACE, LIP
  ~ holder CAN
  enchilada ~ SALSA
  fish ~ ALEC
  Mexican ~ MOLE
  tend the ~ STIR
  Tex-Mex ~ SALSA

___ sauce CHILI, CLAM, CREAM,
  HARD, HOT, SOY

saucepan POT

saucer DISH, PLATE
  flying ~ UFO

sauciness NERVE

saucy ARCH, PERT, RUDE, SASSY,
  SMART

___ Saud IBN

Saudi ARAB
  ~ gulf ADEN
  ~ neighbor OMANI
  ~ robe ABA

Saudi ___ ARABIA

Saudi Arabia
  ~ et al. OPEC
  ~ neighbor IRAQ, OMAN,
    YEMEN

sauerbraten MEAT

Sauk TRIBE

Saul
  ~ cousin ABNER

Sault ___ Marie, Mich. STE

sauna BATH
  ~ output STEAM
  ~ site SPA
  ~ wood CEDAR

saunter LAG, MOVE, PACE, STEP

sausage MEAT
  ~ seasoning SAGE
  spiced ~ SALAMI

sauté FRY, HEAT

Sauterne WINE

Sauternes
  see French

Sauvignon Blanc WINE

savage ANIMAL, BEAST, CRUEL,
  FERAL, MAIM, MAUL

Savage DOC, FRED

"Savage ___, The" EYE

Savalas, Telly
  like ~ BALD

savanna DESERT, LEA, MOOR
  ~ dweller GNU
  ~ sound ROAR

Savannah CITY, PORT
~ **zone** EDT, EST

savant SAGE

savarin
~ **ingredient** RUM

save AMASS, BAR, HELP, KEEP, ONLY
~ **alternative** SPEND
~ **as coupons** CLIP
~ **methodically** FILE

saved
it's ~ **for a rainy day** TARP

"saved Christmas"
he ~ ERNEST

save for a ___ day RAINY

saver
~ **of fable** ANT
damsel ~ HERO
knee ~ RUG

saves
what a certain stitch ~ NINE

"Save the ___" TIGER

"Save the Last ___ for Me" DANCE

Saville, Victor
~ **film of 1950** KIM

___-saving FACE

savings STORE
~ **acct. addition** INT
~ **accts.** CDS
long-term ~ **acct.** IRA

savings and ___ LOAN

"Saviors of the Forest"
~ **director** DAY

Savoie
see French

savoir-faire POISE, TACT

savor LIKE, LOVE, TASTE
~ **the warmth** BASK

savoriness TASTE

savory RICH
~ **jelly** ASPIC

Savoy HOTEL

savvy GRASP, HEP, HIP, SENSE, SMART, TACT, WISE
~ **about** ONTO, UPON

"Savvy?" DIG

saw ADAGE, CUT, GNOME, MOT, TOOL
~ **logs** SLEEP, SNORE
~ **part** TOOTH
~ **wood** SNORE

saw ___ HORSE, LOG

___ saw BAND, BOW, FRET, PIT

Sawatch RANGE

sawbuck HORSE, TEN
~ **fraction** ONE
half a ~ FIN

sawbucks
ten ~ CEE, CNOTE

"Sawdust ___ Tinsel" AND

sawed-off SMALL

"___ saw Elba" EREI

sawhorse REST

sawing
~ **logs** ABED

"___-Saw, Margery Daw" SEE

sawmill
~ **machine** EDGER

saw-whet ___ OWL

Sawyer DIANE, TOM
~ **craft** RAFT

Sawyer, Tom
~ **half brother** SID

sax REED

___ sax ALTO, TENOR

Sax STEVE

saxes
some ~ ALTOS

saxhorn TUBA

saxophone PIPE, REED
~ **range** ALTO, TENOR

saxophones
some ~ ALTOS

say AVER, AVOW, PUT, RELATE, STATE, TALK, UTTER
~ **again** ECHO
~ **cheese** GRIN, SMILE
~ **confidently** ASSERT, AVER, AVOW
~ **"fo'c'sle"** ELIDE
~ **for sure** AVER, AVOW
~ **further** ADD
~ **goodbye** LEAVE, PART
~ **grace** PRAY
~ **hello** GREET, NOD
~ **imperfectly** LISP
~ **indistinctly** SLUR
~ **it isn't so** DENY
~ **more** ADD
~ **"not guilty"** PLEAD
~ **no to** DENY
~ **OK to** ALLOW
~ **"pretty please"** BEG
~ **the rosary** PRAY
~ **the wrong thing** ERR
~ **through the nose** SNORT
~ **uncle** LOSE
~ **under oath** ATTEST
~ **what you think** OPINE
~ **with a gravelly voice** RASP
~ **wrongly** LIE
~ **yea or nay** VOTE
~ **yes** OKAY
~ **you're coming** RSVP
have a ~ VOTE
have one's ~ AVER, STATE
unable to ~ **no** MEEK
what they ~ RUMOR

say ___ UNCLE

"___ say!" ILL

"Say ___" AAH, SISI

"Say ___ My Girl" YOURE

"Say ___ only a paper moon" ITS

"Say ___, Somebody" AMEN

"Say Anything"
~ **actress** SKYE

"___ Say Die" NEVER

Sayer LEO

Sayers GALE

saying ADAGE, GNOME, MOT, SAW

sayings
collected ~ ANA

"Say It ___ So" ISNT

"...say, not as ___" IDO

"Sayonara!" BYE, LATER, TATA
~ **in French** ADIEU
~ **in Hawaiian** ALOHA
~ **in Italian** CIAO
~ **in Latin** AVE, VALE
~ **in Spanish** ADIOS

"___ Say (Oom Dooby Doom)" SHE

Sb ELEM
51 **for ~** ATNO

SBLI
part of ~ INS, LIFE

Sc ELEM
21 **for ~** ATNO

S.C.
see South Carolina

scabbard CASE

scad HEAP, PILE

scads ACRES, ALOT, ATON, LOTS, MASS, OCEAN, RAFT, SEA, TON

scaffold CAGE, STAGE

scaffolding RACK

scald HEAT

scalding ACID, HOT

scale ARISE, LEAF, RANGE, RISE
~ **allowance** TARE
~ **down** PARE
~ **drawing** PLAN
~ **meas.** LBS
~ **note** SOL
~ **notes** DOS, LAS, MIS, RES, TIS
~ **part** PAN
~ **segment** NOTE, TONE
~ **type** MAJOR
~ **unit** OUNCE
bottom of a ~ ONE
bump on the ~ BLIP
top of a ~ TEN

___ scale WAGE

___-scale LARGE, SMALL

scaleless
~ **fish** EEL

___ scale of one to ten ONA

Scales
the ~ SIGN

scallion
~ **cousin** LEEK, ONION

scaloppine MEAT
~ **ingredient** VEAL

scalp SKIN

scalpel LANCE

scam CON

scamp CAD, DOG, IMP

scamper DART, HIE, RACE, RUN, SPEED
~ **off** FLEE

scan EYE, READ
brain ~ EEG

___ scan CAT, PET

Scand.
~ **nation** DEN, NOR

scandal DIRT, FLAP, LIE, RUMOR, SHAME

scandal ___ SHEET

scandalize TAINT

scandalous BAD

"___ Scandals" ROMAN

Scandinavian DANE, LAPP, NORSE
~ **city** OSLO
~ **epic** EDDA
~ **flier** SAS
~ **god** ODIN, THOR
~ **royal name** ERIK, OLAF, OLAV

scandium METAL

scanner
high-tech ~ CAT, PET

scanning
~ **acronym** CAT, PET

scant FEW, MEAN, MERE, POOR, THIN

scantling BEAM, STUD

scanty BARE, LEAN, MEAN, RARE, SMALL, SPARSE, THIN

scapegrace CUR, DOG

scapula BONE

scapular ROBE

scar LINE, MAR, TAINT
car ~ DENT

scarce LEAN, RARE, THIN
make oneself ~ AVOID, ELUDE, EVADE, HIDE

scarce as ___ teeth HENS

scarcely
~ **any** FEW

scarceness WANT

scarcer
~ **than hen's teeth** RARE

scarcity WANT
  Sahara ~ WATER

scare ALARM, AWE, COW
  ~ away SHOO
  ~ off DETER
  ~ up AMASS
  ~ word BOO

scarecrow IMAGE
  ~ innards STRAW

"Scarecrow and ___ King" MRS

scared
  be ~ FEAR
  looking ~ ASHEN, ASHY, PALE

"___ Scared Stupid" ERNEST

scarf WRAP
  ~ down EAT
  deacon's ~ STOLE
  English ~ ASCOT
  feathery ~ BOA
  make a ~ KNIT

"Scarface"
  ~ actor MUNI, RAFT

Scaria EMIL

Scarlatti
  ~ staple ARIA

scarlet COLOR, RED
  ~ runner BEAN

"Scarlet ___, The" CLAW

Scarlet Pimpernel HERO

"Scarlet Street"
  ~ director LANG

Scarlett BELLE, OHARA
  ~ home TARA
  ~ mother ELLEN
  daughter of ~ ELLA

scarp CRAG

scary BAD, EERIE, EERY
  ~ feeling FEAR

scat
  ~ queen ELLA
  do ~ SING

"Scat!" OUT, SCRAM, SHOO

scathing ACID, ACRID, BAD

scatter CAST, DOT, PART, ROUT, SIFT, THIN
  ~ as grass TED
  ~ seeds SOW

scatter ___ PIN, RUG

scatterbrained DAFT, MAD

scattered RARE, SPARSE, THIN

scattering FEW

scavenger
  ~ hunt GAME
  ~ shark NURSE
  doglike ~ HYENA
  sea ~ ERN, ERNE
  Serengeti ~ HYENA

scenario PLOT, SETUP

scene ADO, ARENA, SITE, SPOT, TODO
  ~ locale SET
  ~ of action ARENA, SPHERE, STAGE
  ~ splicer EDITOR
  ~ stealer HAM
  do a ~ ACT
  homophone for ~ SEEN
  make a ~ ACT, RAGE, RANT
  make the ~ ARRIVE, COME
  member of a crowd ~ EXTRA
  mob ~ RIOT
  play a ~ ACT
  quit the ~ FLEE, LEAVE, RUN
  sleep ~ DREAM
  steal a ~ EMOTE
  when the ~ is set ACTI

___ scene MOB

scène
  mise en ~ SET

scenery SET
  ~ chewer HAM
  bit of ~ DROP
  chew the ~ EMOTE
  Mojave ~ CACTI
  oater ~ RANCH
  stage ~ DECOR

scenes
  collection of ~ ACT

"Scenes From a ___" MALL

"Scenes From a Mall"
  ~ star ALLEN

scent AROMA, BALM, ESSENCE, NOSE, ODOR, TRAIL
  air-freshener ~ LILAC, PINE
  throw someone off the ~ ELUDE, LIE

"Scent ___ Woman" OFA

scented SWEET

scents
  it makes ~ ATTAR

scepter MACE, ROD, SIGN, WAND
  ~ partner ORB
  wield the ~ REIGN, RULE

sch.
  ~ before junior high ELEM
  ~ group PTA
  ~ subject ALG, BIO, ECON, ENG, MATH, MUS, SCI
  ~ year SESS
  kind of ~ ELEM, MED
  not in ~ ABS
  primary ~ ELEM

schedule AGENDA, BILL, LIST, PLAN, SET, SLATE, TIME
  ~ abbr. ARR, ETA
  ~ of food DIET, MENU
  ~ position SLOT
  ahead of ~ EARLY
  behind ~ LATE

scheduled DUE, ONTAP

scheelite ORE

Scheherazade
  ~ hero ALI

~ specialty TALE
~ subject ROC

Scheib EARL

Scheider ROY

Schell MARIA

scheme AIM, ANGLE, ART, CABAL, CADRE, GAME, IDEA, MAP, PLAN, PLOT, RUSE, WILE
  crooked ~ CON, SCAM
  deceptive ~ SETUP
  rhyme ~ ABBA
  room ~ DECOR

schemers CABAL

scheming DEEP, SLY

Schepisi FRED

"Scherzo ___ Flat Minor" INE

Schiaparelli ELSA

Schick BELA, TEST

Schifrin LALO

Schiller, Johann von POET
  ~ hero TELL
  see also poet

schilling COIN

"Schindler's ___" LIST

schism RENT, SPLIT

schismatic REBEL

schlemiel CLOD, LOSER, OAF

schlep HAUL, TOTE

Schliemann
  ~ discovery TROY

schmaltz CORN

schmo DOLT, OAF, SAP
  like a ~ INEPT

schmooze CHAT, GAB, TALK

schnapps GIN

schnauzer DOG, PET
  ~ feature BEARD

Schneider PAUL, ROB

schnook DUPE

schnoz NOSE

schnozz
  ~ ender OLA

Schoenberg
  like ~'s music ATONAL

scholar SAGE
  Benedictine ~ BEDE

"___ Scholar" ROAD

scholarly WISE
  ~ dissertation ESSAY
  ~ org. INST

scholarship AWARD, LORE
  ~ criterion NEED

scholium NOTE

school GENRE, MASS, TRAIN
  ~ bag KIT

~ before jr. high ELEM
~ dance PROM
~ founded in 1440 ETON
~ furniture DESK
~ group CLASS
~ in French ECOLE
~ of fish SHOAL
~ of thought ISM
~ on the Thames ETON
~ ordeal EXAM, TEST
~ org. PTA
~ paper ESSAY, THEME
~ period TERM
~ reformer MANN
~ session TERM
~ subj. ALG, BIO, ECON, ENG, MATH, MUS, SCI
~ tool RULER
~ vehicle BUS
~ VIP DEAN
~ worker NURSE
~ yr. SESS
boarding ~ PREP
British prep ~ ETON
divinity ~ subj. REL
doc's ~ MED
dolphin ~ POD
do well in ~ LEARN
eng. ~ TECH
go to ~ LEARN
of the old ~ PASSE
prim. ~ ELEM

school ___ BUS, DAY, YEAR

___ school DAY, MED, OLD, PREP, TRADE

"School ___" DAZE

"School ___ Scoundrels" FOR

schoolbook TEXT

schoolboy LAD

schoolchild GIRL

"School Daze"
  ~ director LEE

schoolmarmish PRIM

schoolmaster
  Sleepy Hollow ~ CRANE

"Schoolmistress, The" POEM

school of ___ knocks HARD

schoolroom
  ~ item PASTE
  ~ stick RULER

schools
  like most ~ COED

schoolyard
  ~ challenge DARE

school zone
  ~ sign SLOW

"School Zone" SIGN

schooner BOAT, SHIP
  ~ contents ALE, BEER
  ~ feature MAST
  ~ team OXEN

schottische DANCE, STEP

Schrader PAUL

Schroeder PAT

Schubert
~ **composition** LIED
~ **string work** OCTET
see also German

Schultz CARL
see also German

Schultz, Dutch ALIAS

Schulz AXEL

Schumann CLARA

schuss SKI

schusser
~ **lift** TBAR

Schwarzenegger
~ **film** ERASER
Mrs. ~ MARIA

Schwarzkopf
~ **rank** GEN
like Gen. ~ RET

sci.
~ **class** ANAT, BIO, LAB
environmental ~ ECOL
social ~ ECO, ECON

science
~ **center** LAB
~ **magazine** OMNI
~ **starter** OMNI, PRE
PBS ~ program NOVA

___ **science** EARTH, LIFE

science fiction
~ **award** HUGO

"Science Guy, The"
~ **on PBS** NYE

sciences
~ **partner** ARTS

scientific
~ **principle** LAW

scientist
~ **workplace** LAB

___ **scientist** MAD

sci-fi GENRE
~ **award** HUGO
~ **character** ALIEN
~ **classic** DUNE, THEM
~ **film of 1979** ALIEN
~ **film of 1982** TRON
~ **invaders** ETS
~ **storm material** ION
~ **vehicle** UFO
~ **weapon** LASER
Czech ~ drama RUR
Doctor of ~ WHO

scimitar STEEL
~ **cousin** SABER

scintilla ATOM, IOTA, JOT, MOTE, SHADE, SHRED, TRACE

scintillate BEAM, FLARE, SHINE

scion HEIR, PLANT, SHOOT, SLIP

scions ISSUE

Scipio ROMAN
rival of ~ CATO

scissors
use the ~ CLIP, SNIP

scoff GIBE, HOOT, SNEER
~ **up** EAT

scoffing SNIDE

Scofield PAUL

scold BASTE, LACE, LASH, NAG, RAG, RAIL, RANT, TRIM

scolding
~ **words** NONO

sconce DOME

scone
~ **partner** TEA

Scooby-Doo DOG

scoop BAIL, DIG, DIP, DIRT, DISH, DOPE, INFO, LADLE, NEWS
~ **out** MINE
~ **receptacle** CONE
~ **up** DIP, LADE
get the ~ HEAR, LEARN
serving ~ LADLE
the ~ FACT, INFO

scoop ___ NECK

scoot DART, DASH, HIE, RACE, RUN, SPEED, TEAR

___ **scooter** MOTOR

scop BARD, POET

scope AREA, RANGE, SIZE
~ **out** CASE
~ **starter** ENDO, OTO, PERI, TELE
enough ~ ROOM
limited in ~ SMALL
of great ~ BIG, LARGE, VAST
use a ~ AIM

scorch CHAR, HEAT, ROAST, SEAR

scorched ARID, DRY, SERE

scorched- ___ **policy** EARTH

scorching HOT

score DEBT, DOPE, GASH, GOAL, RATE, SLASH
~ **fewer points** LOSE
~ **in tennis** ACE
~ **more than** BEAT
~ **100** ACE
baseball ~ RUN
bowling ~ SPARE
court ~ ADIN
equal ~ TIE
even the ~ AVENGE, PAY, TIE
final ~ SUM, TOTAL
football ~ GOAL
golf ~ EAGLE
half a ~ TEN
settle the ~ AVENGE
zero ~ in tennis LOVE

scoreboard
~ **statistic** ERROR, HIT, RUN
~ **tally** OUT

scorecard
~ **abbr.** YDS
~ **word** OUT, PAR

scores HEAP, PILE
football ~ TDS

scoria LAVA, SLAG, STONE

scorn ABHOR, CUT, SNEER
laugh to ~ HOOT
show ~ SNORT

Scorpio SIGN

Scorpius
~ **neighbor** ARA

scot- ___ FREE

Scot CELT, GAEL
~ **family** CLAN
~ **headwear** TAM
young ~ LAD
see also Scottish

Scot.
~ **neighbor** ENG, IRE

scotch STOP

Scotch
~ **partner** SODA
~ **product** TAPE
~ **relative** RYE
like ~ AGED
store ~ AGE
see also Highland, Scottish

Scotch ___ PINE, TAPE

Scotch and ___ SODA

scoter BIRD

scot-free CLEAR

___ **Scotia** NOVA

Scotland
island off ~ IONA, SKYE
lake in ~ AWE
river in ~ AWE, DEE
see also Highland, Scottish

Scotland ___ YARD

Scotland Yard
~ **(abbr.)** CID

Scott DRED, TONY
see also Scottish

"___ Scott!" GREAT

___ **Scott Decision** DRED

Scott, Dred SLAVE

Scott, George C.
~ **film** RAGE

Scottie
FDR ~ FALA

Scottish
~ **accent** BURR
~ **adverb** NAE, SYNE
~ **bonnet** TAM
~ **goblet** TASS
~ **hill** BRAE
~ **household** CLAN
~ **inventor** WATT
~ **landowner** LAIRD
~ **miss** LASS

~ **name prefix** MAC
~ **number** ANE, TWA
~ **tongue** ERSE
ago, in ~ SYNE
alder, in ~ ARN
askew, in ~ AGEE
John, in ~ IAN
no, in ~ NAE
non, in ~ NAE
one, in ~ ANE
part of many ~ names MAC
since, in ~ SYNE
to, in ~ TAE
two, in ~ TWA
yes, in ~ AYE
see also Highland

Scottish Fold CAT, PET

Scotto, Renata DIVA
~ **solo** ARIA

Scott, Ridley
~ **film of 1979** ALIEN

Scott, Steve MILER

Scott, Walter SIR

Scotty
~ **colleague** SULU

scoundrel CAD, CUR, DOG, RAKE, RAT, SNEAK

scoundrelly BAD, BASE, LOW

scour ABRADE, CLEAN, HUNT, RAKE, SEEK

scoured CLEAN

scourge BANE, BEAT, LASH

"scourge of mortals"
Homer's ~ ARES

scourings WASTE

scouse STEW

scout ROAM, ROVE, SPY
~ **act** DEED
~ **destination** CAMP
~ **handiwork** KNOT
~ **out** HUNT, SEEK
~ **recitation** OATH
~ **shelter** TENT
~ **unit** DEN, TROOP

Scout HORSE, PINTO, STEED
~ **mother** MARE
~ **rider** TONTO

___ **Scout** EAGLE, GIRL

scoutmaster
~ **often** DAD

scow BOAT, SHIP

scowl GLARE

scrabble
~ **up** RISE

Scrabble GAME
~ **1-pointer** ESS, TEE
~ **1-pointers** ARS, ELS, ENS
~ **2-pointer** DEE, GEE
~ **3-pointer** BEE, CEE
~ **3-pointers** EMS
~ **4-pointer** VEE
~ **5-pointer** KAY

scraggy
~ **10-pointer** ZEE
~ **piece** TILE
~ **prop** RACK

scraggy LANK, THIN

scram EVADE, FLEE, HIE, LEAVE, RACE, RUN, SCAT

"Scram!" AWAY, GIT, SCAT, SHOO

scramble DART, MELD, SNARL, STIR
~ **as a message** ENCODE
~ **up** RISE

scrambled ___ EGGS

Scranton
~ **st.** PENN

scrap ATOM, BIT, CHIP, MELEE, PART, ROW, SETTO, SHRED, SNIP
~ **a mission** ABORT
~ **of cloth** RAG
table ~ ORT

scrap ___ HEAP

scrapbook
~ **pastings** ANA
add to a ~ PASTE

scrape ABRADE, EKE, ERODE, GRATE, GRIT, HOLE, RASP, SKIN
~ **away at** ERODE
~ **by** EKE
~ **off** SCALE
~ **together** RAISE
bow and ~ BEND, KNEEL

scraping
plate ~ ORT

scraps WASTE

scratch CASH, CHIP, CLAW, EKE, EMEND, LOOT, MAR, MOOLA, NIL, RASP, SCORE
~ **an itch** REACT
~ **out** ERASE
~ **out a living** EKE
~ **the surface** DIP, MAR
~ **to NASA** ABORT
from ~ ANEW, OVER
rock ~ STRIA

scratch ___ PAD, PAPER

scrawl WRITE

scrawny LANK, LEAN, THIN

scream BLARE, CALL, CRY, NOISE, RAGE, RANT, RAVE, REACT, ROAR, YELL
cartoon ~ EEK

"Scream of ___" FEAR

screech BAWL, BLARE, CRY, HOOT, NOISE, PIPE

screech ___ OWL

screen BLUR, HIDE, MASK, MESH, NET, SHADE, SIFT
~ **again** RERUN
~ **partner** STAGE
computer ~ CRT
computer-selection ~ MENU
radar ~ GRID

screen ___ PASS, TEST

___ screen FIRE

Screen ___ (former film studio) GEMS

screening MESH

screenplay DRAMA

"Screens, The"
~ **author** GENET

screwball NUT

screw-cutting
~ **tool** DIE

screwdriver TOOL
impromptu ~ DIME

screws
put the ~ to IMPEL, MAKE, MOVE

screwy DAFT, MAD

scribble PEN, WRITE
~ **(down)** JOT

scribe PEN, WRITE
Biblical ~ EZRA
Dead Sea Scrolls ~ ESSENE

scrimmage MEET, SCRAP
~ **starter** SNAP

scrimp SAVE, STINT

scrimshaw
~ **material** IVORY

script HAND
~ **direction** ENTER, EXIT, FADE
~ **ender** URE
~ **starter** ACTI
alter the ~ EDIT
ignore the ~ ADLIB

scroll ROLL
~ **holder** ARK
synagogue ~ TORAH

scroll ___ SAW

Scrooge
~ **comment** BAH
play ~ STINT

scrounge STEAL

scrub CLEAN, ERASE, WASH
~ **to NASA** ABORT
~ **up** BATHE, LAVE

scrubbed CLEAN

scrubby LOW, SMALL

scrubland MOOR

scrub-up BATH

scruff NAPE, NECK

scruffy MEAN, SEEDY

Scruggs EARL

scrumptious GOOD

scruple PANG

scruples
three ~ DRAM
without ~ AMORAL

scrutinize AUDIT, EYE, PEER, PORE, READ, SCAN, SIFT, TEST

scrutiny TEST
withstand ~ WASH

"SCTV"
~ **actress** OHARA

scuba
~ **diver's weapon** SPEAR
~ **gear** TANK
~ **tank supply** AIR

scud DART, RACE, RUN, SAIL

scudo COIN

scuff MAR

scuffle HOE, MELEE, ROW, SCRAP

scull OAR
~ **squad** CREW

sculler
~ **implement** OAR

sculpt CAST, CUT, HEW, MODEL, MOLD

sculpted
~ **heads island** EASTER

sculptor
~ **material** CLAY, ICE, JADE, STONE
~ **subject** TORSO
French ~ ARP

sculptors
funding source for ~ NEA

sculpture ART, IMAGE, MOLD
1498 ~ PIETA
kind of ~ TORSO
Parthenon ~ ATHENA

scupper HOLE

scurrilous LEWD, LOW, RANK

scurry ADO, DART, HIE, RACE, RIP, RUN, SPEED
~ **about** FLIT
~ **off** FLEE

scurvy BAD, MEAN

scut TAIL

scuttle DART, HIE, PAIL, RUN, SINK
~ **load** COAL
coal ~ HOD

scuttlebutt DIRT, NEWS, RUMOR, TALE, TALK

scutum PLATE

Scylla PERIL

scythe MOW
use a ~ REAP

S. Dak.
~ **neighbor** IOWA, NDAK, NEB, NEBR
see also South Dakota

SDS
object of ~ protests SSS

___ se PER

Se ELEM
34 for ~ ATNO

sea HEAP, MASS, OCEAN
~ **animals** OCTOPI
~ **bottom** BED
~ **captain's command** AVAST
~ **dog** GOB, SALT, TAR
~ **duck** COOT
~ **eagle** ERN, ERNE
~ **ender** BED, BIRD, PLANE, PORT, SHORE, SIDE, WATER
~ **extension** ARM
~ **green** AQUA
~ **greenery** ALGA
~ **greeting** AHOY
~ **in French** MER
~ **in Latin** MARE
~ **life** ALGAE
~ **lion** ANIMAL
~ **motion** TIDE
~ **nymph** SIREN
~ **plea** SOS
~ **resort** LIDO
~ **shade** BLUE
~ **shocker** EEL
~ **shout** AVAST
~ **swallow** TERN
~ **swirl** EDDY
~ **wall** LEVEE, MOLE
Antarctic ~ ROSS
arm of the ~ COVE, INLET
Asian ~ ARAL
at ~ LOST
Celtic ~ god LER
chicken of the ~ TUNA
crosswise, at ~ ABEAM
dot in the ~ ISLE
fasten at ~ LASH
go to ~ SAIL
halt, at ~ AVAST
inclined, at ~ ALIST
inland ~ ARAL
jewel from the ~ PEARL
Kazakhstan ~ ARAL
lunar ~ MARE
move unsteadily, at ~ YAW
mythical ~ nymph IONE
not at ~ ASHORE
Pacific ~ CORAL
put to ~ SAIL
shielded, at ~ ALEE
shrinking ~ ARAL
the fish of the ~ LIFE

sea ___ BASS, COW, DOG, EAGLE, GATE, HORSE, LEGS, LION, OTTER, SALT, STAR

___-sea DEEP

___ Sea ARAL, CORAL, IRISH, RED, ROSS

"___ Sea, The" CRUEL

"Sea Around Us, The"
~ **director** ALLEN

seabird ERN, ERNE, MEW, TERN
Northern ~ AUK

Seabiscuit HORSE

seaboard SHORE

seacoast SHORE

sea dog GOB, SALT, TAR
  ~ **hello** AHOY
  ~ **tale** YARN

sea dogs CREW

seafarer GOB, SALT, TAR
  ~ **shout** AVAST

seafarers CREW

seafood CLAM, COD, CRAB, EEL, ROE, SCROD, SOLE
  ~ **garnish** LEMON

seagirt
  ~ **land** ISLE

seagoing NAVAL
  ~ **initials** USS
  ~ **speed unit** KNOT
  ~ **staff** CREW

seagull MEW
  ~ **cousin** TERN
  ~ **hangout** PIER

Seahawks ELEVEN, TEAM
  ~ **org.** NFL

seal ANIMAL, CAP, CLOSE, GLUE, SHUT, STAMP, TAPE
  ~ **baby** CALF
  ~ **in the juices** SEAR
  ~ **point** CAT
  affix a ~ STAMP
  anagram of ~ ALES, ELSA, LEAS, SALE
  movie ~ ANDRE
  official ~ STAMP

___ **seal** EARED, FUR

Seal
  ~ **org.** USN

sealant
  roofing ~ TAR

sealed SURE

"Sealed With a ___" KISS

sealer
  package ~ TAPE

sea level
  hgt. above ~ ALT, ELEV

sea-level LOW

Seal Harbor
  ~ **site** MAINE

seals
  group of ~ POD
  like some ~ EARED

seam BED, LINE, LODE, SEW
  make a ~ SEW
  tapered ~ DART

seaman GOB, RANK, SALT, TAR
  ~ **libation** RUM
  ~ **saint** ELMO
  ~ **shout** AHOY, AVAST

seams
  join at the ~ SEW

Sean PENN

séance
  ~ **sound** RAP
  like a ~ EERIE, EERY

"Séance ___ Wet Afternoon" ONA

"Séance on a ___ Afternoon" WET

"Sea of ___" LOVE

Sea of Azov
  ~ **feeder** DON

Sea of Okhotsk
  ~ **feeder** AMUR

Sea of Tranquillity
  ~ **site** MOON

sear CHAR, DRY, HEAT, ROAST

search COMB, DIG, HUNT
  ~ **for** SEEK
  ~ **for a missing person** TRACE
  ~ **for apples** BOB
  ~ **out** ROOT, TRACE
  ~ **party** POSSE
  ~ **(through)** SIFT
  ~ **vigorously** RIFLE
  go in ~ **of** SEEK
  in ~ **of** AFTER

"___ Search for Meaning" MANS

"Search for the ___, The" NILE

"Search for Tomorrow" SOAP

___-searching SOUL

"Searching ___ Bobby Fischer" FOR

searchlight LAMP

searing HOT

seas
  high ~ MAIN
  like some ~ CALM

___ seas SEVEN

seascape
  ~ **artist** HOMER

"Seascape"
  ~ **author** ALBEE

seashore LAND
  ~ **recess** INLET

seaside SHORE
  ~ **sidler** CRAB
  ~ **town** PORT

season AGE, ENURE, INURE, RIPEN, SALT, TIME
  Ash Wednesday's ~ LENT
  holiday ~ NOEL, YULE

___ season OPEN

___-season OFF, POST

seasonal
  ~ **song** CAROL, NOEL
  ~ **visitor** SANTA

seasoned RIPE

seasoning SAGE, SALT
  Cajun ~ FILE
  lamb ~ MINT
  spaghetti-sauce ~ HERB

seasons
  four ~ YEAR

"Seasons, The" POEM

"Seasons of the Soul"
  ~ **poet** TATE

seat REST
  ~ **belt** STRAP
  ~ **for a tot** KNEE, LAP
  ~ **for several** SETTEE, SOFA
  ~ **material** CANE
  ~ **of feelings** SOUL
  baby's ~ LAP
  be in the driver's ~ LEAD, PILOT
  chicken's ~ ROOST
  church ~ PEW
  driver's ~ REINS
  leave one's ~ ARISE, RISE
  on the edge of one's ~ AGOG
  reserved ~ SPACE
  show to a ~ USHER
  take a back ~ **(to)** DEFER
  weave a chair ~ CANE

seat ___ BELT

___ seat AISLE, CAR, DROP, HOT, LOVE

seater
  stadium ~ USHER

___-seater TWO

seating
  ~ **for several** SETTEE, SOFA
  ~ **request** AISLE, LOGE
  cathedral ~ PEW
  theater ~ ROW

SEATO PACT
  ~ **counterpart** NATO
  part of ~ ASIA, ORG

seats
  section of ~ TIER

Seattle CITY, PORT
  ~ **arena** KEY
  ~ **hoopster** SONIC
  ~ **st.** WASH
  ~ **time zone** PDT, PST

Seattle ___ SLEW

Seattle Slew
  ~ **to Swale** SIRE

Seaver TOM

seawater
  mineral in ~ SALT

seaway CANAL

seaweed ALGA, ALGAE, KELP
  ~ **product** AGAR

Sea World
  ~ **attraction** SEAL

sebaceous FAT, OILY

Sebastian COE, CRAB

Sebring
  ~ **entry** CAR, RACER

sec DRY

___ sec INA

SEC
  ~ **member** ALA, LSU

___ secant ARC

Seckel PEAR
  ~ **cousin** BOSC

secluded
  ~ **hollow** DELL
  ~ **spot** NOOK, VALE
  ~ **valley** GLEN

second ABET, AIDE, BASE, HELP
  ~ **(abbr.)** ASST
  ~ **brightest star in a constellation** BETA
  ~ **draft** REDO
  ~ **in a series** BETA
  ~ **letter** BEE
  ~ **man** CAIN
  ~ **nature** HABIT
  ~ **of three virtues** HOPE
  ~ **person** EVE, YOU
  ~ **president** ADAMS
  ~ **self** TWIN
  ~ **showing** RERUN
  ~ **sight** ESP
  ~ **smallest st.** DEL
  ~ **son** ABEL
  ~ **starter** NANO
  ~ **to none** AONE, BEST, FIRST, TOP, TOPS
  ~ **X or O** TAC
  any ~ ANON, SOON
  a ~ **time** AGAIN, ANEW
  be in one's ~ **childhood** DOTE
  come in ~ LOSE
  have ~ **thoughts** FEAR
  split ~ HAIR

second ___ BASE, BEST, CLASS, ESTATE, GEAR, HAND, MATE

second-___ RATE

___ second SPLIT

"Second ___" BEST

Second Amendment
  ~ **supporter** NRA
  ~ **word** ARMS

secondary LESS

second-class ___ MAIL

secondhand USED
  ~ **purchase** RESALE

"Second Hand ___" ROSE

second-in-command
  naval ~ EXEC

second-largest
  ~ **bird** EMU

second-place
  ~ **finisher** LOSER

second-rate LESS, MEAN, POOR

seconds
  where ~ **are important** DUEL

second-sequel
  ~ **letters** III

second-stringer SUB

secrecy
  breach of ~ LEAK

secret DEEP, INNER
  ~ **agent** SPY
  ~ **ender** IVE
  ~ **idiom** ARGOT
  ~ **meeting** TRYST
  ~ **message** CODE
  ~ **motive** ANGLE
  ~ **plan** PLOT
  ~ **society** BAND, CABAL,
    ORDER, RING
  ~ **store** STASH
  blonde's ~ DYE
  center of ~ **activity** DEN
  Chinese ~ **society** TONG
  divulge a ~ BLAB, TELL
  hardly ~ OPEN, OVERT
  make a ~ **message** ENCODE
  not keep a ~ TELL
  Zsa Zsa's ~ AGE

secret ___ AGENT

___ secret OPEN, STATE, TRADE

___-secret TOP

Secret
  ~ **rival** BAN

"Secret ___" AGENT, HONOR,
  LOVE

"Secret ___, The" LAND, STORM

"___ Secret" STATE

secretarial
  ~ **work** MEMO

secretary AIDE, DESK, TABLE
  ~ **(abbr.)** ASST
  ~ **at times** STENO
  press ~ AIDE

secretary of state
  Reagan ~ HAIG

secrete EMIT, HIDE, OOZE, STASH

"Secret Love"
  ~ **singer** DAY

secretly APART

"Secret of ___ Inish, The" ROAN

"___ Secrets" THREE

Secret Service
  ~ **agt.** TMAN

"Secrets of ___" LIFE

"Secret Storm, The" SOAP

secs.
  60 ~ MIN

sect ORDER
  Buddhist ~ ZEN
  Mennonite ~ AMISH

sectarian
  ~ **suffix** IST, ITE

section AREA, CLASS, LAND,
  PANEL, PART, SLICE, ZONE
  ~ **of earth's crust** PLATE
  cement ~ SLAB
  choral ~ ALTOS
  church ~ NAVE

curriculum ~ UNIT
drainpipe ~ TRAP
grocery ~ AISLE, DELI
magazine ~ ROTO
newspaper ~ METRO
orchestra ~ BRASS
poem ~ STAVE
rocket ~ STAGE
SAT ~ MATH
stadium ~ LOGE, TIER
theater ~ LOGE, TIER
wall ~ PANEL

sectional LOCAL, SOFA

sector AREA, PART, ZONE

secular LAIC, LAY

secure BAR, BIND, CLASP, CLOSE,
  FAST, GAIN, GET, HIRE, KNOT,
  LACE, LAND, LASH, MOOR, NAIL,
  PASTE, PIN, RIVET, SAFE, SEAL,
  SURE, TAKE, WIN
  ~ **a boat** MOOR
  ~ **a package** TIE
  ~ **as a contract** LAND
  ~ **informally** ICE
  ~ **together** SEW

securities
  new ~ **offering** ISSUE

security BAIL, EASE
  ~ **agreement** LIEN
  ~ **breach** LEAK
  ~ **equipment** CAMERA
  ~ **org.** CIA
  ~ **problem** LEAK

Security Council
  ~ **denial** VETO
  former ~ **member** USSR

secy. ASST

Sedaka NEIL

sedan AUTO, CAR, MOTOR
  large ~ LIMO

Sedan CITY
  see also French

sedate CALM, COOL, SOBER, STAID

sedative OPIATE

Seder
  ~ **mainstay** LAMB

Sedgwick EDIE

sediment OOZE, SILT
  earthy ~ SILT
  wine ~ LEES

seduce BAIT, DRAW, LURE, RUIN

see DATE, ESPY, EYE, GET, GRASP,
  KNOW, NOTE, SENSE, SPOT, SPY
  ~ **after** ATTEND
  ~ **eye to eye** AGREE, MEET
  ~ **fit** LIKE
  ~ **(in)** USHER
  ~ **in a vision** DREAM
  ~ **(out)** USHER
  ~ **partner** WAIT
  ~ **red** BOIL
  ~ **socially** DATE
  ~ **the light** LEARN

cause to ~ **red** ANGER, IRK,
  PEEVE, RILE, UPSET
fail to ~ MISS
how others ~ **us** IMAGE
make someone ~ **red** ANGER,
  RILE
plain to ~ OVERT
what you ~ IMAGE

see ___ (be angry) RED

see ___ (be dazed) STARS

see ___ (investigate) ABOUT

see ___ (tend to) AFTER

"See ___, Private Hargrove"
  HERE

"See ___ run" SPOT

"___ See Clearly Now" ICAN

seed GERM, ISSUE, NUT, PIT, SOW,
  SPORE, STONE
  ~ **container** POD
  ~ **covering** ARIL
  ~ **destination** SOIL
  ~ **remover** GIN
  aromatic ~ ANISE
  edible ~ NUT
  flavorful ~ SESAME
  fruit ~ PIP
  gone to ~ PASSE
  go to ~ LAPSE, ROT
  scatter ~ SOW
  winged ~ MAPLE

"seed"
  bacteria ~ SPORE

seed ___ COAT, PEARL

"___ Seed" DEMON

seedbed SOIL

seedcase POD

seeded
  ~ **bread** RYE
  ~ **player's perk** BYE

seedling PLANT, TREE
  ~ **container** FLAT, TRAY

seedy MEAN, POOR

"___ See for Miles" ICAN

Seeger ALAN, PETE

"___ see here!" NOW

seeing SENSE
  ~ **red** IRATE, MAD, SORE

Seeing ___ dog EYE

"___ seeing things?" AMI

"___ See It" ASI, ICAN

seek AIM, CHASE, HUNT, TRACE
  ~ **alms** BEG
  ~ **excitement** GAD
  ~ **gold** PAN
  ~ **information** ASK
  ~ **office** RUN
  ~ **redress** SUE
  ~ **to win** WOO

seeker
  asylum ~ ALIEN

evade the ~ HIDE
movie revenge ~ NERD
Nirvana ~ HINDU
vote ~ POL

seekers
  re-election ~ INS

seeking AFTER

seem
  ~ **weary** SAG

seemly APT, FIT, GOOD, MEET, NICE

"Seems ___ Old Times" LIKE

"Seems Like ___ Times" OLD

seen
  easily ~ OPEN, OVERT
  not often ~ RARE

"See No ___" EVIL

seep BLEED, DRIP, DROP, ISSUE,
  LEAK, OOZE, RUN
  ~ **out** LEAK, OOZE

seer ORACLE
  ~ **asset** ESP
  ~ **card** TAROT
  ~ **discovery** OMEN
  ~ **ender** ESS
  ~ **gift** ESP

seesaw TEETER
  ~ **quorum** TWO

seethe BOIL, RAGE, STEW

seething HOT, IRATE

see-through THIN

"See You ___, Alligator" LATER

"See you later!" ADIEU, ADIOS,
  BYE, TATA
  ~ **in French** ADIEU
  ~ **in Hawaiian** ALOHA
  ~ **in Italian** CIAO
  ~ **in Latin** AVE, VALE
  ~ **in Spanish** ADIOS

Sega
  ~ **rival** ATARI

Segal ALEX

Segar
  ~ **surname** OYL

segment LEG, PART

sego lily
  ~ **state** UTAH

Segovia
  see Spanish

segregate PART

segregated APART

seigneur LIEGE, LORD, PEER

Seiler LEWIS

seine NET

Seine
  ~ **landscapist** MONET
  ~ **tributary** OISE
  city on the ~ PARIS
  see also French

Seinfeld WIT

"Seinfeld"
~ **role** ELAINE

seismograph
~ **reading** TREMOR

seize ARREST, CLASP, GET, GRAB, GRASP, GRIP, HOLD, NAB, NAIL, TAKE
~ **the day** LIVE

seized
~ **item** REPO

"Seize the ___" DAY

seizure TAKE

Sekely STEVE

Selassie HAILE
~ **ctry.** ETH

seldom
~ **encountered** RARE

select AONE, BEST, DRAW, ELECT, FINE, FIRST, GOOD, OPT, TAKE, TAP, TOPS
~ **at random** DRAW
~ **for admission** TAP
~ **from a menu** ORDER
~ **group** ALIST, ELITE

selected
~ **at random** ANY

Selene
~ **in Latin** LUNA
~ **realm** MOON
sister of ~ EOS

self EGO
~ **(prefix)** AUTO
~ **pride** EGO
inner ~ SOUL
second ~ TWIN

self-___ ESTEEM, HELP, IMAGE, MADE

self-___ man MADE

self-admiration PRIDE

self-admiring VAIN

self-adulation PRIDE

self-assertive
not ~ MEEK

self-assurance BRASS, FACE

self-centered VAIN

self-concept EGO

self-confidence POISE

self-confident
~ **words** ICAN

self-conscious SHY
make ~ ABASH

self-control CALM, POISE

self-controlled COOL, SEDATE, SOBER

self-defense
~ **spray** MACE

self-esteem EGO, PRIDE

self-evident
~ **truth** LAW

self-glorification PRIDE

self-image EGO, PRIDE

self-important SMUG
~ **one** ASS

selfish AVID, MEAN, SMALL
be ~ HOG

"Selfish Gene, The"
~ **topic** DNA

self-possessed CALM, COOL, SEDATE, SERENE

self-possession CALM, POISE

self-regard EGO

self-respect PRIDE

self-righteous SMUG
~ **person** PRIG

self-satisfaction PRIDE

self-satisfied SMUG, VAIN

Selima CAT, PET

Selkirk RANGE

Selkirk, Alexander SCOT

sell VEND
~ **down the river** DESERT
~ **for** COST, RUN
buy and ~ DEAL, TRADE

sell ___ (liquidate) OFF

___ sell HARD

sell a ___ of goods BILL

Selleck TOM

seller
~ **caveat** ASIS
~ **spots** ADS

Sellers PETER

selling
~ **feature** ASSET

sellout HIT
~ **notice** SRO

"___ sells seashells..." SHE

seltzer SODA
make ~ AERATE

selvage END

semaphore CODE, SIGN

Semarang
~ **island** JAVA

"___ Sematary" PET

semblance AIR, CAST, FACE, GARB, IMAGE, MIEN

semester TERM
~ **ender** EXAM, TEST

semesters
two ~ YEAR

semi MOTOR, RIG
~ **compartment** CAB
drive a ~ HAUL

semi- HALF

semibreve NOTE

semicircle ARC, BOW

semi-diameters RADII

seminar CLASS

seminarian
~ **subj.** REL

Seminole TRIBE

semiprecious
~ **stone** ONYX, OPAL

semiquaver NOTE

semisolid GEL

Semite ARAB

Semitic
~ **deity** BAAL

semolina
~ **product** PASTA

"Semper Fidelis"
~ **composer** SOUSA

"___ semper tyrannis" SIC

___ Semple McPherson AIMEE

sen COIN

Sen. POL

senate DIET

Senate
~ **assistant** AIDE, PAGE
~ **garb** TOGA
~ **output** LAW
~ **vote** AYE, NAY, YEA
former ~ **leader** DOLE

senator
ancient ~ ROMAN

"Senator ___ Indiscreet, The" WAS

senators
six years, for ~ TERM

Senators SIX, TEAM
~ **milieu** ICE, RINK
~ **org.** NHL

send ELATE, MAIL, REFER, REMIT, ROUTE
~ **a check** REMIT
~ **a letter** MAIL
~ **a message to** WIRE
~ **a package** MAIL, SHIP
~ **away** EXILE
~ **back to Congress** VETO
~ **down** RAIN
~ **forth** CAST, EJECT, EMIT
~ **into shock** STUN
~ **on a wild-goose chase** STALL
~ **one to sleep** BORE
~ **packing** CAN, EXILE, FIRE, OUST
~ **to another** REFER
~ **to Coventry** SHUN, TABOO, TABU
~ **to the bottom** SINK
~ **up** ERUPT
~ **up a flare** ALARM, ALERT

send ___ (summon) FOR

send-___ UPS

"Send in the Clowns"
~ **starter** ISNT

"___ Send Me" YOU

sendoff START

sends
~ **down for the count** KOS

Seneca LAKE, ROMAN, TRIBE
~ **enemy** ERIE
~ **neighbor** ERIE
~ **student** NERO

Senegal
~ **city** DAKAR
~ **neighbor** MALI

senescent AGED, OLD

senhor MAN, TITLE

senhora DONA, LADY, MADAM, TITLE

senhorita LADY, TITLE

senior ELDER, FIRST, OLD, OLDER, YEAR
~ **member** DEAN
former ~ ALUM, GRAD

seniority
having more ~ OLDER

senior year
~ **highlight** PROM

sennit ROPE

señor MAN, TITLE
~ **in German** HERR
~ **shawl** SERAPE
~ **squiggle** TILDE
see also Spanish

señora LADY, TITLE
~ **mark** TILDE
see also Spanish

señorita LADY, TITLE
~ **mark** TILDE
see also Spanish

sensation STIR
annoying ~ ITCH
painful ~ ACHE
rank ~ ODOR
subjective ~ AURA
warm ~ GLOW

"___ Sensational" YOURE

sense FEEL, KNOW, TENOR
~ **of humor** WIT
~ **of smell** NOSE
~ **organ** EAR, EYE
a ~ TASTE
common ~ TACT
general ~ TENOR
good ~ TACT, WIT
of a ~ AURAL
sixth ~ ESP
with no ~ **of ethics** AMORAL

sense ___ ORGAN

___ sense HORSE, INA, TALK

"Sense ___ Sensibility" AND

"Sense and Sensibility"
  ~ **director** LEE

senseless DAFT, INANE, MAD

"Sense of ___, A" LOSS

sensibilities EGO

sensibility HEART

sensible SAGE, SANE, SOBER, SOLID, WISE
  ~ **of** AWARE

sensing
  ~ **device** RADAR, SONAR

sensitive EDGY, KEEN, SORE

sensitivity TACT
  film ~ SPEED

sensor
  bloodhound ~ NOSE

sensory
  ~ **organ** EAR, EYE, NOSE

sensualist ROUE

sentence RAP, TERM
  ~ **break** DASH
  ~ **ender** DOT
  analyze a ~ PARSE
  boot-camp ~ **ender** SIR

sententious MORAL

sentient AWARE

sentiment
  public ~ PULSE

sentimental SWEET

sentimentality GOO

sentimentalize EMOTE

sentinel
  ~ **command** HALT

sentry
  ~ **order** HALT
  like a good ~ ALERT

Seoul CITY
  ~ **site** KOREA

sepal LEAF

separate ALONE, APART, COMB, LONE, OTHER, PART, RAVEL, SIFT, SORT, SPLIT
  ~ **from** LEAVE
  ~ **the laundry** SORT
  go ~ **ways** SPLIT
  in a ~ **place** ASIDE

separated ALONE, APART, LONE

separately ALONE, APART, EACH, ONLY

"Separate Tables"
  ~ **actress** KERR
  ~ **director** MANN

separation GAP

separator
  continental ~ ATL, PAC
  pew ~ AISLE

separators
  continental ~ URALS

sepia COLOR, INK

Sept.
  ~ **follower** OCT
  ~ **predecessor** AUG

"___ September" COME

septet
  briny ~ SEAS

septi-
  ~ **successor** OCTO

septic BAD

septicity TAINT

septuagenarian ELDER

seq. SER

sequel EVENT
  ~ **letters** III
  ~ **title starter** SON

sequence LINE, ORDER, ROW, SCALE, TRAIN
  alphabetic ~ ABC, RST, STU
  C-to-C ~ SCALE

sequentially NEXT

___ sequitur NON

sequoia TREE

seraglio HAREM
  ~ **chamber** ODA

serai INN
  ~ **site** OASIS

serape WRAP

seraph ANGEL

Serb SLAV

sere ARID, DRY

serenade SING, SONG

serenader
  ~ **instrument** LUTE

serene CALM, CLEAR, EVEN, MILD, SEDATE

Serengeti
  ~ **animal** ELAND, HYENA, LION
  ~ **group** PRIDE

serenity CALM, EASE, PEACE

serf ESNE, LIEGE, PEON, SLAVE

serge
  ~ **bane** LINT

sergeant RANK
  ~ **call** HEP
  ~ **command** ATEASE, HALT

sergeant at ___ ARMS

Sergei
  see Russian

Sergio LEONE

seria
  it may be ~ OPERA

serial PART

series LINE, RANGE, ROW, RUN, TRAIN
  ~ **ender** ETC

  ~ **of problems** SIEGE
  ~ **of rows** TIER
  ~ **of steps** STAIR
  ~ **starter** MINI
  first of a ~ ALPHA
  last of a ~ OMEGA, ZEE

___ serif SANS

serious ACUTE, BAD, DEEP, DIRE, SOBER
  ~ **book** TEXT
  ~ **in character** SOLID
  ~ **play** DRAMA
  make ~ SOBER
  unflappably ~ STAID
  unpleasantly ~ STERN

Serious YAHOO

serious-minded STAID

Serling ROD

sermon TALK, TRACT
  ~ **ender** AMEN, ETTE
  ~ **passage** TEXT
  ~ **subject** EVIL, SIN

sermonize ORATE, RANT, TALK

sermonizer ORATOR

serpent ADDER, ASP, SNAKE
  ~ **ender** INE
  ~ **home** EDEN
  ~ **sound** HISS

___ serpent SEA

"Serpent and the Rainbow, The"
  ~ **setting** HAITI

serpentine
  ~ **form** ESS

Serra da Estrela RANGE

Serra, Junípero
  ~ **title** PADRE

serval ANIMAL, CAT

servant HELP, MAID, PAGE, VALET
  bond ~ SLAVE
  civil ~ AGENT
  lord's ~ SERF
  rani's ~ AMA, AMAH

servants HELP

serve ACT, AID, ATTEND, FEED
  ~ **a meal** FEED
  ~ **as a model** POSE
  ~ **as a witness** ATTEST
  ~ **drinks** POUR
  ~ **food** WAIT
  ~ **the purpose** AVAIL
  ~ **well** ACE
  ~ **with a summons** CITE
  voided ~ LET

served
  where shots are ~ BAR

server TRAY
  ~ **handout** MENU
  chili ~ LADLE
  ice-cream ~ SCOOP
  patio ~ CART
  soup ~ LADLE

serves
  ~ **the purpose** DOES

service HELP, PLATE, RITE, USE
  ~ **award** TIP
  ~ **charge** FEE
  ~ **chow** MESS
  ~ **div.** USA, USN
  ~ **grp.** USO
  ~ **mail drop** APO
  ~ **winner** ACE
  bank ~ LOAN
  be of ~ STEAD
  church ~ MASS
  fine ~ ACE
  garage ~ LUBE
  in ~ **to** LIEGE
  lip ~ CANT
  news ~ PRESS
  of ~ UTILE
  perfect ~ ACE
  press into ~ USE
  road ~ TOW
  Sunday ~ MASS
  TV ~ CABLE

service ___ ACE, MEDAL, ROAD

___ service LIP, MAID, TEA

___-service SELF

"___ Service" ROOM

serviceability USE

serviceable UTILE

service club
  ~ **member** ELK, LION

Service, Robert POET
  see also poet

services
  pay for ~ HIRE
  wire ~ MEDIA, PRESS

service station
  ~ **job** LUBE
  ~ **purchase** GAS

servile BASE

serving DISH
  ~ **a purpose** UTILE
  ~ **customers** OPEN
  ~ **piece** PLATE, TRAY
  ~ **scoop** LADLE
  butter ~ PAT
  coffee ~ CUP
  collation ~ TEA
  corn ~ EAR
  food ~ MEAL
  ham ~ SLICE
  ice-cream ~ DIP
  margarine ~ PAT
  pub ~ PINT
  salmon ~ STEAK
  sommelier's ~ WINE
  Tabard Inn ~ ALE

___-serving SELF

sesame
  ~ **plant** TIL
  ~ **product** SEED

"___ sesame!" OPEN

Sesame
~ and others STS

"Sesame Street"
~ character ERNIE
~ giggler ELMO
~ grouch OSCAR
~ junk robot SAM
~ subject ABCS
it's big on ~ BIRD

session CLASS, TERM
be in ~ SIT
bull ~ site DORM
court ~ TRIAL
have a ~ MEET
jazz ~ JAM
rap ~ TALK

___ **session** JAM, RAP

sesterce COIN

set BAND, CLAN, CLOT, DIP, GANG,
GEL, HARD, KIT, LAY, MOLD,
NEST, POSE, RIPE, SOLID
~ a fine ASSESS
~ a goal AIM
~ apart ALLOT, ALLOW, SPACE
~ a price ASK
~ aside ALLOT, ANNUL, SAVE,
TABLE
~ at odds PIT
~ a trap BAIT
~ by HOLD
~ down ALIT, LAND, LAY, LIT,
NOTE, PUT, WRITE
~ fire to HEAT, LIT
~ for a skirmish ARMED
~ forth ASSERT, POSE, STATE
~ free CLEAR, LOOSE, UNTIE
~ in motion ACT, START
~ loose UNTIE
~ of beliefs CREDO
~ of drawers CHEST
~ off to advantage ADORN
~ of laws CODE
~ of players TEAM
~ of squares GRID
~ on a pedestal ADORE
~ one back COST, RUN
~ one's cap for WOO
~ one's heart on LONG, PINE,
WANT
~ one's mind to BEND
~ one's sights AIM
~ one's sights on TRAIN
~ on its way SEND
~ on one's feet HELP
~ out MOVE, START
~ out to ESSAY
~ period of time TERM
~ right AMEND, CURE, MEND
~ sail LEAVE, SHIP, START
~ sights AIM
~ straight ORIENT
~ the itinerary ROUTE
~ the pace LEAD
~ the sights AIM
~ the stage with
props DRESS
~ the table LAY
~ time DAY
~ up ERECT, RIG
~ upon LACE
~ upright RAISE

~ up shop OPEN
favored ~ ALIST
jet ~ ELITE
leaders ~ it PACE
matched ~ PAIR
nail ~ TOOL
scene ~ ACT
signal on the ~ CUE
start a ~ SERVE
tool ~ KIT
VIP on the ~ STAR
when the scene is ~ ACTI

set ___ (attack) UPON

set ___ (leave) SAIL

set ___ (reserve) ASIDE

set ___ (start) ABOUT, OFF

set ___ by (esteem) STORE

___ **set** JET, NAIL

"___ Set" DESK

setback LOSS

Seth
~ brother ABEL
~ father ADAM
~ mother EVE
~ sib CAIN
~ to Eve SON
son of ~ ENOS

set one's ___ for CAP

sette
number after ~ OTTO

sètte
~ follower OTTO
~ preceder SEI

settee SOFA

___ **setter** IRISH

set the ___ PACE

set the ___ for STAGE

setting SITE, SPOT, STAGE

settings
switch ~ ONS

settle ABIDE, CLEAR, CLOSE, END,
PAY, SEAL, SINK
~ a deal ICE
~ a debt PAY, REMIT
~ on ELECT
~ on, with "for" OPT
~ the score AVENGE
~ up PAY
~ upon TAKE

settled ALIT, LIT, STAID

settlement BASE, FINE, PEACE
arrive at a ~ AGREE

settler TENANT
~ migration TREK

set-to MELEE, ROW, SCRAP, SPAT
saber ~ DUEL

set up ___ SHOP

"Set-Up, The"
~ director WISE
~ star RYAN

___ **seul** PAS

Seurat, Georges
~ spot DOT
see also French
see also French

Seuss
~ and others DRS

Sevareid ERIC

Sevastopol CITY, PORT

seven
~ days WEEK
~ in French SEPT
biggest of ~ ASIA
city of ~ hills ROME
man has ~ of them AGES
one of ~ SEA
the ~ seas MAIN

seven ___, the SEAS

"Seven ___ Ache" YEAR

"Seven ___ From Now" MEN

"Seven ___ in May" DAYS

"Seven ___ Itch, The" YEAR

"Seven ___ to Noon" DAYS

"Seven-___-Cent Solution, The"
PER

"Seven Angry ___" MEN

"Seven Days in ___" MAY

"Seven Days to ___" NOON

Seven Dwarfs
~ workplace MINE
one of the ~ DOC

Seven Hills of ___ ROME

"Seven Men From ___" NOW

"Seven-Per-___ Solution, The"
CENT

"Seven-Per-Cent Solution, The"
~ director ROSS

seventeenth
~ state OHIO

"Seventh ___, The" SEAL

seventh day
~ activity REST

seven-up GAME

"Seven Year ___" ACHE

"Seven Year ___, The" ITCH

Seven Years' ___ WAR

sever CHOP, CUT, HACK, HEW, LOP,
REND, SLICE, SPLIT

several SOME
seating for ~ SETTEE, SOFA

severally EACH

severe ACUTE, BAD, BARE, CRUEL,
DOUR, DRY, SOBER, STERN
more ~ WORSE

severed CUT

Severinsen DOC

severity RIGOR

Severn
river to the ~ AVON

Severus CAESAR, ROMAN

Seville CITY, ORANGE, PORT
~ setting SPAIN
see also Spanish

Sèvres
see French

"Se vuol ballare" ARIA

sew MEND
~ loosely BASTE
~ up ICE

Seward
~ purchase ALASKA

Seward Peninsula
~ cape NOME
~ city NOME

"Seward's Folly" ALASKA

Sewell ANNA, JOE, RIP

sewer MAIN
famous ~ ROSS

sewing ___ KIT

sewing kit ETUI
~ item AWL, NEEDLE

sexagenarian ELDER

sexes
for both ~ COED

sext HOUR

Sexton, Anne POET
see also poet

"Sexy ___" SADIE

Seymour JANE

S.F.
~ setting PDT, PST

SFO
~ stat ARR, ETA

sgt. NCO
~ address APO
like a ~ ENL

"Sgt. Bilko"
~ director LYNN

"Sha ___" NANA

shabby MEAN, POOR, SAD, SEEDY

shack COT, HOLE, HOME, SHED
tumbledown ~ ABODE

"Shack ___ on 101" OUT

Shackelford TED

shackle BIND, IRON, TIE
~ site ANKLE

shackles IRONS

Shackleton, Ernest Henry SIR

shad
~ product ROE

shade COLOR, DASH, DYE, HUE, SOUL, TINGE, TINT, TONE
  change ~ DYE
  light ~ ECRU
  sun ~ TAN
  see also color, hue

shade ___ TREE

shader
  house ~ ELM

shades MANES
  reason for ~ GLARE

shading TINT

shadow BLUR, SHADE, SPY, TAG, TAIL, TRAIL
  ~ locale LID
  beyond a ~ of a doubt CLEAR
  dark ~ PALL
  five o'clock ~ BEARD

___ shadow EYE

"Shadow ___ Doubt" OFA

shadowbox SPAR

"Shadowland"
  ~ singer LANG

"Shadowlands"
  ~ director STONE
  ~ subject LEWIS

"Shadow of the ___ Man" THIN

"Shadow of the Thin ___" MAN

shadows MANES
  when ~ are shortest NOON

Shadow, The
  ~ garment CAPE
  ~ medium RADIO
  ~ nemesis EVIL

shadowy DIM

shady
  ~ area ARBOR
  ~ walk MALL

Shadyac TOM

SHAEF
  ~ commander DDE
  ~ sector ETO

Shaffer PETER
  ~ specialty DRAMA, PLAY

shaft ABYSS, ARROW, AXIS, AXLE, BAT, BEAM, HILT, HOLE, LANCE, MINE, PIT, POST, RAY, ROD
  ~ auto AXLE
  auto ~ CAM
  end of a ~ ADIT
  feathered ~ ARROW
  light ~ BEAM, RAY
  mine ~ PIT
  wheel ~ AXLE

"Shaft's ___ Score!" BIG

"Shaft's Big ___!" SCORE

shag CHASE, PILE, RUG
  ~ cousin BOB

shagbark TREE

shaggy
  ~ animal BEAR
  ~ bovine BISON
  ~ coat HAIR
  ~ dog story LIE, TALE
  ~ hairdo MANE
  ~ mammal YAK

shagreen SKIN

shah EXILE, RULER, TITLE

Shah
  ~ land IRAN

Shah Jahan
  ~ building site AGRA

Shah Mosque
  home of the ~ IRAN

Shahn BEN

shake ELUDE, JAR, LOSE, MOVE, WAG
  ~ a finger WAG
  ~ a leg HIE, MOVE, STIR
  ~ hands with GREET, MEET
  ~ in a way LOSE
  ~ in one's boots FEAR
  ~ off CAST, ELUDE, EVADE, LOSE, REPEL, RID
  ~ up ADDLE, ALARM, JAR, ROUSE, SCARE, STUN

shake ___ (reject) OFF

___ shake FAIR

"Shake ___!" ALEG

"Shake a ___!" LEG

"Shake It Up"
  ~ band CARS

shaken
  it may be ~ LEG

shaker
  ~ contents SALT
  mover and ~ DOER

Shaker ___, Oh. HTS

Shakers SECT

shakes
  in two ~ of a lamb's tail ANON, SOON
  no great ~ MEAN, SOSO

Shakespeare BARD, POET
  ~ wife ANNE
  see also poet

Shakespearean
  ~ adverb ANON
  ~ cry FIE
  ~ device ASIDE
  ~ epithet BARD
  ~ forest ARDEN
  ~ forte DRAMA
  ~ hero CAESAR
  ~ king LEAR
  ~ "Move it!" HIE
  ~ muse ERATO
  ~ plaint ALAS
  ~ point NIB
  ~ prankster ARIEL
  ~ prince HAL
  ~ product PLAY

  ~ river AVON
  ~ segment ACT
  ~ shrew KATE
  ~ sprite ARIEL
  ~ suffix EST, ETH
  ~ teen ROMEO
  ~ title start ALLS
  ~ "very foolish fond old man" LEAR
  ~ villain IAGO

"Shakespeare in ___" LOVE

shaking TREMOR

shako CAP, HAT

shale STONE
  ~ product OIL
  rock formed from ~ SLATE

shale ___ OIL

Shalit GENE

shall
  so ~ it be AMEN

"___ Shall Escape" NONE

"Shall I compare ___ to a summer's day?" THEE

"Shall I compare thee to a summer's day?" POEM

shallot ONION
  ~ relative LEEK

shallow INANE, SHOAL
  ~ pan TIN
  ~ receptacle TRAY

shallows REEF

"Shall we?"
  response to ~ LETS

"Shall We ___?" DANCE

shalom PEACE
  ~ in Hawaii ALOHA

sham ACT, FAKE, FALSE, POSE

shaman
  ~ need OMEN
  ~ wisdom LORE

Shamash SUN

shamble DRAG, LIMP, PLOD, RUIN

shame ABASE, ABASH, FIE, TAINT
  for ~ TSK, TUT

"Shame!" TSK, TUT

"___ Shame" ITSA

shameful BAD, BASE, EVIL, UGLY

shameless LEWD

Shamir
  ~ country ISRAEL

shampoo BATHE, CLEAN, WASH
  ~ bottle word RINSE
  ~ ingredient ALOE
  ~ name PERT

shampooing WASH

shamrock
  ~ isle EIRE, ERIN

Shamsky ART

Shamu ORCA

shamus TEC

___ Shan TAI

Sha Na Na
  ~ number OLDIE
  Lennie's instrument in ~ SAX

shandy
  part of a ~ ALE

"Shane" OATER
  ~ actor LADD

shanghai ROB, STEAL

Shanghai CITY
  ~ resident ASIAN

Shangri-La EDEN
  ~ cleric LAMA
  ~ land TIBET
  ~ locale ASIA

shank LEG, MEAT, SHIN, STEM

Shankar RAVI
  ~ genre RAGA
  ~ instrument SITAR

shank's mare LEG
  by ~ AFOOT

___ Shan mountain range NAN

Shanna REED

Shannon DEL
  ~ coach BELA
  land of the ~ EIRE, ERIN

shanty ABODE, COT, CRIB, HOLE, HOME

shape BEAT, CAST, MAKE, MODEL, MOLD, PLAN
  ~ a course PLAN
  ~ clay MODEL
  ankh's ~ TAU
  bent out of ~ IRATE, UPSET
  bullion ~ BAR
  cameo ~ OVAL
  candy ~ DROP
  chart ~ PIE
  chevron ~ VEE
  chocolate ~ BAR
  cracker ~ ANIMAL
  dunce-cap ~ CONE
  elongated ~ OVAL
  eyebrow ~ ARC
  face ~ OVAL
  gem ~ OVAL
  get in ~ HONE, TONE, TRAIN
  igloo ~ DOME
  in good ~ ABLE, FIT, HALE, LEAN, SAFE, TRIM
  Italy's ~ BOOT
  locket ~ HEART
  macaroni ~ ELBOW
  medal ~ STAR
  neckline ~ VEE
  ogee ~ ESS
  orbit ~ OVAL
  out of ~ BENT
  parenthesis ~ ARC
  pothook ~ ESS
  put into ~ RENEW

right-angle ~ ELBOW, ELL
snaky ~ COIL, ESS
Snickers ~ BAR
take ~ GEL
traffic-sign ~ ARROW
volcano ~ CONE
watermelon ~ OVAL

___-shape SHIP

shaped
~ like a rainbow ARCED

shaper
gelatin ~ MOLD
nail ~ FILE
wood ~ ADZE

shapes
right-angle ~ ELS

"Shape up or ___ out!" SHIP

shaping
~ machine LATHE
~ tool DIE

Shapiro ARTIE
~ métier LAW

Shapiro, Karl POET
see also poet

Shaq ONEAL
~ alma mater LSU
~ org. NBA
like ~ TALL

Shaquille ONEAL

Shaquille O'___ NEAL

Shar-___ (wrinkly dog) PEI

shard BIT, CHIP

share ALLOT, CLAIM, CUT, DOLE,
LEND, LOT, PART, POOL, SLICE,
SPLIT, STAKE, STINT
~ a side with ABUT
~ a view AGREE
~ in ENTER
~ the load HELP
fair ~ HALF
individual ~ ANTE
lion's ~ ALL, MOST
not ~ HOG
pay one's ~ ANTE
pig's ~ ALL

___ share LIONS

___-share TIME

share and share ___ ALIKE

sharecropper TENANT
~ stock MULE

shared
~ resource POOL

shareholder OWNER

sharers
~ word OUR, OURS
harness ~ TEAM

Shari LEWIS

Sharif OMAR
~ role of 1969 CHE

shark ACE, MAKO
~ feature FIN

scavenger ~ NURSE

___ shark SAND, TIGER

"___ Shark" TIGER

"___ Sharkey" CPO

sharks
~ environment OCEAN, SEA

Sharks GANG, SIX, TEAM
~ milieu ICE, RINK
~ org. NHL

Sharman BILL

Sharon ARIEL, STONE, TATE
~ country ISRAEL

sharp ACE, ACID, ACRID, ACUTE,
ALERT, AWARE, CHIC, CLEAR,
CRISP, KEEN, RACY, RAW, RUDE,
SOUR, TART
~ ache PANG
~ as a tack ACUTE, KEEN,
SMART
~ cold NIP
~ corner ANGLE
~ flavor TANG
~ increase HIKE
~ part EDGE
~ put-down SLAP
~ rejoinder NIP
~ sound SNAP
~ tool AWL
~ turn ELBOW
~ weapon EPEE
intellectually ~ KEEN
make ~ HONE
make a ~ turn VEER
not ~ FLAT, MILD

sharp ___ tack ASA

sharp-___ EYED

Sharp DON

sharp-edged KEEN
~ grasses SEDGE

sharpen EDGE, HONE
~ a cheddar AGE

sharpened
finely ~ KEEN

sharp-eyed ALERT

sharpness EDGE, SALT, SENSE

sharpshooter
~ org. NRA

sharp-smelling ACRID

Sharpsteen BEN

sharp-tongued ACID, ACRID,
SASSY, TART, TESTY

sharp-witted ACUTE

Shasta LAKE, TRIBE

Shatt-Al-___ ARAB

Shatt-al-Arab
port on the ~ BASRA

shatter DASH, REND, RUIN, SMASH

shave CUT, MOW, PARE, TRIM

___ shave CLOSE

"Shave ___ haircut..." ANDA

shaven BALD, BARE

___-shaven CLEAN

shaver
little ~ KID, LAD, TAD, TOT,
TYKE
wood ~ PLANE

shaving BIT, CHIP, SHRED
~ aid FOAM
~ site SINK

shaving cream
~ additive ALOE
kind of ~ FOAM, GEL

shavings WASTE

Shaw ARTIE

shawl CAPE, WRAP
prayer ~ SCARF
señor's ~ SERAPE

shawm
~ descendant OBOE

Shawn ESTES, TED

Shawnee TRIBE

Shayne, Michael
~ portrayer NOLAN

she
~ in French ELLE
~ in Spanish ELLA
~ objectively HER

"She ___ a Yellow Ribbon"
WORE

"She ___ Her Man" GETS

"She ___ Him Wrong" DONE

"She ___ Someone to Hold Her"
NEEDS

shear BARE, BOB, CHOP, CLIP, CUT,
LOP, MOW, NIP, PARE, TRIM

Shearer MOIRA, NORMA

shearing
~ candidate EWE

shearwater BIRD

Shea Stadium ARENA
~ player MET
~ sack BASE
~ team METS

sheath CASE, DRESS

sheathe DRAPE

sheathed
~ with metal CLAD

Sheba
~ creator INGE
~ locale ARABIA
~ today YEMEN

shebang
the whole ~ ALL

Shebat
~ follower ADAR

"She Couldn't ___ It" TAKE

shed ABODE, CAST, DROP, EMIT,
LOSE, RID
~ light SHINE
~ light on CLEAR, RAVEL
~ pounds DIET, SLIM
~ tears CRY, SOB, WEEP
something to ~ TEAR

"She Done ___ Wrong" HIM

"She Done Him Wrong"
Cary's ~ costar MAE

Sheedy ALLY

Sheehan NEIL

sheen GLARE

"Sheena, Queen of the Jungle"
chimp in ~ NEAL

Sheen, Martin
~ to Charlie DAD
~ to Emilio Estevez DAD

sheep ANIMAL
~ shed COTE
~ sound BAA, MAA
count ~ REST, SLEEP
female ~ EWE
herd ~ TEND
look at with ~'s eyes OGLE
male ~ RAM
wolf in ~'s clothing SHAM
young ~ LAMB

sheepdogs
what ~ do HERD

sheepfold COTE

sheepish OVINE, RED
~ call BAA, MAA

sheepshank KNOT
make a ~ TIE

sheepskin
~ holder ALUM, GRAD
~ leather ROAN

sheer BALD, CLEAR, FINE, PURE,
RANK, SKEW, STEEP, THIN,
TOTAL, UTTER
~ fabric TOILE

sheet LEAF, PAGE, PANE, PAPER,
PLATE, PLY
~ material SATIN, SILK
~ of ice FLOE
~ of metal PLATE
~ of paper LEAF
~ of stamps PANE
balance ~ examination AUDIT
cheat ~ CRIB, TROT
cookie ~ TIN
dental ~ DAM
glass ~ PANE
ice ~ FLOE
plywood ~ PANEL

sheet ___ KNOT, METAL

___ sheet DOPE, RAP, STYLE, TIME

sheets LINEN
come down in ~ POUR
deal on ~ SALE

"She Gets ___ Man" HER

"She Gets Her ___" MAN

sheik ARAB, LORD, MALE, RULER
~ **domain** ARABIA
~ **peer** AMIR, EMEER, EMIR
~ **robe** ABA
~ **wives** HAREM

"Sheila"
~ **singer** ROE

shekel COIN
~ **fraction** AGORA

shekels GELT
where ~ are spent ISRAEL

shelf LEDGE, REST, TABLE
on a ~ ATOP
put on the ~ DEFER, TABLE
take off the ~ USE

shelf ___ LIFE

shell BOAT, CASE, FIRE, PARE, PLATE, POD, SKIN
~ **lining** NACRE
~ **out** PAY, SPEND
~ **tool** OAR
propel a ~ OAR, ROW
tortoise ~ MAIL

shell ___ BEAN, GAME, STEAK

shell ___ (pay) OUT

___ shell BAND

Shell ART
~ **product** GAS
former ~ rival ESSO

shellac BEAT, CREAM, PAINT, RESIN, ROUT

shellacking BATH, ROUT

shellback SALT

shellbacks CREW

___-shell clam HARD

___-shell crab HARD

Shelley LONG, POET
~ **alma mater** ETON
~ **biography by Maurois** ARIEL
~ **on "Cheers"** DIANE
~ **work** ODE, POEM
see also poet

shellfish CLAM, CRAB
~ **eater** OTTER

shells AMMO, PASTA

"___ She Lovely" ISNT

she loves
~ **in Latin** AMAT

"She loves me"
~ **unit** PETAL

"She Loves Me ___" NOT

"She Loves You"
~ **word** YEAH

shelter HAVEN, HOME, LEE, NEST, NOOK, REST, SHED
animal ~ BARN, COTE
bird ~ NEST
campground ~ TENT
farm ~ SHED

Fox ~ TEPEE
jamboree ~ TENT
latticework ~ ARBOR
leafy ~ ARBOR
livestock ~ BARN
marine ~ COVE
scout ~ TENT
temporary ~ TENT
toward ~ ALEE

___ shelter ANIMAL

sheltered SAFE
~ **nautically** ALEE
~ **spot** COVE, DALE

Shelton RON

shelve DEFER, TABLE

Shem
~ **eldest son** ELAM

Shemp
~ **brother** MOE

shenanigan ANTIC, CAPER, LARK

Shepard ALAN, SAM

Shepard, Alan
~ **org.** NASA

"Shepeardes Calendar" POEM

shepherd DOG, PET, TEND
~ **god** PAN
~ **locale** LEA
Biblical ~ ABEL
first ~ ABEL

shepherd's ___ PIE

shepherd's purse WEED

"___ sher!" FER

Sheraton STYLE

sherbet ICE
~ **flavor** LEMON, LIME

Shere Khan CAT, TIGER

Sheridan ANN

sheriff
~ **band** POSSE
~ **symbol** STAR
TV ~ LOBO

Sherlock
~ **clue** ASH
~ **girlfriend** IRENE
~ **need** CLUE
~ **work** CASE

Sherman ALLIE, TANK
~ **was his veep** TAFT

Sherman ___, Calif. OAKS

Sherpa
~ **home** NEPAL
~ **sighting** YETI

Sherr LYNN

sherry WINE

Sheryl CROW

"She's ___ There" NOT

"She's a ___" LADY

"She's a Lady"
~ **lyricist** ANKA

"___ She's a Lady, The" LINER

"She's Gotta ___ It" HAVE

"She's Gotta Have It"
~ **director** LEE

"She stood in tears amid the ___ corn" ALIEN

"___ She Sweet?" AINT

Shetland
~ **pony** HORSE

Shevat
~ **follower** ADAR

"She Was a Phantom of Delight" POEM

"She Wore a Yellow Ribbon" OATER

shibboleth CRY, SAW

shield AEGIS, ARMOR, EGIS, MASK
~ **border** ORLE
~ **from** AVERT
Athena's ~ AEGIS, EGIS
medieval ~ ECU

shielded
~ **at sea** ALEE

shift ALTER, BOUT, GANG, MOVE, STIR, VEER
~ **a log** TONG
popular ~ DAY
work ~ DAYS

shift ___ KEY

___ shift DAY

Shift
~ **neighbor** ALT, ENTER, TAB

shiftless IDLE
~ **one** IDLER

shift-6 CARET

shifty FALSE, SLY

Shih Tzu DOG, PET, TOY

Shi'ite ARAB
~ **caliph** ALI
~ **deity** ALLAH
~ **faith** ISLAM
~ **holy man** IMAM
~ **land** IRAN

Shi'ites SECT

shikar HUNT

Shikoku
see Japanese

shill PLANT

shillelagh
~ **land** EIRE, ERIN

shilling BOB, COIN

Shillong
~ **region** ASSAM

shilly-shally DRAG, EVADE, HANG

Shimizu CITY, PORT

shimmer BEAM, FLARE, GLARE, GLOW, SHEEN, SHINE

shimmier
~ **of song** KATE

shimmy DANCE, STEP

Shimon PERES

shin LEG
~ **neighbor** ANKLE
~ **topper** KNEE

shinbone TIBIA

shindig BASH, DANCE, GALA, HOP
Honolulu ~ LUAU

shindy MELEE

shine BEAM, FLARE, GLARE, GLOW, RATE, SHEEN
~ **alternative** RAIN
~ **forth** SHED
~ **partner** RISE
~ **(upon)** SMILE
take a ~ to LIKE

___-shine SPIT

"Shine a Little Love"
~ **band** ELO

"___, shine, for thy light is come..." ARISE

shiner MOUSE

"___ Shines Bright, The" SUN

shingle SIGN
~ **letters** DDS
~ **site** ROOF
hang up one's ~ OPEN, SETTLE

shining CLEAR, LIT
~ **example** HERO, IDEAL

Shinnecock Hills
~ **shout** FORE

shinny
~ **up** RISE

Shinto REL

shiny SLEEK
~ **fabric** LAME, SATIN
~ **surface** ENAMEL
not ~ MAT, MATTE

"Shiny Happy People"
~ **band** REM

ship BOAT, HAUL, KEEL, LINER, MAIL, SEND
~ **beam** KEEL
~ **canvas** SAIL
~ **capacity measure** TON
~ **journal** LOG
~ **officer** MATE
~ **of the desert** CAMEL
~ **origin** PORT
~ **out** LEAVE, SAIL
~ **personnel** CREW
~ **plank** WALE
~ **pole** BOOM, MAST, SPAR
~ **position** ALEE
~ **prow** NOSE
~ **slot** SLIP
~ **storage area** HOLD

~ that brought the Statue of Liberty ISERE
~ timber MAST
~ to a poet KEEL
~ to Colchis ARGO
~ wheel HELM
~ wood TEAK
1492 ~ NINA
Amer. ~ designation USS
any ~ HER, SHE
behind, on a ~ AFT
cargo ~ OILER
clumsy ~ ARK, TUB
cruise ~ LINER
en route on a ~ ASEA, ATSEA
fictional ~ CAINE
fleece-seeking ~ ARGO
give up the ~ BOW
go by ~ SAIL
left, on a ~ PORT
memorable ~ MAINE
off the ~ ASHORE
WWII ~ LST
see also boat

"Ship ___!" AHOY

"___ Ship" SLAVE

shipboard
~ buddy MATE
~ direction AFT
~ position ABEAM

shipmates CREW

shipment LOAD, LOT
prepare for ~ WRAP

shipping
~ abbr. COD
~ hazard FLOE, REEF
~ route LANE
~ shortcut CANAL
~ unit TON

ships
group of ~ FLEET
of ~ NAVAL
where ~ run aground REEF

shipshape NEAT, TAUT, TRIM

ship to ___ SHORE

shipwreck
~ cause REEF

Shiraz
~ native IRANI
where ~ is IRAN

shirk AVOID, EVADE, LOAF, OMIT, SKIP

shirker DRONE

Shirley ___ Grau ANN

shirr BAKE

shirred
~ item EGG

shirt TOP
~ accessory TIE
~ measurement NECK
~ part ARM
~ size LARGE
~ starter RED, UNDER
alligator on a ~ LOGO

keep one's ~ on WAIT
kind of ~ TEE
stuffed ~ SNOB

___ shirt HAIR, POLO, TEE

shish kebab MEAT
~ necessity SPIT

Shiva
~ believer HINDU

shivaree BLAST

shiver BEAT, CHOP, DASH, FEAR, SMASH, STAVE

shivering
fit of ~ AGUE

shiver-producing EERIE, EERY

Shmoo
creator of the ~ CAPP

shoal BAR, FLAT, LAND, REEF
long ~ SPIT

shoaled ASHORE

shoat HOG
~ home STY

shock AMAZE, AWE, JAR, MAT, STUN, WOW
~ absorber PAD
express ~ GASP
in ~ AGOG
send into ~ STUN
sound of ~ GASP
white with ~ ASHEN

shocked
~ sound GASP
act ~ START
in a ~ state AGAPE

shocker
sea ~ EEL

shocking OUTRE
~ word BOO

shoddy MEAN, POOR, SEEDY

shoe
~ bottom SOLE
~ clerk query SIZE
~ ender HORN, LACE, SHINE, TREE
~ filler FOOT
~ form LAST
~ impression, maybe CLUE
~ insert FOOT, TREE
~ material SUEDE
~ part ARCH, HEEL, TOE
~ preserver TREE
~ spike CLEAT
~ starter HORSE, OVER, SNOW
~ string LACE
~ width AAA, EEE
ankle-high ~ BAL
cowpuncher's ~ BOOT
fix a ~ SOLE
folk-dance ~ CLOG
narrow ~ AAA
soldier's ~ BOOT
tighten a ~ RETIE
walking ~ FLAT
Western ~ BOOT
wide ~ EEE

woman's ~ FLAT
wooden ~ CLOG

shoebox
~ letters AAA, EEE

shoelace TIE
~ feature KNOT
fix a ~ RETIE

shoemaker
~ bottle DYE
~ device LAST
~ helper ELF
~ mold LAST
~ tool AWL

shoe polish
~ brand KIWI

shoes
like ~ SOLED
like Elvis' ~ SUEDE
wearing ~ SHOD

"___ Shoes" IGOT

"___ Shoes, The" RED

"Shoes of the Fisherman, The"
~ author WEST

shoestring LACE

___ shoestring ONA

shogi GAME
~ master DAN

shogun
~ capital EDO

"Shogun"
~ apparel OBI

Sholokhov
~ title river DON

"Shoo!" AWAY, GIT, SCAT, SCRAM

"shooby-doo"
go ~ SCAT

shoofly ___ PIE

shook
~ up AGOG

"___ Shook Up" ALL

shoot BAG, FIRE, HIT, JET, SCION, SPEED, SPIRE, SPRIG, WAND, ZAP
~ craps BET, GAME, PLAY
~ down VETO
~ forth ERUPT, JET, SPEW
~ for the green CHIP
~ from ambush SNIPE
~ off one's mouth BRAG, RANT, YAK
~ out EMIT
~ the breeze BLAB, CHAT, GAB, PRATE, RAP, TALK
~ up GROW, LEAP, RISE, SOAR
asparagus ~ SPEAR
director's ~ TAKE
movie ~ SCENE
plant ~ SPIRE
slender ~ WAND

"Shoot!" DARN, DRAT

shoot-'em-up OATER

shooter GUN
~ ammo PEA
~ of thunderbolts THOR
~ request SMILE
sidewalk ~ AGATE, TAW

___ shooter PEA

___-shooter SIX

shoot from the ___ HIP

shooting
~ area RANGE
~ game SKEET
~ iron GUN, RIFLE, ROD
~ marble AGATE, TAW
~ pain PANG, STAB
~ position PRONE
clay-pigeon ~ SKEET
end of ~ WRAP

shooting ___ IRON, STAR

___ shooting TRAP

shooting range
~ shout AIM

shooting star
~ path ARC

"Shootist, The" OATER

shootout DUEL
~ statement DRAW
1881 ~ participant EARP

"Shoot the ___" MOON

"Shoot the ___ Player" PIANO

shop MART, PLANT, STORE, TRADE
~ fixture LATHE
~ tool AWL, LATHE
chic ~ SALON
sandwich ~ DELI
set up ~ OPEN

___ shop TALK, UNION

"Shop ___ You Drop" TIL

shopaholic
~ hangout MALL

shoplift ROB, STEAL, TAKE

"Shop on ___ Street, The" MAIN

shoppe
~ descriptor OLDE

shopper
~ aid CART, LIST
~ burden BAG
~ favorite word FREE
~ lure SALE
~ stop MALL, MART, STORE
former ~ mecca AGORA
souk ~ ARAB

shopping
~ center MALL, MART
~ extravaganza SPREE
~ gallery ARCADE
~ prop CART
~ take-along LIST
go ~ SPEND

shopping ___ BAG, CART, MALL, SPREE

shopping list

shopping list
~ **notation** ITEM

shoptalk ARGOT, CANT

"Shop Til You __" DROP

shopworn STALE, TRITE

"Shopworn __, The" ANGEL

shore LAND, SANDS
~ **feature** COVE
~ **find** SHELL
~ **recess** INLET
~ **up** PROP
leave ~ SAIL
make ~ LAND

shore __ LEAVE

__ shore LEE

Shore DINAH, ERNIE

shorebird ERN, ERNE, HERON, STILT, TERN

shoreline
~ **indentation** COVE
~ **scavenger** ERN, ERNE

shorelines
~ **do it** ERODE

shorn BARE

short LOW, NEEDY, SHY, SMALL, TERSE
~ **angry utterance** SNAP
~ **breath** GASP
~ **composition** ESSAY
~ **cut** BOB, LANE, PATH
~ **distance** HOP, INCH, STEP
~ **drink** BELT, TOT
~ **drive** SPIN
~ **ender** AGE, CAKE, CUT, HAIR, HAND, STOP
~ **flight** HOP
~ **hairdo** BOB
~ **jaunt** HOP
~ **letter** NOTE
~ **of cash** NEEDY, POOR
~ **pithy expression** GNOME
~ **play** ACT, SKIT
~ **run** DASH
~ **shot** SNORT
~ **skirt** MINI
~ **story** GENRE, PROSE
~ **street** LANE
~ **swim** DIP
be ~ SNAP
come up ~ LOSE, MISS, OWE
cut ~ BOB, CLIP, CROP, END, LOP, NIP, STOP, TRIM
in a ~ **time** ANON, SOON
in ~ **supply** RARE, SPARSE, THIN
not ~ LONG

short __ FUSE, LIST, ORDER, RIBS, TON

short-__ TERM

__ short (briefly) FOR

__ short (disparage) SELL

__ short (terminate) CUT

"Short __" EYES

shortage WANT

shortcoming DEBIT, WANT

shortcut
shipping ~ CANAL

shorten CLIP, CUT, LOP, TRIM
~ **a garment** ALTER, HEM
~ **perhaps** EDIT

shortening LARD, OIL

shorter
make ~ CLIP, TRIM

shortfall NEED

short-fused IRATE

shorthair CAT

shorthand
~ **expert** STENO

shortie RUNT

shortly ANON, SOON

short-order
~ **cook** CHEF

shortstop
Ebbets Field ~ REESE

short-tempered TESTY

shortwave BAND, RADIO
~ **broadcaster** HAM

short-winded TERSE

"__ Shorty" GET

Shoshone TRIBE, UTE
~ **structure** TEPEE

Shoshone Falls
~ **locale** IDAHO

shot AMMO, BALL, BANG, BBS, DRAM, LEAD, NIP, SNORT, TIRED, TRY
~ **ender** GUN
~ **from the air** AERIAL
~ **in the dark** BET, STAB
~ **put** EVENT
~ **starter** BIRD, BOW, EAR, GUN, HOT, OUT, OVER, SNAP, UNDER
a ~ EACH
bar ~ SNORT
be off like a ~ HIE, RACE, RUN
big ~ LION, NABOB, NAME, NOB
billiards ~ CAROM
film-set ~ TAKE
give it a ~ ESSAY, TRY
go like a ~ HIE, RACE, RUN, SPEED
long ~ BET, RISK
parting ~ TAG
prepare to be ~ POSE
quick ~ SNORT
small ~ DRAM
straight ~ ARROW
sure ~ ACE
take a ~ **at** TRY
take a long ~ BET
tennis ~ LOB, SMASH
wide ~ MISS

shot __ PUT

__ shot BIG, CHIP, DROP, LONG, POT, RIM, SLAP

"__ Shot" SLAP

shot in the __ ARM

"Shot in the Dark, A"
~ **name** ELKE

shots
call the ~ BOSS, LEAD, RULE, RUN
where ~ **are served** BAR

"__ Shots!" HOT

shoulder BEAR, MEAT, PROP
~ **enhancer** PAD
cold ~ SNUB
stand shoulder to ~ BAND

shoulder __ BAG, STRAP

shoulders
be head and ~ **above** BEAT, BEST, TOP

shout BAWL, CALL, CRY, HAIL, HOOT, NOISE, RANT, RAVE, YELL
auction ~ BID
fairway ~ FORE
lab ~ AHA
paper vendor's ~ EXTRA
revival ~ AMEN
solver's ~ AHA

shouting
engage in a ~ **match** ARGUE, SCRAP

shove ELBOW, IMPEL, JAM, MOVE, PRESS, PROD
~ **around** BOSS
~ **in** CRAM
~ **off** LEAVE, SPLIT

shove __ (leave) OFF

shovel DIG, TOOL
~ **cousin** SPADE
~ **in** EAT
~ **relative** SCOOP
use a ~ DIG

shovel __ HAT

__ shovel STEAM

shoveler BIRD

show AIR, ARGUE, ATTEST, BARE, FAIR, MODEL, PLAY, POMP
~ **a clean pair of heels** FLEE
~ **affection** KISS
~ **agreement** NOD
~ **alarm** START
~ **amusement** GRIN
~ **approval** CLAP, NOD
~ **astonishment** GAPE
~ **courage** DARE
~ **curiosity** ASK
~ **delight** BEAM, GLOW, GRIN, SMILE
~ **disapproval** BOO, HISS
~ **emotion** REACT
~ **ender** TIME
~ **fallibility** ERR
~ **fatigue** NOD
~ **favoritism** ROOT
~ **fear** RUN

~ **feelings** EMOTE
~ **for short** EXPO
~ **(in)** USHER
~ **itself** EMERGE, OCCUR
~ **neglect** ROT
~ **off** BRAG, CROW, PARADE, POSE
~ **offense, perhaps** SLAP
~ **of hands** VOTE
~ **one's age** DATE
~ **one's face** RISE
~ **one's heels** HIE, RUN
~ **one's teeth** DARE
~ **(out)** USHER
~ **partner** TELL
~ **patience** ABIDE, AWAIT
~ **penitence** ATONE
~ **place** ARENA
~ **respect** BOW, HONOR
~ **reverence** KNEEL
~ **sadness** BAWL, CRY, SOB, WEEP
~ **some muscle** EXERT
~ **starter** ACTI, SONG
~ **sudden interest** PERK
~ **team spirit** ROOT
~ **teeth** SNARL
~ **the door to** OUST
~ **the pearly whites** SMILE
~ **the way** LEAD, USHER
~ **the world** BARE
~ **to a seat** USHER
~ **up** ARRIVE, ATTEND, COME, ENTER
~ **use** WEAR
boffo ~ HIT
dealers' ~ FAIR
ender ~ BOAT, CASE, MAN, ROOM
fail to ~ LOSE
false ~ ACT
get the ~ **on the road** START
give a ~ ACT
horse ~ FAIR
horse ~ **locale** ARENA
industrial ~ EXPO
light ~ AURORA
livestock ~ FAIR
long-running ~ HIT
make a ~ PARADE
put on a ~ ACT, AMUSE, STAGE
run the ~ RULE
short ~ ACT, SKIT
SRO ~ HIT, SMASH
stage ~ DRAMA, PLAY
starter ~ SIDE
Western ~ OATER
Wild West ~ RODEO

show __ BILL, OFF

__ show GAME, HORSE, ICE, LATE, ROAD, TALK

"Show __" BOAT

"Show __ No Mercy!" THEM

"__ Show, The" LATE

show and __ TELL

show biz
~ **award** OBIE, OSCAR, TONY
~ **group** ACT
~ **headliner** STAR

"Show Boat"
  ~ captain ANDY
  ~ prop BALE
  ~ tune BILL
  Julie in ~ AVA

showcase ARRAY
  big ~ EXPO

showdown DUEL, MEET

shower BATHE, CLEAN, HAIL, HEAP, LAVE, PELT, PLY, RAIN, RINSE, WASH
  ~ affection DOTE
  ~ alternative BATH, TUB
  ~ head JET
  ~ mo. APR
  ~ with love ADORE
  take a ~ BATHE, LAVE

showering BATH, RAINY, WASH

showery WET
  ~ month APRIL

showing
  ~ good judgment SANE
  ~ wonder AGAPE
  aft. movie ~ MAT
  product ~ DEMO
  second ~ RERUN

showman
  American ~ COHAN

showmanship DRAMA

"Show Me the Way"
  ~ band STYX

showoff HAM

showpiece ART

showroom
  ~ car DEMO
  ~ caveat ASIS

show-stopper
  Met ~ ARIA, SOLO

Showtime
  ~ rival HBO

showy ARTY, GALA, GAY, LOUD, ORNATE
  ~ display ECLAT
  ~ flower ASTER, IRIS, TULIP
  ~ parrot MACAW

shoyu
  ~ ingredient SOY

shred ATOM, BIT, CHIP, GRATE, IOTA, PART, RAG, REND, RIP, SCRAP, TEAR
  ~ cheese GRATE

shreds
  in ~ TORN
  pull to ~ TEAR

Shreveport
  ~ inst. LSU

shrew ANIMAL, NAG
  Shakespearean ~ KATE

shrewd ACUTE, CUTE, SLY, SMART, WISE

shrewdness SENSE, TACT

shrewish TESTY

shriek BLARE, BLAST, CRY, NOISE, ROAR, YELL
  comic-strip ~ EEK

shrike BIRD

shrikes
  like ~ AVIAN

shrill PIPE, REEDY
  ~ bark YAP

shrine ALTAR
  Texas ~ ALAMO

shrink DRAW, FEAR, SHY, START
  ~ from ABHOR, HATE, SHUN

shrinker
  skin ~ ALUM

shrinking AVERSE, SHY
  ~ sea ARAL

shrive ATONE

shrivel DRY, SEAR

shriveled ARID, DRY, SERE

Shriver MARIA, PAM

Shropshire
  ~ cry BAA
  ~ she EWE
  ~ youth LAD
  see also British, English

"Shropshire ___, A" LAD

"Shropshire Lad, A" POEM

shroud BLUR, DRAPE, HIDE, MASK, PALL

Shrove
  ~ ender TIDE

"Shrovetide Revelers"
  ~ artist HALS

Shrove Tuesday
  ~ follower LENT

Shroyer, Sonny
  ~ role ENOS

shrub PLANT
  Andes ~ COCA
  evergreen ~ ERICA
  flowering ~ LILAC
  gray-green ~ SAGE
  landscaper's ~ ROSE
  prickly ~ BRIAR
  see also plant

shrubbery
  ~ tool EDGER
  neaten the ~ CLIP

shrubby
  ~ herb SAGE

shrug ___ (disregard) OFF

"___ Shrugged" ATLAS

shrunken DRY, SERE, SMALL

shtick ACT

shuck PARE, PEEL, SHELL, SKIN

"Shucks!" DARN, DRAT, RATS

shudder FEAR, TREMOR
  ~ at ABHOR, HATE
  make one ~ REPEL

shuffle ALTER, DANCE, DRAG, EVADE, LAG, LIMP, MOVE, PLOD, STEP
  ~ follower CUT, DEAL
  ~ one's feet DANCE

"___ Shuffle" LIDO

shuffleboard GAME

shuffling SLOW

shul
  ~ scroll TORAH

Shula DON

Shumway, Gordon
  ~ alias ALF

shun ABHOR, AVOID, CUT, EVADE, SNUB

shut CLASP, CLOSE
  ~ down CEASE, HALT
  ~ forcefully SLAM
  ~ in CAGE, CLOSE, PEN, PENT
  ~ off CLOSE, STEM
  ~ out BAN, BAR, TABOO, TABU
  ~ tight CLOSE, SEAL
  almost ~ AJAR
  not ~ OPEN
  not ~, to a poet OPE

shuteye NAP, SLEEP

shutout ROUT

shutterbug
  ~ device CAMERA

shuttle
  ~ environs SPACE
  ~ org. NASA
  airport ~ BUS
  Armstrong's ~ LEM
  pilot the ~ ORBIT
  use a ~ TAT

___ shuttle SPACE

shuttlecock BIRD

shy FEAR, START
  ~ away REACT
  ~ away from AVOID, SHUN
  ~ of UNDER
  be ~ OWE
  make ~ ABASH

___-shy CAMERA, GUN

"___ Shy" GIRL

sí YES
  ~ in French OUI

Si ELEM
  14 for ~ ATNO

"S.I." MAG

Siam
  ~ ender ESE
  King of ~'s governess ANNA

siamang APE

Siamese CAT, TAI, THAI
  ~ remark MEOW, MEW
  ~ twin ENG

sib REL
  ~ child NIECE
  bro's ~ SIS
  sis's ~ BRO

Siberia
  ~ site ASIA
  see also Russian

Siberian
  ~ citizen TATAR
  ~ river LENA

sibilance HISS, LISP

sibilant ESS, HISS
  ~ sound SSS

sibling BRO, SIS
  having no ~ ONLY
  victim of ~ rivalry ABEL

sibs KIN

Sibuyan SEA

sibyl ORACLE, SEER

sic THUS

Sicily ISLE
  ~ (abbr.) ISL
  ~ neighbor MALTA
  mountain in ~ ETNA
  see also Italian

sick ILL
  ~ at heart SAD
  ~ partner TIRED
  be ~ of HATE
  feel ~ AIL

sick ___ LEAVE

sick and ___ TIRED

sicken AIL, REPEL

sickle TOOL
  swing a ~ REAP

sickly ILL, PALE

sickness EVIL

Sid CAESAR, STONE

"Sid ___ Nancy" AND

"Siddhartha"
  ~ author HESSE

Siddons SARAH

side HAND, PHASE, TEAM
  ~ ender BAR, CAR, LINE, LONG, SHOW, SLIP, SPIN, STEP
  ~ starter BED, FIRE, LAKE, OFF, OUT, POOL, PORT, RING, ROAD, SEA, STATE, SUB, TRAIL, UNDER
  ~ street LANE, ROAD
  ~ that cuts EDGE
  ~ track AVERT
  ~ (with) AGREE
  at one ~ of (prefix) PARA
  by the ~ of ALONG
  checkers ~ RED
  Civil War ~ BLUE, GRAY, UNION
  Cold War ~ WEST
  debate ~ CON, FOR, PRO
  lean to one ~ LIST
  look on the bright ~ HOPE
  off to one ~ APART

side ___

on Mom's ~ ENATE
on the sheltered ~ ALEE
on the wild ~ RACY
other ~ ENEMY, FOE
port ~ LEFT
side by ~ ALONG
the dark ~ EVIL
the other ~ of PAST
thorn in one's ~ BANE, PAIN, PEST
to one ~ APART, AWRY
to one ~ of (prefix) PARA
wrong ~ up OVER

side ___ ARM, BET, DISH

___ side FLIP

"___ Side, The" FAR

sidearm GUN

sideboard TABLE

sideburns BEARD

sidecar
~ occupant RIDER

___-sided ONE, SOBER

side dish RICE, SALAD, SLAW

sidekick AIDE, MATE, PAL

sidelight LAMP

sideline TABLE
~ shout RAH

sidelong
~ glance LEER

sideman
~ instrument AXE

"___ Side of Midnight, The" OTHER

___ side of the coin, the OTHER

___-Sider TOP

sidereal ___ DAY, YEAR

siderite ORE
~ constituent IRON

sides
cricket ~ ONS
slopping over the ~ AWASH

___ sides (be partial) TAKE

sideshow
~ attraction LURE

sideslip SKID, SLIDE, VEER

"___ Sides Now" BOTH

"___ Sides of the Law" BOTH

side-splitter RIOT

sidestep AVERT, AVOID, EDGE, ELUDE, EVADE, MISS, SHUN

"___ Side Story" WEST

"Side Street"
~ director MANN

sidetrack AVERT

sidewalk PATH
~ activity SALE
~ hazard GRATE

~ shooter AGATE, TAW
~ stand offering ADE
lay a ~ PAVE

sidewalk ___ CAFE

"Sidewalk Stories"
~ director LANE

sidewall
~ protection EAVE

sideways AWRY
move ~ EDGE

"___ Side, West Side" EAST

sidewinder SNAKE

sidewise
walk ~ CRAB

siding SPUR

sidle EASE, EDGE, INCH, SNEAK

sidler CRAB

Sidney, Philip POET, SIR
see also poet

Siegel DON

Siegfried HERO

"Siegfried" OPERA
~ piece ARIA

Siegmeister ELIE

sienna COLOR

___ sienna RAW

Siepi, Cesare BASS

sierra RANGE

Sierra ___ LEONE

Sierra Club
~ pioneer MUIR

Sierra Madre RANGE
~ treasure ORO
see also Spanish

Sierra Maestra
~ country CUBA

Sierra Nevada RANGE
~ resort TAHOE

siesta NAP, REST, SLEEP

siete
~ follower OCHO

sieve MESH, NET
pass through a ~ SIFT

sievelike OPEN

sift
~ (for) PAN
~ (through) COMB

Sig ARNO

sigh MOAN, STIR
~ (for) LONG, PINE
~ of relief PHEW
~ of satisfaction AAH
verbal ~ ALAS

sighs AHS

sight AIM, ESPY, KEN, SENSE
~ related OPTIC

sight-___ READ

___-sighted FAR, LONG

"Sighted sub, sank ___" SAME

sight for ___ eyes, a SORE

sighting
mysterious ~ UFO
sailor's ~ LAND
Sherpa ~ YETI

sights
set one's ~ AIM
set one's ~ on TRAIN
take in the ~ TOUR

sightsee TOUR

sightseer
~ need CAMERA, MAP

sigma ESS
~ follower TAU
~ preceder RHO

Sigma ___ (frat of songdom) CHI

sigmatism LISP

sigmoid
~ curve ESS

Sigmund
~ daughter ANNA

sign CLUE, OMEN, TOKEN, WRITE
~ a contract INK
~ away CEDE
~ by a door EXIT
~ ender POST
~ in COME
~ of approval NOD
~ of caution SLO
~ off END
~ off on OKAY
~ of healing SCAB
~ of joy, maybe TEAR
~ of life PULSE
~ of remorse TEAR
~ of sanctity HALO
~ of spring ARIES, THAW
~ of strain ACHE
~ of summer LEO
~ of the future OMEN
~ of the ram ARIES
~ of winter SLEET, SNOW
~ on HIRE
~ on the dotted line AGREE
~ over CEDE
~ up ENROL, ENTER
advertising ~ NEON
apartment ~ TOLET
arithmetic ~ PLUS
August ~ LEO
bad ~ OMEN
bar ~ ONTAP
barber's ~ POLE
beanery ~ EATS
bus ~ LOCAL
cinema ~ EXIT
conspicuous ~ NEON
corner ~ STOP
diner ~ NEON
direction ~ ARROW
dollar ~ basically ESS
doorway ~ EXIT
electric ~ NEON

equinox ~ ARIES
fire ~ ARIES
first ~ ONSET
flat ~ TOLET
gaudy ~ NEON
give a high ~ ALERT, WARN
hash-house ~ EATS
high ~ HINT
highway ~ EATS, EXIT, GAS, SLO, SLOW, YIELD
hotel ~ EXIT
July ~ CRAB
make a ~ NOD
March ~ ARIES
packed-house ~ SRO
parking garage ~ ENTER
positive ~ PLUS
radio-studio ~ ONAIR
rail-crossing ~ STOP
red-letter ~ EXIT
rental ~ TOLET
road ~ EATS, EXIT, GAS, SLO, SLOW, STOP, YIELD
store-window ~ OPEN
street ~ ARROW, SLOW, YIELD
telltale ~ ODOR
theater ~ EXIT
triangular ~ YIELD
TV studio ~ ONAIR
two-finger ~ VEE
V ~ PEACE
vacancy ~ TOLET
victory ~ VEE
yard-sale ~ ASIS
zodiac ~ ARIES, CRAB, LEO, RAM

___ sign CALL, PEACE, PLUS, STOP

signal ALERT, CALL, CRY, CUE, FEED, FLAG, FLARE, LAMP, NOD, SIGN
~ a cab HAIL
~ booster AMP
~ in a way RING
~ light LAMP
~ on the set CUE
~ to retire TAPS
~ to slow AMBER
actor's ~ CUE
danger ~ ALARM, ALERT, RED
directional ~ ARROW
distress ~ FLARE, SOS
early ~ ALERT
emergency ~ FLARE, SOS
game-show ~ DING
hand ~ CLAP
military ~ TAPS
quarterback's ~ HIKE
ref's ~ TEE
sonar ~ ECHO
stage ~ CUE
telecast ~ AUDIO
thespian's ~ CUE
transmit a ~ BEAM
turn ~ ARROW
TV ~ component AUDIO
TV ~ receiver DISH
warning ~ HORN

___ signal HAND, TURN

signature HAND, NAME
~ song THEME
flower's ~ ODOR

signatures
~ **for some** EXES

signer
~ **need** PEN

signet SEAL, STAMP

signet ___ RING

significance NOTE, SENSE, STRESS, TENOR

significant DEEP, MAJOR
~ **other** MATE
~ **time** EPOCH, ERA
highly ~ MAJOR

significant ___ OTHER

signify ARGUE, BODE, MEAN

sign language
~ **pioneer** EPEE

sign-off
~ **word** LOVE, OVER

signor LORD, PEER, TITLE

signora LADY, MADAM, TITLE

Signoret
see French

signorina LADY, TITLE
see also Italian

signs
~ **off on** OKS
decelerate, on ~ SLO
gas for ~ NEON
indicate by ~ BODE
read the ~ CAST

___ signum ECCE

sign up
~ **(abbr.)** ENL

Sigurd HERO
~ **successor** ATLI

"Sigurd the Volsung" EPIC, POEM

sika DEER

Sikh ASIAN

Sikkim
~ **locale** ASIA

Sikorsky IGOR

silage OATS

Silas PAUL

"Silas Marner"
~ **author** ELIOT

silence CEASE, GAG, PEACE, REST

silencer GAG

silent MUTE, TACIT
~ **approval** NOD
~ **bid** NOD
~ **communication** ESP
~ **flier** OWL
~ **language** SIGN
~ **one** CLAM
~ **president** CAL
~ **projectile** ARROW
~ **star** HARPO

not ~ ALOUD
strike ~ AMAZE, AWE, STUN, WOW

silent ___ ALARM

"Silent ___" CAL

"Silent Clowns, The"
~ **author** KERR

silent film ERA
~ **accompaniment** ORGAN

"Silent Night" NOEL
~ **word** SLEEP

"Silent Partner, The"
~ **playwright** ODETS

"Silent Running"
~ **actor** DERN

silent screen
~ **actress** BARA
~ **persona** SIREN
~ **star** HARPO

"Silent Spring"
~ **subject** DDT

Silenus SATYR

Silesian
~ **river** ODER

silhouette FACE, LINE

"Silhouettes" OLDIE
~ **singers** RAYS

silica
form of ~ OPAL

silica ___ GEL

silicate
~ **mineral** MICA
magnesium ~ TALC

"___ Silja, The" MAID

silk
~ **in French** SOIE
~ **replacement** NYLON
~ **shade** ECRU
watered ~ MOIRE

silk ___ HAT

___ silk CORN

"___ & Silk" IRON

silk-cotton TREE

silken SLEEK

silk-making
~ **region** ASSAM

silk-stocking BARON, DUDE, ELITE, PEER

"Silkwood"
~ **actress** CHER

silkworm
Assam ~ ERI

sill LEDGE, REST
~ **sitter** PLANT

Sills DIVA, SAM
~ **former company** MET
~ **solo** ARIA

silly DAFT, GOOSE, INANE, INEPT, MAD
~ **laugh** TEHEE
~ **one** ASS, GOOSE, IDIOT

Silly Putty
~ **holder** EGG

silo
~ **neighbor** BARN

silt DIRT, OOZE, SOIL
~ **deposit** DELTA
windblown ~ LOESS

silver COIN, COLOR, METAL
~ **certificate** BILL
~ **dollars** CACTI
~ **ender** WARE
~ **fabric** LAME
~ **fox** FUR
~ **meas.** STER
~ **source** MINE, ORE
bar of ~ INGOT
coat with ~ PLATE
lad with ~ **skates** HANS

silver ___ PLATE

Silver HORSE, RON, STEED
~ **mother** MARE
~ **St.** NEV
~ **stopper** WHOA

"Silverado"
Danny Glover role in ~ MAL

Silver Comet TRAIN

Silverdome ARENA

silver-gray ASH

Silverheels
~ **partner** MOORE
~ **role** TONTO

___ Silverman (Beverly Sills) BELLE

Silvers PHIL

Silver Springs
town near ~ OCALA

Silver Star MEDAL

Silver State NEV
~ **city** RENO

silvertip BEAR

silver-tongued GLIB

silvery
~ **fish** SMELT
~ **gray** ASH
~ **metal** TIN

Simba LION
~ **and company** PRIDE
~ **pride** MANE
~ **uncle** SCAR
sound like ~ ROAR

___ Simbel ABU

Simcoe LAKE

Simenon
see French

___ Simeon, Calif. SAN

simian APE, ORANG
Sumatra ~ ORANG

similar AKIN, ALIKE, CLOSE, SAME
~ **(prefix)** SYN
~ **to** LIKE
~ **to (prefix)** PARA

similarly ALSO

simile
~ **center** ASA, ASAN
~ **word** LIKE

simmer BOIL, HEAT, STEW
~ **down** ABATE

simmering HOT

Simmons
~ **and others** ALS

Simms PHIL

simoleon CLAM

simoleons CASH, KALE, MOOLA

simon-___ PURE

Simon ESTES, NEIL, PAUL

Simon ___ PETER

"Simon ___" SAYS

Simon and Garfunkel DUO

"Simon Boccanegra" OPERA
~ **setting** GENOA

Simone NINA
see also French

Simonides of Ceos POET
see also poet

Simon, Mrs. Paul EDIE

Simon, Neil
~ **character** OSCAR
~ **nickname** DOC
division for ~ ACT
like ~**'s couple** ODD

"Simon of the ___" DESERT

"Simon Says"
~ **player** APER
play ~ APE

simper SMILE

simpering
~ **sound** TEHEE

simple CLEAN, EASY, INANE, MERE, NAIVE, RUDE, SLOW
~ **answer** AYE, YES
~ **stuff** ABC
~ **tool** LEVER
something ~ SNAP

___ simple FEE

"Simple ___" MEN

simple as ___ ABC

Simple Simon
~ **treat** PIE

simpleton ASS, DODO, DOLT, GOOSE, IDIOT, OAF

simplicity EASE
epitome of ~ ABC

simplify EASE

simply MERE, ONLY

Simpson ABE, ADELE, ALAN, HOMER, LISA

Simpson, Bart BRAT
~ **dad** HOMER
~ **sister** LISA

Simpson, Homer
~ **dad** ABE

Simpson, Lisa
~ **dad** HOMER

Simpson, Marge
~ **hair color** BLUE
~ **husband** HOMER
~ **kid** LISA

"Simpsons, The"
~ **bartender** MOE
~ **bus driver** OTTO
~ **neighbor** NED

simulacrum ICON, IMAGE

simulate ACT, APE, FAKE

simulated FALSE, SHAM

sin ERR, EVIL
deadly ~ ANGER, LUST

Sinai
~ **dweller** ARAB

Sinatra IDOL, TINA

Sinatra, Mrs.
the second ~ AVA

Sinbad HERO
~ **transport** ROC
emulate ~ ROVE
number of voyages of
~ SEVEN

"Sinbad and the Eye of the ___" TIGER

since ASOF, FOR
~ **in French** DES
~ **in Scottish** SYNE

"Since ___ Went Away" YOU

sincere DEEP, HONEST, OPEN, REAL, TRUE, WARM
be ~ MEAN

"Since you ___..." ASKED

"Since You ___ Me" ASKED

"Since You Went ___" AWAY

Sinclair LEWIS
~ **rival** ESSO

Sinclair, Upton
~ **novel** OIL

sine RATIO

sine ___ DIE

___ sine ARC

sine qua ___ NON

sine qua non ESSENCE, GIST, NEED

sinew CORD, NERVE

sinewy HALE

sinful BAD, EVIL, VILE

sing BLAB, CAROL
~ **falsetto** YODEL
~ **like Satchmo** RASP
~ **one's own praises** BRAG, CROW
~ **out** CALL
~ **the blues** MOPE
~ **the praises of** LAUD
~ **tremulously** YODEL

sing-___ ALONG, SONG

"Sing, ___ Sinners" YOU

___ Sing ("Bonanza" cook) HOP

"Sing a ___" (Earth, Wind & Fire tune) SONG

Singapore CITY
~ **resident** ASIAN

Singapore sling
~ **ingredient** GIN

Singaraja
its capital is ~ BALI

singe CHAR, HEAT, SEAR

singer ALTO, BASS, BASSO, TENOR
oft-impersonated ~ ELVIS

Singer MARC

"Sing, goddess, the wrath of Peleus' son..."
~ **source** ILIAD

singing
~ **bird** LARK
~ **sounds** LALA
~ **voice** ALTO, BASS, BASSO, TENOR

Singing ___, The NUN

"Singin' in the ___" RAIN

single ALONE, HIT, LONE, ONE, ONLY
~ **file** LINE
~ **no more** WED
~ **out** CITE, DRAW, ELECT, OPT
~ **(prefix)** MON, UNI
~ **thing** ITEM, UNIT
~ **time** ONCE
in ~ **file** AROW

single ___ FILE

single-___ SPACE

single-gender
not ~ COED

single-handedly ALONE, SOLO

single-masted
~ **boat** SLOOP

single-name
~ **actress** CHER
~ **supermodel** IMAN

single-purpose ADHOC

singles
new ~ EXES

singles ___ BAR

singleton LONER

singly ALONE, EACH

Sing Sing
~ **resident** CON

singspiel OPERA

"___ Sings the Blues" LADY

singular LONE, ODD, RARE

singularity TRAIT

sinister BAD, DIRE, EVIL, LEFT
~ **look** LEER

___ sinister BAR

sinistral LEFT

sink BATH, BORE, DIP, DROP, EBB, LAPSE, SAG, SETTLE, SLIP
~ **alternative** SWIM
~ **deeply** ROOT
~ **down** MIRE, SAG
~ **feature** TRAP
~ **in mud** MIRE
~ **in the west** SET
~ **one's teeth into** BITE
~ **to the bottom** SETTLE

sinker
~ **material** LEAD

sinking ship
~ **deserter** RAT

sink trap
~ **shape** ESS

Sinn Fein
~ **land** EIRE
~ **org.** IRA

Sinope MOON

Sino-Russian
~ **river** AMUR

sinuate BEND, COIL

sinuous LITHE
~ **shape** ESS

sinus BEND, BOW, HOLE

Siouan OTO, OTOE, UTE
~ **language** OSAGE
~ **tongue** IOWA
~ **tribe** OMAHA

Sioux TRIBE
~ **speaker** OTO, OTOE

Sioux City
~ **state** IOWA

"Sioux City ___" SUE

Sioux Falls
~ **st.** SDAK

sip BIT, LAP, TASTE
~ **slowly** NURSE

siphon DRAW, TAP

sipper STRAW

sir MALE, MAN
~ **counterpart** MAAM, MADAM
~ **in India** SAHIB
~ **in Spanish** SENOR

"___, sir!" YES

Sir TITLE

sire BREED, DAD, HORSE, PAPA
~ **mate** DAM

siren ALARM, ALERT, HORN
behave like a ~ LURE
screen ~ BARA

siren ___ SONG

"Sir Galahad" POEM

Sirius STAR
~ **owner** ORION

sirloin MEAT, STEAK

sis REL
~ **sib** BRO

sisal AGAVE

Siskel GENE
~ **cohort** EBERT
emulate ~ RATE

siskin BIRD

___ siskin PINE

sissy ___ BAR

sister NUN
madre's ~ TIA
padre's ~ TIA

___ sister SOB, SOUL

Sister ___ ("Guys and Dolls" role) SARAH

"Sister ___" ACT

"Sister Act"
~ **extra** NUN

sisterhood ORDER

sister-in-___ LAW

"Sisters"
~ **sister** ALEX
~ **star** WARD

"___ Sisters" THREE

"___ Sisters From Boston" TWO

Sisters of Charity
~ **founder** SETON

Sistine Chapel
~ **location** ITALY

Sisyphean ETERNAL

sit ABIDE, POSE, REST
~ **around** LOAF
~ **down** REST, SEAT, SETTLE
~ **down with** SEE
~ **inelegantly** PLOP
~ **in on** ATTEND, AUDIT
~ **in the cellar** AGE
~ **in the sun** BASK
~ **on the throne** REIGN, RULE
~ **still for** ABIDE, ALLOW, LET
~ **tight** STAY, WAIT
~ **up for** AWAIT
cozy place to ~ LAP
how some ~ **by** IDLY
not ~ STAND
place to ~ SOFA
where honored guests
~ DAIS

sit-___ UPS

"Sit ___!" ONIT

Sita
~ **husband** RAMA

sitar
~ **motif** RAGA

sitcom
~ **demo** PILOT
~ **diner** MELS
~ **ET** ALF
~ **of the 1970s** ARNIE
ABC ~ ELLEN
classic ~ MAMA, MRED
FOX ~ ROC
long-running ~ MASH

sitcoms
legendary name in ~ DESI

site AREA, SCENE, SPOT, STAGE
home ~ PLOT

Sitka EMIL
~ **state** ALASKA

sitter POSER
~ **bane** BRAT
~ **creation** LAP
sill ~ PLANT

___ **sitter** AISLE

sitting IDLE
~ **duck** DUPE, PREY, SAP
~ **on** ATOP
~ **place** ROOST
instrument played ~
down CELLO

sitting ___ ROOM

Sitting Bull
~ **st.** SDAK

"Sitting Pretty"
~ **director** LANG

"Sittin' on the Dock of the ___"
BAY

situate LAY, ORIENT, PLANT, POSE,
POST, PUT, SET, SPOT

situated
be ~ LIE
get ~ ORIENT, ROOST

situation CASE, ESTATE, SCORE,
STATE
difficult ~ BIND, SPOT
dull ~ DRAG
overtime ~ TIE
readiness ~ ALERT
unpleasant ~ MESS

"___ sit under the apple tree..."
DONT

sit-up
~ **benefactors** ABS

Sitwell DAME, EDITH, POET
see also poet

sitz ___ BATH

Siva
~ **worshiper** HINDU

Sivash SEA

Siwalik Hills RANGE

six
~ **games in tennis** SET
~ **in Italian** SEI
~ **years, for senators** TERM
coach and ~ RIG
name of ~ **popes** PAUL

___-**six** DEEP

"Six ___ Kind" OFA

"___ Six, The" DEEP

Six Day War
~ **site** SINAI

Sixers FIVE, TEAM
~ **org.** NBA

Six Flags
~ **attraction** RIDE

six-pack
~ **unit** CAN

"Six-Pack ___" ANNIE

six-packs
four ~ CASE

sixpence COIN

sixpenny ___ NAIL

six-pointers TDS

six-shooter GUN, ROD

six-sided
~ **crystals** SNOW

"Sixteen ___" TONS

"___ Sixteen" YOURE

sixteenth-century
~ **Council city** TRENT

sixth
~ **notes** LAS
~ **president** ADAMS
~ **sense** ESP

sixth ___ SENSE

sixty
~ **grains** DRAM
~ **minutes** HOUR

"Sixty Glorious ___" YEARS

"Six Weeks"
~ **actor** MOORE
~ **actress** MOORE

sizable BIG, LARGE, TALL

size RATE
~ **(abbr.)** MED
~ **of type** AGATE
~ **up** ASSAY, ASSESS, EYE,
RATE
adjust the ~ **of** ALTER
bed ~ TWIN
circle ~ AREA
clothing ~ LARGE, MED,
SMALL
coal ~ PEA
comparative ~ RATIO
economy ~ LARGE
garment ~ **(abbr.)** MED
gem ~ CARAT
junior dress ~ NINE

newspaper type ~ AGATE
of great ~ EPIC
paper ~ LEGAL
poodle ~ TOY
soda-bottle ~ LITER
suburban plot ~ ACRE
suit ~ LONG
T-shirt ~ LARGE, MED, SMALL
type ~ AGATE, PICA

___-**size** LIFE, TWIN

___-**sized** BITE, GOOD, PINT

___-**sized hail** PEA

___ **size fits all** ONE

sizing FIT

sizzle BOIL, HISS, RAGE, STEW

sizzling HOT

Skagerrak
~ **port** OSLO

Skagit TRIBE

Skagway
~ **state** ALASKA

skald BARD, POET

Skaneateles LAKE

skat GAME
low card in ~ SEVEN

skate RAY, SLIDE
~ **blade part** EDGE
~ **on thin ice** BEARD, RISK

___ **skate** BOB, ICE

skater
~ **hangout** RINK
~ **leap** AXEL
~ **requirement** ICE, RINK
~ **spin** CAMEL
fictional ~ HANS

skates
lad with silver ~ HANS

skating
figure ~ **event** PAIRS
pairs ~ **event** EVENT

___ **skating** SPEED

Skaw CAPE

sked
~ **abbr.** ARR
~ **approximation** ETA

skedaddle DART, DASH, FLEE, HIE,
LAM, LEAVE, RACE, RUN, SCAT,
SCRAM, SPEED

"Skedaddle!" GIT, SCAT, SCRAM,
SHOO

skeet GAME

skein
~ **unit** GOOSE

skeletal LANK, LEAN
~ **material** BONE

skeleton BONE, CAGE, SHELL
~ **crew** CADRE
~ **starter** ENDO

skeleton ___ KEY

"Skeleton ___" CREW

skelter
helter ~ ABOUT

Skelton RED
~ **character** CLEM
~ **persona** HOBO
~ **script-writing wife** EDNA

skeptic
~ **remark** BAH

skeptical LEERY

skerrick BIT

sketch DRAW, MAP, PLAN, TRACE
comic ~ SKIT
literary ~ CAMEO
thumbnail ~ BIO

skew BEND, SLANT, TILT, VEER

skewbald HORSE

skewer PIN, STAB
kabob ~ SPIT

ski SLIDE
~ **gear** BIB, POLE
~ **maneuver** STEM
~ **resort** ALTA, ASPEN, TAHOE
~ **resort equipment** TBAR
~ **resort need** SNOW
~ **run** TRAIL
~ **slope** RUN
~ **slope machine** TOW
~ **tow** TBAR
~ **wood** ASH
downhill ~ **run** SLOPE

ski ___ BOOT, MASK, POLE, RUN,
TOW

___ **ski** WATER

___-**ski** APRES

___ **Ski** JET

skid SLEW, SLIDE, SLIP, SLUE
~ **starter** ANTI, NON

skid-prone ICY

skier
~ **auto adjunct** RACK
~ **destination** ALPS, ALTA,
ASPEN, TAHOE
~ **milieu** SLOPE
~ **need** SNOW
~ **peak** ALP
~ **snow** CORN
~ **transport** TBAR
~ **turn** STEM
Olympian ~ MOE

"___ Skies" BLUE

**"skies they were ___ and sober,
The"** ASHEN

skiff BOAT
~ **tool** OAR
use a ~ ROW

skiing
~ **spot** ALPS, ALTA, ASPEN,
TAHOE

skill TRADE
~ **in Italian** ARTE
~ **(suffix)** SHIP
creative ~ ART
empath's ~ ESP
having ~ ABLE
mediator's ~ TACT
office ~ STENO
unexplained ~ ESP

skilled ABLE, ADEPT
~ **team** CADRE
~ **worker** TECH
~ **workmanship** ART
highly ~ DEFT

skillet DISH, PAN
use a ~ FRY, SAUTE

skillful ABLE, ADEPT, APT, DEFT, GOOD

skillfulness EASE

skills
basic ~ ABCS
improve, as ~ HONE

ski lodge
~ **instructor** PRO

skim DIP, FLIT, READ, SAIL, SKIP, SLIDE
~ **along** FLIT, MOVE
~ **through** SCAN

skimmer HAT
what a ~ **skims** CREAM, FAT

skim milk
~ **lack** FAT

skimp EKE, STINT

skimpy FEW, MEAN, POOR, SMALL, SPARSE

skin CASE, FUR, HIDE, ORGAN, PARE, PEEL, PELT, RIND
~ **and bones** LANK, POOR, SPARE, THIN
~ **cream** TONER
~ **feature** PORE
~ **lotion ingredient** ALOE
~ **problem** ACNE, RASH
~ **shrinker** ALUM
~ **starter** DOE, KID
animal ~ HIDE, PELT
animal ~ **sometimes** RUG
get under someone's
~ ANGER, IRK, PEEVE, RILE, UPSET
hardened ~ HORN

skin-___ DEEP

"Skin ___" GAME

skinflinty MEAN, SMALL

skinned RAW

___-skinned THIN

Skinner OTIS

"___ Skinner Blues" MULE

skinny DIRT, INFO, LANK, LEAN, REEDY, SPARE, THIN

"Skin of ___ Teeth, The" OUR

skins
tent of ~ TEPEE

'Skins ELEVEN, TEAM
~ **org.** NFL

skintight CLOSE

skip CAPER, DANCE, EVADE, HOP, LEAP, LEAVE, LOPE, MISS, OMIT, ROMP, RUN
~ **about** LARK
~ **meals** FAST
~ **over** CLEAR, PASS
~ **past commercials** ZAP
~ **sweets** DIET
~ **syllables** ELIDE
~ **town** ELOPE, FLEE, LEAVE, RUN

skip ___ BAIL, ROPE

___, skip, and a jump HOP

skipper LEAD
~ **of song** LOU
~ **okay** AYE
~ **place** HELM

"Skip to My ___" LOU

skirl PIPE

skirmish MELEE, RAID, ROW, SETTO, TILT
set for a ~ ARMED
verbal ~ SPAT

skirt AVOID, EDGE, EVADE, FLAP
~ **accessory** BELT
~ **edge** HEM
~ **feature** DART, GORE, PLEAT, SLIT
~ **length** MIDI, MINI
~ **part** GORE
~ **starter** MINI
~ **style** ALINE
alter a ~ SEW
short ~ MINI
shorten a ~ ALTER
work on a ~ HEM

"Skirts ___" AHOY

skit ACT

skitter SKID

skittish EDGY, LEERY, SHY

skittles GAME
beer and ~ PLAY

"Skoal!" TOAST

skosh BIT, IOTA, TAD

skua BIRD

skulk CREEP, SLIP, SNEAK, STEAL
~ **about** SNEAK

skull BONE

skullcap HAT
mad-dog ~ PLANT

skunk ANIMAL, ROUT
~ **defense** ODOR, SCENT

Skunk River
city on the ~ AMES

sky SPACE
~ **blue** AZURE

~ **color** AZURE, BLUE
~ **ender** CAP, LARK, LINE
~ **light** MOON, STAR, SUN
~ **pilot** PADRE
~ **sign** ARIES
~ **to a poet** ETHER
blow ~ **high** BLAST
clear ~ ETHER
Egyptian ~ **goddess** NUT
fall from the ~ HAIL, RAIN, SNOW
the ~ **maybe** LIMIT
toward the ~ ABOVE
up in the ~ AERIAL

sky ___ BLUE, PILOT

sky-___ CAM

"___ Sky" BLUE

"___ Sky, The" BIG

"___ Sky at Morning" RED

skycap
~ **concern** BAG

SkyDome ARENA

Skye IONE, ISLE

sky-high AERIAL, ALOFT, TALL

skyjack STEAL

Skylab
~ **org.** NASA

skylark BIRD, PLAY
emulate a ~ SOAR

Skylark AUTO, CAR

"___ Skylark" TOA

skylarking PLAY

skylight
~ **site** ROOF

skylighted
~ **areas** ATRIA

skyline
~ **feature** SPIRE

skylit
~ **courts** ATRIA

skyrocket RISE, SOAR

skyscraper
like a ~ TALL

"Sky's the ___, The" LIMIT

Skywalker, Luke HERO

skyward ALOFT

S&L
~ **deposit** ACCT
~ **device** ATM
~ **offering** IRA
~ **offerings** CDS
~ **payment** INT
part of ~ LOAN

slab SLICE

slack COAL, EASE, LIMP, LOOSE, SLOW
~ **off** EBB, LOAF, REST
lacking ~ TAUT

slacken ABATE, ALLAY, DROP, EASE, FADE, LAG, REMIT
~ **off** ABATE

slacker
~ **opposite** DOER

slack-jawed AGAPE, AGOG

slacks
~ **specification** LONG

slake ABATE, ALLAY

slalom EVENT, RACE
~ **curve** ESS
~ **marker** GATE
~ **need** SKI
~ **site** SLOPE

___ slalom GIANT

slam BANG, CLAP, DASH, HIT
grand ~ HOMER

slam ___ DANCE

slam-___ BANG

slam dunk SHOT

slammer CAN, PEN, STIR
the ~ STIR

"Slammin' Sammy" SNEAD

slander LIBEL, SHAME, SLUR, SMEAR, TAINT

slang ARGOT, CANT, IDIOM
criminals' ~ ARGOT

slangy
~ **suffix** AROO, EROO, ESE, OLA

slant ANGLE, BIAS, COLOR, HEEL, LEAN, LIE, LIST, PHASE, SKEW, SLOPE, TILT
~ **down** DIP
~ **upward** RISE
on a ~ AWRY

slanted
~ **type** ITAL

slanting ATILT, AWRY
~ **cut** BIAS
~ **surface** RAMP

slap BANG, BAT, BEAT, HIT, SLAM, SMITE
~ **in the face** BARB, CUT, DIG, SNUB
~ **on** ADD, CLAP, DAUB, TAG
~ **someone's face** BEARD
~ **the cuffs on** ARREST, NAB
~ **together** MAKE, REAR

"Slap ___" SHOT

slapdash LOOSE

slapper
high-five ~ PALM

___-slapper KNEE

slapstick GENRE
~ **prop** PIE

slash CLAW, CUT, EMEND, GASH, HACK, MAIM, PARE, RENT, RIP, SCORE, SLIT

slash ___ PINE

slat LATH, PALE

slate AGENDA, COLOR, LIST, STONE
~ **once** SHALE
clean ~ **need** ERASER
make a clean ~ ERASE

slated DUE

Slaughter ENOS

"Slaughterhouse ___" FIVE

"Slaughter on ___ Avenue" TENTH

Slav SERB

slave
~ **away** LABOR, TOIL
~ **relative** SERF
ancient ~ ESNE
operatic ~ AIDA
work like a ~ PLOD

slave ___ ANT

slaver SPIT

Slavic
~ **sovereign** TSAR

___ **slaw** COLE

sleazeball SLIME

sleazy LOW, MEAN, POOR, SEEDY

sled SLIDE, TOY

sled ___ DOG

sledding
~ **surface** SLOPE, SNOW

sledge MAUL, SKID, SLED

sledgehammer RAM

sleek TRIM
~ **in car lingo** AERO
~ **plane** SST

sleep NAP, REST
~ **at one's post** LOAF
~ **cycle** REM
~ **disturber** NOISE
~ **in a tent** CAMP
~ **inducer** OPIATE
~ **noisily** SNORE
~ **out** CAMP
~ **restlessly** TOSS
~ **scene** DREAM
~ **spoiler** ALARM
deep ~ COMA
go to ~ BED, NOD
place to ~ BED, INN
put to ~ BORE

sleep ___ ONIT

___ **sleep** REM

"___ Sleep, The" BIG

sleeper CAR, TRAIN
~ **maybe** SOFA
~ **racket** SNORE
legendary ~ RIP

"Sleeper"
~ **director** ALLEN

sleeping ABED
~ **place** BED
no longer ~ ASTIR

sleeping ___ BAG, CAR

"Sleeping ___, The" TIGER

"___ Sleeping Beauty" TOA

sleeping sickness
~ **carrier** TSETSE

"___ Sleep in the Subway" DONT

"Sleepless in Seattle"
~ **actress** RYAN
Tom's ~ **costar** MEG

sleep like ___ ATOP

sleep like a ___ TOP

"Sleep My ___" LOVE

"___ Sleeps Tonight, The" LION

sleepy TIRED
get ~ NOD

Sleepy
~ **colleague** DOC

Sleepy Hollow
~ **schoolmaster** CRANE

"Sleepy" John ESTES

"___ Sleepy People" TWO

"Sleepy Time ___" GAL

sleet ICE, STORM
~ **essentially** ICE

sleeve
~ **edge** HEM
~ **filler** ARM
it may be up one's ~ ACE
wear one's heart on one's
~ ADORE

sleeveful
cheater's ~ ACE

sleeveless
~ **blouse** SHELL
~ **cloak** ABA
~ **top** VEST

sleeves
roll up one's ~ START

sleigh SLED
~ **driver** SANTA

sleight of ___ HAND

Sleipnir HORSE, STEED
~ **owner** ODIN

slender FINE, LANK, LEAN, SLIM, SMALL, THIN, TRIM
~ **shoot** WAND

slept like ___ ATOP

slept like a ___ TOP

sleuth TEC
~ **cry** AHA
~ **find** CLUE
~ **game** CLUE
~ **job** CASE
four-legged ~ ASTA
Keene ~ DREW

kiddie-lit ~ DREW

slew HEAP, LOT, OCEAN, PILE, RAFT, SEA, WADS

"___ Slew-Foot" OLE

slice CHIP, CHOP, CUT, GASH, HACK, PART
~ **(off)** LOP
generous ~ SLAB
unpopular ~ END

slice of ___ LIFE

slicer
~ **place** DELI

slick GLIB, ICY, NEAT, OILY, PAT, SLEEK, SLY, SUAVE
~ **contents** OIL
~ **publication** MAG
not ~ CRASS

___ **slick** OIL

slicker COAT, MAC, WRAP
city ~ DUDE
Soho ~ MAC

___ **slicker** CITY

"___ Slickers" CITY

slide LAPSE, SKATE, SKID, SLIP, STEAL
~ **by** ELAPSE
~ **on snow** SKI
~ **over** ELIDE
let ~ OMIT

slide ___ RULE

slider
~ **objective** BASE

"___ Slidin' Away" SLIP

slight CUT, FINE, MERE, SLIM, SLUR, SMALL, SNUB, THIN, TINY, TOKEN
~ **amount** HINT
~ **coloring** TINT
~ **degree** SHADE, TINGE
~ **depression** DIP
~ **fight** SPAT
~ **impression** DENT
~ **progress** DENT
~ **sound** PEEP
~ **trace** SCENT, TINGE

"Slight ___ of Murder, A" CASE

slightest LEAST
~ **suggestion** HINT

Sligo
~ **locale** EIRE, ERIN

slim LEAN, SMALL, THIN, TRIM
~ **down** DIET, LOSE
~ **pickings** FEW

slime DIRT, GOO, MIRE, OOZE, SLOP

sling CAST, DASH, HANG, HURL
~ **mud** SLUR

slingshot
~ **part** STRAP

slink EDGE, SLIP, SNEAK, STEAL

slinker
silent-screen ~ SIREN

Slinky COIL, TOY

slip CLAY, ERR, ERROR, KNOT, LAPSE, PLANT, SHOOT, SKID, SLIDE, STEAL, TRIP
~ **a cog** ERR
~ **away from** ELUDE
~ **behind** LAG
~ **by** ELAPSE, PASS
~ **ender** CASE, KNOT, OVER, SHOD, STREAM
~ **into** DON, DRESS, WEAR
~ **of the pen** ERROR
~ **one over on** DUPE
~ **past** ELUDE
~ **starter** COW, SIDE
~ **up** ERR, LAPSE, MISS, NOD
give the ~ **to** AVOID, ELUDE, EVADE, LOSE
let ~ BLAB, LEAK, MISS, TELL
let ~ **through one's fingers** LOSE
moral ~ LAPSE
pink ~ SACK

slip- ___ UPS

___ **slip (divulge)** LET

slip a ___ COG

slipknot NOOSE

slipped
it's sometimes ~ COG

slipper SHOE
backless ~ MULE

"Slipper and the ___, The" ROSE

slippery EELY, OILY, SLY
~ **coating** SLIME
~ **in a way** ICY
~ **one** EEL
~ **surface** ICE
make ~ OIL

slippery ___ ELM, SLOPE

slippery ___ **eel** ASAN

slippery as an ___ EEL

slipshod LOOSE, MESSY, POOR

"Slip Slidin' ___" AWAY

slip-up ERROR, LAPSE

slit CUT, GAP, GASH, HOLE, LANCE, RENT, RIP, SCORE, SLASH, SPLIT

slither SLIDE, SLIP, STEAL
~ **slyly** SIDLE

slitherer SNAKE
African ~ ASP

slithery EELY
~ **swimmer** EEL

sliver BIT, CHIP, CUT, PART, SCRAP, SHRED, TAG

"Sliver"
~ **actress** STONE

slivovitz
~ **maker** SERB

slob BOOR, LOUT

slobber SPIT

sloe ___ fizz GIN

slog PATH, STEP, TRAIL, TREAD, WADE
  ~ along PLOD
  ~ through WADE

slogan CRY, SAW
  ~ maker ADMAN

sloop BOAT, SHIP
  ~ pole MAST
  yon ~ HER, SHE

slop DIRT, OOZE

slope LEAN, LIST, RAMP, RISE, SLANT, TILT
  ~ downward DIP
  ~ transportation TBAR
  bare rocky ~ SCAR
  gentle ~ RISE
  Highlands ~ BRAE
  hill ~ SIDE
  ski ~ RUN

sloped
  ~ pathway RAMP

slopes
  hit the ~ SKI
  negotiate the ~ SLED

sloping AWRY
  sharply ~ STEEP

slopping
  ~ over the sides AWASH

sloppy MESSY, POOR
  ~ brushstroke SMEAR
  ~ spot STY
  ~ stuff GOO

sloppy ___ JOE

slosh DASH, LAP
  ~ about WADE

slot HOLE
  ~ filler TAB
  appointment-book ~ HOUR
  cast ~ ROLE
  radio ~ STA
  ship's ~ SLIP

sloth ANIMAL, BEAR, SIN
  ~ home TREE
  two-toed ~ UNAU

slothful IDLE

sloths AIS

slot machine
  ~ feature ARM
  ~ input COIN

slots
  ~ city RENO

slotted
  ~ box CRATE

slouch BOOR, LEAN, LIE, LOLL

slouching
  not ~ ERECT

slough MIRE
  ~ off DROP, SHED

Slovak SLAV

slovenly MESSY

slow DENSE, LATE
  ~ down CLOG, DETER, LAG, STEM, TIRE
  ~ in music LENTO
  ~ mover SNAIL
  ~ moving beasts OXEN
  ~ on the uptake DENSE, DIM
  ~ pitch LOB
  ~ run TROT
  ~ tempo LENTO
  ~ train LOCAL
  ~ up CLOG, LAG
  go ~ PLOD
  its pace is ~ SNAIL
  on a ~ boat to China ASEA, ATSEA
  signal to ~ AMBER

"Slow" SIGN

"___ Slow Boat to China" ONA

slow burn
  do a ~ REACT, STEW

slower
  ~ than andante LENTO

slowness
  epitome of ~ SNAIL

slowpoke SNAIL
  ~ opposite RACER

slow-witted DENSE, DIM

sludge DIRT, OOZE, SLIME, SLOP

slue VEER

slug BALL, BANG, BAT, BEAT, HIT, JAB, LAM, PEST, SHOT, SLAP, SMITE
  ~ cousin SNAIL
  ~ of hooch BELT

slugabed DRONE, IDLER

sluggard DRONE, IDLER

slugger AARON, OTT, RUTH
  ~ stat HRS, RBI
  ~ tool BAT

Slugger
  Louisville ~ BAT

sluggish IDLE, INERT, SLOW

sluggishness ENNUI

sluice RACE, RUN, STREAM

slumber NAP, REST, SLEEP

slumbering ABED

slumgullion HASH, STEW

slump FLAG, LAPSE, LEAN, LIE, LOLL, SAG, SINK, SLIP

slums
  ~ Mother TERESA

slur DIG, LIBEL, SHAME, SMEAR, TAINT
  ~ over ELIDE

slurp LAP

slush SLOP

sly ARCH, FALSE
  ~ look LEER

Sly STONE

Slyne Head
  ~ locale EIRE

sm.
  bigger than ~ MED

Sm ELEM
  62 for ~ ATNO

sma WEE

smack BAT, BEAT, BELT, BOAT, CHOP, CLAP, CLIP, DASH, HIT, KISS, PELT, SAVOR, SHIP, SLAM, SLAP, SMASH, SMITE, TASTE
  ~ ender EROO

smack-___ DAB

smack-dab BANG

smackeroo BANG

smackeroos
  five ~ FIN

small MEAN, SIZE, SLIM, TEENY, WEE
  ~ (prefix) MINI, NANO
  ~ (suffix) ETTE, LET, ULE

small ___ FRY, TALK

small-___ SCALE

"Small Back ___, The" ROOM

smaller LESS
  ~ than UNDER

smallest LEAST
  ~ pup RUNT

"Smallest ___ on Earth, The" SHOW

"Smallest Show on ___, The" EARTH

small-minded MEAN

smallmouth ___ BASS

small-time MEAN

small-town LOCAL

"Small Town ___" GIRL

"Small world, ___ it?" ISNT

"___ Small World" ITSA

smaltite ORE

smarmy OILY

smart ABLE, ACHE, ACUTE, CHIC, KEEN, NEW, PAIN, PANG, STING
  ~ dully ACHE
  ~ talk SASS
  more than ~ ACHE
  not ~ DENSE, DIM, SLOW
  unusually ~ APT

smart ___ ALEC, CARD

smart ___ whip ASA

"___ Smart" GET

smart-alecky FLIP, PERT, SASSY

"___ Smart Girls" THREE

smarting SORE
  ~ off LIP

Smart, Maxwell AGENT, SPY
  ~ portrayer ADAMS

smartness STYLE

smarts SENSE

smash DASH, HIT, MASH, RAM, RAZE, ROUT, RUIN, SHOT, SLAM, STAVE
  ~ ender EROO
  ~ into RAM
  ~ letters SRO
  box-office ~ HIT

___ smasher ATOM

"___ Smasher" (1940s serial) SPY

smashing
  find ~ ADORE, LOVE

smattering FEW, TINGE

smear BLUR, DAB, DAUB, LIBEL, SHAME, SOIL, SPOT, TAINT
  ~ in print LIBEL
  dirty ~ SMUT
  ink ~ BLOT

Smee MATE

smell AROMA, ODOR, SCENT, SENSE
  ~ detector NOSE
  bad ~ REEK
  sense of ~ NOSE
  sweet ~ BALM

smell ___ (be suspicious) ARAT

smelling ___ SALTS

"___ Smell of Success" SWEET

"Smells Like ___ Spirit" TEEN

smelly RANK

smelt FIRE, FUSE, HEAT

smeltery
  ~ input ORE
  ~ leftover SLAG

smew BIRD

smidgen ATOM, BIT, DAB, DASH, DROP, IOTA, JOT, MITE, SNIP, TAD, TINGE, TRACE

smile BEAM, GRIN
  ~ at GREET
  ~ upon BLESS
  a certain ~ LEER
  bring a ~ to AMUSE
  derisive ~ SNEER

"Smile"
  ~ actor DERN

"___ Smile" SARA

"Smiles ___ Summer Night" OFA

Smiley AGENT, SPY

Smiley, Jane
  ~ novel of 1995 MOO

smiling RIANT

smirch BLOT, DAUB, SLUR, SMEAR, TAINT

smirk SMILE, SNEER
~ **cousin** LEER

smitch BIT

smite BANG, BEAT, HIT, SLAP, SLAY, ZAP

smith
~ **starter** GUN, SONG, TIN
did a ~'s job SHOD

Smith ADAM, BOB, IAN, KATE, LEE, RED, STAN
~ **and others** ALS

Smith, Adam SCOT

"___ Smith and Jones" ALIAS

Smith Brother
~ **feature** BEARD

Smith Brothers
~ **unit** DROP

smithereen ATOM, SCRAP

smithereens ATOMS

Smith, Hannibal
~ **and company** ATEAM

Smith, John
~ **perhaps** ALIAS

Smith, Lee
stat for ~ ERA

Smith, Maggie DAME

Smithsonian
~ **diamond** HOPE
part of the ~ INST
work in the ~ maybe RESTORE

smithsonite ORE

Smith & Wesson GUN

smithy
~ **item** SHOE

smitten
~ **(with)** TAKEN
be ~ LOVE

smock APRON, COAT, WRAP

smog DIRT
sans ~ CLEAR

smoke COLOR, CURE, DIRT, GAS, SPEED, TREE
~ **detector** ALARM
~ **out** PRY
go up in ~ LOSE

"Smoke ___ in Your Eyes" GETS

smoked
~ **meat** HAM
~ **salmon** NOVA

"Smoke Gets in Your ___" EYES

smoker
~ **item** PIPE
~ **relative** STAG

smokestack PIPE

Smokey BEAR

"Smokey ___ the Bandit" AND

smoking ___ GUN

"Smoking or ___?" NON

smoky
~ **quartz** GEM

smoky-smelling ACRID

smolder BOIL

smoldering LIVE
~ **remnant** EMBER

smooch CARESS, KISS, NECK

smooth BALD, CALM, COMB, EASE, EASY, EVEN, FILE, FLAT, GLIB, IRON, PAT, PLANE, RAKE, SAND, SLEEK, SUAVE
~ **dessert** FLAN
~ **out** EVEN, IRON
~ **sailing** EASY
~ **the way** EASE
~ **wood** SAND
make ~ OIL, SAND

smooth as ___ SATIN, SILK

smoother ADZE

smoothness
exemplar of ~ SATIN, SILK

"Smooth Operator"
~ **singer** SADE

smooth-pated BALD

smooth-talking OILY

smooth-tongued GLIB

smorgasbord MEAL
~ **fan** EATER
~ **item** HAM, PASTA, ROAST, SALAD
enjoy a ~ EAT

smother DAMP, GAG

Smothers TOM

Smothers Brothers DUO, PAIR

Smothers, Tom
~ **hobby** YOYO

smudge BLOT, BLUR, DAUB, DIRT, SMEAR, SMUT, SOIL, SPOT, TAINT
Lenten forehead ~ ASH

smudged INKY

smug
~ **one** PRIG

smuggle RUN, SNEAK, STEAL

smugness PRIDE

smut DIRT, MOLD

smutch BLOT, TAINT

Smuts, Jan BOER

Smyrna
site of ancient ~ IONIA

Sn ELEM
50 for ~ ATNO

snack BITE, NOSH
~ **joint** DELI
~ **on** EAT

aardvark ~ ANT
black-and-white ~ OREO
cantina ~ TACO
chipmunk ~ ACORN
crunchy ~ CHIP
dog ~ BONE
have a ~ EAT
more than a ~ MEAL
pangolin's ~ ANT
squirrel ~ ACORN
sunflower ~ SEED

snack ___ BAR, TABLE

snafu ERROR, MESS, SNARL

snag GRAB, NAB, RUN, SNARL, SPUR
hidden ~ TRAP
stocking ~ RUN

snail
~ **home** SHELL
going at a ~'s pace SLOW
like a ~ SLOW
move at a ~'s pace DRAG, LAG

___ snail SEA, TREE

___ snail's pace ATA

snake ADDER, ASP, BOA, COBRA, RACER
~ **charmer's partner** COBRA
~ **covering** SCALE
~ **dancers** HOPI
~ **on Pharaoh's headdress** ASP
~ **shape** ESS
~ **sound** HISS, SSS
African ~ ASP, COBRA
hooded ~ COBRA
jungle ~ BOA
make like a ~ COIL
milk ~ ADDER
Old World ~ ASP, COBRA
poisonous ~ ADDER, ASP, COBRA
quick ~ RACER

snake ___ DANCE, EYES, OIL, PIT, PLANT

___ snake CORAL

"Snake ___, The" PIT

"Snake Eater"
~ **actor** LAMAS

snake eyes
~ **maker** DICE
roll ~ LOSE

snakelike EELY
~ **fish** EEL

snake oil
~ **purportedly** CURE

Snake River
~ **state** IDAHO

snaky
~ **character** ESS
~ **shape** COIL
~ **swimmer** EEL

snap BEAN, BITE, CLASP, ELAN, NIP, SHOOT, SHOT
~ **a picture** TAKE
~ **(at)** SNARL
a ~ EASY

snap-brim HAT

snapper
photo ~ CAMERA

___ snapper RED

snappish BAD, EDGY, IRATE, TART, TESTY, UPSET

snappy CRISP, PERT, RACY, SMART
make it ~ HIE, SPEED

snapshot IMAGE

snare BAG, GIN, NAB, NOOSE, TRAP, WEB

snarl GNAR, KNOT, RAVEL, ROAR
freeway ~ JAM

snarling EDGY, RUDE, TESTY

snatch GET, GRAB, GRASP, NAB, ROB, STEAL

snazzy CHIC, POSH

Snead SAM
~ **org.** PGA

sneak CREEP, SLIP, STEAL
~ **along** SIDLE
~ **a look** PEEP
~ **a peek** PRY
~ **off** DESERT, EVADE
~ **something to eat** NOSH

sneaker SHOE
~ **brand** PUMA
~ **need** LACE
~ **part** SOLE, TOE

sneakers
open, as ~ UNTIE

"Sneak Previews"
~ **critic** EBERT

sneaky SLY

sneaky ___ PETE

sneer HOOT
~ **at** GIBE

sneeze
react to a ~ BLESS

Sneezy
~ **colleague** DOC

snick CHIP, SNIP

snick-a-___ SNEE

snicker SNEER, TEHEE
~ **ender** SNEE

Snickers BAR

snick or ___ SNEE

snide
~ **comment** BARB

Snider DEE
~ **teammate** REESE

sniff SCENT
~ **around** NOSE, PRY
~ **out** SEEK

sniffed
  something ~ AROMA, ODOR

sniffle SOB

sniffles
  have the ~ AIL

sniggler
  ~ quarry EEL

snip CUT, LOP, NIP, TAG
  ~ and tuck ALTER

snipe BIRD
  ~ (at) FIRE

snippet BIT, CHIP, CLIP, PART,
  SCRAP, SHRED, SNIP, TAG
  alphabet ~ ABC, RST, STU

snit
  in a ~ IRATE, MAD, SORE,
  UPSET
  put in a ~ ANGER, IRK, PEEVE,
  RILE, UPSET

snitch BLAB, NIP, RAT, RATON, ROB,
  SING, STEAL, TELL

snivel BAWL, CRY, MOAN, SOB,
  WEEP

SNL
  part of ~ LIVE

Sno-___ CAT, CONE

snobbery AIRS

snobs
  ~ put-on AIRS

snood NET
  ~ site HAIR

snooker CON, DUPE, GAME, POOL
  ~ requirement CUE

snookums DEAR, HON

snoop NOSE, PRY, SPY
  prone to ~ NOSY

Snoop Doggy Dogg
  ~ music RAP

snoopy NOSY

Snoopy
  ~ aviator enemy BARON
  ~ brother OLAF
  ~ sister BELLE

"Snoopy, ___ Home" COME

"Snoopy, Come ___" HOME

snoot NOSE

snootiness AIRS

snooty ALOOF
  ~ attitude AIRS
  ~ sort SNOB

snooze NAP, REST, SLEEP
  take a ~ REST

snoozing ABED

snore
  ~ symbol ZEE

Snorkel SGT

snorkeler
  ~ view CORAL

Snorkel, Sergeant
  ~ bulldog OTTO

snort GASP, NIP, REACT, SHOT
  ~ of derision HAH
  ~ of disgust UGH

snorting
  ~ starter RIP

snout NOSE

snouted
  ~ beast TAPIR

snow DUPE, STORM
  ~ ender BALL, BIRD, CAP,
  DROP, MAN, MELT, SHOE,
  STORM, SUIT
  ~ glider SLED
  ~ job LIE, TALE
  ~ leopard OUNCE
  ~ remover PLOW
  ~ runner SKI
  ~ toy SLED
  like driven ~ PURE
  navigate on ~ SKI
  skier's ~ CORN

snow ___ CONE, CRAB, DAY,
  GOOSE, LINE, PEA, TIRE

snow ___ (overwhelm) UNDER

___ snow CORN

Snow ___ BELT

snowball GROW, RISE
  ~ sometimes AMMO

"Snow-Bound" POEM

snow country
  ~ transport SKI

snowfall STORM
  ~ measure INCH

"Snow Maiden, The" OPERA

snowman
  ~ wear HAT, PIPE, SCARF
  abominable ~ YETI

Snowmass
  enjoy ~ SKI

snowmobiler RIDER

snowshoe
  ~ alternative SKI

"Snowstorm, The" POEM

Snow White
  ~ friend DOC

**"Snow White and the ___
  Dwarfs"** SEVEN

snowy CLEAN, PURE

snowy ___ EGRET, OWL

snub CUT, SHUN

snub-___ NOSED

snub-nosed
  ~ dog PEKE

snuff
  bring back to ~ REHAB
  not be up to ~ AIL
  not up to ~ ILL, OFF, POOR
  up to ~ ABLE, FIT

___ snuff UPTO

snuffle SNORT

"Snuffy Smith"
  ~ baby TATER

snug CLOSE
  ~ bug locale RUG
  ~ spot NEST

"Snug ___ bug..." ASA

snuggle CARESS, PET, PRESS

Snyder TOM

so ERGO, THEN, THUS
  ~ in Latin SIC
  ~ much as EVEN
  ~ to Descartes ERGO

so ___ (yet) FAR

___ so (exceedingly) EVER

"___ so!" TAINT

___-so (authority) SAY

"...so ___ as a day in June?"
  RARE

"So ___" BIG, FINE

"So ___" (Jimmy Dorsey tune)
  RARE

"So ___!" LONG

"So ___ and yet..." NEAR

"So ___ at the Fair" LONG

"So ___ Is New York" THIS

"So ___ Is Paris" THIS

"So ___ My Love" EVIL

"So ___ Our Night" ENDS

"So ___ to My Heart" DEAR

"So!" AHA

soak BATHE, BREW, DIP, ROOK,
  STEEP, STING, WET
  ~ fibers RET
  ~ through SEEP
  ~ up BLOT, SOP
  ~ up some sun BASK

soaked WET

soaking BATH

soap CLEAN
  ~ additive ALOE
  ~ bar CAKE
  ~ bubbles FOAM
  ~ enemy DIRT
  ~ ingredient LYE
  ~ opera DRAMA
  ~ unit BAR, CAKE
  big name in ~ IVORY
  NBC ~ to fans DAYS
  remove ~ RINSE
  TV ~ DRAMA

soap ___ OPERA, PLANT

"Soap"
  ~ family name TATE

soapbark TREE

soapbox
  ~ derby RACE
  mount a ~ ORATE

Soap Box Derby
  ~ site AKRON

soapmaker
  ~ need LYE

soap opera
  ~ (abbr.) SER

soapstone TALC

soar ARISE, KITE, LEAP, LOOM,
  RISE, SAIL

soarer
  sea ~ ERN, ERNE

soaring AERIAL, ALOFT

soave WINE
  land of ~ ITALY
  like ~ SEC

sob BAWL, CRY, MOAN, WEEP

"So be it" AMEN

sober STAID

"So Big"
  ~ director WISE

sobriquet LABEL, NAME, TAG

soc. ASSN

soccer
  ~ goal NET
  ~ score GOAL
  ~ squad ELEVEN
  ~ star of Brazil PELE
  ~ target GOAL

soccer game
  ~ fraction HALF

soccer shoe
  ~ feature CLEAT

sociable SWEET

social
  ~ asset TACT
  ~ calendar LIST
  ~ climber SNOB
  ~ elite ALIST, CREAM
  ~ ender ISM, IST, ITE
  ~ gathering BEE, DANCE,
  LEVEE, SOIREE
  ~ group CLAN, GANG, SET
  ~ insect ANT, BEE
  ~ misfit NERD
  ~ occasion TEA
  ~ pariah CREEP
  ~ presentee DEB
  ~ sci. ECO, ECON
  ~ starter ANTI
  ~ status ESTATE
  ~ stink FLAP
  ~ stratum CASTE, CLASS,
  ELITE, SPHERE
  ~ wedge ENTREE
  box ~ EVENT

Socialist
five-time ~ candidate DEBS

socialistic LEFT

socialite
teen ~ DEB

socialize
~ with KNOW

Social Register LIST
~ folk ALIST, CREAM, ELITE
~ word NEE

societal
~ unit CLAN

society CLAN, ORDER
~ (abbr.) ASSN
~ girl DEB
Chinese secret ~ TONG
dregs of ~ MOB
high ~ ELITE
secret ~ BAND, CABAL, ORDER,
RING

___ society CAFE, HONOR

___ Society (LBJ program) GREAT

society column
~ word NEE

"Society's Child"
~ singer IAN

sock BANG, BAT, BEAT, BELT, CHOP,
HIT, JAB, LAM, SLAP, SMITE
~ away HIDE, SAVE
~ ender EROO
~ hop DANCE
~ material LISLE
~ part FOOT, HEEL, TOE

sock ___ HOP

___ sock CREW, KNEE

sockdolager END, LULU, ONER

socket
it fits in a ~ EYE

**"Sock it ___!" ("Laugh-In" catch
phrase)** TOME

socks HOSE
~ purchase PAIR
fix ~ DARN, MEND
knock one's ~ off AMAZE,
AWE, STUN, WOW

___ socks KNEE

Socks CAT, PET
~ sound MEOW, MEW
~ to Chelsea CAT, PET

socle BASE, FOOT, REST

"___ So Cold" SHES

Socrates
~ pupil PLATO
see also Greek

Socratic ___ IRONY

Soc. Sec.
~ collectors SRS
on ~ RET

sod EARTH, LAND

soda POP
~ accessory STRAW
~ buy CAN, CASE, LITER
**~ fountain, in New
England** SPA
~ order DIET
~ pop COLA

soda ___ ASH, POP, WATER

___ soda CREAM, DIET, SAL

soda fountain
~ treat COLA, MALT

sodality BAND, CLAN, ORDER

sodden DAMP, WET

"So Dear to My ___" HEART

sodium METAL
~ chloride SALT
~ hydroxide LYE

Sodom
~ escapee LOT

"___ So Easy" ITS

"So Ends ___ Night" OUR

"So Evil My ___" LOVE

"So Evil My Love"
~ director ALLEN

sofa SEAT
~ part ARM
converted ~ BED
medium-sized ~ SETTEE

sofa ___ BED

"So far ___ can tell..." ASI

"so few"
Churchill's ~ RAF

"___ So Few" NEVER

"___ Soffel" MRS

soffit
~ location EAVE

Sofia CITY

"___ So Fine" HES

soft LIMP, LOW, MILD, RIPE
~ approach SELL
~ cheese BRIE, FETA
~ color LILAC
~ drink ADE, COLA, POP, SODA,
TAB
~ ender WARE
~ hat BERET, TAM
~ in French BAS
~ in music PIANO
~ light GLOW
~ metal TIN
~ mineral TALC
~ radiance GLOW
~ sound COO
~ spot in one's heart LOVE
~ stroke CARESS, PAT
~ topper BERET, TAM
~ touch DUPE
go ~ MELT, THAW
have a ~ spot for LIKE
not ~ HARD

soft ___ COAL, LENS, LINE, NEWS,
PEDAL, SELL, SOAP, SPOT,
WATER

soft-___ SHELL, SHOE, TOP

softball GAME
~ path ARC
~ team NINE

soften ABATE, ALLAY, CALM, EASE,
MELT, MOVE, MUTE, RIPEN,
TAME, THAW
~ for tanning BATE

softening
~ agent ALOE

soft-hearted MILD
become ~ MELT, THAW

softie LAMB

soft-shell CLAM, CRAB

"___ Soft Shoe, The" OLD

software
~ option list MENU
~ purchaser USER
~ test BETA
~ tycoon GATES

soggy DAMP, WET
not ~ CRISP
not quite ~ DAMP

Soglow OTTO

Soho
~ co. LTD
~ raincoat MAC
~ rental FLAT
~ stroller PRAM
see also British, English

soigné SMART

soil BLOT, DIRT, DUST, EARTH,
LAND, MAR, SMEAR, TAINT
~ additive LIME
~ aerator ROOT
~ component CLAY
~ conditioner PEAT
~ mixture LOAM
~ sweetener LIME
~ turner HOE
kind of ~ CLAY, LOAM
loose ~ DIRT
till the ~ DRESS
turn the ~ AERATE
windborne ~ LOESS

soiree BALL, FETE, GALA, LEVEE,
ROUT

Soissons
see French

sojourn ABIDE, ABODE, BIDE,
CALL, REST, STAY, STOP

sojourner TENANT

Sokolov IVAN

sol COIN, NOTE
~ followers LAS

Sol STAR, SUN

solace EASE

solar
~ cycle YEAR

~ deity ATEN, ATON
~ flare GAS
~ outburst FLARE
~ output HEAT
Egyptian ~ disk ATEN, ATON

solar ___ FLARE, PANEL

"Solar Barque"
~ author NIN

"Solaris"
~ author LEM

solar wind
~ particle ION
~ phenomenon AURORA

Soldati MARIO

solder FUSE
~ material TIN

soldering
~ tool IRON

soldier
~ addr. APO
~ break LEAVE
~ grp. USO
~ home BASE
~ in gray REB
~ position POST
~ shoe BOOT
~ wd. AWOL
**abbreviation for a former
~** RET
certain ~ ANT
Civil War ~ REB
Confederate ~ GRAY
retired ~ VET
tin ~ TOY

___ soldier FOOT

Soldier Field ARENA

"Soldier in the ___" RAIN

soldiers ARMY, GIS
body of ~ TROOP

"Soldiers ___" THREE

soldiers of fortune
~ group ATEAM

"sold out"
~ sign SRO

sole LONE, ONE, ONLY
~ attachment CLEAT
~ part TREAD
~ protector TAP

___ sole HALF

solecism ERROR
popular ~ AINT

___ Soleil (Louis XIV) LEROI

solely ALONE

solemn SEDATE, SOBER, STAID
~ assent AMEN
~ assurance OATH
~ ceremony RITE
~ word OATH
give one's ~ word ATTEST,
AVOW

solemnity POMP, STATE

solemnization RITE

solicit ASK, BEG, HIT, PLEAD
~ **information** ASK

solicitation CARE, CRY

solicitors BAR

solicitous
be ~ CARE

solicitude CARE, FEAR, LOVE

solid DENSE, GOOD, HARD, REAL, SOBER, SURE
~ **ground** EARTH, LAND
~ **hit, in baseball** LINER
~ **in physics** STATE
~ **(prefix)** STEREO
on ~ **ground** SAFE
semirigid ~ GEL

solid-___ STATE

"Solid ___ Cadillac, The" GOLD

"Solid Gold"
~ **host** DEES

solidify CAKE, CLOT, GEL, SET

solidifying
~ **agent** AGAR

solidity
lose ~ MELT, THAW

solidus COIN

soliloquist
like a ~ ALONE

soliloquize ORATE

soliloquy
~ **phrase** TOBE
sung ~ ARIA

solipsist
~ **preoccupation** SELF

solitaire GAME, GEM
how to play ~ ALONE

solitary ALONE, ALOOF, LONE, ONE, ONLY
~ **person** LONER

solleret ARMOR

solo ALONE, ARIA, LONE, SONG
~ **performer** DIVA
~ **practitioner** LONER
opera ~ ARIA

"solo"
anagram for ~ OSLO

Solo AGENT, HAN

Solo, Han HERO

Solomon
~ **queen** SHEBA
~ **to Bathsheba** SON
~ **to David** SON
like ~ WISE

"Solomon and ___" SHEBA

"Solomon and Sheba"
Yul's ~ **costar** GINA

Solon POET, SAGE
see also poet

Solo, Napoleon AGENT, HERO, SPY

"___ So Lonely" IGET

"So long!" ADIEU, BYE, CIAO, LATER, TATA
~ **in French** ADIEU
~ **in Hawaiian** ALOHA
~ **in Italian** CIAO
~ **in Latin** AVE, VALE
~ **in Spanish** ADIOS

"So Long at the ___" FAIR

Solothurn
~ **river** AAR, AARE

___-soluble FAT, WATER

solus ALONE

solution
~ **(abbr.)** ANS
acid ~ BATH
darkroom ~ TONER
hair-coloring ~ RINSE
hydroxide ~ LYE
NaOH ~ LYE

solvent
strong ~ ACID

solver
~ **need** ERASER
~ **shout** AHA

Solway Firth
~ **tributary** EDEN

Solzhenitsyn
~ **formerly** EXILE

Som.
neighbor of ~ ETH

Somalia
gulf north of ~ ADEN

somber SAD, SOBER, STAID, STERN

somberness PALL

sombrero HAT

some ANY, PART
~ **are rough** EDGES
~ **in French** DES

"Some ___ It Hot" LIKE

"Some ___ Running" CAME

"Somebody Up ___ Likes Me" THERE

"Somebody Up There Likes Me"
~ **director** WISE

somehow or ___ OTHER

"Some Like It ___" HOT

"Some of ___ Days" THESE

"Someone to Watch ___ Me" OVER

"Someone to Watch Over Me"
~ **director** SCOTT

somersault FLIP, ROLL

"___ Some Sugar on Me" POUR

something ___ ELSE

something ___ (bride's need) BLUE, NEW, OLD

___ something (scheming) UPTO

"___ something I said?" ISIT

sometime EVER, PAST

somewhat
~ **(prefix)** SEMI
~ **(suffix)** ISH

somewhere
get ~ ARRIVE

"Somewhere ___ the Line" ALONG

"Somewhere My Love"
~ **dedicatee** LARA

Somme
see French

sommelier
~ **cooler** ICER
~ **serving** WINE

Sommer ELKE

"Sommersby"
~ **actor** GERE

Sommers, Jamie
~ **bionic implant** EAR

"...so much ___ by so many to so few" OWED

son KID, LAD, MALE
~ **in Gaelic** MAC
Jr.'s ~ **perhaps** III

son ___ gun OFA

"Son ___ Sailor" OFA

"Son-___ Preacher Man" OFA

sonance TONE

sonar
~ **signal** ECHO

sonata
~ **ender** CODA
~ **movement** TRIO

song AIR, PSALM, TUNE
~ **of the 1940s** OLDIE
eighteenth-century part ~ GLEE
German art ~ LIED
syncopated ~ RAG

___ song ART, SIREN, SWAN, THEME

"___ Song" LUTE

"___ Song" (Ringo Starr tune) NONO

"___ Song, The" (Romberg work) DESERT

song and ___ DANCE

songbird CHAT, LARK, ORIOLE, WREN
colorful ~ ORIOLE

"Song Is ___, The" ENDED

"Song of Hiawatha, The" POEM

"Song of India"
~ **actor** SABU

"Song of Myself" POEM

"Song of Old Hawaii, A"
~ **accompaniment** UKE

"Song of Roland" EPIC

"Song of the Islands"
~ **director** LANG

"Song of the Open Road" POEM

"Song of the South"
~ **title** BRER

songster BIRD, LARK

songstresses
some ~ ALTOS

"Song Sung ___" BLUE

songwriter
~ **org.** ASCAP

sonic
~ **rebound** ECHO
~ **starter** ULTRA

sonic ___ BOOM

sonic boom
~ **source** SST

Sonics FIVE, TEAM
~ **org.** NBA

son-in-___ LAW

sonnet POEM
~ **cousin** ODE
~ **ender** EER
~ **measure** IAMB
~ **stanza** OCTET

sonneteer BARD

sonny KID, LAD, MALE

Sonny BONO

Sonny and Cher
~ **once** DUO, TEAM

son of
~ **in Arabic** IBN

"Son of ___ Cristo, The" MONTE

"Sonofagun!" DARN, DRAT

"Son-of-a Preacher ___" MAN

"Son of Frankenstein"
~ **director** LEE

"Son of Monte Cristo, The"
~ **director** LEE

Sonoma
~ **neighbor** NAPA

Sonora
see Spanish

sonority TONE

sonorous BASS, DEEP, LOUD, RICH

sonorously ALOUD

sonorousness TONE

"Sons and Lovers"
~ **actress** URE

"Sons of Katie ___, The" ELDER

"Sons of Katie Elder, The" OATER

"Sons of the ___" DESERT

Sontag, Susan
~ piece ESSAY

Sony
~ rival RCA

Sonya
~ to Vanya NIECE

sooey CALL
~ responder HOG, SOW

soon ANON, NOW
~ afterward THEN
as ~ as ONCE
too ~ EARLY
very ~ after UPON

___ so on AND

sooner FIRST
~ opposite LATER
~ or later ANON

Sooner
~ city ADA, ENID

soot DIRT, GRIT
~ particle SMUT
smudged with ~ ASHY

soothe ABATE, ALLAY, CALM, EASE, HELP, PAT, SETTLE

soother BALM
baby ~ TALC
skin ~ ALOE

soothing
~ cream BALM
~ plant ALOE
~ word THERE

soothsayer ORACLE, SEER
~ observance OMEN

sooty INKY
~ residue ASH

sop BLOT

SOP MODE
part of ~ STD

Sophia LOREN
~ contemporary GINA

sophisticated AWARE, CHIC, HEP, HIP, SUAVE
~ gathering SALON
~ miss DEB
~ quality CLASS, STYLE

sophistication CHIC, CLASS, STYLE

Sophocles
~ forte DRAMA

sophomore YEAR

sopor SLEEP

soporific OPIATE

sopping WET

soprano RANGE
~ part AIR

~ solo ARIA
between ~ and tenor ALTO
Catfish Row ~ BESS
famous ~ HORNE

soprano ___ SAX

"So Proudly We ___!" HAIL

Sopwith ___ CAMEL

sora BIRD, RAIL

sorbet ICE

Sorbonne
~ site PARIS
see also French

sorcerers MAGI

sorceress
~ of Greek myth MEDEA
African ~ of fiction SHE

sordid BAD, BASE, LOW, VILE

sordidness DIRT

sore ACHY, IRATE, UPSET
~ spot ACHE
be ~ ACHE
make ~ ANGER, IRE, IRK, PEEVE, RILE, UPSET

sorehead BEAR
~ perhaps LOSER

soreness ACHE, PAIN

sorghum
~ structure SILO

sorority ORDER
~ letter ALPHA, BETA, CHI, DELTA, ETA, IOTA, OMEGA, PHI, PSI, RHO, TAU, THETA
~ letters MUS
~ member COED
see also Greek

sorrel BAY, COLOR, HORSE, ROAN
wood ~ OCA

Sorrento CITY, PORT
see also Italian

sorrow ACHE, BANE, CARE, EVIL, PAIN, WOE
show ~ SOB
sign of ~ TEAR
word of ~ ALAS

"Sorrow ___ the Pity, The" AND

sorrowful LOW, SAD, SORE
~ cry MOAN

sorry BAD, MEAN, POOR, SAD
feel ~ about RUE

"Sorry!" OOPS

sort CAST, CLASS, CUT, GENRE, ILK, LIKE, LINE, LOT, MAKE, MOLD, ORDER, RANGE, RANK, RATE, STAMP, STYLE, TYPE
~ of (suffix) ISH

sortie RAID

sorts
feel out of ~ AIL
out of ~ ILL, TESTY

SOS HELP
~ response AID
motorist's ~ FLARE

"S.O.S."
~ band ABBA

"___ So Shy" HES

so-so FAIR
~ grade CEE

sostenuto PEDAL

sot
~ spot BAR
~ syllable HIC

"Sot-___ Factor, The" WEED

"So that's it!" AHA, ISEE

Sotheby's
signal at ~ NOD

"So there!" HAH

Sothern ANN

"So This Is ___" PARIS

"So This Is ___ York" NEW

Soto ___ ZEN

"___ so to bed" AND

sotto voce
~ remark ASIDE
not ~ ALOUD

sou
without a ~ NEEDY, POOR

soubise
~ ingredient ONION

soubrette GIRL, LASS, MAID

souchong TEA

___ souci SANS

Souez INA

soufflé
~ ingredient EGG
like a ~ AIRY

sough DRONE, MOAN

sought
~ after HOT

souk
~ shopper ARAB

soul ESSENCE, GIST, HEART, LIFE
~ in French AME
~ in Spanish ALMA
~ mate PAL
gentle ~ LAMB
nary a ~ NONE, NOONE
solitary ~ LONER

soul ___ MATE

"Soul ___" ONICE, TRAIN

Soule OLAN

"___ soul man" (Blues Brothers lyric) IMA

soulmate PAL

"Souls ___" ATSEA

"Souls at ___" SEA

___ Souls' Day ALL

sound ARM, AUDIO, GOOD, INLET, NOISE, SOBER, SOLID, SURE, TONE
~ booster AMP
~ component AUDIO
~ stage SET
~ unit BEL
deflating ~ SSS

sound ___ BITE, STAGE

sound ___ (boast) OFF

sound bite
~ cousin CLIP

sounded ORAL

sound effect
cartoon ~ THUD

soundness TONE

"Sound of Music, The"
~ director WISE
~ extra NUN
~ heroine MARIA
~ locale ALPS

soundproofing
~ unit SABIN

soup
~ and fish DRESS
~ bean LIMA
~ container CAN
~ herb DILL
~ ingredient BEAN, BEET, CORN, LEEK, OKRA, ONION, PEA
~ order CUP
~ server LADLE
~ staple BONE
~ up RAISE
thick ~ PUREE

soup-___-fish AND

___ soup PEA

soup-and-fish TAILS

soupçon DAB, DASH, IOTA, SHADE, TANG, TASTE, TINGE, TRACE

souped-up
~ auto RACER

___ soup fog PEA

Soupy SALES

"___ soup yet?" ISIT

Soupy Sales EMCEE, HOST
~ missile PIE

sour ACID, ACRID, BAD, DOUR, EVIL, MEAN, SPOIL
~ compound ACID
~ cream DIP
~ expression SNEER
~ flavor LEMON
~ gum TREE
go ~ TURN
it may be ~ CREAM, MASH, NOTE

sour ___ CREAM, MASH

source

source BASE, CAUSE, FONT, GERM, HEAD, MINE, ROOT, SEED
  ~ to a poet FONT

___-source SOLE

sources
  info ~ MEDIA

sourdough
  ~ gear PAN
  ~ quest CLAIM, GOLD, ORE

"Sour grapes"
  ~ author AESOP

sourpuss CRAB
  like a ~ DOUR

soursop TREE

sour-tasting TART

sous-___ CHEF

Sousa
  ~ group BAND

sousaphone BRASS, HORN
  ~ relative TUBA

souse DIP, SOAK, STEEP

soused LIT

south
  ~ ender ERN
  ~ in Spanish SUR

South ___ POLE

South ___ (Pacific area) SEAS

South ___, Ind. BEND

___ South DEEP

South African
  ~ bishop TUTU
  ~ currency RAND
  ~ golfer ELS
  ~ province NATAL
  ~ river ORANGE
  ~ village STAD

South American
  ~ animal LLAMA, TAPIR
  ~ cape HORN
  ~ capital LIMA
  ~ dance TANGO
  ~ Indian INCA
  ~ mountains ANDES
  ~ nation PERU
  ~ parrot MACAW
  ~ port RIO

Southampton CITY, EARL, PORT

South Bend
  ~ st. IND

South Carolina STATE

South China SEA

South Dakota STATE
  ~ neighbor IOWA

Southeast Asian LAO, TAI, THAI
  ~ land LAOS

Southeastern Conference
  ~ sch. ALA, LSU

Southern
  ~ bread PONE

  ~ constellation ARGO
  ~ sch. ALA, LSU
  ~ st. ALA, ARK, FLA, MISS, TENN, TEX

Southern ___ ALPS, BELLE, CAL

southernmost
  ~ US city HILO

Southey, Robert POET
  see also poet

Southfork RANCH
  ~ matriarch ELLIE

south-of-the-border
  ~ coin PESO
  ~ order TACO
  see also Mexican, Spanish

"South of the Border" OATER

South Pacific
  ~ island ATOLL, EASTER
  ~ islands SAMOA
  ~ port APIA
  ~ spot ISLE

"South Pacific"
  ~ character EMILE
  ~ locale BALI

southpaw
  ~ stat. ERA

South Seas
  ~ feature ATOLL, ISLE
  ~ island BALI
  ~ staple TARO

Southwest Conf.
  ~ member SMU

Southwestern
  ~ building material ADOBE
  ~ dwelling ADOBE
  ~ lizard UTA
  ~ predator PUMA
  ~ sight CACTI, DESERT, MESA
  ~ tree ALAMO
  ~ tribe HOPI

souvenir RELIC, TOKEN

souvlaki
  ~ ingredient LAMB

sou'wester HAT

"___ So Vain" YOURE

sovereign ACE, BEST, COIN, LORD, MAIN, REGAL, RULER, TOPS
  ~ decree EDICT
  Slavic ~ TSAR

sovereignty RULE
  emblem of ~ ORB

Soviet
  ~ political div. SSR
  ~ spacecraft LUNA, MIR
  first ~ premier LENIN
  former ~ first lady RAISA
  former ~ press arm TASS
  see also Russian

sow ANIMAL, CAST, GROW, HOG, PLANT, SEED, SHE
  ~ chow SLOP
  ~ home PEN, STY
  ~ mate BOAR

  ~ opposite REAP
  ~ syllable OINK
  ~ wild oats REVEL

"So what ___ is new?" ELSE

sown
  reap what one has ~ PAY

so written SIC

sow wild ___ OATS

Sox
  ~ city BOS, CHI

soybean
  ~ product OIL, TOFU

soybeans CROP

Soyuz
  ~ launcher USSR

Sp. LANG
  see also Spanish

SP
  ~ quarry AWOL

spa BATH
  ~ feature SAUNA
  English ~ BATH
  German ~ EMS

space AREA, GAP, HOLE, PLAY, ROOM
  ~ between teeth GAP
  ~ chimp ENOS
  ~ starter AERO, HEAD
  ~ station supply AIR
  ~ to a poet ETHER
  ~ vehicle APOLLO
  breathing ~ PORE
  confining ~ CELL
  deep ~ ABYSS
  first American woman in ~ RIDE
  like outer ~ VAST
  living ~ AREA
  open ~ ROOM
  open ~ in a forest GLADE
  outer ~ SKY
  parking ~ STALL
  railroad's parking ~ YARD
  sight from ~ EARTH
  swell, in ~ AOK
  upper regions of ~ ETHER
  visitor from ~ ALIEN

space ___ SHIP, SUIT

___ space AIR, DEEP, FREE, OUTER

Space ___ AGE

Space Age
  ~ acronym NASA

space bar
  ~ neighbor ALT

spacecraft SHIP
  ~ compartment POD
  alien ~ UFO
  Soviet ~ LUNA

spaced
  ~ out SPARSE

Space Flight Center
  ~ st. ALA

Space Invaders
  ~ producer ATARI

Spacek, Sissy
  ~ drama MARIE
  ~ role LYNN

spaces
  lofty ~ ATRIA

space shuttle
  ~ assent AOK

space station
  ~ org. NASA
  Russian ~ MIR

spacewalk EVA

spacey
  ~ state DAZE

spacious AIRY, AMPLE, BIG, LARGE, OPEN, VAST, WIDE

spaciousness ROOM

spade TOOL
  one ~ perhaps BID
  use a ~ DIG

Spade SAM
  ~ work CASE

spadefoot TOAD

spades SUIT

spadille
  ~ sometimes ACE

spaghetti PASTA

spaghettini PASTA

spaghetti sauce
  ~ seasoning HERB

Spain
  castle in ~ DREAM
  city in ~ AVILA, LEON, TOLEDO
  eighth-century invader of ~ MOOR
  former queen of ~ ENA
  honorific of ~ DONA
  longest river in ~ EBRO
  Portugal and ~ IBERIA
  princess of ~ ELENA
  province of ~ LEON
  region of ~ AVILA
  where ~ is IBERIA
  see also Spanish

"___ Spake Zarathustra" THUS

Spam MEAT

span EPOCH, ERA, PAIR, RANGE, SPACE
  ~ in years AGE

___ span LIFE

Span.
  see Spanish

Spandau
  last prisoner at ~ HESS

spangle ADORN, STAR

"___ Spangled Girl" STAR

"___ Spangled Rhythm" STAR

___ spaniel WATER

Spanish
~ **acclamation** OLE
~ **adverb** MAS, NADA
~ **affirmatives** SISI
~ **article** LAS, LOS, UNA, UNO
~ **cheer** OLE
~ **compass point** ESTE, SUR
~ **conjunction** MAS
~ **dessert** FLAN
~ **diminutive suffix** ITA, ITO
~ **female** ELLA
~ **gentleman** DON
~ **hero, with "El"** CID
~ **lady** DONA
~ **marking** TILDE
~ **month** ENERO
~ **number** DOS, OCTO, TRES, UNO
~ **painter** MIRO
~ **preposition** ENTRE
~ **priest** PADRE
~ **pronoun** ELLA, ESTA, ESTE, TODO
~ **province** AVILA
~ **river** EBRO
~ **stewpot** OLLA
~ **surrealist** DALI, MIRO
~ **title** DON, SENOR, SRA
~ **verb** ESTA
abode, in ~ CASA
"Absolutely!" in ~ SISI
a, in ~ UNA, UNO
alias, in ~ MOTE
all, in ~ TODO
among, in ~ ENTRE
another, in ~ OTRA
are, in ~ ESTA
aunt, in ~ TIA
bear, in ~ OSO
be, in ~ SER
between, in ~ ENTRE
boss, in ~ AMO
"Bravo!" in ~ OLE
buddy, in ~ AMIGO
bull, in ~ TORO
but, in ~ MAS
chamber, in ~ SALA
child, in ~ NINA, NINO
chum, in ~ AMIGO
definitely, in ~ SISI
domicile, in ~ CASA
east, in ~ ESTE
eight, in ~ OCHO
everything, in ~ TODO
face, in ~ CARA
father, in ~ PADRE
fellow, in ~ SENOR
fingernail, in ~ UNA
friend, in ~ AMIGO
gentleman, in ~ SENOR
gold, in ~ ORO
"Goodbye!" in ~ ADIOS
hall, in ~ SALA
Helen, in ~ ELENA
home, in ~ CASA
hour, in ~ HORA
house, in ~ CASA
how, in ~ COMO
is, in ~ ESTA
January, in ~ ENERO
kid, in ~ NINA, NINO
king, in ~ REY
lady, in ~ SRA

love, in ~ AMOR
matador foe, in ~ TORO
meat, in ~ CARNE
Miss, in ~ SRTA
mister, in ~ SENOR
mit, in ~ CON
monarch, in ~ REY
monsieur, in ~ SENOR
more, in ~ MAS
most, in ~ MAS
Mr., in ~ SENOR
Mrs., in ~ SRA
Ms., in ~ SRTA
nickname, in ~ MOTE
nil, in ~ NADA
nothing, in ~ NADA
octet, in ~ OCHO
old ~ coin REAL
one, in ~ UNA, UNO
other, in ~ OTRA
"Oui, oui", in ~ SISI
ourselves, in ~ NOS
pal, in ~ AMIGO
plus, in ~ MAS
potato, in ~ PAPA
river, in ~ RIO
room, in ~ SALA
route, in ~ VIA
60 minutes, in ~ HORA
she, in ~ ELLA
sir, in ~ SENOR
soul, in ~ ALMA
south, in ~ SUR
sun, in ~ SOL
the, in ~ LAS, LOS
this, in ~ ESTA, ESTE
three, in ~ TRES
to be, in ~ SER
tot, in ~ NINA, NINO
track, in ~ VIA
two, in ~ DOS
uncle, in ~ TIO
us, in ~ NOS
walk, in ~ ANDA
water, in ~ AGUA
waterway, in ~ RIO
wave, in ~ OLA
way, in ~ VIA
will be, in ~ SERA
winter month, in ~ ENERO
with, in ~ CON
yeses, in ~ SIS
youngster, in ~ NINA, NINO
zilch, in ~ NADA
see also Spain

Spanish ___ MAIN, MOSS, OMELET, ONION, RICE, STEPS

Spanish-American WAR

"Spanish Guitar Player"
~ **artist** MANET

Spanish Main
~ **cargo** ORO
~ **coin** REAL

Spanish Steps
~ **city** ROME

spank BEAT, HIT, LACE, SLAP, TAN

spanker MAST, SAIL

spanking FAST, FINE, RAPID

spar ARGUE, BAR, BEAM, BOOM, BOUT, MAST, MILL, POLE
long ~ YARD

spare BARE, CLEAN, EXTRA, LANK, LEAN, OTHER, OVER, REMIT, SLIM, THIN, TIRE
~ **unit** PIN
difficult ~ SPLIT
room to ~ PLAY

spare ___ PART, TIRE

spared
it may be ~ ROD

spareribs MEAT

"Spare the ___..." ROD

sparing
be ~ STINT

spark ARC, BEAU, CHASE, DUDE, FIRE, FLARE, HEAT, IOTA
~ **in older slang** WOO
ignite the ~ AROUSE
inventor's ~ IDEA

sparkle BEAM, FLARE, GLARE, GLOW, LIFE, PEP, SHINE, SNAP, WIT

sparkler GEM
jewel-box ~ RING, TIARA

sparklers ICE

sparkling ALIVE, CLEAR, CRISP

sparkling ___ WATER, WINE

sparkling wine
~ **spot** ASTI

Spark, Muriel SCOT

Sparks NED
~ **agreement** ROGER
~ **post** RADIO
~ **st.** NEV
city west of ~ RENO

Sparky
~ **post** RADIO

sparling SMELT

sparrow BIRD

sparse LEAN, POOR, RARE, SCANT, THIN

Sparta
ally of ~ ELIS
see also Greek

Spartacus SLAVE
spot for ~ ARENA

"Spartacus"
~ **author** FAST

Spartan BARE, DOUR, STERN

spasm TIC
~ **of distress** PANG

Spassky BORIS

spat ADO, ROW, SCRAP, SETTO, TILT, TODO
~ **spot** ANKLE
public ~ SCENE

spate JET, POUR, RASH
~ **of activity** SPASM

spatter DASH, SLOP, SPOT

spatula
use a ~ FLIP

spawn BEAR, ISSUE

spawner
salt-water ~ EEL
upstream ~ SHAD

speak ORATE, SAY, TALK, UTTER
~ **an untruth** LIE
~ **at arraignment** PLEAD
~ **at length** DRAG
~ **bombastically** ORATE
~ **for the doctor** AAH
~ **hesitantly** HAW
~ **highly of** LAUD
~ **highly of oneself** BRAG, CROW
~ **ill of** ABASE, LIBEL, SLUR
~ **imperfectly** LISP
~ **in a monotone** DRONE
~ **interrogatively** ASK
~ **in the Senate** ORATE
~ **irritably** SNAP
~ **lovingly** COO
~ **out** AVER, AVOW, YELL
~ **publicly** ORATE
~ **roughly** RASP
~ **rudely** SASS
~ **unclearly** SLUR
~ **well of** ESTEEM
~ **wildly** RAGE, RANT, RAVE, ROAR, STORM, YELL
~ **with** MEET, SEE
~ **with forked tongue** LIE
~ **with one's hands** SIGN
~ **without notes** ADLIB
as we ~ LIVE
chance to ~ SAY
effectiveness, so to ~ TEETH

speakeasy BAR

speaker ORATOR
~ **alert** AHEM
~ **asset** WIT
~ **need** INTRO
~ **part** AMP
~ **pauses** ERS
~ **spot** DAIS
~ **starter** LOUD
~ **system** STEREO
Latin ~ ROMAN
public ~ ORATOR
Sioux ~ OTO, OTOE

speaking
manner of ~ IDIOM, TONE, USAGE
plain ~ PROSE

spear LANCE, SPIRE
~ **tip** PIKE
fish ~ GIG
whaler's ~ LANCE

spear ___ GUN

spear carrier EXTRA

spearhead LEAD

spearmint HERB

spec
~ recording DEMO

spec. STD

special RARE, SALE
~ delivery MAIL
~ ender IST
~ pleasure TREAT
~ vocabulary ARGOT
make a ~ point of STRESS
newspaper's ~ edition EXTRA
nothing ~ USUAL
something ~ ONER

special ___ AGENT

Special Forces
~ cap BERET
~ unit ATEAM

special interest
~ group BLOC
~ grp. ASSN, ORG

specialist ACE, ADEPT

specialized
~ lingo ARGOT

specialty AREA, LINE, SPHERE

specie CASH, COIN

species CLASS, ORDER, RACE,
SORT, TYPE
~ division SEX
endangered ~ enemy MAN

specific ITEM, LOCAL

specifications
safety ~ CODE

specify CITE, LIMIT, NAME, SET

specimen CASE

specious FAKE, FALSE

speck ATOM, BEAD, BIT, BLOT, DAB,
DOT, DROP, IOTA, JOT, MITE,
MOTE, SHRED, SPOT, TAD, TAINT,
TRACE
~ in the ocean ISLE, ISLET
not a ~ NONE

speckle BLOT, DASH, DOT, SPOT

specklebelly GOOSE

speckled
~ fish TROUT
~ horse ROAN

speckless CLEAN

specs
~ support EAR

spectacle PARADE, PLAY, POMP,
SCENE, SHOW

spectacles
~ support EAR

spectacular EPIC, GALA

spectator FAN

"Spectator, The"
~ writer STEELE

specter SHADE, SOUL

Specter ARLEN

"Specter of the ___" ROSE

specters MANES

spectral EERIE, EERY

spectrum RANGE
~ band BLUE, ORANGE, RED
~ zone HUE

Spectrum
Philadelphia's ~ ARENA

speculate BET, MUSE, RISK

speculations IFS

speech TALK
~ characteristic LISP
~ fumbles ERS
~ pattern TONE
~ site DAIS
figure of ~ IMAGE
fumble one's ~ SLUR
like some ~ NASAL
make a ~ ORATE, TALK
of ~ ORAL
part of ~ NOUN
sparkling, as ~ CRISP
violent ~ RANT

___ speech FREE

speechify ORATE, RANT

speechless AWED, MUTE, TACIT
render ~ AMAZE, AWE, STUN,
WOW

speechmaker ORATOR

speed CLIP, DART, DASH, HASTE,
HIE, PACE, RACE, RATE, RIP,
RUN, TEAR, TEMPO
~ burst DASH
~ contest RACE
~ demon RACER
~ ender BOAT, STER
~ off FLEE
~ up AID, EASE, SPUR
at top ~ APACE
burst of ~ RUN
high ~ electron BETA
it's built for ~ SST
measure ~ TIME
rate of ~ CLIP, PACE
record ~ RPM
reduce ~ SLOW
run at a low ~ IDLE
seagoing ~ unit KNOT
with ~ APACE

speed ___ LIMIT, SKATE, TRAP

speed-___ READ

___-speed TEN

"Speed"
~ vehicle BUS

speeder
~ nemesis COP, RADAR

speedily APACE, FAST, SOON

speed limit
~ letters MPH

speedometer
~ part NEEDLE
~ reading MPH

speed-read SCAN

speedster DEMON

___ Speedwagon REO

speedway PIKE, ROAD, ROUTE
~ area PIT

speedy FAST, FLEET, RAPID

Speedy Gonzales MOUSE

Speke, John
river explored by ~ NILE

speleology
~ topic CAVE

spell BOUT, FIT, TIME
bad ~ BOUT
breathing ~ PEACE
cold ~ AGUE, SNAP
put a ~ on ZAP
warm ~ THAW

spellbind GRIP, HOLD, RIVET

spellbinder ORATOR

spellbinders
~ do it ORATE

spellbound AGAPE, RAPT

spelldown BEE

spelling
~ contest BEE

spelling ___ BEE

Spelling AARON

Spelling, Tori
~ father AARON

spelunker
~ hat attachment LAMP
~ milieu CAVE

spencer COAT

spend EXERT, PAY, USE
~ money PAY
~ recklessly WASTE
place to ~ the night INN

Spender, Stephen POET, SIR
see also poet

spending
~ limit CAP

Spenser, Edmund POET
~ heroine UNA
~ specialty POEM
see also poet

"Spenser: For ___" HIRE

spent DONE, LIMP, SHOT, TIRED

spermatophyte PLANT

Sperry ELMER
~ partner RAND

spew EMIT, ERUPT, JET, SPIT
~ out EGEST
Mount Saint Helens ~ ASH

sphagnum MOSS, PEAT

sphalerite ORE

sphere BALL, CASTE, CLASS,
EARTH, ORB, ORBIT, REALM,
SUN
~ of conflict ARENA
~ of influence AREA, ORBIT
~ starter BIO, ECO, HEMI
tiny ~ BEAD

spherical
~ do AFRO

spheroid BEAD, DROP

spherule BEAD

sphinx
a ~ has its body LION

Sphinx
answer to the ~'s riddle MAN

sphinxlike DEEP

Spica STAR

spice AROMA, MACE
~ starter ALL

spice ___ RACK

spiced
~ sausage SALAMI

Spice Girls
one of the ~ POSH

spiceless MILD

spice rack
~ item DILL, MACE, SAGE

spick-and-___ SPAN

spicule BARB, NEEDLE

spicy HOT, RACY, RICH
~ cuisine THAI
~ jelly ASPIC
~ stew OLLA
not ~ MILD

spider PAN
~ handiwork WEB
~ web NET
fly, to a ~ PREY

spider ___ LILY

Spider-Man HERO

spiders
what ~ do SPIN

"Spiders!" EEK

"___ Spiegel" DER

spiel LINE, TALK
ad ~ HYPE

Spielberg
~ alien and others ETS

"Spies ___ Us" LIKE

spiffy NEAT, SMART

spigot TAP

spike EAR, LACE, NAIL, PEG, STEM
~ the punch LACE
grain ~ AWN, EAR
shoe ~ CLEAT

spike ___ HEEL

Spike LEE

spile PEG, TAP
  ~ fluid SAP

spill OPEN, SLOP, STREAM
  ~ coffee on, perhaps SCALD
  ~ over RUN
  ~ the beans BLAB, LEAK,
    LETON, RAT, SING, TALK,
    TELL
  take a ~ SLIP, TRIP

spillway RACE

spin FLIP, REEL, RIDE, ROLL, TURN
  ~ a yarn RELATE, TELL
  ~ doctor's concern IMAGE
  ~ one's wheels STALL
  ~ out DRAG
  ~ starter TAIL, TOP
  ~ the bottle GAME
  go for a ~ RIDE
  skater's ~ CAMEL
  where to go for a ~ RINK

spin ___ bottle THE

"Spin ___" CITY

spinach ___ PIE

spinal ___ CORD

spindle AXIS, AXLE, REEL

spindle-legged LANK, THIN

spine BARB, BONE
  ~ item TITLE

spineless LIMP

Spiner, Brent
  ~ role DATA

spinet ORGAN, PIANO

spine-tingling EERIE, EERY

Spinks LEON
  ~ defeater ALI
  ~ stat TKO

spin like ___ ATOP

spinnaker SAIL, SHEET
  ~ support MAST

spinner LURE, TOP
  world ~ LOVE

spinneret ORGAN

spinning
  ~ toy TOP, YOYO

spinous ACUTE

spins
  part that ~ ROTOR

spiny
  ~ houseplant ALOE

spiny-leaved
  ~ plant AGAVE

spiracle HOLE

spiral BEND, COIL, LOOP, RISE,
  SOAR
  ~ molecule DNA

spiral-horned
  ~ animal ELAND

spirals PASTA

spire PEAK

spirit ANGEL, ARDOR, AROMA,
  AURA, ELAN, ESSENCE, FIRE,
  GRIT, HEART, LIFE, MOOD, PEP,
  SHADE, SOUL, TONE, VIM
  ~ away SNEAK
  ~ in French AME
  ~ of a culture ETHOS
  benevolent household ~ LAR
  evil ~ DEMON
  guardian ~ ANGEL
  indomitable ~ GRIT
  lively ~ VIM
  magic ~ GENIE
  show team ~ ROOT
  vital ~ SOUL

___ spirit FREE

spirited ALIVE, CRISP, GAME, LIVE,
  PERT, RACY
  ~ equine STEED

___-spirited MEAN

spiritless DAMP, DRAB, FLAT, MEEK,
  TAME

spirits MANES
  high ~ ELAN, GLEE
  in good ~ RIANT
  in high ~ ELATED, GAY
  in low ~ BLUE, SAD
  lift the ~ of ELATE
  like some ~ EVIL

**"Spirits that ___ on mortal
  thoughts"** TEND

spiritual INNER, SONG
  ~ discipline YOGA
  ~ formula CREDO
  ~ guide GURU
  ~ leader LAMA
  word in a ~ AMEN

spiritualist SEER

spirogyra ALGA, ALGAE

spit BAR, EMIT, ROD

spit-___ SHINE

spitchcock EEL

spiteful BAD, MEAN, UGLY

Spitfire
  ~ org. RAF

spitting ___ IMAGE

spitting image TWIN

Spitz, Mark
  emulate ~ SWIM

splash BATHE, LAP, LAVE, SLOP
  ~ around WADE
  ~ down LAND
  make a ~ RATE

"Splat!"
  ~ cousin PLOP

splatter SLOP
  ~ safeguard APRON

spleen ANGER, HATE, IRE, ORGAN,
  SPITE
  vent one's ~ RAGE

spleenwort FERN

splendid FINE, GALA, GAY, KEEN,
  REGAL, RICH

splendor ECLAT, POMP, STATE

"Splendor in the Grass"
  ~ screenwriter INGE

splenetic ACID, RUDE, TART, TESTY

splice
  ~ film EDIT
  thing to ~ GENE

spliced
  get ~ WED

splicer
  ~ material GENE
  scene ~ EDITOR

spline LATH

splinter BIT, CHIP, CHOP, HACK,
  REND, SCRAP, SHRED, SMASH,
  STAVE
  ~ group BLOC, SECT

___ splints SHIN

"Splish Splash"
  ~ locale BATH

split APART, AXE, CHAP, CHOP, CUT,
  EXIT, FLEE, GAP, GASH, HACK,
  LAM, LEAVE, MOVE, PART, REND,
  RENT, RIP, RUN, TEAR
  ~ component PIN
  ~ hairs ARGUE
  ~ second HAIR
  ~ the difference SHARE
  ~ the ears DIN
  ~ up APART, PART
  ~ veggie PEA
  easily ~ rock SHALE
  it may be ~ ATOM
  they may be ~ ENDS

split ___ END

split ___ soup PEA

"Split ___" IMAGE

splittable
  ~ thing ATOM

splitter
  hair ~ PART
  timber ~ SAW
  wood ~ MAUL

splotch DROP, SMEAR, SPOT,
  TAINT

splotchy
  ~ as a horse PIED

splurge SHOP, SPEND, SPREE

splutter BOIL, TALK

Spock
  ~ and others ETS, MDS
  ~ colleague SCOTT, SULU
  ~ mother AMANDA
  ~ org. AMA
  ~ successor DATA
  Mr. ~ ALIEN

spoil DASH, DOTE, HARM, MAR,
  ROT, RUIN, TAINT, WASTE
  ~ with "on" DOTE

spoilage WASTE

spoiled BAD, OFF, RANK, SOUR
  ~ kid BRAT

spoiler BANE, LOUSE
  perfect-game ~ HIT
  picnic ~ RAIN
  winning-streak ~ LOSS

spoils HAUL, LOOT, STAKE, SWAG

Spokane
  ~ event of 1974 EXPO
  ~ st. WASH

spoke
  umbrella ~ RIB

spoken ALOUD, ORAL, PUT
  ~ for TAKEN
  ~ in French DIT
  not ~ TACIT
  not ~ for SPARE
  not ~ of TABOO, TABU

___-spoken FAIR, FREE

spokes RADII

spoliate WASTE

spoliation WASTE

spondee FOOT

sponge BATH, BATHE, CAKE,
  CLEAN, PASTE, RINSE, STEAL
  ~ off BEG
  use a ~ SOP

sponge ___ BATH, CAKE

sponger DRONE

spongy DAMP
  ~ rubber FOAM

sponsor ANGEL
  words from the ~ ADS

sponsorship AEGIS, EGIS

spontaneity ELAN

spontaneous FREE

spontaneously ADLIB

spontoon LANCE, PIKE

spoof TEASE

spook SCARE, SPY

spooky EERIE, EERY
  ~ sound MOAN

spool REEL, ROLL

spoon IRON, KISS, LURE, NECK
  ~ companion, in rhyme DISH
  greasy ~ patron EATER
  serving ~ LADLE

spoon-___ FED, FEED

spoonbill BIRD
  ~ relative IBIS

spoonful SCOOP

spoon-playing
  ~ locale KNEE

spoons
 forks and ~ WARE

spoor LEAD, SCENT, SIGN, TRAIL

sporadic FEW

spore
 ~ **essentially** SEED
 ~ **producer** FERN
 ~ **starter** ENDO

sporran BAG
 ~ **sporter** SCOT

sport CAPER, CHAP, GAME, LARK, PARADE, PLAY, WEAR
 ~ **fish** BASS
 ~ **played to three points** EPEE
 ~ **with masked players** EPEE
 be a ~ PAY, TREAT
 clay-target ~ SKEET
 enjoy a winter ~ SKATE, SKI, SLED
 equestrian ~ POLO
 one-on-one ~ EPEE
 rowing ~ CREW
 royal ~ POLO
 Sapporo ~ SUMO
 water ~ POLO

sport-___ UTE

"___ sport!" BEA

sporting
 ~ **event** GAME, INDY, MEET, RACE

Sporting Life
 ~ **friend** BESS

"___ Sporting Life" THIS

sportive GAY

sports
 ~ **arbiter** REF, UMP
 ~ **car** MOTOR
 ~ **car of old** GTO
 ~ **center** ARENA
 ~ **championship** TITLE
 ~ **commentator's patter** COLOR
 ~ **deal** TRADE
 ~ **ender** CAST, WEAR
 ~ **enthusiast** FAN
 ~ **event** GAME, INDY, MEET, RACE
 ~ **group** TEAM
 ~ **org.** NBA, NFL
 ~ **period** HALF
 ~ **prelim** TRIAL
 ~ **surprise** UPSET
 college ~ **org.** NCAA
 coll. ~ **event** NIT
 like some ~ **fans** RABID
 nip, in ~ EDGE
 unguarded, in ~ OPEN
 winter ~ **item** SKI
 winter ~ **locale** ALPS

sports ___ CAR

sports car
 ~ **initials** GTO
 ~ **noseguard** BRA

sportscaster
 ~ **shout** YES
 hockey ~ **cry** SCORE

sportsmanlike CLEAN

sports page
 ~ **item** STAT

sports schedule
 ~ **word** AWAY

sports shoe
 ~ **attachment** CLEAT

spot BLOT, DAB, DOT, DROP, ESPY, LAMP, SCENE, SEE, SITE, SMEAR, SPY, TAINT
 mooring ~ PIER
 perfect ~ EDEN

___ spot HOT, INA

Spot
 one of ~'s owners JANE

spotless CLEAN, PURE

spotlight LAMP
 ~ **filter** GEL

"___ Spot run" SEE

spots
 seller's ~ ADS

spotted PIED
 ~ **feline** GENET
 ~ **horse** PAINT
 ~ **wildcat** OCELOT

spotted ___ OWL

Spottiswoode ROGER

spouse BRIDE, LADY, LOVE, MATE
 ~ **family member** INLAW
 ~ **title** MRS
 begum's ~ AGA, AGHA

spouses
 former ~ EXES
 sultan's ~ HAREM

spout ERUPT, JET, ORATE, POUR, PRATE, STREAM, TALK
 ~ **off** YAK

___ spout EAVE

spouter
 lava ~ ETNA

"___ Sprach Zarathustra" ALSO

sprag BAR, POLE

sprain
 ~ **site** ANKLE
 treat a ~ ICE

Sprat, Jack
 ~ **diet** LEAN
 ~ **no-no** FAT

Sprat, Mrs.
 ~ **diet** FAT
 ~ **no-no** LEAN

Sprats
 either of the ~ EATER

sprawl LIE, LOLL, SIT
 urban ~ CITY

spray JET
 ~ **graffiti on** MAR
 ~ **perhaps** AROMA
 banned bug ~ DDT
 banned fruit ~ ALAR
 defensive ~ MACE
 fine ~ MIST
 small ~ SPRIG

___ spray HAIR

spread ABODE, FEED, GROW, LAY, MANOR, MEAL, PART, RANCH, RISE, SCALE, SMEAR, SOW
 ~ **around** SHARE
 ~ **cement** PAVE
 ~ **for drying** TED
 ~ **gossip** YAK
 ~ **(out)** FAN
 ~ **outward** FLARE
 ~ **perfume** CENSE
 ~ **rumors** NOISE, TALK
 ~ **thin** SPARSE
 ~ **unchecked** RAGE
 bread ~ JAM, OLEO
 canapé ~ PATE
 cattleman's ~ RANCH
 cracker ~ BRIE, PATE
 fancy ~ ROE
 foyer ~ RUG
 hot-dog ~ CHILI
 luau ~ TARO
 nondairy ~ OLEO
 party ~ BRIE, PATE
 ritzy ~ ESTATE
 salty ~ ROE

spread ___ EAGLE

spread-eagle FLAT

spreader
 pollen ~ BEE

spread-out WIDE

spreadsheet
 ~ **material** DATA
 ~ **pro** CPA
 ~ **unit** CELL
 ~ **worker** USER

spree CAPER, LARK, ORGY, ROMP, TEAR, TOOT
 go on a ~ SPEND
 place for a ~ MALL

___ spree ONA

sprig BRAT, KID, LAD, SHOOT, SLIP

sprightliness PEP

sprightly AGILE, AIRY, ALERT, ALIVE, CRISP, ELFIN, GAY, PERT, SPRY

spring ARISE, BAIL, CAPER, COIL, DART, DASH, HOP, ISSUE, LEAP, LOPE, SKIP, START, TIDE
 ~ **back** REACT, SHY
 ~ **bloom** IRIS, LILAC, PANSY, TULIP
 ~ **ender** TIDE, TIME
 ~ **event** THAW
 ~ **feast** SEDER
 ~ **feast day** EASTER
 ~ **forth** ARISE, EMERGE, START

~ (from) COME
 ~ **holiday** EASTER
 ~ **mo.** APR, MAR
 ~ **month** APRIL, MAY
 ~ **observance** EASTER, LENT
 ~ **playoffs org.** NBA
 ~ **sign** ARIES
 ~ **starter** BED, HAND, INNER, MAIN, OFF
 ~ **to a poet** FONT
 ~ **up** ARISE, EMERGE, GROW, OCCUR, RISE, SHOOT
 hot ~ SPA
 sign of ~ ARIES, THAW

spring ___ ROLL, TIDE

"Spring ___" PARADE

"Spring ___; fall back" AHEAD

"Spring ahead"
 ~ **abbr.** DST

"Spring and ___ Wine" PORT

"Spring and Port ___" WINE

springbok ANIMAL

spring break
 ~ **time** EASTER

springe NOOSE, SNARE, TRAP

Springfield RIFLE
 ~ **st.** ILL

springiness LIFE

"Spring is like a perhaps hand" POEM

springlike MILD

spring month
 ~ **in French** MAI

"___ Spring of Mrs. Stone, The" ROMAN

springs
 it ~ **eternal** HOPE
 it may have ~ BED
 mineral ~ SPA

___ Springs, Australia ALICE

___ Springs, Calif. PALM

"___ springs eternal" HOPE

___ Springs, Fla. CORAL

___ Springs National Park HOT

springtime
 ~ **holiday** EASTER

spring training
 ~ **loc.** FLA

springy AGILE, LIVE

sprinkle DASH, DOT, DRIP, DROP, DUST, RAIN, SIFT, SOW, WATER

sprinkler JET

sprinkling DAB, RAINY, SHADE, TINGE

sprint DART, DASH, RACE, RUN, SPEED
 ~ **need** TAPE

sprinter RACER
~ event DASH
~ goal TAPE
~ must SPEED
~ path LANE

sprite ELF, GNOME, IMP
Persian ~ PERI
Shakespearean ~ ARIEL

___ sprite WATER

spritelike ELFIN

spritz JET

spritzer
~ ingredient SODA, WINE

sprocket COG, TOOTH

sprout GROW, LAD, SHOOT, SLIP,
SPIRE, SPRIG, START
plant ~ SPEAR

___ sprouts BEAN

spruce CHIC, CLEAN, COLOR, NEAT,
SMART, TAUT, TREE, TRIM
~ cousin FIR
~ in London TRIG
~ up ADORN, DRESS

"Spruce ___" GOOSE

spruced
~ up NEAT

"Spruce Goose" PLANE

spruceness TRIM

spry AGILE

spud TATER
~ bud EYE
~ country IDAHO
~ covering SKIN
~ st. IDA

___ spumante ASTI

spume BOIL, FOAM

spun
~ out LONG
it's ~ YARN

___-spun FINE

spunk GRIT, NERVE, SAND

spunky GAME

spur ABET, AROUSE, BARB, EGG,
GOAD, IMPEL, MOVE, PRESS,
PROD, ROUSE, STING, URGE
~ on ABET, EGG, ROOT
~ sporter BOOT
rocky ~ ARETE

spurious BAD, FAKE, FALSE, SHAM
~ thing FAKE, SHAM

spurn ABHOR, REPEL, SHUN, SNUB

spur-of-the-moment ADLIB

Spurs FIVE, TEAM
~ former org. ABA
~ org. NBA

spurt EMIT, ERUPT, ISSUE, JET,
POUR, SHOOT, SPEW, STREAM
sudden ~ SPASM

"Sputnik"
~ actor AUER

sputter BOIL, SPIT, TALK

spy AGENT, MOLE, PRY, SEE, SPOT
~ name HARI, MATA
~ of 1776 HALE
~ on TAIL, TRAIL
~ org. CIA
~ writing CODE
fictional ~ HELM
first name in ~ stories IAN
kind of ~ MOLE, PLANT
Revolutionary War ~ ANDRE,
HALE

"Spy ___ Came in From the Cold,
The" WHO

"Spy ___ Loved Me, The" WHO

spyglass
~ part LENS

spying NOSY

"Spy in the House of Love, A"
~ author NIN

"Spy Who ___ in From the Cold,
The" CAME

"Spy Who Loved Me, The"
~ actress BACH

squabble ADO, MELEE, ROW,
SCRAP, SPAT, TILT

squad BAND, CREW, GANG, TEAM
lacrosse ~ TEN
yacht ~ CREW

squad ___ CAR

___ squad RIOT, TAXI

"___ Squad, The" MOD

squad car
~ device SIREN

squadron FLEET, UNIT

squalid MEAN, SEEDY, VILE
~ quarters STY

squall BAWL, BLAST, CRY, GALE,
NOISE, RAIN, ROAR, STORM

squall ___ LINE

___ squall LINE

squalor DIRT

squama SCALE

squander LOSE, SPEND, WASTE

squandered LOST

"Squanto: A Warrior's ___" TALE

square AGREE, CLEAR, EVEN, FAIR,
HONEST, KNOT
~ footage AREA, SIZE
~ off against DARE, FACE
~ one NERD, START
~ quartet SIDES
~ (with) AGREE
~ with the facts HOLD
calendar ~ DAY
ceramic ~ TILE

from ~ one AGAIN, ANEW,
OVER
game-board ~ START
glass ~ PANE
Greek ~ AGORA
half the ~ dancers GALS
it may be ~ DANCE, KNOT,
MEAL, ROOT
many ~ rods ACRES
not ~ HEP, HIP

square ___ DANCE, KNOT, MEAL,
ONE, ROOT

square ___ (prepare) AWAY

___ square (carpenter's tool)
TRY

___-square (statistical distribu-
tion) CHI

___ Square (London locale)
SOHO

squared
~ away EVEN
three ~ NINE

square dance
~ call GEE
~ group OCTET
~ partner GAL
~ site BARN

"Square Egg, The"
~ author SAKI

square-ended
~ boat PRAM

square root
~ of eighty-one NINE
~ of forty-nine SEVEN
~ of four TWO
~ of nine THREE
~ of one hundred TEN
~ of one hundred twenty-
one ELEVEN

squares
one of three ~ MEAL
set of ~ GRID

___ squares (statistical method)
LEAST

squash GAME, MASH, TREAD
~ coat RIND
~ shot CAROM

___ squash ACORN

squat BEND, LOW, SIT

squatter TENANT

"Squaw ___, The" MAN

squawk CRY, FRET, YAP

squeak PEEP, PIPE
~ by NOSE
~ past, in sports EDGE
fix a ~ OIL

squeaker MOUSE, RAT

squeaky-___ CLEAN

squeal BAWL, BLAB, CRY, PIPE,
RAT, SING, TELL, YELP
comic-book ~ EEK

squealer
be a ~ RATON

squeamish PRIM

squeeze BLEED, CLASP, CRAM,
HOLE, JAM, MAKE, PRESS
~ by EKE

squeeze ___ PLAY

"Squeeze Box"
~ band WHO

squeezer
animal ~ BOA
cider ~ BOOR

squelch END, HALT, STOP

squib
news ~ ITEM

squid
~ cousins OCTOPI
~ weapon INK

squiggle
señor's ~ TILDE

squint
~ (at) PEER

squire ATTEND, DATE, GENT, LORD,
MAN, PEER, RANK

squirrel ANIMAL
~ abode TREE
~ away AMASS, HEAP, SAVE,
STASH, STORE, STOW
~ food ACORN, NUT
~ hangout OAK

squirrelly DAFT, MAD, ODD

squirt EMIT, JET, KID, SPEW,
STREAM
~ gun TOY

squirt ___ GUN

squishy WET

sr.
former ~ GRAD

Sr ELEM
38 for ~ ATNO

sra.
~ in French MME

Sri Lanka
~ (abbr.) ISL
~ crop TEA
~ export PEKOE
~ neighbor INDIA
wood from ~ EBONY

SRO
~ presentation HIT
~ show SMASH
part of ~ ONLY, ROOM

SS
~ recipients SRS

SSE
~ opposite NNW

s-shaped
~ curve OGEE

SSN's IDS

SSS
  ~ classification ONEA

SST JET, PLANE
  ~ crossing ATL
  ~ height ALT
  part of ~ SONIC

SSW
  ~ opposite NNE

st. RTE
  ~ crosser AVE

St.
  see Saint

"St. ___" (Bronson film) IVES

stab ESSAY, HARM, JAB, SHOT, STING, TRY
  take a ~ at ESSAY, TRY

stabbing BAD

Stabile
  ~ and others EDS

stability POISE, REST

stabilize SETTLE, TAME, TRIM

stabilizer TAIL
  food ~ AGAR
  plane's ~ FIN
  sailboat's ~ KEEL

stabilizer ___ BAR

stable ETERNAL, EVEN, SANE, SET, SHED, SOLID, STALL, SURE
  ~ area MEWS
  ~ baby FOAL
  ~ bed STRAW
  ~ home BARN
  ~ kid COLT
  ~ newborn FOAL
  ~ parent DAM, MARE, SIRE
  ~ sound SNORT
  ~ sustenance FEED, OATS
  ~ unit STALL

stables
  Augean ~ MESS

staccato
  ~ mark DOT

stack HEAP, MASS, PILE, RAFT
  ~ material HAY
  ~ of firewood CORD
  ~ starter HAY
  ~ up AMASS, STORE
  bank ~ ONES, TENS
  blow one's ~ RAGE, STORM

stacked ___ HEEL

Stack, Robert
  ~ TV role NESS

stacks
  frequent the ~ READ

stadium ARENA
  ~ area GATE, LOGE, TIER
  ~ employee USHER
  ~ feature DOME
  ~ habitué FAN
  ~ instrument ORGAN
  ~ lumber BAT
  ~ near Shea ASHE
  ~ roar BOO, HISS, RAH, RAHS

  ~ sound ROAR
  ~ walkway RAMP
  Mets' ~ SHEA
  U.S. Open ~ ASHE

staff BAT, CANE, HELP, MACE, MAN, ROD, STAVE, WAND
  ~ figure NOTE
  ~ of a regiment CADRE
  ~ officer AIDE
  ~ of office MACE
  ~ symbol CLEF
  add to ~ HIRE
  ceremonial ~ MACE
  seagoing ~ CREW
  take on ~ MAN

staffer AIDE
  estate ~ CHEF, MAID
  nonpermanent ~ TEMP
  zoo ~ VET

staffing
  provide ~ for MAN

staff of ___ LIFE

stag ALONE, ANIMAL, DEER, HART, MALE
  ~ attendees HES, MALES, MEN
  ~ mate DOE

stage ARENA, PHASE, STEP
  ~ area APRON
  ~ award OBIE, TONY
  ~ beginning ACTI
  ~ curtain ARRAS
  ~ decor SET
  ~ direction ENTER, EXIT
  ~ gizmo PROP
  ~ name ALIAS
  ~ of life ADULT, AGE
  ~ performer ACTOR
  ~ platform RISER
  ~ production DRAMA, PLAY
  ~ scenery DECOR
  ~ setting SCENE
  ~ signal CUE
  ~ strap REIN
  ~ success HIT
  ~ whisper ASIDE
  central ~ ARENA
  Freudian ~ ORAL
  get off the ~ EXIT
  go on ~ ENTER
  go on the ~ ACT
  highest ~ ACME
  initial ~ ONSET
  set the ~ with props DRESS
  sound ~ SET
  "terrible" age ~ TWOS
  tourney ~ SEMIS
  US ~ org. ANTA

"Stage ___" DOOR

stagecoach
  ~ puller TEAM

"Stagecoach" OATER

stagecraft DRAMA

stage door
  ~ symbol STAR

"Stage Door"
  ~ actress ARDEN

stagehand GRIP
  ~ concern PROP, SET

stagehands CREW

stage light
  ~ covering GEL

"Stage to Mesa City" OATER

Stagg AMOS

stagger AMAZE, DAZE, LIMP, MOVE, REEL, STUN, TEETER, WOW

staggering BIG, LARGE

staghorn FERN

staghorn ___ CORAL

stagnant STALE
  ~ water POOL

stagnate SIT

stagnation RUT
  sign of ~ ALGAE

stag party
  ~ attendee MALE, MAN

stags HES, MALES, MEN

staid SEDATE, SOBER

stain BLOT, COLOR, DIRT, DYE, MAR, PAINT, SLUR, SMEAR, SOIL, SPOT, TAINT
  driveway ~ OIL
  escutcheon ~ BLOT
  shirt pocket ~ INK

stained glass
  ~ figure ANGEL

stainless CLEAN, CLEAR, PURE

stainless ___ STEEL

stair
  ~ alternative RAMP
  ~ part RAIL, RISER, STEP
  ~ post NEWEL

"Stairway to the ___" STARS

stake ANTE, BAR, BET, PALE, POST, PROP, ROD
  gambling ~ ANTE
  poker ~ BET
  something to ~ CLAIM

stake ___ (surveil) OUT

stakes POOL
  pull up ~ LEAVE, MOVE
  put down ~ ABIDE, STAY
  up the ~ RAISE

stalactite
  form a ~ DRIP

stalagmite
  form a ~ DRIP

"Stalag 17"
  ~ role ANIMAL

stale ARID, BANAL, CLOSE, DATED, DRY, FLAT, HARD, OLD, PASSE, TIRED, TRITE

stalemate DRAW, HANG, PASS, TIE

Stalin RED
  ~ predecessor LENIN

  ~ realm USSR

Stalingrad
  see Russian

stalk CANE, CHASE, HUNT, REED, STEM
  ~ food CORN
  ~ of bananas HAND, STEM
  grass ~ REED

___ stalk CORN

stalking-___ HORSE

stall ARREST, CRIB, DEFER, DETER, PEN, STAND, STOP
  cattle ~ CRIB

staller
  plan ~ SNAG

stalling
  stop ~ ACT

stallion HORSE, MALE, SIRE
  ~ mate MARE
  ~ sound SNORT
  ~ stopper WHOA
  future ~ COLT

"___ Stallion" ROAN

Stallone
  ~ film COBRA, OSCAR
  ~ nickname SLY

stalwart BIG, FIT, HALE, IRON, LARGE

stamen ORGAN

stamina GRIT, SINEW

stammers ERS

stamp CLASS, DIE, LABEL, MOLD, ORDER, SEAL, SORT
  ~ backing GLUE
  ~ out COIN, MINT, RID
  ~ purchase SHEET
  ~ sheet PANE
  coin ~ DIE
  Easter ~ SEAL
  office ~ PAID, VOID
  ornamental ~ SEAL
  passport ~ VISA
  subject of 1993 ~ ELVIS

Stamp ___ ACT

stampede
  ~ cause FEAR, PANIC
  ~ group HERD

stamping
  ~ ground HOME
  ~ machine DIE
  ~ need PAD

stamps
  ~ of approval OKS
  food ~ DOLE
  roll of postage ~ COIL
  sheet of ~ PANE

Stan LEE
  ~ and Ollie foul-up MESS
  ~ cohort OLLIE

stance POSE
  rider's ~ SEAT

stanch CEASE, STEM, STOP

stanchion PILE, POST, STAY

stand ABIDE, ALLOW, ARISE, BASE, BEAR, RACK, REST, STALL, TAKE
  ~ aghast PALE
  ~ aloof SNUB
  ~ around IDLE, LOAF
  ~ before FACE
  ~ behind ATTEST, AVOW
  ~ by ADHERE, AWAIT, WAIT
  ~ for ABIDE, ALLOW, LET, MEAN
  ~ in awe of FEAR
  ~ in good stead AID, HELP
  ~ in line WAIT
  ~ in the way of BAR, CLOG
  ~ out SHINE
  ~ pat STAY
  ~ shoulder to shoulder BAND
  ~ side by side ABUT
  ~ the test of time LAST
  ~ together UNITE
  ~ up ERECT, LAST, RAISE, RISE
  ~ up against BEARD, PROP
  ~ up to DARE, FACE, MEET
  ~ vehicle CAB
  ~ wide-open GAPE
  art ~ EASEL
  can't ~ ABHOR, HATE
  Crockett's last ~ ALAMO
  flip-chart ~ EASEL
  football ~ TEE
  let it ~ STET
  magazine ~ RACK
  make one's hair ~ on end REPEL, SCARE
  one way to ~ PAT, TALL
  three-legged ~ EASEL

stand ___ PAT, TALL

stand ___ by IDLY

stand-___ computer ALONE

___ stand TAXI

"Stand ___ Deliver!" AND

stand-alone UNIT

standard CODE, FLAG, IDEAL, NORM, PAR, RULE, USUAL
  ~ operating procedure MODE
  below ~ POOR
  flying ~ FLAG
  moral ~ ETHIC

___ standard GOLD

Standard
  ~ partner POOR

Standard Oil of New Jersey
  ~ for short ESSO

standards ETHOS
  lacking ~ AMORAL

standee
  ~ lack LAP

stand-in SUB, TEMP

standing CASTE, CLASS, ERECT, ESTATE, NAME, RANK, RATE
  ~ around IDLE
  ~ at home, maybe ATBAT
  have ~ RANK, RATE
  in good ~ SOLID

just ~ around IDLE
official ~ RANK
of long ~ OLD
of longer ~ ELDER
social ~ CASTE, ESTATE

standing ___ ARMY

stand in good ___ STEAD

standings
  ~ column LOSE, LOSS, LOST, WIN, WON

Standish
  stand-in for ~ ALDEN

"Stand like Druids of ___..." ELD

standoff TIE
  like a ~ TENSE

standoffish ALOOF, COOL, ICY
  ~ person SNOB

standout ACE, ONER

standpoint ANGLE

___ stands ASIT

standstill HALT, PASS, REST
  bring to a ~ ARREST
  come to a ~ CEASE, STALL, STOP

___ standstill ATA

stand up ___ (support) FOR

Stanford
  ~ rival UCLA

Stanislaw LEM

Stanley ___ CUP

Stanley Cup AWARD
  ~ org. NHL

___ Stanley Gardner ERLE

Stanley, Henry Morton SIR

Stanley Steamer AUTO, CAR
  ~ contemporary REO

stannite ORE

stannous
  ~ element TIN

stannum TIN

Stansfield LISA

Stan the Man
  ~ teammate ENOS

stanza PART
  sonnet ~ OCTET

stapes BONE

staple
  cooking ~ OLEO
  Italian ~ PASTA
  mixologist's ~ GIN
  Polynesian ~ POI
  sushi ~ TUNA

Staple Singers
  one of the ~ CLEO

star ACE, LEAD, MEDAL, NAME, ORB, SPHERE, SUN
  ~ car LIMO

~ environment SPACE
~ followers MAGI
~ place SKY
~ (prefix) ASTRO
~ starter ALL
air-battle ~ ACE
constellation's brightest ~ ALPHA
Earth's ~ SOL, SUN
exploding ~ NOVA
hitch one's wagon to a ~ AIM
kind of ~ ALPHA, BETA, NOVA
look like a ~ SHINE
mound ~ ACE
movie ~ union SAG
variable ~ NOVA

star-___ mole NOSED

"Star ___" TREK

"___ Star" POLAR

"___ Star, The" TIN

___ Star (Sirius) DOG

Starbuck MATE
  ~ captain AHAB

starch GRIT, NERVE
  ~ source CORN, TARO

starched PRIM, STAID
  not ~ LIMP

starchy
  ~ root TARO
  ~ vegetable TATER, YAM

"Stardust Memories"
  ~ director ALLEN

stare GAPE, OGLE, SEE
  ~ at EYE, OGLE
  ~ down BEARD
  one way to ~ AGAPE
  piercing ~ GLARE
  villainous ~ LEER

stares
  like some ~ ICY

"___ Star Final" FIVE

starfish
  ~ part ARM, RAY

stargaze DREAM, MOON

stargazer SEER
  ~ sight NOVA

stargazers
  Biblical ~ MAGI

staring AGAPE

"Star Is Born, A"
  ~ actor MASON
  Barbra's ~ costar KRIS

stark BALD, PURE, UTTER
  ~ horror PANIC
  ~ raving mad RABID

starkers BARE, NUDE

Star-Kist TUNA

starlet
  ~ quest ROLE

starlike
  ~ flower ASTER

starling BIRD
  ~ relative MYNA

Starman ALIEN

___-Star Pictures TRI

Starr BELLE, KAY, KEN

___-starred ILL

starring
  ~ role LEAD

starry-___ EYED

"Starry Night" OIL

stars
  give ~ to RATE
  of ~ (prefix) ASTRO

___ stars (be dazed) SEE

Stars SIX, TEAM
  ~ milieu ICE, RINK
  ~ org. NHL

Stars and ___ BARS

Stars and Bars FLAG
  ~ holder MAST
  ~ inits. CSA

Stars and Stripes FLAG

"Stars and Stripes Forever"
  ~ composer SOUSA

"Starsky and Hutch"
  ~ actor SOUL

"Stars Look Down, The"
  ~ director REED

"Star-Spangled Banner, The"
  ~ contraction OER

___ Star State LONE

start ARISE, ENTER, ONSET, OPEN, REACT, ROOT, SHOOT, SHY
  ~ a card game DEAL
  ~ a handball game SERVE
  ~ for a playwright ACTI

start-___ UPS

___ start HEAD

___-starter SELF

___ starters FOR

starting NEW
  ~ from ASOF
  ~ gate POST
  ~ point BASE, BASIS
  leaf's ~ point NODE, STEM

starting ___ GATE, LINE, OVER

startle ALARM, DAZE, JAR, ROUSE, SCARE

startling
  ~ report BANG

"Star Trek"
  ~ engineer SCOTT
  ~ navigator SULU
  ~ weapon setting STUN
  ~ yeoman RAND
  rank on ~ ENS

"Star Trek ___: The Search for Spock" III

"Star Trek: First Contact"
~ **villains** BORG

"Star Trek II: The Wrath of ___"
KHAN

"Star Trek IV: The Voyage ___"
HOME

"Star Trek: The Next Generation"
~ **character** DATA, WES

starve
~ **(for)** ACHE, LONG, PINE

"Star Wars"
~ **captain** SOLO
~ **pilot** ACE
~ **weapon** LASER
aka ~ SDI
Harrison, in ~ HAN

starwort ASTER

stash HIDE, MINT, STOW
~ **away** AMASS, SAVE
cash ~ IRA

stasis POISE

stat ASAP
~ **starter** AERO

state AVER, AVOW, CLAIM, SAY
~ **confidently** ASSERT
~ **in French** ETAT
~ **starter** INTER
~ **(suffix)** ENCE, ISM, NESS, SHIP
turn ~'s evidence SING
US ~ ALA, ALAS, ARK, CAL, DEL, FLA, IDA, ILL, IND, IOWA, KAN, KEN, MASS, MISS, NDAK, NEB, NEBR, NEV, OHIO, ORE, OREGON, PENN, SDAK, TENN, TEX, UTAH, WASH

___-**state** CITY, SOLID

"State ___" FAIR

___ **State (Big Ten school)** PENN

___ **State (Hawaii)** ALOHA

___ **State (Idaho)** GEM

___ **State (Letterman's alma mater)** BALL

___ **State (Massachuetts)** BAY

___ **State (Ohio school)** KENT

"State Fair"
~ **director** LANG
~ **state** IOWA

stately REGAL
~ **home** MANOR

statement BILL, NEWS
~ **entry** DEBIT
~ **of belief** CREDO
authoritative ~ EDICT
brief ~ NOTE
false ~ LIE, TALE
fashion ~ DRESS
itemized ~ BILL
make a ~ AVER, SAY
mudslinger's ~ SLUR
profit and loss ~

entry ASSET
shootout ~ DRAW

"State of Grace"
~ **actor** PENN

state of the ___ ART

"State of the ___" UNION

"State of the Union"
~ **director** CAPRA

stater COIN

___ **statesman** ELDER

static INERT, NOISE

station BASE, CASTE, ESTATE, LAY, LOT, ORDER, PLANT, POST, PUT, RANK, SPHERE, SPOT, STATE, STOP
~ **abbr.** ARR, ETA
~ **wagon** AUTO, CAR, MOTOR
Army ~ BASE
bus ~ DEPOT
captain's ~ HELM
"Deep Space Nine" ~ OPS
military ~ POST
railroad ~ STOP
train ~ DEPOT

___ **station** BUS, FIRE, GAS, SPACE, TRAIN

"Station ___" WEST

___ **Station** PENN, UNION

stationary FAST, INERT

stationery PAPER

stations
radio ~ MEDIA

"___ Station Zebra" ICE

statistic
scoreboard ~ ERROR, HIT, RUN
vital ~ AGE

statistical
~ **abbr.** PCT
~ **info** DATA
~ **pattern** TREND
~ **term** MEAN, MODE

statistician
~ **no-no** BIAS

statistics DATA
~ **(abbr.)** NOS

stator
~ **partner** ROTOR

stats
vital ~ BIO

statue IMAGE
~ **of a god** IDOL
~ **site** APSE
~ **stone** JADE
~ **support** BASE
headless ~ TORSO
Piccadilly ~ EROS

Statue of Liberty
ship that brought the
~ ISERE

statues
island of large ~ EASTER

statuesque TALL
~ **model** IMAN

statuette
coveted ~ OSCAR

stature MERIT
gain ~ GROW

status CASTE, CLASS, MODE, RANK, RATE, STATE
~ **(suffix)** SHIP
Army ~ RANK
call-up ~ ONEA
have ~ RATE
raise in ~ EXALT
social ~ CASTE, ESTATE
suburban ~ symbol POOL
tennis ~ BYE

statute ACT, EDICT, LAW, ORDER, RULE

statutory LEGAL

Staubach ROGER

staunch STEM, STOP, TRUE

Stautner ERNIE

stave
~ **off** AVERT, DEFER, DETER, FEND, REPEL

Stavros
~ **rival** ARI

stay ABIDE, ABODE, ARREST, BIDE, DEFER, HALT, LAST, REIN, SHORE, STEM, STOP, TABLE
~ **afloat** SWIM
~ **around** LAST
~ **attached** ADHERE
~ **awake nights** STEW
~ **away from** AVOID, MISS, SHUN
~ **behind** LAG
~ **for** AWAIT
~ **fresh** KEEP
~ **home for dinner** EATIN
~ **in touch** WRITE
~ **put** HOLD
~ **unsettled** PEND
~ **with** TAIL, TRAIL
~ **with a contract** RENEW
don't ~ fast RUN
extended ~ ABODE

stay ___ (don't move) PUT

"Stay ___, Joe" AWAY

stay-at-home LONER

stayed BEEN

"Stayin' ___" ALIVE

stead LIEU
stand in good ~ AID

steadfast SET, SOLID, SURE, TRUE
be ~ ABIDE, LAST

steady DATE, SAME, SURE, TRUE
~ **succession** STREAM
go ~ DATE, PIN

"Steady as ___ goes" SHE

steak MEAT
~ **cut** LOIN, TBONE
~ **on the hoof** STEER
~ **style** DIANE
like prime ~ AGED
prepare a ~ SEAR

steak ___ DIANE

steakhouse
~ **offering** TBONE
~ **order** RARE

steaks
like some ~ AGED

steak sauce
~ **name** LEA

steak tartare
like ~ RAW

steal COP, CRIB, NIP, SNEAK, TAKE
~ **a march on** LEAD
~ **a scene** EMOTE
~ **(away)** SLIP
~ **by** ELAPSE
~ **from** ROB
what hams try to ~ SCENE

"___ Steal, The" BIG

stealer
scene ~ HAM

___-**stealer** SCENE

stealthy SLY

steam ANGER, BOAT, BOIL, GAS, HEAT, SAIL, UPSET
~ **bath** BATH, SAUNA
~ **conveyor** PIPE
~ **up** ANGER, ENRAGE, RILE
cook with ~ SCALD
give off ~ REEK
let off ~ YELL
run out of ~ PETER
sound of ~ HISS
under one's own ~ ALONE

steam ___ BATH

steam ___ (appliance) IRON

"Steamboat ___, Jr." BILL

"Steamboat 'Round the ___" BEND

steamed IRATE, SORE, UPSET
~ **seafood** CLAM
get ~ up BOIL

steam engine
~ **developer** WATT

steamer BOAT, CLAM, LINER, PAN, SHIP

steamer ___ RUG

steaming ATSEA, HOT, IRATE, UPSET

steamroom
~ **site** SPA

steamship BOAT, LINER

steamy DAMP, HOT

stearate ESTER, SALT

stearin ESTER

steatite TALC

Steber, Eleanor
~ **role** ELSA

steed ARAB, HORSE, MARE, PACER
~ **stopper** WHOA

Steed, John
~ **partner** EMMA, GALE, PEEL

steel METAL, NERVE
~ **base** IRON
~ **by-product** SLAG
~ **ender** HEAD, YARD
~ **factory** MILL
~ **plow inventor** DEERE
curved ~ **tool** ADZE
fine ~ TOLEDO
German ~ **center** ESSEN, RUHR

steel ___ BAND, BLUE, GRAY, TRAP

Steel ___ (Atlantic City site) PIER

steel-belted
~ **buy** TIRE

Steel, Danielle
~ **bestseller** STAR

Steele, Richard SIR

Steelers ELEVEN, TEAM
~ **org.** NFL

___ steel guitar PEDAL

steelhead TROUT

steelie
~ **alternative** AGATE

"Steel Magnolias"
~ **director** ROSS

steel plow
~ **inventor** DEERE

steelworkers
former ~ **chief** ABEL

steely COOL, HARD

Steely ___ DAN

steenbok ANIMAL

Steenburgen, Mary
~ **role in "Back to the Future III"** CLARA
~ **sitcom** INK

steep BATHE, BREW, DEAR, RET, RICH, SOAK, SOP
~ **cliff** CRAG

steepen RISE

steeple SPIRE
~ **adornment** EPI

steeplechase RACE

steer HEAD, PILOT, RUN, SAIL
~ **clear of** AVOID, EVADE, SHUN
~ **(for)** AIM, TRY
anagram of ~ ESTER, RESET, TREES
give someone a bum ~ LIE
throw a ~ ROPE

steering
~ **apparatus** HELM

Steffi
score for ~ ADIN
see also German

Steiger ROD

stein
~ **contents** ALE, BEER, LAGER

Stein
part of a ~ **quote** AROSE, ISA, ROSE

Steinbeck
~ **topic** PEARL

steinful ALE

Stein, Jean
~ **book** EDIE

"Stein Song"
~ **town** ORONO

Steinway PIANO

stela STONE

Stella ADLER

Stella d'___ ORO

stellar
~ **(prefix)** ASTRO
~ **wind** GAS

"St. Elmo's ___" FIRE

stem AXIS, CANE, HALT, ISSUE, SPRIG, STOP
~ **(from)** ARISE, COME
~ **joint** NODE
~ **opposite** STERN
from ~ **to stern** OVER
raspberry ~ CANE

stem-to-stern
~ **timber** KEEL

Sten ANNA
~ **role** NANA

stench ODOR, REEK
~ **feedback** GAG

stencil TRACE

Stengel, Mrs. EDNA

steno
~ **boss** EXEC
~ **item** PAD

stentorian LOUD

stentoriously ALOUD

step GAIT, MOVE, TREAD
~ **backward** LOSS
~ **forward** GAIN
~ **in French** PAS
~ **lightly** TRIP
~ **lively** RACE, STIR
~ **on** TREAD
~ **on it** HIE, RACE, RUN, SPEED
~ **part** RISER
~ **starter** DOOR, FOOT, OVER, SIDE
~ **through water** WADE
~ **to the music** DANCE
~ **up** RAISE, RISE
~ **up the RPMs** REV
~ **up to the plate** BAT
a ~ **up** STAIR

ballerina's ~ PAS
car-wash ~ RINSE
measured ~ PACE
quick ~ TROT
take the first ~ START
tango ~ DIP

step ___ ASIDE

step-___ UPS

___ step GOOSE

___-step ONE, TWO

"Step ___!" ONIT

Stephen CRANE, REA

Stephen, King
~ **mother** ADELA

Stephen Vincent ___ BENET

step on the ___ GAS

steppe DESERT, LEA, MOOR
~ **cousin** LLANO

"Steppenwolf"
~ **author** HESSE

"Step right in!" ENTER

steps
~ **over a fence** STILE
series of ~ STAIR
take ~ ACT, PACE

step to the ___ REAR

step up to the ___ BAR

-ster
~ **cousin** IST, ITE

stereo
~ **input** TAPE
~ **knob** BASS
run the ~ PLAY

stereotype LABEL, PEG

stereotyped BANAL, STALE

stereotypes
use ~ LABEL

stereotypical USUAL

sterile ARID, DESERT, DRY

sterilized PURE

sterling ACE, BEST, FINE, GOOD, PURE

stern AFT, CRUEL, DOUR, IRON, REAR
~ **opposite** STEM
from stem to ~ OVER
toward the ~ AFT

Stern ISAAC
~ **need** RESIN
~ **stick** BOW

"___ Stern" DER

sternness RIGOR

sternum BONE

sternward AFT

stet
~ **opposite** DELE

Stetson HAT

Stettin
~ **river** ODER

Steve ALLEN, RASH, SAX

"Steve Allen Show"
~ **regular** NYE

stevedore LADE
~ **org.** ILA

___-steven EVEN

Stevens APRIL, ART, CAT, RAY, RISE

Stevens, George
~ **film of 1953** SHANE
~ **film of 1956** GIANT

Stevenson ADLAI

Stevenson, Robert Louis
~ **character** HYDE
~ **home** SAMOA

Stevens, Ray
~ **Ahab** ARAB
~ **Arab** AHAB

Stevens, Wallace POET
see also poet

Steverino ALLEN

stew BOIL, FRET, HEAT, OLIO, PET, RAGE
~ **ingredient** MEAT, VEAL
~ **pod** OKRA
~ **vegetable** ONION
spicy ~ OLLA

___ stew INA, IRISH

steward AGENT
~ **ender** ESS

Stewart ROD

Stewart, Jackie RACER, SCOT

Stewart, James
~ **thriller** ROPE

stewpot
Spanish ~ OLLA

stibnite ORE

stich LINE
~ **starter** HEMI

Stich, Michael
~ **specialty** ACE

stick BAT, CANE, GLUE, HOLD, JAM, ROD, STAB, STAKE, WAND
~ **around** ABIDE, BIDE, LAST, STAY, WAIT
~ **ender** PIN, UPS
~ **fast** ADHERE
~ **in one's craw** IRK, PEEVE, REPEL, RILE
~ **in the dugout** BAT
~ **in the mud** MIRE
~ **it out** BEAR, STAY
~ **like glue** ADHERE
~ **on** ADD
~ **one's head out** EMERGE
~ **one's neck out** BET, CRANE, RISK
~ **one's nose in** PRY

stick ___

~ out a hand for ABET, AID, HELP
~ starter CHOP, DIP, FLAG, LIP, NON, SLAP, YARD
~ together BIND, GLUE, PASTE
~ up ROB
~ up for AID, HELP
~ with it PEG, PLOD
billiards ~ CUE
burn a joss ~ CENSE
fiddle ~ BOW
J-shaped ~ CANE
lick and ~ SEAL
on the ~ ALERT
pogo ~ TOY
pointed ~ GOAD
riding ~ CROP
schoolroom ~ RULER
swagger ~ CANE
walking ~ CANE, STAVE

stick ___ (protrude) OUT

___ stick BIG, ORANGE, POGO

___ Stick CHAP

stickball
~ marker SEWER

sticker BARB, LABEL, NEEDLE, PIN, SEAL, STAMP, TAG
decorative ~ SEAL
window ~ DECAL

stickers
big ~ CACTI

stick in one's ___ CRAW

stick-on LABEL
~ design DECAL

stick one's ___ out NECK

stickshift
~ selection GEAR

stick-to-itiveness GRIT

stickum GLUE, PASTE

stick up ___ (support) FOR

sticky DAMP
~ fruit DATE
~ material GLUE, GOO
~ mud SLIME
~ place MIRE
~ strip TAPE

Stieglitz
~ need CAMERA, LENS

stiff HARD, STAID
~ in the joints ACHY
~ wind BLAST, GALE
having a ~ upper lip STOIC
not at all ~ LIMP

stiff ___ board ASA

stiff-backed ERECT

stiffen TENSE

stiffener
collar ~ STAY

stiff-necked PRIM

stiffness RIGOR

stiff upper ___ LIP

stifle DAMP, GAG, STOP

stifling CLOSE
not ~ AIRY

stigma SHAME, TAINT

stigmatize LIBEL, PEG, SLUR, TAINT
~ socially SNUB

stile GATE

stiletto
use a ~ STAB

still ALLAY, CALM, CLEAR, GAG, IDLE, INERT, STOP, YET
~ asleep ABED
~ in the game ALIVE
~ in use LIVE
~ kicking AGILE, SPRY
~ water POND, POOL
be ~ REST
lying ~ INERT
sit ~ for ABIDE, ALLOW

still ___ LIFE, WATER

Stiller BEN
~ mother ANNE, MEARA

Stiller and ___ MEARA

still life
~ subject EWER, PEAR

stillness CALM, PEACE

stilt BIRD
~ cousin EGRET

stilts TOY

Stimpy CAT
~ pal REN

stimulant TONIC

stimulate AROUSE, PROD, ROUSE, SPUR, URGE

stimulated
be ~ REACT

stimulating RACY, TONIC

stimulus CAUSE, CUE, GOAD, SPUR
nose ~ ODOR
olfactory ~ AROMA
respond to ~ REACT

sting BITE, ITCH, PAIN, ROOK, SCAM, SMART
~ operation CON, SETUP, TRAP
~ org. FBI

Sting
1984 ~ film DUNE

stinger BARB, BEE

stinging ACID, ACRID, SORE, TART
~ comment BARB
~ insect BEE

"Sting like ___" ABEE

"Sting like a bee"
~ boxer ALI

stingo BEER

stingy MEAN, NEAR

stink ODOR, REEK
~ ender AROO, EROO
social ~ FLAP

stinker LOUSE

stinking BAD

"___ Stinks" LOVE

stinky RANK

stint BOUT, TASK

stipend DOLE, FEE, WAGE

stipple DOT

stipulate ORDER

stipulation TERM
added ~ AND
seller's ~ ASIS

stipulations IFS

stir ADO, ARISE, AROUSE, BEAT, FIRE, MOVE, PEN, ROUSE, ROW, SWAY, TODO
~ in ADD
~ the air FAN
~ to action GOAD, PROD, URGE
~ up GOAD, PROD, RAISE, RILE, ROIL, ROUSE
don't ~ SIT

stir-___ FRY

Stirling MOSS

stirred
~ up AGOG, EAGER

stirring ABOUT, AFOOT, LIVE

stirrup BONE
~ site EAR

stitch CABLE, MEND, PAIN, PANG, SEW
~ loosely BASTE
pick up a ~ KNIT
what a certain ~ saves NINE
without a ~ BARE, NUDE

stitches
line of ~ SEAM

stiver COIN

"...St. Ives, ___ a man..." IMET

stock ASSET, BANAL, CLAN, KEEP, LINE, ORDER, PLANT
~ (abbr.) MDSE
~ broker's directive SELL
~ car MOTOR, RACER
~ diet HAY
~ ender ADE, YARD
~ holding LOT
~ in trade ASSET
~ of goods LINE
~ option CALL, PUT
~ starter ROOT
~ statistic YIELD
~ ticker output TAPE
~ unit SHARE
~ up AMASS, STORE
~ volatility
measurement BETA
arsenal ~ ARMS
decline, as ~ prices SAG

dispensary ~ SERA
have in ~ SELL
take ~ of ASSESS, AUDIT

stock ___ CAR

___ stock OPEN, SEED, TAKE

stockade PALE

stock exchange
~ membership SEAT

Stockholm CITY, PORT
~ resident SWEDE
airline to ~ SAS

stock in ___ TRADE

stocking
~ cap HAT
~ filler LEG
~ in French BAS
~ material LISLE, MESH, SILK
~ part FOOT, TOE
~ shade ECRU
~ snag RUN
~ stuffer TOY
~ stuffer, perhaps COAL
~ style MESH

stocking ___ CAP

stockings HOSE
make ~ KNIT

"stockings ___ hung..., The" WERE

"___ Stockings" SILK

stockpile AMASS, HEAP, SAVE, STORE

stock ticker
~ inventor EDISON

Stockwell DEAN

stocky BIG, LARGE

stockyard
~ group HERD

stoical CALM

stoicism
practice ~ INURE

stoke FEED

Stoke-on-___, England TRENT

stole FUR, SCARF, WRAP
~ material SABLE
feather ~ BOA

stolen HOT
~ goods LOOT, SWAG

stolid DENSE, SLOW

Stoller ILONA

Stoloff BEN

stolon SHOOT

Stoltz ERIC

Stolze LENA

stoma PORE

stomach ABIDE, BEAR, CRAW, TAKE
~ ender ACHE

~ muscles, for short ABS
~ problem ACID, GAS
animal ~ CRAW
can't ~ ABHOR, HATE
on one's ~ PRONE
turn one's ~ REPEL

stomp DANCE, STAMP, STORM
~ around RAGE

"Stompin' at ___ Savoy" THE

stone PELT, PIT, SEED
~ broke POOR
~ ender CHAT, CROP, MASON, WARE, WASH
~ monument STELE
~ piece SLAB
~ starter FLAG, FREE, GEM, HAIL, IRON, KEY, LIME, LODE, MILE, MILL, MOON, PIPE, RHINE, SAND, SOAP
~ throw STEP
a ~'s throw away NEAR
banded ~ AGATE
cameo ~ ONYX
carver's ~ JADE
cherry ~ PIT
fiery ~ OPAL
hollow ~ GEODE
intaglio ~ ONYX
layered ~ ONYX
leave no ~ unturned DIG, HUNT, RAKE, SEEK
precious ~ GEM
rolling ~ HOBO, NOMAD
semiprecious ~ ONYX, OPAL
statue ~ JADE
striped ~ AGATE
whitish ~ OPAL

stone ___ CRAB

Stone AGE, EZRA, SLY

Stone ___ AGE

"Stone Boy, The"
~ director CAIN

stonechat BIRD

Stonehenge
~ builder CELT
reaction to ~ AWE
river near ~ AVON

Stone of ___ SCONE

stones
lay ~ PAVE
throw ~ at PELT

stonewall DETER, STALL

stoneware CLAY

stone-wash ABRADE

stoneworker MASON

stonewort ALGA

stony COOL, CRUEL, HARD

stony ___ CORAL

"stony British ___, a" STARE

stood
~ up AROSE, ROSE

stooge TOOL

Stooge MOE
~ count THREE

Stooges TRIO

Stookey PAUL

stool SEAT
~ part LEG
~ pigeon RAT
~ starter BAR, STEP

stoolie RAT
play ~ BLAB, RATON, SING

stoop BEND, BOW, OBEY, STEP

stooped BENT

"___ Stoops to Conquer" SHE

stop ABIDE, ARREST, CEASE, CLOG, END, HALT, LAPSE, REST, STALL, STAND
~ aboard ship AVAST
~ a launch ABORT
~ at ABUT
~ stalling ACT
~ starter DOOR, NON
~ the leak STEM
~ up CLOG, DAM
~ working REST, STALL
camel ~ OASIS
cruise ~ ISLE, PORT, RIO
El ~ STA
lunchtime ~ DELI
put a ~ to ARREST, CEASE
roadside ~ INN
RR ~ STA
shopper's ~ MALL, MART
toll ~ STILE
try to ~ DETER

stop ___ SIGN

stop ___ dime ONA

___ stop PIT, REST

"Stop!" HALT, WHOA
director's ~ CUT

"___ Stop" BUS

"STOP" SIGN

"___ Stop, Greenwich Village" NEXT

"Stop! in the ___ of Love" NAME

stoplight
~ color AMBER, RED

"Stop Making ___" SENSE

stop on a ___ DIME

stopover CALL, STAY
~ site HOTEL
desert ~ OASIS
rustic ~ CAMP, INN

Stoppard TOM

stopper CAP, LID, PEG, TOP
dogie ~ NOOSE
horse ~ WHOA
knock ~ OCTANE
match ~ TKO
parade ~ RAIN
parking-scofflaw ~ BOOT
sash ~ SILL

stopping
~ point LIMIT

"Stopping by Woods ___ Snowy Evening" ONA

"Stopping by Woods on a Snowy Evening" POEM

stopple LID, PEG

"Stop that!" DONT

stopwatch
~ button RESET
use a ~ TIME

storage
~ area ATTIC, DEPOT, SHED
~ bin CRIB, SILO
~ container BIN, CHEST
put in cold ~ DEFER
ship's ~ area HOLD

store KEEP, MART, MINE, PILE, SAVE, SHOP, STOW
~ away STOW
~ inventory ASSET
~ liquor AGE
~ of knowledge LORE
~ up AMASS, SAVE
be in ~ LOOM
be in ~ for AWAIT
department ~ event SALE
food ~ DELI
health-food ~ buy BRAN, KELP, OATS
in ~ ONTAP
makeshift ~ STAND
retail ~ SHOP
run a ~ SELL
secret ~ STASH

___ store DIME

___ store by SET

storefront
~ sign OPEN

storehouse MINE

storeroom ATTIC
~ item BIN

store window
~ light NEON
~ sign OPEN
~ word SALE

stories
handed-down ~ LORE

stork BIRD
~ cousin CRANE, EGRET, HERON, IBIS

storm BESET, BOIL, DOOR, GALE, HAIL, RAGE, RAMP, RANT, RAVE
~ center EYE
~ drain SEWER
~ heading ENE, ESE, NNE, NNW, SSE, SSW, WNW, WSW
~ pellets HAIL, SLEET
~ posting ALERT
~ preceder CALM
~ starter BARN
~ the ramparts ARISE, RISE
~ warning ALERT
electrical ~ RAIN
electromagnetic ~ AURORA

gathering ~ PERIL
port in a ~ HOME
sci-fi ~ material ION

storm ___ DOOR

___ storm DUST, ICE

Storm GALE, GEO

storming MAD

stormless CALM, CLEAR

stormy BAD, RAINY, UGLY
~ weather GALE

"Stormy Weather"
~ composer ARLEN
~ director STONE
~ singer HORNE

Storting
where the ~ meets OSLO

story LIE, TALE, YARN
~ going around RUMOR
~ inconsistency HOLE
~ line PLOT
~ name TITLE
adventure ~ GEST, GESTE
cock-and-bull ~ ALIBI, LIE, TALE, YARN
common ~ subject LOVE
fish ~ LIE, TALE, YARN
heroic ~ EPIC, GEST, GESTE
inside ~ DOPE, SCOOP
life ~ BIO
long ~ EPIC, SAGA
main ~ PLOT
shaggy dog ~ LIE, TALE, YARN
short ~ GENRE, PROSE
suspect's ~ ALIBI
tall ~ LIE, TALE, YARN
top ~ ATTIC
trumped-up ~ TALE

story ___ LINE

___ story LEAD, SOB

"___ Story" LOVE, TOY

"___ Story, The" FBI, NUNS

"Story of ___ H, The" ADELE

"Story of ___ Loves, The" THREE

"Story of Vernon & ___ Castle, The" IRENE

"Story on ___ One, The" PAGE

"Story on Page ___, The" ONE

"Story on Page One, The"
~ director ODETS

storyteller LIAR
ancient ~ AESOP

storytelling
~ dance HULA

storytime
~ Mother GOOSE

stout BIG, FAT, LARGE, OBESE
~ cousin ALE, BEER
~ ingredient MALT

Stout REX
~ sleuth NERO

stout-hearted
~ **one** HERO

"Stouthearted ___" MEN

stout-heartedness NERVE

stove RANGE
~ **part** OVEN
right off the ~ HOT

stovepipe HAT, LID

stovetop
~ **item** PAN, POT

stow LADE
~ **away** HIDE, SAVE
~ **on board** LADE

Stowe
~ **character** EVA, TOM
~ **equipment** SKI
~ **novel** DRED
~ **sight** SLOPE, SNOW, TBAR, TOW

Strad
~ **relative** AMATI

straddle SIT, SPAN

straddle-legged ACROSS

straddling ACROSS, ATOP

Stradivari
~ **teacher** AMATI

straggle DRAG, LAG, TAIL

straight CLEAN, ERECT, GOOD, NEAR
~ **drive** LINER
~ **line** ROW
~ **shot** ARROW
~ **up** NEAT
look ~ in the eye DARE, FACE
make ~ lines RULE
not ~ ATILT, WRY
the ~ goods FACT

straight ___ ARROW, FACE, MAN, PIN

straight ___ (immediately) OFF

straight ___ arrow ASAN

straight-___ ARM, LACED, OUT

___ straight SET

"Straight ___" TIME

straightaway ANON, NOW, SOON

straightedge RULER

straighten ALINE, ERECT, EVEN, TRUE
~ **out** DRESS, SETTLE

straightener
collar ~ IRON

straightforward CLEAR, HONEST, OPEN

straight-grained
tough ~ wood ASH

straightness
symbol of ~ ARROW

straight-out FLAT, TOTAL

strain AIR, ARIA, EXERT, SONG, STRESS, TASK, TUNE, TYPE
~ **as the neck** CRANE
~ **oneself** LABOR
mental ~ STRESS
muscle ~ ACHE
subject to ~ TRY
Swiss ~ YODEL
under a ~ EDGY, TENSE

strain ___ gnat ATA

strain at a ___ GNAT

strained TAUT, TENSE

strainer MESH

strait ARM, CANAL, INLET, NECK

strait-___ LACED

___ Strait (Arctic channel) RAE

___ Strait (Asian waterway) KOREA

straitened POOR

"Strait Is the Gate"
~ **author** GIDE

strait-laced PRIM, STAID, STERN

Strait of Belle ___ ISLE

straits NEED, PASS
in dire ~ NEEDY
like some ~ DIRE

___ straits DIRE

strand CABLE, CORD, DESERT, SANDS, SHORE

stranded ASHORE

strange ALIEN, EERIE, EERY, NEW, ODD, OFF

"Strange ___, The" ONE

"Strange Affair of ___ Harry, The" UNCLE

strange as it ___ seem MAY

Strange, Curtis
~ **org.** PGA

"Strange Impersonation"
~ **director** MANN

Strangelove
~ **and others** DRS

"Strange Magic"
~ **band** ELO

stranger ALIEN

"Stranger ___ Paradise" THAN

"Stranger on the ___" SHORE

"Strangers ___ Train" ONA

"Stranger's ___, The" HAND

"___ Strangers" THREE

"Strangers in ___ Company" GOOD

"Strangers in Good Company"
~ **director** SCOTT

"Strangers on a ___" TRAIN

strap BAND, BEAT, BELT, BIND, HIT, LASH, LEASH, SMITE, TAB
harness ~ TRACE
leather ~ REIN
parachutist's ~ RISER

straphanger RIDER
~ **purchase** TOKEN

strapped NEEDY, POOR

strapping BIG, FIT, HALE, LARGE

Strasberg LEE

Strasbourg
~ **river** ILL
see also French

Strastny PETER

stratagem ART, GAME, LURE, MOVE, RUSE, STALL, TRAP, WILE
Alexander's ~ SIEGE
basketball ~ PRESS

Stratas TERESA

strategize PLAN

strategy PATH, PLAN
~ **game** RISK

Stratford
~ **river** AVON

stratum BED, CLASS, RANK, TIER
social ~ CASTE, CLASS, ELITE, SPHERE
thin ~ SEAM

Strauss LEVI
~ **work** OPERA

Stravinsky IGOR

straw COLOR, HAY, PIPE
~ **in the wind** OMEN
~ **product** MAT
~ **unit** BALE
~ **vote** POLL
~ **wear** HAT
last ~ LIMIT
use a ~ SIP

straw ___ BOSS, HAT, MAN, VOTE

___ straw LAST

strawberry PIE, RED

strawberry ___ ROAN

Strawberry
~ **once** MET

strawberry-blonde FAIR

"Straw Dogs"
Peter, in ~ ARNE

straws
drink with ~ MALT, SODA

stray CUR, ERR, ROAM, ROVE
~ **from the path** SIN

"Stray ___" DOG

"Stray ___ Strut" CAT

streak BAND, BAR, BEAM, LINE, RAY, SPEED, STRIA
like a blue ~ RAPID
on a ~ HOT
winning ~ RUN

___ streak BLUE

streaking FAD

stream ISSUE, POUR, RAIN, RAY, RILL, RUN, SAIL
~ **forth** EMERGE, EMIT
~ **from** TRAIL
~ **starter** MAIN, MILL
factory on a ~ MILL
forceful ~ JET

___ stream JET

streamer FLAG, RAY

streamlined SLEEK, TRIM

street LANE, PATH, ROAD, ROUTE
~ **address abbr.** AVE
~ **band** GANG
~ **guide** MAP
~ **in French** RUE
~ **in Italian** VIA
~ **language** SLANG
~ **noise** SIREN
~ **posting** SIGN
~ **prohibiting cars** MALL
~ **salutation** BRO
~ **sign** ARROW, SLOW, YIELD
~ **urchin** IMP, LAD
back ~ ALLEY
British ~ MEWS
common ~ name ELM, MAIN, MAPLE
desirable ~ EASY
put on the ~ BAIL
roll down the ~ SKATE
side ~ LANE

street-___ SMART

___ street EASY

Street DELLA
~ **boss** MASON
~ **portrayer** HALE

"Street ___" ANGEL, SCENE

"___ Street" EASY, LIME, MAIN, SESAME, SIDE

___ Street (journalism center) FLEET

streetcar
~ **building** BARN
~ **charge** FARE
London ~ TRAM

"Streetcar"
~ **role** STAN

"Streetcar ___ Desire, A" NAMED

street corner
~ **call** TAXI

street fighting RIOT

Street, Picabo
emulate ~ SKI
lift for ~ TBAR

streets
like wintry ~ ICY

"___ Streets" CITY, MEAN

"Street Scene"
~ **author** RICE

street-sign
~ abbr. AVE

"Streets of ___" FIRE

___ Street, USA MAIN

streetwise ONTO

"Street With No ___, The" NAME

Streisand
~ film NUTS
emulate ~ SING

strength ASSET, MAIN, SINEW
~ of mind METAL
lose ~ FADE
test for ~ STRESS
trial of ~ BOUT

strengthening TONIC

strenuous HARD

strenuously HARD

strepitous LOUD

stress ASSERT
~ perhaps AGER
~ result, maybe ULCER
feeling no ~ ATEASE
syllable ~ TONE

stressed
~ out TENSE

stress-free CALM

stretch AREA, COLOR, CRANE, EKE, RANGE, RUN, TERM, TIME, TRACT
~ auto LIMO
~ of good luck RUN
~ one's legs PACE
~ out DRAG, LIE, PAD, REST, SPIN, TRAIL
~ over SPAN
~ pennies EKE
~ the neck CRANE
~ the truth LIE

stretched
~ out LONG
fully ~ TAUT

stretch one's ___ LEGS

strew CAST

striate LINE

striation BAND

strict CRUEL, DOUR, HARD, SOBER, STERN

strictness RIGOR

stride GAIT, PACE, STEP, TREAD
easy ~ LOPE

strident
~ sound BLARE, DIN

strides
make rapid ~ HIE, MOVE, RUN, SPEED

stridulate GRATE

stridulation NOISE, RASP

strife ROW
personification of ~ ERIS

strigine
~ youngster OWLET

strike BAT, BEAT, BELT, CHOP, CLIP, DASH, HIT, OCCUR, PELT, RAM, SLAP
~ an attitude POSE
~ a pose MODEL
~ a rail CAROM
~ at RAID
~ caller UMP
~ down SMITE
~ ignorer SCAB
~ lightly TAP
~ one as SEEM
~ out DELE, ERASE, FAN
~ sharply HIT, RAP
~ silent AMAZE, AWE, DAZE, STUN, WOW
~ terror into SCARE
~ together CLAP
~ with force RAM
~ zone ALLEY
~ zone's lower boundary KNEE
air ~ RAID
end a ~ SETTLE
hunger ~ FAST
Klondike ~ GOLD
on ~ OUT
sourdough's ~ GOLD, LODE

strike ___ ZONE

___ strike AIR

strike a ___ POSE

strikebreaker SCAB

strike it ___ RICH

strikeout
all-time ~ king RYAN

strikes
three ~ OUT

"___ Strikes Back, The" SAINT

"___ Strikes Out" FEAR

"Strike Up the Band"
~ song SOON

striking LOUD

Strindberg SWEDE

string BEAN, CORD, FILE, LINE, ROW, RUN
~ along DUPE
~ along (with) AGREE
~ fastening KNOT
~ instrument BASS, CELLO, HARP, LUTE, LYRE, SITAR, UKE, VIOL
~ player CAT
piece on a ~ BEAD
shoe ~ LACE
toy on a ~ YOYO

string ___ ALONG, BASS, BEAN, TIE

___ string APRON, ONA

___-string FIRST

stringbean
like a ~ LANK

stringed
~ instrument of India SITAR
ancient ~ instrument LYRE

stringency RIGOR

stringent SOUR

string quartet
~ member CELLO

strings
apron ~ TIES
celestial ~ HARP
hula ~ UKE
medieval ~ LUTE
tighten the purse ~ STINT

strip BAND, BAR, BARE, BELT, LANE, PEEL, ROAD, ROB, ROUTE, SHED, SHRED, TAPE
~ down PEEL
~ of wood LATH, SLAT
carpenter's ~ LATH
freeway ~ LANE
lattice ~ LATH
median ~ MALL
narrow ~ SHRED
sticky ~ TAPE
toothed ~ COMB
wooden ~ LATH

strip-___ MINE

___ strip DRAG

stripe BAND, BAR, BELT, CAST, CLASS, ILK, LINE, SORT, STAMP
~ starter PIN
of the same ~ ALIKE

striped
~ cat TIGER
~ stone AGATE

stripes
person in ~ REF

Stripes
Stars and ~ FLAG

stripling KID, LAD

stripped BARE

stripping BAND

strips
make ~ TEAR

Stritch ELAINE

strive ASSAY, ESSAY, EXERT, LABOR, TRY, TUG, VIE
~ (for) AIM

strobilus CONE

stroke BEAT, PET
~ gently CARESS, PET
ax ~ CHOP
badminton ~ LOB
barber's ~ SNIP
golf ~ CHIP
head ~ PAT
keyboard ~ TAP
letter ~ SERIF
light ~ DAB
master ~ FEAT
tennis ~ CHOP

stroll HIKE, MOVE, ROAM, STEP

stroller
~ occupant TOT
London ~ PRAM

strong ABLE, BAD, DEEP, FIT, HALE, HARD, IRON, RICH
~ bug ANT
~ cleaner LYE
~ emotion ANGER, FEAR, HATE, IRE, LOVE
~ fiber SISAL
~ inclination URGE, YEN
~ point ASSET
~ rope CABLE
~ solvent ACID
~ suds ALE
~ suit ARMOR
~ temptation URGE
~ thread LISLE
~ twine CORD
~ wind GALE

strong ___ SUIT

strong ___ ox ASAN

strong-___ ARM

"Strong ___, The" MAN

strong-arm MAKE, PRESS, ROB

strongbox CHEST, SAFE, TILL

"Stronger ___ the Sun" THAN

"Stronger Than the ___" SUN

stronghold KEEP, LAIR
castle ~ KEEP
mountain ~ AERIE

strongman
mythical ~ ATLAS

"Strong Man, The"
~ director CAPRA

strong silent ___, the TYPE

strong-smelling RANK

strontianite ORE

strontium METAL

strop BAND, EDGE, HONE

struck
~ again RELIT
~ a match LIT

structure MAKE, ORDER
backyard ~ SHED
baglike ~ SAC
boardwalk ~ PIER
cylindrical ~ SILO
elevated ~ ALTAR
hockey ~ CAGE
river ~ LEVEE
rural ~ BARN
Shoshone ~ TEPEE
skeletal ~ BONE
sorghum ~ SILO

struggle LABOR, PLOD, ROW, VIE, WAR
~ for air GASP
long ~ SIEGE

strung
~ out LONG
highly ~ TAUT, TENSE

strut BRAG, CROW, MOVE, PARADE, POST, SHORE, STAY

sts. RDS, RTES

Stuart MEL
    last ~ monarch ANNE

Stuart __ Flexner BERG

Stuart, Corey
    ~ on "Lassie" BRAY

Stuart, J.E.B. REB

Stuart, Mary SCOT

stub END, TAG, TAIL
    ~ one's toe ERR

stubble BEARD
    ~ site CHIN

stubborn SET
    ~ one ASS, MULE

stubborn __ mule ASA

stubborn as a __ MULE

Stubbs LEVI

stubby LOW

stuck
    ~ in place SET
    be ~ on DOTE
    place to be ~ RUT

stuck in __ ARUT

stuck-up VAIN
    ~ person SNOB

stud BEAM, DOT, HORSE, MALE
    ~ progeny FOAL
    ~ site EAR, LOBE

studded BESET

Studebaker AUTO, CAR

student
    ~ concern TEXT
    ~ hurdle ORAL
    ~ in French ELEVE
    ~ ordeal EXAM, TEST
    ~ paper ESSAY
    ~ quarters DORM
    ~ seat DESK
    ~ vehicle BUS
    certain ~ COED
    Colorado Springs ~ CADET
    former ~ ALUM, GRAD
    military ~ CADET
    New Haven ~ ELI
    second-year ~ SOPH
    West Point ~ CADET
    Yale ~ ELI

"Student Prince in __ Heidelberg, The" OLD

students
    final-yr. ~ SRS

studio FLAT, SHOP
    ~ couch SOFA
    ~ feature EASEL, SET
    movie ~ LOT
    TV ~ sign ONAIR

study CON, DEN, EYE, READ, ROOM, SCAN, TAKE
    ~ hard CRAM

    ~ intently PORE
brown ~ MUSE
main course of ~ MAJOR
musical ~ ETUDE

study __ HALL

__ study CASE, HOME

__-study SELF

stuff CRAM, GEAR, GLUT, ITEMS, JAM, PAD, RAM, SATE

__ stuff HOT, KID

stuffed DENSE
    ~ shirt PRIG, SNOB
    ~ tortilla TACO

stuffer
    stocking ~ TOY
    stocking ~ perhaps COAL

stuffing
    ~ flavoring SAGE

stuffy CLOSE, PRIM, STAID, STALE

stumble ERR, REEL, SLIP, TRIP
    ~ upon LEARN, MEET

stumblebum BOOR, LOUT, OAF

stumbling
    ~ block BAR, SNAG

stump POSE, STUB
    take the ~ ORATE

stumped ASEA, ATSEA

stumper POSER

stumpy LOW

stun AMAZE, AWE, DAZE, JAR, WOW

stung
    be ~ with remorse SMART

"__ Stung" IGOT

stunned AGOG
    appear ~ GAPE

stunt ANTIC, ARREST, DEED, FEAT
    ~ man's concern RISK

"Stunt __, The" MAN

stunted LOW, SMALL
    ~ animal RUNT
    ~ branch SPUR

stunt plane
    ~ maneuver LOOP, ROLL

stupefaction AWE, DAZE

stupefied AGAPE

stupefy AMAZE, AWE, DAZE, STUN

stupendous BIG, LARGE, VAST

stupid DIM, INANE, INEPT, MAD, SLOW
    ~ person ASS, CLOD, GOOSE, OAF

Stupid __ Tricks PET

stupor DAZE

sturdy FIT, HALE, IRON

sturgeon
    ~ product ROE

Sturluson, Snorri
    ~ compilation EDDA

Sturm und Drang DRAMA

Stuttgart CITY
    see also German

Stutz Bearcat AUTO, CAR
    ~ contemporary REO

__ St. Vincent Millay EDNA

sty ABODE, PEN
    ~ cry OINK
    ~ fare SLOP
    ~ occupant HOG, SOW

Stygian BAD, DIM, EVIL

style CALL, CAST, CHIC, CLASS, CUT, DASH, ELAN, FAD, GENRE, LABEL, MIEN, MODE, PEN, RAGE, STATE, TACT, TASTE, TONE, TREND
    1960s ~ MOD
    art ~ DECO, GENRE
    artistic ~ IDIOM
    auto ~ SEDAN
    chicken ~ KIEV
    coat ~ ALINE
    déjà-vu clothing ~ RETRO
    dress ~ ALINE, MINI, TENT
    Erte's ~ DECO
    Greek architectural ~ IONIC
    house ~ RANCH
    in ~ CHIC, MOD
    in the ~ of AFTER, ALA
    jacket ~ ETON, MAO, NEHRU
    jazz ~ BOP
    music ~ RAP
    no longer in ~ OUT
    nostalgic clothes ~ RETRO
    out of ~ DATED, PASSE
    salami ~ GENOA
    sardonic ~ IRONY
    skirt ~ ALINE
    steak ~ DIANE
    stocking ~ MESH
    tonsorial ~ AFRO
    type ~ ELITE, FONT, ROMAN

styled
    ~ like ALA

__-styled SELF

styling
    ~ preparation GEL

stylish CHIC, MOD, NEW, NOW, SMART, TONY
    ~ cut ALINE
    ~ place SALON
    too ~ ARTY

stylishness CHIC, TASTE, TON

stylist
    ~ supply GEL
    hair ~ sometimes DYER

stylite LONER

stylus NEEDLE, PEN
    ~ holder ARM

stymie DETER, TREE

styptic ALUM

suave COOL, EASY, GLIB, OILY, SLEEK

Suave
    ~ rival PERT

sub HERO, TEMP, UBOAT
    ~ detector SONAR
    ~ medium OCEAN, SEA
    ~ outlet DELI

sub __ ROSA

"__ Sub" OMEGA

subaltern RANK

subcontinent
    ~ prefix INDO

subcontract LEASE

subdivision TRACT
    dramatic ~ ACT
    Indian ~ TRIBE
    military ~ UNIT
    phylum ~ CLASS

subdue BEAT, BEND, BOW, COW, TAME

subdued MEEK, SOBER, TAME
    ~ color ASH

subjacent UNDER

subject NOUN, PRONE, THEME, TOPIC
    loyal ~ LIEGE
    sensitive ~, for some AGE

"Subject __ Roses, The" WAS

subjective
    ~ sensation AURA

subjectivity BIAS

subjects
    chief's ~ TRIBE

"Subject Was __, The" ROSES

"Subject Was Roses, The"
    ~ actress NEAL

subjoin ADD

subjugate BEND, BOW, REIGN, TAME, TREAD

subjunctive
    ~ word WERE

sublease LET, RELET, RENT

sublet LEASE, RENT

sublime GREAT, REGAL

submarine BOAT, HERO, SHIP
    ~ device SONAR
    ~ on sonar BLIP
    ~ part SALAMI
    ~ sandwich HERO
    ~ staffer CPO

submerge BATHE, DIP, SINK

submerged LOW

submerse BATHE, DIP, SINK

submission
    contest ~ ENTRY

record-company ~ DEMO

submissions
editorial ~ MSS

submissive EASY, LIMP, MEEK, TAME

submit ARGUE, BEND, BOW, DEFER, OBEY, POSE, REFER, YIELD
~ to BEAR, LET

subordinate ASST

suborn OIL

Subotica
~ citizen SERB

subpoena CITE, ORDER, WRIT

subs
where ~ are found ASEA, ATSEA, DELI

subscribe
~ again RENEW
~ (to) AGREE

subscription
~ unit ISSUE
extend a ~ RENEW

subsequent LATER, NEXT
~ to AFTER

subsequently AFTER, ANON, LATER, SINCE, THEN

subservient MEEK
~ to UNDER

subside ABATE, DROP, EBB, FADE, FLAG, LAPSE, REMIT, SETTLE, SINK, WANE

subsidiary
~ (prefix) PARA

subsidize HELP, KEEP

subsidy AID, ALMS, DOLE

subsist LAST, LIVE

subsistence KEEP

subsoil EARTH, LAND

substance ESSENCE, GIST, HEART, MEAT
~ partner SUM
lacking ~ INANE, THIN
man of ~ NOB
sum and ~ CORE, ESSENCE, SENSE

substandard OFF
~ contraction AINT

substantial BIG, GOOD, LARGE, REAL
~ content MEAT

substantiate ATTEST, SHOW

substantiation TRIAL

substantive NOUN

substitute SWAP, TEMP, TRADE

substitution
word of ~ LIEU

substructure ROOT

subterfuge RUSE, TRAP, WILE

subterrane CAVE

subterranean DEEP
~ dweller BAT, GNOME, MOLE

subtle DEEP, FINE, NICE
~ atmosphere AURA
~ indication HINT
~ sarcasm IRONY
~ suggestion CUE

subtlety
lack of ~ CAMP

subtract TAKE

subtraction
~ word LESS

suburban
~ ender ITE
~ grass LAWN
~ plot size ACRE
~ status symbol POOL

suburbia
symbol of ~ MALL

Suburu AUTO, CAR

subway TRAIN
~ access STILE
~ alternative BUS, TAXI
~ fare TOKEN
~ power source RAIL
~ station STOP
~ token cost FARE
DC ~ METRO
Montreal ~ METRO
Paris ~ METRO
Washington ~ METRO

succeed ARRIVE, ENSUE, RISE, WIN

succeeding AFTER, NEXT
~ (prefix) EPI

success HIT, SMASH, WIN
achieve ~ ARRIVE
assure ~ ICE
assured of ~ ONICE
big ~ HIT
dazzling ~ ECLAT
sign of ~ SRO

"Success at ___ Price" ANY

successful
~ at-bat HIT
~ auditioners CAST
~ candidates INS

succession LINE, PARADE, RASH, ROW, RUN, SCALE, STREAM, TRAIN
in ~ to AFTER
steady ~ STREAM

successive LATER

successively AROW

successor HEIR

succinct CRISP, TERSE

succor ABET, AID, HELP

succotash
~ ingredient CORN, LIMA

succubus DEMON

succulent AGAVE, ALOE, RICH
~ houseplant ALOE

succulents CACTI

succumb BEND, LOSE, OBEY
~ (to) BOW

such
~ as LIKE
as ~ PERSE

"Such ___ Friends" GOOD

suchness ESSENCE

suck
~ in DRAW, GASP, TRAP
~ wind PANT

sucker DUPE, SAP, SPRIG
play for a ~ USE
sap ~ APHID

"___, sucker!" HELLO

Suckling, John POET
see also poet

Sucre
see Spanish

Sudan
~ neighbor CHAD
~ river NILE
most of ~ SAHARA

Sudanese Republic
~ today MALI

sudatorium BATH, SAUNA

Sudbury
~ prov. ONT

sudden ACUTE, RAPID, RASH
~ attack RAID
~ contraction SPASM
~ fear ALARM
~ flight LAM
~ gust BLAST
~ motion DART
~ outpouring SPATE
~ sound BANG
~ spurt SPASM
~ start SHY
~ transition LEAP
all of a ~ BANG
feel ~ fright PANIC
show ~ interest PERK

"Sudden ___" FEAR

suddenly BANG

"Suddenly"
~ director ALLEN
~ singer OCEAN

"Suddenly, ___ Summer" LAST

suds BEER, FOAM, HEAD, SOAP
get rid of the ~ RINSE
strong ~ ALE

sue ASK, BEG, CLAIM, PLEAD, PRAY

Sue ___ Langdon ANE

"___, Sue and Bob Too" RITA

"___ Suede Shoes" BLUE

suet FAT
~ cousin LARD

Suetonius ROMAN

___ suey CHOP

Suez CANAL, CITY, PORT

Suez Canal
~ fueling station ADEN
opera written for the opening of the ~ AIDA

suffer ACHE, AIL, ALLOW, BEAR, FEEL, LET
~ defeat LOSE
~ the consequences PAY

suffering COST, EVIL, HARM, PAIN, RACK, WOE

suffice SERVE

sufficient AMPLE, DUE
~ to a poet ENOW

___-sufficient SELF

suffix ADD, TAG

suffrage VOTE

"Suffragette ___" CITY

suffragist
~ quest VOTE

suffuse BATHE, DYE, STEEP

sugar HON
~ qty. TSP
~ source BEET, CANE, MAPLE
~ (suffix) OSE

sugar ___ BEET, CANE, CONE, MAPLE, PINE

___ sugar CANE, CORN, MALT, MAPLE, SPUN

Sugar ___ Leonard RAY

Sugar ___ Mountain LOAF

Sugar ___ Robinson RAY

sugarbush
~ unit MAPLE

sugar cane
~ liquor RUM

sugar-coat EASE

Sugar Loaf Mountain
~ locale RIO

Sugar Ray
~ stat KOS, TKO

sugary SWEET

suggest EVOKE, HINT, MEAN, MOVE, OPINE, RUMOR
~ strongly URGE

suggestion CLUE, CUE, DAB, DASH, HINT, JOT, LEAD, SHADE, SIGN, TASTE, TINGE, TIP, TRACE
~ starter AUTO
AAA ~ ROUTE, RTE

suggestion box
~ opening SLOT

suggestive BLUE, LEWD, RACY
  more than ~ LEWD

sui generis RARE

suit ADAPT, ATTIRE, CLAIM, DRESS, FIT, HIT, PLEA
  ~ accompaniment TIE
  ~ adjunct VEST
  ~ feature LAPEL
  ~ grounds LIBEL
  ~ material SERGE
  ~ size LONG
  ~ so to speak EXEC
  ~ the purpose SERVE
  ~ up DRESS
  alter to ~ ADAPT
  follow ~ APE, ECHO
  grounds for a ~ TORT
  in one's birthday ~ BARE, NUDE
  legal ~ CASE
  monkey ~ DRESS, TAILS
  one of a ~ HEART, SPADE
  strong ~ ARMOR

suit ___ tee TOA

___ suit DRESS, LONG, MAO, TANK, UNION, WET

suitable APT, FIT, MEET, NICE
  ~ for cacti ARID, DRY
  ~ for dieters LOCAL
  absolutely ~ IDEAL
  make ~ ADAPT

suit and ___ TIE

suitcase BAG
  small ~ GRIP

suit changer
  fictional ~ KENT

suite
  ~ locale HOTEL
  ~ piece BED

suited
  ~ to its purpose APT
  more ~ ABLER

suiter
  zoot ~ DUDE

suitor BEAU, LOVE, ROMEO
  act the ~ WOO
  colonial ~ ALDEN
  pussycat's ~ OWL

suitors
  what ~ pitch WOO

suit to ___ ATEE

suit to a ___ TEE

sukkah TENT

sulfate SALT

sulfide
  hydrogen ~ GAS

sulfite SALT

sulfuric ACID

sulk FRET, MOPE, STEW

sulky CART

Sulla ROMAN

sullen DOUR, TESTY

Sullivan ANNE
  ~ and others EDS

Sullivan, Arthur SIR

Sullivan, Ed EMCEE, HOST
  ~ had a "really big" one SHOW
  ~ network CBS

sully BLOT, BLUR, LIBEL, MAR, SHAME, SLUR, SMEAR, SOIL, TAINT

sultan RULER
  ~ cousin AMIR, EMEER, EMIR
  ~ spouses HAREM

sultanate REALM
  Gulf ~ OMAN
  Ruth's ~ SWAT

"Sultan of ___, The" SWAT

"Sultan of Sulu, The"
  ~ author ADE

"Sultan of Swat, The" BABE, RUTH

sultriness HEAT

sultry HOT

Sulu SEA

sum ADD, ALL, TOTAL
  ~ and substance CORE, ESSENCE, SENSE
  ~ of one's virtues, to the Greeks ARETE
  ~ up ADD, CAST, RECAP
  goodly ~ PILE
  trifling ~ SOU

"sum"
  ~ in "Cogito, ergo sum" IAM

___ sum DIM

sumac TREE

Sumatra ISLE
  ~ setting ASIA
  ~ simian ORANG

sum, es, ___ EST

summarize CUT

summary GIST, RECAP

summer ADDER
  ~ appliance FAN
  ~ beverage ADE
  ~ cabin site LAKE
  ~ clock setting EDT
  ~ confection CONE
  ~ cooler FAN, ICE, SODA
  ~ drink ADE
  ~ escape CAMP
  ~ fabric LINEN
  ~ feature HEAT
  ~ fruit MELON
  ~ hrs. DST
  ~ in French ETE
  ~ mo. AUG
  ~ retreat SHADE
  ~ shade TAN
  ~ theater, often BARN
  ~ top TEE
  ~ TV fare RERUN
  late ~ flower ASTER
  sign of ~ LEO

summer ___ CAMP

"Summer ___" STORM

"___ Summer" LAST

Summerall PAT

"Summer and Smoke"
  ~ heroine ALMA

summer camp
  do a ~ activity HIKE, ROW, SWIM

"Summer in the ___" CITY

"Summer of '42"
  ~ pianist NERO

Summer Olympics
  1900 ~ site PARIS
  1904 ~ site USA
  1924 ~ site PARIS
  1932 ~ site USA
  1960 ~ site ITALY, ROME
  1980 ~ site USSR
  1984 ~ site USA
  1988 ~ site KOREA
  1992 ~ site SPAIN
  1996 ~ site ATLANTA, USA
  see also Olympics

"Summer Place, A"
  ~ actor EGAN

Summers MARC

summertime
  ~ cooler ADE

"Summertime" ARIA
  ~ director LEAN

Summerville SLIM

summery HOT, MILD

summit ACME, APEX, CAP, CREST, PEAK, SPIRE, TIP, TOP
  at the ~ of ATOP
  Italian ~ MONTE

Summit
  ~ in Houston ARENA

summon ASK, BID, CALL, CITE, EVOKE, HAIL, PAGE, RING, ROUSE
  ~ a taxi FLAG
  ~ up TAP

summons CALL, ORDER, WRIT
  chanticleer's ~ CROW
  discreet ~ PSST, PST
  urgent ~ SOS

sumo
  like ~ wrestlers OBESE

sumptuous GALA, ORNATE, POSH, RICH

sun AGER, BAKE, ORB, SOL, SPHERE, STAR
  ~ block SHADE
  ~ disk ATEN, ATON
  ~ ender BATH, BEAM, DIAL, DOG, DRESS, LESS, LIT, RISE, ROOF, ROOM, SET, SHADE, SHINE, SPOT, TAN, UPS
  ~ in Latin SOL
  ~ in Spanish SOL
  ~ oneself BASK
  ~ worshiper of old INCA
  bask in the ~ TAN
  blue-to-white ~ ASTAR
  climb, as the ~ ARISE
  dry in the ~ BAKE
  Egyptian ~ god ATEN, ATON
  emulate the ~ SHINE
  erstwhile ~ dancer UTE
  full ~ DAY
  hang in the ~ AIR
  lie in the ~ BASK, BATHE, TAN
  name for the ~ SOL
  of the ~ SOLAR
  once around the ~ YEAR
  sit in the ~ BASK
  toward the rising ~ EAST
  toward the setting ~ WEST

sun ___ DANCE, GOD, LAMP

Sun ___ BELT

"Sun ___ Rises, The" ALSO

Sun.
  ~ discourse SER

"Sun Also ___, The" RISES

sunbathe BASK, TAN

sunbeam RAY

sunblock
  ~ ingredient ALOE

sunbonnet HAT

sunbow IRIS

sunburn
  ~ remedy ALOE

sunburned RED

sundae
  ~ topping NUTS

Sundance
  ~ girlfriend ETTA

Sundance ___ KID

Sundance Film Festival
  ~ locale UTAH

Sunday
  ~ best BEST, DRESS
  ~ closing AMEN
  ~ dinner ROAST
  ~ drive SPIN
  ~ service MASS

Sunday ___ BEST

___ Sunday PALM

"___ Sunday Afternoon" ONA, ONE

"Sunday Dinner ___ a Soldier" FOR

Sunday-go-to-meeting DRESS

"Sunday in ___ York" NEW

"Sunday Morning" POEM

sunder CHOP, CUT, HACK, LOP, REND

sundered APART

Sun Devils
~ **home** TEMPE
~ **sch.** ASU

sundial
~ **numeral** III

sundowner HOBO

"Sundowners, The"
~ **actress** KERR

sundries
~ **case** ETUI

sundry
all and ~ EACH

sunflower COLOR
~ **center** DISC
~ **family member** ASTER
~ **product** OIL
~ **snack** SEED
~ **support** STEM

Sunflower
~ **St.** KAN

"Sunflowers" OIL

sung
~ **soliloquy** ARIA

"___ Sung Blue" SONG

sunglasses
what ~ **cut** GLARE

sunk
~ **in oblivion** LOST

sunken LOW
~ **fence** HAHA

sunless COOL

sunlight DAY

Sun Myung ___ MOON

Sunni
~ **faith** ISLAM

sunny CLEAR, FAIR, GAY, GLAD, MILD, WARM

"Sunny ___ Up" SIDE

"Sunny Side of the Street"
~ **singer** LAINE

sunny-side up
~ **item** EGG

sunrise
~ **goddess** AURORA
~ **locale** EAST
~ **to sunset** DAY

suns
~ **do it** RISE, SET

Suns FIVE, TEAM
~ **org.** NBA

sunset
~ **direction** WEST
~ **hue** RED
sunrise to ~ DAY
toward ~ WEST

"___ Sunset, The" LAST

Sunset Limited TRAIN

sunshine DAY
enjoy the ~ BASK, TAN

Sunshine
~ **St.** FLA

"Sunshine Boys, The"
~ **director** ROSS

"Sunshine of Your Love"
~ **band** CREAM

sunshiny CLEAR

suntan ___ OIL

suntan lotion
~ **ingredient** ALOE

sunup
~ **direction** EAST
at ~ EARLY

Sun Valley
~ **site** IDAHO
~ **st.** IDA
enjoy ~ SKI

Sun Yat-___ SEN

sup DINE, EAT, FARE
~ **at home** EATIN

super ACE, AONE, BEST, GOOD, GREAT, RAD, TOPS

super ___ slalom GIANT

"Super ___, The" COPS

"Super!" FINE, GREAT, WOW

superabound TEEM

superabundance OCEAN, PLUS, SEA

superabundant AMPLE

superannuated OLD

superb AONE, BEST, FINE, FIRST, GREAT, REGAL

Super Bowl EVENT
~ **org.** NFL
~ **won by Jets** III

Superboy
~ **girlfriend** LANA, LANG

Super Chief TRAIN

superciliousness AIRS

superconfident SMUG

super-duper ACE, AONE, FIRST, GREAT, TOPS

superficial TOKEN
not ~ SOLID

superfluity GLUT

superfluous EXTRA

"Superfly"
~ **director** ONEAL

Super G
~ **segment** ESS

Supergirl HERO
~ **hometown** ARGO

superhero
~ **wear** CAPE
diminutive comics ~ **with "The"** ATOM

superhighway PIKE, ROAD, ROUTE

superhuman EPIC

superimpose ADD

superimposed ATOP

superintend HEAD, LEAD, RUN
~ **ender** ENT

superintendency CARE

superintendent BOSS, HEAD
ancient ~ EDILE

superior ABBOT, ABLE, ABOVE, AONE, BEST, FINE, GOOD, GREAT, RARE, TOPS
~ **in rank** ABOVE
~ **(prefix)** FORE

Superior LAKE

superlative ACE, AONE, BEST, TOP, TOPS
~ **suffix** EST

superliner TRAIN

Superman HERO
~ **alias** KENT
~ **attire** CAPE
~ **girlfriend** LANE, LOIS
~ **mother** LARA
~ **portrayer** CAIN, REEVE
~ **symbol** ESS
~ **to Jimmy Olsen** IDOL
~ **to Lex Luthor** ENEMY

"Superman"
~ **actor** REEVE
Ned Beatty's ~ **role** OTIS
Valerie Perrine's ~ **role** EVE

"Superman ___" III

supermarket STORE
~ **freebie** BAG
~ **phenomenon** LINE
~ **section** AISLE
~ **vehicle** CART
like ~ **milk** DATED
work at the ~ BAG
see also grocery

supermodel
single-name ~ IMAN

supernal AERIAL

supernatural EERIE, EERY

supernova STAR

supernumerary EXTRA, SPARE

superpower
former ~ USSR

SuperSonics FIVE, TEAM
~ **org.** NBA

superstar IDOL, NAME
~ **of a sort** NOVA

superstation
~ **familiarly** TBS

supervene ENSUE

supervise BOSS, LEAD, RUN

supervision CARE

supervisor BOSS, HEAD

supine FLAT
~ **opposite** PRONE
be ~ LIE
not ~ ERECT

supper MEAL
fix ~ EATIN
have ~ DINE, EAT

___ Supper LAST

"Supper Club"
~ **radio host** COMO

supplant OUST

supple AGILE, LITHE

supplement ADD, EKE, EXTRA, TAG
dietary ~ IRON
nutritional ~ YEAST

supplemental MORE
~ **worker** TEMP

supplementary ADDED, NEW, OTHER

supplicate ADORE, ASK, BEG, PLEAD, PRAY, SUE

supplication CRY, PLEA, SUIT

supplies GEAR
weapon ~ AMMO

supply CATER, ENDOW, FIT, LEND, SELL, STORE
~ **food** CATER
~ **troops to** MAN
~ **weapons to** ARM
full ~ GLUT
hidden ~ STASH
in short ~ RARE, SCANT, SPARSE, THIN
rich ~ LODE

___ Supply AIR

support ABET, ABUT, AEGIS, AID, ARM, BASE, BASIS, BEAR, CITE, EGIS, FEED, HELP, HOLD, KEEP, LEG, MAST, POST, PROP, SHORE, STAY
~ **in wrongdoing** ABET
~ **unit** BEAM, STUD
aerial ~ MAST, SPAR
arch ~ PIER
avid ~ ZEAL
beach-house ~ STILT
blossom ~ STEM
boom ~ MAST
bridge ~ PIER
building ~ BEAM
canvas ~ MAST, SPAR
dock ~ PILE
drapery ~ ROD
eyeglasses ~ EAR
fence ~ POST
get ~ **for, as an idea** SELL
give ~ **to** ABET, ENDOW
hanger ~ ROD
head ~ NECK

___ support

jib ~ MAST, SPAR
lend moral ~ ROOT
mast ~ STAY
mattress ~ SLAT
means of ~ LABOR
proposer's ~ KNEE
rail ~ TIE
rigging ~ MAST, SPAR
sail ~ MAST, SPAR
specs ~ EAR
statue ~ BASE
sunflower ~ STEM
tech ~ HELP
tomato-plant ~ STAKE
transverse ~ BEAM
use timber for ~ SHORE
word of ~ AYE, YES

___ support MORAL

supporter ALLY, ANGEL, DONOR, FAN
art ~ EASEL
world ~ ATLAS

supporters
union ~ LABOR

supporting FOR, PRO, UNDER
~ factor BASIS
~ (prefix) PRO

supportive FOR

"Support Your ___ Gunfighter" LOCAL

"Support Your ___ Sheriff" LOCAL

"Support Your Local Gun- fighter"
~ actor ELAM

suppose DEEM, DRAW, DREAM, OPINE

supposition IDEA

suppositions IFS

suppress ELIDE, GAG, HIDE, STOP

supremacy LEAD, RULE, SWAY

supreme ACE, BEST, BIG, FIRST, GREAT, IDEAL, MAIN, TOP

Supreme Court
~ complement NINE
~ position SEAT

Supremes, The TRIO
~ lead singer DIANA, ROSS

___ Sur, Calif. BIG

surcharge EXTRA, FEE

surcingle BAND, BELT

sure FAST, SAFE, TRUE, YEAH, YEP, YES
~ 'nuff YEAH, YEP
~ shot ACE
~ thing YEAH, YEP, YES
feel ~ of RELY
too ~ of oneself SMUG

___ sure (definitely) FOR

"___, sure!" YEAH

Sure
~ rival BAN

"Sure ___" FIRE

"Sure!" OKAY

___ Sure ALB

sure-enough REAL

surefooted AGILE
~ animal GOAT

surely AYE, YES

surety AEGIS, BAIL, EGIS
give ~ BAIL

surf FOAM, RIDE
~ and turf DUO, MEAL
~ motion TIDE
~ murmur ROTE
~ sound ROAR
place to ~ NET
walk in the ~ WADE

surf ___ CLAM

"Surf ___" CITY

surface AREA, ARISE, EMERGE, FACE, PAVE
~ measurement AREA
~ transport AUTO, BUS, CAB, CAR, LIMO, TAXI, TRAIN
Alps ~ SNOW
Arctic ~ ICE
beach ~ SAND
below the ~ INNER
bowling ~ LAWN
carpet ~ NAP, PILE
desert ~ SAND
die ~ FACE, SIDE
downy ~ NAP, PILE
dull ~ MAT, MATTE
dune buggy's ~ SAND
earth's ~ LAND
flat ~ PLANE
frozen ~ ICE
fuzzy ~ NAP, PILE
gym ~ MAT
having a dull ~ MAT, MATTE
hockey ~ ICE
metric ~ measure ARE
painting ~ GESSO
perpendicular ~ SIDE
ring ~ MAT
rink ~ ICE
sandpaper ~ GRIT
scratch the ~ DIP
shiny ~ ENAMEL
slanting ~ RAMP
sledder's ~ SLOPE, SNOW
slippery ~ ICE
tennis ~ LAWN
two-dimensional ~ AREA
velvety ~ NAP, PILE
Wimbledon ~ LAWN
wrestling ~ MAT

surfboard
use a ~ RIDE

surfeit GLUT, SATE

surfer RIDER
~ challenge CREST
~ hangout NET
~ place CREST

Internet ~ USER

surfers
channel ~ zap past them ADS

"Surfin' ___" USA

surfing
~ site SHORE, WEB

surge LEAP, MOB, ROLL
ocean ~ TIDE

surgeon
~ word STAT

___ surgeon TREE

surgical
modern ~ tool LASER

"Sur la plage"
~ painter DEGAS

surly BAD, MEAN, SOUR, TART, UGLY

surmise DEEM, EDUCE, IDEA, OPINE

surmount RISE, TOP

surmounting ATOP, UPON

surpass BEAT, CAP, LEAD, TOP

surpassing ABOVE, OVER
~ (prefix) PRE

surplice ROBE

surplus EXTRA, FAT, GLUT, OVER, PLUS, REST
~ plant WEED

surprise AMAZE, AWE, DAZE, JAR, STUN
~ win UPSET
comment of ~ GEE
cry of ~ EEK
exclamation of ~ AHA, LORD, OHO, OOH, WOW
exclamations of ~ AHS, OHS
pleasant ~ TREAT
reaction of ~ GASP
react with ~ START

"Surprise!" BOO

surprised AGAPE

surrealism
~ predecessor DADA

surrealist
German ~ ERNST
Spanish ~ DALI, MIRO
Swiss ~ KLEE

surrender BEND, CEDE, DEFER, YIELD
cry of ~ UNCLE

surreptitious SLY

Surrey SHIRE
~ town EPSOM

surround BATHE, RING, WRAP

surrounded
~ by AMID, AMONG

surrounding ABOUT, LOCAL

surroundings AREA, SITE

surveillance
~ item CAMERA

survey CASE, EYE, MAP, POLL, SCAN, SEE, SPY
~ input DATA

surveyor
~ item TAPE
~ map PLAT

survive ABIDE, LAST, LIVE

surviving
~ trace RELIC

survivor
flood ~ HAM, NOAH

___ survivor SOLE

Susa
~ kingdom ELAM

Susan ANTON, DEY, ROOK
lazy ~ TRAY

Susanin IVAN

"___ Susan Williams" STOP

susceptibility PERIL, RISK

susceptible PRONE

sushi
~ fish EEL, TUNA
~ ingredient RICE
~ selections OCTOPI
like ~ RAW

suslik ANIMAL

suspect FEAR
~ need ALIBI

"Suspect"
~ actress CHER

suspend CEASE, DEFER, DRAPE, HANG, STAY, TABLE

suspended
hang ~ POISE

suspenders
~ alternative BELT

suspension STAY
~ of hostilities PEACE

suspicion DASH, FEAR, HINT, IDEA, NOTE, TASTE, TINGE, TRACE
above ~ PURE

"___ Suspicion" ABOVE

suspicious LEERY, WARY

suspire DRAW

Susquehanna TRIBE

Susskind, David EMCEE, HOST

sustain BEAR, FEED

sustained LONG
be ~ by LEAN

sustenance DIET, FARE, MEAL
take ~ DINE, EAT

"Sustineo ___" ALAS

Sutcliffe STU

Sutherland DIVA
   solo for ~ ARIA

Sutherland, Joan DAME

Sutter's ___ MILL

Sutton HAL

Sutton, Willie
   emulate ~ ROB

suture SEW
   ~ material SILK

suzerain LIEGE, LORD, RULER

suzerainty REIGN, RULE

___ suzette CREPE

Suzette
   see French

Suzy AMIS

svelte SLIM, THIN, TRIM
   hardly ~ OBESE

Svenson
   ~ and others BOS

svgs. ___ ACCT

swab BATHE, CLEAN, DRY, GOB,
   SALT, TAR, WASH
   ~ salutation AHOY

swabber
   ~ need PAIL, WATER

swabbie GOB, SALT, TAR

swaddle DRAPE, WRAP

swag HAUL, LOOT, TAKE

swagger BRAG, CROW, STEP
   ~ stick CANE

Swahili BANTU

swain BEAU, DATE, LOVE, MALE
   ~ offering ROSE
   legendary ~ ROMEO

SWAK
   part of ~ KISS

swallow BEAR, BIRD, TAKE
   sea ~ TERN

___ swallow BARN, SEA

**"___ swallow does not make a
summer"** ONE

swami HINDU, SEER

swamp FEN, MIRE, SINK, WASH
   ~ buggy MOTOR
   ~ dweller CROC, EGRET,
     HERON
   ~ grass SEDGE
   ~ whooper CRANE

swamp ___ GAS

swamped AWASH

swampland MIRE

swampy DAMP
   ~ area MIRE

___ Swampy CAMP

swan BIRD
   ~ song END

female ~ PEN
male ~ COB

swan ___ SONG

___ swan MUTE

swank CHIC, POSH, TONY
   ~ up DRESS

swanky CHIC, POSH

"Swan Lake"
   ~ costume TUTU

Swann LYNN

"___ swans a-swimming..."
   SEVEN

Swansea CITY, PORT
   where ~ is WALES

Swanson, Gloria
   ~ role of 1928 SADIE
   ~ role of 1950 NORMA

swap TRADE

swap ___ MEET

sward LAWN, LEA

swarm ARMY, BAND, HIVE, HORDE,
   HOST, MASS, MOB, NEST, PILE,
   PRESS, TROOP
   ~ home HIVE
   ~ with TEEM

"Swarm, The"
   ~ attacker BEE

swarming RIFE

swarthy
   far from ~ PALE

swash BRAG, DASH, LAP

swashbuckling
   ~ actor ERROL

swat BAT, SLAP, ZAP

swatch
   ~ of material SNIP

swath CUT, LINE

swathe BIND, DRAPE, DRESS,
   WRAP

sway ARM, BEND, BIAS, DANCE,
   LEAD, REEL, REIGN, ROLL, RULE,
   TEETER, TOSS
   ~ about REEL
   hold ~ RULE

sway ___ BAR

swear ATTEST, AVER, AVOW, STATE
   ~ by HOLD, LEAN, RELY
   ~ in SEAT
   ~ to ASSERT, AVER, AVOW
   ~ (to) ATTEST
   something to ~ by OATH

swear ___ (give up) OFF

swearword OATH

sweat LABOR, OOZE, PLOD, STEW
   ~ bullets STEW
   ~ it out BEAR
   ~ of one's brow LABOR
   bit of ~ BEAD

break out in a cold ~ PANIC
no ~ EASY

sweat ___ (await) OUT

sweater WRAP
   ~ eater MOTH
   ~ letter ALPHA, BETA, CHI,
     DELTA, ETA, IOTA, OMEGA,
     PHI, PSI, RHO, TAU, THETA
   ~ letters MUS
   ~ part ARM
   make a ~ KNIT

sweatshirt
   ~ part, maybe HOOD

sweatshop PLANT

Swed.
   ~ neighbor DEN, FIN, NOR

Swede
   ~ neighbor DANE
   certain ~ LAPP
   Turku, to a ~ ABO

Sweden
   ~ native LAPP

Swedish
   ~ bath SAUNA
   ~ netman BORG
   ~ rock group ABBA

Swee' ___ PEA

sweep AREA, CLEAN, RANGE
   ~ across COMB
   ~ of time LAPSE
   ~ target SOOT
   ~ up SCOOP
   ~ upward RISE
   radar ~ SCAN

sweeping BIG, EPIC, LARGE,
   TOTAL, WIDE
   ~ hairstyle UPDO
   ~ motion SLASH

sweepings DIRT, TRASH, WASTE
   barber's ~ HAIR

sweepstakes
   enter the ~ BET

___ Sweepstakes IRISH

sweet NICE, TREAT
   ~ bread CAKE
   ~ girl of song SUE
   ~ potato PIE, YAM
   ~ smell BALM
   ~ starter SEMI
   ~ suffix OSE
   home ~ home ABODE
   not ~ DRY, SEC, SOUR, TART

sweet ___ BAY, CIDER, CORN, PEA,
   TALK, TOOTH

"Sweet"
   ~ place HOME

"Sweet ___ of Youth" BIRD

sweet-and-___ SOUR

"Sweet are the ___ of adversity"
   USES

"Sweet as apple cider"
   ~ girl IDA

sweetbrier ROSE

"Sweet Dreams"
   ~ actress LANGE

sweeten EASE

sweetened
   ~ drink ADE

sweetener
   request ~ PLEASE

"Sweeter ___ You" THAN

"sweetest nymph"
   Milton's ~ ECHO

"Sweetest Taboo, The"
   ~ singer SADE

sweetheart BEAU, DEAR, GIRL,
   LOVE, PET
   be a ~ WOO

"Sweetheart of Sigma ___, The"
   CHI

sweetie BEAU, DEAR, HON
   cowboy's ~ GAL

sweetie ___ PIE

"Sweet Liberty"
   ~ actor ALDA

sweet nothings
   whisper ~ COO, WOO

sweets
   skip ~ DIET

"Sweet 16"
   ~ org. NCAA

sweetsop TREE

"Sweet Swan of ___!" AVON

swell BEAU, DUDE, FINE, GREAT,
   GROW, KEEN, NICE, RAD, RISE,
   SEA
   ~ in space AOK
   ~ out BAG
   ~ time GAS

"___ Swell" THOU

swelled
   ~ head EGO

swelled ___ HEAD

swell-headed BIG

swelling CREST, EDEMA, NODE
   plant ~ EDEMA

swelter BOIL, HEAT, ROAST, STEW

sweltering CLOSE, HOT

Swenson INGA

swept CLEAN

"Swept ___" AWAY

swerve CUT, SKEW, TURN, VEER,
   YAW

swift AGILE, BIRD, FAST, FLEET,
   RAPID

Swift KAY, TOM
   ~ colleague POPE, TOM
   ~ creature YAHOO
   ~ friend STEELE

swift-footed FLEET

swiftly APACE, FAST

swiftness HASTE, PACE, SPEED

swig BELT
quick ~ SNORT
small ~ SIP

swill SLOP, TRASH

swim BATHE
~ **alternative** SINK
~ **competition** MEET
brief ~ DIP
make one's head ~ STUN
nonconformists ~ against
it TIDE
place to ~ POOL

swimmer
~ **measure** LAP
Bering Sea ~ SEAL
elongated ~ EEL
long-snouted ~ GAR
Nile ~ CROC
playful ~ OTTER

swimmers
armed ~ OCTOPI

swimming
~ **hole** POND, POOL
~ **spot** HOLE
~ **unit** LAP
go ~ BATHE

swimming pool
~ **problem** ALGAE

swimsuit
~ **part** BRA

Swinburne, Algernon POET
~ **work** ODE
see also poet

swindle CLIP, CON, DUPE, HAVE,
ROB, ROOK, SCAM, SKIN, STING

swindle ___ SHEET

swine ANIMAL, BOAR, HOG, SOW
~ **food** SLOP
~ **place** PEN, STY

swine ___ FLU

swing DANCE, FLAP, HANG, SWAY
~ **around** AVERT, SLEW, SLUE,
TURN
~ **around, as a ship** YAW
~ **a sickle** REAP
~ **a thurible** CENSE
~ **freely** HANG
~ **loosely** FLAP
~ **partner** SWAY
ersatz ~ TIRE
full ~ PLAY
half a ~ FRO
ready to ~ ATBAT
rhythmic ~ LILT

swing and ___ SWAY

swinger RAKE
~ **perhaps** DOOR
barn ~ VANE
jungle ~ APE
wrecking-ball ~ CRANE

"Swinging on ___" ASTAR

"Swinging on a ___" STAR

swings
thing that ~ DOOR

swinish
~ **remark** OINK

swipe COP, NIP, ROB, STEAL, TAKE
take a ~ at SWAT

swirl EDDY

Swiss
~ **artist** KLEE
~ **canton** BERN, URI
~ **city** BERN
~ **mathematician** EULER
~ **mountain** ALP
~ **partner** HAM
~ **peak** ALP
~ **river** AAR, AARE
~ **strain** YODEL
~ **topper** RYE
legendary ~ **hero** TELL

Swiss ___ ALPS, STEAK

Swit
~ **costar** ALDA, FARR
~ **played one** NURSE
~ **sitcom** MASH

switch BEAT, CANE, HIT, LACE,
ROD, SWAP, TRADE, WAG
~ **activator** CLAP
~ **ender** EROO
~ **partner** BAIT
~ **position** OFF
~ **settings** ONS
electric ~ RELAY

switchback ROAD
~ **shape** ESS

Swithin SAINT

Switz.
~ **neighbor** GER, ITAL

Switzerland
~ **capital** BERN
mountain in ~ ALP

swivel SPIN

swiveler
hip ~ ELVIS

swizzle STIR
~ **ingredient** RUM

Swoboda RON

swollen BIG, LARGE

swoon DROP, REACT

swoop DROP, KITE
~ **down upon** RAID

swooped
~ **down** DOVE

swooper
sea ~ ERN, ERNE

swoosh
Nike ~ LOGO

sword FERN, STEEL
~ **fight** DUEL
~ **handle** HILT

Arthurian ~ **holder** STONE
blunted ~ EPEE
cut-and-slash ~ SABER
fine-tempered ~ TOLEDO
hold, like a ~ WIELD
light ~ EPEE

sword ___ CANE, DANCE

"Sword and the ___, The" ROSE

"Sword in the ___, The" STONE

swordplay EPEE

swords
cross ~ ARGUE, CLOSE

sworn
~ **statement** OATH

sybarite
~ **delight** EASE

sycamore TREE

sycophant
~ **answer** YES

Sydney CITY, PORT
see also Australian

Sykes PETER

syllable
~ **stress** TONE
chorus ~ TRA
dance ~ CHA
giggler's ~ HEE
miss a ~ ELIDE
musical ~ SOL
poetry ~ FOOT
singer's ~ TRA
sot's ~ HIC
sow ~ OINK
verse ~ FOOT

syllables
~ **of comprehension** OHS
carol ~ FALA, LALA
hesitater's ~ ERS
laugh-track ~ HAHA
refrain ~ FALA, LALA
skip ~ ELIDE

syllabub
~ **ingredient** CIDER, CREAM,
WINE

syllabus LIST, PLAN

syllogism
~ **word** ERGO
~ **words** ISTO

"___ Sylphides" LES

sylvan
~ **deity** PAN, SATYR

"Sylvan historian,"
~ **to Keats** URN

sylvanite ORE

Sylvester CAT
~ **to Tweety** TAT

Sylvia FINE, SASS

sylvite ORE

symbol ICON, IMAGE, LOGO, SIGN,
TOKEN, TOTEM

___ symbol PEACE

symbolic TOKEN
~ **puzzle** REBUS

symbolize MEAN

Symington STU

symmetrical CLEAN, EVEN

symmetry ORDER
line of ~ AXIS

sympathetic GOOD, MILD, NICE
be ~ CARE

sympathize BLEED, FEEL

sympathy BALM, LOVE
feel ~ ACHE

"Symphonie espagnole"
~ **composer** LALO

symphony OPUS

"Symphony No. 7 ___" INE

"Symphony No. 2 ___ minor"
INE

Symposium
subject of Plato's ~ EROS

"Symposium"
~ **man** PLATO

symptom SIGN
~ **for a dentist** ACHE
flu ~ ACHE, AGUE
poison-ivy ~ ITCH, RASH

syn.
~ **opposite** ANT

synagogue
~ **container** ARK
~ **scroll** TORAH

synapse GAP

sync
out of ~ OFF
put in ~ PHASE

___-synch LIP

synchronize SET, TIME

synchronous ___ ORBIT

syndicate BLOC, MELD, MOB,
POOL, RING, UNITE
~ **head** DON

syndication
air in ~ RERUN

syne
auld lang ~ PAST

synod DIET

synonym
~ **opp.** ANT

synonymist
famous ~ ROGET

synonymous ALIKE, SAME

synthetic FAKE, FALSE, SHAM
~ **fabric** NYLON

Syr.
Egypt and ~, once UAR
neighbor of ~ ISR

Syracuse
~ **team color** ORANGE
city east of ~ UTICA
city near ~ ONEIDA
lake near ~ ONEIDA

Syria
~ **neighbor** IRAQ, ISRAEL
~ **president** ASSAD
ancient ~ ARAM

Syrian ARAB, DESERT

Syrian ___ Republic ARAB

syrup
~ **flavoring** MAPLE
~ **source** CORN, SAP

___ syrup CORN, MAPLE

syrupy SWEET

system ISM, MODE, PLAN
~ **starter** ECO

___ system HONOR, MERIT, SOLAR

___ system (blood typing) ABO

systematic CLEAN, NEAT

systematize FILE, ORDER, SORT

systemized
~ **(abbr.)** ORG

___ Systems (PostScript authors)
ADOBE

systole
~ **and diastole** PULSE

1

2.0
~ grade CEE

2
multiple of ~ EVEN

2-pointer
Scrabble ~ DEE, GEE

2.5
about ~ centimeters INCH

3.0
~ grade BEE

3
~ on a par 5 EAGLE

"3 ___ and a Baby" MEN

"3 ___ Men" BAD

3-___ Oil INONE

"3 Bad ___" MEN

"3 Men ___ Baby" ANDA

3-pointer
Scrabble ~ BEE, CEE

3-pointers
Scrabble ~ EMS

3.78
~ lit. GAL

10
~ ccs. DOSE

10
~ on the Beaufort
    scale GALE
one who gets ~ pct. AGT

$10
~ coin EAGLE

"10"
~ composer RAVEL

___-10 conference PAC

10K RACE, RUN
~ competitor RACER

10-pointer
Scrabble ~ ZEE

"___-12" ADAM

"12 Angry ___" MEN

12th-graders SRS

13th
~ often IDES

"13 ___ Madeleine" RUE

"___ 13" APOLLO

"13 Days to Glory"
~ subject ALAMO

20
~ quires REAM

20th
~ st. MISS

"20/20"
~ network ABC

20-game
~ winner ACE

20K RACE

"20 Million Miles to ___" EARTH

21
~ and over ADULT

21st
~ st. ILL

21%
it's ~ oxygen AIR

"___ 21" OVER

22nd
~ st. ALA

23rd
~ state MAINE

"23 ___ to Baker Street" PACES

24
~ bottles CASE
~ hours DAY

24-book
~ poem ILIAD

24-hour
~ service ATM

24-hour ___ FLU

24-k
the k in ~ KARAT

25th
~ st. ARK

26
element ~ IRON

27th
~ st. FLA

28th
~ st. TEX

28.35
~ grams OUNCE

29th
~ state IOWA

30
~ minutes of football HALF

"30 ___ of Fun" YEARS

30-day
~ mo. APR, APRIL, NOV, SEPT

31st
~ st. CAL

33 RPM

33rd
~ Pres. HST

33
~ rpm records LPS

33rd
~ st. ORE

34th
~ Pres. DDE
~ st. KAN

35mm CAMERA

36th
~ st. NEV

'36
campaign name of ~ ALF

37th
~ st. NEB, NEBR

38th
~ st. COL

38th parallel
~ country KOREA

39
~ for Jack Benny AGE

39th
~ st. NDAK

39+
~ inches METER

"39 ___, The" STEPS

200
~ milligrams CARAT

212
go over ~ degrees BOIL

237
~ milliliters CUP

252
~ cals. BTU
~ gallons TUN

1040
~ org. IRS
~ time APRIL
Form ~ expert CPA

1300
~ hours ONE

2000
~ pounds TON

"2001"
~ computer HAL

"2001: A ___ Odyssey" SPACE

$10,000
portrait on a ~ bill CHASE

"20,000 ___ in Sing Sing" YEARS

"20,000 Leagues ___ the Sea"
UNDER

"20,000 Leagues Under the ___"
SEA

"20,000 Leagues Under the Sea"
~ captain NEMO
~ seal ESME

32,000
~ ounces TON

3,000,000,000
home to over ~ ASIA

T
~ to ham operators TANGO
~ to Morse DAH, DASH

T ___ "Tom" ASIN

T-___ BAR, BILL, BONE

T. ___ REX

T. ___ Pickens BOONE

___ T MODEL

"___ T, The" TALL

___-T ICE

Ta ELEM
   73 for ~ ATNO

"Ta-___-Boom-De-Re" RARA

Taal LAKE

tab BILL, FLAP, IOU, LABEL
   pick up the ~ PAY, TREAT
   run up a ~ OWE

Tab KEY

Tabard CAPE, INN

Tabard Inn
   ~ serving ALE

Tabasco
   see Spanish

tabbouleh SALAD

tabby CAT, PET
   ~ mate TOM
   ~ sound MEOW, MEW, PURR

"___ Ta Be My Girl" USE

tabernacle
   ~ singer ALTO, BASS, TENOR

Tabitha
   ~ "Bewitched" brother ADAM

Tabitha Twitchit CAT

table DEFER, FARE, KEY, MEAL,
   STALL, STAND
   ~ accessory LAMP
   ~ cover SCARF
   ~ d'hôte MEAL
   ~ ender LAND, WARE
   ~ insert LEAF
   ~ material DATA
   ~ of contents LIST
   ~ part LEG
   ~ scrap ORT
   ~ staple SALT
   ~ tennis GAME
   ~ wine RED, ROSE
   baccarat ~ item SHOE
   communion ~ ALTAR
   place at the ~ SEAT
   prepare the ~ SET
   remove dishes from the
      ~ BUS
   roast ~ DAIS
   set the ~ LAY
   tea ~ CART
   temple ~ ALTAR
   TV dinner ~ TRAY
   writing ~ DESK

table ___ LAMP, LINEN, SALT, SAW,
   WINE

table-___ HOP

___ table END, POOL, WATER

"Table ___ Five" FOR

tablecloth
   ~ material LINEN

table d'hôte MEAL

"Table for ___" FIVE

tableland MESA

tables
   attend ~ SERVE
   clear ~ BUS

tablet DOSE, PAD, PILL, SLATE

tableware DISH

tabloid PAPER, RAG, SHEET
   ~ boss EDITOR
   ~ flier UFO
   ~ items DIRT
   ~ subject ALIEN

tabloids
   ~ take them ADS

taboo BAN, BAR
   it's ~ NONO
   vegan ~ MEAT

Tabriz
   ~ citizen IRANI
   ~ country IRAN

___ tabs on KEEP

tabulate ADD, LIST

tabulation BILL, POLL

"___ Tac Dough" TIC

tach
   ~ reading REV, RPM

taciturn CLOSE, MUTE, STERN
   ~ one CLAM
   ~ president CAL

Tacitus ROMAN

tack BASTE, BEAT, CHOP, CUT,
   GEAR, LINE, NAIL, RIG, SEW
   ~ on ADD, AMEND, TAG
   ~ up POST
   ~ up a hem BASTE
   tie ~ PIN, STUD

___ tack TIE

tackle CRANE, ESSAY, GEAR, KIT,
   MEET, ROPE, TRY
   ~ teammate END
   ~ the quarterback SACK

tackle box
   ~ item LINE, LURE, REEL

___ tacks BRASS

tacky
   ~ product GLUE

taco
   ~ topping SALSA

Tacoma CITY, PORT
   ~ st. WASH

taconite ORE

tact ASSET
   ~ ender ILE

tactful MILD, SUAVE, WISE

tactfulness TASTE

tactic ART, MOVE, RUSE
   campaign ~ SMEAR
   dilatory ~ STALL
   hockey ~ ICING
   military ~ SIEGE
   sly ~ RUSE

tactics PLAN
   ___ **tactics** SCARE

tactless RUDE
   ___-**tac-toe** TIC

tad DASH, IOTA, JOT, KID, LAD,
   MITE, TINGE, TYKE
   ~ ender POLE

Tad
   father of ~ ABE

"Ta-da!" THERE

tadpole
   ~ cousin EFT

Tadzhikistan
   ~ once SSR

TAE
   part of ~ ALVA, EDISON

taffrail
   toward the ~ AFT

tafia RUM

___ Taft Benson EZRA

Taft, William Howard
   ~ state OHIO

tag GAME, IDS, LABEL, NAME, PEG,
   RATE, STYLE
   ~ after HEEL, TAIL, TRAIL
   ~ along COME
   ~ end LAST, TAIL
   ~ on ADD
   ~ words ASIS
   baseball ~ OUT
   ID ~ LABEL
   manufacturer's ~ LABEL
   red ~ event SALE

tag ___ ALONG, END, LINE, SALE,
   TEAM

tag ___ with ALONG

___ tag DOG

"Tag! ___ it!" YOURE

Taggard, Genevieve POET
   see also poet

Tagliabue, Paul
   ~ org. NFL

tag-on
   ~ abbr. ETC

Tagore, Rabindranath POET, SIR
   see also poet

tags
   dog ~ IDS

Tagus
   city on the ~ TOLEDO
   where the ~ flows IBERIA

tahini
   ~ base SESAME

Tahiti ILE
   novel set in ~ OMOO
   see also French

Tahitian
   ~ dish TARO

Tahoe LAKE

tai ___ CHI

___ tai MAI

Tai
   ~ language LAO

"Tai-___" PAN

tail DOG, END, HUNT, SPY, STERN,
   TAG, TRACE, TRAIL
   ~ end HEEL, LAST, REAR,
      STUB, TAG
   ~ ender BONE, GATE, SPIN
   ~ starter BOB, CAT, CUR,
      DOVE, FAN, PIN, RING
   burro's ~ PLANT
   in two shakes of a lamb's
      ~ ANON, SOON
   shake a ~ LOSE
   toy with a ~ KITE
   turn ~ DESERT, FLEE, RUN
   twist the lion's ~ DARE

tail ___ (wane) OFF

___ tail TURN

___-tail MARES

tailed
   ~ amphibian NEWT

___-tailed RING

tailgate TAG

tailless
   ~ mammal APE

taillight LAMP

tailor ADAPT
   ~ cut ALINE
   ~ measurer TAPE
   ~ need IRON
   ~ of song SAM
   ~ tool NEEDLE, PIN
   ~ work HEM, PLEAT, SEAM

tailor-___ MADE

tailoring
   do ~ ALTER, FIT, HEM, PLEAT

"___ Tailors, The" NINE

tailpiece TAG

tails DRESS, SUIT
   ~ accompaniment TIE
   make heads or ~ of LEARN
   white tie and ~ DRESS

tailward AFT

taint BLOT, LIBEL, ROT, SHAME,
   SMEAR, SPOT

'tain't
   opposite of ~ TIS

tainted BAD, OFF, RANK

taipan SNAKE

Taipei CITY

Taiwan
   ~ ender ESE

Taiwanese ASIAN
   ~ computer company ACER

Taj Mahal TOMB
   ~ city AGRA

~ feature DOME

Tajo ITALO

taka COIN

Takamatsu CITY, PORT

take GATE, GET, GRAB, GRASP, HAUL, HAVE, NET, STAKE
~ aback ABASH, JAR
~ a back seat (to) DEFER
~ a bath WASH
~ a bough LOP
~ a bow out UNTIE
~ a break CEASE, DEFER, HALT, REST
~ a cab RIDE
~ a carbon-14 measurement DATE
~ a chair SIT
~ a chance BET, DARE, RISK
~ a crack at ESSAY, TRY
~ action MOVE
~ action against SUE
~ a dip SWIM
~ a dive LOSE
~ advantage AVAIL
~ advantage of ABUSE, HAVE, USE
~ advice HEED
~ a fancy to LIKE
~ a flier DARE, RISK
~ a gander EYE, PEER, SEE
~ a header TRIP
~ a hike LEAVE, SCAT, SCRAM
~ a humble position KNEEL
~ alarm PALE, SHY
~ a limo RIDE
~ a load off SIT
~ a long hard look PORE, STARE
~ a long shot BET
~ a look at EYE, NOTE, SEE
~ a loss on EAT
~ a meal EAT
~ a nap REST
~ an apartment LET, RENT
~ an arm STEER, USHER
~ an exam SIT
~ apart RAVEL, UNDO
~ a picture SHOOT, SNAP
~ a plunge DIP
~ a potshot SNIPE
~ a powder EXIT, FLEE, LAM, LEAVE, SCAT, SCRAM
~ a pratfall MISS, SLIP, TRIP
~ a quick look SCAN
~ a raincheck MISS
~ a ride MOTOR
~ a role ACT
~ as a course ELECT
~ a shine to LIKE
~ a shot at ESSAY, TRY
~ a shower BATHE, LAVE
~ a snooze NAP, REST
~ as one's own ADOPT
~ a spill SLIP
~ a spouse WED
~ as testimony HEAR
~ a total ADD, SUM
~ a trip MOTOR
~ a tumble TRIP
~ away CLEAR, LESS, STRIP
~ a wrong turn ERR
~ back DENY

~ by the hand AID, LEAD
~ care of ATTEND, DEAL, FEED, MEET, SEETO
~ charge BOSS, LEAD, RULE, STEER
~ control LEAD
~ countermeasures REACT
~ delight (in) REVEL
~ different paths PART
~ down RAZE, UNDO, WRITE
~ down a peg ABASE
~ effect ENURE, INURE
~ everything HOG
~ first place LEAD, WIN
~ five REST
~ flight FLEE, JET, LAM, SCRAM
~ for a ride CON, DUPE, SCAM
~ for non-credit AUDIT
~ for one's own ADOPT
~ French leave DESERT, RUN
~ heart HOPE
~ heed HEAR
~ home CLEAR, EARN, MAKE, NET
~ home a trophy WIN
~ in ADMIT, ADOPT, ALTER, CON, DUPE, EARN, EAT, EYE, HEAR, KID, LEARN, NOTE, SEE, SEW
~ in the sights TOUR
~ into account ALLOW, HEED, NOTE
~ into custody ARREST, NAB, NAIL
~ in tow DRAG, HELP
~ it ABIDE, BEAR
~ it easy IDLE, LOAF, LOLL, REST, SIT, SLIDE
~ it from the top REDO
~ it on the chin BEAR
~ kindly to LIKE
~ leave PART
~ lodgings LET, RENT
~ lots DRAW
~ measures ACT
~ no note of CUT, SNUB
~ note HEED
~ note of SEE
~ notes JOT
~ notice HEED
~ odds BET
~ off CUT, DASH, ELOPE, EXIT, FLEE, HIE, LEAVE, MOVE, RISE, RUN, SHED, SOAR, SPEED, SPLIT, START
~ off after CHASE
~ off pounds DIET
~ off the shelf USE
~ off the top CLEAR
~ on ADD, ADOPT, EMOTE, HIRE
~ on cargo LADE
~ one's breath away AMAZE, AWE, STUN, WOW
~ one's ease REST
~ oneself away LEAVE
~ one's medicine PAY
~ on staff HIRE, MAN
~ on water LEAK
~ out DATE, DELE, DRAW
~ out a mortgage OWE
~ out of the freezer THAW
~ out to dinner TREAT

~ over ADOPT
~ part in SHARE
~ part in a biathlon SKI
~ place OCCUR
~ pleasure in ADORE, BASK, LIKE, REVEL, SAVOR
~ precedence RANK
~ pride PREEN
~ quickly GRAB
~ revenge on GET
~ satisfaction AVENGE
~ second place LOSE
~ shape GEL
~ sick leave AIL
~ steps ACT, PACE
~ stock of ASSESS, AUDIT
~ surreptitiously PALM
~ sustenance DINE, EAT
~ ten REST
~ the bait BITE, REACT
~ the bull by the horns BEARD, DARE
~ the bus RIDE
~ the cake WIN
~ the count LOSE
~ the first step START
~ the floor ORATE, TALK
~ the heat off EASE
~ the helm LEAD, STEER
~ the law into one's own hands AVENGE
~ the lead HEAD
~ the measure of ASSAY, ASSESS
~ the money and run FLEE
~ the mound HURL
~ the offensive LEAD
~ the plunge DARE, START, WED
~ the podium ORATE
~ the prize WIN
~ the reins STEER
~ the stage ACT
~ the stump ORATE
~ the tiller STEER
~ the trolley RIDE
~ the van LEAD
~ the wheel STEER
~ the wraps off OPEN
~ the wrong road ERR
~ time off REST
~ to AGREE, LIKE
~ to a seat USHER
~ to court SUE
~ to flight FLEE
~ to heart HEED
~ to mean READ
~ to one's heels DESERT, FLEE, HIE, RUN
~ to task RAG
~ to the air AVIATE
~ to the woods RUN
~ up ADOPT, ALTER
~ up, as a cause ADOPT
~ up quarters ABIDE
~ wing AVIATE, FLEE, JET, SOAR
agent's ~ FEE, TENTH
agt.'s ~ PCT
burglar's ~ LOOT, SWAG
give and ~ SWAP, TRADE
give or ~ a little LIKE
prepare to ~ off TAXI
the ~ GATE, LOOT

winner's ~ ALL

take ___ (assume to be) FOR
take ___ (delete) OUT
take ___ (dismantle) APART
take ___ (emulate) AFTER
take ___ (enroot) HOLD
take ___ (jump into a debate) SIDES
take ___ (remove) OFF
take ___ (rest) FIVE, TEN
take ___ account INTO
take ___ a ride FOR
take ___ granted FOR
take ___ on ATOLL
take ___ the chin ITON
take ___ the lam ITON
"Take ___!" THAT
"Take ___ leave it!" ITOR
take a ___ BATH, STAND
take a ___ at (try) STAB
take a ___ to (like) SHINE
"Take a ___!" HIKE
"Take a Chance on Me" ~ band ABBA
take a crack ___ ATIT
take-along shopping ~ LIST
take-back dealer's ~ REPO
take by ___ STORM
take down a ___ PEG
take for a ___ RIDE
"Take Good Care of My Baby" ~ singer VEE
"Take Her, ___ Mine" SHES
take-home NET
take-home ___ PAY
Takei, George ~ role SULU
take it like ___ AMAN
take it on the ___ CHIN
take it or leave it ASIS
"___ Take It to Heart" DONT
"___ Take Manhattan" ILL
"Take Me ___" ALONG
"Take Me ___ Am" ASI
"Take Me ___ to the Ball Game" OUT
"Take Me as ___" IAM
"Take Me Home" ~ singer CHER

"Take Me Out to the ___ Game" BALL

"Take Me Out to the Ball ___" GAME

taken
~ alone PERSE
~ for granted TACIT
~ with INTO
amount ~ in GATE
be ~ aback START
be ~ with ADORE
easily ~ in NAIVE
not ~ in by ONTO

taken-back
~ item REPO

takeoff
~ artist APER
do a ~ APE

take one's ___ TIME

"Take On Me"
~ band AHA

takeout
~ shop DELI
call for ~ ORDER
for ~ TOGO
get ~ perhaps EATIN

taker
letter ~ STENO
SAT ~ TEEN
token ~ SLOT

"___ takers?" ANY

takes
~ action DOES
~ a turn GOES
~ one's leave GOES
it ~ a licking STAMP

"___ Takes a Chance, A" LADY

take the ___ CAKE, HEAT, RAP

"Take the Money and ___" RUN

"Take the Money and Run"
~ director ALLEN

take to ___ HEART, TASK

take with a grain of ___ SALT

taking
~ a cruise ASEA, ATSEA
~ after ALA

"Taking ___" OFF

"Taking ___ of Business" CARE

"Taking of Pelham ___ Two Three, The" ONE

"Taking of Pelham One ___ Three, The" TWO

"Taking of Pelham One Two ___, The" THREE

takings HAUL

Taklamakan DESERT

talaria
like ~ ALAR

Talbot NITA

"Talcum is walcum"
~ poet NASH

tale LIE
~ teller LIAR
fairy ~ LIE, YARN
heroic ~ EDDA, EPIC, GEST, GESTE, SAGA
Homeric ~ ILIAD
medieval ~ GEST, GESTE
tall ~ LIE, YARN
tell a ~ SPIN

___ tale TALL

"Tale ___ Tub, A" OFA

talent ASSET, BENT, FEEL, TURN
endow, as with ~ BLESS
mind reader's ~ ESP
possessing ~ ABLE

talent ___ SHOW

talented ABLE, ADEPT, SMART

talent scout AGENT, REP

tale of ___ WOE

"Tale of ___ Cities, A" TWO

"Tale of ___ Saltan, The" TSAR

tales
old wives' ~ LORE

Talese GAY

"Tales From Shakespeare"
~ author ELIA, LAMB

"Tales From the ___" HOOD

"Tales From the Crypt"
like ~ EERIE, EERY

"Tales of Hoffmann" OPERA

"Tales of Terror"
~ star LORRE

"tale told by an ___, A" IDIOT

Talia SHIRE

talipot PALM, TREE

talk GAB, NOISE, RAP, RUMOR, SAY, YAK
~ about AIR
~ amorously COO
~ at length GAB, YAK
~ back to SASS
~ big BRAG, CROW, ORATE
~ excessively GAS
~ fondly COO
~ hoarsely RASP
~ idly BLAB
~ incessantly GAB, YAP
~ into CON, GOAD
~ irrationally RAGE, RANT, RAVE, STORM
~ like APE
~ like a child LISP
~ like Daffy Duck LISP
~ on and on DRONE
~ one's head off BORE
~ out SETTLE
~ out of ARGUE, DETER
~ over, with "out" HASH
~ rhythmically RAP
~ through one's hat LIE
~ unclearly SLUR

~ up BOOM
~ wildly RANT, RAVE
baby ~ GOO, MAMA, PAPA
back ~ ECHO, LIP, SASS
chick ~ PEEP
eccl. ~ SER
empty ~ CANT, GAS, PAP, PRATE
foolish ~ YAP
fresh ~ LIP, SASS
friendly ~ CHAT
idle ~ GAB, GAS, NEWS, PRATE, TRASH, YAP
insider's ~ ARGOT
insincere ~ CANT
kiddie ~ LISP
mule ~ BRAY
ordinary ~ PROSE
pig ~ OINK
small ~ CHAT, GAB
smart ~ LIP, SASS
thieves' ~ ARGOT

talk ___ BIG, OVER, RADIO, SENSE, SHOP, SHOW

___ talk GIRL, PEP, SMALL, SWEET

___-talk FAST

talking
~ bird MYNA
~ point ASSET
TV's ~ horse MRED

"___ Talking" ENTER

talk it ___ OVER

talks
SALT ~ subject ARMS

talk show
~ host LENO
former ~ host ALLEN, DINAH, PAAR

talk through one's ___ HAT

tall BIG, LANK, LARGE, SIZE
~ and skinny LANK
~ bird CRANE
~ bloomer GLAD, IRIS
~ in Tampico ALTO
~ peak SPIRE
~ story ATTIC, LIE, TALE
~ tale LIE, YARN
it may be ~ ORDER, TALE
like ~ grass REEDY

tall ___ ORDER, TALE

Tallahassee
~ st. FLA

taller
get ~ GROW

"Tall in the Saddle" OATER

tallow FAT, LARD, SUET
~ source SUET

tall tale LIE, YARN
~ teller LIAR

"Tall Target, The"
~ director MANN

tally ADD, AGREE, BILL, POLL, SCORE, SUIT, SUM

tallyho CRY

Talmadge NORMA

talon CLAW, NAIL

talus ANKLE, SCREE

tam CAP, HAT
~ cousin BERET
~ wearer SCOT

___ tamale HOT

tamarack TREE

tamarau
~ relative BISON

tamarin ANIMAL

tamarind TREE

"Tamarind ___, The" SEED

tame MEEK, MILD, PET, SAFE
not ~ FERAL

"Tamerlane"
~ poet POE

Tamiami ___ TRAIL

Tamil ASIAN

tam-o'-shanter CAP, HAT

tamp RAM, STEM

Tampa BAY, CITY, PORT
~ clock setting EDT, EST

Tampa ___ Buccaneers BAY

tamper
~ with RIG, SKEW
~ with dice LOAD
~ with odometers RESET

Tampico CITY, PORT
see also Spanish

tampion PEG

tan COLOR, ECRU, SUN, TAUPE
~ leather CURE
~ oneself BASK
~ someone's hide BEAT, CANE
get a ~ SUN
light ~ ECRU

___-tan FAN

Tan AMY

Tana LAKE

tanager BIRD

tandem BIKE

tandoor OVEN

tang BITE, NIP, SAVOR

Tanganyika LAKE

tangelo UGLI

tangent RATIO
~ cousin SINE

___ tangent ARC

tangential
~ remark ASIDE

tangerine COLOR, TREE

tangible REAL

Tangier CITY, PORT

tangle KNOT, MAT, RAVEL, SNAG
  ~ **up** SNAG
  ~ **(with)** CLOSE

tangled
  get ~ MAT, SNARL

tango DANCE
  ~ **feature** DIP
  ~ **requirement** DUO, TWO

"Tango and ___" CASH

"___ Tango in Paris" LAST

Tanguay EVA

Tanguy YVES

tangy RACY, TART
  ~ **flavor** MINT

Tanith LEE

tank VAT
  ~ **filler** GAS
  ~ **starter** ANTI

tank ___ TOP

tankard CUP, POT
  ~ **contents** ALE

tanker BOAT, OILER, SHIP
  ~ **cargo** OIL
  ~ **insignia, once** ESSO

tankful GAS

tanned
  ~ **skin** KID
  not ~ PALE

"Tannenbaum"
  ~ **literally** FIR

Tanners
  the ~ alien live-in ALF

Tannhäuser HERO

"Tannhäuser" OPERA

tannic ACID

tanning
  ~ **agent** SUN
  ~ **need** HIDE
  ~ **solution** BATE

tantalite ORE

tantalize BAIT, LURE, TEASE

tantalum METAL

tantamount ALIKE

tantara BLARE

tantivy APACE, RAPID

tantrum FIT, RAGE, SCENE, SNIT
  ~ **thrower** BRAT
  throw a ~ RAGE, STORM

"Tantum ___" ERGO

tao
  ~ **literally** PATH

Tao
  ~ **ender** ISM

Taoism REL

Taormina
  ~ **mount** ETNA

tap BORE, CLAP, DAB, DRAW, FLIP,
  HIT, OPEN, PAT, RAP
  ~ **choice** ALE, BEER
  ~ **gently** DAB
  ~ **problem** DRIP, LEAK
  ~ **product** ALE, BEER
  ~ **word** HOT
  light ~ PAT

tap ___ DANCE, INTO, WATER

tape BIND, CORD, GOAL, SEAL
  ~ **up** MEND, SEAL
  clear a ~ ERASE
  cut through red ~ AID
  degauss a ~ ERASE
  put on ~ CUT
  sample ~ DEMO

___ tape RED

tape deck
  ~ **button** REC
  ~ **option** ERASE

taper LAMP
  ~ **off** ABATE, DROP, FADE,
  FLAG, SLOW, WANE

tapered
  ~ **boat** CANOE

tapestry ARRAS, DRAPE

tapir ANIMAL

Tappan ___ Bridge ZEE

tapped
  ~ **item** KEG
  it may be ~ MAPLE

taproom BAR, INN

"Taps"
  ~ **time, at times** TEN

tapster
  ~ **unit** KEG

tar GOB, PAVE, SALT
  ~ **affirmative** AYE
  ~ **saint** ELMO
  ~ **shout** AHOY, AVAST
  ~ **source** COAL, PINE
  cover with ~ PAVE
  on leave, to a ~ ASHORE

___ tar COAL, PINE

Tar ___ (North Carolinian) HEEL

Tara ESTATE
  ~ **family name** OHARA
  land of ~ EIRE, ERIN

taradiddle LIE, TALE

taradiddler LIAR

tarantella DANCE

Taranto CITY
  ~ **locale** ITALY
  see also Italian

"Ta-Ra-Ra-___-De-Re" BOOM

Tarbell IDA

tarboosh CAP, HAT

tardy LATE

tare WEED

Tarentum
  see Latin

targe ARMOR

target AIM, PREY
  face the ~ AIM
  on ~ APT

target ___ DATE

"___ Target, The" TALL

targeter
  apple ~ TELL

target practice
  ~ **game** SKEET

tariff COST, FEE, TOLL
  turnpike ~ TOLL

Tarkenton FRAN

Tarkington, Booth
  ~ **character** ADAMS, ALICE

tarmac
  ~ **area** APRON
  lay down ~ PAVE
  reached ~ **the** ALIT
  roll on the ~ TAXI

tarn LAKE, POOL

tarnish BLOT, LIBEL, SHAME,
  SMEAR, SOIL, TAINT

taro
  ~ **product** POI

tarot
  ~ **reader** SEER

tarry ABIDE, BIDE, LAG, STAY, STOP,
  WAIT
  ~ **for** AWAIT

tars CREW

tarsus ANKLE, BONE

tart ACID, ACRID, PIE, RACY, SOUR,
  TESTY
  ~ **fruit** LEMON, SLOE
  ~ **relative** PIE
  ~ **substance** ACID

tartan
  ~ **wearer** CLAN, SCOT

___ tartare STEAK

tartaric ACID

tartar sauce
  ~ **ingredient** CAPER

tartlike
  ~ **pastry** FLAN

tartness NIP

tartrate ESTER, SALT

tart-tasting ACID

Tarzan HERO
  ~ **associate** APE
  ~ **love** JANE
  ~ **mother** ALICE
  ~ **portrayer** ELY
  ~ **transport** LIANA

"Tarzan and ___ Mate" HIS

"Tarzan and His ___" MATE

"Tarzan Finds a ___!" SON

"Tarzan, the ___ Man" APE

"Tarzan, the Ape ___" MAN

Taschhorn ALP

Tashkent CITY

task LABOR, STINT
  simple ~ SNAP
  unpleasant ~ ONUS

taskmaster BOSS

Tasman ABEL, SEA

Tasmania
  ~ **(abbr.)** ISL

Tasmanian
  ~ **devil** ANIMAL
  ~ **mountain** OSSA

tasse ARMOR
  ~ **starter** DEMI

tassel
  corn ~ SILK

tasseled
  ~ **cap** TAM

Tasso, Torquato POET
  patron of ~ ESTE
  see also poet

taste BITE, DASH, EAT, SAVOR,
  SENSE, STYLE, TACT, TRY
  ~ **stimulus** AROMA
  get a ~ **of** TRY
  in good ~ NICE
  minty ~ TANG
  preserve the ~ SAVOR
  small ~ BITE, NIP, SIP

"___ Taste" BAD

tasteful NICE

tasteless BLAH, FLAT, LOUD, STALE

tasty GOOD, SWEET

___-tat RATA

"Ta-ta!" BYE, LATER
  ~ **in French** ADIEU
  ~ **in Hawaiian** ALOHA
  ~ **in Italian** CIAO
  ~ **in Latin** AVE, VALE
  ~ **in Spanish** ADIOS

tatami MAT
  ~ **material** STRAW

Tatar
  ~ **chief** KHAN

Tatar Strait
  river into the ~ AMUR

Tate ALLEN, LAURA

Tate, Allen POET
  see also poet

Tate Gallery
  ~ **display** ART

Tate, Nahum POET
  see also poet

"Tatler, The"
  ~ **essayist** STEELE

___-tat-tat RATA

tatter SHRED, TEAR

Tattered Tom
  ~ creator ALGER

tatters
  in ~ SHOT, TORN

tatting LACE

tattle BLAB, RAT, TALK, TELL

tattler RAT

tattletale ___ GRAY

tattoo
  ~ place ARM
  popular ~ MOM

"___ Tattoo, The" ROSE

Tatum ART, ONEAL
  ~ dad RYAN

taught
  be ~ LEARN
  where Zeno ~ STOA

___-taught SELF

taunt BAIT, DIG, EGG, GIBE, HISS,
  HOOT, RAG, SNEER, TEASE,
  TWIT

taupe COLOR

Taurus AUTO, CAR, RANGE, SIGN
  ~ preceder ARIES
  nebula in ~ CRAB
  neighbor of ~ ORION

taut TENSE

tautness STRESS
  lose ~ SAG

tautomeric
  ~ compound ENOL

tavern BAR, HOTEL, INN
  ~ fare ALE, BEER, LAGER
  ~ sign ONTAP

tawdry LOUD

tawny COLOR, ECRU
  ~ cat LION

tax ASSESS, ONUS, STRESS, TASK,
  TOLL, TRY
  ~ expert CPA
  ~ mo. APR
  ~ once SESS
  ~ org. IRS
  ~ rolls POLL
  ~ shelter IRA
  ~ someone's patience BORE,
  TRY
  ~ time APRIL

tax ___ CODE, LIEN

tax-___ FREE

___ tax ESTATE, GAS, POLL, SALES,
  SIN

___-tax AFTER

**"Taxation without representa-
tion"**
  ~ coiner OTIS

Taxco
  see Spanish

taxes
  after ~ NET
  earn after ~ CLEAR

tax-free
  ~ bond, briefly MUNI

taxi CAB, HACK, MOTOR, RIDE
  ~ device METER
  ~ fee FARE
  ~ passenger FARE
  go by ~ RIDE
  summon a ~ FLAG, HAIL

taxi ___ STAND

___ taxi AIR

"Taxi"
  ~ actress KANE
  ~ role ALEX, TONY
  Marilu's ~ role ELAINE

taxicab
  typical ~ SEDAN

taximeter
  ~ reading FARE

taxonomic
  ~ suffix ELLA

taxpayer
  ~ fear AUDIT

Taylor DON, LILI, RENEE, RIP, ROD,
  SAM
  **he ran against ~ in
  1848** CASS

Taylor, Andy
  ~ aunt BEE
  ~ son OPIE

Taylor, Bee
  Mayberry's ~ AUNT

Taylor, Liz
  1963 ~ role CLEO

Tb ELEM
  65 for ~ ATNO

T-bar
  ~ terrain SLOPE

Tbilisi CITY

T-bone STEAK
  ~ source LOIN

tbsp. AMT
  one-third ~ TSP

Tc ELEM
  43 for ~ ATNO

TCU
  ~ rival SMU

TD STAT

TDs STAT

Te ELEM
  52 for ~ ATNO

tea MEAL
  ~ brewer URN
  ~ herb MINT
  ~ holder BAG, CUP
  ~ in French THE

~ ingredient HERB
~ quantity SPOT
~ rose COLOR
~ table CART
Chinese ~ CHA
high ~ MEAL
Indian ~ source ASSAM
make ~ BREW, STEEP
one's cup of ~ BAG
serve ~ POUR
type of ~ PEKOE

tea ___ BAG, BALL, DANCE, ROSE,
TRAY

___ tea HERB, HOT, ICED

"Tea ___ Sympathy" AND

"Tea and Sympathy"
  ~ actress KERR

teacake SCONE

teach PLANT, SHOW, TRAIN

teacher
  ~ charge CLASS
  ~ deg. EDD, MED
  ~ figuratively LAMP
  ~ need DESK, ERASER, MAP,
  PAPER, PEN, RULER
  ~ org. AFT, NEA
  ~ roster ROLL
  Hindu ~ GURU, SWAMI
  Mahayana ~ LAMA
  private-school ~ NUN
  Siam ~ ANNA
  tennis ~ PRO
  turbaned ~ SWAMI

"Teachers ___" ONLY

"Teacher's ___" PET

teaching
  ~ tool MAP, RULER
  inflexible ~ DOGMA

teachings DOGMA
  early ~ ABCS

teacup
  ~ handle EAR
  ~ rim LIP
  like a ~ EARED

"Tea for ___" TWO

"Tea for Two" DUET

tea-growing
  ~ state ASSAM

Teague LEWIS

**"Teahouse of the August ___,
The"** MOON

**"Teahouse of the August Moon,
The"**
  ~ director MANN

teak COLOR, TREE

teakettle
  ~ sound HISS

"___ Teakettle" USS

teal BIRD, COLOR

team CREW, GANG, SIDE
  ~ and wagon RIG

~ ender MATE, STER
~ goal WIN
~ member HORSE
~ of horses SPAN
~ of oxen SPAN
~-supporting word RAH
~ up ALLY, BAND, HELP, UNITE
baseball ~ NINE, TEN
basketball ~ FIVE
be on a ~ PLAY
bridge ~ DUO, PAIR
drop from the ~ CUT
football ~ ELEVEN
fresh ~ of horses RELAY
hockey ~ SIX
lacrosse ~ TEN
police ~ SWAT
rowing ~ CREW
schooner ~ OXEN
show ~ spirit ROOT
skilled ~ CADRE
softball ~ NINE
the other ~ ENEMY, FOE
West Point ~ ARMY

___ team (assault unit) DELTA,
SWAT

"___, team!" YEA

team player
  not a ~ LONER, REBEL

teams
  one of two ~ HOME

Teamster
  ~ unit LOCAL, SEMI

teamwork
  ~ obstacles EGOS

tea party
  ~ attendee ALICE
  host a ~ POUR

teapot
  tempest in a ~ ADO

Teapot ___ scandal DOME

teapoy TABLE

tear CLAW, DROP, GASH, HIE,
  RACE, RENT, RIP, RUN, SHOOT,
  SHRED, SPEED, SPLIT, SPREE,
  WEEP
  ~ along HIE, RACE, RUN,
  SPEED
  ~ apart REND
  ~ around RAMP
  ~ down RAZE, RUIN
  ~ ender DROP
  ~ gas MACE
  ~ holder SAC
  ~ (into) LACE
  ~ off HIE, RACE, RIP, RUN,
  SPEED
  ~ partner WEAR
  garment ~ RENT
  go on a ~ RAGE, STORM
  small ~ SLIT
  wear and ~ LOSS

tear ___ GAS

tear ___ (attack) INTO

tear ___ (do quickly) OFF

___ tear ONA

tearjerker DRAMA
  kitchen ~ ONION

tearoom
  ~ cousin CAFE

tears
  crocodile ~ POSE
  Job's ~ PLANT
  like crocodile ~ FALSE
  move to ~ GET
  shed ~ BAWL, CRY, SOB, WEEP

"Tears ___ Clown, The" OFA

"Tears in the Rain"
  ~ actress STONE

teary-___ EYED

Teasdale POET, SARA
  see also poet

tease BAIT, GIBE, KID, NEEDLE,
PLAY, RAG, RIB, RIDE, TWIT

teaser
  ~ of a sort BAIT

teaspoon
  use a ~ STIR

teatime
  ~ treat SCONE

Teatro ___ Scala ALLA

Teatro alla ___ SCALA

Tebaldi DIVA
  ~ role TOSCA
  medium for ~ OPERA

tech
  ~ talk ARGOT

___-tech LOW

___ Tech CAL

"___ Te Ching" TAO

technical
  ~ sch. INST
  ~ word TERM

technique ART, MODE
  cinematic ~ FADE
  fade-out ~ IRIS

technology
  ~ (abbr.) SCI

___ tectonics PLATE

Ted KEY, POST, ROSS
  TV logo for ~ TBS, TNT

TED
  ~ defeater HST

teddy BEAR
  ~ bear TOY

Teddy
  ~ mom ROSE

tedious ARID, BANAL, DRY, FLAT,
HARD, LONG, SLOW, STALE,
TAME
  ~ one BORE

tedium ENNUI

"___ & Ted's Excellent Adventure" BILL

tee PEG
  ~ off ANGER, ENRAGE, IRK,
PEEVE, RILE, START, STEAM,
UPSET
  ~ preceder ESS

tee-___ HEE

teed
  ~ off IRATE, MAD, SORE,
UPSET

teeming DENSE, LIVE, RIFE

teen
  ~ ender AGER
  ~ exclamation RAD
  ~ fave IDOL
  ~ hangout ARCADE, MALL
  ~ language SLANG
  ~ room, often MESS
  ~ socialite DEB
  ~ woe ACNE
  former ~ ADULT

teen ___ IDOL

"Teen ___" ANGEL

"Teenage Mutant Ninja Turtles"
  ~ lady APRIL

**"Teenage Mutant Ninja Turtles
II: The Secret of the ___"**
OOZE

teenager KID
  ~ desire AUTO, CAR

teens
  big night for ~ PROM
  like many ~ rooms MESSY

teensy WEE

teenybopper FAN, GIRL, MISS

teeny-weeny SMALL, TINY

teeter REEL, SWAY

teeth
  bare one's ~ DARE, SNARL
  scarcer than hen's ~ RARE
  tool with ~ RAKE, SAW
  use one's ~ BITE, GNAW

teetotaler DRY

Tegucigalpa CITY
  see also Spanish

tegument CASE

Tehachapi RANGE

Teheran CITY
  ~ locale IRAN
  ~ resident IRANI
  ~ VIP IMAM

Tehuantepec
  see Spanish

Te Kanawa, Kiri DAME, DIVA,
MAORI
  ~ solo ARIA

Tel ___ AVIV

telamon ATLAS, POST

Tel Aviv
  ~ loc. ISR
  ~ locale ISRAEL

telecast
  ~ signal AUDIO

telecasts
  like some ~ LIVE

telecommunications
  ~ co. ITT

telegram CABLE, WIRE
  ~ word STOP

telegraph CABLE, SEND, WIRE
  ~ datum DASH, DOT
  ~ inventor MORSE
  ~ part KEY, RELAY

telegraph ___ PLANT

Telemachus
  ~ to Odysseus SON
  ~ to Penelope SON

"Télémaque" EPIC

telepathist SEER

telepathy ESP, PSI

telephone CALL, DIAL, HORN, RING
  ~ ABC TWO
  ~ book LIST
  ~ button ABC, STAR
  ~ charge TOLL
  ~ DEF THREE
  ~ greeting HELLO
  ~ JKL FIVE
  ~ line CORD
  ~ MNO SIX
  ~ PRS SEVEN
  ~ WXY NINE
  wait on the ~ HOLD
  see also phone

"Telephone Line"
  ~ band ELO

telephonic
  ~ two ABC

telescope
  ~ lens OPTIC
  ~ part LENS

___ telescope RADIO

Telescopium
  ~ neighbor ARA

telesthesia ESP

Telesto MOON

Teletubbies
  ~ fan KID, TOT

televise AIR, SEND

television
  ~ receiver SET
  ~ signal component AUDIO
  ~ tube component NEON
  ~ tuner DIAL
  like early ~ LIVE
  see also TV

___ television CABLE

"Television, Mr." BERLE

telex SEND

tell ADMIT, LEAK, OWN, RELATE,
SAY, SPIN, STATE, TALK
  ~ a falsehood LIE

  ~ a lie FAKE
  ~ all BARE, BLAB, SING
  ~ a tale SPIN
  ~ jokes AMUSE
  ~ on BLAB, RAT, SING
  ~ partner KISS, SHOW
  ~ the judge PLEAD
  ~ the world AIR

tell ___ (scold) OFF

tell ___ glance ATA

"___ tell!" PRAY

"Tell ___" HIM

"Tell ___!" ALL

"Tell ___ About It" HER

"Tell ___ I Love Her" LAURA

"Tell ___ Willie Boy Is Here"
THEM

teller
  ~ cry NEXT
  fortune ~ SEER
  tale ~ LIAR

Teller
  ~ partner PENN

"___ telling me!" YOURE

"Tell it like ___!" ITIS

**"Tell Me ___ You Love Me, Junie
Moon"** THAT

**"Tell Me That ___ Love Me, Junie
Moon"** YOU

**"Tell Me That You ___ Me, Junie
Moon"** LOVE

**"Tell Me That You Love Me,
Junie ___"** MOON

telltale SIGN
  ~ sign ODOR

"Tell-Tale ___, The" HEART

"Tell-Tale Heart, The"
  ~ author POE

"Tell Them Willie Boy Is ___"
HERE

Telluride
  enjoy ~ SKI

tellurium METAL

Tell, William
  ~ home URI
  ~ target APPLE
  ~ weapon ARROW, BOW

"Telly"
  ~ network BBC

___ tem PRO

temblor TREMOR

temp
  December ~ SANTA

Tempe
  ~ river SALT
  ~ sch. ASU

temper ABATE, ADAPT, ALLAY,

ANGER, BILE, IRE, IRISH, MOOD, TONE
~ tantrum PET, RAGE, SNIT
display of ~ FIT, SCENE
fit of ~ PET, RAGE, SNIT
lose one's ~ RAGE, RANT, RAVE, ROAR, SNARL, STORM, YELL

temperament MOOD, TONE

temperamental TESTY

temperate EASY, EVEN, MILD, SOBER, ZONE

Temperate ZONE

temperature HEAT
~ extreme LOW
~ inversion problem SMOG
overnight ~ usually LOW

___ temperature MEAN, ROOM

temperatures
freezing ~ TEENS

___-tempered EVEN, GOOD, HOT, ILL

tempest GALE, STORM
~ in a teapot ADO

tempest ___ teacup INA

tempest ___ teapot INA

Tempest MARIE

"Tempest, The"
~ character ARIEL
~ start ACTI

tempestuous UGLY

Templar, Simon SAINT
~ portrayer MOORE

temple
~ image IDOL
~ table ALTAR
Greek ~ detail ANTA

temple ___ ORANGE

Temple, Shirley
~ costar of 1936 EBSEN
~ first husband AGAR

Templeton ALEC

Temple University
~ athlete OWL

tempo BEAT, PACE, RATE, TIME
slow ~ LENTO

temporal LAIC, LAY

temporary
~ failure LAPSE
~ gift LOAN
~ job GIG
~ lodgings CAMP
~ resident TENANT
~ shelter TENT
~ tint RINSE
grant ~ use of LEASE

___ tempore PRO

temporize DEFER

tempt BAIT, DRAW, LURE
~ fate DARE, RISK

temptation BAIT, URGE
Eve's ~ APPLE

temptress SIREN

ten
~ rin SEN
~ sawbucks CEE
hang ~ RIDE
take ~ REST

ten-___ SPOT

ten-___ bicycle SPEED

___ ten HANG, TAKE

___ ten (rating scale) ONETO

tenaciously FAST, HARD

tenacity GRIT

tenant
~ pact LEASE
find a ~ RENT
joint ~ CON
mall ~ STORE
marina ~ BOAT

tenantless OPEN

tenants
find new ~ RELET

"Ten Cents a ___" DANCE

Ten Commandments
~ recipient MOSES
~ repository ARK

"Ten Commandments, The" EPIC
~ role AARON, MOSES

tend LEAN, NURSE, SEETO, SIT
~ the houseplants WATER
~ the kids SIT
~ the lawn MOW
~ the sauce STIR
~ the turkey BASTE
~ the yard RAKE
~ to NURSE
~ to the radiator BLEED
~ (towards) LEAN

"Ten Days That Shook the World"
~ author REED

tendency BENT, BIAS, CAST, HABIT, SLANT, TENOR, TIDE, TREND, TURN
~ (suffix) IVE
general ~ STYLE
have a ~ LEAN

tender BID, BILL, BOAT, CEDE, MILD, RAW, RED, SHIP, SORE
~ an offer BID
~ passion LOVE
~ starter BAR, GOAL
legal ~ BILL, CASH, NOTE, PAPER

___ tender LEGAL

"Tender ___, The" TRAP

tenderfoot BABE, DUDE

Tenderfoot
~ org. BSA

tender-hearted MILD

"Tender Land, The" OPERA

tenderloin MEAT

tenderness LOVE

tending APT
~ to (suffix) ISH
~ toward PRONE

tendon CORD, SINEW

tendril COIL, STEM

tenebrous DIM

tenebrousness SHADE

tenement ABODE

tenet DOGMA, ISM, LAW, RULE

tenets DOGMA
group ~ ETHOS

"Ten From Your ___ of Shows" SHOW

ten-gallon ___ HAT

"Ten Gentlemen From ___ Point" WEST

"___ Ten List" TOP

Tenn.
~ neighbor ALA, ARK, KEN, MISS
see also Tennessee

tenner
half a ~ FIN

Tennessee STATE
~ state flower IRIS

Tennessee ___ Ford ERNIE

Tennessee River
~ tributary ELK

Tennessee walking ___ HORSE

Tennille TONI

tennis GAME
~ call LET
~ edge ADIN
~ match division SET
~ official REF
~ referee's cry LONG
~ requirement NET
~ score LOVE
~ scores ADS
~ shot LOB, SMASH
~ status BYE
~ stroke CHOP
~ surface LAWN
~ teacher PRO
~ term ACE, ADIN, ALL, LOVE
~ winner ACE
backspin a ~ ball SLICE
score in ~ ACE
six games in ~ SET
start a ~ game SERVE
table ~ GAME
zero score in ~ LOVE

tennis ___ BALL, ELBOW, SHOE

___ tennis LAWN, TABLE

tennis elbow
~ site ULNA

"Ten North Frederick"
~ author OHARA

Tennyson LORD, POET
~ heroine ENID
~ maid ELAINE
~ princess IDA
see also poet

tenor CLEF, LINE, MALE, RANGE, SENSE, TIDE, TONE, TREND
between soprano and ~ ALTO
"The Flying Dutchman" ~ ERIK

tenpenny ___ NAIL

ten-percenter AGENT, AGT, REP

tenpins GAME

ten-point
~ type ELITE

tenrec ANIMAL

tense EDGY, TAUT
have the same ~ AGREE
kind of ~ PAST
vb. ~ PRES

___ tense PAST

tenseness STRESS

tension DRAMA, STRESS
lose ~ SAG
muscle ~ TONE

ten-speed BIKE
~ bike RACER
~ part GEAR

"Tenspeed and Brown ___" SHOE

tent DRESS, TEPEE
~ area CAMP
~ caterpillar PEST
~ dweller NOMAD
~ holder PEG, STAKE
~ out CAMP
pitch a ~ ABIDE, CAMP, STAY

tentacle ARM, ORGAN

tentacled
~ mollusks OCTOPI

tentative TRIAL

tenterhook NAIL

tenterhooks
on ~ TENSE

tenth century
~ explorer ERIC

"Tentmaker"
~ of poetry OMAR

ten to one ODDS

tenuous AERIAL

tenure TERM, TIME

"Ten Who ___" DARED

tepee ABODE, TENT

tepid MILD, WARM

tequila
~ source AGAVE

terbium METAL

terce HOUR

Tercel AUTO, CAR

Terence ROMAN, STAMP

Terence ___ D'Arby TRENT

Teresa, Mother NUN

Teresa, Saint
~ town AVILA

tergiversate EVADE

Terhune
~ canine LAD

teriyaki MEAT

term LABEL, NAME, PEG, RUN, STYLE, TIME
~ terminator EXAM, TEST
Cong. ~ SESS

___-term LONG

termagant NAG

terminal ANODE, END, STOP
~ abbr. ARR, ETA
approach the ~ TAXI
bus ~ STA
current ~ ANODE
railroad ~ DEPOT

"Terminal ___, The" MAN

"Terminal Man, The"
~ actor SEGAL

terminate ABORT, ANNUL, CEASE, EJECT, END, HALT, STOP

terminated DONE, OVER

termination CLOSE, END, TAIL

terminology CANT

terminus END

termite
~ kin ANT

term paper
~ abbr. ETAL, IBID
~ need TOPIC

terms
~ of sale ASIS
be on good ~ with KNOW
come to ~ AGREE, CLOSE, DEAL, SETTLE
two ~ for some YEAR

tern BIRD

Terpsichore MUSE
~ sister CLIO, ERATO

terra EARTH, LAND

terrace PATIO

"Terrace at Le Havre"
~ painter MONET

terra cotta CLAY

terra firma EARTH, LAND, SHORE

terrain AREA, LAND

___-terrain vehicle ALL

terrarium
~ plant FERN

Terre Haute
~ st. IND

terrene EARTH

terrible BAD, DIRE, VILE
~ twos PHASE

"terrible"
~ age TWOS

"Terrible"
~ czar IVAN
~ title TSAR

terrier
fictional ~ ASTA
kind of ~ SKYE

terrific FINE, GREAT
~ time BALL, BLAST

"Terrific!" FINE, GREAT, WOW

terrified ASHEN

terrify AWE, COW, SCARE

terrifying DIRE

territory AREA, LAND, PALE, REALM, SITE, SPHERE, TRACT, ZONE

terror FEAR, PANIC
holy ~ BRAT, IMP
strike ~ into SCARE

"___ Terror" CRY

terrorize ALARM

Terry ELI, ELLEN

terse
~ affirmation IDO
~ assent YEP
~ president CAL

Tesh
~ former colleague HART

Tessie O'___ SHEA

"Tess of the D'Urbervilles"
~ cad ALEC

test ASSAY, ESSAY, EXAM, PILOT, SIP, TRIAL, TRY
~ answer FALSE, TRUE
~ car DEMO
~ for strength STRESS
~ response ANS
~ the patience of TRY
~ venue LAB
kind of ~ ORAL
kind of ~ question ESSAY
medical ~ XRAY
ore ~ ASSAY
software ~ BETA
stand the ~ of time LAST

test ___ CASE

test-___ treaty BAN

___ test ACID, ROAD, STRESS, TASTE

"Test ___" PILOT

testa
~ cousin ARIL

___-tested TIME

tester COIN
~ output SCENT

testify SAY, STATE
~ to ASSERT

testimony
~ preceder OATH

tests
F, on some ~ FALSE
T, on some ~ TRUE

test tube
~ relative VIAL

testy EDGY, IRATE, TART
~ mood SNIT

Tet
~ locale NAM

tetchy TESTY

tête-à-tête CHAT, TALK
have a ~ SEE

tether BIND, LEASH, MOOR, ROPE, STAKE, TIE

tetherball GAME

Tethys MOON, TITAN

Tetley
~ product TEA

Teton TRIBE

Tetons RANGE

tetr-
~ successor PENT

tetra
neon ~ PET

tetra-
~ doubled OCTO
~ predecessor TRI

___ tetra (tropical fish) NEON

tetrahedrite ORE

tetrarch LORD, RULER

Tetzlaff TED

Teut. GER

Teutonic
~ earth goddess ERDA
see also German

Tevere
city on the ~ ROMA

Tevye
~ portrayer ZERO

Tewksbury PETER

Tex.
see Texas

___-Tex GORE

Texaco
former ~ rival ESSO

"Texaco Star Theater"
~ star BERLE

Texas STATE
~ baseballer ASTRO
~ city ODESSA, WACO

~ dish CHILI
~ river PECOS
~ state tree PECAN
~ tourist site ALAMO
~ university RICE

Texas ___ (Lubbock school) TECH

Texas ___ (oil) TEA

"Texas ___ the River" ACROSS

Texas A&M
~ rival SMU

"Texas Chain ___ Massacre, The" SAW

"Texas tea" OIL

Tex-Mex
~ item TACO
~ sauce SALSA
~ specialty CHILI

text THEME, TOPIC
~ mistakes ERRATA
~ reviewer EDITOR
change ~ EDIT, EMEND

textbook
~ heading UNIT

textile
~ machine LOOM
~ worker DYER

texts
orig. ~ MSS

texture FEEL, NAP
fabric ~ WALE
rug ~ NAP

TGIF
part of ~ FRI, ITS

Th ELEM
90 for ~ ATNO

Thai ASIAN
~ language LAO
~ neighbor LAO

___ Thai ("The Elvis of Vietnam") TAI

Thailand
~ coin ATT
~ export TEAK
~ native LAO
~ neighbor LAOS
~ royal name RAMA
old name for ~ SIAM

"Thaïs" OPERA

Thalia MUSE
~ sister CLIO, ERATO

___ T. Hall TOM

thallium METAL

Thames
~ leave-taking TATA
school on the ~ ETON
see also British, English

___ than (except) OTHER

"Thanatopsis" POEM

thane PEER, TITLE

Thanet ISLE

"Thank ___ All Very Much" YOU

"Thank ___ and Good Night!" YOU

"Thank ___, Mr. Moto" YOU

thanks
   Londoner's ~ TAS

"Thanks ___!" ALOT

"Thanks a ___!" LOT

"Thanks a Million"
   ~ director RUTH

Thanksgiving
   ~ feature BIRD
   ~ mo. NOV
   ~ offering YAM

Thanksgiving Day
   ~ tradition PARADE

Thanksgiving Parade
   ~ participant SANTA

thank you
   ~ item NOTE

"Thank You ___ Good Night!"
   AND

"Thank You ___ Very Much" ALL

"Thank You and ___ Night!"
   GOOD

"Thank Your Lucky ___" STARS

Thar DESERT

"Thar ___ blows!" SHE

that
   ~ being the case THEN
   ~ boat HER, SHE
   ~ man HIM
   ~ man's HIS
   ~ partner THIS
   ~ thing's ITS
   ~ woman HER, SHE
   ~ woman's HERS
   after ~ time SINCE
   at ~ place THERE, YON
   at ~ time THEN
   be ~ as it may YET
   failing ~ ELSE
   for fear ~ LEST
   for ~ reason ERGO, THEN, THUS
   in ~ case THEN
   in ~ place THERE
   in ~ way ERGO, THUS
   more than ~ ALSO
   not ~ THIS
   not ~ great SOSO
   this and ~ ANA, BOTH

that ___ say ISTO

"That ___" GIRL

"That ___ Black Magic" OLD

"That ___ Cat!" DARN

"That ___ is, so was he made"
   ASHE

"That ___ it all!" SAYS

"That ___ no lady, that..." WAS

"That ___ Rock" WAS

"That ___ Then, This Is Now"
   WAS

"That ain't ___!" HAY

"___ That a Shame" AINT

"___ That Ate Paris, The" CARS

"thataway"
   it often went ~ POSSE

___ that broke the camel's back,
   the STRAW

thatch HAIR, MAT

"That Championship Season"
   ~ actor DERN

Thatcher, Margaret TORY
   ~ successor MAJOR

thatching
   ~ material REED

"___ That Co-ed" HOLD

"That Darn ___!" CAT

"That feels good!" AAH

"___ That Ghost" HOLD

"That Girl"
   ~ role ANN, DON, HELEN,
      LEON, LOU, MARIE, PETE,
      RUTH

"___ that has gits" THEM

"___ That Heaven Allows" ALL

"___ That I Marry, The" GIRL

that is
   ~ in Latin IDEST

"___ That Jazz" ALL

"That'll Be the ___" DAY

"...that married dear old ___"
   DAD

"___ that men do..., The" EVIL

"___ That Never Sleeps" CITY

"That Old Black Magic"
   ~ composer ARLEN

"___ That Ring on My Finger"
   PUT

"___ That Roared, The" MOUSE

"That's ___" AMORE

"That's ___!" AGAS, ALIE, ALL, LIFE

"That's ___, folks!" ALL

"That's ___ she wrote" ALL

"That's a ___!" NONO, WRAP

"That's a joke, ___!" SON

"That's a laugh!" HAHA

"That's all ___ wrote!" SHE

"That's All Right, ___" MAMA

"That's amazing!" GEE, WOW

"That's a pity" TSK

"That's a riot!" HAHA

"That's it!" AHA

"That's My Desire"
   ~ singer LAINE

"That's not the ___ of it" HALF

"That's one small ___ for a
   man..." STEP

"That's one small step for ___..."
   AMAN

"That's the last ___!" STRAW

"That's the truth!" HONEST

"That Summer in ___" PARIS

"That's what you think!" HAH

"That's wonderful!" AAH

"That Thing You Do"
   ~ setting ERIE

"___ That Time Forgot, The"
   LAND

"___ That Tune" NAME

"___ that which is evil" ABHOR

"___ That You Love, The" ONE

thaw MELT, RUN, WARM

thawed OPEN

the
   ~ in French LES
   ~ in German DAS, DER, DIE
   ~ in Spanish LAS, LOS

___, the (all) LOT

___, the (big cheese) MAN

___, the (regular's order) USUAL

"...the ___ are getting fat"
   GEESE

___, The (rock band) WHO

___, The (Springsteen) BOSS

"___ the Angels Sing" AND

"___ the Arab" AHAB

theater ARENA, ART, HALL, STAGE
   ~ abbr. SRO
   ~ acronym ANTA
   ~ area LOGE, TIER
   ~ award OBIE, TONY
   ~ company REP
   ~ employee USHER
   ~ in French CINE
   ~ light NEON
   ~ offering DRAMA, PLAY,
      SHOW
   ~ org. ANTA
   ~ passage AISLE
   ~ seating ROW
   ~ section LOGE, TIER
   ~ sign EXIT
   ~ souvenir STUB
   cultural ~ OPERA
   Harlem ~ APOLLO
   movie ~ CINE
   summer ~ often BARN
   see also Broadway

theaters
   ancient ~ ODEA

theatrical CAMP, FAKE, FALSE
   ~ alert CALL
   ~ award OBIE, TONY
   ~ bit ACT, SKIT
   ~ lament ALAS
   ~ org. ANTA
   ~ performance DRAMA, PLAY,
      SHOW
   ~ success HIT
   be ~ HAM
   overly ~ ARTY

theatrically
   behave ~ EMOTE

theatricals DRAMA

"___, the Bad, and the Ugly,
   The" GOOD

"___ the Ball Is Over" AFTER

___ the ball rolling KEEP

Thebe MOON

"___ the Beasts and Children"
   BLESS

"___ the Beat Goes On" AND

"___, the Beloved Country" CRY

___ the bench WARM

Thebes
   river at ~ NILE

___ the bill FOOT

___ the birds FOR

"___ the Bismarck!" SINK

"___ the Blame on Mame" PUT

___ the blues SING

"___ the Blues When It Rains"
   IGET

___-the-board ACROSS

___ the boards (act) TREAD

"___ the Boardwalk" UNDER

"___ the bomb" BAN

___ the books HIT

___ the bottle (party game) SPIN

___ the breeze SHOOT

___ the buck PASS

"___ the Bullet" BITE

theca SAC

"___ the calmly gathered
   thought" UNTO

___ the ceiling HIT

"___ the Cherry Moon" UNDER

"___ the Children" SAVE

"___ the Clock" BEAT

"___ the Clouds Roll By" TILL

"___ the Conquering Hero" HAIL

___-the-counter OVER

___ the course

___ the course STAY
___ the Cow ELSIE
___ the cuff OFF
Theda BARA
___ the day RUE
"___ the Day Break" UNTIL
"___, the Dead Speak to Us" YES
"___ the Devil" BEAT
___ the dirt DISH
"___ the Dog" WAG
"___ the Dragon" ENTER
"___ the Drum Slowly" BANG
___ the dust BITE
thee
    fare ~ well ADIEU, ADIOS, BYE, CIAO, TATA
"___ the Earth Caught Fire, The" DAY
"___ the Earth Stood Still, The" DAY
"___ the Edge" OVER
"___ the End of Time" TILL
___-thee-well FARE
"___ the faith" KEEP
"___ the Family" ALLIN
___ the field PLAY
"___ the fields we go..." OER
"___, the final frontier..." SPACE
___ the finger on PUT
"___ the Force be with you!" MAY
theft
    baseball ~ BASE, HOME
___ the Giant ANDRE
"___ the Good Times Roll" LET
___ the Great HEROD, PETER
"___ the Great" ELMER
"___ the Great Divide" ACROSS
"___ the greatest!" YOURE
"___ the Great Pumpkin, Charlie Brown" ITS
___ the Grouch OSCAR
___ the ground running HIT
___ the gun UNDER
___ the hay HIT
"___ the High Country" RIDE
"___ the High Ground" TAKE
___ the high spots HIT
___-the-hill OVER
___ the hook OFF

"___ the housetop reindeer pause..." UPON
___ the Hyena LENA
their
    not ~ OUR
theirs
    not ~ OURS
"Theirs ___ to reason why..." NOT
"___ the King's Men" ALL
___ the kitty FEED
___ the knot TIE
"___ the land of the free" OER
"___ the Last Dance for Me" SAVE
"___ the Last Rose of Summer" TIS
"___ the Law" IAM
"___ the lifeboats!" MAN
___ the light SEE
___ the light fantastic TRIP
___ the line (conform) TOE
"Thelma & Louise"
    ~ director SCOTT
"___ the Lonely" ONLY
"___ the Love of Benji" FOR
"___ the Lovin'" AFTER
them ENEMY
    belonging to ~ THEIR
"them"
    ~ or "us" SIDE
    ~ to "us" ENEMY, FOE
"Them"
    ~ author OATES
"Them!"
    ~ creature ANT
___ the Man STAN
"___, the Man" EDISON
"...___ the Marbles" ALL
___ the mark TOE
theme ESSAY, TEXT, TOPIC
theme ___ SONG
theme park
    ~ feature RIDE
"___ the merrier!, The" MORE
___-the-minute UPTO
"___ Them No Mercy!" SHOW
"___ the Money and Run" TAKE
"___ the Mood for Love" IMIN
"___ the Moon" ISEE, SHOOT
"___ the music!" STOP
"___ Them Willie Boy Is Here" TELL

then ERGO, THUS
    as of ~ UNTIL
    back ~ ONCE, PAST
    between ~ and now SINCE
    enough and ~ some AMPLE
"Then ___ Bronson" CAME
"Then ___ will guide the planets..." PEACE
"Then ___ You" CAME
___ the nail on the head HIT
then and ___ THERE
thenar PALM
"___ the Nation" FACE
thence ERGO
"___ the Night" INTO
"___ the Night Away" DANCE
"___ the night before Christmas..." TWAS
"___ then I wrote..." AND
"Then punctual as ___..." ASTAR
"___ Then There Were None" AND
"___ Then You Kissed Me" AND
Theocritus POET
    see also poet
"Theodora ___ Wild" GOES
Théodore
    see French
theologian
    ~ belief DOGMA
theology
    ~ subj. REL
"___ the One" SHES
theorem RULE
    ~ initials QED
theoretical PURE
theorize IDEATE
theory IDEA, ISM
___ the other cheek TURN
___ the phone HOLD
"___ the Piano Player" SHOOT
"___ the Pink Horse" RIDE
___ the piper PAY
"___ the President's Men" ALL
"___ the Press" MEET
___ the question POP
___-the-rack OFF
"___ the Rainbow" OVER
"___ the ramparts we..." OER
therapeutic
    ~ plant ALOE
___ the rapids SHOOT

therapy CURE
    ~ for short REHAB
    ~ starter AROMA
___ therapy GENE
there
    ~ for the ride ALONG
    ~ partner HERE, THEN
    all ~ SANE
    all ~ is SUM, TOTAL
    almost ~ CLOSE, NEAR
    get ~ ARRIVE, ATTEND
    go here and ~ ROAM, ROVE
    hang in ~ TRY
    here and ~ ABOUT
    means of getting ~ ROAD, ROUTE
    not ~ HERE
    not all ~ DAFT, MAD
    over ~ AFAR, YON
    the one ~ THAT
    the ones over ~ THOSE
    up ~ ALOFT
___ there (sane) ALL
"There ___ a Crooked Man..." WAS
"There ___ My Baby" GOES
"There ___ My Heart" GOES
"There ___ tide..." ISA
"There! ___ Said It Again" IVE
"___ There" (1954 song) HEY
"___ There" (Cohan tune) OVER
thereabouts ORSO
thereafter THEN
"Thereby hangs ___" ATALE
___ the Red ERIC
"___ the Red Lantern" RAISE
"___ there, done that" BEEN
"___ There Eyes" THEM
therefore ERGO, THEN, THUS
    ~ in Latin ERGO
"There Goes My ___" HEART
"There Is Nothin' Like a ___" DAME
"There oughta be ___!" ALAW
"There oughta be a ___!" LAW
"There's ___ here but..." NOONE
"There's ___ Moon Over My Shoulder" ANEW
"...there's a ___ of us!" PAIR
Theresa
    ~ of Avila NUN, SAINT
"There's Always a Woman"
    ~ director HALL
Theresa, Saint
    ~ birthplace AVILA
Thérèse STE
    see also French
"There's no future ___" INIT

"___ the Revolution Without Me" START

"There was ___ danced..." ASTAR

"There Was a Crooked ___..." MAN

"___ There Was You" TILL

"There you are!" AHA

___ the riot act READ

thermal
~ starter GEO

___ thermometer ORAL

___ the road HIT

"___ the Road Jack" HIT

___ the roof HIT, RAISE

"___ the Roof" UPON

Theroux PAUL

___ the sack HIT

"___ the Santa Fe Trail" ALONG

thesaurus
~ compiler ROGET
~ detail SYN

___ the score EVEN

these
not ~ THOSE
one of ~ days SOON

"These ___" THREE

"These ___ the times..." ARE

"___ the Sea" UNDER

"...___ the season..." TIS

"___ the seas run dry..." TIL

"These Boots Are ___ for Walkin'" MADE

Theseus HERO
~ stepmother MEDEA

___ the Sham SAM

"___ the Ship Sails On" AND

thesis ESSAY, THEME
~ starter SYN

"___, the Sixth of June" DDAY

"___ the Southern Moon" NEATH

thespian ACTOR
~ art DRAMA
~ org. SAG
~ quest PART, ROLE
~ signal CUE
~ workplace STAGE

Thespis POET
see also poet

Thessaloníki CITY, PORT

Thessaly
mountain in ~ OSSA

"___ the Stars Get in My Eyes" ILET

"___—The Story of Michelangelo" TITAN

"___ the Strong Survive" ONLY

"___ the Sun in the Morning" IGOT

theta
~ follower IOTA
~ preceder ETA

___ the table UNDER

___-the-table UNDER

"___ the Tail on the Donkey" PIN

___ the Terrible IVAN

"___ the Thin Man" AFTER

"___ the Top" YOURE

___ the town red PAINT

___ the transom OVER

"___ the twain shall meet" NEER, NEVER

"___ the Valley" INTO

"___ the Vermeers in New York" ALL

"___ the Volcano" UNDER

thew SINEW

___ the wall OFF

"___ the Walrus" IAM

"___ the Water to Charlie" OER

___ the way PAVE

"___ the Way Home" ALL

___ the weather UNDER

"___ The West" INTO

___ the whip SNAP

"___ the Wild Wind" REAP

"___ the Woods" INTO

they
~ in Italian ESSE, ESSO
what ~ say RUMOR

"They ___ by Night" LIVE

"They ___ Expendable" WERE

"They ___ Horses, Don't They?" SHOOT

"They ___ serve..." ALSO

"They ___ What They Wanted" KNEW

"___ the Yankees Lost the Pennant, The" YEAR

"They called her frivolous ___" SAL

"They Call the Wind ___" MARIA

"They Died With ___ Boots On" THEIR

"They Learned ___ Women" ABOUT

"They Live by Night"
~ director RAY

"___ the Young Men" ALL

"They're Biting"
~ painter KLEE

"___ They Robbed the Bank of England, The" DAY

"They Shall ___ Music" HAVE

"They Shoot Horses, ___ They?" DONT

"They Won't Forget"
~ director LEROY

"They worshipped from ___" AFAR

thick CRASS, DENSE, FAT, LARGE, RIFE
~ as thieves CLOSE
~ cord ROPE
~ hair MANE
~ piece SLAB
~ pile SHAG
~ soup PUREE
get ~ GEL
in the ~ of AMID, AMONG
lay it on ~ BRAG, LIE
the ~ of things MIDST

thick-___ SOLED

thick and ___ THIN

Thicke ALAN

thicken CAKE, CLOT, GEL, SET

thickener
food ~ AGAR
novel ~ PLOT

thicket STAND

thickhead CLOD, OAF, SAP

thickheaded DENSE, SLOW

thickness PLY

thickset BIG, LARGE

thief
~ take LOOT, SWAG
be a ~ LOOT, ROB, SACK, STEAL, STRIP
jewel ~ term ICE
pig ~ of rhyme TOM

"Thief"
~ actor CAAN
~ director MANN

"Thief of ___, The" PARIS

"Thief of Bad Gags, The" BERLE

"Thief of Bagdad, The"
~ actor SABU

thieve ROB, STEAL

thieves
~ hangout DEN
~ talk ARGOT
thick as ~ CLOSE

"Thieves ___ Us" LIKE

"___ Thieves" SEVEN

thigh LEG
it's above the ~ HIP

thimbleful SIP

"Thimble Theatre"
~ name OLIVE, OYL

thin CUT, FINE, LAME, LANK, LEAN, SLIM, SPARE, SPARSE
~ board SLAT
~ coin DIME
~ cut SLIT
~ metal overlay WASH
~ out LOP
~ stratum SEAM
~ strip of wood LATH
skate on ~ ice BEARD, DARE, RISK
spread ~ SPARSE
worn ~ BARE

___ thin WEAR

___-thin PAPER

"Thin ___, The" MAN

"Thin ___ Line, The" BLUE

thin as a ___ RAIL, REED

"Thin Blue ___, The" LINE

"Thine ___" ALONE

thing
~ in Latin RES
~ of value ASSET
~ on a ring KEY
~ on a string YOYO
~ starter ANY, PLAY, SOME
~ that swings DOOR, GATE
~ to be hedged BET
~ to save FACE
~ to splice CABLE, GENE, ROPE
any ~ NOUN
forbidden ~ NONO
latest ~ FAD, MODE, RAGE, STYLE
lawyer's ~ RES
no big ~ BLIP
not a ~ NONE
play ~ PROP
remarkable ~ LULU, ONER
single ~ ITEM, UNIT
sure ~ YEAH, YEP, YES
that ~'s ITS
the latest ~ NEW
tiresome ~ BORE, DRAG

___ thing FIRST, SURE

"Thing"
Addams Family's ~ HAND

"___ Thing Called Love" THIS

things GEAR
~ to do AGENDA
~ to eat FARE
one of those ~ THAT
real ~, in philosophy ENS
run ~ RULE
sign of ~ to come OMEN
the ~ nearby THESE
thick of ~ MIDST
work ~ out COPE
yonder ~ THOSE

"Things could be ___!" WORSE

"Things to ___" COME

think DEEM, HOLD, IDEATE, OPINE, PLAN
~ alike AGREE
~ best LEAN
~ better of RUE
~ hard RACK
~ highly of ADORE, ESTEEM, LIKE
~ over MUSE
~ piece ESSAY
~ the world of LOVE
~ up BREW, COIN
not ~ of OMIT
say what you ~ OPINE

think ___ TANK

"Think ___, Mr. Moto" FAST

thinker
~ opposite, perhaps DOER
positive ~ PEALE

thinking ___ CAP

think tank
~ name RAND
~ output IDEA

"Thin Man, The"
~ dog ASTA
~ wife NORA

"Thin Man ___ Home, The" GOES

"Thin Man Goes ___, The" HOME

Thinnes ROY

thinness
epitome of ~ RAIL

thin-skinned TESTY

thin-voiced REEDY

third BASE, PART
~ Arabic letters TAS
~ degree PHD
~ in line CEE
~ man ABEL
~ man in the ring REF
~ of a yard FOOT
~ of thrice ONCE
~ planet from the sun EARTH
~ son SETH
~ Vice President BURR
finish ~ SHOW
give the ~ degree ASK

third ___ BASE, ESTATE, GEAR, MATE, RAIL

third-___ CLASS, RATE

"Third ___, The" KEY, MAN

"Third ___ on the Mountain" MAN

third-class POOR

third-class ___ MAIL

"Third Man, The"
~ director REED
~ role LIME

third-rate MEAN, POOR
~ newspaper RAG

Third, the III

thirst ITCH, LONG, YEN
~ (for) LONG, LUST, PANT, PINE, WANT
~ quencher ADE, ALE, BEER, COLA, SODA, TEA, WATER
allay, as ~ SLAKE

thirsty ARID, AVID, DESERT, DRY

"___ Thirteen" THESE

thirteenth-century
~ invader TATAR
~ traveler POLO

thirtieth
~ pres. CAL

"Thirty Seconds ___ Tokyo" OVER

"Thirty Seconds Over Tokyo"
~ director LEROY

"thirtysomething"
~ actor OLIN

this
~ and that ANA, BOTH
~ being the case ERGO, THEN, THUS
~ can't be OHNO
~ in Latin HIC
~ in Spanish ESTA, ESTE
~ instant NOW
~ place HERE
at ~ time NOW
before ~ time AGO
for ~ reason ERGO, THEN, THUS
from ~ place AWAY
in ~ day and age NOW
in ~ fashion THUS
not ~ THAT
out of ~ world ALIEN, EERIE, EERY
to ~ point YET

this ___ of tears VALE

"This ___ All" ABOVE

"This ___ and Age" DAY

"This ___ be!" CANT

"This ___ fine how-do-you-do!" ISA

"This ___ for Hire" GUN

"This ___ man, he played two..." OLD

"This ___ Navy" MANS

"This ___ of Innocence" SIDE

"This ___ stickup!" ISA

"This ___ test" ISA

"This Above ___" ALL

this and ___ THAT

"___ This and Heaven Too" ALL

"This Boy's ___" LIFE

"This can't be!" OHNO

this day and ___ AGE

"This Gun ___ Hire" FOR

"This Gun for ___" HIRE

"This Gun for Hire"
~ actor LADD
Ladd costar in ~ LAKE

"This Happy ___" BREED

"This Happy Breed"
~ director LEAN

"This is ___-brainer!" ANO

"This Is ___ Ask" ALLI

"This Island ___" EARTH

"This is only ___" ATEST

"This Is Spinal ___" TAP

"This Is the ___" ARMY

"This is the dawning of the ___..." AGE

"This is the thanks ___?" IGET

"This Is Your ___" LIFE

"This means ___!" WAR

"This must weigh ___!" ATON

"This must weigh a ___!" TON

this one
~ in Spanish ESTA, ESTE

"...this sceptred ___" ISLE

"This Sporting ___" LIFE

"This Thing Called ___" LOVE

"This Thing Called Love"
~ director HALL

thistle BURR, WEED

"This way in"
~ sign ARROW, ENTER

"This weighs ___!" ATON

"This weighs a ___!" TON

thith
thpeak like ~ LISP

thither THERE
hither and ~ ABOUT
move hither and ~ GAD, RANGE, ROAM, ROVE

thither and ___ YON

thole PEG, PIN
~ insert OAR

tholos DOME

Thomas ARNE, CAL, GRAY, HELEN, IRA, IRMA, MANN, NAST, SETH

Thomas ___ Edison ALVA

Thomas Alva ___ EDISON

Thomas, Debi
~ milieu ICE, RINK
emulate ~ SKATE
maneuver for ~ AXEL

Thomas, Dylan POET
~ home WALES
see also poet

Thomas, Lowell
~ milieu RADIO

Thomas Stearns ___ ELIOT

"Thomas the Rhymer" SEER

Thompson EMMA, ERNEST, KAY, LEA, SADA

___ Thompson (Maugham character) SADIE

Thompson, Francis POET
see also poet

Thompson Twins, The TRIO

thong BAND, LEASH, STRAP, STRIP

Thor GOD
~ father ODIN
re ~ NORSE

thorax CHEST, PART

Thoreau
Walden, to ~ POND

thorite ORE

thorium METAL

thorn BARB, BRIAR, NEEDLE
~ in one's side BANE, PAIN, PEST
be a ~ IRK, PEEVE, RILE, UPSET

"Thorn Birds, The"
~ actress WARD

Thornburgh
~ predecessor MEESE

Thorndike, Sybil DAME

Thornfield
~ governess EYRE

thorny HARD, MESSY
~ blossom ROSE

thorough ENTIRE, TOTAL

thoroughbred PURE
~ mother DAM, MARE

Thoroughbred HORSE
~ trial RACE

thoroughfare ROAD, ROUTE
~ abbr. AVE
~ in French RUE

thoroughfares RDS, STS

thoroughgoing ENTIRE

those THEM
~ in power INS
not ~ THESE
one of ~ things THAT

"Those ___ the Days" WERE

"Those ___, Those Eyes" LIPS

"Those Lazy, Hazy, Crazy ___ of Summer" DAYS

"Those Lips, Those ___" EYES

"Those Magnificent ___ in Their Flying Machines" MEN

"Those Magnificent Men in ___ Flying Machines" THEIR

"Those Were the ___" DAYS

Thoth, the ___-headed god IBIS

thou GEE
~ objectively THEE
~ today YOU

thought IDEA, IMAGE
~ (prefix) IDEO
be lost in ~ DREAM, MUSE
course of ~ TENOR
give ~ to SEE
have a ~ IDEATE
lost in ~ RAPT
venture a ~ OPINE
without much ~ IDLY

thoughtful DEEP

thoughtfulness CARE

thoughtless CRASS, RASH

thought provoker MUSE

thought-provoking DEEP

thoughts
have second ~ FEAR
offer one's ~ OPINE

thousand
~ bucks GEE
a ~ G's MIL

Thousand ___, Calif. OAKS

"Thousand ___, A" ACRES

"Thousand and ___ Nights, A"
ONE

"thousand and one ___, A"
USES

"Thousand Clowns, A"
~ director COE

"Thousand Days"
~ queen ANNE

"___ Thousand Hills" THESE

Thousand Island
~ alternative RANCH

"...thou vain world, ___" ADIEU

"Thou would'st still be ___"
ADORED

thpeak
~ like thith LISP

thrall ESNE, LIEGE, PEON, SERF,
SLAVE

thrash BASTE, BEAT, CANE, HIDE,
HIT, LACE, LAM, ROUT, SMITE,
STRAP, TAN, TAR, TRIM
~ out ARGUE

thrasher BIRD

thread CORD, LINE, YARN
bits of ~ LINT
cotton ~ LISLE
metal ~ WIRE

threadlike FINE

threads ARRAY, ATTIRE, DRESS,
GARB
heavy ~ ARRAY, DRESS, SUIT
loose ~ LINT

threat PERIL
~ ender ELSE
urban ~ GANG

threaten COW, LOOM, SCARE

threatening ACUTE, BAD, UGLY

three
~ feet YARD
~ in cards TREY
~ in German DREI
~ in Italian TRE
~ in Spanish TRES
~ (prefix) TER, TRI
~ scruples DRAM
~ squared NINE
~ strikes OUT
~ to Caesar III
group of ~ TRIAD
one of ~ squares MEAL
work for ~ TRIO

three ___ kind OFA

three-___ circus RING

three-___ hit BASE

three-___ limit MILE

three-___ monte CARD

three-___ sloth TOED

Three ___ Night DOG

"Three ___" AGES

"Three ___ Girls" SMART

"Three ___ Home" CAME

"Three ___ in Search of a Bolt"
NUTS

"Three ___ Match" ONA

"Three ___ of the Condor" DAYS

"Three ___ on a Horse" MEN

"___ Three" THESE

Three Bears
one of the ~ MAMA, PAPA

"Three Blind ___" MICE

"Three Came ___" HOME

three-card ___ MONTE

three-card monte CON, GAME,
SCAM

"three cheers"
~ recipient HERO

"Three-Cornered ___" MOON

"Three-Cornered ___, The" HAT

three-dimensional SOLID
~ (prefix) STEREO

Three Dog Night
~ song ONE

"three-faced"
~ Woodward role EVE

"Three Faces of ___, The" EVE

three-legged
~ stand EASEL

three-legged ___ RACE

"Three Little Girls in ___" BLUE

"Three Little Words"
one of the ~ YOU

"Three Lives"
~ author STEIN

"___ Three Lives" ILED

"three men ___ tub..." INA

"Three Men ___ Horse" ONA

"Three Men on a ___" HORSE

"Three Men on a Horse"
~ director LEROY

three-mile ___ LIMIT

"Three Musketeers, The"
~ character ATHOS
~ Dumas PERE
~ motto starter ALL

"Three on a Match"
~ director LEROY

"Threepenny ___, The" OPERA

Three Rivers ARENA

three-seater SOFA

"Three Secrets"
~ actress NEAL
~ director WISE

"Three Sisters"
one of Chekhov's ~ OLGA

"Three Smart Girls ___ Up"
GROW

threesome TRIO

three-spot TREY

Three Stooges
one of the ~ MOE

"Three Tall Women"
~ author ALBEE

three-year-old KID, TOT, TYKE

thresh BEAT, HIT, TAN

threshold DOOR, EVE, LINE,
ONSET, RIM, SILL

thrice
~ in prescriptions TER
a third of ~ ONCE

thrift shop STORE
~ transaction RESALE

thrill BANG, ELATE, REACT, SEND,
STIR, WOW

"Thrilla in Manila"
~ victor ALI

thrilled AGOG, ELATED, GLAD

"Thriller"
~ sequel BAD

thrilling
not ~ BLAH

"Thrill of It ___, The" ALL

thrive BOOM, GROW, LIVE

throat NECK
~ clearer AHEM

~ infection STREP
frog in one's ~ RASP
jump down someone's
~ LACE

throat-clearing
~ sound AHEM

throb ACHE, BEAT, PAIN, PULSE,
STAB

throbbing ACHY, LOUD

throe ACHE, SPASM, STAB
emotional ~ PANG

thrombus CLOT

throne
~ locale DAIS
sit on the ~ REIGN, RULE

throng ARMY, BAND, CREW, HERD,
HORDE, HOST, MASS, MOB,
PRESS, TROOP

throttle GAG

through DONE, ENDED, OVER,
PER, VIA

___ through (persevere with)
SEE

___ through (rehearse) RUN

___ through (succeed) COME

"___ Through the Night" ALL

throw CAST, DASH, HURL, LOB,
PASS, PELT, SHOOT, TOSS
~ a bash HOST
~ a curve DUPE
~ a damper on DASH
~ a fit RAGE, RAMP, RANT,
RAVE, STORM, YELL
~ a steer ROPE
~ caution to the
winds DARE, RISK
~ dust in the eyes of DUPE
~ forth ERUPT, SPEW
~ good money after
bad WASTE
~ in ADD
~ in the towel BEND, BOW,
LOSE, YIELD
~ into panic ALARM, SCARE
~ into the shade LEAD
~ light on SHOW
~ money around SPEND
~ money away WASTE
~ mud on LIBEL, SLUR
~ off CAST, EMIT, SHED
~ off balance UPSET
~ off the scent LIE
~ oneself at the feet of BOW
~ on the pile ADD
~ out BAN, CAST, EJECT, EMIT,
SCRAP, WASTE
~ out, as lava SPEW
~ out of whack SKEW
~ over DESERT, DROP
~ someone off the
scent ELUDE
~ speedily FIRE
~ stones at PELT
~ together MAKE, MELD
a stone's ~ away CLOSE,
NEAR

throw ___
baseball ~ PEG
basketball ~ SHOT
dice ~ ELEVEN, NINE, SEVEN, TEN, THREE, TWO
hammer ~ EVENT
pub ~ DART
quarterback's ~ PASS
slow ~ LOB
stone's ~ STEP

throw ___ RUG

throw ___ (confuse) OFF

throw ___ (discard) AWAY, OUT

___ throw FREE

throw a ___ FIT

throwaway
melon ~ RIND

___ thrower SNOW

___-throw line FREE

"Throw Momma From the ___" TRAIN

thrown
they're ~ in Atlantic City DICE

thrush BIRD

thrust DIG, JAB, PRESS, PROD, RUN, STAB
~ back REPEL
~ out EJECT

thrusting
~ weapon EPEE, SPEAR

thruway
~ entrance RAMP
~ warning SLO

thud BANG, PLOP

thug GOON

Thule
ultima ~ POLE

thumb FEEL, LEAF
~ one's nose at SNEER
~ (through) LEAF, PAGE, READ, SCAN
rule of ~ LAW

___ Thumb TOM

thumb a ___ RIDE

Thumbelina GIRL

thumbnail
~ sketch BIO

thumbs
~ down NAY
~ up AYE, YEA, YES
all ~ INEPT
turn ~ down to DENY, VETO
twiddle one's ~ LOAF

___ thumbs (clumsy) ALL

thumbs-down
~ critic EBERT
~ vote NAY
~ voter ANTI
~ votes NOES, NOS
give a ~ RATE

slangy ~ NAH, NOPE
vocal ~ BOO, HISS

thumbs-up
~ critic EBERT
~ vote AYE, YEA, YES
give a ~ RATE
gives a ~ OKS
NASA ~ AOK
slangy ~ YEAH, YEP

thump BANG, BASH, BAT, BEAT, CLAP, HIT, PELT, PLOP, PULSE, RAP, TAN, THUD

thumping BIG, LARGE

Thun LAKE
~ river AAR, AARE

thunder BLARE, BLAST, BOOM, DIN, NOISE, PEAL, RAVE, ROAR, ROLL, STORM
~ and lightning STORM
~ god THOR
~ sound BOOM, CLAP
~ unit PEAL

Thunder BAY

"Thunder ___" ROAD

"Thunder Alley"
~ actor ASNER
~ character GIL

Thunder Bay CITY, PORT
~ prov. ONT

"Thunder Bay"
~ director MANN

"Thunderbolt ___ Lightfoot" AND

thunderbolts
shooter of ~ THOR

thunderclap BANG, DIN

"Thunderer, The"
~ composer SOUSA

thundering BIG, GREAT, LARGE, LOUD
~ group HERD

"Thunder in Paradise"
~ actress ALT

"Thunder in the ___" CITY

thundershower STORM

thunderstorm RAIN
~ product OZONE

thunderstruck AGAPE, AWED
~ reaction AWE

Thurber
like ~'s animal MALE

thurible
use a ~ CENSE

Thürigen
see German

Thuringia
see German

Thurman UMA

Thurmond NATE

Thurmond, Strom SEN

Thurs.
~ follower FRI

Thursday
~ eponym THOR

thus ERGO, THEN
~ far YET
~ in Latin SIC

thwack BANG, BAT, BEAT, CHOP, CLAP, HIT, PELT, SMITE

thwart DASH, DETER, STOP

thyme HERB

ti NOTE
~ preceders LAS

Ti ELEM
22 for ~ ATNO

Tiant LUIS

Tibbets, Col.
~ mom ENOLA

Tiber
~ city ROME

Tiberius CAESAR, ROMAN
see also Latin

Tibet
~ capital LHASA
~ location ASIA
~ neighbor INDIA, NEPAL

Tibetan ASIAN
~ creature YETI
~ gazelle GOA
~ monk LAMA
~ ox YAK
~ rare mammal PANDA

tibia BONE, SHIN
~ neighbor ANKLE

Tibullus, Albius POET
see also poet

tic SPASM

tic-___-toe TAC

"Tic ___ Dough" TAC

tick BEAT, PEST, RUN
~ away ELAPSF
~ off ANGER, ENRAGE, IRE, IRK, PEEVE, RILE, STEAM, UPSET

tickbird ANI

ticked
~ off IRATE, MAD, SORE, UPSET

ticker HEART

ticker ___ TAPE

ticket CITE, ENTREE, LABEL, PASS, TAG
~ info ROW, SEAT, TIER
~ leftover STUB
~ office sign SRO
~ punishment FINE
choose a ~ VOTE
free ~ PASS
price ~ TAG

risk a ~ SPEED
word on a ~ ADMIT
word on a track ~ SHOW, WIN

___ ticket MEAL

___-ticket item BIG

tickets
overcharge for ~ SCALP

"Ticket to ___" RIDE

"Ticket to Tomahawk, A"
~ director SALE

tickle ELATE, ITCH, PLEASE
~ one's fancy AMUSE
~ pink AMUSE, SUIT
~ response TEHEE
~ the ivories PLAY

tickled
~ pink ELATED, GLAD
it may be ~ RIB

tickled-pink
~ feeling GLEE

"Tickle Me"
~ doll ELMO

___-tickling RIB

ticklish MESSY

tic-tac-___ TOE

tic-tac-toe GAME
~ result DRAW

tidal
~ motion EBB
~ wave BORE

tidbit
almanac ~ FACT
gossip ~ ITEM, RUMOR
try a ~ TASTE

tiddlywinks GAME

tide
~ cause MOON
~ ender WATER
~ of events LIFE
~ over AID, HELP
~ starter EVEN, NOON, RIP
kind of ~ EBB, NEAP
lapped by the ~ AWASH
low ~ EBB
turn the ~ HELP

___ tide EBB, LOW, NEAP, RED

Tide
~ rival ALL, ERA

tides
~ do it EBB

tidewater WASH

tidiness TRIM

tidings NEWS

tidy CLEAN, GOOD, NEAT, ORDER, TAUT, TRIM
~ up CLEAN, DUST

tie BELT, BIND, DRAW, KNOT, LACE, LASH, ROPE, STAKE, STRAP
~ adornment PIN, STUD, TAC
~ down LASH

~ fabric REP, SILK
~ feature KNOT
~ holder CLASP, PIN, STUD
~ in with RELATE
~ on the feedbag EAT
~ place NECK
~ tack PIN, STUD
~ the knot MATE, UNITE, WED
~ together UNITE
~ up CLOG, CORD, LEASH, MOOR, STOP
~ up the phone CHAT, GAB, RAP, TALK, YAK
black ~ DRESS
broad ~ ASCOT
kimono ~ OBI
white ~ and tails DRESS

tie ___ BEAM, CLASP, ROD, TAC

tie-___ DYE, UPS

___ tie BOW

"Tie a Yellow Ribbon"
~ tree OAK

"Tie a Yellow Ribbon Round the ___ Oak Tree" OLE

tieback
~ locale DRAPE

tied EVEN
fit to be ~ IRATE, MAD, RILED, UPSET
not ~ down FREE, LOOSE
where knots get ~ ALTAR

Tien Shan RANGE

Tientsin CITY

tier BED, RANK, ROW

tierce HOUR

Tierney GENE

Tierney, Gene
~ film LAURA

Tierra ___ Fuego DEL

Tierra del Fuego
~ co-owner ARG
~ native ONA
~ range ANDES

ties
family ~ KIN
like some ~ LOUD

tie the ___ KNOT

tie-up JAM, SNARL

tiff ADO, PET, ROW, SCRAP, SETTO, SPAT, TILT

tiffin MEAL
take ~ EAT

tiger ANIMAL, BEAST, CAT
blind ~ BAR
cereal-eating ~ TONY

tiger ___ CAT, LILY, MOTH

___ tiger PAPER

Tiger
~ org. PGA

"Tiger ___" BAY, BEAT

"Tiger Beat"
~ reader TEEN

"Tiger in your tank"
~ company ESSO

Tigers TEAM, TEN

tiger's-eye GEM

Tigger
~ creator MILNE
~ pal OWL, POOH, ROO

tight CLOSE, DENSE, MEAN, SMALL, TAUT
~ closure SEAL
~ corner PASS
~ spot HOLE, JAM, SNARL
draw ~ TENSE
drawn ~ TAUT, TENSE
hold ~ CLASP
not ~ LOOSE
pack ~ CRAM
shut ~ CLOSE
sit ~ STAY, WAIT
they may be ~ ENDS

tight ___ END, SPOT

tight ___ drum ASA

___ tight SIT

___ tight budget ONA

tighten EMEND, TENSE
~ a shoe RETIE
~ one's belt SAVE, STINT

tighten ___ belt ONES

___-tightening BELT

tighten one's ___ BELT

tight-fisted MEAN, NEAR

tight-fitting CLOSE

tight-lipped MUTE, TACIT

tightrope
walk a ~ DARE, RISK

tights HOSE

Tigris
where the ~ flows IRAQ

"Tigris" BOAT, SHIP

Tijuana
~ change PESO
~ locale BAJA
~ title SENOR
see also Spanish

"Tijuana ___" TAXI

tiki IDOL

til SESAME

tilbury CART

Tilden BILL

tile PAVE
install ~ LAY

tiler MASON

till CHEST, GROW, HOE, PLOW, UPTO
~ compartment ONES, TENS
~ the soil DRESS

Till ERIC

tillage BED

tiller HELM
~ locale AFT
~ tool HOE
early ~ CAIN

___-tiller ROTO

Tillie OLSEN

"Tillie ___ Gus" AND

tilling
~ tool HOE

Tillis MEL, PAM

Tillis, Pam
~ pop MEL

Tillstrom BURR

"Till the ___ of Time" END

till the cows ___ home COME

"Till the End of ___" TIME

"Till We Meet Again"
~ songwriter EGAN

Tilly MEG

tilt CANT, HEEL, LEAN, LIST, SLANT, SLOPE, TIP

Tilt-a-Whirl RIDE

tilted ALIST, AWRY

"___ 'Til the Sun Shines, Nellie" WAIT

tilting ALIST

Tim ALLEN

___ Tim TINY

timber
~ hitch KNOT
~ piece BEAM
~ splitter SAW
~ tool ADZE, AXE
~ tree ASH
~ wolf LOBO
cut ~ LOG
foundation ~ SILL
ship ~ MAST
ship's bottom ~ KEEL
use ~ for support SHORE

"___ Timberlane" CASS

Timberwolves FIVE, TEAM
~ org. NBA

timbre NOTE, TONE

Timbuktu
~ locale MALI

time AGER, HOUR
~ and time again OFT, OFTEN
~ being NONCE
~ can do it HEAL
~ delay LAG
~ div. MIN
~ divs. HRS
~ ender CARD, LESS, TABLE
~ for a whistle NOON
~ for one revolution YEAR
~ of day HOUR, NOON

~ off LEAVE, REST
~ partner TIDE
~ period DAY, EON, EPOCH, ERA, HOUR, SPAN, WEEK, YEAR
~ starter AIR, ANY, BED, DAY, HALF, NOON, OVER, RAG, SOME, TEA
~ teller DIAL
~ to remember EPOCH, ERA
~ zone abbr. CDT, CST, EDT, EST, MDT, MST, PDT, PST
action ~ DDAY
after that ~ SINCE
ahead of ~ EARLY
ahead of its ~ NEW
all the ~, to a poet EER
a long ~ EON, YEARS
a long ~ ago ONCE
another ~ AGAIN, ANEW, OVER
anticipatory ~ EVE
any ~ now ANON, SOON
appointed ~ DAY, HOUR
a second ~ AGAIN, ANEW, OVER
at a future ~ AFTER, LATER
at any ~ EVER
at no ~ NEVER
at no ~, to a poet NEER
at that ~ THEN
at the present ~ NOW, YET
at the same ~ (prefix) SYN
at this ~ NOW
back in ~ AGO
before the appointed ~ EARLY
behind ~ LATE
bide one's ~ WAIT
bit of ~ SEC
correct the ~ RESET
egg-rolling ~ EASTER
fast ~ LENT
flowering ~ MAY
fool away ~ IDLE
for all ~ EVER
for the ~ being NOW
fossil's ~ PAST
further in ~ LATER
gain ~ DEFER, STALL
galactic ~ period EON
geological ~ division AGE, EON
great ~ BALL, BLAST, GAS
Haggadah-reading ~ SEDER
hands-up ~ NOON
have a good ~ PLAY
high ~ NOON
high old ~ LARK
holiday ~ YULE
immeasurable ~ EON
important ~ AGE, ERA
in a short ~ ANON, SOON
in good ~ ANON, EARLY, SOON
in jig ~ NOW
in ~ past AGO
in plenty of ~ EARLY
in ~ to come LATER
keep ~ manually CLAP
kill ~ ABIDE, IDLE, LOAF, WAIT
limited ~ TERM
long ~ AGE, AGES, EON
major ~ division EPOCH, ERA
mark ~ SIT, WAIT

measure of ~ DAY, HOUR, WEEK, YEAR
news ~ ELEVEN, SEVEN
Normandy ~ DDAY
nostalgic ~ YORE
notable ~ ERA
not on ~ LATE
of a ~ ERAL
one more ~ AGAIN, ANEW, OVER
palindromic ~ NOON
pass, as ~ SPEND
pass the ~ of day CHAT
period of ~ SPACE, TERM
play for ~ STALL
point in ~ DATE, DAY, HOUR
response ~ LAG
set ~ DATE, DAY, HOUR
significant ~ ERA
single ~ ONCE
some ~ ago ONCE
spring-break ~ EASTER
stand the test of ~ LAST
sweep of ~ LAPSE
swell ~ BALL, BLAST, GAS
take ~ off REST
tax ~ APRIL
to the end of ~ EVER
transitory ~ PHASE
twilight ~ EEN
very long ~ EON
waste no ~ DASH, FLEE, HIE, RACE, RUN, SPEED, TEAR
wild ~ SPREE
work against ~ PRESS

time ___ LAG, LIMIT, LINE, SHEET, ZONE

time ___ half ANDA

time-___ LAPSE, SHARE

time-___ photography LAPSE

___ time ATNO, BIG, HANG, MAKE, PLAY, POST, REAL, SPARE, TEE

___-time ALL, LEAD, LONG, OLD, ONE, PART, SMALL

"Time"
   film critic of ~ AGEE

"Time ___" LIMIT

"Time ___ and Time Remembered" LOST

"Time ___ Bottle" INA

"Time ___ Time" AFTER

"___ Time" BIG, PLAY

"___ Time, The" FIRST

time and ___ AGAIN, TIDE

time and a ___ HALF

"___ Time at All" ANY

time-consuming LONG

___-timed ILL

time-honored OLD, USUAL

"___ Time I Saw Paris, The" LAST

timeless ETERNAL

time limit
   ~ word UNTIL

timely EARLY, RIPE

time machine
   ~ destination PAST

"Time Machine, The"
   ~ director PAL

"Time Must Have a ___" STOP

"___ Time, Next Year" SAME

"___ time no see!" LONG

"Time of ___ Lives, The" THEIR

time-out HALT, LAPSE, REST
   tot's ~ NAP

timer
   ~ filler SAND

___ timer EGG

times ERA
   ~ past YORE
   boom ~ UPS
   keep up with the ~ ADAPT
   length ~ width AREA
   many ~ OFT, OFTEN
   old ~ PAST
   olden ~ YORE

Times FONT

"___ Times" HARD

"Time's Arrow"
   ~ author AMIS

"___ Times at Ridgemont High" FAST

timesaver TOOL

timesaving
   ~ mark DITTO

time-setting
   ~ phrase ASOF

time-share LEASE

"Times of Your Life"
   ~ singer ANKA

"___ Times With Bill Moyers" OUR

timetable AGENDA
   ~ abbr. ARR, ETA

time-tested OLD

"Time the devourer of all things"
   ~ writer OVID

"___ Time We Love" NEXT

timeworn OLD

timid MEEK, SHY

timidity FEAR

Timor SEA

timorous SHY

timothy HAY

tin CAN, METAL
   ~ anniversary TENTH
   ~ lizzie AUTO, CAR
   ~ organ EAR

~ soldier TOY
~ soldier's prop RIFLE

tin ___ EAR, GOD, PLATE

Tin ___ Alley PAN

"Tin ___" CUP, MEN

"Tin ___, The" STAR

tin can
   ~ eater GOAT

tinct DYE, HUE

tincture COLOR, DYE

"Tin Cup"
   Kevin's costar in ~ RENE

tine BARB

tinge BIT, COLOR, DAB, DASH, DYE, SHADE, TASTE, TRACE

tingle GLOW, ITCH, SMART, STING

tingling RED

tinhorn SMALL

tinker PLAY

Tinker-Chance
   ~ middleman EVERS

"Tinker, Tailor, Soldier, ___" SPY

tinkle NOISE, RING

Tin Man
   ~ need HEART, OIL
   ~ tool AXE

Tin Pan ___ ALLEY

Tin Pan Alley
   ~ org. ASCAP
   ~ product SONG, TUNE

"Tin Pan Alley"
   ~ director LANG

tinsel TRIM
   ~ time NOEL, YULE

"Tin Star, The"
   ~ director MANN

tint CAST, COLOR, DYE, HUE, PAINT, RINSE, SHADE, TONE
   ~ starter AQUA
   auburn ~ HENNA
   hair ~ HENNA
   photo ~ SEPIA
   temporary ~ RINSE
   watery ~ AQUA

Tintagel Head CAPE

tinted
   ~ windows reduce it GLARE

"Tin Tin ___" DEO

___ Tin Tin RIN

tintinnabulate PEAL, RING

tintinnabulation NOISE, PEAL

tintype
   ~ color SEPIA

tinware
   painted ~ TOLE

Tin Woodman
   ~ desire HEART
   ~ need OIL
   ~ tool AXE

tiny SMALL, WEE
   ~ amount BIT, DAB, JOT
   ~ aperture PORE
   ~ bit IOTA, MOTE
   ~ bug ANT, GNAT, MITE
   ~ circle DOT
   ~ container VIAL
   ~ fish SMELT
   ~ imperfection NIT
   ~ particle ATOM
   ~ (prefix) MINI, NANO
   ~ shriek EEK
   ~ sphere BEAD
   ~ (suffix) ULE
   ~ taste SIP

"Tiny"
   ~ Albee character ALICE

Tiny ___ TIM

"Tiny Alice"
   ~ author ALBEE

Tiny Tim
   ~ favorite flower TULIP
   ~ instrument UKE
   ~ last word ONE

tip ACME, APEX, CLUE, CREST, CUE, END, EXTRA, FEE, HEEL, HINT, LEAD, LEAN, LIST, NIB, PAY, SPIRE, STEER, TAG, TAIL
   ~ ender STER, TOE
   ~ off ALERT, TELL, WARN
   ~ over CANT, UPEND, UPSET
   ~ (over) KEEL
   ~ to one side LIST
   a good ~, once DIME
   cigar ~ ASH
   pyramid ~ APEX
   spear ~ PIKE
   triangle ~ APEX
   trident ~ TINE

Tiphys
   ~ ship ARGO

tip-off CLUE, HINT, LEAD, SIGN

tipped
   ~ over UPSET
   be ~ off LEARN

Tipper GORE

Tipperary
   ~ locale EIRE, ERIN

tippet CAPE, SCARF

tippler SOT
   Mayberry ~ OTIS

tippy
   ~ boat CANOE

tip the ___ SCALE

tiptoe STEAL
   on ~ AGOG

tiptop ACME, AONE, APEX, BAD, BEST, FIRST, PEAK

tirade RANT, TALK
   deliver a ~ RAGE, RANT, RAVE, STORM, YELL

tire BORE, FLAG, JADE, PALL, SAP, STRESS, WEAR
   ~ contents AIR
   ~ fastener LUG
   ~ holder RIM
   ~ part BELT
   ~ pressure meas. PSI
   ~ rubber TREAD
   ~ town AKRON
   ~ track RUT
   ~ trouble FLAT
   extra ~ SPARE
   fixed-up ~ RECAP

___ tire SNOW, SPARE

tired ALLIN, BEAT, LIMP, SPENT, STALE
   be ~ of HATE
   get ~ FADE, FLAG, PETER

tires
   equipped with ~ SHOD
   like worn ~ BALD

Tiresias SEER

tiresome ARID, DRY, FLAT, SLOW
   ~ person BORE, PEST, PILL
   ~ thing DRAG
   become ~ BORE, PALL, WEAR

Tiriac ION

Tirtoff, Romain de
   alias of ~ ERTE

'tis
   ~ in the past TWAS

"'Tis a pity!" ALAS

"'Tis good to keep ___ egg" ANEST

"...'tis of ___" THEE

tissue
   ~ additive ALOE
   ~ target TEAR
   adipose ~ FAT
   build new ~ HEAL

tissue ___ PAPER

"___, 'tis true I have gone here and there" ALAS

tit ___ tat FOR

titan GIANT

Titan MOON
   ~ locale SILO
   burdened ~ ATLAS

Titania MOON
   ~ spouse OBERON

titanic BIG, GREAT, LARGE, VAST

"Titanic" BOAT, LINER, SHIP
   ~ award OSCAR
   ~ undoing BERG

titanium METAL

Titans
   mother of the ~ GAEA

tit for ___ TAT

tit for tat
   ~ object EYE

tithe TENTH

titian COLOR, RED

Titian
   ~ work ART

Titicaca LAKE

titillate AMUSE, AROUSE

titivate PREEN

title CLAIM, NAME, PAPER, TAG
   former ~ in India SAHIB
   gentleman's ~ EARL, LORD, SIR
   Japanese ~ SAN
   proof of ~ DEED

title ___ BOUT, DEED, PAGE

titled
   ~ man EARL, LORD
   ~ person PEER
   ~ woman DAME

titmouse BIRD

titter TEHEE

tittle ATOM, BIT, DOT, IOTA, JOT, MITE

tittle-tattle NEWS, RUMOR, TALE, TALK

Tittle, Y.A. GIANT

Titus CAESAR, ROMAN

"Titus Andronicus"
   ~ villain AARON

tizzy FIT, FLAP, SNIT, STEW
   in a ~ AGOG, UPSET

___ tizzy INA

TKO
   ~ caller REF

Tl ELEM
   81 for ~ ATNO

___ T. Lardbottom NASAL

TLC
   ~ provider NURSE
   ~ providers RNS
   overdo ~ DOTE
   part of ~ CARE

Tlingit TRIBE
   ~ home ALASKA

Tm ELEM
   69 for ~ ATNO

T-man AGT, FED

"T-Men"
   ~ director MANN

T, Mr.
   ~ group ATEAM

TN
   see Tennessee

TNT
   one T of ~ TRI
   use ~ BLAST

to
   ~ in Scottish TAE

to ___ (also) BOOT

to ___ (exactly) ATEE

to ___ (namely) WIT

to ___ (unanimously) AMAN

___ to (awaken) COME

___ to (cite) REFER

___ to (deceive) LIE

___ to (like) TAKE

___ to (must) HAS

___ to (take care of) SEE

___ to (try to please) CATER

___-to LEAN, SET

"To ___ and Have Not" HAVE

"To ___ His Dulcinea" EACH

"To ___ His Own" EACH

"To ___ is human" ERR

"To ___ their golden eyes" OPE

"To ___ With Anger" SLEEP

"To ___, With Love" SIR

to a ___ (exactly) TEE

to a ___ (perfectly) TURN

to a ___ (unamimously) MAN

___ to account CALL

___ to a customer ONE

toad
   ~ abode POND

___ toad TREE

toadflax WEED

toads
   group of ~ KNOT

toadstool PLANT

"To Althea, From Prison" POEM

"To a Mouse" POEM
   ~ starter WEE

to and ___ FRO

"___ to a Nightingale" ODE

"To a Poor Old Woman" POEM

"To a Skylark" ODE, POEM

toast BAKE, HEAT, ROAST, TAN
   ~ of the town LION, STAR
   ~ oneself BASK, TAN
   ~ starter HERES
   ~ topper JAM, OLEO
   end of Rick's ~ KID
   like ~ CRISP

"To a Steam Roller"
   ~ poet MOORE

toastmaster EMCEE, HOST

"Toast of New York, The"
   ~ director LEE

toasts
   where ~ are proposed DAIS

toasty WARM

___ to a turn DONE

"To Autumn" POEM

"To a Waterfowl" POEM

tobacco
   ~ dryer OAST
   coarse ~ SHAG

"Tobacco ___" ROAD

Tobago ISLE
   ~ (abbr.) ISL

"___ to Bali" ROAD

to be
   ~ in French ETRE
   ~ in Italian SER
   ~ in Latin ESSE
   ~ in Spanish SER

"to be"
   part of ~ ARE, BEEN, WAS, WERE

"To Be a Lover"
   ~ singer IDOL

"___ to Beauty" ODE

"___ to bed..." EARLY

"___ to Be Home" GLAD

"To Be or ___ to Be" NOT

"To Be or Not ___" TOBE

"Tobermory"
   ~ author SAKI

"___ to be tied FIT

"___ to Billie Joe" ODE

"___ to Blue" USED

toboggan SLED
   go by ~ SLIDE

"___ to Bountiful, The" TRIP

toby
   ~ contents ALE

"___ to Creation" ODE

tocsin ALARM, ALERT, CALL

today NOW

"___ Today" USA

"Today I ___ man!" AMA

"Today I am ___" AMAN

today's
   ~ paper NEWS

Todd ANN, TONY

toddler KID, TOT, TYKE
   ~ perch KNEE, LAP
   watch a ~ SIT
   words to a ~ NOES, NOS

Todd, Mary
   ~ man ABE

Todd, Sweeney
   ~ street FLEET

toddy PALM

___ **toddy** HOT

"to do"
~ **list** AGENDA

to-do ADO, FLAP, MELEE, ROW, STIR

toe
~ **in the water** TEST
~ **the line** OBEY
~ **topper** ENAMEL, NAIL
~ **woe** CORN
hurt one's ~ STUB

toe ___ DANCE, LOOP

"To Each ___ Own" HIS

"To Each His ___" OWN

"To Earthward" POEM

___-**toed sloth** THREE, TWO

toe loop
where to do a ~ ICE, RINK

toes
on one's ~ ALERT, WARY
tread on someone's ~ IRK, PEEVE, RILE

toe the ___ LINE

toff DUDE

"To Find ___" AMAN

"To Find a ___" MAN

"___ to Five" NINE

___-**to-fiver** NINE

"To form ___ perfect Union..." AMORE

tofu
~ **base** SOY

toga ROBE

toga party
~ **venue** FRAT

"___ to Get" HARD

together ASONE, ATONE, CALM, ONE, SANE
~ **(prefix)** SYN

___-**together** GET

"Together ___" AGAIN

"___ to get ready..." THREE

toggery DRESS

"___ to Glory, The" ROAD

to-go
~ **choice** BLT

___ **to grips with** COME

___ **to grow on** ONE

togs ATTIRE, DRESS, GARB, GEAR

"To Have ___ Have Not" AND

"To Have and ___ Not" HAVE

"To Have and Have ___" NOT

"To Helen" POEM

"To Hell ___ Back" AND

toheroa CLAM

"___ to Himself" ODE

"To His Coy Mistress" POEM

"___ to Home" CLOSE

"To Homer" POEM

toil LABOR, PLOD, SLAVE, SLOG, TUG

toiler
indentured ~ ESNE, SERF

toiletries
~ **case** ETUI

toilet water SCENT

toiling
~ **away** ATIT

___ **to it** GET, HOP, SEE

"___ to Joy" ODE

Tokay WINE

token CHIP, COIN, OMEN, SIGN
~ **taker** SLOT
~ **user** FARE

"To Kill a Mockingbird"
~ **author** LEE
~ **character** BOO

Toklas ALICE
~ **biographer** STEIN
~ **friend** STEIN

"To Know Him ___ Love Him" ISTO

Tokugawa
~ **shogunate capital** EDO

Tokushima CITY, PORT

Tokyo CITY, PORT
~ **former name** EDO
~ **potable** SAKE, SAKI
airline to ~ ANA
see also Japanese

"Tokyo Rose" ALIAS

told
do as ~ OBEY

"___ told by an idiot" ATALE

tole
~ **material** TIN

"___ to leap tall buildings..." ABLE

Toledo
~ **lake** ERIE
~ **locale** OHIO, SPAIN
~ **product** STEEL
see also Spanish

tolerable FAIR, SOSO

tolerant LOOSE

tolerate ABIDE, ALLOW, BEAR, BIDE, LET, STAND, TAKE

tolerated ABODE

"___ to Liberty" ODE

___-**to-life** TRUE

"___ to Life" TRUE

___ **to light** COME

"___ to live..." EAT

"___ to Live, A" RAGE

Tolkien
~ **creature** ENT
~ **monster** ORC

toll FARE, FEE, PEAL, PIKE, RATE, RING
~ **road** PIKE, ROUTE
~ **stop** STILE

"Toll ___, The" GATE

tollbooth PIKE
~ **part** BAR

tollgate PIKE

"___ to Love" EASY

Tolstoy LEO
~ **character** IVAN
~ **heroine** ANNA
~ **title word** PEACE, WAR

"To Lucasta, Going to the Wars" POEM

___ **to lunch** OUT

tom CAT, MALE
~ **mate** HEN

Tom KITE, UNCLE
~ **Dick or Harry** MALE

"Tom"
he was ~ **to Paul's "Jerry"** ART

tomahawk AXE

Tom and Jerry
~ **ingredient** EGG, RUM

tomato
~ **container** CAN
~ **jelly** ASPIC
~ **louse** APHID
~ **plant support** STAKE
~ **product** PASTE, PUREE

tomato sauce
~ **ingredient** PUREE

Tomba
emulate ~ SKI

tomboy GIRL, KID, LASS

Tombstone
~ **marshal** EARP

tomcat MALE

Tom Collins
~ **ingredient** GIN, LEMON, LIME, SODA

"Tom Corbett, Space Cadet"
Venusian crewman on ~ ASTRO

Tom, Dick, and Harry MALES, TRIO

tome OPUS
Mercator's ~ ATLAS

"___ to Me" (Etting favorite) MEAN

___ **Tomé and Principe** SAO

___ **to mention** NOT

tomfool IDIOT

tomfoolery PLAY

Tomlin LILY

Tommie AARON, AGEE

Tommy LEE, MOE, SANDS, TUNE

"Tommy" OPERA
~ **band, with "The"** WHO

Tommy gun STEN

tommyrot TRASH

"___ to Morocco" ROAD

"Tomorrow"
~ **musical** ANNIE
~ **singer** ANNIE

"___ Tomorrow" UNTIL

"Tomorrow and Tomorrow and Tomorrow"
~ **hero** REN

___-**to-mouth** HAND

"tom thumb"
~ **director** PAL

Tom Thumb
like ~ SMALL

"Tom, Tom, the Piper's ___" SON

"___ to My Heart" CLOSE

ton RAFT
~ **starter** MEGA
bon ~ CHIC, CLASS, DASH, STYLE, TASTE
hit like a ~ **of bricks** STUN

___ **ton** BON

"___ to Napoleon" ODE

tone AURA, CAST, COLOR, DYE, FEEL, HUE, NOTE
~ **down** MUTE, TAME
copper ~ RED
earth ~ OCHER, OCHRE
emotional ~ MOOD
gray ~ SLATE
sense of ~ EAR
soft ~ AQUA, CREAM, IVORY, LILAC
sound of the ~ BEEP

___ **tone** DIAL, EARTH

toned
~ **down** DIM, LOW, SOBER

toneless PALE

Tone Loc
~ **music** RAP

toner
hair ~ RINSE

tong RING

tongs CLAW

tongue ARGOT, CAPE, LAP, NECK, ORGAN
~ **covering** COAT
adder's ~ FERN

African ~ BANTU
Alaskan ~ ALEUT
Asian ~ LAO
Highlands ~ ERSE
one with a forked ~ LIAR
Siouan ~ IOWA
speak with forked ~ LIE
see also language

tongue-___ LASH, TIE

___ tongue ACID

tongue-clicking
~ sound TSK

tongue-depressee
~ word AAH

tongue-lash CARP, HARP, LACE,
NAG, RAG

tongues
~ do it LASH, WAG

tonic SODA
~ amount DOSE
~ companion GIN
~ starter ISO

"Tonight Show, The"
~ host LENO
~ starter, formerly HERES
first ~ host ALLEN
former ~ regular NYE
Hall of ~ EDD
old ~ theme composer ANKA

tonka BEAN
~ bean TREE

Tonka
~ product TOY

Tonkin
~ delta city HANOI

Tonle Sap LAKE

to no ___ AVAIL

___ to none SLIM

tons ALOT, HEAP, MASS, OCEAN,
PILE, SCAD, SEA

tonsorial
~ procedure CLIP, CUT, TRIM
~ style AFRO

___ ton soup WON

tonsure BARE

tonsured BALD

tontine PACT

Tonto HERO

tony CHIC

Tony AWARD, BILL, SCOTT
~ of cereal fame TIGER
~ relative OBIE

"Tony ___" ROME

Tony the Tiger
~ favorite word GREAT

Tony winner
1998 ~ ART

too ALSO
~ big OBESE

~ funny for words RICH
~ glib OILY
~ interested NOSY
~ little SMALL
~ many to count SCAD
~ much advertising HYPE
~ quick RASH
~ rococo ARTY
~ showy ORNATE
~ soon EARLY
~ stylish ARTY
~ sure of oneself SMUG
be ~ fond DOTE
before ~ long LATER
cut ~ close SCALP
drive ~ fast SPEED
feed ~ well SATE
fill ~ tightly CRAM
get ~ personal PRY
look ~ long OGLE, STARE
not ~ bad SOSO
not ~ many SOME
remind ~ often NAG

too ___ to handle HOT

"Too ___ the Hero" LATE

"Too ___ the Phalarope" LATE

"Too bad!" ALAS

too clever by ___ HALF

"Too Close for Comfort"
~ daughter SARA

"Toodle-oo!" ADIEU, ADIOS, BYE,
CIAO, TATA

Toody, Gunther
~ portrayer ROSS
~ uncle IGOR

tool ADZE, AWL, AXE, DUPE,
EDGER, HOE, LEVER, PLANE,
RAKE, RASP, SAW, SPADE, SPIN
~ around MOTOR
~ building SHED
~ partner DIE
~ set KIT
axlike ~ ADZE
beltmaker's ~ AWL
boring ~ AWL
carpenter's ~ ADZE, PLANE,
SAW
chef's ~ MILL, RICER
chopping ~ AXE
cooper's ~ ADZE
crewel ~ NEEDLE
croupier's ~ RAKE
cutting ~ ADZE, AXE, SAW
digging ~ SPADE
dowser's ~ ROD
embossing ~ SEAL
farm ~ HOE
farrier's ~ RASP
fire-fighting ~ AXE
forestry ~ AXE, SAW
garden ~ EDGER, HOE, HOSE,
RAKE, SPADE
high-tech FBI ~ DNA
leather ~ AWL
logger's ~ AXE, SAW
medical ~ LASER
metalworking ~ LATHE
plumber's ~ SNAKE
pointed ~ AWL

prehistoric ~ ADZE, AXE
prospector's ~ PAN
prying ~ LEVER
punching ~ AWL
rancher's ~ PROD
saddler's ~ AWL
shaping ~ ADZE, DIE
sharp ~ AWL
shell ~ OAR
shoemaker's ~ AWL
shop ~ LATHE, PLANE, SAW
shrubbery ~ EDGER
simple ~ LEVER
skiff ~ OAR
slugger's ~ BAT
tailor's ~ NEEDLE, PIN, TAPE
teaching ~ RULER
tiller's ~ HOE
timber-dressing ~ ADZE
toothed ~ RAKE, SAW
tree ~ AXE
trimming ~ EDGER
turning ~ LATHE
vocational school ~ LATHE,
PLANE, SAW
weeding ~ HOE
woodworking ~ ADZE, LATHE,
PLANE, RASP
writer's ~ ERASER, PEN
yard ~ EDGER, RAKE
see also implement

tool ___ KIT

"___ Too Late" ITS

"Too Late the ___" HERO

toolbox
~ item AWL, FILE, NAIL, RASP

toolhouse SHED

tools GEAR

toolshed
~ item HOE, SPADE

too many ___ in the fire IRONS

toon TREE
~ Chihuahua REN
~ rabbit ROGER

to one's ___ (agreeable) TASTE

___ to one's word TRUE

"___ Too Proud to Beg" AINT

___-to-order MADE

"___ to Order" MAID

toot BEEP, BLAST, SPREE, TEAR
~ one's own horn BRAG,
CROW

tooth
~ doctor's deg. DDS
~ doctor's org. ADA
~ ender ACHE, PASTE, SOME
~ material ENAMEL
~ on a wheel COG
~ part ROOT
~ partner NAIL
~ starter EYE
~ topper CAP
~ trouble ACHE
gear ~ COG
kind of ~ MOLAR

long in the ~ AGED
pitchfork ~ TINE

___ tooth SWEET

toothed
~ device COMB
~ tool RAKE, SAW
~ wheel GEAR

___-toothed SAW

___-toothed comb FINE

___-toothed tiger SABER

toothpaste
kind of ~ GEL

toothpaste approving
~ org. ADA

tootle PIPE

too-too ULTRA

toots HON

tootsie DOG, FOOT

"Tootsie"
~ actress LANGE
Dustin ~ costar BILL, TERI

tootsy FOOT

top ACE, ACME, APEX, BEAT, BEST,
CAP, CREST, END, FIRST, HEAD,
LID, LIMIT, LOP, PEAK, ROOF, TOY
~ a cake ICE
~ card ACE
~ digit NINE
~ draw STAR
~ drawer ABLE, ACE, AONE,
BEST, FINE, GREAT
~ ender COAT, KNOT, MAST,
SAIL, SIDE, SOIL
~ executive BARON, LION
~ flight ABLE
~ group ALIST, ELITE
~ honor ACE
~ level ACME
~ of one's head PATE
~ of the line AONE, BEST
~ of the mountain ACME
~ ornament EPI
~ performer ACE
~ rating TEN
~ spot LEAD
~ starter FLAT, HARD, LAP,
RAG, RED, TABLE, TIP, TREE
~ story ATTIC
~ tune HIT
at ~ speed APACE
at the ~ of one's
lungs ALOUD
bathing-suit ~ BRA
be on ~ REIGN, RULE
big ~ TENT
blow one's ~ BOIL, ERUPT,
RAGE, RAMP
bottle ~ CAP, NECK
box ~ LID
come out on ~ ACE, WIN
decorative ~ EPI
frizzy ~ AFRO
from the ~ ANEW, OVER
get ~ billing STAR
house ~ ATTIC
jar ~ LID

mountain ~ CREST
off the ~ of one's head ADLIB
on ~ of ABOVE, OVER, UPON
on ~ of the world ELATED
on ~ of, to a poet OER
pot ~ LID
reach the ~ SCALE
rocket ~ NOSE
room at the ~ ATTIC
round ~ DOME
sleeveless ~ VEST
summer ~ TEE
take it from the ~ REDO
take off the ~ CLEAR
the ~ ACE, AONE, BEST

top ___ DOG

top ___ (complete) OFF

___ top BIG, TANK

___-top POP

"Top ___" HAT

"Top ___" (Arnold Stang cartoon) CAT

"Top ___, White Tie and Tails" HAT

___ to pass (happen) COME

topaz COLOR, GEM
~ mo. NOV

"Topaz"
~ author URIS

top banana STAR

top-billed
~ one STAR

top-class ELITE

top-drawer AAA, ACE, AONE, BEST, ELITE, FINE, GREAT, ONEA

Topeka
~ st. KAN

toper SOT

top-40 music POP

topflight AAA, ACE, AONE, BEST, ELITE, FINE, GREAT, ONEA

top-grade AONE, BEST

topi HAT

topic ISSUE, TEXT, THEME
Biblical ~ EVIL, SIN
hot ~ ISSUE
oenology ~ AROMA, NOSE
speleology ~ CAVE
tout's ~ ODDS

topical NEW

___ to pick BONE

topknot COMB, CREST

topless OPEN

topnotch ABLE, ACE, AONE, BEST, FIRST, GOOD

top-of-the-line AONE, BEST, FINE, FIRST, GREAT

topographer
~ high pts. MTS

topographic
~ feature CAPE, LAKE, SPIT
~ map info ELEV

toponym NAME

topper CAP, HAT
angelic ~ HALO
barn ~ VANE
beatnik ~ BERET
burger ~ ONION
canapé ~ ROE
Capitol ~ DOME
casual ~ BERET, CAP, TAM
chopper ~ ROTOR
Christmas-tree ~ ANGEL, STAR
cracker ~ DIP
cupola ~ VANE
flagpole ~ EAGLE
French ~ BERET
jar ~ LID
king ~ ACE
pizza ~ ONION
popcorn ~ SALT
Pope's ~ TIARA
present ~ BOW
roof ~ AERIAL
saltbox ~ ROOF
shin ~ KNEE
soft ~ BERET, TAM
Swiss ~ RYE
toast ~ JAM, OLEO
toe ~ NAIL
tooth ~ CAP
torso ~ HEAD
wicket ~ BAIL
see also hat

"Topper"
~ dog NEIL

"Topper ___ a Trip" TAKES

"Topper Returns"
~ director RUTH

"Topper Takes a ___" TRIP

topping ABOVE
canapé ~ PATE
chip ~ DIP
cookie ~ ICING
hot-dog ~ CHILI
road ~ TAR
roll ~ SEED, SESAME
roof ~ EPI
sundae ~ NUTS
taco ~ SALSA
tress ~ TIARA

topple OUST, RAZE, RUIN, UPEND, UPSET
~ (over) TIP

toppled UPSET

top-rated AAA, AONE, BEST, FINE, FIRST, GREAT, ONEA

tops
~ in seniority ELDEST
what ~ do SPIN

topsoil EARTH, LAND

Topsy
~ friend EVA

"___ to Psyche" ODE

topsy-turvy MESSY, UPSET
turn ~ UPEND

"Top Ten"
Letterman's ~ LIST

toque HAT

tor CRAG, PEAK
~ lodging AERIE
cousin to a ~ CRAG

Torah
~ repository ARK

torch FLARE, LAMP
~ bearer DIME
~ crime ARSON
carry the ~ for ADORE, PINE

torch ___ SONG

"Torch ___ Trilogy" SONG

torched LIT

"Toreador Song" ARIA

___ to reason STAND

"Torero Saluting"
~ painter MANET

___ to rest PUT

Tori AMOS
~ father AARON

___ to riches RAGS

torii GATE

Torino
see Italian

"___ to Rio" ROAD

Torme MEL
~ technique SCAT
~ tune AGAIN

torment BAIT, BANE, HARM, PAIN, RIDE, TEASE, TRY
teenage ~ ACNE

tormenting BAD

torn RENT

Torn RIP

tornado STORM
~ warning ALERT

Torne LAKE

Toronto CITY, PORT
~ prov. ONT
inc., in ~ LTD

Toronto ___ Jays BLUE

Toronto ___ Leafs MAPLE

torpid INERT

torpor COMA, REST, SLEEP

torque RING

Torre JOE

torrefy BAKE

Torrens LAKE

torrent POUR, RAIN, RASH, SPATE, STORM, STREAM

torrid HOT

"Torrid ___" ZONE

Torrijos OMAR

torso
~ area HIP
~ topper HEAD

torte CAKE
~ ingredient NUT
like a ~ RICH
sacher ~ CAKE

tortellini PASTA

tortilla
~ topper SALSA
like a ~ FLAT
stuffed ~ TACO

"Tortilla ___" FLAT

tortoise
~ opponent HARE
~ pace SLOW

"Tortoise and the Hare, The"
~ author AESOP

tortoiseshell CAT

___ Tortugas DRY

torture ABUSE, PAIN, RACK

torturer OGRE

torturous HARD

torus RING

Torvill
~ partner DEAN

to say the ___ LEAST

"Tosca" OPERA
~ has three ACTS
~ piece ARIA
~ role MARIO

tosh TRASH

"___ to Singapore" ROAD

"To Sir, With ___" LOVE

"To Sir, With Love"
~ singer LULU

"To Sleep With ___" ANGER

toss CAST, FLIP, HURL, LOB, PASS, ROLL
~ a coin FLIP
~ and turn FRET, STEW
~ around HASH
~ out EJECT, SCRAP
dice ~ ELEVEN, NINE, ROLL, SEVEN, THREE, TWO
soft ~ LOB

tossed
~ item SALAD

tosspot SOT

tostada
~ cousin TACO

___ to stand on, a LEG

___ to stern STEM

tot ADD, DRAM, KID, MITE, SNORT, SUM
~ coverup BIB

~ first word DADA, MAMA
~ holder CRIB
~ in Spanish NINA, NINO
~ of whiskey DRAM
~ perch LAP
~ time-out NAP
~ up ADD, SUM

total ADD, ALL, CAST, ENTIRE, PURE, RAZE, RUIN, RUN, SUM, UTTER
~ indifference ENNUI
~ receipts GATE
~ wealth ESTATE
it's often ~ LOSS

totality ALL, SUM

totalizer
~ numbers ODDS

totally ALL, CLEAN

"Total Recall"
~ actress STONE
~ planet MARS

___ to task CALL

tote BEAR, CART, LUG, TAKE
~ tots BUS
~ up ADD

tote ___ BAG

___ to tears BORE

tote board
~ numbers ODDS

"To Tell the Truth"
~ contestant LIAR
~ panelist BEAN, CASS, ORSON

totem ___ POLE

totem pole
low man on the ~ PEON

___ to terms COME

to the ___ (completely) HILT

to the ___ (fully) TEETH

to the ___ degree NTH

to the ___ of the earth ENDS

"___ to the Chief" HAIL

___ to the occasion RISE

"___ to the Stable" COME

___ to the teeth ARMED

"To the Virgins to Make Much of Time" POEM

"___ to the West Wind" ODE

"To thine own ___..." SELF

"To thine own self be ___" TRUE

toting
~ a gun ARMED

toto
in ~ ALL

tots
tend ~ SIT
tote ~ BUS

___ Tots TATER

totter LEAN, LIMP, REEL, SWAY

___-totter TEETER

toucan BIRD, PET
~ feature BILL

touch ABUT, BIT, CARESS, DAB, DASH, FEEL, GET, HINT, MELT, MITE, MOVE, RELATE, SENSE, SHADE, STIR, SWAY, TAG, TANG, TAP
~ a chord MELT
~ at one end ABUT
~ down LAND
~ home plate SCORE
~ off AROUSE, ROUSE, SPUR, START
~ on ABUT, RAISE, REFER
~ one's heart MELT
~ softly PAT, PET
~ up EDIT, EMEND, MEND
~ up against ABUT
~ up articles EDIT
finishing ~ HEM
light ~ KISS, PAT, TAP
loving ~ CARESS
man with a golden ~ MIDAS
Midas ~ GOLD
out of ~ APART
soft ~ DUPE
stay in ~ CALL, PHONE, WRITE

touch ___ (initiate) OFF

touch ___ (mention) UPON

touch ___ with BASE

touch-___ TONE, TYPE

___ touch MIDAS

touchdown GOAL
make a ~ SCORE

touched DAFT, MAD
~ down ALIT, LIT
~ off LIT

"Touched by an Angel"
~ actress REESE, ROMA
~ network CBS
Della, in ~ TESS

touching ABOUT, NEAR
~ on OVER
not ~ APART

touch-me-___ NOT

"Touch of ___" EVIL

"Touch of ___, A" CLASS

touchstone TEST

touch-tone
~ two ABC

touchy EDGY, IRATE, SORE, TESTY

tough HARD, HOOD
~ it out BEAR
~ nut to crack POSER
~ situation BIND, JAM
~ to resolve MESSY
get ~ ENURE, INURE
hang ~ DARE

tough ___ to hoe, a ROW

"___-Tough" SEMI

tough as ___ NAILS

toughen ADAPT, ENURE, INURE

toughie POSER

toughness GRIT, METAL, SAND, SINEW

"___ Tough to Be Famous" ITS

Toulon CITY, PORT
see also French

Toulouse CITY
see also French

toupee RUG

tour MOTOR, TRIP
~ de force FEAT
~ guide MAP, PILOT
~ of duty STINT
~ part STOP
~ participant PRO
~ planning org. AAA
~ segment LEG
~ vehicle BUS

touraco BIRD

tour de force FEAT

Tour de France RACE
~ need BIKE
~ participant RACER

touring car SEDAN

tourist
~ accommodation HOTEL, INN
~ gadget CAMERA
~ magnet MECCA
~ need MAP, VISA

tourist ___ CLASS, TRAP

tourmaline GEM

tournament GAME, MEET
~ attire ARMOR
~ favorite SEED
~ pass BYE
~ round SEMIS
basketball ~ NIT
kind of ~ OPEN

Tours
~ topper BERET
river of ~ LOIRE
see also French

tousle MESS, SNARL

tousled MESSY

tout
~ interest BET
~ offering TIP
~ post RAIL
~ topic ODDS

tout de suite ANON, SOON

"___ to Utopia" ROAD

tow DRAG, DRAW, HAUL, LUG, ROPE
ski ~ TBAR
take in ~ DRAG, HELP

tow-___ zone AWAY

___ tow ROPE, SKI

towage RATE

"Toward Freedom"
~ autobiographer NEHRU

towards
~ the rear ASTERN
act ~ TREAT
move ~, with "for" HEAD
turn ~ ORIENT

towel
~ (off) DRY
~ word HERS, HIS
throw in the ~ BEND, BOW, LOSE, YIELD

towels LINEN

tower LOOM, RISE, SOAR
~ above LEAD, REAR, SHINE
~ cap SPIRE
~ material IVORY
~ (over) LOOM
~ town PISA
emulate Pisa's ~ LEAN
rural ~ SILO
TV ~ MAST

___ tower FIRE, IVORY, WATER

___ Tower (Chicago landmark) SEARS

towering BIG, GREAT, LARGE, TALL

Tower of ___ HANOI

Tower of Pisa
like the ~ ATILT

town CITY
Canadian ~ official REEVE

town ___ HALL

___ town COW

___ town (leave) SKIP

___ Town CAPE

"___ Town" BOOM, OUR

"___ Town Girl" SMALL

townhouse ABODE

townie LOCAL

"Town Like ___, A" ALICE

Townshend PETE

Townshend ___ ACTS

townsman LOCAL

"___ Town Too" HER

"___ to worry!" NOT

towpath LANE

toxic EVIL
org. overseeing ~ cleanups EPA

toxin BANE
~ starter ANTI

toxophilite
~ weapon ARROW, BOW
famous ~ TELL

toy PLAY
~ gun ammo CAP
~ holder CHEST

"___ to Yesterday, The"
~ **maker** ELF
~ **on a string** YOYO
~ **with** KID, TEASE, USE
~ **with a tail** KITE
bathtub ~ BOAT
beach ~ PAIL
cat ~ YARN
child's ~ BALL, TOP
flying ~ KITE
snow ~ SLED
spinning ~ YOYO

"___ to Yesterday, The" ROAD

Toyland
~ **visitor** BABE

toymaker ELF

Toyota AUTO, CAR

"___ to you!" HERES

"To your health!" TOAST

toys
~ **place** ATTIC
name in ~ IDEAL

Toys for ___ TOTS

"Toys in the ___" ATTIC

"___ to Zanzibar" ROAD

tpks. RTE

tra ___ LALA

trace BIT, CAST, CLUE, DAB, DASH, DRAW, DROP, HINT, IOTA, SHADE, SHRED, TANG, TRAIL
~ **down** HUNT
not a ~ NONE
retriever's ~ SCENT
slight ~ SCENT, TANG, TINGE
surviving ~ RELIC

"Tracer of Lost Persons"
radio's ~ KEEN

tracery NET

traces
kick over the ~ REBEL

track CHASE, DOG, HUNT, LANE, ORBIT, PATH, ROAD, ROUTE, RUN, RUT, SCENT, SIGN, TAIL, TRACE, TRAIL
~ **action** BET
~ **athlete** MILER
~ **circuit** LAP
~ **contest** EVENT
~ **distance** MILE
~ **division** LANE
~ **down** SEEK, TRACE
~ **event** DASH, MEET, RELAY
~ **figures** ODDS
~ **in Spanish** VIA
~ **path** LANE
~ **shape** OVAL
~ **starter** RACE, SIDE
~ **trial** HEAT
~ **unit** METER, YARD
Amtrak ~ RAIL
car ~ RUT
half a ~ RAIL
hurricane ~ PATH
moon ~ ORBIT
muddy ~ RUT
off the ~ ASEA, ATSEA, LOST

side ~ SPUR
tire ~ RUT
word on a ~ **ticket** SHOW, WIN

track ___ MEET, SHOE, SUIT

___ track FAST

___-track ONE

trackball
~ **relative** MOUSE

___-track betting OFF

tracker
airplane ~ RADAR
underwater ~ SONAR

___ Tracker GEO

___-track mind ONE

tracks
cover another's ~ ABET
make ~ FLEE, HIE, RACE, RUN, SPEED, TEAR

___ tracks (rush) MAKE

tract AREA, ESSAY, LAND, LOT, PLAT, THEME, ZONE
homesteader's ~ CLAIM
open ~ LLANO

tractable EASY, MEEK, TAME

traction
lose ~ SKID, SLIDE

tractor
~ **housing** BARN
~ **maker** DEERE
big ~ CAT

tractor ___ FEED

tractor-trailer RIG, SEMI

Tracy, Dick
~ **wife** TESS

trade DEAL, LINE, POST, SWAP
~ **center** MART
~ **in** SELL
~ **journal** ORGAN
~ **org.** ASSN
~ **(suffix)** IER
~ **upon** USE
carry on a ~ PLY
horse ~ DEAL
ply one's ~ LABOR

trade ___ NAME, ROUTE, SHOW

trade-___ OFF

___ trade FREE, HORSE, RAG

___-trade agreement FAIR

trademark LABEL, MAKE, NAME, SIGN, STAMP, TRAIT
~ **design** LOGO

trader
~ **order** SELL

"Trader ___" HORN

trade show
~ **presentation** DEMO

trading
~ **center** MART

~ **vessel** BOAT, SHIP

trading ___ CARD, POST, STAMP

___-trading HORSE

tradition HABIT, USAGE
Thanksgiving Day ~ PARADE
wedding ~ TOAST
Yuletide ~ CAROL, NOG, TREE

___ tradition ORAL

traditional OLD, USUAL
~ **knowledge** LORE

traduce LIBEL, SLUR

Trafalgar CAPE
~ **site** SPAIN

traffic DEAL, TRADE
~ **caution** SLO, SLOW
~ **director** ARROW, COP
~ **in** SELL, TRADE
~ **jam** SNARL
~ **jam noise** BLARE, HORN
~ **jam unit** AUTO, CAR
~ **light** LAMP
~ **pylon** CONE
~ **sign** STOP, YIELD
~ **sound** BEEP
~ **trouble** JAM
what the ~ **will bear** COST

traffic ___ JAM

"Traffic"
~ **actor** TATI

traffic light
~ **color** AMBER, RED

traffic report
~ **source** RADIO

traffic sign
~ **shape** ARROW

tragedy BANE, DRAMA, GENRE, PLAY

"Tragedy of ___, The" NAN

tragic BAD, SAD
~ **fate** DOOM
~ **monarch** LEAR

tragicomedy DRAMA

trail HEEL, HUNT, LAG, LANE, PASS, PATH, ROAD, ROUTE, SCENT, TAG, TRACE
~ **behind** DRAG
~ **persistently** DOG
~ **the field** LOSE
blaze a ~ LEAD
hit the ~ START
hound's ~ ODOR, SCENT

trail ___ BIKE

___ trail PAPER

"___ Trail, The" BIG

trailbike MOTOR

Trail Blazers FIVE, TEAM
~ **org.** NBA

trailer ABODE, HOME, TAG
kind of ~ SEMI

trailing LAST

"Trail of the Lonesome ___, The" PINE

train AIM, PARADE, RAIL, ROW, TAIL, TOY
~ **for a fight** SPAR
~ **fuel** COAL
~ **lines** RRS
~ **patron** RIDER
~ **station** DEPOT
~ **unit** CAR
go by ~ RIDE
kind of ~ LOCAL

"___ Train" PEACE

trained FIT

trainer
lion ~ TAMER

"___ Train From Gun Hill" LAST

"___ Train From Madrid, The" LAST

___ training BASIC

training room
~ **complaint** ACHE

"___ Train Robbery, The" GREAT

trains
aboveground ~ ELS
like some ~ LATE
"The Bob Newhart Show" ~ ELS

"___ Train to Clarksville" LAST

traipse GAD, HIKE, MOVE, ROAM, ROVE

trait
~ **carrier** GENE
~ **transmitter** DNA
desirable ~ ASSET

traitor RAT, REBEL, SNAKE
turn ~ DESERT

traitorous BAD

traits
good character ~ ARETE

Trajan CAESAR, ROMAN
year in ~'s reign CII
see also Latin

trajectory ORBIT, PATH
curved ~ ARC
in a ~ ARCED

Tralee
~ **locale** EIRE, ERIN

tram CAR
~ **cargo** ORE

Trammell ALAN

tramp HIKE, HOBO, MOVE, NOMAD, PLOD, ROAM, ROVE, SLOG, STAMP, STEP, TREK
~ **steamer** BOAT, SHIP
~ **upon** TREAD

trample BEAT, ROUT, STAMP, TREAD

trampoline
~ **surface** BED
like a ~ TAUT

trance DAZE, SLEEP
  be in a ~ MUSE

"Trancers"
  ~ director BAND

tranquil CALM, CLEAR, EASY, EVEN, MILD, SERENE

tranquillity CALM, EASE, PEACE

Tranquillity
  ~ on the moon SEA

Trans ___ Range ALAI

transaction DEAL, SALE, TRADE
  cashless ~ SWAP, TRADE
  flea-market ~ RESALE
  library ~ LOAN
  thrift-shop ~ RESALE
  Vegas ~ BET

Trans Alai RANGE

transceiver
  ~ button SEND

transcend LEAD

transcending ABOVE, OVER

transcript TEXT

transfer CEDE, MOVE, PASS, REFER
  ~ art DECAL
  ~ property DEED
  ~ title to SELL

transfer ___ RNA

transferable
  ~ design DECAL

transfigure ALTER

transfix AWE, NAIL, PIN, SPEAR, STAB

transfixed RAPT

transform ALTER, TURN

transformation TURN

transformer
  ~ part CORE
  ~ unit WATT

transfusion
  ~ liquids SERA

transgression ERROR, SIN

transient HOBO, NOMAD

transistor RADIO

transit
  airport ~ CAB
  city ~ BUS, ELS

___ transit RAPID

"___ transit gloria mundi" SIC

transition
  film ~ FADE
  logician's ~ ERGO
  sudden ~ LEAP

transitory
  ~ fancy FAD
  ~ time PHASE

translate PUT, READ

translation CRIB

translucent CLEAR
  ~ mineral MICA, OPAL
  not ~ DENSE

transmission
  ~ choice GEAR, LOW
  understand a ~ READ

transmit MAIL, PASS, RADIO, SEND, SHIP
  ~ a signal BEAM

transmitter
  trait ~ DNA

transmute ALTER, TURN

transparency
  photo ~ SLIDE

transparent CLEAR
  ~ fabric TOILE

transpicuous CLEAR

transpire ELAPSE, OCCUR, OOZE

transplant
  ~ need DONOR
  ~ patient DONEE

transport BEAR, BOAT, BUS, CART, EJECT, HAUL, LINER, LUG, RUN, SEND, SHIP, TAKE
  Algonquin ~ CANOE
  Aspen ~ TBAR, TOW
  back-country ~ BURRO, HORSE, LLAMA, MULE
  Bedouin ~ CAMEL
  bloke's ~ TRAM
  castaway's ~ RAFT
  frontier ~ STAGE
  Grand Canyon ~ BURRO
  means of ~ AUTO, BOAT, BUS, CAB, CAR, FOOT, JET, LINER, PLANE, RAIL, SHIP, TRAIN
  metered ~ CAB
  prom-night ~ LIMO
  public ~ BUS
  river ~ RAFT
  Saharan ~ CAMEL
  skier's ~ TBAR, TOW
  snow-country ~ SKI
  urban ~ BUS, CAB, HACK, TAXI
  VIP ~ SST
  whitewater ~ RAFT
  winter ~ SKATE, SKI, SLED

transportation RIDE
  ~ system LINE
  form of ~ BOAT, LINER, RAIL, SHIP
  use public ~ RIDE

Transportation Dept.
  ~ concern RRS

transported ELATED, RAPT

transpose ALTER, SWAP

transude OOZE, SEEP

Transvaal
  ~ resident BOER

transverse SPAN
  ~ support BEAM

transversely ACROSS

trap ADORN, BAG, CART, DOOR, GIN, SETUP, SNARE, WEB
  ~ filler SAND
  ~ fodder BAIT
  ~ out ATTIRE
  ~ starter CLAP
  bear ~ SNARE
  booby ~ MINE, SNARE
  fish ~ NET, SEINE, WEIR
  fly ~ WEB
  lobster ~ POT
  set a ~ BAIT, LURE

___ trap RADAR, SAND, SETA, SPEED

trapdoor DROP, EXIT

"Trapeze"
  ~ director REED

trapezium BONE

trapezoid BONE

trapper
  ~ commodity HIDE
  ~ transport CANOE
  ~ trophy PELT

Trapper John
  ~ and others MDS

trappings DRESS, GARB, GEAR

___ Trapps ("The Sound of Music" family) VON

traps
  ~ game SKEET

trapshooting SKEET

trash CAST, DIRT, RAZE, RUIN, WASTE
  ~ hauler SCOW

trash ___ BIN, CAN

trashy POOR

Trasimeno LAKE

___ Trask
  ~ ("East of Eden" character) ADAM, ARON, CAL

trattoria
  ~ staple PASTA

Traubel HELEN

trauma HARM, STRESS
  ~ aftermath SCAR
  ~ sites ERS

traumatize SCAR, UPSET

traumatized UPSET

travail PAIN, TASK, TOIL, WOE

travel LOG, MOTOR, RANGE, RIDE, ROAM, ROVE, STEP, TOUR, WEND
  ~ abbr. ARR, ETA
  ~ account LOG
  ~ a curved path ARC
  ~ aimlessly GAD, ROAM, ROVE
  ~ around RING
  ~ document VISA
  ~ on ice SKATE
  ~ on runners SKI, SLED

~ org. AAA
~ reference ATLAS, MAP
customary line of ~ ROUTE
mode of ~ AUTO, BOAT, BUS, CAB, CAR, FOOT, JET, LINER, PLANE, RAIL, SHIP, TRAIN

travel agent
  ~ offering TOUR

traveler NOMAD, RIDER
  ~ burden BAG
  ~ choice AUTO, BOAT, BUS, CAR, JET, LINER, PLANE, ROUTE, SHIP, TRAIN
  ~ from space ALIEN
  ~ lodging HOTEL, INN
  ~ need MAP, VISA
  ~ piece GRIP
  air ~ bane WAIT
  thirteenth-century ~ POLO

travelers
  Biblical ~ MAGI

traveling
  ~ salesman AGENT

Traveller HORSE, MARE, STEED
  ~ owner LEE

travels GOES

"Travels in Hyperreality"
  ~ author ECO

"Travels With My ___" AUNT

traverse ACROSS, CUT, PLY, SPAN
  ~ the ocean SAIL

travesty SHAM

trawl DRAG

trawler
  ~ equipment NET, SEINE

tray CASE, DISH
  ~ filler ASH
  construction site ~ HOD
  kind of ~ ASH
  printer's ~ FONT

___ tray TEA

Traynor PIE

tre
  ~ preceder DUE

treacherous BAD, BASE, FALSE, ICY

treachery EVIL

treacly SWEET

tread GAIT, PACE, PLOD, STEP
  ~ on someone's toes ANGER, IRK, PEEVE, RILE, UPSET
  ~ the boards ACT, PLAY
  ~ upon the heels of TAG, TAIL, TRAIL
  ~ water SWIM
  riser plus ~ STAIR

treading
  ~ on air ELATED

treadless BALD

treadmill RUT

"___ Tread On Me" DONT

Treas. EXEC

treasure ADORE, ESTEEM, GEM, GOLD, LOVE, PEARL
~ **finder** MAP
~ **guarder** GNOME
~ **holder** CHEST, SAFE
~ **hunt** GAME
~ **hunter's aid** SONAR
~ **map features** EXES
basilica ~ ICON
El Dorado ~ ORO
Vatican ~ PIETA

treasure ___ HUNT

treasured DEAR, PET

treasure hunt
~ **aid** CLUE, MAP

"Treasure Island"
~ **character** PEW
~ **monogram** RLS
~ **prop** MAP

treasury CHEST, MINE

Treasury
~ **agent** TMAN
~ **offering** BILL, NOTE

Treasury ___ BILL, NOTE

Treasury Dept.
~ **org.** IRS

treat CURE, DOSE, HEAL, NURSE
~ **an icy road** SAND
~ **as a wound** DRESS
~ **a sprain** ICE
~ **badly** ABUSE
~ **clouds** SEED
~ **crops** DUST
~ **ender** ISE
~ **hair** RINSE
~ **hides** CURE, TAN
~ **impolitely** DIS
~ **leniently** SPARE
~ **like a pariah** SHUN
~ **meat** CORN, CURE
~ **roughly** MAUL
~ **too well** SPOIL
~ **with gas** AERATE
after-school ~ OREO
soda fountain ~ MALT
teatime ~ SCONE

___-treat ILL

treatise ESSAY, THEME, TRACT

"Treat Me ___" NICE

treatment USAGE, USE
bad ~ ABUSE
remedial ~ CURE
special ~ TLC

treaty
~ **alliance** NATO
~ **initials** SEATO
former international ~ PACT
nonproliferation ~ SALT
party to a ~ ALLY

___ treaty PEACE

Trebek ALEX, EMCEE, HOST
answer ~ ASK

treble CLEF

tree ALDER, ASH, ASPEN, BALSA, CEDAR, EBONY, ELM, FIR, LEMON, LIME, MAPLE, OAK, ORANGE, PALM, PEAR, PECAN, PINE, PLANT, ROOST, TEAK
~ **anchor** ROOT
~ **cutter** AXE, SAW
~ **feller** AXE, SAW
~ **genus** ACER
~ **graft site** NODE
~ **growth** LEAF
~ **house** NEST
~ **juice** SAP
~ **of Lebanon** CEDAR
~ **ornament** ANGEL, STAR
~ **product** RESIN
~ **trunk** BOLE
~ **with catkins** ALDER
aromatic ~ CEDAR, FIR, PINE
barking up the wrong ~ OFF
bark up the wrong ~ ERR
bee ~ HIVE
berry ~ ELDER
bump on a ~ KNOT
Canadian ~ MAPLE
Christmas ~ FIR, PINE
citrus ~ LEMON, LIME, ORANGE
clothes ~ RACK
cone-bearing ~ ALDER, CEDAR, FIR, PINE
controversial ~ **spray** ALAR
date ~ PALM
decorate the ~ TRIM
endangered ~ ELM
fallen ~ LOG
flat-needled ~ FIR
fragrant ~ CEDAR, FIR, PINE
gum ~ **denizen** BEE
hardwood ~ ASH, EBONY
hat ~ RACK
honeysuckle ~ ELDER
Maine state ~ PINE
Maryland state ~ OAK
Massachusetts state ~ ELM
mighty ~ OAK
New Haven ~ ELM
oleaceous ~ ASH
out of one's ~ MAD
partridge's ~ PEAR
quaking ~ ASPEN
rubber ~ ULE
shade ~ ASH, ELM, MAPLE, OAK
Southwestern ~ ALAMO
stately ~ ELM
sugar ~ MAPLE
Texas state ~ PECAN
timber ~ ASH
trim a ~ LOP
Vermont ~ MAPLE

tree ___ LINE, TOAD

___ tree BEE, COAT, SHADE

"Tree at My Window" POEM

tree-dwelling
~ **marsupial** KOALA

treeless BALD
~ **plain** LLANO

tree of life
~ **location** EDEN

trees
cut down ~ LOG
group of ~ STAND
remove ~ CLEAR

tree-to-be ACORN, SEED

trek HIKE, MOVE, ROAM, ROVE, SLOG, TOUR, TRIP

"___ Trek" STAR

trellis ARBOR
~ **piece** LATH

tremble BEAT, FEAR, STIR

trembling
fear and ~ AWE

tremendous BIG, GREAT, LARGE, VAST

trench CUT, GAP, MOAT
like an ocean ~ DEEP

trench ___ COAT

trenchancy EDGE

trenchant ACID, ACRID, EDGED, KEEN, TART

trencher PLATE

trencherman EATER, HOG

trend MODE, STYLE, TENOR
be the present ~ REIGN
hot ~ FAD, RAGE

trendy CHIC, NEW, NOW, OUT, TONY
~ **edible** TOFU
no longer ~ PASSE

Trento
see Italian

trepan BORE

trepidation ALARM, AWE, FEAR, PANIC

tres
~ **preceder** DOS

trespass ENTER, RAID, SIN, TORT

tress TAIL
~ **topping** TIARA

tresses HAIR
Dobbin's ~ MANE

trestle BEAM, HORSE, REST

Trevi
~ **coin count** TRE
see also Italian

Trevi Fountain
~ **city** ROME
~ **coin** LIRA
~ **coins** LIRE

Trevino LEE, PRO
~ **org.** PGA
see also golf

T. Rex
"Jurassic Park'"s ~ CLONE

trey CARD

triad ATOM

triage
~ **locs.** ERS

trial ESSAY, MEET, PAIN, TEST, WOE
~ **balloon** TEST
~ **companion** ERROR
~ **evidence** DNA
~ **of strength** BOUT
~ **precursor** ARREST
~ **record** DEMO
~ **ritual** PLEA
~ **VIPs** DAS
bring to ~ SUE
put to ~ ASSAY
1692 ~ **site** SALEM
thoroughbred ~ RACE
track ~ HEAT

trial ___ RUN

trial and ___ ERROR

___ trial basis ONA

trial by ___ FIRE

trials WOE
~ **and tribulations** LIFE

triangle
~ **part** BASE, LEG, SIDE
~ **ratio** SINE
~ **shape** DELTA
~ **tip** APEX
kind of ~ ACUTE

triangular
~ **letter** DELTA
~ **sign** YIELD

triathlete
~ **need** BIKE

triathlon EVENT
~ **event** SWIM

tribal
~ **division** CLAN
~ **leader** ELDER

"Tribal-Love Rock Musical, The" HAIR

tribe BAND, BANTU, CLAN, CREE, CROW, ERIE, HOPI, HORDE, HOST, KIN, LEVI, OMAHA, ONEIDA, OSAGE, OTO, OTOE, RACE, REE, UTE
~ **of Israel** GAD
African ~ BANTU
Biblical ~ LEVI
Canadian ~ CREE
Dakota ~ REE
Hudson Bay ~ CREE
Iroquois ~ ONEIDA
Midwest ~ OSAGE
Mohawk River Valley ~ ONEIDA
Mongol ~ HORDE
Nebraska ~ OMAHA
Oklahoma ~ OTO, OTOE
Rocky Mountain ~ UTE
Siouan ~ OMAHA
Western ~ CROW, HOPI, UTE

tribulations CARE, WOE
trials and ~ LIFE

tribunal BAR
prelates' ~ ROTA

tributary STREAM

tribute AWARD
    metrical ~ ODE
    pay ~ to CITE, HAIL, HONOR, LAUD

"Tribute to a Bad ___" MAN

"Tribute to a Bad Man"
    ~ director WISE

triceps
    ~ locale ARM

Tricia and Julie
    ~ mom PAT

trick ACT, CAPER, CON, DUPE, GAME, HAVE, MOVE, RUSE, STALL, TRAP, WILE
    ~ alternative TREAT
    ~ ender STER
    ~ out ADORN, ARRAY, ATTIRE, DRESS, RIG
    ~ winner ACE
    do the ~ AVAIL
    dumb ~ ERROR
    playful ~ ANTIC, LARK

___ trick CARD, HAT

trickery ART
    piece of ~ RUSE

trickle DRIP, DROP, OOZE, RUN, SEEP

"Trick or ___!" TREAT

"___-Trick Pony" ONE

tricks of the ___ TRADE

trick-winning
    ~ feat SLAM

tricky BAD, FALSE, SLY
    ~ problem POSER

tricolor FLAG

tricorn HAT

trident SPEAR
    ~ part TINE

tried-and-___ TRUE

tried and true LIEGE, SAFE, SURE

Trier
    see German

Trieste CITY, PORT
    see also Italian

trifecta BET

trifle BIT, CAKE, DAB, JOT, LOAF, PIN, PLAY, TOY
    ~ away LOSE

trifling MEAN, MERE, SLIM, SMALL, TINY, VAIN

trig CLEAN, MATH, NEAT, SMART, TRIM
    ~ cousin ALG
    ~ function COS, COT, SIN, TAN
    ~ ratio SINE

trigger CAUSE
    pull the ~ FIRE

___ trigger HAIR

Trigger HORSE, STEED
    ~ guidance system REINS
    ~ rider ROY

triglyceride ESTER

trilby HAT
    ~ material FELT

trill ROLL, SING

Trillin, Calvin
    ~ piece ESSAY

trim ADORN, BEAD, BIND, BOB, CLIP, CUT, DRESS, EDGE, EDIT, FILE, LACE, LEAN, LOP, MOW, NEAT, PARE, PREEN, SLASH, SMART, SNIP, TAUT
    ~ a photo CROP
    ~ feathers PREEN
    ~ (off) LOP
    ~ the fairway MOW
    ~ the hedge CLIP, SNIP
    in ~ TAUT
    robe ~ ERMINE

trimmed
    it's often ~ HAIR, SAIL

trimmer EDGER
    wood ~ ADZE

trimming LACE
    ~ tool EDGER

Trinidad ISLE
    ~ (abbr.) ISL

Trinidad ___ Tobago AND

Trinity
    ~ member SON

"Trinity"
    ~ author URIS

trinket PIN, TOY

trio THREE
    first-grader's ~ ABC
    Latin ~ III
    Yuletide ~ MAGI

trip ERR, ERRAND, RIDE, SLIP, SPIN, TOUR
    ~ around the world ORBIT
    ~ delayer FLAT
    ~ record LOG
    ~ segment LEG
    ~ the light fantastic DANCE
    ~ to the grocery ERRAND
    boat ~ SAIL
    brief ~ ERRAND
    motor ~ SPIN
    quick ~ ERRAND, HOP, RUN, SPIN
    round ~ LAP
    sightseeing ~ TOUR
    take a ~ MOTOR

___ trip EGO

tripe TRASH

triphosphate ESTER

triple GROW, HIT

triple ___ AXEL, PLAY, SEC

Triple Alliance
    ~ country ITALY

Triple Crown AWARD
    ~ event RACE
    1935 ~ winner OMAHA

triple-decker
    ~ perhaps BLT

"___ Triplex" (RLS essay) AES

tripod EASEL
    ~ part LEG

Tripoli CITY, PORT
    old ~ governor DEY

___-tripper EGO

"___ Tripper" DAY

trippet CAM

tripping AGILE

trip-routing
    ~ org. AAA

Triptik
    ~ org. AAA

trireme BOAT, SHIP
    ~ complement CREW
    ~ unit OAR
    ~ weapon RAM

Tristan
    Mark, to ~ UNCLE

"Tristan und Isolde" OPERA

triste SAD

trite BANAL, HACK, STALE, TIRED
    not as ~ NEWER

Triton GOD, MOON
    ~ to Poseidon SON

triturate ABRADE

triumph HIT, SCORE, WIN
    ~ over BEAT, UPSET
    boxing ~ TKO
    cry of ~ AAH, AHA, HAH, OHO

triumphant ELATED

triumphs
    boxing ~ KOS

trivet REST, TABLE

trivia
    ~ collection ANA
    historical ~ DATE

trivial IDLE, MEAN, VAIN
    ~ detail NIT
    seem ~ PALE

Trivial Pursuit
    ~ need DICE

-trix
    ~ cousin ESS

Trixie
    ~ sitcom friend ALICE

Troche ROSE

troglodyte ANIMAL, LONER

troika SLED, TRIAD

Troilus
    ~ to Priam SON

"Troilus and Cressida" PLAY

"Troilus and Criseyde" POEM

Trois Rivières CITY, PORT

Trojan
    ~ ally ARES
    ~ prince PARIS
    ~ princess of a Mozart opera ILIA
    work like a ~ LABOR, PLOD, SLAVE, TOIL

Trojan ___ HORSE, WAR

Trojan horse RUSE

Trojan War
    ~ cause HELEN
    ~ epic ILIAD
    ~ instigator ERIS
    ~ lure APPLE

troll ANGLE, DEMON, DRAG, ELF, OGRE
    ~ cousin GNOME
    whence the word ~ NORSE

"___ Troll" (Heine poem) ATTA

trolley
    ~ garage BARN
    ~ passage FARE
    dessert ~ CART
    off one's ~ BATS, MAD
    Piccadilly ~ TRAM
    take the ~ RIDE

Trollope
    ~ lady ANNA

trombone HORN
    ~ accessory MUTE
    ~ part SLIDE

trombones BRASS

tromp STAMP

Trondheim
    from ~ NORSE

Troon SPA
    ~ resident SCOT

troop ARMY, BAND, GANG, HORDE, HOST, LOT, MOB, PRESS
    ~ carrier LST
    ~ group UNIT
    ~ org. BSA
    ~ the colors PARADE
    ~ troupe USO

trooper
    ~ aid RADAR
    ~ bulletin APB
    ~ concern MPH
    ~ starter PARA

troops
    supply ~ to MAN

___-Tropez SAINT

trophy AWARD, CUP, MEDAL
    ~ room DEN
    AMPAS ~ OSCAR
    Broadway ~ TONY
    champ's ~ BELT
    Off-Broadway ~ OBIE
    take home a ~ WIN
    trapper's ~ PELT

tropical RANK
  ~ spot ATOLL, ISLE

tropophyte PLANT

trot GAIT, HIE, MOVE, PACE, POST, RUN
  ~ out SHOW
  fox ~ DANCE
  turkey ~ DANCE

troth OATH

Trotsky LEON, RED
  ~ foe LENIN
  ~ realm USSR

trotter FOOT, HORSE, PACER, RACER

troubadour BARD
  ~ prop LUTE

trouble ADO, AIL, BANE, BESET, CARE, ILL, IRK, PEEVE, TODO, TRIAL, UPSET, WOE
  ~ partner TOIL
  destine for ~ DOOM
  have ~ with esses LISP
  prolonged period of ~ SIEGE
  skin ~ ACNE
  tooth ~ ACHE
  traffic ~ JAM
  tummy ~ ACHE

"Trouble ___ Two" FOR

"___ Trouble" CAR

troubled BESET, UPSET
  feel ~ AIL

"Trouble for ___" TWO

troubleless EASY

troublemaker IMP
  Olympus ~ ERIS

troublesome BAD

trouble spot
  athlete's ~ KNEE

troubling BAD

trough
  ~ contents FEED
  mortar ~ HOD

___ trough EAVE

trounce BASTE, BEAT, LAM, MAUL, ROUT, TRIM

troupe CAST, CREW, TEAM

trouper ACTOR

trouser
  ~ part KNEE, LEG, LOOP

trout
  Arctic ~ CHAR

"___ Trout" PARIS

trouveur BARD

trowel TOOL

Troy
  mountain near ~ IDA

"Tru"
  Tony-winner for ~ MORSE

truant
  ~ soldier AWOL
  play ~ EVADE

truce PACT, PEACE

truck CART, MOTOR, SEMI, VAN
  ~ attachment PLOW
  ~ complement FLEET
  ~ ender STOP
  ~ floor BED
  ~ front CAB
  ~ part AXLE
  all-purpose ~ UTE
  big ~ RIG
  ore ~ TRAM
  pickup ~ MOTOR
  send by ~ SHIP
  word on a ~ TARE

truck ___ STOP

___ truck HAND, PANEL, TOW

Truckee
  city on the ~ RENO

trucker
  ~ amount LOAD
  ~ charge RIG, SEMI
  ~ choice GEAR
  ~ radios CBS
  ~ unit TON

truckers
  ~ do it HAUL

truckful LOAD

truckle
  ~ (to) BEND, OBEY

truckle ___ BED

truckload LOTS

truck stop
  ~ fare HASH
  ~ sight RIG, SEMI
  ~ sign EATS

truculent CRUEL, FERAL

trudge DRAG, HIKE, MOVE, PLOD, SLOG, STEP, TREK
  ~ (on) PRESS

true ALINE, GOOD, REAL
  ~ (abbr.) ANS
  be ~ ADHERE
  it can't be ~ OHNO
  not ~ FALSE
  state as ~ AVER, AVOW
  tried and ~ LIEGE, SAFE, SURE

"true"
  name that means ~ VERA

true ___ BILL, RIB

true-___ BLUE, LIFE

___ true COME, RING

"True ___" GRIT, LIES, LOVE

true-crime
  ~ TV show COPS

true-false EXAM, TEST

"True Grit" OATER

Trueheart TESS

truehearted PURE

truelove DEAR

"True to ___" LIFE

true-to-life REAL

"___ True What They Say About Dixie?" ISIT

Truffaut
  ~ subject ADELE

truism ADAGE, FACT, GNOME, SAW

truly AMEN

Truman, Bess, ___ Wallace NEE

Truman, Margaret
  ~ mother BESS

"Truman Show, The"
  ~ director WEIR

trump
  high ~ ACE

trump ___ CARD

trumped-up FALSE
  ~ story LIE, TALE

trumpery TRASH

trumpet BLAST, BRAG, CROW, HORN, POST, STATE
  ~ accessory MUTE
  ~ sound BLARE, BLAST
  blow one's ~ BRAG, CROW

___ trumpet EAR

trumpeter BIRD, SWAN

trumpets BRASS

truncate CHOP, CUT, LOP, TRIM

truncated LOW

truncheon BAT

trundle BED, ROLL

trundle ___ BED

trunk AXIS, CASE, CHEST, LOG, NOSE, PART, STEM, TORSO
  ~ chambers ATRIA
  ~ feature KNOT
  ~ item SPARE, TIRE
  Rolls Royce ~ BOOT
  tree ~ BOLE

trunk ___ LINE

truss BALE, BIND, LACE, LASH, PROP, STAY, STRAP

trust HOPE
  ~, with "on" RELY

trusted
  not to be ~ FALSE, SLY

trusting NAIVE

trustworthy GOOD, HONEST, SAFE, SOLID, SURE, TRUE

trusty SURE

truth FACT
  ~ alternative DARE
  ~ twister LIAR
  devoid of ~ FALSE
  general ~ LAW, RULE

in ~ NAY, YEA
  moment of ~ TEST
  twist the ~ LIE
  universal ~ LAW

truth ___ SERUM

___-truth HALF

"Truth ___ Spring, The" ABOUT

truthful HONEST

Truthful James
  ~ creator HARTE

truthfulness HONOR

truth-in-lending
  ~ stat. APR

"Truth or ___" DARE

try ASSAY, ESSAY, RISK, SHOT, STAB, TASTE
  ~ a case HEAR
  ~ a contest ENTER
  ~ again REDO
  ~ a tidbit TASTE
  ~ (for) AIM, ANGLE
  ~ for a fish CAST
  ~ for office RUN
  ~ hard EXERT
  ~ one's hand at ESSAY
  ~ one's luck GAME, PLAY
  ~ out ESSAY, TEST
  ~ someone's patience IRK, PEEVE, RILE, TEST
  ~ to discern PEER
  ~ to elude, perhaps HIDE
  ~ to find HUNT, SEEK
  ~ to get answers ASK
  ~ to influence PLEAD, PRESS, URGE
  ~ to learn ASK
  ~ to lose weight DIET
  ~ to stop DETER
  ~ to win, in a way WOO
  ready to ~ GAME
  what hams ~ to steal SCENE

"Try ___ Get Me!" AND

"Try and ___ Me!" GET

Trygve LIE
  ~ successor DAG

trying BAD, HARD
  ~ for a homer ATBAT
  keep ~ LABOR

Tryon TOM
  ~ novel, with "The" OTHER

tryout TEST

tryst DATE

T.S. ELIOT

Tsana LAKE

tsar MALE

___-tse LAO

___ Tse-tung MAO

T-shirt
  ~ size LARGE, MED, SMALL

tsk ALAS, TUT

___ Tso (salt lake of Tibet) NAM

tsp. AMT

"___ tu" (Verdi aria) ERI

tuan SIR

tub BATH, KEEL
~ **ritual** BATH
~ **toy** BOAT
hot ~ SPA
industrial ~ VAT
lie in the ~ SOAK
old ~ SCOW
use the ~ BATHE

___ tub HOT

tuba BRASS, HORN

Tubb ERNEST

Tubbs
~ **beat** MIAMI

Tubby
~ **girlfriend, in the comics** LULU

"Tubby the ___" TUBA

tube CANAL, HOSE, PIPE
~ **part** ANODE
boob ~ SET
daytime ~ **fare** SOAP
flexible ~ HOSE
light in a ~ NEON
put on the ~ AIR

___ tube INNER, TEST

tubeless ___ TIRE

tuber
~ **ender** OSE
~ **for short** TATER
Andes ~ OCA
Polynesian ~ TARO
sweet ~ YAM

tubes
down the ~ GONE, LOST, NOGO

tubing HOSE

tuck PLEAT, STOW
~ **away** EAT
~ **in** BED
~ **into** EAT
~ **partner** NIP
nip and ~ CLOSE
sewer's ~ DART
snip and ~ ALTER

tuckahoe PLANT

tucked
~ **in** ABED

tucker
best bib and ~ ATTIRE

tuckered
~ **out** ALLIN, BEAT, DONE, SPENT, TIRED

"Tucker: The ___ and His Dream" MAN

"Tucker: The Man and His ___" DREAM

Tuck, Friar
~ **quaff** ALE

Tues.
~ **preceder** MON

___ Tuesday (rock group) TIL

tuft COMB, CREST

tug BOAT, DRAG, DRAW, HAUL, LUG, SHIP
~ **chore** TOW
~ **on the heartstrings** MOVE

tugboat
~ **sound** TOOT

"Tugboat ___" ANNIE

tug of ___ WAR

tuille ARMOR

tuition FEE

___ tulip LADY

___ Tully Hall ALICE

Tulsa
city near ~ ADA
city west of ~ ENID

Tulsidas POET
see also poet

tumble ROLL, SLIP
~ **the wash** DRY
take a ~ TRIP

tumble-___ DRY

tumbledown
~ **building** RUIN

tumbler CUP
~ **contents** ICE, SODA, WATER
~ **movement** SPLIT
~ **pad** MAT
~ **turner** KEY

tumbrel CART

tummy
~ **trouble** ACHE

Tums
~ **target** ACID, GAS

tumult ADO, DIN, MELEE, NOISE, RIOT, ROW, STIR, STORM, TODO, YEAST

tumulus PILE

tun VAT

Tun.
neighbor of ~ ALG

tuna
~ **anagram** AUNT
~ **catcher** NET, SEINE
~ **holder** CAN

tuna ___ SALAD

"Tuna-Fishing"
~ **artist** DALI

tunas CACTI

___ Tunas, Cuba LAS

Tunbridge Wells SPA

tundra DESERT, LAND, MOOR
~ **animal** ELK

tune AIR, LILT, SONG
1960s ~ OLDIE
happy ~ LILT

___-tune FINE

tuned
~ **in** AWARE, HEP, HIP

tuner
radio ~ KNOB

Tune, Tommy
~ **musical** NINE

tung OIL

tungsten METAL
~ **light** LAMP

tunic ROBE
eye ~ UVEA
kind of ~ ALB

Tunis CITY

Tunisian
former ~ **ruler** DEY

tunnel BORE, CUT, DIG, HOLE, MINE, PASS
~ **builder** ANT
~ **maker** MOLE
make a ~ BORE, DIG

tunneler
small ~ ANT

"Tunnel of ___, The" LOVE

Tunney GENE

Tu-144 SST

tupelo TREE

Tupelo
singer from ~ ELVIS

Tupolev SST

tuppence COIN

Tupper AMOS

tuque CAP, HAT

"Turandot" OPERA
~ **tune** ARIA

turban HAT

turbaned
~ **teacher** SWAMI

turbine MOTOR
~ **blade** VANE
~ **part** ROTOR

turbulence CHOP, RAGE

Turcotte RON

tureen DISH, POT
~ **accessory** LADLE

turf EARTH, LAND, LAWN, SOD, SOIL
~ **grabber** CLEAT
~ **material** PEAT
~ **starter** ASTRO
~ **warriors** GANG
surf and ~ MEAL

Turgenev IVAN
~ **birthplace** OREL
~ **lady** ELENA

Turin ADELA, CITY
city near ~ ASTI
Shroud of ~ RELIC
see also Italian

Turing ALAN

Turk ASIAN
~ **neighbor** IRANI

Turkana LAKE

turkey BIRD, DUD, LEMON
~ **part** LEG
~ **roaster** OVEN
~ **trot** DANCE
female ~ HEN
male ~ TOM
tend the ~ BASTE

turkey ___ RED, TROT

___ turkey TALK

Turkey
~ **highest point** ARARAT
~ **locale** ASIA
~ **neighbor** IRAN, IRAQ, SYRIA
lake in ~ VAN

turkey trot DANCE

Turkic
~ **language** TATAR

Turkish
~ **bath** SAUNA
~ **currency** LIRA
~ **leader** AGA, AGHA
~ **mountain** ARARAT
~ **staple** SESAME
~ **title** AGA, AGHA, AMIR, EMEER, EMIR, PASHA

Turkish ___ BATH

___-Turkish War ITALO

Turkmenistan
~ **once** SSR
neighbor of ~ IRAN

Turk's-___ lily CAP

Turk's-head KNOT

Turku
~ **to a Swede** ABO

turmoil ADO, DUST, MELEE, NOISE, ROW, STIR, TODO, YEAST
mental ~ PANIC

turn ACT, ANGLE, BEND, BOUT, CAST, LEAF, LOOP, SNAKE, SOUR, SPIN, SPOIL, STINT, TREND, VEER
~ **about** SLEW, SLUE
~ **a deaf ear to** DENY
~ **aside** AVERT, REPEL, VEER
~ **away** SHUN
~ **bad** ROT, SPOIL
~ **down** DENY, DIM
~ **(from)** DETER
~ **gray** AGE
~ **in** SLEEP
~ **indicator** LAMP
~ **inside-out** EVERT
~ **left** HAW
~ **loose** UNTIE
~ **obliquely** SKEW
~ **of phrase** IDIOM

turn ___

~ **on** AROUSE, ELATE, ENABLE, SEND
~ **one's back on** AVOID, CUT, DESERT, SHUN
~ **out** ENSUE, FARE
~ **over** CEDE, FLIP, ROLL, UPEND, UPSET
~ **over earth** PLOW
~ **pages** FLIP
~ **partner** TOSS
~ **right** GEE
~ **round and round** REEL
~ **signal** ARROW
~ **state's evidence** SING
~ **suddenly** VEER
~ **tail** DESERT, FLEE, RUN
~ **the soil** AERATE
~ **the tide** HELP
~ **thumbs down** DENY
~ **(to)** REFER
~ **to account** AVAIL
~ **to a page** OPEN
~ **to cinders** CHAR
~ **topsy-turvy** UPEND
~ **toward** FACE, ORIENT
~ **traitor** DESERT
~ **turtle** KEEL
~ **up** ARISE, ARRIVE, COME, OCCUR, PLOW
~ **up one's nose** SNEER
~ **up one's nose at** SNUB
do a good ~ SERVE
full ~ COIL
good ~ HELP
hairpin ~ BEND
make a sharp ~ VEER
race course ~ ESS
sharp ~ ELBOW
skier's ~ STEM
takes a ~ GOES
toss and ~ STEW
vaudeville ~ SOLO

turn ___ (alienate) OFF

turn ___ (appear) OUT

turn ___ (flee) TAIL

turn ___ (invert) OVER

turn ___ (start making money) PRO

turn a ___ ear to DEAF

"Turn Around, Look ___" ATME

turncoat REBEL

turndown
emphatic ~ NEVER
slangy ~ NAH, NOPE
White House ~ VETO

turndowns NOES, NOS

turned BAD
~ **back on** RELIT
~ **on** ELATED, LIT
~ **the clock back** RESET

turned-up SNUB

turner
~ **device** LATHE
soil ~ HOE
tumbler ~ KEY

___-turner PAGE

Turner IKE, LANA, NAT, ODESSA, TED, TINA
~ **network** TBS, TNT

Turner Field
~ **site** ATLANTA

Turner, Nat REBEL, SLAVE

Turner, Tina
~ **ex** IKE

turning
~ **point** AXIS, AXLE, HEAD
~ **tool** LATHE
earth's ~ **point** AXIS
WWII ~ **point** DDAY

"Turning to ___" STONE

"Turning to Stone"
~ **director** TILL

turnip ROOT

turnoff EXIT

turn-of-the-century
~ **fighter** BOER

"Turn of the Screw, The"
~ **girl** FLORA

turnover
home ~ RESALE

turn over ___ leaf ANEW

turnpike PATH, ROAD, ROUTE
~ **access** RAMP
~ **tariff** TOLL

turns
it often ~ TIDE

turnstile GATE
~ **drop-in** TOKEN
~ **opening** SLOT

turntable
~ **abbr.** RPM
~ **extension** ARM

turn the ___ cheek OTHER

"Turn to Stone"
~ **band** ELO

turpentine
~ **source** PINE

Turpin BEN

turpitude SHAME

turquoise AQUA, BLUE, COLOR, GEM

turtle PET
~ **home** SHELL
about to turn ~ ALIST
turn ~ KEEL

___ turtle TURN

turtledove BIRD, LOVE

"___ turtledoves..." TWO

turtles
group of ~ BALE

Turturro AIDA

Turturro, John
~ **film of 1992** MAC

Tuscaloosa
~ **st.** ALA

Tuscan ORDER

Tuscany
river in ~ ARNO

Tushingham RITA

tusk TOOTH
~ **material** IVORY
narwhal ~ HORN

tusker BOAR, HOG

tusks IVORY

___ Tussaud's Wax Museum MME

tussle MELEE, PLAY, ROW, SCRAP

tutelage CARE

tutelary
~ **deity** LAR

tutor TRAIN
Oxford ~ DON
Thai ~ ANNA

"Tutte le feste" ARIA

Tuttlingen
see German

tut-tut POOH, TSK

tux ATTIRE, DRESS

tuxedo DRESS, SUIT
~ **junction** SEAM

TV SET
~ **antenna** AERIAL
~ **band** UHF
~ **breaks** ADS
~ **commercial** SPOT
~ **control** KNOB
~ **dinner** MEAL
~ **drama** PLAY
~ **feature** STEREO
~ **inits.** ABC, CBS
~ **knob** DIAL, TINT
~ **melodrama** SOAP
~ **messages** ADS
~ **mfr.** RCA
~ **network** ABC, CBS
~ **networks** MEDIA
~ **nuisance** SNOW
~ **option** CABLE
~ **remote-control button** MUTE
~ **room** DEN
~ **screen** CRT
~ **service** CABLE
~ **signal component** AUDIO
~ **signal receiver** DISH
~ **soap** DRAMA
~ **studio sign** ONAIR
~ **tower** MAST
part of ~ TELE
pay ~ CABLE
put on ~ AIR
summer ~ **fare** RERUN

TVA
~ **product** ELEC
~ **project** DAM
part of ~ TENN

TV dinner
~ **table** TRAY

"TV Guide" MAG
~ **time span** WEEK

twa
~ **preceder** ANE

TWA
~ **abbr.** ARR, ETA
~ **rival** DELTA

twaddle PAP, PRATE, ROT, TALK, YAK

twain BOTH, DUO, PAIR, TWO

Twain, Mark PILOT

twangy NASAL

tweak NIP, RAG

Tweed BOSS
~ **nemesis** NAST

"Tweedle ___" DEE

tweet CALL, PEEP, PIPE, SING

Tweety BIRD
~ **home** CAGE

twelfth
~ **letter** ELL

Twelfth ___ (January 6) DAY

twelve NOON
~ **months** YEAR
game with ~ **wild cards** CANASTA

Twelve ___ ("GWTW" locale) OAKS

"Twelve Days of Christmas, The"
~ **gift** GEESE

twelvemonth YEAR

Twelve Oaks
~ **neighbor** TARA

"Twelve O'Clock High"
~ **org.** USAF

twenty SCORE
change for a ~ TENS

twenty-four
~ **carat** FINE, SOLID
one of ~ HOUR

"Twenty Questions"
~ **category** ANIMAL
~ **reply** YES

twenty-seventh
~ **President** TAFT

"Twenty Years on Broadway"
~ **autobiographer** COHAN

twerp CREEP, NERD

twice
~ **halved** ONCE
occurring ~ **(prefix)** SEMI

"...twice ___" SHY

"Twice ___ a Time" UPON

"Twice ___ Lifetime" INA

"Twice-___ Tales" TOLD

twice-told OLD

"Twice-Told ___" TALES

"Twice Upon a ___" TIME

"Twicknam Garden"
  ~ **poet** DONNE

twiddle ROLL
  ~ **one's thumbs** IDLE, LOAF

twig PART, ROOST, SCION, SHOOT, SPRIG, STEM

twiggy LEAN, THIN

Twiggy MODEL
  emulate ~ MODEL, POSE, SIT

twilight
  ~ **to a poet** EEN

"Twilight ___, The" ZONE

"Twilight Zone, The"
  ~ **name** ROD
  like ~ EERIE, EERY

twilled
  ~ **cloth** SERGE

twin BED, DUAL, IMAGE, KIN, MATE, SAME
  Biblical ~ ESAU

twin ___ BED, BILL

twin-___ SIZE

twine COIL, CORD, LINE
  ~ **material** SISAL
  strong ~ CORD

Twin Falls
  ~ **state** IDAHO

twinge ACHE, PAIN, PANG, SMART, STAB

twinkle BEAM, FLARE, GLOW, SHINE, SNAP
  it may ~ EYE

twinkler STAR

twinkle-toed AGILE

"Twinkle, Twinkle, Little ___" STAR

twinkling
  in the ~ **of an eye** ANON, SOON

"Twin Peaks" SOAP
  ~ **character** DALE, LAURA, PETE, SARAH
  ~ **state** IDAHO

twins DUO, PAIR

Twins TEAM, TEN
  ~ **follower** CRAB
  the ~ SIGN

twirl LOOP, REEL, SPIN

twirler
  tuner ~ KNOB

twirling
  ~ **feat** FLIP

twist BEND, CAST, COIL, DANCE, FLIP, LIE, LOOP, RAVEL, SKEW, SNAKE, TURN
  ~ **someone's arm** LEAD
  ~ **the lion's tail** DARE
  ~ **the truth** LIE

plot ~ IRONY

___-twist ARM

"Twist"
  ~ **director** MANN

"___ Twist Again" LETS

twisted AWRY, BENT, VILE, WRY

twister STORM
  truth ~ LIAR

twist of ___, a FATE

Twist, Oliver
  ~ **request** MORE

twit DOLT, GIBE, PIPE, RAG, TEASE

twitch PANG, STIR, TIC
  muscle ~ SPASM

twitter PEEP

"Twittering Machine, The"
  ~ **artist** KLEE

'twixt AMID, AMONG
  something ~ **cup and lip** SLIP

two DUO, PAIR
  ~ **cents' worth** SAY
  ~ **cups** PINT
  ~ **diamonds** BID
  ~ **ender** FER
  ~ **gridiron periods** HALF
  ~ **in Italian** DUE
  ~ **in Scottish** TWA
  ~ **in Spanish** DOS
  ~ **nickels** DIME
  ~ **of a kind** ALIKE
  ~ **semesters** YEAR
  ~ **under par** EAGLE
  carriage for ~ SHAY
  cut in ~ SPLIT
  eagle plus ~ PAR
  for ~ DUAL
  having ~ **parts** DUAL
  in ~ APART
  in ~ **shakes of a lamb's tail** SOON
  it takes ~ TANGO
  multiple of ~ EVEN
  not divisible by ~ ODD
  one of ~ **teams** HOME
  one or ~ FEW
  put one's ~ **cents in** ADD
  put two and ~ **together** ADD
  song for ~ DUET
  telephonic ~ ABC
  the ~ BOTH

two ___ (25 cents) BITS

two ___ kind OFA

two ___ time ATA

two ___ worth CENTS

two-___ BIT, PLY, SPOT, STEP, TONE

two-___ hit BASE

two-___ sloth TOED

"Two ___ Bananas" TOP

"Two ___ Before the Mast" YEARS

"Two ___ the Road" FOR

"Two ___ the Seesaw" FOR

"Two-___ Blacktop" LANE

"___ two aspirin and..." TAKE

two-bit MEAN, SMALL

"___, two, buckle my shoe" ONE

two-by-four BEAM

two-by-two
  ~ **vessel** ARK

"Two by Two"
  ~ **character** NOAH

two cents
  put one's ~ **in** OPINE

two cents worth SAY

"Two Cities"
  one of Dickens' ~ PARIS

two-dimensional PLANE
  ~ **measure** AREA

two-faced FALSE

two-finger
  ~ **sign** VEE

"___ Two Flags" UNDER

twofold DUAL

"Two for the ___" ROAD

"Two for the Seesaw"
  ~ **director** WISE

"Two Gentlemen of Verona, The"
  ~ **character** SPEED

"Two Girls ___ Sailor" ANDA

"Two hearts that beat ___" ASONE

two-L
  Nash's ~ **beast** LLAMA

"Two mints ___" INONE

"Two Mules ___ Sister Sara" FOR

"Two Mules for Sister ___" SARA

"Two Mules for Sister Sara" OATER

two-part DUAL

twopence COIN

two-person DUAL

two-piece
  ~ **part** BRA

___-two punch ONE

two-seater AUTO, CAR, MOTOR

two-sided DUAL

twosome DUET, DUO, PAIR, SPAN

twosomes
  place for ~ ARK

two-step DANCE

two-striper
  ~ **(abbr.)** NCO

"___, Two, Three" ONE

two-time
  ~ **loser of the 1950s** AES

two-timer CAD

two-toed
  ~ **sloth** UNAU

"Two-ton" ___ **Galento** TONY

two to one ODDS, RATIO

two-track STEREO

"Two Way Stretch"
  ~ **director** DAY

two-wheeled
  ~ **vehicle** CART

two-wheeler BIKE

"Two Women"
  ~ **actress** LOREN

two-year-old KID, TOT, TYKE

"Two Years Before the ___" MAST

"Two Years Before the Mast"
  ~ **author** DANA

TX
  ~ **school** SMU
  see also Texas

tycoon BARON, NABOB
  ~ **home** ESTATE
  fur ~ ASTOR
  Greek ~**'s sobriquet** ARI
  software ~ GATES

"___ Tycoon, The" LAST

"Tyger, The" POEM

tyke KID, TAD, TOT

Tylenol
  ~ **target** ACHE

Tyler ANNE, LIV

Tynan, Joe
  ~ **portrayer** ALDA

Tyndareus
  wife of ~ LEDA

Tynemouth CITY, PORT

type CAST, CLASS, CUT, GENRE, ILK, LIKE, LINE, LOT, MAKE, MOLD, ORDER, RANK, SORT, STAMP, STYLE
  ~ **assortment** FONT
  ~ **starter** STEREO, TELE
  ~ **style** ITAL
  ~ **widths** EMS, ENS
  size of ~ AGATE
  typewriter ~ ELITE, PICA

typecast PEG

"Typee"
  ~ **sequel** OMOO

typeface FONT
  ~ **detail** SERIF

typesetter
  ~ **selection** FONT

typesetters
  ~ **measures** EMS, ENS

typesetting

typesetting
~ **boo-boos** ERRATA

typewriter
~ **key** TAB
~ **part** KEY
~ **type** ELITE, PICA
former ~ accessory ERASER

typhoon STORM

typical USUAL
~ **of** LIKE
~ **Russian** IVAN
~ **taxicab** SEDAN

"Typical ___" MALE

typist
~ **colleague** STENO

typo ERROR
~ **list** ERRATA

typographic
~ **flourish** SERIF

typographical ___ ERROR

typos ERRATA
make some ~ ERR

Tyr
~ **to Odin** SON

tyrannical STERN

tyrannize REIGN

Tyrannosaurus ___ REX

tyranny ROD

tyrant LORD, OGRE, TSAR
~ **of yore** TSAR
Ugandan ~ AMIN

Tyre CITY, PORT
Qinault's queen of ~ ELISE

tyro BABE
military ~ CADET

Tyrol
~ **locale** ALPS
see also German

Tyrolean
~ **peak** ALP
~ **song** YODEL

Tyrrhenian SEA

Tyson
~ **move** JAB
~ **specialty** TKO
~ **stat** KOS

Tzara, Tristan
~ **movement** DADA

___-tzu LAO

U ELEM
92 for ~ ATNO

U-___ BOAT, TURN

UAE
~ honcho AMIR, EMEER, EMIR
part of ~ ARAB

UAR
half of the ~ SYR
part of ~ ARAB

UB40 OCTET

ubiquitous RIFE

U-boat SUB

UCLA
part of ~ CAL, LOS

Udall, Nicholas
~ school ETON

udder BAG

___-Ude, Russia ULAN

Uffizi
~ contents ART

UFO
~ crew member ALIEN
~ occupants ETS
~ pilots ETS

Ugandan
~ exile AMIN

ugly duckling
ex ~ SWAN

uh
~ cousins ERS

UHF
part of ~ ULTRA

"Uh-huh" ISEE, YEAH, YEP, YES

Uhland, Johann Ludwig POET
see also poet

"Uh-oh!" OOPS

"Uh-uh" NAH, NAY, NOPE

Uinta RANGE

Uinta Range
~ state UTAH

UK
~ defenders RAF
~ money, once LSD

~ network BBC
fast way to the ~ SST
inc. in the ~ LTD
part of the ~ ENG, IRE, SCOT

ukase EDICT, FIAT, ORDER

Ukraine
~ capital KIEV
~ once SSR
~ port ODESSA
~ seaport YALTA

Ukrainian SLAV

ukulele
~ feature FRET

Ukulele ___ IKE

"Ulalume" POEM
~ author POE
like the skies in ~ ASHEN

Ulanov IGOR

Ullman NORM

Ullmann LIV

Ullsten OLA

Ulm
see German

ulna BONE
~ neighbors RADII
~ site ARM

ulster COAT, WRAP

ultimate IDEAL, LAST, NTH
~ objective END

ultimatum DARE, ORDER
~ ending ELSE

ultra MOST
ne plus ~ APEX, MODEL, PEAK, TOP

ultramarine BLUE, COLOR

ultramodern NEW, STYLE

ultrasound TEST

ululate BAY, CRY, KEEN, MOAN, WEEP

ululation BAY, NOISE

Ulyanov, Vladimir LENIN

"Ulysses"
last word of ~ YES

"Ulzana's ___" RAID

um
~ cousins ERS

umber COLOR

Umberto ECO
see also Italian

umbra SHADE

umbrage ANGER, IRE, SHADE

umbrella AEGIS, EGIS, PALM, SHADE, TREE
~ of song SMILE
~ spoke RIB
picnic ~ TREE

umbrella ___ PLANT, TREE

umbrette
~ relative HERON

Umbria
from ~ ITAL

Umbrian
~ commune ASSISI
~ (prefix) ITALO

Umbriel MOON

umiak BOAT
~ home ALASKA
~ relative CANOE

umlaut
half an ~ DOT

umpire
~ call FAIR, OUT, SAFE
~ purview PLATE
~ relative REF
ride the ~ BOO

UMW
~ opening ADIT

UN
~ agcy. ILO
~ Day mo. OCT
~ member ALB, ALG, ARG, CHAD, COL, CUBA, DEN, ENG, ETH, FIN, GER, HAITI, IND, IRE, ISR, ITAL, LAOS, LAT, MALI, NOR, PAN, PERU, POL, PORT, ROM, SYR, TOGO, TUN, USA
~ observer grp. PLO
name in ~ history DAG, LIE

unabashed COOL

unable
~ to decide TORN
~ to say no MEEK

unabridged ENTIRE
~ dictionary TOME

unacceptable POOR

unaccommodating MEAN, STERN

unaccompanied ALONE, LONE, SOLO, STAG

unaccompanined SOLO

unaccounted-for
~ GI MIA

unaccustomed NEW

"Unaccustomed ___ am..." ASI

unadmired
~ one LOSER, NERD

unadorned BALD, BARE, DRY, HONEST, PURE, SOBER

unadulterated MERE, NEAT, PURE

unaffected NAIVE

unaffectedness EASE

unaffiliated
~ (abbr.) IND

unafraid GAME, TAME

unaggressive MEEK
~ one LAMB

unagi
~ at a Japanese restaurant EEL

unagitated CALM, CLEAR

unaided ALONE, SOLO

Unalaska
~ resident ALEUT

unallowed TABOO, TABU

unalloyed PURE, SOLID

unaltered SAME

unambiguous CLEAR, HONEST

unambitious
~ one IDLER

unamicable COOL, ICY

Unamuno, Miguel de POET
see also poet

unanimous ASONE, ATONE, SOLID

unanimously ASONE, ATONE

"Unanswered Question, The"
~ composer IVES

unappareled BARE, NUDE

unappetizing BLAH, FLAT

unapproachable ALOOF, COOL

unassisted ALONE, SOLO

unassuming MEEK, MILD

unattached FREE, LONE, LOOSE
~ male STAG

unattended ALONE, LONE

unattired BARE, NUDE

unattributed
~ (abbr.) ANON

unavailing VAIN

"Una voce poco fa" ARIA

unbalanced DAFT, MAD
~ at sea ALIST

unbarred FREE, OPEN

unbearable BAD, HARD

"Unbearable Bassington, The"
~ author SAKI

"Unbearable Lightness of Being, The"
~ actress OLIN

"Un bel di" ARIA

unbend OPEN

unbending IRON, STERN

unbendingness RIGOR

unbiased BIG, EVEN, FAIR

unbilled
~ performer EXTRA

unbind LOOSE

unblemished CLEAR, PURE

unblenching GAME

unblock CLEAR, OPEN

unblocked OPEN

unbolt OPEN

unbooked OPEN

unbosom OPEN

unbound FREE, LOOSE

unbounded BIG, LARGE, OPEN

unbribed CLEAN, HONEST

unbridled FREE

unbroken ENTIRE, FLAT, PLANE, SOLID

unbuckle LOOSE, OPEN

unbuild RAZE

unburden EASE, RID
~ oneself TELL

unburdensome EASY

unbuttered DRY

unbuttoned LOOSE

uncanny EERIE, EERY

uncap OPEN

Uncas
craft for ~ CANOE

unceasing ETERNAL

unceasingly EVER

unceremonious EASY, FREE, RUDE
~ dismissal BOOT

unceremoniousness EASE

uncertain ASEA, ATSEA, DIM, LEERY, OPEN, WARY
~ amount ANY, FEW, SOME

"___ Uncertain Feeling" THAT

uncertainty PERIL, RISK
sounds of ~ ERS

unchain FREE

unchained LOOSE

unchallenged ALONE
go ~ PASS

unchanged ASIS, SAME

unchanging ETERNAL, SAME

uncharitable SMALL

uncharted NEW

unchecked
spread ~ RAGE

uncivil CRASS, PERT, RUDE

uncivilized RUDE
~ one ANIMAL

unclad BARE, NUDE

unclaimed OPEN

unclasp LOOSE

unclassifiable ODD

uncle KIN, MALE, MAN
~ (abbr.) REL
~ brother, maybe DAD
~ in Spanish TIO
~ kid NIECE
~ mom GRAM, NANA
~ sister, maybe MOM
~ wife AUNT
cry ~ YIELD
everybody's ~ SAM
say ~ LOSE

___ uncle CRY, SAY

Uncle ___ SAM

Uncle ___ (rice brand) BENS

U.N.C.L.E.
~ agent SOLO

unclean
make ~ TAINT

unclear DIM

unclench OPEN

"Uncle Remus"
~ epithet BRER

Uncle Sam
~ feature BEARD, HAT
agent of ~ FED

"Uncle Tom's Cabin"
~ character EVA

unclog CLEAR, OPEN

unclose OPEN
~ to a poet OPE

unclosed AJAR

unclothe PEEL

unclothed BARE, NUDE

unclouded CLEAR

uncluttered NEAT

uncolored BARE

uncomfortable
be ~ ACHE
vaguely ~ ACHY

uncommitted OPEN

uncommon ODD, RARE, SPARSE
~ conjunction LEST
~ in Latin RARA
~ sense ESP

uncommonly EXTRA

uncommunicative CLOSE, MUTE

uncomplaining STOIC

uncomplicate EASE

uncomplicated EASY

uncompromised TOTAL

uncompromising STERN
~ response NEVER

unconcealed CLEAR, OVERT

unconcerned ALOOF, COOL

unconditional OPEN, TOTAL, UTTER

unconditioned ENTIRE, FREE

unconfining EASY

unconfused CLEAR

unconnected LOOSE

unconscious OUT

unconstrained EASY, LOOSE

unconstraint EASE

uncontaminated CLEAN, PURE

uncontrollable AMOK

unconventional FAST, ODD, OUTRE

unconversant NAIVE

unconvincing LAME, POOR

uncooked RAW

uncool
~ one NERD

uncordial COOL

uncork OPEN, POP

uncorrectness ERROR

uncourtly RUDE

uncouth CRASS, LOUD, RAW, RUDE
~ one APE, BOOR, CLOD, OAF

uncover BARE, LEARN, TRACE
~ to a poet OPE

uncovered BALD, BARE, NUDE, OPEN

uncrowded OPEN, SPARSE

unctuous OILY, SLEEK

uncultivable ARID, DESERT

uncultured RUDE
~ one BOOR, CLOD, OAF, SLOB

uncurbed FREE

uncustomary RARE

uncut ENTIRE, NEAT, RAW

undamaged ENTIRE, SAFE

undampened DRY

undaunted GAME

undecided TORN
remain ~ PEND

undeclared TACIT

undecorated BARE

undefiled CLEAN, PURE

undelayed EARLY

undemanding EASY, MEEK

undemonstrative CALM, COOL

undeniable CLEAR, TRUE
it's ~ FACT

under NEATH
~ sail ASEA, ATSEA
~ the covers ABED
~ to a poet NEATH
~ way AFOOT

under ___ (embattled) FIRE

under ___ (sworn) OATH

___ under (overwhelm) SNOW

"Under ___" FIRE, SIEGE

"Under ___ Flags" TWO

"Under a Glass Bell"
~ author NIN

undercoat PAINT
artist's ~ GESSO

undercover
~ agent MOLE, PLANT, SPY
~ cop AGENT, NARC
~ operation STING
~ org. CIA
go ~ HIDE, SPY
recognize, as an ~ cop MAKE

"Undercover ___, The" MAN

"Undercover Man, The"
~ director LEWIS

undercut ERODE

underdog
~ **often** LOSER

underdone RARE

underestimate ERR

underfed LEAN

"Under Fire"
~ **star** NOLTE

underfoot
it may be ~ MAT, RUG
it's ~ SOLE

undergo BEAR
~ **nivation** ERODE

undergrad SOPH
~ **degs.** BAS

underground LOW
~ **chamber** CAVE
~ **conduit** SEWER
~ **dweller of folklore** GNOME
~ **find** ORE
~ **growth** ROOT
~ **passage** SEWER
~ **rodent** MOLE
go ~ HIDE

"Underground ___" USA

underhand SLY
~ **throw** LOB

underhanded SLY
~ **fellow** SNEAK

"Under Hawaiian Skies"
~ **accompaniment** UKE

underline STRESS
~ **equiv.** ITAL

underling AIDE, COG, HELP

underlying BASIC
~ **sentiment** PULSE

undermine ERODE, RUIN, SAP

undernourished LEAN, POOR

under one's ___ BELT

underpaid
~ **employee** PEON

underpin BEAR

underpinning BASE, LEG, PROP
foliage ~ STEM

underprivileged NEEDY, POOR

underscore LINE, STRESS

underseller BEAR

undershirt TEE
~ **size** LARGE, MED, SMALL

underside KEEL

undersized SMALL
~ **one** RUNT

understand DIG, FEEL, GET,
GRASP, KNOW, LEARN, SEE
~ **a transmission** READ
easy to ~ CLEAR

understandable CLEAR

understanding GRIP, IDEA, KEN
~ **words** OHS
phrase of ~ ISEE

understood ROGER, TACIT
not easily ~ DEEP

"Understood!" ISEE

understructure BASE

understudy ACTOR

undertake ENTER, ESSAY, START,
TRY, WAGE

undertaking DEED, MOVE, TASK

under the ___ (just in time)
WIRE

under the ___ (pressured) GUN

under the ___ (secretly) TABLE

"Under the ___" SEA

___ under the bridge WATER

___ under the collar HOT

**"Under the hawthorne in the
___"** DALE

"___ under the haystack..." HES

"___ Under the Sun" EVIL

"Under the Yum Yum ___" TREE

undertow STREAM

underwater LOW
~ **boat** SUB
~ **cave dweller** EEL
~ **shelf** LEDGE
~ **tracker** SONAR
go ~ SINK

underway AFOOT

underweight LANK, LEAN, THIN

Underwood RON

underworld ABYSS
~ **figure** DON, SATAN
~ **lingo** ARGOT
~ **river** STYX
~ **weapon** GAT
Roman god of the ~ DIS

underwrite ENDOW, HELP

undesirable CREEP

undeveloped NEW

undiluted NEAT, RAW

undiminished ENTIRE

undisguised BALD, BARE, CLEAR,
OPEN, OVERT

undismayed GAME, SERENE

undisputed CLEAR

undistinguished SOSO

undisturbed CALM, CLEAR,
SERENE

undivided ENTIRE, ONE
~ **attention** EAR
~ **whole** UNIT

undo ANNUL, LOOSE, OPEN,
RAVEL, RUIN
~ **a dele** STET
~ **(prefix)** DIS

undocumented
~ **person, perhaps** ALIEN

undoing RUIN
pigeon's ~ SCAM
Pompeii's ~ LAVA
rat's ~ TRAP
"Titanic" ~ BERG

undomesticated FERAL

undone LOST
leave ~ OMIT, SKIP
remain ~ WAIT
wish ~ RUE

undoubtedly AYE, YES

undoubting SURE

undrape BARE, SHOW, STRIP

Undset, Sigrid DANE

"___ und Tabu" TOTEM

undulate BATHE, ROLL, SWAY

unduly TOO
~ **quick** RASH

unearth LEARN, ROOT, TRACE

unearthly ALIEN, EERIE, EERY

uneasiness ALARM, FEAR

uneasy EDGY

unelected
~ **group** OUTS

unelevated LOW

unembellished BALD, BARE,
CLEAN

unemotional CALM, COOL, DRY,
HARD, STOIC

unemployed IDLE

unencouraging
~ **reply** NAH, NAY, NOPE

unencumbered CLEAR, FREE

unending ETERNAL, EVER

unendurable HARD

unenergetic LIMP, TIRED

unenthusiastic DAMP, TEPID

unequaled ALONE, AONE, BEST,
TOP, TOPS

unequivocal CLEAR, HONEST,
TOTAL, UTTER

unerring SURE, TRUE

unescorted ALONE, LONE, SOLO,
STAG

unethical LOW, SLY
~ **one** LOUSE

uneven AWRY, EROSE
~ **as leaf edges** EROSE
~ **gait** LIMP

unevenly AWRY

unexacting EASY, LOOSE

unexampled RARE

unexcelled ALONE, AONE, BEST,
TOPS

unexceptional SOSO

unexcitable CALM, COOL, SERENE

unexciting BLAH, FLAT, TAME

unexpected ODD
~ **pleasure** TREAT
~ **problem** SNAG

unexplainable EERIE, EERY

unexplained ODD
~ **sighting** UFO

unexploded LIVE

unexplored NEW

unexpressed TACIT

unexpurgated ENTIRE

unextinguished ALIVE, LIVE

unfaceted
~ **gem** OPAL, PEARL

unfailing SAFE, SURE, TRUE

unfairness BIAS

unfaithful FALSE

unfaltering ETERNAL, SURE

unfamiliar ALIEN, NEW, RARE

unfashionable OUT, PASSE

unfasten LOOSE, OPEN

unfastened LOOSE

unfathomable DEEP
it's ~ ABYSS

unfavorable BAD, DIRE, ILL
more ~ WORSE

unfavorably ILL

unfazed CALM, COOL, SERENE

unfeeling CRASS, CRUEL, HARD,
IRON, STERN

unfeigned HONEST, PURE, REAL

unfenced OPEN

unfertile ARID, DESERT, DRY, SERE

unfetter FREE

unfettered FREE, LOOSE

unfinished
~ **room** ATTIC

"Unfinished Business"
~ **director** OWEN

unfirm LIMP

unfit
~ **for farming** ARID, SERE

unfixed ASIS

unflappable CALM, COOL,
SEDATE, SERENE

unflattering SNIDE

unfledged NEW, RAW

unflinching STOIC

unfluctuating EVEN

unflustered CALM, COOL, SERENE

unfold BARE, EMERGE, OPEN
~ **to a poet** OPE

unforced EASY, FREE

"Unforgettable"
~ **singer** COLE, NAT

unforgiving MEAN, STERN

unfortunate BAD, POOR, SAD

unfoul CLEAN

unfounded IDLE
~ **report** RUMOR

unfreeze MELT, THAW

unfriendly COOL, ICY
~ **one** ENEMY, FOE
~ **sound** SNARL

unfruitful ARID

unfurl FAN, OPEN

unfurnished BARE

ungainly INEPT

ungallant RUDE

ungenerous MEAN, SMALL

ungentle RUDE, STERN

ungentlemanly RUDE

Unger, Felix
like ~ NEAT
no ~ SLOB

unginned
like ~ **cotton** SEEDY

unglued MAD
come ~ RAVE

ungraceful INEPT

ungracious COOL, RUDE

ungrip DROP

unguarded OPEN

unguent BALM, CREAM, OIL

unguinous OILY

unguis CLAW, NAIL

ungulate
South American ~ TAPIR

Unh ELEM
106 for ~ ATNO

unhallow TAINT

unhampered FREE

unhappiness EVIL, PAIN, WOE

unhappy BLUE, LOW, SAD

unhatched
~ **fish** ROE

unhealthful BAD
~ **atmosphere** SMOG
~ **rain component** ACID

unhealthy ILL, LOW

unheard-of NEW, RARE

unhearing DEAF

unheated COOL

unheeding DEAF

unhesitating SURE

unhidden CLEAR

unhinge UPSET

unhinged BATS, DAFT, LOCO, MAD, UPSET

unhip
~ **one** NERD

unhitched FREE

unholy EVIL

"Unholy Partners"
~ **director** LEROY

unhurried EASY, SLOW

unhurt SAFE

uni-
~ **cousin** MON

unicorn ANIMAL
~ **feature** HORN

unicorn ___ PLANT

unified ASONE
~ **group** CADRE

uniform ALIKE, ATTIRE, DRESS, EVEN, GARB, PLANE, SAME
~ **extra** SASH
~ **(prefix)** ISO

uniformed
~ **group** TEAM

uniforms GARB

unify WED

unimaginative ARID, BANAL, STALE, TRITE

unimpeded FREE

unimportant MEAN, MERE, SMALL, TINY, VAIN

unimproved ASIS
~ **land** LOT

uninformed NAIVE

uninhibited FREE

uninjured
leave ~ SPARE

uninspired BANAL, DRAB, FLAT, STALE, TRITE

uninspiring ARID

unintelligent
~ **one** ASS, CLOD, DOLT

unintelligible
~ **speech** SLUR

uninteresting ARID, BLAH, DRAB, DRY, FLAT, STALE, TAME

uninterrupted ETERNAL, SOLID

"Uninvited, The"
~ **director** ALLEN

uninviting COOL

uninvolved ALOOF, COOL

union BLOC
~ **bane** SCAB
~ **branch** LOCAL
~ **supporters** LABOR
dockworkers' ~ ILA
educ. ~ AFT, NEA
form a ~ WED
movie ~ SAG

___ union LABOR, TRADE

Union STA
~ **member** STATE
~ **opp.** CSA

"Union ___" DEPOT

unionize ALLY

Union Jack FLAG
~ **holder** MAST

Union Pacific
~ **terminus** OMAHA

unique ALONE, LONE, NEW, ODD, ONLY, RARE, SOLE
~ **thing** ONER

unison TUNE
be in ~ AGREE
in ~ ASONE
work in ~ SYNC

unit ITEM, ONE
~ **for a poet** FOOT, IAMB

unite ADD, ALLY, BAND, BIND, FUSE, MASS, MELD, TIE, WED

united ASONE, ATONE, ONE
~ **group** BLOC
~ **(prefix)** SYN

United
~ **rival** DELTA, TWA

United ___ Emirates ARAB

United Federation of Planets
~ **member** EARTH

United Kingdom
~ **division** WALES

units
dol. ~ CTS

units, ___, hundreds TENS

unity PEACE

___ Unit Zappa MOON

Univers FONT

universal BIG, ENTIRE, LARGE, TOTAL
~ **(prefix)** OMNI
~ **truth** LAW
~ **wish** PEACE
be ~ REIGN
philosopher's ~ TAO

universal ___ (type O) DONOR

Universal
~ **workplace** LOT

universality ALL

universe SPACE
bit of the ~ ATOM

university
~ **deg.** MBA
~ **degs.** ABS, BAS, MAS
~ **department** ART, DRAMA, MATH
~ **maj.** BIO, ECO, ECON, ENG, GEO, MUS
~ **major** ART, DRAMA, MATH
~ **sports org.** NCAA
~ **woman** COED
Houston ~ RICE

New York ~ PACE

University of Maine
~ **locale** ORONO

University of Nevada
~ **locale** RENO

unkempt MESSY, SEEDY
~ **one** SLOB

unkeyed ATONAL

unkind CRUEL, EVIL, STERN

unkindly ILL

unknown NEW
~ **author** ANON
legal ~ DOE, ROE

"Unknown Eros, The" POEM

unlace LOOSE

unladylike RUDE

unlatch OPEN
~ **to a poet** OPE

unlatched AJAR

unlawful
~ **act** TORT

"Unlawful ___" ENTRY

unleaded GAS

unleash
~ **one's anger** ERUPT, RAGE

unleashed LOOSE

unlidded OPEN

unlike ALIEN, OTHER

unlikely RARE

unlimited BIG, ENTIRE, LARGE

unlit
~ **buoy** NUN

unload DROP, SELL

unlock OPEN
~ **to a poet** OPE

unlucky ILL, POOR

UNLV
part of ~ LAS, NEV

unmannered CRASS

unmannerly PERT, RUDE

unmarried LONE
~ **woman** MAID

"Unmarried Woman, An"
~ **role** ERICA

unmask BARE, LEAK

unmatched ODD

unmentionable TABOO, TABU

unmentioned TACIT

unmindful DEAF

unmingled PURE

unmistakable CLEAR

unmitigated ENTIRE, RANK, TOTAL, UTTER

unmixed CLEAN, PURE, SOLID

unmoved CALM, COOL, DEAF, SERENE

unmoving INERT

unmuzzled FREE

unnatural EERIE, EERY

unnaturalized ALIEN

unnerve ALARM, UPSET

unnerved UPSET

unnerving BAD, EERIE, EERY

unnoticed
　go ~ PASS

uno
　~ follower DOS, DUE

unobstructed CLEAR, OPEN

unoccupied IDLE, OPEN, SPARE

uno, due, ___ TRE

unoppressive EASY

unorganized LOOSE

unoriginal BANAL, STALE, TRITE
　be ~ APE, ECHO

unornamented BARE

unorthodox
　opp. of ~ STD

Unp ELEM
　105 for ~ ATNO

unpackaged LOOSE

unpaid DUE
　~ worker SERF

unpalatable VILE

unparalleled ALONE, BEST, FIRST, LONE, RARE, TOP

unpartnered ALONE, LONE

unpasteurized RAW

unpermissable TABOO, TABU

unperturbed CALM, COOL, SEDATE

unpin FREE, LOOSE

unplanned ADLIB, LOOSE

unpleasant BAD, MEAN, MESSY, RAW, SOUR
　~ odor REEK
　~ person PEST, PILL
　~ situation MESS
　~ task ONUS
　more than ~ RUDE

unplentiful THIN

unpolished CRASS, RUDE

unpolluted CLEAN, PURE

unprecedented FIRST, NEW

unpredictability RISK

unprejudiced FAIR

unpremeditated ADLIB

unprestigious
　~ publication RAG

unpretended REAL, TRUE

unpretentious SMALL

unprincipled AMORAL, BAD, BASE
　~ one CAD

unprocessed RAW

unproductive ARID, DESERT, DRY, POOR, SERE, STALE, VAIN

unprofessional POOR

unpromising BAD

unpronounced MUTE

unpropitious BAD, DIRE, EVIL, ILL

unproven
　~ facility ESP

unpunctual LATE

Unq ELEM
　104 for ~ ATNO

unqualified PURE, RANK, TOTAL, UTTER

unquenchable AVID
　~ desire PANG

unquestionable CLEAR, SOLID, SURE, TRUE

unquestionably AYE, YES

unravel RAVEL, RUN

unraveled
　become ~ RUN

unreactive INERT

unreal AERIAL, EERIE, EERY, FAKE

unreasonable DAFT, MAD

unreasonably TOO

unreasoning
　~ terror PANIC

unrefined CRASS, LOUD, RAW, RUDE

unregulated LOOSE

unrelenting CRUEL, STERN

unreliable
　~ source LIAR

unrelieved SOLID

unremitting ETERNAL

unremittingly EVER

unreserved EASY, TOTAL

unreservedness EASE

unresisting LIMP, MEEK, TAME

unresponsive ALOOF, COOL

unrest
　civil ~ RIOT
　major ~ WAR

unrestrained EASY, FAST, FREE

unrestraint EASE

unrestricted FREE, OPEN
　~ use PLAY

unrestricting EASY

unruffled CALM, COOL, EVEN, SEDATE, SERENE

Uns ELEM
　107 for ~ ATNO

"Unsafe at ___ Speed" ANY

"Unsafe at Any Speed"
　~ author NADER

unsaid TACIT

unsalvageable LOST

unsatisfactorily ILL

unsatisfactory BAD, ILL, LAME, POOR

unsavory BAD, FLAT

unsay DENY

unscathed SAFE

unscripted
　~ line ADLIB

unscrupulous BAD, EVIL
　~ scheme SCAM

unseal OPEN
　~ to a poet OPE

unseasoned RAW

unseemly BAD, RAW

unseen
　~ substance GAS

Unseld WES

unselfish BIG, GREAT

unseparated ONE

Unser RACER
　~ and others ALS

unsettle JAR, UPSET

unsettled EDGY, UPSET
　be ~ HANG, PEND

unsettling BAD

unshackle FREE

unshackled LOOSE

unshakable SURE

unsheathe DRAW

unskilled
　~ laborer PEON

unskillful INEPT

unsmiling DOUR

unsnap LOOSE

unsnarl COMB

unsociable ALOOF, COOL, SHY

unsoiled CLEAN, PURE

unsophisticate BABE, LAMB

unsophisticated NAIVE

unsound FALSE, ILL
　of ~ mind DAFT, MAD

unsparing STERN

unspeakable DIRE, EVIL

unspeaking MUTE, TACIT

unspecified
　~ amount ANY, FEW, SOME
　~ degree NTH

unspoiled CLEAN, NAIVE

unspoken TACIT

unspotted CLEAN

unstained CLEAN

unstated TACIT

unsteady
　~ light FLARE
　make ~ TIP

unstick LOOSE

unstiffened LIMP

unstinted AMPLE

unstinting FREE

unstop CLEAR, OPEN
　~ to a poet OPE

unstoppable SURE

unsubstantial AERIAL, THIN

unsuccessful VAIN
　be ~ LOSE, MISS

unsuitable AMISS

unsullied CLEAN, PURE

unsure ASEA, ATSEA, LEERY, LOST

unsurpassed ALONE, AONE, BEST, FIRST, TOPS

unsuspecting NAIVE

unswerving TRUE

unsympathetic ALOOF, COOL, HARD, STERN

untainted PURE

untamed FERAL

untangle COMB, RAVEL

untapped NEW

unter
　~ opposite UBER

untested NEW, RAW

unthinking INANE

unthreatened SAFE

unthreatening TAME

untidiness MESS

untidy MESSY
　~ spot MESS
　~ type SLOB

untie FREE, LOOSE

untied LOOSE

until UPTO
　~ now SINCE

"___ Until Dark" WAIT

untimely EARLY

untold
　~ centuries EON

___ unto oneself, a LAW

untouchable TABOO, TABU

untouchables CASTE

"Untouchables, The"
~ agt. TMAN
~ character NESS

untouched NEW

untoward BAD, DIRE

untraditional
musically ~ ATONAL

untrained NEW, RAW

untrammeled FREE

untried NEW

untrodden NEW

untroubled CLEAR, EASY, SERENE

untrue FALSE, NOT
declare ~ DENY
make ~ BELIE

untrustworthy BAD, FALSE
~ sort LIAR, SNEAK

untruth LIBEL, LIE, TALE
speak an ~ LIE

untruthful
~ one LIAR

unturned
leave no stone ~ DIG, HUNT, RAKE, SEEK

untwist RAVEL

unum
what ~ means ONE

unusable
become ~ ROT, SPOIL

unused IDLE, NEW
go ~ SIT

unusual EERIE, EERY, NEW, ODD, OUTRE, RARE
~ in Latin RARA
~ person ONER

unusually EXTRA

unvaried SAME

unvarnished BALD, BARE, HONEST, PURE, RAW
~ truth FACT

unvarying EVEN, SAME

unveil BARE, LEAK, SHOW
~ to a poet OPE

unversed NAIVE, RAW

unvoiced TACIT

unwanted
~ guest PEST
~ layer DUST
~ plant WEED
~ pool visitor ALGA

unwarmed COOL

unwashed
great ~ MOB

unwavering ETERNAL, SURE, TRUE

unweave RAVEL

unwell ILL
feel ~ AIL

unwheeled
~ vehicle SLED

unwholesome BAD

unwilling AVERSE
~ to listen DEAF

unwilted CRISP

unwind REEL, REST

unwonted RARE

unworldly NAIVE

unworthiness
feeling of ~ SHAME

unwrap OPEN
~ to a poet OPE

unwritten ORAL

unyielding AVERSE, DEAF, DOUR, HARD, IRON, STERN

up ALOFT, ASTIR, RISEN
~ for grabs OPEN
~ (prefix) ANO
~ to one's ears AWASH
neither ~ nor down EVEN

up ___ grabs FOR

up-___ CLOSE

___ up (absorb) SOAK, SOP

___ up (admit) FESS, OWN

___ up (ahead) ONE

___ up (amass) RUN

___ up (appear) TURN

___ up (arrive) SHOW

___ up (bungle) LOUSE, MESS

___ up (busy) TIED

___ up (buy immediately) SNAP

___ up (cancel) TEAR

___ up (clean one's plate) EAT

___ up (collaborate) TEAM

___ up (confess) OWN

___ up (confide) OPEN

___ up (consume) EAT, USE

___ up (cram) BONE

___ up (delay) HOLD

___ up (devise) DREAM

___ up (disgusted) FED

___ up (ease) LET

___ up (endure) BEAR

___ up (enliven) PEP, PERK

___ up (enroll) SIGN

___ up (evaluate) SIZE

___ up (fabricate) MAKE

___ up (fill the tank) GAS

___ up (finalize) SEW

___ up (find) SCARE

___ up (get gas) TANK

___ up (get into shape) TONE

___ up (get ready to drive) TEE

___ up (hide) HOLE

___ up (incite) RILE, STIR

___ up (increase) STEP

___ up (intensify) HEAT

___ up (maintain) KEEP

___ up (make sense) ADD

___ up (mature) GROW

___ up (misbehave) ACT

___ up (monopolize) SEW

___ up (parody) SEND

___ up (pay) ANTE

___ up (prepare) GEAR

___ up (profit) CLEAN

___ up (publicize) PLAY

___ up (recap) SUM

___ up (reinforce) SHORE

___ up (reject) PASS

___ up (relent) EASE

___ up (relish) EAT, LAP

___ up (rise) GET

___ up (talk) PIPE

___ up (uncover) DIG, RAKE, ROOT

___-up BANG, BEAT, CHIN, CLOSE, FLARE, HANG, JAM, LAY, MADE, NIP, ONE, PILE, POP, PUT, SEND, SIT, SLIP, START, STEP, TIE, TUNE, WARM, WRAP, WRITE

"Up ___ & Personal" CLOSE

"___-Up, The" SET

U.P.
~ and others RRS

up a ___ TREE

up and ___ ABOUT

up and around ABOUT

up-and-coming EAGER
~ one DOER

up-and-down
~ toy YOYO

___-up-and-go GET

up-and-up
on the ~ SAFE

Upanishads
~ studier HINDU

upbeat ALIVE, ROSY

upbraid LACE, LASH, RAG, RATE, TWIT

UPC
~ element BAR
part of ~ CODE

update REDO
~ a watch RESET

___ manuscripts EMEND
evening ~ NEWS

___-up demand PENT

upend RAISE, STAND, UPSET

___ up for (support) STAND

upfront
not ~ SLY

up-front HONEST, OPEN
~ money ANTE

upgrade RAISE
~ text EMEND
hi-fi ~ STEREO

upheaval RIOT, STIR, STORM
emotional ~ SPASM

uphill HARD
go ~ RISE

uphold ASSERT, BEAR, KEEP

upholsterer
~ tool AWL

UPI
part of ~ PRESS

up in ___ ARMS

"Up in Mabel's ___" ROOM

"Up in Smoke"
~ director ADLER

up in the ___ AIR

upland MOOR

uplift EXALT, RAISE

uplifting TONIC

___-upmanship ONE

UPN
~ rival ABC, CBS

Upolu
~ port APIA

upon ABOVE, ATOP, NEAR, ONTO, OVER
~ in French SUR
~ (prefix) EPI, SUR

___ upon (meet) COME

___ upon (summon) CALL

___ up on (learn about) READ

"___ upon a time..." ONCE

"___ Upon a Time in America" ONCE

"___ Upon a Time in the West" ONCE

___ up one's act CLEAN

___ up one's mind MAKE

"Up on the ___" ROOF

"___ up or shut up!" PUT

upper ABOVE
~ atmosphere SKY
~ crust CREAM, ELITE
~ garment VEST
~ hand EDGE
~ house SENATE
~ part TOP

~ (prefix) ANO
~ regions of space ETHER
gain the ~ hand BEND
have the ~ hand LEAD
having a stiff ~ lip STOIC

upper ___ CLASS, HAND

Upper ___ Side EAST

uppercut JAB
~ target CHIN

upper house
~ mem. SEN

Upper Klamath LAKE

uppermost FIRST, LEAD, MAIN, TOP

uppers
on one's ~ POOR

"Upperworld"
~ director RUTH

uppity
~ one SNIP, SNOB
act ~ SNAP

upright CLEAN, ERECT, GOOD, HONEST, MORAL, PIANO, PILE, POST, PROP, PURE, STAKE
lift ~ REAR
not ~ ATILT
remain ~ STAND
set ~ RAISE

upriser
~ for short REB

uprising RIOT

uproar ADO, DIN, MELEE, NOISE, ROW, STIR, TODO
climatic ~ STORM

___ uproar (chaotic) INAN

uproarious LOUD

uproot EXILE

ups
~ and downs LIFE

UPS
~ units LBS

upscale POSH, TONY
~ shop SALON

upset ADO, ALARM, ANGER, BEAT, ENRAGE, IRATE, IRE, JAR, MAD, RILE, SCARE, TIP
~ state SNIT
not ~ CALM, COOL, SERENE

upsetting BAD

upshot END, EVENT, ISSUE

upside
~ down OVER

upside-down CAKE

upsilon
~ follower PHI
~ preceder TAU

upstager
chronic ~ HAM

upstairs ABOVE
go ~ RISE

"Upstairs, Downstairs"
~ role MAID

upstanding ERECT, GOOD, HONEST, MORAL

upstart YAHOO

upstream
~ spawner SHAD

upswing RISE

___ upswing ONAN

uptake
fast on the ~ ALERT, APT, KEEN, SMART
slow on the ~ DENSE, DIM

upthrust RAISE

uptight EDGY, TAUT, TENSE

up to ___ PAR, SPEED

up-to-date AWARE, LATE, LIVE, MOD, NEW
make ~ RENEW

up-to-the-minute CHIC, LAST, LATE, MOD

"Uptown New York"
~ actor OAKIE

upturn RISE
brief ~ BLIP
economic ~ BOOM

"Up-Up and ___" AWAY

upward
~ extension RISE
~ of OVER
~ (prefix) ANO
move ~ ARISE, RISE

___ up with (devise) COME

___ up with (endure) PUT

Ur
~ locale IRAQ

uraeus ASP

Ural RANGE

Urals
area W of the ~ EUR
it's east of the ~ ASIA

Urania MUSE
~ sister CLIO, ERATO

uraninite ORE

uranium METAL

Uranus
~ daughter RHEA
~ to Gaea SON
child of ~ TITAN
moon of ~ ARIEL, OBERON
wife of ~ GAEA

urban
~ blight SMOG
~ district WARD
~ for short METRO
~ opposite RURAL
~ rte. AVE
~ rtes. STS
~ sprawl CITY
~ threat GANG

~ transport BUS, CAB, ELS, HACK, TAXI, TRAM
~ wailer SIREN
not ~ RURAL

Urban POPE

urbane AWARE, EASY, SUAVE

urbaneness STYLE

urchin BRAT, KID
street ~ IMP, LAD

___ urchin SEA

urethane ESTER

urge ABET, AROUSE, ASK, EGG, GOAD, IMPEL, ITCH, PLEAD, PRAY, PRESS, ROUSE, WARN, YEN
~ Fido on SIC
~ forward IMPEL
~ on ABET, EGG, MOVE, PROD, ROOT, SPUR

urgency HASTE, PRESS, STRESS
without ~ IDLY

urgent ACUTE, DIRE, LOUD
~ appeal PLEA
~ call SOS
~ letters ASAP
~ summons SOS

urges
primitive ~ IDS

Uriel ANGEL
~ instrument HARP

Uris LEON
~ character ARI

Urmia LAKE

urn EWER, JAR, POT, VASE
~ protuberance EAR
homophone for ~ EARN, ERN, ERNE

Urquhart, Sir Thomas SCOT

Ursa Major BEAR

Ursa Minor BEAR

Uru.
~ neighbor ARG

Uruguay
see Spanish

Uruguayan
~ coin PESO

us
~ according to Pogo ENEMY
~ in German UNS
~ in Spanish NOS
belonging to ~ OUR
how others see ~ IMAGE
not ~ THEM
with ~ ALIVE, HERE

"us"
"them," to ~ ENEMY, FOE

"Us" MAG

US
~ 1 RTE
~ alliance OAS
~ citizen AMER
~ leader PRES

~ missile TITAN
~ national flower ROSE
~ rocket ATLAS
Britain, to ~ ALLY
from the ~ AMER
southernmost ~ city HILO

"U.S. ___" (Jim Davis comic) ACRES

USA
~ ally ENG
~ competitor TNT
~ resident AMER
part of ~ AMER

US 95
~ terminus MIAMI

usable
make ~ ADAPT

USAF
~ bigwig GEN
~ unit SAC

USAF Academy
~ st. COL

usage HABIT, ORDER
~ fee TOLL
informal ~ SLANG

US Airways
~ rival TWA

"Us and ___" THEM

USAR
part of ~ RES

"___ us a son is given" UNTO

USA/UK
~ divider ATL

USC
~ rival UCLA

USCG
~ officer ENS
~ signal SOS

use AVAIL, PLY, TAKE, WEAR
~ a backhoe DIG
~ a ballpoint PEN, WRITE
~ a blender PUREE
~ a blower DRY, STYLE
~ a branding iron SEAR
~ a bucket BAIL
~ a calculator ADD, TOTE
~ a camcorder TAPE
~ a CB RADIO
~ acid ETCH
~ a cipher ENCODE
~ a compass ORIENT
~ a crayon COLOR, DRAW
~ a crowbar PRY
~ a cue CAROM
~ a dipper LADE
~ a door ENTER, EXIT, LEAVE
~ a doorbell RING
~ a dory OAR, ROW
~ a ewer POUR
~ a finger bowl RINSE
~ a fork EAT
~ a four-wheeler SKATE
~ a gimlet BORE
~ a glider SOAR
~ a gun SHOOT
~ a hammock LOAF, LOLL

~ **a harpoon** SPEAR
~ **a harvester** REAP
~ **a hatchet** CHOP, CUT, HEW
~ **a joystick** AVIATE
~ **a keyboard** ENTER, PLAY, TYPE
~ **a kiddie pool** WADE
~ **a kiln** BAKE, DRY
~ **a knife** CHOP, CUT, DICE, HACK, PARE, SLASH, SLICE, SLIT
~ **a letter opener** SLIT
~ **a lever** PRY
~ **a loophole** EVADE
~ **a mangle** IRON, PRESS
~ **a mattock** DIG
~ **Ameslan** SIGN
~ **a microwave** HEAT, THAW, WARM, ZAP
~ **a mouse** DRAG
~ **an abacus** ADD, TOTE
~ **an axe** CHOP, CUT, HEW, SPLIT
~ **an intercom** PAGE
~ **an oven** BAKE, HEAT, ROAST
~ **a paper towel** DRY, SOP
~ **a pencil** JOT, NOTE, WRITE
~ **a pew** SIT
~ **a plus sign** ADD
~ **a pool** SWIM
~ **a postscript** ADD
~ **a powder puff** DAB, PAT
~ **a prie-dieu** KNEEL
~ **a ray gun** ZAP
~ **a rink** SKATE
~ **a rudder** PILOT, SAIL, STEER
~ **as an excuse** PLEAD
~ **as a reference** CITE
~ **a sari** DRAPE
~ **a scope** AIM
~ **a scythe** CUT, REAP
~ **a shovel** DIG
~ **a shuttle** TAT
~ **a Singer** HEM, SEW
~ **a skiff** OAR, ROW, SAIL
~ **a skillet** FRY, SAUTE
~ **a spade** DIG
~ **a spatula** FLIP
~ **a sponge** DRY, SOP, WET
~ **a spyglass** PEER, SEE, SPOT
~ **a stiletto** STAB
~ **a stopwatch** TIME
~ **a straw** SIP
~ **a surfboard** RIDE
~ **a teaspoon** STIR
~ **a thurible** CENSE
~ **a touch-tone** CALL, RING
~ **a tub** BATHE, RINSE, SOAK, WASH
~ **a VCR** TAPE
~ **a weapon** WIELD
~ **a whetstone** HONE
~ **binoculars** EYE, PEER, SPOT, SPY
~ **Braille** READ
~ **carets** ADD, AMEND, EDIT, EMEND
~ **charcoal** DRAW

~ **coupons** SAVE
~ **crayons** COLOR
~ **credit** OWE
~ **dynamite on** BLAST
~ **effectively** WIELD
~ **force** EXERT
~ **freeways** MOTOR
~ **grindstones** HONE
~ **leverage** PRY, SWAY
~ **litmus** TEST
~ **one's fingertips** FEEL
~ **one's peepers** ESPY, EYE, SEE, SPOT, STARE
~ **one's teeth** BITE, EAT, GNAW
~ **plastic** OWE
~ **poor judgment** ERR
~ **public transportation** RIDE
~ **rollers** SET
~ **rope** BIND, LASH, LASSO, TIE
~ **sights** AIM
~ **skillfully** WIELD
~ **solder** FUSE
~ **sparingly** EKE, STINT
~ **stereotypes** LABEL
~ **the dotted line** INK
~ **the gray matter** IDEATE
~ **the scissors** CLIP, CUT, SNIP, TRIM
~ **the soft pedal** MUTE
~ **timber for support** SHORE
~ **TNT** BLAST
~ **to best advantage** AVAIL
~ **unnecessarily** WASTE
~ **up** SPEND
be of ~ AVAIL, SERVE
deny ~ BAN
grant temporary ~ **of** LEASE
have no ~ **for** ABHOR, HATE
let ~ LEND, SHARE
make ~ **of** AVAIL, TAKE, WIELD
not in ~ IDLE
pay for the ~ **of** LEASE, RENT
put to ~ AVAIL, EXERT, PLY, WIELD
show ~ WEAR
still in ~ LIVE
temporary ~ LOAN
unrestricted ~ PLAY

used OLD
~ **a candle** LIT
~ **to be** WAS, WERE
~ **up** DONE, GONE, SHOT
become ~ **(to)** ENURE, INURE
gets ~ **up** GOES
get ~ **to** ENURE, INURE, ORIENT
get ~ **to change** ADAPT
much ~ TRITE
no longer ~ DATED
not ~ NEW
previously ~ OLD
"Used ___" CARS
used car
~ **deal** RESALE
useful
~ **article** THE

~ **item** AID
~ **quality** ASSET
prove ~ AID, AVAIL, HELP
useless INEPT, NULL, VOID
make ~ SPOIL
___ user END
user-friendly
~ **feature** ICON
ush SEAT
usher BEAR, LEAD, PAGE, SEAT, SEE, SHOW
~ **ender** ETTE
~ **in** GREET, HAIL, RING, START
~ **offering** ARM
~ **out** RING
~ **route** AISLE
USMC
~ **poster word** FEW
~ **vessel** LST
USN
~ **offense** AWOL
~ **rank** CPO, ENS
USNA
~ **grad** ENS
~ **rank** CPO
part of ~ NAVAL
USO
~ **stalwart** HOPE
~ **visitors** GIS
US Open
~ **champ of 1968** ASHE
~ **org.** PGA
~ **stadium** ASHE
six-time ~ **champ** EVERT
Uspallata PASS
___ U.S. Pat. Off. REG
USPS
~ **circuit** RTE
~ **letters** RFD
~ **rival** EMAIL
~ **units** LBS
USSR
first head of the ~ LENIN
"___ Us the Waves" ABOVE
Ustinov PETER, SIR
usual
the ~ NORM
usually OFT, OFTEN
usurp GRAB, ROB, STEAL, TAKE
US-USSR
~ **pact** SALT
US Virgin Islands TER, TERR
USX
~ **product** STEEL
Ut.
see Utah

U2
~ **producer** ENO
~ **singer** BONO
~ **song** ONE
Utah STATE
~ **city** ALTA, OGDEN
~ **mountains** UINTA
~ **national forest** UINTA
~ **neighbor** IDAHO
~ **resort** ALTA
~ **state flower** SEGO
Ute TRIBE
utensil DISH, TOOL
~ **point** TINE
kitchen ~ LADLE, PAN, POT, RICER
utensils GEAR
util.
a ~ ELEC, TEL
1930s ~ **program** REA
utility
~ **building** SHED
~ **device** METER
utilize TAKE, TAP, WIELD
~ **as strength** EXERT
utilized
not ~ IDLE
utmost BEST, IDEAL, NTH, TOP
utopia EDEN
"Utopia" ESSAY
~ **author** MORE
Utopian IDEAL
Utrecht CITY
~ **neighbor** EDE
see also Dutch
utricle BAG, SAC
Utrillo
~ **contemporary** MONET
Uttar Pradesh
city in ~ AGRA
utter CRY, ENTIRE, PURE, RANK, RELATE, SAY, STATE, TALK, TELL, TOTAL
~ **defeat** ROUT
~ **loudly** BRAY
~ **sharply** RAP
utterance CRY
uttered ORAL
utterly CLEAN, FLAT
uttermost PEAK
Utu SUN
Uzbek
~ **once** SSR
Uzi GUN

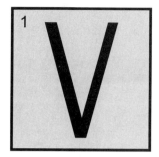

V ELEM, FIVE
  ~ sign PEACE
  ~ to a Roman FIVE
  23 for ~ ATNO
  inverted ~ CARET

"V"
  ~ villain ALIEN

V ___ SIGN

V ___ "Victor" ASIN

V ___ "victory" ASIN

V-___ NECK

Va.
  ~ neighbor KEN
  see also Virginia

vacancy VOID
  ~ sign TOLET
  motel ~ ROOM

vacant FREE, IDLE, INANE, OPEN, VOID
  make ~ CLEAR

vacate DESERT, EXIT, LEAVE, MOVE, SPLIT

vacation LEAVE, REST, STAY
  ~ mo. AUG
  ~ option TRIP
  ~ spot CAMP, CAPE, SHORE
  military ~ LEAVE
  on ~ AWAY, OFF

vacationer
  ~ goal REST, TAN

vacationing AWAY

vaccination SHOT

vaccine SERUM
  kind of ~ ORAL
  place to get a ~ ARM
  polio ~ developer SABIN, SALK

___ vaccine ORAL, SALK

vaccines SERA

vacillate EVADE, HANG, TEETER, YOYO

vacillating TORN

vacuous INANE

vacuum CLEAN, GAP, SPACE, VOID
  ~ part BAG, HOSE
  ~ target DIRT

Vader, Darth
  ~ foe SOLO
  like ~ EVIL

Vadim ROGER

vagabond HOBO, NOMAD

vagary DREAM

vagrant HOBO, NOMAD

vague DIM, LOOSE
  ~ amount SOME
  ~ idea CLUE

Vague VERA

Vail
  ~ conveyor TBAR, TOW
  enjoy ~ SKI

vain IDLE, SMUG, VOID
  be ~ POSE

vainglory POMP

Val d'___ (1992 Olympics venue) ISERE

Valdez LUIS
  ~ product OIL
  ~ state ALASKA

vale ADIEU, DALE, DELL

Valencia CITY, PORT
  see also Spanish

Valenciennes LACE

valentine HEART
  ~ color RED
  ~ purchase ROSE

Valentine's Day
  ~ figure AMOR, EROS

Valerian ROMAN

Valéry, Paul POET
  see also poet

valet HELP, MAN

Valhalla HALL
  ~ dweller ODIN, THOR

valiant GAME

Valiant, Prince HERO
  ~ son ARN

valid GOOD, LEGAL, REAL, SOLID, TRUE
  allow as ~ ADMIT
  not ~ VOID
  remain ~ HOLD

validate ATTEST, PASS, SIGN, VET

valise BAG, GRIP

Valkyries
  ~ lord ODIN
  ~ mother ERDA

Valletta
  ~ is its capital MALTA

valley DALE, GLEN, PASS, VALE
  California wine ~ NAPA
  European river ~ SAAR
  French wine ~ LOIRE
  German ~ RUHR
  lunar ~ RILL

___ Valley NAPA

"___ Valley" DEEP

___ Valley, Calif. NAPA

Valley Forge
  ~ st. PENN

___ Valley, Idaho SUN

"Valley of the ___" SUN

"___ Valley Serenade" SUN

Vallone RAF

Valmiki POET
  see also poet

valor HEART, NERVE

Valova ELENA

Valparaiso CITY, PORT
  see also Spanish

valuable ASSET, DEAR, RICH
  ~ dust GOLD
  ~ fur SABLE
  ~ possession ASSET
  ~ rock ORE

valuables LOOT, SWAG
  place for ~ SAFE

valuation EST, RATE

value MERIT, RATE
  ~ highly ESTEEM
  ~ system CODE, ETHIC

determine the ~ of ASSESS
dollar ~ COST
grocery coupon ~ CENTS
having practical ~ UTILE
item of ~ ASSET
market ~ COST
put a ~ on RATE

value-___ ADDED

___ value FACE, PAR, RESALE

Value ___ LINE

"Value ___ Money" FOR

valued DEAR
  ~ vein LODE

valueless NULL, VAIN

values
  ~ of a people ETHOS
  group ~ ETHIC

valve STOP
  ~ part STEM

vambrace ARMOR

vamoose AVOID, CUT, FLEE, LEAVE, RUN, SCAT, SCRAM

"Vamoose!" GIT, SCAT, SCRAM, SHOO

vamoosed GONE

vamp SIREN
  movie ~ BARA

"___ Vamp From East Broadway" IMA

vampire DEMON, OGRE
  ~ bane STAKE

vampire ___ BAT

vampires
  ~ do it BITE

van LEAD, MOTOR
  ~ starter MINI
  in the ~ AHEAD, FIRST
  take the ~ LEAD

van ___ Waals forces DER

Van LAKE

vanadinite ORE

vanadium METAL

Van Allen ___ BELT

Van Brocklin NORM

Vance AFB
 home of ~ ENID

Vancouver CITY, PORT
 ~ st. WASH

vandal
 ~ missile EGG

Vandal HUN

vandalize MAR, RUIN, TRASH

Vanderbilt AMY

Vanderbilt, Gloria
 ~ logo SWAN

Van Diemen's ___ LAND

Van Dine, S.S. ALIAS

Van Doren, Mark POET
 see also poet

Van Duyn MONA

Vandyke BEARD, SIR
 ~ site CHIN

vane SAIL
 ~ direction EAST, WEST
 ~ pointer ARROW

Vänern LAKE

Vanessa
 ~ sister LYNN

van Gogh
 ~ forte ART
 ~ locale ARLES
 ~ medium OIL
 ~ painting IRISES

"Van Gogh in ___" ARLES

vanguard HEAD, LEAD

Van Halen ALEX, EDDIE

vanilla BEAN

Vanilla ___ ICE

vanish DIE, END, FADE, FLEE, FLIT, MELT

vanish ___ thin air INTO

vanished GONE, LOST

"___ Vanishes, The" LADY

vanish into thin ___ AIR

vanity EGO, PRIDE
 ~ case BAG

Vanna HOST
 ~ boss MERV
 ~ cohost PAT
 ~ turnover ANA, ANE, ANI, ANO

Van Owen
 ~ player on "L.A. Law" DEY

Van Peebles MARIO

vanquish BEAT, BEST, REPEL, TRIM, UNDO, ZAP
 ~ a dragon SLAY

vanquished
 the ~ LOSER

vans
 company of moving ~ FLEET

Van Slyke ANDY

Van Winkle RIP
 emulate ~ NAP
 pull a ~ SLEEP

Vanya UNCLE

vapid ARID, BANAL, FLAT, INANE, STALE, TAME, VAIN

vapor GAS, MIST, STEAM
 ~ (prefix) ATM
 mine ~ DAMP

vapor ___ TRAIL

___ vapor WATER

vaporous DAMP

Vardon Trophy
 ~ awarder PGA

Varens
 ~ ("Jane Eyre" girl) ADELE

___ Vargas Llosa MARIO

vargueno DESK

variable
 ~ star NOVA

variable-interest
 ~ home loan ARM

variance
 at ~ AJAR

variant OTHER

variation TURN
 color ~ TONE
 extent of ~ RANGE
 poker ~ STUD

variegated PIED, SHOT
 ~ stone AGATE

variety CLASS, GENRE, ILK, LOT, OLIO, ORDER, RANGE, SORT, STAMP, TYPE

variety show
 ~ segment ACT, SKIT

varlet CAD

varmint ANIMAL

Varney, Jim
 ~ persona ERNEST

varnish ADORN, COAT, COLOR, LIE, PAINT
 ~ base ELEMI
 ~ ingredient ELEMI, LAC, RESIN

varsity ATEAM, TEAM

"Varsity ___" SHOW

"Varsity ___, The" DRAG

vary ALTER

vasculum CASE

vase
 ~ cousin JAR
 decorative ~ URN

Vasily
 see Russian

vassal LIEGE, SERF

vast AMPLE, BIG, DEEP, EPIC, GREAT, LARGE, WIDE
 ~ amount LOTS, OCEAN, SEA, SLEW, TONS
 ~ assortment ARRAY

vastness ROOM
 symbol of ~ OCEAN, SEA

vasty
 the ~ deep MAIN

vat CASE, TANK, TUB
 ~ worker DYER
 brewer's ~ TUN

VAT
 part of ~ ADDED

Vatican City
 ~ head POPE
 ~ money LIRA, LIRE
 ~ name LEO, PAUL, PIUS
 ~ site ROME
 ~ treasure PIETA

vaticinator SEER

Vättern LAKE

vaudeville
 ~ routine ACT, OLIO, SKIT
 ~ turn SOLO

vaudevillian
 ~ prop CANE

Vaughan SARAH
 ~ nickname SASSY

Vaughan, Henry POET
 see also poet

Vaughn, Robert
 ~ role SOLO

vault ARCH, BOW, CAGE, HOP, LEAP, SAFE, TOMB
 ~ of heaven BLUE
 ~ over CLEAR
 cloistered ~ ARCH
 place for a ~ APSE
 pole ~ LEAP

___ vault POLE

vaulted
 ~ alcove APSE

vaunt BOOM, BRAG

vb.
 ~ tense PRES
 ~ type INT

VCR
 ~ button EJECT, PLAY, REC, RESET, STOP
 ~ format BETA
 ~ function ERASE
 ~ input TAPE
 ~ maker RCA
 place for a ~ DEN
 use a ~ TAPE

veal MEAT
 ~ cut CHOP
 ~ source CALF

Veda
 ~ believer HINDU

Vedanta
 ~ adherent HINDU

veejay
 ~ cousin EMCEE

veep EXEC
 see also vice president

veer BEND, CUT, HEEL, SKEW, TREND, TURN, YAW

Vega STAR

vegan
 ~ taboo MEAT

Vegas
 ~ action BET
 ~ alternative RENO, TAHOE
 ~ area STRIP
 ~ cubes DICE
 ~ game FARO, KENO
 ~ headliner ANKA
 ~ machine SLOT
 ~ natural ELEVEN, SEVEN
 ~ posting ODDS
 ~ roller DIE
 work in ~ DEAL

___ Vegas, Nev. LAS

vegetable BEAN, BEET, KALE, LEEK, OKRA, ONION, PEA, PLANT, TATER, YAM
 ~ eater APHID
 ~ holder CAN
 ~ processor RICER
 Creole ~ OKRA
 curly-leafed ~ KALE
 green ~ PEA
 hashhouse ~ TATER
 leafy green ~ KALE
 orange ~ YAM
 pungent ~ LEEK
 red ~ BEET
 starchy ~ YAM
 stew ~ ONION

vegetable ___ OIL

vegetarian
 ~ no-no MEAT

vegetate IDLE, LOAF, LOLL, SIT, SLEEP

vegetation FLORA, LEAF, PLANT, TREE
 green ~ LAWN
 wetlands ~ SEDGE
 without ~ BARE

veggies
 prepare ~ CREAM, STEAM

veggie tray
 ~ item DIP, OLIVE

vehemence ARDOR, FIRE, HEAT, RAGE

vehement HOT

vehicle AUTO, BIKE, BOAT, BUS, CAB, CANOE, CAR, CART, HACK, LIMO, LINER, MOTOR, ORGAN, PLANE, PLAY, PRAM, RAFT, SHAY, SHIP, SLED, TANK, TAXI, TRAIN, UTE, VAN
 ~ sticker DECAL
 airport ~ LIMO
 all-purpose ~ UTE
 amphibious ~ LST
 Arctic ~ SLED

Army ~ TANK
celeb's ~ LIMO
city ~ BUS, CAB, HACK, TAXI
commuter ~ BUS, TRAIN
defective ~ LEMON
emergency ~ RAFT
escape ~ POD
ET ~ UFO
family ~ AUTO, CAR, VAN
farm ~ CART
golfer's ~ CART
gravity-powered ~ SLED
Hyde Park ~ PRAM
messenger's ~ BIKE
mil. landing ~ LST
moving ~ VAN
one-hoss ~ SHAY
passenger ~ AUTO, CAR
recreational ~ CANOE
Santa's ~ SLED
school ~ BUS
sci-fi ~ UFO
supermarket ~ CART
tour ~ BUS
two-wheeled ~ CART
unwheeled ~ SLED
vintage ~ NASH, REO

vehicles
commuter ~ ELS

veil BLUR, DRAPE, HIDE, MASK

"___ Veil, The" BLUE

veiling NET

veil of ___ ISIS

vein BED, CAST, MINE, MOOD, RUN, SEAM, STYLE
~ deposit ORE
leaf ~ RIB
mineral ~ LODE

Velcro
~ alternative LACE, SNAP

veldt LAND
~ beast ELAND, GNU, HYENA, LION
~ sound ROAR

vellum PAPER, SKIN

velocipede
~ need GEAR, TIRE

velocity PACE, RATE, SPEED, TEMPO
~ abbr. MPH

___ Velva AQUA

velvet
~ ender EEN

velvet ___ PLANT

"___ Velvet" BLUE

"Velvet Fog, The" MEL

velvety
~ surface NAP

vena cava
~ counterpart AORTA

vend SELL, TRADE

vending machine
~ part SLOT

vendition SALE

veneer COAT, FACE, SHEET, SKIN

venerable AGED, OLD
~ one ELDER

"Venerable"
~ writer BEDE

venerate ADORE, ESTEEM, EXALT, HONOR, LAUD

venerated DEAR

veneration AWE, ESTEEM, LOVE
object of ~ ICON, IDOL

Venetian
~ artery CANAL
~ blind SHADE
~ official DOGE
~ resort LIDO
~ traveler POLO

venetian blind
~ component SLAT
~ wood TEAK

___ Veneto VIA

Venezuela
~ falls ANGEL
~ org. OPEC
island near ~ ARUBA
see also Spanish

"Vengeance is ___..." MINE

vengefulness SPITE

Venice CITY, PORT
~ beach LIDO
~ feature CANAL
~ locale ITALY
old ruler of ~ DOGE
symbol of ~ LION
villain of ~ IAGO
see also Italian

"Venice of Japan, The" OSAKA

venison GAME, MEAT
~ source DEER

"___ Venner" ELSIE

venom BANE, BILE, HATE, IRONY, SPITE

venomous BAD, EVIL
~ snake ASP

vent EMIT, HOLE, SLIT, TALK
~ contempt SNEER
~ one's spleen RAGE
dermal ~ PORE
give ~ to POUR

ventail ARMOR

venter CRAW

ventilate AERATE, AIR

ventilated AIRY

ventilation AIR

ventilator FAN

Ventnor AVE

ventral FIN

ventricle
~ neighbor AORTA
~ neighbors ATRIA

ventriculus CRAW

Ventura ACE

venture DARE, ESSAY, RISK, SINK, STAKE, TRY
~ a thought OPINE

venue SITE, SPOT

Venus DEA, ORB, SPHERE
~ son AMOR

"Venus d'___" ARLES

Venus de Milo
~ lack ARMS

Venusian ALIEN
~ crewman on "Tom Corbett, Space Cadet" ASTRO

Venusians ETS

Venus's-flytrap PLANT

Venus's-hair FERN

Venus's-looking-glass PLANT

___ vera ALOE

Vera-___ ELLEN

veracious TRUE

Veracruz CITY, PORT
see also Spanish

veranda LANAI

verb
~ ender OSE
~ for a poet OPE
~ tense PRES
~ type INT

verbal ORAL
~ attack SLAM
~ blow LASH
~ sigh ALAS
~ skirmish SPAT

verbalize SAY, STATE, UTTER
~ anger RANT

verbalized ORAL

verbally ALOUD

verbose LONG

verboten TABOO, TABU

verde
palo ~ TREE

___ Verde National Park MESA

___ Verde, Senegal CAPE

Verdi
~ baritone IAGO
~ highlight ARIA
~ home ITALY
~ opera AIDA
~ work OPERA
see also Italian

Verdon, Gwen
~ role LOLA

Verdugo ELENA

Verdun
see French

verdure LAWN, LEAF

verdureless BARE

verecund SHY

Vereen BEN

verge EDGE, LIMIT, LIP, RIM
~ upon ABUT
on the ~ of ABOUT, NEAR

Verhoeven PAUL

verifiable REAL, TRUE

verification TEST, TRIAL

verify AUDIT

"___, verily!" YEA

"Verily!" AMEN, YEA

veritable REAL, TRUE

verity FACT

Verlaine, Paul POET
see also poet

vermicelli PASTA

vermilion COLOR, RED

vermin MOUSE

Vermont STATE
~ harvest SAP
~ tree MAPLE

vermouth WINE

vernacular ARGOT, CANT, IDIOM, SLANG

vernal NEW

Verne, Jules
~ captain NEMO

Verona CITY
~ locale ITALY
see also Italian

Veronica LAKE

Versailles
see French

versatile
~ truck UTE

versatility RANGE

verse LINE, PSALM
~ alternative PROSE
~ form ODE
~ part STAVE
~ reciter BARD
~ syllable FOOT
~ writer POET
analyze ~ SCAN
ancient Greek ~ form EPOS
light ~ creator NASH

___ verse FREE

versed ABLE, ADEPT, AWARE

versifier BARD, POET

version
abbreviated ~ MINI

verso LEAF, LEFT, PAGE, SHEET

vert COLOR

vertebra BONE
~ neighbor DISC
head-supporting ~ ATLAS

vertex ACME, CAP, NODE, PEAK, TIP

vertical AXIS, ERECT, STEEP
 be ~ STAND
 make ~ RAISE
 nearly ~ STEEP

verve ARDOR, DASH, ELAN, FIRE, LIFE, PEP, VIM, ZEAL
 sans ~ BLAH

very MOST
 ~ in French TRES

"very ___!, The" IDEA

"very foolish fond old man"
 Shakespeare's ~ LEAR

"Very funny!" HAHA

vesica SAC

vesicle SAC

Vespasian CAESAR, ROMAN

vespers HOUR

vespertilian BAT

vespiary NEST

vessel BOAT, DISH, EWER, JAR, KEEL, LINER, PAIL, POT, SHIP, TANK
 Arab ~ DHOW
 blood ~ AORTA
 chemist's ~ ETNA
 cook's ~ PAN, POT
 drinking ~ CUP
 floral ~ VASE
 Genesis ~ ARK
 glass ~ VIAL
 Golden Fleece ~ ARGO
 heating ~ ETNA
 Indian Ocean ~ DHOW
 Jason's ~ ARGO
 large ~ VAT
 light ~ LAMP
 museum ~ URN
 ocean ~ BOAT, LINER, SHIP
 OPEC ~ OILER
 passenger ~ BOAT, LINER, SHIP
 Red Sea ~ DHOW
 regatta ~ SHELL
 river ~ CANOE
 sailing ~ BOAT, SHIP, SLOOP
 spouted ~ EWER
 WWII ~ LST
 see also boat, ship

vest ATTIRE, DON, DRESS, ROBE

vestal PURE

vestibule ENTRY, HALL

vestige RELIC, SHRED, TRACE
 leave no ~ of RAZE

vestiges ASHES

"Vesti la giubba" ARIA

vestment ROBE
 church ~ ALB, COPE

vestments ARRAY, ATTIRE, DRESS, GARB
 certain ~ HABIT

vest-pocket TINY

Vesuvius
 ~ output LAVA

vet DOC
 ~ patient CALF, CAT, COW, DOG, EWE, GOAT, HOG, HORSE, KID, LAMB, MARE, MULE, PET, RAM, SOW
 case for a ~ LICE

vetch ERS, TARE

veteran ACE, ADEPT
 abbreviation for a ~ RET
 government ~ POL

veterans
 Civil War ~ org. GAR

Veterans Day
 ~ mo. NOV

veto BAN, DENY, TABOO, TABU

vetoed TABOO, TABU

vetos NOES, NOS

vex ANGER, FRET, GET, IRE, IRK, PEEVE, RILE, ROIL, TEASE

vexation ANGER, TRIAL

vexed IRATE, MAD, SORE, UPSET

vexillum FLAG

VHS
 ~ alternative BETA

VI SIX
 ~ halved III

via PER, USING

Via Appia
 ~ terminus ROME

viable LIVE

viands DIET, FARE, FEED, MEAL, MEAT

Via Veneto
 ~ auto FIAT
 see also Italian

vibes FEEL, MOOD
 bad ~ OMEN
 have ~ SENSE

___ vibes BAD

vibrancy COLOR

vibrant ALIVE, DEEP, SPRY

vibrate BEAT, RING

vibration JAR, PULSE, TREMOR

vibrations AURA, FEEL

Vic
 ~ radio wife SADE

vicar PADRE
 ~ residence MANSE

vicarage MANSE

vice EVIL, HARM, SIN

"___ Vice" MIAMI

___ Vicente, Brazil SAO

vice president
 FDR's last ~ HST
 first ~ ADAMS

Warren's ~ CAL

viceroy RULER

vice squad
 ~ action RAID

Vichy SPA
 see also French

Vichy ___ WATER

vichyssoise
 ~ ingredient LEEK

vicinage AREA

vicinity AREA, SITE
 in the ~ NEAR
 in the ~, to a poet ANEAR

vicious BAD, CRUEL, FERAL, MEAN

Vicious SID

viciousness SIN, SPITE

vicissitude TURN

vicissitudes LIFE

Vickers, Jon TENOR

Vicki VALE

Vicksburg
 ~ event SIEGE
 ~ st. MISS

victim GOAT, PREY
 ~ of deflation EGO
 asp ~ CLEO
 blight ~ ELM
 collar ~ FLEA
 conquistador ~ INCA
 curiosity ~ CAT
 razzing ~ GOAT

victimize DUPE, HAVE, ROB

Victor HUGO, MOORE

Victor ___ Hugo MARIE

Victor ___ Yung SEN

___ Victor RCA

Victoria LAKE, RULER, STA
 ~ to William IV NIECE
 one of ~'s prime ministers PEEL

Victoria Cross MEDAL

Victorian AGE, ERA, PRIG, STYLE

Victoria, Queen
 granddaughter of ~ ENA

"Victoria the ___" GREAT

victorious
 be ~ over UPSET
 emerge ~ WIN

victors
 November ~ INS

victory WIN
 ~ opposite LOSS
 ~ sign VEE
 goddess of ~ NIKE
 mat ~ PIN
 overwhelming ~ ROUT

"___ victory!" ONTO

"Victory ___" ATSEA

"Victory at ___" SEA

Victrola
 ~ descendant STEREO
 ~ maker RCA
 ~ part HORN

victual CATER

victuals DIET, EATS, FARE, FEED, MEAL, MEAT

vicuña ANIMAL
 ~ cousin CAMEL, LLAMA
 ~ home ANDES

Vida BLUE

Vidal GORE

Vidalia ___ ONION

video TAPE
 ~ arcade name ATARI
 ~ award AVA
 ~ companion AUDIO
 ~ room DEN
 make a ~ TAPE

"video"
 what ~ means ISEE

video ___ CAMERA, GAME

___ video HOME

video game
 ~ center ARCADE
 ~ hedgehog SONIC
 ~ hero MARIO
 ~ pioneer ATARI

videotape
 borrow a ~ RENT

vie PLAY
 ~ for office RUN

"___ Vie" UNE

Vienna CITY
 see also German

Vientiane
 ~ country LAOS
 capital NE of ~ HANOI

vier
 ~ preceder DREI

Vietnam
 ~ ender ESE
 ~ neighbor LAOS
 capital of ~ HANOI

Vietnamese ASIAN
 ~ city HUE
 ~ festival TET
 former ~ president DIEM

view DEEM, ESTEEM, EYE, IDEA, SCENE, SEE
 ~ as CALL
 ~ with horror ABHOR, HATE
 come into ~ EMERGE, LOOM, RISE, SHOW
 end in ~ GOAL
 express a ~ OPINE
 have in ~ AIM, MEAN
 hold in ~ SEE
 in full ~ OPEN, OVERT, SEEN
 mind's-eye ~ IMAGE
 point of ~ ANGLE, SIDE
 share a ~ AGREE

within ~ NEAR

"View of ___" TOLEDO

viewpoint ANGLE, PHASE, SLANT, STAND
  personal ~ SLANT

views
  state one's ~ OPINE

vigilance CARE

vigilant ALERT, AWARE, CLOSE, WARY
  highly ~ ALERT

vigilantes POSSE

Vigny, Alfred Victor de POET
  see also poet

Vigoda ABE

vigor ARDOR, DASH, ELAN, FIRE, LIFE, PEP, SINEW, TEETH, TONE, VIM
  full of vim and ~ HALE
  lose ~ FADE
  with fresh ~ ANEW

vigorous ALIVE, FIT, HALE, RACY, SPRY

vigorously HARD

VII SEVEN

VIII OCTO

Viking
  ~ reading EDDA
  ~ sortie RAID
  ~ touchdown site MARS
  ~ weapon AXE

Vikings ELEVEN, NORSE, TEAM
  ~ org. NFL

Vikki CARR

Vila BOB

vile BAD, BASE, EVIL, LOW, RANK

vileness DIRT

vilify ABUSE, LIBEL, SHAME, SLUR, SMEAR, TAINT

vilipend LIBEL, SLUR

villa ABODE, ESTATE, HOME
  ~ features ATRIA

Villa d'___ ESTE

"Village ___" TALE

"Village Voice"
  ~ award OBIE

villain CAD, CUR, OGRE
  ~ foe HERO
  ~ laugh HAH
  ~ visage SNEER
  greet the ~ BOO, HISS
  New Testament ~ HEROD
  opera ~, often BASS, BASSO
  Shakespearean ~ IAGO

villainess
  opera ~, often ALTO

villainous BAD, BASE, EVIL, LOW
  ~ stare LEER

villainy EVIL

villanella SONG

villanelle POEM

Villa, Pancho
  ~ coin PESO
  emulate ~ RAID
  see also Spanish

villein LIEGE, SERF

Villon, François POET
  see also poet

villus HAIR

vim ELAN, FIRE, LIFE, PEP
  full of ~ and vigor HALE

Vimy
  see French

Viña ___ Mar, Chile DEL

Viña del ___, Chile MAR

"Vincent, François, ___ and the Others" PAUL

"Vincent, François, Paul ___ the Others" AND

vinculum CORD, TIE

Vindhya ___ RANGE

vindicate AVENGE, CLEAR, FREE

vine PLANT
  ~ ender YARD
  ~ fruit MELON
  ornamental ~ IVY
  tropical ~ LIANA

vinegar ACID
  ~ partner OIL
  ~ source CIDER
  full of ~ SASSY

vinegar ___ EEL

vinegar-to-be CIDER

vinegary ACID, SOUR, TART

vines
  place for ~ ARBOR

"___ Vines Have Tender Grapes" OUR

vino
  ~ region ASTI

vintage OLD, WINE, YEAR
  ~ song OLDIE
  ~ vehicle NASH, REO

vintner
  ~ need VAT

vinyl
  ~ records LPS

viol
  ~ feature FRET

___ viol BASS

viola
  ~ cousin CELLO

violate TAINT

violating
  ~ propriety OUTRE

violation
  ~ of privileges ABUSE

violent FERAL, RABID
  ~ speech RANT
  ~ weather STORM

"Violent ___, The" ENEMY

violet COLOR
  ~ relative PANSY
  ~ starter ULTRA

violin
  ~ attachment MUTE
  ~ cousin CELLO
  ~ knob PEG
  ~ part NECK
  fine ~ AMATI

violinist
  ~ need BOW

violin maker
  Italian ~ AMATI

VIP EXEC, LION, STAR

viper ADDER, ASP, COBRA, SNAKE

___ viper PIT

virago HAG

Virgil POET, ROMAN
  ~ genre EPOS
  see also Latin, poet

Virgin
  the ~ SIGN

Virginia DARE, STATE
  ~ reel DANCE
  famous family of ~ LEES
  New World baby ~ DARE

Virginia ___ DARE, REEL

Virginia City
  ~ neighbor RENO

"___, Virginia, there is a Santa Claus" YES

"...Virginia Woolf"
  ~ author ALBEE

"Virgin in a Tree"
  ~ etcher KLEE

Virgo SIGN
  ~ preceder LEO
  mo. for ~ SEPT

virgule LINE, SLASH

virile MALE

virtual ___ IMAGE

virtually ABOUT, NEAR

virtue ASSET, GOOD, MERIT
  model of ~ SAINT
  symbol of ~ HALO

"Virtue is ___ own reward" ITS

virtueless BAD, EVIL

virtues
  second of three ~ HOPE
  sum of one's ~ to the Greeks ARETE

virtuoso ACE, ADEPT
  ~ performance ECLAT

virtuous CLEAN, GOOD, MORAL, NICE, PURE
  ~ one SAINT

path of ~ conduct TAO

virulence ANGER, EDGE, IRE, SPITE

virulent ACID, ACRID, EVIL

virus BANE, GERM

visa PASS

Visa
  ~ charge DEBT

visage FACE, MIEN
  villain's ~ SNEER

visceral INNER

viscid
  ~ substance GOO

viscount LORD, PEER, RANK, TITLE
  ~ superior EARL

Viscount TITLE

viscountess LADY, RANK

viscous
  ~ liquid OIL
  ~ substance SLIME, TAR

Viscuso SAL

Vishnu
  ~ worshiper HINDU
  avatar of ~ RAMA

visibility
  ~ hazard MIST

visible CLEAR, OPEN, OVERT
  be ~ SHOW
  become ~ EMERGE, LOOM

Visigoth
  ~ foe HUN

vision DREAM, EYE, IMAGE
  ~ starter TELE
  of ~ OPTIC
  range of ~ KEN
  see in a ~ DREAM

___ vision XRAY

visionary AERIAL, IDEAL, SEER

visit CALL, COME, SEE, STAY, STOP, TOUR
  ~ dreamland SLEEP
  ~ Nod SLEEP
  ~ the market SHOP
  Dr.'s ~ APPT
  hotel ~ STAY
  icebox ~ RAID

"Visit ___ Small Planet" TOA

"Visit From St. Nicholas, A"
  ~ opener TWAS

visiting ___ NURSE

visitor
  ~ from space ALIEN
  ~ room SALON
  annual ~ SANTA
  Ararat ~ NOAH
  birdhouse ~ WREN
  Cathay ~ POLO
  Emerald City ~ TOTO
  flower ~ BEE
  Oz ~ LION
  receive a ~ SEE

Visitor
Toyland ~ BABE
unwelcome Asian ~ FLU

Visitor NANA

visitors
~ from afar ETS
home or ~ TEAM
manger ~ MAGI

visor ARMOR, BILL, PEAK

visorless
~ cap BERET

"Vissi d'___" ARTE

"Vissi d'arte"
~ singer TOSCA

vista SCENE
planetarium ~ SKY

___ Vista ALTA

VISTA
part of ~ AMER

visual OPTIC

visual ___ AID, ARTS

visualize DREAM, SEE

vitae
lignum ~ TREE

vital ACUTE, ALIVE, BASIC, LIVE,
MAIN
~ body fluids SERA
~ fluid SAP
~ part COG
~ sign PULSE
~ spirit SOUL
~ statistic AGE
~ stats BIO
élan ~ LIFE

vitality DASH, ELAN, LIFE, PEP,
TONE, VIM
have ~ LIVE

vitalizing TONIC

vitamin
~ abbr. RDA
~ amount DOSE
~ monitors FDA
~ starter MEGA
~ unit PILL

vitamin A
~ source KALE

vitamin C ACID
~ drink ADE
~ source LIME, ORANGE

vitiate ABASE, CUT, HARM, MAR,
TAINT

vitiation TAINT

vitriol ACID

vitriolic ACID

vittles FEED, MEAT
have ~ EAT

Vittorio
see Italian

vituperate ABUSE, LIBEL, RAIL

vituperation RANT

viva
~ voce ALOUD, ORAL

"Viva ___ Vegas" LAS

vivace TEMPO

vivacious ALIVE

"Vivacious ___" LADY

vivaciousness ELAN

vivacity DASH, ELAN, FIRE, LIFE,
PEP

___ vivant BON

vive
on the qui ~ ALERT, AWARE,
WARY

"Vive ___!" LEROI

"Vive le ___!" ROI

vivid ALIVE, CLEAR, DEEP, GAY,
RICH
~ display RIOT
~ quality COLOR
not ~ PALE

vividness COLOR

vivify AROUSE, RESTORE, ROUSE

vivifying TONIC

vixen ANIMAL
~ home DEN
~ offspring KIT

vizard MASK

vizier
~ superior AGA, AGHA

Vladimir
see Russian

Vladivostok CITY, PORT

vocabulary
special ~ ARGOT

vocal ORAL
~ ender IST
~ gaffe SLIP
~ group OCTET, TRIO
~ music SONG
~ offering ARIA
~ range ALTO, BASS, TENOR
~ thumbs-down BOO

vocalize SAY, SING, TALK, UTTER
~ displeasure BOO

vocalized
~ pauses ERS

vocally ALOUD

vocation LINE, TRADE

voce
sotto ~ remark ASIDE
viva ~ ALOUD, ORAL

___ voce UNA

"___ voce poco fa" UNA

vociferate CALL, CRY, RANT, TELL,
YELL

vociferation CRY, DIN, NOISE

vociferous LOUD

vociferously ALOUD

vodka
~ cousin GIN

___ V of Norway OLAF, OLAV

vogue FAD, MODE, RAGE, STYLE,
TON, TREND
be in ~ REIGN
in ~ CHIC, HOT, NEW, NOW
no longer in ~ DATED, OUT,
PASSE

"Vogue"
~ rival ELLE

voice ALTO, BASS, SAY, TALK,
TENOR, UTTER
~ a conviction ASSERT
~ an opinion SAY
~ an opinion,
perhaps ARGUE
~ inflection TONE
~ of Charlie EDGAR
~ of Mortimer EDGAR
~ vote AYE, NAY, YEA
deep ~ BASS
gravelly ~ RASP
operatic ~ BASSO
organ ~ OBOE
raise one's ~ YELL

voice-___ OVER

voiced ALOUD, ORAL

voiceless MUTE, TACIT

"Voice of Israel"
~ author EBAN

voices
choral ~ ALTI
eight ~ OCTET
three ~ TRIO

void ABYSS, ANNUL, BARE, CLEAN,
CLEAR, EGEST, GAP, HOLE,
SPACE
~ partner NULL
declare null and ~ ANNUL

voided
~ serve LET

voila THERE

"Voina i ___" MIR

voiture MOTOR

volatility
~ measure, on Wall
Street BETA

volcanic
~ formation CONE
~ matter SLAG
~ product ASH
~ rock LAVA

volcano CONE
~ goddess PELE
~ output ASH, LAVA
~ residue ASH
~ shape CONE
Caribbean ~ PELEE
Mindanao ~ APO
Sicilian ~ ETNA

volcanoes
~ do it SPEW

vole ANIMAL
~ cousin MOUSE
~ relative RAT

___ volente DEO

Volga
see Russian

Volga River
~ denizen TATAR

Volgograd
see Russian

volitate FLIT

volley BLAST, FIRE, STORM,
STREAM

volleyball GAME
~ need NET

Vols
~ loc. TENN

Volstead
~ opponent WET

"Völsunga ___" SAGA

"Volsunga Saga"
~ king ATLI

Volta
~ subj. ELEC

voltaic cell
~ part ANODE

voluble GLIB

volume MASS, OPUS, SIZE, STORE
~ measure LITER
~ setting LOW
~ unit STERE
increase the ~ BLARE
lacking ~ THIN
scholarly ~ TOME

voluminous AMPLE, BIG, GREAT,
LARGE

voluntary FREE

volunteer
~ words ICAN

"Volunteer"
~ author AGEE

Volunteer St. TENN

vomer BONE

von Behring EMIL

von Bulow
~ portrayer IRONS

von Bulow, Sunny
~ portrayer CLOSE

von Fürstenberg DIANE

von Richthofen ACE, BARON

Von Ryan's Express TRAIN

Von Sydow, Max SWEDE

von Trapp MARIA

voodoo
~ country HAITI

voracious AVID

voracity LUST

"-vore"
 what ~ means EATER

Vork
 ~ country EIRE, ERIN

vortex EDDY

Vosges RANGE

"___ vostra salute" ALLA

vote ELECT, POLL, SAY
 ~ **against** CON, NAY
 ~ **for** ADOPT, AYE, YEA, YES
 ~ **in** ELECT
 ~ **seeker** POL
 straw ~ POLL

___ vote STRAW

votes
 group that ~ **alike** BLOC
 negative ~ NOES, NOS

vote with one's ___ FEET

voting
 ~ **district** WARD
 ~ **group** BLOC
 ~ **list** POLL

voting booth
 ~ **closer** LEVER

___ votre permission AVEC

vouch ATTEST, AVER, AVOW, SAY
 ~ **for** ASSERT

voucher ALIBI, PAPER

___ vous plaît SIL

Vouvray WINE

vow OATH
 ~ **giver** MATE
 marriage ~ IDO
 pronoun in a wedding
  ~ THEE
 solemnly ~ AVER

vowel
 Greek ~ ETA, IOTA, OMEGA

vows
 ~ **venue** ALTAR
 make ~ WED

voyage TRIP
 bon ~ ADIEU
 embark on a ~ SAIL
 on a ~ ASEA, ATSEA

"___ voyage!" BON

"___ Voyage, The" LAST

"___ Voyage, Charlie Brown" BON

"___ Voyage Home, The" LONG

"Voyager"
 ~ **org.** NASA
 home of ~ EARTH

"___, Voyager" NOW

"Voyagers"
 Phineas Bogg's time travel device in ~ OMNI

voyages
 number of ~ **of Sinbad** SEVEN

"Voyage to the Bottom of the ___" SEA

"Voyage to the Bottom of the Sea"
 ~ **director** ALLEN

voyaging ASEA, ATSEA

Vronsky
 ~ **girl** ANNA

vroom ROAR

"___ vs. the Flying Saucers" EARTH

___ vs. Wade ROE

Vt.
 ~ **clock setting** EDT, EST
 ~ **neighbor** MASS
 see also Vermont

Vulcan GOD

vulcanize BAKE

vulcanologist
 ~ **concern** LAVA

Vulcan's
 ~ **forge** ETNA

vulgar BLUE, CRASS, LEWD, LOW, RACY
 ~ **masses** MOB

vulgarian BOOR

vulnerability PERIL, RISK

vulpine SLY

vulture BIRD

VW
 ~ **preceders** STU

W ELEM
74 for ~ ATNO

"W" MAG

WA
clock setting in ~ PDT, PST
see also Washington

Wabash
~ st. IND

Wabash Cannonball TRAIN

wabbit
~ antagonist ELMER

"Wackiest ___ in the Army, The"
SHIP

"Wackiest Ship in the ___, The"
ARMY

wacko MAD

wacky BATS, DAFT, LOCO, MAD,
ODD
not ~ SANE

wad CLOD, GOB, MINT, PILE, ROLL
one of a ~ CNOTE

wadding PAD

wade
~ through PORE, READ, SLOG

Wade
~ opponent ROE

wader BOOT
marsh ~ EGRET, HERON
Nile ~ IBIS

wadi STREAM

wading
~ bird CRANE, EGRET, HERON,
IBIS, RAIL, STILT

waferlike THIN

waffle EVADE, SWAY

waffle ___ IRON

waft AROMA, STREAM
~ over KISS
it may ~ AROMA

wag CARD, LASH, WIT
~ remark PUN

wage FEE

wage ___ SCALE

wager BET, GAME, LAY, PUT, STAKE
lay a ~ BET, PLAY
minimum ~ CHIP
opening ~ ANTE
place a ~ BET

wages PAY
collect ~ EARN

wagger TAIL

waggish ARCH

waggishness WIT

waggle BOB, FLAP

Wagner
~ character ERDA
~ cycle RING
~ earth goddess ERDA
~ heroine ELSA, EVA, SENTA
~ work OPERA
TV role for ~ HART
see also German

Wagner, Honus
like a ~ baseball card RARE

wagon CART
~ load HAY
~ part AXLE
hitch one's ~ to a star AIM
station ~ AUTO, CAR, MOTOR
team and ~ RIG

wagon ___ TRAIN

wagon- ___ LIT

___ wagon TEA

"___ Wagon, The" BAND, LAST,
WAR

wagon-lit CAR, TRAIN

wagon train
~ direction WEST
~ puller MULE

"Wagon Train"
~ character SETH

wahine
~ dance HULA
~ feast LUAU
~ instrument UKE
~ wear LEI
~ welcome ALOHA

wahoo TREE

Waianae RANGE

Waikiki
~ feast LUAU
~ island OAHU
~ music maker UKE
~ wear LEI
~ welcome ALOHA
see also Hawaiian

wail BAWL, CRY, KEEN, MOAN,
NOISE, SOB, WEEP

wailer
urban ~ SIREN

wailing
~ instrument SAX

wainscot PANEL

wainscoting PANEL

waist
~ band SASH
~ neighbor HIP

waistcoat VEST

wait ABIDE, BIDE, DEFER, SIT, STAY
~ in line STAND
~ on ATTEND, SERVE
~ on the telephone HOLD
~ partner SEE
~ upon SERVE
not ~ ACT
where passengers ~ DEPOT

"Wait ___ Dark" UNTIL

"Wait ___ the Sun Shines, Nellie"
TIL

"Wait a ___!" SEC

"Wait a minute!" HEY

wait and ___ SEE

waited BODE

waiter
~ at times ADDER
~ burden TRAY
~ offering MENU
~ request ORDER
~ reward TIP
~ starter HEAD
help a ~ BUS
one way to call a ~ AHEM

**"Waiter and the Porter and the
Upstairs ___, The"** MAID

waiting
~ in the wings ONTAP

waiting ___ GAME, LIST, ROOM

"Waiting for Godot"
~ actor LAHR

"Waiting for Lefty"
~ playwright ODETS

"Waiting for the Robert ___"
ELEE

waiting room
~ cry NEXT
~ reading MAG

waitress
~ at Mel's ALICE, FLO, VERA
initials for a ~ BLT

waits
it ~ for no man TIME

"Wait 'Til the ___ Shines, Nellie"
SUN

Waitz, Grete
~ birthplace OSLO

waive CEDE, DROP, YIELD

wake TAIL, TRACE, TRAIL
~ location ASTERN
~ up ARISE, AROUSE, ROUSE,
STIR
boat's ~ WASH
in the ~ of AFTER

"Wake Me Up Before You ___"
GOGO

"Wake Me When ___ Over" ITS

"Wake Me When It's ___" OVER

"Wake Me When It's Over"
~ director LEROY

waken AROUSE, CALL, RAISE, RISE

waker-upper ALARM

wake-up
~ call ALARM
~ times AMS
farmer's ~ call CROW

"Wake Up ___ Live" AND

"Wake Up and ___" LIVE

waking
~ up ASTIR

wanting NEEDY, POOR

"___ want is a room somewhere..." ALLI

wanton FAST, LEWD, LOOSE
~ **look** LEER
~ **revelry** ORGY

wantonness LUST

"___ Wants Mink, The" LADY

wapiti ANIMAL, DEER, ELK

war GAME
~ **club** MACE
~ **game** TEST
~ **hero** ACE
~ **partner** ALLY
~ **starter** ANTI
1960s ~ zone NAM
goddess of ~ ATHENA
Greek ~ god ARES
Norse ~ god ODIN
old ~ story ILIAD
prepare for ~ ARM
Roman ~ god MARS

war ___ BRIDE, CHEST, CRY, DANCE, GAME, PAINT, ZONE

war-___ HORSE

"War ___, The" GAME, LORD, ROOM

"War ___ Peace" AND

___ War (1899-1902) BOER

"___ & War" LOVE

"War and ___" PEACE

"War and ___" PEACE

"War and Peace" EPIC

"War As I ___ It" KNEW

warble PIPE, SING, YODEL

warbler BIRD, WREN

___ warbler PINE

Warbucks, Daddy
~ **underling** ASP
~ **ward** ANNIE
like ~ RICH

ward
~ **heeler** POL
~ **off** AVERT, STEM
~ **(off)** FEND

Ward
~ **to the Beaver** DAD

Ward, Artemus
~ **birthplace** MAINE

___ warden GAME

wardrobe ATTIRE, GARB

warehouse DEPOT, STORE, STOW
~ **platform** SKID
~ **receptacle** BIN
~ **unit** TON

wares
~ **(abbr.)** MDSE
butcher's ~ MEAT

warfare
lack of ~ PEACE

Warhol ANDY
~ **film** TRASH
~ **subject** CAN, MAO
~ **work** ART

Waring FRED

warlock MALE

warm CLOSE, MILD, NEAR, RICH
~ **greeting** KISS
~ **oneself** BASK
~ **sensation** GLOW
~ **so to speak** NEAR
~ **spell** THAW
~ **up** HEAT, MELT, THAW
moderately ~ TEPID

warm-___ UPS

warmed-over BANAL, FLAT, STALE, TIRED, TRITE

warmer
bench ~ SUB
neck ~ SCARF
winter ~ COAT, COCOA

warm-hearted NICE

warmonger
Greek ~ ARES
Roman ~ MARS

Warm Springs SPA

warmth ARDOR, COLOR, GLOW, HEART, HEAT, LIFE, LOVE
~ **of feeling** ARDOR
savor the ~ BASK
source of ~ SUN

warm-up PREP

warn ALARM, ALERT

Warner Bros.
one of the ~ ABE

warning ALARM, ALERT, HINT, OMEN, SIGN, SIREN
~ **light** FLARE
~ **signal** HORN
~ **sound** SIREN
~ **to baby** NONO
canine ~ GNAR, SNARL
fairway ~ FORE
floor-model ~ ASIS
highway ~ SLO
merchandise ~ ASIS
police-car ~ SIREN
ring a ~ bell ALARM
road-repair ~ SLOW
roadside ~ FLARE
road-sign ~ DIP
storm ~ ALERT
thruway ~ SLO
without any ~ BANG
word of ~ DONT

___ warning STORM

"Warning ___" SHOT

___-warning system EARLY

War of 1812
~ **battle site** ERIE

"War of the ___, The" ROSES

"War of the Worlds"
~ **planet** MARS

warp BEND, CAST, LIE

___ warp TIME

warped BENT

warrant ATTEST, EARN, LET, MERIT, OATH, WRIT
~ **officer** RANK

warranted DUE

warranty
without a ~ ASIS

warren
~ **female** DOE

Warren EARL, MOON, OATES
~ **V.P.** CAL

Warren, Mrs.
~ **creator** SHAW

Warren, Robert Penn POET
see also poet

"___ Warren's Profession" MRS

warrior
fifth-century ~ HUN
intrepid ~ LION
Wednesday's ~ ODIN

"___ Warrior" ROAD

warriors
turf ~ GANG

Warriors FIVE, TEAM
~ **org.** NBA

war-room
~ **fixture** MAP

"___ Wars" STAR

Warsaw CITY, PACT
~ **native** POLE

Warsaw ___ PACT

Warsaw Pact
~ **leader** USSR
~ **opposite** NATO

warship
~ **initials** USS

warships
of ~ NAVAL

"Warszawa"
~ **instrumentalist** ENO

wart NODE
~ **ender** HOG

warthog ANIMAL

warts
~ **and all** ASIS

warty
~ **critter** TOAD

"War Wagon, The" OATER

Warwick
~ **river** AVON

wary ALERT, AWARE, LEERY, SHY

"___ was a child and I was a child..." SHE

"___ Was a Crooked Man..." THERE

"___ was a cunning hunter" ESAU

"___ was a man!" THIS

"___ Was a Rollin' Stone" PAPA

Wasatch RANGE
~ **ski resort** ALTA
~ **state** UTAH

"...was blind but now ___" ISEE

"___ was going to St. Ives..." ASI

wash BATHE, CLEAN, LAVE, PAINT, SWAB
~ **against** BATHE, LAP, LAVE
~ **away** ABRADE, ERODE
~ **cycle** RINSE, SOAK, SPIN
~ **down** HOSE
~ **ender** ABLE, DAY, RAG, STAND, TUB
~ **off** RINSE
~ **out** ERODE, FADE
~ **over** SLOP
~ **water** BATH
get ruined in the ~ RUN

wash ___ (fail) OUT

___ wash CAR

Wash
~ **tributary** OUSE

Wash.
~ **neighbor** IDA, ORE
see also Washington

"___ Wash" CAR

wash-and-___ WEAR

wash-and-wear
~ **material** NYLON

Washbourne MONA

washbowl SINK

washcloths LINEN

washed CLEAN
~ **out** PALE
~ **up** DONE

___-washed ACID

washed-out PALE

washer RING
~ **contents** LOAD
~ **cycle** RINSE, SOAK, SPIN
~ **fuzz** LINT
gully ~ RAIN

washing BATH

washing ___ SODA

Washington DINAH, LAKE, NED, STATE
~ **(abbr.)** PRES
~ **and others** MTS
~ **bill** ONE
~ **couldn't tell it** ALIE
~ **helper** AIDE
~ **hostess** MESTA
~ **hundred** SENATE
~ **neighbor** IDAHO, OREGON
~ **paper** POST
~ **portraitist** PEALE
~ **subway** METRO
~ **successor** ADAMS

bane for ~ LIE
part of ~'s signature GEO

"Washington ___ here" SLEPT

Washington, George
~ no-no LIE
~ opponent HOWE

Washoe TRIBE

washout DUD, LOSER

washroom BATH

washstand
~ item EWER

wash-up BATH

wasn't
~ colorfast BLED
~ it HID
~ kidding MEANT

"___ was only a bird..." SHE

wasp PEST
~ colony NEST
~ prey ANT

waspish SOUR, TART, TESTY

Wass TED

wassail
~ ingredient WINE

wassailer
~ song CAROL

"___ was saying,..." ASI

waste DESERT, DIRT, HARM, PINE,
SLAY, SLOP
~ allowance TRET
~ away ERODE, FADE, FLAG,
PINE
~ maker HASTE
~ material SCRAP
~ no time DASH, FLEE, HIE,
RACE, RUN, SPEED
~ time IDLE, LAG, LOAF
go to ~ LOSE
lay ~ BLAST, RAID, RAZE, RUIN,
SACK

"Waste ___, The" LAND

wasted LOST

wasteland DESERT, MOOR

"Waste Land, The" POEM
~ author ELIOT
~ mo. APR
~ monogram TSE
~ month APRIL

"___ Was That Lady?" WHO

"___ was the sky so deep a hue"
NEER

watch EYE, NOTE, SEE, STARE
~ a toddler SIT
~ ender BAND, DOG
~ feature ALARM
~ for AWAIT
~ intently STARE
~ one's intake DIET
~ over ATTEND, SIT, TEND
~ part DIAL, FACE, HAND,
STEM
~ secretly SPY, TAIL

~ starter STOP
~ the birdie SMILE
~ the river flow LOAF
on a whale ~ perhaps ASEA,
ATSEA
on the ~ ALERT
something to ~ STEP
update a ~ RESET

watch ___ CAP

watch ___ (be careful) OUT

watch ___ (tend) OVER

watchband STRAP

watcher
ardent ~ FAN

___ watcher BIRD

watchful ALERT, AWARE, LEERY,
WARY

watchfulness CARE

"Watch on the ___" RHINE

watchword SIGN

"Watch your ___!" STEP

water TEAR, WET
~ barrier DAM
~ bird COOT
~ buffalos OXEN
~ carrier HOSE, PAIL, PIPE
~ closet BATH, LOO
~ color AQUA
~ colors PAINT
~ container CUP, EWER, OLLA,
PAIL, PAN, POT, URN, VASE
~ cooler ICE
~ craft BOAT, CANOE, DHOW,
LINER, SHIP, SLOOP
~ down CUT, THIN, WET
~ droplets DEW
~ ender BED, COLOR, CRESS,
LOG, MELON, SHED
~ form STEAM
~ hole LAKE, POND, POOL
~ in French EAU
~ in Latin AQUA
~ in Spanish AGUA
~ lily leaf PAD
~ main PIPE
~ moccasin SNAKE
~ mover OAR
~ nymph NAIAD
~ organism ALGA
~ pipe MAIN
~ pistol TOY
~ pitcher EWER
~ plant ALGA
~ polo GAME
~ (prefix) AQUA
~ receptacle SINK
~ source TAP
~ sport POLO
~ starter DISH, FIRE, HEAD,
LIME, RAIN, UNDER
~ tester TOE
~ thoroughly SOAK
add ~ to THIN
body of ~ LAKE, OCEAN,
POND, POOL, SEA, TARN
cook in ~ BOIL
covered with ~ AWASH
empty of ~ BAIL

frozen ~ ICE
get ~ from a well DRAW
glide on ~ SKI
go by ~ SAIL
heat ~ BOIL
hold ~ WASH
hot ~ HOLE
it'll hold ~ CUP, EWER, OLLA,
PAIL, PAN, POT, VASE
keep one's head above
~ TREAD
leave the ~ EMERGE
low ~ EBB
moisten with ~ WASH
of the first ~ RARE
out of the ~ ASHORE
play in the ~ BATHE, SWIM,
WADE
quinine ~ TONIC
ring of ~ MOAT
salt ~ BAY, OCEAN, SEA
solid ~ ICE
stagnant ~ POOL
step through ~ WADE
still ~ POND, POOL
take on ~ LEAK
toilet ~ SCENT
tread ~ SWIM
wash ~ BATH
without ~ ARID, DRY, NEAT,
SERE

water ___ BED, BIRD, DOG, GAP,
GUN, HOLE, LILY, LINE, MAIN,
MILL, PIPE, POLO, RAT, SKI,
TABLE, TAXI

water ___ the bridge UNDER

___ water BATH, HOT, ICE, ROSE,
SODA, TAP, TREAD

**Water ___ ("Wind in the
Willows" character)** RAT

"___ Water" HOT

Water Bearer
the ~ SIGN

watercolor ART, PAINT
~ application WASH

watercolorist
marine ~ HOMER

watercolors MEDIA

watercourse CANAL, RACE
dry ~ WADI

watercraft BOAT, CANOE, DHOW,
LINER, SHELL, SHIP, SLOOP

watercress
~ unit SPRIG

watered
~ down TAME
~ silk MOIRE

watered-down FLAT, THIN
~ ideas PAP

"___ Waterfowl" TOA

waterfront
~ org. ILA
beyond the ~ ASEA, ATSEA
city with a ~ PORT

Watergate
~ acronym CREEP
~ record TAPE
~ witness DEAN

watering
~ hole BAR, OASIS, POND

watering ___ CAN, HOLE

watering can
~ alternative HOSE

waterless ARID, DESERT, DRY,
SERE

"Water Lilies"
~ painter MONET

waterlogged WET

Waterloo
~ site IOWA
meet one's ~ LOSE

"Waterloo"
~ band ABBA

"Waterloo ___" ROAD

"Waterloo Bridge"
~ director LEROY
~ painter MONET

Waterman
~ filler INK
~ invention PEN

watermelon
~ covering RIND
~ shape OVAL
like ~ SEEDY

water park
~ feature SLIDE

water power
~ org. TVA

waterproof
make ~ SEAL

waters
healing ~ SPA
like still ~ DEEP

Waters ALICE, ETHEL

"___ Waters" MATT

Waters, Ethel
~ song DINAH

"Watership Down"
~ author ADAMS

waterside LAND, SHORE

Waterston SAM

___ water taffy SALT

waterway STREAM
~ in Spanish RIO
narrow ~ CANAL

"Waterworld"
~ girl ENOLA

watery DAMP, THIN, WET
~ expanse OCEAN, SEA
~ tint AQUA
~ trench MOAT

Watkins PETER

Watkins ___, N.Y. GLEN

WATS
part of ~ AREA, WIDE

Watson
~ and others MDS
~ to Bell ASST

Watson and Crick
~ concern DNA

watt
~ starter MEGA

Watts ANDRE
~ instrument PIANO

Watusi DANCE

Waugh ALEC

wave FLAP, SET, SIGN, STREAM
~ a red flag ENRAGE
~ away SHOO
~ destination SHORE
~ down FLAG, HAIL
~ in Spanish OLA
~ part CREST
~ phenomenon CHOP
big ~ SEA
catch a ~ RIDE
certain ~ PERM

___ wave HEAT, NEW, RADIO, SINE, TIDAL

wavelength
on the same ~ ALIKE

waveless CALM

wavelike
~ pattern MOIRE

waver HANG, TEETER
flag ~ GALE

___-waver FLAG

"Waverley"
~ author SCOTT

waves
braving the ~ ASEA, ATSEA
it makes ~ OCEAN, SEA
ride the ~ SAIL
sound of ~ ROAR
wash against, as ~ LAP

___ waves MAKE

waves of grain
~ color AMBER

wavy
~ design MOIRE

___ Wawa (Radner character) BABA

wax BOOM, GROW, RISE, SHINE
~ closure SEAL
~ ecstatic RAVE
~ eloquent EMOTE, ORATE
~ maker BEE
~ producer EAR
apply ~ to SEAL
opposite of ~ WANE

wax ___ BEAN, PALM, PAPER, PLANT

waxbill BIRD

waxen PALE

Waxman
~ and others ALS

way HABIT, LANE, MODE, PATH, ROAD, STYLE
~ about one AIR
~ back when ONCE, PAST, YORE
~ down DEEP, LOW
~ down yonder FAR
~ ender BILL, LAY, SIDE
~ in DOOR, ENTRY, GATE
~ in Italian VIA
~ in Latin ITER
~ in Spanish VIA
~ off AFAR, FAR, RAMP, YON
~ of walking GAIT
~ on RAMP
~ out DOOR, EXIT, GATE
~ starter ALLEY, ARCH, AREA, BIKE, DOOR, FAIR, FREE, GANG, HALF, HALL, HEAD, LEE, RAIL, ROAD, ROLL, RUN, SLIP, SOME, STAIR, SUB, WATER
~ through PASS
~ to go ROUTE
~ to the altar AISLE
~ up STAIR
~ up the slope TBAR, TOW
~ west TRAIL
~ with a no. RTE
~ with words TACT
a long ~ off AFAR, FAR
back ~ ALLEY
be on one's ~ MOVE, RUN
by ~ of VIA
feel one's ~ ORIENT
force one's ~ in ENTER
forest ~ PATH
get in the ~ DETER
get out of the ~ EVADE
get the old-fashioned ~ EARN
give ~ BEND, LAPSE, YIELD
give ~ (to) DEFER
in a different ~ ANEW
in a lazy ~ IDLY
in no ~ NONE
in that ~ ERGO, THEN, THUS
in the same ~ as LIKE
make (one's ~) WEND
middle ~ MEAN
on one's ~ OFF
on the ~ out OLD, PASSE
out of harm's ~ ALEE, SAFE
out of the ~ ASIDE, FAR
paper deliverer's ~ ROUTE
pave the ~ AID, EASE, HELP
pick one's ~ FEEL
rub the wrong ~ FRET, IRE, IRK, PEEVE, RILE
rustic ~ LANE
set on its ~ SEND
show the ~ LEAD, USHER
smooth the ~ EASE
stand in the ~ BAR, CLOG
the ~ the ball bounces LOT
trodden ~ PATH
walk a long ~ HIKE, TREK
wing one's ~ SOAR
work one's ~ up RISE

___ way (sort of) INA

"Way ___, The" AHEAD

"Way ___ West" OUT

"___ Way, The" HARD

"___ Way" (Sinatra bio) HIS

"Way Ahead, The"
~ director REED

___-way chili FIVE

"Way Down ___" EAST

wayfarer
~ refuge INN

"___ Way for Tomorrow" MAKE

waylay ROB

Wayne DYER

Wayne, Anthony
epithet for ~ MAD

Wayne, Bruce
~ dog ACE
~ home MANOR

Wayne, John
~ birthplace IOWA
~ film, with "The" ALAMO

"Wayne's World"
~ catchword NOT
~ town AURORA

"Way Out ___" WEST

"Way Out West"
~ director HORNE

"___ Way Passage" ONE

ways
a ~ away AFAR, FAR
change one's ~ MEND
go separate ~ SPLIT

"___ Ways" EVIL

___-way street ONE, TWO

"___ Way Stretch" TWO

"Way to ___, The" LOVE

"way to a ___ heart..., The" MANS

"___ way to go!" ATTA

"Way to the ___, The" STARS

wayward
~ ice BERG

"Way We ___, The" WERE

"Way West, The"
~ actor ELAM

WBA ASSN
~ decision TKO

W.C. Fields
~ costar MAE
~ persona SOT

"W.C. Fields ___ Me" AND

we
as ~ speak LIVE
what have ~ here OHO

"We ___ Family" ARE

"We ___ Need Another Hero" DONT

"We ___ Not Alone" ARE

"We ___ not amused" ARE

"We ___ no thin red 'eroes" ARENT

"We ___ Strangers" WERE

"We ___ the Champions" ARE

"We ___ the World" ARE

"We ___ to please" AIM

weak DIM, FLAT, PALE
~ as an excuse LAME

weaken ABATE, CUT, DIE, ERODE, FADE, FLAG, PINE, SAG, SAP, THIN, WANE

weakening WANE

weaker
~ ones PREY

weak-kneed LIMP

weak-minded DAFT

weakness
have a ~ for LIKE

weak-willed
~ one SOP

weal GOOD

"___ We All?" ARENT

wealth ASSET, EASE, ESTATE, GOLD, MINE, PILE
total ~ ESTATE

wealthy FAT, RICH
~ one HAVE

weapon ARM, ARROW, BOW, GUN, SPEAR
archer's ~ ARROW, BOW
boxer's ~ JAB
Cupid ~ ARROW, BOW
dueler's ~ EPEE
jousting ~ LANCE
lobster's ~ CLAW
picador's ~ LANCE
underworld ~ GAT, ROD

weaponless CLEAN

weaponry ARMS

weapons
equip with ~ ARM
lge. caliber ~ ARTY
provide with new ~ REARM

wear ATTIRE, DON, ERODE, MODEL

wear ___ THIN

wear and ___ TEAR

"We are ___ amused" NOT

wearisome DRY
become ~ PALL

weary ALLIN, BORE, JADE, LIMP, SPENT
grow ~ FLAG, SAG, TIRE

weasel ANIMAL, ERMINE, SNEAK, STOAT
~ cousin OTTER, SABLE
~ out of EVADE
~ word POP

weather BEAR, LAST, STAND
  ~ forecast CLEAR, COOL, DAMP, DRY, FAIR, GALE, HAIL, HOT, MILD, RAIN, SLEET, SNOW, STORM, WARM, WET
  ~ indicator VANE
  ~ phenomenon STORM
  ~ system LOW
  away from the ~ ALEE
  feel under the ~ AIL
  inclement ~ GALE, RAIN, SLEET, SNOW
  like autumn ~ CRISP
  stormy ~ GALE
  under the ~ ACHY, ILL
  violent ~ GALE, STORM
  wet ~ RAIN, SLEET, SNOW
  winter ~ SLEET, SNOW

weather ___ EYE, MAP, STRIP

weather-___ WISE

weather-beaten AGED, EROSE, OLD

weathercock VANE

___-weather friend FAIR

weatherworn EROSE

weave BIND, KNIT, SPIN
  ~ a chair seat CANE
  ~ mate BOB
  ~ together KNIT
  glossy ~ SATIN
  hammock ~ NET

weaver
  ~ device LOOM
  ~ hitch KNOT

___ weaver ORB

Weaver EARL

Weaver, Sigourney
  1979 ~ film ALIEN

"Weavers: Wasn't ___ a Time!, The" THAT

"Weavers: Wasn't That a ___!, The" TIME

web MESH, SNARE
  make a ~ SPIN
  spider ~ NET

webbing LACE, MESH, NET

Weber
  ~ opera OBERON

web-footed
  ~ bird AUK
  ~ mammal OTTER

web site
  ~ language JAVA

Webster NOAH

Webster, Daniel ORATOR

Webster, Noah
  ~ alma mater YALE

Web, the
  exchange words on ~ CHAT

"___ We Can Can" YES

"We Can Work It ___" OUT

wed ALLY, MATE, MELD, TIE, UNITE
  ~ in haste ELOPE

wedded ONE

Weddell SEA

wedding UNION
  ~ band RING
  ~ conveyance LIMO
  ~ dessert CAKE
  ~ finery LACE, SATIN
  ~ guest INLAW
  ~ party member BRIDE, USHER
  ~ party members KIN
  ~ phrase IDO
  ~ route AISLE
  ~ site ALTAR
  ~ tradition TOAST
  avoid a big ~ ELOPE
  old-fashioned ~ word OBEY
  pronoun in a ~ vow THEE

wedding ___ BAND, CAKE, RING

wedding announcement
  ~ word NEE

wedding cake STYLE
  ~ figurine BRIDE
  ~ layer TIER

wedding gown
  ~ fabric LACE, SATIN

"___ Wedding Journey" THEIR

wedding song
  ~ start HERE

wedeln
  perform a ~ SKI

wedge IRON, SLICE, STOW
  ~ in JAM
  social ~ ENTREE

Wedgeworth ANN

wedgie SHOE

"We Didn't ___ the Fire" START

Wednesday
  ~ warrior ODIN

___ Wednesday ASH

"___ Wednesday" ANY

"We Don't Need Another ___" HERO

"We Do Our Part"
  ~ org. NRA

wee ELFIN, SMALL, TEENY, TINY
  ~ amount BIT
  ~ bit IOTA
  ~ hour ONE, TWO
  ~ one TOT, TYKE
  ~ worker ANT
  a ~ drop DRAM
  until the ~ hours LATE

weed HOE, PLANT, RAKE
  ~ chopper HOE
  ~ out COMB, ROOT, THIN
  ~ starter RAG
  Biblical ~ TARE
  grow like a ~ RIOT

___ weed LOCO

weeding
  ~ tool HOE

weedy LANK, THIN

wee hours
  in the ~ LATE

week
  ~ component DAY

weekday
  ~ abbr. FRI, MON, WED

"___ Weekend, The" LOST

"Weekend in Havana"
  ~ director LANG

weekly ORGAN, PAPER, SHEET

weeks
  ~ per annum LII
  fifty-two ~ YEAR

"___ Weeks in Another Town" TWO

Weems TED

ween DEEM

weeny SMALL, TINY

___-weeny TEENY

weep BAWL, CRY, MOAN, OOZE, RAIN, SEEP, SOB
  ~ (for) FEEL
  ~ over RUE

weeper
  ~ perhaps LOSER

weevil PEST

"___ we forget..." LEST

"___ We Got Fun?" AINT

"___! We Have No Bananas" YES

"___ we having fun yet?" ARE

"We hold ___ truths..." THESE

weigh ASSAY, ASSESS, MUSE, RATE
  ~ anchor LEAVE, SAIL
  ~ down LADE, LOAD, TASK
  ~ the merits of ASSESS
  ~ upon PRESS

weighed
  ~ down LADEN

weight LOAD, ONUS, RANK, STRESS
  ~ allowance TRET
  ~ deduction TARE
  ~ off one's mind LOAD
  ~ starter OVER, PAPER
  ~ system TROY
  ~ unit CARAT, DRAM
  ~ units LBS
  Asian ~ TAEL
  carry ~ RATE
  empty-vehicle ~ TARE
  freight ~ TON
  gemstone ~ CARAT
  gold ~ GRAM
  have ~ RANK
  heavy ~ TON
  Indian ~ SER
  jeweler's ~ CARAT, KARAT
  lab ~ GRAM

light ~ OUNCE
  lose ~ DIET, SLIM
  metric ~ GRAM, TON
  pharmacist's ~ DRAM, GRAM
  put on ~ GAIN
  unit of ~ GRAM, OUNCE, TON

weightlifter
  ~ muscles ABS
  ~ pride TORSO
  ~ unit REP

weight loss
  ~ program DIET

weighty BIG, DEEP, GREAT, LARGE, SOBER
  ~ reading TOME

Weimar
  see German

weir DAM

Weir PETER

weird EERIE, EERY, ODD

"Weird Al"
  ~ Yankovic film UHF

weirdo BIRD, NUT

Weis DON

Weisberg ROGER

Weisshorn ALP

Welby, Marcus
  ~ and others DRS, MDS
  ~ org. AMA

welcome ADMIT, AVE, GREET, HAIL, MEET, SEE
  ~ item MAT
  ~ mat RUG
  ~ order from the D.I. ATEASE
  ~ uncivilly BOO, HISS
  Honolulu ~ ALOHA, LEI

welcome ___ MAT

"Welcome to ___ Times" HARD

welcoming
  ~ word ENTER

weld ARC, FUSE, UNITE

welfare AID, DOLE, GOOD, SAKE

welkin BLUE

Welk, Lawrence
  ~ intro AONE
  one-two link for ~ ANDA

well FIT, SAFE
  ~ contents INK, OIL, WATER
  ~ forth STREAM
  ~ out OOZE
  ~ partner ALIVE
  ~ qualified ABLE
  ~ starter FARE, INK, SPEED, STAIR
  ~ thought-out SANE
  alive and ~ SAFE
  as ~ ALSO, THEN, TOO
  as ~ as ALONG, ALSO, AND
  be not ~ AIL
  do ~ ACE
  do ~ in school LEARN
  fare thee ~ ADIEU, ADIOS, BYE, LATER, TATA

well-___

488

feed too ~ SATE
get ~ HEAL, MEND
get water from a ~ DRAW
less ~ WORSE
make ~ CURE, HEAL, MEND
not ~ ILL
perform ~ SHINE
serve ~ ACE
speak ~ of ESTEEM
think ~ of LIKE
very ~ GOOD, YES
wear ~ LAST

well-___ BRED, DONE, OFF, READ, TODO

___ well DRY, OIL

"___ well!" ALLS

"Well, The"
~ director ROUSE

"Well, ___ be!" ILL

well-aged RIPE

Welland CANAL, CITY, PORT

Welland Canal
~ terminus ERIE

"Wellaway!" ALAS

well-behaved GOOD
~ kid ANGEL

well-being GOOD, SAKE

well-built BIG, LARGE, SOLID

___-well card GET

well-cared-for SLEEK

well-constructed SOLID

well-coordinated AGILE

well-defined CLEAR, NICE

well-done
not ~ RARE

well-dressed SMART, TRIM

well-earned DUE

Welles ORSON

Wellesley
~ student COED

Welles, Orson
~ film, with "The" TRIAL
~ role KANE, LIME

well-favored FAIR

well-fixed RICH

well-founded SOBER

well-groomed CLEAN, NEAT, SLEEK, SMART, TRIM

well-grounded FIT, READ, SANE, SOLID, SURE

well-handled DEFT

well-heeled RICH

"Well, I'll be!" GEE

well-informed UPON

Wellington BOOT
~ alma mater ETON
~ to Napoleon ENEMY, FOE

well-kept CLEAN, NEAT, TRIM

well-known BIG, GREAT, NOTED

well-maintained NEAT, TRIM

well-mannered GOOD

well-marked CLEAR

well-matched CLOSE

well-nigh ABOUT, CLOSE

well-off RICH

well-ordered NEAT
not ~ MESSY

well-organized NEAT, TRIM

well-pleased EASY

well-practiced ADEPT

well-protected SAFE

well-put APT

well-reasoned SANE

Wells IDA

Wells Fargo
~ transport STAGE

wellspring HEAD
~ to a poet FONT

well-stocked RICH

well-suited FIT

"Well-Tempered Clavier"
~ composer BACH

"___ Well That Ends Well" ALLS

well-thought-out SANE

well-to-do RICH

well-trained
~ one ADEPT

well-used OLD

well-versed ADEPT, READ

well-wisher
~ gesture TOAST

Welsh
~ product COAL
~ river DEE
~ symbol LEEK
John, in ~ EVAN

Welshman CELT

Weltschmerz ENNUI

"___ We Meet Again" TILL

wen NODE

___ Wences SENOR

wend MOVE

Wendkos PAUL

Wendy's
go to ~ EAT

went
~ for BIT
~ up AROSE, ROSE

"___ Went Over the Mountain, The" BEAR

___ were (so to speak) ASIT

"We're ___ Dressing" NOT

"We're ___ Married" NOT

"___ Were a Carpenter" IFI

"___ Were a Rich Man" IFI

"___ Were King" IFI

"___ Were King of the Forest" IFI

"___ Were Meant for Me" YOU

"___ Were Never Lovelier" YOU

"We're number ___!" ONE

"___ Were the Days" THOSE

werewolf DEMON, OGRE

"___ were you..." IFI

Werner PETER
see also German

Wernher ___ Braun VON

"Wes Craven's ___ Nightmare" NEW

weskit VEST

west
~ ender ERN
land ~ of Nod EDEN
sink in the ~ SET
way ~ TRAIL

West ADAM, KEY, MAE
the ~ had one CODE

West ___ Beach, Fla. PALM

West ___, Conn. HAVEN

"West ___ Story" SIDE

"West, ___, and You, The" ANEST

___ West FAR

West, Adam
part of ~ costume CAPE

West African
~ capital ACCRA
~ port DAKAR
~ republic TOGO

West Bank
~ grp. PLO

West Coast
~ campus UCLA
~ st. CAL, ORE, WASH

West, Dame Rebecca ALIAS

'wester
~ starter NOR, SOU

western ___ OMELET

Western OATER
~ airline ALOHA
~ alliance NATO
~ Athletic Conference player UTE
~ author GREY, HARTE
~ beast BISON
~ capital BOISE, SALEM
~ hero EARP
~ shoe BOOT
~ show OATER, RODEO
~ state IDAHO, UTAH
~ tribe CROW, HOPI, UTE

~ wear VEST

Western ___ SAMOA

"Western ___" UNION

Western Hemisphere
~ abbr. AMER

western omelet
~ ingredient EGG, HAM, ONION

___ Western Reserve University CASE

Westerns
backdrop in ~ MESA
first name in ~ ZANE

Western Samoa
capital of ~ APIA

"Western Star"
~ poet BENET

Western Union
use ~ WIRE

"Western Union"
~ director LANG

___ West, Fla. KEY

Westheimer RUTH

West Indies
~ island ARUBA
~ islet CAY, KEY
~ republic HAITI

Westinghouse
~ rival AMANA

West, Mae
~ feathers BOA
~ role LIL

Westminster
~ district SOHO

Westmore ERN

"West of the ___" PECOS

Westphalian
~ city ESSEN

West Point
~ byword HONOR
~ mascot MULE
~ meal MESS
~ student CADET
~ subject WAR
~ team ARMY

West, Rebecca DAME

"West Side Story"
~ character TONY
~ director WISE
~ gang member JET
~ girl ANITA
~ heroine MARIA
~ song MARIA
Anita in ~ RITA

West Virginia STATE
~ resource COAL

wet BATHE, DAMP, RAINY, WATER
~ behind the ears NAIVE, NEW, RAW
~ blanket BORE, DRAG, DRIP
~ down DIP, HOSE, SOAK
~ earth CLAY

~ **expanse** OCEAN, SEA
~ **mud** SLOP
~ **slightly** DIP
~ **weather** RAIN
all ~ FALSE
become thoroughly ~ SOP
get one's feet ~ START, WADE
like a ~ **noodle** LIMP
mad as a ~ **hen** IRATE
somewhat ~ DAMP

wet ___ CELL, SUIT

___ wet ALL

wet behind the ___ EARS

"We, the People"
~ **playwright** RICE

"___ we there yet?" ARE

"We Think the World of ___"
YOU

wetlands
~ **vegetation** SEDGE

wet noodle
~ **stroke** LASH

"We try harder"
~ **company** AVIS

"We would all be ___ if we could" IDLE

Weymouth TINA

whack BANG, BAT, BEAT, CHOP, CLAP, HIT, PELT, SLAP, SMITE, SWAT
~ **down** HEW
~ **old-style** SMITE
out of ~ ATILT, AWRY
take a ~ **at** ESSAY, TRY
throw out of ~ SKEW

whacking BIG, LARGE

whale ANIMAL, BEAT, CANE, HIT, LACE, SMITE
~ **home** OCEAN, SEA
~ **the tar out of** CREAM
female ~ COW
killer ~ ORC, ORCA
on a ~ **watch, perhaps** ASEA, ATSEA
type of ~ SEI
young ~ CALF

___ whale BLUE, PILOT

whale hunter
~ **of fiction** AHAB

whalelike BIG, LARGE

whaler BOAT, SHIP
obsessed ~ AHAB

Whalers SIX, TEAM
~ **milieu** ICE, RINK
~ **org.** NHL

whales
group of ~ GAM, POD

"Wham!" BANG, BOOM

wharf HAVEN, MOLE, PIER
~ **workers' org.** ILA

wharfage RATE

Wharton EDITH
~ **character** ETHAN
~ **degree** MBA
~ **subj.** ECON

what
~ **have I done** OHNO
~ **have we here** OHO
~ **they say** RUMOR
~ **you eat** DIET
~ **you see** IMAGE
~ **you wear** GARB
beyond ~'s required EXTRA
do ~ **one can** TRY
give someone ~ **for** BEAT

what-___ NOT

"___ what?" SAY

"What ___?" NOW, TODO

"What ___, a mind reader?" AMI

"What ___ bid?" AMI

"What ___ Bob?" ABOUT

"What ___ can I say?" ELSE, MORE

"What ___, chopped liver?" AMI

"What ___ doing here?" AMI

"What ___ Happened to Baby Jane?" EVER

"What ___ mind reader?" AMIA

"What ___ My Love" NOW

"What ___ of baloney!" ALOT

"What ___ to Go!" AWAY

"What ___ You Do in the War, Daddy?" DID

"What ___ you say?" DID

"What?"
say ~ ASK

"What About ___?" BOB

"What a good boy ___!" AMI

"What a piece of work is ___"
MAN

"What a pity!" ALAS

"What a rare mood ___" IMIN

"What a shame!" ALAS

"What a Way ___!" TOGO

"What color is an ___?" ORANGE

"What'd ___" ISAY

"What Did ___ Do in the War, Daddy?" YOU

"What did I tell you?" SEE

"What Did You Do in the ___, Daddy?" WAR

"What else?" AND

whatever ANY

"Whatever ___ Wants" LOLA

"Whatever Happened to ___ Alice?" AUNT

"Whatever Happened to Aunt ___?" ALICE

"What Ever Happened to Baby ___?" JANE

"What happened ___?" THEN

"What Happened ___..." WAS

"What hath ___ wrought" GOD

"What have I done!" OHNO

"What have we here?" OHO

"What have you been ___?" UPTO

"What ho!" AHA

"What I ___" (Sublime song) GOT

"What I ___ for Love" DID

"What in ___ Hill...?" SAM

"What Is ___ Thing Called Love?" THIS

"What is so ___..." RARE

"What Kind of Fool ___?" AMI

"What'll ___?" IDO

"What, me worry?"
~ **magazine** MAD

"What's ___?" NEW

"What's ___ for me?" INIT

"What's ___ Got to Do With It"
LOVE

"What's ___ name?" INA

"What's ___ Pussycat?" NEW

"What's ___ use?" THE

"What's a Grecian ___?" URN

"What's in ___?" ANAME

"What's It All About?"
~ **author** CAINE

"What's Love ___ to Do With It"
GOT

"What's Love Got ___ With It"
TODO

"What's Missing?"
~ **artist** KLEE

what's more ALSO, AND

"What's My ___?" LINE

"What's My Line?"
~ **group** PANEL
~ **panelist** ARLENE

"What's the ___!" USE

"What's the ___ of Wond'rin'?"
USE

"What's the big ___?" IDEA

"What's the Frequency, Kenneth?"
~ **band** REM

"What's the Matter With ___?"
HELEN

"What's up, ___?" DOC

"What's Up, ___ Lily?" TIGER

"What's Up, Tiger ___?" LILY

"What's Up, Tiger Lily?"
~ **director** ALLEN

"What's Your ___" NAME

"What this country ___..."
NEEDS

"What was ___ do?" ITO

"What was ___ think?" ITO

wheat
~ **beard** AWN
~ **center** GERM
~ **husk** BRAN
~ **product** PASTA

wheat ___ GERM

Wheatley, Phillis POET
see also poet

wheedle PLY, PROD

wheel HELM, ROLL
~ **around** TURN
~ **bolt holder** LUG
~ **cover** MAG
~ **ender** BASE
~ **hub** NAVE
~ **part** RIM
~ **partner** DEAL
~ **rod** AXLE
~ **spokes** RADII
~ **starter** CART, COG, PIN
be at the ~ PILOT
big ~ HEAD, NABOB, NAME, NOB
eccentric ~ CAM
emery ~ HONE
fifth ~ SPARE
hot-rod ~ MAG
play the ~ BET, GAME
potter's ~ **kin** LATHE
projection on a ~ CAM
shaft ~ CAM
ship's ~ HELM
take the ~ STEER
toothed ~ GEAR
tooth on a ~ COG

___ wheel BIG, MAG, WATER

wheel and ___ AXLE, DEAL

wheelbarrow CART

___-wheeler THREE, TWO

Wheeler ANNE

wheeler-dealer DOER

___ Wheeler Wilcox ELLA

Wheeling
~ **river** OHIO

"Wheel of Fortune"
~ **buy** ANA, ANE, ANI, ANO
~ **category** TITLE
~ **prize** CAR, CASH, TRIP
~ **singer** STARR

wheels AUTO, CAR, MOTOR
fancy ~ LIMO
grease the ~ EASE, OIL
kid's ~ BIKE
spin one's ~ STALL

"wheels" AUTO, CAR

___ **wheels** MAG

"___ Wheels" STEEL

wheeze GASP, PANT

Whelan TIM

whelp BEAR, BRAT, DOG, LAD

W. Hemisphere
~ **alliance** OAS
of the ~ AMER

when
way back ~ ONCE, PAST, YORE

"When ___ door not a door?" ISA

"When ___ Eyes Are Smiling" IRISH

"When ___ Loves a Woman" AMAN

"When?"
~ **reply** SOON

"When Comedy ___ King" WAS

"When Dinosaurs Ruled the ___" EARTH

"When Doves ___" CRY

"When elephants fly!" NEVER

"When Harry ___ Sally..." MET

"When I ___ my lips" OPE

"When I ___ Up" GROW

"When I Grow Too Old to ___" DREAM

"When I Heard the Learn'd Astronomer" POEM

"___ When I Laugh" ONLY

"When in ___..." ROME

"When Irish ___ Are Smiling" EYES

"When I Take My Sugar to ___" TEA

"When I was a ___..." LAD

"When Ladies ___" MEET

"When My Baby Smiles ___" ATME

"When pigs fly!" NEVER

"When the Daltons ___" RODE

"When the Frost Is on the Punkin" POEM
~ **author** RILEY

"When the Legends ___" DIE

"When the moon hits your eye..." AMORE

"When the West ___ Young" WAS

"When We ___ Fab" WAS

"When We Were Kings"
~ **subject** ALI

"When We Were Very Young"
~ **author** MILNE

"When Worlds Collide"
~ **director** MATE

"When You Wish Upon ___" ASTAR

where
~ **starter** ANY, ELSE

where ___ at ITS

"Where ___?" AMI

"Where ___ All the Flowers Gone" HAVE

"Where ___ I?" WAS

whereabouts SITE

"Where Eagles ___" DARE

"Where Eagles Dare"
~ **actress** URE
~ **weapon** STEN

"Where'er I ___..." ROAM

wherefore
why and ~ CAUSE

"Wherefore ___ thou..." ART

"Wherefore art thou ___?" ROMEO

"Where Is the Life That Late ___?" ILED

"Where or When"
~ **lyricist** HART

"Where's Daddy?"
~ **author** INGE

"Where's Poppa?"
~ **actor** SEGAL

"Where the ___ Fern Grows" RED

"Where the Boys ___" ARE

"...where the buffalo ___" ROAM

"Where the Red ___ Grows" FERN

"Where There's ___..." LIFE

"Where the Sidewalk ___" ENDS

"Where the Spies ___" ARE

wherever
~ **you are** HERE

wherewithal GELT
has the ~ CAN
having the ~ ABLE

wherry
~ **implement** OAR

whet AROUSE, EDGE, HONE
~ **the appetite** LURE

"Whether ___ nobler..." TIS

whetstone
use a ~ HONE

whey SERA, SERUM

whey-faced ASHEN, ASHY, PALE, WAN

which
~ **person** WHO
besides ~ AND
river for ~ **a dog was named** AIRE

"Which came first?"
~ **choice** EGG

whichever ANY

whichway
every ~ MESSY

"___ Which Way You Can" ANY

whiff AROMA, FAN, ODOR, SCENT, TRACE
not a ~ NONE
sniffer's ~ ODOR

Whiffenpoof ELI
~ **word** BAA

whiffle EVADE

while
~ **away** SPEND, WASTE
~ **away the hours** TOY
a ~ **back** ONCE
in a ~ ANON, LATER, SOON
little ~ BIT
prefix for ~ ERST
quite a ~ AGES, DAYS

"___ While I'm Around" NOT

"While the ___ Sleeps" CITY

"While the City Sleeps"
~ **director** LANG

"___ whillikers!" GEE

whilom ERST, PAST

whim LARK, URGE

___ whim ONA

whimper BAWL, CRY, MEW, MOAN, NOISE, SOB, WEEP
~ **alternative** BANG

whine BAWL, CRY, FRET, NAG, NOISE

whinny CRY, NOISE
~ **companion** SNORT

whip BEAT, BEST, CANE, CUT, HIT, LACE, LASH, MILL, STRAP, TAN
~ **along** RACE, SPEED
~ **around** CHOP
~ **end** LASH
~ **hand** EDGE
~ **handle** CROP
~ **soundly** TAR
~ **up** BREW, FAN, MAKE, SEW, SPUR
crack the ~ GAME, LEAD
have the ~ **hand** LEAD

whip ___ SNAKE

Whiplash, Snidely
like ~ EVIL

whippersnapper BRAT, KID

whipping
~ **boy** GOAT

"Whipping ___" POST

whippoorwill BIRD

whir DRONE, NOISE

whirl EDDY, REEL, SPIN, STAB, STIR, TURN
give it a ~ ESSAY, TRY

whirligig TOY

whirling
~ **current** EDDY

whirlpool EDDY, SPA

Whirlpool
~ **rival** AMANA

whirlybird
~ **blade** ROTOR

whisk BEAT, CLEAN, MILL

whisker HAIR
barley ~ AWN

whiskers BEARD
where ~ **grow** CHIN

whiskey RYE
~ **grain** CORN, RYE
~ **source** MASH
ounce of ~ SHOT
tot of ~ DRAM

whiskey ___ SOUR

___ whiskey IRISH

Whisky Rebellion
~ **suppressor** LEE

whisper ASIDE, HINT, RUMOR, SAY, STIR, TALK
~ **sweet nothings** COO
actor's ~ ASIDE
furtive ~ PSST, PST
not in a ~ ALOUD

___ whisper STAGE

whispered LOW
not ~ ALOUD

whistle ALARM, NOISE, PIPE, SIREN
~ **sound** TOOT
after the ~ LATE
blow the ~ TELL
boatswain's ~ PIPE
time for a ~ NOON

whistle ___ STOP

Whistler
~ **work** ART

whistling
~ **sound** ESS

whit ATOM, BIT, IOTA, JOT, MITE, SCRAP, SHRED
not a ~ NONE

white COLOR, PURE, WINE
~ **alternative** RYE
~ **as a sheet** ASHEN, ASHY, PALE, WAN
~ **belt** RANK
~ **bird** SWAN
~ **Christmas need** SNOW
~ **cloud** PET
~ **fish** SCROD
~ **gem** OPAL, PEARL
~ **knight** HERO
~ **mouse** PET
~ **poplar** ASPEN

~ sheet FLOE
~ starter BOB
~ stuff SNOW
~ tie and tails DRESS
~ wader EGRET
~ weasel ERMINE
~ with shock ASHEN, ASHY, PALE
black plus ~ GRAY, GREY
clown ~ PAINT
craft for ~ water CANOE
go ~ PALE
grayish ~ ASHEN
shade of ~ BONE, IVORY
type of ~ wine RHINE
woman in ~ BRIDE

white ___ ANT, BASS, BELT, CEDAR, CELL, FLAG, GOLD, HEAT, HOLE, HOPE, LEAD, LIE, MEAT, NOISE, OAK, PAGES, PAPER, PINE, RAT, SALE, TIE, WATER, WINE

white ___ ghost ASA

white-___ HOT

___ white EGG

___-white OFF, SNOW

White RANGE, SEA
~ or Blue river NILE

White ___, N. Mex. SANDS

"White ___" HEAT

"White ___ Can't Jump" MEN

"White ___ Fever" LINE

"___ White and the Seven Dwarfs" SNOW

whitebark ___ PINE

white buck shoes
~ singer BOONE

whitecaps FOAM
form ~ COMB

White, E.B.
~ piece ESSAY

white-faced PALE

White Fang
~ creator SALES

white-footed ___ MOUSE

white hat
~ wearer CHEF, HERO, NURSE
~ wearers RNS

"___ White Hope, The" GREAT

white-hot AVID

White House
~ area LAWN
~ dog FALA, HER, HIM
~ initials DDE, HST
~ kid of the 1970s AMY
~ name of the 1860s TAD
~ nickname ABE, BILL, CAL, IKE
~ office OVAL
~ room EAST
~ staffer AIDE
~ turndown VETO
Betty's ~ predecessor PAT

"White Hunter, Black ___" HEART

"White Men ___ Jump" CANT

whiten FADE, PALE

"White of the ___" EYE

White, Perry BOSS, EDITOR
emulate ~ EDIT

"Whiter ___ of Pale, A" SHADE

White Rabbit
~ associate ALICE
like the ~ LATE

"White Room"
~ band CREAM

"Whiter Shade of ___" PALE

whites
show the pearly ~ SMILE

white sale
~ grouping LINEN
~ item SHEET

White Sands
~ county OTERO

___ white shark GREAT

"White Silver ___" SANDS

White Sox TEAM, TEN

"White Squall"
~ director SCOTT

whitetail DEER

white-tailed ___ DEER

White, Vanna HOST

whitewall TIRE

whitewash COAT, HIDE, PAINT
~ ingredient LIME

white water
~ craft CANOE, RAFT

"Whitewater ___" SAM

"White Wedding"
~ singer IDOL

whiting
Northern ~ HAKE

whitish
~ stone OPAL

Whitman POET, SLIM
~ bloomer LILAC

Whitman, Walt POET
see also poet

Whitney ELI
~ invention GIN

Whittier CITY, POET
~ work POEM
see also poet

whittle CHIP, CUT, HEW, SLICE, TRIM
~ away ERODE
~ down PARE

Whitty MAY

Whitty, May DAME

whiz ACE, RACE, RUN, SHOOT, SPEED
computer ~ impolitely NERD

whiz ___ KID

whiz-___ BANG

"___ whiz!" GEE

whiz-bang ABLE, ACE, ADEPT

whizzo ABLE

who
one ~ (suffix) IST

"who"
~ sayer OWL

"___ who?" SAYS

"Who ___?" ISIT

"Who ___ I Can't Ride a Rainbow?" SAYS

"Who ___ it?" NEEDS

"Who ___ It?" DONE

"Who ___ kidding?" AMI

"Who ___ Seen the Wind" HAS

"Who ___ That Lady?" WAS

"Who ___ that masked man?" WAS

"Who ___ there?" GOES

"Who ___ to say?" AMI

"Who ___ You?" ARE

"Whoa!" HALT, STOP

"Who am ___ argue?" ITO

"Who am ___ say?" ITO

"___ Who Came In From the Cold, The" SPY

"___ Who Came to Dinner, The" MAN

whodunit GENRE
~ award EDGAR
~ board game CLUE
~ item CLUE
~ need PLOT
~ story ALIBI

whodunits
first name in ~ ERLE

"___ Who Fell to Earth, The" MAN

"Who Framed ___ Rabbit" ROGER

"Who goes there?"
~ preceder HALT

"Who Is Killing the ___ Chefs of Europe?" GREAT

"___ Who Knew Too Much, The" MAN

whole ALL, ENTIRE, TOTAL
~ bunch LOT, LOTS, RAFT, SCAD, SLEW, TON
~ kit and caboodle ALL
become ~ KNIT
make ~ CURE, HELP, MEND
make out of ~ cloth LIE

"Who's minding the ___?"
part of the ~ UNIT
the ~ story FACT
the ~ world EARTH
undivided ~ UNIT

whole ___ NOTE

whole ___ and caboodle, the KIT

whole-___ HOG

"Whole ___ of Shakin' Going On" LOT

wholehearted EAGER

wholesale MASS, SELL
~ quantity CRATE
buy ~ SAVE

wholesome CLEAN, FIT, GOOD, PURE, SANE, SWEET

"Who'll ___ the Rain" STOP

"Who'll Stop the ___" RAIN

"Who'll Stop the Rain"
~ actor NOLTE

wholly ALL, CLEAN, CLEAR

"___ Who Loved Cat Dancing, The" MAN

"___ Who Loved Me, The" SPY

whomp BANG, BEAT, CHOP, HIT, SMITE, TAN

"___ Whom the Bell Tolls" FOR

whoop BAWL, CRY, DIN, HOOT, NOISE
~ it up PLAY, REVEL, ROMP

whoop-de-do ADO

whoopee
make ~ REVEL

whooper
swamp ~ CRANE

Whoopi
~ disguise NUN

whoosh NOISE, SPEED

whop BANG, BAT

whopper GIANT, LIE, LULU, TALE, YARN
~ teller LIAR

whopping BIG, LARGE

whorl COIL, LOOP

"Who's ___ eating my porridge?" BEEN

"Who's ___ Knocking at My Door?" THAT

"Who's Afraid of Virginia Woolf?"
~ author ALBEE

"Whose ___ Is It Anyway?" LIFE

"Whose Life ___ Anyway?" ISIT

"___ Who Shot Liberty Valance, The" MAN

"Who Slew Auntie ___?" ROO

"Who's minding the ___?" STORE

"Who's Minding the ___?"

"Who's Minding the ___?" MINT
"Who's on ___?" FIRST
"Who's Sorry ___?" NOW
"Who's That ___?" GIRL
"Who's That Knocking at My ___?" DOOR
"Who's the ___?" BOSS
"Who's the Boss?"
   ~ grandma MONA
"Who's Who"
   ~ entry BIO
"Who Was ___ Lady?" THAT
"Who Was That ___?" LADY
"___ Who Would Be King, The" MAN
why
   ~ and wherefore CAUSE
   ~ not YES
"Why ___ the Teacher?" SHOOT
"Why not?" LETS, SURE
WI
   see Wisconsin
Wicca REL
Wichita TRIBE
   ~ st. KAN
wick FUSE
wicked BAD, BASE, EVIL, HARD, ILL, VILE
   ~ thing SIN
wickedness EVIL, HARM, SIN
Wicked Wasp of Twickenham POPE
Wicked Witch of the ___ WEST
wicker
   ~ basket CREEL
   ~ material OSIER
"Wicker ___, The" MAN
wicket GATE
   ~ material WIRE
   ~ topper BAIL
   cricket ~ END
   sticky ~ PASS
wickiup TEPEE
wide AMPLE, BIG, LARGE, VAST
   ~ awake ALERT
   ~ berth PLAY, ROOM
   ~ divergence GAP
   ~ neckwear ASCOT
   ~ of the mark FALSE
   ~ open AGAPE
   ~ partner FAR
   ~ rd. AVE
   ~ receiver END
   ~ shoe EEE
   ~ shot MISS
   be ~ of the mark ERR
   go ~ of AVOID
   open ~ GAPE
   the ~ world EARTH
wide-angle LENS

wide-awake ACUTE, AWARE
wide berth
   give a ~ to SHUN
wide-eyed AGAPE, AGOG, ALERT, NAIVE
   ~ remark GEE, WOW
wide-mouthed
   ~ jar OLLA
   ~ jug EWER
widen FLARE, GROW
   ~ a hole REAM
   ~ the gap GAIN
wide-open AGAPE
wider
   get ~ FLARE
wide-ranging BIG, LARGE
widespread ABOUT, BIG, LARGE, RIFE
   ~ alarm PANIC
   be ~ REIGN, RULE
   not ~ LOCAL
widest
   ~ part BEAM
widgeon BIRD
widow's ___ MITE, PEAK
width
   length times ~ AREA
   shoe ~ AAA, EEE
widths
   typesetters' ~ EMS, ENS
Wiedersehen
   auf ~ ADIEU, ADIOS, BYE, CIAO, LATER, TATA
wield EXERT, PLY, USE
   ~ a baton LEAD
   ~ a brush PAINT
   ~ a fork EAT
   ~ authority REIGN, RULE
wielder
   blue-pencil ~ EDITOR
Wien
   see German
wiener
   ~ wrapping SKIN
Wiener schnitzel
   ~ base VEAL
Wienerwald RANGE
Wiesbaden SPA
   ~ state HESSE
   see also German
Wiesel ELIE
wife BRIDE, LADY, MATE
"___ Wife" HIRED
"Wife, Husband ___ Friend" AND
Wife of ___ BATH
wig
   ~ starter EAR, PERI
Wiggily UNCLE

"___ Wiggs of the Cabbage Patch" MRS
Wight ISLE
   ~ (abbr.) ISL
Wightman ___ CUP
wigwag SIGN
wigwam TENT
   ~ cousin TEPEE
Wilander MATS, SWEDE
Wilbur POET, POST
___ wilco ROGER
wild DESERT, FAST, FERAL, FREE, RAD, RANK
   ~ about INTO
   ~ and crazy guy YAHOO
   ~ animal BEAST, GAME
   ~ blue yonder ETHER, SKY, SPACE
   ~ bovine BISON
   ~ bunch MOB
   ~ cat PUMA
   ~ donkey ASS
   ~ guess SHOT, STAB
   ~ mountain goat IBEX
   ~ party BLAST
   ~ pig BOAR
   ~ plum SLOE
   ~ time SPREE
   go ~ about RAVE
   make less ~ TAME
   on the ~ side RACY
   run ~ RIOT
   running ~ AMOK
   sow ~ oats REVEL
   they may be ~ OATS
wild ___ BOAR, CARD, OATS, RICE, ROSE
wild-___ EYED
wild-___ chase GOOSE
___-wild HOG
Wild ___ WEST
"Wild ___, The" ONE, SEED
"Wild Animals I Have Known"
   ~ author SETON
"Wild at Heart"
   ~ actress DERN
Wild Bill
   ~ girl ANNIE
"Wild Blue Yonder"
   ~ org. USAF
"Wild Boys of the ___" ROAD
wildcat ANIMAL, OCELOT
wildcatter
   ~ quest OIL
"Wild Duck, The"
   ~ author IBSEN
Wilde OSCAR, TED
wildebeest ANIMAL, GNU
   ~ hunter LION
Wilde, Oscar POET, WIT
   see also poet

Wilder ALEC, GENE
wilderness DESERT
   ~ home CAMP
   ~ path TRACE
   ~ trek HIKE
wilderness ___ AREA
"___ Wilderness, The" NEON
Wilderness Road
   ~ blazer BOONE
wild-eyed MAD, RABID
wildflower
   ~ site LEA
wild-goose
   send on a ~ chase STALL
wild-goose ___ CHASE
"Wild Hearts ___ Be Broken" CANT
wilding PLANT
wildlife
   ~ staple ACORN
wildly AMOK
Wild West
   ~ show RODEO
"Wild Wild ___, The" WEST
wile ART, RUSE
   ~ away the hours LOAF
wiles ART
Wiley POST
Wilfred OWEN
Wilfrid ___-White HYDE
Wilhelm
   see German
wiliness ART
Wilkens LEN
Wilkes-Barre
   ~ st. PENN
Wilkins ROY
will ENDOW, LEAVE
   ~ designee HEIR
   ~ power GRIT
   ~ subject ESTATE
   exert one's ~ OPT
   good ~ ASSET
   ill ~ ANGER, HATE, IRE, SPITE
   it ~ pass TIME
   subject of a ~ ESTATE
   what the traffic ~ bear COST
___ will FREE, ILL
Will
   ~ river AVON
   ~ wife ANNE
   word for ~ BARD
"___ Will" IRON
Willamette
   ~ University site SALEM
Willard EMMA, ESPY, SCOTT
   ~ pet RAT

"Willard"
  ~ sequel BEN

will be
  ~ in Spanish SERA

"___ Will Be" THIS

"___ will believe me!" NOONE

"___ Will Dawn, The" DAY

"___ will dwell..." ANDI

willemite ORE

willful
  ~ destruction ABUSE

William DEAR, INGE, PENN, ROTH, TELL
  ~ to Charles SON

William ___ White ALLEN

___ William SWEET

William H. ___ HOWE

William Howard ___ TAFT

William III
  ~ successor ANNE
  house of ~ ORANGE

William IV
  Victoria, to ~ NIECE

William of ___ ORANGE

William of Baskerville
  ~ creator ECO

William Rose ___ BENET

Williams AMIR, ANDY, CARA, ESTHER, JOE, OTIS, PAUL, REMO, ROGER, TED, TREAT

"___ Williams" REMO

Williams, Esther
  ~ ex LAMAS

Williams, Robin
  ~ film TOYS
  ~ forte ADLIB
  ~ role GENIE

Williams, Tennessee
  part of a ~ title IGUANA

Williams, William Carlos POET
  see also poet

"William Tell" OPERA

William the Conqueror
  daughter of ~ ADELA

Willie
  ~ and others GIS

"Willie ___ Phil" AND

"Willie and ___" PHIL

"Willie Dynamite"
  ~ director MOSES

Willie "Say ___" Mays HEY

"___ Willie Winkie" WEE

willing GAME, GLAD
  ~ partner ABLE
  ~ to listen OPEN
  more than ~ AVID, EAGER, KEEN
  not ~ AVERSE

ready and ~ KEEN
very ~ GLAD

willingly
  more ~ FIRST

Willis REED

Willis, Mrs. Bruce DEMI

williwaw GALE, STORM

will-o'-the-wisp DREAM

willow OSIER, TREE

willowy LITHE, SLIM, TALL, TRIM

Wills HELEN

"Will Success ___ Rock Hunter?" SPOIL

Willy ORCA

"___ Willy" FREE

"___, Will You Talk?" MADAM

Willys-Knight
  ~ contemporary REO

willy-willy STORM

Wilma
  ~ husband FRED

Wilson ANN, FLIP, HACK, MARIE, PETE
  ~ predecessor TAFT

Wilson, Marie
  ~ TV role IRMA

wilt DRY, SAG

wilted LIMP

Wilt the ___ STILT

wily ACUTE, SLY

Wimbledon
  ~ blast ACE, SMASH
  ~ call LET, OUT
  ~ champ of 1975 ASHE
  ~ champ of 1977 WADE
  ~ opener SERVE
  ~ rating SEED
  ~ surface LAWN
  five-time ~ champ BORG
  three-time ~ champ EVERT
  see also tennis

wimp
  ~ cousin NERD
  ~ word CANT

wimple
  ~ wearer NUN

Wimsey PETER

Wimsey, Peter LORD
  ~ alma mater ETON
  work for ~ CASE

win GAIN, GET, LAND, REAP, SCORE, TAKE
  ~ against BEAT, BEST
  ~ at chess MATE
  ~ barely EDGE
  ~ by a hair's breadth NOSE
  ~ in wrestling PIN
  ~ over ENDEAR, SWAY
  fail to ~ LOSE
  lopsided ~ ROMP, ROUT

seek to ~ WOO
surprise ~ UPSET

"Win, ___, or Draw" LOSE

win by a ___ NOSE

wince START

winch CRANE

Winchester RIFLE

"Winchester '73"
  ~ director MANN

wind BEND, COIL, GALE, LOOP, REEL, ROLL, SCENT, STORM
  ~ around COIL, LAP
  ~ catcher SAIL
  ~ dir. ENE, ESE, NNE, NNW, SSE, SSW, WNW, WSW
  ~ down END, SLOW, WANE
  ~ essentially AIR
  ~ indicator VANE
  ~ instrument HORN, OBOE, PIPE
  ~ resistance DRAG
  ~ up CLOSE, END, LAND, STOP
  ~ up a case SETTLE
  away from the ~ ALEE
  bend in the ~ SWAY
  get ~ of HEAR, LEARN
  go like the ~ DASH, HIE, RACE, RUN, SPEED, TEAR
  gust of ~ BLAST
  move with the ~ SAIL
  out of the ~ ALEE
  outstrip the ~ RACE, RUN, SPEED
  rainy ~ direction EAST
  sail before the ~ SCUD
  stellar ~ GAS
  stiff ~ BLAST
  straw in the ~ OMEN
  strong ~ GALE
  suck ~ PANT

wind ___ CAVE, HARP, ROSE, TEE

___ wind HEAD, ILL, SOLAR, TAIL, TRADE

Wind ___ National Park CAVE

___, Wind and Fire EARTH

windbag BORE

windborne
  ~ soil LOESS
  ~ toy KITE

Windbreaker COAT, WRAP

windburned ROSY

winded
  be ~ PANT
  become ~ TIRE

___-winded LONG

___-winder STEM

Windermere LAKE

windfall MELON

"Windhover, The" POEM

winding
  ~ device STEM
  river ~ ESS

___-winding watch SELF

"Wind in the Willows, The"
  ~ character MOLE, OTTER, TOAD

windjammer BOAT, SHIP
  ride a ~ SAIL

windlass CRANE

windless CALM

windmill
  ~ blade VANE

___ wind of GET

"Windom's Way"
  ~ actress URE

window
  ~ covering DRAPE, SHADE
  ~ dressing TRIM
  ~ ender PANE
  ~ frame SASH
  ~ molding LEDGE
  ~ part PANE
  ~ seat BAY
  ~ sticker DECAL
  bay ~ ORIEL
  gaze out the ~ DREAM
  out the ~ GONE, LOST
  projecting ~ ORIEL

window ___ SEAT, SHADE, SILL

window-___ SHOP

___ window BAY, BOW, ROSE, STORM

"___ Window" ATA, REAR

window box
  place for a ~ LEDGE

window frame
  ~ part SILL

window-rattling LOUD

windows
  tinted ~ prevent it GLARE

Windows
  ~ alternative DOS
  ~ owner USER

window-shop GAD

wind-powered
  ~ toy KITE

Wind River RANGE

winds
  goddess of gentle ~ AURA
  heavy ~ STORM
  it ~ things up REEL

"___ Winds" TRADE

windshield
  ~ annoyance SLEET
  ~ attachment DECAL
  ~ option TINT

Windsor
  ~ prov. ONT
  racetrack near ~ ASCOT

Windsor Castle
  school near ~ ETON

"Windsor Forest"
  ~ poet POPE

windup CLOSE, END
  ~ **device** REEL
  benediction ~ AMEN
  director's ~ WRAP

windward
  not ~ ALEE

wind-worn EROSE

windy COOL
  be ~ BRAG
  hardly ~ TERSE
  not ~ CALM

Windy City
  ~ **(abbr.)** CHI
  ~ **airport** OHARE
  ~ **transports** ELS

wine COLOR
  ~ **accompaniment** DINE
  ~ **and dine** FEED, FETE, WOO
  ~ **bouquet** AROMA, NOSE
  ~ **category** RED
  ~ **container** SKIN, TUN, VAT
  ~ **cooler** ICE
  ~ **label info** YEAR
  ~ **list** MENU
  ~ **(prefix)** ENO
  ~ **sediment** LEES
  ~ **served warm** SAKE, SAKI
  ~ **word** DRY, SEC
  California ~ **valley** NAPA
  dry, as ~ SEC
  French ~ **valley** LOIRE
  German ~ **region** RHINE
  improve, as ~ AGE
  Italian ~ **region** ASTI
  Japanese ~ SAKE, SAKI
  like some ~ AGED, DRY
  nonvine ~ **source** ELDER
  rice ~ SAKE, SAKI
  serve ~ POUR
  sparkling ~ ASTI
  type of ~ PORT, RED, ROSE
  type of white ~ RHINE

___ wine POP, RHINE, TABLE

"___ Wine" MAY

wine and ___ DINE

wine bottle
  ~ **datum** YEAR

wine-colored RED

wine cooler
  ~ **base** ADE

wine festival
  ~ **mo.** OCT

wineglass
  ~ **feature** STEM

winemaking
  ~ **device** PRESS

wine-producing
  ~ **region** ASTI, LOIRE, RHINE

wines
  like some ~ AGED, DRY, SEC, SWEET

Winesap APPLE

"Winesburg, ___" OHIO

Winfield DAVE, SCOTT

wing ALA, ARMY, ELL, ORGAN, PART
  ~ **it** ADLIB, SOAR
  ~ **one's way** SOAR
  ~ **shape** DELTA
  build a ~ ADD
  building ~ ELL
  house ~ ELL
  of a ~ ALAR
  take ~ AVIATE, FLEE, JET, SOAR

wing ___ NUT, TIP

"Wing ___ a Prayer" AND

"Wing ___ Prayer" ANDA

wingding BASH, GALA, SPREE

winged AGILE, ALAR, ALATE, FLEET, RAPID
  ~ **child** EROS
  ~ **one** ANGEL
  ~ **seed** MAPLE

Winged Victory NIKE

Winger
  ~ **costar** GERE

wing it ADLIB

winglike ALAR

wings
  ~ **in Latin** ALAE
  ~ **to a botanist** ALAE
  beat, as ~ FLAP
  clip one's ~ LIMIT
  flutter ~ BATE
  having ~ ALAR, ALATE
  insect ~ ALAE
  waiting in the ~ ONTAP

___ wings WATER

wing-shaped ALAR

wingspread SPAN

wingtip SHOE

wink BAT, SIGN
  in a ~ ANON, SOON

winks
  forty ~ NAP, REST, SLEEP

"Win, Lose, or ___" DRAW

Winnebago LAKE, TRIBE

winner HIT, SMASH
  Derby ~ **flower** ROSE
  20-game ~ **perhaps** ACE

winners
  ~ **color** BLUE
  election ~ INS

winner take ___ ALL

"Winnie ___" MAE

Winnie-the-___ POOH

"Winnie-the-Pooh"
  ~ **author** MILNE
  ~ **character** OWL, ROO

winning AHEAD, NICE
  ~ **margin** NOSE
  ~ **streak** RUN

Winningham MARE

winnings STAKE, TAKE
  game-show ~ LOOT
  poker ~ POT

Winnipeg CITY
  ~ **hockey player** JET

Winnipesaukee LAKE

winnow FAN, SIFT

wino SOT
  ~ **problem** DTS

___-win situation ANO

Winslow HOMER, OLA

winsome NICE

Winsor
  ~ **heroine** AMBER

Winston RON

Winston-___, N.C. SALEM

Winston Cup
  ~ **entry** AUTO, CAR, RACER

winter
  ~ **ailment** AGUE, FLU, STREP
  ~ **air** CAROL
  ~ **blahs** SAD
  ~ **festival** YULE
  ~ **hazard** ICE
  ~ **quarters** DEN
  ~ **runner** SKATE, SKI
  ~ **sports locale** ALPS
  ~ **transportation** SLED, TBAR, TOW
  ~ **warmer** COAT, COCOA
  ~ **wear** COAT, SCARF
  ~ **weather** SLEET, SNOW
  ~ **woe** AGUE, FLU
  enjoy a ~ **sport** SKATE, SKI, SLED
  fall in ~ SNOW
  like ~ **roads** ICY
  sign of ~ ICE, SLEET, SNOW

Winter ___, Fla. HAVEN

"Winter ___ too long in country towns..." LIES

"___ Winterbourne" MRS

winterize
  ~ **a raincoat** LINE

"Winter Landscape With a Bird ___" TRAP

winter month
  ~ **in Spanish** ENERO

"Winter of Artifice"
  ~ **author** NIN

Winter Olympics
  1932 ~ **site** USA
  1952 ~ **site** OSLO
  1956 ~ **site** ITALY
  1960 ~ **site** USA
  1980 ~ **site** USA
  2002 ~ **site** USA
  see also Olympics

"Winter on Majorca, A"
  ~ **author** SAND

Winter Palace
  ~ **dweller** TSAR

"Winter's ___, The" TALE

wintry
  ~ **forecast** SLEET, SNOW
  ~ **weather word** ICY

Winwood STEVE

wipe CLEAN
  ~ **clean** CLEAR
  ~ **lightly** DAB
  ~ **off** DRY, SWAB
  ~ **off the books** ANNUL
  ~ **out** BLAST, END, ERASE, ROUT, SLAY
  ~ **out an old score** AVENGE
  ~ **the woodwork** DUST

wiped
  ~ **out** ALLIN, LOST, POOR, TIRED

wipe off the ___ MAP

wipeout ROUT

wiper
  foot ~ MAT

wire CABLE, CORD, LINE, SEND
  ~ **enclosure** CAGE
  ~ **for help** SOS
  ~ **measure** MIL
  ~ **service** UPI
  ~ **services** MEDIA, PRESS
  chicken ~ MESH
  electrical ~ CORD
  radio ~ AERIAL

___ wire LIVE

wired EDGY, TENSE

___-wired HARD

wirehair
  ~ **of film** ASTA

wireless RADIO

wiry SPRY

Wis.
  see Wisconsin

Wisc.
  ~ **neighbor** ILL, IOWA
  see also Wisconsin

Wisconsin STATE
  ~ **neighbor** IOWA

wisdom
  ~ **tooth** MOLAR
  Greek goddess of ~ ATHENA
  morsel of ~ PEARL
  traditional ~ LORE
  words of ~ ADAGE, SAW

"Wisdom of Eve, The"
  ~ **author** ORR

wise DEEP, HEP, HIP, MODE, ONTO, SAGE, SMART
  ~ **bird** OWL
  ~ **ender** ACRE
  ~ **goddess** ATHENA
  ~ **guy** GURU, SAGE, WAG
  ~ **man** HEP, HIP
  ~ **men** MAGI
  ~ **starter** CRAB, EDGE, END, LIKE, OTHER, SIDE
  ~ **to** AWARE, HEP, HIP, INON
  get ~ **to** LEARN

wise ___ owl ASAN

"___ wise child..." ITSA

wisecrack DIG, GAG, GIBE, MOT, PUN

wisecracker WAG, WIT

Wiseman ADELE

wisent BISON

wiser
~ maybe OLDER

wish AIM, HOPE, PLEASE, WANT
~ ardently ACHE
~ for LONG, PINE, WANT, YEARN
~ granter GENIE
~ the best for BLESS
~ undone RUE
~ you hadn't RUE
devoutly ~ PRAY
fervent ~ HOPE
something to ~ on STAR
universal ~ PEACE

wish ___ LIST

"Wish ___ Were Here" YOU

wishful EAGER

"Wish You ___ Here" WERE

"Wish You Were ___" HERE

Wisk
~ rival ALL, ERA, TIDE

wisp SHRED

wispy THIN

Wister OWEN

wisteria VINE

wistful
~ word ALAS

wit CARD, IRONY, SALT, WAG
~ starter NIT
biting ~ IRONY
like some ~ DRY
pointed, as ~ ACID

witch
~ creation BREW
~ familiar CAT
~ to Shakespeare HAG

witches' ___ BREW

witches' brew
~ need NEWT

witch hunt
~ locale SALEM

"Witch of ___, The" COOS

"Witch of Eastwick, The"
~ star CHER

with AMONG
~ in French AVEC
~ in German MIT
~ in Spanish CON
~ it CHIC, HEP, HIP
~ nothing left out ENTIRE
~ (prefix) SYN

with ___ arms OPEN

with ___ gloves KID

___ with (charmed by) TAKEN

___ with (full of) ALIVE

___ with (handle) DEAL

___ with (support) SIDE

___ with (tease) TOY

___ with (try to influence) PLEAD

"...with ___-foot pole!" ATEN

"With ___ ring..." THIS

"With ___ You Get Eggroll" SIX

"With a ___ in My Heart" SONG

"...with a banjo on my ___" KNEE

"___ With a Cloak, The" MAN

with an ___ to EYE

"With a Song in My ___" HEART

"With a Song in My Heart"
~ director LANG

"___ With a Stranger" DANCE

"___ With a View, A" ROOM

"___ with Bob Costas" LATER

withdraw EBB, EXIT, LEAVE
~ from DESERT, DROP

withdrawn ALOOF, SHY

wither DIE, DRY, FADE, SEAR

withered DRY, SERE

Witherspoon REESE

"___ With Father" LIFE

withhold DENY, KEEP

within
~ (prefix) ENDO, ENTO, INTER, INTRO

within ___ (audible) HAIL

within an ___ of ACE, INCH

___ with it GET

"With malice toward ___" NONE

"___ With Me" ABIDE

with might and ___ MAIN

"___ With Mikey" LIFE

"___ With No Name, A" HORSE

with open ___ ARMS

without SANS
~ a record CLEAN
~ delay APACE, ASAP, STAT
~ in French SANS
~ in Latin SINE
~ much thought IDLY
~ plans FREE
~ purpose IDLY
~ (suffix) LESS
~ warranty ASIS

without ___ to stand on ALEG

"Without ___" LOVE

without a ___ SOU

without a ___ to stand on LEG

"___ Without a Cause" REBEL

"___ Without a Face, The" MAN

"___ Without a Head, The" HORSE

"___ Without a Star, The" MAN

"___ Without a World, The" MAN

without further ___ ADO

"___ Without My Daughter" NOT

"___ Without Pity" TIME

"Without Reservations"
~ director LEROY

"___ Without Thunder" RAIN

"With Reagan: The Inside Story"
~ author MEESE

withstand BEAR, ENURE, INURE, REPEL, TAKE

"___ With the Golden Arm, The" MAN

"___ With the Golden Gun, The" MAN

"...with the greatest of ___" EASE

"___ With the Proper Stranger" LOVE

___ with the punches ROLL

"___ With the Wind" GONE

"___ With Two Brains, The" MAN

witless DAFT, INANE

witness ATTEST, ESPY, NOTE, SEE, SIGN
~ box STAND
~ reply IDO
~ statement OATH
be a ~ ATTEST, AVER
bear ~ ATTEST, SAY
bear false ~ LIE
false ~ LIAR
Watergate ~ DEAN

witness ___ STAND

"Witness"
~ director WEIR
~ group AMISH

"Witness ___ the Prosecution" FOR

"___ Witness" STAR

Wittenberg
see German

___ Witter DEAN

witticism MOT, PUN

Witt, Katarina
~ maneuver AXEL, CAMEL, SPIN
~ milieu ICE, RINK
emulate ~ SKATE

witty SMART
~ person CARD, WAG
~ saying MOT

wives
former ~ EXES
sheik's ~ HAREM

wives'
old ~ tales LORE

___ wives' tale OLD

wiz
financial ~ ACCT
no. ~ CPA

"Wiz, The"
~ actor ROSS
~ actress HORNE, ROSS
~ name DIANA, LENA
Dorothy, in ~ DIANA, ROSS

wizard ACE, ADEPT, SEER, TOPS

"Wizard"
~ monogram TAE

Wizard, Mr.
~ subj. SCI

"Wizard of Menlo Park, The" EDISON

"Wizard of Oz, The"
~ actor LAHR
~ dog TOTO
~ producer LEROY
~ prop AXE
~ setting KAN
last word of ~ HOME

Wizards FIVE, TEAM
~ org. NBA

wizened DRY, SERE

WJC PRES

WJM
~ anchorman TED

WKRP STA
~ medium RADIO
~ sign ONAIR

"WKRP"
~ character LES
Jennifer on ~ LONI

WNW
~ opposite ESE

Wo-___ ("Hawaii Five-O" villain) FAT

woad DYE

wobble SWAY, TEETER

Wobegon LAKE

"___ Wobegon Days" LAKE

woe BANE, EVIL, HARM, ILL, PAIN, TRIAL
expression of ~ ALAS
muscle ~ ACHE
washday ~ SPOT

woebegone LOW, SAD

woeful BAD, SAD
~ word ALAS

"Woe is me!" ALAS

Wohl IRA

wok PAN

wold LAND, MOOR

Wolds RANGE

wolf ANIMAL, DOG, RAKE, SATYR
~ **down** CRAM, EAT, SCARF
~ **expression** LEER
~ **in sheep's clothing** FAKE, SHAM
~ **pack member** UBOAT
~ **starter** WERE
keep the ~ from the door EARN, TOIL
like a ~'s howl EERIE, EERY
timber ~ LOBO

___ **wolf** CRY, LONE

___-**wolf** SHE

Wolf ___ ("Li'l Abner" character) GAL

"**Wolf** ___, **The**" MAN

"___ **Wolf**" TEEN

"___ **Wolf, The**" SEA

Wolf Creek ___ PASS

Wolfe NERO

Wolfe, Nero
like ~ OBESE

Wolfert IRA

Wolfgang
see German

___ **wolfhound** IRISH

wolfman DEMON

Wolfman Jack
~ **records** LPS

wolf pack
~ **member** UBOAT

"___ **Wolf Returns, The**" LONE

"___ **Wolf Spy Hunt, The**" LONE

"___ **Wolf Too**" TEEN

Wolitzer MEG

Wollaston LAKE

Wolsey
~ **successor** MORE

wolverine ANIMAL

Wolves FIVE, TEAM
~ **org.** NBA

"___ **Wolves, The**" SEA

woman ADULT, LADY
~ **title** MRS
~ **to Mike Hammer** DAME
French holy ~ STE
sacrée ~ STE
that ~ HER, SHE
titled ~ LADY
tomorrow's ~ GIRL

"**Woman** ___ **Dressing Gown**" INA

"___ **Woman**" COBRA, EVIL, IAM, IMA, SMART

"___, **Woman and Child**" MAN

"___ **Woman Blues**" MEAN

"**Woman in** ___, **The**" RED

"**Woman in the Dunes, The**"
~ **author** ABE

"**Woman in the Window, The**"
~ **director** LANG

womanizer RAKE, ROUE, SATYR

"**Woman of** ___, **A**" PARIS

"**Woman of the** ___" YEAR

"**Woman on the** ___" RUN

woman's
that ~ HER, HERS

"**Woman's** ___, **A**" FACE

"**Woman Times** ___" SEVEN

wombat ANIMAL
~ **relative** KOALA

women
for men and ~ COED
magazine for ~ ELLE, SELF
org. for ~ DAR, NOW

"___ **Women**" TWO

"___, **Women, and Song**" WINE

"**Women in** ___" LOVE

"**Women Ironing**"
~ **artist** DEGAS

"**Women of** ___, **The**" ARLES

"**Women's** ___ **Daily**" WEAR

"**Women Who Run With the Wolves**"
~ **author** ESTES

won
~ **homophone** ONE
as good as ~ ONICE

won ___ **soup** TON

wonder AWE
~ **aloud** ASK
fill with ~ AMAZE
showing ~ AGAPE
word of ~ GEE, OOH, WOW

"**Wonder** ___" MAN

"**Wonder** ___, **The**" YEARS

wonderful FINE, GREAT, RAD, RARE

"**Wonderful!**" AAH, FINE, GREAT, RAD

"___ **Wonderful Life**" ITSA

"**wonderful one-hoss** ___, **The**" SHAY

"___ **Wonderful World**" ITSA

"**Wonderful World of the Brothers Grimm, The**"
~ **director** PAL

Wonderland
~ **bird** DODO
~ **character** HARE
~ **drink** TEA
~ **girl** ALICE

wonderment AWE

___ **wonders of the world** SEVEN

Wonder, Stevie
~ **instrument** PIANO

Wonder Woman
~ **secret identity** DIANA

"**Wonder Years, The**"
~ **years** TEENS

Wonka
~ **creator** DAHL

wont HABIT, MODE, RULE

wonted USUAL

"**Won't Get Fooled Again**"
~ **band** WHO

woo SEE

wood
~ **chopper** AXE
~ **ender** CUT, PILE, SHED
~ **from India** EBONY
~ **measure** CORD
~ **piece** SLAB
~ **processor** MILL, SAW
~ **product** TAR
~ **residue** ASH
~ **shaper** ADZE
~ **shaver** PLANE
~ **sorrel** OCA
~ **splitter** MAUL
~ **trimmer** ADZE
aromatic ~ CEDAR
barrel-hoop ~ ELM
baseball bat ~ ASH
black ~ EBONY
bucket ~ OAK
cabin ~ PINE
cabinet ~ ALDER, EBONY
chest ~ CEDAR
chop ~ HEW
cigar-box ~ CEDAR
close-grained ~ MAPLE
closet ~ CEDAR
cut ~ SAW
dartboard ~ ELM
durable ~ CEDAR, TEAK
fragrant ~ ALOE, CEDAR
furniture ~ ALDER, EBONY, MAPLE, OAK, PINE, TEAK
glider ~ BALSA
hard ~ ASH, CEDAR, MAPLE, TEAK
hobbyist's ~ BALSA
hockey-stick ~ ASH
knotty ~ PINE
light ~ BALSA
like some ~ AGED
modeling ~ BALSA
moth-repellent ~ CEDAR
oar ~ ASH
parquetry ~ OAK
pencil ~ CEDAR
piano-key ~ EBONY
place for ~ SHED
raft ~ BALSA
salad-bowl ~ TEAK
sauna ~ CEDAR
saw ~ SNORE
shipbuilder's ~ TEAK
ski ~ ASH
sliver of ~ CHIP
smooth ~ SAND
strip of ~ LATH, SLAT
sturdy ~ ASH

tool-handle ~ ASH
tropical ~ BALSA, EBONY, TEAK
venetian-blind ~ TEAK

wood ___ IBIS, LOT, TAR

___ **wood (snore)** SAW

Wood LANA, SAM
~ **and others** EDS

wood ash
~ **product** LYE

"**Woodchopper's** ___" BALL

woodchuck ANIMAL

woodcutter SAW
~ **in a children's story** ALI

wooded
~ **valley** DELL

wooden
~ **nickel** FAKE, SHAM
~ **pin** PEG
~ **post** STAKE
~ **shoe** CLOG
~ **strip** LATH
travel on ~ runners SKI

"**Wooden** ___, **The**" HORSE

"**Wooden Horse, The**"
~ **director** LEE

wooden shoe
~ **sailor** NOD

Wood, Grant
~ **home** IOWA

Woodhouse EMMA

wood joint
~ **feature** TENON

woodland
~ **creature** DEER
~ **deity** SATYR
~ **plant** MOSS, TREE

"**Woodman Spare That** ___" TREE

Wood, Natalie
~ **sister** LANA

woodpecker BIRD

Wood, Peggy
~ **TV role** MAMA

woods STAND
neck of the ~ AREA
out of the ~ SAFE

Woods REN, TIGER

woodshaping
~ **tool** ADZE

woodshop
~ **tool** LATHE

woodsman
~ **implement** AXE

___ **Woods National Monument** MUIR

Woods, Tiger
~ **org.** PGA
see also golf

woodsy
~ **area** GLADE
~ **home** CAMP

wood-turning
~ **tool** LATHE

Woodward, Joanne
~ **role** EVE

woodwind OBOE, REED, SAX

woodwork
do ~ SAND
wipe the ~ DUST

woodworking
~ **machine** LATHE
~ **tool** ADZE, PLANE, RASP

Woody ALLEN
~ **frequent costar** MIA
~ **perennial used in medicine** RUE
~ **son** ARLO

Woody Herman's "Thundering ___" HERD

wooer BEAU, LOVE

woof ARF, CRY, NOISE

wooing SUIT

wool HAIR, PELT
~ **producer** EWE, LLAMA, RAM
coarse ~ **fabric** ABA
pull the ~ **over someone's eyes** LIE

___ **wool** STEEL

Wool ABBE

woolen
~ **fabric** FELT

Woolf, Virginia
~ **piece** ESSAY

Woollcott WIT

woolly ___ BEAR

Woolsey, James
~ **former org.** CIA

"Wooly Bully"
opening word of ~ UNO

Woosnam IAN

word DOPE, NEWS
~ **in French** MOT

___ **word** CODE, GOOD, KEY, LAST, LOAN

worded PUT

wording STYLE, TEXT

wordless MUTE, TACIT

word-of-mouth ORAL

wordplay PUN

word processor
~ **alternative** PEN
~ **command** CUT, EDIT, PASTE, SORT

words ROW
~ **from the sponsor** ADS
~ **on the cover** TITLE

~ **to live by** ADAGE, CREDO, CREED
bandy ~ ARGUE, TALK
contest of ~ BEE
duel with ~ SPAR
good with ~ GLIB
have ~ SCRAP
in other ~ IDEST
last ~ TAG
muddle one's ~ SLUR
of few ~ TERSE
opening ~ INTRO
play on ~ PUN
put into ~ RELATE, SAY, STATE, TALK, UTTER
put ~ **to music** SET
run ~ **together** SLUR
too funny for ~ RICH
way with ~ TACT

"___ words were never spoken" TRUER

Wordsworth, William POET
~ **piece** POEM
~ **work** ODE
see also poet

wordy LONG

"___ Wore a Yellow Ribbon" SHE

"___ Wore Black, The" BRIDE

Worf ALIEN

work DRAMA, OPUS, TASK
~ **against time** PRESS
~ **alone** SOLO
~ **antithesis** PLAY
~ **area** DESK
~ **around** AVOID
~ **as a salesman** VEND
~ **as a tailor** SEW
~ **assignment** TASK
~ **as yeast** RISE
~ **at the supermarket** BAG
~ **clothing** APRON, DRESS, SUIT
~ **day and night** LABOR
~ **ender** DAY, HORSE, LOAD, ROOM, SHOP, WEEK
~ **for** EARN
~ **for a bondsman** BAIL
~ **for a musician** GIG
~ **force** HELP
~ **for the MPAA** RATE
~ **for three** TRIO
~ **group** CREW, TEAM
~ **hard** LABOR, PLOD, SLAVE, SLOG, TOIL
~ **horse** HACK
~ **in a leaking boat** BAIL
~ **in an office** TYPE
~ **in the garden** HOE, WEED
~ **in the mailroom** SORT
~ **in the Smithsonian, maybe** RESTORE
~ **in unison** SYNC
~ **like a dog** LABOR, PLOD, SLAVE, TOIL
~ **like a Trojan** LABOR, PLOD, SLAVE, TOIL
~ **on an old painting, perhaps** RESTORE
~ **on a skirt** HEM

~ **one's fingers to the bone** LABOR, PLOD, SLAVE, TOIL
~ **one's muscles** EXERT
~ **one's way up** RISE
~ **on hides** TAN
~ **out** EDUCE, SETTLE
~ **out in the gym** SPAR
~ **out on ice** SKATE
~ **over** BEAT, HARM, LAM, REDO
~ **period** WEEK
~ **pick and shovel** DIG
~ **(prefix)** ERGO
~ **shift** DAYS
~ **starter** ART, BEAD, CUT, FIRE, FOOT, HOME, LEG, NET, OPEN, OVER, ROAD, TEAM
~ **surface, sometimes** LAP
~ **the land** DRESS, HOE, PLOW, TILL
~ **things out** COPE
~ **to do** AGENDA
~ **up** ANGER, ENRAGE, IRK, PEEVE, RILE, UPSET
~ **well together** MESH
~ **with acid** ETCH
~ **with antiques** RESTORE
~ **with art** RESTORE
~ **with clay** MODEL
~ **with leather** TOOL
~ **with oils** PAINT
~ **without a net** DARE
~ **with thread** SEW
artistic ~ OPUS
back from ~ HOME
bit of ~ ERG
chamber ~ OCTET
dedicatory ~ ODE
detective ~ CASE
do detective ~ TRACE
do dock ~ LADE
do lawn ~ WEED
do post-office ~ SORT
do postproduction ~ EDIT
do road ~ PAVE, TAR
fine ~ ART
get to ~ START
important ~ OPUS
late for ~ ABED
line of ~ TRADE
literary ~ ESSAY, OPUS
lyric ~ POEM
major ~ OPUS
make sad ~ **of** HASH
math ~ AREA
menial ~ LABOR
not ~ **out** LOSE
numbered ~ OPUS
off from ~ IDLE
piece of ~ TASK
prepare for ~ DRESS
put to ~ HIRE, USE
romantic ~ POEM
secretarial ~ MEMO
tailor's ~ SEAM
theater ~ SHOW
unit of ~ ERG

work ___ CAMP, ETHIC, SHEET

work ___ (fulfill) OFF

workaday USUAL

workaholic SLAVE

work as ___ ATEAM

workbench TABLE
~ **item** ADZE, NAIL, NUT, TOOL

worked
~ **up** AGOG, IRATE, MAD, TENSE, UPSET
get all ~ **up** ANGER, IRK, PEEVE, RANT, RAVE, RILE, UPSET

worker ANT, BEE, DOER, HAND
~ **protection org.** OSHA
~ **with an apron** CHEF
feudal ~ ESNE
off. ~ ASST
worldwide ~ **grp.** ILO

worker ___ ANT, BEE

workers CREW, LABOR
~ **group** UNION

"Workers of the world ___!" UNITE

workhorse SLAVE

workhorses
like ~ SHOD

working
~ **class** LABOR
~ **diligently** ATIT
~ **or not** ASIS
not ~ IDLE, OFF, OUT
stop ~ REST

working ___ ASSET, CLASS, DAY, DOG

"Working ___" GIRL

"Working ___, The" MAN

"___ Working" MEN

workings PIT
inner ~ CORE

workload
detective's ~ CASES

workmanship ART

work of ___ ART

workout
~ **aftermath** ACHE
~ **site** SPA
~ **target** ABS

workplace DESK
acrobat's ~ RING
gaffer's ~ SET
gladiator's ~ ARENA
Ice Capades ~ RINK
Mesabi ~ MINE
movie ~ LOT, SET
scientist's ~ LAB
Seven Dwarfs' ~ MINE

workroom
manual-arts ~ SHOP

works GOES, MILL, PLANT
give someone the ~ BEAT
great ~ OPERA
in the ~ AFOOT
the ~ ALL, ENTIRE

work safety
  ~ agcy. OSHA

workshop
  ~ hardware NAIL, NUT
  ~ tool FILE, LATHE, PLANE, RASP, SAW

"works, the"
  part of ~ ONION

workweek
  ~ part FRI, MON, WED

work without ___ ANET

world
  ~ book ATLAS
  ~ relief group CARE
  ~ supporter ATLAS
  come up in the ~ RISE
  it makes the ~ go round LOVE
  most of the ~ OCEAN, SEA
  on top of the ~ ELATED
  out of this ~ ALIEN, EERIE, EERY
  show the ~ BARE
  tell the ~ AIR
  the wide ~ EARTH
  think the ~ of ADORE, LOVE
  trip around the ~ ORBIT

world ___, the OVER

world-___ CLASS

___ world SMALL, WIDE

"World ___ See It, The" ASI

___ World NEW, OLD

"___ World" SMALL

"World Changes, The"
  ~ director LEROY

world-class AONE, BEST, FINE, GREAT

World Cup
  ~ objective GOAL, SCORE
  three-time ~ winner ITALY

"World in ___ Arms, The" HIS

"World in His ___, The" ARMS

worldly LAIC, LAY, SUAVE
  ~ starter OTHER

worldly-___ WISE

worldly-wise AWARE

"World of Henry ___, The" ORIENT

"World of Tomorrow, The"
  ~ director BIRD

world's
  ~ largest democracy INDIA
  ~ largest desert SAHARA
  ~ longest river NILE

World Series EVENT
  ~ mo. OCT
  1969 ~ champs METS
  1986 ~ champs METS
  1997 ~ city MIAMI

World Series of Golf
  ~ site AKRON

___ World Service BBC

World's Fair EXPO
  1970 ~ site OSAKA

"___ Worlds of Angelita, The" TWO

world-weary
  ~ feeling ENNUI

worldwide BIG, LARGE, RIFE

World Wide ___ WEB

World Wildlife Fund
  ~ symbol PANDA

"World Without ___" SUN

"World Without End, ___" AMEN

worm BAIT, CAD, STEAL
  ~ along EDGE
  ~ ender HOLE
  ~ in DRAG
  ~ out LEARN
  ~ product SILK
  ~ starter ARMY, CUT, EARTH, FLAT, GLOW, INCH, SHIP, SILK

worm-___ EATEN

worm-catching
  like a ~ bird EARLY

worms BAIT
  can of ~ MESS

worm's-___ view EYE

Worms
  see German

worn OLD
  ~ out BEAT, OLD, SPENT, TIRED, TRITE
  ~ thin BARE
  ~ to a frazzle ALLIN, BEAT, TENSE, TIRED
  irregularly ~ EROSE
  like ~ tires BALD

worn-down
  ~ pencil STUB

worn-out OLD, SHOT, SPENT, STALE

Worrell ERNEST

worried UPSET
  act ~ PACE

worrier
  ~ risk ULCER

worry BAIT, CARE, EAT, FEAR, FRET, STEW, STRESS, TEASE, UPSET
  ~ (about) CARE
  ~ perhaps AGER
  cause of ~ PERIL, RISK

worsen SINK

worship ADORE, HONOR, LAUD, LOVE, PRAY
  object of ~ GOD, ICON, IDOL
  place of ~ ALTAR

___ worship HERO

worshiped
  ~ one IDOL

worship from ___ AFAR

worst BEAT
  get the ~ of LOSE

worst-___ scenario CASE

"Worst ___ in London, The" PIES

worsted YARN
  ~ fabric SERGE

wort PLANT

worth COST, ESTATE, MERIT, USE
  ~ a bundle RICH
  determine ~ ASSESS
  of some ~ UTILE
  play it for all it's ~ HAM
  two cents' ~ SAY

___ worth NET

Worth IRENE

worthiest BEST

worthiness MERIT

worthless MEAN, NIL, NULL, POOR, VAIN
  ~ coin SOU

worth one's ___ SALT

worthwhile GOOD
  be ~ PAY

worthy
  be ~ of EARN, MERIT, RATE

Wotan ODIN

Wouk, Herman
  ~ ship CAINE
  ~ topic WAR

"Would ___ to you?" ILIE

wound ABUSE, BITE, CLAW, CUT, GASH, HARM, MAIM, MAR, PAIN, SPITE
  ~ up TAUT, TENSE

Wounded ___, S. Dak. KNEE

woven
  ~ fabric KNIT, LINEN, MESH

wow AMAZE, AWE, MAN

___-wow BOW

"Wow!" GEE, OOH

Wozniak STEVE
  ~ company APPLE

"Wozzeck" OPERA
  ~ composer BERG

WPA
  ~ project ROAD

wpm
  part of ~ MIN, PER

wrack RUIN

___-wracking NERVE

wraith SOUL

Wrangell RANGE
  ~ state ALASKA

wrangle ARGUE, MELEE, ROW, SCRAP, SETTO, SPAR, SPAT

wrap BIND, BOA, CAPE, COAT, DRAPE, PAPER, SERAPE, STOLE
  ~ around COIL, ROLL

  ~ name GLAD
  ~ up CEASE, CLOSE, END, TAPE
  clear ~ CELLO
  colorful ~ SERAPE
  Delhi ~ SARI
  evening ~ STOLE
  food ~ CELLO
  gift ~ PAPER
  glamorous ~ BOA
  kind of ~ FUR
  kitchen ~ SARAN
  maharani's ~ SARI
  Rajput ~ SARI
  ranchero's ~ SERAPE

___ wrap SARAN

"wrapped"
  homophone for ~ RAPT

wrapper CASE, ROBE
  ham ~ RYE
  sandwich ~ SARAN

wraps
  keep under ~ HIDE
  kept under ~ PENT
  take the ~ off OPEN

wrath ANGER, IRE, RAGE

Wrath CAPE

wrathful IRATE, MAD

wreak
  ~ havoc RAGE
  ~ havoc upon RAID, RUIN, UNDO, WASTE
  ~ vengeance GET

wreath AWARD, LEI
  ~ ornamental CONE
  laurel ~ substitute MEDAL

wreathe LOOP
  ~ with laurel HONOR

wreck MAR, RAZE, RUIN, SMASH, SPOIL, TOTAL, TRASH, UNDO

wreckage LOSS, RUIN

wrecked LOST, SHOT

wrecker TOW

wrecking ___ BAR, CREW

wrecking ball
  ~ swinger CRANE

wrecking bar
  ~ end CLAW

wren BIRD

wrench PRY, TEAR, TOOL, TUG, TURN

___ wrench ALLEN, PIPE

Wren, Christopher SIR

___-wrestle ARM

Wrestle
  ~ ender MANIA

wrestler
  kind of ~ SUMO

wrestlers
  like sumo ~ OBESE

wrestling
~ **grip** HOLD
~ **locale** ARENA
~ **maneuver** PIN, SLAM
~ **match** BOUT
~ **official** REF
~ **result** DRAW
~ **surface** MAT
Japanese ~ SUMO
win, in ~ PIN

wretch DOG

wretched BAD, MEAN, POOR, SAD, SEEDY, VILE

wretchedness WOE

wriggler EEL

wriggly EELY

Wright TERESA

Wrigley Field ARENA
~ **home** CHI

wring PRY

wrinkle KNIT, LINE, SEAM

wrinkles
remove ~ IRON, PRESS

wrist
~ **extension** HAND

writ BAN, PAPER
serve with a ~ CITE

write NOTE, PEN
~ **a check** DRAW
~ **a postscript** ADD
~ **bad checks** KITE
~ **down** LIST, NOTE
~ **hastily** DASH, JOT
~ **on metal** ETCH
nothing to ~ **home**
about MEAN, SOSO

write-___ UPS

writer
~ **need** EDITOR, PAPER, PEN
~ **org.** ASCAP, PEN
jingle ~ ADMAN
unskilled ~ HACK

writing
~ **fluid** INK
~ **table** DESK
~ **tool** PEN

amatory ~ ODE
gushy ~ SLOP
kind of ~ PROSE
put down in ~ PEN
spy ~ CODE
style of ~ GENRE

writing ___ PAPER

written
~ **exercise** THEME
~ **part** TEXT
~ **permission** PASS
~ **reminder** MEMO
not ~ ORAL
produce as ~ CITE

Wroclaw
~ **river** ODER

wrong ABUSE, AMISS, AWRY, BAD, ERROR, EVIL, HARM, ILL, OFF, SIN
~ **move** ERROR
~ **(prefix)** MAL, MIS
~ **side up** OVER
actionable ~ TORT
all ~ FALSE
back the ~ **horse** LOSE
barking up the ~ **tree** OFF
bark up the ~ **tree** ERR
do ~ ERR, SIN
get the ~ **idea** MISS
have something ~ AIL
make a ~ **move** ERR
morally ~ EVIL
rub the ~ **way** ANGER, FRET, IRE, IRK, PEEVE, RILE
take the ~ **road** ERR

"___ wrong?" AMI

"Wrong ___, The" MAN

"Wrong ___ of the Law, The" ARM

"Wrong Arm of the ___, The" LAW

"Wrong Arm of the Law, The"
~ **director** OWEN

wrongdoing EVIL, HARM
aid in ~ ABET
legal ~ TORT

wrongful
~ **act, in law** TORT

wrongly AMISS, AWRY

wroth IRATE

wrought
highly ~ ORNATE
it may be ~ IRON

wrought ___ IRON

wrought-up TENSE

wry
~ **face** MOUE

WSW
~ **opposite** ENE

wt.
~ **units** CTS, LBS
~ **units for a jeweler** CTS

wulfenite ORE

wunderbar GREAT

"Wuthering Heights"
~ **actress** OBERON
~ **character** EDGAR
~ **locale** MOOR

W. Va.
~ **neighbor** KEN, OHIO, PENN
~ **setting** EDT, EST
see also West Virginia

WWI
~ **battle site** YSER
~ **fliers** RAF
~ **German admiral** SPEE
~ **venue** EUR

WWII
~ **address** APO
~ **alliance** AXIS
~ **arena** ETO
~ **battle site** CAEN, STLO
~ **conference site** YALTA
~ **craft** LST
~ **fliers** RAF
~ **foe** AXIS
~ **general** DDE
~ **gun** STEN
~ **intelligence agency** OSS
~ **journalist** PYLE
~ **nickname** IKE
~ **Pope** PIUS
~ **soldiers** GIS
~ **turning point** DDAY

~ **vessel** LST, UBOAT
Ike's ~ **command** ETO

"www"
part of ~ WEB, WIDE

WXY
telephone's ~ NINE

WY
see Wyoming

Wyandot TRIBE
~ **cousin** ERIE

Wyandotte CAVE

Wyatt EARP, JANE
cohort of ~ DOC

wych ___ ELM

Wyche SAM

wye
~ **follower** ZEE
~ **preceders** EXES
~ **predecessors** EXES

Wyle NOAH

Wylie PAUL

Wylie, Elinor POET
see also poet

Wylie, Philip
~ **target** MOM

Wyman JANE

Wyndham LEWIS

Wynken, Blynken, and ___ NOD

Wynken, Blynken, and Nod TRIO

Wynn BOB, EARLY
~ **and others** EDS

Wynonna
~ **mother** NAOMI

Wynter DANA

Wyo.
~ **neighbor** IDA, NEB, NEBR, SDAK, UTAH
see also Wyoming

Wyoming STATE
~ **neighbor** IDAHO, UTAH
~ **peak** TETON

1

x AXIS
  ~ **may mark it** SPOT

x ___ "xylophone" ASIN

X
  ~ **in Greek** CHI
  ~ **to Caesar** TEN
  first ~ TIC
  Greek ~ CHI
  second ~ TAC
  third ~ TOE

"___ X" MME

"Xanadu"
  ~ **band** ELO

Xanthippe NAG

Xanthus HORSE, STEED

xat POLE, TOTEM

Xavier
  ~ **ex** ABBE

Xe ELEM
  54 for ~ ATNO

xebec BOAT, SHIP

Xenia
  ~ **state** OHIO

xenon GAS

xenophobe
  ~ **fear** ALIEN

xerography
  ~ **powder** TONER

xerophagy FAST

xerophyte PLANT

xerophytes
  American ~ CACTI

Xerxes
  ~ **wife** ESTHER

"X-Files, The"
  ~ **character** DANA
  ~ **extra** ALIEN
  ~ **phenomenon** UFO
  ~ **subjects** ETS
  like ~ EERIE, EERY

Xiamen CITY, PORT

XIII
  ~ **quadrupled** LII

XL SIZE

Xmas
  ~ **gift recipient** DAD, MOM,
    SON
  ~ **mo.** DEC
  ~ **time** YULE

X-rated ADULT

x-ray
  ~ **blocker** LEAD
  ~ **dose** REM
  ~ **unit** RAD

XXVI
  twice ~ LII

XXX
  ~ **center** TAC
  ~ **drink** ALE
  ~ **end** TOE
  ~ **start** TIC

xylem
  ~ **source** TREE

y AXIS
    comparative of ~ IER

y ___ "Yolanda" ASIN

-y
    ~ equivalent ISH

Y ELEM
    39 for ~ ATNO
    having a ~
        chromosome MALE
    X and ~ to a
        mathematician AXES

"Y"
    ~ wearer ELI

yacht BOAT, SHIP
    ~ squad CREW
    yon ~ HER, SHE

yachting ASEA, ATSEA

yackety-yak BLAB, CHAT, CHIN,
GAB, GAS, PRATE, RAP, TALK

yadda yadda yadda ETC

yahoo BOOR, LOUT

Yahtzee
    ~ need DICE

Yahweh LORD

yak ANIMAL, BLAB, CHAT, CHIN,
GAB, GAS, PRATE, RAP, TALK
    ~ habitat TIBET
    like the ~ ASIAN

"Yakety ___" SAX, YAK

"Yakety Yak" OLDIE

Yakima TRIBE

yaks OXEN

Yakutsk CITY, PORT
    ~ river LENA

Yale
    ~ student ELI

Yalie ELI

Yalta CITY, PORT

Yamaguchi, Kristi
    ~ maneuver AXEL, CAMEL,
        SPIN
    ~ milieu ICE, RINK
    emulate ~ SKATE

yammer BLAB, CHAT, CHIN, GAB,
GAS, PRATE, RAP

yang
    ~ partner YIN
    pert. to ~ MASC

Yangon CITY
    ~ resident ASIAN

yank DRAW, LUG, TUG

Yank
    ~ foe REB
    ~ to a Reb ENEMY, FOE

"Yank at ___, A" ETON

Yankee
    ~ nickname BABE, YOGI
    legendary ~ RUTH

Yankee Clipper TRAIN
    ~ brother DOM

"Yankee Doodle Dandy"
    ~ composer COHAN

"___ Yankee Doodle Dandy" IMA

Yankees TEAM, TEN

"Yank in the ___, A" RAF

Yankovic
    ~ and others ALS

Yankovic, "Weird Al"
    ~ movie UHF

Yanks TEAM, TEN
    ~ home USA

"Yanks"
    ~ actor GERE

Yannick NOAH

yap NOISE, TALK

yard LAND, MAST
    ~ covering LAWN
    ~ fraction FOOT
    ~ pest MOLE
    ~ tool RAKE
    European ~ METER
    prison ~ PALE
    tend the ~ RAKE

yard ___ SALE

yardage
    first-down ~ TEN
    football ~ GAIN

yard of ___ ALE

yard sale
    ~ sign ASIS
    bought at a ~ USED

yardstick NORM, RULER, SCALE

yarmulke CAP, HAT

yarn CORD, LIE, LINE, TALE
    ~ difficulty KNOT
    ~ unit PLY
    make ~ SPIN
    spin a ~ RELATE

Yasmin
    ~ mother RITA

Yasmin ___ Khan AGA

Yastrzemski CARL

Yates PETER

yaw HEEL, SWAY, TURN

yawl BOAT, SHIP
    ~ pole MAST

yawn GAPE, SPLIT
    ~ follow-up NOD
    ~ inducer BORE

yawner
    ~ feeling ENNUI

yawning AGAPE, DEEP, OPEN

Yb ELEM
    70 for ~ ATNO

yclept NAMED

ye
    ~ follower OLDE

"Ye ___ Curiosity Shoppe" OLDE

yea AYE

Yeager, Chuck PILOT
    emulate ~ AVIATE

yeah OKAY
    opposite of ~ NAH

"Yeah, right!" SURE

yeanling
    ~ mother EWE

year
    part of a ~ DAY, WEEK

year ___ day, a ANDA

"year ___ day, A" ANDA

___ year LEAP, OFF

___-year MAN

Year
    Rookie of the ~ AWARD

yearbook
    ~ classmates SRS

year-end
    ~ abbr. DEC
    ~ drink NOG
    ~ helper ELF
    ~ tune CAROL, NOEL

"___ Year Itch, The" SEVEN

yearling HORSE

"Yearling, The"
    ~ mother ORA
    ~ pet DEER

yearn ACHE, ITCH, PANT, PINE, YEN
    ~ for LOVE, MISS, NEED, WANT
    ~ (for) ACHE, LONG

yearning ACHE, EAGER, TASTE,
URGE, YEN
    have a ~ ACHE

**"Year of Living Dangerously,
The"**
    ~ director WEIR

years AGE
    ~ and years AGES
    ~ in French ANS
    ~ to date AGE
    along in ~ AGED
    countless ~ AGES
    formative ~ TEENS
    four ~ for a President TERM
    millions of ~ EON
    not in a million ~ NEVER
    of greater ~ ELDER
    one billion ~ in geology EON
    put on ~ AGE
    six ~ for senators TERM
    up in ~ OLD
    years and ~ AGES, EON

___ Year's Day NEW

"___ Years of Our Lives, The"
BEST

yeas
    ~ and nays VOTE

yeast
   work, as ~ RISE

Yeats IRISH, POET
   ~ **contemporary** ELIOT
   ~ **home** EIRE, ERIN

Yeats, William Butler POET
   see also poet

"Yecch!" UGH

yegg
   ~ **excuse** ALIBI
   ~ **target** SAFE

yell BAWL, CALL, CRY, NOISE, RAVE, ROAR
   ~ **oneself hoarse** ROOT
   cardplayer's ~ GIN
   director's ~ CUT
   driver's ~ FORE
   football ~ RAH
   umpire's ~ OUT, SAFE, TIME

___ yell REBEL

"___ Yeller" OLD

yellow
   ~ **jacket** PEST
   ~ **journalism** LIBEL
   ~ **ocher** SIL
   ~ **orange** OCHER, OCHRE
   ~ **pages** LIST
   ~ **shade** STRAW
   ~ **vehicle** CAB
   dark ~ OCHER, OCHRE
   greenish ~ LIME
   pale ~ LEMON
   pinkish ~ CORAL

yellow ___ PAGES, PINE

Yellow SEA

Yellow ___ CAB

"Yellow ___" BIRD, SKY

"Yellow ___, The" KID

"Yellow ___ Man, The" CAB

"Yellow ___ of Texas, The" ROSE

Yellow Brick ___ ROAD

"Yellow Cab ___, The" MAN

yellowcake ORE

yellowfin TUNA

yellowhammer BIRD

Yellowhammer
   ~ **St.** ALA

yellowish AMBER
   ~ **brown** AMBER
   ~ **red** CORAL
   ~ **white** CREAM

Yellow Pages
   ~ **entries** ADS
   ~ **orgs.** COS

Yellow Sea
   ~ **land** KOREA

Yellowstone LAKE
   ~ **animal** BEAR, BISON, ELK, MOOSE

yelp CRY, NOISE, YAP

Yeltsin BORIS
   see also Russian

Yemana, Nick
   ~ **portrayer** SOO

Yemen
   ~ **capital** SANA
   ~ **city** ADEN
   ~ **neighbor** OMAN
   ~ **of old** SHEBA
   ~ **peninsula** ARABIA
   gulf near ~ ADEN

Yemeni ARAB
   ~ **neighbor** OMANI

yen ACHE, COIN, ITCH, URGE
   ~ **fraction** SEN
   have a ~ **for** LONG, WANT

yenta
   like a ~ NOSY

yeoman LIEGE, RANK

yep
   ~ **opposite** NOPE

yerba maté TEA

yerk BEAT

Yertle the Turtle
   ~ **creator** SEUSS
   ~ **home** POND

yes AYE
   ~ **at the altar** IDO
   ~ **ender** SIREE
   ~ **in French** OUI
   ~ **in Japanese** HAI
   ~ **in Scottish** AYE
   ~ **vote** AYE, YEA
   say ~ OKAY

"yes"
   address after ~ MAAM, SIR
   gesture meaning ~ NOD

yes-___ MAN

"Yes ___!" SIR, SIREE

"Yes ___ Bob!" SIREE

"Yes, ___" (Davis autobiography) ICAN

"Yes, ___!" MAAM

"Yes, I ___" CAN

yesterday PAST
   born ~ NAIVE, RAW

"___ Yesterday" ONLY

"Yesterday, Today ___ Tomorrow" AND

yesteryear ELD, PAST, YORE

yet
   ~ **to a poet** EEN
   ~ **to be decided** OPEN

"Yet here's a ___" (Lady Macbeth line) SPOT

Yevtushenko, Yevgeny POET
   see also poet

Yggdrasil TREE

yield AGREE, BEAR, BEND, BOW, CEDE, CROP, DEFER, EARN, GAIN, LET, MELT, PAY, REFER
   ~ **passage to** ADMIT
   ~ **possession of** CEDE
   ~ **to fatigue** SAG
   bank acct. ~ INT
   farm ~ CROP
   fishing boat's ~ HAUL
   galena ~ LEAD
   mine ~ ORE

"Yield" SIGN

yielding LIMP, MEEK

"Yikes!" EEK, EGAD, EGADS

yin
   pert. to ~ FEM

YMCA
   part of ~ ASSN

"Yo!" AHOY, HEY

Yoda ALIEN

yodel
   place to ~ ALPS

yodeler
   ~ **perch** ALP
   ~ **return** ECHO

___ Yoelson (Al Jolson's real name) ASA

yoga
   ~ **practitioner** HINDU

Yogi BEAR

yogurt shop
   ~ **order** CONE

yo-ho CRY

"Yo-ho-ho, and a bottle of ___" RUM

yoicks CRY

yoke BIND, PAIR, TIE, UNITE, WED
   ~ **sharers** TEAM

yokel BOOR, CLOD, OAF, YAHOO

Yoko ONO

Yokohama CITY, PORT
   ~ **moola** YEN
   see also Japanese

Yokum ABNER
   ~ **creator** CAPP

Yokum, Mammy PANSY
   ~ **prop** PIPE

"Yolanta" OPERA

Yom Kippur
   observe ~ ATONE, FAST

yon THERE
   ~ **maiden** HER, SHE
   ~ **sloop** HER, SHE
   hither and ~ ABOUT

"Yond Cassius has a ___ and hungry look" LEAN

yonder AFAR, THERE
   ~ **folks** THEM
   ~ **things** THOSE
   over ~ THERE
   way down ~ FAR

wild blue ~ ETHER, SKY, SPACE

"Yoo-hoo!" HEY

yore
   of ~ AGO

Yorick
   ~ **skull** PROP
   lament for ~ ALAS

York CAPE, SGT
   House of ~ **symbol** ROSE

Yorkshire
   ~ **river** AIRE, OUSE, URE

Yosemite ___ SAM

"Yo te ___" AMO

Yothers TINA

you SELF
   ~ **bet** SURE, YEP, YES
   ~ **once** THEE, THOU
   before ~ **know it** ANON, SOON
   here's looking at ~ TOAST
   I caught ~ AHA
   may I help ~ YES
   see ~ **later** ADIEU
   what ~ **see** IMAGE
   what ~ **used to be** THEE, THOU
   what ~ **wear** GARB
   where ~ **live** ABODE
   wherever ~ **are** HERE

"___ you!" SAYS

"___ you..." (polite rejoinder) AFTER

"You ___" (Glenn Miller tune) ANDI

"You ___" (Richie tune) ARE

"You ___!" BET

"You ___?" RANG

"You ___ a Mouthful" SAID

"You ___ Can Tell" NEVER

"You ___ Cheat an Honest Man" CANT

"You ___ for It" ASKED

"You ___ Have Everything" CANT

"You ___ heard nothin' yet!" AINT

"You ___ here" ARE

"You ___ it!" SAID

"You ___ kidding!" ARENT

"You ___ Live Once" ONLY

"You ___ Live Twice" ONLY

"You ___ Love" ARE

"You ___ Me" SEND

"You ___ Meant for Me" WERE

"You ___ Me Love You" MADE

"You ___ my day!" MADE

"You ___ My Sunshine" ARE

yucca AGAVE
  ~ cousin AGAVE, ALOE

"Yuck!" UGH

Yug.
  ~ neighbor ALB

Yugoslav
  ~ coin PARA
  former ~ leader TITO

Yuko ITO

Yukon
  ~ (abbr.) TER, TERR
  ~ discovery GOLD
  ~ home IGLOO
  ~ neighbor ALASKA

  ~ vehicle SLED

Yul
  ~ "Solomon and Sheba"
    costar GINA

YUL
  ~ abbr. ARR, ETA

yule ___ LOG

Yule
  ~ ender TIDE
  ~ mo. DEC

Yuletide NOEL
  ~ burner LOG
  ~ buy TREE
  ~ figure SANTA

  ~ quaff NOG
  ~ song CAROL, NOEL
  ~ tree FIR
  ~ trio MAGI

Yuma TRIBE

yummy GOOD

Yum-Yum
  sash for ~ OBI

"Yup!" YES

yuppie
  ~ farewell CIAO

Yuri
  ~ love LARA

  see also Russian

yurt TENT

Yves
  see French

Yvette
  see French

YWCA
  part of ~ ASSN

YYZ
  ~ abbr. ARR, ETA

Yzerman STEVE

0
   ~ on the Beaufort scale CALM

z AXIS

z ___ "zebra" ASIN

___ z (the gamut) ATO

Z
   A to ~ ENTIRE, TOTAL

"Z,"
   ~ in comics SNORE

zabaglione
   ~ base EGG
   ~ ingredient WINE

Zadora PIA

zag VEER

Zagreb CITY

Zagros RANGE

Zagros Mountains
   ~ site IRAN

Zaharias BABE

Zahn PAULA

Zamboni
   ~ creation ICE
   where to see a ~ RINK

Zampi MARIO

"Zandalee"
   ~ actor CAGE

Zane GREY

Zanzibar CITY, PORT

zap BANG, HIT
   channel surfers ~ them ADS

Zapata
   see Spanish

zapateado DANCE

Zapopan
   see Spanish

Zaragoza
   ~ river EBRO
   see also Spanish

zarf CUP

Zatopek EMIL

zax TOOL

Zayak ELAINE

zeal ARDOR, HEAT, VIM

Zealander DANE

zealot FAN, NUT, ULTRA

zealous AFIRE, AVID, EAGER, HOT, KEEN
   beyond ~ RABID

zebra ANIMAL
   ~ fish PET
   ~ group HERD
   young ~ COLT

"zebra"
   football ~ REF

zebras
   ~ to lions PREY

zebrawood TREE

zebu ANIMAL

Zebulon PIKE

zed ZEE

___ zed ATO

"Zed & ___ Noughts, A" TWO

Zedong MAO

Zeena
   ~ spouse ETHAN

Zeitgeist TONE

"Zelig"
   ~ director ALLEN

Zellweger RENEE

zenana HAREM
   ~ room ODA

zenith ACME, APEX, DAY, NOON, PEAK, TIP, TOP
   ~ opposite NADIR
   at the ~ ATOP

Zenith
   ~ rival RCA

Zeno
   follower of ~ STOIC
   where ~ taught STOA

Zenobia
   ~ husband ETHAN

zephyr AIR

Zephyr
   ~ mother EOS

___ Zeppelin LED

Zermatt
   ~ locale ALPS

zero NADA, NARY, NIL, NONE, NULL
   ~ in on AIM, HOME
   ~ people NOONE
   ~ score in tennis LOVE
   greater than ~ PLUS
   like ~ OVAL
   put back to ~ RESET

zero ___ HOUR

zero-___ game SUM

"Zero ___ Conduct" FOR

zero-shaped OVAL

zest ARDOR, DASH, ELAN, LIFE, LUST, NIP, PEP, SALT, SAVOR, SNAP, TANG, TASTE, VIM
   ~ ingredient PEEL, RIND

Zest
   ~ rival DIAL

zesty RACY

zeta
   ~ follower ETA

Zetterling MAI

Zeus GOD
   ~ changed her into a spring AURA
   ~ mother RHEA
   ~ offspring ATE
   ~ shield AEGIS, EGIS
   ~ son APOLLO, ARES
   ~ to Cronus SON
   ~ wife HERA
   daughter of ~ ATHENA, CLIO, ERATO, HELEN, MUSE
   mount where ~ was worshiped IDA
   Norse ~ ODIN
   sister of ~ HERA
   whom ~ visited as a swan LEDA

Zheng He
   ~ landed here in 1416 ADEN

Zhou ___ ENLAI

zibet CAT

Ziegfeld FLO

"Ziegfeld ___" GIRL

"___ Ziegfeld, The" GREAT

"Ziegfeld Girl"
   Hedy's ~ costar LANA

Ziering IAN

zig VEER

"Zigeunerliebe"
   ~ composer LEHAR

zigzag BEND

zilch NADA, NIL, NONE, ZERO
   ~ in Spanish NADA
   ~ in tennis LOVE

zillion OCEAN, SEA, SLEW

zillions ALOT, SCAD

Zimbalist, Efrem
   ~ teacher AUER

Zimbalist, Jr., Efrem
   ~ mother ALMA
   ~ role GMAN
   ~ series, with "The" FBI

zinc METAL

zincite ORE

zincograph PLATE

zinfandel WINE
   like ~ DRY

zing DASH, ELAN, LIFE, PEP, SALT, SNAP

zinger BARB, MOT

zingy TART

Zinnemann FRED

Zion ISRAEL

Zion National Park
   ~ location UTAH

zip ELAN, FLIT, NADA, NIL, NIP, NONE, PEP, RACE, RIP, RUN, SALT, SNAP, SPEED, TANG, VIM, ZERO
   ~ along TEAR
   ~ over the ice SKATE
   give ~ to SAVOR

ZIP CODE

"Zip-a-___-Doo-Dah" DEE

"Zip-a-Dee-Doo-___" DAH

Ziploc
~ rival GLAD

zipper
transatlantic ~ SST

zipping
~ along APACE

zippo NIL

zippy KEEN, SPRY

zircon GEM

zirconium METAL

ziti PASTA

Zn ELEM
30 for ~ ATNO

zodiac BELT
~ animal CRAB, GOAT, LION, RAM
~ constellation ARIES, LEO
Chinese ~ animal DOG, GOAT, HARE, HORSE, RAT, SNAKE, TIGER
Chinese ~ animals OXEN

Zoeller, Fuzzy
~ org. PGA

Zola EMILE
~ novel NANA
~ portraitist MANET
~ portrayer MUNI
see also French

zombie
~ ingredient RUM

"Zombie"
~ author OATES

Zona GALE

zone AREA, BAND, BELT, LAND, REALM, SPOT, TRACT
combat ~ ARENA
strike ~ ALLEY
time ~ abbr. CDT, CST, EDT, EST, MDT, MST, PDT, PST

___ zone END, TIME

"___ Zone" LOVE

zoning
~ unit ACRE

zoo
~ animal APE, BEAR, EMU, KOALA, LION, MACAW, PANDA, SEAL, TIGER
~ barrier MOAT
~ enclosure CAGE
~ sound ROAR

~ staffer VET

"Zoo ___" PARADE

zoochore PLANT

zooid ANIMAL

"Zoo in Budapest"
~ director LEE

zookeeper
early ~ NOAH

zoom FLIT, LENS, MOVE, RACE, RIP, RUN, SPEED, TEAR

zooming APACE

zoophilist
~ org. SPCA

"Zoo Story, The"
~ author ALBEE

"Zoot ___" SUIT

zoot suiter DUDE

"Zorba the Greek"
~ setting CRETE

Zorina VERA

Zorro HERO
~ wear CAPE
see also Spanish

"Zounds!" EGAD

Zr ELEM
40 for ~ ATNO

z's
catch some ~ NAP, REST, SLEEP
make ~ SNORE

Zsa Zsa
~ real name SARI
~ secret AGE
~ sister EVA

zucchetto CAP, HAT

Zug LAKE

Zuider ___ ZEE

Zulu BANTU

Zumwalt ELMO

Zuni TRIBE

Zurich CITY, LAKE
~ money maven GNOME
~ peak ALP
city SW of ~ BERN

zwei
~ follower DREI

zygoma BONE